$2.50

D0221170

FUNDAMENTALS OF CORPORATE FINANCE

FUNDAMENTALS OF CORPORATE FINANCE

SECOND CANADIAN EDITION

Stephen A. Ross
Yale University

Randolph W. Westerfield
University of Southern California

Bradford D. Jordan
University of Missouri—Columbia

Gordon S. Roberts
York University

IRWIN

Chicago • Bogotá • Boston • Buenos Aires • Caracas
London • Madrid • Mexico City • Sydney • Toronto

Cover photograph: Robert Serveri
Cover designer: Stuart Paterson, Image House Inc.
© The McGraw-Hill Companies, Inc., 1993 and 1996

All rights reserved. No part of this publication may be reproduced, stored in a retrieval system, or transmitted, in any form or by any means, electronic, mechanical, photocopying, recording, or otherwise, without the prior written permission of the publisher.

Irwin Book Team
Publisher: *Roderick T. Banister*
Sponsoring editor: *Evelyn Veitch*
Developmental editor: *Karen Conlin*
Marketing manager: *Murray Moman*
Project editor: *Rebecca Dodson*
Production supervisor: *Dina L. Genovese*
Designer: *Larry J. Cope*
Cover designer: *Stuart Paterson, Image House, Inc.*
Cover photograph: *Robert Serveri*
Compositor: *Carlisle Communications, Ltd.*
Typeface: *10/12 Times Roman*
Printer: *Von Hoffman Press, Inc.*

ISBN 0-256-18335-X

Library of Congress Catalog Number 95-79287

Printed in the United States of America
 2 3 4 5 6 7 8 9 0 VH 3 2 1 0 9 8 7

To our parents, families, and friends with love and gratitude.

S.A.R.
R.W.W.
B.D.J.

To Sonita who encouraged me to tackle this book.

G.S.R.

Stephen A. Ross, *Yale University*

Stephen Ross has held the position of Sterling Professor of Economics and Finance at Yale University since 1985. One of the most widely published authors in finance and economics, Professor Ross is recognized for his work in developing the Arbitrage Pricing Theory. He has also made substantial contributions to the discipline through his research in signalling, agency theory, options, and the theory of the term structure of interest rates. Previously the president of the American Finance Association, he serves as an associate editor of the *Journal of Finance* and the *Journal of Economic Theory.* He is co-chairman of Roll and Ross Asset Management Corporation.

Randolph W. Westerfield, *University of Southern California*

Dr. Randolph W. Westerfield is dean of the University of Southern California School of Business Administration and holder of the Robert R. Dockson Dean's Chair of Business Administration.

Dr. Westerfield came to USC from the Wharton School, University of Pennsylvania, where he was the chairman of the finance department and senior associate at the Rodney L. White Center for Financial Research at Wharton. He has taught at Stanford University, The Claremont Graduate School, and the University of Lisbon.

His research interests are in corporate financial policy, investment management and analysis, mergers and acquisitions, and stock market price behavior.

Dr. Westerfield has served as a member of the Continental Bank trust committee. He has also been consultant to a number of corporations, including AT&T, Mobil Oil, and Pacific Enterprises, as well as to the United Nations, the U.S. Departments of Justice and Labor, and the State of California. He has served on the editorial review board of the *Journal of Banking and Finance* and the *Financial Review.*

Bradford D. Jordan, *University of Missouri—Columbia*

Bradford Jordan is associate professor of finance at the University of Missouri. He has a long-standing interest in both applied and theoretical issues in corporate finance, and he has extensive experience teaching all levels of corporate finance and financial management policy. Professor Jordan has published numerous articles on issues such as cost of capital, capital structure, and the behavior of security prices. He is Ph.D. coordinator for the Finance Department at the University of Missouri.

Gordon S. Roberts, *York University*

Gordon Roberts is Director, Financial Services Program, and Canadian Imperial Bank of Commerce Professor of Finance, at York University. His extensive teaching experience includes finance classes for undergraduate and MBA students, managers, and bankers under the auspices of the Institute of Canadian Bankers. Professor Roberts conducts research on duration models for bond portfolio management, corporate finance, and banking. He has served on the editorial boards of *The Financial Review, Journal of Financial Research, Canadian Investment Review,* and *Canadian Journal of Administrative Sciences.*

P R E F A C E

In the 1990s, the challenge of financial management is greater than ever. The previous decade brought fundamental changes in financial markets and instruments, and the practice of corporate finance continues to evolve rapidly. Often, what was yesterday's state of the art is commonplace today, and it is essential that our finance courses and finance texts do not get left behind. *Fundamentals of Corporate Finance,* Second Canadian Edition, provides what we believe is a modern, unified treatment of financial management in Canada that is suitable for beginning students.

The Underlying Philosophy

Rapid and extensive changes place new burdens on the teaching of corporate finance. On the one hand, it is much more difficult to keep materials up to date. On the other, the permanent must be distinguished from the temporary to avoid following what is merely the latest fad. Our solution is to stress the modern fundamentals of finance and to make the subject come alive with contemporary Canadian examples. As we emphasize throughout this book, we view the subject of corporate finance as the working of a small number of integrated and very powerful intuitions.

From our survey of existing introductory textbooks, including the ones we have used, this commonsense approach seems to be the exception rather than the rule. All too often, the beginning student views corporate finance as a collection of unrelated topics that are unified by virtue of being bound together between the covers of one book. In many cases, this perception is only natural because the subject is treated in a way that is both topic oriented and procedural. Commonly, emphasis is placed on detailed and specific "solutions" to certain narrowly posed problems. How often have we heard students exclaim that they could solve a particular problem if only they knew which formula to use?

We think this approach misses the forest for the trees. As time passes, the details fade, and what remains, if we are successful, is a sound grasp of the underlying principles. This is why our overriding concern, from the first page to the last, is with the basic logic of financial decision making.

Distinctive Features

Our general philosophy is apparent in the following ways:

An Emphasis on Intuition   We are always careful to separate and explain the principles at work on an intuitive level before launching into any specifics. The underlying ideas are discussed first in very general terms and then by way of examples that illustrate in more concrete terms how a financial manager might proceed in a given situation.

A Unified Valuation Approach   Many texts pay only lip service to net present value (NPV) as the basic concept of corporate finance and stop short of consistently integrating this important principle. The most basic notion, that NPV represents the excess of market value over cost, tends to get lost in an overly mechanical approach to NPV that emphasizes computation at the expense of understanding. Every subject covered in *Fundamentals of Corporate Finance* is firmly rooted in valuation, and care is taken throughout to explain how particular decisions have valuation effects.

A Managerial Focus   Students won't lose sight of the fact that financial management concerns *management*. Throughout the text, the role of the financial manager as decision maker is emphasized, and the need for managerial input and judgment is stressed. "Black box" approaches to finance are consciously avoided.

In *Fundamentals of Corporate Finance,* these three themes work together to provide consistent treatment, a sound foundation, and a practical, workable understanding of how to evaluate financial decisions.

Intended Audience

This text is designed and developed explicitly for a first course in business or corporate finance. The typical student will not have previously taken a course in finance, and no previous knowledge of finance is assumed. Since this course is frequently part of a common business core, the text is intended for majors and nonmajors alike. In terms of background or prerequisites, the book is nearly self-contained. Some familiarity with basic accounting principles is assumed, but even these are reviewed very early on. The only other tool the student needs is basic algebra. As a result, students with very different backgrounds will find the text very accessible.

Coverage

From the start, *Fundamentals of Corporate Finance* contains innovative coverage on a wide variety of subjects. For example, Chapter 4, on long-term financial planning, contains a thorough discussion of the sustainable growth rate as a planning tool. Chapter 9, on project analysis and evaluation, contains an extensive discussion of how to evaluate NPV estimates. Chapter 10, on capital market history, discusses in detail the famous Ibbotson-Sinquefield study and related Canadian studies and the nature of capital market risks and returns. Chapter 13, on selling securities to the public, contains an up-to-date discussion of IPOs and the costs of going public in Canada.

This is just a sampling. Because *Fundamentals of Corporate Finance* is not a "me-too" book, we have taken a very close look at what is likely to be relevant in the 1990s, and we have taken a fresh, modern approach to many traditional subjects. In doing so, we eliminated topics of dubious relevance, downplayed purely theoretical issues, and minimized the use of extensive and elaborate computations to illustrate points that are either intuitively obvious or of limited practical use.

Unlike virtually any other introductory text, *Fundamentals of Corporate Finance* provides extensive real-world practical advice and guidance. We try to go beyond just presenting dry, standard textbook material to show how to actually use the tools discussed in the text. When necessary, the approximate, pragmatic nature of some types of financial analysis is made explicit, possible pitfalls are described, and limitations are outlined.

Attention to Pedagogy

In addition to illustrating pertinent concepts and presenting up-to-date coverage, *Fundamentals of Corporate Finance* strives to present the material in a way that makes it coherent and easy to understand. To meet the varied needs of its intended audience, *Fundamentals of Corporate Finance* is rich in valuable learning tools, including:

Extensive Examples, Questions, and Problems

1. *Examples.* Every chapter contains a variety of detailed, worked-out examples. These examples are found both in the main body of the text and separately as numbered examples that correspond to the main text. Based on our classroom testing, these examples are among the most useful learnings aids because they provide both detail and explanation.

2. *Concept questions.* Chapter sections are kept relatively short and are followed by a series of concept questions that provide a quick check concerning the material just covered. Because they highlight key concepts, we have found that students rely heavily on them when reviewing chapter material.

3. *Self-test questions.* At the end of each chapter, comprehensive self-test questions appear, along with detailed solutions and comments on the solutions. These frequently combine topics covered in the chapter to illustrate how they fit together.

4. *End-of-chapter problems.* Finally, we have found that students learn better when they have plenty of opportunity for practice. In the second edition, we therefore provide completely revised, extensive end of chapter questions and problems of varying degrees of difficulty.

Appendix B   Found at the back of the book, this appendix provides concise answers to selected chapter-end problems to allow students to check their understanding.

The questions and problems range in difficulty from relatively easy practice problems to thought-provoking "challenge" problems designed to intrigue enthusiastic students. All problems are fully annotated in the margins so that students and instructors can readily identify particular types. Throughout the text, we have worked to supply interesting problems that illustrate real-world applications of chapter material.

Boxed Essays   A unique series of brief essays entitled "In Their Own Words" are written by distinguished scholars and by Canadian practitioners on key topics in the text. To name just a few, these include essays by Merton Miller on capital structure, Richard Roll on security prices, and F. Anthony Comper on the future of the financial services industry. In all cases, the essays are enlightening, informative, and entertaining.

Other Chapter Features   Several other features, designed to promote learning, include:

1. *Key terms.* Within each chapter, key terms are highlighted in **boldface** type the first time they appear. Key terms are defined in the text, and there is a running glossary in the margins of the text for quick reminders. For reference there is a comprehensive list of key terms at the end of each chapter and a full glossary at the back with page references for each term.

2. *Chapter reviews and summaries.* Each chapter ends with a summary that enumerates the key points and provides an overall perspective on the chapter material. Summary tables succinctly restate key principles. They appear whenever it is useful to emphasize and summarize a group of key concepts.

3. *Suggested readings.* A short, annotated list of books and articles to which the interested reader may refer for additional information follows each chapter.

4. *Writing style.* To better engage the reader, the writing style in *Fundamentals of Corporate Finance* is informal. Throughout, we try to convey our considerable enthusiasm for the subject. Students consistently find the relaxed style approachable and likable.

Supporting Materials

Fundamentals of Corporate Finance, Second Canadian Edition, comes with a full package of supporting materials that reinforce the pedagogical strengths of the text.

Study Guide   A complete Study Guide, authored by Jeannette Switzer, Concordia University, elaborates on and expands the material in the text. It includes study outlines and further review questions including additional challenge questions. Consistent with the text's emphasis on using Lotus 1-2-3® spreadsheets, the Study Guide includes software. It offers detailed explanations and examples of how to use spreadsheets in solving financial management problems.

FAST Templates   Financial Analysis Spreadsheet Template (FAST) applications correspond with selected problems from the text.

Instructor's Manual   A complete instructor's manual, prepared by the authors, includes detailed answers to all questions and problems at the end of chapters. For the second edition, independent problem checkers verified all solutions. The Instructor's Manual also contains lecture outlines and a set of transparency masters.

Test Bank   A stand-alone Test Bank includes multiple-choice and true-false questions of varying levels of difficulty. Irwin's testing system, Computest 3, is available in a 3 1/2″ format. Up to 99 versions of the same test can be generated using this software.

Organization of the Text

We have found that the phrase "so much to do, so little time" accurately describes an introductory finance course. For this reason, we designed *Fundamentals of Corporate Finance* to be as flexible and modular as possible. There are nine parts, and, in broad terms, the instructor is free to decide the particular sequence. Further, within each part, the first chapter generally contains a broad overview and survey. Thus, when time is limited, subsequent chapters can be omitted. Finally, the sections placed early in each chapter are generally the most important, and later sections frequently can be omitted without loss of continuity. For these reasons, the instructor has great control over the topics covered, the sequence in which they are covered, and the depth of coverage.

Part One of the text contains two chapters. Chapter 1 considers the goal of the corporation, the corporate form of organization, the agency problem, and, briefly, money and capital markets. Chapter 2 succinctly discusses cash flow versus accounting income, market value versus book value, and taxes. It also provides a useful review of financial statements.

After Part One, either Part Two, on financial statements analysis, long-range planning, and corporate growth, or Part Three, on time value and stock and bond valuation, follow naturally. Part Two can be omitted if desired. After Part Three, most instructors will probably want to move directly into Part Four, which covers net present value, discounted cash flow valuation, and capital budgeting.

Part Five contains two chapters on risk and return. The first one, on market history, is designed to give students a feel for typical rates of return on risky assets. The second one discusses the expected return/risk trade-off, and it develops the security market line in a highly intuitive way that bypasses much of the usual portfolio theory and statistics.

The first chapter of Part Six introduces long-term financing by discussing the essential features of debt and equity instruments. Important elements of bankruptcy and reorganization are covered briefly as well. The second chapter in Part Six covers selling securities to the public with an emphasis on the role of the investment banker and the costs of going public. Because both chapters contain a fair amount of descriptive material, they can easily be assigned as out-of-class reading as time constraints dictate.

Cost of capital, capital structure, and dividend policy are covered in the three consecutive chapters of Part Seven. The chapter on dividends can be covered independently, if desired, and the chapter on capital structure can be omitted without creating loss of continuity.

Part Eight covers issues in contemporary short-term financial management. The first of the three chapters is a general survey of short-term management, which is very useful when time does not permit a more in-depth treatment. The next two chapters provide greater detail on cash, credit, and inventory management.

Last, Part Nine covers four important topics: options and optionlike securities, mergers, international finance, and leasing. These chapters contain somewhat greater depth of coverage than the basic text chapters and may be covered partially in courses where time is constrained or completely in courses that give special emphasis to these topics.

Acknowledgments

We never would have completed this book without the incredible amount of help and support we received from colleagues, editors, family members, and friends. We would like to thank, without implicating, all of you.

For starters, a great many of our colleagues read the drafts of our first and current editions. The fact that this book has so little in common with those drafts is a reflection of the value we placed on the many comments and suggestions that we received. Our reviewers continued to keep us working on improving the content, organization, exposition, and Canadian content of our text. To the following reviewers, we are grateful for their many contributions to the Second Canadian Edition:

William J. McNally	*University of Victoria*
Jeannette Switzer	*Concordia University*
Jack Schnabel	*Wilfrid Laurier University*
Ian Feltmate	*Acadia University*
Sylvie Bequet	*Bishop's University*
Merv Michaels	*Kwantlen College*
Lachlan Whatley	*University College of Fraser Valley*
Said Elfakhani	*University of Saskatchewan*
Charles Priester	*British Columbia Institute of Technology*

We would also like to express our appreciation to the following individuals for their detailed proofing of the problem material:

Devashis Mitro	*University of New Brunswick*
Sylvie Bequet	*Bishop's University*

Several of our most respected colleagues contributed essays, which are entitled "In Their Own Words" and appear in selected chapters. To these individuals we extend a special thanks:

Edward I. Altman	*New York University*
Trevor Chamberlain	*McMaster University*
F. Anthony Comper	*Bank of Montreal*
Jean-Claude Delorme	*Caisse de depot et placement du Quebec*
Esben Eckbo	*University of British Columbia*
Myron Gordon	*University of Toronto* (Ret.)
Roger Ibbotson	*Yale University*
Stephen Jarislowsky	*Jarislowsky, Fraser and Company*
Andre Kleynhans	*NutriSystem Ltd.*
Richard M. Levich	*New York University*
Robert C. Merton	*Harvard University*
Merton H. Miller	*University of Chicago*
David Rogers	*London Life*
Richard Roll	*University of California at Los Angeles*

Also deserving of special mention are Ronald Manurung and Kenneth Stanton, Ph.D. students at York University. Working as research assistants, they developed examples and problems, checked calculations and solutions, and furnished editorial assistance. Esther Maciuk, York University, provided valuable typing and editorial assistance.

Finally, in every phase of this project, we have been privileged to have had the complete and unwavering support of a great organization: Richard D. Irwin and Times Mirror Professional Publishing. We are deeply grateful to the select group of professionals who served as the development team for the Second Canadian Edition. Alphabetically, they are: Rod Banister, Karen Conlin, Mike Junior, and Evelyn Veitch.

Of this group, two deserve particular mention. First, with understanding, tact, and flexibility, Evelyn Veitch, sponsoring editor, guided the work on the Second Canadian Edition. Second, Rod Banister, publisher, oversaw the process and provided encouragement at key points along the way. Others at Irwin, too numerous to list here, have improved this book in countless ways.

Through the development of this edition, we have taken great care to discover and eliminate errors. Our goal is to provide the best Canadian textbook available on the subject. Please write and tell us how to make this a better text. Forward your comments to: Professor Gordon S. Roberts, Schulich School of Business, York University, 4700 Keele Street, North York, Ontario M3J IP3.

Stephen A. Ross
Randolph W. Westerfield
Bradford D. Jordan
Gordon S. Roberts

Note to Students

Study Guide   The Study Guide to accompany this textbook has been designed with you in mind and will help in your understanding of the material that you will cover in this course. It includes page-referenced chapter outlines, concept test questions, and further review questions including additional challenge questions. In addition, a disk that is designed for Lotus 1-2-3 or any compatible spreadsheet is included to complement spreadsheet cases that allow you to do programming to solve a variety of financial applications.

For additional information on how to order a copy of the Study Guide, please contact your local bookstore.

Study Guide ISBN: 0-256-19517-X

To the Student,

"Why are textbook prices so high?"

This is, by far, the most frequently asked question heard in the publishing industry. There are many factors that influence the price of your new textbook. Here are just a few:

- **The cost of instructor support materials:** Your instructor may be using teaching supplements, many of which are provided by the publisher. Teaching supplements include videos, colour transparencies, instructor's manuals, software, computerized testing materials, and more. These supplements are designed as part of a learning package to enhance your educational experience.
- **Developmental costs:** These are costs associated with the extensive development of your textbook. Expenses include permissions fees, manuscript review costs, artwork, typesetting, printing and binding costs, and more.
- **Author royalties:** Authors are paid based on a percentage of new book sales and **do not** receive royalties on the sale of a used book. They are also deprived of their rightful royalties when their books are illegally photocopied.
- **Marketing costs:** Instructors need to be made aware of new textbooks. Marketing costs include academic conventions, remuneration of the publisher's representatives, promotional advertising pieces, and the provision of instructor's examination copies.
- **Bookstore markups:** In order to stay in business, your local bookstore must cover its costs. A textbook is a commodity, just like any other item your bookstore may sell, and bookstores are the most effective way to get the textbook from the publisher to you.
- **Publisher profits:** In order to continue to supply students with quality textbooks, publishers must make a profit to stay in business. Like the authors, publishers **do not** receive any compensation from the sale of a used book or the illegal photocopying of their textbooks.

We at Times Mirror Professional Publishing hope you will find this information useful and that it addresses some of your concerns. We also thank you for your purchase of this new textbook. If you have any questions that we can answer, please write to us at:

> Times Mirror Professional Publishing
> College Division
> 130 Flaska Drive
> Markham, Ontario
> L6G 1B8

B R I E F   C O N T E N T S

CONTENTS

OVERVIEW OF CORPORATE FINANCE

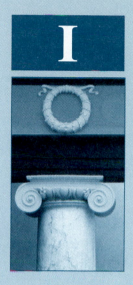

Introduction to Corporate Finance

To begin our study of modern corporate finance and financial management, we need to address two central issues: First, what is corporate finance, and what is the role of the financial manager in the corporation? Second, what is the goal of financial management? To describe the financial management environment, we look at the corporate form of organization and discuss some conflicts that can arise within the corporation. We also take a brief look at financial institutions and financial markets in Canada.

1.1 | CORPORATE FINANCE AND THE FINANCIAL MANAGER

In this section, we discuss where the financial manager fits in the corporation. We start by looking at what corporate finance is and what the financial manager does.

What Is Corporate Finance?

Imagine that you were to start your own business. No matter what type you started, you would have to answer the following three questions in some form or another:

1. What long-term investments should you take on? That is, what lines of business will you be in and what sorts of buildings, machinery, equipment, and research and development facilities will you need?
2. Where will you get the long-term financing to pay for your investment? Will you bring in other owners or will you borrow the money?
3. How will you manage your everyday financial activities such as collecting from customers and paying suppliers?

These are not the only questions by any means, but they are among the most important. Corporate finance, broadly speaking, is the study of ways to answer these three questions. Accordingly, we'll be looking at each of them in the chapters ahead. Though our discussion focusses on the role of the financial manager, these three questions are important to managers in all areas of the corporation. For example, selecting the firm's lines of business (Question 1) shapes the jobs of managers in production, marketing, and management information systems. As a result, most large corporations centralize their finance function and use it to measure performance in other areas. Most CEOs have significant financial management experience.

The Financial Manager

A striking feature of large corporations is that the owners (the shareholders) are usually not directly involved in making business decisions, particularly on a day-to-day basis. Instead, the corporation employs managers to represent the owners' interests and make decisions on their behalf. In a large corporation, the financial manager is in charge of answering the three questions we raised earlier.

It is a challenging task because changes in the firm's operations and shifts in Canadian and global financial markets mean that the best answers for each firm are changing, sometimes quite rapidly. Globalization of markets, advanced communications and computer technology, as well as increased volatility of interest rates and foreign exchange rates have raised the stakes in financial management decisions. We discuss these major trends after we introduce you to some of the basics of corporate financial decisions.

The financial management function is usually associated with a top officer of the firm, such as a vice president of finance or some other chief financial officer (CFO). Figure 1.1 is a simplified organization chart that highlights the finance activity in a large firm. The chief financial officer (CFO) reports to the president, who is the chief operating officer (COO) in charge of day-to-day operations. The COO reports to the chairman who is usually chief executive officer. The CEO has overall responsibility to the board. As shown, the vice president of finance coordinates the activities of the treasurer and the controller. The controller's office handles cost and financial accounting, tax payments, and management information systems. The treasurer's office is responsible for managing the firm's cash, its financial planning, and its capital expenditures. These treasury activities are all related to the three general questions raised earlier, and the chapters ahead deal primarily with these issues. Our study thus bears mostly on activities usually associated with the treasurer's office.

Financial Management Decisions

As our discussion suggests, the financial manager must be concerned with three basic types of questions. We consider these in greater detail next.

Capital Budgeting   The first question concerns the firm's long-term investments. The process of planning and managing a firm's long-term investments is called **capital budgeting.** In capital budgeting, the financial manager tries to identify investment opportunities worth more to the firm than they cost to acquire. Loosely speaking, this means that the value of the cash flow generated by an asset exceeds the cost of that asset.

capital budgeting
The process of planning and managing a firm's investment in fixed assets.

Financial managers must be concerned not only with how much cash they expect to receive, but also with when they expect to receive it and how likely they are to receive it. Evaluating the size, timing, and risk of future cash flows is the essence of capital budgeting. We discuss how to do this in detail in the chapters ahead.

Capital Structure   The second major question for the financial manager concerns how the firm should obtain and manage the long-term financing it needs to support its long-term investments. A firm's **capital structure** (or financial structure) refers to the specific mixture of long-term debt and equity the firm uses to finance its operations. The financial manager has two concerns in this area. First, how much should the firm borrow; that is, what mixture is best? The mixture chosen affects both the risk and value of the firm. Second, what are the least expensive sources of funds for the firm?

capital structure
The mix of debt and equity maintained by a firm.

F I G U R E 1.1

*A simplified
organization chart.
The exact titles and
organization differ
from company to
company.*

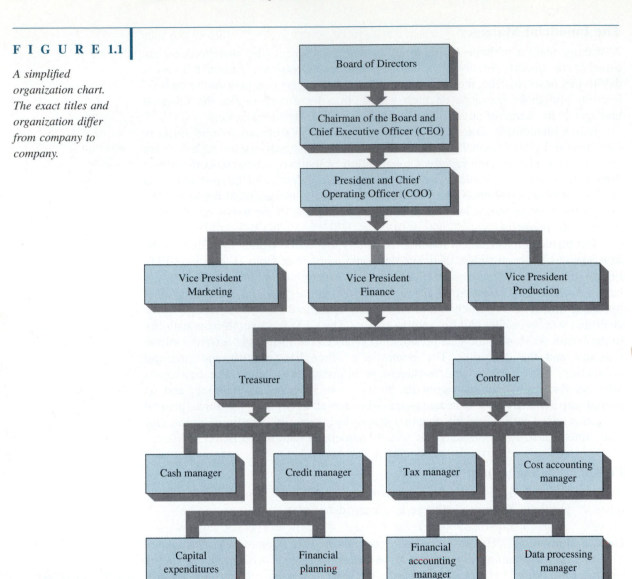

If we picture the firm as a pie, then the firm's capital structure determines how that pie is sliced. In other words, what percentage of the firm's cash flow goes to creditors and what percentage goes to shareholders? Management has a great deal of flexibility in choosing a firm's financial structure. Whether one structure is better than any other for a particular firm is the heart of the capital structure issue.

In addition to deciding on the financing mix, the financial manager has to decide exactly how and where to raise the money. The expenses associated with raising long-term financing can be considerable, so different possibilities must be carefully evaluated. Also, corporations borrow money from a variety of lenders tapping both Canadian and international debt markets, in a number of different—and sometimes exotic—ways. Choosing among lenders and among loan types is another of the jobs handled by the financial manager.

Working Capital Management The third major question concerns **working capital management.** The phrase *working capital* refers to a firm's short-term assets, such as inventory, and its short-term liabilities, such as money owed to suppliers. Managing the firm's working capital is a day-to-day activity that ensures the firm has sufficient resources to continue its operations and avoid costly interruptions. This involves a number of activities all related to the firm's receipt and disbursement of cash.

working capital management
Planning and managing the firm's current assets and liabilities.

Some of the questions about working capital that must be answered are: (1) How much cash and inventory should we keep on hand? (2) Should we sell on credit? If so, what terms should we offer, and to whom should we extend them? (3) How do we obtain any needed short-term financing? Will we purchase on credit or borrow short-term and pay cash? If we borrow short-term, how and when should we do it? This is just a small sample of the issues that arise in managing a firm's working capital.

The three areas of corporate financial management we have described—capital budgeting, capital structure, and working capital management—are very broad categories. Each includes a rich variety of topics; we have indicated only a few of the questions that arise in the different areas. The following chapters contain greater detail.

> **CONCEPT QUESTIONS**
> 1. What is the capital budgeting decision?
> 2. Into what category of financial management does cash management fall?
> 3. What do you call the specific mixture of long-term debt and equity that a firm chooses to use?

1.2 | THE CORPORATE FORM OF BUSINESS ORGANIZATION

Large firms in Canada, such as CIBC and Canadian Pacific Enterprises, are almost all organized as corporations. We examine the three different legal forms of business organization—sole proprietorship, partnership, and corporation—to see why this is so. Each of the three forms has distinct advantages and disadvantages in the life of the business, the ability of the business to raise cash, and taxes. A key observation is that, as a firm grows, the advantages of the corporate form may come to outweigh the disadvantages.

Sole Proprietorship

A **sole proprietorship** is a business owned by one person. This is the simplest type of business to start and is the least regulated form of organization. Depending on where you live, you can start up a proprietorship by doing little more than getting a business licence and opening your doors. For this reason, many businesses that later become large corporations start out as small proprietorships. There are more proprietorships than any other type of business.

sole proprietorship
A business owned by a single individual.

As the owner of a sole proprietorship, you keep all the profits. That's the good news. The bad news is that the owner has *unlimited liability* for business debts. This means that creditors can look beyond assets to the proprietor's personal assets for payment. Similarly, there is no distinction between personal and business income, so all business income is taxed as personal income.

The life of a sole proprietorship is limited to the owner's life span, and, importantly, the amount of equity that can be raised is limited to the proprietor's personal wealth. This limitation often means that the business cannot exploit new opportunities because of insufficient capital. Ownership of a sole proprietorship may be difficult to transfer since this requires the sale of the entire business to a new owner.

Partnership

partnership

A business formed by two or more co-owners.

A **partnership** is similar to a proprietorship, except that there are two or more owners (partners). In a *general partnership,* all the partners share in gains or losses, and all have unlimited liability for all partnership debts, not just some particular share. The way partnership gains (and losses) are divided is described in the *partnership agreement.* This agreement can be an informal oral agreement, such as "Let's start a lawn mowing business," or a lengthy, formal written document.

In a *limited partnership,* one or more *general partners* has unlimited liability and runs the business for one or more *limited partners* who do not actively participate in the business. A limited partner's liability for business debts is limited to the amount contributed to the partnership. This form of organization is common in real estate ventures, for example.

The advantages and disadvantages of a partnership are basically the same as those for a proprietorship. Partnerships based on a relatively informal agreement are easy and inexpensive to form. General partners have unlimited liability for partnership debts, and the partnership terminates when a general partner wishes to sell out or dies. All income is taxed as personal income to the partners, and the amount of equity that can be raised is limited to the partners' combined wealth. Ownership by a general partner is not easily transferred because a new partnership must be formed. A limited partner's interest can be sold without dissolving the partnership. But finding a buyer may be difficult, because there is no organized market in limited partnerships.

Based on our discussion, the primary disadvantages of sole proprietorship and partnership as forms of business organization are (1) unlimited liability for business debts on the part of the owners, (2) limited life of the business, and (3) difficulty of transferring ownership. These three disadvantages add up to a single, central problem: the ability of such businesses to grow can be seriously limited by an inability to raise cash for investment.

Corporation

corporation

A business created as a distinct legal entity composed of one or more individuals or entities.

In terms of size, the **corporation** is the most important form of business organization in Canada. A corporation is a legal entity separate and distinct from its owners; it has many of the rights, duties, and privileges of an actual person. Corporations can borrow money and own property, can sue and be sued, and can enter into contracts. A corporation can even be a general partner or a limited partner in a partnership, and a corporation can own stock in another corporation.

Not surprisingly, starting a corporation is somewhat more complicated than starting the other forms of business organization, but not greatly so for a small business. Forming a corporation involves preparing *articles of incorporation* (or a charter) and a set of *bylaws.* The articles of incorporation must contain a number of things, including the corporation's name, its intended life (which can be forever), its business purpose, and the number of shares that can be issued. This information must be supplied to regulators in the jurisdiction in which the firm is incorporated.

Canadian firms can be incorporated under either the federal Canada Business Corporation Act or provincial law.[1]

The bylaws are rules describing how the corporation regulates its own existence. For example, the bylaws describe how directors are elected. These bylaws may be a very simple statement of a few rules and procedures, or they may be quite extensive for a large corporation. The bylaws may be amended or extended from time to time by the shareholders.

In a large corporation, the shareholders and the management are usually separate groups. The shareholders elect the board of directors that then selects the managers. Management is charged with running the corporation's affairs in the shareholders' interest. In principle, shareholders control the corporation because they elect the directors.

As a result of the separation of ownership and management, the corporate form has several advantages. Ownership (represented by shares of stock) can be readily transferred, and the life of the corporation is therefore not limited. The corporation borrows money in its own name. As a result, the shareholders in a corporation have limited liability for corporate debts. The most they can lose is what they have invested.[2]

While limited liability makes the corporate form attractive to equity investors, lenders sometimes view the limited liability feature as a disadvantage. If the borrower experiences financial distress and is unable to repay its debt, limited liability blocks lenders' access to the owners' personal assets. For this reason, chartered banks often circumvent limited liability by requiring owners of small businesses to provide personal guarantees of company debt.

The relative ease of transferring ownership, the limited liability for business debts, and the unlimited life of the business are the reasons why the corporate form is superior when it comes to raising cash. If a corporation needs new equity, for example, it can sell new shares of stock and attract new investors. The number of owners can be huge; larger corporations have many thousands or even millions of shareholders. In a recent year, for example, Bell Canada Enterprises had more than 277,000 shareholders and Bombardier had about 10,000. In such cases, ownership can change continuously without affecting the continuity of the business.

The corporate form has a significant disadvantage. Because a corporation is a legal entity, it must pay taxes. Moreover, money paid out to shareholders in dividends is taxed again as income to those shareholders. This is *double taxation,* meaning that corporate profits are taxed twice—at the corporate level when they are earned and again at the personal level when they are paid out.[3]

As the discussion in this section illustrates, the need of large businesses for outside investors and creditors is such that the corporate form generally is best for such firms. We focus on corporations in the chapters ahead because of the importance of the corporate form in the Canadian and world economies. Also, a few important financial management issues, such as dividend policy, are unique to corporations. However, businesses of all types and sizes need financial management, so the majority of the subjects we discuss bear on all forms of business.

---

[1] In some provinces, the legal documents of incorporation are called letters patent or a memorandum of association.

[2] An important exception is negligence by a corporate director. If this can be proven, for example in a case of environmental damage, the director may be liable for more than the original investment.

[3] The dividend tax credit for individual shareholders and a corporate dividend exclusion reduce the bite of double taxation for Canadian corporations. These tax provisions are discussed in Chapter 2.

T A B L E 1.1 | *International corporations*

Company	Country of Origin	Type of Company	Translation
Porsche AG	Germany	Aktiengesellschaft	Corporation
Bayerische Moteren Werke (BMW) AG			
Dornier GmBH		Gesellschaft mit	
	Germany	Beschraenkter Haftung	Cooperative with limited liability
Rolls-Royce PLC	United Kingdom	Public limited company	Public limited company
Shell UK LTD	United Kingdom	Limited	Corporation
Unilever NV	Netherlands	Naamloze Vennootschap	Limited liability company
Fiat SpA	Italy	Sociéta per Azioni	Public limited company
Volvo AB	Sweden	Aktiebolag	Joint stock company
Peugeot SA	France	Société Anonyme	Joint stock company

A Corporation by Another Name   The corporate form of organization has many variations around the world. The exact laws and regulations differ from country to country, of course, but the essential features of public ownership and limited liability remain. These firms are often designated as joint stock companies, public limited companies, or limited liability companies, depending on the specific nature of the firm and the country of origin.

Table 1.1 gives the names of a few well-known international corporations, their country of origin, and a translation of the abbreviation that follows the company name.

CONCEPT QUESTIONS
1. What are the three forms of business organization?
2. What are the primary advantages and disadvantages of a sole proprietorship or partnership?
3. What is the difference between a general and a limited partnership?
4. Why is the corporate form superior when it comes to raising cash?

1.3 | THE GOAL OF FINANCIAL MANAGEMENT

Assuming that we restrict ourselves to for-profit businesses, the goal of financial management is to make money or add value for the owners. This goal is a little vague, of course, so we examine some different ways of formulating it to come up with a more precise definition. Such a definition is important because it leads to an objective basis for making and evaluating financial decisions.

Possible Goals

If we were to consider possible financial goals, we might come up with some ideas like the following:

Survive in business.

Avoid financial distress and bankruptcy.

Beat the competition.

Maximize sales or market share.

Minimize costs.

Maximize profits.

Maintain steady earnings growth.

These are only a few of the goals we could list. Furthermore, each of these possibilities presents problems as a goal for a financial manager.

For example, it's easy to increase market share or unit sales; all we have to do is lower our prices or relax our credit terms. Similarly, we can always cut costs simply by doing away with things such as research and development. We can avoid bankruptcy by never borrowing any money or taking any risks, and so on. It's not clear that any of these actions is in the shareholders' best interests.

Profit maximization would probably be the most commonly cited goal, but even this is not a very precise objective. Do we mean profits this year? If so, then actions such as deferring maintenance, letting inventories run down, and other short-run cost-cutting measures tend to increase profits now, but these activities aren't necessarily desirable.

The goal of maximizing profits may refer to some sort of long-run or average profits, but it's still unclear exactly what this means. First, do we mean something like accounting net income or earnings per share? As we see in more detail in the next chapter, these accounting numbers may have little to do with what is good or bad for the firm. Second, what do we mean by the long run? As a famous economist once remarked, in the long run, we're all dead! More to the point, this goal doesn't tell us what the appropriate trade-off is between current and future profits.

Although the goals we've just listed are all different, they fall into two classes: The first of these relates to profitability. The goals involving sales, market share, and cost control all relate, at least potentially, to different ways of earning or increasing profits. The second group, involving bankruptcy avoidance, stability, and safety, relates in some way to controlling risk. Unfortunately, these two types of goals are somewhat contradictory. The pursuit of profit normally involves some element of risk, so it isn't really possible to maximize both safety and profit. What we need, therefore, is a goal that encompasses both these factors.

The Goal of Financial Management

The financial manager in a corporation makes decisions for the shareholders of the firm. Given this, instead of listing possible goals for the financial manager, we really need to answer a more fundamental question: From the shareholders' point of view, what is a good financial management decision?

If we assume that shareholders buy stock because they seek to gain financially, the answer is obvious: Good decisions increase the value of the stock, and poor decisions decrease it.

Given our observation, it follows that the financial manager acts in the shareholders' best interests by making decisions that increase the value of the stock. The appropriate goal for the financial manager can thus be stated quite easily: The goal of financial management is to maximize the current value per share of existing stock.

The goal of maximizing the value of the stock avoids the problems associated with the different goals we listed earlier. There is no ambiguity in the criterion, and there is no short-run versus long-run issue. We explicitly mean that our goal is to maximize the current stock value.

Because the goal of financial management is to maximize the value of the stock, we need to learn how to identify those investments and financing arrangements that favourably impact the value of the stock. This is precisely what we are studying. In fact, we could have defined corporate finance as the study of the relationship between business decisions and the value of the stock in the business.

To make the market value of the stock a valid measure of financial decisions requires an *efficient capital market*. In an efficient capital market, security prices fully reflect available information. The market sets the stock price to give the firm an accurate report card on its decisions. We return to capital market efficiency in Part Five.

A More General Goal

Given our goal of maximizing the value of the stock, an obvious question comes up: What is the appropriate goal when the firm is privately owned and has no traded stock? Corporations are certainly not the only type of business, and the stock in many corporations rarely changes hands, so it's difficult to say what the value per share is at any given time.

To complicate things further, some large Canadian companies such as Irving are privately owned. Many large firms in Canada are subsidiaries of foreign multinationals, while others are controlled by a single domestic shareholder.

Recognizing these complications, as long as we are dealing with for-profit businesses, only a slight modification is needed. The total value of the stock in a corporation is simply equal to the value of the owners' equity. Therefore, a more general way of stating our goal is to maximize the market value of the owners' equity. This market value can be measured by a business appraiser or by investment bankers if the firm eventually goes public.

With this in mind, it doesn't matter whether the business is a proprietorship, a partnership, or a corporation. For each of these, good financial decisions increase the market value of the owners equity and poor financial decisions decrease it. In fact, although we choose to focus on corporations in the chapters ahead, the principles we develop apply to all forms of business. Many of them even apply to the not-for-profit sector.

Finally, our goal does not imply that the financial manager should take illegal or unethical actions in the hope of increasing the value of the equity in the firm. What we mean is that the financial manager best serves the owners of the business by identifying goods and services that add to the firm because they are desired and valued in the free marketplace.

> CONCEPT QUESTIONS
> 1. What is the goal of financial management?
> 2. What are some shortcomings of the goal of profit maximization?
> 3. How would you define corporate finance?

1.4 | THE AGENCY PROBLEM AND CONTROL OF THE CORPORATION

We've seen that the financial manager acts in the best interest of the shareholders by taking actions that increase the value of the stock. However, we've also seen that in large corporations ownership can be spread over a huge number of shareholders. Or a large shareholder may own a whole block of shares with large minority blocks owned by pension funds. In either case, this dispersion of ownership arguably means that management effectively controls the firm. In this case, will management necessarily act in the best interests of the shareholders? Put another way, might not management pursue its own goals at the shareholders' expense? We briefly consider some of the arguments next.

Agency Relationships

The relationship between shareholders and management is called an *agency relationship*. Such a relationship exists whenever someone (the principal) hires another (the agent) to represent his or her interests. For example, you might hire someone (an agent) to sell a car that you own. In all such relationships, there is a possibility of conflict of interest between the principal and the agent. Such conflict is called an **agency problem.**

In hiring someone to sell your car, you agree to pay a flat fee when the car sells. The agent's incentive is to make the sale, not necessarily to get you the best price. If you paid a commission of, say, 10 percent of the sale price instead of a flat fee, this problem might not exist. This example illustrates that the way an agent is compensated is one factor that affects agency problems.

agency problem
The possibility of conflicts of interest between the shareholders and management of a firm.

Management Goals

To see how management and shareholders' interests might differ, imagine that the firm has a new investment under consideration. The new investment favourably impacts the share value, but it is a relatively risky venture. The owners of the firm may wish to take the investment because the stock value will rise, but management may not because of the possibility that things will turn out badly and management jobs will be lost. If management does not take the investment, the shareholders may have lost a valuable opportunity. This is one example of an *agency cost.*

More generally, agency costs refer to the costs of the conflict of interests between shareholders and management. These costs can be indirect or direct. An indirect agency cost is a lost opportunity such as the one we have just described.

Direct agency costs come in two forms: The first is a corporate expenditure that benefits management but costs the shareholders. Perhaps the purchase of a luxurious and unneeded corporate jet would fall under this heading. The second direct agency cost is an expense that arises from the need to monitor management actions. Paying outside auditors to assess the accuracy of financial statement information is one example.

Some argue that if left to themselves, managers would maximize the amount of resources over which they have control or, more generally, corporate power or wealth. This goal could lead to an overemphasis on corporate size or growth. For example, cases where management is accused of overpaying to buy up another company just to increase the size of the business or to demonstrate corporate power are not uncommon. Obviously, if overpayment does take place, such a purchase does not benefit the shareholders.

Our discussion indicates that management may tend to overemphasize organizational survival to protect job security. Also, management may dislike outside interference, so independence and corporate self-sufficiency may be important goals.[4]

---

[4] A survey of CEOs identified these factors. See G. Donaldson, *Managing Corporate Wealth: The Operations of a Comprehensive Goals System* (New York: Praeger Publishers, 1984).

Do Managers Act in the Shareholders' Interests?

Whether managers do, in fact, act in the best interest of shareholders depends on two factors. First, how closely are management goals aligned with shareholder goals? This question relates to the way managers are compensated. Second, can managers be replaced if they do not pursue shareholder goals? This issue relates to control of the firm. As we discuss, there are a number of reasons to think that, even in the largest firms, management has a significant incentive to act in the interest of shareholders.

Managerial Compensation   Management frequently has a significant economic incentive to increase share value for two reasons: First, managerial compensation, particularly at the top, is usually tied to financial performance in general and often to the share value in particular. For example, managers are frequently given the option to buy stock at bargain prices. The more the stock is worth, the more valuable is this option. The second incentive managers have relates to job prospects. Better performers within the firm get promoted. More generally, those managers who are successful in pursuing shareholder goals are in greater demand in the labour market and thus command higher salaries.

Control of the Firm   Control of the firm ultimately rests with shareholders. They elect the board of directors, who, in turn, hire and fire management. Management can be replaced by a takeover. Poorly managed firms are more attractive as acquisitions than well-managed firms because a greater turnaround potential exists. Thus, avoiding a takeover by another firm gives management another incentive to act in the shareholders' interest.

The available theory and evidence substantiate that shareholders control the firm and that shareholder wealth maximization is the relevant goal of the corporation. Even so, at times management goals are undoubtedly pursued at the expense of the shareholders, at least temporarily. For example, management may try to avoid the discipline of a potential takeover by instituting "poison pill" provisions to make the stock unattractive. Or the firm may issue non-voting stock to thwart a takeover attempt. Canadian shareholders, particularly pension funds and other institutional investors, are becoming increasingly active in campaigning against such management actions.[5]

Stakeholders   Our discussion thus far implies that management and shareholders are the only parties with an interest in the firm's decisions. This is an oversimplification, of course. Employees, customers, suppliers, and various levels of government all have financial interests in the firm.

stakeholder
Anyone who potentially has a claim on a firm.

Taken together, these various groups are called **stakeholders** in the firm. In general, a stakeholder is a shareholder, creditor, or other individual (or group) that potentially has a claim on the cash flows of the firm. Such groups also attempt to exert control over the firm by introducing alternate, socially oriented goals such as preserving the environment or creating employment equity. Even though stakeholder pressures may create additional costs for owners, almost all major corporations pay close attention to stakeholders. Table 1.2 summarizes concerns of various stakeholders.

Well-managed large corporations seek to maintain a reputation as good corporate citizens with detailed policies on important social issues. For example, major chartered banks require a favourable audit of a client's impact on the environment as

---

[5] We discuss takeovers and pension managers' activism in monitoring management activities in Chapter 21.

Inventory of typical stakeholders and issues | **T A B L E 1.2**

Company	Employees		Shareholders	Customers	Suppliers	Public Stakeholders	Competitors
Company history	General policy	Benefits	General policy	General policy	General policy	Public health, safety, and protection	General policy
Industry background	Compensation and rewards	Training and development	Shareholder communications and complaints	Customer communications	Relative power	Environmental issues	
Organization structure	Career planning	Employee assistance program	Shareholder advocacy	Product safety	Other supplier issues	Public policy involvement	
Economic performance	Health promotion	Absenteeism and turnover	Shareholder rights	Customer complaints		Community relations	
Competitive environment	Leaves of absence	Relationships with unions	Other shareholder issues	Special customer services		Social investment and donations	
Mission or purpose	Dismissal and appeal	Termination, layoff, and redundancy		Other customer issues			
Corporate codes	Retirement and termination counselling	Employment equity and discrimination					
Stakeholder and social issues	Women in management and on the board	Day care and family accommodation					
Management	Employee communication	Occupational health and safety					
	Part-time temporary, or contract employees	Other employee or human resource issues					

Source: M. B. E. Clarkson, "Analyzing Corporate Performance: A New Approach," *Canadian Investment Review,* Fall 1991, p. 70.

a condition for lending. Investors are becoming increasingly concerned about social issues and may seek the services of a Toronto-based consultant who tracks Canada's 1,500 largest companies on selected issues including policies on hiring and promotion, day care, and job creation.[6] Ethical investment funds offer an opportunity to buy shares in a portfolio of companies that meet stated criteria. Critics of ethical investing argue that it tends to produce lower financial returns because it is not driven by profit maximization. Ethical investors counter that they do better by backing firms that, because they act responsibly, perform well over the long run. Various studies reveal that sometimes ethical investing pays, sometimes it does not. All indications are that the trend toward paying increasing attention to stakeholders will continue.

CONCEPT QUESTIONS
1. What is an agency relationship?
2. What are agency problems and how do they come about? What are agency costs?
3. What incentives do managers in large corporations have to maximize share value?
4. What role do stakeholders play in determining corporate goals?

---

[6] A. Morantz, "Capitalism's Halo Effect," *Business Journal,* November 1989, p. 13.

1.5 | FINANCIAL INSTITUTIONS, FINANCIAL MARKETS, AND THE CORPORATION

We've seen that the primary advantages of the corporate form of organization are that ownership can be transferred more quickly and easily than with other forms and that money can be raised more readily. Both of these advantages are significantly enhanced by the existence of financial institutions and markets. Financial markets play an extremely important role in corporate finance.

The interplay between the corporation and the financial markets is extensive. Suppose we start with the firm selling shares of stock and borrowing money to raise cash. Cash flows to the firm from the financial market. The firm invests the cash in current and fixed assets. These assets generate some cash, some of which goes to pay corporate taxes. After taxes are paid, some of this cash flow is reinvested in the firm. The rest goes back to the financial markets as cash paid to creditors and shareholders.

The financial market, like any market, is just a way of bringing buyers and sellers together. In financial markets, debt and equity securities are bought and sold. As in other markets, financial markets are driven by supply and demand. As our discussion illustrates, when financial market participants with surplus funds invest in securities issued by a firm, they are *supplying* funds to the firm. In the same terminology, the firm is *demanding* funds from financial market participants.

Financial Institutions

Financial institutions act as *intermediaries* between investors (funds suppliers) and firms raising funds. (Federal and provincial governments and individuals also raise funds in financial markets, but our examples focus on firms.) Financial institutions justify their existence by providing a variety of services that promote the efficient allocation of funds. Canadian financial institutions include *chartered banks* and other *depository institutions-trust companies, credit unions, investment dealers, insurance companies, pension funds,* and *mutual funds.*

Table 1.3 shows the top 10 deposit-taking financial institutions in 1993. They include the Big Six chartered banks, one credit union (Mouvement Desjardins), and

TABLE 1.3 *Market share in the deposit-taking sector in 1993*	Total Worldwide Assets 1993 ($billion)	Share of Total Assets in Canada (1991)	Share of Total Assets in Canada (1993)
Royal Bank	$164.9	15%	18%
CIBC	141.3	13	15
Bank of Nova Scotia	121.7	8	10
Bank of Montreal	116.9	9	10
Toronto-Dominion	85.0	8	9
Mouvement Desjardins	74.7	6	10
CT Financial	46.1	5	5
National Bank	42.7	4	5
National Trustco	15.8	2	2
HongKong Bank of Canada	13.5	1	2
		Top 4—45%	Top 4—53%
		Top 10—71%	Top 10—86%

Note: Total deposit-taking assets includes banks, trust and loan companies, and credit unions. Bank of Nova Scotia 1993 figures include corporate assets of Montreal Trust.

Source: "Report on Business," *Globe and Mail,* December 7, 1994, p. B6. Used with permission.

a financial holding company (CT Financial, parent of Canada Trust). Because they are allowed to diversify by operating in all provinces, Canada's chartered banks are good sized on an international scale. Table 1.3 shows that the chartered banks hold the top five slots domestically.

Chartered banks operate under federal regulation, accepting deposits from suppliers of funds and making commercial loans to mid-sized businesses, corporate loans to large companies, and personal loans and mortgages to individuals. Banks make the majority of their income from the *spread* between the interest paid on deposits and the higher rate earned on loans. This process is called *indirect finance* because banks receive funds in the form of deposits and engage in a separate lending contract with funds demanders. Figure 1.2 illustrates indirect finance.

Chartered banks also provide other services that generate fees instead of spread income. For example, a large corporate customer seeking short-term debt funding can borrow *directly* from another large corporation with funds supplied through a *bankers acceptance.* This is an interest-bearing IOU stamped by a bank guaranteeing the borrower's credit. Instead of spread income, the bank receives a *stamping fee.* Bankers acceptances are an example of *direct finance* illustrated in Figure 1.2. Notice that the key difference between direct finance and indirect finance is that in direct finance funds do not pass through the bank's balance sheet in the form of a deposit and loan. Often called *securitization* because a security (the bankers acceptance) is created, direct finance is growing rapidly. Several major Canadian chartered banks have set the goal of receiving half of their income from fees generated from direct finance by the year 2000.

Trust companies also accept deposits and make loans. In addition, trust companies engage in fiduciary activities—managing assets for estates, registered retirement savings plans, and so on. Like trust companies, credit unions also accept deposits and make loans. In recent years, most large trust companies have been acquired by chartered banks.

Investment dealers are non-depository institutions that assist firms in issuing new securities in exchange for fee income. Investment dealers also aid investors in buying and selling securities. Chartered banks own majority stakes in 5 of Canada's top 15 investment dealers.

Insurance companies include property and casualty insurance and health and life insurance companies. Life insurance companies engage in indirect finance by accepting funds in a form similar to deposits and making loans.

Pension funds invest contributions from employers and employees in securities offered by financial markets. Mutual funds pool individual investments to purchase a diversified portfolio of securities.

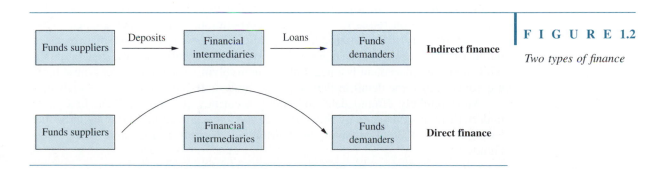

F I G U R E 1.2

Two types of finance

We base this survey of the principal activities of financial institutions on their main activities today. Recent deregulation now allows chartered banks, trust companies, insurance companies, and investment dealers to engage in most of the activities of the others with one exception: Chartered banks are not allowed to sell life insurance through their branch networks. This is likely to become allowed in the next Bank Act revision in 1997. Although not every institution plans to become a one-stop financial supermarket, the different types of institutions are likely to continue to become more alike.

Like financial institutions, financial markets differ. The principal differences concern the types of securities that are traded, how trading is conducted, and who the buyers and sellers are. Some of these differences are discussed next.

Money versus Capital Markets

money markets

Financial markets where short-term debt securities are bought and sold.

capital markets

Financial markets where long-term debt and equity securities are bought and sold.

Financial markets can be classified as either **money markets** or **capital markets.** Short-term debt securities of many varieties are bought and sold in money markets. These short-term debt securities are often called money-market instruments and are essentially IOUs. For example, a bankers acceptance represents short-term borrowing by large corporations and is a money-market instrument. Treasury bills are an IOU of the government of Canada. Capital markets are the markets for long-term debt and shares of stock, so the Toronto Stock Exchange, for example, is a capital market.

The money market is a dealer market. Generally, dealers buy and sell something for themselves, at their own risk. A car dealer, for example, buys and sells automobiles. In contrast, brokers and agents match buyers and sellers, but they do not actually own the commodity. A real estate agent or broker, for example, does not normally buy and sell houses.

The largest money-market dealers are chartered banks and investment dealers. Their trading facilities, along with other market participants, are connected electronically via telephone and computer, so the money market has no actual physical location.

Primary versus Secondary Markets

Financial markets function as both primary and secondary markets for debt and equity securities. The term *primary markets* are where these securities are bought and sold after the original sale. Equities are, of course, issued solely by corporations. Debt securities are issued by both governments and corporations. In the following discussion, we focus only on corporate securities.

Primary Markets   In a primary market transaction, the corporation is the seller, and the transaction raises money for the corporation. Corporations engage in two types of primary market transactions: public offerings and private placements. A public offering, as the name suggests, involves selling securities to the general public, while a private placement is a negotiated sale involving a specific buyer. These topics are covered in some detail in Part VI, so we only introduce the bare essentials here.

Most publicly offered debt and equity securities are underwritten. In Canada, underwriting is conducted by *investment dealers* specialized in marketing securities. Examples are RBC Dominion, ScotiaMcLeod, Nesbitt Burns, and CIBC Wood Gundy.

When a public offering is underwritten, an investment dealer or a group of investment dealers (called a *syndicate*) typically purchases the securities from the firm and markets them to the public. The underwriters hope to profit by reselling the securities to investors at a higher price than they pay the firm.

By law, public offerings of debt and equity must be registered with provincial authorities, of which the most important is the Ontario Securities Commission (OSC). Registration requires the firm to disclose a great deal of information before selling any securities. The accounting, legal, and underwriting costs of public offerings can be considerable.

Partly to avoid the various regulatory requirements and the expense of public offerings, debt and equity are often sold privately to large financial institutions such as life insurance companies or mutual funds. Such private placements do not have to be registered with the OSC and do not require the involvement of underwriters.

Secondary Markets   A secondary market transaction involves one owner or creditor selling to another. Therefore, the secondary markets provide the means for transferring ownership of corporate securities. There are two kinds of secondary markets: *auction* markets and *dealer* markets.

Dealer markets in stocks and long-term debt are called *over-the-counter* (OTC) markets. Trading in debt securities takes place over the counter. The expression *over the counter* refers to days of old when securities were literally bought and sold at counters in offices around the country. Today, like the money market, a significant fraction of the market for stocks and all of the market for long-term debt have no central location; the many dealers are connected electronically.

The equity shares of most of the large firms in Canada trade in organized auction and dealer markets. The largest stock market in Canada is the Toronto Stock Exchange (TSE). Table 1.4 shows the top 20 stock exchanges in the world in 1994; the TSE ranked number 12. Smaller stock exchanges in Canada include the Montreal Stock Exchange and the Vancouver Stock Exchange.

Auction markets differ from dealer markets in two ways: First, an auction market or exchange, unlike a dealer market, has a physical location (like Bay Street or Wall Street). Second, in a dealer market, most of the buying and selling is done by the dealer. The primary purpose of an auction market, on the other hand, is to match those who wish to sell with those who wish to buy. Dealers play a limited role. The TSE offers both floor trading and trading on a wide-area computer network. This technological shift makes the TSE a hybrid of auction and dealer markets.[7]

Listing   Stocks that trade on an organized exchange are said to be listed on that exchange. To be listed, firms must meet certain minimum criteria concerning, for example, asset size and number of shareholders. These criteria differ for various exchanges.

The TSE has the most stringent requirements of the exchanges in Canada. For example, to be listed on the TSE, a company is expected to have a market value for its publicly held shares of at least $2 million and a total of at least 300 shareholders with at least 100 shares each. There are additional minimums on earnings, assets, and number of shares outstanding.

---

[7] S. McHale, "TSE Votes to Computerize Floor Trading," *Globe and Mail,* February 13, 1992, p. B7.

T A B L E 1.4 | *World equity trading summary of top 20 exchanges (millions of U.S. dollars)*

	Equity Trading		Market Capitalization Domestic Shares Only	
Exchanges	1994 Jan.–June	1993 Jan.–Dec.	1994 Jan.–June	1993 Jan.–Dec.
New York	$1,270,365.5	$2,283,389.6	$4,164,759.9	$4,220,974.3
London	538,597.7	857,330.9	1,118,771.5	1,198,554.1
Tokyo	502,981.9	792,976.7	3,851,728.4	2,906,298.7
Germany	362,022.1	594,943.1	464,626.7	460,753.6
Taiwan	324,389.0	352,624.4	208,961.7	193,251.5
Switzerland	136,644.0	209,884.5	276,254.9	270,879.1
Korea	132,286.8	211,968.4	159,445.3	139,583.9
Paris	108,130.2	171,780.1	434,822.9	455,484.6
Osaka	95,165.3	131,998.8	3,219,684.6	N/A
Italy	84,946.4	66,035.7	184,341.5	144,045.0
Hong Kong	75,378.8	132,286.6	289,884.7	385,042.7
Toronto	**70,462.2**	**110,634.3**	**300,859.4**	**325,246.8**
Kuala Lumpur	54,195.5	145,528.8	173,838.6	219,758.7
Australia	50,425.3	67,791.8	209,590.5	199,891.4
Mexico	47,122.6	63,733.1	174,324.4	200,865.2
Amsterdam	47,013.1	67,019.7	201,375.1	182,628.5
Buenos Aires	46,180.9	49,690.3	41,390.4	44,055.1
Thailand	41,314.1	83,842.8	112,014.9	127,473.7
Singapore	40,714.7	83,529.4	129,844.6	132,677.8
Stockholm	38,864.9	42,753.4	103,532.4	106,968.0

Source: *TSE Review,* September 1994.

CONCEPT QUESTIONS
1. What are the principal financial institutions in Canada? What is the principal role of each?
2. What are direct and indirect finance? How do they differ?
3. How are money and capital markets different?
4. What is a dealer market? How do dealer and auction markets differ?
5. What is the largest auction market in Canada?

1.6 | TRENDS IN FINANCIAL MARKETS AND FINANCIAL MANAGEMENT

Like all markets, financial markets are experiencing rapid globalization. For example, shares of Canadian firms like Bank of Montreal and Seagram trade on the New York Stock Exchange along with other non-U.S. companies like Telmex, the Mexican telecommunications giant. Globalization also makes it harder for investors to shelter their portfolios from financial shocks in other countries. In late 1994 and early 1995, the peso devaluation caused Telmex to lose almost two-thirds of its value in U.S. dollars. At the same time, interest rates, foreign exchange rates, and other macroeconomic variables have become more volatile. The toolkit of available financial management techniques has expanded rapidly in response to a need to control increased risk from volatility and to track complexities arising from dealings in many countries. Computer technology improvements are making new **financial engineering** applications practical.

financial engineering
Creation of new securities or financial processes.

When financial managers or investment dealers design new securities or financial processes, their efforts are referred to as financial engineering. Successful financial engineering reduces and controls risk and minimizes taxes. Financial engineering creates a variety of debt securities and reinforces the trend toward securitization of credit introduced earlier. A controversial example is the invention and rapid growth of trading in options, futures, and other **derivative securities.** Derivative securities are very useful in controlling risk, but they have also produced large losses when mishandled. At the time of writing, the largest financial accident with derivatives was a loss of $1.5 billion in futures that bankrupted Barings, a venerable British merchant bank in 1995.

Financial engineering also seeks to reduce financing costs of issuing securities as well as the costs of complying with rules laid down by regulatory authorities. An example is the Prompt Offering Prospectus (POP) allowing firms that frequently issue new equity to bypass most of the OSC registration requirements.

In addition to financial engineering, advances in computer technology also created opportunities to combine different types of financial institutions to take advantage of economies of scale and scope. For example, Royal Bank, Canada's largest chartered bank, owns Royal Trust and RBC Dominion Securities. Such large institutions operate in all provinces and internationally and enjoy more lax regulations in some jurisdictions than in others. Financial institutions pressure authorities to deregulate in a push-pull process called the **regulatory dialectic.**

For example, in the mid-1980s Quebec removed almost all restrictions on combining different types of financial institutions. As a result, Quebec-based institutions grew much faster than their competitors outside the province. At this time, Quebec was the only province that allowed chartered banks to own investment dealers. Quebec's example pressured regulators to allow chartered banks this power in other provinces.

More broadly, the regulatory dialectic has produced Canada's current regulations that allow financial institutions almost unlimited scope to enter each others' traditional businesses.[8]

These trends have made financial management a much more complex and technical activity. For this reason, many students of business find introductory finance one of their most challenging subjects. The trends we reviewed have also increased the stakes. In the face of increased global competition, the payoff for good financial management is great. The finance function is also becoming important in corporate strategic planning. The good news is that career opportunities (and compensation) in financial positions are quite attractive.

derivative securities
Options, futures, and other securities whose value derives from the price of another, underlying, asset.

regulatory dialectic
The pressures financial institutions and regulatory bodies exert on each other.

1.7 | OUTLINE OF THE TEXT

Now that we've completed a quick tour of the concerns of corporate finance, we can take a closer look at the organization of this book. The text is organized into the following nine parts:

Part I: Overview of Corporate Finance
Part II: Financial Statements and Long-Term Financial Planning
Part III: Valuation of Future Cash Flows
Part IV: Capital Budgeting

---

[8] This discussion draws on L. Kryzanowski and G. S. Roberts, "Bank Structure in Canada," in *Banking Structure in Major Countries,* ed., G. G. Kaufman (Boston: Kluwer Academic Publishers, 1992).

F. Anthony Comper on Financial Trends

Today's financial services industry is profoundly different from yesterday's. Tomorrow's promises even more change.

Boundaries separating the traditional four pillars of the financial services industry in Canada—the banks, the trusts, the insurance companies, and the investment dealers—have all but disappeared. Banks can now engage in trust and insurance business; trust companies can now own schedule II banks; banks can own investment dealers; insurance companies can compete in the traditional business activities of the other three. In short, all the pillars can play in each other's backyards.

In consequence of the removal of barriers separating the four pillars, the financial services industry has become intensely more competitive—to the benefit of consumers of financial services: With economies from enlarged scales of operation and greater efficiencies from the distribution side, today's financial institutions have been able to provide greater value at lower costs.

Consumers have also benefitted from—and the financial services industry in Canada has also had to respond to—intensely greater competition in the global arena for financial services. International capital controls—which long acted to protect and insulate domestic

financial institutions from global competition—are now dramatically less prevalent than they once were.

Finally, explosive advances in computerization have increased dramatically the processing capacities of today's financial institutions, permitting both more rapid responses to near instantaneous flows of information and the proliferation of new products and services ever more attuned to the needs of consumers. From swaps, bankers acceptances, and asset-backed securities, to image processing, voice-recognition, and "smart" cards, the range of options in today's marketplace is almost bewildering.

Expect even more change in the years ahead. Advances in information and computer technology can be expected to continue at breakneck speed; barriers to competition—both domestically and internationally—will continue to fall. New frontiers in the financial services industry will open up in consequence of economic and political reforms in Latin America, Eastern Europe, the former Soviet Union, and the Far East.

With intensified competition and seemingly ever greater complexity in financial arrangements, there will continue to be development of a plethora of new products whose precise characteristics we can only vaguely discern at this point in our history.

Although many aspects of the future of the financial services industry are cloudy, two features seem abundantly clear at this juncture. First, although the demands for various financial services will proliferate, advances in computer technology are bound to cause processing capacity to grow even faster in an industry already plagued by excess capacity. When this is combined with what promises to be an even more competitive environment, the stage is set for greater consolidation and rationalization, the result of which is likely to be fewer and larger institutions offering an even larger menu of financial services.

Second, intensified competition will inevitably result in financial institutions being even more customer-driven. Poor financial results, and even failure, will be the outcome for those financial institutions that fail to provide superior customer service.

F. Anthony Comper is president and chief operating officer of the Bank of Montreal. Over the years, Comper has held executive positions in virtually every major area of the bank, both in Canada and abroad. Prior to becoming chief operating officer on July 1, 1989, he served as executive vice president of operations; as a senior vice president in personal banking, treasury, and corporate and government banking, which included a posting as manager of the London (England) branch; and as vice president of systems development.

Part V: Risk and Return
Part VI: Long-Term Financing
Part VII: Cost of Capital and Long-Term Financial Policy
Part VIII: Short-Term Financial Planning and Management
Part IX: Topics in Corporate Finance

Part I of the text contains some introductory material and goes on to explain the relationship between accounting and cash flow. Part II explores financial statements and how they are used in finance in greater depth.

Parts III and IV contain our core discussion on valuation. In Part III, we develop the basic procedures for valuing future cash flows with particular emphasis on stocks and bonds. Part IV draws on this material and deals with capital budgeting and the effect of long-term investment decisions on the firm.

In Part V, we develop some tools for evaluating risk. We then discuss how to evaluate the risks associated with long-term investments by the firm. The emphasis in this section is on coming up with a benchmark for making investment decisions.

Parts VI and VII deal with the related issues of long-term financing, dividend policy, and capital structure. We discuss corporate securities in some detail and describe the procedures used to raise capital and sell securities to the public. We also introduce and describe the important concept of the cost of capital. We go on to examine dividends and dividend policy and important considerations in determining a capital structure.

The working capital question is addressed in Part VIII. The subjects of short-term financial planning, cash management, and credit management are covered.

The final part, Part IX, contains several important special topics. There is a chapter on the subject of options and optionlike securities such as warrants and convertible bonds, a chapter on mergers and acquisitions, and a chapter on international aspects of corporate finance.

1.8 | SUMMARY AND CONCLUSIONS

This chapter has introduced you to some of the basic ideas in corporate finance. In it, we saw that:

1. Corporate finance has three main areas of concern:
   a. What long-term investments should the firm take? This is the capital budgeting decision.
   b. Where will the firm get the long-term financing to pay for its investment? In other words, what mixture of debt and equity should we use to fund our operations? This is the capital structure decision.
   c. How should the firm manage its everyday financial activities? This is the working capital decision.
2. The goal of financial management in a for-profit business is to make decisions that increase the value of the stock or, more generally, increase the market value of the equity.
3. The corporate form of organization is superior to other forms when it comes to raising money and transferring ownership interest, but it has the disadvantage of double taxation.

4. There is the possibility of conflicts between shareholders and management in a large corporation. We called these conflicts agency problems and discussed how they might be controlled and reduced.

5. The advantages of the corporate form are enhanced by the existence of financial markets. Financial institutions function to promote the efficiency of financial markets. Financial markets function as both primary and secondary markets for corporate securities and can be organized as either dealer or auction markets. Globalization, deregulation, and financial engineering are important forces shaping financial markets and the practice of financial management.

Of the topics we've discussed thus far, the most important is the goal of financial management: maximizing the value of the stock. Throughout the text, as we analyze financial decisions, we always ask the same question: How does the decision under consideration affect the value of the shares?

Key Terms

capital budgeting (page 3)

capital structure (page 3)

working capital management (page 5)

sole proprietorship (page 5)

partnership (page 6)

corporation (page 6)

agency problem (page 11)

stakeholder (page 12)

money markets (page 16)

capital markets (page 16)

financial engineering (page 18)

derivative securities (page 19)

regulatory dialectic (page 19)

Questions and Problems

**Basic
(Questions 1–8)**

1. **The Financial Management Decision Process**   What are the three types of financial management decisions? For each type of decision, give an example of a business transaction that would be relevant.

2. **Sole Proprietorships and Partnerships**   What are the four primary disadvantages to the sole proprietorship and partnership forms of business organization? What benefits are there to these types of business organization as opposed to the corporate form?

3. **Corporate Organization**   What is the primary disadvantage of the corporate form of organization? Name at least two of the advantages of corporate organization.

4. **Corporate Finance Organizational Structure**   In a large corporation, what are the two distinct groups that report to the chief financial officer? Which group is the focus of corporate finance?

5. **The Goal of Financial Management**   What goal should always motivate the actions of the firm's financial manager?

6. **Corporate Agency Issues**   Who owns a corporation? Describe the process whereby the owners control the firm's management. What is the main reason that an agency relationship exists in the corporate form of organization? In this context, what kind of problems can arise?

7. **Financial Markets**   An initial public offering (IPO) of a company's securities is a term you've probably noticed in the financial press. Is an IPO a primary market transaction or a secondary market transaction?

Basic
(Continued)

8. **Financial Markets**   What does it mean when we say the Toronto Stock Exchange is both an auction market and a dealer market? How are auction markets different from dealer markets? What kind of market is NASDAQ?

9. **Not-for-Profit Firm Goals**   Suppose you were the financial manager of a not-for-profit business (a not-for-profit hospital, perhaps). What kinds of goals do you think would be appropriate?

Intermediate
(Questions 9–17)

10. **Firm Goals and Stock Value**   Evaluate the following statement: "Managers should not focus on the current stock value because doing so will lead to an overemphasis on short-term profits at the expense of long-term profits."

11. **Firm Goals and Ethics**   Can our goal of maximizing the value of the stock conflict with other goals, such as avoiding unethical or illegal behavior? In particular, do you think subjects like customer and employee safety, the environment, and the general good of society fit in this framework, or are they essentially ignored? Try to think of some specific scenarios to illustrate your answer.

12. **Firm Goals and Multinational Firms**   Would our goal of maximizing the value of the stock be different if we were thinking about financial management in a foreign country? Why or why not?

13. **Agency Issues and Corporate Control**   Suppose you own stock in a company. The current price per share is $25. Another company has just announced that it wants to buy your company and will pay $35 per share to acquire all the outstanding stock. Your company's management immediately begins fighting off this hostile bid. Is management acting in the shareholders' best interests? Why or why not?

14. **Agency Issues and International Finance**   Corporate ownership varies around the world. Historically, individuals have owned the majority of shares in public corporations in the United States. In Canada this is also the case, but ownership is more often concentrated in the hands of a majority shareholder. In Germany and Japan, banks, other financial institutions, and large companies own most of the shares in public corporations. How do you think these ownership differences affect the severity of agency costs in different countries?

15. **Major Institutions and Markets**   What are the major types of financial institutions and financial markets in Canada?

16. **Direct versus Indirect Finance**   What is the difference between direct and indirect finance? Give an example of each.

17. **Current Major Trends**   What are some of the major trends in Canadian financial markets? Explain how these trends affect the practice of financial management in Canada.

Suggested Readings

A survey of trends affecting chartered banks and other Canadian financial institutions is:

Kryzanowski, L., and G. S. Roberts. "Bank Structure in Canada." In *Banking Structure in Major Countries,* ed. G. G. Kaufman. Boston: Kluwer Academic Publishers, 1992.

Two nontechnical discussions of financial engineering and trends are:

Finnerty, J. D. "Financial Engineering in Corporate Finance: An Overview." In *The Handbook of Financial Engineering,* eds. C. W. Smith and C. W. Smithson. Grand Rapids: Harper Business, 1990.

Lessard, D. R. "Global Competition and Corporate Finance in the 1990s." *Journal of Applied Corporate Finance,* Winter 1991, pp. 59–72.

Financial Statements, Taxes, and Cash Flow

In this chapter, we examine financial statements, cash flow, and taxes. Our emphasis is not on preparing financial statements. Instead, we recognize that financial statements are frequently a key source of information for financial decisions, so our goal is to briefly examine such statements and point out some of their more relevant features along with a few limitations. We pay special attention to some of the practical details of cash flow.

One very important topic is taxes because cash flows are measured after taxes. Our discussion looks at how corporate and individual taxes are computed and at how investors are taxed on different types of income. A basic understanding of the Canadian tax system is essential for success in applying the tools of financial management.

2.1 | THE BALANCE SHEET

The **balance sheet** is a snapshot of the firm. it is a convenient means of organizing and summarizing what a firm owns (its *assets*), what a firm owes (its *liabilities*), and the difference between the two (the firm's *equity*) at a given time. Figure 2.1 illustrates how the balance sheet is constructed. As shown, the left-hand side lists the assets of the firm, and the right-hand side lists the liabilities and equity.

balance sheet
Financial statement showing a firm's accounting value on a particular date.

Assets: The Left-Hand Side

Assets are classified as either *current* or *fixed.* A fixed asset is one that has a relatively long life. Fixed assets can either be *tangible,* such as a truck or a computer, or *intangible,* such as a trademark or patent. Accountants refer to these assets as *capital assets*. A current asset has a life of less than one year. This means that the asset will convert to cash within 12 months. For example, inventory would normally be purchased and sold within a year and is thus classified as a current asset. Obviously, cash itself is a current asset. Accounts receivable (money owed to the firm by its customers) is also a current asset.

Liabilities and Owners' Equity: The Right-Hand Side

The firm's liabilities are the first thing listed on the right-hand side of the balance sheet. These are classified as either *current* or *long-term.* Current liabilities, like

F I G U R E 2.1

The balance sheet model of the firm. Left side lists total value of assets. Right side, or total value of the firm to investors, determines how the value is distributed.

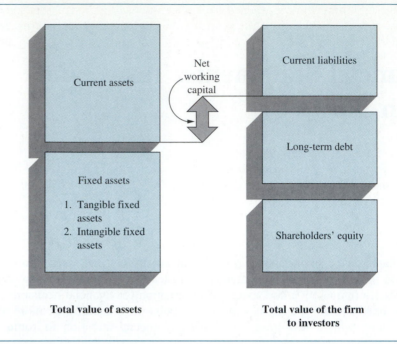

Total value of assets   Total value of the firm
                                                       to investors

current assets, have a life of less than one year (meaning they must be paid within the year) and are listed before long-term liabilities. Accounts payable (money the firm owes to its suppliers) is one example of a current liability.

A debt that is not due in the coming year is a long-term liability. A loan that the firm will pay off in five years is one such long-term debt. Firms borrow long-term from a variety of sources. We use the terms *bond* and *bondholders* generically to refer to long-term debt and long-term creditors, respectively.

Finally, by definition, the difference between the total value of the assets (current and fixed) and the total value of the liabilities (current and long-term) is the *shareholders' equity,* also called *common equity* or *owners' equity.* This feature of the balance sheet is intended to reflect the fact that, if the firm were to sell all of its assets and use the money to pay off its debts, whatever residual value remained would belong to the shareholders. So, the balance sheet balances because the value of the left-hand side always equals the value of the right-hand side. That is, the value of the firm's assets is equal to the sum of liabilities and shareholders' equity:[1]

Assets = Liabilities + Shareholders' equity   [2.1]

This is the balance sheet identity or equation, and it always holds because shareholders' equity is defined as the difference between assets and liabilities.

Net Working Capital

As shown in Figure 2.1, the difference between a firm's current assets and its current liabilities is called *net working capital.* Net working capital is positive when current

---

[1] The terms *owners' equity* and *shareholders' equity* are used interchangeably to refer to the equity in a corporation. The term *net worth* is also used. Variations exist in addition to these.

assets exceed current liabilities. Based on the definitions of current assets and current liabilities, this means that the cash available over the next 12 months exceeds the cash that must be paid over that same period. For this reason, net working capital is usually positive in a healthy firm.

E X A M P L E | **2.1**   **Building the Balance Sheet**

A firm has current assets of $100, fixed assets of $500, short-term debt of $70, and long-term debt of $200. What does the balance sheet look like? What is shareholders' equity? What is net working capital?

In this case, total assets are $100 + 500 = $600 and total liabilities are $70 + 200 = $270, so shareholders' equity is the difference: $600 − 270 = $330. The balance sheet would thus look like:

Assets		Liabilities	
Current assets	$100	Current liabilities	$ 70
Fixed assets	500	Long-term debt	200
		Shareholders' equity	330
Total assets	$600	Total liabilities and shareholders' equity	$600

Net working capital is the difference between current assets and current liabilities, or $100 − 70 = $30.

Table 2.1A shows a simplified balance sheet for Canadian Enterprises Limited. The assets in the balance sheet are listed in order of the length of time it takes for them to convert to cash in the normal course of business. Similarly, the liabilities are listed in the order in which they would normally be paid.

The structure of the assets for a particular firm reflects the line of business that the firm is in and also managerial decisions about how much cash and inventory to maintain and about credit policy, fixed asset acquisition, and so on.

The liabilities side of the balance sheet primarily reflects managerial decisions about capital structure and the use of short-term debt. For example, in 1995, total long-term debt for Canadian Enterprises was $454 and total equity was $640 + 1,629 = $2,269, so total long-term financing was $454 + 2,269 = $2,723. Of this amount, $454/2,723 = 16.67% was long-term debt. This percentage reflects capital structure decisions made in the past by the management of Canadian.

				T A B L E 2.1A	
CANADIAN ENTERPRISES Balance Sheets as of December 31, 1994 and 1995 ($ in millions)					
	1994	1995		1994	1995
Assets			*Liabilities and Owners' Equity*		
Current assets			Current liabilities		
Cash	$ 114	$ 160	Accounts payable	$ 232	$ 266
Accounts recievable	445	688	Notes payable	196	123
Inventory	553	555	Total	$ 428	$ 389
Total	$1,112	$1,403			
			Long-term debt	$ 408	$ 454
Fixed assets			Owners' equity		
Net, plant and equipment	$1,644	$1,709	Common shares	600	640
			Retained earnings	1,320	1,629
			Total	$1,920	$2,269
Total assets	$2,756	$3,112	Total liabilities and owners' equity	$2,756	$3,112

Three particularly important things to keep in mind when examining a balance sheet are liquidity, debt versus equity, and market value versus book value.[2]

Liquidity

Liquidity refers to the speed and ease with which an asset can be converted to cash. Gold is a relatively liquid asset; a custom manufacturing facility is not. Liquidity really has two dimensions: ease of conversion versus loss of value. Any asset can be converted to cash quickly if we cut the price enough. A highly liquid asset is therefore one that can be quickly sold without significant loss of value. An illiquid asset is one that cannot be quickly converted to cash without a substantial price reduction.

Assets are normally listed on the balance sheet in order of decreasing liquidity, meaning that the most liquid assets are listed first. Current assets are relatively liquid and include cash and those assets that we expect to convert to cash over the next 12 months. Accounts receivable, for example, represents amounts not yet collected from customers on sales already made. Naturally, we hope these will convert to cash in the near future. Inventory is probably the least liquid of the current assets, at least for many businesses.

Fixed assets are, for the most part, relatively illiquid. These consist of tangible things such as buildings and equipment. Intangible assets, such as a trademark, have no physical existence but can be very valuable. Like tangible fixed assets, they won't ordinarily convert to cash and are generally considered illiquid.

Liquidity is valuable. The more liquid a business is, the less likely it is to experience financial distress (that is, difficulty in paying debts or buying needed assets). Unfortunately, liquid assets are generally less profitable to hold. For example, cash holdings are the most liquid of all investments, but they sometimes earn no return at all—they just sit there. Therefore, the trade-off is between the advantages of liquidity and forgone potential profits. We discuss this trade-off further in the rest of the book.

Debt versus Equity

To the extent that a firm borrows money, it usually gives creditors first claim to the firm's cash flow. Equity holders are only entitled to the residual value, the portion left after creditors are paid. The value of this residual portion is the shareholders' equity in the firm and is simply the asset value less the value of the firm's liabilities:

$$\text{Shareholders' equity} = \text{Assets} - \text{Liabilities}$$

This is true in an accounting sense because shareholders' equity is defined as this residual portion. More importantly, it is true in an economic sense: If the firm sells its assets and pays its debts, whatever cash is left belongs to the shareholders.

The use of debt in a firm's capital structure is called *financial leverage*. The more debt a firm has (as a percentage of assets), the greater is its degree of financial leverage. As we discuss in later chapters, debt acts like a lever in the sense that using it can greatly magnify both gains and losses. So financial leverage increases the potential reward to shareholders, but it also increases the potential for financial distress and business failure.

Market Value versus Book Value

The values shown on the balance sheet for the firm's assets are *book values* and generally are not what the assets are actually worth. Under **Generally Accepted**

generally accepted accounting principles (GAAP)
The common set of standards and procedures by which audited financial statements are prepared.

---

[2] Chapters 3 and 4 expand on financial statement analysis.

Accounting Principles (GAAP), audited financial statements show assets at *historical cost.* In other words, assets are carried on the books at what the firm paid for them, no matter how long ago they were purchased or how much they are worth today.

For current assets, market value and book value might be somewhat similar because current assets are bought and converted to cash over a relatively short span of time. In other circumstances, they might differ quite a bit. Moreover, for fixed assets, it would be purely a coincidence if the actual market value of an asset (what the asset could be sold for) were equal to its book value. For example, a railroad might own enormous tracts of land purchased a century or more ago. What the railroad paid for that land could be hundreds or thousands of times less than it is worth today. The balance sheet would nonetheless show the historical cost.

Since book values are seldom what assets are worth today, you might wonder why accountants use them. Their rationale is linked to two accounting principles: *objectivity* and *conservatism.* Book values are objective as they are a matter of record and not subject to opinion. Due to inflation, book values generally understate the market values of assets and so are conservative. When they know that asset market values are significantly *below* book values, accountants write down assets. A well-known example is the major write-down of assets in the form of Third World loans by all major Canadian chartered banks in the late 1980s.[3]

The balance sheet is potentially useful to many different parties. A supplier might look at the size of accounts payable relative to total purchases to see how promptly the firm pays its bills. A potential creditor would examine the liquidity and degree of financial leverage. Managers within the firm can track things like the amount of cash and the amount of inventory that the firm keeps on hand. Uses such as these are discussed in more detail in Chapter 3.

Managers and investors are frequently interested in knowing the value of the firm. This information is not on the balance sheet. The fact that balance sheet assets are listed at cost means that there is no necessary connection between the total assets shown and the value of the firm. Indeed, many of the most valuable assets that a firm might have—good management, a good reputation, talented employees—don't appear on the balance sheet at all.

Similarly, the shareholders' equity figure on the balance sheet and the true value of the stock need not be related. For financial managers, then, the accounting value of the stock is not an especially important concern; it is the market value that matters. Henceforth, whenever we speak of the value of an asset or the value of the firm, we normally mean its *market value.* So, for example, when we say the goal of the financial manager is to increase the value of the stock, we mean the market value of the stock.

E X A M P L E | 2.2   **Market versus Book Values**

The Quebec Corporation has fixed assets with a book value of $700 and an appraised market value of about $1,000. Net working capital is $400 on the books, but approximately $600 would be realized if all the current accounts were liquidated. Quebec Corporation has $500 in long-term debt, both book value and market value. What is the book value of the equity? What is the market value?

We can construct two simplified balance sheets, one in accounting (book value) terms and one in economic (market value) terms:

---

[3] In such cases, the asset is recorded at the lesser of market or book value.

QUEBEC CORPORATION
Balance Sheets
Market Value versus Book Value

	Book	Market		Book	Market
Assets			*Liabilities*		
Net working capital	$ 400	$ 600	Long-term debt	$ 500	$ 500
Net fixed assets	700	1,000	Shareholders' equity	600	1,100
	$1,100	$1,600		$1,100	$1,600

In this example, shareholders' equity is actually worth almost twice as much as what is shown on the books. The distinction between book and market values is important precisely because book values can be so different from true economic value.

CONCEPT QUESTIONS

1. What is the balance sheet identity?
2. What is liquidity? Why is it important?
3. What do we mean by financial leverage?
4. Explain the difference between accounting value and market value. Which is more important to the financial manager? Why?

2.2 | THE INCOME STATEMENT

income statement

Financial statement summarizing a firm's performance over a period of time.

The **income statement** measures performance over some period of time, usually a year. The income statement equation is

Revenues − Expenses = Income   [2.1]

If you think of the balance sheet as a snapshot, then you can think of the income statement as a video recording covering the period between before and after pictures. Table 2.1B gives a simplified income statement for Canadian Enterprises.

The initial thing reported on an income statement would usually be revenue and expenses from the firm's principal operations. Subsequent parts include, among other things, financing expenses such as interest paid. Taxes paid are reported separately. The last item is *net income* (the so-called bottom line). Net income is often expressed on a per-share basis and called *earnings per share (EPS)*.

T A B L E 2.1B

CANADIAN ENTERPRISES
1995 Income Statement
($ in millions)

Net sales		$1,509
Cost of goods sold		750
Depreciation		65
Earnings before interest and taxes		$ 694
Interest paid		70
Taxable income		$ 624
Taxes		250
Net income		$ 374
Addition to retained earnings	$ 309	
Dividends	65	

As indicated, Canadian paid cash dividends of $65. The difference between net income and cash dividends, $309, is the addition to retained earnings for the year. This amount is added to the cumulative retained earnings account on the balance sheet. If you'll look back at the two balance sheets for Canadian, you'll see that retained earnings did go up by this amount, $1,320 + 309 = $1,629.

E X A M P L E | 2.3   **Calculating Earnings and Dividends per Share**

Suppose that Canadian had 200 million shares outstanding at the end of 1995. Based on the preceding income statement, what was Canadian's EPS? What were the dividends per share?

From the income statement, Canadian had a net income of $374 million for the year. Since 200 million shares were outstanding, EPS was $374/200 = $1.87 per share. Similarly, dividends per share were $65/200 = $.325 per share.

When looking at an income statement, the financial manager needs to keep three things in mind: GAAP, cash versus non-cash items, and time and costs. |

GAAP and the Income Statement

An income statement prepared using GAAP shows revenue when it accrues. This is not necessarily when the cash comes in. The general rule (the realization principle) is to recognize revenue when the earnings process is virtually complete and the value of an exchange of goods or services is known or can be reliably determined. In practice, this principle usually means that revenue is recognized at the time of sale, which need not be the same as the time of collection.

Costs shown on the income statement are based on the matching principle. The basic idea here is first to determine revenues as just described and then match those revenues with the costs associated with producing them. So, if we manufacture and then sell a product on credit, the revenue is realized at the time of sale. The production and other costs associated with the sale of that product would likewise be recognized at that time. Once again, the actual cash outflows may have occurred at some very different time.

As a result of the way revenues and costs are realized, the figures shown on the income statement may not be at all representative of the actual cash inflows and outflows that occurred during a particular period.

Non-Cash Items

A primary reason that accounting income differs from cash flow is that an income statement contains **non-cash items.** The most important of these is *depreciation*. Suppose a firm purchases an asset for $5,000 and pays in cash. Obviously, the firm has a $5,000 cash outflow at the time of purchase. However, instead of deducting the $5,000 as an expense, an accountant might depreciate the asset over a five-year period.

If the depreciation is straight-line and the asset is written down to zero over that period, $5,000/5 = $1,000 would be deducted each year as an expense.[4] The important thing to recognize is that this $1,000 deduction isn't cash—it's an accounting number. The actual cash outflow occurred when the asset was purchased.

non-cash items *Expenses charged against revenues that do not directly affect cash flow, such as depreciation.*

---

[4] By straight-line, we mean that the depreciation deduction is the same every year. By written down to zero, we mean that the asset is assumed to have no value at the end of five years. Tax depreciation is discussed in more detail later in the chapter.

The depreciation deduction is simply another application of the matching principle in accounting. The revenues associated with an asset would generally occur over some length of time. So the accountant seeks to match the expense of purchasing the asset with the benefits produced from owning it.

As we shall see, for the financial manager, the actual timing of cash inflows and outflows is critical in coming up with a reasonable estimate of market value, so we need to learn how to separate the cash flows from the non-cash accounting entries.

Time and Costs

It is often useful to think of the future as having two distinct parts: the short run and the long run. These are not precise time periods. The distinction has to do with whether costs are fixed or variable. In the long run, all business costs are variable. Given sufficient time, assets can be sold, debts can be paid, and so on.

If our time horizon is relatively short, however, some costs are effectively fixed—they must be paid no matter what (property taxes, for example). Other costs, such as wages to workers and payments to suppliers, are still variable. As a result, even in the short run, the firm can vary its output level by varying expenditures in these areas.

The distinction between fixed and variable costs is important, at times, to the financial manager, but the way costs are reported on the income statement is not a good guide as to which costs are which. The reason is that, in practice, accountants tend to classify costs as either product costs or period costs.

Product costs include such things as raw materials, direct labour expense, and manufacturing overhead. These are reported on the income statements as costs of goods sold, but they include both fixed and variable costs. Similarly, period costs are incurred during a particular time period and are reported as selling, general, and administrative expenses. Once again, some of these period costs may be fixed and others may be variable. The company president's salary, for example, is a period cost and is probably fixed, at least in the short run.

CONCEPT QUESTIONS

1. What is the income statement equation?
2. What are three things to keep in mind when looking at an income statement?
3. Why is accounting income not the same as cash flow? Give two reasons.

2.3 | CASH FLOW

At this point, we are ready to discuss one of the most important pieces of financial information that can be gleaned from financial statements: cash flow. By cash flow, we simply mean the difference between the number of dollars that come in and the number that go out. A crucial input to sound financial management, cash flow analysis is used throughout the book. For example, bankers lending to businesses are looking increasingly at borrowers' cash flows as the most reliable measures of each company's ability to repay its loans. In another example, most large companies base their capital budgets for investments in plant and equipment on analysis of cash flow. As a result, there is an excellent payoff in later chapters for knowledge of cash flow.

There is no standard financial statement for presenting this information in the way that we wish. Therefore, we discuss how to calculate cash flow for Canadian

Enterprises and point out how the result differs from standard financial statement calculations. There is a standard accounting statement called the statement of cash flows, but it is concerned with a somewhat different issue and should not be confused with what is discussed in this section. The accounting statement of cash flows is discussed in Chapter 3.

From the balance sheet identity, we know that the value of a firm's assets is equal to the value of its liabilities plus the value of its equity. Similarly, the cash flow from assets must equal the sum of the cash flow to bondholders (or creditors) plus the cash flow to shareholders (or owners):

$$\text{Cash flow from assets} = \text{Cash flow to bondholders} \qquad [2.3]$$
$$+ \text{Cash flow to shareholders}$$

This is the cash flow identity. It says that the cash flow from the firm's assets is equal to the cash flow paid to suppliers of capital to the firm. A firm generates cash through its various activities; that cash is either used to pay creditors or paid out to the owners of the firm.

Cash Flow from Assets

Cash flow from assets involves three components: operating cash flow, capital spending, and additions to net working capital. *Operating cash flow* refers to the cash flow that results from the firm's day-to-day activities of producing and selling. Expenses associated with the firm's financing of its assets are not included because they are not operating expenses.

As we discussed in Chapter 1, some portion of the firm's cash flow is reinvested in the firm. *Capital spending* refers to the net spending on fixed assets (purchases of fixed assets less sales of fixed assets). Finally, *additions to net working capital* is the amount spent on net working capital. It is measured as the change in net working capital over the period being examined and represents the net increase in current assets over current liabilities. The three components of cash flow are examined in more detail next.

cash flow from assets
The total of cash flow to bondholders and cash flow to shareholders, consisting of: operating cash flow, capital spending, and additions to net working capital.

Operating Cash Flow   To calculate **operating cash flow,** we want to calculate revenues minus costs, but we don't want to include depreciation since it's not a cash outflow, and we don't want to include interest because it's a financing expense. We do want to include taxes, because taxes are, unfortunately, paid in cash.

If we look at the income statement in Table 2.1B, Canadian Enterprises had earnings before interest and taxes (EBIT) of $694. This is almost what we want since it doesn't include interest paid. We need to make two adjustments: First, recall that depreciation is a non-cash expense. To get cash flow, we first add back the $65 in depreciation since it wasn't a cash deduction. The second adjustment is to subtract the $250 in taxes since these were paid in cash. The result is operating cash flow:

Canadian Enterprises thus had a 1995 operating cash flow of $509.

There is an unpleasant possibility for confusion when we speak of operating cash flow. In accounting practice, operating cash flow is often defined as net income plus depreciation. For Canadian Enterprises in Table 2.2, this would amount to $374 + 65 = $439.

The accounting definition of operating cash flow differs from ours in one important way: Interest is deducted when net income is computed. Notice that the difference between the $509 operating cash flow we calculated and this $439 is $70, the amount of interest paid for the year.

operating cash flow
Cash generated from a firm's normal business activities.

T A B L E 2.2

CANADIAN ENTERPRISES LTD.
1995 Operating Cash Flow

Earnings before interest and taxes	$694
+ Depreciation	65
− Taxes	250
Operating cash flow	$509

This definition of cash flow thus considers interest paid to be an operating expense. Our definition treats it properly as a financing expense. If there were no interest expense, the two definitions would be the same.

To finish our calculations of cash flow from assets for Canadian Enterprises, we need to consider how much of the $509 operating cash flow was reinvested in the firm. We consider spending on fixed assets first.

Capital Spending   Net capital spending is just money spent on fixed assets less money received from the sale of fixed assets. At the end of 1994, net fixed assets were $1,644. During the year, we wrote off (depreciated) $65 worth of fixed assets on the income statement. So, if we didn't purchase any new fixed assets, we would have had $1,644 − 65 = $1,579 at year's end. The 1995 balance sheet shows $1,709 in net fixed assets, so we must have spent a total of $1,709 − 1,579 = $130 on fixed assets during the year:

Ending fixed assets	$1,709
− Beginning fixed assets	1,644
+ Depreciation	65
Net investment in fixed assets	$ 130

This $130 is our net capital spending for 1995.

Could net capital spending be negative? The answer is yes. This would happen if the firm sold more assets than it purchased. The net here refers to purchases of fixed assets net of any sales.

Additions to Net Working Capital   In addition to investing in fixed assets, a firm also invests in current assets. For example, going back to the balance sheet in Table 2.1A, we see that, at the end of 1995, Canadian had current assets of $1,403. At the end of 1991, current assets were $1,112, so, during the year, Canadian invested $1,403 − 1,112 = $291 in current assets.

As the firm changes its investment in current assets, its current liabilities usually change as well. To determine the additions to net working capital, the easiest approach is just to take the difference between the beginning and ending net working capital (NWC) figures. Net working capital at the end of 1995 was $1,403 − 389 = $1,014. Similarly, at the end of 1994, net working capital was $1,112 − 428 = $684. So, given these figures, we have:

Ending NWC	$1,014
− Beginning NWC	684
Addition to NWC	$ 330

Net working capital thus increased by $330. Put another way, Canadian Enterprises had a net investment of $330 in NWC for the year.

Cash Flow from Assets   Given the figures we've come up with, we're ready to calculate cash flow from assets. The total cash flow from assets is given by operating cash flow less the amounts invested in fixed assets and net working capital. So, for Canadian Enterprises we have:

CANADIAN ENTERPRISES
1995 Cash Flow from Assets

Operating cash flow	$509
− Net capital spending	130
− Additions to NWC	330
Cash flow from assets	$ 49

From the preceding cash flow identity, this $49 cash flow from assets equals the sum of the firm's cash flow to creditors and cash flow to shareholders. We consider these next.

It wouldn't be at all unusual for a growing corporation to have a negative cash flow. As we see next, the negative cash flow means that the firm raised more money by borrowing and selling shares than it paid out to creditors and shareholders that year.

Cash Flow to Creditors and Shareholders

The cash flows to creditors and shareholders represent the net payments to creditors and owners during the year. They are calculated in a similar way. **Cash flow to creditors** is interest paid less net new borrowing; **cash flow to shareholders** is dividends less net new equity raised.

cash flow to creditors
A firm's interest payments to creditors less net new borrowings.

cash flow to shareholders
Dividends paid out by a firm less net new equity raised.

Cash Flow to Creditors   Looking at the income statement in Table 2.1B, Canadian paid $70 in interest to creditors. From the balance sheets in Table 2.1A, long-term debt rose by $454 − 408 = $46. So, Canadian Enterprises paid out $70 in interest, but it borrowed an additional $46. Net cash flow to creditors is thus:

CANADIAN ENTERPRISES
1995 Cash Flow to Creditors

Interest paid	$70
− Net new borrowing	46
Cash flow to creditors	$24

Cash flow to creditors is sometimes called cash flow to bondholders; we use these interchangeably.

Cash Flow to Shareholders   From the income statement, we see that dividends paid to shareholders amount to $65. To calculate net new equity raised, we need to look at the common share account. This account tells us how many shares the company has sold. During the year, this account rose by $40, so $40 in net new equity was raised. Given this, we have:

CANADIAN ENTERPRISES
1995 Cash Flow to Shareholders

Dividends paid	$65
− Net new equity	40
Cash flow to shareholders	$25

The cash flow to shareholders for 1995 was thus $25.

The last thing that we need to do is to check what the cash flow identity holds to be sure that we didn't make any mistakes. Earlier we found the cash flow from assets is $49. Cash flow to creditors and shareholders is $24 + 25 = $49, so everything checks out. Table 2.3 contains a summary of the various cash flow calculations for future reference.

Two important observations can be drawn from our discussion of cash flow: First, several types of cash flow are relevant to understanding the financial situation of the firm. *Operating cash flow,* defined as earnings before interest and depreciation minus taxes, measures the cash generated from operations not counting capital spending or working capital requirements. It should usually be positive; a firm is in trouble if operating cash flow is negative for a long time because the firm is not generating enough cash to pay operating costs. *Total cash flow* of the firm includes capital spending and additions to net working capital. It will frequently be negative. When a firm is growing at a rapid rate, the spending on inventory and fixed assets can be higher than cash flow from sales.

Second, net income is not cash flow. The net income of Canadian Enterprises in 1995 was $374 million, whereas total cash flow from assets was $49 million. The two numbers are not usually the same. In determining the economic and financial condition of a firm, cash flow is more revealing.

E X A M P L E | 2.4   Cash Flows for Dole Cola

During the year, Dole Cola, Ltd., had sales and costs of $600 and $300, respectively. Depreciation was $150 and interest paid was $30. Taxes were calculated at a straight

---

T A B L E 2.3

Cash flow summary

The cash flow identity
  Cash flow from assets   = Cash flow to creditors (or bondholders)
                              + Cash flow to shareholders (or owners)

Cash flow from assets
  Cash flow from assets   = Operating cash flow
                              − Net capital spending
                              − Additions to net working capital (NWC)

  where:
  a. Operating cash flow   = Earnings before interest and taxes (EBIT)
                              + Depreciation
                              − Taxes

  b. Net capital spending = Ending net fixed assets
                              − Beginning net fixed assets
                              + Depreciation

  c. Additions to NWC   = Ending NWC
                              − Beginning NWC

Cash flow to creditors (bondholders)
  Cash flow to creditors = Interest paid − Net new borrowing

Cash flow to shareholders (owners)
  Cash flow to shareholders = Dividends paid − Net new equity raised

40 percent. Dividends were $30. All figures are in millions of dollars. What was the operating cash flow for Dole? Why is this different from net income?

The easiest thing to do here is to create an income statement. We can then fill in the numbers we need. Dole Cola's income statement follows:

DOLE COLA
1995 Income Statement
($ in millions)

Net sales	$600
Cost of goods sold	300
Depreciation	150
Earnings before interest and taxes	$150
Interest paid	30
Taxable income	$120
Taxes	48
Net income	$ 72
Retained earnings	$42
Dividends	30

Net income for Dole is thus $72. We now have all the numbers we need; so referring back to the Canadian Enterprises example, we have:

DOLE COLA
1995 Operating Cash Flow
($ in millions)

Earnings before interest and taxes	$150
+ Depreciation	150
− Taxes	48
Operating cash flow	$252

As this example illustrates, operating cash flow is not the same as net income, because depreciation and interest are subtracted out when net income is calculated. If you recall our earlier discussion, we don't subtract these out in computing operating cash flow because depreciation is not a cash expense and interest paid is a financing expense, not an operating expense.

Net Capital Spending

Suppose that beginning net fixed assets were $500 and ending net fixed assets were $750. What was the net capital spending for the year?

From the income statement for Dole, depreciation for the year was $150. Net fixed assets rose by $250. We thus spent $150 to cover the depreciation and an additional $250 as well, for a total of $400.

Change in NWC and Cash Flow from Assets

Suppose that Dole Cola started the year with $2,130 in current assets and $1,620 in current liabilities. The corresponding ending figures were $2,260 and $1,710. What was the addition to NWC during the year? What was cash flow from assets? How does this compare to net income?

Net working capital started out as $2,130 − 1,620 = $510 and ended up at $2,260 − 1,710 = $550. The addition to NWC was thus $550 − 510 = $40. Putting together all the information for Dole we have:

DOLE COLA
1995 Cash Flow from Assets

Operating cash flow	$252
− Net capital spending	400
− Additions to NWC	40
Cash flow from assets	−$188

Dole had a cash flow from assets of negative $188. Net income was positive at $72. Is the fact that cash flow from assets is negative a cause for alarm? Not necessarily. The cash flow here is negative primarily because of a large investment in fixed assets. If these are good investments, the resulting negative cash flow is not a worry.

Cash Flow to Creditors and Shareholders

We saw that Dole Cola had cash flow from assets of −$188. The fact that this is negative means that Dole raised more money in the form of new debt and equity than it paid out for the year. For example, suppose we know that Dole didn't sell any new equity for the year. What was cash flow to shareholders? To bondholders?

Because it didn't raise any new equity, Dole's cash flow to shareholders is just equal to the cash dividend paid:

DOLE COLA
1995 Cash Flow to Shareholders

Dividends paid	$30
− Net new equity	0
Cash flow to shareholders	$30

Now, from the cash flow identity the total cash paid to bondholders and shareholders was −$188. Cash flow to shareholders is $30, so cash flow to bondholders must be equal to −$188 − $30 = −$218:

Cash flow to bondholders + Cash flow to shareholders = −$188
Cash flow to bondholders + $30   = −$188
Cash flow to bondholders   = −$218

From the income statement, interest paid is $30. We can determine net new borrowing as follows:

DOLE COLA
1995 Cash Flow to Bondholders

Interest paid	$ 30
− Net new borrowing	−248
Cash flow to bondholders	−$ 218

As indicated, since cash flow to bondholders is −$218 and interest paid is $30, Dole must have borrowed $248 during the year to help finance the fixed asset expansion.

CONCEPT QUESTIONS

1. What is the cash flow identity? Explain what it says.
2. What are the components of operating cash flow?
3. Why is interest paid not a component of operating cash flow?

2.4 | TAXES

Taxes are very important because, as we just saw, cash flows are measured after taxes. In this section, we examine corporate and personal tax rates and how taxes are calculated. We apply this knowledge to see how different types of income are taxed in the hands of individuals and corporations.

The size of the tax bill is determined through tax laws and regulations in the annual budgets of the federal government (administered by Revenue Canada) and provincial governments. If the various rules of taxation seem a little bizarre or convoluted to you, keep in mind that tax law is the result of political, as well as economic, forces. According to economic theory, an ideal tax system has three features. First, it should distribute the tax burden equitably, with each taxpayer shouldering a "fair share." Second, the tax system should not change the efficient allocation of resources by markets. If this happened, such distortions would reduce economic welfare. Third, the system should be easy to administer.

The tax law is continually evolving so our discussion cannot make you a tax expert. Rather it gives you an understanding of the tax principles important for financial management along with the ability to ask the right questions when consulting a tax expert.

For example, in the federal budget of 1995, the finance minister increased corporate surtax and large corporation tax rates and proposed no increases to individual tax rates. The government said the plan was necessary to increase tax fairness. Our discussion of taxes can help you understand how.

Individual Tax Rates

Individual tax rates in effect for federal and provincial taxes for 1994 are shown in Table 2.4 These rates apply to income from employment (wages and salary) and from unincorporated businesses. Investment income is also taxable. Interest income is taxed at the same rates as employment income, but special provisions reduce the taxes payable on dividends and capital gains. We discuss these in detail later in the chapter.

Federal				Provincial	
Taxable Income	Tax	Rate on Excess		Resident of	Percentage of Basic Federal Tax
$ 1	$ —	17%		Alberta	45.5%
29,590	5,030	26		British Columbia	52.5
59,180	12,724	29		Manitoba	52.0
				New Brunswick	62.0
				Newfoundland	69.0
	Quebec			Nova Scotia	59.5
Taxable Income	Tax	Rate on Excess		Ontario	58.0
				Prince Edward Island	59.5
$ 1	$ —	16%		Saskatchewan	50.0
7,000	1,120	19		Northwest Territories	45.0
14,000	2,450	21		Yukon Territory	50.0
23,000	4,340	23		Non-residents	52.0
50,000	10,550	24			

T A B L E 2.4

Individual income tax rates—1994

Source: *General Income Tax Guide 1994* and *Canadian Income Tax Act 1993, CCH.*

With the exception of Quebec residents, taxpayers file one tax return. In computing your tax, you find the federal tax and then calculate the provincial tax as a percentage of the federal tax. For example, if you live in Ontario, and had a taxable income of more than $59,180, your tax on the next dollar is:[5]

45.82% = Federal tax rate × (1 + Provincial tax rate) = .29 × (1 + .58)

To get the rates for Quebec, first find the federal tax and subtract a 16.5 percent abatement.[6] Provincial tax is due at the rates shown in Table 2.4 multiplied by taxable income.

Average versus Marginal Tax Rates

In making financial decisions, it is frequently important to distinguish between average and marginal tax rates. Your **average tax rate** is your tax bill divided by your taxable income; in other words, the percentage of your income that goes to pay taxes. Your **marginal tax rate** is the extra tax you would pay if you earned one more dollar. The percentage tax rates shown in Table 2.4 are all marginal rates. To put it another way, the tax rates in Table 2.4 apply to the part of income in the indicated range only, not all income.

average tax rate
Total taxes paid divided by total taxable income.

marginal tax rate
Amount of tax payable on the next dollar earned.

E X A M P L E | 2.5   **Taxes at the Margin**

Suppose you have a taxable income of $250,000 and live in Noval Scotia. What is your tax bill? From Table 2.4, we can figure your tax bill as follows:[7]

Federal tax: $12,724 on the first $59,180 plus 29% of ($250,000 − $59,180) = $12,724 + $55,338 = $68,062.

Provincial tax: 59.5% of federal tax = $68,062 × .595 = $40,497

Total tax: $68,062 + $40,497 = $108,559

In our example, what is the average tax rate? Taxable income is $250,000 and the tax bill is $108,559 so the average tax rate is $108,559/$250,000 = 43.42%. What is the marginal tax rate? If you made one more dollar, the tax on that dollar would be 46.3 cents = 29% (1 + .595). Our marginal rate is 46.3 percent. |

Our example illustrates the workings of marginal and average tax rates. Notice that the marginal and average rates were very close. This occurred because the income amount far exceeded the floor of the top bracket so most of it was taxed at the marginal rate.

Following the equity principle, individual taxes are designed to be progressive with higher incomes taxed at a higher rate. In contrast, with a flat rate tax, there is only one tax rate, and this rate is the same for all income levels. With such a tax, the marginal tax rate is always the same as the average tax rate. As it stands now, individual taxation in Canada is progressive but approaches a flat rate for the highest incomes.

---

[5] Actual rates are a little higher as our analysis ignores surtaxes that apply in higher brackets. Our example shows the marginal combined tax rate for Ontario residents in the top bracket as 44.4 percent. With surtaxes, it rises to 48.84 percent.
[6] Multiply by .835.
[7] Actually, your tax bill would be slightly higher due to the federal surtax we ignore here.

Normally, the marginal tax rate is relevant for decision making. Any new cash flows are taxed at that marginal rate. Since financial decisions usually involve new cash flows or changes in existing ones, this rate tells us the marginal effect on our tax bill.

Taxes on Investment Income

When introducing the topic of taxes, we warned that tax laws are not always logical. The treatment of dividends in Canada is at least a partial exception because there are two clear goals: First, corporations pay dividends from aftertax income so tax laws shelter dividends from full tax in the hands of shareholders. This avoids double taxation, which would violate the principle of equitable taxation. Second, tax shelters for dividends apply only to dividends paid by Canadian corporations. This is to encourage Canadian investors to invest in Canadian firms as opposed to foreign companies.[8]

To see how dividends are taxed, we start with common shares held by individual investors. Table 2.5 shows how the **dividend tax credit** of the three federal tax brackets. The steps follow the instructions on federal tax returns. Actual dividends are grossed up by 25 percent and federal tax is calculated on the grossed up figure. A dividend tax credit of 16 2/3 percent of the actual dividend is subtracted from the federal tax to get the federal tax payable. The provincial tax (for Ontario in this example) is calculated and added.

As an alternative to the calculations in Table 2.5, the following equation represents the marginal tax rate on dividends:[9]

Effective tax rate on dividends =
1.25 [(Federal tax rate) − .1333] [1 + (Provincial tax rate)]

The result is that dividends are taxed far more lightly than ordinary income for investors in all tax brackets. The difference is most dramatic for investors in the lowest bracket where dividends are subject to a tax rate of only 7.24 percent.

dividend tax credit
Tax formula that reduces the effective tax rate on dividends.

Federal Tax Rate	17%	26%	29%
Dividends	$1,000.00	$1,000.00	$1,000.00
Gross up at 25%	250.00	250.00	250.00
Grossed up dividends	$1,250.00	$1,250.00	$1,250.00
Federal tax	212.50	325.00	362.50
Less dividend tax credit (.1667 × $1,000)	(166.70)	(166.70)	(166.70)
Federal tax payable	$ 45.80	$ 158.30	$ 195.80
Provincial tax at 58% of federal tax	26.56	91.81	113.56
Total Tax	$ 72.36	$ 250.11	$ 309.36
Effective combined tax rates			
Dividends	7.24%	25.01%	30.94%
Ordinary income	26.86%	41.08%	45.82%
Capital gains	20.15%	30.81%	34.37%

T A B L E 2.5

Dividend tax credit for Ontario residents

---

[8] Evidence that the dividend tax credit causes investors to favour Canadian stocks is provided in L. Booth, "The Dividend Tax Credit and Canadian Ownership Objectives," *Canadian Journal of Economics* 20 (May 1987).
[9] A. H. R. Davis and G. E. Pinches, *Canadian Financial Management,* 2nd ed. (New York: Harper Collins, 1991), p. 26.

42 PART I | Overview of Corporate Finance

capital gains
*The increase in value
of an investment over
its purchase price.*

Individual Canadian investors also benefit from a tax reduction for **capital gains.** Capital gains arise when an investment increases in value above its purchase price. For capital gains, taxes apply at 75 percent of the applicable marginal rate. For example, individuals in the highest bracket in Table 2.5 would pay taxes on capital gains at a nominal rate of 34.37 percent = 45.82% × .75.

realized capital gains
*The increase in value
of an investment,
when converted to
cash.*

In practice, capital gains are lightly taxed because individuals pay taxes on **realized capital gains** only when stock is sold. Because many individuals hold shares for a long time (have unrealized capital gains), the time value of money dramatically reduces the effective tax rate on capital gains.[10]

E X A M P L E | 2.6   **Comparing Aftertax Investment Income**

You have $10,000 in a chartered bank earning interest at an effective annual rate of 6 percent. An Ontario resident, you are in the top tax bracket. If you invest instead in Canadian common shares, the dividends you receive would qualify for the dividend tax credit. The stock portfolio you are considering pays dividends at a rate of 5 percent. Ignoring the possibility of capital gains or losses from the shares, which investment would produce the larger aftertax cash flow?

The interest you receive is fully taxable at your marginal rate of 45.82 percent. Aftertax interest income is:

$10,000 × .06 (1 − .4582) = $325.08

Effective tax rate on dividends:

= 1.25 [(Federal tax rate) − .1333] [1 + (Provincial tax rate)]

= 1.25 [.29 − .1333] [1 + .58]

= 30.95%

Aftertax dividends = $10,000 × .05 × (1 − .3095) = $345.25

So you would have $345.25 in aftertax dividends and only $325.08 in aftertax interest. Of course, before investing in stocks, you would have to consider the added risk. We have a lot more to say on this in Chapter 10. |

Corporate Taxes

Canadian corporations, like individuals, are subject to taxes levied by the federal and provincial governments. Corporate taxes are passed on to consumers through higher prices, to workers through lower wages, or to investors through lower returns.

Table 2.6 shows corporate tax rates using Ontario as an example. You can see from the table that small corporations (income less than $200,000) and, to a lesser degree, manufacturing and processing companies, receive a tax break in the form of lower rates.

Comparing the rates in Table 2.6 with the personal tax rates in Table 2.4 appears to reveal a tax advantage for small businesses and professionals that form corporations. The tax rate on corporate income of, say, $150,000 is less than the personal tax

---

[10] D. Booth and D. J. Johnston, "The Ex-Dividend Day Behavior of Canadian Stock Prices: Tax Changes and Clientele Effects," *Journal of Finance* 39 (June 1984). Booth and Johnston find a "very low effective tax rate on capital gains" in the 1970s before the introduction of the current lifetime exemption. They compare their results with a U.S. study that found an effective tax rate on capital gains under 7 percent.

	Federal	Ontario	Combined
Basic corporations	28.0%	15.5%	43.5%
Manufacturing and processing	21.0%	14.5%	35.5%
All small corporations with a taxable income less than $200,000	12.0%	10.0%	22.0%

T A B L E 2.6

Corporate tax rates in percentages in 1993

rate assessed on the income of unincorporated businesses. But this is oversimplified because dividends paid to the owners are also taxed, as we saw earlier.

Taxable Income

In Section 2.2 we discussed the income statement for Canadian Enterprises (Table 2.1B); it includes both dividends and interest paid. An important difference is that interest paid is deducted from EBIT in calculating taxable income but dividends paid are not. Because interest is a tax-deductible expense, debt financing has a tax advantage over financing with common shares. To illustrate, Table 2.1B shows that Canadian Enterprises paid $250 million in taxes on taxable income of $624 million. The firm's tax rate is $250/624 = 40%. This means that to pay another $1 in dividends, Canadian Enterprises must increase EBIT by $1.67. Of the marginal $1.67 EBIT, 40 percent, or 67 cents goes in taxes, leaving $1 to increase dividends. In general, a taxable firm must earn $1/(1 − $ Tax rate) in additional EBIT for each extra dollar of dividends. Because interest is tax deductible, Canadian Enterprises needs to earn only $1 more in EBIT to be able to pay $1 in added interest.

The tables are turned when we contrast interest and dividends earned by the firm. Interest earned is fully taxable just like any other form of ordinary income. Dividends on common shares received from other Canadian corporations qualify for a 100 percent exemption and are received tax free.[11]

Capital Gains and Carry-forward and Carry-back

When a firm disposes of an asset for more than it paid originally, the difference is a capital gain. As with individuals, firms receive favorable tax treatment on capital gains. At the time of writing, capital gains received by corporations are taxed at 75 percent of the marginal tax rate.

When calculating capital gains for tax purposes, a firm nets out all capital losses in the same year. If capital losses exceed capital gains, the net capital loss may be carried back to reduce taxable capital gains in the three prior years. Under the **carry-back** feature, a firm files a revised tax return and receives a refund of prior years' taxes. For example, suppose Canadian Enterprises experienced a net capital loss of $1 million in 1994 and net capital gains of $300,000 in 1993, $200,000 in 1992, and $150,000 in 1991. Canadian could carry back a total of $650,000 to get a refund on its taxes. The remaining $350,000 can be **carried forward** indefinitely to reduce future taxes on capital gains.

A similar carry-forward provision applies to operating losses. The carry-back period is three years and carry-forward is allowed up to seven years.

loss carry-forward, carry-back
Using a year's capital losses to offset capital gains in past or future years.

---

[11] The situation is more complicated for preferred stock dividends as we discuss in Chapter 12.

2.5 | CAPITAL COST ALLOWANCE

capital cost
allowance (CCA)
*Depreciation for tax
purposes, not
necessarily the same
as depreciation under
GAAP.*

Capital cost allowance (CCA) is depreciation for tax purposes in Canada. Capital cost allowance is deducted in determining taxable income. Because the tax law reflects various political compromises, CCA is not the same as depreciation under GAAP so there is no reason calculation of a firm's income under tax rules has to be the same as under GAAP. For example, taxable corporate income may often be lower than accounting income because the company is allowed to use accelerated capital cost allowance rules in computing depreciation for Revenue Canada while using straight-line depreciation for GAAP reporting.[12]

CCA calculation begins by assigning every capital asset to a particular class. An asset's class establishes its maximum CCA rate for tax purposes. Intangible assets like leasehold improvements in Table 2.7 follow straight-line depreciation for CCA. For all other assets, CCA follows the declining balance method. The CCA for each year is computed by multiplying the asset's book value for tax purposes, called undepreciated capital cost (UCC), by the appropriate rate.

The CCA system is unique to Canada and differs in many respects from the ACRS depreciation method used in the United States. One key difference is that in the Canadian system, the expected salvage value (what we think the asset will be worth when we dispose of it) and the actual expected economic life (how long we expect the asset to be in service) are not explicitly considered in the calculation of capital cost allowance. Some typical CCA classes and their respective CCA rates are described in Table 2.7.

To illustrate how capital cost allowance is calculated, suppose your firm is considering buying a van costing $30,000, including any setup costs that must (by law) be capitalized. (No rational business would capitalize, for tax purposes, anything that could legally be expensed.) Table 2.7 shows that vans fall in Class 10 with a 30 percent CCA rate. To calculate the CCA, we follow Revenue Canada's **half-year rule** that allows us to figure CCA on only half of the asset's installed cost in the first year it is put in use. Table 2.8 shows the CCA for our van for the first five years.

half-year rule
*Revenue Canada's
requirement to figure
CCA on only one-half
of an asset's installed
cost for its first year
of use.*

As we pointed out, in calculating CCA under current tax law, the economic life and future market value of the asset are not an issue. As a result, the UCC of an asset can differ substantially from its actual market value. With our $30,000 van, UCC after the first year is $15,000 less the first year's CCA of $4,500, or $10,500. The

T A B L E 2.7

*Common capital cost
allowance classes*

Class	Rate	Assets
3	5%	Brick buildings
6	10	Fences, frame buildings
7	15	Canoes, boats, ships
8	20	Manufacturing and processing equipment
9	25	Electrical equipment and aircraft
10	30	Vans, trucks, tractors, and computer equipment
13	Straight-line	Leasehold improvements
16	40	Taxicabs and rental cars
22	50	Excavating equipment

[12] Where taxable income is less than accounting income, the difference goes into a long-term liability account on the balance sheet labelled deferred taxes.

Year	Beginning UCC	CCA	Ending UCC
1	$15,000*	$4,500	$10,500
2	25,500†	7,650	17,850
3	17,850	5,355	12,495
4	12,495	3,748	8,747
5	8,747	2,624	6,123

T A B L E 2.8

Capital cost allowance for a van

*One-half of $30,000.
†Year 1 ending balance + Remaining half of $30,000.

remaining UCC values are summarized in Table 2.8. After five years, the undepreciated capital cost of the van is $6,123.

E X A M P L E | 2.7   **Capital Cost Allowance Incentives in Practice**

Since capital cost allowance is deducted in computing taxable income, larger CCA rates reduce taxes and increase cash flows. As we pointed out earlier, finance ministers sometimes tinker with the CCA rates to create incentives. For example, in the *1992 Federal Budget,* the minister announced an increase in CCA rates from 20 to 25 percent for manufacturing and processing assets. The combined federal/provincial corporate tax rate for this sector is 36.5 percent.

Mississauga Manufacturing was planning to acquire new processing equipment to enhance efficiency and its ability to compete with U.S. firms. The equipment had an installed cost of $1 million. How much additional tax will the new measure save Mississauga in the first year the equipment is put into use?

Under the half-year rule, UCC for the first year is $1/2 \times \$1$ million = $500,000. The CCA deductions under the old and new rates are:

Old rate: CCA = $.20 \times \$500,000 = \$100,000$

New rate: CCA = $.25 \times \$500,000 = \$125,000$

Because the firm deducts CCA in figuring taxable income, taxable income will be reduced by the incremental CCA of $25,000. With $25,000 less in taxable income, Mississauga Manufacturing's combined tax bill would drop by $25,000 \times .365 = $9,125.

Asset Purchases and Sales

When an asset is sold, the UCC in its asset class (or pool) is reduced by what is realized on the asset or by its original cost, whichever is less. This amount is called the adjusted cost of disposal. Suppose we wanted to sell the van in our earlier example after five years. Based on historical averages of resale prices, it will be worth, say, 25 percent of the purchase price or $.25 \times \$30,000 = \$7,500$. Since the price of $7,500 is less than the original cost, the adjusted cost of disposal is $7,500 and the UCC in Class 10 is reduced by this amount.

Table 2.8 shows that the van has a UCC after five years of $6,123. The $7,500 removed from the pool is $1,377 more than the undepreciated capital cost of the van we are selling, and future CCA deductions will be reduced as the pool continues. On the other hand, if we had sold the van for, say, $4,000, the UCC in Class 10 would be reduced by $4,000 and the $2,123 excess of UCC over the sale price would remain in the pool. Then, future CCA increases as the declining balance calculations depreciate the $2,123 excess UCC to infinity.

So far we focussed on CCA calculations for one asset. In practice, firms often buy and sell assets from a given class in the course of a year. In this case, we apply the **net acquisitions** rule. From the total installed cost of all acquisitions, we subtract the adjusted cost of disposal of all assets in the pool. The result is net acquisitions for the asset class. If net acquisitions is positive, we apply the half-year rule and calculate CCA as we did earlier. If net acquisitions is negative, there is no adjustment for the half-year rule.

net acquisitions
Total installed cost of capital acquisitions minus adjusted cost of any disposals within an asset pool.

When an Asset Pool Is Terminated   Suppose your firm decides to contract out all transport and to sell all company vehicles. If the company owns no other Class 10 assets, the asset pool in this class is terminated. As before, the adjusted cost of disposal is the net sales proceeds or the total installed cost of all the pool assets, whichever is less. This adjusted cost of disposal is subtracted from the total UCC in the pool. So far, the steps are exactly the same as in our van example where the pool continued. What happens next is different. Unless the adjusted cost of disposal just happens to equal the UCC exactly, a positive or negative UCC balance remains and this has tax implications.

A positive UCC balance remains when the adjusted cost of disposal is less than UCC before the sale. In this case, the firm has a **terminal loss** equal to the remaining UCC. This loss is deductible from income for the year. For example, if we sell the van after two years for $10,000, the UCC of $17,850 in Table 2.8 exceeds the market value by $7,850. The terminal loss of $7,850 gives rise to a tax saving of .40 × $7,850 = $3,140. (We assume the tax rate is 40 percent.)

terminal loss
The difference between UCC and adjusted cost of disposal when the UCC is greater.

A negative UCC balance occurs when the adjusted cost of disposal exceeds UCC, in the pool. To illustrate, return to our van example and suppose that this van is the only Class 10 asset our company owns when it sells the pool for $7,500 after five years. There is a $1,377 excess of adjusted cost of disposal (7,500 − 6,123) over UCC, so the final UCC balance is $1,377.

The company must pay tax at its ordinary tax rate on this balance. The reason that taxes must be paid is that the difference in adjusted cost of disposal and UCC is excess CCA **recaptured** when the asset is sold. We overdepreciated the asset by $7,500 − $6,123 = $1,377. Because we deducted $1,377 too much in CCA, we paid $550.80 too little in taxes (at 40 percent), and we simply have to make up the difference.

recaptured depreciation
The taxable difference between adjusted cost of disposal and UCC when UCC is greater.

Notice that this is *not* a tax on a capital gain. As a general rule, a capital gain only occurs if the market price exceeds the original cost. To illustrate a capital gain, suppose that instead of buying the van, our firm purchased a classic car for $50,000. After five years, the classic car will be sold for $75,000. The sales price would exceed the purchase price, so the adjusted cost of disposal is $50,000 and UCC pool is reduced by this amount. The total negative balance left in the UCC pool is $50,000 − $6,123 = $43,877 and this is recaptured CCA. In addition, the firm has a taxable capital gain of $75,000 − $50,000 = $25,000, the difference between the sales price and the original cost.[13]

---

[13] This example shows that it is possible to have a recapture of CCA without closing out a pool if the UCC balance goes negative.

Year	Beginning UCC	CCA	Ending UCC
1	$ 80,000*	$24,000	$56,000
2	136,000†	40,800	95,200
3	95,200	28,560	66,640
4	66,640	19,992	46,648

*One-half of $160,000.
†Year 1 ending balance + Remaining half of $160,000.

T A B L E 2.9

CCA for computer system

E X A M P L E | 2.8   CCA Calculations

Staple Supply Ltd. has just purchased a new computerized information system with an installed cost of $160,000. The computer is in Class 10 for CCA purposes. What are the yearly capital cost allowances? Based on historical experience, we think that the system will be worth only $10,000 when we get rid of it in four years. What will be the tax consequences of the sale if the company has several other computers still in use in four years? Now suppose that Staple Supply will sell all its assets and wind up the company in four years. What is the total aftertax cash flow from the sale?

In Table 2.9, at the end of Year 4, the remaining balance for the specific computer system mentioned would be $46,648.[14] The pool is reduced by $10,000, but it will continue to be depreciated. There are no tax consequences in Year 4. This is only the case when the pool is active. If this were the only computer system, we would have been closing the pool and would have been able to claim a terminal loss of $46,648 − $10,000 = $36,648.

CONCEPT QUESTIONS

1. What is the difference between capital cost allowance and GAAP depreciation?
2. Why do governments sometimes increase CCA rates?
3. Reconsider the 1992 CCA increase discussed in example 2.7. How effective do you think it was in stimulating investment? Why?

2.6 | SUMMARY AND CONCLUSIONS

This chapter has introduced you to some of the basics of financial statements, taxes, and cash flow. In it we saw that:

1. The book values on an accounting balance sheet can be very different from market values. The goal of financial management is to maximize the market value of the stock, not its book value.
2. Net income as it is computed on the income statement is not cash flow. A primary reason is that depreciation, a non-cash expense, is deducted when net income is computed.
3. Marginal and average tax rates can be different; the marginal tax rate is relevant for most financial decisions.

---

[14] In actuality, the capital cost allowance for the entire pool will be calculated at once, without specific identification of each computer system.

4. There is a cash flow identity much like the balance sheet identity. It says that cash flow from assets equals cash flow to bondholders and shareholders. The calculation of cash flow from financial statements isn't difficult. Care must be taken in handling non-cash expenses, such as depreciation, and in not confusing operating costs with financial costs. Most of all, it is important not to confuse book values with market values and accounting income with cash flow.

5. Different types of Canadian investment income, dividends, interest, and capital gains are taxed differently.

6. Corporate income taxes create a tax advantage for debt financing (paying tax-deductible interest) over equity financing (paying dividends). Chapter 15 discusses this in depth.

7. Capital cost allowance (CCA) is depreciation for tax purposes in Canada. CCA calculations are important for determining cash flows.

Key Terms

balance sheet (page 25)
generally accepted accounting
principles (GAAP) (page 28)
income statement (page 30)
non-cash items (page 31)
cash flow from assets (page 33)
operating cash flow (page 33)
cash flow to creditors (page 35)
cash flow to shareholders (page 35)
average tax rate (page 40)
marginal tax rate (page 40)
dividend tax credit (page 41)

capital gains (page 42)
realized capital gains (page 42)
loss carry-forward, carry-back (page 43)
capital cost allowance (CCA) (page 44)
half-year rule (page 44)
net acquisitions (page 46)
terminal loss (page 46)
recaptured depreciation (page 46)

Chapter Review Problem and Self-Test

2.1 **Cash Flow for B. C. Resources Ltd.** This problem will give you some practice working with financial statements and figuring cash flow. Based on the following information for B. C. Resources Ltd., prepare an income statement for 1995 and balance sheets for 1994 and 1995. Next, following our Canadian Enterprises examples in the chapter, calculate cash flow for B. C. Resources, cash flow to bondholders, and cash flow to shareholders for 1995. Use a 40 percent tax rate throughout. You can check your answers in the next section.

	1994	1995
Sales	$3,790	$3,990
Costs	2,043	2,137
Depreciation	975	1,018
Interest	225	267
Dividends	200	205
Current assets	2,140	2,346
Fixed assets	6,770	7,087
Current liabilities	994	1,126
Long-term debt	2,869	2,956

Answer to Self-Test Problem

2.1   In preparing the balance sheets, remember that shareholders' equity is the residual and can be found using the equation:

Total assets = Total liabilities + Total equity

With this mind, B. C. Resources's balance sheets are as follows:

B. C. RESOURCES LTD.
Balance Sheets as of December 31, 1994 and 1995

	1994	1995		1994	1995
Current assets	$2,140	$2,346	Current liabilities	$ 994	$1,126
Net fixed assets	6,770	7,087	Long-term debt	2,869	2,956
			Equity	5,047	5,351
Total assets	$8,910	$9,433	Total liabilities and owners' equity	$8,910	$9,433

The income statement is straightforward:

B. C. RESOURCES LTD.
1995 Income Statement

Sales	$3,990
Costs	2,137
Depreciation	1,018
Earnings before interest and taxes	$ 835
Interest paid	267
Taxable income	$ 568
Taxes	227
Net income	$ 341
Addition to retained earnings	$136
Dividends	205

Notice that we've used a flat 40 percent tax rate. Also notice that retained earnings are just net income less cash dividends. We can now pick up the figures we need to get operating cash flow:

B. C. RESOURCES LTD.
1995 Operating Cash Flow

Earnings before interest and taxes	$ 835
+ Depreciation	1,018
− Current taxes	227
Operating cash flow	$1,626

Next, we get the capital spending for the year by looking at the change in fixed assets, remembering to account for the depreciation:

Ending fixed assets	$7,087
− beginning fixed assets	6,770
+ Depreciation	1,018
Net investment in fixed assets	$1,335

After calculating beginning and ending NWC, we take the difference to get the addition to NWC:

Ending NWC	$1,220
− Beginning NWC	1,146
Addition to NWC	$ 74

We now combine operating cash flow, net capital spending, and the addition to net working capital to get the total cash flow from assets:

B. C. RESOURCES LTD.
1995 Cash Flow from Assets

Operating cash flow	$1,626
− Net capital spending	1,335
− Additions to NWC	74
Cash flow from assets	$ 217

To get cash flow to creditors, notice that long-term borrowing increased by $87 during the year and that interest paid was $267:

B. C. RESOURCES LTD.
1995 Cash Flow to Creditors

Interest paid	$267
− Net new borrowing	87
Cash flow to bondholders	$180

Finally, dividends paid were $205. To get net new equity, we have to do some extra calculating. Total equity was found by balancing the balance sheets. During 1995, equity increased by $5,351 − 5,047 = $304. Of this increase, $136 was from additions to retained earnings, so $168 in new equity was raised during the year. Cash flow to shareholders was thus:

B. C. RESOURCES LTD.
1995 Cash Flow to Shareholders

Dividends paid	$205
− Net new equity	168
Cash flow to shareholders	$ 37

As a check, notice that cash flow from assets, $217, does equal cash flow to creditors plus cash flow to shareholders ($180 + 37 = $217).

Questions and Problems

**Basic
(Questions 1–13)**

1. **Building a Balance Sheet**   XYZ, Inc., has current assets of $1,000, net fixed assets of $4,500, current liabilities of $500, and long-term debt of $1,200. What is the shareholders' equity account for this firm? How much is net working capital?

2. **Building an Income Statement**   Kuipers Manufacturing Co. has sales of $300,000, costs of $175,000, depreciation expense of $25,000, interest expense of $30,000, and a tax rate of 34 percent. What is the net income for this firm?

3. **Dividends and Retained Earnings**   Suppose the firm in Problem 2 paid out $20,000 in cash dividends. What is the addition to retained earnings?

4. **Per Share Earnings and Dividends**   Suppose the firm in Problem 3 had 30,000 shares of common stock outstanding. What is the earnings per share (EPS) figure? What is the dividends per share figure?

5. **Market Values and Book Values**   Klingon Widgets, Inc., purchased new machinery three years ago for $3 million. The machinery can be sold to the Romulans today for $2 million. Klingon's current balance sheet shows net fixed assets of $1.5 million, current liabilities of $500,000, and net working capital of $500,000. If all the current accounts were liquidated today, the company would

receive $1.2 million cash. What is the book value of Klingon's assets today? What is the market value?

Basic
(Continued)

6. **Calculating OCF** Cyclone Water Works, Inc., has sales of $5,000, costs of $3,000, depreciation expense of $450, and interest expense of $250. If the tax rate is 35 percent, what is the operating cash flow (OCF)?

7. **Calculating Net Capital Spending** The Maxwell Hammer Co.'s December 31, 1993, balance sheet showed net fixed assets of $3.4 million, and the December 31, 1994, balance sheet showed net fixed assets of $3.5 million. The company's 1994 income statement showed a depreciation expense of $400,000. What was Maxwell's net capital spending for 1994?

8. **Calculating Tax Rates** The Canadian Shield Company, a non-manufacturing corporation located in Ontario, had a taxable income of $140,000 in 1995. Based on Table 2.6 in the chapter, calculate the actual tax bill for the year. What is the average tax rate? The marginal tax rate?

9. **Calculating Tax Rates** In Problem 8, what would the answers be if taxable income were $640,000?

10. **Incorporation and Tax** Find the tax advantage to the owner of incorporating the Canadian Shield Company if it was a sole proprietorship, for both income figures. Refer back to Table 2.4.

11. **Cash Flow to Bondholders** ABC, Inc.'s December 31, 1994, balance sheet showed long-term debt of $5 million, and the December 31, 1995, balance sheet showed long-term debt of $5.9 million. The 1995 income statement showed an interest expense of $575,000. What was ABC's cash flow to bondholders during 1995?

12. **Cash Flow to Stockholders** ABC, Inc.'s December 31, 1994, balance sheet showed $300,000 in the common stock account, and $5,700,000 in the additional paid-in surplus account. The December 31, 1995, balance sheet showed $325,000 and $5,975,000 in the same two accounts. If the company paid out $450,000 in cash dividends during 1995, what was the cash flow to stockholders for the year?

13. **Calculating Total Cash Flows** Given the information for ABC, Inc., in Problems 11 and 12, suppose you also know that the firm made $750,000 in new capital spending investments during 1995, and that the firm reduced its net working capital investment by $75,000. What was ABC, Inc.'s, 1995 operating cash flow (OCF)?

14. **Calculating Total Cash Flows** MBI, Inc., shows the following information on its 1995 income statement: sales = $50,000; costs = $30,000; other expenses = $2,500; depreciation expense = $2,500; interest expense = $5,000; taxes paid = $3,400; dividends paid = $3,200. In addition, you're told that the firm issued $500 in new equity during 1995, and redeemed $1,000 in outstanding long-term debt.

Intermediate
(Questions 14–23)

    a. What is the 1995 cash flow from operations?
    b. What is the 1995 cash flow to bondholders?
    c. What is the 1995 cash flow to stockholders?
    d. If net fixed assets increased by $2,900 during the year, what were the additions to NWC?

15. **Using Income Statements** Given the following information, calculate the depreciation expense: sales = $10,000; costs = $6,000; additions to retained earnings = $1,000; dividends paid = $625; interest expense = $500; tax rate = 35 percent.

16. **Market Value versus Book Value**   Explain the difference between market value and book value. Which is more relevant? Why?

17. **Residual Claims**   OnTheBrink, Inc., is obligated to pay its creditors $1,700 during the year. What is the value of the shareholders' equity if assets equal $1,800? What if assets equal $1,500?

18. **Marginal versus Average Tax Rates**   (Refer to Table 2.6.) Corporation X has $80,000 in taxable income, and Corporation Y, a manufacturer, has $800,000 in taxable income.

    a. What is the tax bill for each firm?

    b. Suppose both firms have identified a new project that will increase taxable income by $10,000. How much in additional taxes will each firm pay? Why isn't this amount the same?

19. **OCF and Net Income**   During 1995, My Money, Inc., had sales of $750,000. Cost of goods sold, administrative and selling expenses, and depreciation expenses were $500,000, $150,000, and $50,000, respectively. In addition, the company had an interest expense of $75,000 and a tax rate of 35 percent. (Ignore any tax loss carry-back or carry-forward provisions.)

    a. What is My Money's net income for 1995?

    b. What is its operating cash flow?

    c. Explain your results in *(a)* and *(b)*.

20. **Taxes on Investment Income**   Mary Song, a Vancouver investor, receives $1,000 in dividends from B. C. Forest Products shares, $1,000 in interest from a deposit in a chartered bank, and a $1,000 capital gain from central B. C. Mines shares. Use the information in Table 2.4 to calculate the aftertax cash flow from each investment. Ms. Song's federal tax rate is 17 percent.

21. **Calculating Cash Flows**   Tiger Paw Corporation had the following operating results for 1995: sales = $4,000; cost of goods sold = $2,000; depreciation expense = $1,000; interest expense = $300; dividends paid = $250. At the beginning of the year, net fixed assets were $3,000, current assets were $2,000, and current liabilities were $1,000. At the end of the year, net fixed assets were $3,600, current assets were $2,750, and current liabilities were $1,250. The tax rate for 1995 was 34 percent.

    a. What is net income for 1995?

    b. What is the operating cash flow for 1995?

    c. What is the cash flow from assets for 1995? Is this possible? Explain.

    d. If no new debt was issued during the year, what is the cash flow to bondholders? What is the cash flow to stockholders? Explain and interpret the positive and negative signs of your answers in *(a)* through *(d)*.

22. **Calculating Cash Flows**   Consider the following abbreviated financial statements for Jumbo, Inc.:

Jumbo, Inc. Partial Balance Sheets as of December 31, 1994 and 1995					
	1994	1995		1994	1995
Assets			*Liabilities and Owners' Equity*		
Current assets	$ 354	$ 465	Current liabilities	$ 171	$ 205
Net fixed assets	1,800	1,995	Long-term debt	1,150	1,190

Jumbo, Inc. 1995 Income Statement	
Sales	$5,125
Costs	1,478
Depreciation	540
Interest	259

   a. What is owners' equity for 1994 and 1995?

   b. What is the addition to net working capital for 1995?

c. In 1995, Jumbo purchased $1,000 in new fixed assets. How much in fixed assets did Jumbo sell? What is the cash flow from assets for the year? (The tax rate is 35 percent.)

d. During 1995, Jumbo raised $100 in new long-term debt. How much long-term debt must Jumbo have paid off during the year? What is the cash flow to bondholders?

Intermediate (Continued)

23. **Liquidity** What does liquidity measure? Explain the trade-off the firm faces between high liquidity and low liquidity levels.

24. **Net Fixed Assets and Depreciation** On the balance sheet, the net fixed assets (NFA) account is equal to the gross fixed assets (FA) account, which records the acquisition cost of fixed assets, minus the accumulated depreciation (AD) account, which records the total depreciation taken by the firm against its fixed assets. Using the fact that NFA = FA − AD, show that the expression given in the chapter for increases in capital spending, $NFA_{end} - NFA_{beg} + D$ (where D is the depreciation expense during the year), is equivalent to $FA_{end} - FA_{beg}$.

Challenge (Questions 24–35)

Use the following information for Flies Right, Inc., to work Problems 25 and 26 (the tax rate is 34 percent):

	1994	1995
Sales	$1,745	$1,900
Depreciation	184	184
Cost of goods sold	690	770
Other expenses	165	150
Interest	122	148
Cash	955	1,190
Receivables	1,444	1,555
Short-term notes payable	179	149
Long-term debt	3,475	4,300
Net fixed assets	8,106	8,315
Accounts payable	1,050	1,000
Inventory	2,188	2,275
Dividends	150	165

25. **Financial Statements** Draw up an income statement and balance sheet for this company for 1994 and 1995.

26. **Calculating Cash Flow** For 1995, calculate the cash flow from assets, cash flow to bondholders, and cash flow to stockholders.

27. **Investment Income** Assuming that Song's cash flows in Problem 20 came from equal investments of $20,000 each, find her *aftertax* rate of return on each investment.

28. **CCA** Mississauga Manufacturing Ltd. just invested in some new processing machinery to take advantage of more favourable CCA rates in a new federal budget. The machinery qualifies for 25 percent CCA rate and has an installed cost of $1,600,000. Calculate the CCA and UCC for the first five years.

29. **UCC** A piece of newly purchased industrial equipment costs $368,000. It is Class 8 property. Calculate the annual depreciation allowances and end-of-year book values (UCC) for the first five years.

30. **CCA and UCC** Our new computer system cost us $160,000. We will outgrow it in three years. When we sell it, we will probably get only 20 percent of the purchase price. CCA on the computer will be calculated at a 30 percent rate (Class 10). Calculate the CCA and UCC values for five years. What will be

**Challenge
(Continued)**

the aftertax proceeds from the sale assuming the asset class is continued? Assume a 40 percent tax rate.

31. **CCA** Trans Canada Industries bought new manufacturing equipment (Class 8) for $500,000 in 1995 and then paid $50,000 for installation it capitalized in Class 8. The firm also invested $1 million in a new brick building (Class 3). During 1995, Trans Canada finished the project and put it in use. Find the total CCA for Trans Canada for 1995 and 1996.

32. **UCC** Tor-Van Construction specializes in large projects in Toronto and Vancouver. In 1995, Tor-Van invested $300,000 in new excavating equipment (Class 22). At the same time, the firm sold some older equipment on the secondhand market for $50,000. When it was purchased in 1992, the older equipment cost $150,000. Calculate the UCC for the asset pool in Class 22 in each year from 1992 through 1996.

33. **Income Tax** A resident of Alberta has taxable income from employment of $85,000. This individual is considering three investments of equal risk and wishes to determine the aftertax income for each:

    a. $40,000 worth of bonds with a coupon rate of 9.5 percent.
    b. 500 shares of stock that will pay a dividend at the end of the year of $7 per share.
    c. 1,000 shares of another stock that is expected to increase in value by $3 per share during the year.

34. **Tax Loss Carry-back and Carry-forward** The Three R Company experienced an operating loss of $450,000 in 1992. Taxable income figures for recent years are given below. Show how the firm can maximize its tax refunds.

	1989	1990	1991	1992	1993	1994	1995
Taxable income ($1,000)	$58	$70	$84	($300)	$20	$20	$20

35. **UCC** A proposed cost-saving device has an installed cost of $59,400. It is in Class 9 for CCA purposes. It will actually function for five years, at which time it will have no value.

    a. Calculate UCC at the end of five years.
    b. What are the tax implications when the asset is sold?

Suggested Readings

There are many excellent textbooks on accounting and financial statements. One that we have found helpful is:

Garrison, R. H.; G. R. Chesley; and R. G. Carroll. *Managerial Accounting,* 2nd Canadian ed. Homewood, IL: Richard D. Irwin, Inc., 1993.

FINANCIAL STATEMENTS AND LONG-TERM FINANCIAL PLANNING

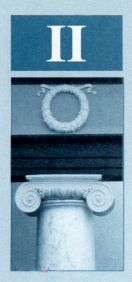

II

CHAPTER 3 | Working with Financial Statements

This chapter discusses different aspects of financial statements, including how the statement of cash flows is constructed, how to standardize financial statements, and how to determine and interpret some common financial ratios.

CHAPTER 4 | Long-Term Financial Planning and Corporate Growth

Chapter 4 examines the basic elements of financial planning. It introduces the concept of sustainable growth that can be a very useful tool in financial planning.

Working with Financial Statements

In Chapter 2, we discussed some of the essential concepts of financial statements and cash flows. Part II, this chapter and the next, continues where our earlier discussion left off. Our goal here is to expand your understanding of the uses (and abuses) of financial statement information.

Financial statement information crops up in various places in the remainder of our book. Part II is not essential for understanding this material, but it helps give you an overall perspective on the role of financial statement information in corporate finance.

A good working knowledge of financial statements is desirable simply because such statements, and numbers derived from those statements, are the primary means of communicating financial information both within the firm and outside the firm. In short, much of the language of corporate finance is rooted in the ideas we discuss in this chapter.

Furthermore, as we shall see, there are many different ways of using financial statement information and many different types of users. This diversity reflects the fact that financial statement information plays an important part in many types of decisions.

In the best of all worlds, the financial manager has full market value information about all the firm's assets. This rarely (if ever) happens. So the reason we rely on accounting figures for much of our financial information is that we almost always cannot obtain all (or even part) of the market information that we want. The only meaningful metrestick for evaluating business decisions is whether or not they create economic value (see Chapter 1). However, in many important situations, it is not possible to make this judgment directly because we can't see the market value effects.

We recognize that accounting numbers are often just pale reflections of economic reality, but they frequently are the best available information. For privately held corporations, not-for-profit businesses, and smaller firms, for example, very little direct market value information exists. The accountant's reporting function is crucial in these circumstances.

Clearly, one important goal of the accountant is to report financial information to the user in a form useful for decision making. Ironically, the information frequently does not come to the user in such a form. In other words, financial statements don't come with a user's guide. This chapter and the next are first steps in filling this gap.

3.1 | CASH FLOW AND FINANCIAL STATEMENTS: A CLOSER LOOK

At the most fundamental level, firms do two different things: They generate cash and they spend it. Cash is generated by selling a product, an asset, or a security. Selling a security involves either borrowing or selling an equity interest (i.e., shares of stock) in the firm. Cash is spent by paying for materials and labor to produce a product and by purchasing assets. Payments to creditors and owners also require spending cash.

In Chapter 2, we saw that the cash activities of a firm could be summarized by a simple identity:

Cash flow from assets = Cash flow to creditors + Cash flow to owners

This cash flow identity summarizes the total cash result of all the transactions the firm engaged in during the year. In this section, we return to the subject of cash flows by taking a closer look at the cash events during the year that lead to these total figures.

Sources and Uses of Cash

Those activities that bring in cash are called **sources of cash.** Those activities that involve spending cash are called **uses** (or applications) **of cash.** What we need to do is to trace the changes in the firm's balance sheet to see how the firm obtained its cash and how the firm spent its cash during some time period.

To get started, consider the balance sheets for the Prufrock Corporation in Table 3.1. Notice that we have calculated the changes in each of the items on the balance sheet over the year from the end of 1994 to the end of 1995.

sources of cash
A firm's activities that generate cash.

uses of cash
A firm's activities in which cash is spent.

TABLE 3.1

PRUFROCK CORPORATION
Balance Sheets as of December 31, 1994 and 1995
($ in thousands)

	1994	1995	Change
Assets			
Current assets			
Cash	$ 84	$ 98	+$ 14
Accounts receivable	165	188	+ 23
Inventory	393	422	+ 29
Total	$ 642	$ 708	+$ 66
Fixed assets			
Net plant and equipment	2,731	2,880	+ 149
Total assets	$3,373	$3,588	+$ 215
Liabilities and Owners' Equity			
Current liabilities			
Accounts payable	$ 312	$ 344	+$ 32
Notes payable	231	196	− 35
Total	$ 543	$ 540	−$ 3
Long-term debt	$ 531	$ 457	−$ 74
Owners' equity			
Common stock	500	550	+ 50
Retained earnings	1,799	2,041	+ 242
Total	$2,299	$2,591	+$ 292
Total liabilities and owners' equity	$3,373	$3,588	+$ 215

Looking over the balance sheets for Prufrock, we see that quite a few things changed during the year. For example, Prufrock increased its net fixed assets by $149,000 and its inventory by $29,000. Where did the money come from? To answer this and related questions, we must identify those changes that used up cash (uses) and those that brought cash in (sources). A little common sense is useful here. A firm uses cash by either buying assets or making payments. So, loosely speaking, an increase in an asset account means the firm bought some net assets, a use of cash. If an asset account went down, then, on a net basis, the firm sold some assets. This would be a net source. Similarly, if a liability account goes down, then the firm has made a net payment, a use of cash.

Given this reasoning, there is a simple, albeit mechanical, definition that you may find useful. An increase in a left-hand side (asset) account or a decrease in a right-hand side (liability or equity) account is a use of cash. Likewise, a decrease in an asset account or an increase in a liability (or equity) account is a source of cash.

Looking back at Prufrock, we see that inventory rose by $29. This is a net use since Prufrock effectively paid out $29 to increase inventories. Accounts payable rose by $32. This is a source of cash since Prufrock effectively has borrowed an additional $32 by the end of the year. Notes payable, on the other hand, went down by $35, so Prufrock effectively paid off $35 worth of short-term debt—a use of cash.

Based on our discussion, we can summarize the sources and uses from the balance sheet as follows:

Sources of cash:	
Increase in accounts payable	$ 32
Increase in common stock	50
Increase in retained earnings	242
Total sources	$324
Uses of cash:	
Increase in accounts receivable	$ 23
Increase in inventory	29
Decrease in notes payable	35
Decrease in long-term debt	74
Net fixed asset acquisitions	149
Total uses	$310
Net addition to cash	$ 14

The net addition to cash is just the difference between sources and uses, and our $14 result here agrees with the $14 change shown on the balance sheet.

This simple statement tells us much of what happened during the year, but it doesn't tell the whole story. For example, the increase in retained earnings is net income (a source of funds) less dividends (a use of funds). It would be more enlightening to have these reported separately so we could see the breakdown. Also, we have only considered net fixed asset acquisitions. Total or gross spending would be more interesting to know.

To further trace the flow of cash through the firm during the year, we need an income statement. For Prufrock, the results for these two years are shown in Table 3.2. Because we are looking at cash flow during calendar year 1995, we focus on the 1995 income statement.

Notice here that the $242 addition to retained earnings we calculated from the balance sheet is just the difference between the 1994 net income of $363 and that year's dividend of $121.

PRUFROCK CORPORATION
Income Statements
($ in thousands)

	1995		1994
Sales	$2,311		$2,070
Cost of goods sold	1,344		1,291
Depreciation	276		250
Earnings before interest and taxes	$ 691		$ 529
Interest paid	141		127
Taxable income	$ 550		$ 402
Taxes	187		161
Net income	$ 363		$ 241
Addition to retained earnings	$242		$120
Dividends	121		121

The Statement of Changes in Financial Position

There is some flexibility in summarizing the sources and uses of cash in the form of a financial statement. However it is presented, the result is called the **statement of changes in financial position.**

We present a particular format in Table 3.3 for this statement. The basic idea is to group all the changes into one of three categories: operating activities, financing activities, and investment activities. The exact form differs in detail from one preparer to the next.

Don't be surprised if you come across different arrangements. The types of information presented may be very similar, but the exact order can differ. The key thing to remember is that we started out with $84 in cash and ended up with $98, for a net increase of $14. We're just trying to see what events led to this change.

Going back to Chapter 2, there is a slight conceptual problem here. Interest paid should really go under financing activities, but, unfortunately, that's not the way the accounting is handled. The reason, you may recall, is that interest is deducted as an expense when net income is computed. Also, notice that our net purchase of fixed assets was $149. Since we wrote off $276 worth (the depreciation), we must have actually spent a total of $149 + 276 = $425 on fixed assets.

Once we have this statement, it might seem appropriate to express the change in cash on a per-share basis, much as we did for net income. Although standard accounting practice does not report this information, it is often calculated by financial analysts. The reason is that accountants believe that cash flow (or some component of cash flow) is not an alternative to accounting income, so only earnings per share are to be reported.

Now that we have the various cash pieces in place, we can get a good idea of what happened during the year. Prufrock's major cash outlays were fixed asset acquisitions and cash dividends. The firm paid for these activities primarily with cash generated from operations.

Prufrock also retired some long-term debt and increased current assets. Finally, current liabilities were virtually unchanged, and a relatively small amount of new

statement of changes in financial position

A firm's financial statement that summarizes its sources and uses of cash over a specified period.

T A B L E 3.3	PRUFROCK CORPORATION 1995 Statement of Changes in Financial Position	
	Operating activities	
	Net income	$ 363
	Plus:	
	Depreciation	276
	Increase in accounts payable	32
	Less:	
	Increase in accounts receivable	−23
	Increase in inventory	−29
	Net cash from operating activity	$ 619
	Investment activities:	
	Fixed asset acquisitions	−$ 425
	Net cash from investment activity	−$ 425
	Financing activities:	
	Decrease in notes payable	−$ 35
	Decrease in long-term debt	−74
	Dividends paid	−121
	Increase in common stock	50
	Net cash from financing activity	−$ 180
	Net increase in cash	$ 14

equity was sold. Altogether, this short sketch captures Prufrock's major sources and uses of cash for the year.

> CONCEPT QUESTIONS
> 1. What is a source of cash? Give three examples.
> 2. What is a use or application of cash? Give three examples.

3.2 | STANDARDIZED FINANCIAL STATEMENTS

The next thing we might want to do with Prufrock's financial statements is to compare them to those of other, similar companies. We would immediately have a problem, however. It's almost impossible to directly compare the financial statements for two companies because of differences in size. In Canada, this problem is compounded because some companies are one of a kind. Canadian Pacific Enterprises and Northern Telecom are examples. Further, large Canadian companies usually span two, three, or more industries, making comparisons extremely difficult.

common-size statement
A standardized financial statement presenting all items in percentage terms. Balance sheets are shown as a percentage of assets and income statements as a percentage of sales.

To start making comparisons, one obvious thing we might try to do is to somehow standardize the financial statements. One very common and useful way of doing this is to work with percentages instead of total dollars. In this section, we describe two different ways of standardizing financial statements along these lines.

Common-Size Statements

To get started, a useful way of standardizing financial statements is to express the balance sheet as a percentage of assets and to express the income statement as a percentage of sales. Such financial statements are called **common-size statements.** We consider these next.

Common-Size Balance Sheets   One way, but not the only way, to construct a common-size balance sheet is to express each item as a percentage of total assets. Prufrock's 1994 and 1995 common-size balance sheets are shown in Table 3.4.

Notice that some of the totals don't check exactly because of rounding errors. Also, notice that the total change has to be zero since the beginning and ending numbers must add up to 100 percent.

In this form, financial statements are relatively easy to read and compare. For example, just looking at the two balance sheets for Prufrock, we see that current assets were 19.7 percent of total assets in 1995, up from 19 percent in 1994. Current liabilities declined from 16.1 percent to 15.1 percent of total liabilities over that same time. Similarly, total equity rose from 68.2 percent of total liabilities to 72.2 percent.

Overall, Prufrock's liquidity, as measured by current assets compared to current liabilities, increased over the year. Simultaneously, Prufrock's indebtedness diminished as a percentage of total assets. We might be tempted to conclude that the balance sheet has grown stronger. We say more about this later.

Common-Size Income Statements   A useful way of standardizing income statements is to express each item as a percentage of total sales, as illustrated for Prufrock in Table 3.5.

Common-size income statements tell us what happens to each dollar in sales. For Prufrock in 1995 for example, interest expense eats up $.061 out of every sales dollar and taxes take another $.081. When all is said and done, $.157 of each dollar flows through to the bottom line (net income), and that amount is split into $.105 retained in the business and $.052 paid out in dividends.

T A B L E 3.4

PRUFROCK CORPORATION
Common-Size Balance Sheets
December 31, 1994 and 1995

	1994	1995	Change
Assets			
Current assets			
Cash	2.5%	2.7%	+.2%
Accounts receivable	4.9	5.2	+.3
Inventory	11.7	11.8	+.1
Total	19.0	19.7	+.7
Fixed assets			
Net plant and equipment	81.0	80.3	−.7
Total assets	100.0%	100.0%	0 %
Liabilities and Owners' Equity			
Current liabilities			
Accounts payable	9.2%	9.6%	+.4%
Notes payable	6.8	5.5	−1.3
Total	16.1	15.1	−1.0
Long-term debt	15.7	12.7	−3.0
Owners' equity			
Common stock	14.8	15.3	+.5
Retained earnings	53.3	56.9	+3.6
Total	68.2	72.2	+4.0
Total liabilities and owners' equity	100.0%	100.0%	0 %

T A B L E 3.5

PRUFROCK CORPORATION
Common-Size Income Statements

		1994		1995
Sales		100.0%		100.0%
Cost of goods sold		62.4		58.2
Depreciation		12.0		11.9
Earnings before interest and taxes		25.6		29.9
Interest paid		6.2		6.1
Taxable income		19.4		23.8
Taxes		7.8		8.1
Net income		11.6%		15.7%
Addition to retained earnings	5.8%		10.5%	
Dividends	5.8%		5.2%	

These percentages are very useful in comparisons. For example, a very relevant figure is the cost percentage. For Prufrock, $.582 of each $1.00 in sales goes to pay for goods sold in 1995 as compared to $.624 in 1994. The reduction likely signals improved cost controls in 1995. To pursue this point, it would be interesting to compute the same percentage for Prufrock's main competitors to see how Prufrock's improved cost control in 1995 stacks up.

Although we have not presented it here, it is also possible and useful to prepare a common-size statement of cash flows. Unfortunately, with the current statement of cash flows, there is no obvious denominator such as total assets or total sales. However, when the information is arranged similarly to Table 3.5, each item can be expressed as a percentage of total sources (or total uses). The results can then be interpreted as the percentage of total sources of cash supplied or as the percentage of total uses of cash for a particular item.

Common-Base-Year Financial Statements: Trend Analysis

Imagine that we were given balance sheets for the last 10 years for some company and we were trying to investigate trends in the firm's pattern of operations. Does the firm use more or less debt? Has the firm grown more or less liquid? A useful way of standardizing financial statements is to choose a base year and then express each item relative to the base amount. We call such statements **common-base-year statements.**

common-base-year statement
A standardized financial statement presenting all items relative to a certain base year amount.

For example, Prufrock's inventory rose from $393 to $422. If we pick 1994 as our base year, then we would set inventory equal to 1.00 for that year. For the next year, we would calculate inventory relative to the base year as $422/$393 = 1.07. We could say that inventory grew by about 7 percent during the year. If we had multiple years, we would just divide each one by $393. The resulting series is very easy to plot, and it is then very easy to compare two or more different companies. Table 3.6 summarizes these calculations for the asset side of the balance sheet.

Combined Common-Size and Base-Year Analysis   The trend analysis we have been discussing can be combined with the common-size analysis discussed earlier. The reason for doing this is that as total assets grow, most of the other accounts must grow as well. By first forming the common-size statements, we eliminate the effect of this overall growth.

	Assets		Common Size		Common Base Year	Combined Common-Size and Base-Year
	1994	1995	1994	1995	1995	1995
Current assets						
Cash	$ 84	$ 98	2.5%	2.7%	1.17	1.08
Accounts receivable	165	188	4.9	5.2	1.14	1.06
Inventory	393	422	11.7	11.8	1.07	1.01
Total current assets	$ 642	$ 708	19.0	19.7	1.10	1.04
Fixed assets						
Net plant and equipment	2,731	2,880	81.0	80.3	1.05	0.99
Total assets	$3,373	$3,588	100 %	100 %	1.06	1.00

PRUFROCK CORPORATION
Summary of Standardized Balance Sheets (Asset side only)
($ in thousands)

T A B L E 3.6

The common-size numbers are calculated by dividing each item by total assets for that year. For example, the 1994 common-size cash amount is $84/$3,373 = 2.5%. The common-base-year numbers are calculated by dividing each 1995 item by the base-year dollar (1994) amount. The common-base cash is thus $98/$84 = 1.17, representing a 17 percent increase. The combined common-size and base-year figures are calculated by dividing each common-size amount by the base-year (1994) common-size amount. The cash figure is therefore 2.7%/2.5% = 1.08, representing an 8 percent increase in cash holdings as a percentage of total assets.

For example, Prufrock's accounts receivable were $165, or 4.9 percent of total assets in 1994. In 1995, they had risen to $188, which is 5.2 percent of total assets. If we do our trend analysis in terms of dollars, the 1995 figure would be $188/$165 = 1.14, a 14 percent increase in receivables. However, if we work with the common-size statements, the 1995 figure would be 5.2%/4.9% = 1.06. This tells us that accounts receivable, as a percentage of total assets, grew by 6 percent. Roughly speaking, what we see is that of the 14 percent total increase, about 8 percent (14% − 6%) is attributable simply to growth in total assets. Table 3.6 summarizes this discussion for Prufrock's assets.

CONCEPT QUESTIONS

1. Why is it often necessary to standardize financial statements?

2. Name two types of standardized statements and describe how each is formed.

3.3 | RATIO ANALYSIS

Another way of avoiding the problem of comparing companies of different sizes is to calculate and compare **financial ratios.** Such ratios are ways of comparing and investigating the relationships between different pieces of financial information. Using ratios eliminates the size problem since the size effectively divides out. We're then left with percentages, multiples, or time periods.

There is a problem in discussing financial ratios. Since a ratio is simply one number divided by another, and since there is a substantial quantity of accounting numbers out there, there are a huge number of possible ratios we could examine. Everybody has a favorite, so we've restricted ourselves to a representative sampling. We chose the sample to be consistent with the practice of experienced financial analysts. Another way to see which ratios are used most often in practice is to look at the output of commercially available software that generates ratios.

financial ratios
Relationships determined from a firm's financial information and used for comparison purposes.

Once you have gained experience in ratio analysis, you will find that 20 ratios do not tell you twice as much as 10. You are looking for problem areas, not an exhaustive list of ratios so you don't have to worry about including every possible ratio.

What you do need to worry about is the fact that different people and different sources frequently don't compute these ratios in exactly the same way, and this leads to much confusion. The specific definitions we use here may or may not be the same as ones you have seen or will see elsewhere. When you are using ratios as a tool for analysis, you should be careful to document how you calculate each one.

We defer much of our discussion of how ratios are used and some problems that come up with using them to the next section. For now, for each of the ratios we discuss, several questions come to mind:

1. How is it computed?
2. What is it intended to measure, and why might we be interested?
3. What might a high or low value be telling us? How might such values be misleading?
4. How could this measure be improved?

Financial ratios are traditionally grouped into the following categories:

1. Short-term solvency or liquidity ratios.
2. Long-term solvency or financial leverage ratios.
3. Asset management or turnover ratios.
4. Profitability ratios.
5. Market value ratios.

We consider each of these in turn. To illustrate ratio calculations for Prufrock, we use the ending balance sheet (1995) figures unless we explicitly say otherwise. After calculating the 1995 ratios, we illustrated the inferences you can make from ratios by making two comparisons for each ratio. The comparisons draw on numbers in Table 3.7 that summarize each ratio's 1995 value and also present corresponding values for Prufrock in 1994 and for the industry average.[1]

Short-Term Solvency or Liquidity Measures

As the name suggests, short-term solvency ratios as a group are intended to provide information about a firm's liquidity, and these ratios are sometimes called liquidity measures. The primary concern is the firm's ability to pay its bills over the short run without undue stress. Consequently, these ratios focus on current assets and current liabilities.

For obvious reasons, liquidity ratios are particularly interesting to short-term creditors. Since financial managers are constantly working with banks and other short-term lenders, an understanding of these ratios is essential.

One advantage of looking at current assets and liabilities is that their book values and market values are likely to be similar. Often (but not always), these assets and liabilities just don't live long enough for the two to get seriously out of step. This is true for a going concern that has no problems in selling inventory (turning it into

---

[1] In this case the industry average figures are hypothetical. We will discuss industry average ratios in some detail later.

Short-Term Solvency (Liquidity)	1994	1995	Industry	Rating
Current ratio	1.18	1.31	1.25	OK
Quick ratio	0.46	0.53	0.60	—
Cash ratio	0.15	0.18	0.20	OK
Net working capital	2.9 %	4.7 %	5.2 %	OK
Interval measure (days)	182	192	202	OK
Turnover				
Inventory turnover	3.3	3.3	4.0	—
Days' sales in inventory	111	114	91	—
Receivables turnover	12.5	12.3	11.5	OK
Days' sales in receivables	29	30	32	OK
NWC turnover	20.9	13.8	14.6	—
Fixed asset turnover	0.76	0.80	0.90	OK
Total asset turnover	0.61	0.64	0.71	OK
Financial Leverage				
Total debt ratio	0.32	0.28	0.42	++
Debt/equity	0.47	0.39	0.72	++
Equity multiplier	1.47	1.39	1.72	+
Long-term debt ratio	0.16	0.15	0.16	+
Times interest earned	4.2	4.9	2.8	++
Cash coverage ratio	6.2	6.9	4.2	++
Profitability				
Profit margin	11.6 %	15.7 %	10.7 %	++
Return on assets (ROA)	7.1 %	10.1 %	7.6 %	+
Return on equity (ROE)	10.5 %	14.0 %	13.1 %	+
Market Value Ratios				
Price-earnings ratio (P/E)	7.0	8.0	7.1	+
Market-to-book ratio	0.73	1.12	0.92	+

T A B L E 3.7

Selected financial ratios for Prufrock

Comments: Company shows strength relative to industry in avoiding increased leverage. Profitability is above average. Company carries more inventory than the industry causing weakness in related ratios. Market value ratios are strong.

receivables) and then collecting the receivable, all at book values. Even in a going concern, all inventory may not be liquid since some may be held permanently as a buffer against unforeseen delays.

On the other hand, like any type of near-cash, current assets and liabilities can and do change fairly rapidly, so today's amounts may not be a reliable guide to the future. For example, when a firm experiences financial distress and undergoes a loan workout or liquidation, obsolete inventory and overdue receivables often have market values well below their book values.

Current Ratio   One of the best known and most widely used ratios is the *current ratio*. As you might guess, the current ratio is defined as:

$$\text{Current ratio} = \text{Current assets/Current liabilities} \qquad [3.1]$$

For Prufrock, the 1995 current ratio is:

$$\text{Current ratio} = \$708/540 = 1.31$$

Because current assets and liabilities are, in principle, converted to cash over the following 12 months, the current ratio is a measure of short-term liquidity. The unit of measurement is either dollars or times. So, we could say that Prufrock has $1.31 in current assets for every $1 in current liabilities, or we could say that Prufrock has its current liabilities covered 1.31 times over. To a creditor, particularly a short-term creditor such as a supplier, the higher the current ratio, the better. To the firm, a high current ratio indicates liquidity, but it also may indicate an inefficient use of cash and other short-term assets. Absent some extraordinary circumstances, we would expect to see a current ratio of at least 1, because a current ratio of less than 1 would mean that net working capital (current assets less current liabilities) is negative. This would be unusual in a healthy firm, at least for most types of business. Some analysts use a rule of thumb that the current ratio should be at least 2.0 but this can be misleading for many industries.

Applying this to Prufrock, we see from Table 3.7 that the current ratio of 1.31 for 1995 is higher than the 1.18 recorded for 1994 and slightly above the industry average. For this reason, the analyst has recorded an OK rating for this ratio.

In general, the current ratio, like any ratio, is affected by various types of transactions. For example, suppose the firm borrows long term to raise money. The short-run effect would be an increase in cash from the issue proceeds and an increase in long-term debt. Current liabilities would not be affected, so the current ratio would rise.

Finally, note that an apparently low current ratio may not be a bad sign for a company with a large reserve of untapped borrowing power.

E X A M P L E | **3.1**   **Current Events**

Suppose a firm were to pay off some of its suppliers and short-term creditors. What would happen to the current ratio? Suppose a firm buys some inventory for cash. What happens in this case? What happens if a firm sells some merchandise?

The first case is a trick question. What happens is that the current ratio moves away from 1. If it is greater than 1 (the usual case), it gets bigger; but if it is less than one, it gets smaller. To see this, suppose the firm has $4 in current assets and $2 in current liabilities for a current ratio of 2. If we use $1 in cash to reduce current liabilities, then the new current ratio is ($4 - $1)/($2 - $1) = 3. If we reverse this to $2 in current assets and $4 in current liabilities, the current ratio would fall to ⅓ from ½.

The second case in not quite as tricky. Nothing happens to the current ratio because cash goes down while inventory goes up—total current assets are unaffected.

In the third case, the current ratio would usually rise because inventory is normally shown at cost and the sale would normally be at something greater than cost (the difference is the markup). The increase in either cash or receivables is therefore greater than the decrease in inventory. This increases current assets, and the current ratio rises. ▐

The Quick (or Acid-Test) Ratio   Inventory is often the least liquid current asset. It's also the one for which the book values are least reliable as measures of market value, since the quality of the inventory isn't considered. Some of it may be damaged, obsolete, or lost.

More to the point, relatively large inventories are often a sign of short-term trouble. The firm may have overestimated sales and overbought or overproduced as a result. In this case, the firm may have a substantial portion of its liquidity tied up in slow-moving inventory.

To further evaluate liquidity, the *quick* or *acid-test ratio* is computed just like the current ratio, except inventory is omitted:

$$\text{Quick ratio} = \frac{\text{Current assets} - \text{Inventory}}{\text{Current liabilities}} \qquad [3.2]$$

Notice that using cash to buy inventory does not affect the current ratio, but it reduces the quick ratio. Again, the idea is that inventory is relatively illiquid compared to cash.

For Prufrock, this ratio in 1995 was:

$$\text{Quick ratio} = [\$708 - 422]/\$540 = .53$$

The quick ratio here tells a somewhat different story from the current ratio, because inventory accounts for more than half of Prufrock's current assets. To exaggerate the point, if this inventory consisted of, say, unsold nuclear power plants, this is a cause for concern.

Table 3.7 provides more information. The quick ratio has improved from 1994 to 1995, but it is still less than the industry average. At a minimum, this suggests Prufrock still is carrying relatively more inventory than its competitors. We need more information to know if this is a problem.

Other Liquidity Ratios

We briefly mention three other measures of liquidity. A very short-term creditor might be interested in the *cash ratio:*

$$\text{Cash ratio} = \text{Cash/Current liabilities} \qquad [3.3]$$

You can verify that this works out to be .18 for Prufrock in 1995. According to Table 3.7, this is a slight improvement over 1994 and around the industry average. Cash adequacy does not seem to be a problem for Prufrock.

Because net working capital (NWC) is frequently viewed as the amount of short-term liquidity a firm has, we can measure the ratio of *NWC to total assets:*

$$\text{Net working capital to total assets} = \text{Net working capital/Total assets} \qquad [3.4]$$

A relatively low value might indicate relatively low levels of liquidity. For Prufrock in 1995, this ratio works out to be ($708 − 540)/$3,588 = 4.7%. As with the cash ratio, comparisons with 1994 and the industry average indicate no problems.

Finally, imagine that Prufrock is facing a strike and cash inflows are beginning to dry up. How long could the business keep running? One answer is given by the *interval measure:*

$$\text{Interval measure} = \text{Current assets/Average daily operating costs} \qquad [3.5]$$

Total costs for the year 1995, excluding depreciation and interest, were $1,344. The average daily cost was $1,344/365 = $3.68 per day. The interval measure is thus $708/$3.68 = 192 days. Based on this, Prufrock could hang on for six months or so, about in line with its competitors.[2]

---

[2] Sometimes depreciation and/or interest is included in calculating average daily costs. Depreciation isn't a cash expense, so this doesn't make a lot of sense. Interest is a financing cost, so we excluded it by definition (we only looked at operating costs). We could, of course, define a different ratio that included interest expense.

Long-Term Solvency Measures

This group of ratios is intended to address the firm's long-run ability to meet its obligations or, more generally, its financial leverage. These are sometimes called *financial leverage ratios* or just *leverage ratios*. We consider three commonly used measures and some variations. These ratios all measure debt, equity, and assets at book values. As we stressed at the beginning, market values would be far better but these are often not available.

Total Debt Ratio   The *total debt ratio* takes into account all debts of all maturities to all creditors. It can be defined in several ways, the easiest of which is:

$$\text{Total debt ratio} = [\text{Total assets} - \text{Total equity}]/\text{Total assets} \qquad [3.6]$$
$$= [\$3,588 - 2,591]/\$3,588 = .28$$

In this case, an analyst might say that Prufrock uses 28 percent debt.[3] There has been a large volume of theoretical research on how much debt is optimal, and we discuss this in Part VII. Taking a more pragmatic view here, most financial analysts would note that Prufrock's use of debt has declined slightly from 1994 and is considerably less than the industry average. To find out if this is good or bad, we would look for more information on the financial health of Prufrock's competitors. Firms in many industries took on excessive debt in the 1980s—especially in the United States. The rating and comment in Table 3.7 suggest that competitors are overleveraged and that Prufrock's more moderate use of debt is a strength.

Regardless of the interpretation, the total debt ratio shows that Prufrock has $.28 in debt for every $1 in assets in 1992. Therefore, there is $.72 in equity ($1 − $.28) for every $.28 in debt. With this in mind, we can define two useful variations on the total debt ratio, the *debt/equity ratio* and the *equity multiplier*. We illustrate each Prufrock for 1995:

$$\text{Debt/equity ratio} = \text{Total debt}/\text{Total equity} \qquad [3.7]$$
$$= \$.28/\$.72 = .39$$
$$\text{Equity multiplier} = \text{Total assets}/\text{Total equity} \qquad [3.8]$$
$$= \$1/\$.72 = 1.39$$

The fact that the equity multiplier is 1 plus the debt/equity ratio is not a coincidence:

$$\text{Equity multiplier} = \text{Total assets}/\text{Total equity} = \$1/\$.72 = 1.39$$
$$= (\text{Total equity} + \text{Total debt})/\text{Total equity}$$
$$= 1 + \text{Debt/Equity ratio} = 1.39$$

The thing to notice here is that given any one of these three ratios, you can immediately calculate the other two, so they all say exactly the same thing. You can verify this by looking at the comparisons in Table 3.7.

A Brief Digression: Total Capitalization versus Total Assets   Frequently, financial analysts are more concerned with the firm's long-term debt than its short-term debt because the short-term debt is constantly changing. Also, a firm's accounts payable may be more a reflection of trade practice than debt management policy. For these reasons, the *long-term debt ratio* is often calculated as:

---

[3] Total equity here includes preferred stock (discussed in Chapter 12 and elsewhere), if there is any. An equivalent numerator in this ratio would be (Current liabilities + Long-term debt).

$$\text{Long-term debt ratio} = \frac{\text{Long-term debt}}{\text{Long-term debt} + \text{Total equity}} \qquad [3.9]$$

$$= \$457/[\$457 + 2{,}591] = \$457/\$3{,}048 = .15$$

The $3,048 in total long-term debt and equity is sometimes called the firm's *total capitalization,* and the financial manager frequently focusses on this quantity rather than total assets. As you can see from Table 3.7, the long-term debt ratio follows the same trend as the other financial leverage ratios.

To complicate matters, different people (and different books) mean different things by the term *debt ratio.* Some mean total debt, and some mean long-term debt only, and, unfortunately, a substantial number are simply vague about which one they mean.

This is a source of confusion, so we choose to give two separate names to the two measures. The same problem comes up in discussing the debt/equity ratio. Financial analysts frequently calculate this ratio using only long-term debt.

Times Interest Earned   Another common measure of long-term solvency is the *times interest earned* (TIE) *ratio.* Once again, there are several possible (and common) definitions, but we'll stick with the most traditional:

$$\text{Times interest earned ratio} = \text{EBIT/Interest} \qquad [3.10]$$

$$= \$691/\$141 = 4.9 \text{ times}$$

As the name suggests, this ratio measures how well a company has its interest obligations covered. For Prufrock, the interest bill is covered 4.9 times over in 1995. Table 3.7 shows that TIE increased slightly over 1994 and exceeds the industry average. This reinforces the signal of the other debt ratios.

Cash Coverage   A problem with the TIE ratio is that it is based on EBIT, which is not really a measure of cash available to pay interest. The reason is that depreciation, a non-cash expense, has been deducted out. Since interest is most definitely a cash outflow (to creditors), one way to define the *cash coverage ratio* is:

$$\text{Cash coverage ratio} = [\text{EBIT} + \text{Depreciation}]/\text{Interest} \qquad [3.11]$$

$$= [\$691 + 276]/\$141 = \$967/\$141 = 6.9 \text{ times}$$

The numerator here, EBIT plus depreciation, is often abbreviated EBDIT (earnings before depreciation, interest, and taxes). It is a basic measure of the firm's ability to generate cash from operations, and it is frequently used as a measure of cash flow available to meet financial obligations. If depreciation changed dramatically from one year to the next, cash coverage could give a different signal than TIE. In the case of Prufrock, the signals are reinforcing as you can see in Table 3.7.[4]

Asset Management or Turnover Measures

We next turn our attention to the efficiency with which Prufrock uses its assets. The measures in this section are sometimes called *asset utilization ratios.* The specific ratios we discuss can all be interpreted as measures of turnover. What they are intended to describe is how efficiently or intensively a firm uses its assets to generate sales. We first look at two important current assets, inventory and receivables.

---

[4] Any onetime transactions, such as capital gains or losses, should be netted out of EBIT before calculating cash coverage.

Inventory Turnover and Days' Sales in Inventory   During 1995, Prufrock had a cost of goods sold of $1,344. Inventory at the end of the year was $422. With these numbers, *inventory turnover* can be calculated as:

$$\text{Inventory turnover} = \text{Cost of goods sold/Inventory} \qquad\qquad [3.12]$$
$$= \$1,344/\$422 = 3.2 \text{ times}$$

In a sense, the company sold or turned over the entire inventory 3.2 times.[5] As long as Prufrock is not running out of stock and thereby forgoing sales, the higher this ratio is, the more efficiently it is managing inventory.

If we turned our inventory over 3.2 times during the year, then we can immediately figure out how long it took us to turn it over on average. The result is the average *days' sales in inventory:*

$$\text{Days' sales in inventory} = 365 \text{ days/Inventory turnover} \qquad\qquad [3.13]$$
$$= 365/3.2 = 114 \text{ days}$$

This tells us that, roughly speaking, inventory sits 114 days on average in 1995 before it is sold. Alternatively, assuming we used the most recent inventory and cost figures, it should take about 114 days to work off our current inventory.

Looking at Table 3.7, it would be fair to state that Prufrock has a 114 days' supply of inventory. Ninety-one days is considered normal. This means that, at current daily sales, it would take 114 days to deplete the available inventory. We could also say that we have 114 days of sales in inventory. Table 3.7 registers a negative rating for inventory because Prufrock is carrying more than the industry average. This could be a sign of poor financial management in overinvesting in inventory that will eventually be sold at a normal markup. Worse, it could be that some of Prufrock's inventory is obsolete and should be marked down. Or it could be that Prufrock is simply selling a different product mix than its competitors and nothing is wrong. What the ratio tells us is that we should investigate further.

Returning to ratio calculation, it might make more sense to use the average inventory in calculating turnover. Inventory turnover would then be $1,344/[($393 + $422)/2] = 3.3 times.[6] It really depends on the purpose of the calculation. If we are interested in how long it will take us to sell our current inventory, then using the ending figure (as we did initially) is probably better.

In many of the ratios we discuss next, average figures could just as well be used. Again, it really depends on whether we are worried about the past when averages are appropriate, or the future, when ending figures might be better. Also, using ending figures is very common in reporting industry averages; so, for comparison purposes, ending figures should be used. In any event, using ending figures is definitely less work, so we'll continue to use them.

Receivables Turnover and Days in Receivables   Our inventory measures give some indications of how fast we can sell products. We now look at how fast we collect on those sales. The *receivables turnover* is defined in the same way as inventory turnover:

---

[5] Notice that we used cost of goods sold in the top of this ratio. For some purposes, it might be more useful to use sales instead of costs. For example, if we wanted to know the amount of sales generated per dollar of inventory, then we could just replace the cost of goods sold with sales.

[6] Notice we have calculated the average as (Beginning value + Ending value)/2.

Receivables turnover = Sales/Accounts receivable   [3.14]

= $2,311/$188 = 12.3 times

Loosely speaking, we collected our outstanding credit accounts and reloaned the money 12.3 times during 1995.[7]

This ratio makes more sense if we convert it to days, so the *days' sales in receivables* is:

Days' sales in receivables = 365 days/Receivables turnover   [3.15]

= 365/12.3 = 30 days

Therefore, on average, we collect on our credit sales in 30 days in 1995. For this reason, this ratio is very frequently called the *average collection period (ACP).*

Also, note that if we are using the most recent figures, we could also say that we have 30 days' worth of sales that are currently uncollected. Turning to Table 3.7, we see that Prufrock's average collection period is holding steadily on the industry average so no problem is indicated. You will learn more about this subject when we discuss credit policy in Chapter 19.

E X A M P L E | **3.2**   **Payables Turnover**

Here is a variation on the receivables collection period. How long, on average, does it take for Prufrock Corporation to pay its bills in 1995? To answer, we need to calculate the accounts payable turnover rate using cost of goods sold.[8] We assume that Prufrock purchases everything on credit.

The cost of goods sold is $1,344, and accounts payable are $344. The turnover is therefore $1,344/$344 = 3.9 times. So payables turned over about every 365/3.9 = 94 days. On average then, Prufrock takes 94 days to pay. As a potential creditor, we might take note of this fact. |

Asset Turnover Ratios   Moving away from specific accounts like inventory or receivables, we can consider several "big picture" ratios. For example, *NWC turnover* is:

NWC turnover = Sales/NWC   [3.16]

= $2,311/($708 − $540) = 13.8 times

Looking in Table 3.7, you can see that NWC turnover is smaller than the industry average. Is this good or bad? This ratio measures how much work we get out of our working capital. Once again, assuming that we aren't missing out on sales, a high value is preferred. Likely, sluggish inventory turnover causes the lower value for Prufrock.

Similarly, *fixed asset turnover* is:

Fixed asset turnover = Sales/Net fixed assets   [3.17]

= $2,311/$2,880 = .80 times

With this ratio, we see that, for every dollar in fixed assets, we generated $.80 in sales.

---

[7] Here we have implicitly assumed that all sales are credit sales. If they are not, then we would simply use total credit sales in these calculations, not total sales.

[8] This calculation could be refined by changing the denominator from cost of goods sold to purchases.

Our final asset management ratio, the *total asset turnover,* comes up quite a bit. We see it later in this chapter and in the next chapter. As the name suggests, the total asset turnover is:

$$\text{Total asset turnover} = \text{Sales/Total assets} \qquad\qquad [3.18]$$
$$= \$2,311/\$3,588 = .64 \text{ times}$$

In other words, for every dollar in assets, we generate $.64 in sales in 1995. Comparisons with 1994 and with the industry norm reveal no problem with fixed asset turnover. Because the total asset turnover is slower than the industry average, this points to current assets—and in this case, inventory—as the source of a possible problem.

E X A M P L E | 3.3   **More Turnover**

Suppose you find that a particular company generates $.40 in sales for every dollar in total assets. How often does this company turn over its total assets?

The total asset turnover here is .40 times per year. It takes $1/.40 = 2.5$ years to turn them over completely. |

Profitability Measures

The three measures we discuss in this section are probably the best known and most widely used of all financial ratios. In one form or another, they are intended to measure how efficiently the firm uses its assets and how efficiently the firm manages its operations. The focus in this group is on the bottom line, net income.

Profit Margin   Companies pay a great deal of attention to their *profit margins:*

$$\text{Profit margin} = \text{Net income/Sales} \qquad\qquad [3.19]$$
$$= \$363/\$2,311 = 15.7\%$$

This tells us that Prufrock, in an accounting sense, generates a little less than 16 cents in profit for every dollar in sales in 1995. This is an improvement over 1994 and exceeds the industry average.

All other things being equal, a relatively high profit margin is obviously desirable. This situation corresponds to low expense ratios relative to sales. However, we hasten to add that other things are often not equal.

For example, lowering our sales price normally increases unit volume, but profit margins normally shrink. Total profit (or more importantly, operating cash flow) may go up or down; so the fact that margins are smaller isn't necessarily bad. After all, isn't it possible that, as the saying goes, "Our prices are so low that we lose money on everything we sell, but we make it up in volume!"[9]

Return on Assets   *Return on assets* (ROA) is a measure of profit per dollar of assets. It can be defined several ways, but the most common is:[10]

$$\text{Return on assets} = \text{Net income/Total assets} \qquad\qquad [3.20]$$
$$= \$363/\$3,588 = 10.12\%$$

---

[9] No, it's not.

[10] An alternate definition abstracting from financing costs of debt and preferred shares is in R. H. Garrison, G. R. Chesley, and R. F. Carroll, *Managerial Accounting,* 2nd Canadian ed. (Homewood, IL: Richard D. Irwin, 1993), chap. 17.

Return on Equity   *Return on equity* (ROE) is a measure of how the shareholders fared during the year. Since benefiting shareholders is our goal, ROE is, in an accounting sense, the true bottom-line measure of performance. ROE is usually measured as:

$$\text{Return on equity} = \text{Net income/Total equity} \qquad [3.21]$$
$$= \$363/\$2,591 = 14\%$$

For every dollar in equity, therefore, Prufrock generated 14 cents in profit, but, again, this is only correct in accounting terms.

Because ROA and ROE are such commonly cited numbers, we stress that they are accounting rates of return. For this reason, these measures should properly be called return on *book* assets and return on *book* equity. In fact, ROE is sometimes called return on net worth. Whatever it's called, it would be inappropriate to compare the result to, for example, an interest rate observed in the financial markets. We have more to say about accounting rates of return in later chapters.

From Table 3.7, you can see that both ROA and ROE are more than the industry average. The fact that ROE exceeds ROA reflects Prufrock's use of financial leverage. We examine the relationship between these two measures in more detail next.

E X A M P L E | 3.4   ROE and ROA

Because ROE and ROA are usually intended to measure performance over a prior period, it makes a certain amount of sense to base them on average equity and average assets, respectively. For Prufrock, how would you calculate these for 1995?

We begin by calculating average assets and average equity:

Average assets = ($3,373 + $3,588)/2 = $3,481
Average equity = ($2,299 + $2,591)/2 = $2,445

With these averages, we can recalculate ROA and ROE as follows:

ROA = $363/$3,481 = 10.43%
ROE = $363/$2,445 = 14.85% |

These are slightly higher than our previous calculations because assets grew during the year, with the result that the average is less than the ending value.

Market Value Measures

Our final group of measures is based, in part, on information that is not necessarily contained in financial statements—the market price per share of the stock. Obviously, these measures can only be calculated directly for publicly traded companies.

We assume that Prufrock has 33,000 shares outstanding at the end of 1995 and the stock sold for $88 per share at the end of the year. If we recall Prufrock's net income was $363,000, its earnings per share (EPS) are:

EPS = $363/33 = $11

Price/Earning Ratio   The first of our market value measures, the *price/earning (P/E) ratio* (or multiple) is defined as:

$$\text{P/E ratio} = \text{Price per share/Earnings per share} \qquad [3.22]$$
$$= \$88/\$11 = 8 \text{ times}$$

In the vernacular, we would say that Prufrock shares sell for 8 times earnings, or we might say that Prufrock shares have or carry a P/E multiple of 8. In 1994, the P/E ratio was 7 times, the same as the industry average.

Because the P/E ratio measures how much investors are willing to pay per dollar of current earnings, higher P/Es are often taken to mean that the firm has significant prospects for future growth. Of course, if a firm had no or almost no earnings, its P/E would probably be quite large; so, as always, care is needed in interpreting this ratio.

Market-to-Book Ratio and the Q Ratio   A second commonly quoted measure is the *market-to-book ratio:*

$$\text{Market-to-book ratio} = \text{Market value per share/Book value per share} \qquad [3.23]$$
$$= \$88/(\$2,591/33) = \$88/\$78.5 = 1.12 \text{ times}$$

Notice that book value per share is total equity (not just common stock) divided by the number of shares outstanding. Table 3.7 shows that the market-to-book ratio was 0.73 in 1994.

Since book value per share is an accounting number, it reflects historical costs. In a loose sense, the market-to-book ratio therefore compares the market value of the firm's investments to their cost. A value less than 1 could mean that the firm has not been successful overall in creating value for its shareholders. Prufrock's market-to-book ratio exceeds 1.0 and this is a positive indication.

There is another ratio, called *Tobin's Q,* that is very much like the market-to-book ratio. Tobin's Q ratio divides the market value of all the firm's debt plus equity by the replacement value of the firm's assets. The Q ratios for several U.S. firms are:[11]

		Q Ratio
High Q's	Coca Cola Company	4.2
	IBM	4.2
Low Q's	National Steel Corporation	0.53
	USX	0.61

The Q Ratio differs from the market-to-book ratio in that the Q ratio uses market value of the debt plus equity. It also uses the replacement value of all assets and not the historical cost value.

A firm that has a Q ratio above 1 has an incentive to invest that is probably greater than a firm's with a Q ratio below 1. Firms with high Q ratios tend to be those firms with attractive investment opportunities or a significant competitive advantage.

This completes our definitions of some common ratios. We could tell you about more of them, but these are enough for now. We'll leave it here and go on to discuss in detail some ways of using these ratios in practice. Table 3.8 summarizes the formulas for the ratios that we discussed.

CONCEPT QUESTIONS

1. What are the five groups of ratios? Give two or three examples of each kind.
2. Turnover ratios all have one of two figures as numerators. What are they? What do these ratios measure? How do you interpret the results?
3. Profitability ratios all have the same figure in the numerator. What is it? What do these ratios measure? How do you interpret the results?

---

[11] E. B. Lindberg, and S. Ross, "Tobin's Q and Industrial Organization," *Journal of Business* 54 (January 1981).

Common financial ratios

T A B L E 3.8

I. Short-Term Solvency or Liquidity Ratios

$$\text{Current ratio} = \frac{\text{Current assets}}{\text{Current liabilities}}$$

$$\text{Quick ratio} = \frac{\text{Current assets} - \text{Inventory}}{\text{Current liabilities}}$$

$$\text{Cash ratio} = \frac{\text{Cash}}{\text{Current liabilities}}$$

$$\text{Net working capital to total assets} = \frac{\text{Net working capital}}{\text{Total assets}}$$

$$\text{Interval measure} = \frac{\text{Current assets}}{\text{Average daily operating costs}}$$

III. Asset Utilization Turnover Ratios

$$\text{Inventory turnover} = \frac{\text{Cost of goods sold}}{\text{Inventory}}$$

$$\text{Days' sales in inventory} = \frac{365 \text{ days}}{\text{Inventory turnover}}$$

$$\text{Receivables turnover} = \frac{\text{Sales}}{\text{Accounts receivable}}$$

$$\text{Days' sales in receivables} = \frac{365 \text{ days}}{\text{Receivables turnover}}$$

$$\text{NWC turnover} = \frac{\text{Sales}}{\text{NWC}}$$

$$\text{Fixed asset turnover} = \frac{\text{Sales}}{\text{Net fixed assets}}$$

$$\text{Total asset turnover} = \frac{\text{Sales}}{\text{Total assets}}$$

II. Long-Term Solvency or Financial Leverage Ratios

$$\text{Total debt ratio} = \frac{\text{Total assets} - \text{Total equity}}{\text{Total assets}}$$

$$\text{Debt/equity ratio} = \text{Total debt/Total equity}$$

$$\text{Equity multiplier} = \text{Total assets/Total equity}$$

$$\text{Long-term debt ratio} = \frac{\text{Long-term debt}}{\text{Long-term debt} + \text{Total equity}}$$

$$\text{Times interest earned} = \frac{\text{EBIT}}{\text{Interest}}$$

$$\text{Cash coverage ratio} = \frac{\text{EBIT} + \text{Depreciation}}{\text{Interest}}$$

IV. Profitability Ratios

$$\text{Profit margin} = \frac{\text{Net income}}{\text{Sales}}$$

$$\text{Return on assets (ROA)} = \frac{\text{Net income}}{\text{Total assets}}$$

$$\text{Return on equity (ROE)} = \frac{\text{Net income}}{\text{Total equity}}$$

$$\text{ROE} = \frac{\text{Net income}}{\text{Sales}} \times \frac{\text{Sales}}{\text{Assets}} \times \frac{\text{Assets}}{\text{Equity}}$$

V. Market Value Ratios

$$\text{Price/earning ratio} = \frac{\text{Price per share}}{\text{Earnings per share}}$$

$$\text{Market-to-book ratio} = \frac{\text{Market value per share}}{\text{Book value per share}}$$

3.4 | THE DU PONT IDENTITY

As we mentioned in discussing ROA and ROE, the difference between these two profitability measures is a reflection of the use of debt financing or financial leverage. We illustrate the relationship between these measures in this section by investigating a famous way of decomposing ROE into its component parts.

To begin, let's recall the definition of ROE:

Return on equity = Net income/Total equity

If we were so inclined, we could multiply this ratio by Assets/Assets without changing anything:

Return on equity = Net income/Total equity × Assets/Assets

= Net income/Assets × Assets/Equity

Notice that we have expressed the return on equity as the product of two other ratios—return on assets and the equity multiplier:

ROE = ROA × Equity multiplier = ROA × (1 + Debt/equity ratio)

Looking back at Prufrock in 1995, for example, the debt/equity ratio was .39 and ROA was 10.12 percent. Our work here implies that Prufrock's return on equity, as we previously calculated, is:

ROE = 10.12% × 1.39 = 14%

We can further decompose ROE by multiplying the top and bottom by total sales:

ROE = Sales/Sales × Net income/Assets × Assets/Equity

If we rearrange things a bit, ROE is:

$$ROE = \frac{\text{Net income/Sales} \times \text{Sales/Assets} \times \text{Assets/Equity}}{\text{Return on assets}} \qquad [3.24]$$

= Profit margin × Total asset turnover × Equity multiplier

Du Pont identity

Popular expression breaking ROE into three parts: profit margin, total asset turnover, and financial leverage.

What we have now done is to partition the return on assets into its two component parts, profit margin and total asset turnover. This last expression is called the **Du Pont identity**, after E. I. Du Pont de Nemours & Company, which popularized its use.

We can check this relationship for Prufrock by noting that in 1995 the profit margin was 15.7 percent and the total asset turnover was .64. ROE should thus be:

ROE = Profit margin × Total asset turnover × Equity multiplier

= 15.7%   ×   .64   ×   1.39

= 14%

This 14 percent ROE is exactly what we had before.

The Du Pont identity tells us that ROE is affected by three things:

1. Operating efficiency (as measured by profit margin).
2. Asset use efficiency (as measured by total asset turnover).
3. Financial leverage (as measured by the equity multiplier).

Weakness in either operating or asset use efficiency (or both) shows up in a diminished return on assets, which translates into a lower ROE.

Considering the Du Pont identity, it appears that the ROE could be leveraged up by increasing the amount of debt in the firm. It turns out that this only happens when the firm's ROA exceeds the interest rate on the debt. More importantly, the use of debt financing has a number of other effects, and, as we discuss at some length in Part VII, the amount of leverage a firm uses is governed by its capital structure policy.

The decomposition of ROE we've discussed in this section is a convenient way of systematically approaching financial statement analysis. If ROE is unsatisfactory by some measure, then the Du Pont identity tells you where to start looking for the reasons. To illustrate, we know from Table 3.7, that ROE for Prufrock increased from 10.4 percent in 1994 to 14 percent in 1995. The Du Pont identity can tell us why. After decomposing ROE for 1994, we can compare the parts with what we found earlier for 1995. For 1994:

ROE = 10.4% = Profit margin × Total asset turnover × Equity multiplier

=   11.6%   ×   .61   ×   1.47

For 1995:

ROE = 14% =   15.7%   ×   .64   ×   1.39

This comparison shows that the improvement in ROE for Prufrock was caused mainly by the higher profit margin.

E X A M P L E | **3.5**   **Food versus Variety Stores**

Table 3.9 shows the ratios of the Du Pont identity for food and variety stores. The return on equity ratios (ROEs) for the two industries are roughly comparable. This is

Industry	Profit Margin	Total Asset Turnover	Equity Multiplier	Return on Equity	T A B L E 3.9
Food stores	1.0%	3.56	3.04	10.8%	*Du Pont identity ratios for food and variety stores*
Variety stores	1.8	2.60	2.58	12.1	

The Du Pont analysis   F I G U R E 3.1

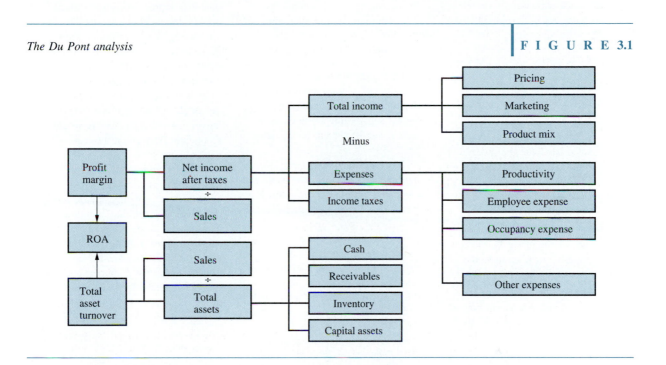

despite the higher profit margin achieved by variety stores. To overcome their lower profit margin, food stores turn over their assets faster and use more financial leverage. Du Pont analysis allows us to go further by asking why food stores have higher total asset turnover. The reason is higher inventory turnover—15.4 times for food stores versus 4.9 times for variety stores. Figure 3.1 shows the interaction of balance sheet and income statement items through the Du Pont analysis.

CONCEPT QUESTIONS
1. Return on assets (ROA) can be expressed as the product of two ratios. Which two?
2. Return on equity (ROE) can be expressed as the product of three ratios. Which three?

3.5 | USING FINANCIAL STATEMENT INFORMATION

Our last task in this chapter is to discuss in more detail some practical aspects of financial statement analysis. In particular, we look at reasons for doing financial statement analysis, how to get benchmark information, and some of the problems that come up in the process.

Prudent investors who shun speculative issues are naturally on the lookout for stocks that provide one or all of the following:

A reasonable trading price in terms of the company's profitability—otherwise known as the price/earnings ratio.

An attractive dividend yield that rivals what the investor could earn on a Canada savings bond or one-year guaranteed investment certificate.

The potential for a capital gain, as suggested by the current price in relation to the 52-week high.

The ease of buying or selling when the occasion arises. This is known as liquidity.

A decent book value, meaning that the shares trade

at or near the value of the company's assets minus its liabilities; that is, shareholders' equity divided by the number of shares outstanding.

One company that comes close to fitting all of those criteria is BC Sugar Refinery Ltd., which is the largest sugar company in Canada with about 70 percent of the market.

Its shares, at $9.87, trade at a multiple of 13.7 times earnings, compared with the Toronto Stock Exchange blue-chip average of 41.7. They yield a dividend of 4 percent, compared with the average of 2.9 percent. Furthermore, the current price suggests lots of room for capital appreciation, because the shares have traded for as much as $11.62 in the past six months. And BC Sugar is a fairly liquid stock, with trading volume on the TSE frequently exceeding 100,000 shares.

According to the most recent quarterly report, BC Sugar's share book value is $7.40. Shares thus are trading at a premium of about 30 percent over book, which is not at all out of line with other companies in the food industry.

It is fair to say, therefore, that the stock fits into parameters that most conservative investors would recognize. How about the company itself?

Besides being dominant in Canada, BC Sugar is the third-largest sugar company in North America, with refining operations in one U.S. and five Canadian cities. Its market is defined as containing 75 million potential customers in the two countries. Its product is relatively recession-proof.

Edward Clifford writes the "Stock Scene" column in the *Globe and Mail*. His comments are reproduced with permission from the October 29, 1993, edition.

Why Evaluate Financial Statements?

As we have discussed, the primary reason for looking at accounting information is that we don't have, and can't reasonably expect to get, market value information. Remember that whenever we have market information, we would use it instead of accounting data. Also, when accounting and market data conflict, market data should be given precedence.

Financial statement analysis is essentially an application of management by exception. In many cases, as we illustrated with our hypothetical company, Prufrock, such analysis boils down to comparing ratios for one business with some kind of average or representative ratios. Those ratios that differ the most from the averages are tagged for further study.

Internal Uses   Financial information has a variety of uses within a firm. Among the most important of these is performance evaluation. For example, managers are frequently evaluated and compensated on the basis of accounting measures of performances such as profit margin and return on equity. Also, firms with multiple divisions frequently compare the performance of those divisions using financial statement information.

Another important internal use that we explore in the next chapter is planning for the future. As we see, historical financial statement information is very useful for generating projections about the future and for checking the realism of assumptions made in those projections.

External Uses   Financial statements are useful to parties outside the firm, including short-term and long-term creditors and potential investors. For example, we would find such information quite useful in deciding whether or not to grant credit to a new customer. Chapter 19 shows how statistical models based on ratios are used in credit analysis in predicting insolvency.

If your firm borrows from a chartered bank, you can expect your loan agreement to require you to submit financial statements periodically. Most bankers use computer software to prepare common-size statements and to calculate ratios for their accounts. Standard software produces output in the format of Table 3.7. More advanced software generates a preliminary diagnosis of the account by comparing the company's ratios against benchmark parameters selected by the banker.

We would also find such information useful in evaluating our main competitors. We might be thinking of launching a new product. A prime concern would be whether the competition would jump in shortly thereafter. Thus, we would be interested in our competitors' financial strength to see if they can afford the necessary development.

Finally, we might be thinking of acquiring another firm. Financial statement information would be essential in identifying potential targets and deciding what to offer.

Choosing a Benchmark

Given that we want to evaluate a division or a firm based on its financial statements, a basic problem immediately comes up. How do we choose a benchmark or a standard of comparison? We describe some ways of getting started in this section.

Time-Trend Analysis   One standard we could use is history. In our Prufrock example, we looked at two years of data. More generally, suppose we find that the current ratio for a particular firm is 2.4 based on the most recent financial statement information. Looking back over the last 10 years, we might find that this ratio has declined fairly steadily.

Based on this, we might wonder if the liquidity position of the firm has deteriorated. It could be, of course, that the firm has made changes to use its current assets more efficiently, that the nature of the firm's business has changed, or that business practices have changed. If we investigate, these are all possible explanations. This is an example of what we mean by management by exception—a deteriorating time trend may not be bad, but it does merit investigation.

Peer Group Analysis   The second means of establishing a benchmark is to identify firms that are similar in the sense that they compete in the same markets, have similar assets, and operate in similar ways. In other words, we need to identify a *peer group*. In our analysis of Prufrock, we used an industry average without worrying about where it came from. In practice, matters are not so simple because no two companies are identical. Ultimately, the choice of which companies to use as a basis for comparison involves judgment on the part of the analyst.

F I G U R E 3.2 *Key business ratios of Canadian businesses (1989) Dun & Bradstreet*

KEY BUSINESS RATIOS CANADA-CORPORATIONS
PRINCIPAUX COEFFICIENTS RELATIFS AUX ENTREPRISES CANADIENNES

LINE OF BUSINESS (and number of concerns reporting) DOMAINE D'EXPLOITATION (et nombre d'entreprises étudiées)	Cost of Goods Sold Coût des marchandises vendues Per Cent Pour cent	Gross Margin Marge bénéficiaire brute Per Cent Pour cent	Current Assets to Current Debt Coefficient du fonds de roulement Times Fois	Profits on Sales Coefficient du profit sur les ventes Per Cent Pour cent	Profits on Equity Coefficient du profit sur l'avoir Per Cent Pour cent	Sales to Equity Coefficient des ventes sur l'avoir Times Fois	Collection Period Période de recouvrement Days Jours	Sales to Inventory Coefficient des ventes sur les stocks Times Fois	Fixed Assets Equity Coefficient des immobilisations sur l'avoir Per Cent Pour cent	Current Debt Equity Coefficient des exigibilités sur l'avoir Per Cent Pour cent	Total Debt Equity Coefficient de la dette totale sur l'avoir Per Cent Pour cent
ALL COMPANIES TOUTES LES COMPAGNIES* 606,562	66.9%	33.1%	1.0	7.1%	11.3%	1.6		7.6	65.0%	124.5%	223.1%
RETAIL TRADE COMMERCE DE DÉTAIL 90,373	74.3%	25.7%	1.4	2.5%	20.9%	8.2		6.4	66.4%	142.5%	217.2%
Auto Acc. & Parts Pièces et accessoires d'automobiles 3,136	70.9%	29.1%	1.5	2.2%	20.6%	9.3		5.4	61.3%	174.8%	257.6%
Book & Stat. Stores Livres et papeterie 1,221	62.6%	37.4%	1.3	2.3%	22.0%	9.4		5.0	90.3%	216.9%	304.7%
Clothing, Men's Vêtements pour hommes 1,914	58.9%	41.1%	1.6	3.5%	12.9%	3.7		4.8	25.7%	79.4%	115.5%
Clothing, Women's Vêtements pour dames 3,706	57.0%	43.0%	1.5	1.9%	12.8%	6.6		5.6	74.4%	139.8%	206.4%
Dept. Stores Magasins à rayons 45	69.0%	31.0%	1.7	1.4%	5.0%	3.6		5.0	29.0%	74.0%	112.5%
Drug Stores Pharmacies 3,788	72.6%	27.4%	1.5	2.2%	20.7%	9.2		5.3	41.3%	161.6%	215.6%
Dry Goods Merceries 2,798	60.6%	39.4%	1.6	1.3%	9.8%	7.3		4.4	77.2%	144.1%	246.1%
Elec. Appliances Repair Appareils électriques, réparation 1,042	57.0%	43.0%	1.7	1.9%	11.9%	6.2		8.3	45.6%	126.7%	179.5%
Florists Fleuristes 1,405	46.4%	53.6%	1.2	2.6%	24.0%	9.2		10.6	115.4%	166.7%	270.9%
Food Stores Magasins d'alimentation 13,460	77.7%	22.3%	1.1	1.0%	10.8%	10.9		15.4	95.9%	113.1%	203.6%
Fuel Dealers Vendeurs d'huile 371	79.3%	20.7%	1.5	3.9%	21.1%	5.4		14.4	72.3%	84.6%	114.8%
Furniture & Appliance Ameublement et appareils ménagers 9,344	69.3%	30.7%	1.5	1.9%	13.0%	6.7		4.7	38.1%	150.8%	200.0%
Gas. Serv. Stns. Stations-service 7,214	81.4%	18.6%	1.2	1.4%	23.1%	16.3		27.3	145.9%	133.9%	277.6%
General Mdse. Marchandises générales 1,195	79.1%	20.9%	1.3	1.7%	13.6%	8.0		7.6	77.5%	117.1%	197.7%
Hardware Quincaillerie 3,371	68.5%	31.5%	1.8	2.6%	14.5%	5.7		4.2	47.1%	110.2%	177.9%
Jewellery store Bijouterie 2,378	54.0%	46.0%	1.8	2.9%	8.3%	2.9		2.2	25.1%	105.0%	168.0%
Motor Veh. Dealers Concessionnaires automobiles 6,405	88.0%	12.0%	1.2	-0.7%	-11.7%	16.9		5.5	125.5%	337.6%	466.9%
Motor Veh. Repairs Réparation des véhicules 9,179	58.8%	41.2%	1.3	2.9%	21.6%	7.4		11.0	109.1%	123.7%	221.1%
Shoe Stores Magasins de chaussures 1,333	57.1%	42.9%	1.5	1.8%	8.1%	4.6		3.5	44.3%	112.8%	139.5%
Tobacconists Tabagies 398	61.0%	39.0%	2.1	-2.0%	-21.4%	10.6		8.3	162.1%	103.8%	1668.6%
Variety Stores Magasins d'articles variés 1,008	71.9%	28.1%	1.6	1.8%	12.1%	6.9		4.9	47.1%	121.8%	158.2%
WHOLESALE TRADE COMMERCE DE GROS 53,026	81.8%	18.2%	1.3	1.9%	14.0%	7.3	39	7.4	39.9%	171.0%	219.0%
App. & Dry Goods Mercerie et habillement 2,608	79.6%	20.4%	1.4	2.0%	15.3%	7.6	49	6.2	23.3%	189.6%	236.4%
Coal & Coke Charbon et coke 19	-103.8%	203.8%	2.2	-0.2%	1.2%	(4.8)	-38	(4.6)	1.2%	80.2%	77.9%
Drug & Toilet Prep. Pharmacie et produits de beauté 770	79.7%	20.3%	1.5	2.0%	15.4%	7.9	45	7.4	30.1%	159.6%	190.2%
Food Alimentation 4,211	87.3%	12.7%	1.3	1.9%	21.4%	11.4	20	16.6	40.4%	137.1%	183.7%
Furn. & Furnishings Meubles et ameublement 1,083	76.5%	23.5%	1.6	1.9%	14.2%	7.5	48	5.8	22.3%	162.0%	205.3%

Not applicable
Non applicable

( ) Loss
( ) Perte

1990 /   Copyright© Dun & Bradstreet Canada Limited. Permission to reprint or reproduce in any form whatsoever in whole or in part should be obtained from Dun & Bradstreet Canada Limited, P.O. Box 6200, Station 'A', Mississauga, Ontario L5A 4G4.

1990 /   Copyright© Dun & Bradstreet Canada Limitée. Le permission de réimprimer ou reproduire les présentes, en tout ou en partie, et sous quelque forme que ce soit, doit être obtenue de Dun & Bradstreet Canada Limitée, P.O. Box 6200, Station 'A', Mississauga, Ontario L5A 4G4.

(concluded)

LINE OF BUSINESS (and number of concerns reporting) DOMAINE D'EXPLOITATION (et nombre d'entreprises étudiées)		Cost of Goods Sold Coût des marchandises vendues	Gross Margin Marge bénéficiaire brute	Current Assets to Current Debt Coefficient du fonds de roulement	Profits on Sales Coefficient du profit sur les ventes	Profits on Equity Coefficient du profit sur l'avoir	Sales to Equity Coefficient des ventes sur l'avoir	Collection Period Période de recouvrement	Sales to Inventory Coefficient des ventes sur les stocks	Fixed Assets Equity Coefficient des immobi-lisations sur l'avoir	Current Debt Equity Coefficient des exigibilités sur l'avoir	Total Debt Equity Coefficient de la dette totale sur l'avoir
		Per Cent Pour cent	Per Cent Pour cent	Times Fois	Per Cent Pour cent	Per Cent Pour cent	Times Fois	Days Jours	Times Fois	Per Cent Pour cent	Per Cent Pour cent	Per Cent Pour cent
General Mdse. Marchandises générales	291	93.2%	6.8%	1.2	1.0%	16.0%	15.3	21	14.7	15.2%	413.7%	447.1%
Grain Grains	180	92.3%	7.7%	0.4	0.7%	8.1%	12.2	16	5.1	74.6%	882.5%	928.7%
Hdwe. Plmbg. & Hting Quincaillerie, plomberie et chauffage	2,098	81.6%	18.4%	1.5	1.9%	15.9%	8.4	40	6.5	30.5%	172.8%	251.9%
Livestock Bétail	635	92.6%	7.4%	1.2	1.2%	21.4%	17.6	19	30.3	93.2%	177.2%	277.1%
Lmbr. & Bldg. Prod. Bois et matériaux de construction	4,970	82.1%	17.9%	1.4	2.3%	19.8%	8.6	37	8.0	44.0%	164.9%	211.4%
Machy., Electrical Machinerie électrique	4,081	71.2%	28.8%	1.5	2.6%	12.0%	4.5	68	6.6	37.0%	129.2%	167.0%
Machy., Farm Machinerie agricole	2,250	84.5%	15.5%	1.4	1.2%	7.1%	6.0	34	2.6	38.0%	226.3%	290.0%
Machy., Industrial Machinerie industrielle	9,797	72.4%	27.6%	1.4	2.5%	12.9%	5.1	59	5.0	41.8%	160.5%	213.4%
Metal Products Produits métalliques	658	84.4%	15.6%	1.3	2.5%	19.4%	7.7	53	6.3	32.3%	204.8%	253.6%
Motor Veh. & Parts Véhicules et pièces	3,460	81.8%	18.2%	1.4	1.2%	7.5%	6.4	29	5.6	44.1%	141.0%	176.4%
Paper Papier	737	85.4%	14.6%	1.4	1.3%	18.3%	13.6	46	12.3	32.7%	249.1%	330.1%
Petroleum Products Produits du pétrole	2,188	89.4%	10.6%	1.1	1.7%	8.7%	5.1	30	28.5	38.6%	91.6%	131.8%
Scrap & Waste Dealers Produits de rebut	1,269	75.0%	25.0%	1.4	2.9%	18.6%	6.3	43	10.4	80.9%	130.7%	196.0%
Tobacco Tabac	118	93.8%	6.2%	1.1	-0.2%	-5.0%	22.4	25	28.1	45.9%	248.8%	364.5%
Other Wholesalers Autres grossistes	11,603	80.0%	20.0%	1.4	2.1%	16.1%	7.6	49	6.9	35.8%	185.4%	241.0%
MANUFACTURERS MANUFACTURIERS	44,324	77.3%	22.7%	1.5	4.5%	12.4%	2.8	42	7.2	74.2%	64.2%	119.7%
Agric. Implements Instruments aratoires	241	82.4%	17.6%	1.3	-0.9%	-3.7%	4.3	48	3.8	118.6%	194.0%	337.8%
Aircraft & Parts Avions et pièces	230	74.2%	25.8%	1.3	-1.6%	-4.0%	2.5	59	2.7	40.9%	120.4%	138.8%
Appliances, Major Appareils électroménagers	33	80.9%	19.1%	1.7	3.3%	12.0%	3.6	50	5.1	36.2%	79.7%	92.4%
Appliances, Small Petits appareils électriques	65	71.7%	28.3%	2.2	7.5%	18.4%	2.5	62	5.3	26.3%	57.8%	76.9%
Bakery Products Pâtisseries	1,235	70.0%	30.0%	1.2	5.3%	17.8%	3.4	20	28.0	61.6%	49.1%	89.2%
Batteries Piles	26	269.5%	-169.5%	1.3	-4.1%	-7.4%	1.8		1.3	125.1%	232.1%	360.0%
Boiler & Plate Fournaises et plaques	91	85.4%	14.6%	1.4	0.6%	2.5%	4.0	82	4.9	49.3%	148.2%	188.5%
Breweries Brasseries	28	53.6%	46.4%	1.3	4.5%	17.7%	3.9	26	8.4	143.7%	93.6%	238.6%
Brooms, Brushes & Mops Balais, brosses et vadrouilles	38	75.6%	24.4%	1.7	10.0%	39.6%	4.0	26	6.2	69.6%	67.1%	160.4%
Cement Ciment	25	73.8%	26.2%	1.4	3.3%	4.3%	1.3	55	7.5	54.9%	31.0%	127.9%
Chemicals, Industrial Produits chimiques, industriels	136	73.9%	26.1%	1.6	9.1%	22.7%	2.5	38	8.9	137.5%	53.6%	197.0%
Chemicals, Other Produits chimiques, autres	468	73.8%	26.2%	1.7	5.1%	14.8%	2.9	48	7.3	75.3%	64.4%	122.9%
Clay Products Produits en argile	173	73.4%	26.6%	1.8	5.7%	13.3%	2.3	39	4.4	106.1%	55.9%	145.9%
Clothing, Men's Vêtements pour hommes	764	72.8%	27.2%	1.8	3.5%	14.3%	4.1	69	4.6	26.6%	111.3%	136.3%
Clothing, Women's Vêtements pour dames	1,445	77.4%	22.6%	1.6	2.8%	16.8%	6.0	58	5.7	23.6%	144.3%	171.4%
Clothing, Other Vêtements, autres	426	77.3%	22.7%	2.0	3.7%	13.4%	3.6	53	3.9	22.5%	103.5%	137.0%
Coffins & Caskets Cercueils et urnes funéraires	34	77.7%	22.3%	1.5	3.8%	15.3%	4.0	54	3.9	89.0%	128.0%	190.7%

Various benchmarks are available.[12] Statistics Canada publications include typical balance sheets, income statements, and selected ratios for firms in about 180 industries. Dun & Bradstreet Canada provides key business ratios for Canadian corporations. An example for retail companies is shown in Figure 3.2. Other sources of benchmarks for Canadian companies include financial data bases available from the *Financial Post and InfoGlobe*.[13] Several financial institutions gather their own financial ratio data bases by compiling information on their loan customers. In this way, they seek to obtain more up-to-date information than is available from services like Statistics Canada and Dun & Bradstreet.

Obtaining current information is not the only challenge facing the financial analyst. Most large Canadian corporations do business in several industries so the analyst must often compare the company against several industry averages. Also keep in mind that the industry average is not necessarily where firms would like to be. For example, agricultural analysts know that farmers are suffering with painfully low average profitability coupled with excessive debt. Despite these shortcomings, the industry average is a useful benchmark for the management by exception approach we advocate for ratio analysis.

Problems with Financial Statement Analysis

We close our chapter on financial statements by discussing some additional problems that can arise in using financial statements. In one way or another, the basic problem with financial statement analysis is there is no underlying theory to help us identify which quantities to look at and to guide us in establishing benchmarks.

As we discuss in other chapters, there are many cases where financial theory and economic logic provide guidance to making judgments about value and risk. Very little such help exists with financial statements. This is why we can't say which ratios matter the most and what a high or low value might be.

One particularly severe problem is that many firms are conglomerates, owning more-or-less unrelated lines of business. The consolidated financial statements for such firms don't really fit any neat industry category. For example, Sears has an SIC code of 6710 (Holding Offices) because of its diverse financial and retailing operations. More generally, the kind of peer group analysis we have been describing is going to work best when the firms are strictly in the same line of business, the industry is competitive, and there is only one way of operating.

Another problem that is becoming increasingly common is major competitors and natural peer group members in an industry may be scattered around the globe. The automobile industry is an obvious example. The problem here is that financial statements from outside Canada and the United States do not necessarily conform to GAAP. The existence of different standards and procedures makes it very difficult to compare financial statements across national borders.

Even companies that are clearly in the same line of business may not be comparable. For example, electric utilities engaged primarily in power generation are all classified in the same group (SIC 4911). This group is often thought to be relatively homogeneous. However, utilities generally operate as regulated monopolies, so they don't compete with each other. Many have stockholders, and many are

---

[12] This discussion draws on L. Kryznaowski, M-C. To and R. Seguin, *Business Solvency Risk Analysis,* Institute of Canadian Bankers, 1990, chap. 3.

[13] Analysts examining U.S. companies will find comparable information available from Robert Morris Associates.

organized as cooperatives with no stockholders. There are several different ways of generating power, ranging from hydroelectric to nuclear, so their operating activities can differ quite a bit. Finally, profitability is strongly affected by regulatory environment, so utilities in different locations can be very similar but show very different profits.

Several other general problems frequently crop up. First, different firms use different accounting procedures for inventory, for example. This makes it difficult to compare statements. Second, different firms end their fiscal years at different times. For firms in seasonal businesses (such as a retailer with a large Christmas season), this can lead to difficulties in comparing balance sheets because of fluctuations in accounts during the year. Finally, for any particular firm, unusual or transient events, such as a onetime profit from an asset sale, may affect financial performance. In comparing firms, such events can give misleading signals.

CONCEPT QUESTIONS

1. What are some uses for financial statement analysis?

2. Where do industry average ratios come from and how might they be useful?

3. Why do we say that financial statement analysis is management by exception?

4. What are some problems that can come up with financial statement analysis?

3.6 | SUMMARY AND CONCLUSIONS

This chapter has discussed aspects of financial statement analysis:

1. Sources and uses of cash. We discussed how to identify the ways that businesses obtain and use cash, and we described how to trace the flow of cash through the business over the course of the year. We briefly looked at the statement of cash flows.

2. Standardized financial statements. We explained that differences in size make it difficult to compare financial statements, and we discussed how to form common-size and common-base-period statements to make comparisons easier.

3. Ratio analysis. Evaluating ratios of accounting numbers is another way of comparing financial statement information. We therefore defined and discussed a number of the most commonly reported and used financial ratios. We also developed the famous Du Pont identity as a way of analyzing financial performance.

4. Using financial statements. We described how to establish benchmarks for comparison purposes and discussed some of the types of available information. We then examined some of the problems that can arise.

After you study this chapter, we hope that you will have some perspective on the uses and abuses of financial statements. You should also find that your vocabulary of business and financial terms has grown substantially.

Key Terms

sources of cash (page 57)

uses of cash (page 57)

statement of changes in financial position (page 59)

common-size statement (page 60)

common-base-year statement (page 62)

financial ratios (page 63; Table 3.8, p. 75)

Du Pont identity (page 76)

Chapter Review Problems and Self-Test

3.1   Sources and Uses of Cash   Consider the following balance sheets for the Wildhack Corporation. Calculate the changes and, where applicable, identify the change as a source or use of cash. What were the major sources and uses of cash? Did the company become more or less liquid during the year? What happened to cash during the year?

WILDHACK CORPORATION
Balance Sheets as of December 31, 1994 and 1995
($ in millions)

	1994	1995
Assets		
Current assets		
Cash	$ 120	$ 88
Accounts receivable	224	192
Inventory	424	368
Total	$ 768	$ 648
Fixed assets		
Net plant and equipment	5,228	5,354
Total assets	$5,996	$6,002
Liabilities and Owners' Equity		
Current liabilities		
Accounts payable	$ 124	$ 144
Notes payable	1,412	1,039
Total	$1,536	$1,183
Long-term debt	1,804	2,077
Owners' equity		
Common stock	300	300
Retained earnings	2,356	2,442
Total	$2,656	$2,742
Total liabilities and owners' equity	$5,996	$6,002

3.2   Common-Size Statements   The most recent income statement for Wildhack follows. Prepare a common-size income statement based on this information. How do you interpret the standardized net income? What percentage of sales goes to cost of goods sold?

WILDHACK CORPORATION
1995 Income Statement
($ in millions)

Sales	$3,756
Cost of goods sold	2,453
Depreciation	490
Earnings before interest and taxes	$ 813
Interest paid	613
Taxable income	$ 200
Taxes	68
Net income	$ 132
Additions to retained earnings	$ 86
Dividends	46

3.3   Financial Ratios   Based on the balance sheets and income statements in the previous two problems, calculate the following ratios for 1995:

Current ratio	Days in receivables
Quick ratio	Total debt ratio
Cash ratio	Long-term debt ratio
Inventory turnover	Times interest earned ratio
Receivables turnover	Cash coverage ratio
Days in inventory	

3.4   ROE and the Du Pont Identity   Calculate the 1995 ROE for the Wildhack Corporation and then break down your answer into its component parts using the Du Pont identity.

Answers to Self-Test Problems

3.1   We've filled in the following answers. Remember, increases in assets and decreases in liabilities indicate we spent some cash. Decreases in assets and increases in liabilities are ways of getting cash.

WILDHACK CORPORATION
Balance Sheets as of December 31, 1994 and 1995
($ in millions)

	1994	1995	Change	Source/Use of cash
Assets				
Current assets				
Cash	$ 120	$ 88	−$ 32	
Accounts receivable	224	192	−32	Source
Inventory	424	368	−56	Source
Total	$ 768	$ 648	−$ 120	
Fixed assets				
Net plant and equipment	5,228	5,354	+126	Use
Total assets	$5,996	$6,002	+$ 6	
Liabilities and Owners' Equity				
Current liabilities				
Accounts payable	$ 124	$ 144	+$ 20	Source
Notes payable	1,412	1,039	−373	Use
Total	$1,536	$1,183	−$ 353	
Long-term debt	1,804	2,077	+273	Source
Owners' equity				
Common stock	300	300	+0	—
Retained earnings	2,356	2,442	+86	Source
Total	$2,656	$2,742	+86	
Total liabilities and owners' equity	$5,996	$6,002	+$ 6	

Wildhack used its cash primarily to purchase fixed assets and to pay off short-term debt. The major sources of cash to do this were additional long-term borrowing, and, to a larger extent, reductions in current assets and additions to retained earnings.

   The current ratio went from $768/$1,536 = .5 to $648/$1,183 = .55; so, the firm's liquidity appears to have improved somewhat, primarily because of the large reduction in short-term debt. Overall, however, the amount of cash on hand declined by $32.

3.2   We've calculated the following common-size income statement. Remember that we simply divide each item by total sales.

WILDHACK CORPORATION
1992 Common-Size Income Statement

Sales	100.0%
Cost of goods sold	65.3
Depreciation	13.0
Earnings before interest and taxes	21.6
Interest paid	16.3
Taxable income	5.3
Taxes	1.8
Net income	3.5%
Addition to retained earnings	2.3%
Dividends	1.2

Net income is 3.5 percent of sales. Since this is the percentage of each sales dollar that makes its way to the bottom line, the standardized net income is the firm's profit margin. Cost of goods sold is 65.3 percent of sales.

3.3   We've calculated the following ratios based on the ending figures. If you don't remember a definition, refer back to Table 3.8.

Current ratio	$648/$1,183	= .55
Quick ratio	$280/$1,183	= .24
Cash ratio	$88/$1,183	= .07
Inventory turnover	$2,453/$368	= 6.7 times
Receivables turnover	$3,756/$192	= 19.6 times
Days in inventory	365/6.7	= 54.5 days
Days in receivables	365/19.6	= 18.6 days
Total debt ratio	$3,260/$6,002	= 54.3%
Long-term debt ratio	$2,077/$4,819	= 43.1%
Times interest earned ratio	$813/$613	= 1.33 times
Cash coverage ratio	$1,303/$613	= 2.13 times

3.4   The return on equity is the ratio of net income to total equity. For Wildhack, this is $132/$2,742 = 4.8%, which is not outstanding.

Given the Du Pont identity, ROE can be written as:

$$\text{ROE} = \text{Profit margin} \times \text{Total asset turnover} \times \text{Equity multiplier}$$
$$= \$132/\$3,756 \times \$3,756/\$6,002 \times \$6,002/\$2,742$$
$$= 3.5\% \times .626 \times 2.19$$
$$= 4.8\%$$

Notice that return on assets, ROA, is 3.5% × .626 = 2.2%.

Questions and Problems

Basic
(Questions 1–21)

1. **Changes in the Current Ratio**   What effect would the following actions have on a firm's current ratio? Assume that net working capital is positive.

a. Inventory is purchased.
b. A supplier is paid.
c. A short-term bank loan is repaid.
d. A long-term debt is paid off early.
e. A customer pays off a credit account.
f. Inventory is sold at cost.
g. Inventory is sold for a profit.

2. **Liquidity and Ratios**   In recent years, Dixie Co. has greatly increased its current ratio. At the same time, the quick ratio has fallen. What has happened? Has the liquidity of the company improved?

3. **Current Ratio** Explain what it means for a firm to have a current ratio equal to 0.50. Would the firm be better off if the current ratio was 1.50? What if it was 15.0? Explain your answers.

Basic
(Continued)

4. **Interpreting Financial Ratios** Fully explain the kind of information the following financial ratios provide about a firm:

   a. Quick ratio
   b. Cash ratio
   c. Interval measure
   d. Total asset turnover
   e. Equity multiplier
   f. Long-term debt ratio
   g. Times interest earned ratio
   h. Profit margin
   i. Return on assets
   j. Return on equity
   k. Price/earnings ratio

5. **Calculating Liquidity Ratios** A firm has net working capital of $500, current liabilities of $1,800, and inventory of $600. What is the current ratio? What is the quick ratio?

6. **Calculating Profitability Ratios** A firm has sales of $5 million, total assets of $9 million, and total debt of $3 million. If the profit margin is 11 percent, what is net income? What is ROA? What is ROE?

7. **Calculating the Average Collection Period** Fred's Print Shop has a current accounts receivable balance of $13,565. Credit sales for the year just ended were $94,300. What is the receivables turnover? The days' sales in receivables? How long did it take on average for credit customers to pay off their accounts during the past year?

8. **Calculating Inventory Turnover** Mary's Print Shop has a current inventory of $46,325, and cost of goods sold for the year just ended was $147,750. What is the inventory turnover? The days' sales in inventory? How long on average did a unit of inventory sit on the shelf before it was sold?

9. **Calculating Leverage Ratios** A firm has a total debt ratio of 0.60. What is its debt/equity ratio? What is its equity multiplier?

10. **Calculating Market Value Ratios** MegaWidgets Co. had additions to retained earnings for the year just ended of $170,000. The firm paid out $80,000 in cash dividends and it has total equity of $4 million. If MegaWidgets currently has 120,000 shares of common stock outstanding, what is earnings per share? Dividends per share? Book value per share? If the stock currently sells for $50 per share, what is the market-to-book ratio? The price/earnings ratio?

11. **Du Pont Identity** If a firm has an equity multiplier of 2.0, total asset turnover of 1.25, and a profit margin of 8 percent, what is its ROE?

12. **Du Pont Identity** Smith Manufacturing has a profit margin of 9 percent, total asset turnover of 1.5, and ROE of 20.25 percent. What is this firm's debt/equity ratio?

13. **Sources and Uses of Cash** Based only on the following information for the SemiPhonics Corp., did cash go up or down? By how much? Classify each event as a source or a use of cash.

Decrease in inventory	$350
Decrease in accounts payable	175
Decrease in notes payable	400
Increase in accounts receivable	600

14.   **Calculating Average Payables Period**   For 1994, DRK, Inc., had cost of goods sold of $8,325. At the end of the year, the accounts payable balance was $1,100. How long on average did it take the company to pay off its suppliers last year? What might a large value for this ratio imply?

15.   **Cash Flow and Capital Spending**   For the year just ended, AWOI Co. shows an increase in its net fixed assets account of $370. The company took $130 in depreciation expense for the year. How much did AWOI spend on new fixed assets? Is this a source or use of cash?

16.   **Equity Multiplier and Return on Equity**   Folker Fried Chicken Company has a debt/equity ratio of 1.10. Return on assets is 6.5 percent, and total equity is $210,000. What is the equity multiplier? Return on equity? Net income?

Manitoba Dental Floss Company reports the following balance sheet information for 1994 and 1995. Use this information to work Problems 17 through 21.

MANITOBA DENTAL FLOSS CORPORATION
Balance Sheets as of December 31, 1994 and 1995

	1994	1995
Assets		
Current assets		
Cash	$ 9,320	$ 10,050
Accounts receivable	29,720	31,525
Inventory	58,500	66,710
Total	$ 97,540	$108,285
Fixed assets		
Net plant and equipment	248,060	269,460
Total assets	$345,600	$377,745
Liabilities and Owners' Equity		
Current liabilities		
Accounts payable	$ 56,250	$ 51,900
Notes payable	26,200	30,000
Total	$ 82,450	$ 81,900
Long-term debt	$ 50,000	$ 35,000
Owners' equity		
Common stock and paid-in surplus	$ 62,600	$ 62,600
Accumulated retained earnings	150,550	198,245
Total	$213,150	$260,845
Total liabilities and owners' equity	$345,600	$377,745

17.   **Preparing Standardized Financial Statements**   Prepare the 1994 and 1995 common-size balance sheets for Manitoba Dental Floss.

18.   **Preparing Standardized Financial Statements**   Prepare the 1995 common-base-year balance sheet for Manitoba Dental Floss.

19.   **Preparing Standardized Financial Statements**   Prepare the 1995 combined common-size/common-base-year balance sheet for Manitoba Dental Floss.

20.   **Sources and Uses of Cash**   For each account on this company's balance sheet, show the change in the account during 1995 and note whether this

change was a source or use of cash. Do your numbers add up and make sense? Explain your answer for total assets compared to your answer for total liabilities and owners' equity.

**Basic
(Continued)**

21. **Calculating Financial Ratios**   Based on the balance sheets given for Manitoba Dental Floss, calculate the following ratios for each year:
    a. Current ratio
    b. Quick ratio
    c. Cash ratio
    d. NWC/TA ratio
    e. Debt/equity ratio, and equity multiplier
    f. Total debt ratio and long-term debt ratio

22. **Using Standardized Financial Statements**   What types of information do common-size financial statements reveal about the firm? What is the best use for these common-size statements? What purpose do common-base-year statements have? When would you use them?

**Intermediate
(Questions 22–37)**

23. **Using Financial Ratios**   Explain what peer group analysis means. As a financial manager, how could you use the results of peer group analysis to evaluate the performance of your firm? How is a peer group different from an aspirant group?

24. **Interpreting the Du Pont Identity**   Why is the Du Pont identity a valuable tool for analyzing the performance of a firm? Discuss the types of information it reveals compared to the ROE ratio considered by itself.

25. **Using the Du Pont Identity**   A firm has sales of $500, total assets of $300, and a debt/equity ratio of 1.00. If its return on equity is 15 percent, what is its net income?

26. **Sources and Uses of Cash**   If accounts payable on the balance sheet increase by $4,000 from the beginning of the year to the end of the year, is this a source or a use of cash? Explain your answer.

27. **Ratios and Fixed Assets**   XYZ Company has a long-term debt ratio of 0.75 and a current ratio of 1.50. Current liabilities are $500, sales are $2,500, profit margin is 8 percent, and ROE is 22.5 percent. What is the firm's net fixed assets?

28. **Profit Margin**   In response to complaints about high prices, a grocery store chain runs the following advertising campaign: "If you pay your child 75 cents to go buy $25 worth of groceries, then your child makes twice as much on the trip as we do." You've collected the following information from the grocery chain's financial statements:

Sales	$225 million
Net income	$3.375 million
Total assets	$40 million
Total debt	$17 million

Evaluate the grocery chain's claim. What is the basis for the statement? Is this claim misleading? Why or why not?

29. **Using the Du Pont Identity**   The Jordan Company has net income of $47,500. There are currently 16.60 days' sales in receivables. Total assets are $527,000, total receivables are $61,000, and the debt/equity ratio is 0.85. What is Jordan's profit margin? Its total asset turnover? Its ROE?

**Intermediate
(Continued)**

30. **Calculating the Cash Coverage Ratio**   Super Duper, Inc.'s net income for the most recent year was $4,950. The tax rate was 34 percent. The firm paid $1,200 in total interest expense and deducted $1,300 in depreciation expense. What was Super Duper's cash coverage ratio for the year?

31. **Calculating the Times Interest Earned Ratio**   For the most recent year, a firm had sales of $110,000, cost of goods sold of $45,000, depreciation expense of $15,000, and additions to retained earnings of $12,800. The firm currently has 5,000 shares of common stock outstanding, and last year, dividends per share were $1.40. What was the times interest earned ratio?

32. **Ratios and Foreign Companies**   The London Bridge Company PLC had 1995 net income of £6,211 on sales of £479,650 (both in thousands of pounds). What was the company's profit margin? Does the fact that these figures are quoted in a foreign currency make any difference? Why? In thousands of dollars, sales were $767,440. What was net income in dollars?

Some recent financial statement information for Kuipers Enterprises are given below. Use this information to work Problems 33 through 38.

KUIPERS ENTERPRISES
1995 Income Statement

Sales	$9,000
Cost of goods sold	4,500
Depreciation	700
EBIT	$3,800
Interest paid	600
Taxable income	$3,200
Taxes (34%)	1,088
Net income	$2,112
Addition to retained earnings	$1,512
Dividends	600

KUIPERS ENTERPRISES
Balance sheets ending December 31, 1994 and 1995

	1994	1995		1994	1995
Assets			*Liabilities and Owners' Equity*		
Current assets			Current liabilities		
Cash	$ 404	$ 247	Accounts payable	$ 650	$ 679
Receivables	1,115	1,616	Notes payable	375	400
Inventory	2,870	4,225	Other	219	250
			Total	$ 1,244	$ 1,329
Fixed assets			Long-term debt	$ 3,400	$ 3,150
Net plant and equipment	$ 8,452	$ 8,100	Owners' equity		
			Common stock	$ 500	$ 500
			Capital surplus	1,300	1,300
			Retained earnings	6,397	7,909
			Total	$ 8,197	$ 9,709
Total	$12,841	$14,188	Total	$12,841	$14,188

33. **Calculating Financial Ratios**   Find the following financial ratios for Kuipers Enterprises (use year-end figures rather than average values where appropriate):

Intermediate
(Continued)

Short-term solvency ratios

Current ratio _____

Quick ratio _____

Cash ratio _____

Asset management ratios

Total asset turnover _____

Inventory turnover _____

Receivables turnover _____

Long-term solvency ratios

Debt ratio _____

Debt/equity ratio _____

Equity multiplier _____

Times interest earned ratio _____

Cash coverage ratio _____

Profitability ratios

Profit margin _____

Return on assets _____

Return on equity _____

34. **Du Pont Identity** Construct the Du Pont identity for Kuipers Enterprises.

35. **Calculating the Interval Measure** For how many days could Kuipers Enterprises continue if its operations were suddenly suspended?

36. **Statement of Cash Flows** Prepare the 1995 statement of cash flows for Kuipers Enterprises.

37. **Market Value Ratios** Kuipers has 400 shares of common stock outstanding, and the market price for a share of stock at the end of 1995 is $52. What is the price/earnings ratio? What is the dividends per share? What is the market-to-book ratio at the end of 1995?

38. **Stock Market Acceptance** A typical competitor has a price-earnings ratio of 8 times and a market-book value ratio of 1.5 times. What does this suggest about the attractiveness of Kuipers' stock?

ATLANTIC LUMBER TRADERS

CASE   **3A**

On April 20, 1989, Lynn Thomas put down the phone and looked at the notes before her. Gail Hall, one of the owners of Atlantic Lumber Traders, had just given Lynn the final details she needed. As credit assistant to Harry Sarson of the Maritime Bank in Saint John, New Brunswick, Lynn had been asked to review the file of Atlantic Lumber Traders. Her job was to decide if Gail Hall's explanation of what had gone wrong was plausible, then to predict risks to the bank under various projections of the company's future. Finally, Lynn was to make recommendations for action by the bank. In the worst instance, if a turnaround was not possible, it was Lynn Thomas's

This case was prepared with Linda P. Hendry, finance lecturer at Dalhousie University for the Atlantic Entrepreneurial Institute, as a basis for classroom discussion and is not meant to illustrate either effective or ineffective management. Some elements of this case have been disguised. Copyright © 1991, the Atlantic Entrepreneurial Institute, an Atlantic Canada Opportunities Agency funded organization. Used with permission.

job to recommend the best course for the orderly wind-up of Atlantic Lumber Traders.

The file indicated that Atlantic Lumber Traders had been established in 1983 in Saint John to wholesale lumber in the Atlantic provinces. Major shareholders were brother and sister Edward and Gail Hall, members of a wealthy and respected family with a long entrepreneurial history in New Brunswick.

After four years of profitable operations, the company showed an operating loss of $219,666 and a net loss of $174,216 on sales of $17 million for the year ending December 31, 1988. This loss was an urgent concern to the Halls and to the Maritime Bank, which had extended the company a $1.3 million revolving line of credit (at prime plus 1 percent).

When the third quarter results were in, Gail Hall felt she needed to personally take charge of the company. In October of 1988, she therefore put aside her lucrative law practice (she had netted $140,000 in 1988) to devote her full attention to the company. She first had to identify its main problems, then take corrective action.

Company History

Edward and Gail Hall, both lawyers in their mid-30s, had set up Atlantic Lumber Traders in 1983 to wholesale lumber. Atlantic Lumber Traders had sales territories in the four Atlantic provinces, Quebec, and Ontario and, secondarily, in the United States. Approximately 80 percent of sales were generated in the Atlantic provinces, 19 percent in Quebec and Ontario, and 1 percent in the United States. Shares had been owned by Edward and Gail, and also by David Lawson, who had managed the company until October 1988. At that time he was released and Edward and Gail had purchased his shares for $1. Lawson was blamed for the company's poor performance in late 1987 and 1988. The Halls, however, admitted they should have been more involved.

With the exception of 1988, the operation had enjoyed significant sales increases from $3 million for the first year of operation (1984), to $19 million for fiscal 1987 (Exhibit 2). Net income had reached a high of $128,000 (after a $48,000 loss from a rental operation). The rental operation consisted of two 16-unit apartment buildings acquired by the company in 1987. The rental operation loss was intended to offset income from the lumber operation. During 1988, due in part to the poor performance of Atlantic Lumber traders, the rental property was sold (at book value) to another company operated by the Halls. According to Gail, the rental operation now broke even because she stepped in, did some refurbishing, changed property managers, and thus increased occupancy.

The lumber operation was straightforward. At the end of 1988, Atlantic Lumber Traders had a sales team of four—three full-time traders and a general manager who did some selling—to wholesale lumber to a customer base of 50 to 100 large retailers. The sales staff were paid a commission of 1.8 percent and the mark-up ranged between 4.5 percent and 5.5 percent. No inventory for the bulk of sales was required, as orders were placed with the mills as received and wood was transported from the mill directly to the purchaser. Atlantic Lumber Traders had a small administrative staff of two to three people to handle accounting. Terms with most mills were net 10 days, with an average collection period on receivables of 22 days in 1987 (37 days for the industry, see Exhibit 3). The company thus needed to finance about 40 days' sales on average, which required a large capital base. A small inventory of uncommon lengths was maintained for special orders; approximate inventory value was $200,000.

ATLANTIC LUMBER TRADERS
Balance Sheet ($000s)—December 31

	1985[1]	1986[2]	1987[2]	1988[2]
Assets				
Current				
Cash	$ 0	$ 0	$ 0	$ 0
Trade receivables (Net)	645	938	1,174	688
Other receivables (Net)	2	39	79	101
Inventory	99	184	570	262
Prepaid expenses	0	0	12	5
Due from shareholders	0	33	0	0
Income tax refund	0	0	1	71
Total current assets	$746	$1,194	$1,836	$1,127
Fixed assets				
Land & buildings	0	0	1,150	0
Equipment & machinery	6	6	58	19
Leasehold improvements	9	9	10	13
Accumulated depreciation	(4)	(6)	(69)	(20)
Total fixed assets	$ 11	$ 9	$1,149	$ 12
Other assets				
Intangible assets	18	0	0	0
Investments in/Due from	0	60	180	0
Deferred gtee charges	0	0	11	0
Notes receivable	0	0	0	328
Total other assets	$ 18	$ 60	$ 191	$ 328
Total assets	$775	$1,263	$3,176	$1,467
Liabilities & shareholder equity				
Current liabilities				
Bank	$471	$ 668	$ 985	$ 886
Trade payables	207	425	933	467
Income tax payable	14	11	0	0
Current portion LTD	12	12	44	0
Total current liabilities	$704	$1,116	$1,962	$1,353
Long-term liabilities				
Bank LTD	29	17	501	0
Other LTD to related Co. 1	0	0	225	0
Other LTD to related Co. 2	0	0	200	0
Due to shareholders[3]	0	0	30	30
Total long-term liabilities	$ 29	$ 17	$ 956	$ 30
Total liabilities	$733	$1,133	$2,918	$1,383
Shareholder equity				
Common Shares	1	1	1	1
Retained Earnings	41	129	257	83
Total shareholder equity	$ 42	$ 130	$ 258	$ 84
Total liabilities & shareholder equity	$775	$1,263	$3,176	$1,467

[1]Unaudited.
[2]Audited.
[3]Deferred.

Source: Company records and bank files.

E X H I B I T 2

ATLANTIC LUMBER TRADERS
Income Statement ($000s)
Year Ended December 31

	1985[1]	1986[2]	1987[2]	1988[2]
Sales	$7,507	$12,540	$19,049	$16,853
Cost of goods sold	7,148	11,936	18,121	16,095
Gross profit	$ 359	$ 604	$ 928	$ 758
Operating expenses				
Depreciation	2	2	4	9
Bad debt expense	12	3	2	16
Interest expense	31	54	82	130
Salaries	102	237	419	489
Telephone	42	60	94	100
Travel	25	46	80	66
Rent	12	16	18	20
Start-up costs (amortization)	18	0	0	0
Other[3]	29	76	85	46
Total operating expenses	$ 273	$ 494	$ 784	$ 876
Operating income (loss)	86	110	144	(118)
Other income (expense)				
Rental division loss	0	0	(48)	(102)
Affiliated company	0	0	54	22
Miscellaneous	4	0	0	0
Income (loss) before tax	$ 90	$ 110	$ 150	$ (198)
Income taxes (recovery)	14	22	32	(46)
Extraordinary gain (loss)	0	0	10	(22)
Net income (loss)	$ 76	$ 88	$ 128	$ (174)
Opening retained earnings	(35)	$ 41	$ 129	$ 257
Closing retained earnings	$ 41	$ 129	$ 257	$ 83

Financial statement comments: Sales down $2,200M from previous year due to internal management problems and restructuring. Loss incurred ($174M), after income tax recovery ($46M) and extraordinary loss on sale of investment in associated company ($22M). This loss attributed to drop in gross margin of 0.4% ($75M) due to inefficient purchasing by previous manager, i.e., inventory purchased on speculation, then disposed at less than normal margin. This area now under control of owners, who now manage. Total expenses up 1.1% ($185M) due to excessive spending on non-essential items (expense accounts, administration staff, etc). Since year end, five staff released and all expense items reduced to essential (sales do not seem to have suffered to date).
[1]Unaudited.
[2]Audited.
[3]Selling, general and administrative expenses.
Source: Company records and bank files.

During 1988, David Lawson had speculated on purchases both for resale and inventory, which at one point exceeded $600,000. In making these purchases, for which there was no firm order, Lawson had attempted to take advantage of swings in market prices.

During 1987 and 1988, the number of employees had reached a high of 11 with the office staff of 16 exceeding the sales force of 5. To satisfy customers, Lawson had sold lumber in irregular lots, rather than follow the industry practice of requiring customers to buy full lots. As a result, the company was left with a considerable stock of less popular lengths, which required a write-down in inventory once this practice was discovered.

According to Gail Hall, these practices ended when she took over the day-to-day operation of the company. Her efforts produced a small profit of $16,000 for the first

E X H I B I T 3

Atlantic Lumber Traders' selected industry ratios

	Industry Ratios 1987
Liquidity	
Current ratio	1.50
Quick ratio	0.70
Average collection period	36.80
Average payment period	10.55
Sales/Working capital	14.90
Leverage ratios	
Debt to equity	2.10
Debt to tangible net worth	2.10
Net fixed assets/TNW	0.51
Coverage ratios	
EBIT/Interest	2.50
Profitability ratios (%)	
Gross profit/Sales	5.00
Gross cash profit/Sales	3.00
Profit pretax/Sales	2.58
Net profit/Sales	2.30
Profit pretax/Total assets	5.30

Source: Bank files

quarter of 1989. According to her, this showed that the company had turned around because the first quarter of the year was traditionally the company's worst.

The Principals in the Company

Although Atlantic Lumber Traders was founded in 1983, the Hall family had been involved in the wood/lumber industry for more than half a century. Hall Investments Ltd., a holding company set up in 1984 by Edward and Gail, had two wholly owned subsidiaries, one in transportation and the other in a lumber-related business. The companies dealt with all the major banks. The Halls felt they knew the lumber industry, and that they had the required contacts to generate substantial sales. Edward Hall had never taken an active role in the business and Gail agreed she neglected it in favour of her law practice. Gail appeared knowledgeable and was prepared to assist in a sales effort if necessary.

Because the Halls were very influential in the New Brunswick marketplace, Lynn knew that her boss, Harry Sarson, wished to maintain their goodwill. However, he also wanted to ensure the safety of the bank's investment.

The Banker's Risk Assessment of the Company in April 1989

Lynn Thomas identified four areas where the company significantly risked the bank's capital: (1) operating losses sustained to date; (2) debt to equity at 17:1 for year-end 1988, down to 4:1 when subordinated loans[1] and liquid security were included for the first quarter of 1989; (3) competition; and (4) inability to sustain any further losses.

According to Lynn, there were mitigating circumstances for each risk factor. The improvement in performance since year-end 1988 seemed to indicate that problem

---

[1] Subordinate to the bank debt. Also called a postponement of shareholders' claims. In this case, the Halls had injected $200,000 (a subordinated shareholders' loan) into the company since year-end 1988.

areas had been identified and corrected. In-house financial statements were monitored closely by Gail Hall. Lynn did not consider the Canada-U.S. Free Trade Agreement a significant risk; Gail assured her it would have little impact on the 1 percent of company sales to the United States.

Personal guarantees in the amount of $316,000 from the Halls partly offset the debt to equity position.

Atlantic Lumber Traders had an established client base; the Hall name had been synonymous with lumber for over 50 years. Lynn felt that reluctance to tarnish the Hall family name would prompt Gail to cooperate with the bank. Gail had indicated that to forestall losses, she would close down operations if there was any sign of a downturn.

Economic Forecast

As part of her background analysis of the business, Lynn had reviewed the economic forecast prepared by the bank's Economics Department in early 1989. The forecast surveyed leading economic indicators and showed that the economy would begin to slow down during the second quarter. The bank's economists believed that interest rates would remain high as long as John Crow, governor of the Bank of Canada, tried to reduce inflation.

The economic report argued that the Canadian dollar was overvalued relative to the U.S. dollar as a result of high interest rates and the unusually wide spread in interest rates between the two currencies. The Canadian dollar was expected to fall to around 81 cents U.S. by the end of 1989.

An economic slowdown was also forecast for the Atlantic region. This would have a negative effect on Atlantic Lumber Traders' sales. The Goods and Services Tax (GST) was to come into effect in January 1991, and because of additional record-keeping costs, was expected to have a significant impact on this low margin industry.

Industry Scan

Lumber traders' customers were usually independent supply stores, general contractors working on large projects (cutting out the middleman), or large end users such as mobile home manufacturers.

Without the service that a lumber trader provided, the customer (wholesaler or retailer) would have to go through a time-consuming process to purchase lumber. Wholesalers and retailers avoided the time necessary to purchase directly from the sawmill or to purchase partial loads by giving up a percentage of gross margin (usually 5 percent to 6 percent) to have the purchasing done by lumber traders.

Lumber traders needed experience to buy at low cost and to know which sawmills were producing given species, dimensions, and grades of lumber at any given time. It was also important to know the reputation for quality and reliability of each mill. The trader also had to arrange for transportation of lumber from the mill to its destination. If a purchaser did not want a full load, as was often the case, the cost of transporting a partial load could make the order uneconomical. Low cost was a critical factor in the lumber business because it operated on low margins.

There were risks inherent in the lumber trading business; the most significant was bad debts. The trader was responsible for paying the mill regardless of whether the customer paid on time, late, or not at all. If the customer did not pay, the resulting loss could bankrupt the trader. The trader also had the responsibility to deliver the stated quantity and quality of product on time. Buying off-grade lumber or having late deliveries could hurt customer relations and affect receivables collection.

The Atlantic provinces constituted the major market of Atlantic Lumber Traders; this market consumed approximately 1.2 billion board feet of lumber per year. The company's market share was about 5 percent in a fiercely competitive industry where they competed with other well-established families and interests such as the Irvings, another influential New Brunswick family. Atlantic Lumber Traders had to recover quickly if it was to maintain its competitive position.

Environmental factors could negatively affect the supply of lumber. Spruce budworm damage and the controversial forest spraying program had hurt the public image of the forestry industry and the profits of individual companies. Also, sawmills recognized the need to control pollution and the costs of doing so would be passed on to customers. This would put additional pressure on lumber traders' margins and might cause some customers to deal directly with mills to reduce costs.

The Situation in April 1989

Since year-end 1988, the Halls had injected an additional $200,000 into Atlantic Lumber Traders and the bank had reduced the available line of credit from $1.3 to $1 million. The availability of funds under the operating line of credit was subject to a maximum of: 75 percent of the bank's valuation of assigned accounts receivable after deducting receivables 60 days or more past due; plus 50 percent of the bank's valuation of free and clear assigned inventory to a maximum value of $125,000. The bank asked for, and received, a Section 178 lien over inventory in March 1989. The lien effectively meant that if the company failed, the goods covered by the lien could be liquidated only against the debt owed by the company to the bank, and not to other creditors. The bank also had an assignment of book debts (accounts receivable).

Action taken by Gail Hall included reducing staff from 11 to 6. The inefficient in-house accounting system was replaced by a simple, effective computer program. Sales personnel were put on commission only and lost their commission on accounts unpaid after 60 days. Inventory levels were cut from the $500,000 to $850,000 range to below $150,000. According to Gail, these changes went a long way toward reestablishing profitability.

With its reduced staff, the company expected to sell about $10 million of lumber in 1989, compared to $16.9 million in 1988. A gross margin of 5 percent was expected for 1989. Based on past performance, on the company's budget for 1989, and on industry benchmarks, Lynn projected variable costs for a wholesale lumber company at about 3 percent of sales. She also estimated that fixed costs for the company were between $14,000 and $15,000 per month. She used her estimates to calculate break-even sales levels and then prepared a spreadsheet to determine the combined effect (on break-even sales and net income) of changing each of her estimates in turn—recalculating with gross margin, variable costs, and fixed costs above and below the expected values.

The Alternatives for Management and the Bank

At their last meeting, Gail had given Lynn a proposal. Based on the improvements since year end, Gail hoped to negotiate an increase in the line of credit from $1 to $1.4 million. This would allow for increased sales to about $14.5 million rather than the $10 million expected. Based on historical sales and the improvements in the first quarter, Gail felt this figure more clearly reflected the ability of the company. According to Gail there was space available in the office for another trader, and the administrative capacity to support the added business. She pointed out that past history had shown the market could support the higher sales. Therefore, if the main constraint of working capital was overcome, Gail felt that Atlantic Lumber Traders was a viable operation.

A more conservative plan, already in the back of Lynn's mind, consisted of two parts: (1) increase the interest rate by 1 percent (cost to the company $10,000 per year) to cover additional monitoring costs, and (2) eliminate the margin available on inventory (50 percent up to $125,000). Besides covering the additional costs incurred in monitoring the account, this plan would reduce the bank's exposure. The lost margin on inventory would have a direct effect on the sales potential for Atlantic Lumber Traders.

Lynn knew that at worst, she could recommend that the Halls close their operations in an orderly fashion, one sales territory at a time, so that they and the bank would recover their investments.

Final Preparations

Lynn took a mouthful of coffee and turned to her computer to prepare the report Harry needed before tomorrow morning's meeting with Gail Hall. She knew that since Gail Hall's efforts had resulted in some improvement in company performance in the first quarter of 1989, and Gail had cooperated with the bank in its review, calling the loan was not an option at this point.

Case Questions

1. Conduct a financial ratio analysis of Atlantic Lumber Traders for 1987 and 1988. Compare the ratios to the industry averages in Exhibit 3. Comment on the company's strengths and weaknesses and compare your comments with the views expressed by Gail Hall and Lynn Thomas.

2. Examine how the changes introduced by Gail Hall in 1989 would improve the picture.

3. As advisor to Lynn Thomas, what action do you advise?

Suggested Readings

There are many excellent textbooks on financial statement analysis. Three that we have found helpful are:

Garrison, R. H., G. R. Chesley, and R. F. Carroll. *Managerial Accounting,* 2nd Canadian ed. Homewood, IL: Richard D. Irwin, 1993, chap. 17.

Gibson, C. H., and P. A. Frishkoff. *Financial Statement Analysis.* Boston: Kent Publishing, 1986.

Viscione, J. A. *Financial Analysis: Tools and Concepts.* New York: National Association of Credit Management, 1984.

Long-Term Financial Planning and Corporate Growth

A lack of effective long-range planning is a commonly cited reason for financial distress and failure. This is especially true for small businesses—a sector vital to the creation of future jobs in Canada. As we develop in this chapter, long-range planning is a means of systematically thinking about the future and anticipating possible problems before they arrive. There are no magic mirrors, of course, so the best we can hope for is a logical and organized procedure for exploring the unknown. As one member of General Motors Corporation's board was heard to say, "Planning is a process that at best helps the firm avoid stumbling into the future backwards."

Financial planning establishes guidelines for change and growth in a firm. It normally focusses on the "big picture." This means it is concerned with the major elements of a firm's financial and investment policies without examining the individual components of those policies in detail.

Our primary goal in this chapter is to discuss financial planning and to illustrate the interrelatedness of the various investment and financing decisions that a firm makes. In the chapters ahead, we examine in much more detail how these decisions are made.

We begin by describing what is usually meant by financial planning. For the most part, we talk about long-term planning. Short-term financial planning is discussed in Chapter 17. We examine what the firm can accomplish by developing a long-term financial plan. To do this, we develop a simple, but very useful, long-range planning technique: the percentage of sales approach. We describe how to apply this approach in some simple cases, and we discuss some extensions.

To develop an explicit financial plan, management must establish certain elements of the firm's financial policy. These basic policy elements of financial planning are:

1. The firm's needed investment in new assets. This arises from the investment opportunities that the firm chooses to undertake, and it is the result of the firm's capital budgeting decisions.

2. The degree of financial leverage the firm chooses to employ. This determines the amount of borrowing the firm uses to finance its investments in real assets. This is the firm's capital structure policy.

3. The amount of cash the firm thinks is necessary and appropriate to pay shareholders. This is the firm's dividend policy.

4. The amount of liquidity and working capital the firm needs on an ongoing basis. This is the firm's net working capital decision.

As we shall see, the decisions that a firm makes in these four areas directly affect its future profitability, its need for external financing, and its opportunities for growth.

A key lesson from this chapter is that the firm's investment and financing policies interact and thus cannot truly be considered in isolation from one another. The types and amounts of assets that the firm plans on purchasing must be considered along with the firm's ability to raise the necessary capital to fund those investments.

Financial planning forces the corporation to think about goals. A goal frequently espoused by corporations is growth, and almost all firms use an explicit, company-wide growth rate as a major component of their long-run financial planning. In the mid-1980s, IBM's stated growth goal was simple but typical (and optimistic): to match the growth of the computer industry, which it projected would be 15 percent per year through 1995.[1]

There are direct connections between the growth that a company can achieve and its financial policy. In the following sections, we show that financial planning models can help you better understand how growth is achieved. We also show how such models can be used to establish limits on possible growth. This analysis can help companies avoid the sometimes fatal mistake of growing too fast.

4.1 | WHAT IS FINANCIAL PLANNING?

Financial planning formulates the way financial goals are to be achieved. A financial plan is thus a statement of what is to be done in the future. Most decisions have long lead times, which means they take a long time to implement. In an uncertain world, this requires that decisions be made far in advance of their implementation. A firm that wants to build a factory in 1997, for example, might have to begin lining up contractors and financing in 1995, or even earlier.

Growth as a Financial Management Goal

Because we discuss the subject of growth in various places in this chapter, we start out with an important warning: Growth, by itself, is *not* an appropriate goal for the financial manager. For example, if a firm reinvests 50 percent of its earnings and earns 10 percent on the investment, all else constant, its earnings grow by $.50 \times 10\%$ = 5%. However, if the investor could invest elsewhere at 15 percent in projects with similar risks, the firm's stock price would fall. As we discuss in Chapter 1, the appropriate goal is increasing the market value of the owners' equity. Of course, if a firm is successful in doing this, growth usually results.

Growth may thus be a desirable consequence of good decision making, but it is not an end unto itself. We discuss growth simply because growth rates are so commonly used in the planning process. As we see, growth is a convenient means of summarizing various aspects of a firm's financial and investment policies. Also, if we think of growth as growth in the market value of the equity in the firm, then the goals of growth and increasing the market value of the equity in the firm are not all that different.

---

[1] See *The Wall Street Journal*, June 12, 1985.

Dimensions of Financial Planning

It is often useful for planning purposes to think of the future as having a short run and a long run. The short run, in practice, is usually the coming 12 months. We focus our attention on financial planning over the long run, which is usually taken to be the coming two to five years. This is called the **planning horizon**, and it is the first dimension of the planning process that must be established.[2]

In drawing up a financial plan, all of the individual projects and investments that the firm undertakes are combined to determine the total needed investment. In effect, the smaller investment proposals of each operational unit are added up and treated as one big project. This process is called **aggregation**. This is the second dimension of the planning process.

Once the planning horizon and level of aggregation are established, a financial plan would need inputs in the form of alternative sets of assumptions about important variables. For example, suppose a company has two separate divisions: one for consumer products and one for gas turbine engines. The financial planning process might require each division to prepare three alternative business plans for the next three years.

1. A worst case. This plan would require making the worst possible assumptions about the company's products and the state of the economy. This kind of disaster planning would emphasize a division's ability to withstand significant economic adversity, and it would require details concerning cost cutting, and even divestiture and liquidation.

2. A normal case. This plan would require making most likely assumptions about the company and the economy.

3. A best case. Each division would be required to work out a case based on the most optimistic assumptions. It could involve new products and expansion and then would detail the financing needed to fund the expansion.

In this example, business activities are aggregated along divisional lines and the planning horizon is three years.

What Can Planning Accomplish?

Because the company is likely to spend a lot of time examining the different scenarios that could become the basis for the company's financial plan, it seems reasonable to ask what the planning process will accomplish.

Interactions   As we discuss in greater detail later, the financial plan must make explicit the linkages between investment proposals for the different operating activities of the firm and the financing choices available to the firm. In other words, if the firm is planning on expanding and undertaking new investments and projects, where will the financing be obtained to pay for this activity?

Options   The financial plan provides the opportunity for the firm to develop, analyze, and compare many different scenarios in a consistent way. Various investment and financing options can be explored, and their impact on the firm's shareholders can be evaluated. Questions concerning the firm's future lines of

planning horizon
The long-range time period the financial planning process focusses on, usually the next two to five years.

aggregation
Process by which smaller investment proposals of each of a firm's operational units are added up and treated as one big project.

---

[2] The techniques we present can also be used for short-term financial planning.

business and questions of what financing arrangements are optimal are addressed. Options such as marketing new products or closing plants might be evaluated.

Avoiding Surprises   Financial planning should identify what may happen to the firm if different events take place. In particular, it should address what actions the firm would take if things go seriously wrong or, more generally, if assumptions made today about the future are seriously in error. Thus, one of the purposes of financial planning is to avoid surprises and develop contingency plans.

Feasibility and Internal Consistency   Beyond a specific goal of creating value, a firm normally has many specific goals. Such goals might be couched in market share, return on equity, financial leverage, and so on. At times, the linkages between different goals and different aspects of a firm's business are difficult to see. Not only does a financial plan make explicit these linkages, but it also imposes a unified structure for reconciling differing goals and objectives. In other words, financial planning is a way of checking that the goals and plans made with regard to specific areas of a firm's operations are feasible and internally consistent. Conflicting goals often exist. To generate a coherent plan, goals and objectives have to be modified therefore, and priorities have to be established.

For example, one goal a firm might have is 12 percent growth in unit sales per year. Another goal might be to reduce the firm's total debt ratio from 40 percent to 20 percent. Are these two goals compatible? Can they be accomplished simultaneously? Maybe yes, maybe no. As we discuss later, financial planning is a way of finding out just what is possible, and, by implication, what is not possible.

The fact that planning forces management to think about goals and to establish priorities is probably the most important result of the process. In fact, conventional business wisdom says that plans can't work, but planning does. The future is inherently unknown. What we can do is establish the direction that we want to travel and take some educated guesses about what we will find along the way. If we do a good job, we won't be caught off guard when the future rolls around.

Communication with Investors and Lenders   Our discussion to this point has tried to convince you that financial planning is essential to good management. Because good management controls the riskiness of a firm, equity investors and lenders are very interested in studying a firm's financial plan. As discussed in Chapter 13, securities regulators require that firms issuing new shares or debt file a detailed financial plan as part of the *prospectus* describing the new issue. Chartered banks and other financial institutions that make loans to businesses almost always require prospective borrowers to provide a financial plan. In small businesses with limited resources for planning, pressure from lenders is often the main motivator for engaging in financial planning.

CONCEPT QUESTIONS
1. What are the two dimensions of the financial planning process?
2. Why should firms draw up financial plans?

4.2 | FINANCIAL PLANNING MODELS: A FIRST LOOK

Just as companies differ in size and products, the financial planning process differs from firm to firm. In this section, we discuss some common elements in financial plans and develop a basic model to illustrate these elements.

A Financial Planning Model: The Ingredients

Most financial planning models require the user to specify some assumptions about the future. Based on those assumptions, the model generates predicted values for a large number of variables. Models can vary quite a bit in their complexity, but almost all would have the following elements:

Sales Forecast Almost all financial plans require an externally supplied sales forecast. In the models that follow, for example, the sales forecast is the driver, meaning that the user of the planning model supplies this value and all other values are calculated based on it. This arrangement would be common for many types of business; planning focusses on projected future sales and the assets and financing needed to support those sales.

Frequently, the sales forecast is given as a growth rate in sales rather than as an explicit sales figure. These two approaches are essentially the same because we can calculate projected sales once we know the growth rate. Perfect sales forecasts are not possible, of course, because sales depend on the uncertain future state of the economy and on industry conditions.

For example, the recession in 1990–92 caused many firms to scale down their sales forecasts. Some industries were hit particularly hard. Two examples were airlines (economic slowdown and the Persian Gulf War) and retail (economic slowdown and cross-border shopping). To help firms come up with such projections, some economic consulting firms specialize in macroeconomic and industry projections. Economic and industry forecasts are also available free from the economic research departments of chartered banks.

As we discussed earlier, we are frequently interested in evaluating alternative scenarios, so it isn't necessarily crucial that the sales forecast be accurate. Our goal is to examine the interplay between investment and financing needs at different possible sales levels, not to pinpoint what we expect to happen.

Pro Forma Statements A financial plan has a forecasted balance sheet, an income statement, and a statement of cash flows. These are called pro forma statements, or pro formas for short. The phrase *pro forma* literally means "as a matter of form." This means that the financial statements are the forms we use to summarize the different events projected for the future. At a minimum, a financial planning model generates these statements based on projections of key items such as sales.

In the planning models we describe later, the pro formas are the output from the financial planning model. The user supplies a sales figure, and the model generates the resulting income statement and balance sheet.

Asset Requirements The plan describes projected capital spending. At a minimum, the projected balance sheets contain changes in total fixed assets and net working capital. These changes are effectively the firm's total capital budget. Proposed capital spending in different areas must thus be reconciled with the overall increases contained in the long-range plan.

Financial Requirements The plan includes a section on the financial arrangements that are necessary. This part of the plan should discuss dividend policy and debt policy. Sometimes firms expect to raise cash by selling new shares of stock or by borrowing. Then, the plan has to spell out what kinds of securities have to be sold and what methods of issuance are most appropriate. These are subjects we consider in Parts VI and VII when we discuss long-term financing, capital structure, and dividend policy.

The Plug   After the firm has a sales forecast and an estimate of the required spending on assets, some amount of new financing is often necessary because projected total assets exceed projected total liabilities and equity. In other words, the balance sheet no longer balances.

Because new financing may be necessary to cover all the projected capital spending, a financial "plug" variable must be designated. The plug is the designated source or sources of external financing needed to deal with any shortfall (or surplus) in financing and thereby to bring the balance sheet into balance.

For example, a firm with a great number of investment opportunities and limited cash flow may have to raise new equity. Other firms with few growth opportunities and ample cash flow have a surplus and thus might pay an extra dividend. In the first case, external equity is the plug variable. In the second, the dividend is used.

Economic Assumptions   The plan has to explicitly describe the economic environment in which the firm expects to reside over the life of the plan. Among the more important economic assumptions that have to be made are the level of interest rates and the firm's tax rate as well as sales forecasts, as discussed earlier.

A Simple Financial Planning Model

We begin our discussion of long-term planning models with a relatively simple example.[3] The Computerfield Corporation's financial statements from the most recent year are as follows:

COMPUTERFIELD CORPORATION
Financial Statements

Income Statement			Balance Sheet			
Sales	$1,000		Assets	$500	Debt	$250
Costs	800				Equity	250
Net income	$ 200		Total	$500	Total	$500

Unless otherwise stated, the financial planners at Computerfield assume that all variables are tied directly to sales and that current relationships are optimal. This means that all items grow at exactly the same rate as sales. This is obviously oversimplified; we use this assumption only to make a point.

Suppose that sales increase by 20 percent, rising from $1,000 to $1,200. Then planners would also forecast a 20 percent increase in costs, from $800 to $800 × 1.2 = $960. The pro forma income statement would thus be:

Pro Forma Income Statement	
Sales	$1,200
Costs	960
Net income	$ 240

The assumption that all variables would grow by 20 percent enables us to easily construct the pro forma balance sheet as well:

---

[3] Computer spreadsheets are the standard way to execute this and the other examples we present. Appendix 8B gives an overview of spreadsheets and how they are used in planning with capital budgeting as the application.

Pro Forma Balance Sheet

Assets	$600 (+100)	Debt	$300 (+50)
		Equity	300 (+50)
Total	$600 (+100)	Total	$600 (+100)

Notice that we have simply increased every item by 20 percent. The numbers in parentheses are the dollar changes for the different items.

Now we have to reconcile these two pro formas. How, for example, can net income be equal to $240 and equity increase by only $50? The answer is that Computerfield must have paid out the difference of $240 − 50 = $190, possibly as a cash dividend. In this case, dividends are the plug variable.

Suppose Computerfield does not pay out the $190. Here, the addition to retained earnings is the full $240. Computerfield's equity thus grows to $250 (the starting amount) + 240 (net income) = $490, and debt must be retired to keep total assets equal to $600.

With $600 in total assets and $490 in equity, debt has to be $600 − 490 = $110. Since we started with $250 in debt, Computerfield has to retire $250 − 110 = $140 in debt. The resulting pro forma balance sheet would look like this:

Pro Forma Balance Sheet

Assets	$600 (+100)	Debt	$110 (−140)
		Equity	490 (+240)
Total	$600 (+100)	Total	$600 (+100)

In this case, debt is the plug variable used to balance out projected total assets and liabilities.

This example shows the interaction between sales growth and financial policy. As sales increase, so do total assets. This occurs because the firm must invest in net working capital and fixed assets to support higher sales levels. Since assets are growing, total liabilities and equity, the right-hand side of the balance sheet, grow as well.

The thing to notice from our simple example is that the way the liabilities and owners' equity change depends on the firm's financing policy and its dividend policy. The growth in assets requires that the firm decide on how to finance that growth. This is strictly a managerial decision. Also, in our example the firm needed no outside funds. As this isn't usually the case, we explore a more detailed situation in the next section.

CONCEPT QUESTIONS

1. What are the basic concepts of a financial plan?
2. Why is it necessary to designate a plug in a financial planning model?

4.3 | THE PERCENTAGE OF SALES APPROACH

In the previous section, we described a simple planning model in which every item increased at the same rate as sales. This may be a reasonable assumption for some elements. For others, such as long-term borrowing, it probably is not, because the amount of long-term borrowing is something set by management, and it does not necessarily relate directly to the level of sales.

In this section, we describe an extended version of our simple model. The basic idea is to separate the income statement and balance sheet accounts into two groups, those that do vary directly with sales and those that do not. Given a sales forecast, we are able to calculate how much financing the firm needs to support the predicted sales level.

An Illustration of the Percentage of Sales Approach

percentage of sales approach
Financial planning method in which accounts are projected depending on a firm's predicted sales level.

The financial planning model we describe next is based on the **percentage of sales approach**. Our goal here is to develop a quick and practical way of generating pro forma statements. We defer discussion of some bells and whistles to a later section.

The Income Statement   We start with the most recent income statement for the Rosengarten Corporation, as shown in Table 4.1. Notice that we have still simplified things by including costs, depreciation, and interest in a single cost figure. We separate these out in Appendix 4A at the end of this chapter.

Rosengarten has projected a 25 percent increase in sales for the coming year, so we are anticipating sales of $1,000 × 1.25 = $1,250. To generate a pro forma income statement, we assume that total costs continue to run at $800/$1,000 = 80% of sales. With this assumption, Rosengarten's pro forma income statement is as shown in Table 4.2. The effect here of assuming that costs are a constant percentage of sales is to assume that the profit margin is constant. To check this, notice that the profit margin was $132/$1,000 = 13.2%. In our pro forma, the profit margin is $165/$1,250 = 13.2%; so it is unchanged.

Next, we need to project the dividend payment. This amount is up to Rosengarten's management. We assume that Rosengarten has a policy of paying out a constant fraction of net income in the form of a cash dividend. From the most recent year, the **dividend payout ratio** was:

dividend payout ratio
Amount of cash paid out to shareholders divided by net income.

$$\text{Dividend payout ratio} = \text{Cash dividends/Net income} \qquad [4.1]$$
$$= \$44/\$132$$
$$= 33\tfrac{1}{3}\%$$

We can also calculate the ratio of the addition to retained earnings to net income as:

retention ratio or plowback ratio
Retained earnings divided by net income.

$$\text{Retained earnings/Net income} = \$88/\$132 = 66\tfrac{2}{3}\%.$$

This ratio is called the **retention ratio** or **plowback ratio**, and it is equal to 1 minus the dividend payout ratio because everything not paid out is retained. Assuming that

T A B L E 4.1

ROSENGARTEN CORPORATION
Income Statement

Sales		$1,000
Costs		800
Taxable income		$ 200
Taxes		68
Net income		$ 132
Addition to retained earnings	$88	
Dividends	$44	

T A B L E 4.2

ROSENGARTEN CORPORATION
Pro Forma Income Statement

Sales (projected)	$1,250
Costs (80% of sales)	1,000
Taxable income	$ 250
Taxes	85
Net income	$ 165

the payout and retention ratios are constant, the projected dividends and addition to retained earnings would be:

Projected addition to retained earnings $= \$165 \times \frac{2}{3} = \$110$

Projected dividends paid to shareholders $= \$165 \times \frac{1}{3} = \underline{\quad 55}$

$$\text{Net income} \quad \underline{\$165}$$

The Balance Sheet   To generate a pro forma balance sheet, we start with the most recent statement in Table 4.3. On our balance sheet, we assume that some of the items vary directly with sales while others do not. For those items that do vary with sales, we express each as a percentage of sales for the year just completed. When an item does not vary directly with sales, we write "n/a" for "not applicable."

For example, on the asset side, inventory is equal to 60 percent of sales ($600/$1,000) for the year just ended. We assume that this percentage applies to the coming year, so for each $1 increase in sales, inventory rises by $.60. More generally, the ratio of total assets to sales for the year just ended is $3,000/$1,000 = 3, or 300%.

This ratio of total assets to sales is sometimes called the **capital intensity ratio**. It tells us the assets needed to generate $1 in sales; so the higher the ratio is, the more

capital intensity ratio
A firm's total assets divided by its sales, or the amount of assets needed to generate $1 in sales.

T A B L E 4.3

ROSENGARTEN CORPORATION
Balance Sheet

	($)	(%)		($)	(%)
Assets			*Liabilities and Owners' Equity*		
Current assets			Current liabilities		
Cash	$ 160	16%	Accounts payable	$ 300	30%
Accounts			Notes payable	100	n/a
receivable	440	44			
Inventory	600	60	Total	$ 400	n/a
Total	$1,200	120%			
			Long-term debt	$ 800	n/a
Fixed assets			Owners' equity		
Net plant and			Common stock	$ 800	n/a
equipment	$1,800	180%	Retained earnings	1,000	n/a
			Total	$1,800	n/a
Total assets	$3,000	300%	Total liabilities and owners' equity	$3,000	n/a

capital intensive is the firm. Notice also that this ratio is just the reciprocal of the total asset turnover ratio we defined in the last chapter.

For Rosengarten, assuming this ratio is constant, it takes $3 in total assets to generate $1 in sales (apparently Rosengarten is in a relatively capital intensive business). Therefore, if sales are to increase by $100, Rosengarten has to increase total assets by three times this amount, or $300.

On the liability side of the balance sheet, we show accounts payable varying with sales. The reason is that we expect to place more orders with our suppliers as sales volume increases, so payables should change spontaneously with sales. Notes payable, on the other hand, represent short-term debt such as bank borrowing. These would not vary unless we take specific actions to change the amount, so we mark them as n/a.

Similarly, we use n/a for long-term debt because it won't automatically change with sales. The same is true for common stock. The last item on the right-hand side, retained earnings, varies with sales, but it won't be a simple percentage of sales. Instead, we explicitly calculate the change in retained earnings based on our projected net income and dividends.

We can now construct a partial pro forma balance sheet for Rosengarten. We do this by using the percentages we calculated earlier wherever possible to calculate the projected amounts. For example, fixed assets are 180 percent of sales; so, with a new sales level of $1,250, the fixed asset amount is 1.80 × $1,250 = $2,250, an increase of $2,250 − 1,800 = $450 in plant and equipment. Importantly, for those items that don't vary directly with sales, we initially assume no change and simply write in the original amounts. The result is the pro forma balance sheet in Table 4.4. Notice that the change in retained earnings is equal to the $110 addition to retained earnings that we calculated earlier.

Inspecting our pro forma balance sheet, we notice that assets are projected to increase by $750. However, without additional financing, liabilities and equity only increase by $185, leaving a shortfall of $750 − 185 = $565. We label this amount *external financing needed* (EFN).

T A B L E 4.4

ROSENGARTEN CORPORATION
Partial Pro Forma Balance Sheet

	Present Year	Change from Previous Year		Present Year	Change from Previous Year
Assets			*Liabilities and Owners' Equity*		
Current assets			Current liabilities		
Cash	$ 200	$ 40	Accounts payable	$ 375	$ 75
Accounts			Notes payable	100	0
receivable	550	110	Total	$ 475	$ 75
Inventory	750	150			
Total	$1,500	$300	Long-term debt	$ 800	$ 0
Fixed assets			Owners' equity		
Net plant and			Common stock	$ 800	$ 0
equipment	$2,250	$450	Retained earnings	1,110	110
			Total	$1,910	$110
Total assets	$3,750	$750	Total liabilities		
			and owners' equity	$3,185	$185
			External		
			financing needed	$ 565	

A Particular Scenario   Our financial planning model now reminds us of one of those good news/bad news jokes. The good news is that we're projecting a 25 percent increase in sales. The bad news is that this isn't going to happen unless we can somehow raise $565 in new financing.

This is a good example of how the planning process can point out problems and potential conflicts. If, for example, Rosengarten has a goal of not borrowing any additional funds and not selling any new equity, a 25 percent increase in sales is probably not feasible.

When we take the need for $565 in new financing as a given, Rosengarten has three possible sources: short-term borrowing, long-term borrowing, and new equity. The choice of a combination among these three is up to management; we illustrate only one of the many possibilities.

Suppose that Rosengarten decides to borrow the needed funds. The firm might choose to borrow some short-term and some long-term. For example, current assets increased by $300 while current liabilities rose by only $75. Rosengarten could borrow $300 − 75 = $225 in short-term notes payable in the form of a loan from a chartered bank. This would leave total net working capital unchanged. With $565 needed, the remaining $565 − 225 = $340 would have to come from long-term debt. Two examples of long-term debt discussed in Chapter 13 are a bond issue and a term loan from a chartered bank or insurance company. Table 4.5 shows the completed pro forma balance sheet for Rosengarten.

Even though we used a combination of short- and long-term debt as the plug here, we emphasize that this is just one possible strategy; it is not necessarily the best one by any means. There are many other scenarios that we could (and should) investigate.

Now that we have finished our balance sheet, we have all of the projected sources and uses of cash. We could finish off our pro formas by drawing up the projected statement of changes in financial position along the lines discussed in Chapter 3. We leave this as an exercise and instead investigate an important alternative scenario.

ROSENGARTEN CORPORATION
Pro Forma Balance Sheet

T A B L E 4.5

	Present Year	Change from Previous Year		Present Year	Change from Previous Year
	Assets		*Liabilities and Owners' Equity*		
Current assets			Current liabilities		
Cash	$ 200	$ 40	Accounts payable	$ 375	$ 75
Accounts			Notes payable	325	225
receivable	550	110	Total	$ 700	$300
Inventory	750	150	Long-term debt	$1,140	$340
Total	$1,500	$300	Owners' equity		
Fixed assets			Common stock	$ 800	$ 0
Net plant and			Retained earnings	1,110	110
equipment	$2,250	$450	Total	$1,910	$110
Total assets	$3,750	$750	Total liabilities and owners' equity	$3,750	$750

An Alternative Scenario   The assumption that assets are a fixed percentage of sales is convenient, but it may not be suitable in many cases. For example, we effectively assumed that Rosengarten was using its fixed assets at 100 percent of capacity because any increase in sales led to an increase in fixed assets. For most businesses, there would be some slack or excess capacity, and production could be increased by, perhaps, running an extra shift.

If we assume that Rosengarten is only operating at 70 percent of capacity, the need for external funds would be quite different. By 70 percent of capacity, we mean that the current sales level is 70 percent of the full capacity sales level:

Current sales = $1,000 = .70 × Full capacity sales

Full capacity sales = $1,000/.70 = $1,429

This tells us that sales could increase by almost 43 percent—from $1,000 to $1,429—before any new fixed assets were needed.

In our previous scenario, we assumed it would be necessary to add $450 in net fixed assets. In the current scenario, no spending on net fixed assets is needed, because sales are projected to rise to $1,250, which is substantially less than the $1,429 full capacity level.

As a result, our original estimate of $565 in external funds needed is too high. We estimated that $450 in net new fixed assets would be needed. Instead, no spending on new net fixed assets is necessary. Thus, if we are currently operating at 70 percent capacity, we only need $565 − 450 = $115 in external funds. The excess capacity thus makes a considerable difference in our projections.

E X A M P L E │ 4.1   EFN and Capacity Usage

Suppose Rosengarten were operating at 90 percent capacity. What would be sales at full capacity? What is the capital intensity ratio at full capacity? What is EFN in this case?

Full capacity sales would be $1,000/.90 = $1,111. From Table 4.3, fixed assets are $1,800. At full capacity, the ratio of fixed assets to sales is thus:

Fixed assets/Full capacity sales = $1,800/$1,111 = 1.62

This tells us that we need $1.62 in fixed assets for every $1 in sales once we reach full capacity. At the projected sales level of $1,250, we need $1,250 × 1.62 = $2,025 in fixed assets. Compared to the $2,250 we originally projected, this is $225 less, so EFN is $565 − 225 = $340.

Current assets would still be $1,500, so total assets would be $1,500 + 2,025 = $3,525. The capital intensity ratio would thus be $3,525/$1,250 = 2.82, less than our original value of 3 because of the excess capacity. │

These alternative scenarios illustrate that it is inappropriate to manipulate financial statement information blindly in the planning process. The output of any model is only as good as the input assumptions or, as is said in the computer field, GIGO: garbage in, garbage out. Results depend critically on the assumptions made about the relationships between sales and asset needs. We return to this point later.

CONCEPT QUESTIONS
1. What is the basic idea behind the percentage of sales approach?
2. Unless it is modified, what does the percentage of sales approach assume about fixed asset capacity usage?

4.4 | EXTERNAL FINANCING AND GROWTH

External financing needed and growth are obviously related. All other things being the same, the higher the rate of growth in sales or assets, the greater will be the need for external financing. In the previous section, we took a growth rate as a given, and then we determined the amount of external financing needed to support the growth. In this section, we turn things around a bit. We take the firm's financial policy as a given and then examine the relationship between that financial policy and the firm's ability to finance new investments and thereby grow.

This approach can be very useful because, as you have already seen, growth in sales requires financing, so it follows that growth that is too fast can cause a company to grow broke.[4] Companies that neglect to plan for financing growth can fail even when production and marketing are on track. From a positive perspective, planning growth that is financially sustainable can help an excellent company achieve its potential. This is why managers, along with their bankers and other suppliers of funds, need to look at sustainable growth.

EFN and Growth

To begin, we must establish the relationship between EFN and growth. To do this, we introduce Table 4.6, a simplified income statement and balance sheet for the Hoffman Company. Notice that we have simplified the balance sheet by combining short-term and long-term debt into a single total debt figure. Effectively, we are assuming that none of the current liabilities varies spontaneously with sales. This assumption isn't as restrictive as it sounds. If any current liabilities (such as accounts payable) vary

---

[4] This phrase and the following discussion draws heavily on R. C. Higgins, "How Much Growth Can a Firm Afford?" *Financial Management* 6, Fall 1977, pp. 7–16.

HOFFMAN COMPANY
Income Statement and Balance Sheet

TABLE 4.6

Income Statement

Sales	$500
Costs	400
Taxable income	$100
Taxes	34
Net income	$ 66

Addition to retained earnings	$44
Dividends	$22

Balance Sheet

	$	% of Sales		$	% of Sales
Assets			*Liabilities*		
Current assets	$200	40%	Total debt	$250	n/a
Net fixed assets	300	60%	Owners' equity	250	n/a
Total assets	$500	100%	Total liabilities and owners' equity	$500	n/a

with sales, we can assume they have been netted out in current assets. Also, we continue to combine depreciation, interest, and costs on the income statement.

The following symbols are useful:

S = Previous year's sales = $500
A = Total assets = $500
D = *Total debt = $250*
E = Total equity = $250

In addition, based on our earlier discussions of financial ratios, we can calculate the following:

p = Profit margin = $66/$500 = 13.2%
R = Retention ratio = $44/$66 = 2/3
ROA = Return on assets = $66/$500 = 13.2%
ROE = Return on equity = $66/$250 = 26.4%
D/E = Debt/equity ratio = $250/$250 = 1.0

Suppose the Hoffman Company is forecasting next year's sales level at $600, a $100 increase. The capital intensity ratio is $500/$500 = 1, so assets need to rise by 1 × $100 = $100 (assuming full capacity usage). Notice that the percentage increase in sales is $100/$500 = 20%. The percentage increase in assets is also 20 percent: 100/$500 = 20%. As this illustrates, assuming a constant capital intensity ratio, the increase in total assets is simply A × g, where g is growth rate in sales:

Increase in total assets = $A \times g$
$= \$500 \times 20\%$
$= \$100$

In other words, the growth rate in sales can also be interpreted as the rate of increase in the firm's total assets.

Some of the financing necessary to cover the increase in total assets comes from internally generated funds and shows up in the form of the addition to retained earnings. This amount is equal to net income multiplied by the plowback or retention ratio, R. Projected net income is equal to the profit margin, p, multiplied by projected sales, $S \times (1 + g)$. The projected addition to retained earnings for Hoffman can thus be written as:

Addition to retained earnings = $p(S)R \times (1 + g)$
$= .132(\$500)(\frac{2}{3}) \times 1.20$
$= \$44 \times 1.20$
$= \$52.80$

Notice that this is equal to last year's addition to retained earnings, $44, multiplied by $(1 + g)$.

Putting this information together, we need A × g = $100 in new financing. We generate $p(S)R \times (1 + g)$ = $52.80 internally, so the difference is what we need to raise. In other words, we find that EFN can be written as:

EFN = Increase in total assets − Addition to retained earnings   [4.2]
$= A(g) - p(S)R \times (1 + g)$

For Hoffman, this works out to be

EFN = $500(.20) − .132($500)(⅔) × 1.20

= $100 − $52.80

= $47.20

We can check that this is correct by filling in a pro forma income statement and balance sheet as in Table 4.7. As we calculated, Hoffman needs to raise $47.20.

Looking at our equation for EFN, we see that EFN depends directly on g. Rearranging things to highlight this relationship, we get:

$$EFN = -p(S)R + [A - p(S)R] \times g \qquad [4.3]$$

Plugging in the numbers for Hoffman, the relationship between EFN and g is:

EFN = −.132($500)(⅔) + [$500 − .132($500)(⅔)] × g

= −44 + 456 × g

Notice that this is the equation of a straight line with a vertical intercept of −$44 and a slope of $456.

The relationship between growth and EFN is illustrated in Figure 4.1. The y-axis intercept of our line, −$44, is equal to last year's addition to retained earnings. This makes sense because, if the growth in sales is zero, then retained earnings are $44, the same as last year. Furthermore, with no growth, no net investment in assets is needed, so we run a surplus equal to the addition to retained earnings, which is why we have a negative sign.

The slope of the line in Figure 4.1 tells us that for every .01 (1 percent) in sales growth, we need an additional $456 × .01 = $4.56 in external financing to support that growth.

TABLE 4.7

HOFFMAN COMPANY
Pro Forma Income Statement and Balance Sheet

Income Statement

Sales	$600.0
Costs (80% of sales)	480.0
Taxable income	$120.0
Taxes	40.8
Net income	$ 79.2
Addition to retained earnings	$52.8
Dividends	$26.4

Balance Sheet

Assets	$	% of Sales	Liabilities	$	% of Sales
Current assets	$240.0	40%	Total debt	$250.0	n/a
Net fixed assets	360.0	60	Owners' equity	302.8	n/a
Total assets	$600.0	100%	Total liabilities	$552.8	n/a
			External funds needed	$ 47.2	

FIGURE 4.1

External financing needed and growth in sales for the Hoffman Company.

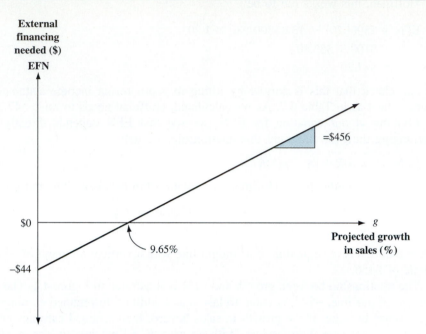

The relationship between external financing needed (EFN) and growth in sales (*g*) for Hoffman is given by

$$EFN = -44 + 456 \times g$$

As illustrated, Hoffman can grow at 9.65% with no external financing (debt or equity).

Internal Growth Rate

internal growth rate

The growth rate a firm can maintain with only internal financing.

Looking at Figure 4.1, there is one growth rate of obvious interest. What growth rate can we achieve with no external financing? We call this the **internal growth rate** because it is the rate the firm can maintain with only internal financing. This growth rate corresponds to the point where our line crosses the horizontal axis, that is, the point where EFN is zero. At this point, the required increase in assets is exactly equal to the addition to retained earnings, and EFN is therefore zero. Figure 4.1 shows that this rate is just under 10 percent.

We can easily calculate this rate by setting EFN equal to zero:

$$EFN = -p(S)R + [A - p(S)R] \times g \qquad [4.4]$$
$$g = pS(R)/[A - pS(R)]$$
$$= .132(\$500)(\tfrac{2}{3})/[\$500 - .132(\$500)(\tfrac{2}{3})]$$
$$= 44/[500 - 44]$$
$$= 44/456 = 9.65\%$$

Hoffman can therefore grow at a 9.65 percent rate before any external financing is required. With a little algebra, we can restate the expression for the internal growth rate (Equation 4.4) as:[5]

---

[5] To derive Equation 4.5 from (4.4) divide through by A and recognize that ROA = $p(S)/A$.

$$\text{Internal growth rate} = \frac{ROA \times R}{1 - ROA \times R} \qquad [4.5]$$

For Hoffman, we can check this by recomputing the 9.65% internal growth rate

$$= \frac{.132 \times \frac{2}{3}}{1 - .132 \times \frac{2}{3}}$$

Financial Policy and Growth

Suppose Hoffman, for whatever reason, does not wish to sell any new equity. As we discuss in Chapter 13, one possible reason is simply that new equity sales can be very expensive. Alternatively, the current owners may not wish to bring in new owners or contribute additional equity themselves. For a small business or a start-up, the reason may be even more compelling: All sources of new equity have likely already been tapped and the only way to increase equity is through additions to retained earnings.

In addition, we assume that Hoffman wishes to maintain its current debt/equity ratio. To be more specific, Hoffman (and its lenders) regard its current debt policy as optimal. We discuss why a particular mixture of debt and equity might be better than any other in Chapters 14 and 15. For now, we say that Hoffman has a fixed **debt capacity** relative to total equity. If the debt/equity ratio declines, Hoffman has excess debt capacity and can comfortably borrow additional funds.

debt capacity
The ability to borrow to increase firm value.

Assuming that Hoffman does borrow to its debt capacity, what growth rate can be achieved? The answer is the **sustainable growth rate**, the maximum growth rate a firm can achieve with no external *equity* financing while it maintains a constant debt/equity ratio. To find the sustainable growth rate, we go back to Equation 4.2 and add another term for new borrowings (up to debt capacity). One way to see where the amount of new borrowings comes from is to relate it to the addition to retained earnings. Because this addition increases equity, it reduces the debt/equity ratio. Since sustainable growth is based on a constant debt/equity ratio, we use new borrowings to top up debt. Now EFN refers to outside equity only. Because no new outside equity is available, EFN = 0.

sustainable growth rate
The growth rate a firm can maintain given its debt capacity, ROE, and retention ratio.

$$\text{EFN} = \text{Increase in total assets} - \text{Addition to retained earnings} \qquad [4.6]$$
$$\qquad - \text{New borrowing}$$
$$= A(g) - p(S)R \times (1 + g) - pS(R) \times (1 + g)[D/E]$$
$$\text{EFN} = 0$$

With some algebra we can solve for the sustainable growth rate.[6]

$$g^* = ROE \times R/[1 - ROE \times R] \qquad [4.7]$$

This growth rate is called the firm's sustainable growth rate (SGR).

For example, for the Hoffman Company, we already know that the ROE is 26.4 percent and the retention ratio, R, is $\frac{2}{3}$. The sustainable growth rate is thus:

$$g^* = (ROE \times R)/(1 - ROE \times R)$$
$$= .176/.824$$
$$= 21.3\%$$

---

[6] The derivation of the sustainable growth rate is shown in Appendix 4B.

This tells us that Hoffman can increase its sales and assets at a rate of 21.3 percent per year without selling any additional equity and without changing its debt ratio or payout ratio. If a growth rate in excess of this is desired or predicted, something has to give.

To better see that the SGR is 21.3 percent (and to check our answer), we can fill out the pro forma financial statements assuming that Hoffman's sales increase at exactly the SGR. We do this to verify that if Hoffman's sales do grow at 21.3 percent, all needed financing can be obtained without the need to sell new equity, and, at the same time, the debt/equity ratio can be maintained at its current level of 1.0.

To get started, sales increase from $500 to $500 × (1 + .213) = $606. Assuming, as before, that costs are proportional to sales, the income statement would be:

HOFFMAN COMPANY
Pro Forma Income Statement

Sales	$606
Costs (80% of sales)	485
Taxable income	$121
Taxes	41
Net income	$ 80

Given that the retention ratio, R, stays at ⅔, the addition to retained earnings is $80 × (⅔) = $53, and the dividend paid is $80 − 53 = $27.

We fill out the pro forma balance sheet (Table 4.8) just as we did earlier. Note that the owners' equity rises from $250 to $303 because the addition to retained earnings is $53. As illustrated, EFN is $53. If Hoffman borrows this amount, its total debt rises to $250 + 53 = $303. The debt/equity ratio therefore is $303/$303 = 1.0 as desired, thereby verifying our earlier calculations. At any other growth rate, something would have to change.

E X A M P L E | 4.2   Growing Bankrupt

Suppose the management of Hoffman Company is not satisfied with a growth rate of 21 percent. Instead, the company wants to expand rapidly and double its sales to $1,000 next year. What will happen? To answer this question we go back to the starting point of our previous example.

We know that the sustainable growth rate for Hoffman is 21.3 percent so doubling sales (100 percent growth) is not possible unless the company obtains outside equity financing or allows its debt/equity ratio to balloon beyond 1.0. We can prove this with simple pro forma statements.

T A B L E 4.8

HOFFMAN COMPANY
Pro Forma Balance Sheet

	$	% of Sales		$	% of Sales
Current assets	$242	40	Total debt	$250	n/a
Net fixed assets	364	60	Owners' equity	303	n/a
Total assets	$606	100	Total liabilities	$553	n/a
			External funds needed	$ 53	

Pro Forma Income Statement

Sales		$1,000
Costs (80% of sales)		800
Taxable income		$ 200
Taxes		68
Net income		$ 132
Dividends (⅓)	$44	
Addition to retained earnings	88	

Pro Forma Balance Sheet

Current assets	$ 400	Total debt	$250
Fixed assets	600	Owners' equity	338
Total assets	$1,000	Total liabilities	$588
		External funds needed	$412

To maintain the debt/equity ratio at 1.0, Hoffman can increase debt to $338. This leaves $588 − $338 = $250 to be raised by external equity. If this is not available, Hoffman could try to raise the full $412 in additional debt. This would rocket the debt/equity ratio to ($250 + $412)/$338 = 1.96, basically doubling the target amount.

Given that the firm's bankers and other external lenders likely had considerable say over the target D/E in the first place, it is highly unlikely that Hoffman could obtain this much additional debt. The most likely outcome is that if Hoffman insists on doubling sales, the firm would grow bankrupt.

Determinants of Growth

In the last chapter, we saw that the return on equity could be decomposed into its various components using the Du Pont identity. Because ROE appears prominently in the determination of the SGR, the important factors in determining ROE are also important determinants of growth. To see this, recall that from the Du Pont identity, ROE can be written as:

ROE = Profit margin × Total asset turnover × Equity multiplier

Using our current symbols for these ratios,[7]

ROE = $p(S/A)(1 + D/E)$

If we substitute this into our expression for g^* (SGR), we see that the sustainable growth rate can be written in greater detail as:

$$g^* = \frac{p(S/A)(1 + D/E) \times R}{1 - p(S/A)(1 + D/E) \times R} \qquad [4.8]$$

Writing the SGR out in this way makes it look a little complicated, but it does highlight the various important factors determining the ability of a firm to grow.

Examining our expression for the SGR, we see that growth depends on the following four factors:

1. Profit margin. An increase in profit margin, p, increases the firm's ability to generate funds internally and thereby increase its sustainable growth.

---

[7] Remember that the equity multiplier is the same as 1 plus the debt/equity ratio. Appendix 4B shows the derivation in detail.

2. Dividend policy. A decrease in the percentage of net income paid out as dividends increases the retention ratio, R. This increases internally generated equity and thus increases sustainable growth.

3. Financial policy. An increase in the debt/equity ratio, D/E, increases the firm's financial leverage. Since this makes additional debt financing available, it increases the sustainable growth rate.

4. Total asset turnover. An increase in the firm's total asset turnover, S/A, increases the sales generated for each dollar in assets. This decreases the firm's need for new assets as sales grow and thereby increases the sustainable growth rate. Notice that increasing total asset turnover is the same thing as the decreasing capital intensity.

The sustainable growth rate is a very useful planning number. What it illustrates is the explicit relationship between the firm's four major areas of concern: its operating efficiency as measured by p, its asset use efficiency as measured by S/A, its dividend policy as measured by R, and its financial policy as measured by D/E.

Given values for all four of these, only one growth rate can be achieved. This is an important point, so it bears restating:

> If a firm does not wish to sell new equity and its profit margin, dividend policy, financial policy, and total asset turnover (or capital intensity) are all fixed, there is only one possible maximum growth rate.

As we described early in this chapter, one of the primary benefits to financial planning is to ensure internal consistency among the firm's various goals. The sustainable growth rate captures this element nicely. For this reason, sustainable growth is included in the Fast™ and Turbofast™ software used by commercial lenders at several Canadian chartered banks in analyzing their accounts.

Also, we now see how to use a financial planning model to test the feasibility of a planned growth rate. If sales are to grow at a rate higher than the sustainable growth rate, the firm must increase profit margins, increase total asset turnover, increase financial leverage, increase earnings retention, or sell new shares.

At the other extreme, suppose the firm is losing money (has a negative profit margin) or is paying out more than 100 percent of earnings in dividends so that R is negative. In each of these cases, the negative SGR signals the rate at which sales and assets must shrink. Firms can achieve negative growth by selling assets and closing divisions. The cash generated by selling assets is often used to pay down excessive debt taken on earlier to fund rapid expansion. Campeau Corporation and Central Capital are examples of Canadian firms that have undergone this painful deleveraging process.

E X A M P L E | 4.3   **Sustainable Growth**

The Sandar Company has a debt/equity ratio of .5, a profit margin of 3 percent, a dividend payout of 40 percent, and a capital intensity ratio of 1. What is its sustainable growth rate? If Sandar desires a 10 percent SGR and plans to achieve this goal by improving profit margins, what would you think?

The sustainable growth rate is:

$$g^* = .03(1)(1 + .5)(1 - .40)/[1 - .03 (1) (1 + .5)(1 - .40)] = 2.77\%$$

IN THEIR OWN WORDS . . .

Robert C. Higgins on Sustainable Growth

Most financial officers know intuitively that it takes money to make money. Rapid sales growth requires increased assets in the form of accounts receivable, inventory, and fixed plant, which, in turn, require money to pay for assets. They also know that if their company does not have the money when needed, it can literally "grow broke." The sustainable growth equation states these intuitive truths explicitly.

Sustainable growth is often used by bankers and other external analysts to assess a company's creditworthiness. They are aided in this exercise by several sophisticated computer software packages that provide detailed analyses of the company's past financial performance, including its annual sustainable growth rate.

Bankers use this information in several ways. Quick comparison of a company's actual growth rate to its sustainable rate tells the banker what issues will be at the top of management's financial agenda. If actual growth consistently exceeds sustainable growth, management's problem will be where to get the cash to finance growth. The banker thus can anticipate interest in loan products. Conversely, if sustainable growth consistently exceeds actual, the banker had best be prepared to talk about investment products, because management's problem will be what to do with all the cash that keeps piling up in the till.

Bankers also find the sustainable growth equation useful for explaining to financially inexperienced small business owners and overly optimistic entrepreneurs that, for the long-run viability of their business, it is necessary to keep growth and profitability in proper balance.

Finally, comparison of actual to sustainable growth rates helps a banker understand why a loan applicant needs money and for how long the need might continue. In one instance, a loan applicant requested $100,000 to pay off several insistent suppliers and promised to repay in a few months when he collected some accounts receivable that were coming due. A sustainable growth analysis revealed that the firm had been growing at four to six times its sustainable growth rate and that this pattern was likely to continue in the foreseeable future. This alerted the banker that impatient suppliers were only a symptom of the much more fundamental disease of overly rapid growth, and that a $100,000 loan would likely prove to be only the down payment on a much larger, multiyear commitment.

Robert C. Higgins is professor of finance at the University of Washington. He pioneered the use of sustainable growth as a tool for financial analysis.

To achieve a 10 percent growth rate, the profit margin has to rise. To see this, assume that g^* is equal to 10 percent and then solve for p:

$.10 = p(1.5)(.6)/[1 - p(1.5)(.6)]$

$p = .1/.99 = 10.1\%$

For the plan to succeed, the necessary increase in profit margin is substantial, from 3 percent to about 10 percent. This may not be feasible.

CONCEPT QUESTIONS

1. What are the determinants of growth?
2. How is a firm's sustainable growth related to its accounting return on equity (ROE)?
3. What does it mean if a firm's sustainable growth rate is negative?

4.5 | SOME CAVEATS ON FINANCIAL PLANNING MODELS

Financial planning models do not always ask the right questions. A primary reason is that they tend to rely on accounting relationships and not financial relationships. In particular, the three basic elements of firm value tend to get left out, namely, cash flow size, risk, and timing.

Because of this, financial planning models sometimes do not produce output that gives the user many meaningful clues about what strategies would lead to increases in value. Instead, they divert the user's attention to questions concerning the association of, say, the debt/equity ratio and firm growth.

The financial model we used for the Hoffman Company was simple, in fact, too simple. Our model, like many in use today, is really an accounting statement generator at heart. Such models are useful for pointing out inconsistencies and reminding us of financial needs, but they offer very little guidance concerning what to do about these problems.

In closing our discussion, we should add that financial planning is an iterative process. Plans are created, examined, and modified over and over. The final plan is a negotiated result between all the different parties to the process. In practice, long-term financial planning in some corporations relies too much on a top-down approach. Senior management has a growth target in mind and it is up to the planning staff to rework and ultimately deliver a plan to meet that target. Such plans are often made feasible (on paper or a computer screen) by unrealistically optimistic assumptions on sales growth and target debt/equity ratios. The plans collapse when lower sales make it impossible to service debt. This is what happened to Campeau's takeover of Federated Department Stores as we discuss in Chapter 21.

As a negotiated result, the final plan implicitly contains different goals in different areas and also satisfies many constraints. For this reason, such a plan need not be a dispassionate assessment of what we think the future will bring; it may instead be a means of reconciling the planned activities of different groups and a way of setting common goals for the future.

> CONCEPT QUESTIONS
>
> 1. What are some important elements often missing in financial planning models?
> 2. Why do we say that planning is an iterative process?

4.6 | SUMMARY AND CONCLUSIONS

Financial planning forces the firm to think about the future. We have examined a number of features of the planning process. We describe what financial planning can accomplish and the components of a financial model. We go on to develop the relationship between growth and financing needs. Two growth rates, internal and sustainable, are summarized in Table 4.9. We discuss how a financial planning model is useful in exploring that relationship.

Corporate financial planning should not become a purely mechanical activity. When it does, it probably focusses on the wrong things. In particular, plans all too often are formulated in terms of a growth target with no explicit linkage to value creation, and they frequently are overly concerned with accounting statements. Nevertheless, the alternative to financial planning is stumbling into the future backwards.

I. Internal Growth Rate	T A B L E 4.9

$$\text{Internal growth rate} = \frac{\text{ROA} \times R}{1 - \text{ROA} \times R}$$

where

ROA = Return on assets = Net income/Total assets
 R = Plowback (retention) ratio
   = Addition to retained earnings/Net income

The internal growth rate is the maximum growth rate than can be achieved with no external financing of any kind.

II.   Sustainable Growth Rate

$$\text{Sustainable growth rate} = \frac{\text{ROE} \times R}{1 - \text{ROE} \times R}$$

where

ROE = Return on equity = Net income/Total equity
 R = Plowback (retention) ratio
   = Addition to retained earnings/Net income

The sustainable growth rate is the maximum growth rate than can be achieved with no external equity financing while maintaining a constant debt/equity ratio.

Summary of internal and sustainable growth rates

Key Terms

planning horizon (page 101)
aggregation (page 101)
percentage of sales approach (page 106)
dividend payout ratio (page 106)
retention ratio or plowback ratio (page 106)

capital intensity ratio (page 107)
internal growth rate (page 114)
debt capacity (page 115)
sustainable growth rate (page 115)

Chapter Review Problems and Self-Test

4.1   Calculating EFN   Based on the following information for the Corwin Company, what is EFN, if sales are predicted to grow by 20 percent?

CORWIN COMPANY
Financial Statements

Income Statement		Balance Sheet			
Sales	$2,750	Current assets	$ 600	Long-term debt	$ 200
Cost of sales	2,400	Net fixed assets	800	Equity	1,200
Tax	119	Total	$1,400	Total	$1,400
Net income	$ 231				
Dividends	$ 77				

4.2   **EFN and Capacity Use**   Based on the information in Problem 4.1, what is EFN, assuming 75 percent capacity usage for net fixed assets? 90 percent capacity?

4.3   **Sustainable Growth**   Based on the information in Problem 4.1, what growth rate can Corwin maintain if no external financing is used? What is the sustainable growth rate?

Answers to Self-Test Problems

4.1   **EFN can be calculated easily as:**

$$EFN = -p(S)R + [A - p(S)R] \times g$$
$$= -154 + (1{,}400 - 154) \times g$$
$$= -154 + (1{,}246 \times .20)$$
$$= \$95.20$$

We can check this by preparing the pro forma statements using the percentage of sales approach. Note that sales are forecast to be $2,750 × 1.2 = $3,300.

CORWIN COMPANY
Financial Statements

Income Statement

Sales	$3,300.0	Forecast
Cost of sales	2,880.0	87.27% of sales
Tax	142.8	
Net income	$ 277.2	
Dividends	$ 92.4	33.33% of net income

Balance Sheet

Current assets	$ 720	21.81% of sales	Long-term debt	$ 200.0
Net fixed assets	960	29.09% of sales	Equity	1,384.8
Total	$1,680	50.90% of sales	Total	$1,584.8
			EFN	$ 95.2

4.2   Full capacity sales are equal to current sales divided by the capacity utilization. At 75 percent of capacity:

$2,750 = .75 × Full capacity sales

$3,667 = Full capacity sales

With a sales level of $3,300, no net new fixed assets are needed, so our earlier estimate is too high. We estimated an increase in fixed assets of $960 − 800 = $160. The new EFN would thus be $95.2 − 160 = −$64.8, a surplus. No external financing is needed in this case.

At 90 percent capacity, full capacity sales are $3,056. The ratio of fixed assets to full capacity sales is thus $800/$3,056 = .262. At a sales level of $3,300, we thus need $3,300 × .262 = $864 in net fixed assets, an increase of $64. This is $160 − 64 = $96 less than we originally predicted, so the EFN is now $95.2 − 96 = −$.80, a small surplus. No additional financing is needed.

4.3   Corwin retains R = (1 − .33) = .67 of net income.   Return on equity for Corwin is $231/$1,200 = 19.25%, so we can calculate the sustainable growth rate as $(ROE \times R)/(1 - ROE \times R) = (.1925 \times .67)/(1 - .1925 \times .67) = 14.81\%$.

From Self-Test Problem 4.1, we saw that EFN can be written:

$$EFN = -154 + 1{,}246 \times g$$

If we set this equal to zero and solve for g, we get:

$$g = 154/1{,}246$$
$$= 12.36\%$$

Questions and Problems

1. **Pro Forma Statements**   Consider the following simplified financial statements for the Goldfinch Corporation:

Basic
(Questions 1–17)

Income Statement		Balance Sheet			
Sales	$7,000	Assets	$3,500	Debt	$1,750
Costs	6,000			Equity	1,750
Net income	$1,000	Total	$3,500	Total	$3,500

Goldfinch has predicted a sales increase of 25 percent. It has also predicted that every item on the balance sheet will increase by 25 percent as well. Create the pro forma statements and reconcile them. What is the plug variable here?

2. **Pro Forma Statements and EFN**   In the previous question, assume that Goldfinch pays out half of net income in the form of a cash dividend. Costs and assets vary with sales, but debt and equity do not. Prepare the pro forma statements and determine the external financing needed.

3. **Calculating EFN**   The most recent financial statements for Gletglen Co. are shown below:

Income Statement		Balance Sheet			
Sales	$2,000	Assets	$5,000	Debt	$3,000
Costs	850			Equity	2,000
Net income	$1,150	Total	$5,000	Total	$5,000

Assets and costs are proportional to sales. Debt is not. No dividends are paid. Next year's sales are projected to be $2,300. What is the external financing needed (EFN)?

4. **EFN**   The most recent financial statements for REM Co. are shown below:

Income Statement		Balance Sheet			
Sales	$10,000	Assets	$40,000	Debt	$15,000
Costs	4,000			Equity	25,000
EBIT	$ 6,000	Total	$40,000	Total	$40,000
Taxes	2,400				
Net income	$ 3,600				

Assets and costs are proportional to sales. Debt is not. A dividend of $2,000 was paid, and REM wishes to maintain a constant payout. Next year's sales are projected to be $12,000. What is the external financing needed (EFN)?

5. **EFN**   The most recent financial statements for Aprostate Co. are shown below:

Income Statement		Balance Sheet			
Sales	$2,500	Current assets	$2,000	Current liabilities	$ 800
Costs	2,000	Fixed assets	4,000	Long-term debt	1,200
Taxes	200			Equity	4,000
Net income	$ 300	Total	$6,000	Total	$6,000

Assets, costs, and current liabilities are proportional to sales. Long-term debt is not. Aprostate maintains a constant 60 percent dividend payout. Next year's sales are projected to be $2,900. What is the external financing needed (EFN)?

6. **Calculating Internal Growth**   The most recent financial statements for Piltdown Co. are shown below:

Income Statement		Balance Sheet			
Sales	$4,750	Current assets	$ 5,500	Debt	$20,000
Costs	2,900	Fixed assets	27,500	Equity	13,000
Taxes	740	Total	$33,000	Total	$33,000
Net income	$1,110				

Assets and costs are proportional to sales. Debt is not. Piltdown maintains a constant 30 percent dividend payout. No equity external financing is possible. What is the internal growth rate?

7. **Calculating Sustainable Growth**   For the company in the previous problem, what is the sustainable growth rate?

8. **Growth as a Firm Goal**   Explain why growth by itself is not an appropriate goal for financial management. In particular, describe a scenario under which the goals of growth and owner wealth maximization could be in conflict.

9. **Sales and Growth**   The most recent financial statements for Fiddich Co. are shown below:

Income Statement		Balance Sheet			
Sales	$19,000	Net working capital	$17,475	Long-term debt	$55,820
Costs	14,700	Fixed assets	75,000	Equity	36,655
Taxes	1,720	Total	$92,475	Total	$92,475
Net income	$ 2,580				

Assets and costs are proportional to sales. Fiddich maintains a constant 40 percent dividend payout and a constant debt/equity ratio. What is the maximum increase in sales that can be sustained assuming no new equity is issued?

10. **Calculating Retained Earnings from Pro Forma Income**   Consider the following income statement for the Folker Corporation:

FOLKER CORPORATION
Income Statement

Sales	$9,000
Costs	6,000
Taxable income	$3,000
Taxes (34%)	1,020
Net income	$1,980
Dividends	$500

A 15 percent growth rate in sales is projected. Prepare a pro forma income statement assuming costs vary with sales and the dividend payout ratio is constant. What is the projected addition to retained earnings?

11. **Applying Percentage of Sales**   The balance sheet for the Folker Corporation is shown below. Based on this information and the income statement in the previous problem, supply the missing information using the percentage of sales approach. Assume that accounts payable vary with sales while notes payable do not. Put "n/a" where needed.

FOLKER CORPORATION
Balance Sheet

Basic
(Continued)

	$	%		$	%
Assets			*Liabilities and Owners' Equity*		
Current assets			Current liabilities		
Cash	$ 1,500	_____	Accounts payable	$ 3,000	_____
Accounts receivable	3,000	_____	Notes payable	2,000	_____
Inventory	3,000	_____	Total	$ 5,000	_____
Total	$ 7,500	_____	Long-term debt	$ 3,000	_____
Fixed assets			Owners' equity		
Net plant and			Common stock and		
equipment	$10,000	_____	paid-in surplus	$ 2,500	_____
			Retained earnings	7,000	_____
			Total	$ 9,500	_____
			Total liabilities and owners'		
Total assets	$17,500	_____	equity	$17,500	_____

12. **EFN and Sales**   From the previous two questions, prepare a pro forma balance sheet showing EFN, assuming a 15 percent increase in sales and no new external debt or equity financing.

13. **Calculating ROA and ROE**   From the previous question, what is the projected ROA? ROE?

14. **Internal Growth**   If a firm has a 12 percent ROA and a 60 percent payout ratio, what is its internal growth rate?

15. **Sustainable Growth**   If a firm has a 25 percent ROE and a 45 percent payout ratio, what is its sustainable growth rate?

16. **Sustainable Growth**   Based on the following information, calculate the sustainable growth rate:

> Profit margin = 6%
> Capital intensity ratio = 0.5
> Debt/equity ratio = 0.8
> Net income = $20,000
> Dividends = $5,000

What is the ROE here?

17. **Sustainable Growth**   Assuming the following ratios are constant, what is the sustainable growth rate?

> Total asset turnover = 1.0
> Profit margin = 4%
> Equity multiplier = 2.5
> Payout ratio = 30%

18. **Full Capacity Sales**   UR Slack, Inc., is currently operating at only 80 percent of fixed asset capacity. Current sales are $100,000. How fast can sales grow before any new fixed assets are needed?

Intermediate
(Questions 18-28)

19. **Fixed Assets and Capacity Usage**   For the company in the previous problem, suppose fixed assets are $170,000 and sales are projected to grow to $130,000. How much in new fixed assets are required to support this growth in sales?

20. **Percentage of Sales Issues**   What are the advantages and disadvantages of the percentage of sales approach? In particular, is the assumption that many of the firm's costs and assets are directly proportional to sales a reasonable assumption? Does your answer depend on the time horizon being considered?

21. **Growth and Profit Margin**   A firm wishes to maintain a growth rate of 12 percent a year, a debt/equity ratio of 0.6, and a dividend payout of 40 percent. The ratio of total assets to sales is constant at 1.1. What profit margin must the firm achieve?

22. **Growth and Debt/Equity Ratio**   A firm wishes to maintain a growth rate of 15 percent and a dividend payout of 30 percent. The ratio of total assets to sales is constant at 1.5, and profit margin is 8 percent. If the firm also wishes to maintain a constant debt/equity ratio, what must it be?

23. **Growth and Assets**   A firm wishes to maintain a growth rate of 6 percent and a dividend payout of 70 percent. The current profit margin is 10 percent and the firm uses no external financing sources. What must the current total asset turnover be?

24. **Sustainable Growth**   Based on the following information, calculate the sustainable growth rate:

   Profit margin = 5%
   Total asset turnover = 1.2
   Total debt ratio = 0.6
   Payout ratio = 40%

   What is ROA here?

25. **Sustainable Growth and Outside Financing**   You've collected the following information about the Wutzup Corporation:

   Sales = $25,000
   Net income = $1,000
   Dividends = $400
   Total debt = $30,000
   Total equity = $40,000

   What is the sustainable growth rate for Wutzup? If it does grow at this rate, how much borrowing will take place in the coming year? What rate could be supported with no outside financing at all?

26. **Calculating EFN**   The most recent financial statements for Hi Grow, Inc., are shown below. 1996 sales are projected to grow by 25 percent. Depreciation expense and interest expense will remain constant; the tax rate and the payout rate will also remain constant. Costs, other expenses, current assets, and accounts payable increase spontaneously with sales. If the firm is operating at full capacity and no new debt or equity is issued, what is the external financing needed (EFN) to support the 25 percent growth rate in sales?

HI GROW, INC.
1995 Income Statement

Sales	$600,000
Costs	450,000
Other expenses	25,000
EBDIT	$125,000
Depreciation	25,000
EBIT	$100,000
Interest	10,000
Taxable income	$ 90,000
Taxes (34%)	30,600
Net income	$ 59,400
Dividends	$ 12,500
Retained earnings	46,900

HI GROW, INC.
Balance Sheet as of December 31, 1995

Assets		Liabilities and Owners' Equity	
Current assets		Current liabilities	
Cash	$ 10,000	Accounts payable	$ 40,000
Accounts receivable	40,000	Notes payable	10,000
Inventory	50,000	Total	$ 50,000
Total	$100,000	Long-term debt	75,000
Fixed assets		Total liabilities	$125,000
Net plant and		Owners' equity	
equipment	250,000	Common stock and	
		paid-in surplus	$ 25,000
		Retained earnings	200,000
		Total	$225,000
		Total liabilities and	
Total assets	$350,000	owners' equity	$350,000

27. **Capacity Usage and Growth**   In the previous problem, suppose the firm is operating at only 90 percent capacity in 1995. What is EFN now?

28. **Calculating EFN**   In Problem 26, suppose the firm wishes to keep its debt/equity ratio constant. What is EFN now?

29. **EFN and Internal Growth**   Redo Problem 26 using sales growth rates of 15 and 20 percent in addition to 25 percent. Illustrate graphically the relationship between EFN and the growth rate, and use this graph to determine the relationship between them. At what growth rate is the EFN equal to zero? Why is this internal growth rate different from that found by using the equation in the text?

30. **EFN and Sustainable Growth**   Redo Problem 28 using sales growth rates of 30 and 35 percent in addition to 25 percent. Illustrate graphically the relationship between EFN and the growth rate, and use this graph to determine the relationship between them. At what growth rate is the EFN equal to zero? Why is this sustainable growth rate different from that found by using the equation in the text?

31. **Constraints on Growth**   A firm wishes to maintain a growth rate of 10 percent per year and a debt/equity ratio of 0.40. Profit margin is 5 percent, and the ratio of total assets to sales is constant at 1.75. Is this growth rate possible?

To answer, determine what the dividend payout must be. How do you interpret the result?

32. **EFN Intuition**   Feels Right, Inc., uses no external financing and maintains a positive retention ratio. When sales grow by 15 percent, the firm has a negative projected EFN. What does this tell you about the firm's internal growth rate? How about the sustainable growth rate? At this same level of sales growth, what will happen to the projected EFN if the retention ratio is increased? What if the retention ratio is decreased? What happens to the projected EFN if the firm pays out all its earnings in the form of dividends?

33. **EFN Intuition**   Sleight Manufacturing, Inc., maintains a positive retention ratio and keeps its debt/equity ratio constant every year. When sales grow by 20 percent, the firm has a negative projected EFN. What does this tell you about the firm's sustainable growth rate? Do you know if the internal growth rate is greater than or less than 20 percent with certainty? Why? What happens to the projected EFN if the retention ratio is increased? What if the retention ratio is decreased? What if the retention ratio is zero?

34. **EFN**   Define the following:

    S = Previous year's sales

    A = Total assets

    D = Total debt

    E = Total equity

    g = Projected growth in sales

    p = Profit margin

    R = Retention (plowback) ratio

    Show that EFN can be written as:

    $$\text{EFN} = -\,p(S)R + (A - p(S)R) \times g.$$

    Hint: Asset needs will equal $A \times g$. The addition to retained earnings will equal $p(S)R \times (1 + g)$.

35. **Growth Rates**   Based on the result in Problem 34, show that the internal and sustainable growth rates are as given in the chapter. Hint: For the internal growth rate, set EFN equal to zero and solve for g.

Suggested Readings

Approaches to building a financial planning model are contained in:

Carleton, W. T.; D. H. Downes; and C. L. Dick, Jr. "Financial Policy Models: Theory and Practice." *Journal of Financial and Quantitative Analysis* 8, 1973.

Francis, J. C., and D. R. Rowell. "A Simultaneous-Equation Model of the Firm for Financial Analysis and Planning." *Financial Management* 7, Spring 1978.

Myers, S. C., and G. A. Pogue. "A Programming Approach to Corporate Financial Management." *Journal of Finance* 29, May 1974.

Warren, J. M., and J. R. Shelton. "A Simultaneous-Equation Approach to Financial Planning." *Journal of Finance* 26, December 1971.

Two textbooks on financial planning are:

Lee, C. F. *Financial Analysis and Planning: Theory and Application.* Reading, MA: Addison-Wesley, 1985.

Viscione, J. A. *Financial Analysis: Tools and Concepts.* New York: National Association of Credit Management, 1984.

Sustainable growth is discussed in:

Higgins, R. C. "Sustainable Growth under Inflation." *Financial Management* 10, Autumn 1981.

For a critical discussion of sustainable growth, see:

Rappaport, A. *Creating Shareholder Value: The New Standard for Business Performance.* New York: Free Press, 1986.

A Financial Planning Model for the Hoffman Company   APPENDIX   4A

In this appendix, we discuss how to get started with building a financial planning model in somewhat greater detail.[8] Our goal is to build a simple model for the Hoffman Company, incorporating some features commonly found in planning models. This model includes our earlier percentage of sales approach as a special case, but it is more flexible and a little more realistic. It is by no means complete, but it should give you a good idea of how to proceed.

Table 4A.1 shows the financial statements for the Hoffman Company in slightly more detail than we had before. Primarily, we have separated out depreciation and interest. We have also included some abbreviations that we use to refer to the various items on these statements.

As we have discussed, it is necessary to designate a plug. We use new borrowing as the plug in our model, and we assume Hoffman does not issue new equity. This means our model allows the debt/equity ratio to change if needed. Our model takes a sales forecast as its input and supplies the pro forma financial statements as its output.

To create our model, we take the financial statements and replace the numbers with formulas describing their relationships. In addition to the preceding symbols, we use E_0 to stand for the beginning equity.

In Table 4A.2, the symbols a_1 through a_7 are called the *model parameters*. These describe the relationships among the variables. For example, a_7 is the relationship between sales and total assets, and it can be interpreted as the capital intensity ratio:

$$TA = a_7 \times S$$

$$a_7 = TA/S = \text{Capital intensity ratio}$$

---

[8] This appendix draws, in part, from R. A. Brealey and S. C. Myers, *Principles of Corporate Finance,* 3rd ed. (New York: McGraw-Hill Book Company, 1984), chap. 28.

HOFFMAN COMPANY
Income Statement and Balance Sheet

Income Statement

Sales	(S)		$500
Costs	(C)		235
Depreciation	(DEP)		120
Interest	(INT)		45
Taxable income	(TI)		$100
Taxes	(T)		34
Net income	(NI)		$ 66
Addition to retained earnings	(ARE)	$22	
Dividends	(DIV)	$44	

Balance Sheet

Assets			Liabilities		
Current assets	(CA)	$ 400	Total debt	(D)	$ 450
Net fixed assets	(FA)	600	Owners' equity	(E)	550
Total assets	(TA)	$1,000	Total liabilities	(L)	$1,000

Similarly, a_3 is the relationship between total debt and interest paid, so a_3 can be interpreted as an overall interest rate. The tax rate is given by a_4, and a_5 is the dividend payout ratio.

This model uses new borrowing as the plug by first setting total liabilities and owners' equity equal to total assets. Next, the ending amount for owners' equity is calculated as the beginning amount, E_0, plus the addition to retained earnings, ARE. The difference between these amounts, $TA - E$, is the new total debt needed to balance the balance sheet.

The primary difference between this model and our earlier EFN approach is that we have separated out depreciation and interest. Notice that a_2 expresses depreciation as a fraction of beginning fixed assets. This, along with the assumption that the interest paid depends on total debt, is a more realistic approach than we used earlier. However, since interest and depreciation now do not necessarily vary directly with sales, we no longer have a constant profit margin.

Model parameters a_1 to a_7 can be based on a simple percentage of sales approach, or they can be determined by any other means that the model builder wishes. For example, they might be based on average values for the last several years, industry standards, subjective estimates, or even company targets. Alternatively, sophisticated statistical techniques can be used to estimate them.

We finish this discussion by estimating the model parameters for Hoffman using simple percentages and then generating pro forma statements for a $600 predicted sales level. We estimate the parameters as:

$a_1 = \$235/500 = .47 =$ Cost percentage

$a_2 = \$120/600 = .20 =$ Depreciation rate

HOFFMAN COMPANY
Long-Term Financial Planning Model

Income Statement

Sales	$S = \text{Input by user}$
Costs	$C = a_1 \times S$
Depreciation	$DEP = a_2 \times FA$
Interest	$INT = a_3 \times D$
Taxable income	$TI = S - C - DEP - INT$
Taxes	$T = a_4 \times TI$
Net income	$NI = TI - T$
Addition to retained earnings	$ARE = NI - DIV$
Dividends	$DIV = a_5 \times NI$

Balance Sheet

Assets		Liabilities	
Current assets	$CA = TA - FA$	Total debt	$D = TA - E$
Net fixed assets	$FA = a_6 \times TA$	Owners' equity	$E = E_0 \times ARE$
Total assets	$TA = a_7 \times S$	Total liabilities	$L = TA$

$a_3 = \$45/450 = .10 = \text{Interest rate}$

$a_4 = \$34/100 = .34 = \text{Tax rate}$

$a_5 = \$44/66 = \frac{2}{3} = \text{Payout ratio}$

$a_6 = \$600/1{,}000 = .60 = \text{Fixed assets/Total assets}$

$a_7 = \$1{,}000/500 = 2 = \text{Capital intensity ratio}$

With these parameters and a sales forecast of $600, our pro forma financial statements are shown in Table 4A.3.[9]

What our model is now telling us is that a sales increase of $100 requires $200 in net new assets (since the capital intensity ratio is 2). To finance this, we use $24 in internally generated funds. The balance of $200 − $24 = $176 has to be borrowed. This amount is the increase in total debt on the balance sheet: $626 − $450 = $176. If we pursue this plan, our profit margin would decline somewhat and the debt/equity ratio would rise.

---

[9] If you put this model in a standard computer spreadsheet (as we did to generate the numbers), the software may "complain" that a "circular" reference exists, because the amount of new borrowing depends on the addition to retained earnings, the addition to retained earnings depends on the interest paid, the interest paid depends on the borrowing, and so on. This isn't really a problem; we can have the spreadsheet recalculated a few times until the numbers stop changing.

There really is no circular problem with this model because there is only one unknown, the ending total debt, which we can solve for explicitly. This will usually be the case as long as there is a single plug variable. The algebra can get to be somewhat tedious, however. See the problems at the end of this appendix for more information.

T A B L E 4A.3

HOFFMAN COMPANY
Pro Forma Financial Statements

Income Statement

Sales	(S)	$600	= Input
Cost of sales	(C)	282	= .47 × $600
Depreciation	(DEP)	144	= .20 × $720
Interest	(INT)	63	= .10 × $626
Taxable income	(TI)	$111	= $600 − 282 − 144 − 63
Taxes	(T)	38	= .34 × $111
Net income	(NI)	$ 73	= $111 − 38

Appendix Questions and Problems

A.1 Consider the following simplified financial statements from the Dotsa Lot Company.

DOTSA LOT COMPANY
Income Statement and Balance Sheet

Income Statement

Sales		$1,500
Costs		1,200
Taxable income		$ 300
Taxes		102
Net income		$ 198
Addition to retained earnings	$ 66	
Dividends	$132	

Balance Sheet

Assets		Liabilities	
Current assets	$1,200	Total debt	$1,350
Net fixed assets	1,800	Owners' equity	1,650
Total assets	$3,000	Total liabilities	$3,000

Prepare a financial planning model along the lines of our model for the Hoffman Company. Estimate the values for the model parameters using percentages calculated from these statements. Prepare the pro forma statements by recalculating the model by hand three or four times.

A.2 Modify the model in the previous question so that borrowing doesn't change and new equity sales are the plug.

A.3 This is a challenge question. How would you modify the model for Hoffman Company if you wanted to maintain a constant debt/equity ratio?

A.4 This is a challenge question. In our financial planning model for Hoffman, show that it is possible to solve algebraically for the amount of new borrowing. Can you interpret the resulting expression?

Derivation of the Sustainable Growth Formula

$$\text{EFN} = \text{Increase in total assets} - \text{Addition to retained earnings} \quad [4A.1]$$
$$\qquad - \text{New borrowing}$$
$$= A(g) - p(S)R \times (1 + g) - pS(R) \times (1 + g)[D/E]$$

Since

$$\text{EFN} = 0$$
$$0 = A(g) - pS(R)(1 + g)[1 + D/E]$$
$$= -pS(R)[1 + D/E] + [A - pS(R) \times (1 + D/E)]g$$

Dividing through by A gives:

$$= -p(S/A)(R)[1 + D/E] + [1 - p(S/A)(R) \times (1 + D/E)]g$$
$$g^* = \frac{p(S/A)(R)[1 + D/E]}{1 - p(S/A)(R)[1 + D/E]}$$

In the last chapter, we saw that the return on equity could be decomposed into its various components using the Du Pont identity. Recall that from the Du Pont identity, ROE can be written as:

$$\text{ROE} = \text{Profit margin} \times \text{Total asset turnover} \times \text{Equity multiplier}$$

Using our current symbols for these ratios, ROE is:

$$\text{ROE} = p(S/A)(1 + D/E) \quad [4A.2]$$
$$g^* = \frac{ROE \times R}{1 - ROE \times R}$$

P A R T

VALUATION OF FUTURE CASH FLOWS

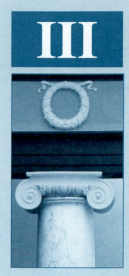

CHAPTER 5 | First Principles of Valuation: The Time Value of Money

This chapter introduces the basic principles of present value and discounted cash flow. Time value of money is treated in depth. The concepts in this chapter are important building blocks for chapters to come.

CHAPTER 6 | Valuing Stocks and Bonds

Chapter 6 shows how to extend the concepts of present value and discounted cash flow to valuing bonds and stocks.

First Principles of Valuation:
The Time Value of Money

One of the basic problems faced by financial managers is how to determine the value today of cash flows that are expected in the future. For example, suppose your province's finance minister asked your advice on overhauling the provincial lottery with a view toward increasing revenues to help balance the budget. One attractive idea is to increase the size of the prizes while easing the strain on the treasury by spreading out the payments over time. Instead of offering $1 million paid immediately, the new lottery would pay $1 million in 10 annual payments of $100,000. How much would this save the province? The answer depends on the time value of money, the subject of this chapter.

In the most general sense, the phrase *time value of money* refers to the fact that a dollar in hand today is worth more than a dollar promised at some time in the future. On a practical level, the reason for this is that you could earn interest while you waited; so a dollar today would grow to more than a dollar later. The trade-off between money now and money later thus depends on, among other things, the rate you can earn by investing.

nominal rate of interest

The stated rate of interest applied to your investment.

real interest rate

The nominal interest rate minus the rate of inflation.

The difference between the **nominal rate of interest** (the rate you earn) and the inflation rate is called the **real interest rate**. Whether your money grows in real purchasing power depends on whether the nominal interest rate exceeds inflation. We have a lot more to say about interest rates and inflation in Chapter 10. Our goal in this chapter is to explicitly evaluate this trade-off between dollars today and dollars at some future time.

In this chapter, we look at the basic mechanics of common financial calculations. When you finish this chapter, you should have some very practical skills. For example, you will know how to calculate your own car payments or student loan payments. You will also be able to determine how long it will take to pay off a loan. We show you how to compare interest rates to determine which are the highest and which are the lowest. We will also show you how interest rates can be quoted in different, and at times confusing, ways.

The financial calculations we introduce in this chapter are used every day by investors and financial managers. A thorough understanding of the material in this chapter is critical to understanding material in subsequent chapters, so you should study it with particular care. We present a large number of examples in this chapter. In many problems, your answer may differ from ours somewhat. This can happen because of rounding and is not a cause for concern.

5.1 | FUTURE VALUE AND COMPOUNDING

We begin by studying future value. **Future value** refers to the amount of money an investment would grow to over some length of time at some given interest rate. Put another way, future value is the cash value of an investment sometime in the future. We start out by considering the simplest case, a single period investment.

future value (FV)
The amount an investment is worth after one or more periods. Also compound value.

Investing for a Single Period

Suppose you were to invest $100 in a savings account that pays 10 percent interest per year. How much will you have in one year? You would have $110. This $110 is equal to your original *principal* of $100 plus $10 in interest that you earn. We say that $110 is the future value (FV) of $100 invested for one year at 10 percent, and we simply mean that $100 today is worth $110 in one year, given that 10 percent is the interest rate.

In general, if you invest for one period at an interest rate of *r,* your investment grows to $(1 + r)$ per dollar invested. In our example, *r* is 10 percent, so your investment grows to $(1 + .10) = 1.1$ dollars per dollar invested. You invested $100 in this case, so you ended up with $100 \times (1.10) = 110.

You might wonder if the single period in this example has to be a year. The answer is no. For example, if the interest rate were 2 percent per quarter, your $100 would grow to $100 \times (1 + .02) = 102 by the end of the quarter. You might also wonder if 2 percent every quarter is the same as 8 percent per year. The answer is again no, and we'll explain why a little later.

Investing for More than One Period

Going back to our $100 investment, what will you have after two years, assuming the interest rate doesn't change? If you leave the entire $110 in the bank, you will earn $110 \times .10 = 11 in interest during the second year, so you will have a total of $110 + 11 = 121. This $121 is the future value of $100 in two years at 10 percent. Another way of looking at it is that one year from now you are effectively investing $110 at 10 percent for a year. This is a single period problem, so you'll end up with $1.1 for every dollar invested or $110 \times 1.1 = 121 total.

This $121 has four parts. The first part is the $100 original principal. The second part is the $10 in interest you earned in the first year along with another $10 (the third part) you earn in the second year, for a total of $120. The last $1 you end up with (the fourth part) is interest you earn in the second year on the interest paid in the first year: $10 \times .10 = 1.

This process of leaving your money and any accumulated interest in an investment for more than one period, thereby *reinvesting* the interest, is called **compounding**. Compounding the interest means earning **interest on interest**, so we call the result **compound interest**. With **simple interest**, the interest is not reinvested, so interest is earned each period only on the original principal.

compounding
The process of accumulating interest in an investment over time to earn more interest.

interest on interest
Interest earned on the reinvestment of previous interest payments.

compound interest
Interest earned on both the initial principal and the interest reinvested from prior periods.

simple interest
Interest earned only on the original principal amount invested.

E X A M P L E | 5.1   Interest on Interest

Suppose you locate a two-year investment that pays 14 percent per year. If you invest $325, how much will you have at the end of the two years? How much of this is simple interest? How much is compound interest?

At the end of the first year, you would have $325 \times (1 + .14) = 370.50. If you reinvest this entire amount and thereby compound the interest, you would have

$370.50 \times 1.14 = \$422.37$ at the end of the second year. The total interest you earn is thus $422.37 - 325 = \$97.37$. Your $325 original principal earns $325 \times .14 = \$45.50$ in interest each year, for a two-year total of $91 in simple interest. The remaining $97.37 - 91 = \$6.37$ results from compounding. You can check this by noting that the interest earned in the first year is $45.50. The interest on interest earned in the second year thus amounts to $45.50 \times .14 = \$6.37$, as we calculated. |

We now take a closer look at how we calculated the $121 future value. We multiplied $110 by 1.1 to get $121. The $110, however, was $100 also multiplied by 1.1. In other words:

$$\begin{aligned} \$121 &= \$110 \times 1.1 \\ &= (\$100 \times 1.1) \times 1.1 \\ &= \$100 \times (1.1 \times 1.1) \\ &= \$100 \times 1.1^2 \\ &= \$100 \times 1.21 \end{aligned}$$

As our example suggests, the future value of $1 invested for t periods at a rate of r per period is:

$$\text{Future value} = \$1 \times (1 + r)^t \qquad [5.1]$$

The expression $(1 + r)^t$ is sometimes called the *future value interest factor* (or just future value factor) for $1 invested at r percent for t periods and can be abbreviated as FVIF (r,t).

In our example, what would your $100 be worth after five years? We can first compute the relevant future value factor as:

$$(1 + r)^t = (1 + .10)^5 = 1.1^5 = 1.6105$$

Your $100 would thus grow to:

$$\$100 \times 1.6105 = \$161.05$$

The growth of your $100 each year is illustrated in Table 5.1. As shown, the interest earned in each year is equal to the beginning amount multiplied by the interest rate of 10 percent.

In Table 5.1, notice that the total interest you earn is $61.05. Over the five-year span of this investment, the simple interest is $100 \times .10 = \$10$ per year, so you accumulate $50 this way. The other $11.05 is from compounding.

	Year	Beginning Amount		Interest Earned	Ending Amount
T A B L E 5.1	1	$100.00		$10.00	$110.00
Future values of $100	2	110.00		11.00	121.00
at 10 percent	3	121.00		12.10	133.10
	4	133.10		13.31	146.41
	5	146.41		14.64	161.05
			Total interest	$61.05	

Figure 5.1 illustrates the growth of the compound interest in Table 5.1. Notice how the simple interest is constant each year, but the compound interest you earn gets bigger every year. The size of the compound interest keeps increasing because more and more interest builds up and there is thus more to compound.

Future values depend critically on the assumed interest rate, particularly for long-lived investments. Figure 5.2 illustrates this relationship by plotting the growth of $1 for different rates and lengths of time. Notice that the future value of $1 after 10 years is about $6.20 at a 20 percent rate, but it is only about $2.60 at 10 percent. In this case, doubling the interest rate more than doubles the future value.

To solve future value problems, we need to come up with the relevant future value factors. There are several different ways of doing this. In our example, we could have multiplied 1.1 by itself five times. This will work just fine, but it would get to be very tedious for, say, a 30-year investment.

Fortunately, there are several easier ways to get future value factors. Most calculators have a key labelled y^x. You can usually just enter 1.1, press this key, enter 5, and press the = key to get the answer. This is an easy way to calculate future value factors because it's quick and accurate.

Alternatively, you can use a table that contains future value factors for some common interest rates and time periods. Table 5.2 contains some of these factors. Table A.1 in the Appendix at the end of the book contains a much larger set. To use

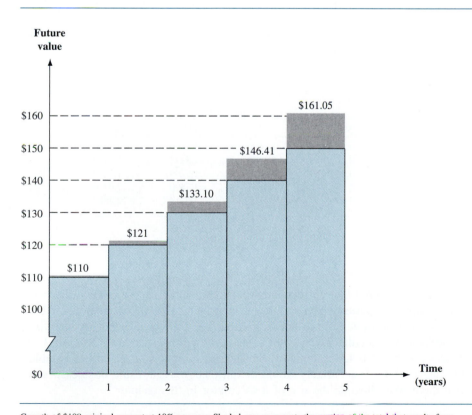

FIGURE 5.1

Future value, simple interest, and compound interest

Growth of $100 original amount at 10% per year. Shaded area represents the portion of the total that results from compounding of interest.

FIGURE 5.2

Future value of $1 for different periods and rates

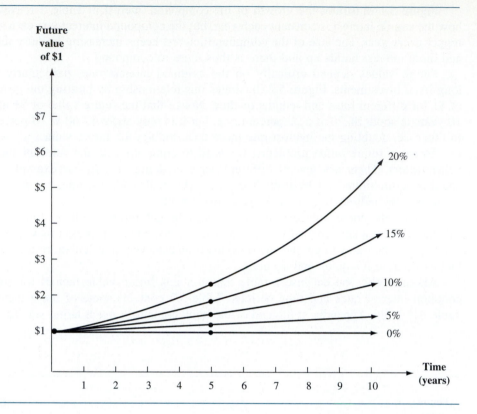

TABLE 5.2

Future value interest factors

	Interest rate			
Periods	5%	10%	15%	20%
1	1.0500	1.1000	1.1500	1.2000
2	1.1025	1.2100	1.3225	1.4400
3	1.1576	1.3310	1.5209	1.7280
4	1.2155	1.4641	1.7490	2.0736
5	1.2763	1.6105	2.0114	2.4883

the table, find the column that corresponds to 10 percent. Then look down the rows until you come to five periods. You should find the factor that we calculated, 1.6105.

Tables similar to Table 5.2 are not as common as they once were because they predate inexpensive calculators and spreadsheet programs such as Lotus 1–2–3. Interest rates are often quoted to three or four decimal points, so the number of tables needed to deal with these accurately would be quite large. As a result, businesspeople rarely use them. We illustrate the use of a calculator in this chapter.[1]

---

[1] Selected chapter problems incorporate the use of Lotus 1–2–3.

These tables still serve a useful purpose. To make sure that you are doing the calculations correctly, pick a factor from the table and then calculate it yourself to see that you get the same answer. There are plenty of numbers to choose from.

E X A M P L E | **5.2**   **Compound Interest**

You've located an investment that pays 12 percent. That rate sounds good to you, so you invest $400. How much will you have in three years? How much will you have in seven years? At the end of seven years, how much interest have you earned? How much of that interest results from compounding?

Based on our discussion, we can calculate the future value factor for 12 percent and three years as:

$$(1 + r)^t = 1.12^3 = 1.4049$$

Your $400 thus grows to:

$$\$400 \times 1.4049 = \$561.97$$

After seven years, you would have:

$$\$400 \times 1.12^7 = \$400 \times 2.2107 = \$884.27$$

Thus, you more than double your money over seven years.

Since you invested $400, the interest in the $884.27 future value is $884.27 − 400 = $484.27. At 12 percent, your $400 investment earns $400 × .12 = $48 in simple interest every year. Over seven years, the simple interest thus totals 7 × $48 = $336. The other $484.27 − 336 = $148.27 is from compounding.

The effect of compounding is not great over short time periods, but it really starts to add up as the horizon grows. To take an extreme case, suppose one of your more frugal ancestors had invested $5 for you at a 6 percent interest 200 years ago, how much would you have today? The future value factor is a substantial $(1.06)^{200} = 115,125.90$ (you won't find this one in a table), so you would have $5 × 115,125.90 = $575,629.52. Notice that the simple interest is just $5 × 0.6 = $.30 per year. After 200 years, this amounts to $60. The rest is from reinvesting. Such is the power of compound interest!

E X A M P L E | **5.3**   **How Much for that Cup?**

To further illustrate the effect of compounding for long horizons, consider the case of the Stanley Cup. The cup, the oldest team trophy in North America, was originally purchased by the governor general of Canada, Sir Frederick Arthur Stanley, in 1893. Lord Stanley paid $48.67 for the cup over 100 years ago. The Hockey Hall of Fame in Toronto values the cup at $75,000, although to millions of hockey fans across Canada, it is priceless.[2] What would the sum Lord Stanley paid for the cup be worth today if he had invested it at 10 percent rather than purchasing the cup?

In 100 years, at 10 percent, $48.67 grows by quite a bit. How much? The future value factor is approximately:

$$(1 + r)^t = (1.10)100 = 13,780.61$$
$$FV = \$48.67 \times 13,780.61 = \$670,702.40$$

---

[2] When this value for the Stanley Cup was reported in 1991, the practice of compounding interest was already more than 600 years old.

Well, $670,000 is a lot of money, significantly more than $75,000; with it you could buy seven or eight cups now!

This example is something of an exaggeration, of course. In 1893, it would not have been easy to locate an investment that would pay 10 percent every year without fail for the next 100 years. ▌

A Note on Compound Growth

If you are considering depositing money in an interest-bearing account, the interest rate on that account is just the rate at which your money grows, assuming you don't remove any of it. If that rate is 10 percent, each year you simply have 10 percent more money than you had the year before. In this case, the interest rate is just an example of a compound growth rate.

The way we calculated future values is actually quite general and lets you answer some other types of questions related to growth. For example, your company currently has 10,000 employees. You've estimated that the number of employees grows by 3 percent per year. How many employees will there be in five years? Here, we start with 10,000 people instead of dollars, and we don't think of the growth rate as an interest rate, but the calculation is exactly the same:

$$10,000 \times (1.03)^5 = 10,000 \times 1.1593 = 11,593 \text{ employees}$$

There will be about 1,593 net new hires over the coming five years.

E X A M P L E | **5.4**   **Dividend Growth**

Over the 10 years ending in 1991, the Royal Bank of Canada's dividend grew from $0.63 to $1.16, an average annual growth rate of 6.3 percent.[3] Assuming this growth continues, what will the dividend be in 1996?

Here we have a cash dividend growing because it is being increased by management, but, once again, the calculation is the same:

$$\text{Future values} = \$1.16 \times (1.063)^5 = \$1.16 \times (1.3569) = \$1.57$$

The dividend will grow by $0.41 over that period. Dividend growth is a subject we return to in a later chapter. ▌

> CONCEPT QUESTIONS
>
> 1. What do we mean by the future value of an investment?
> 2. What does it mean to compound interest? How does compound interest differ from simple interest?
> 3. In general, what is the future value of $1 invested at r per period for t periods?

---

[3] $\$1.16 = \$0.63 \times (1 + r)^{10}$
   $1.84 = (1 + r)^{10}$
   $(1.84)^{1/10} = 1 + r$
   $1.0629 = 1 + r$
   $r = 6.3\%$

5.2 | PRESENT VALUE AND DISCOUNTING

When we discuss future value, we are thinking of questions such as, What will my $2,000 investment grow to if it earns a 6.5 percent return every year for the next six years? The answer to this question is what we called the future value of $2,000 invested at 6.5 percent for six years (check that the answer is about $2,918).

Another type of question that comes up even more often in financial management is obviously related to future value. Suppose you need to have $10,000 in 10 years, and you can earn 6.5 percent on your money. How much do you have to invest today to reach your goal? You can verify that the answer is $5,327.26. How do we know this? Read on.

The Single Period Case

We've seen that the future value of $1 invested for one year at 10 percent is $1.10. We now ask a slightly different question: How much do we have to invest today at 10 percent to get $1 in one year? In other words, we know the future value here is $1, but what is the **present value (PV)**? The answer isn't too hard to figure out. Whatever we invest today will be 1.1 times bigger at the end of the year. Since we need $1 at the end of the year:

> Present value $\times$ 1.1 = $1

Or:

> Present value = $1/1.1 = $.909

present value (PV)
The current value of future cash flows discounted at the appropriate discount rate.

This present value is the answer to the following question: What amount, invested today, will grow to $1 in one year if the interest rate is 10 percent? Present value is thus just the reverse of future value. Instead of compounding the money forward into the future, we **discount** it back to the present.

discount
Calculate the present value of some future amount.

E X A M P L E | 5.5   Single Period PV

Suppose you need $400 to buy textbooks next year. You can earn 7 percent on your money. How much do you have to put up today?

We need to know the PV of $400 in one year at 7 percent. Proceeding as we just did:

> Present value $\times$ 1.07 = $400

We can now solve for the present value:

> Present value = $400 $\times$ [1/1.07] = $373.83

Thus, $373.83 is the present value. Again, this just means that investing this amount for one year at 7 percent results in your having a future value of $400. ▌

From our examples, the present value of $1 to be received in one period is generally given as:

> PV = $1 $\times$ [1/(1 + r)]

We next examine how to get the present value of an amount to be paid in two or more periods into the future.

Present Values for Multiple Periods

Suppose you needed to have $1,000 in two years. If you can earn 7 percent, how much do you have to invest to make sure that you have the $1,000 when you need it? In other words, what is the present value of $1,000 in two years if the relevant rate is 7 percent?

Based on your knowledge of future values, we know that the amount invested must grow to $1,000 over the two years. In other words, it must be the case that:

$$\$1,000 = PV \times 1.07^2$$
$$= PV \times 1.1449$$

Given this, we can solve for the present value as:

Present value $= \$1,000/1.1449 = \$873.44$

Therefore, $873.44 is the amount you must invest to achieve your goal.

E X A M P L E | 5.6   Saving Up

You would like to buy a new automobile. You have about $50,000 or so, but the car costs $68,500. If you can earn 9 percent, how much do you have to invest today to buy the car in two years? Do you have enough? Assume the price will stay the same.

What we need to know is the present value of $68,500 to be paid in two years, assuming a 9 percent rate. Based on our discussion, this is:

$$PV = \$68,500/1.09^2 = \$68,500/1.1881 = \$57,655.08$$

You're still about $7,655 short, even if you're willing to wait two years. |

As you have probably recognized by now, calculating present values is quite similar to calculating future values, and the general result looks much the same. The present value of $1 to be received t periods in the future at a discount rate of r is:

$$PV = \$1 \times [1/(1 + r)^t] = \$1/(1 + r)^t \qquad [5.2]$$

discount rate

The rate used to calculate the present value of future cash flows.

The quantity in brackets, $1/(1 + r)^t$, goes by several different names. Since it's used to discount a future cash flow, it is often called a *discount factor*. With this name, it is not surprising that the rate used in the calculation is often called the **discount rate**. We tend to call it this in talking about present values. The quantity in brackets is also called the *present value interest factor* for $1 at r percent for t periods and is sometimes abbreviated as PVIF(r,t). Finally, calculating the present value of a future cash flow to determine its worth today is commonly called *discounted cash flow (DCF)* valuation.

To illustrate, suppose you needed $1,000 in three years. You can earn 15 percent on your money. How much do you have to invest today? To find out, we have to determine the present value of $1,000 in three years at 15 percent. We do this by discounting $1,000 back three periods at 15 percent. With these numbers, the discount factor is:

$$1/(1 + .15)^3 = 1/1.5209 = .6575$$

The amount you must invest is thus?

$$\$1,000 \times .6575 = \$657.50$$

We say that $657.50 is the present or discounted value of $1,000 to be received in three years at 15 percent.

There are tables for present value factors just as there are tables for future value factors, and you use them in the same way (if you use them at all). Table 5.3 contains a small set. A much larger set can be found in Table A.2 in the book's Appendix.

In Table 5.3, the discount factor we just calculated (.6575) can be found by looking down the column labelled 15% until you come to the third row.

E X A M P L E | **5.7   Stripped Bonds**

Canadian investment dealers purchase government of Canada bonds and resell the coupons and principal repayment separately. This process is called *bond stripping* because the coupons are stripped off. Such stripped coupons may be attractive to investors because they compound automatically with no reinvestment risk. An investor who buys a stripped coupon receives no payments before the coupon date.[4] So the price of a 25-year coupon with a face value of $10,000 is simply the present value of $10,000 in 25 years. Suppose the price of this coupon is $915.10. This discount rate, or the yield, of this bond issue is:

$$\$915.10 = \$10,000/(1 + r)^{25}$$
$$(1 + r)^{25} = 10.9278$$
$$1 + r = 1.1004$$

The discount rate, r, is found to be 10.04 percent. A dollar in 25 years is worth a little more than nine cents today, assuming a 10.04 percent discount rate. Zero coupon bonds are discussed in more detail in Chapter 12.

As the length of time until payment grows, present values decline. As Example 5.7 illustrates, present values tend to become small as the time horizon grows. If you look out far enough, they will always get close to zero. Also, for a given length of time, the higher the discount rate is, the lower is the present value. Put another way, present values and discount rates are inversely related. Increasing the discount rate decreases the PV and vice versa.

The relationship between time, discount rates, and present values is illustrated in Figure 5.3. Notice that by the time we get to 10 years, the present values are all substantially smaller than the future amounts.

Periods	Interest Rate			
	5%	10%	15%	20%
1	.9524	.9091	.8696	.8333
2	.9070	.8264	.7561	.6944
3	.8638	.7513	.6575	.5787
4	.8227	.6830	.5718	.4823
5	.7835	.6209	.4972	.4019

T A B L E 5.3

Present value interest factors

---

[4] ScotiaMcLeod, "Bearer Coupons and Bond Residues; Investment Attributes," October 1988.

F I G U R E 5.3

Present value of $1 for different periods and rates

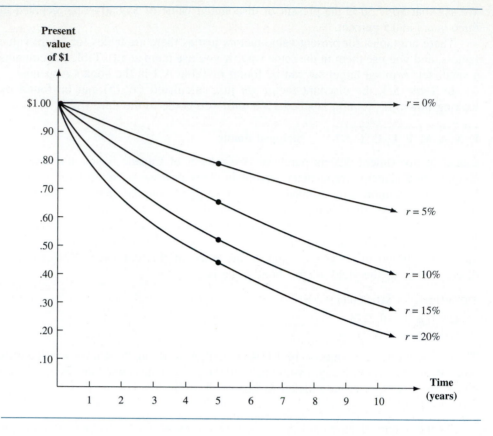

CONCEPT QUESTIONS

1. What do we mean by the present value of an investment?

2. The process of discounting a future amount back to the present is the opposite of doing what?

3. What do we mean by the discounted cash flow or DCF approach?

5.3 I MORE ON PRESENT AND FUTURE VALUES

Look back at the expressions that we came up with for present and future values, and you will see a very simple relationship between the two. We explore this relationship and some related issues in this section.

Present versus Future Value

What we called the present value factor is just the reciprocal of (that is, 1 divided by) the future value factor:

Future value factor $= (1 + r)^t$

Present value factor $= 1/(1 + r)^t$

In fact, the easy way to calculate a present value factor on many calculators is to first calculate the future value factor and then press the *1/x* key to flip it over.

If we let FV_t stand for the future value after t periods, the relationship between future value and present value can be written very simply as one of the following:

$$PV \times (1 + r)^t = FV_t \qquad\qquad [5.3]$$
$$PV = FV_t/(1 + r)^t = FV_t \times [1/(1 + r)^t]$$

This last result we call the *basic present value equation*. We use it throughout the text. There are a number of variations that come up, but this simple equation underlies many of the most important ideas in corporate finance.

E X A M P L E | 5.8   **Evaluating Investments**

To give you an idea of how we use present and future values, consider the following simple investment. Your company proposes to buy an asset of $355,000. This investment is very safe. You will sell the asset in three years for $400,000. You know that you could invest the $335,000 elsewhere at 10 percent with very little risk. What do you think of the proposed investment?

This is not a good investment. Why not? Because you can invest the $335,000 elsewhere at 10 percent. If you do, after three years it would grow to:

$$\$335,000 \times (1 + r)^t = \$335,000 \times 1.1^3$$
$$= \$335,000 \times 1.331$$
$$= \$445,885$$

Because the proposed investment pays out only $400,000, it is not as good as other alternatives that we have. Another way of saying the same thing is to notice that the present value of $400,000 in three years at 10 percent is:

$$\$400,000 \times [1/(1 + r)^t] = \$400,000/1.1^3 = \$400,000/1.331 = \$300,526$$

This tells us that we only have to invest about $300,000 to get $400,000 in three years, not $335,000. We return to this type of analysis later. ▌

Determining the Discount Rate

Frequently, we need to determine what discount rate is implicit in an investment. We can do this by looking at the basic present value equation:

$$PV = FV_t/(1 + r)^t$$

There are only four parts to this equation: the present value (PV), the future value (FV_t), the discount rate (r), and the life of the investment (t). Given any three of these, we can always find the fourth.

E X A M P L E | 5.9   **Finding *r* for a Single Period Investment**

You are considering a one-year investment. If you put up $1,250, you would get back $1,350. What rate is this investment paying?

First, in this single period case, the answer is fairly obvious. You are getting a total of $100 in addition to your $1,250. The rate of return on this investment is thus $100/1,250 = 8$ percent.

More formally, from the basic present value equation, the present value (the amount you must put up today) is $1,250. The future value (what the present value grows to) is $1,350. The time involved is one period, so we have:

$$\$1,250 = \$1,350/(1 + r)^1$$
$$(1 + r) = \$1,350/1,250 = 1.08$$
$$r = 8\%$$

In this simple case, of course, there was no need to go through this calculation, but, as we describe later, it gets a little harder when there is more than one period. |

For example, we might be offered an investment that cost us $100 and doubles our money in eight years. To compare this to other investments, we would like to know what discount rate is implicit in these numbers. This discount rate is called the *rate of return* or sometimes just *return* for the investment. We have a present value of $100, a future value of $200 (double our money), and an eight-year life. To calculate the return, we can write the basic present value equation as:

$$PV = FV_t/(1 + r)^t$$
$$\$100 = \$200/(1 + r)^8$$

It could also be written as:

$$(1 + r)^8 = 200/100 = 2$$

We now need to solve for r. There are three ways we could do it:

1. Use a financial calculator.
2. Solve the equation for $1 + r$ by taking the eighth root of both sides. Since this is the same thing as raising both sides to the power of ⅛ or .125, this is actually easy to do with the y^x key on a calculator. Just enter 2, then press y^x, enter .125, and press the = key. The eighth root should be about 1.09, which implies that r is 9 percent.
3. Use a future value table. The future value factor after eight years is equal to 2. Look across the row corresponding to eight periods in Table A.1 to see that a future value factor of 2 corresponds to the 9 percent column, again implying that the return here is 9 percent.[5]

E X A M P L E | **5.10**   **Saving for University**

Many Canadian universities are increasing their tuition and fees. You estimate that you will need about $65,000 to send your child to a university in eight years. You have about $25,000 now. If you can earn 15 percent, will you make it? At what rate will you just reach your goal?

---

[5] There is a useful "back of the envelope" means of solving for r—the Rule of 72. For reasonable rates of return, the time it takes to double your money is given approximately by $72/r\%$. In our example, this is $72/r\% = 8$ years, implying that r is 9 percent as we calculated. This rule is fairly accurate for discount rates in the 5 percent to 20 percent range.

If you can earn 15 percent, the future value of your $25,000 in eight years would be:

$$FV = \$25{,}000 \times (1.15)^8 = \$25{,}000 \times 3.0590 = \$76{,}475.57$$

So you will make it easily. The minimum rate is the unknown r in the following:

$$FV = \$25{,}000 \times (1 + r)^8 = \$65{,}000$$
$$(1 + r)^8 = \$65{,}000/25{,}000 = 2.6000$$

Therefore, the future value factor is 2.6000. Looking at the row in Table A.1 that corresponds to eight periods, our future value factor is partway between the ones shown for 12 percent (2.4760) and 14 percent (2.8526), so you would just reach your goal if you earn slightly greater than 12 percent. To get the exact answer, we could use a financial calculator or we can solve for r:

$$(1 + r)^8 = \$65{,}000/25{,}000 = 2.6000$$
$$(1 + r) = 2.6000^{(1/8)} = 2.6000^{.125} = 1.1269$$
$$r = 12.69\%$$

E X A M P L E | 5.11   **Only 10,956 Days to Retirement**

You would like to retire in 30 years as a millionaire. If you have $10,000 today, what rate of return do you need to earn to achieve your goal?

The future value is $1 million. The present value is $10,000, and there are 30 years until payment. We need to calculate the unknown discount rate in the following:

$$\$10{,}000 = \$1{,}000{,}000/(1 + r)^{30}$$
$$(1 + r)^{30} = 100$$

The future value factor is thus 100. You can verify that the implicit rate is about 16.59 percent.

Finding the Number of Periods

Suppose we were interested in purchasing an asset that costs $50,000. We currently have $25,000. If we can earn 12 percent on this $25,000, how long until we have the $50,000? The answer involves solving for the last variable in the basic present value equation, the number of periods. You already know how to get an approximate answer to this particular problem. Notice that we need to double our money. From the Rule of 72, this would take $72/12 = 6$ years at 12 percent.

To come up with the exact answer, we can again manipulate the basic present value equation. The present value is $25,000, and the future value is $50,000. With a 12 percent discount rate, the basic equation takes one of the following forms:

$$\$25{,}000 = \$50{,}000/(1.12)^t$$
$$\$50{,}000/25{,}000 = (1.12)^t = 2$$

We thus have a future value factor of 2 for a 12 percent rate. We now need to solve for t. In Table A.1, if you look down the column that corresponds to 12 percent, you will see that a future value factor of 1.9738 occurs at six periods. Thus, it takes about six years as we calculated. To get the exact answer, we have to explicitly solve for t

(or use a financial calculator). If you do this, the answer is 6.1163 years, so our approximation was quite close in this case.[6]

E X A M P L E | 5.12   Waiting for Godot

You've been saving to buy the Godot Company. The total cost will be $10 million. You currently have about $2.3 million. If you can earn 5 percent on your money, how long will you have to wait? At 16 percent, how long must you wait?

At 5 percent, you'll have to wait a long time. From the basic present value equation:

How To Calculate

$$\$2.3 = 10/(1.05)^t$$
$$1.05^t = 4.33$$
$$t = 30 \text{ years}$$

At 16 percent, things are a little better. Check for yourself that it would take about 10 years. ▮

CONCEPT QUESTIONS

1. What is the basic present value equation?
2. In general, what is the present value of $1 to be received in t periods, assuming a discount rate of r per period?

5.4 | PRESENT AND FUTURE VALUES OF MULTIPLE CASH FLOWS

Thus far, we have restricted our attention to either the future value of a lump-sum present amount or the present value of some single future cash flow. In this section, we extend these basic results to handle any number of cash flows. We start with future value.

Future Value with Multiple Cash Flows

Suppose you deposit $100 today in an account paying 8 percent. In one year, you will deposit another $100. How much will you have in two years? This particular problem is relatively easy. At the end of the first year, you will have $108 plus the second $100 you deposit for a total of $208. You leave this $208 on deposit at 8 percent for another year. At the end of this second year, it is worth:

$$\$208 \times 1.08 = \$224.64$$

Figure 5.4 is a *time line* that illustrates the process of calculating the future value of these two $100 deposits. Figures such as this one are very useful for solving

---

[6] To solve for t, we have to take the logarithm of both sides of the equation:

$$1.12^t = 2$$
$$\log 1.12^t = \log 2$$
$$t \log 1.12 = \log 2$$

We can then solve for t explicitly:

$$t = \log 2/\log 1.12$$
$$= 6.1163$$

Almost all calculators can determine a logarithm; look for a key labelled *log* or *ln*. If both are present, use either one.

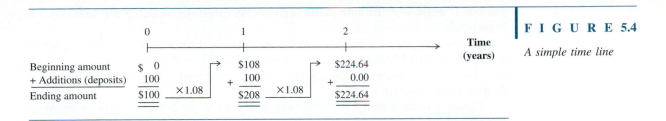

F I G U R E 5.4

A simple time line

complicated problems. Anytime you are having trouble with a present or future value problem, drawing a time line can usually help you to see what is happening.

E X A M P L E | 5.13   Saving Up Revisited

You think that you will be able to deposit $4,000 at the end of each of the next three years in a bank account paying 8 percent interest. You currently have $7,000 in the account. How much will you have in three years? In four years?

At the end of the first year, you will have:

$7,000 × (1.08) + $4,000 = $11,560

At the end of the second year, you will have:

$11,560 × (1.08) + $4,000 = $16,484.80

Repeating this for the third year gives:

$16,484.8 × (1.08) + $4,000 = $21,803.58

Therefore, you will have $21,803.58 in three years. If you leave this on deposit for one more year and don't add to it, at the end of the fourth year you'll have:

$21,803.58 × (1.08) = $23,547.87 ❙

When we calculated the future value of the two $100 deposits, we simply calculated the balance as of the beginning of each year and then rolled that amount forward to the next year. We could have done it another, quicker way. The first $100 was on deposit for two years at 8 percent, so its future value is:

$100 × (1.08)^2 = $100 × 1.1664 = $116.64

The second $100 was on deposit for one year at 8 percent, and its future value is thus:

$100 × 1.08 = $108.00

The total future value, as we previously calculated, is equal to the sum of these two future values:

$116.64 + 108 = $224.64

Based on this example, there are two ways to calculate future values for multiple cash flows: (1) Compound the accumulated balance forward one year at a time or (2) calculate the future value of each cash flow first and then add them up. These give the same answer, so you can do it either way.

To illustrate the two different ways of calculating future values, consider the future value of $2,000 invested at the end of each of the next five years. The current balance is zero, and the rate is 10 percent. We begin by drawing the time line in Figure 5.5.

On the time line, notice that nothing happens until the end of the first year when we make the first $2,000 investment. This first $2,000 earns interest for the next four (not five) years. Also notice that the last $2,000 is invested at the end of the fifth year, so it earns no interest.

Figure 5.6 illustrates the calculations involved if we compound the investment one period at a time. As illustrated, the future value is $12,210.20.

Figure 5.7 goes through the same calculations, but the second technique is used. Naturally, the answer is the same.

E X A M P L E | 5.14   Saving Up Once Again

If you deposit $100 in one year, $200 in two years, and $300 in three years, how much will you have in three years? How much of this is interest? How much will you have in five years if you don't add additional amounts? Assume a 7 percent interest rate throughout.

We calculate the future value of each amount in three years. Notice that the $100 earns interest for two years, and the $200 earns interest for one year. The final $300 earns no interest. The future values are thus:

$$\begin{aligned}
\$100 \times 1.07^2 &= \$114.49 \\
\$200 \times 1.07 &= 214.00 \\
+\$300 &= \underline{\ 300.00} \\
\text{Total future value} &= \underline{\$628.49}
\end{aligned}$$

The future value is thus $628.49. The total interest is:

$$\$628.49 - (\$100 + 200 + 300) = \$28.49$$

How much will you have in five years? We know that you will have $628.49 in three years. If you leave that in for two more years, it will grow to:

$$\$628.49 \times (1.07)^2 = \$628.49 \times 1.1449 = \$719.56$$

Notice that we could have calculated the future value of each amount separately. Once again, be careful about the lengths of time. As we previously calculated, the first $100 earns interest for only four years, the second deposit earns three years' interest, and the last earns two years' interest:

$$\begin{aligned}
\$100 \times (1.07)^4 &= \$100 \times 1.3108 = \$131.08 \\
\$200 \times (1.07)^3 &= \$200 \times 1.2250 = 245.01 \\
+\$300 \times (1.07)^2 &= \$300 \times 1.1449 = \underline{\ 343.47} \\
&\ \ \text{Total future value} \quad \underline{\$719.56}
\end{aligned}$$

F I G U R E 5.5

Time line for $2,000 per year for five years

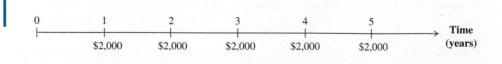

Future value calculated by compounding forward one period at a time

FIGURE 5.6

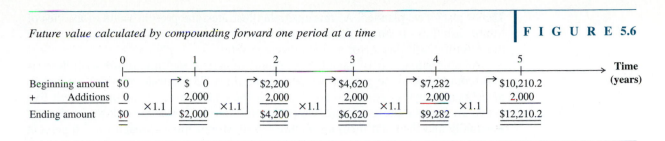

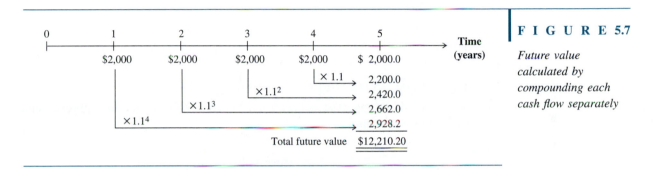

FIGURE 5.7

Future value calculated by compounding each cash flow separately

Present Value with Multiple Cash Flows

Very often we need to determine the present value of a series of future cash flows. As with future values, there are two ways we can do it. We can either discount back one period at a time, or we can just calculate the present values individually and add them up.

Suppose you needed $1,000 in one year and $2,000 more in two years. If you can earn 9 percent on your money, how much do you have to put up today to exactly cover these amounts in the future? In other words, what is the present value of the two cash flows at 9 percent?

The present value of $2,000 in two years at 9 percent is:

$2,000/1.09^2 = $1,683.36

The present value of $1,000 in one year is:

$1,000/1.09 = $917.43

Therefore, the total present value is:

$1,683.36 + 917.43 = $2,600.79

To see why $2,600.79 is the right answer, we can check to see that after the $2,000 is paid out in two years, there is no money left. By investing $2,600.79 for one year at 9 percent, we have:

$2,600.79 × 1.09 = $2,834.86

We take out $1,000, leaving $1,834.86. This amount earns 9 percent for another year, leaving us with:

$1,834.86 × 1.09 = $2,000

This is just as we planned. As this example illustrates, the present value of a series of future cash flows is simply the amount that you would need today to exactly duplicate those future cash flows (for a given discount rate).

An alternative way of calculating present values for multiple future cash flows is to discount back to the present one period at a time. To illustrate, suppose we had an investment that was going to pay $1,000 at the end of every year for the next five years. To find the present value, we could discount each $1,000 back to the present separately and then add them up. Figure 5.8 illustrates this approach for a 6 percent discount rate.

As Figure 5.8 shows, the answer is $4,212.37 (ignoring a small rounding error). Alternatively, we could discount the last cash flow back one period and add it to the next-to-the-last cash flow:

$$\$1,000/1.06 + 1,000 = \$943.40 + 1,000 = \$1,943.40$$

We could then discount this amount back one period and add it to the year-three cash flow:

$$\$1,943.40/1.06 + 1,000 = \$1,833.39 + 1,000 = \$2,833.39$$

This process could be repeated as necessary. Figure 5.9 illustrates this approach and the remaining calculations.

E X A M P L E | 5.15   How Much Is It Worth?

You are offered an investment that will pay you $200 in one year, $400 the next, $600 the next, and $800 at the end of the last year. You can earn 12 percent on very similar investments. What is the most you should pay for this one?

We need to calculate the present value of these cash flows at 12 percent. Taking them one at a time gives:

$$\$200 \times 1/1.12^1 = \$200/1.1200 = \$178.57$$
$$\$400 \times 1/1.12^2 = \$400/1.2544 = 318.88$$
$$\$600 \times 1/1.12^3 = \$600/1.4049 = 427.07$$
$$\$800 \times 1/1.12^4 = \$800/1.5735 = \underline{508.41}$$
$$\text{Total present value} \qquad \underline{\underline{\$1,432.93}}$$

If you can earn 12 percent on your money, you can duplicate this investment's cash flows for $1,432.93, so this is the most you should be willing to pay. |

F I G U R E 5.8

Present value calculated by discounting each cash flow separately

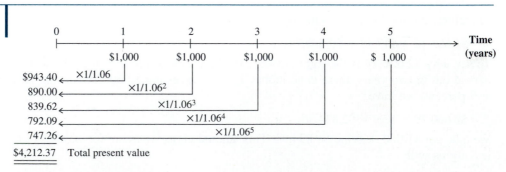

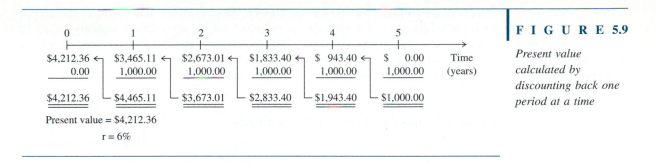

FIGURE 5.9

Present value calculated by discounting back one period at a time

---

E X A M P L E | **5.16**   **How Much Is It Worth? Part 2**

You are offered an investment that will make three $5,000 payments. The first payment will occur four years from today. The second will occur in five years, the third will follow in six years. If you can earn 11 percent, what is the most this investment is worth today? What is the future value of the cash flows?

We answer the questions in reverse order to illustrate a point. The future value of the cash flows in six years is:

$$\$5,000 \times (1.11)^2 + 5,000 \times (1.11) + 5,000 = \$6,160.50 + 5,550 + 5,000$$
$$= \$16,710.50$$

The present value must be:

$$\$16,710.50/1.11^6 = \$8,934.12$$

Let's check this. Taking them one at a time, the PV of the cash flows is:

$$\$5,000 \times (1/1.11^6) = \$5,000/1.8704 = \$2,673.20$$
$$+\$5,000 \times (1/1.11^5) = \$5,000/1.6851 = \$2,967.26$$
$$+\$5,000 \times (1/1.11^4) = \$5,000/1.5181 = \underline{\$3,293.65}$$
$$\text{Total present value} \quad \underline{\$8,934.12}$$

This is as we previously calculated. The point we want to make is that we can calculate present and future values in any order and convert between them using whatever way seems most convenient. The answers are always the same as long as we stick with the same discount rate and are careful to keep track of the right number of periods.

CONCEPT QUESTIONS

1. Describe how to calculate the present value of a series of cash flows.
2. Describe how to calculate the future value of a series of cash flows.

5.5 | VALUING LEVEL CASH FLOWS: ANNUITIES AND PERPETUITIES

We frequently encounter situations where we have multiple cash flows that are all the same amount. For example, a very common type of loan repayment plan calls for the borrower to repay the loan by making a series of equal payments for some length of time. Almost all consumer loans (such as car loans) and home mortgages feature equal payments, usually made each month.

annuity

A level stream of cash flows for a fixed period of time.

More generally, a series of constant or level cash flows that occurs at the end of each period for some fixed number of periods is called an ordinary **annuity**, or, more correctly, the cash flows are said to be in *ordinary annuity form*. Annuities appear very frequently in financial arrangements, and there are some useful shortcuts for determining their values. We consider these next.

Present Value for Annuity Cash Flows

Suppose we were examining an asset that promised to pay $500 at the end of each of the next three years. The cash flows from this asset are in the form of a three-year, $500 annuity. If we wanted to earn 10 percent on our money, how much would we offer for this annuity?

From the previous section, we can discount each of these $500 payments back to the present at 10 percent to determine the total present value:

$$\text{Present value} = \$500/1.1^1 + 500/1.1^2 + 500/1.1^3$$
$$= \$500/1.10 + 500/1.21 + 500/1.1331$$
$$= \$454.55 + 413.22 + 375.66$$
$$= \$1,243.43$$

This approach works just fine. However, we often encounter situations where the number of cash flows is quite large. For example, a typical car loan calls for monthly payments over three or more years for a total of a least 36 payments. If we were trying to determine the present value of those payments, it would be useful to have a shortcut.

Since the cash flows on an annuity are all the same, we can come up with a very useful variation on the basic present value equation. It turns out that the present value of an annuity of C dollars per period for t periods when the rate of return or interest rate per period is r is given by:[7]

$$\text{Annuity present value} = C \times (1 - \text{Present value factor})/r \qquad [5.4]$$
$$= C \times [1 - \{1/(1 + r)^t\}]/r$$

The term following the multiplication sign is sometimes called the present value interest factor for annuities and abbreviated PVIFA(r,t).

The expression for the annuity present value may look a little complicated, but it isn't difficult to use. Notice that the term in curly braces, $\{1/(1 + r)^t\}$, is the same present value factor we've been calculating. In our preceding example, the interest rate is 10 percent and there are three years involved. The usual present value factor is thus:

$$\text{Present value factor} = 1/1.1^3 = 1/1.331 = .75131$$

To calculate the annuity present value factor, we just plug this in:

$$\text{Annuity present value factor} = (1 - \text{Present value factor})/r$$
$$= (1 - .75131)/.10$$
$$= .248685/.10 = 2.48685$$

---
[7] We give the proof of this formula in Appendix 5A at the end of the chapter.

Just as we calculated before, the present value of our $500 annuity is then:[8]

Annuity present value = $500 × 2.48685 = $1,243.43

E X A M P L E | **5.17**   **How Much Can You Afford?**

After carefully going over your budget, you have demonstrated you can afford to pay $632 per month toward a new sports car. You call your bank branch and find out that the going rate is 1 percent per month for 48 months. How much can you borrow?

To determine how much you can borrow, we need to calculate the present value of $632 per month for 48 months at 1 percent per month. The loan payments are in ordinary annuity form, so the annuity present value factor is:

$$\text{Annuity PV factor} = (1 - \text{Present value factor})/r$$
$$= [1 - (1/(1.01)^{48})]/.01$$
$$= (1 - .6203)/.01 = 37.9740$$

With this factor, we can calculate the present value of the 48 payments of $632 each as:

Present value = $632 × 37.9740 = $24,000

Therefore, $24,000 is what you can afford to borrow and repay. |

Annuity Tables   Just as there are tables for ordinary present value factors, there are tables for annuity factors as well. Table 5.4 contains a few such factors; Table A.3 in the Appendix to the book contains a larger set. To find the annuity present value factor we just calculated, look for the row corresponding to three periods and then find the column for 10 percent. The number you see at that intersection should be 2.4869, as we calculated. Once again, try calculating a few of these factors yourself and compare your answers to the ones in the table to make sure you know how to do

T A B L E 5.4

Annuity present value interest factors

Periods	5%	10%	15%	20%
		Interest Rate		
1	.9524	.9091	.8696	.8333
2	1.8594	1.7355	1.6257	1.5278
3	2.7232	2.4869	2.2832	2.1065
4	3.5460	3.1699	2.8550	2.5887
5	4.3295	3.7908	3.3522	2.9906

---

[8] To solve this problem on a common financial calculator, you would need to do the following:
1. Enter the payment of C = $500 and press *PMT.*
2. Enter the interest rate of r = 10 percent as 10 (not .10) and press *i.*
3. Enter the number of periods as 3 and press *n.*
4. Ask the calculator for the PV by pressing the *compute* or *solve* key and then pressing *PV.*
   Here is a useful tip: Many financial calculators have the feature of "constant memory." As a practical matter, what this can mean is that the calculator will remember your mistakes, even if you turn it off. You need to be sure to press the appropriate key(s) to clear out the calculator's memory before you begin. If you make a mistake, it is usually better to clear the memory and start over. Otherwise, you may learn the hard way what GIGO stands for.

it. If you are using a financial calculator, just enter $1 as the payment and calculate the present value; the result should be the annuity present value factor.

Finding the Payment   Suppose you wished to start a new business that specializes in the latest of health food trends, frozen yak milk. To produce and market your product, Yakkee Yogurt, you need to borrow $100,000. Because it strikes you as unlikely that this particular fad will be long-lived, you propose to pay off the loan quickly by making five equal annual payments. If the interest rate is 18 percent, what will the payment be?

We know the present value is $100,000, the interest rate is 18 percent, and there are five years. The payments are all equal, so we need to find the relevant annuity factor and solve for the unknown cash flow:

$$\text{Annuity present value} = \$100,000 = C \times (1 - \text{Present value factor})/r$$
$$\$100,000 = C \times (1 - 1/1.18^5)/.18$$
$$= C \times (1 - .4371)/.18$$
$$= C \times (3.1272)$$
$$C = \$31,977$$

Therefore, you'll make five payments of just under $32,000 each.

E X A M P L E | 5.18   Finding the Number of Payments

You ran a little short on your spring break vacation, so you charged $1,000 on your credit card. You can only afford to make the minimum payment of $20 per month. The interest rate on the credit card is 1.5 percent per month. How long will you need to pay off the $1,000?

What we have here is an annuity of $20 per month at 1.5 percent per month for some unknown length of time. The present value is $1,000 (the amount you owe today). We need to do a little algebra:

$$\$1,000 = \$20 \times (1 - \text{Present value factor})/.015$$
$$(\$1,000/20) \times .015 = 1 - \text{Present value factor}$$
$$\text{Present value factor} = .25 = 1/(1 + r)^t$$
$$(1.015)^t = 1/.25 = 4$$

At this point, the problem boils down to the question: How long does it take for your money to quadruple at 1.5 percent per month? Based on the previous sections, the answer is about 93 months:

$$1.015^{93} = 3.99 = 4$$

It will take you about 93/12 = 7.75 years at this rate. |

Finding the Rate   The last question we might want to ask concerns the interest rate implicit in an annuity. For example, an insurance company offers to pay you $1,000 per year for 10 years if you will pay $6,710 up front. What rate is implicit in this 10-year annuity?

We know the present value ($6,710), the cash flows ($1,000 per year), and the life of the investment (10 years). What we don't know is the discount rate:

$$\$6,710 = \$1,000 \times (1 - \text{Present value factor})/r$$
$$\$6,710/1,000 = 6.71 = (1 - \{1/1(1 + r)^{10}\})/r$$

So, the annuity factor for 10 periods is equal to 6.71, and we need to solve this equation for the unknown value of r. Unfortunately, this is mathematically impossible to do directly. The only way to do it is to use a table or trial and error to find a value for r.[9]

In Table A.3, look across the row corresponding to 10 periods for a factor of 6.7101 under 8 percent. Right away, we know that the insurance company is offering just about 8 percent. Alternatively, we could just start trying different values until we get very close to the answer. Using this trial-and-error approach can be a little tedious, but, fortunately, machines are good at that sort of thing.

To illustrate how to find the answer by trial and error, suppose a relative of yours wants to borrow $3,000. She offers to repay you $1,000 every year for four years. What interest rate are you being offered?

The cash flows here have the form of a four-year $1,000 annuity. The present value is $3,000. We need to find the discount rate, r. Our goal in doing so is primarily to give you a feel for the relationship between annuity values and discount rates.

We need to start somewhere, so 10 percent is probably as good a place as any to begin. At 10 percent, the annuity factor is:

Annuity present value factor $= (1 - 1/1.10^4)/.10 = 3.1699$

The present value of the cash flows at 10 percent is thus:

Present value $= \$1,000 \times 3.1699 = \$3,169.90$

You can see that we're already in the right ballpark.

Is 10 percent too high or too low? Recall that present values and discount rates move in opposite directions: Increasing the discount rate lowers the PV and vice versa. Our present value here is too high, so the discount rate is too low. If we try 12 percent:

Present value $= \$1,000 \times (1 - 1/1.12^4)/.12 = \$3,037.35$

Now we're almost there. We are still a little low on the discount rate (because the PV is a little high), so we'll try 13 percent:

Present value $= \$1,000 \times (1 - 1/1.13^4)/.13 = \$2,974.47$

This is less than $3,000, so we now know that the answer is between 12 percent and 13 percent, and it looks to be about 12.5 percent. For practice, work at it for a while longer and see if you find that the answer is about 12.59 percent.

Future Value for Annuities

On occasion, it's also handy to know a shortcut for calculating the future value of an annuity. For example, suppose you plan to contribute $2,000 every year into a Registered Retirement Savings Plan (RRSP) paying 8 percent. If you retire in 30 years, how much will you have?

One way to answer this particular problem is to calculate the present value of a $2,000, 30-year annuity at 8 percent to convert it to a lump sum, and then calculate the future value of that lump sum:

---

[9] Financial calculators rely on trial and error to find the answer. That's why they sometimes appear to be "thinking" before coming up with the answer. Actually, it is possible to directly solve for r if there are less than five periods, but it's usually not worth the trouble.

Annuity present value = $2,000 × (1 − 1/1.08^{30})/.08
= $2,000 × 11.2578
= $22,515.57

The future value of this amount in 30 years is:

Future value = $22,516 × 1.08^{30} = $22,515.57 × 10.0627 = $226,566.40

We could have done this calculation in one step:

Annuity future value = Annuity present value × $(1.08)^{30}$
= $2,000 × (1 − 1/1.08^{30})/.08 × $(1.08)^{30}$
= $2,000 × (1.08^{30} − 1)/.08
= $2,000 × (10.0627 − 1)/.08
= $2,000 × 113.2832 = $226,566.4

As this example illustrates, there are future value factors for annuities as well as present value factors. In general, the future value factor for an annuity is given by:

Annuity FV factor = (Future value factor − 1)/r   [5.5]
= ({$(1 + r)^t$} − 1)/r

For example, True North Distillers has just placed a shipment of Canadian whiskey in a bonded warehouse where it will age for the next eight years. An exporter plans to buy $1 million worth of whiskey in eight years. If the exporter annually deposits $95,000 at year-end in a bank account paying 8 percent interest, would there be enough to pay for the whiskey?

In this case, the annuity future value factor is given by:

Annuity FV factor = (Future value factor − 1)/r
= $(1.08^8 − 1)/.08$
= (1.8509 − 1)/.08
= 10.6366

The future value of this eight-year, $95,000 annuity is thus:

Annuity future value = $95,000 × 10.6366
= $1,010,480

Thus, the exporter would make it with $10,480 to spare.

In our example, notice that the first deposit occurs in one year and the last in eight years. As we discussed earlier, the first deposit earns seven years' interest; the last deposit earns none.

Annuity Due   Annuity contracts sometimes specify payments at the beginning of the period. Leases are a common example of such an **annuity due**. To illustrate, suppose that True North Distillers from our previous example decides to make the payments for the bonded whiskey at the beginning of each year. How much would the payments be for this annuity due given that the future value must still be $1 million?

Because the payments would now be made at the beginning of the period, each payment earns interest at r percent for one additional period. It follows that:

Annuity due FV factor = Annuity FV factor × (1 + r)   [5.6]
Annuity due future value = Payment × Annuity FV factor × (1 + .08)
$1,000,000 = Payment × 10.6366 × (1.08)
Payment = $87,051

annuity due
Annuity contract specification of payments at the beginning of each period.

By making the payments at the beginning of the period, True North has reduced the necessary payments to just over $87,000.[10]

E X A M P L E | **5.19**   **Early Bird RRSPs**

Every February, financial institutions advertise their various RRSP products. While most people contribute just before the deadline, RRSP sellers point out the advantages of contributing early—greater returns because of compounding.[11] In our example of the future value of annuities, we found that contributing $2,000 each year at the end of the year would compound to $226,566 in 30 years at 8 percent. Suppose you made the contribution at the beginning of each year. How much more would you have after 30 years?

$$\text{Annuity due future value} = \text{Payment} \times \text{Annuity FV factor} \times (1 + r)$$
$$= \$2,000 \times (1.08^8 - 1)/.08 \times (1.08)$$
$$= \$244,692$$

You would have $244,692 - $226,566 = $18,126 more. |

Perpetuities

We've seen that a series of level cash flows can be valued by treating those cash flows as an annuity. An important special case of an annuity arises when the level stream of cash flows continues forever. Such an asset is called a **perpetuity** because the cash flows are perpetual. Perpetuities are also called **consols**.

    Since a perpetuity has an infinite number of cash flows, we obviously can't compute its value by discounting each one. Fortunately, valuing a perpetuity turns out to be the easiest possible case. Consider a perpetuity that costs $1,000 and offers a 12 percent rate of return with payments at the end of each period. The cash flow each year must be $1,000 × .12 = $120. More generally, the present value of a perpetuity (PV = $1,000) multiplied by the rate (r = 12%) must equal the cash flow (C = $120):

$$\text{Perpetuity present value} \times \text{Rate} = \text{Cash flow}$$
$$PV \times r = C$$

Therefore, given a cash flow and a rate of return, we can compute the present value very easily:

$$PV \text{ for a perpetuity} = C/r = C \times (1/r)$$

For example, an investment offers a perpetual cash flow of $500 every year. The return you require on such an investment is 8 percent. What is the value of this investment? The value of this perpetuity is:

$$\text{Perpetuity PV} = C \times (1/r) = \$500/.08 = \$6,250$$

Another way of seeing why a perpetuity's value is so easy to determine is to take a look at the expression for an annuity present value factor:

$$\text{Annuity present value factor} = (1 - \text{Present value factor})/r$$
$$= (1/r) \times (1 - \text{Present value factor})$$

perpetuity
An annuity in which the cash flows continue forever.

consol
A perpetual bond.

---

[10] The present value of an annuity due is found in the same way: Annuity due present value = Payment × Annuity PV factor × (1 + r).

[11] "How to Give Your RRSP Extra Punch," *Mackenzie Insight,* Winter 1992.

As we have seen, when the number of periods involved gets very large, the present value factor gets very small. As a result, the annuity factor gets closer and closer to $1/r$. At 10 percent, for example, the annuity present value factor for 100 years is:

$$\text{Annuity present value factor} = (1/.10) \times (1 - 1/1.10^{100})$$
$$= (1/.10) \times (1 - .000073)$$
$$\approx (1/.10)$$

E X A M P L E | 5.20   Preferred Stock

Fixed rate preferred stock is an important example of a perpetuity.[12] When a corporation sells fixed rate preferred, the buyer is promised a fixed cash dividend every period (usually every quarter) forever. This dividend must be paid before any dividend can be paid to regular shareholders, hence the term *preferred*.

Suppose the Home Bank of Canada wants to sell preferred stock at $100 per share. A very similar issue of preferred stock already outstanding has a price of $40 per share and offers a dividend of $1 every quarter. What dividend would the Home Bank have to offer if the preferred stock is going to sell?

The issue that is already out has a present value of $40 and a cash flow of $1 every quarter forever. Since this is a perpetuity:

$$\text{Present value} = \$40 = \$1 \times (1/r)$$
$$r = 2.5\%$$

To be competitive, the new Home Bank issue would also have to offer 2.5 percent *per quarter;* so, if the present value is to be $100, the dividend must be such that:

$$\text{Present value} = \$100 = C \times (1/.025)$$
$$C = \$2.50 \text{ (per quarter)}$$

CONCEPT QUESTIONS

1. In general, what is the present value of an annuity of C dollars per period at a discount rate of r per period? The future value?
2. In general, what is the present value of a perpetuity? The future value?

5.6 | COMPARING RATES: THE EFFECT OF COMPOUNDING PERIODS

The last issue we need to discuss has to do with the way interest rates are quoted. This subject causes a fair amount of confusion because rates are quoted in many different ways. Sometimes the way a rate is quoted is the result of tradition, and sometimes it's the result of legislation. Unfortunately, at times, borrowers and investors don't understand rate quotations. We discuss these topics in this section.

Effective Annual Rates and Compounding

If a rate is quoted as 10 percent compounded semiannually, the investment actually pays 5 percent every six months. A natural question then arises: Is 5 percent every six months the same thing as 10 percent per year? It's easy to see that it is not. If you invest $1 at 10 percent per year, you will have $1.10 at the end of the year. If you

---

[12] Corporations also issue floating rate preferred stock as we discuss in Chapter 12.

invest at 5 percent every six months, then you'll have the future value of $1 at 5 percent for two periods, or:

$$\$1 \times (1.05)^2 = \$1.1025$$

This is .0025 more. The reason is very simple. What has occurred is that your account is credited with $1 × .05 = 5 cents in interest after six months. In the following six months, you earned 5 percent on that nickel, for an extra 5 × .05 = .25 cents.

As our example illustrates, 10 percent compounded semiannually is actually equivalent to 10.25 percent per year. Put another way, we would be indifferent between 10 percent compounded semiannually and 10.25 percent compounded annually. Anytime we have compounding during the year, we need to be concerned about what the rate really is.

In our example, the 10 percent is called a **stated** or **quoted interest rate**. Other names are used as well. The 10.25 percent, which is actually the rate that you earn, is called the **effective annual rate (EAR)**. To compare different investments or interest rates, we always need to convert to effective rates. Some general procedures for doing this are discussed next.

stated or quoted interest rate
The interest rate expressed in terms of the interest payment made each period. Also quoted interest rate.

effective annual rate (EAR)
The interest rate expressed as if it were compounded once per year.

Calculating and Comparing Effective Annual Rates

To see why it is important to work only with effective rates, suppose that you've shopped around and come up with the following three rates.

Bank A: 15 percent, compounded daily

Bank B: 15.5 percent, compounded quarterly

Trust Company C: 16 percent compounded annually

Which of these is the best if you are thinking of opening a savings account? Which of these is best if they represent loan rates?

To begin, Trust Company C is offering 16 percent per year. Because there is no compounding during the year, this is the effective rate. Bank B is actually paying .155/4 = .03875 or 3.875 percent per quarter. At this rate, an investment of $1 for four quarters would grow to:

$$\$1 \times (1.03875)^4 = \$1.1642$$

The EAR, therefore, is 16.42 percent. For a saver, this is much better than the 16 percent rate Trust Company C is offering; for a borrower, it's worse.

Bank A is compounding every day. This may seem a little extreme, but it is very common to calculate interest daily. This interest rate is actually:

$$.15/365 = .000411$$

At .0411 percent per day, an investment of $1 for 365 periods would grow to:

$$\$1 \times (1.000411)^{365} = \$1.1618$$

The EAR is 16.18 percent. This is not as good as Bank B's 16.42 percent for a saver.

This example illustrates two things: First, the highest quoted rate is not necessarily the best. Second, the compounding during the year can lead to a significant difference between the quoted rate and the effective rate. Remember that the *effective* rate is what you get or what you pay.

If you look at our examples, we computed the EARs in three steps. We first divided the quoted rate by the number of times that the interest is compounded. We then added 1 to the result and raised it to the power of the number of times the interest is compounded. Finally, we subtracted the 1. If we let m be the number of times the interest is compounded, these steps can be summarized simply as:

$$\text{EAR} = [1 + (\text{Quoted rate})/m]^m - 1 \qquad [5.7]$$

For example, suppose you were offered 12 percent compounded monthly. In this case, the interest is compounded 12 times a year; so m is 12. You can calculate the effective rate as:

$$
\begin{aligned}
\text{EAR} &= [1 + (\text{Quoted rate})/m]^m - 1 \\
&= [1 + .12/12]^{12} - 1 \\
&= 1.01^{12} - 1 \\
&= 1.126825 - 1 \\
&= 12.6825\%
\end{aligned}
$$

E X A M P L E | 5.21   What's the EAR?

A bank is offering 12 percent compounded quarterly. If you put $100 in an account, how much will you have at the end of one year? What's the EAR? How much will you have at the end of two years?

    The bank is effectively offering 12%/4 = 3% every quarter. If you invest $100 for four periods at 3 percent per period, the future value is:

$$
\begin{aligned}
\text{Future value} &= \$100 \times (1.03)^4 \\
&= \$100 \times (1.1255) \\
&= \$112.55
\end{aligned}
$$

The EAR is 12.55 percent ($100 $\times$ [1 + .1255] = $112.55).[13]

    We can determine what you have at the end of two years in two different ways: The first way is to recognize that two years is the same as eight quarters. At 3 percent per quarter, after eight quarters, you would have:

$$\$100 \times (1.03)^8 = \$100 \times 1.2668 = \$126.68$$

The second way recognizes that the interest rate is effectively 12.55 percent per year; so after two years you would have:

$$\$100 \times (1.1255)^2 = \$100 \times 1.2688 = \$126.68$$

Thus, the two calculations produce the same answer. This illustrates an important point. Anytime we do a present or future value calculation, the rate we use must be an actual or effective rate. In this case, the actual rate is 3 percent per quarter. The effective annual rate is 12.55 percent. It doesn't matter which one we use once we know the EAR. |

---

[13] To solve this problem on a common financial calculator, you use the *Effective Rate* (EFF) key. First clear the calculator and then:
1. Enter the number of compounding periods per years = 4 and press *2ndF*.
2. Press *EFF* and then enter the quoted interest rate = 12.
3. Ask the calculator for the effective annual rate by pressing the = key.

E X A M P L E | **5.22**   **Quoting a Rate**

Now that you know how to convert a quoted rate to an EAR, consider going the other way. As a lender, you know that you want to actually earn 18 percent on a particular loan. You want to quote a rate that features monthly compounding. What rate do you quote?

We know the EAR is 18 percent, and we know that this is the result of monthly compounding. Let q stand for the quoted rate. We thus have:

$$\text{EAR} = [1 + (\text{Quoted rate})/m]^m - 1$$
$$.18 = [1 + q/12]^{12} - 1$$
$$1.18 = [1 + q/12]^{12}$$

We need to solve this equation for the quoted rate. This calculation is the same as the ones we did to find an unknown interest rate in Section 5.3:

$$1.18^{(1/12)} = [1 + q/12]$$
$$1.18^{.08333} = 1 + q/12$$
$$1.0139 = 1 + q/12$$
$$.0139 = q/12.$$

This is the monthly quoted rate. On an annual basis, the rate you would quote is $1.39\% \times 12 = 16.68\%$, compounded monthly. |

Mortgages

Mortgages are a very common example of an annuity with monthly payments. To understand mortgage calculations, keep in mind two institutional arrangements: First, although payments are monthly, regulations for Canadian financial institutions require that mortgage rates be quoted with semiannual compounding. Second, financial institutions offer mortgages with interest rates fixed for various periods generally up to five years. As the borrower, you must choose the period for which the rate is fixed. (We offer some guidance in Example 5.24.) In any case, payments on conventional mortgages are calculated to maturity (usually after 25 years).

E X A M P L E | **5.23**   **What Are Your Payments?**

A financial institution is offering a $100,000 mortgage at a quoted rate of 12 percent. To find the payments, we need to find the quoted monthly rate. To do this, we convert the quoted semiannual rate to an EAR:[14]

$$\text{EAR} = [1 + \text{Quoted rate}/m]^m - 1$$
$$= [1 + .12/2]^2 - 1$$
$$= 1.06^2 - 1$$
$$= 12.36\%$$

Then we follow Example 5.22 to find the quoted monthly rate used to calculate the payments:

---

[14] Chartered banks use 10 decimal places for all calculations; this causes some rounding differences when calculating this problem.

$$\text{Quoted rate}/m = (EAR + 1)^{1/m} - 1$$
$$\text{Quoted rate}/12 = (1.1236)^{1/12} - 1$$
$$= 1.0098 - 1 = 0.98\%$$

The quoted monthly rate is 0.98 percent and there are $12 \times 25 = 300$ payments. To find the payment, we use the annuity present value formula:

$$\text{Annuity present value} = \$100,000 = C \times (1 - \text{Present value factor})/r$$
$$\$100,000 = C \times (1 - 1/1.0098^{300})/.0098$$
$$= C \times (1 - .0536)/.0098$$
$$= C \times 96.5741$$
$$C = \$1,035.50$$

Your monthly payments will be $1,035.50. |

E X A M P L E | 5.24   **Choosing the Mortgage Term**

Earlier we pointed out that while mortgages are amortized over 300 months, the rate is fixed for a shorter period usually no longer than five years. Suppose the rate of 12 percent in Example 5.23 is fixed for five years and you are wondering whether to lock in this rate or to take a lower rate of 10 percent fixed for only one year. If you chose the one-year rate, how much lower would your payments be for the first year?

The payments at 10 percent are $894.49, a reduction of $141.01 per month. If you choose to take the shorter-term mortgage with lower payments, you are betting that rates will not take a big jump over the next year leaving you with a new rate after one year much higher than 12 percent. While the mortgage formula cannot make this decision for you (it depends on risk and return discussed in Chapter 10), it does give you the risk you are facing in higher monthly payments. In 1981, mortgage rates were around 20 percent! |

EARs and APRs

annual percentage rate (APR)

The interest rate charged per period multiplied by the number of periods per year.

Sometimes it's not clear whether a rate is an effective annual rate. A case in point concerns what is called the **annual percentage rate (APR)** on a loan. Cost of borrowing disclosure regulations (part of the Bank Act) in Canada require that lenders disclose an APR on virtually all consumer loans. This rate must be displayed on a loan document in a prominent and unambiguous way.

Given that an APR must be calculated and displayed, an obvious question arises: Is an APR an effective annual rate? Put another way, if a bank quotes a car loan at 12 percent APR, is the consumer actually paying 12 percent interest? Surprisingly, the answer is no. There is some confusion over this point, which we discuss next.

The confusion over APRs arises because lenders are required by law to compute the APR in a particular way. By law, the APR is simply equal to the interest rate per period multiplied by the number of periods in a year. For example, if a bank is charging 1.2 percent per month on car loans, then the APR that must be reported is $1.2\% \times 12 = 14.4\%$. So, an APR is, in fact, a quoted or stated rate in the sense we've been discussing. For example, an APR of 12 percent on a loan calling for monthly payments is really 1 percent per month. The EAR on such a loan is thus:

$$EAR = [1 + APR/12]^{12} - 1 \qquad\qquad [5.8]$$
$$= 1.01^{12} - 1 = 12.6825\%$$

E X A M P L E | 5.25   **What Rate Are You Paying?**

Depending on the issuer, a typical credit card agreement quotes an interest rate of 18 percent APR. Monthly payments are required. What is the actual interest rate you pay on such a credit card?

Based on our discussion, an APR of 18 percent with monthly payments is really .18/12 = .015 or 1.5 percent per month. The EAR is thus:

$$\text{EAR} = [1 + .18/12]^{12} - 1$$
$$= 1.015^{12} - 1$$
$$= 1.1956 - 1$$
$$= 19.56\%$$

This is the rate you actually pay. |

The difference between an APR and an EAR probably won't be all that great, but it is somewhat ironic that the cost of borrowing disclosure regulations sometimes require lenders to be untruthful about the actual rate on a loan.

Taking It to the Limit: A Note on Continuous Compounding

If you made a deposit in a savings account, how often could your money be compounded during the year? If you think about it, there isn't really any upper limit. We've seen that daily compounding, for example, isn't a problem. There is no reason to stop here, however. We could compound every hour or minute or second. How high would the EAR get in this case? Table 5.5 illustrates the EARs that would result as 10 percent is compounded at shorter and shorter intervals. Notice that the EARs do keep getting larger, but the differences get very small.

As the numbers in Table 5.5 suggest, there is an upper limit to the EAR. If we let q stand for the quoted rate, then, as the number of times the interest is compounded gets extremely large, the EAR approaches:

$$\text{EAR} = e^q - 1 \qquad\qquad\qquad [5.9]$$

where e is Euler's (rhymes with *toiler's*) constant, 2.71828 (look for a key labelled e^x on your calculator). For example, with our 10 percent rate, the highest possible EAR is:

$$\text{EAR} = e^q - 1$$
$$= (2.71828)^{.10} - 1$$
$$= 1.1051709 - 1$$
$$= 10.51709\%$$

Compounding Periods	Times Compounded	Effective Annual Rate
Year	1	10.00000%
Quarter	4	10.38129
Month	12	10.47131
Week	52	10.50648
Day	365	10.51558
Hour	8,760	10.51703
Minute	525,600	10.51709

T A B L E 5.5

Compounding frequency and effective annual rates

In this case, the money is continuously or instantaneously compounded. What is happening is that interest is credited the instant it is earned, so the amount of interest grows continuously.

> ### CONCEPT QUESTIONS
> 1. If an interest rate is given as 12 percent, compounded daily, what do we call this rate?
> 2. What is an APR? What is an EAR? Are they the same thing?
> 3. In general, what is the relationship between a stated interest rate and an effective interest rate? Which is more relevant for financial decisions?
> 4. How does a mortgage in Canada differ from an ordinary annuity?
> 5. What does continuous compounding mean?

5.7 | LOAN TYPES AND LOAN AMORTIZATION

Whenever a lender extends a loan, some provision is made for repayment of the principal (the original loan amount). A loan might be repaid in equal installments, for example, or it might be repaid in a single lump sum. Because the way that the principal and interest are paid is up to the parties involved, the number of possibilities is actually unlimited.

A few forms of repayment are used quite often, and more complicated forms can usually be built up from these. The three basic types are pure discount loans, interest-only loans, and amortized loans. As we see, working with these loans is a very straightforward application of the present value principles that we have already developed.

Pure Discount Loans

The pure discount loan is the simplest form. With such a loan, the borrower receives money today and repays a single lump sum at some time in the future. A one-year, 10 percent pure discount loan, for example, would require the borrower to repay $1.10 in one year for every dollar borrowed today.

Because a pure discount loan is so simple, we already know how to value one. Suppose a borrower was able to repay $25,000 in five years. If we, acting as the lender, wanted a 12 percent interest rate on the loan, how much would we be willing to lend? Put another way, what value would we assign today to that $25,000 to be repaid in five years? Based on our work in this chapter, we know that the answer is just the present value of $25,000 at 12 percent for five years.

$$\text{Present value} = \$25,000/1.12^5$$
$$= \$25,000/1.7623$$
$$= \$14,186$$

Pure discount loans are very common when the loan term is short, say, a year or less. In recent years, they have become increasingly common for much longer periods.

E X A M P L E | **5.26** **Treasury Bills**

When the government of Canada borrows money on a short-term basis (a year or less), it does so by selling what are called Treasury bills or T-bills for short. A T-bill is a promise by the government to repay a fixed amount at some time in the future, for example, 3 or 12 months.

Treasury bills are pure discount loans. If a T-bill promises to repay $10,000 in 12 months, and the market interest rate is 7 percent, how much does the bill sell for in the market?

Since the going rate is 7 percent, the T-bill sells for the present value of $10,000 to be paid in one year at 7 percent, or:

Present value = $10,000/1.07 = $9,345.79

In recent years, the government of Canada has emphasized T-bills over Canada Savings Bonds when seeking short-term financing. T-bills are originally issued in denominations of $1 million. Investment dealers buy T-bills and break them up into smaller denominations, some as small as $1,000, for resale to individual investors.[15]

Interest-Only Loans

A second type of loan repayment plan calls for the borrower to pay interest each period and to repay the entire principal (the original loan amount) at some point in the future. Such loans are called *interest-only loans*. Notice that if there is just one period, a pure discount loan and an interest-only loan are the same thing.

For example, with a three-year, 10 percent interest-only loan of $1,000, the borrower would pay $1,000 × .10 = $100 in interest at the end of the first and second years. At the end of the third year, the borrower would return the $1,000 along with another $100 in interest for that year. Similarly, a 50-year interest-only loan would call for the borrower to pay interest every year for the next 50 years and then repay the principal. In the extreme, the borrower pays the interest every period forever and never repays any principal. As we discussed in the chapter, the result is a perpetuity.

Most bonds issued by the government of Canada, the provinces, and corporations have the general form of an interest-only loan. Because we consider bonds in some detail in the next chapter, we defer a further discussion of them for now.

Amortized Loans

With a pure discount or interest-only loan, the principal is repaid all at once. An alternative is an *amortized loan* where the lender may require the borrower to repay parts of the loan amount over time. The process of paying off a loan by making regular principal reductions is called *amortizing* the loan.

A simple way of amortizing a loan is to have the borrower pay the interest each period plus some fixed amount. This approach is common with consumer loans and is used for some medium-term business loans. For example, suppose a business takes out a $5,000, five-year loan at 9 percent. The loan agreement calls for the borrower to pay the interest on the loan balance each year and to reduce the loan balance each year by $1,000. Since the loan amount declines by $1,000 each year, it is fully paid in five years.

In the loan we are considering, notice that the total payment declines each year. The reason is that the loan balance goes down, resulting in a lower interest charge each year, while the $1,000 principal reduction is constant. For example, the interest in the first year is $5,000 × .09 = $450. The total payment is $1,000 + 450 = $1,450. In the second year, the loan balance is $4,000, so the interest is $4,000 × .09 = $360,

---

[15] The smallest denomination of T-bill offered varies across financial institutions.

and the total payment is \$1,360. We can calculate the total payment in each of the remaining years by preparing a simple *amortization schedule* as follows:

Year	Beginning Balance	Total Payment	Interest Paid	Principal Paid	Ending Balance
1	\$5,000	\$1,450	\$ 450	\$1,000	\$4,000
2	4,000	1,360	360	1,000	3,000
3	3,000	1,270	270	1,000	2,000
4	2,000	1,180	180	1,000	1,000
5	1,000	1,090	90	1,000	0
Totals		\$6,350	\$1,350	\$5,000	

Notice that, in each year, the interest paid is just given by the beginning balance multiplied by the interest rate. Also notice that the beginning balance is given by the ending balance from the previous year.

Probably the most common way of amortizing a loan is for the borrower to make a single, fixed payment every period. Almost all consumer loans (such as car loans) and mortgages work this way. For example, suppose our five-year, 9 percent, \$5,000 loan was amortized this way. How would the amortization schedule look?

We first need to determine the payment. From our discussion in the chapter, we know that the loan's cash flows are in the form of an ordinary annuity, so we can solve for the payment as follows:

$$\$5,000 = C \times (1 - 1/1.09^5)/.09$$
$$= C \times (1 - .6499)/.09$$

This gives us:

$$C = \$5,000/3.8897$$
$$= \$1,285.46$$

The borrower therefore makes five equal payments of \$1,285.46. Will this pay off the loan? We can check by filling in an amortization schedule.

In our previous example, we knew the principal reduction each year. We then calculated the interest owed to get the total payment. In this example, we know the total payment. We thus calculate the interest and then subtract it from the total payment to calculate the principal portion in each payment.

In the first year, the interest is \$450 as we calculated before. Since the total payment is \$1,285.46, the principal paid in the first year must be:

$$\text{Principal paid} = \$1,285.46 - 450 = \$835.46$$

The ending loan balance is thus:

$$\text{Ending balance} = \$5,000 - 835.46 = \$4,164.54$$

The interest in the second year is \$4,164.54 × .09 = \$374.81, and the loan balance declines by \$1,285.46 − 374.81 = \$910.65. We can summarize all of the relevant calculations in the following schedule.[16]

---

[16] The amortization of loan payments may be determined using your calculator once you have mastered the calculation of the loan payment (see footnote 8). Once you have completed the four-step procedure to find the loan payment, you can find the amortization of any payment.
  1. Input the payment number and press *AMRT*. This initially gives you the principal returned. For example, input 1.0 and press *AMRT*. You get \$835.46.
  2. Pressing *AMRT* again gives the interest paid.
  3. Pressing *AMRT* a third time gives you the balance of principal.
  On Hewlett-Packard calculators, simply press *AMRT* when you are in the TVM mode and then input the number of payments to amortize by pressing the soft key corresponding to *#P*.

Year	Beginning Balance	Total Payment	Interest Paid	Principal Paid	Ending Balance
1	$5,000.00	$1,285.46	$ 450.00	$ 835.46	$4,164.54
2	4,164.54	1,285.46	374.81	910.65	3,253.88
3	3,253.88	1,285.46	292.85	992.61	2,261.27
4	2,261.27	1,285.46	203.51	1,081.95	1,179.32
5	1,179.32	1,285.46	106.14	1,179.32	0.00
Totals		$6,427.31	$1,427.31	$5,000.00	

Since the loan balance declines to zero, the five equal payments do pay off the loan. Notice that the interest paid declines each period. This isn't surprising because the loan balance is going down. Given that the total payment is fixed, the principal paid must be rising each period.

Finally, notice that when we use the annuity present value formula to calculate loan payments, we automatically obtain an amortization schedule with two properties. Interest is computed on the declining balance and the loan is fully amortized over its life.

If you compare the two loan amortizations in this section, you see that the total interest is greater for the equal total payment case, $1,427.31 versus $1,350. The reason for this is that the loan is repaid more slowly early on, so the interest is somewhat higher. This doesn't mean that one loan is better than the other; it simply means that one is effectively paid off faster than the other. For example, the principal reduction in the first year is $835.46 in the equal total payment case compared to $1,000 in the first case.

E X A M P L E | 5.27   Partial Amortization or "Bite the Bullet" Mortgages

As we explained earlier, real estate lending usually involves mortgages with a loan period far shorter than the mortgage life. A common example might call for a 5-year loan with, say, a 15-year amortization. This means the borrower makes a payment every month of a fixed amount based on a 15-year amortization. However, after 60 months, the borrower either negotiates a new five-year loan or makes a single, much larger payment called a *balloon* or *bullet* to pay off the loan. Balloon payments are common in commercial mortgages. In either case, because the monthly payments don't fully pay off the loan, the loan is said to be partially amortized.

Suppose we have a $100,000 commercial mortgage with a 12 percent rate compounded semiannually and a 20-year (240-month) amortization. Further suppose that the mortgage has a five-year balloon. What will the monthly payment be? How big will the balloon payment be?

The monthly payment can be calculated based on an ordinary annuity with a present value of $100,000. To find the monthly rate, we first have to find the EAR and then convert it to a quoted monthly rate. To do this, we convert the quoted semiannual rate to an EAR.

$$\text{EAR} = [1 + \text{Quoted rate}/m]^m - 1$$
$$= [1 + .12/2]^2 - 1$$
$$= 1.06^2 - 1$$
$$= 12.36\%$$

Then, we follow Example 5.22 to find the quoted monthly rate used to calculate the payments:

$$\text{Quoted rate}/m = (\text{EAR} + 1)^{1/m} - 1$$
$$\text{Quoted rate}/12 = (1.1236)^{1/12} - 1$$
$$= 1.0098 - 1 = 0.98\%$$

EFFECTIVE

The ~~quoted~~ monthly rate is 0.98 percent and there are $12 \times 20 = 240$ payments. To find the payment amount, we use the annuity present value formula.

$$\text{Annuity present value} = \$100,000 = C \times (1 - \text{Present value factor})/r$$
$$\$100,000 = C \times (1 - 1/1.0098^{240})/.0098$$
$$= C \times (1 - .0972)/.0098$$
$$= C \times 92.5092$$
$$C = \$1,080.97$$

Your monthly payments will be \$1,080.97.

Now, there is an easy way and a hard way to determine the balloon payment. The hard way is to actually amortize the loan for 60 months to see what the balance is at that time. The easy way is to recognize that after 60 months, we have a $240 - 60 = 180$-month loan. The payment is still \$1,080.97 per month, and the interest rate is still .98 percent per month. The loan balance is thus the present value of the remaining payments:

$$\text{Loan balance} = \$1,080.97 \times (1 - 1/1.0098^{180})/.0098$$
$$= \$1,080.97 \times 84.6303$$
$$= \$91,482.84[17]$$

The balloon payment is a substantial \$91,483. Why is it so large? To get an idea, consider the first payment on the mortgage. The interest in the first month is $\$100,000 \times .0098 = \$975.88$ (rounding difference). Your payment is \$1,080.97, so the loan balance declines by only \$105.09. Since the loan balance declines so slowly, the cumulative pay down over five years is not great. |

CONCEPT QUESTIONS

1. What are the basic loan types? Give an example of each.
2. Some home owners believe it is unfair that mortgage payments are almost all interest in the early years. Do you agree?

5.8 | SUMMARY AND CONCLUSIONS

This chapter has introduced you to the basic principles of present value and discounted cash flow valuation. Table 5.6 contains a summary of the basic calculations we describe. In the chapter, we explain a number of things about the time value of money, including:

1. For a given rate of return, the value at some point in the future of an investment made today can be determined by calculating the future value of that investment.
2. The current worth of a future cash flow or a series of cash flows can be determined for a given rate of return by calculating the present value of the cash flow(s) involved.
3. The relationship between present value (PV) and future value (FV) for a given rate r and time t is given by the basic present value equation:

$$PV = FV_t/(1 + r)^t$$

---

[17]When using a calculator with an amortization function, the value is found to be \$91,483.18.

I. Symbols:

PV = Present value, what future cash flows are worth today
FV_t = Future value, what cash flows are worth in the future
r = Interest rate, rate of return, or discount rate per period—typically, but not always, one year
t = Number of periods—typically, but not always, the number of years
C = Cash amount

II. Future value of C invested at r percent per period for t periods:

$$FV_t = C \times (1 + r)^t$$

The term $(1 + r)^t$ is called the *future value factor.*

III. Present value of C to be received in t periods at r percent per period:

$$PV = C/(1 + r)^t$$

The term $1/(1 + r)^t$ is called the *present value factor.*

IV. Future value of C per period for t periods at r percent per period:

$$FV_t = C \times [(1 + r)^t - 1]/r$$

A series of identical cash flows is called an *annuity,* and the term $[(1 + r)^t - 1]/r$ is called the *annuity future value factor.*

V. Present value of C per period for t periods at r percent per period:

$$PV = C \times [1 - \{1/(1 + r)^t\}]/r$$

The term $\{1 - \{1/(1 + r)^t\}\}/r$ is called the *annuity present value factor.*

VI. Present value of a perpetuity of C per period:

$$PV = C/r$$

A *perpetuity* has the same cash flow every year forever.

As we have shown, it is possible to find any one of the four components (PV, FV_t, r, t) given the other three.

4. A series of constant cash flows that arrive or are paid at the end of each period is called an ordinary annuity, and we describe some useful shortcuts for determining the present and future values of annuities.

5. Interest rates can be quoted in a variety of ways. When making financial decisions, any rates being compared must be converted to effective rates. The relationship between a quoted rate, such as an annual percentage rate (APR), and an effective annual rate (EAR) is given by:

$$EAR = [1 + \text{Quoted rate}/m]^m - 1$$

where m is the number of times during the year the money is compounded or, equivalently, the number of payments during the year.

The principles developed in this chapter figure prominently in the chapters to come. The reason for this is that most investments, whether they involve real assets or financial assets, can be analyzed using the discounted cash flow (DCF) approach. As a result, the DCF approach is broadly applicable and widely used in practice. For example, the next chapter shows how to value bonds and stocks using an extension of the techniques presented in this chapter. Before going on, however, you might want to do some of the following problems.

Many students find it useful to consider two questions when solving time value problems:

1. Is the answer sought in present or future value?
2. Do the cash flows involved represent annuities, single sums, or a combination?

Key Terms

nominal rate of interest (page 136)

real interest rate (page 136)

future value (FV) (page 137)

compounding (page 137)

interest on interest (page 137)

compound interest (page 137)

simple interest (page 137)

present value (PV) (page 143)

discount (page 143)

discount rate (page 144)

annuity (page 156)

annuity due (page 160)

perpetuity (page 161)

consol (page 161)

stated or quoted interest rate (page 163)

effective annual rate (EAR) (page 163)

annual percentage rate (APR) (page 166)

Chapter Review Problems and Self-Test

5.1   **Compound Interest**   In 1867, George Edward Lee found an astrolabe (a 17th-century navigating device) originally lost by Samuel de Champlain on his property in Ontario. Lee sold the astrolabe to a stranger for $10. In 1989 the Canadian Museum of Civilization purchased the astrolabe for $250,000 from the New York Historical Society. (How it got there is a long story.) It appears that Lee has been swindled; however, suppose he had invested the $10 at 10 percent. How much would it be worth in 1995?

5.2   **Calculating Future Values**   Assume that you deposit $1,000 today in an account that pays 8 percent interest. How much will you have in four years? How much will you have if the 8 percent is compounded quarterly? How much will you have in 4½ years?

5.3   **Calculating Present Values**   Suppose you have just celebrated your 19th birthday. A rich uncle set up a trust fund for you that will pay you $100,000 when you turn 25. If the relevant discount rate is 11 percent, how much is this fund worth today?

5.4   **More Present Values**   A first-round draft choice quarterback has been signed to a three-year, $10 million contract. The details provided for an immediate cash bonus of $1 million. The player is to receive $2 million in salary at the end of the first year, $3 million the next, and $4 million at the end of the last year. Assuming a 10 percent discount rate, is this package worth $10 million? How much is it worth?

5.5   **Future Value with Multiple Cash Flows**   You plan to make a series of deposits in an interest-bearing account. You deposit $1,000 today, $2,000 in two years, and $8,000 in five years. If you withdrew $3,000 in three years and $5,000 in seven years, how much will you have after eight years if the interest rate is 9 percent? What is the present value of these cash flows?

5.6 **Annuity Present Value** You are looking into an investment that would pay you $12,000 per year for the next 10 years. If you require a 15 percent return, what is the most you would pay for this investment?

5.7 **Payments** A family is going to finance a new home with a 25-year mortgage for $75,000. The financial institution has offered to lend the $75,000 at a quoted rate of 12 percent APR (remember semiannual compounding). At this interest rate, what will the monthly payments be?

5.8 **APR versus EAR** The going rate on student loans is quoted as 9 percent APR. The terms of the loan call for monthly payments. What is the effective annual rate (EAR) on such a student loan?

Answers to Self-Test Problems

5.1 At 10 percent, the $10 would have grown quite a bit over 128 years. The future value factor is:

$$(1 + r)^t = 1.1^{128} = \$198,730.12$$

The future value is thus on the order of:

$$\$10 \times 198,730.12 = \$1,987,301.$$

5.2 We need to calculate the future value of $1,000 at 8 percent for four years. The future value factor is:

$$1.08^4 = 1.3605$$

The future value is thus $1,000 × 1.3605 = $1,360.50. If the 8 percent is compounded quarterly, the rate is actually 2 percent per quarter. In four years, there are 16 quarters; so the future value factor is now:

$$1.02^{16} = 1.3728$$

The future value of your $1,000 is thus $1,372.80, which is a little more than before because of the extra compounding. Notice that we could have calculated the EAR first:

$$EAR = [1 + .08/4]^4 - 1 = 8.24322\%$$

The future value factor would then be:

$$1.0824322^4 = 1.3728$$

This is just as we calculated. To find the future value after 4½ years, we could either use the actual quarterly rate with 18 quarters or the effective annual rate with 4.5 years. We'll do both:

$$\text{Future value} = \$1,000 \times (1.02)^{18} = \$1,000 \times 1.42825 = \$1,428.25$$

Or:

$$\text{Future value} = \$1,000 \times (1.0824322)^{4.5} = \$1,000 \times 1.42825$$
$$= \$1,428.25$$

5.3 We need the present value of $100,000 to be paid in six years at 11 percent. The discount factor is:

$$1/1.11^6 + 1/1.8704 = .5346$$

The present value is about $53,460.

5.4   Obviously, the package is not worth $10 million because the payments are spread out over three years. The bonus is paid today, so it's worth $1 million. The present values for the three subsequent salary payments are:

$$\$2/1.1 + 3/1.1^2 + 4/1.1^3 = \$2/1.1 + 3/1.21 + 4/1.3310 = \$7.3028$$

The package is worth a total of $8.3028 million.

5.5   We calculate the future values for each of the cash flows separately and then add them up. Notice that we treat the withdrawals as negative cash flows:

$\$1,000 \times 1.09^8 =$	$\$1,000 \times 1.9926 =$	$\$\ 1,992.60$
$\$2,000 \times 1.09^6 =$	$\$2,000 \times 1.6771 =$	$\$\ 3,354.20$
$-\$3,000 \times 1.09^5 =$	$\$3,000 \times 1.5386 =$	$-\$\ 4,615.87$
$\$8,000 \times 1.09^3 =$	$\$8,000 \times 1.2950 =$	$\$10,360.23$
$-\$5,000 \times 1.09^1 =$	$-\$5,000 \times 1.0900 =$	$-\$\ 5,450.00$
	Total future value	$\$\ 5,641.12$

This value includes a small rounding error.

To calculate the present value, we could discount each cash flow back to the present or we could discount back a single year at a time. However, since we already know that the future value in eight years is $5,641.12, the easy way to get the PV is just to discount this amount back eight years:

$$\text{Present value} = \$5,641.12/1.09^8 = \$5,641.12/1.9926 = \$2,831.03$$

We again ignore a small rounding error. For practice, you can verify that this is what you get if you discount each cash flow back separately.

5.6   The most you would be willing to pay is the present value of $12,000 per year for 10 years at a 15 percent discount rate. The cash flows here are in ordinary annuity form, so the relevant present value factor is:

$$\begin{aligned}
\text{Annuity present value factor} &= (1 - (1/1.15^{10}))/.15 \\
&= (1 - .2472)/.15 \\
&= 5.0188
\end{aligned}$$

The present value of the 10 cash flows is thus:

$$\begin{aligned}
\text{Present value} &= \$12,000 \times 5.0188 \\
&= \$60,225
\end{aligned}$$

This is the most you would pay.

5.7   At 12 percent APR, the payments are calculated by finding the relevant monthly interest rate as follows:

$$\begin{aligned}
\text{EAR} &= [1 + \text{Quoted Rate}/2]^2 - 1 \\
&= [1 + .12/2]^2 - 1 \\
&= 12.36\% \\
\text{monthly rate} &= (1.1236)^{1/12} - 1 \\
&= 0.98\% \\
C &= \text{Present value/annuity present value factor} \\
&= \text{PV}/(1 - (1/1.0098^{300}))/.0098 \\
&= \$75,000/96.9087 \\
&= \$773.92
\end{aligned}$$

5.8   A rate of 9 percent APR with monthly payments is actually 9%/12 = .75% per month. The EAR is thus:

$$\text{EAR} = [1 + .09/12]^{12} - 1 = 9.38\%$$

Questions and Problems

Basic
(Questions 1–38)

1. **Simple Interest versus Compound Interest** Simpleton Bank pays 5 percent simple interest on its savings account balances, while Complexity Bank pays 5 percent interest compounded annually. If you made a $10,000 deposit in each bank, how much additional money would you earn from your Complexity Bank account at the end of 12 years?

2. **Calculating Future Values** For each of the following, compute the future value:

Present Value	Years	Interest Rate	Future Value
$ 570	15	9%	
$ 8,922	9	18%	
$ 61,133	3	12%	
$219,850	10	4%	

3. **Calculating Present Values** For each of the following, compute the present value:

Future Value	Years	Interest Rate	Present Value
$ 349	5	6%	
$ 5,227	20	2%	
$ 48,950	12	25%	
$612,511	7	33%	

4. **Calculating Interest Rates** Solve for the unknown interest rate in each of the following:

Present Value	Years	Interest Rate	Future Value
$ 475	4		$ 615
$ 7,350	7		$ 18,350
$27,175	11		$ 65,000
$93,412	19		$200,000

5. **Calculating the Number of Periods** Solve for the unknown number of years in each of the following:

Present Value	Years	Interest Rate	Future Value
$ 1,200		8%	$ 2,550
$ 16,310		12%	$ 21,225
$ 75,000		3%	$175,000
$183,650		29%	$912,475

6. **Calculating Interest Rates** Assume the total cost of a university education will be $50,000 when your child enters university in 18 years. You presently have $5,000 to invest. What rate of interest must you earn on your investment to cover the cost of your child's university education?

7. **Calculating the Number of Periods** At 9 percent interest, how long does it take to double your money? To triple? *roughly 8*

8. **Calculating Interest Rates** You are offered an investment that requires you to put up $4,000 today in exchange for $10,000 eight years from now. What is the rate of return on this investment?

9. **Calculating the Number of Periods** You're trying to save to buy a new $20,000 speedboat to take to the lake. You have $16,000 today that can be

invested at your bank. The bank pays 6 percent annual interest on its accounts. How long will it be before you have enough to buy the speedboat?

10. **Calculating Present Value**   Rarely Prudent, Inc., has an unfunded pension liability of $225 million that must be paid in 17 years. To assess the value of the firm's stock, financial analysts want to discount this liability back to the present. If the relevant discount rate is 8.5 percent, what is the present value of this liability?

11. **Present Value and Multiple Cash Flows**   Looking Good Co. has identified an investment project with the following cash flows. If the discount rate is 10 percent, what is the present value of these cash flows? What is the present value at 14 percent? At 20 percent?

Year	Cash Flow
1	$500
2	$700
3	$600
4	$300

12. **Present Value and Multiple Cash Flows**   Investment X offers to pay you $2,000 per year for four years, while Investment Y offers to pay you $2,500 per year for three years. Which of these cash flow streams has the higher present value if the discount rate is 5 percent? If the discount rate is 20 percent?

13. **Future Value and Multiple Cash Flows**   ABC Co. has identified an investment project with the following cash flows. If the discount rate is 6 percent, what is the future value of these cash flows in Years 4? What is the future value at a discount rate of 8 percent? At 16 percent?

Year	Cash Flow
1	$900
2	$800
3	$700
4	$600

14. **Calculating Annuity Present Value**   An investment offers $1,500 per year for 12 years, with the first payment occurring one year from now. If the required return is 12 percent, what is the value of the investment? What would the value be if the payments occurred for 35 years? 60 years? Forever?

15. **Calculating Annuity Cash Flows**   If you put up $55,000 today in exchange for a 9 percent, 7-year annuity, what will the annual cash flow be?

16. **Calculating Annuity Values**   Your company will generate $27,000 annual payments each year for the next eight years from a new information data base. The computer system needed to set up the data base costs $180,000. If you can borrow the money to buy the computer system at 7 percent annual interest, can you afford the new system?

17. **Annuity Values**   If you deposit $600 at the end of the next 10 years into an account paying 9.5 percent interest, how much money will you have in the account in 10 years? How much will you have in 13 years?

18. **Annuity Values**   You want to have $17,000 in your savings account six years from now, and you're prepared to make equal annual deposits into the account at the end of each year. If the account pays 8 percent interest, what amount must you deposit each year?

PVA

19. **Annuity Values**   Betty's Bank offers you a $7,000 six-year term loan at 10 percent annual interest. What will your annual loan payment be?

Basic (Continued)

20. **Perpetuity Values**   Bob's Life Insurance Co. is trying to sell you an investment policy that will pay you and your heirs $700 per year forever. If the required return on this investment is 12 percent, how much will you pay for the policy?

21. **Perpetuity Values**   In the previous problem, suppose Bob told you the policy costs $8,500. At what interest rate would this be a fair deal?

22. **Calculating EAR**   Find the EAR in each of the cases below:

Stated Rate (APR)	Number of Times Compounded	Effective Rate (EAR)
10%	Quarterly	
16	Monthly	
9	Daily	
21	Infinite	

23. **Calculating APR**   Find the APR or stated rate in each of the cases below:

Stated Rate (APR)	Number of Times Compounded	Effective Rate (EAR)
	Semiannually	8%
	Monthly	12
	Weekly	17
	Infinite	24

24. **Calculating EAR**   The Bank of Upper Canada charges 8 percent, compounded quarterly, on its business loans. The Bank of New Brunswick charges 8.5 percent compounded semiannually. As a potential borrower, which bank would you go to for a new loan?

25. **Calculating APR**   Colossus Banken Corp. wants to earn an effective annual return on its consumer loans of 9 percent per year. The bank uses monthly compounding on its loans. What interest rate is the bank required by law to report to potential borrowers? Explain why this rate is misleading to an uninformed borrower.

26. **Calculating Future Value**   What is the future value of $900 in 16 years assuming an interest rate of 11 percent compounded quarterly?

27. **Calculating Future Value**   Kommisar's Kredit Bank is offering 4 percent compounded daily on its savings accounts. If you deposit $300 today, how much will you have in the account in 3 years? In 4 years? In 20 years?

28. **Calculating Present Value**   An investment will pay you $34,000 in four years. If the appropriate discount rate is 11 percent compounded daily, what is the present value?

29. **EAR versus APR**   Roger Ripov's Pawn Shop charges an interest rate of 25 percent per month on loans to its customers. Like all lenders, Roger Ripov must report an APR to consumers. What rate should the shop report? What is the effective annual rate?

30. **Calculating Loan Payments**   You want to buy a new sports coupe for $26,500, and the finance office at the dealership has quoted you an 11.9 percent APR loan for 60 months to buy the car. What will your monthly payments be? What is the effective annual rate on this loan?

31. **Calculating Number of Periods**   One of your customers is delinquent on his accounts payable balance. You've mutually agreed to a repayment schedule of

log question (ln)

$263 per month. You will charge 1.2 percent per month interest on the overdue balance. If the current balance is $8,794.29, how long will it take for the account to be paid off?

32. **Calculating EAR**   A local loan shark offers you "three for four or I knock on your door." This means you get $3 today and repay $4 when you get your paycheck in five days (or else). What's the effective annual return the loan shark earns on his lending business? If you're brave enough to ask him, what APR would he say you're paying?

33. **Valuing Perpetuities**   Lollapalooza Life Insurance Co. is selling a perpetual annuity contract that pays $500 monthly. The contract currently sells for $60,000. What is the monthly return on this investment vehicle? What is the APR? The effective annual return?

34. **Calculating Annuity Future Values**   You make monthly deposits of $50 into a retirement account that pays 15 percent interest compounded monthly. If your first deposit will be made one month from now, how large will your retirement account be in 20 years?

35. **Calculating Annuity Future Values**   In the previous problem, suppose you make $750 annual deposits into the same retirement account. How large will your account balance be in 15 years?

36. **Calculating Annuity Present Values**   Beginning three months from now, you want to be able to withdraw $1,000 each quarter from your bank account to cover university expenses over the next three years. If the account pays 3 percent interest per quarter, how much do you need to have in your bank account today to meet your expense needs over the next three years?

37. **Discounted Cash Flow Analysis**   If the appropriate discount rate for the following cash flows is 12 percent compounded quarterly, what is the present value of the cash flows?

Year	Cash Flow
1	$3,500
2	$4,900
3	$ 0
4	$5,500

38. **Discounted Cash Flow Analysis**   If the appropriate discount rate for the following cash flows is 9.8 percent per year, what is the present value of the cash flows?

Year	Cash Flow
1	$800
2	$ 0
3	$450
4	$650

39. **Simple Interest versus Compound Interest**   Simpleton Bank pays 8 percent simple interest on its investment accounts. If Complexity Bank pays interest on its accounts compounded annually, what rate should the bank set if it wants to match Simpleton Bank over an investment horizon of 10 years?

40. **Calculating EAR**   You are looking at an investment that has an effective annual rate of 16 percent. What is the effective semiannual return? The effective quarterly return? The effective monthly return?

41. **Comparing Cash Flow Streams**   You've just joined the investment banking firm of Godel, Esher, and Bock. They've offered you two different salary arrangements. You can have $40,000 per year for the next two years or $20,000 per year for the next two years, along with a $30,000 signing bonus today. If the interest rate is 14 percent compounded monthly, which do you prefer?

Intermediate
(Continued)

42. **Calculating Present Value of Annuities**   Bill Broker wants to sell you an investment contract that pays equal $5,000 payments at the end of each of the next eight years. If you require an effective annual return of 18 percent on this investment, how much will you pay for the contract today?

43. **Calculating Rates of Return**   You're trying to choose between two different investments, both of which have up-front costs of $25,000. Investment G returns $40,000 in six years. Investment H returns $60,000 in 11 years. Which of these investments has the higher return?

44. **Present Value and Interest Rates**   What is the relationship between the value of an annuity and the level of interest rates? Suppose you just bought an eight-year annuity of $400 per year when interest rates are 10 percent per year. What happens to the value of your investment if interest rates suddenly drop to 6 percent? What if interest rates suddenly rise to 14 percent?

45. **Calculating Annuity Future Values**   You're prepared to make monthly payments of $75.21, beginning next month, into an account that pays 16 percent interest compounded monthly. How many payments will you have made when your account balance reaches $10,000?

46. **Calculating Annuity Present Values**   You want to borrow $12,000 from your local bank to buy a new sailboat. You can afford to make monthly payments of $325, but no more. Assuming monthly compounding, what is the highest 48-month APR loan you can afford to take out?

47. **Mortgage payments**   A stock promoter in Vancouver is contemplating buying a new condominium. The condo is worth $540,000 and a bank has offered a mortgage of $405,000 at 12 percent APR (remember semiannual quotes) for 25 years. What is the monthly payment at this interest rate?

48. **Mortgage term**   An entrepreneur is considering the purchase of an office in a new high-rise complex. The office is worth $450,000 and a bank is offering a mortgage for $330,000 at 12 percent APR. If the entrepreneur's budget allows payments of $3,750 a month, how long will it take to pay off the purchase?

49. **Present Value and Break-Even Interest**   Consider a firm with a contract to sell an asset for $50,000 three years from now. The asset costs $42,000 to produce today. Given a relevant discount rate on this asset of 9 percent per year, will the firm make a profit on this asset? At what rate does the firm just break even?

50. **Present Value and Interest Rates**   On a trip to Florida you've just won the U.S. MegaLottery. Lottery officials offer you the choice of two alternative payouts: either $1 million today, or $2 million six years from now. Which payout will you choose if the relevant discount rate is 0 percent? 10 percent? 20 percent? Ignore taxes.

51. **Calculating Present Value of Annuities**   Congratulations! You've just won the $10 million first prize in the Editor's Clearingworld Sweepstakes. Unfortunately, the sweepstakes will actually give you the $10 million in $250,000 annual installments over the next 40 years, beginning next year. If your appropriate discount rate is 7 percent per year, how much money did you really win?

52. **Present Value and Multiple Cash Flows**   What is the present value of $300 per year payments, at a discount rate of 12 percent, if the first payment is received 4 years from now and the last payment is received 25 years from now?

53. **Variable Interest Rates**   A 12-year annuity pays $1,000 per month, and payments are made at the end of each month. If the interest rate is 16 percent compounded monthly for the first four years, and 10 percent compounded monthly thereafter, what is the value of the annuity?

54. **Comparing Cash Flow Streams**   You have your choice of two investment accounts. Investment A is a seven-year annuity that features end-of-month $100 payments and has an interest rate of 17 percent compounded monthly. Investment B is a 12 percent continuously compounded lump-sum investment, also good for seven years. How much money would you need to invest in B today so it is worth as much as Investment A seven years from now?

55. **Present Value of a Perpetuity**   Given an interest rate of 6.6 percent per year, what is the value at date $t = 9$ of a perpetual stream of $300 payments that begin at date $t = 14$?

56. **Calculating EAR**   A local finance company quotes a 23 percent interest rate on one-year loans. So, if you borrow $10,000, the interest for the year will be $2,300. Since you must repay a total of $12,300 in one year, the finance company requires you to pay $12,300/12 or $1,025 per month over the next 12 months. Is this a 23 percent loan? What rate would legally have to be quoted? What is the effective annual rate?

57. **Calculating Future Values**   If today is Year 0, what is the future value of the following cash flows 6 years from now? What is the future value 12 years from now? Assume a discount rate of 8 percent per year.

Year	Cash Flow
2	$30,000
3	$60,000
5	$75,000

58. **Calculating Present Values**   A 5-year annuity of 10 $7,000 semiannual payments will begin 9 years from now, with the first payment coming 9.5 years from now. If the discount rate is 13 percent compounded monthly, what is the present value of this annuity at the date five years from now? What is the present value at the date two years from now? What is the current present value of the annuity?

59. **Calculating Annuities Due**   As discussed in the text, an ordinary annuity assumes equal payments at the end of each period over the life of the annuity. An *annuity due* is the same thing except the payments occur at the beginning of each period instead. Thus, a three-year annual annuity due would have periodic payment cash flows occurring at Years 0, 1, and 2, while a three-year annual ordinary annuity would have periodic payment cash flows occurring at Years 1, 2, and 3.

    a. At a 7 percent annual discount rate, find the present value of a four-year ordinary annuity contract of $500 payments.
    b. Find the present value of the same contract if it is an annuity due.

60. **Calculating Annuities Due**   You want to lease a new car from Mary's Motorworks for $13,000. The lease contract is in the form of a 24-month annuity due at a 10.5 percent APR. What will your monthly lease payment be?

61. **Discount Interest Loans**   This question illustrates what is known as *discount interest*. Imagine you are discussing a loan with a somewhat unscrupulous lender. You want to borrow $17,500 for one year. The interest rate is 10 percent. You and the lender agree that the interest on the loan will be .10 × $17,500 = $1,750. So the lender deducts this interest amount from the loan up front and gives you $15,750. In this case, we say that the discount is $1,750. What's wrong here?

**Challenge
(Questions 61–73)**

62. **Calculating EAR with Discount Interest**   You are considering a one-year loan of $18,000. The interest rate is quoted on a discount basis (see the previous problem) as 16 percent. What is the effective annual rate?

63. **Mortgage APR and EAR**   This challenge problem is much easier if you have a financial calculator or use Lotus 1–2–3. A young bond trader on Bay Street has just purchased a condominium and taken out a mortgage for $400,000. The financing calls for monthly payments of $4,500 over the 25-year life of the mortgage. What is the APR of the investment? (Remember how mortgages are quoted.) What is the EAR?

64. **Calculating EAR with Add-On Interest**   This problem illustrates a deceptive way of quoting interest rates called add-on interest. Imagine that you see an advertisement for Ripov Retailing that reads something like: "$1,000 Instant Credit! 10% Simple Interest! Three Years to Pay! Low, Low Monthly Payments!" You're not exactly sure what all this means and somebody spilled ink over the APR on the loan contract, so you ask the manager for clarification.

    Roger Ripov explains that if you borrow $1,000 for three years at 10 percent interest, in three years you will owe:

    $$\$1,000 \times 1.10^3 = \$1,000 \times 1.331 = \$1,331.$$

    Now, Roger recognizes that coming up with $1,331 all at once might be a strain, so he lets you make "low, low monthly payments" of $1,331/36 = $36.97 per month, even though this is extra bookkeeping work for him.

    Is this a 10 percent loan? Why or why not? What is the APR on this loan? What is the EAR? Why do you think this is called "add-on" interest?

65. **Calculating Annuity Payments**   This is a classic "retirement" problem. A time line will help in solving it. Your friend is celebrating her 35th birthday today and wants to start saving for her anticipated retirement at age 65. She wants to be able to withdraw $15,000 from her savings account on each birthday for 12 years following her retirement; the first withdrawal will be on her 66th birthday. Your friend intends to invest her money in the local credit union, which offers 9 percent interest per year. She wants to make equal, annual payments on each birthday into the account established at the credit union for her retirement fund.

    a. If she starts making these deposits on her 36th birthday and continues to make deposits until she is 65 (the last deposit will be on her 65th birthday), what amount must she deposit annually to be able to make the desired withdrawals at retirement?

    b. Suppose your friend has just inherited a large sum of money. Rather than making equal annual payments, she has decided to make one lump-sum payment on her 36th birthday to cover her retirement needs. What amount would she have to deposit?

    c. Suppose your friend's employer will contribute $250 into the account every year as part of the company's profit-sharing plan. In addition, your friend

Challenge
(Continued)

expects a $10,000 distribution from a family trust fund on her 55th birthday, which she will also put into the retirement account. What amount must she deposit annually now to be able to make the desired withdrawals at retirement?

66. **Present Value with Multiple Cash Flows**   In January 1984, Richard "Goose" Gossage signed a contract to play for the San Diego Padres that guaranteed him a minimum of $9,955,000. The guaranteed payments were $875,000 for 1984, $650,000 for 1985, $800,000 for 1986, $1 million for 1987, $1 million for 1988, and $300,000 for 1989. In addition, the contract called for $5,330,000 in deferred money payable at the rate of $240,000 per year from 1990 through 2006 and then $125,000 a year from 2007 through 2016. If the relevant rate of interest is 9 percent and all payments are made on July 1 of each year, beginning on July 1, 1984, what would the present value of these guaranteed payments be on January 1, 1984? If he were to receive an equal annual salary at the end of each of the five years from 1984 through 1988, what would his equivalent annual salary be? Ignore any tax consequences throughout this problem.

67. **Future Value and Multiple Cash Flows**   An insurance company is offering a new policy to its customers. Typically, the policy is bought by a parent or grandparent for a child at the child's birth. The details of the policy are as follows: The purchaser (say, the parent) makes the following six payments to the insurance company:

1st birthday	$1,000
2nd birthday	$1,000
3rd birthday	$1,000
4th birthday	$1,250
5th birthday	$1,250
6th birthday	$1,250

After the child's sixth birthday, no more payments are made. When the child reaches age 65, he or she receives $120,000. If the relevant interest rate is 8 percent for the first six years and 5 percent for all subsequent years, is the policy worth buying?

68. **Calculating Interest Rates**   A financial planning service offers a university savings program. The plan calls for you to make six annual payments of $2,000 each, with the first payment occurring today, your child's 12th birthday. Beginning on your child's 18th birthday, the plan will provide $7,000 per year for four years. What return is this investment offering?

69. **Break-Even Investment Returns**   Your financial planner offers you two different investment plans. Plan X is a $3,000 annual perpetuity. Plan Y is a 10-year, $10,000 annual annuity. Both plans will make their first payment one year from today. At what discount rate would you be indifferent between these two plans?

70. **Perpetual Cash Flows**   What is the value of an investment that pays $5,000 every *other* year forever, if the first payment occurs one year from today and the discount rate is 9 percent compounded daily? What would the value be today if the first payment occurs four years from today?

71. **Ordinary Annuities and Annuities Due**   As discussed in the text, an annuity due is identical to an ordinary annuity except that the periodic payments occur at the beginning of each period and not at the end of the period (see Problem 59). Show that the relationship between the value of an ordinary annuity and the value of an otherwise equivalent annuity due is: (see Problem 59)

   Challenge (Continued)

$$\text{Annuity due value} = \text{Ordinary annuity value} \times (1 + r)$$

   Show this for both present and future values.

72. **Calculating Annuities Due**   A six-year annual annuity due with the first payment occurring at date $t = 7$ has a current value of \$17,500. If the discount rate is 13 percent per year, what is the annuity payment amount?

73. **Calculating EAR**   A cheque-cashing store is in the business of making personal loans to walk-up customers. The store makes only one-week loans at 10 percent interest per week.

   a. What APR must the store report to its customers? What is the EAR that the customers are actually paying?

   b. Now suppose the store makes one-week loans at 10 percent discount interest per week (see Problem 61). What's the APR now? The EAR?

   c. The cheque cashing store also makes one-month, add-on interest loans at 10 percent discount interest per week. Thus, if you borrow \$100 for one month (four weeks), the interest would be $\$100 \times 1.10^4 - \$100 = \$46.41$. Since this is discounter interest, your net loan proceeds today will be \$53.59. You must then repay the store \$100 at the end of the month. To help you out, though, the store lets you pay off this \$100 in \$25 per week installments. What is the APR of this loan? What is the EAR?

Suggested Readings

One of the best places to learn more about the mathematics of present value is the owner's manual that comes with a financial calculator. One of the best is the one that comes with the Hewlett-Packard 12C calculator:

Hewlett-Packard HP-12C. *Owner's Handbook and Problem Solving Guide,* latest edition.

Hewlett-Packard HP-12C. *Solutions Handbook,* latest edition.

Other useful references are:

Texas Instruments. *Business Analyst/Guidebook,* latest edition.

Sharp. Business/Financial Calculator EL-731SL. *Instruction Guide and Application Manual.*

PROOF OF ANNUITY PRESENT VALUE FORMULA | APPENDIX   5A

An *annuity* is a level stream of regular payments that lasts for a fixed number of periods. Not surprisingly, annuities are among the most common kinds of financial instruments. The pensions that people receive when they retire are often in the form of an annuity. Leases, mortgages, and pension plans are also annuities.

To figure out the present value of an annuity, we need to evaluate the following equation:

$$\frac{C}{1 + r} + \frac{C}{(1 + r)^2} + \frac{C}{(1 + r)^3} + \ldots + \frac{C}{(1 + r)^T}$$

The present value of only receiving the coupons for T periods must be less than the present value of a consol, but how much less? To answer this, we have to look at consols a bit more closely.

Consider the following time chart:

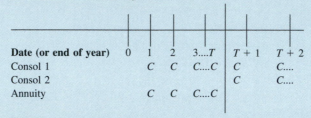

Date (or end of year)	0	1	2	3....T	$T + 1$	$T + 2$
Consol 1		C	C	C....C	C	C....
Consol 2					C	C....
Annuity		C	C	C....C		

Consol 1 is a normal consol with its first payment at date 1. The first payment of consol 2 occurs at date $T + 1$.

The present value of having cash flow of C at each of T dates is equal to the present value of consol 1 minus the present value of consol 2. The present value of consol 1 is given by

$$PV = \frac{C}{r}$$

Consol 2 is just a consol with its first payment at date $T + 1$. From the perpetuity formula, this consol will be worth C/r at date T.[18] However, we do not want the value at date T. We want the value now; in other words, the present value at date 0. We must discount C/r back by T periods. Therefore, the present value of consol 2 is

$$PV = \frac{C}{r} \left[\frac{1}{(1 + r)^T} \right]$$

The present value of having cash flows for T years is the present value of a consol with its first payment at date 1 minus the present value of a consol with its first payment at date $T+1$. Thus, the present value of an annuity is the first formula minus the second formula. This can be written as

$$\frac{C}{r} - \frac{C}{r} \left[\frac{1}{(1 + r)^T} \right]$$

This simplifies to the formula for present value of annuity:

$$PV = C \left[\frac{1}{r} - \frac{1}{r(1 + r)^T} \right]$$
$$= C \left[1 - \{ 1/(1 + r)^T \} \right]/r$$

---

[18]Students frequently think that C/r is the present value at date $T + 1$ because consol's first payment is at date $T + 1$. However, the formula values the annuity as of one period before the first payment.

Valuing Stocks and Bonds

Chapter 5 introduced you to the basic procedures used to value future cash flows. In this chapter, we show you how to use those procedures to value stocks and bonds. Along the way, we introduce you to some of the terminology that commonly appears in these areas, and we also describe how the prices for these assets are reported in the financial press.

Throughout this and the next several chapters, we generally assume that we know the appropriate discount rate. The question of what determines this discount rate and how we might go about measuring it is sufficiently important that we devote several chapters to it later in the text. For now, we focus on the relevant cash flows from financial assets and how to value them, given a suitable discount rate.

6.1 | BONDS AND BOND VALUATION

When a corporation or government wishes to borrow money from the public on a long-term basis, it usually does so by issuing or selling debt securities that are generically called bonds. In this section, we describe the various features of corporate bonds and some of the terminology associated with bonds. These subjects are discussed in greater detail in Parts VI and VIII when we examine long-term financing and capital structure; we examine only the essentials in this chapter. We then discuss the cash flows associated with a bond and how bonds can be valued using our discounted cash flow procedure. We next show how bond prices are quoted in the financial press. The final part of this section shows how selected bond pricing principles are applied by investors and bond traders.

Bond Features and Prices

A bond is normally an interest-only loan, meaning the borrower pays the interest every period, but none of the principal is repaid until the end of the loan. For example, suppose Alcan wants to borrow $1,000 for 30 years and that the interest rate on similar debt issued by similar corporations is 12 percent. Alcan thus pays $.12 \times \$1,000 = \$120$ in interest every year for 30 years. At the end of 30 years, Alcan repays the $1,000. As this example suggests, a bond is a fairly simple financing arrangement. There is, however, a rich jargon associated with bonds, so we use this example to define some of the more important terms.

coupons

The stated interest payments made on a bond.

In our example, the $120 regular interest payments that Alcan promises to make are called the bond's **coupons**. Because the coupon is constant and paid every year, the type of bond we are describing is sometimes called a *level coupon bond*. The amount repaid at the end of the loan is called the bond's **face value** or **par value**. As in our example, this par value is usually $1,000 for corporate bonds, and a bond that sells for its par value is called a *par bond*. Government of Canada and provincial bonds frequently have much larger face or par values. Finally, the annual coupon divided by the face value is called the **coupon rate** on the bond, which is $120/1,000 = 12%; so the bond has a 12 percent coupon rate.

face value

The principal amount of a bond that is repaid at the end of the term. Also par value.

The number of years until the face value is paid is called the bond's time to **maturity**. A corporate bond would frequently have a maturity of 30 years when it is originally issued, but this varies. Once the bond has been issued, the number of years to maturity declines as time goes by.

coupon rate

The annual coupon divided by the face value of a bond.

Bond Values and Yields

As time passes, interest rates change in the marketplace. The cash flows from a bond, however, stay the same because the coupon rate and maturity date are specified when it is issued. As a result, the value of the bond fluctuates. When interest rates rise, the present value of the bond's remaining cash flows declines, and the bond is worth less. When interest rates fall, the bond is worth more.

maturity

Specified date at which the principal amount of a bond is paid.

yield to maturity (YTM)

The market interest rate that equates a bond's present value of interest payments and principal repayment with its price.

To determine the value of a bond on a particular date, we need to know the number of periods remaining until maturity, the face value, the coupon, and the market interest rate for bonds with similar features. This interest rate required in the market on a bond is called the bond's **yield to maturity (YTM)**. This rate is sometimes called the bond's *yield* for short. Given this information, we can calculate the present value of the cash flows as an estimate of the bond's current market value.

For example, suppose B. C. Telephone were to issue a bond with 10 years to maturity. The B. C. Telephone bond has an annual coupon of $100. Suppose similar bonds have a yield to maturity of 10 percent.[1] Based on our previous discussion, the B. C. Telephone bond pays $100 per year for the next 10 years in coupon interest. In 10 years, B. C. Telephone pays $1,000 to the owner of the bond. The cash flows from the bond are shown in Figure 6.1. What would this bond sell for?

As illustrated in Figure 6.1, the B. C. Telephone bond's cash flows have an annuity component (the coupons) and a lump sum (the face value paid at maturity). We thus estimate the market value of the bond by calculating the present value of these two components separately and adding the results together. First, at the going rate of 10 percent, the present value of the $1,000 paid in 10 years is:

Present value = $1,000/1.10^{10} = $1,000/2.5937 = $385.55

Second, the bond offers $100 per year for 10 years, so the present value of this annuity stream is:

$$\text{Annuity present value} = \$100 \times (1 - 1/1.10^{10})/.10$$
$$= \$100 \times (1 - 1/2.5937)/.10$$
$$= \$100 \times 6.1445$$
$$= \$614.45$$

---

[1] At the time of writing in February 1995, B. C. Telephone long-term bonds carried a market yield of around 9.8 percent.

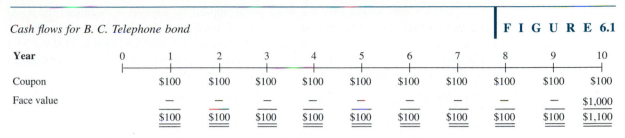

Cash flows for B. C. Telephone bond

Year	0	1	2	3	4	5	6	7	8	9	10
Coupon		$100	$100	$100	$100	$100	$100	$100	$100	$100	$100
Face value		—	—	—	—	—	—	—	—	—	$1,000
		$100	$100	$100	$100	$100	$100	$100	$100	$100	$1,100

As shown, the B.C Telephone bond has an annual coupon of $100 and a face or par value of $1,000 paid at maturity in 10 years.

We can now add the values for the two parts together to get the bond's value:

Total bond value = $385.55 + 614.45 = $1,000.00

This bond sells for its exact face value. This is not a coincidence. The going interest rate in the market is 10 percent. Considered as an interest-only loan, what interest rate does this bond have? With a $100 coupon, this bond pays exactly 10 percent interest only when it sells for $1,000.

To illustrate what happens as interest rates change, suppose a year has gone by. The B. C. Telephone bond now has nine years to maturity. If the interest rate in the market had risen to 12 percent, what would the bond be worth? To find out, we repeat the present value calculations with 9 years instead of 10, and a 12 percent yield instead of a 10 percent yield. First, the present value of the $1,000 paid in nine years at 12 percent is:

Present value = $1,000/1.12^9 = $1,000/2.7731 = $360.61

Second, the bond now offers $100 per year for nine years, so the present value of this annuity stream at 12 percent is:

$$\begin{aligned}
\text{Annuity present value} &= \$100 \times (1 - 1/1.12^9)/.12 \\
&= \$100 \times (1 - 1/2.7731)/.12 \\
&= \$100 \times 5.3282 \\
&= \$532.83
\end{aligned}$$

We can now add the values for the two parts together to get the bond's value:

Total bond value = $360.61 + 532.83 = $893.44

Therefore, the bond should sell for about $894. In the vernacular, we say this bond, with its 10 percent coupon, is priced to yield 12 percent at $894.

The B. C. Telephone bond now sells for less than its $1,000 face value. Why? The market interest rate is 12 percent. Considered as an interest-only loan of $1,000, this bond pays only 10 percent, its coupon rate. Because this bond pays less than the going rate, investors are only willing to lend something less than the $1,000 promised repayment. A bond that sells for less than face value is a *discount bond.*

The only way to get the interest rate up to 12 percent is for the price to be less than $1,000 so that the purchaser, in effect, has a built-in gain. For the B. C. Telephone bond, the price of $894 is $106 less than the face value, so an investor who purchased and kept the bond would get $100 per year and would have a $106 gain at maturity as well. This gain compensates the lender for the below-market coupon rate.

Another way to see why the bond is discounted by $106 is to note that the $100 coupon is $20 below the coupon on a newly issued par value bond, based on current market conditions. By this we mean the bond would be worth $1,000 only if it had a coupon of $120 per year. In a sense, an investor who buys and keeps the bond gives up $20 per year for nine years. At 12 percent, this annuity stream is worth:

$$\text{Annuity present value} = \$20 \times (1 - 1/1.12^9)/.12$$
$$= \$20 \times 5.3282$$
$$= \$106.56$$

This is just the amount of the discount.

What would the B. C. Telephone bond sell for if interest rates had dropped by 2 percent instead of rising by 2 percent? As you might guess, the bond would sell for more than $1,000. Such a bond is said to sell at a *premium* and is called a *premium bond.*

This case is just the opposite of a discount bond. The B. C. Telephone bond still has a coupon rate of 10 percent when the market rate is only 8 percent. Investors are willing to pay a premium to get this extra coupon. The relevant discount rate is 8 percent, and there are nine years remaining. The present value of the $1,000 face amount is:

$$\text{Present value} = \$1,000/1.08^9 = \$1,000/1.9990 = \$500.25$$

The present value of the coupon stream is:

$$\text{Annuity present value} = \$100 \times (1 - 1/1.08^9)/.08$$
$$= \$100 \times (1 - 1/1.990)/.08$$
$$= \$100 \times 6.2469$$
$$= \$624.69$$

We can now add the values for the two parts together to get the bond's value:

$$\text{Total bond value} = \$500.25 + 624.69 = \$1,124.94$$

Total bond value is, therefore, about $125 in excess of par value. Once again, we can verify this amount by noting that the coupon is now $20 too high. The present value of $20 per year for nine years at 8 percent is:

$$\text{Annuity present value} = \$20 \times (1 - 1/1.08^9)/.08$$
$$= \$20 \times 6.2469$$
$$= \$124.94$$

This is just as we calculated.

Based on our examples, we can now write the general expression for the value of a bond. If a bond has (1) a face value of F paid at maturity, (2) a coupon of C paid per period, (3) t periods to maturity, and (4) a yield of r per period, its value is:

$$\text{Bond value} = C \times (1 - 1/(1 + r)^t)/r + F/(1 + r)^t \qquad [6.1]$$

$$\text{Bond value} = \frac{\text{Present value}}{\text{of the coupons}} + \frac{\text{Present value}}{\text{of the face amount}}$$

E X A M P L E | 6.1   Semiannual Coupons

In practice, bonds issued in Canada usually make coupon payments twice a year. So, if an ordinary bond has a coupon rate of 14 percent, the owner gets a total of $140 per year, but this $140 comes in two payments of $70 each. Suppose we were examining such a bond. The yield to maturity is quoted at 16 percent.

Bond yields are quoted like APRs; the quoted rate is equal to the actual rate per period multiplied by the number of periods. With a 16 percent quoted yield and semiannual payments, the true yield is 8 percent per six months. The bond matures in seven years. What is the bond's price? What is the effective annual yield on this bond?

Based on our discussion, we know the bond would sell at a discount because it has a coupon rate of 7 percent every six months when the market requires 8 percent every six months. So, if our answer exceeds $1,000, we know that we made a mistake.

To get the exact price, we first calculate the present value of the bond's face value of $1,000 paid in seven years. This seven years has 14 periods of six months each. At 8 percent per period, the value is:

Present value = $1,000/1.08^{14} = $1,000/2.9372 = $340.46

The coupons can be viewed as a 14-period annuity of $70 per period. At an 8 percent discount rate, the present value of such an annuity is:

$$\text{Annuity present value} = \$70 \times (1 - 1/1.08^{14})/.08$$
$$= \$70 \times (1 - .3405)/.08$$
$$= \$70 \times 8.2442$$
$$= \$577.10$$

The total present value gives us what the bond should sell for:

Total present value = $340.46 + 577.10 = $917.56

To calculate the effective yield on this bond, note that 8 percent every six months is equivalent to:

Effective annual rate = $(1 + .08)^2 - 1 = 16.64\%$

The effective yield, therefore, is 16.64 percent.

As we have illustrated in this section, bond prices and interest rates (or market yields) always move in opposite directions like the ends of a seesaw. Most bonds are issued at par with the coupon rate set equal to the prevailing market yield or interest rate. When interest rates rise, a bond's value, like any other present value, declines. When interest rates are more than the bond's coupon rate, the bond sells at a discount. Similarly, when interest rates fall, bond values rise. Interest rates less than the bond's coupon rate cause the bond to sell at a premium. Even if we are considering a bond that is riskless in the sense that the borrower is certain to make all the payments, there is still risk in owning a bond. We discuss this next.

Interest Rate Risk

The risk that arises for bond owners from fluctuating interest rates (market yields) is called *interest rate risk*. How much interest risk a bond has depends on how sensitive its price is to interest rate changes. This sensitivity directly depends on two things: the time to maturity and the coupon rate. Keep the following in mind when looking at a bond:

1. All other things being equal, the longer the time to maturity, the greater the interest rate risk.

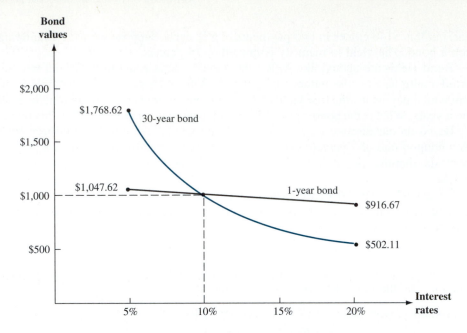

Value of a Bond with a 10% Coupon Rate for Different Interest Rates and Maturities

	Time to Maturity	
Interest Rate	1 Year	30 Years
5%	$1,047.62	$1,768.62
10%	1,000.00	1,000.00
15%	956.52	671.70
20%	916.67	502.11

2. All other things being equal, the lower the coupon rate, the greater the interest
    rate risk.

We illustrate the first of these two points in Figure 6.2. As shown, we compute
and plot prices under different interest rate scenarios for 10 percent coupon bonds
with maturities of 1 year and 30 years. Notice how the slope of the line connecting
the prices is much steeper for the 30-year maturity than it is for the 1-year maturity.[2]
This tells us that a relatively small change in interest rates could lead to a substantial
change in the bond's value. In comparison, the one-year bond's price is relatively
insensitive to interest rate changes.

Intuitively, the reason that longer-term bonds have greater interest rate sensitivity
is that a large portion of a bond's value comes from the $1,000 face amount. The
present value of this amount isn't greatly affected by a small change in interest rates
if it is to be received in one year. If it is to be received in 30 years, however, even a
small change in the interest rate can have a significant effect once it is compounded
for 30 years. The present value of the face amount becomes much more volatile with
a longer-term bond as a result.

---

[2] We explain a more precise measure of this slope, called duration, in Appendix 6A. Our example assumes
that yields of 1-year and 30-year bonds are the same. Appendix 6B discusses the term structure of interest
rates.

The reason that bonds with lower coupons have greater interest rate risk is essentially the same. As we just discussed, the value of a bond depends on the present value of its coupons and the present value of the face amount. If two bonds with different coupon rates have the same maturity, the value of the one with the lower coupon is proportionately more dependent on the face amount to be received at maturity. As a result, all other things being equal, its value fluctuates more as interest rates change. Put another way, the bond with the higher coupon has a larger cash flow early in its life, so its value is less sensitive to changes in the discount rate.

Finding the Yield to Maturity

Frequently, we know a bond's price, coupon rate, and maturity date, but not its yield to maturity. For example, suppose we were interested in a six-year, 8 percent coupon bond. A broker quotes a price of $955.14. What is the yield on this bond?

We've seen that the price of a bond can be written as the sum of its annuity and lump-sum components. With an $80 coupon for six years and a $1,000 face value, this price is:

$$\$955.14 = \$80 \times (1 - 1/(1 + r)^6)/r + \$1{,}000/(1 + r)^6$$

where r is the unknown discount rate or yield to maturity. We have one equation here and one unknown, but we cannot solve it for r explicitly. The only way to find the answer exactly is to use trial and error.[3]

This problem is essentially identical to the one we examined in the last chapter when we tried to find the unknown interest rate on an annuity. However, finding the rate (or yield) on a bond is even more complicated because of the $1,000 face amount.

We can speed up the trial-and-error process by using what we know about bond prices and yields: The bond has an $80 coupon and is selling at a discount. We thus know that the yield is greater than 8 percent. If we compute the price at 10 percent:

$$\begin{aligned}
\text{Bond value} &= \$80 \times (1 - 1/1.10^6)/.10 + \$1{,}000/1.10^6 \\
&= \$80 \times (4.3553) + \$1{,}000/1.7716 \\
&= \$912.89
\end{aligned}$$

At 10 percent, the value we calculate is lower than the actual price, so 10 percent is too high. The true yield must be somewhere between 8 percent and 10 percent. At this point, it's "plug and chug" to find the answer. You would probably want to try 9 percent next. If you do, you will see that this is, in fact, the bond's yield to maturity.

There is a shortcut to guessing the yield on a bond:

$$\text{Yield} = \frac{[\text{Coupon} + (\text{Face value} - \text{Price})/\text{Maturity}]}{(\text{Price} + \text{Face value})/2}$$

In the preceding example, we could approximate the trial yield as:

$$\begin{aligned}
\text{Yield} &= \frac{[\$80 + (\$1{,}000 - \$955.14)/6]}{(\$955.14 + \$1{,}000)/2} \\
&= \frac{[\$80 + 7.48]}{\$977.57} \\
&= 8.95\%
\end{aligned}$$

---

[3] Appendix 6C shows how to find a bond's yield to maturity using a financial calculator.

T A B L E 6.1

Summary of bond valuation

I. Finding the Value of a Bond:

Bond value $= C \times (1 - 1/(1 + r)^t)/r + F/(1 + r)^t$

where:

C = the coupon paid each period
r = the rate per period
t = the number of periods
F = the bond's face value

II. Finding the Yield on a Bond:

Given a bond value, coupon, time to maturity, and face value, it is possible to find the implicit discount rate or yield to maturity by trial and error only. To do this, try different discount rates until the calculated bond value equals the given value. Remember that increasing the rate decreases the bond value.

The approximation formula divides the average cash flow by the average amount invested in the bond. It is useful in saving time by giving a starting point for trial and error calculations. The approximation formula can never replace the present value calculations. This is because the approximation ignores the time value of money and can be seriously off from the true yield when the bond is selling at a large premium or discount. Our discussion of bond valuation is summarized in Table 6.1.

E X A M P L E | 6.2   Bond Yields

You're looking at two bonds identical in every way except for their coupons and, of course, their prices. Both have 12 years to maturity. The first bond has a 10 percent coupon rate and sells for $935.08. The second has a 12 percent coupon rate. What do you think it would sell for?

Because the two bonds are very similar, they are priced to yield about the same rate. We begin by calculating the yield on the 10 percent coupon bond. The approximation formula gives 10.89 percent as the trial yield.

$$\text{Yield} = \frac{[\$100 + (\$1,000 - \$935.08)/12]}{(\$935.08 + \$1,000)/2}$$

$$= \frac{\$105.41}{\$967.54}$$

$$\text{Yield} = 10.89\%$$

A little trial and error reveals that the yield is actually 11 percent:

Bond value $= \$100 \times (1 - 1/1.11^{12})/.11 + \$1,000/1.11^{12}$
$= \$100 \times 6.4924 + \$1,000/3.4985$
$= \$649.24 + 285.84$
$= \$935.08$

With an 11 percent yield, the second bond sells at a premium because of its $120 coupon. Its value is:

Bond value $= \$120 \times (1 - 1/1.11^{12})/.11 + \$1,000/1.11^{12}$
$= \$120 \times 6.4924 + \$1,000/3.4985$
$= \$779.08 + 285.84$
$= \$1,064.92$

What we did in pricing the second bond is what bond traders do. Bonds trade over the counter in a secondary market made by investment dealers and banks. Suppose a bond trader at, say, Nesbitt Burns receives a request for a selling price on the second bond from another trader at, say, ScotiaMcLeod. Suppose further that the second bond has not traded recently. The trader prices it off the first actively traded bond.

Bond Price Reporting

If you were to look in the *Globe and Mail* (or similar financial newspaper), you would see information on various bonds issued by the government of Canada, the provinces and provincial crown corporations, and large corporations. Figure 6.3 reproduces the bond quotations from February 2, 1995. If you look down the list under Corporate, you come to an entry marked "ROYAL BANK 10.50 1 MAR 02." This tells us the bond was issued by Royal Bank and it will mature on March 1, 2002. The 10.50 is the bond's coupon rate, so the coupon is 10.50 percent of the face value. Assuming the face value is $1,000, the annual coupon on this bond is .1050 × $1,000 = $105.00.

The column marked Price gives us the last available price on the bond at close of business the day before. This price was supplied by RBC Dominion Securities. As with the coupon, the price is quoted as a percentage of face value; so, again assuming a face value of $1,000, this bond last sold for 104.500 percent of $1,000 or $1,045.00. Because this bond is selling for about 104.50 percent of its par value, it is trading at a premium. The last column, marked $Chg, indicates there was $0.375 increase in the closing price of the previous trading day.

The column marked Yield gives the going market yield to maturity on the Royal Bank bond as 9.605 percent. This yield is lower than the coupon rate of 10.50 percent, which explains why the bond is selling above its par value. The market yield falls below the coupon rate by .895 percent, or 89.5 basis points. (In bond trader's jargon, one basis point equals 1/100 of 1 percent.) This causes the price premium above par.[4]

E X A M P L E | 6.3   **Bond Pricing in Action**

Investment managers who specialize in bonds use bond pricing principles to try to make money for their clients by buying bonds whose prices they expect to rise. An interest rate anticipation strategy starts with a forecast for the level of interest rates. Such forecasts are extremely difficult to make consistently. In Chapter 10, we discuss in detail how difficult it is to beat the market.

Suppose a manager had predicted a significant drop in interest rates in 1995. How should such a manager have invested?

This manager would have invested heavily in bonds with the greatest price sensitivity; that is, in bonds whose prices would rise the most as rates fell. Based on the earlier discussion, you should recall that such price-sensitive bonds have longer times to maturity and low coupons.

Suppose you wanted to bet on the expectation that interest rates were going to fall significantly using the bond quotations in Figure 6.3. Suppose further that your client wanted to invest only in government of Canada bonds. Which would you buy?

---

[4] If you have a financial calculator, you can easily check the bond quotation for the Royal Bank example. Using semiannual coupons, and the following Appendix 6C, it comes out to 104.50.

F I G U R E 6.3

Sample bond quotation

CANADIAN BONDS

Selected quotations, with changes since the previous day, on actively traded bond issues, provided by RBC Dominion Securities. Yields are calculated to full maturity, unless marked C to indicate callable date. Price is the midpoint between final bid and ask quotations Feb. 2, 1995.

Issuer	Coupon	Maturity	Price	Yield	$ Chg
GOVERNMENT OF CANADA					
CANADA	6.50	1 AUG 96	96.945	8.735	+0.150
CANADA	7.75	15 SEP 96	98.625	8.679	+0.150
CANADA	8.00	15 MAR 97	98.560	8.757	+0.192
CANADA	7.50	1 JUL 97	97.045	8.888	+0.240
CANADA	6.25	1 FEB 98	92.965	8.988	+0.250
CANADA	6.50	1 SEP 98	92.445	9.029	+0.270
CANADA	5.75	1 MAR 99	89.020	9.043	+0.260
CANADA	7.75	1 SEP 99	95.250	9.043	+0.300
CANADA	9.25	1 DEC 99	100.680	9.066	+0.321
CANADA	8.50	1 MAR 00	97.910	9.022	+0.330
CANADA	9.75	1 JUN 01	102.907	9.128	+0.378
CANADA	9.50	1 OCT 01	101.775	9.133	+0.400
CANADA	9.75	1 DEC 01	103.050	9.133	+0.400
CANADA	8.50	1 APR 02	96.700	9.136	+0.400
CANADA	7.25	1 JUN 03	89.007	9.166	+0.381
CANADA	7.50	1 DEC 03	90.003	9.176	+0.398
CANADA	10.25	1 FEB 04	106.352	9.195	+0.470
CANADA	6.50	1 JUN 04	83.530	9.165	+0.405
CANADA	9.00	1 DEC 04	98.983	9.156	+0.489
CANADA	10.00	1 JUN 08	106.000	9.205	+0.550
CANADA	9.50	1 JUN 10	102.250	9.220	+0.600
CANADA	9.00	1 MAR 11	98.150	9.222	+0.600
CANADA	10.25	15 MAR 14	109.200	9.215	+0.750
CANADA	9.75	1 JUN 21	105.200	9.219	+0.800
CANADA	8.00	1 JUN 23	87.850	9.212	+0.700
CMHC	8.80	1 MAR 00	98.469	9.183	+0.330
REAL RETURNS	4.25	1 DEC 21	89.325	4.975	+0.075
PROVINCIAL					
ALBERTA	7.00	20 AUG 97	95.650	8.958	+0.200
ALBERTA	8.50	1 SEP 99	97.625	9.147	+0.300
ALBERTA	6.38	1 JUN 04	81.975	9.310	+0.400
B C	7.00	9 JUN 99	92.500	9.131	+0.250
B C	9.00	9 JAN 02	98.200	9.356	+0.400
B C	9.00	21 JUN 04	97.350	9.429	+0.350
B C	8.50	23 AUG 13	91.100	9.531	+0.650
B C	8.00	8 SEP 23	85.025	9.534	+0.650
HYDRO QUEBEC	9.25	2 DEC 96	100.425	8.976	+0.200
HYDRO QUEBEC	10.88	25 JUL 01	104.725	9.866	+0.400
HYDRO QUEBEC	11.00	15 AUG 20	107.525	10.168	+0.550
HYDRO QUEBEC	9.63	15 JUL 22	94.875	10.182	+0.500
MANITOBA	6.75	24 AUG 95	99.095	8.487	NC
MANITOBA	7.00	19 APR 99	92.350	9.238	+0.250
MANITOBA	7.88	7 APR 03	90.850	9.509	+0.400
MANITOBA	10.50	5 MAR 31	108.700	9.631	+0.850
NEW BRUNSWIC	7.00	17 MAR 98	94.225	9.178	+0.250
NEW BRUNSWIC	8.38	26 AUG 02	93.800	9.545	+0.400

Issuer	Coupon	Maturity	Price	Yield	$ Chg
NEW BRUNSWIC	8.50	28 JUN 13	89.925	9.681	+0.600
NEWFOUNDLAND	10.13	22 NOV 14	99.475	10.184	+0.650
NOVA SCOTIA	9.60	30 JAN 22	97.325	9.885	+0.850
ONTARIO HYD	10.88	8 JAN 96	101.810	8.747	NC
ONTARIO HYD	7.25	31 MAR 98	94.775	9.199	+0.250
ONTARIO HYD	9.63	3 AUG 99	100.950	9.360	+0.300
ONTARIO HYD	8.63	6 FEB 02	95.175	9.588	+0.400
ONTARIO HYD	9.00	24 JUN 02	96.875	9.597	+0.400
ONTARIO	8.75	16 APR 97	99.325	9.086	+0.200
ONTARIO	9.00	15 SEP 04	95.975	9.650	+0.450
ONTARIO	7.50	7 FEB 24	78.375	9.751	+0.600
P E I	9.75	30 APR 02	99.875	9.769	+0.400
P E I	11.00	19 SEP 11	108.600	9.930	+0.850
QUEBEC	8.00	30 MAR 98	96.125	9.450	+0.200
QUEBEC	10.25	7 APR 98	102.075	9.465	+0.200
QUEBEC	10.25	15 OCT 01	101.750	9.880	+0.350
QUEBEC	9.38	16 JAN 23	92.525	10.186	+0.500
SASKATCHEWAN	9.88	6 JUL 99	101.575	9.425	+0.300
SASKATCHEWAN	9.50	16 AUG 04	98.675	9.716	+0.450
SASKATCHEWAN	9.60	4 FEB 22	97.950	9.817	+0.750
TORONTO -MET	10.38	4 SEP 01	104.125	9.513	+0.400
CORPORATE					
AGT LIMITED	9.50	24 AUG 04	99.125	9.641	+0.375
AVCO FIN	8.50	8 SEP 97	98.000	9.387	+0.250
BELL CANADA	9.20	1 JUN 99	99.500	9.337	+0.375
BELL CANADA	9.50	15 JUN 02	99.625	9.568	+0.500
BELL CANADA	9.70	15 DEC 32	98.875	9.811	+0.750
BC TELEPHONE	9.65	8 APR 22	98.875	9.766	+0.750
CDN IMP BANK	7.10	10 MAR 04	84.875	9.635	+0.375
CDN IMP BANK	9.65	31 OCT 14	98.250	9.850	+0.750
CDN UTIL	9.40	1 MAY 23	96.750	9.737	+0.750
IMASCO LTD	8.38	23 JUN 03	92.000	9.794	+0.375
INTERPRV PIP	8.20	15 FEB 24	84.375	9.838	+0.625
MOLSON BREW	8.20	11 MAR 03	91.250	9.789	+0.375
MOLSON BREW	8.40	7 DEC 18	85.500	10.005	+0.625
NVA SCOT PWR	6.50	15 DEC 98	90.625	9.459	+0.250
NVA SCOT PWR	9.75	2 AUG 19	98.250	9.941	+0.625
NOVA GAS	8.30	15 JUL 03	91.500	9.803	+0.375
NOVA GAS	9.90	16 DEC 24	99.750	9.924	+0.750
ROYAL BANK	10.50	1 MAR 02	104.500	9.605	+0.375
TALISMAN	9.45	22 DEC 99	99.250	9.641	+0.375
TALISMAN	9.80	22 DEC 04	98.875	9.978	+0.500
THOMSON CORP	9.15	6 JUL 04	96.000	9.808	+0.375
TRANSCDA PIP	9.45	20 MAR 18	95.875	9.905	+0.625
UNION GAS	9.75	13 DEC 04	99.875	9.766	+0.500
WSTCOAST ENE	9.50	10 JAN 00	99.875	9.528	+0.250
WSTCOAST ENE	9.70	15 NOV 04	99.500	9.776	+0.500
WSTCOAST ENE	9.90	10 JAN 20	99.625	9.939	+0.750

BOND INDEX
ScotiaMcLeod Bond Indexes

Index	Close	% chg	Yield	Chg	52 wk High	52 wk Low
Short	227.92	0.19	9.027	-0.07	231.25	215.83
Mid	240.16	0.31	9.367	-0.06	257.42	223.77
Long	252.79	0.48	9.542	-0.06	281.17	232.20
Universe	242.25	0.31	9.279	-0.06	257.08	226.21

BENCHMARK INTERNATIONAL BONDS

Issuer	Coupon	Maturity	Price	Yield	$ chg
U.S. Treasury	7.5	Nov/24	97 5/32	7.74	+1/32
British gilt	6.75	Oct/04	88 3/32	8.55	-4/32.
German	7.375	Mar/05	99.39	7.46	-0.19
Japan #164	4.5	Jun/03	96.18	4.710	-0.13

Reprinted with permission of the *Globe and Mail*, February 3, 1995, p. B13.

CONCEPT QUESTIONS

1. What are the cash flows associated with a bond?
2. What is the general expression for the value of a bond?
3. Is it true that the only risk associated with owning a bond is that the issuer will not make all the payments? Explain.

6.2 | COMMON STOCK VALUATION

A share of common stock is more difficult to value in practice than a bond for at least three reasons: First, not even the promised cash flows are known in advance. Second, the life of the investment is essentially forever because common stock has no maturity. Third, there is no way to easily observe the rate of return that the market requires. Nonetheless, there are cases under which we can come up with the present value of the future cash flows for a share of stock and thus determine its value.

Common Stock Cash Flows

Imagine that you are buying a share of stock today. You plan to sell the stock in one year. You somehow know that the stock will be worth $70 at that time. You predict that the stock will also pay a $10 per share dividend at the end of the year. If you require a 25 percent return on your investment, what is the most you would pay for the stock? In other words, what is the present value of the $10 dividend along with the $70 ending value at 25 percent?

If you buy the stock today and sell it at the end of the year, you will have a total of $80 in cash. At 25 percent:

Present value = ($10 + 70)/1.25 = $64

Therefore, $64 is the value you would assign to the stock today.

More generally, let P_0 be the current price of the stock, and define P_1 to be the price in one period. If D_1 is the cash dividend paid at the end of the period, then:

$$P_0 = (D_1 + P_1)/(1 + r) \qquad [6.2]$$

where r is the required return in the market on this investment.

Notice that we really haven't said much so far. If we wanted to determine the value of a share of stock today (P_0), we would have to come up with its value in one year (P_1). This is even harder to do in the first place, so we've only made the problem more complicated.[5]

What is the price in one period, P_1? We don't know in general. Instead, suppose that we somehow knew the price in two periods, P_2. Given a predicted dividend in two periods, D_2, the stock price in one period would be:

$$P_1 = (D_2 + P_2)/(1 + r)$$

If we were to substitute this expression for P_1 into our expression for P_0, we would have:

$$P_0 = \frac{D_1 + P_1}{1 + r} = \frac{D_1 + \dfrac{D_2 + P_2}{1 + r}}{1 + r}$$

$$= \frac{D_1}{(1 + r)^1} + \frac{D_2}{(1 + r)^2} + \frac{P_2}{(1 + r)^2}$$

Now we need to get a price in two periods. We don't know this either, so we can procrastinate again and write:

$$P_2 = (D_3 + P_3)/(1 + r)$$

---

5 The only assumption we make about the stock price is that it is a finite number no matter how far away we push it. It can be extremely large, just not infinitely so. Since no one has ever observed an infinite stock price, this assumption is plausible.

If we substitute this back in for P_2, we would have:

$$P_0 = \frac{D_1}{(1+r)^1} + \frac{D_2}{(1+r)^2} + \frac{P_2}{(1+r)^2}$$

$$= \frac{D_1}{(1+r)^1} + \frac{D_2}{(1+r)^2} + \frac{\frac{D_3 + P_3}{1+r}}{(1+r)^2}$$

$$= \frac{D_1}{(1+r)^1} + \frac{D_2}{(1+r)^2} + \frac{D_3}{(1+r)^3} + \frac{P_3}{(1+r)^3}$$

Notice that we can push the problem of coming up with the stock price off into the future forever. Importantly, no matter what the stock price is, the present value is essentially zero if we push it far enough away.[6] What we would be left with is the result that the current price of the stock can be written as the present value of the dividends beginning in one period and extending out forever:

$$P_0 = \frac{D_1}{(1+r)^1} + \frac{D_2}{(1+r)^2} + \frac{D_3}{(1+r)^3} + \frac{D_4}{(1+r)^4} + \frac{D_5}{(1+r)^4} + \cdots$$

We have illustrated here that the price of the stock today is equal to the present value of all the future dividends. How many future dividends are there? In principle, there can be an infinite number. This means we still can't compute a value for the stock because we would have to forecast an infinite number of dividends and then discount them all. In the next section, we consider some special cases where we can get around this problem.

E X A M P L E | 6.4   Growth Stocks

You might be wondering about shares of stock in companies that currently pay no dividends. Small, growing companies frequently plow back everything and thus pay no dividends. Many such companies are in mining and oil and gas. For example, at the time of writing, Sceptre Resources was trading at $8.375 per share and paid no dividends. Are such shares actually worth nothing? When we say that the value of the stock is equal to the present value of the future dividends, we don't rule out the possibility that some number of those dividends are zero. They just can't all be zero.

Imagine a hypothetical company that had a provision in its corporate charter prohibiting the paying of dividends now or ever. The corporation never borrows any money, never pays out any money to shareholders in any form whatsoever, and never sells any assets. Such a corporation couldn't really exist because the shareholders wouldn't stand for it. However, the shareholders could always vote to amend the charter if they wanted to. If it did exist, however, what would the stock be worth?

The stock is worth absolutely nothing. Such a company is a financial black hole. Money goes in, but nothing valuable ever comes out. Because nobody would ever get any return on this investment, the investment has no value. This example is a little absurd, but it illustrates that when we speak of companies that don't pay dividends, what we really mean is that they are not currently paying dividends. ▌

---

[6] One way of solving this problem is the "bigger fool" approach, which asks how much a bigger fool (than you) would pay for the stock. This approach has considerable appeal in explaining speculative bubbles that occur when prices rise to irrational levels and then fall when the bubble bursts. Our discussion focusses on more ordinary times when prices are based on rational factors.

Common Stock Valuation: Some Special Cases

There are a few very useful special circumstances where we can come up with a value for the stock. What we have to do is make some simplifying assumptions about the pattern of future dividends. The three cases we consider are (1) the dividend has a zero growth rate, (2) the dividend grows at a constant rate, and (3) the dividend grows at a constant rate after some length of time. We consider each of these separately.[7]

Zero Growth   The case of zero growth is one we've already seen. A share of common stock in a company with a constant dividend is much like a share of preferred stock. From Example 5.22 in the previous chapter, we know that the dividend on a share of fixed-rate preferred stock has zero growth and thus is constant through time. For a zero growth share of common stock, this implies that:

$$D_1 = D_2 = D_3 = D = \text{constant}$$

So, the value of the stock is:

$$P_0 = \frac{D}{(1 + r)^1} + \frac{D}{(1 + r)^2} + \frac{D}{(1 + r)^3} + \frac{D}{(1 + r)^4} + \frac{D}{(1 + r)^5} + \cdots$$

Since the dividend is always the same, the stock can be viewed as an ordinary perpetuity with a cash flow equal to D every period. The per-share value is thus given by:

$$P_0 = D/r \qquad\qquad [6.3]$$

where r is the required return.

For example, suppose the Eastcoast Energy Company has a policy of paying a $10 per share dividend every year. If this policy is to be continued indefinitely, what is the value of a share of stock if the required return is 20 percent? As it amounts to an ordinary perpetuity, the stock is worth $10/.20 = $50 per share.

Constant Growth   Suppose we knew that the dividend for some company always grows at a steady rate. Call this growth rate g. If we let D_0 be the dividend just paid, then the next dividend, D_1 is:

$$D_1 = D_0 \times (1 + g)$$

The dividend in two periods is:

$$D_2 = D_1 \times (1 + g)$$
$$= [D_0 \times (1 + g)] \times (1 + g)$$
$$= D_0 \times (1 + g)^2$$

We could repeat this process to come up with the dividend at any point in the future. In general, from our discussion of compound growth in the previous chapter, we know that the dividend t periods in the future, D_t, is given by:

$$D_t = D_0 \times (1 + g)^t$$

---

[7] Growth simply compares dollar dividends over time. In Chapter 10, we examine inflation and growth.

An asset with cash flows that grow at a constant rate forever is called a *growing perpetuity*. As we see momentarily, there is a simple expression for determining the value of such an asset.

The assumption of steady dividend growth might strike you as peculiar. Why would the dividend grow at a constant rate? The reason is that, for many companies—chartered banks, for example—steady growth in dividends is an explicit goal. This subject falls under the general heading of dividend policy, so we defer further discussion of it to Chapter 16.

E X A M P L E | 6.5   Dividend Growth Revisited

The Bank of Manitoba has just paid a dividend of $3 per share. The dividend grows at a steady rate of 8 percent per year. Based on this information, what would the dividend be in five years?

Here we have a $3 current amount that grows at 8 percent per year for five years. The future amount is thus:

$$\$3 \times (1.08)^5 = \$3 \times 1.4693 = \$4.41$$

The dividend, therefore, increases by $1.41 over the coming five years. |

If the dividend grows at a steady rate, we have replaced the problem of forecasting an infinite number of future dividends with the problem of coming up with a single growth rate, a considerable simplification. Taking D_0 to be the dividend just paid and g to be the constant growth rate, the value of a share of stock can be written as:

$$P_0 = \frac{D_1}{(1+r)^1} + \frac{D_2}{(1+r)^2} + \frac{D_3}{(1+r)^3} + \cdots$$

$$= \frac{D_0(1+g)^1}{(1+r)^1} + \frac{D_0(1+g)^2}{(1+r)^2} + \frac{D_0(1+g)^3}{(1+r)^3} + \cdots$$

As long as the growth rate, g, is less than the discount rate, r, the present value of this series of cash flows can be written very simply as:

$$P_0 = \frac{D_0 \times (1+g)}{r-g} = \frac{D_1}{r-g} \qquad [6.4]$$

dividend growth model
Model that determines the current price of a stock at its dividend next period divided by the discount rate less the dividend growth rate.

This elegant result goes by a lot of different names. We call it the **dividend growth model**.[8] By any name, it is very easy to use. To illustrate, suppose D_0 is $2.30, r is 13 percent, and g is 5 percent. The price per share is:

$$P_0 = D_0 \times (1+g)/(r-g)$$
$$= \$2.30 \times (1.05)/(.13 - .05)$$
$$= \$2.415/(.08)$$
$$= \$30.19$$

---

[8] It is often called the Gordon Model in honour of Professor Myron Gordon, University of Toronto, its best-known developer.

We can actually use the dividend growth model to get the stock price at any point in time, not just today. In general, the price of the stock as of time t is:

$$P_t = \frac{D_t \times (1 + g)}{r - g} = \frac{D_{t+1}}{r - g} \qquad [6.5]$$

In our example, suppose we were interested in the price of the stock in five years, P_5. We first need the dividend at time 5, D_5. Since the dividend just paid is \$2.30 and the growth rate is 5 percent per year, D_5 is:

$$D_5 = \$2.30 \times (1.05)^5 = \$2.30 \times 1.2763 = \$2.935$$

From the dividend growth model, the price of stock in five years is:

$$P_5 = \frac{D_5 \times (1 + g)}{r - g} = \frac{\$2.935 \times (1.05)}{.13 - .05} = \frac{\$3.0822}{.08} = \$38.53$$

E X A M P L E | 6.6   Bank of Prince Edward Island

The next dividend for the Bank of Prince Edward Island (BPEI) will be \$4.00 per share. Investors require a 16 percent return on companies such as BPEI. The bank's dividend increases by 6 percent every year. Based on the dividend growth model, what is the value of BPEI stock today? What is the value in four years?

The only tricky thing here is that the next dividend, D_1, is given as \$4.00, so we won't multiply this by $(1 + g)$. With this in mind, the price per share is given by:

$$P_0 = D_1/(r - g)$$

$$= \$4.00/(.16 - .06)$$

$$= \$4.00/(.10)$$

$$= \$40.00$$

Because we already have the dividend in one year, the dividend in four years is equal to $D_1 \times (1 + g)^3 = \$4.00 \times (1.06)^3 = \$4.764$. The price in four years is therefore:

$$P_4 = [D_4 \times (1 + g)]/(r - g)$$

$$= [\$4.764 \times 1.06]/(.16 - .06)$$

$$= \$5.05/(.10)$$

$$= \$50.50$$

Notice in this example that P_4 is equal to $P_0 \times (1 + g)^4$:

$$P_4 = \$50.50 = \$40.00 \times (1.06)^4 = P_0 \times (1 + g)^4$$

To see why this is so, notice that:

$$P_4 = D_5/(r - g)$$

However, D_5 is just equal to $D_1 \times (1 + g)^4$, so we can write P_4 as:

$$P_4 = D_1 \times (1 + g)^4/(r - g)$$

$$= \{D_1/(r - g)\} \times (1 + g)^4$$

$$= P_0 \times (1 + g)^4$$

This last example illustrates that the dividend growth model has the implicit assumption that the stock price will grow at the same constant rate as the dividend. This really isn't too surprising. What it tells us is that if the cash flows on an investment grow at a constant rate through time, so does the value of that investment. ▐

You might wonder what would happen with the dividend growth model if the growth rate, g, were greater than the discount rate, r. It looks like we would get a negative stock price because r − g would be less than zero. This is not what would happen.

Instead, if the constant growth rate exceeds the discount rate, the stock price is infinitely large. Why? When the growth rate is bigger than the discount rate, the present value of the dividends keeps on getting bigger and bigger. Essentially, the same is true if the growth rate and the discount rate are equal. In both cases, the simplification that allows us to replace the infinite stream of dividends with the dividend growth model is "illegal," so the answers we get from the dividend growth model are nonsense unless the growth rate is less than the discount rate.

Finally, the expression we came up with for the constant growth case works for any growing perpetuity, not just dividends on common stock. If C_1 is the next cash flow on a growing perpetuity, the present value of the cash flows is given by:

$$\text{Present value} = C_1/(r - g) = C_0(1 + g)/(r - g)$$

Notice that this expression looks like the result for an ordinary perpetuity except that we have $r - g$ on the bottom instead of just r.[9]

Non-constant Growth   The last case we consider is non-constant growth. The main reason to consider this is to allow for supernormal growth rates over some finite length of time. As we discussed earlier, the growth rate cannot exceed the required return indefinitely, but it certainly could do so for some number of years. To avoid the problem of having to forecast and discount an infinite number of dividends, we require that the dividends start growing at a constant rate sometime in the future.

To give a simple example of non-constant growth, consider a company that is not currently paying dividends. You predict that in five years, the company will pay a dividend for the first time. The dividend will be $.50 per share. You expect this dividend to grow at 10 percent indefinitely. The required return on companies such as this one is 20 percent. What is the price of the stock today?

To see what the stock is worth today, we find out what it will be worth once dividends are paid. We can then calculate the present value of that future price to get today's price. The first dividend will be paid in five years, and the dividend will

---

[9] PV is the sum of an infinite geometric series:

$$PV = a(1 + x + x^2 + \ldots)$$

where $a = C_1/(1 + r)$ and $x = (1 + g)/(1 + r)$. The sum of an infinite geometric series is $a/(1 - x)$. Using this result and substituting for a and x, we find

$$PV = C_1/(r - g)$$

Note that this geometric series converges to a finite sum only when x is less than 1. This implies that the growth rate, g, must be less than the interest rate.

grow steadily from then on. Using the dividend growth model, the price in four years will be:

$$P_4 = D_5/(r - g)$$

$$= \$.50/(.20 - .10)$$

$$= \$5.00$$

If the stock will be worth $5.00 in four years, we can get the current value by discounting this back four years at 20 percent:

$$P_0 = \$5.00/(1.20)^4 = \$5.00/2.0736 = \$2.41$$

The stock is therefore worth $2.41 today.

The problem of non-constant growth is only slightly more complicated if the dividends are not zero for the first several years. For example, suppose you have come up with the following dividend forecasts for the next three years:

Year	Expected Dividend
1	$1.00
2	2.00
3	2.50

After the third year, the dividend will grow at a constant rate of 5 percent per year. The required return is 10 percent. What is the value of the stock today?

As always, the value of the stock is the present value of all the future dividends. To calculate this present value, we begin by computing the present value of the stock price three years down the road just as we did previously. We then add in the present value of the dividends paid between now and then. So, the price in three years is:

$$P_3 = D_3 \times (1 + g)/(r - g)$$

$$= \$2.50 \times (1.05)/(.10 - .05)$$

$$= \$52.50$$

We can now calculate the total value of the stock as the present value of the first three dividends plus the present value of the price at time 3, P_3:

$$P_0 = D_1/(1 + r)^1 + D_2/(1 + r)^2 + D_3/(1 + r)^3 + P_3/(1 + r)^3$$

$$= \$1.00/1.10 + \$2.00/1.10^2 + \$2.50/1.10^3 + \$52.50/1.10^3$$

$$= \$0.91 + 1.65 + 1.88 + 39.44$$

$$= \$43.88$$

Thus, the value of the stock today is $43.88.

E X A M P L E | 6.7   **Supernormal Growth**

Genetic Engineering, Ltd., has been growing at a phenomenal rate of 30 percent per year because of its rapid expansion and explosive sales. You believe that this growth rate will last for three more years and then drop to 10 percent per year. If the growth rate remains at 10 percent indefinitely, what is the total value of the stock? Total dividends just paid were $5 million, and the required return is 20 percent.

Genetic Engineering is an example of supernormal growth. It is unlikely that 30 percent growth can be sustained for any extended time. To value the equity in this company, we calculate the total dividends over the supernormal growth period:

Year	Total Dividends (in millions)
1	$5.00 \times (1.3) = \$ 6.500$
2	$6.50 \times (1.3) = 8.450$
3	$8.45 \times (1.3) = 10.985$

The price at time 3 can be calculated as:

$$P_3 = D_3 \times (1 + g)/(r - g)$$

where g is the long-run growth rate. So we have:

$$P_3 = \$10.985 \times (1.10)/(.20 - .10) = \$120.835$$

To determine the value today, we need the present value of this amount plus the present value of the total dividends:

$$P_0 = D_1/(1 + r)^1 + D_2/(1 + r)^2 + D_3/(1 + r)^3 + P_3/(1 + r)^3$$

$$= \$6.50/1.20 + \$8.45/1.20^2 + \$10.985/1.20^3 + \$120.835/1.20^3$$

$$= \$5.42 + 5.87 + 6.36 + 69.93$$

$$= \$87.58$$

The total value of the stock today is thus $87.58 million. If there were, for example, 20 million shares, the stock would be worth $87.58/20 = $4.38 per share.

Changing the Growth Rate

When investment analysts use the dividend valuation model, they generally consider a range of growth scenarios. The way to do this is to set up the model on a spreadsheet and vary the inputs. For example, in our original analysis of Genetic Engineering, Ltd., we chose numbers for the inputs as shown in the baseline scenario in the following table. The model calculated the price per share as $4.38. The table shows two other possible scenarios. In the best case, the supernormal growth rate is 40 percent and continues for five instead of three years. Starting in Year 6, the normal growth rate is higher at 13 percent. In the worst case, normal growth starts immediately and there is no supernormal growth spurt. The required rate of return is 20 percent in all three cases.

The table shows that the model-calculated price is very sensitive to the inputs. In the worst case, the model price drops to $2.50; in the best case, it climbs to $8.14. Of course, there are many other scenarios we could consider with our spreadsheet. But we have done enough to show that the value of a stock depends greatly on expected growth rates and how long they last.

	Baseline	Best Case	Worst Case
Supernormal growth rate	30%	40%	n/a
Supernormal growth period	3 years	5 years	0 years
Normal growth rate	10%	13%	10%
Required rate of return	20%	20%	20%
Model calculated price	$4.38	$8.14	$2.50

Components of the Required Return

Thus far, we have taken the required return or discount rate, r, as given. We have quite a bit to say on this subject in Chapters 10 and 11. For now, we want to examine the implications of the dividend growth model for this required return. Earlier, we calculated P_0 as:

$$P_0 = D_1/(r - g)$$

If we rearrange this to solve for r, we get:

$$(r - g) = D_1/P_0 \qquad\qquad\qquad [6.6]$$
$$r = D_1/P_0 + g$$

This tells us that the total return, r, has two components: The first of these, D_1/P_0, is called the **dividend yield**. Because this is calculated as the expected cash dividend divided by the current price, it is conceptually similar to the current yield on a bond.

The second part of the total return is the growth rate, g. We know that the dividend growth rate is also the rate at which the stock price grows (see Example 6.6). Thus, this growth rate can be interpreted as the **capital gains yield**, that is, the rate at which the value of the investment grows.

To illustrate the components of the required return, suppose we observe a stock selling for $20 per share. The next dividend will be $1 per share. You think that the dividend will grow by 10 percent more or less indefinitely. What return does this stock offer you if this is correct?

dividend yield
A stock's cash dividend divided by its current price.

capital gains yield
The dividend growth rate or the rate at which the value of an investment grows.

The dividend growth model calculates total return as:

$$r = \text{Dividend yield} + \text{Capital gains yield}$$
$$r = D_1/P_0 + g$$

The total return works out to be:

$$r = \$1/\$20 + 10\%$$
$$= 5\% + 10\%$$
$$= 15\%$$

This stock, therefore, has a return of 15 percent.

We can verify this answer by calculating the price in one year, P_1, using 15 percent as the required return. Based on the dividend growth model, this price is:

$$P_1 = D_1 \times (1 + g)/(r - g)$$
$$= \$1 \times (1.10)/(.15 - .10)$$
$$= \$1.1/.05$$
$$= \$22$$

Notice that this $22 is $20 × (1.1), so the stock price has grown by 10 percent as it should. If you pay $20 for the stock today, you would get a $1 dividend at the end of the year and have a $22 − 20 = $2 gain. Your dividend yield is thus $1/$20 = 5%. Your capital gains yield is $2/$20 = 10%, so your total return would be 5% + 10% = 15%. Our discussion of stock valuation is summarized in Table 6.2.

Stock Market Reporting

If you look through the pages of the *Financial Post* or another financial newspaper, you find information on a large number of stocks in several different markets. Figure

T A B L E 6.2

Summary of stock valuation

The General Case

In general, the price today of a share of stock, P_0, is the present value of all of its future dividends, $D_1, D_2, D_3 \ldots$

$$P_0 = \frac{D_1}{(1+r)^1} + \frac{D_2}{(1+r)^2} + \frac{D_3}{(1+r)^3} \cdots$$

where r is the required return.

Constant Growth Case

If the dividend grows at a steady rate, g, the price can be written as:

$$P_0 = \frac{D_1}{(r-g)}$$

This result is called the *dividend growth model*.

Supernormal Growth

If the dividend grows steadily after t periods, the price can be written as:

$$P_0 = \frac{D_1}{(1+r)^1} + \frac{D_2}{(1+r)^2} + \cdots + \frac{D_t}{(1+r)^t} + \frac{P_t}{(1+r)^t}$$

where

$$P_t = \frac{D_t \times (1+g)}{(r-g)}$$

The Required Return

The required return, r, can be written as the sum of two things:

$$R = D_1/P_0 + g$$

where D_1/P_0 is the *dividend yield* and g is the *capital gains yield* (which is the same thing as the growth rate in the dividends for the steady growth case).

6.4 reproduces a small section of the stock page for the Toronto Stock Exchange (TSE) for February 2, 1995. In Figure 6.4, locate the line for Bombardier (Bombrdr A).

The first two numbers, 25 and 18, are the high and low price for the last 52 weeks. Stock prices are quoted in dollars and fractions down to 1/8.[10] The diamond next to the company name indicates that these shares are non-voting stock. We discuss voting rights in Chapter 13.

The .30 is the annual dividend rate. Since Bombardier, like most companies, pays dividends quarterly, this $.30 is actually the last quarterly dividend multiplied by four. So, the last cash dividend paid was $.30/4 = $.075. The column marked Yield % gives the dividend yield based on the current dividend and the closing price. For Bombardier this is $.30/23.75 = 1.3% as shown.

The High, Low, and Close figures are the high, low, and closing prices during the day. The Net Chg of +3/4 tells us the closing price of $23 3/4 per share is $.75 higher than the closing price the day before; so we say that Bombardier was up 3/4 for the day.

The column labelled PE (short for price/earnings or P/E ratio) is the closing price of $23 3/4 divided by annual earnings per share (based on the most recent full fiscal year.) In the jargon of Bay Street, we might say Bombardier "sells for 17.5 times earnings."

---

[10] Earlier we saw that the bond market has evolved a different tradition of quoting in dollars, percents, and basis points. To compare the two, recall that a basis point is 1/100 of 1 percent.

The Financial Post Feb. 3/95 p.26

Toronto Thurs. Feb. 2,1995

	52W high	52W low	Stock	Ticker	Div	Yield %	P/E	Vol 100s	High /ask	Low /bid	Cls/ last	Net chg
x	$29\frac{3}{4}$	$26\frac{5}{8}$	BkofMtl4pf		v2.25	8.3		49	$27\frac{1}{8}$	27	27	$-\frac{5}{8}$
x	$31\frac{3}{4}$	$27\frac{1}{2}$	BkofMtl1pf		2.25	8.2		10	$27\frac{1}{2}$	$27\frac{1}{2}$	$27\frac{1}{2}$	$-\frac{3}{8}$
lx	$28\frac{3}{8}$	$24\frac{1}{4}$	BkofMtl2pf*		u1.68	6.9		110	$24\frac{1}{2}$	$24\frac{1}{4}$	$24\frac{1}{2}$	$-\frac{1}{2}$
	$33\frac{1}{4}$	$23\frac{1}{8}$	BkofNS	BNS	1.24	4.8	14.7	4487	$25\frac{7}{8}$	$25\frac{1}{2}$	$25\frac{7}{8}$	$+\frac{1}{4}$
	$24\frac{1}{4}$	$21\frac{5}{8}$	BkofNS1pf		f1.26	5.7		1129	$22\frac{1}{4}$	$22\frac{1}{8}$	$22\frac{1}{4}$	$+\frac{1}{8}$
	$27\frac{1}{2}$	$25\frac{1}{4}$	BkofNS4pf		v2.25	8.6		17	$26\frac{1}{2}$	$26\frac{1}{4}$	$26\frac{1}{4}$	$-\frac{1}{8}$
	$29\frac{1}{4}$	$26\frac{3}{8}$	BkofNS5pf		2.31	8.7		19	$26\frac{7}{8}$	$26\frac{5}{8}$	$26\frac{5}{8}$	$-\frac{1}{8}$
	$28\frac{1}{2}$	$24\frac{1}{4}$	BkofNS6pf		1.78	7.3		85	$24\frac{5}{8}$	$24\frac{1}{2}$	$24\frac{1}{2}$	$-\frac{1}{8}$
n	$25\frac{1}{4}$	$24\frac{1}{4}$	BkofNS7pf		1.77	7.2		8	$24\frac{1}{2}$	$24\frac{1}{2}$	$24\frac{1}{2}$	
	$40\frac{5}{8}$	$27\frac{1}{4}$	BarrickGld	ARX	u0.10	0.5	25.8	17065	$29\frac{1}{2}$	$28\frac{3}{4}$	$29\frac{3}{8}$	+1
	$7\frac{1}{4}$	3.85	Barrington	BPL			17.3	6	4.15	4.15	4.15	-0.15
	$8\frac{3}{4}$	6	Baton	BNB				nt	$8\frac{1}{8}$	$7\frac{1}{2}$	$7\frac{3}{4}$	
n	3.45	2.60	BaytexA‡	BTE			33.1	47	2.65	2.65	2.65	
n	0.50	0.31	BaytexB♦					nt	0.41	0.38	0.40	
	$14\frac{1}{2}$	$9\frac{1}{4}$	Beamscope	BSP			17.9	5	$13\frac{1}{4}$	$13\frac{1}{4}$	$13\frac{1}{4}$	$-\frac{1}{4}$
	1.25	0.50	BearingPwr	BPO				nt	0.60	0.50	0.50	
	2.59	1.65	BeauCda	BAU			17.0	2492	1.73	1.70	1.70	
	$13\frac{3}{4}$	$7\frac{1}{4}$	BeckerB♦	BEK				19	8	8	8	
n	2.45	1.80	Bedford B♦‡	BED				nt	3.25	2.00	1.90	
	$28\frac{1}{2}$	25	Bell8pf	BC	1.94	7.6		2	$25\frac{1}{2}$	$25\frac{1}{2}$	$25\frac{1}{2}$	
	$27\frac{1}{2}$	$24\frac{1}{8}$	Bell9pf		1.87	7.4		5	$25\frac{1}{4}$	$25\frac{1}{4}$	$25\frac{1}{4}$	
	28	$25\frac{3}{4}$	Bell10pf		1.86			nt	$26\frac{1}{4}$	$25\frac{1}{2}$	$25\frac{3}{4}$	
	3.40	2.05	BemaGld‡	BGO			30.4	201	2.15	2.11	2.13	+0.02
	1.60	1.10	Benson‡	BEN			16.4	40	1.15	1.15	1.15	-0.05
	0.65	0.35	Bethlehem	BTH				725	0.43	0.38	0.41	+0.02
	21	$11\frac{1}{2}$	BioChemPh	BCH				237	$19\frac{3}{4}$	19	$19\frac{1}{8}$	$-\frac{5}{8}$
	$9\frac{1}{2}$	4.65	Biomira	BRA				60	4.80	4.75	4.75	-0.05
↓	4.10	1.70	Bionaire	ION			85.0	5	1.70	1.70	1.70	-0.10
n	4.70	1.60	Bioniche‡	BNC				152	2.00	1.85	1.85	-0.15
	$13\frac{1}{2}$	4.60	Biovail	BVF			6.8	18	$11\frac{1}{2}$	$11\frac{1}{2}$	$11\frac{1}{2}$	$-\frac{1}{2}$
	1.05	0.47	BiHawk‡	BHK				61	0.79	0.77	0.79	+0.04
	0.48	0.12	BiSwan	BSW				975	0.19	0.165	0.175	+0.01
	$11\frac{3}{4}$	$8\frac{1}{8}$	BiRangeA	BBR				nt	$8\frac{3}{8}$	$8\frac{1}{4}$	$8\frac{3}{8}$	
ln	2.75	1.56	BolivarGld‡	BVG				48	1.56	1.56	1.56	-0.14
	25	18	BombrdrA♦	BBD	0.30	1.3	17.5	174	$23\frac{3}{4}$	$23\frac{1}{4}$	$23\frac{3}{4}$	$+\frac{3}{4}$
	$25\frac{1}{4}$	$17\frac{3}{4}$	BombrdrB♦		0.31	1.3	17.5	1207	24	$23\frac{1}{4}$	$23\frac{3}{4}$	$+\frac{5}{8}$
	26	$22\frac{3}{4}$	Bombrdr pf		v1.87			nt	$24\frac{5}{8}$	...	$24\frac{5}{8}$	
	24	20	Bonar	BON	0.20			nt	$23\frac{3}{4}$	20	20	
	1.48	0.90	Bovar	BVR			17.5	2685	1.07	1.00	1.05	+0.05
	0.55	0.105	BowFlex‡	BFX				61	0.40	0.35	0.39	+0.04
	4.70	2.20	Bracknell	BRK				55	3.00	2.80	2.90	-0.10
s	$9\frac{3}{4}$	0.99	Bramalea	BCD			5.2	1183	1.16	1.12	1.15	+0.03
↓	2.90	1.35	BramptnBrA♦	BBL				2	1.45	1.35	1.35	-0.20
	0.45	0.13	Brandevor‡	BVE				150	0.19	0.19	0.19	+0.01
n	1.30	0.55	Brandslt	BNT			14.6	20	0.70	0.65	0.70	+0.10
n	0.25	0.03	BrandsltAwt					nt	0.08	0.03	0.03	
	$40\frac{1}{2}$	$36\frac{5}{8}$	BrascdApf	BCA	f3.62			nt	$38\frac{1}{2}$	37	38	
	$39\frac{1}{2}$	37	BrascdBpf		f3.22			nt	39	$38\frac{1}{4}$	$38\frac{1}{4}$	
	21	$16\frac{3}{4}$	BrascanA	BL	1.04	5.6	22.4	2247	$18\frac{5}{8}$	$18\frac{1}{2}$	$18\frac{5}{8}$	

FIGURE 6.4

Sample stock market quotation from the Financial Post

Reprinted with permission of the *Financial Post,* February 3, 1995, p. 6.

The remaining column, marked Vol 100s, tells us how many shares traded during the day (in hundreds). For example, the 174 for Bombardier tells us that 17,400 shares changed hands. If the average price during the day was $23.50 or so, the dollar volume of transactions was on the order of $23.50 × 17,400 = $408,900 worth of Bombardier stock.

Growth Opportunities

We previously spoke of the growth rate of dividends. We now want to address the related concept of growth opportunities. Imagine a company with a level stream of earnings per share in perpetuity. The company pays all these earnings out to shareholders as dividends. Hence,

EPS = Div

where EPS is *earnings per share* and Div is dividends per share. A company of this type is frequently called a *cash cow*.

From the perpetuity formula of the previous chapter, the value of a share of stock is:

Value of a share of stock when firm acts as a cash cow: $\dfrac{EPS}{r} = \dfrac{Div}{r}$

where r is the discount rate on the firm's stock.

The preceding policy of paying out all earnings as dividends may not be the optimal one. Many firms have growth opportunities, that is, opportunities to invest in profitable projects. Because these projects can represent a significant fraction of the firm's value, it would be foolish to forgo them to pay out all earnings as dividends.

Although management frequently thinks of a set of growth opportunities, let's focus on only one opportunity; that is, the opportunity to invest in a single project. Suppose the firm retains the entire dividend at Date 1 to invest in a particular capital budgeting project. The net present value per share of the project as of Date 0 is NPVGO, which stands for the *net present value (per share) of the growth opportunity*.

What is the price of a share of stock at Date 0 if the firm decides to take on the project at Date 1? Because the per-share value of the project is added to the original stock price, the stock price must now be:

Stock price after firm commits to new project: $\dfrac{EPS}{r} + NPVGO$

This equation indicates that the price of a share of stock can be viewed as the sum of two different items: The first term (EPS/r) is the value of the firm if it rested on its laurels, that is, if it simply distributed all earnings to the shareholders. The second term is the additional value if the firm retains earnings to fund new projects.

Application: The Price Earnings Ratio

Even though our stock valuation formulas focussed on dividends, not earnings, financial analysts often rely on price earnings ratios (P/Es). We saw in Figure 6.4 that financial newspapers report P/Es.

We showed in the previous section that

Price per share $= \dfrac{EPS}{r} + NPVGO$

Dividing by EPS yields

$$\frac{\text{Price per share}}{\text{EPS}} = \frac{1}{r} + \frac{NPVGO}{EPS}$$

The left-hand side is the formula for the price-earnings ratio. The equation shows that the P/E ratio is related to the net present value of growth opportunities. As an example, consider two firms each having just reported earnings per share of $1. However, one firm has many valuable growth opportunities while the other firm has no growth opportunities at all. The firm with growth opportunities should sell at a higher price because an investor is buying both current income of $1 and growth opportunities. Suppose the firm with growth opportunities sells for $16 and the other firm sells for $8. The $1 earnings per share appears in the denominator of the P/E ratio for both firms. Thus, the P/E ratio is 16 for the firm with growth opportunities, but only 8 for the firm without the opportunities.[11]

Our discussion of growth and NPVGO helps explain why Barrick Gold has a higher P/E than Bank of Nova Scotia. Figure 6.4 shows that on February 3, 1995, Bank of Nova Scotia's P/E was 14.7 versus 25.8 for Barrick Gold. Investors likely expect higher growth in EPS for Barrick Gold.

Because P/E ratios are based on earnings and not cash flows, investors comparing CIBC and Barrick Gold should follow up with cash flow analysis using the dividend valuation model. Using a spreadsheet to look at different growth scenarios lets investors quantify projected growth in cash flows.

> CONCEPT QUESTIONS
> 1. What are the relevant cash flows for valuing a share of common stock?
> 2. Does the value of a share of stock depend on how long you expect to keep it?
> 3. How does expected dividend growth impact on the stock price in the dividend valuation model? Is this consistent with the NPVGO approach?

6.3 | SUMMARY AND CONCLUSIONS

This chapter has shown you how to extend the basic present value results of Chapter 5 in some important ways. In our discussion of bonds and stocks, we saw that:

1. Bonds are long-term corporate debts. We examined the cash flows from a corporate bond and found that the present value of the cash flows and, hence, the bond's value can be readily determined. We also introduced some of the terminology associated with bonds, and we discussed how bond prices are reported in the financial press.

2. The cash flows from owning a share of stock come in the form of future dividends. We saw that in certain special cases it is possible to calculate the present value of all the future dividends and thus come up with a value for the stock. We discussed some of the terms associated with common stock, and we also examined how stock price information is reported.

This chapter completes Part III of our book. By now, you should have a good grasp of what we mean by present value. You should also be familiar with how to calculate present values, loan payments, and so on. In Part IV, we cover capital budgeting decisions. As you will see, the techniques you learned in Chapters 5 and 6 form the basis for our approach to evaluating business investment decisions.

Key Terms

coupons (page 188)   yield to maturity (YTM) (page 188)
face value or par value (page 188)   dividend growth model (page 200)
coupon rate (page 188)   dividend yield (page 205)
maturity (page 188)   capital gains yield (page 205)

---

[11] Other factors causing a high P/E are low risk reflected in a low discount rate, *r*, and conservative accounting. Because they are based on earnings and not cash flows, P/E ratios should be compared with caution.

Chapter Review Problems and Self-Test

6.1 **Bond Values**   A Mataborough Industries bond has a 10 percent coupon rate and a $1,000 face value. Interest is paid semiannually, and the bond has 20 years to maturity. If investors require a 12 percent yield, what is the bond's value? What is the effective annual yield on the bond?

6.2 **Bond Yields**   A Macrohard Corporation bond carries an 8 percent coupon, paid semiannually. The par value is $1,000 and the bond matures in six years. If the bond currently sells for $911.37, what is its yield to maturity? What is the effective annual yield?

6.3 **Dividend Growth and Stock Valuation**   The Arro Company has just paid a cash dividend of $2 per share. Investors require a 16 percent return from investments such as this. If the dividend is expected to grow at a steady 8 percent per year, what is the current value of the stock? What would the stock be worth in five years?

6.4 **More Dividend Growth and Stock Valuation**   In the previous problem, what would the stock sell for today if the dividend is expected to grow at 20 percent for the next three years and then settle down to 8 percent per year?

Answers to Self-Test Problems

6.1 Because the bond has a 10 percent coupon yield while investors require a 12 percent return, we know the bond must sell at a discount. Notice that, since the bond pays interest semiannually, the coupons amount to $100/2 = $50 every six months. The required yield is 12%/2 = 6% every six months. Finally, the bond matures in 20 years, so there are a total of 40 six-month periods.

The bond's value is thus equal to the present value of $50 every six months for the next 40 six-month periods plus the present value of the $1,000 face amount:

$$\text{Bond value} = \$50 \times [1 - 1/(1.06)^{40}]/.06 + \$1,000/(1.06)^{40}$$
$$= \$50 \times 15.04630 + \$1,000/10.2857$$
$$= \$849.54$$

Notice that we discounted the $1,000 back 40 periods at 6 percent per period, rather than 20 years at 12 percent. The reason is that the effective annual yield on the bond is $1.06^2 - 1 = 12.36\%$, not 12%. We thus could have used 12.36 percent per year for 20 years when we calculated the present value of the $1,000 face amount, and the answer would have been the same.

6.2 The present value of the bond's cash flows is its current price, $911.37. The coupon is $40 every six months for 12 periods. The face value is $1,000, so the bond's yield is the unknown discount rate in the following:

$$\$911.37 = \$40 \times [1 - 1/(1 + r)^{12}] + \$1,000/(1 + r)^{12}$$

The bond sells at a discount. Since the coupon rate is 8 percent, the yield must be something in excess of that.

If we were to solve this by trial and error, we might try 12 percent (or 6 percent per six months):

$$\text{Bond value} = \$40 \times [1 - 1/1.06^{12}]/.06 + \$1,000/1.06^{12}$$
$$= \$832.32$$

This is less than the actual value, so our discount rate is too high. We now know that the yield is somewhere between 8 and 12 percent. With further trial and error (or a little machine assistance), the yield works out to be 10 percent, or 5 percent every six months.

By convention, the bond's yield to maturity would be quoted as $2 \times 5\% = 10\%$. The effective yield is thus $1.05^2 - 1 = 10.25\%$.

6.3   The last dividend, D_0, was \$2. The dividend is expected to grow steadily at 8 percent. The required return is 16 percent. Based on the dividend growth model, the current price is:

$$P_0 = D_1/(r - g) = D_0 \times (1 + g)/(r - g)$$

$$= \$2 \times (1.08)/(.16 - .08)$$

$$= \$2.16/(.08)$$

$$= \$27$$

We could calculate the price in five years by calculating the dividend in five years and then using the growth model again. Alternatively, we could recognize that the stock price increases by 8 percent per year and calculate the future price directly. We'll do both. First, the dividend in five years would be:

$$D_5 = D_0 \times (1 + g)^5$$

$$= \$2 \times 1.08^5$$

$$= \$2.9387$$

The price in five years would therefore be:

$$P_5 = D_5 \times (1 + g)/(r - g)$$

$$= \$2.9387 \times (1.08)/.08$$

$$= \$3.1738/.08$$

$$= \$39.67$$

Once we understand the dividend model, however, it's easier to notice that:

$$P_5 = P_0 \times (1 + g)^5$$

$$= \$27 \times 1.08^5$$

$$= \$27 \times 1.4693$$

$$= \$39.67$$

Notice that both approaches yield the same price in five years.

6.4   In this scenario, we have supernormal growth for the next three years. We'll need to calculate the dividends during the rapid growth period and the stock price in three years. The dividends are:

$$D_1 = \$2.00 \times 1.20 = \$2.400$$
$$D_2 = \$2.40 \times 1.20 = \$2.880$$
$$D_3 = \$2.88 \times 1.20 = \$3.456$$

After three years, the growth rate falls to 8 percent indefinitely. The price at that time, P_3, is thus:

$$P_3 = D_3 \times (1 + g)/(r - g)$$

$$= \$3.456 \times 1.08/(.16 - .08)$$

$$= \$3.7325/.08$$

$$= \$46.656$$

To complete the calculation of the stock's present value, we have to determine the present value of the three dividends and the future price:

$$P_0 = D_1/(1 + r)^1 + D_2/(1 + r)^2 + D_3/(1 + r)^3 + P_3/(1 + r)^3$$

$$= \$2.40/1.16 + \$2.88/1.16^2 + \$3.456/1.16^3 + 46.656/1.16^3$$

$$= \$2.07 + \$2.14 + \$2.21 + \$29.89$$

$$= \$36.31$$

Questions and Problems

Basic
(Questions 1–20)

1. **Coupon Rates**   How does a bond issuer decide the appropriate coupon rate to set on its bonds? Explain the difference between the coupon rate and the required return on a bond.

2. **Interpreting Bond Yields**   Is the yield to maturity on a bond the same thing as the required return? Is YTM the same thing as the coupon rate? Suppose today a 10 percent coupon bond sells at par. Two years from now, the required return on the same bond is 8 percent. What is the coupon rate on the bond now? The YTM?

3. **Interpreting Bond Yields**   Suppose you buy a 9 percent coupon, 15-year bond today when its first issued. If interest rates suddenly rise to 15 percent, what happens to the value of your bond? Why?

4. **Bond Prices**   CIR, Inc., has 7 percent coupon bonds on the market that have 11 years left to maturity. The bonds make annual payments. If the YTM on these bonds is 8.5 percent, what is the current bond price?

5. **Bond Yields**   N&N Co. has 10.5 percent coupon bonds on the market with eight years left to maturity. The bonds make annual payments. If the bond currently sells for $1,070, what is its YTM?

6. **Coupon Rates**   Merton Enterprises has bonds on the market making annual payments, with 14 years to maturity, and selling for $950. At this price, the bonds yield 7.5 percent. What must the coupon rate be on Merton's bonds?

7. **Bond Prices**   Jane's Pizzeria issued 10-year bonds one year ago at a coupon rate of 8.75 percent. The bonds make semiannual payments. If the YTM on these bonds is 7.25 percent, what is the current bond price?

8. **Bond Yields**   Jerry's Spaghetti Factory issued 12-year bonds two years ago at a coupon rate of 9.5 percent. The bonds make semiannual payments. If these bonds currently sell for 96 percent of par value, what is the YTM?

9. **Coupon Rates**   Dunbar Corporation has bonds on the market with 10.5 years to maturity, a YTM of 10 percent, and a current price of $860. The bonds make semiannual payments. What must the coupon rate be on Dunbar's bonds?

10. **Interpreting Stock Valuations**   Explain the general method for valuing a share of stock. Under what two assumptions can you use the dividend growth model presented in the text? Suppose a stock violates these assumptions. Explain how you could find the price of a share in this case.

11. **Stock Values**   MegaCapital, Inc., just paid a dividend of $2.00 per share on its stock. The dividends are expected to grow at a constant 6 percent per year indefinitely. If investors require a 13 percent return on MegaCapital stock, what is the current price? What will the price be in 3 years? In 15 years?

12. **Stock Values**   SAF Inc.'s next dividend payment will be $3.00 per share. The dividends are anticipated to maintain a 5 percent growth rate forever. If SAF stock currently sells for $70.50 per share, what is the required return?

Basic
(Continued)

13. **Stock Values**   For the company in the previous problem, what is the dividend yield? What is the expected capital gains yield?

14. **Stock Values**   Makin' Copies Corporation will pay a $4.25 per share dividend next year. The company pledges to increase its dividend by 9 percent per year indefinitely. If you require an 18 percent return on your investment, how much will you pay for the company's stock today?

15. **Stock Valuation**   Utopia Power Co. is expected to maintain a constant 5 percent growth rate in its dividends indefinitely. If the company has a dividend yield of 5.5 percent, what is the required return on the power company's stock?

16. **Stock Valuation**   Suppose you know that a company's stock currently sells for $50 per share and the required return on the stock is 15 percent. You also know that the total return on the stock is evenly divided between a capital gains yield and a dividend yield. If it's the company's policy to always maintain a constant growth rate in its dividends, what is the current dividend per share?

17. **Stock Valuation**   Jordan's Jalopies pays a constant $5.00 dividend on its stock. The company will maintain this dividend for the next seven years, and then cease paying any more dividends forever. If the required return on this stock is 12 percent, what is the current share price?

18. **Valuing Preferred Stock**   Always Tranquil, Inc., has an issue of preferred stock outstanding that pays an $8.50 dividend every year in perpetuity. If this issue currently sells for $115.00 per share, what is the required return?

19. **Bond Pricing**   This problem refers to the bond quotes in Figure 6.3. Calculate the price of the CANADA 10.25 1 FEB 04 to prove that it is 106.352 as shown.

20. **Bond Value**   In 1995, Quebec provincial bonds carried a higher yield than comparable Ontario bonds because of investors' uncertainty about the political future of Quebec. Suppose you were an investment manager who thought the market was overplaying these fears. In particular, suppose you thought that yields on Quebec bonds would fall by 50 basis points. Which bonds would you buy or sell? Explain in words. Illustrate with a numerical example showing your potential profit.

21. **Bond Prices versus Yields**
    a. What is the relationship between the price of a bond and its YTM?
    b. Explain why some bonds sell at a premium to par value, and other bonds sell at a discount. What do you know about the relationship between the coupon rate and the YTM for premium bonds? What about for discount bonds? For bonds selling at par value?
    c. What is the relationship between the current yield and YTM for premium bonds? For discount bonds? For bonds selling at par value?

Intermediate
(Questions 21–40)

22. **Bond Price Movements**   Bond X is a premium bond making annual payments. The bond pays a 9 percent coupon, has a YTM of 7 percent, and has 15 years to maturity. Bond Y is a discount bond making annual payments. This bond pays a 6 percent coupon, has a YTM of 9 percent, and also has 15 years to maturity. If interest rates remain unchanged, what do you expect the price of these bonds to be one year from now? In 5 years? In 10 years? In 14 years? In

15 years? What's going on here? Illustrate your answers by graphing bond prices versus time to maturity.

23. **Interest Rate Risk**   Both Bond A and Bond B have 8 percent coupons, make semiannual payments, and are priced at par value. Bond A has 2 years to maturity, while Bond B has 15 years to maturity. If interest rates suddenly rise by 2 percent, what is the percentage change in price of Bond A? Of Bond B? If rates were to suddenly fall by 2 percent instead, what would the percentage change in the price of Bond A be now? Of Bond B? Illustrate your answers by graphing bond prices versus YTM. What does this problem tell you about the interest rate risk of longer-term bonds?

24. **Interest Rate Risk**   Bond J is a 4 percent coupon bond. Bond K is a 10 percent coupon bond. Both bonds have 10 years to maturity, make semiannual payments, and have a YTM of 9 percent. If interest rates suddenly rise by 2 percent, what is the percentage price change of these bonds? What if rates suddenly fall by 2 percent instead? What does this problem tell you about the interest rate risk of lower-coupon bonds?

25. **Bond Yields**   BrainDrain Software has 12 percent coupon bonds on the market with nine years to maturity. The bonds make semiannual payments and currently sell for 110 percent of par. What is the current yield on BrainDrain's bonds? The YTM? The effective annual yield?

26. **Bond Yields**   DRK Co. wants to issue new 10-year bonds for some much-needed expansion projects. The company currently has 8 percent coupon bonds on the market that sell for $1,040, make semiannual payments, and mature in 10 years. What coupon rate should the company set on its new bonds if it wants them to sell at par?

27. **Finding the Bond Maturity**   ABC Co. has 10 percent coupon bonds making annual payments with a YTM of 8.5 percent. The current yield on these bonds is 9.01 percent. How many years do these bonds have left until they mature?

28. **Using Bond Quotes**   Suppose the following bond quote for ISU Corporation appears on the financial page of today's newspaper. If this bond has a face value of $1,000, what closing price appeared in yesterday's newspaper?

Bonds	Cur Yld	Vol	Close	Net Chg
ISU 7⅞s11	8.7	10	??	+½

29. **Finding the Maturity**   You've just found a 10 percent coupon bond on the market that sells for par value. What is the maturity on this bond?

30. **Stock Value Intuition**   Suppose you buy some stock today with the intention of selling it in three years to your brother. Does your expected selling price enter into your valuation of the current stock price? Draw a time line of your cash flows from the stock and a time line of your brother's cash flows to illustrate your answer.

31. **Stock Valuation**   My Money, Inc., just paid a dividend of $2.50 on its stock. The growth rate in dividends is expected to be a constant 6.5 percent per year indefinitely. Investors require a 20 percent return on the stock for the first three years, then a 15 percent return for the next three years, and then a 10 percent return thereafter. What is the current share price for My Money stock?

32. **Non-constant Growth**   Harry's Hat Shop is a young start-up company. No dividends will be paid on the stock over the next five years, because the firm

needs to plow back its earnings to fuel growth. The company will then begin paying a $2.00 per share dividend and will increase the dividend by 7 percent per year thereafter. If the required return on this stock is 14 percent, what is the current share price?

Intermediate
(Continued)

33. **Non-constant Dividends**   Lennen & McKarty, Inc., has an odd dividend policy. The company just paid a dividend of $6.00 per share and has announced it will increase the dividend by $1.00 per share each of the next four years and then never pay another dividend thereafter. If you require an 8 percent return on the company's stock, how much will you pay for a share today?

34. **Non-constant Dividends**   Callaway Corporation is expected to pay the following dividends over the next four years: $2.25, $4.00, $3.00, $1.00. Afterward, the company pledges to maintain a constant 8 percent growth rate in dividends forever. If the required return on the stock is 16 percent, what is the current share price?

35. **Supernormal Growth**   Giant Growth Co. is growing fast. Dividends are expected to grow at a 28 percent rate for the next three years and then fall off to a constant 5 percent growth rate thereafter. If the required return is 20 percent and the company just paid a $1.75 dividend, what is the current share price?

36. **Supernormal Growth**   PerfectSoft Corp. is experiencing rapid growth. Dividends are expected to grow at 30 percent per year during the next three years, 20 percent over the following year, and then 6 percent per year indefinitely. The required return on this stock is 15 percent, and the stock currently sells for $42.50 per share. What is the projected dividend for the coming year?

37. **Negative Growth**   Ancient Items Co. is a mature manufacturing firm. The company just paid a $4.00 dividend, but management expects to reduce this payout by 6 percent per year indefinitely. If you require a 15 percent return on this stock, what will you pay for a share today?

38. **Finding the Dividend**   Carla's Candy Shop stock currently sells for $92 per share. The market requires a 13 percent return on the firm's stock. If the company maintains a constant 10 percent growth rate in dividends, what was the most recent dividend per share paid on the stock?

39. **Valuing Preferred Stock**   Bob's Bank just issued some new preferred stock. The issue will pay a $7.00 annual dividend in perpetuity, beginning four years from now. If the market requires a 6 percent return on this investment, how much does a share of preferred stock cost today?

40. **Using Stock Quotes**   You found the following stock quote for DRK Enterprises, Inc., in the financial pages of today's newspaper. What was the closing price for this stock that appeared in yesterday's paper? If the company currently has one million shares of stock outstanding, what was net income for the most recent four quarters?

52 wk.											
Hi	Lo	Stock	Sym	Div	Yld %	P/E	Vol 100s	Hi	Lo	Close	Net Chg
117	52½	DRK	DRK	3.60	4.6	16	7295	81¾	76	??	−⅜

41. **Components of Bond Returns**   Bond P is a premium bond with a 9.5 percent coupon. Bond D is a 6 percent coupon discount bond. Both bonds make annual

Challenge
(Questions 41–48)

**Challenge
(Continued)**

payments, have a YTM of 8 percent, and have eight years to maturity. What is the current yield for Bond P? For Bond D? If interest rates remain unchanged, what is the expected capital gains yield over the next year for Bond P? For Bond D? Explain your answers and the interrelationship among the various types of yields.

42. **Holding Period Yield** The YTM on a bond is the interest rate you earn on your investment if interest rates don't change. If you actually sell the bond before it matures, your realized return is known as the holding period yield (HPY).

a. Suppose you buy a 10 percent coupon bond making annual payments today for $1,100. The bond has 10 years to maturity. What rate of return do you expect to earn on your investment?

b. Two years from now, the YTM on your bond has declined by 2.5 percent, and you decide to sell. What price will your bond sell for? What is the HPY on your investment? Compare this yield to the YTM when you first bought the bond. Why are they different?

43. **Valuing Bonds** The Tightwad Corporation has two different bonds currently outstanding. Bond M has a face value of $25,000 and matures in 20 years. The bond makes no payments for the first six years, then pays $1,500 semiannually over the subsequent eight years, and finally pays $2,000 semiannually over the last six years. Bond N also has a face value of $25,000 and a maturity of 20 years; it makes no coupon payments over the life of the bond. If the required return on both these bonds is 10 percent compounded semiannually, what is the current price of Bond M? Of Bond N?

44. **Valuing Consol Bonds** Forever Working Co. has a consol bond on the market that just made a $50 coupon payment. The bond makes annual payments in perpetuity that grow at a rate of 5 percent every year. Your required return on these consol bonds is 10 percent.

a. How much would you pay for this bond today?

b. If the bond was issued 20 years ago, what coupon payment was made at the end of the first year the bond was outstanding?

c. If the required return was 12 percent 20 years ago, and Forever Working issued 1,000 of these bonds, what was the company's proceeds from the issuance?

45. **Capital Gains versus Income** Consider four different stocks, all of which have a required return of 18 percent and a most recent dividend of $2.25 per share. Stocks W, X, and Y are expected to maintain constant growth rates in dividends for the foreseeable future of 12 percent, 0 percent, and −10 percent per year, respectively. Stock Z is a growth stock that will increase its dividend by 30 percent for the next two years and then maintain a constant 12 percent growth rate thereafter. What is the dividend yield for each of these four stocks? What is the expected capital gains yield? Discuss the relationship among the various returns that you find for each of these stocks.

46. **Stock Valuation** Most corporations pay quarterly dividends on their common stock rather than annual dividends. Barring any unusual circumstances during the year, the board raises, lowers, or maintains the current dividend once a year and then pays this dividend out in equal quarterly installments to its shareholders.

a. Suppose a company currently pays a $3.00 annual dividend on its common stock in a single annual installment, and management plans on raising this dividend by 10 percent per year indefinitely. If the required return on this stock is 18 percent, what is the current share price?

b. Now suppose the company in (*a*) actually pays its annual dividend in equal quarterly installments; thus this company just paid a $0.75 dividend per share, as it has the previous three quarters. What is your value for the current share price now? (Hint: Find the equivalent annual end-of-year dividend for each year, and the appropriate effective annual discount rate.) Comment on whether you feel this model of stock valuation is appropriate.

47. **Non-constant Growth**   Kardassian Ice Cream Co. just paid a dividend of $6.75 per share. The company will increase its dividend by 25 percent next year and then will reduce this dividend growth rate by 5 percent a year until it reaches the industry average of 5 percent, after which the company will keep a constant growth rate forever. If the required return on Kardassian stock is 13.75 percent, what will a share of stock sell for today?

48. **Non-constant Growth**   This one's a little harder. Suppose the current share price for the firm in the previous problem is $100, and all the dividend information remains the same. What required return must investors be demanding on Kardassian stock? (Hint: Set up the valuation formula with all the relevant cash flows, and use trial and error to find the unknown rate of return.)

**Challenge
(Continued)**

Suggested Readings

The best place to look for additional information about valuing stocks and bonds is in an investments textbook. Some good ones are

Bodie, Z.; A. Kane; A. Marcus; S. Perrakis; and P. Ryan. *Investments,* 1st Canadian ed. Homewood, IL.: Richard D. Irwin, 1993.

Francis, J. C., and E. Kirzner. *Investments: Analysis and Management.* Toronto, Ont.: McGraw-Hill Ryerson Ltd., 1988.

Hatch, J. E., and M. J. Robinson. *Investment Management in Canada,* 2nd ed. Scarborough, Ont.: Prentice Hall Canada Inc., 1989.

For more on duration applications see:

Fooladi, I., and G. S. Roberts. "How Effective Are Duration-Based Bond Strategies in Canada?" *Canadian Investment Review,* Spring 1989, pp. 57–61.

ON DURATION

APPENDIX   6A

Our discussion of interest rate risk and applications explains how bond managers can select bonds to enhance price volatility when interest rates are falling. In this case, we recommended buying long-term, low-coupon bonds. When they apply this advice, Canadian bond managers use *duration*—a measure of a bond's effective maturity incorporating both time to maturity and coupon rate. This appendix explains how duration is calculated and how it is used by bond managers.

Consider a portfolio consisting of two pure discount (zero coupon) bonds. The first bond matures in one year and the second after five years. As pure discount bonds, each provides a cash flow of $100 at maturity and nothing before maturity. Assuming the interest rate is 10 percent across all maturities, the bond prices are:

Value of the one-year discount bond: $\dfrac{\$100}{1.10} = \$90.91$

Value of the five-year discount bond: $\dfrac{\$100}{(1.10)^5} = \$62.09$

Which of these bonds would produce the greater percentage capital gain if rates drop to 8 percent across all maturities? From the text discussion, we know that price volatility increases with maturity and decreases with the coupon rate. Both bonds have the same coupon rate (namely zero), so the five-year bond should produce the larger percentage gain.

To prove this, we calculate the new prices and percentage changes. The one-year bond is now priced at $92.59 and has increased in price by 1.85%.[12] The five-year bond is now priced at $68.06 for a price rise of 9.61 percent. You should be able to prove that the effect works the other way. If interest rates rise to 12 percent across maturities, the five-year bond will have the greater percentage loss.

If all bonds were pure discount bonds, time to maturity would be a precise measure of price volatility. In reality, most bonds bear coupon payments. Duration provides a measure of effective maturity that incorporates the impact of differing coupon rates.

Duration

We begin by noticing that any coupon bond is actually a combination of pure discount bonds. For example, a five-year, 10 percent coupon bond, with a face value of $100, is made up of five pure discount bonds:

1. A pure discount bond paying $10 at the end of Year 1.
2. A pure discount bond paying $10 at the end of Year 2.
3. A pure discount bond paying $10 at the end of Year 3.
4. A pure discount bond paying $10 at the end of Year 4.
5. A pure discount bond paying $110 at the end of Year 5.

Because the price volatility of a pure discount bond is determined only by its maturity, we would like to determine the average maturity of the five pure discount bonds that make up a five-year coupon bond. This leads us to the concept of duration.

We calculate average maturity in three steps for the 10 percent coupon bond:

1. Calculate present value of each payment using the bond's yield to maturity. We do this as

Year	Payment	Present Value of Payment by Discounting at 10%
1	$ 10	$ 9.091
2	10	8.264
3	10	7.513
4	10	6.830
5	110	68.302
Total		$100.000

---

[12] The percentage price increase is: ($92.59 − $90.91)/$90.91 = 1.85%.

2. Express the present value of each payment in relative terms. We calculate the relative value of a single payment as the ratio of the present value of the payment to the value of the bond. The value of the bond is $100. We have

Year	Payment	Present Value of Payment	Relative value = Present Value of Payment ÷ Value of Bond
1	$ 10	$ 9.091	$9.091/$100 = 0.09091
2	10	8.264	0.08264
3	10	7.513	0.07513
4	10	6.830	0.0683
5	110	68.302	0.68302
Total		$100.000	1.00000

The bulk of the relative value, 68.302 percent, occurs at Date 5 because the principal is paid back at that time.

3. Weight the maturity of each payment by its relative value. We have

4.1699 years = 1 year × 0.09091 + 2 years × 0.08264 + 3 years × 0.07513 + 4 years × 0.06830 + 5 years × 0.68302

There are many ways to calculate the average maturity of a bond. We have calculated it by weighting the maturity of each payment by the payment's present value. We find that the effective maturity of the bond is 4.1699 years. *Duration* is a commonly used word for effective maturity. Thus, the bond's duration is 4.1699 years. Note that duration is expressed in units of time.[13]

Because the five-year, 10 percent coupon bond has a duration of 4.1699 years, its percentage price fluctuations should be the same as those of a zero coupon bond with a duration of 4.1699 years.[14] It turns out that a five-year, 1 percent coupon bond has a duration of 4.8742 years. Because the 1 percent coupon bond has a higher duration than the 10 percent bond, the 1 percent coupon bond should be subject to greater price fluctuations. This is exactly what we expected.

Why does the 1 percent bond have a greater duration than the 10 percent bond, even though they both have the same five-year maturity? As mentioned earlier, duration is an average of the maturity of the bond's cash flows, weighted by the present value of each cash flow. The 1 percent coupon bond receives only $1 in each of the first four years. Thus, the weights applied to Years 1 through 4 in the duration formula will be low. Conversely, the 10 percent coupon bond receives $10 in each of the first four years. The weights applied to Years 1 through 4 in the duration formula will be higher.

In general, the percentage price changes of a bond with high duration are greater than the percentage price changes for a bond with low duration. This property is useful to investment managers who seek superior performance. These managers extend portfolio duration when rates are expected to fall and reduce duration in the face of rising rates.

---

[13] Also note that we discounted each payment by the interest rate of 10 percent. This was done because we wanted to calculate the duration of the bond before a change in the interest rate occurred. After a change in the rate to say 8 or 12 percent, all three of our steps would need to reflect the new interest rate. In other words, the duration of a bond is a function of the current interest rate.

[14] Actually, the relationship only exactly holds true in the case of a one-time shift in the flat yield curve, where the change in the spot rate is identical for all different maturities. But duration research finds that the error is small.

Because forecasting rates consistently is almost impossible, other managers hedge their returns by setting the duration of their assets equal to the duration of liabilities. In this way, market values on both sides of the balance sheet adjust in the same direction keeping the market value of net worth constant. Duration hedging is often called portfolio *immunization.*

Current research on government of Canada bond returns shows that duration is a practical way of measuring bond price volatility and an effective tool for hedging interest rate risk.

Appendix Review Questions and Problems

A.1 Why do portfolio managers use duration instead of term to maturity as a measure of a bond's price volatility?

A.2 Calculate the duration of a seven-year Canada bond with an 8 percent coupon.

A.3 You are managing a bond portfolio following a policy of interest-rate anticipation. You think that rates have bottomed and are likely to rise. The average duration of your portfolio is 4.5 years. Which bonds are more attractive for new purchases, those with a 10-year duration or 3-year duration? Explain.

THE TERM STRUCTURE OF INTEREST RATES | APPENDIX   6B

Spot Rates and Yield to Maturity

In the main body of this chapter, we have assumed that the interest rate is constant across all times to maturity. In reality, interest rates vary across times to maturity. This occurs primarily because inflation rates are expected to differ through time.

To illustrate, we consider two zero coupon bonds. Bond A is a one-year bond and Bond B is a two-year bond. Both have face values of $1,000. The one-year interest rate, r_1, is 8 percent. The two-year interest rate, r_2, is 10 percent. These two rates of interest are examples of *spot rates.* Perhaps this inequality in interest rates occurs because inflation is expected to be higher over the second year than over the first year. The two bonds are depicted in the following time chart:

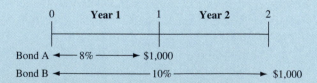

We can easily calculate the present value for Bond A and Bond B as:

$$PV_A = \$925.93 = \frac{\$1,000}{1.08}$$

$$PV_B = \$826.45 = \frac{\$1,000}{(1.10)^2}$$

Of course, if PV_A and PV_B were observable and the spot rates were not, we could determine the spot rates using the PV formula, because

$$PV_A = \$925.93 = \frac{\$1,000}{(1 + r_1)} \rightarrow r_1 = 8\%$$

and

$$PV_B = \$826.45 = \frac{\$1,000}{(1 + r_2)^2} \rightarrow r_2 = 10\%$$

Now we can see how the prices of more complicated bonds are determined. Try to do the next example. It illustrates the difference between spot rates and yields to maturity.

E X A M P L E | **6B.1**

Given the spot rates, r_1 equals 8 percent and r_2 equals 10 percent, what should a 5 percent coupon, two-year bond cost? The cash flows C_1 and C_2 are illustrated in the following time chart:

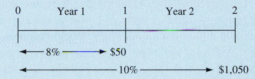

The bond can be viewed as a portfolio of zero coupon bonds with one- and two-year maturities. Therefore,

$$PV = \frac{\$50}{1 + 0.08} + \frac{\$1,050}{(1 + 0.10)^2} = 914.06 \qquad [6B.1]$$

We now want to calculate a single rate for the bond. We do this by solving for y in the following equation:

$$\$914.06 = \frac{\$50}{1 + y} + \frac{\$1,050}{(1 + y)^2} \qquad [6B.2]$$

In (6B.2), y equals 9.95 percent. As explained in the chapter, we call y the *yield to maturity* on the bond.

It is worthwhile to contrast Equation 6B.1 and Equation 6B.2. In 6B.1, we use the marketwide spot rates to determine the price of the bond. Once we get the bond price, we use 6B.2 to calculate its yield to maturity. Because Equation 6B.1 employs two spot rates whereas only one appears in 6B.2, we can think of yield to maturity as some sort of average of the two spot rates.[15]

Using these spot rates, the yield to maturity of a two-year coupon bond whose coupon rate is 12 percent and PV equals \$1,036.73 can be determined by:

$$\$1,036.73 = \frac{\$120}{1 + r} + \frac{\$1,120}{(1 + r)^2} \rightarrow r = 9.89\%$$

---

[15] Yield to maturity is not a simple average of r_1 and r_2. Rather, financial economists speak of it as a time weighted average of r_1 and r_2.

As these calculations show, two bonds with the same maturity usually have different yields to maturity if the coupons differ. ▮

> CONCEPT QUESTION
> 1. What is the difference between a spot interest rate and the yield to maturity?

Explanations of the Term Structure

We now want to explore the relationship between the spot rate and maturity in more detail. We begin by defining a new term, the forward rate. Next, we relate this forward rate to future interest rates. Finally, we consider alternative theories of the term structure.

Definition of Forward Rate   Earlier in this appendix, we developed a two-year example where the spot rate over the first year is 8 percent and the spot rate over the two years is 10 percent. Here, an individual investing $1 in a two-year zero coupon bond would have $1 \times (1.10)^2$ in two years.

To pursue our discussion, it is worthwhile to rewrite[16]

$$\$1 \times (110)^2 = \$1 \times 1.08 \times 1.1204 \qquad \text{[6B.3]}$$

Equation 6B.3 tells us something important about the relationship between one- and two-year rates. When an individual invests in a two-year zero coupon bond yielding 10 percent, his wealth at the end of two years is the same as if he received an 8 percent return over the first year and a 12.04 percent return over the second year. This hypothetical rate over the second year, 12.04 percent, is called the *forward rate*. Thus, we can think of an investor in a two-year zero coupon bond as getting the one-year spot rate of 8 percent and *locking in* 12.04 percent over the second year.

More generally, when given spot rates r_1 and r_2, we can always determine the forward rate, f_2, such that:

$$(1 + r_2)^2 = (1 + r_1) \times (1 + f_2) \qquad \text{[6B.4]}$$

We solve for f_2, yielding:

$$f_2 = \frac{(1 + r_2)^2}{1 + r_1} = 1 \qquad \text{[6B.5]}$$

E X A M P L E | **6B.2**

If the one-year spot rate is 7 percent and the two-year spot rate is 12 percent, what is f_2?

We plug in to (6B.5), yielding

$$f_2 = \frac{(1.12)^2}{1.07} - 1 = 17.23\%$$

Consider an individual investing in a two-year zero coupon bond yielding 12 percent. We say it is as if he receives 7 percent over the first year and simultaneously locks in 17.23 percent over the second year. Note that both the one-year spot rate and the two-year spot rate are known at Date 0. Because the forward rate is calculated from the one-year and two-year spot rates, it can be calculated at Date 0 as well.

---

[16] 12.04 percent is equal to $\{(1.10)^2/1.08\} - 1$ when rounding is performed after four digits.

The material in this appendix is likely to be difficult for students exposed to term structure for the first time. It helps to state what you should know at this point. Given Equation 6B.5, you should be able to calculate a set of forward rates given a set of spot rates. This can simply be viewed as mechanical computation. In addition to the calculations, a student should understand the intuition of this calculation.

We now turn to the relationship between the forward rate and the expected spot rates in the future.

The Relationship between Forward Rates and Expected Spot Rates

An investor wishing to invest $1,000 over a two-period horizon can choose between two investment strategies at Date 0:

1. Buy a two-year pure discount bond. Given the two-year spot rate of 10 percent, the proceeds will be:

$$\$1,000 \times (1.10)^2 = \$1,210$$

2. Buy a one-year bond and reinvest the proceeds after one year. The spot rate for the first year is known to be 8 percent. The reinvestment rate for the second period is r_2. This is the one-year spot rate starting at Date 1 and is unknown at Date 0. Proceeds will be:

$$\$1,000 \times (1.08) \times (1 + r_2) = ?$$

   Assuming the risks are equal, if you were the investor, how would you decide which is the better strategy?

Your choice would depend on your expectation for the one-year spot rate starting at Date 1, r_2. If you think the one-year spot rate will be 13 percent, you should take strategy 2. The expected return on strategy 2 would be:

$$\$1,000 \times (1.08) \times (1.13) = \$1,220.40$$

If you think the one-year spot rate starting at Date 1 will be 11 percent, you should take strategy 1. With r_2 at 11 percent, strategy 2 will produce only:

$$\$1,000 \times (1.08) \times (1.11) = \$1,198.80.$$

   Under what condition would the return from strategy 1 equal the expected return from strategy 2?

The two strategies yield the same expected return only when:

$$12.04\% = \text{spot rate expected over Year 2}$$

In other words, if the forward rate equals the expected spot rate, one would expect to earn the same return over the two years.

The Expectations Hypothesis

It is reasonable that investors would set interest rates in such a way that the forward rate would equal the spot rate expected by the marketplace a year from now.[17]

---

[17] Of course, each individual has different expectations, so the equality cannot hold for all individuals. However, financial economists generally speak of a consensus expectation. This is the expectation of the market as a whole.

Our equation was stated for the specific case where the forward rate was 12.04 percent. We can generalize this to:

Expectations hypothesis: f_2 = Spot rate expected over Year 2   [6B.6]

The forward rate over the second year is set to the spot rate that people expect to prevail over the second year. This is called the *expectations hypothesis*. It states that investors set interest rates so that the forward rate over the second year is equal to the one-year spot rate expected over the second year.

Liquidity Preference Hypothesis

At this point, many students think that Equation 6B.6 must hold. However, note that we developed 6B.6 by assuming that investors were risk-neutral. Suppose, alternatively, that investors are adverse to risk.

Which of the following strategies would appear more risky for an individual who wants to invest for one year (instead of two years as we assumed earlier)?

3. Buy a one-year bond.
4. Buy a two-year bond but sell at the end of one year.

Strategy 3 has no risk because the investor knows that the rate of return must be r_1. Conversely, strategy 4 has much risk; the final return is dependent on what happens to interest rates.

Because strategy 4 has more risk than strategy 3, no risk-averse investor would choose strategy 4 if both strategies have the same expected return. Risk-averse investors can have no preference for one strategy over the other only when the expected return on strategy 4 is *above* the return on strategy 3. Because the two strategies have the same expected return when f_2 equals the spot rate expected over Year 2, strategy 3 can only have a higher rate of return when

Liquidity-preference hypothesis: f_2 = Spot rate expected + Liquidity premium   [6B.7]

That is, to induce investors to hold the riskier two-year bonds, the market sets the forward rate over the second year to be more than the spot rate expected over the second year. Equation 6B.7 is called the *liquidity-preference* hypothesis.

We developed the liquidity-preference hypothesis by assuming that individuals are planning to invest over one year. We pointed out that for these individuals, a two-year bond has extra risk because it must be sold prematurely. What about those individuals who want to invest for two years as we originally assumed? (We call these people investors with a two-year *time horizon*.) They could

1. Buy a two-year zero coupon bond.
2. Buy a one-year bond. When the bond matures, they immediately buy another one-year bond.

Strategy 1 has no risk for an investor with a two-year time horizon, because the proceeds to be received at Date 2 are known as of Date 0. However, strategy 2 has risk since the spot rate over Year 2 is unknown at Date 0. It can be shown that risk-averse investors prefer neither strategy 1 nor strategy 2 over the other when

f_2 = Spot rate − Term premium   [6B.8]

Note that the assumption of risk aversion gives a contrary prediction. Relationship 6B.7 holds for a market dominated by investors with a one-year time horizon. Relationship 6B.8 holds for a market dominated by investors with a two-year time horizon. Financial economists have generally argued that the time horizon of the typical investor is generally much shorter than the maturity of typical bonds in the marketplace. Thus, economists view (6B.7) as the best depiction of equilibrium in the bond market with risk-averse investors.

However, do we have a market of risk-neutral investors or risk-averse investors? In other words, can the expectations hypothesis of Equation 6B.6 or the liquidity-preference hypothesis of equation 6B.7 be expected to hold? As we learn later in this book, economists view investors as being risk-averse for the most part. Yet economists are never satisfied with a casual examination of a theory's assumptions. To them, empirical evidence of a theory's predictions must be the final arbiter.

There has been a great deal of empirical evidence on the term structure of interest rates. Unfortunately (perhaps fortunately for some students), we are not able to present the evidence in any detail. Suffice it to say that, in our opinion, the evidence supports the liquidity-preference hypothesis over the expectations hypothesis.

CONCEPT QUESTIONS

1. Define the forward rate.
2. What is the relationship between the one-year spot rate, the two-year spot rate, and the forward rate over the second year?
3. What is the expectations hypothesis?
4. What is the liquidity-preference hypothesis?

Application of Term Structure Theory

In explaining term structure theory, it was convenient to use examples of zero coupon bonds and spot and forward rates. To see the application, we go back to coupon bonds and yields to maturity the way that actual bond data is presented in the financial press.

Figure 6B.1 shows a yield curve for government of Canada bonds; it plots Canada yields to maturity against time to maturity. Yield curves are observed at a particular date and change shape over time. This yield curve is for February 1995.

Notice that the yield curve is ascending with the long rates above the short rates. Term structure theory tells that there are two reasons the observed yield curve is ascending. Investors expect that rates will rise in the future and the existence of the liquidity premium.

Now suppose you were advising a friend who was renewing a home mortgage as we discussed in Chapter 5. Suppose further that the alternatives were a one-year mortgage at 6.5 percent and a two-year mortgage at 8 percent. We know that on average, over the life of a mortgage, rolling over one-year rates would probably be cheaper because the borrower avoids paying the liquidity premium. But we also know that this approach is riskier because the ascending yield curve for bonds and mortgages suggests that investors believe that rates will rise.

Appendix Review Questions

B.1 Explain the expectations and liquidity-preference theories in your own words.

B.2 Suppose 10-year Canadas yield 9 percent and 1-year Treasury bills yield 7 percent. You are a bond portfolio manager following an interest rate anticipation strategy. Should you invest in 10-year or 1-year securities? Explain your answer.

B.3 Your friend asks you for advice on renewing a home mortgage. The rate for five years is 11 percent and the one-year rate is 9 percent. Your friend is tempted to take the one-year rate but is afraid that rates may rise. What do you advise? Explain your answer.

F I G U R E 6B.1

Term structure of interest rates, February 1995

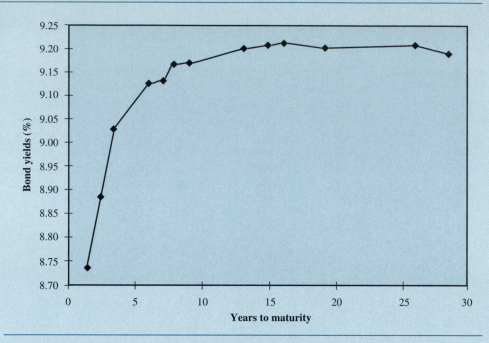

Source: *Globe and Mail,* February 3, 1995, p. B13. Used with permission.

APPENDIX   6C | FINANCIAL CALCULATORS AND BOND ANALYSIS

Financial calculators differ among manufacturers. What we present here is common to most popular brands, but the order of entering data may differ. The examples are from the text discussion of bonds.

To calculate bond prices:

1. Enter the number of periods of $n = 10$ and press n.
2. Enter the yield of $i = 8$ percent as 8 (not .08) and press i.
3. Enter the coupon of 80 and press *PMT.*
4. Enter the face value of 1,000 and press *FV.*
5. Ask the calculator for the price by pressing the compute key and then pressing *PV.*

Most financial calculators find a bond's yield to maturity. A common procedure would involve entering $80 (the coupon) as the payment (*PMT*), 6 as the number of periods (*n*), $955.14 (the current price) as the present value (*PV*), and $1,000 (the face value) as the future value (*FV*). If you solve for the interest rate (*i*), the answer should be 9 percent. On some calculators, either the future value or the payment must be entered with a negative sign.

CAPITAL BUDGETING

CHAPTER 7 | Net Present Value and Other Investment Criteria
The most important subject in this chapter is net present value. Chapter 7 compares and contrasts net present value with other methods for selecting among alternative investment proposals.

CHAPTER 8 | Making Capital Investment Decisions
This chapter describes how to actually do a net present value and discounted cash flow analysis. The primary aim of the chapter is to describe how to identify a project's incremental cash flows. Chapter 8 also discusses how to handle such issues as sunk costs, opportunity costs, financing costs, net working capital, and erosion.

CHAPTER 9 | Project Analysis and Evaluation
This chapter discusses problems regarding the reliability of net present value estimates. It also describes some important tools for project analysis, such as break-even analysis, operating leverage, and sensitivity analysis.

Net Present Value and Other Investment Criteria

In Chapter 1, we identified the three key areas of concern to the financial manager. The first of these was deciding which fixed assets to buy. We called this the capital budgeting decision. In this chapter, we begin to deal with the issues that arise in answering this question.

The process of allocating or budgeting capital is usually more involved than just deciding whether to buy a particular fixed asset. We frequently face broader issues such as whether to launch a new product or enter a new market. Decisions such as these determine the nature of a firm's operations and products for years to come, primarily because fixed asset investments are generally long-lived and not easily reversed once they are made.

The most fundamental decision that a business must make concerns its product line. What services will we offer or what will we sell? In what markets will we compete? What new products will we introduce? The answer to any of these questions requires that the firm commit its scarce and valuable capital to certain types of assets. As a result, all these strategic issues fall under the general heading of capital budgeting. The process of capital budgeting could thus be given a more descriptive (not to mention impressive) name: strategic asset allocation.

For the reasons we have discussed, the capital budgeting question is probably the most important issue in corporate finance. How a firm chooses to finance its operations (the capital structure question) and how a firm manages its short-term operating activities (the working capital question) are certainly issues of concern; however, fixed assets define the business of the firm. Airlines, for example, are airlines because they operate airplanes, regardless of how they finance them.

Any firm possesses a huge number of possible investments. Each of these possible investments is an option available to the firm. Some of these options are valuable and some are not. The essence of successful financial management, of course, is learning to identify which are which. With this in mind, our goal in this chapter is to introduce you to the techniques used to analyze potential business ventures to decide which are worth undertaking.

We present and compare a number of different procedures used in practice. Our primary goal is to acquaint you with the advantages and disadvantages of the various approaches. As we shall see, the most important concept in this area is the idea of net present value. We consider this next.

7.1 | NET PRESENT VALUE

In Chapter 1, we argued that the goal of financial management is to create value for the shareholders. The financial manager must thus examine a potential investment in light of its likely effect on the price of the firm's shares. In this section, we describe a widely used procedure for doing this, the net present value approach.

The Basic Idea

An investment is worth undertaking if it creates value for its owners. In the most general sense, we create value by identifying an investment that is worth more in the marketplace than it costs us to acquire. How can something be worth more than it costs? It's a case of the whole being worth more than the cost of the parts.

For example, suppose you buy a run-down house for $65,000 and spend another $25,000 on painters, plumbers, and so on to get it fixed. Your total investment is $90,000. When the work is completed, you place the house back on the market and find that it's worth $100,000. The market value ($100,000) exceeds the cost ($90,000) by $10,000. What you have done here is to act as a manager and bring together some fixed assets (a house), some labour (plumbers, carpenters, and others), and some materials (carpeting, paint, and so on). The net result is that you have created $10,000 in value. Put another way, this $10,000 is the *value added* by management.

With our house example, it turned out after the fact that $10,000 in value was created. Things thus worked out very nicely. The real challenge, of course, was to somehow identify ahead of time whether or not investing the necessary $90,000 was a good idea. This is what capital budgeting is all about, namely, trying to determine whether a proposed investment or project will be worth more than it costs once it is in place.

For reasons that will be obvious in a moment, the difference between an investment's market value and its cost is called the **net present value (NPV)** of the investment. In other words, net present value is a measure of how much value is created or added today by undertaking an investment. Given our goal of creating value for the shareholders, the capital budgeting process can be viewed as a search for investments with positive net present values.

net present value (NPV)
The difference between an investment's market value and its cost.

With our run-down house, you can probably imagine how we would make the capital budgeting decision. We would first look at what comparable, fixed-up properties were selling for in the market. We would then get estimates of the cost of buying a particular property and bringing it up to market. At this point, we have an estimated total cost and an estimated market value. If the difference is positive, this investment is worth undertaking because it has a positive estimated net present value. There is risk, of course, because there is no guarantee that our estimates will turn out to be correct.

As our example illustrates, investment decisions are greatly simplified when there is a market for assets similar to the investment we are considering. Capital budgeting becomes much more difficult when we cannot observe the market price for at least roughly comparable investments. We are then faced with the problem of estimating the value of an investment using only indirect market information. Unfortunately, this is precisely the situation the financial manager usually encounters. We examine this issue next.

Estimating Net Present Value

Imagine that we are thinking of starting a business to produce and sell a new product, say, organic fertilizer. We can estimate the start-up costs with reasonable accuracy because we know what we need to buy to begin production. Would this be a good investment? Based on our discussion, you know that the answer depends on whether the value of the new business exceeds the cost of starting it. In other words, does this investment have a positive NPV?

This problem is much more difficult than our fixer-upper house example because entire fertilizer companies are not routinely bought and sold in the marketplace; so it is essentially impossible to observe the market value of a similar investment. As a result, we must somehow estimate this value by other means.

Based on our work in Chapters 5 and 6, you may be able to guess how we estimate the value of our fertilizer business. We begin by trying to estimate the future cash flows that we expect the new business to produce. We then apply our basic discounted cash flow procedure to estimate the present value of those cash flows. Once we have this number, we estimate NPV as the difference between the present value of the future cash flows and the cost of the investment. As we mentioned in Chapter 5, this procedure is often called **discounted cash flow (DCF) valuation**.

discounted cash flow (DCF) valuation

The process of valuing an investment by discounting its future cash flows.

To see how we might estimate NPV, suppose we believe that the cash revenues from our fertilizer business will be $20,000 per year, assuming everything goes as expected. Cash costs (including taxes) will be $14,000 per year. We will wind down the business in eight years. The plant, property, and equipment will be worth $2,000 as salvage at that time. The project costs $30,000 to launch. We use a 15 percent discount rate on new projects such as this one. Is this a good investment? If there are 1,000 shares of stock outstanding, what will be the effect on the price per share from taking it?

From a purely mechanical perspective, we need to calculate the present value of the future cash flows at 15 percent. The net cash flow inflow will be $20,000 cash income less $14,000 in costs per year for eight years. These cash flows are illustrated in Figure 7.1. As Figure 7.1 suggests, we effectively have an eight-year annuity of $20,000 − 14,000 = $6,000 per year along with a single lump-sum inflow of $2,000 in eight years. Calculating the present value of the future cash flows thus comes down to the same type of problem we considered in Chapter 5. The total present value is:

$$\text{Present value} = \$6,000 \times (1 - 1/1.15^8)/.15 + 2,000/1.15^8$$
$$= \$6,000 \times 4.4873 + 2,000/3.0590$$
$$= \$26,924 + 654$$
$$= \$27,578$$

When we compare this to the $30,000 estimated cost, the NPV is:

$$\text{NPV} = -\$30,000 + 27,578 = -\$2,422$$

Therefore, this is not a good investment. Based on our estimates, taking it would decrease the total value of the stock by $2,422. With 1,000 shares outstanding, our best estimate of the impact of taking this project is a loss of value of $2,422/1,000 = $2.422 per share.

Our fertilizer example illustrates how NPV estimates can help determine whether or not an investment is desirable. From our example, notice that, if the NPV is negative, the effect on share value would be unfavourable. If the NPV is positive, the effect would be favourable. As a consequence, all we need to know about a particular

Time (years)	0	1	2	3	4	5	6	7	8
Initial cost	−$30								
Inflows		$20	$20	$20	$20	$20	$20	$20	$20
Outflows		− 14	− 14	− 14	− 14	− 14	− 14	− 14	− 14
Net inflow		$ 6	$ 6	$ 6	$ 6	$ 6	$ 6	$ 6	$ 6
Salvage		—	—	—	—	—	—	—	2
Net cash flow	−$30	$ 6	$ 6	$ 6	$ 6	$ 6	$ 6	$ 6	$ 8

FIGURE 7.1

Project cash flows ($000's) (thousands)

proposal for the purpose of making an accept/reject decision is whether the NPV is positive or negative.

Given that the goal of financial management is to increase share value, our discussion in this section leads us to the *net present value rule:*

> An investment should be accepted if the net present value is positive and rejected if it is negative.

In the unlikely event that the net present value turned out to be zero, we would be indifferent to taking the investment or not taking it.

Two comments about our example are in order: First, it is not the rather mechanical process of discounting the cash flows that is important. Once we have the cash flows and the appropriate discount rate, the required calculations are fairly straightforward. The task of coming up with the cash flows and the discount rate in the first place is much more challenging. We have much more to say about this in the next several chapters. For the remainder of this chapter, we take it as given that we have estimates of the cash revenues and costs and, where needed, an appropriate discount rate.

The second thing to keep in mind about our example is that the −$2,422 NPV is an estimate. Like any estimate, it can be high or low. The only way to find out the true NPV would be to place the investment up for sale and see what we could get for it. We generally won't be doing this, so it is important that our estimates be reliable. Once again, we have more to say about this later. For the rest of this chapter, we assume the estimates are accurate.

E X A M P L E | 7.1   Using the NPV Rule

Suppose we are asked to decide whether or not a new consumer product should be launched. Based on projected sales and costs, we expect that the cash flows over the five-year life of the project will be $2,000 in the first two years, $4,000 in the next two, and $5,000 in the last year. It will cost about $10,000 to begin production. We use a 10 percent discount rate to evaluate new products. What should we do here?

Given the cash flows and discount rate, we can calculate the total value of the product by discounting the cash flows back to the present:

$$\text{Present value} = \$2,000/1.1 + 2,000/1.1^2 + 4,000/1.1^3 + 4,000/1.1^4 + 5,000/1.1^5$$
$$= \$1,818 + 1,653 + 3,005 + 2,732 + 3,105$$
$$= \$12,313$$

The present value of the expected cash flows is $12,313, but the cost of getting those cash flows is only $10,000, so the NPV is $12,313 − 10,000 = $2,313. This is positive; so, based on the net present value rule, we should take it.   ▌

As we have seen in this section, estimating NPV is one way of assessing the profitability of a proposed investment. It is certainly not the only way that profitability is assessed, and we now turn to some alternatives. As we shall see, when compared to NPV, each of the ways of assessing profitability that we examine is flawed in some key way; so NPV is the preferred approach in principle, if not always in practice.

CONCEPT QUESTIONS
1. What is the net present value rule?
2. If we say that an investment has an NPV of $1,000, what exactly do we mean?

7.2 I THE PAYBACK RULE

It is very common in practice to talk of the payback on a proposed investment. Loosely, the *payback* is the length of time it takes to recover our initial investment or "get our bait back." Because this idea is widely understood and used, we examine and critique it in some detail.

Defining the Rule

We can illustrate how to calculate a payback with an example. Figure 7.2 shows the cash flows from a proposed investment. How many years do we have to wait until the accumulated cash flows from this investment equal or exceed the cost of the investment? As Figure 7.2 indicates, the initial investment is $50,000. After the first year, the firm has recovered $30,000, leaving $20,000. The cash flow in the second year is exactly $20,000, so this investment pays for itself in exactly two years. Put another way, the **payback period** is two years. If we require a payback of, say, three years or less, then this investment is acceptable. This illustrates the *payback period rule:*

payback period
The amount of time required for an investment to generate cash flows to recover its initial cost.

> An investment is acceptable if its calculated payback is less than some prespecified number of years.

In our example, the payback works out to be exactly two years. This won't usually happen, of course. When the numbers don't work out exactly, it is customary to work with fractional years. For example, suppose the initial investment is $60,000, and the cash flows are $20,000 in the first year and $90,000 in the second. The cash

F I G U R E 7.2

Net project cash flows

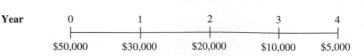

Year	0	1	2	3	4
	$50,000	$30,000	$20,000	$10,000	$5,000

flows over the first two years are $110,000, so the project obviously pays back sometime in the second year. After the first year, the project has paid back $20,000, leaving $40,000 to be recovered. To figure out the fractional year, note that this $40,000 is $40,000/$90,000 = 4/9 of the second year's cash flow. Assuming that the $90,000 cash flow is paid uniformly throughout the year, the payback would thus be 1 4/9 years.

Analyzing the Payback Period Rule

When compared to the NPV rule, the payback period rule has some rather severe shortcomings: First, the payback period is calculated by simply adding the future cash flows. There is no discounting involved, so the time value of money is ignored. Second, a payback rule does not consider risk differences. The payback would be calculated the same way for both very risky and very safe projects.

Perhaps the biggest problem with the payback period rule is coming up with the right cutoff period because we don't really have an objective basis for choosing a particular number. Put another way, there is no economic rationale for looking at payback in the first place, so we have no guide as to how to pick the cutoff. As a result, we end up using a number that is arbitrarily chosen.

Suppose we have somehow decided on an appropriate payback period, say two years or less. As we have seen, the payback period rule ignores the time value of money for the first two years. More seriously, cash flows after the second year are ignored. To see this, consider the two investments, Long and Short, in Table 7.1. Both projects cost $250. Based on our discussion, the payback on Long is 2 + $50/100 = 2.5 years, and the payback on Short is 1 + $150/200 = 1.75 years. With a cutoff of two years, Short is acceptable and Long is not.

Is the payback period rule giving us the right decisions? Maybe not. Suppose again that we require a 15 percent return on this type of investment. We can calculate the NPV for these two investments as:

$$\text{NPV(Short)} = -\$250 + 100/1.15 + 200/1.15^2 = -\$11.81$$
$$\text{NPV(Long)} = -\$250 + 100 \times (1 - 1/1.15^4)/.15 = \$35.50$$

Now we have a problem. The NPV of the shorter-term investment is actually negative, meaning that taking it diminishes the value of the shareholders' equity. The opposite is true for the longer-term investment—it increases share value.

Our example illustrates two primary shortcomings of the payback period rule. First, by ignoring time value, we may be led to take investments (like Short) that actually are worth less than they cost. Second, by ignoring cash flows beyond the cutoff, we may be led to reject profitable long-term investments (like Long). More generally, using a payback period rule tends to bias us toward shorter-term investments.

Year	Long	Short
1	$100	$100
2	100	200
3	100	0
4	100	0

T A B L E 7.1

Investment projected cash flows

Redeeming Qualities

Despite its shortcomings, the payback period rule is often used by small businesses whose managers lack financial skills. It is also used by large and sophisticated companies when making relatively small decisions. There are several reasons for this. The primary reason is that many decisions simply do not warrant detailed analysis because the cost of the analysis would exceed the possible loss from a mistake. As a practical matter, an investment that pays back rapidly and has benefits extending beyond the cutoff period probably has a positive NPV.

Small investment decisions are made by the hundreds every day in large organizations. Moreover, they are made at all levels. As a result, it would not be uncommon for a corporation to require, for example, a two-year payback on all investments of less than $10,000. Investments larger than this are subjected to greater scrutiny. The requirement of a two-year payback is not perfect for reasons we have seen, but it does exercise some control over expenditures and thus limits possible losses.

In addition to its simplicity, the payback rule has several other features to recommend it. First, because it is biased toward short-term projects, it is biased toward liquidity. In other words, a payback rule favours investments that free up cash for other uses more quickly. This could be very important for a small business; it would be less so for a large corporation.

The large corporation could be interested in projects that pay off quickly because management feels the need to produce short-term results. In the corporate takeover binge of the 1980s, companies with poor quarterly earnings (and hence lower stock prices) were regarded as promising takeover targets. It is debatable whether such a short-term focus really serves shareholders; we return to this topic in Chapter 21.

A less controversial positive feature of the payback period is that the cash flows that are expected to occur later in a project's life are probably more uncertain. Arguably, a payback period rule adjusts for the extra riskiness of later cash flows, but it does so in a rather draconian fashion—by ignoring them altogether.

We should note here that some of the apparent simplicity of the payback rule is an illusion. We still must come up with the cash flows first, and, as we discussed previously, this is not easy to do. Thus, it would probably be more accurate to say that the concept of a payback period is both intuitive and easy to understand. The following table lists the pros and cons of the payback period rule:

Payback Period Rule

Advantages	Disadvantages
1. Easy to understand.	1. Ignores the time value of money.
2. Adjusts for uncertainty of later cash flows.	2. Requires an arbitrary cutoff point.
3. Biased toward liquidity.	3. Ignores cash flow beyond the cutoff date.
	4. Biased against long-term projects, such as research and development, and new projects.

discounted payback period

The length of time required for an investment's discounted cash flows to equal its initial cost.

The Discounted Payback Rule

We saw that one of the shortcomings of the payback period rule was that it ignored time value. There is a variation of the payback period, the discounted payback period, that fixes this particular problem. The **discounted payback period** is the length of time until the sum of the discounted cash flows equals the initial investment. The *discounted payback rule* is:

An investment is acceptable if its discounted payback is less than some prescribed number of years.

To see how we might calculate the discounted payback period, suppose we require a 12.5 percent return on new investments. We have an investment that costs $300 and has cash flows of $100 per year for five years. To get the discounted payback, we have to discount each cash flow at 12.5 percent and then start adding them. We do this in Table 7.2. We have both the discounted and the undiscounted cash flows in Table 7.2. Looking at the accumulated cash flows, the regular payback is exactly three years (look for the arrow in Year 3). The discounted cash flows total $300 only after four years, so the discounted payback is four years as shown.[1]

How do we interpret the discounted payback? Recall that the ordinary payback is the time it takes to break even in an accounting sense. Since it includes the time value of money, the discounted payback is the time it takes to break even in an economic or financial sense. Loosely speaking, in our example, we get our money back along with the interest we could have earned elsewhere in four years.

Based on our example, the discounted payback would seem to have much to recommend it. You may be surprised to find out that it is rarely used. Why? Probably because it really isn't any simpler than NPV. To calculate a discounted payback, you have to discount cash flows, add them up, and compare them to the cost, just as you do with NPV. So, unlike an ordinary payback, the discounted payback is not especially simple to calculate.

A discounted payback period rule still has a couple of significant drawbacks. The biggest one is that the cutoff still has to be arbitrarily set and cash flows beyond that point are ignored.[2] As a result, a project with a positive NPV may not be acceptable because the cutoff is too short. Also, just because one project has a shorter discounted payback than another does not mean it has a larger NPV.

All things considered, the discounted payback is a compromise between a regular payback and NPV that lacks the simplicity of the first and the conceptual rigor of the second. Nonetheless, if we need to assess the time it takes to recover the investment required by a project, the discounted payback is better than the ordinary payback because it considers time value. In other words, the discounted payback recognizes that we could have invested the money elsewhere and earned a return on it. The ordinary payback does not take this into account.

	Cash Flow		Accumulated Cash Flow		
Year	Undiscounted	Discounted	Undiscounted	Discounted	
1	$100	$89	$100	$ 89	
2	100	79	200	168	
3	100	70	⇒300	238	
4	100	62	400	⇒300	
5	100	55	500	355	

T A B L E 7.2

Ordinary and discounted payback

[1] In this case, the discounted payback is an even number of years. This won't ordinarily happen, of course. However, calculating a fractional year for the discounted payback period is more involved than it is for the ordinary payback, and it is not commonly done.
[2] If the cutoff were forever, then the discounted payback rule would be the same as the NPV rule. It would also be the same as the profitability index rule considered in a later section.

The advantages and disadvantages of the discounted payback are summarized in the following table:

Discounted Payback Period Rule

Advantages	Disadvantages
1. Includes time value of money.	1. May reject positive NPV investments.
2. Easy to understand.	2. Requires an arbitrary cutoff point.
3. Does not accept negative estimated NPV investments.	3. Ignores cash flows beyond the cutoff date.
4. Biased toward liquidity.	4. Biased against long-term projects, such as research and development, and new projects.

CONCEPT QUESTIONS

1. What is the payback period? The payback period rule?
2. Why do we say that the payback period is, in a sense, an accounting break-even?

7.3 | THE AVERAGE ACCOUNTING RETURN

average accounting return (AAR)

An investment's average net income divided by its average book value.

Another attractive, but flawed, approach to making capital budgeting decisions is the **average accounting return (AAR)**. There are many different definitions of the AAR. However, in one form or another, the AAR is always defined as:

$$\frac{\text{Some measure of average accounting profit}}{\text{Some measure of average accounting value}}$$

The specific definition we use is:

$$\frac{\text{Average net income}}{\text{Average book value}}$$

To see how we might calculate this number, suppose we are deciding whether to open a store in a new shopping mall. The required investment in improvements is $500,000. The store would have a five-year life because everything reverts to the mall owners after that time. The required investment would be 100 percent depreciated (straight-line) over five years, so the depreciation would be $500,000/5 = $100,000 per year. The tax rate for this small business is 25 percent.[3] Table 7.3 contains the projected revenues and expenses. Based on these figures, net income in each year is also shown.

To calculate the average book value for this investment, we note that we started out with a book value of $500,000 (the initial cost) and ended up at $0. The average book value during the life of the investment is thus ($500,000 + 0)/2 = $250,000. As long as we use straight-line depreciation, the average investment is always ½ of the initial investment.[4]

---

[3] These depreciation and tax rates are chosen for simplicity. Leasehold improvements are one of the few assets for which tax depreciation in Canada is straight-line. Chapter 8 discusses depreciation and taxes.

[4] We could, of course, calculate the average of the six book values directly. In thousands, we would have ($500 + 400 + 300 + 200 + 100 + 0)/6 = $250.

	Year 1	Year 2	Year 3	Year 4	Year 5
Revenue	$433,333	$450,000	$266,667	$200,000	$133,333
Expenses	200,000	150,000	100,000	100,000	100,000
Earnings before depreciation	$233,333	$300,000	$166,667	$100,000	$ 33,333
Depreciation	100,000	100,000	100,000	100,000	100,000
Earnings before taxes	$133,333	$200,000	$ 66,667	$ 0	$−66,667
Taxes ($T_c = 0.25$)	33,333	50,000	16,667	0	−16,667
Net income	$100,000	$150,000	$ 50,000	$ 0	−$ 50,000

T A B L E 7.3

Projected yearly revenue and costs for average accounting return

$$\text{Average net income} = \frac{(\$100,000 + 150,000 + 50,000 + 0 - 50,000)}{5} = \$50,000$$

$$\text{Average investment} = \frac{\$500,000 + 0}{2} = \$250,000$$

Looking at Table 7.3, net income is $100,000 in the first year, $150,000 in the second year, $50,000 in the third year, $0 in Year 4, and −$50,000 in Year 5. The average net income, then, is:

[$100,000 + 150,000 + 50,000 + 0 + (−$50,000)]/5 = $50,000

The average accounting return is:

AAR = Average net income/Average book value = $50,000/$250,000

= 20%

If the firm has a target AAR less than 20 percent, this investment is acceptable; otherwise it is not. The *average accounting return rule* is thus:

> A project is acceptable if its average accounting return exceeds a target average accounting return.

As we see in the next section, this rule has a number of problems.

Analyzing the Average Accounting Return Method

You recognize the first drawback to the AAR immediately. Above all else, the AAR is not a rate of return in any meaningful economic sense. Instead, it is the ratio of two accounting numbers, and it is not comparable to the returns offered, for example, in financial markets.[5]

One of the reasons the AAR is not a true rate of return is that it ignores time value. When we average figures that occur at different times, we are treating the near future and the more distant future the same way. There was no discounting involved when we computed the average net income, for example.

The second problem with the AAR is similar to the problem we had with the payback period rule concerning the lack of an objective cutoff period. Since a

---

[5] The AAR is closely related to the return on assets (ROA) discussed in Chapter 3. In practice, the AAR is sometimes computed by first calculating the ROA for each year and then averaging the results. This produces a number that is similar, but not identical, to the one we computed.

calculated AAR is really not comparable to a market return, the target AAR must somehow be specified. There is no generally agreed-on way to do this. One way of doing it is to calculate the AAR for the firm as a whole and use this for a benchmark, but there are lots of other ways as well.

The third, and perhaps worst, flaw in the AAR is that it doesn't even look at the right things. Instead of cash flow and market value, it uses net income and book value. These are both poor substitutes because the value of the firm is the present value of future cash flows. As a result, an AAR doesn't tell us what the effect on share price will be from taking an investment, so it doesn't tell us what we really want to know.

Does the AAR have any redeeming features? About the only one is that it almost always can be computed. The reason is that accounting information is almost always available, both for the project under consideration and for the firm as a whole. We hasten to add that once the accounting information is available, we can always convert it to cash flows, so even this is not a particularly important fact. The AAR is summarized in the following table:

Average Accounting Return Rule

Advantages	Disadvantages
1. Easy to calculate.	1. Not a true rate of return; time value of money is ignored.
2. Needed information is usually available.	2. Uses an arbitrary benchmark cutoff rate.
	3. Based on accounting (book) values, not cash flows and market values.

CONCEPT QUESTIONS

1. What is an accounting rate of return (AAR)?

2. What are the weaknesses of the AAR rule?

7.4 | THE INTERNAL RATE OF RETURN

internal rate of return (IRR)

The discount rate that makes the NPV of an investment zero.

We now come to the most important alternative to NPV, the **internal rate of return**, universally known as the IRR. As we see, the IRR is closely related to NPV. With the IRR, we try to find a single rate of return that summarizes the merits of a project. Furthermore, we want this rate to be an internal rate in the sense that it depends only on the cash flows of a particular investment, not on rates offered elsewhere.

To illustrate the idea behind the IRR, consider a project that costs $100 today and pays $110 in one year. Suppose you were asked, "What is the return on this investment?" What would you say? It seems both natural and obvious to say that the return is 10 percent because, for every dollar we put in, we get $1.10 back. In fact, as we see in a moment, 10 percent is the internal rate of return or IRR on this investment.

Is this project with its 10 percent IRR a good investment? Once again, it would seem apparent that this is a good investment only if our required return is less than 10 percent. This intuition is also correct and illustrates the *IRR rule*:

> An investment is acceptable if the IRR exceeds the required return. It should be rejected otherwise.

Imagine that we wanted to calculate the NPV for our simple investment. At a discount rate of r, the NPV is:

$$NPV = -\$100 + 110/(1 + r)$$

Suppose we didn't know the discount rate. This presents a problem, but we could still ask how high the discount rate would have to be before this project was unacceptable. We know that we are indifferent to taking or not taking this investment when its NPV is just equal to zero. In other words, this investment is economically a break-even proposition when the NPV is zero because value is neither created nor destroyed. To find the break-even discount rate, we set NPV equal to zero and solve for r:

$$NPV = 0 = -\$100 + 110/(1 + r)$$
$$\$100 = \$110/(1 + r)$$
$$1 + r = \$110/100 = 1.10$$
$$r = 10\%$$

This 10 percent is what we already have called the return on this investment. What we have now illustrated is that the internal rate of return on an investment (or just return for short) is the discount rate that makes the NPV equal to zero. This is an important observation, so it bears repeating:

> The IRR on an investment is the required return that results in a zero NPV when it is used as the discount rate.

The fact that the IRR is simply the discount rate that makes the NPV equal to zero is important because it tells us how to calculate the returns on more complicated investments. As we have seen, finding the IRR turns out to be relatively easy for a single period investment. However, suppose you were now looking at an investment with the cash flows shown in Figure 7.3. As illustrated, this investment costs $100 and has a cash flow of $60 per year for two years, so it's only slightly more complicated than our single period example. If you were asked for the return on this investment, what would you say? There doesn't seem to be any obvious answer (at least to us). Based on what we now know, we can set the NPV equal to zero and solve for the discount rate:

$$NPV = 0 = -\$100 + 60/(1 + IRR) + 60/(1 + IRR)^2$$

Unfortunately, the only way to find the IRR in general is by trial and error, either by hand or by calculator. This is precisely the same problem that came up in Chapter 5 when we found the unknown rate for an annuity and in Chapter 6 when we found the yield to maturity on a bond. In fact, we now see that, in both of those cases, we were finding an IRR.

Year	0	1	2
	−$100	+$60	+$60

F I G U R E 7.3

Project cash flows

	Discount Rate	NPV
T A B L E 7.4	0%	$20.00
	5	11.56
NPV at different	10	4.13
discount rates	15	−2.46
	20	−8.33

In this particular case, the cash flows form a two-period, $60 annuity. To find the unknown rate, we can try various different rates until we get the answer. If we were to start with a 0 percent rate, the NPV would obviously be $120 − 100 = $20. At a 10 percent discount rate, we would have:

$$\text{NPV} = -\$100 + 60/1.1 + 60/(1.1)^2 = \$4.13$$

Now, we're getting close. We can summarize these and some other possibilities as shown in Table 7.4. From our calculations, the NPV appears to be zero between 10 and 15 percent, so the IRR is somewhere in that range. With a little more effort, we can find that the IRR is about 13.1 percent.[6] So, if our required return is less than 13.1 percent, we would take this investment. If our required return exceeds 13.1 percent, we would reject it.

By now, you have probably noticed that the IRR rule and the NPV rule appear to be quite similar. In fact, the IRR is sometimes simply called the discounted cash flow or DCF return. The easiest way to illustrate the relationship between NPV and IRR is to plot the numbers we calculated in Table 7.4. On the vertical or y-axis we put the different NPVs. We put discount rates on the horizontal or x-axis. If we had a very large number of points, the resulting picture would be a smooth curve called a **net present value profile**. Figure 7.4 illustrates the NPV profile for this project. Beginning with a 0 percent discount rate, we have $20 plotted directly on the y-axis. As the discount rate increases, the NPV declines smoothly. Where does the curve cut through the x-axis? This occurs where the NPV is just equal to zero, so it happens right at the IRR of 13.1 percent.

net present value profile

A graphical representation of the relationship between an investment's NPVs and various discount rates.

In our example, the NPV rule and the IRR rule lead to identical accept/reject decisions. We accept an investment using the IRR rule if the required return is less than 13.1 percent. As Figure 7.4 illustrates, however, the NPV is positive at any discount rate less than 13.1 percent, so we would accept the investment using the NPV rule as well. The two rules are equivalent in this case.

E X A M P L E | 7.2   Calculating the IRR

A project has a total up-front cost of $435.44. The cash flows are $100 in the first year, $200 in the second year, and $300 in the third year. What's the IRR? If we require an 18 percent return, should we take this investment?

---

[6] With a lot more effort (or a calculator or personal computer), we can find that the IRR is approximately (to 15 decimal points) 13.0662386291808 percent, not that anybody would ever want this many decimal points.

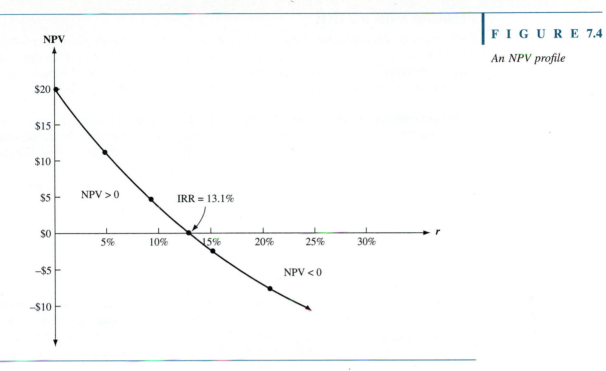

We'll describe the NPV profile and find the IRR by calculating some NPVs at different discount rates. You should check our answers for practice. Beginning with 0 percent, we have:

Discount Rate	NPV
0%	$164.56
5	100.36
10	46.15
15	0.00
20	−39.61

The NPV is zero at 15 percent, so 15 percent is the IRR. If we require an 18 percent return, we should not take the investment. The reason is that the NPV is negative at 18 percent (check that it is −$24.47). The IRR rule tells us the same thing in this case. We shouldn't take this investment because its 15 percent return is less than our required 18 percent return.

At this point, you may be wondering whether the IRR and the NPV rules always lead to identical decisions. The answer is yes as long as two very important conditions are met: First, the project's cash flows must be conventional, meaning that the first cash flow (the initial investment) is negative and all the rest are positive. Second, the project must be independent, meaning the decision to accept or reject this project does not affect the decision to accept or reject any other. The first of these conditions is typically met, but the second often is not. In any case, when one or both of these conditions is not met, problems can arise. We discuss some of these next.

Problems with the IRR

Problems with the IRR come about when the cash flows are not conventional or when we are trying to compare two or more investments to see which is best. In the first case, surprisingly, the simple question—What's the return?—can become very difficult to answer. In the second case, the IRR can be a misleading guide.

Non-conventional Cash Flows   Suppose we have a strip-mining project that requires a $60 investment. Our cash flow in the first year will be $155. In the second year, the mine is depleted, but we have to spend $100 to restore the terrain. As Figure 7.5 illustrates, both the first and third cash flows are negative.

To find the IRR on this project, we can calculate the NPV at various rates:

Discount Rate	NPV
0%	−$ 5.00
10	−1.74
20	−0.28
30	0.06
40	−0.31

The NPV appears to be behaving in a very peculiar fashion here. As the discount rate increases from 0 percent to 30 percent, the NPV starts out negative and becomes positive. This seems backward because the NPV is rising as the discount rate rises. It then starts getting smaller and becomes negative again. What's the IRR? To find out, we draw the NPV profile in Figure 7.6.

In Figure 7.6, notice that the NPV is zero when the discount rate is 25 percent, so this is the IRR. Or is it? The NPV is also zero at 33⅓ percent. Which of these is correct? The answer is both or neither; more precisely, there is no unambiguously correct answer. This is the **multiple rates of return** problem. Many financial computer packages (including the best seller for personal computers) aren't aware of this problem and just report the first IRR that is found. Others report only the smallest positive IRR, even though this answer is no better than any other.

In our current example, the IRR rule breaks down completely. Suppose our required return were 10 percent. Should we take this investment? Both IRRs are greater than 10 percent, so, by the IRR rule, maybe we should. However, as Figure 7.6 shows, the NPV is negative at any discount rate less than 25 percent, so this is not a good investment. When should we take it? Looking at Figure 7.6 one last time, the NPV is positive only if our required return is between 25 and 33⅓ percent.

The moral of the story is that when the cash flows aren't conventional, strange things can start to happen to the IRR. This is not anything to get upset about, however, because the NPV rule, as always, works just fine. This illustrates that, oddly enough, the obvious question—What's the rate of return?—may not always have a good answer.

multiple rates of return

One potential problem in using the IRR method if more than one discount rate makes the NPV of an investment zero.

FIGURE 7.5

Project cash flows

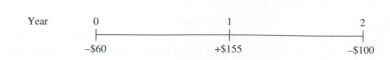

Year	0	1	2
	−$60	+$155	−$100

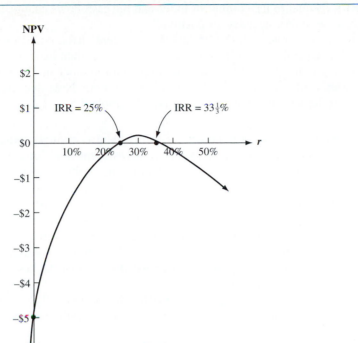

E X A M P L E | 7.3   What's the IRR?

You are looking at an investment that requires you to invest $51 today. You'll get $100 in one year, but you must pay out $50 in two years. What is the IRR on this investment?

    You're on the alert now to the non-conventional cash flow problem, so you probably wouldn't be surprised to see more than one IRR. However, if you start looking for an IRR by trial and error, it will take you a long time. The reason is that there is no IRR. The NPV is negative at every discount rate, so we shouldn't take this investment under any circumstances. What's the return of this investment? Your guess is as good as ours. ▌

**E X A M P L E | 7.4   "I Think; Therefore, I Know How Many IRRs There
                          Can Be."**

We've seen that it's possible to get more than one IRR. If you wanted to make sure that you had found all of the possible IRRs, how could you tell? The answer comes from the great mathematician, philosopher, and financial analyst Descartes (of "I think; therefore I am" fame). Descartes's rule of sign says that the maximum number of IRRs is equal to the number of times that the cash flows change sign from positive to negative and/or negative to positive.[7]

In our example with the 25 and 33⅓ percent IRRs, could there be yet another IRR? The cash flows flip from negative to positive, then back to negative for a total of two sign changes. As a result, the maximum number of IRRs is two, and, from Descartes's rule, we don't need to look for any more. Note that the actual number of IRRs can be less than the maximum (see Example 7.5). |

Mutually Exclusive Investments   Even if there is a single IRR, another problem can arise concerning **mutually exclusive investment decisions**. If two investments, X and Y, are mutually exclusive, then taking one of them means we cannot take the other. For example, if we own one corner lot, we can build a gas station or an apartment building, but not both. These are mutually exclusive alternatives.

Thus far, we have asked whether or not a given investment is worth undertaking. A related question, however, comes up very often: Given two or more mutually exclusive investments, which one is the best? The answer is simple enough: The best one is the one with the largest NPV. Can we also say that the best one has the highest return? As we show, the answer is no.

To illustrate the problem with the IRR rule and mutually exclusive investments, consider the cash flows from the following two mutually exclusive investments:

Year	Investment A	Investment B
0	−$100	−$100
1	50	20
2	40	40
3	40	50
4	30	60
IRR	24%	21%

Since these investments are mutually exclusive, we can take only one of them. Simple intuition suggests that Investment A is better because of its higher return. Unfortunately, simple intuition is not always correct.

To see why investment A is not necessarily the better of the two investments, we've calculated the NPV of these investments for different required returns:

Discount Rate	NPV(A)	NPV(B)
0%	$60.00	$70.00
5	43.13	47.88
10	29.06	29.79
15	17.18	14.82
20	7.06	2.31
25	−1.63	−8.22

The IRR for A (24 percent) is larger than the IRR for B (21 percent). However, if you compare the NPVs, you'll see that which investment has the higher NPV depends on our required return. B has greater total cash flow, but it pays back more slowly than A. As a result, it has a higher NPV at lower discount rates.

[7] To be more precise, the number of IRRs that are bigger than −100 percent is equal to the number of sign changes, or it differs from the number of sign changes by an even number. Thus, for example, if there are five sign changes, there are either five, three, or one IRRs. If there are two sign changes, there are either two IRRs or no IRRs.

mutually exclusive investment decisions
One potential problem in using the IRR method if the acceptance of one project excludes that of another.

In our example, the NPV and IRR rankings conflict for some discount rates. If our required return is 10 percent, for instance, B has the higher NPV and is thus the better of the two even though A has the higher return. If our required return is 15 percent, there is no ranking conflict: A is better.

The conflict between the IRR and NPV for mutually exclusive investments can be illustrated as we have done in Figure 7.7 by plotting their NPV profiles. In Figure 7.7, notice that the NPV profiles cross at about 11 percent. Notice also that at any discount rate less than 11 percent, the NPV for B is higher. In this range, taking B benefits us more than taking A, even though A's IRR is higher. At any rate greater than 11 percent, project A has the greater NPV.

What this example illustrates is that whenever we have mutually exclusive projects, we shouldn't rank them based on their returns. More generally, anytime we are comparing investments to determine which is best, IRRs can be misleading. Instead, we need to look at the relative NPVs to avoid the possibility of choosing incorrectly. Remember, we're ultimately interested in creating value for the shareholders, so the option with the higher NPV is preferred, regardless of the relative returns.

If this seems counterintuitive, think of it this way. Suppose you have two investments. One has a 10 percent return and makes you $100 richer immediately. The other has a 20 percent return and makes you $50 richer immediately. Which one do you like better? We would rather have $100 than $50, regardless of the returns, so we like the first one better.

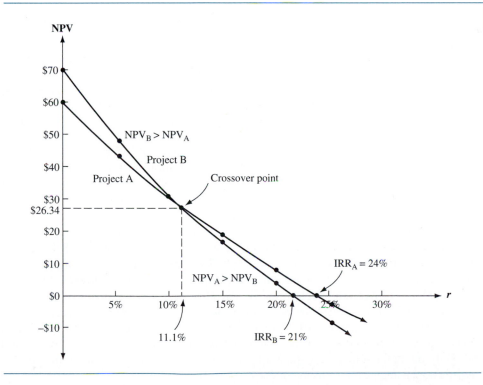

F I G U R E 7.7

NPV and the IRR ranking problem

E X A M P L E | 7.5   **Calculating the Crossover Rate**

In Figure 7.7, the NPV profiles cross at about 11 percent. How can we determine just what this crossover point is? The *crossover rate,* by definition, is the discount rate that makes the NPVs of two projects equal. To illustrate, suppose we have the following two mutually exclusive investments:

Year	Investment A	Investment B
0	−$400	−$500
1	250	320
2	280	340

What's the crossover rate?

To find the crossover, consider moving out of Investment A and into Investment B. If you make the move, you'll have to invest an extra $100 = ($500 − 400). For this $100 investment, you'll get an extra $70 = ($320 − 250) in the first year and an extra $60 = ($340 − 280) in the second year. Is this a good move? In other words, is it worth investing the extra $100?

Based on our discussion, the NPV of the switch, NPV(B − A) is:

$$\text{NPV(B − A)} = -\$100 + \$70/(1 + r) + \$60/(1 + r)^2$$

We can calculate the return on this investment by setting the NPV equal to zero and solving for the IRR;

$$\text{NPV(B − A)} = 0 = -\$100 + \$70/(1 + r) + \$60/(1 + r)^2$$

If you go through this calculation, you will find the IRR is exactly 20 percent. What this tells us is that at a 20 percent discount rate, we are indifferent between the two investments because the NPV of the difference in their cash flows is zero. As a consequence, the two investments have the same value, so this 20 percent is the crossover rate. Check that the NPV at 20 percent is $2.78 for both.

In general, you can find the crossover rate by taking the difference in the cash flows and calculating the IRR using the differences. It doesn't make any difference which one you subtract from which. To see this, find the IRR for (A − B); you'll see it's the same number. Also, for practice, you might want to find the exact crossover in Figure 7.7. (Hint: It's 11.0704 percent.) |

Redeeming Qualities of the IRR

Despite its flaws, the IRR is very popular in practice, more so than even the NPV. It probably survives because it fills a need that the NPV does not. In analyzing investments, people in general and financial analysts in particular seem to prefer talking about rates of return rather than dollar values.

In a similar vein, the IRR also appears to provide a simple way of communicating information about a proposal. One manager might say to another: "Remodeling the clerical wing has a 20 percent return." This may somehow be simpler than saying: "At a 10 percent discount rate, the net present value is $4,000."

Finally, under certain circumstances, the IRR may have a practical advantage over NPV. We can't estimate the NPV unless we know the appropriate discount rate, but we can still estimate the IRR. Suppose we didn't know the required return on an investment, but we found, for example, that it had a 40 percent return. We would probably be inclined to take it since it is very unlikely that the required return is that high. The advantages and disadvantages of the IRR follow:

Internal Rate of Return Rule	
Advantages	Disadvantages
1. Closely related to NPV, generally leading to identical decisions.	1. May result in multiple answers or no answer with non-conventional cash flows.
2. Easy to understand and communicate.	2. May lead to incorrect decisions in comparisons of mutually exclusive investments.

CONCEPT QUESTIONS

1. Under what circumstances will the IRR and NPV rules lead to the same accept/reject decisions? When might they conflict?

2. Is it generally true that an advantage of the IRR rule over the NPV rule is that we don't need to know the required return to use the IRR rule?

7.5 | THE PROFITABILITY INDEX

Another method used to evaluate projects is called the **profitability index (PI)** or **benefit/cost ratio**. This index is defined as the present value of the future cash flows divided by the initial investment. So, if a project costs $200 and the present value of its future cash flows is $220, the profitability index value would be $220/200 = 1.10. Notice that the NPV for this investment is $20, so it is a desirable investment.

More generally, if a project has a positive NPV, the present value of the future cash flows must be bigger than the initial investment. The profitability index would thus be bigger than 1.00 for a positive NPV investment and less than 1.00 for a negative NPV investment.

How do we interpret the profitability index? In our example, the PI was 1.10. This tells us that, per dollar invested, $1.10 in value or $.10 in NPV results. The profitability index thus measures "bang for the buck," that is, the value created per dollar invested. For this reason, it is often proposed as a measure of performance for government or other not-for-profit investments. Also, when capital is scarce, it may make sense to allocate it to those projects with the highest PIs. We return to this issue in a later chapter.

The PI is obviously very similar to the NPV. However, consider an investment that costs $5 and has a $10 present value and an investment that costs $100 with a $150 present value. The first of these investments has an NPV of $5 and a PI of 2. The second has an NPV of $50 and a PI of 1.50. If these were mutually exclusive investments, the second one is preferred even though it has a lower PI. This ranking problem is very similar to the IRR ranking problem we saw in the previous section. In all, there seems to be little reason to rely on the PI instead of the NPV. Our discussion of the PI is summarized in the following table:

profitability index (PI)
The present value of an investment's future cash flows divided by its initial cost. Also benefit/cost ratio.

benefit/cost ratio
The profitability index of an investment project.

Profitability Index Rule	
Advantages	Disadvantages
1. Closely related to NPV, generally leading to identical decisions.	1. May lead to incorrect decisions in comparisons of mutually exclusive investments.
2. Easy to understand and communicate.	
3. May be useful when available investment funds are limited.	

CONCEPT QUESTIONS

1. What does the profitability index measure?

2. How would you state the profitability index rule?

IN THEIR OWN WORDS . . .

Samuel Weaver on Capital Budgeting at Hershey Foods Corporation

The capital program at Hershey Foods Corporation and most Fortune 500/1,000 companies involves a three-phase approach: planning/budgeting, evaluation, and post-completion reviews.

The first phase involves identification of likely projects at strategic planning time. These are selected to support the strategic objectives of the corporation. This identification is generally broad in scope with minimal financial evaluation attached. As the planning process focusses more closely on the short-term plans, major capital expenditures are scrutinized more rigorously. Project costs are more closely honed, and specific projects may be reconsidered.

Each project is then individually reviewed and authorized. Planning, developing, and refining cash flows underlie capital analysis at Hershey Foods. Once the cash flows have been determined, the application of capital evaluation techniques such as net present value, internal rate of return, and payback period is routine. Presentation of the results is enhanced using sensitivity analysis, which plays a major role for management in assessing the critical assumptions and resulting impact.

The final phase relates to post-completion reviews in which the original forecasts of the project's performance are compared to actual results and/or revised expectations.

Capital expenditure analysis is only as good as the assumptions that underlie the project. The old cliché of "GIGO" (garbage in, garbage out) applies in this case. Incremental cash flows primarily result from incremental sales or margin improvements (cost savings). For the most part, a range of incremental cash flows can be identified from marketing research or engineering studies. However, for a number of projects, correctly discerning the implications and the relevant cash flows is analytically challenging. For example, when a new product is introduced and is expected to generate millions of dollars worth of sales, the appropriate analysis focusses on the incremental sales after accounting for cannibalization of existing products.

One of the problems that we face at Hershey Foods deals with the application of net present value (NPV) versus internal rate of return (IRR). NPV offers the correct investment indication when dealing with mutually exclusive alternatives. However, decision makers at all levels sometimes find it difficult to comprehend the result. Specifically, an NPV of, say, $535,000 needs to be interpreted. It is not enough to know that the NPV is positive or even more positive than an alternative. Decision makers seek a level of "comfort" of how profitable the investment is by relating it to other standards.

Although the IRR may provide a misleading indication of which project to select, the result is pro-

vided in a way that can be interpreted by all parties. The resulting IRR can be mentally compared to expected inflation, current borrowing rates, the cost of capital, an equity portfolio's return, and so on. An IRR of, say, 18 percent is readily interpretable by management. Perhaps this ease of understanding is why surveys indicate that most Fortune 500 or Fortune 1,000 companies use the IRR method as a primary evaluation technique.

In addition to the NPV versus IRR problem, there are a limited number of projects for which traditional and capital expenditure analysis is difficult to apply because the cash flows can't be determined. When new computer equipment is purchased, an office building is renovated, or a parking lot is repaved, it is essentially impossible to identify the cash flows, so the use of traditional evaluation techniques is limited. These types of "capital expenditure" decisions are made using other techniques that hinge on management's judgment.

Samuel Weaver, Ph.D., is director, Corporate Financial Planning and Analysis for the Hershey Foods Corporation. He is a certified management accountant, and he currently serves on the board of directors of the Financial Management Association as vice president, practitioner services. His current position combines the theoretical with the pragmatic and involves the analysis of many different facets of finance in addition to capital expenditure analysis.

7.6 | THE PRACTICE OF CAPITAL BUDGETING

A number of surveys have asked executives of large firms what types of investment criteria they actually use. Table 7.5 presents the results of a recent survey of the chief financial officers of Canada's largest industrial corporations. Based on the results, the most frequently used capital budgeting technique is some form of discounted cash flow (such as NPV or IRR). In practice, the payback period is the second most popular approach. Other surveys in both Canada and the United States are consistent with these results. They also show a trend toward increasing use of discounted cash flow methods. The most common practice is to look at NPV or IRR along with nondiscounted cash flow criteria such as payback and AAR. Given our discussion, this is sound practice. For future reference, the various criteria are summarized in Table 7.6.

Given that NPV seems to be telling us directly what we want to know, you might be wondering why there are so many other procedures and why alternative procedures are commonly used. Recall that we are trying to make an investment decision and that we are frequently operating under considerable uncertainty about the future. We can only estimate the NPV of an investment in this case. The resulting estimate can be very soft, meaning that the true NPV might be quite different.

Because the true NPV is unknown, the astute financial manager seeks clues to assess whether the estimated NPV is reliable. For this reason, firms would typically use multiple criteria for evaluating a proposal. For example, suppose we have an investment with a positive estimated NPV. Based on our experience with other projects, this one appears to have a short payback and a very high AAR. In this case, the different indicators seem to agree that it's all systems go. Put another way, the payback and the AAR are consistent with the conclusion that the NPV is positive.

On the other hand, suppose we had a positive estimated NPV, a long payback, and a low AAR. This could still be a good investment, but it looks like we need to be much more careful in making the decision since we are getting conflicting signals. If the estimated NPV is based critically on sales projections, further analysis is probably in order. This is the case because managers in a recent survey state that sales projections, especially for new ventures, are far more likely to be overly optimistic than projections for cost savings.

	NPV	IRR	Payback Period	Accounting ROR	Other
Replacement projects	34.6	46.6	48.9	13.5	12.9
Expansion—existing operations	41.4	61.6	50.0	16.5	7.5
Expansion—new operations	45.1	61.6	47.4	18.8	6.8
Foreign operations	29.3	41.4	30.8	9.0	8.3
Abandonment	29.3	19.6	15.0	11.3	21.8
General & administrative	17.3	19.6	27.8	12.0	21.8
Social expenditures	10.5	8.3	6.8	5.3	40.6
Leases	42.9	36.1	14.3	7.5	13.5

TABLE 7.5

Evaluative methods and types of projects (in percent)

Note: A firm could use several different techniques to evaluate the same project. Again, the percentages above give the frequency of citation of a particular technique as being used for capital budgeting.
Source: V. M. Jog and A. K. Srivastava, "Corporate Financial Decision Making in Canada," *Canadian Journal of Administrative Sciences* 11 (June 1994), pp. 156–76.

T A B L E 7.6

*Summary of
investment criteria*

I. Discounted Cash Flow Criteria

A. Net present value (NPV). The NPV of an investment is the difference between its market value and its cost. The NPV rule is to take a project if its NPV is positive. NPV is frequently estimated by calculating the present value of the future cash flows (to estimate market value) and then subtracting the cost. NPV has no serious flaws; it is the preferred decision criterion.

B. Internal rate of return (IRR). The IRR is the discount rate that makes the estimated NPV of investment equal to zero; it is sometimes called the discounted cash flow (DCF) return. The IRR rule is take a project when its IRR exceeds the required return. IRR is closely related to NPV, and it leads to exactly the same decisions as NPV for conventional, independent projects. When project cash flows are not conventional, there may be no IRR or there may be more than one. More seriously, the IRR cannot be used to rank mutually exclusive projects; the project with the highest IRR is not necessarily the preferred investment.

C. Profitability index. The profitability index, also called the benefit/cost ratio, is the ratio of present value to cost. The profitability index rule is to take an investment if the index exceeds one. The profitability index measures the present value of an investment per dollar invested. It is quite similar to NPV, but, like IRR, it cannot be used to rank mutually exclusive projects. However, it is sometimes used to rank projects when a firm has more positive NPV investments than it can currently finance.

II. Payback Criteria

A. Payback period. The payback period is the length of time until the sum of an investment's cash flows equals its cost. The payback period rule is to take a project if its payback is less than some cutoff. The payback period is a flawed criterion primarily because it ignores risk, the time value of money, and cash flows beyond the cutoff point.

B. Discounted payback period. The discounted payback period is the length of time until the sum of an investment's discounted cash flows equals its cost. The discounted payback period rule is to take an investment if the discounted payback is less than some cutoff. The discounted payback rule is flawed primarily because it ignores cash flows after the cutoff.

III. Accounting Criteria

A. Average accounting return (AAR). The AAR is a measure of accounting profit relative to book value. It is *not* related to the IRR, but it is similar to the accounting return on assets (ROA) measure in Chapter 3. The AAR rule is to take an investment if its AAR exceeds a benchmark AAR. The AAR is seriously flawed for a variety of reasons, and it has little to recommend it.

An extreme case of cash flows being almost entirely dependent on sales is the movie industry. The information that a studio uses to accept or reject a movie idea comes from the pitch. An independent movie producer schedules an extremely brief meeting with a studio to pitch his or her idea for a movie. Consider the following four paragraphs of quotes concerning the pitch from the thoroughly delightful book, *Reel Power:*

"They [studio executives] don't want to know too much," says Ron Simpson. "They want to know concept . . . They want to know what the three-liner is, because they want it to suggest the ad campaign. They want a title . . . They don't want to hear any esoterica. And if the meeting lasts more than five minutes, they're probably not going to do the project."

"A guy comes in and says this is my idea: 'Jaws on a spaceship,' " says writer Clay Frohman (*Under Fire*). "And they say, 'Brilliant, fantastic.' Becomes *Alien.* That is *Jaws* on a spaceship, ultimately . . . And that's it. That's all they want to hear. Their attitude is 'Don't confuse us with the details of the story.' "

"Some high-concept stories are more appealing to the studios than others. The ideas liked best are sufficiently original that the audience will not feel it has already seen the movie, yet similar enough to past hits to reassure executives wary of anything too far-out. Thus, the frequently used shorthand: It's *Flashdance* in the country (*Footloose*) or *High Noon* in outer space *(Outland)*.

"One gambit not to use during a pitch," says executive Barbara Boyle, "is to talk about big box-office grosses your story is sure to make. Executives know as well as anyone that it's impossible to predict how much money a movie will make, and declarations to the contrary are considered pure malarkey."[8]

The authors are not experts on reforming capital budgeting practices in the movie industry in Hollywood or Toronto. Large firms in most other industries do use the techniques we present as you can see in Table 7.5. We consider how to go about this analysis in more detail in the next two chapters.[9]

CONCEPT QUESTIONS

1. What are the most commonly used capital budgeting procedures?
2. Since NPV is conceptually the best procedure for capital budgeting, why do you think that multiple measures are used in practice?

7.7 | SUMMARY AND CONCLUSIONS

This chapter has covered the different criteria used to evaluate proposed investments. The six criteria, in the order we discussed them, are:

1. Net present value (NPV)
2. Payback period
3. Discounted payback period
4. Average accounting return (AAR)
5. Internal rate of return (IRR)
6. Profitability index (PI)

We illustrated how to calculate each of these and discussed the interpretation of the results. We also described the advantages and disadvantages of each of them.

The most important concept in this chapter is net present value (NPV). We return to this idea repeatedly in the chapters to come. We defined NPV as the difference between the market value of an asset or project and its cost. We saw that the financial manager acts in the best interest of the shareholders by identifying and undertaking positive NPV investments.

Finally, we noted that NPVs can't normally be observed in the market; instead, they must be estimated. Because there is always the possibility of a poor estimate, financial managers use multiple criteria for examining projects. These other criteria provide additional information about whether a project truly has a positive NPV.

KEY TERMS

net present value (NPV) (page 229)
discounted cash flow (DCF)
valuation (page 230)
payback period (page 232)
discounted payback period (page 234)
average accounting return (AAR)
(page 236)

internal rate of return (IRR) (page 238)
net present value profile (page 240)
multiple rates of return (page 242)
mutually exclusive investment
decisions (page 244)
profitability index (PI) (page 247)
benefit/cost ratio (page 247)

---

[8] Mark Litwak, *Reel Power: The Struggle for Influence and Success in the New Hollywood* (New York: William Morrow, 1986), pp. 73, 74, and 77.
[9] Chapter 14's appendix discusses the adjusted present value approach to capital budgeting. Capital budgeting by multinational firms is discussed in Chapter 22.

Chapter Review Problems and Self-Test

7.1   Investment Criteria   This problem will give you some practice calculating NPVs, IRRs, and paybacks. A proposed overseas expansion has the following cash flows:

Year	Investment A
0	-$100
1	50
2	40
3	40
4	15

Calculate the payback, the discounted payback, and the NPV at a required return of 15 percent.

7.2   Mutually Exclusive Investments   Consider the following two mutually exclusive investments. Calculate the IRR for each and the crossover rate. Under which circumstances will the IRR and NPV criteria rank the two projects differently?

Year	Investment A	Investment B
0	-$100	-$100
1	50	70
2	70	75
3	40	10

7.3   Average Accounting Return   You are looking at a three-year project with a projected net income of $1,000 in Year 1, $2,000 in Year 2, and $4,000 in Year 3. The cost is $9,000, which will be depreciated straight-line to zero over the three-year life of the project. What is the average accounting return (AAR)?

Answers to Self-Test Problems

7.1   In the following table, we have listed the cash flows, cumulative cash flows, discounted cash flows (at 15%), and cumulative discounted cash flows.

Cash Flows and Accumulated Cash Flows

	Cash Flow		Accumulated Cash Flow	
Year	Undiscounted	Discounted	Undiscounted	Discounted
1	$50	$ 43.5	$ 50	$ 43.5
2	40	30.2	⇒90	73.7
3	40	26.3	⇒130	⇒100.0
4	15	⇒8.6	145	108.6

Recall that the initial investment is $100. When we compare this to accumulated undiscounted cash flows, we see that payback occurs between Years 2 and 3. The cash flows for the first two years are $90 total, so, going into the third year, we are short by $10. The total cash flow in Year 3 is $40, so the payback is 2 + $10/40 = 2¼ years. √

Looking at the accumulated discounted cash flows, we see that the discounted payback occurs right at three years. The sum of the discounted cash flows is $108.6, so the NPV is $8.60. Notice that this is the present value of the cash flows that occur after the discounted payback.

7.2 To calculate the IRR, we might try some guesses as in the following table:

Discount Rate	NPV(A)	NPV(B)
0%	$ 60.00	$55.00
10	33.36	33.13
20	13.43	16.20
30	−1.91	2.78
40	−14.01	−8.09

Several things are immediately apparent from our guesses. First, the IRR on A must be just a little less than 30 percent (why?). With some more effort, we find that it's 28.61 percent. Second, for B, the IRR must be a little more than 30 percent (again, why?); it works out to be 32.37 percent. Third, notice that at 10 percent, the NPVs are very close, indicating that the crossover is in that vicinity.

To find the crossover exactly, we can compute the IRR on the difference in the cash flows. If we take the cash flows from A minus the cash flows from B, the resulting cash flows are:

Year	A − B
0	$ 0
1	−20
2	−5
3	30

These cash flows look a little odd, but the sign only changes once, so we can find an IRR. With some trial and error, you'll see that the NPV is zero at a discount rate of 10.61 percent, so this is the crossover rate.

Now, the IRR for B is always higher. As we've seen, A has the larger NPV for any discount rates less than 10.61 percent, so the NPV and IRR rankings conflict in that range. Remember, if there's a conflict, we go with the higher NPV. Our decision rule is thus very simple: Take A if the required return is less than 10.61 percent; take B if the required return is between 10.61 percent and 32.37 percent (the IRR on B); and take neither if the required return is more than 32.37 percent.

7.3 Here, we need to calculate the ratio of average net income to average book value to get the AAR. Average net income is:

Average net income = ($1,000 + 2,000 + 4,000)/3 = $2,333.33

Average book value is:

Average book value = $9,000/2 = $4,500

So the average accounting return is:

AAR = $2,333.33/4,500 = 51.85%

This is an impressive return. Remember, however, that it isn't really a rate of return like an interest rate or an IRR, so the size doesn't tell us a lot. In particular, our money is probably not going to grow at 51.85 percent per year, sorry to say.

Questions and Problems

1. **Calculating Payback**   What is the payback period for the following set of cash flows?

Year	Cash Flow
0	−$2,000
1	800
2	600
3	900
4	300

2. **Calculating Payback**   An investment project provides annual cash inflows of $750 per year for eight years. What is the project payback period if the initial cost is $2,500? What if the initial cost is $5,000? $7,500?

3. **Calculating Payback**   John's Bakery Products, Inc., imposes a payback cutoff of 2.5 years for its investment projects. If the company has the following two projects available, should it accept either of them?

Year	Cash Flows A	Cash Flows B
0	−$25,000	−$ 72,000
1	16,000	30,000
2	16,000	30,000
3	3,000	15,000
4	3,000	200,000

4. **Calculating Discounted Payback**   An investment project has annual cash inflows of $500, $600, $700, and $800, and a discount rate of 10 percent. What is the discounted payback period for these cash flows if the initial cost is $1,000? What if the initial cost is $1,800? $2,500?

5. **Calculating Discounted Payback**   An investment project costs $3,000 with annual cash flows of $750 for five years. What is the discounted payback period if the discount rate is zero percent? What if the discount rate is 5 percent? 10 percent?

6. **Calculating AAR**   You're trying to determine whether to expand your business by building a new manufacturing plant. The plant has an installation cost of $2 million, which will be depreciated straight-line to zero over its four-year life. If the project has projected net income of $417,000, $329,500, $216,200, and $48,000 over these four years, what is the project's average accounting return (AAR)?

7. **Calculating IRR**   A firm evaluates all of its projects by applying the IRR rule. If the required return is 14 percent, should the firm accept the following project?

Year	Cash Flow
0	−$15,000
1	10,000
2	0
3	10,000

8. **Calculating NPV**   For the cash flows in the previous problem, suppose the firm uses the NPV decision rule. At a required return of 14 percent, should the firm accept this project? What if the required return was 18 percent?

Basic
(Continued)

9. **Calculating NPV and IRR** A project that provides annual cash flows of $200 for seven years costs $1,000 today. Is this a good project if the required return is 7 percent? What if it's 15 percent? At what discount rate would you be indifferent to accepting the project or not?

10. **Calculating IRR** What is the IRR of the following set of cash flows?

Year	Cash Flow
0	−$600
1	200
2	300
3	400

11. **Calculating NPV** For the cash flows in the previous problem, what is the NPV at a discount rate of zero percent? What if the discount rate is 10 percent? 20 percent? 30 percent?

12. **NPV versus IRR** The Heitman Group, Inc., has identified the following two mutually exclusive projects:

Year	Cash Flows L	Cash Flows S
0	−$10,000	−$10,000
1	200	5,000
2	500	6,000
3	8,200	500
4	4,800	500

    a. What is the IRR for each of these projects? If you apply the IRR decision rule, which project should the company accept? Is this decision necessarily correct?
    b. If the required return is 9 percent, what is the NPV for each of these projects? Which project will you choose if you apply the NPV decision rule?
    c. Over what range of discount rates would you choose Project L? Project S? At what discount rate would you be indifferent between these two projects? Explain.

13. **NPV versus IRR** Consider the two mutually exclusive projects below:

Year	Cash Flows M	Cash Flows N
0	−$50	−$50
1	40	5
2	20	5
3	5	65

    Sketch the NPV profiles for M and N over a range of discount rates from zero to 25 percent. What is the crossover rate for these two projects?

14. **Problems with IRR** Friedlich Co. is trying to evaluate a project with the following cash flows:

Year	Cash Flow
0	−$ 900
1	1,200
2	− 200

    a. If the company requires a 10 percent return on its investments, should it accept this project? Why?

b. Compute the IRR for this project. How many IRRs are there? If you apply the IRR decision rule, should you accept the project or not? What's going on here?

15. **Calculating Profitability Index**   What is the profitability index for the following set of cash flows if the relevant discount rate is 8 percent? What if the discount rate is 12 percent? 18 percent?

Year	Cash Flow
0	−$1,400
1	800
2	500
3	500

16. **Problems with Profitability Index**   The Bundy Valve Corporation is trying to choose between the two mutually exclusive projects below.

Year	Cash Flows X	Cash Flows Y
0	−$23,000	−$4,000
1	10,000	2,000
2	10,000	2,000
3	10,000	2,000

a. If the required return is 12 percent and Bundy applies the profitability index decision rule, which project should the firm accept?

b. If the company applies the NPV decision rule, which project should it take?

c. Explain why your answers in *(a)* and *(b)* are different.

17. **Comparing Investment Criteria**   Consider the following two mutually exclusive projects:

Year	Cash Flows A	Cash Flows B
0	−$260,000	−$40,000
1	5,000	45,000
2	15,000	5,000
3	15,000	500
4	425,000	500

Whichever project you choose, if any, you require a 15 percent return on your investment.

a. If you apply the payback criterion, which investment will you choose? Why?

b. If you apply the discounted payback criterion, which investment will you choose? Why?

c. If you apply the NPV criterion, which investment will you choose? Why?

d. If you apply the IRR criterion, which investment will you choose? Why?

e. If you apply the profitability index criterion, which investment will you choose? Why?

f. Based on your answers in *(a)* through *(e),* which project will you finally choose? Why?

 18. **NPV and Discount Rates**   An investment has an installed cost of $176,515. The cash flows over the four-year life of the investment are projected to be $58,675, $63,116, $69,370, and $72,000. If the discount rate is zero, what is the NPV? If the discount rate is infinite, what is the NPV? At what discount rate is the NPV just equal to zero? Sketch the NPV profile for this investment based on these three points.

19. **Payback Intuition**   If a project with conventional cash flows has a payback period less than the project's life, can you definitively state the algebraic sign of NPV? Why or why not? If you know that the discounted payback period is less than the project's life, what can you say about the NPV now? Explain.

Basic (Continued)

20. **Investment Criteria and Their Relationships**   Suppose a project has conventional cash flows and a positive NPV. What do you know about its payback? Its discounted payback? Its profitability index? Its IRR? Explain.

21. **Interpreting Payback**

Intermediate (Questions 21–30)

   a. Describe how the payback period is calculated, and describe the information this measure provides about a sequence of cash flows. What is the payback criterion decision rule?
   b. What are the problems associated with using the payback period as a means of evaluating cash flows?
   c. What are the advantages of using the payback period to evaluate cash flows? Are there any circumstances where using payback might be appropriate? Explain.

22. **Interpreting Discounted Payback**

   a. Describe how the discounted payback period is calculated, and describe the information this measure provides about a sequence of cash flows. What is the discounted payback criterion decision rule?
   b. What are the problems associated with using the discounted payback period as a means of evaluating cash flows?
   c. What conceptual advantage does the discounted payback have over the regular payback method? Can the discounted payback ever be longer than the regular payback? Explain.

23. **Interpreting AAR**

   a. Describe how the average accounting return is usually calculated, and describe the information this measure provides about a sequence of cash flows. What is the AAR criterion decision rule?
   b. What are the problems associated with using AAR as a means of evaluating a project's cash flows? What underlying feature of AAR is most troubling to you from a financial perspective? Does the AAR have any redeeming qualities?

24. **Interpreting NPV**

   a. Describe how NPV is calculated, and describe the information this measure provides about a sequence of cash flows. What is the NPV criterion decision rule?
   b. Why is NPV considered to be a superior method of evaluating the cash flows from a project? Suppose the NPV for a project's cash flows is computed to be $2,500. What does this number represent with respect to the firm's shareholders?

25. **Interpreting IRR**

   a. Describe how IRR is calculated, and describe the information this measure provides about a sequence of cash flows. What is the IRR criterion decision rule?
   b. What is the relationship between IRR and NPV? Are there any situations where you might prefer one method over the other? Explain.
   c. Despite its shortcomings in some situations, why do most financial managers use IRR along with NPV when evaluating projects? Can you think of a

**Intermediate
(Continued)**

situation where IRR might be a more appropriate measure to use than NPV? Explain.

26. **Interpreting Profitability Index**

 a. Describe how the profitability index is calculated, and describe the information this measure provides about a sequence of cash flows. What is the profitability index decision rule?

 b. What is the relationship between the profitability index and NPV? Are there any situations where you might prefer one method over the other? Explain.

27. **Payback and IRR**   A project has perpetual cash flows of $\$C$ per period, a cost of $\$I$, and a required return of r. What is the relationship between the project's payback and its IRR? What implications does your answer have for long-lived projects with relatively constant cash flows?

28. **NPV and the Profitability Index**   If we define the NPV index as the ratio of NPV to cost, what is the relationship between this index and the profitability index?

29. **NPV Intuition**   Projects A and B have the same cost, and both have conventional cash flows. The total undiscounted cash inflows for A are $1,900, and for B the total is $1,500. The IRR for A is 18 percent; the IRR for B is 15 percent. What can you deduce about the NPVs for Projects A and B? What do you know about the crossover rate? Under what circumstances would you choose Project A over Project B? How about B over A?

30. **Cash Flow Intuition**   A project has an inital cost of $\$I$, a required return of r, and pays $\$C$ annually for N years.

 a. Find C in terms of I and N such that the project has a payback period just equal to its life.

 b. Find C in terms of I, N, and r such that this is a profitable project according to the NPV decision rule.

 c. Find C in terms of I, N, and r such that the project has a benefit/cost ratio of 1.5.

**Challenge
(Questions 31–35)**

31. **Payback and NPV**   An investment under consideration has a payback of seven years and a cost of $70,000. If the required return is 16 percent, what is the worst-case NPV? The best-case NPV? Explain.

32. **Multiple IRRs**   This problem is useful for testing the ability of financial calculators and computer software. Consider the following cash flows. How many IRRs can there be? How many are there (hint: search between 20 percent and 70 percent)? When should we take this project?

Year	Cash Flow
0	−$ 252
1	1,431
2	− 3,035
3	2,850
4	− 1,000

33. **NPV Valuation**   The Grim Reaper Corporation wants to set up a private cemetery business. The cemetery project will provide a net cash inflow of $25,000 for the firm during the first year, and these cash flows are projected to grow at a rate of 6 percent per year forever (the Grim Reaper keeps pretty busy). The project requires an initial investment of $400,000.

 a. If the Grim Reaper requires a 12 percent return on investment, should the cemetery business be started?

Challenge (Continued)

b. The company is somewhat unsure about the assumption of a 6 percent growth rate in its cash flows. At what constant growth rate would the company just break even if it still requires a 12 percent return on investment?

34. **Project Choice and NPV Intuition**   Atlantic Megaprojects has a contract to build a tunnel connecting two Atlantic provinces. The contract calls for the firm to complete the tunnel in three years with an annual cash outlay of $100 million at the end of years 1 and 2. At the end of the third year, governments will pay Atlantic Megaprojects $260 million. If it wishes, the firm can exercise an option to build the tunnel in just two years by subcontracting part of the work to a government-sponsored entity designed to create employment in the region. Under this option, Atlantic Megaprojects will make a cash payment of $220 million at the end of the first year and will receive $260 million after the second year.

    a. Suppose Atlantic Megaprojects has a cost of capital of 15 percent. Should the firm subcontract the work?

    b. Now suppose Atlantic Megaprojects can estimate its cost of capital only up to a range. Over what range of discount rates is subcontracting attractive?

35. **Applications of Various Techniques**   Ted Black, chief financial officer of Consumers Cable Ltd. (CCL), is looking at two capital projects designed to correct the company's current restricted ability to service expanding customer demand. Project Refit revolves around upgrading transmission technology to allow an increased number of programs to be supplied over CCL's existing cable network. Because the network is aging, future cost increases will produce a declining stream of cash flows over the project's four-year life. In contrast, Project Hightech would upgrade the cable network to expand capacity beyond immediately projected needs. Project Hightech has cash flows that increase over time as increased demand catches up with supply capabilities. Like Project Refit, Project Hightech has a four-year life as Black expects that a new generation of technology will come in after four years.

    The following estimates include all elements of cash flows in millions.

Year	Project Hightech	Project Refit
0	($33)	($33)
1	3	23
2	20	17
3	27	7
4	35	2

Ted Black's staff conducted risk analysis of the two projects and found that both are similar in risk to what the firm is currently doing. Consequently, both have an assigned cost of capital (discount rate) of 11 percent.

As Ted Black's executive assistant, you are assigned the task of completing the capital budgeting analysis and drafting a memo to the board to go forward over Black's signature. In preparing the memo, be sure to address the following questions.

a. State the rationale for capital budgeting and how it links to the goal of the financial manager—maximizing the value of the shareholders' wealth.

b. Are these projects independent or mutually exclusive and how does this affect your analysis?

c. Calculate the payback period for each project. Which project is better according to this method? Relate the advantages and disadvantages of the payback method in this case.

Challenge
(Continued)

d. Use the NPV method to analyze the projects. Which project(s) should the firm undertake according to this method?

e. Use the IRR method to analyze the projects. Which project(s) should the firm undertake according to this method?

f. Do the NPV and IRR methods give the same recommendations in this case? Use NPV profiles to see whether the two methods ever disagree over these two projects. How would you resolve such a disagreement if it occurred?

g. What is your recommendation to the board? Justify your position.

Suggested Readings

For a discussion of the capital budgeting techniques used by large firms, see:

Bierman, Harold. *Implementing Capital Budgeting Techniques,* rev. ed. The Institutional Investor Series in Finance and Financial Management Association Survey and Synthesis Series. Cambridge, MA: Ballinger Publishing Company, 1988.

Blazouske, J. D.; I. Carlin; and S. H. Kim. "Current Capital Budgeting Practices in Canada," *CMA Magazine,* March 1988, pp. 51–54.

Making Capital Investment Decisions

So far, we've covered various parts of the capital budgeting decision. Our task in this chapter is to start bringing these pieces together. In particular, we show you how to "spread the numbers" for a proposed investment or project and, based on those numbers, make an initial assessment about whether or not the project should be undertaken.

In the discussion that follows, we focus on setting up a discounted cash flow analysis. From the last chapter, we know that the projected future cash flows are the key element in such an evaluation. Accordingly, we emphasize working with financial and accounting information to come up with these figures.

In evaluating a proposed investment, we pay special attention to deciding what information is relevant to the decision at hand and what information is not. As we shall see, it is easy to overlook important pieces of the capital budgeting puzzle.

We wait until the next chapter to describe in detail how to evaluate the results of our discounted cash flow analysis. Also, where needed, we assume that we know the relevant required return or discount rate. We continue to defer discussion of this subject to Part V.

8.1 | PROJECT CASH FLOWS: A FIRST LOOK

The effect of undertaking a project is to change the firm's overall cash flows today and in the future. To evaluate a proposed investment, we must consider these changes in the firm's cash flows and then decide whether they add value to the firm. The most important step, therefore, is to decide which cash flows are relevant and which are not.

Relevant Cash Flows

What is a relevant cash flow for a project? The general principle is simple enough: A relevant cash flow for a project is a change in the firm's overall future cash flow that comes about as a direct consequence of the decision to take that project. Because the relevant cash flows are defined in terms of changes in or increments to the firm's existing cash flow, they are called the **incremental cash flows** associated with the project.

incremental cash flows

The difference between a firm's future cash flows with a project or without the project.

261

The concept of incremental cash flow is central to our analysis, so we state a general definition and refer back to it as needed:

> The incremental cash flows for project evaluation consist of any and all changes in the firm's future cash flows that are a direct consequence of taking the project.

This definition of incremental cash flows has an obvious and important corollary: Any cash flow that exists regardless of whether or not a project is undertaken is not relevant.

The Stand-Alone Principle

stand-alone principle
Evaluation of a project based on the project's incremental cash flows.

In practice, it would be very cumbersome to actually calculate the future total cash flows to the firm with and without a project, especially for a large firm. Fortunately, it is not really necessary to do so. Once we identify the effect of undertaking the proposed project on the firm's cash flows, we need focus only on the resulting project's incremental cash flows. This is called the **stand-alone principle**

What the stand-alone principle says is that, once we have determined the incremental cash flows from undertaking a project, we can view that project as a kind of minifirm with its own future revenues and costs, its own assets, and, of course, its own cash flows. We are then primarily interested in comparing the cash flows from this minifirm to the cost of acquiring it. An important consequence of this approach is that we evaluate the proposed project purely on its own merits, in isolation from any other activities or projects.

CONCEPT QUESTIONS
1. What are the relevant incremental cash flows for project evaluation?
2. What is the stand-alone principle?

8.2 | INCREMENTAL CASH FLOWS

We are concerned here only with those cash flows that are incremental to a project. Looking back at our general definition, it seems easy enough to decide whether a cash flow is incremental or not. Even so, there are a few situations when mistakes are easy to make. In this section, we describe some of these common pitfalls and how to avoid them.

Sunk Costs

sunk cost
A cost that has already been incurred and cannot be removed and therefore should not be considered in an investment decision.

A **sunk cost**, by definition, is a cost we have already paid or have already incurred the liability to pay. Such a cost cannot be changed by the decision today to accept or reject a project. Put another way, the firm has to pay this cost no matter what. Based on our general definition of cash flow, such a cost is clearly not relevant to the decision at hand. So, we are always careful to exclude sunk costs from our analysis.

That a sunk cost is not relevant seems obvious given our discussion. Nonetheless, it's easy to fall prey to the sunk cost fallacy. For example, suppose True North Distillery Ltd. hires a financial consultant to help evaluate whether or not a line of maple sugar liqueur should be launched. When the consultant turns in the report, True North objects to the analysis because the consultant did not include the hefty consulting fee as a cost to the liqueur project.

Who is correct? By now, we know that the consulting fee is a sunk cost, because the consulting fee must be paid whether or not the liqueur line is launched (this is an attractive feature of the consulting business).

A more subtle example of a cost that can sometimes be sunk is overhead. To illustrate, suppose True North Distillery is now considering building a new warehouse to age the maple sugar liqueur. Should a portion of overhead costs be allocated to the proposed warehouse project? If the overhead costs are truly sunk and independent of the project, the answer is no. An example of such an overhead cost is the cost of maintaining a corporate jet for senior executives. But if the new warehouse requires additional reporting, supervision, or legal input, these overheads should be part of the project analysis.

Opportunity Costs

When we think of costs, we normally think of out-of-pocket costs, namely, those that require us to actually spend some amount of cash. An **opportunity cost** is slightly different; it requires us to give up a benefit. A common situation arises where another division of a firm already owns some of the assets that a proposed project will be using. For example, we might be thinking of converting an old rustic water-powered mill that we bought years ago for $100,000 into upscale condominiums.

If we undertake this project, there will be no direct cash outflow associated with buying the old mill since we already own it. For purposes of evaluating the condo project, should we then treat the mill as free? The answer is no. The mill is a valuable resource used by the project. If we didn't use it here, we could do something else with it. Like what? The obvious answer is that, at a minimum, we could sell it. Using the mill for the condo complex thus has an opportunity cost: We give up the valuable opportunity to do something else with it.

There is another issue here. Once we agree that the use of the mill has an opportunity cost, how much should the condo project be charged? Given that we paid $100,000, it might seem we should charge this amount to the condo project. Is this correct? The answer is no, and the reason is based on our discussion concerning sunk costs.

The fact that we paid $100,000 some years ago is irrelevant. It's sunk. At a minimum, the opportunity cost that we charge the project is what it would sell for today (net of any selling costs) because this is the amount that we give up by using it instead of selling it.[1]

> **opportunity cost**
> *The most valuable alternative that is given up if a particular investment is undertaken.*

Side Effects

Remember that the incremental cash flows for a project include all the changes in the *firm's* future cash flows. It would not be unusual for a project to have side or spillover effects, both good and bad. For example, if the Innovative Motors Company (IMC) introduces a new car, some of the sales might come at the expense of other IMC cars. This is called **erosion**, and the same general problem could occur for any multiline

> **erosion**
> *The cash flows of a new project that come at the expense of a firm's existing projects.*

---

[1] Economists sometimes use the acronym TANSTAAFL, which is short for there ain't no such thing as a free lunch, to describe the fact that only very rarely is something truly free. Further, if the asset in question is unique, the opportunity cost might be higher because there might be other valuable projects we could undertake that would use it. However, if the asset in question is of a type that is routinely bought and sold (a used car, perhaps), the opportunity cost is always the going price in the market because that is the cost of buying another one.

consumer producer or seller.[2] In this case, the cash flows from the new line should be adjusted downward to reflect lost cash flows on other lines.

In accounting for erosion, it is important to recognize that any sales lost as a result of our launching a new product might be lost anyway because of future competition. Erosion is only relevant when the sales would not otherwise be lost.

Net Working Capital

Normally, a project requires that the firm invest in net working capital in addition to long-term assets. For example, a project generally needs some amount of cash on hand to pay any expenses that arise. In addition, a project needs an initial investment in inventories and accounts receivable (to cover credit sales). Some of this financing would be in the form of amounts owed to suppliers (accounts payable), but the firm has to supply the balance. This balance represents the investment in net working capital.

It's easy to overlook an important feature of net working capital in capital budgeting. As a project winds down, inventories are sold, receivables are collected, bills are paid, and cash balances can be drawn down. These activities free up the net working capital originally invested. So, the firm's investment in project net working capital closely resembles a loan. The firm supplies working capital at the beginning and recovers it toward the end.

Financing Costs

In analyzing a proposed investment, we do not include interest paid or any other financing costs such as dividends or principal repaid, because we are interested in the cash flow generated by the assets from the project. As we mentioned in Chapter 2, interest paid, for example, is a component of cash flow to creditors, not cash flow from assets.

More generally, our goal in project evaluation is to compare the cash flow from a project to the cost of acquiring that project to estimate NPV. The particular mixture of debt and equity that a firm actually chooses to use in financing a project is a managerial variable and primarily determines how project cash flow is divided between owners and creditors. This is not to say that financing arrangements are unimportant. They are just something to be analyzed separately. We cover this in later chapters.

Inflation

Because capital investment projects generally have long lives, price inflation or deflation is likely to occur during the project's life. It is possible that the impact of inflation will cancel out—changes in the price level will impact all cash flows equally—and that the required rate of return will also shift exactly with inflation. But this is unlikely, so we need to add a brief discussion of how to handle inflation.

As we explain in more detail in Chapter 10, investors form expectations of future inflation. These are included in the discount rate as investors wish to protect themselves against inflation. Rates including inflation premiums are called *nominal rates*. In Brazil, for example, where the inflation rate is very high, discount rates are much higher than in Canada.

---

[2] More colourfully, erosion is sometimes called *piracy* or *cannibalism*.

Given that nominal rates include an adjustment for expected inflation, cash flow estimates must also be adjusted for inflation.[3] Ignoring inflation in estimating the cash inflows would lead to a bias against accepting capital budgeting projects. As we go through detailed examples of capital budgeting, we comment on making these inflation adjustments. Appendix 8A discusses inflation effects further.

Government Intervention

In Canada, various levels of government commonly offer incentives to promote certain types of capital investment. These include grants, investment tax credits, more favourable rates for **capital cost allowance**, and subsidized loans. Since these change a project's cash flows, they must be factored into capital budgeting analysis.

capital cost allowance (CCA) *Depreciation method under Canadian tax law allowing for the accelerated write-off of property under various classifications.*

Other Issues

There are other things to watch for. First, we are interested only in measuring cash flow. Moreover, we are interested in measuring it when it actually occurs, not when it arises in an accounting sense. Second, we are always interested in aftertax cash flow since tax payments are definitely a cash outflow. In fact, whenever we write incremental cash flows, we mean aftertax incremental cash flows. Remember, however, that aftertax cash flow and accounting profit or net income are different things.

CONCEPT QUESTIONS
1. What is a sunk cost? An opportunity cost?
2. Explain what erosion is and why it is relevant.
3. Explain why interest paid is not a relevant cash flow for project valuation.
4. Explain how consideration of inflation comes into capital budgeting.

8.3 | PRO FORMA FINANCIAL STATEMENTS AND PROJECT CASH FLOWS

When we begin evaluating a proposed investment, we need a set of pro forma or projected financial statements. Given these, we can develop the projected cash flows from the project. Once we have the cash flows, we can estimate the value of the project using the techniques we described in the previous chapter.

In calculating the cash flows, we make several simplifying assumptions to avoid bogging down in technical details at the outset. We use straight-line depreciation as opposed to capital cost allowance. We also assume that a full year's depreciation can be taken in the first year. In addition, we construct the example so the project's market value equals its book cost when it is scrapped. Later, we address the real-life complexities of capital cost allowance and salvage values introduced in Chapter 2.

Getting Started: Pro Forma Financial Statements

Pro forma financial statements are a convenient and easily understood means of summarizing much of the relevant information for a project. To prepare these statements, we need estimates of quantities such as unit sales, the selling price per unit, the variable cost per unit, and total fixed costs. We also need to know the total investment required, including any investment in net working capital.

pro forma financial statements *Financial statements projecting future years' operations.*

---
[3] In Chapter 10, we explain how to calculate real discount rates. The term, *real,* in finance and economics means adjusted for inflation, that is, net of the inflation premium. A less common alternative approach uses real discount rates to discount real cash flows.

To illustrate, suppose we think we can sell 50,000 cans of shark attractant per year at a price of $4.30 per can. It costs us about $2.50 per can to make the attractant, and a new product such as this one typically has only a three-year life (perhaps because the customer base dwindles rapidly). We require a 20 percent return on new products.

Fixed operating costs for the project, including such things as rent on the production facility, would run $12,000 per year.[4] Further, we need to invest $90,000 in manufacturing equipment. For simplicity, we assume this $90,000 will be 100 percent depreciated over the three-year life of the project in equal annual amounts.[5] Furthermore, the cost of removing the equipment roughly equals its actual value in three years, so it would be essentially worthless on a market value basis as well. Finally, the project requires a $20,000 investment in net working capital. This amount remains constant over the life of the project.

In Table 8.1, we organize these initial projections by first preparing the pro forma income statements.

Once again, notice that we have not deducted any interest expense. This is always so. As we described earlier, interest paid is a financing expense, not a component of operating cash flow.

We can also prepare a series of abbreviated balance sheets that show the capital requirements for the project as we've done in Table 8.2. Here we have net working capital of $20,000 in each year. Fixed assets are $90,000 at the start of the project's life (Year 0), and they decline by the $30,000 in depreciation each year, ending at zero. Notice that the total investment given here for future years is the total book or accounting value, not market value.

At this point, we need to start converting this accounting information into cash flows. We consider how to do this next.

Project Cash Flows

To develop the cash flows from a project, we need to recall (from Chapter 2) that cash flow from assets has three components: operating cash flow, capital spending, and additions to net working capital. To evaluate a project or minifirm, we need to arrive at estimates for each of these.

T A B L E 8.1

Projected income statement, shark attractant project

Sales (50,000 units at $4.30/unit)	$215,000
Variable costs ($2.50/unit)	125,000
	$ 90,000
Fixed costs	$ 12,000
Depreciation ($90,000/3)	30,000
EBIT	$ 48,000
Taxes (40%)	19,200
Net income	$ 28,800

---

[4] By fixed cost, we literally mean a cash outflow that occurs regardless of the level of sales. This should not be confused with some sort of accounting period charge.
[5] We also assume that a full year's depreciation can be taken in the first year. Together with the use of straight-line depreciation, this unrealistic assumption smoothes the exposition. We bring in real-life complications of capital cost allowance and taxes (introduced in Chapter 2) later in the chapter.

	Year			
	0	1	2	3
Net working capital	$ 20,000	$20,000	$20,000	$20,000
Net fixed assets	90,000	60,000	30,000	0
Total investment	$110,000	$80,000	$50,000	$20,000

T A B L E 8.2

Projected capital requirements, shark attractant project

Once we have estimates of the components of cash flow, we can calculate cash flow for our minifirm just as we did in Chapter 2 for an entire firm:

Project cash flow = Project operating cash flow
 − Project additions to net working capital
 − Project capital spending

We consider these components next.

Project Operating Cash Flow   To determine the operating cash flow associated with a project, recall the definition of operating cash flow:

Operating cash flow = Earnings before interest and taxes (EBIT)
 + Depreciation
 − Taxes

As before, taxes in our equation are taxes assuming that there is no interest expense. To illustrate the calculation of operating cash flow, we use the projected information from the shark attractant project. For ease of reference, Table 8.3 contains the income statement.

Given the income statement in Table 8.3, calculating the operating cash flow is very straightforward. As we see in Table 8.4, projected operating cash flow for the shark attractant project is $58,800.

Project Net Working Capital and Capital Spending   We next need to take care of the fixed asset and net working capital requirements. Based on our preceding balance sheets, the firm must spend $90,000 up front for fixed assets and invest an additional $20,000 in net working capital. The immediate outflow is thus $110,000. At the end of the project's life, the fixed assets are worthless, but the firm recovers the $20,000 tied up in working capital.[6] This leads to a $20,000 inflow in the last year.

On a purely mechanical level, notice that whenever we have an investment in net working capital that investment has to be recovered; in other words, the same number needs to appear with the opposite sign.

Project Total Cash Flow and Value

Given the information we've accumulated, we can finish the preliminary cash flow analysis as illustrated in Table 8.5.

---

[6] In reality, the firm would probably recover something less than 100 percent of this amount because of bad debts, inventory loss, and so on. If we wanted to, we could just assume that, for example, only 90 percent was recovered and proceed from there.

T A B L E 8.3

Projected income statement, shark attractant project

Sales	$215,000
Variable costs	125,000
Fixed costs	12,000
Depreciation	30,000
EBIT	$ 48,000
Taxes (40%)	19,200
Net income	$ 28,800

T A B L E 8.4

Projected operating cash flow, shark attractant project

EBIT	$ 48,000
Depreciation	30,000
Taxes	−19,200
Operating cash flow	$ 58,800

T A B L E 8.5

Projected total cash flows, shark attractant project

	Year			
	0	1	2	3
Operating cash flow	0	$58,800	$58,800	$58,800
Additions to NWC	−$ 20,000	0	0	20,000
Capital spending	−90,000	0	0	0
Total cash flow	−$110,000	$58,800	$58,800	$78,800
DCF	−$110,000	$49,000	$40,833	$45,602
NPV	$ 25,435			

Now that we have cash flow projections, we are ready to apply the various criteria we discussed in the last chapter. The NPV at the 20 percent required return is:

$$NPV = -\$110,000 + \$58,800/1.2 + \$58,800/1.2^2 + 78,800/1.2^3$$
$$= \$25,435$$

So, based on these projections, the project creates more than $25,000 in value and should be accepted. Also, the return on this investment obviously exceeds 20 percent (since the NPV is positive at 20 percent). After some trial and error, we find that the IRR works out to be about 34 percent.

In addition, if required, we could go ahead and calculate the payback and the average accounting return (AAR). Inspection of the cash flows shows that the payback on this project is just a little under two years (check that it's about 1.85 years).[7]

From the last chapter, the AAR is average net income divided by average book value. The net income each year is $28,800. The average (in thousands) of the four

---

[7] We're guilty of a minor inconsistency here. When we calculated the NPV and the IRR, we assumed all the cash flows occurred at end of year. When we calculated the payback, we assumed the cash flow occurred uniformly through the year.

book values (from Table 8.2) for total investment is ($110 + 80 + 50 + 20)/4 = $65, so the AAR is $28,800/65,000 = 44.31 percent.[8] We've already seen that the return on this investment (the IRR) is about 34 percent. The fact that the AAR is larger illustrates again why the AAR cannot be meaningfully interpreted as the return on a project.

CONCEPT QUESTIONS

1. What is the definition of project operating cash flow? How does this differ from net income?
2. In the shark attractant project, why did we add back the firm's net working capital investment in the final year?

8.4 | MORE ON PROJECT CASH FLOW

In this section, we take a closer look at some aspects of project cash flow. In particular, we discuss project net working capital in more detail. We then examine current tax laws regarding depreciation. Finally, we work through a more involved example of the capital investment decision.

A Closer Look at Net Working Capital

In calculating operating cash flow, we did not explicitly consider the fact that some of our sales might be on credit. Also, we may not have actually paid some of the costs shown. In either case, the cash flow has not yet occurred. We show here that these possibilities are not a problem as long as we don't forget to include additions to net working capital in our analysis. This discussion thus emphasizes the importance and the effect of doing so.

Suppose that during a particular year of a project we have the following simplified income statement:

Sales	$500
Costs	310
Net income	$190

Depreciation and taxes are zero. No fixed assets are purchased during the year. Also, to illustrate a point, we assume the only components of net working capital are accounts receivable and payable. The beginning and ending amounts for these accounts are:

	Beginning of Year	End of Year	Change
Accounts receivable	$880	$910	+$ 30
Accounts payable	550	605	+55
Net working capital	$330	$305	−$ 25

Based on this information, what is total cash flow for the year? We can begin by mechanically applying what we have been discussing to come up with the answer. Operating cash flow in this particular case is the same as EBIT since there are no taxes or depreciation; thus, it equals $190. Also, notice that net working capital

---

[8] Notice that the average total book value is not the initial total of $110,000 divided by 2. The reason is that the $20,000 in working capital doesn't depreciate. Notice that the average book value could be calculated as (beginning book value + ending book value)/2 = ($110,000 + 20,000)/2 = $65,000.

actually *declined* by $25, so the addition to net working capital is negative. This just means that $25 was freed up during the year. There was no capital spending, so the total cash flow for the year is:

$$\text{Total cash flow} = \text{Operating cash flow} - \text{Additions to NWC}$$
$$- \text{Capital spending}$$
$$= \$190 - (-\$25) - \$0$$
$$= \$215$$

Now, we know that this $215 total cash flow has to be "dollars in" less "dollars out" for the year. We could, therefore, ask a different question: What were cash revenues for the year? Also, what were cash costs?

To determine cash revenues, we need to look more closely at net working capital. During the year, we had sales of $500. However, accounts receivable rose by $30 over the same time period. What does this mean? The $30 increase tells us that sales exceeded collections by $30. In other words, we haven't yet received the cash from $30 of the $500 in sales. As a result, our cash inflow is $500 − 30 = $470. In general, cash income is sales minus the increase in accounts receivable.

Cash outflows can be similarly determined. We show costs of $310 on the income statement, but accounts payable increased by $55 during the year. This means we have not yet paid $55 of the $310, so cash costs for the period are just $310 − 55 = $255. In other words, in this case, cash costs equal costs less the increase in accounts payable.[9]

Putting this information together, cash inflows less cash outflows is $470 − 255 = $215, just as we had before. Notice that:

$$\text{Cash flow} = \text{Cash inflow} - \text{Cash outflow}$$
$$= (\$500 - 30) - (\$310 - 55)$$
$$= (\$500 - \$310) - (30 - 55)$$
$$= \text{Operating cash flow} - \text{Change in NWC}$$
$$= \$190 - (-25)$$
$$= \$215$$

More generally, this example illustrates that including net working capital changes in our calculations has the effect of adjusting for the discrepancy between accounting sales and costs and actual cash receipts and payments.

E X A M P L E | 8.1   **Cash Collections and Costs**

For the year just completed, Combat Wombat Telestat Ltd. (CWT) reports sales of $998 and costs of $734. You have collected the following beginning and ending balance sheet information:

	Beginning	Ending
Accounts receivable	$100	$110
Inventory	100	80
Accounts payable	100	70
Net working capital	$100	$120

[9] If there were other accounts, we might have to make some further adjustments. For example, a net increase in inventory would be a cash outflow.

Based on these figures, what are cash inflows? Cash outflows? What happened to each? What is net cash flow?

Sales were $998, but receivables rose by $10. So cash collections were $10 less than sales, or $988. Costs were $734, but inventories fell by $20. This means we didn't replace $20 worth of inventory, so cash costs are actually overstated by this amount. Also, payables fell by $30. This means that, on a net basis, we actually paid our suppliers $30 more than the value of what we received from them, resulting in a $30 understatement of cash costs. Adjusting for these events, cash costs are $734 − 20 + 30 = $744. Net cash flow is $988 − 744 = $244.

Finally, notice that net working capital increased by $20 overall. We can check our answer by noting that the original accounting sales less costs of $998 − 734 is $264. In addition, CWT spent $20 on net working capital, so the net result is a cash flow of $264 − 20 = $244, as we calculated. |

Depreciation and Capital Cost Allowance

As we note elsewhere, accounting depreciation is a noncash deduction. As a result, depreciation has cash flow consequences only because it influences the tax bill. The way that depreciation is computed for tax purposes is thus the relevant method for capital investment decisions. Chapter 2 introduced the capital cost allowance (CCA) system—Revenue Canada's version of depreciation. We use CCA in the example that follows.

An Example: The Majestic Mulch and Compost Company (MMCC)

At this point, we want to go through a somewhat more involved capital budgeting analysis. Keep in mind as you read that the basic approach here is exactly the same as that in the earlier shark attractant example. We have only added more real-world detail (and a lot more numbers).

MMCC is investigating the feasibility of a new line of power mulching tools aimed at the growing number of home composters. Based on exploratory conversations with buyers for large garden shops, we project unit sales as follows:

Year	Unit Sales
1	3,000
2	5,000
3	6,000
4	6,500
5	6,000
6	5,000
7	4,000
8	3,000

The new power mulcher would be priced to sell at $120 per unit to start. When the competition catches up after three years, however, we anticipate that the price would drop to $110.[10]

The power mulcher project requires $20,000 in net working capital at the start. Subsequently, total net working capital at the end of each year would be about 15 percent of sales for that year. The variable cost per unit is $60, and total fixed costs are $25,000 per year.

---

[10] To be consistent, these prices include an inflation estimate.

	Year	Unit Price	Unit Sales	Revenues
T A B L E 8.6	1	$120	3,000	$360,000
	2	120	5,000	600,000
Projected revenues,	3	120	6,000	720,000
power mulcher project	4	110	6,500	715,000
	5	110	6,000	660,000
	6	110	5,000	550,000
	7	110	4,000	440,000
	8	110	3,000	330,000

	Year	Beginning UCC	CCA	Ending UCC
T A B L E 8.7	1	$400,000	$ 80,000	$320,000
	2	720,000	144,000	576,000
Annual CCA, power	3	576,000	115,200	460,800
mulcher project (Class	4	460,800	92,160	368,640
8, 20% rate)	5	368,640	73,728	294,912
	6	294,912	58,982	235,930
	7	235,930	47,186	188,744
	8	188,744	37,749	150,995

It costs about $800,000 to buy the equipment necessary to begin production. This investment is primarily in industrial equipment and thus falls in Class 8 with a CCA rate of 20 percent.[11] The equipment will actually be worth about $150,000 in eight years. The relevant tax rate is 40 percent, and the required return is 15 percent. Based on this information, should MMCC proceed?

Operating Cash Flows   There is a lot of information here that we need to organize. The first thing we can do is calculate projected sales. Sales in the first year are projected at 3,000 units at $120 apiece, or $360,000 total. The remaining figures are shown in Table 8.6.

Next, we compute the CCA on the $800,000 investment in Table 8.7. Notice how, under the half-year rule (Chapter 2), UCC is only $400,000 in Year 1.

With this information, we can prepare the pro forma income statements, as shown in Table 8.8.

From here, computing the operating cash flows is straightforward. The results are illustrated in the first part of Table 8.9.

Additions to NWC   Now that we have the operating cash flows, we need to determine the additions to NWC. By assumption, net working capital requirements change as sales change. In each year, we generally either add to or recover some of our project net working capital. Recalling that NWC starts at $20,000 and then rises to 15 percent of sales, we can calculate the amount of NWC for each year as illustrated in Table 8.10.

---

[11] Chapter 2 explains CCA classes.

Projected income statements, power mulcher project

	Year							
	1	2	3	4	5	6	7	8
Unit price	$ 120	$ 120	$ 120	$ 110	$ 110	$ 110	$ 110	$ 110
Unit sales	3,000	5,000	6,000	6,500	6,000	5,000	4,000	3,000
Revenues	$360,000	$600,000	$720,000	$715,000	$660,000	$550,000	$440,000	$330,000
Variable costs	180,000	300,000	360,000	390,000	360,000	300,000	240,000	180,000
Fixed costs	25,000	25,000	25,000	25,000	25,000	25,000	25,000	25,000
CCA	80,000	144,000	115,200	92,160	73,728	58,982	47,186	37,749
EBIT	75,000	131,000	219,800	207,840	201,272	166,018	127,814	87,251
Taxes	30,000	52,400	87,920	83,136	80,509	·66,407	51,126	34,901
Net income	$ 45,000	$ 78,600	$131,880	$124,704	$120,763	$ 99,611	$ 76,688	$ 52,350

Projected cash flows, power mulcher project

	Year								
	0	1	2	3	4	5	6	7	8
				I. Operating Cash Flow					
EBIT		$ 75,000	$131,000	$219,800	$207,840	$201,272	$166,018	$127,814	$ 87,251
CCA		80,000	144,000	115,200	92,160	73,728	58,982	47,186	37,749
Taxes		30,000	52,400	87,920	83,136	80,509	66,407	51,126	34,901
Operating cash flow		$125,000	$222,600	$247,080	$216,864	$194,491	$158,593	$123,874	$ 90,099
				II. Net Working Capital					
Initial NWC									
NWC increases	$ 20,000	$ 34,000	$ 36,000	$ 18,000	–$ 750	–$ 8,250	–$ 16,500	–$ 16,500	–$ 16,500
NWC recovery									–$ 49,500
Additions to NWC	$ 20,000	$ 34,000	$ 36,000	$ 18,000	–$ 750	–$ 8,250	–$ 16,500	–$ 16,500	–$ 66,000
				III. Capital Spending					
Initial outlay	$800,000								
Aftertax salvage									–$150,000
Capital spending	$800,000								–$150,000

As illustrated, during the first year, net working capital grows from $20,000 to .15 × 360,000 = $54,000. The increase in net working capital for the year is thus $54,000 − 20,000 = $34,000. The remaining figures are calculated the same way.

Remember that an increase in net working capital is a cash outflow and a decrease in net working capital is a cash inflow. This means that a negative sign in this table represents net working capital returning to the firm. Thus, for example, $16,500 in NWC flows back to the firm in Year 6. Over the project's life, net working capital builds to a peak of $108,000 and declines from there as sales begin to drop.

We show the result for additions to net working capital in the second part of Table 8.9. Notice that at the end of the project's life there is $49,500 in net working capital still to be recovered. Therefore, in the last year, the project returns $16,500 of NWC during the year and then returns the remaining $49,500 for a total of $66,000 (the addition to NWC is −$66,000).

T A B L E 8.10

Additions to net
working capital,
power mulcher project

Year	Revenues	Net Working Capital	Increase
0		$ 20,000	
1	$360,000	54,000	$ 34,000
2	600,000	90,000	36,000
3	720,000	108,000	18,000
4	715,000	107,250	−750
5	660,000	99,000	−8,250
6	550,000	82,500	−16,500
7	440,000	66,000	−16,500
8	330,000	49,500	−16,500

Finally, we have to account for the long-term capital invested in the project. In this case, we invest $800,000 at Time 0. By assumption, this equipment would be worth $150,000 at the end of the project. It will have an undepreciated capital cost of $150,995 at that time as shown in Table 8.7. As we discussed in Chapter 2, this $995 shortfall of market value below UCC creates a tax refund only if MMCC has no continuing Class 8 assets. However, we assume the company would continue in this line of manufacturing so there is no tax refund. The investment and salvage are shown in the third part of Table 8.9.

Total Cash Flow and Value   We now have all the cash flow pieces, and we put them together in Table 8.11. In addition to the total project cash flows, we have calculated the cumulative cash flows and the discounted cash flows. At this point, it's essentially "plug and chug" to calculate the net present value, internal rate of return, and payback.

If we sum the discounted flows and the initial investment, the net present value (at 15 percent) works out to be $4,604. This is positive, so, based on these preliminary projections, the power mulcher project is acceptable. The internal or DCF rate of return is slightly greater than 15 percent since the NPV is positive. It works out to be 15.15, again indicating that the project is acceptable.[12]

Looking at the cumulative cash flows, we see that the project has almost paid back after four years since the cumulative cash flow is almost zero at that time. As indicated, the fractional year works out to be 96,306/202,741 = .47, so the payback is 4.47 years. We can't say whether or not this is good since we don't have a benchmark for MMCC. This is the usual problem with payback periods.

This completes our preliminary DCF analysis. Where do we go from here? If we have a great deal of confidence in our projections, there is no further analysis to be done. We should begin production and marketing immediately. It is unlikely that this would be the case. For one thing, NPV is not that far above zero and IRR is only marginally more than the 15 percent required rate of return. Remember that the result of our analysis is an estimate of NPV, and we usually have less than complete confidence in our projections. This means we have more work to do. In particular, we almost surely want to evaluate the quality of our estimates. We take up this subject in the next chapter. For now, we look at alternative definitions of operating cash flow, and we illustrate some different cases that arise in capital budgeting.

---

[12] Appendix 8B shows how to analyze Majestic Mulch using Lotus 1-2-3®.

Projected total cash flows, power mulcher project

T A B L E 8.11

					Year				
	0	1	2	3	4	5	6	7	8
Operating cash flow		$125,000	$222,600	$247,080	$216,864	$194,491	$158,593	$123,874	$ 90,099
Additions to NWC	–$ 20,000	–34,000	–36,000	–18,000	750	8,250	16,500	16,500	66,000
Capital spending	–800,000	0	0	0	0	0	0	0	150,000
Total project cash flow	–$ 820,000	$ 91,000	$186,600	$229,080	$217,614	$202,741	$175,093	$140,374	$306,099
Cumulative cash flow	–$ 820,000	–$729,000	–$542,400	–$313,320	–$ 95,706	$107,035	$282,128	$422,503	$728,602
Discounted cash flow @ 15%	–$ 820,000	$ 79,130	$141,096	$150,624	$124,422	$100,798	$ 75,698	$ 52,772	$100,064
NPV	$ 4.604								
IRR	15.15%								
PB	4.47								

CONCEPT QUESTIONS

1. Why is it important to consider additions to net working capital in developing cash flows? What is the effect of doing so?

2. How is depreciation calculated for fixed assets under current tax law? What effect do expected salvage value and estimated economic life have on the calculated capital cost allowance?

8.5 | ALTERNATIVE DEFINITIONS OF OPERATING CASH FLOW

The analysis we have been through in the previous section is quite general and can be adapted to almost any capital investment problem. In the next section, we illustrate some particularly useful variations. Before we do so, we need to discuss the fact that different definitions of project operating cash flow are commonly used, both in practice and in finance texts.

As we see, the different definitions of operating cash flow all measure the same thing. If they are used correctly, they all produce the same answer, and one is not necessarily any better or more useful than another. Unfortunately, the fact that alternative definitions are used sometimes leads to confusion. For this reason, we examine several of these variations next to see how they are related.

In the following discussion, keep in mind that when we speak of cash flow, we literally mean dollars in less dollars out. This is all that we are concerned with. Different definitions of operating cash flow simply amount to different ways of manipulating basic information about sales, costs, depreciation, and taxes to get at cash flow.

To begin, it will be helpful to define the following:

OCF = Project operating cash flow

S = Sales

C = Operating costs

D = Depreciation for tax purposes, i.e., CCA[13]

T_c = Corporate tax rate

---

[13] In this discussion, we use the terms *depreciation* and *CCA* interchangeably.

For a particular project and year under consideration, suppose we have the following estimates:

$$S = \$1,500$$
$$C = \$700$$
$$D = \$600$$
$$T_c = 40\%$$

With these definitions, notice that EBIT is:

$$\begin{aligned}\text{EBIT} &= S - C - D \\ &= \$1,500 - 700 - 600 \\ &= \$200\end{aligned}$$

Once again, we assume no interest is paid, so the tax bill is:

$$\begin{aligned}\text{Taxes} = \text{EBIT} \times T_c &= (S - C - D) \times T_c \\ &= \$200 \times .40 = \$80\end{aligned}$$

When we put all of this together, project operating cash flow (OCF) is:

$$\begin{aligned}\text{OCF} &= \text{EBIT} + D - \text{Taxes} \\ &= (S - C - D) + D - (S - C - D) \times T_c \\ &= \$200 + 600 - 80 = \$720\end{aligned} \qquad [8.1]$$

If we take a closer look at this definition of OCF, we see that there are other definitions that could be used. We consider these next.

The Bottom-Up Approach

Since we are ignoring any financing expenses such as interest in our calculations of project OCF, we can write project net income as:

$$\begin{aligned}\text{Project net income} &= \text{EBIT} - \text{Taxes} \\ &= (S - C - D) - (S - C - D) \times T_c \\ &= (S - C - D) \times (1 - T_c) \\ &= (\$1,500 - 700 - 600) \times (1 - .40) \\ &= \$200 \times .60 \\ &= \$120\end{aligned}$$

With this in mind, we can develop a slightly different and very common approach to the cash flow question by restating Equation (8.1) as follows:

$$\begin{aligned}\text{OCF} &= (S - C - D) + D - (S - C - D) \times T_c \\ &= (S - C - D) \times (1 - T_c) + D \\ &= \text{Project net income} + \text{Depreciation} \\ &= \$120 + 600 \\ &= \$720\end{aligned} \qquad [8.2]$$

This is the bottom-up approach. Here we start with the accountant's bottom line (net income) and add back any non-cash deductions such as depreciation. It is important to remember that this definition of operating cash flow as net income plus depreciation is only equivalent to our definition, and thus correct, when there is no interest expense subtracted in the calculation of net income.

For the shark attractant project, net income was $28,800 and depreciation was $30,000, so the bottom-up calculation is:

OCF = $28,800 + 30,000 = $58,800

This again is the correct answer.

The Top-Down Approach

A closely related, and perhaps more obvious, manipulation of our definition is to cancel the depreciation expense where possible:

$$
\begin{aligned}
\text{OCF} &= (S - C - D) + D - (S - C - D) \times T_c \\
&= (S - C) - (S - C - D) \times T_c \\
&= \text{Sales} - \text{Costs} - \text{Taxes} \\
&= \$1{,}500 - 700 - 80 = \$720
\end{aligned}
$$

[8.3]

This is the top-down approach. Here we start at the top of the income statement with sales and work our way down to net cash flow by subtracting costs, taxes, and other expenses. Along the way, we simply leave out any strictly non-cash items such as depreciation.

For the shark attractant project, the top-down cash flow can be readily calculated. With sales of $240,000, total costs (fixed plus variable) of $162,000, and a tax bill of $19,220, the OCF is:

OCF = $240,000 − 162,000 − 19,220 = $58,800

This is just as we had before.

The Tax Shield Approach

The final variation on our basic definition of OCF is the tax shield approach. This approach will be very useful for some problems we consider in the next section. The tax shield definition of OCF is:

$$
\begin{aligned}
\text{OCF} &= (S - C - D) + D - (S - C - D) \times T_c \\
&= (S - C) \times (1 - T_c) + D \times T_c
\end{aligned}
$$

[8.4]

With our numbers, this works out to be:

$$
\begin{aligned}
&= (S - C) \times (1 - T_c) + D \times T_c \\
&= \$800 \times .60 + \$600 \times .40 \\
&= \$480 + 240 \\
&= \$720
\end{aligned}
$$

This is just as we had before.

This approach views OCF as having two components: The first part, $(S - C) \times (1 - T_c)$, is what the project's cash flow would be if there were no depreciation expense. In this case, this would-have-been cash flow is $480.

The second part of OCF in this expression, $D \times T_c$, is called the **depreciation (CCA) tax shield**. We know that depreciation is a non-cash expense. The only cash flow effect from deducting depreciation is to reduce our taxes, a benefit to us. At the current 40 percent corporate tax rate, every dollar in CCA expense saves us 40 cents in taxes. So, in our example, the $600 in depreciation tax shield saves us $600 × .40 = $240 in taxes.

For the shark attractant project we considered earlier in the chapter, the CCA tax shield would be $30,000 × .40 = $12,000. The aftertax value for sales less costs

depreciation (CCA) tax shield

Tax saving that results from the CCA deduction, calculated as depreciation multiplied by the corporate tax rate.

T A B L E 8.12	Approach	Formula
Alternative definitions of operating cash flow	Basic	OCF = EBIT + Depreciation − Taxes
	Bottom-up	OCF = Net income + Depreciation
	Top-down	OCF = Sales − Costs − Taxes
	Tax shield	OCF = (Sales − Costs) $(1 - T_c)$ + Depreciation × T_c

would be ($240,000 − 162,000) × (1 − .40) = $46,800. Adding these together yields the right answer:

$$OCF = \$46,800 + 12,000 = \$58,800$$

This verifies this approach.

Table 8.12 summarizes the four approaches to computing OCF. Now that we've seen that all these definitions are the same, you're probably wondering why everybody doesn't just agree on one of them. One reason, as we see in the next section, is that different definitions are useful in different circumstances. The best one to use is whichever happens to be the most convenient for the problem at hand.

8.6 | APPLYING THE TAX SHIELD APPROACH TO THE MAJESTIC MULCH AND COMPOST COMPANY PROJECT

If you look back over our analysis of MMCC, you'll see that most of the number crunching involved finding CCA, EBIT, and net income figures. The tax shield approach has the potential to save us considerable time.[14] To realize on that potential, we do the calculations in a different order from Table 8.11. Instead of adding the cash flow components down the columns for each year and finding the present value of the total cash flows, we find the present values of each source of cash flows and add the present values.

The first source of cash flow is $(S - C)(1 - T_c)$ as shown for each year on the first line of Table 8.13. The figure for the first year, $93,000, is the first part of the OCF equation.

$$
\begin{aligned}
OCF &= (S - C)(1 - T_c) + DT_c \\
&= (360,000 - 180,000 - 25,000)(1 - .40) + 80,000(.40) \\
&= 93,000 + 32,000 = \$125,000
\end{aligned}
$$

Calculating the present value of the $93,000 for the first year and adding the present values of the other $(S - C)(1 - T_c)$ figures in Table 8.13 gives a total present value for this source of $645,099 as seen in the lower part of Table 8.13.

The second term is the tax shield on CCA for the first year. Table 8.14 reproduces the first year's tax shield of $32,000 along with the corresponding tax shields for each year. The total present value of the CCA tax shield is shown as $159,649.

The additions to net working capital and capital expenditure are essentially the same as in Table 8.11. Their present values are shown in the lower part of Table 8.13. The NPV is the sum of the present value of the four sources of cash flow. The answer, $4,604 is identical to what we found earlier in Table 8.11.

---

[14] This is particularly true if we set it up using a spreadsheet. See Appendix 8B.

TABLE 8.13

Tax shield solution, power mulcher project

	0	1	2	3	4	5	6	7	8
					Year				
$(S - C)(1 - T_c)$		$93,000	$165,000	$201,000	$180,000	$165,000	$135,000	$105,000	$ 75,000
Additions to NWC	−$ 20,000	−34,000	− 36,000	− 18,000	750	8,250	16,500	16,500	66,000
Capital spending	−800,000								150,000

Totals

PV of $(S - C)(1 - T_c)$	$ 645,099
PV of additions to NWC	−49,179
PV of capital spending	−750,965
PV of CCA tax shield	159,649
NPV	$ 4,604

TABLE 8.14

PV of tax shield on CCA

	Tax Shield		
Year	CCA	.40 × CCA	PV at 15 %
1	$ 80,000	$32,000	$ 27,826
2	144,000	57,600	43,554
3	115,200	46,080	30,298
4	92,160	36,864	21,077
5	73,728	29,491	14,662
6	58,982	23,593	10,200
7	47,186	18,874	7,096
8	37,749	15,100	4,936
	PV of tax shield on CCA		$159,649

Present Value of the Tax Shield on CCA

Further time savings are possible by using a formula that replaces the detailed calculation of yearly CCA. The formula is based on the idea that tax shields from CCA continue in perpetuity as long as there are assets remaining in the CCA class.[15] To calculate the present value of the tax shield on CCA, we find the present value of an infinite stream of tax shields abstracting from two practical implications—the half-year percent rule for CCA and disposal of the asset. We then adjust the formula.

Our derivation uses the following terms:

C = Total capital cost of the asset which is added to the pool

d = CCA rate for the asset class

T_c = Company's marginal tax rate

k = Discount rate

S = Salvage or disposal value of the asset

n = Asset life in years

[15] Strictly speaking, the UCC for a class remains positive as long as there are physical assets in the class and the proceeds from disposal of assets is less than total UCC for the class.

We can use the dividend valuation formula from Chapter 6 to derive the present value of the CCA tax shield. Recall that when dividends grow at a constant rate, g, the stock price is

$$P_0 = \frac{D_1}{k - g}$$

To apply this to the tax shield problem, we recognize that the formula can be generalized for any growing perpetuity where for example, Payment 3 = (Payment 2) × (1 + g)

$$PV = \frac{1\text{st payment}}{(\text{Discount rate}) - (\text{Growth rate})}$$

Since we are temporarily ignoring the half-year rule, the growth rate in CCA payments is equal to $(-d)$. For example, in Table 8.14:

CCA 3 = CCA2 (1 + (−d))
CCA 3 = 144,000 (1 + (−.20))
CCA 3 = 144,000 (.8) = 115,200

Given the growth rate as $(-d)$, we need the 1st payment to complete the formula. This is the first year's tax shield CdT_c. We can now complete the formula:

$$PV(\text{CCA tax shield}) = \frac{1\text{st payment}}{(\text{Discount rate}) - (\text{Growth rate})}$$

$$= \frac{CdT_c}{k - (-d)}$$

$$= \frac{CdT_c}{k + d}$$

The next step is to extend the formula to adjust for Revenue Canada's half-year rule. This rule states that a firm must add one-half of the incremental capital cost of a new project in Year 1 and the other half in Year 2. The result is that we now calculate the present value of the tax shield in two parts: The present value of the stream starting the first year is simply one-half of the original value:

$$PV \text{ of 1st half} = 1/2 \frac{CdT_c}{k + d}$$

The PV of the second half (deferred one year) is the same quantity (bracketed term) discounted back to time zero. The total present value of the tax shield on CCA under the half-year rule is the sum of the two present values.

$$PV \text{ tax shield on CCA} = \frac{1/2 \; CdT_c}{k + d} + \left[\frac{1/2 CdT_c}{k + d}\right]/(1 + k)$$

With a little algebra we can simplify the formula:

$$PV = \frac{1/2 \; CdT_c}{k + d}[1 + 1/(1 + k)] = \frac{1/2 \; CdT_c}{k + d}\left[\frac{1 + k + 1}{1 + k}\right]$$

$$PV = \frac{CdT_c}{k + d}\left[\frac{1 + .5k}{1 + k}\right]$$

The final adjustment for salvage-value begins with the present value in the salvage year, n of future tax shields beginning in Year $n + 1$:

$$\frac{SdT_c}{d + k}$$

We discount this figure back to today and subtract it to get the complete formula.[16]

$$\text{PV tax shield on CCA} = \frac{[CdT_c]}{d + k} \times \frac{[1 + .5k]}{1 + k} - \frac{SdT_c}{d + k} \times \frac{1}{(1 + k)^n}$$

Using the first part of the formula, the present value of the tax shield on MMCC's project is $170,932 assuming the tax shield goes on in perpetuity

$$= \frac{800,000(.20)(.40)}{.20 + .15} \times \frac{1 + .5 \times (.15)}{1 + .15}$$
$$= 182,857 \times 1.08/1.15 = \$170,932.$$

The adjustment for the salvage value is

$$\frac{- 150,000(.20)(.40)}{.20 + .15} \times \frac{1}{(1 + .15)^8}$$
$$= -34,286 \times 1/(1.15)^8 = -\$11,208$$

The present value of the tax shield on CCA is the sum of the two present values.

$$\text{Present value of tax shield from CCA} = \$170,932 - \$11,208$$
$$= \$159,724$$

Salvage Value versus UCC

There is a slight difference between this calculation for the present value of the tax shield on CCA and what we got in Table 8.14 by adding the tax shields over the project life. The difference arises whenever the salvage value of the asset differs from its UCC. The formula solution is more accurate as it takes into account the future CCA on this difference. In this case, the asset was sold for $150,000 and had UCC of $150,995. The $995 left in the pool after eight years creates an infinite stream of CCA. At Time 8, this stream has a present value of [$995(.20)(.40)]/[.20 + .15] = $227.43. At Time 0, the present value of this stream at 15 percent is about $75. To get the precise estimate of the present value of the CCA tax shield, we need to add this to the approximation in Table 8.14: $159,649 + $75 = $159,724.

E X A M P L E | 8.2   **The Ogopogo Paddler**

Harvey Bligh, of Kelowna, British Columbia, is contemplating purchasing a paddle-wheel boat that he will use to give tours of Okanagan Lake in search of the elusive Ogopogo. Bligh has estimated cash flows from the tours and discounted them back over the eight-year expected life of the boat at his 20 percent required rate of return. The summary of his calculations follows:

---

[16] By not adjusting the salvage value for the half-year rule, we assume there will be no new investment in year n.

Investment	−$250,000.00
Working capital	−50,000.00
PV of salvage	11,628.40
PV of NWC recovery	11,628.40
PV of aftertax operating income	251,548.33
PV of CCATS	?
NPV	?

He is struggling with the CCA tax shield calculation and is about to dump the project as it appears to be unprofitable. Is the project as unprofitable as Bligh believes?

The salvage value of the boat is $50,000, the combined federal and provincial corporate tax rate in British Columbia is 43 percent, and the CCA rate is 15 percent on boats.

$$\text{PV tax shield on CCA} = \frac{[CdT_c]}{d+k} \times \frac{[1+.5k]}{1+k} - \frac{SdT_c}{d+k} \times \frac{1}{(1+k)^n}$$

$$\text{1st term} = [(\$250,000 \times .15 \times .43)/(.15+.20)]$$
$$\times [(1+.50 \times .20)/(1+.20)]$$
$$= \$42,232.14$$

$$\text{2nd term} = [(\$50,000 \times .15 \times .43)/(.15+.20)] \times 1/(1+.20)^8$$
$$= \$2,142.95$$

$$\text{PV of CCATS} = \$42,232.14 - 2,142.95 = \$40,089.19$$

The NPV of the investment is $14,894.32. Bligh should pursue this venture.

CONCEPT QUESTIONS

1. What is meant by the term *depreciation (CCA) tax shield?*
2. What are the top-down and bottom-up definitions of operating cash flow?

8.7 | SOME SPECIAL CASES OF DISCOUNTED CASH FLOW ANALYSIS

To finish our chapter, we look at four common cases involving discounted cash flow analysis. The first case involves investments that are primarily aimed at improving efficiency and thereby cutting costs. The second case demonstrates analysis of a replacement decision. The third case arises in choosing between equipment with different economic lives. The fourth and final case we consider comes up when a firm is involved in submitting competitive bids.

There are many other special cases that we should consider, but these four are particularly important because problems similar to these are so common. Also, they illustrate some very diverse applications of cash flow analysis and DCF valuation.

Evaluating Cost-Cutting Proposals

One decision we frequently face is whether to upgrade existing facilities to make them more cost-effective. The issue is whether the cost savings are large enough to justify the necessary capital expenditure.

For example, suppose we are considering automating some part of an existing production process presently performed manually in one of our plants. The necessary equipment costs $80,000 to buy and install. It will save $35,000 per year (pretax) by reducing labour and material costs. The equipment has a five-year life and is in Class 8 with a CCA rate of 20 percent. Due to rapid obsolescence, it will actually be worth nothing in five years. Should we do it? The tax rate is 40 percent, and the discount rate is 10 percent.

As always, the initial step in making this decision is to identify the relevant incremental cash flows. We keep track of these in the following table. First, determining the relevant capital spending is easy enough. The initial cost is $80,000 and the salvage value after five years is zero. Second, there are no working capital consequences here, so we don't need to worry about additions to net working capital.

Operating cash flows are the third component. Buying the new equipment affects our operating cash flows in two ways. First, we save $35,000 pretax every year. In other words, the firm's operating income increases by $35,000, so this is the relevant incremental project operating income. After taxes, this represents an annual cash flow of $21,000 as shown in the following table:

		Year				
	0	1	2	3	4	5
Investment	−$ 80,000					
NWC	0					
Subtotal	−80,000					
Op. income		$35,000	$35,000	$35,000	$35,000	$35,000
Taxes		14,000	14,000	14,000	14,000	14,000
Subtotal		21,000	21,000	21,000	21,000	21,000
Salvage						0
Total	−$ 80,000	$21,000	$21,000	$21,000	$21,000	$21,000

Present value of the tax shield on the CCA:

$$PV = \frac{80,000(.20)(.40)}{.20 + .10} \times \frac{1 + .5(.10)}{1 + .10}$$

$$= \$20,364$$

Present value of the aftertax operating savings:

$$PV = \$21,000 \times (1 - (1/1.10^5))/.10$$

$$= \$21,000 \times 3.7908$$

$$= \$79,607$$

NPV	
Investment	−$80,000
Operating cash flows	79,607
PV of salvage	0
CCATS	20,364
NPV	$19,971

Second, we have a tax shield on the incremental CCA created by the new equipment. This equipment has zero salvage so the formula is simplified as shown. CCA goes on forever and the present value of the tax shield is the sum of an infinite series. The present value is $20,364.

We can now finish our analysis by finding the present value of the $21,000 aftertax operating savings and adding the present values. At 10 percent, it's straightforward to verify that the NPV here is $19,971, so we should go ahead and automate.

E X A M P L E | 8.3   To Buy or Not to Buy

We are considering the purchase of a $200,000 computer-based inventory manage-ment system. It is in Class 10 with a CCA rate of 30 percent. The computer has a four-year life. It will be worth $30,000 at that time. The system would save us $60,000 pretax in inventory-related costs. The relevant tax rate is 43.5 percent. Because the new setup is more efficient than our existing one, we would be able to carry less total inventory and thus free $45,000 in net working capital. What is the NPV at 16 percent? What is the DCF return (the IRR) on this investment?

We begin by calculating the operating cash flow. The aftertax cost savings are $60,000 × (1 − .435) = $33,900. The present value of the tax shield on the CCA is found using the formula we first used in the Majestic Mulch and Compost Company problem.

$$PV = \frac{200,000(.30)(.435)}{.30 + .16} \times \frac{1 + .5(.16)}{1 + .16}$$

$$- \frac{30,000(.30)(.435)}{.30 + .16} \times \frac{1}{(1 + .16)^4}$$

$$= \$48,126$$

The capital spending involves $200,000 up front to buy the system. The salvage is $30,000. Finally, and this is the somewhat tricky part, the initial investment in net working capital is a $45,000 inflow because the system frees working capital. Fur-thermore, we have to put this back in at the end of the project's life. What this really means is simple: While the system is in operation, we have $45,000 to use elsewhere.

To finish our analysis, we can compute the total cash flows:

	Year				
	0	1	2	3	4
Investment	−$200,000				
NWC	45,000				
Subtotal	−155,000				
Operating income		$60,000	$60,000	$60,000	$ 60,000
Taxes		26,100	26,100	26,100	26,100
Aftertax operating income		33,900	33,900	33,900	33,900
NWC returned					−45,000

NPV	
Investment	−$200,000
NWC recovered now	45,000
Operating income	94,858
PV of salvage	16,569
PV of NWC returned	−24,853
CCATS	48,126
NPV	−$ 20,300

At 16 percent, the NPV is −$20,300, so the investment is not attractive. After some trial and error, we find that the NPV is zero when the discount rate is 8.28 percent, so the IRR on this investment is about 8.3 percent.[17]

---

[17] This IRR is tricky to compute without a spreadsheet because the asset is sold for $30,000, which is less than its undepreciated capital cost (after four years) of $48,000. Capital cost allowance on the difference remains in the pool and goes on to infinity. For this reason, we need to solve for the CCATS by trial and error.

Replacing an Asset

Instead of cutting costs by automating a manual production process, companies often need to decide whether it is worthwhile to enhance productivity by replacing existing equipment with newer models or more advanced technology. Suppose the promising numbers we calculated for the automation proposal encourage you to look into buying three more sets of equipment to replace older technology on your company's other production lines. Three new sets of equipment cost $200,000 to buy and install. (Your projected cost is less than the earlier $80,000 per machine because you receive a quantity discount from the manufacturer.)

This time, the analysis is more complex because you are going to replace existing equipment. You bought it four years ago for $150,000 and expect it to last for six more years. Due to rapid technological advances, the existing equipment is only worth $50,000 if you sell it today. The more efficient newer technology would save you $75,000 per year in production costs over its projected six-year life.[18] These savings could be realized through reduced wastage and downtime on the shop floor.

If you retain the current equipment for the rest of its working life, you can expect to realize $10,000 in scrap value after six years. The new equipment, on the other hand, is saleable in the second-hand market and is expected to have a salvage value of $30,000 after six years.

With regard to working capital, the new equipment requires a greater stock of specialized spare parts but offers an offsetting reduction in wastage of work in process. On balance, no change in net working capital is predicted.

You determine that both the existing and new equipment are Class 8 assets with a CCA rate of 20 percent. Your firm requires a return of 15 percent on replacement investments and faces a tax rate of 44 percent. Should you recommend purchase of the new technology?

There is a lot of information here and we organize it in Table 8.15. The first cash flow is the capital outlay—and the difference between the cost of the new and the sale realization on the old equipment. To address CCA, we draw on the discussion in Chapter 2. There will still be undepreciated capital cost in the Class 8 pool because the amount we are adding to the pool (purchase price of new equipment) is greater than the amount we are subtracting (salvage on old equipment). Because we are not creating a negative balance of undepreciated capital cost (recapturing CCA) or selling all the pool's assets, there are no tax adjustments to the net outlay. The incremental salvage in six years is treated in the same way.[19]

The fact that we are making a net addition to the asset pool in Class 8 simplifies calculation of the tax shield on CCA. In this common case, Revenue Canada's half-year rule applies to the net addition to the asset class. So, we simply substitute the incremental outlay for C in the present value of tax shield formula. Finally, we substitute the incremental salvage for S and crank the formula.[20]

---

[18] For simplicity, we assume that both the old and new equipment have six-year remaining lives. Later, we discuss how to analyze cases in which lives differ.

[19] Here we are making an implicit assumption that at the end of six years the deduction of salvage will not exhaust the Class 8 pool. If this were not the case, the excess, recaptured depreciation would be taxable at the firm's tax rate of 44 percent.

[20] The present value of tax shield formula does not adjust the salvage for the half-year rule. This means we are assuming that, while the asset class will continue beyond Year 6, no new assets will be added in that year. We make this and the other tax assumptions to illustrate common situations without bogging down in the fine points of taxes.

T A B L E 8.15 | *Replacement of existing asset (thousands of dollars)*

				Year			
	0	1	2	3	4	5	6
Investment	−$ 200						
Salvage on old	50						
NWC additions	0						
Subtotal	−150						
Op. savings		$75	$75	$75	$75	$75	$ 75
Taxes		33	33	33	33	33	33
Subtotal		42	42	42	42	42	42
Salvage forgone							−10
Salvage							30

NPV	
Investment	−$200,000
Salvage recovered now	50,000
Operating cash flows	158,948
PV of salvage forgone	−4,323
PV of salvage recovered	12,970
CCATS	33,081
NPV	$ 50,676

$$PV = \frac{150,000(.20)(.44)}{.20 + .15} \times \frac{1 + .5(.15)}{1 + .15}$$
$$- \frac{20,000(.20)(.44)}{.20 + .15} \times \frac{1}{(1 + .15)^6}$$
$$= \$33,081$$

Additions to net working capital are not relevant here. Aftertax operating savings are calculated in the same way as in our prior examples. Table 8.15 shows that the replacement proposal has a substantial positive NPV and seems attractive.

E X A M P L E | 8.4   Replacement

Theatreplex Oleum is considering replacing a projector system in one of its cinemas. The new projector has super-holographic sound and is able to project laser-sharp images. These features would increase the attendance at the theatre; and the new projector could cut repair costs dramatically. The new projector costs $250,000 and has a useful life of 15 years, at which time it could be sold for $20,000. The projector currently being used was purchased for $150,000 five years ago and can be sold now for $50,000. In 15 years the old projector would be scrapped for $5,000. The new projector would increase operating income by $50,000 annually; it belongs to Class 9 for CCA calculations. Theatreplex requires a 15 percent return on replacement assets and the corporate tax rate is 43.5 percent. Should Theatreplex replace the projector?

We begin calculating the profitability of such an investment by finding the present value of the increased operating income:

$$\text{Aftertax flow} = \$50,000 \times (1 - .435)$$
$$= \$28,250$$
$$\text{PV} = \$28,250 \times (1 - 1/(1.15)^{15})/.15$$
$$= \$28,250 \times 5.84737$$
$$= \$165,188$$

The next step is to calculate the present value of the net salvage value of the new projector:

$$\text{PV} = (\$20,000 - 5,000) \times 1/(1.15)^{15}$$
$$= \$1,843$$

The last step is to calculate the present value tax shield on the CCA:

$$\text{PV} = \frac{200,000(.25)(.435)}{.25 + .15} \times \frac{1 + .5(.15)}{1 + .15}$$
$$- \frac{15,000(.25)(.435)}{.25 + .15} \times \frac{1}{(1 + .15)^{15}}$$
$$= 54,375 \times 1.075/1.15 - 4,078 \times 1/(1.15)^{15}$$
$$= \$50,829 - \$501$$
$$= \$50,328$$

The NPV is found by adding these present values to the original investment:

Net investment	−$200,000
Increased operating income	165,188
Net salvage	1,843
CCATS	50,328
NPV	$ 17,359

The investment surpasses the required return on investments for Theatreplex Oleum and should be pursued.

Evaluating Equipment with Different Lives

Our previous examples assumed, a bit unrealistically, that competing systems had the same life. The next problem we consider involves choosing among different possible systems, equipment, or procedures with different lives. For example, an automobile fleet manager needs to know whether it is better to replace cars every year or to keep cars until they are five years old. As always, our goal is to maximize net present value. To do this, we place the projects on a common horizon for comparison.

The approach we consider here is only necessary when two special circumstances exist: First, the possibilities under evaluation have different economic lives. Second, and just as important, we need whatever we buy more or less indefinitely. As a result, when it wears out, we buy another one.

We can illustrate this problem with a simple example that holds the benefits constant across different alternatives. This way we can focus on finding the least-cost alternative.[21] Imagine that we are in the business of manufacturing stamped metal

---

[21] Alternatively, in another case, the costs could be constant and the benefits differ. Then we would maximize the equivalent annual benefit.

subassemblies. Whenever a stamping mechanism wears out, we have to replace it with a new one to stay in business. We are considering which of two stamping mechanisms to buy.

Machine A costs $100 to buy and $10 per year to operate. It wears out and must be replaced every two years. Machine B costs $140 to buy and $8 per year to operate. It lasts for three years and must then be replaced. Ignoring taxes, which one should we go with if we use a 10 percent discount rate?

In comparing the two machines, we notice that the first is cheaper to buy, but it costs more to operate and it wears out more quickly. How can we evaluate these trade-offs? We can start by computing the present value of the costs for each:

Machine A: PV = −$100 + −$10/1.1 + −10/1.1^2 = −$117.36

Machine B: PV = −$140 + −$8/1.1 + −$8/1.12 + −$8/1.1^3 = −$159.89

Notice that all the numbers here are costs, so they all have negative signs. If we stopped here, it might appear that A is the more attractive since the PV of the costs is less. However, all we have really discovered so far is that A effectively provides two years' worth of stamping service for $117.36, while B effectively provides three years' worth for $159.89. These are not directly comparable because of the difference in service periods.

We need to somehow work out a cost per year for these two alternatives. To do this, we ask the question: What amount, paid each year over the life of the machine, has the same PV of costs? This amount is called the **equivalent annual cost (EAC)**.

Calculating the EAC involves finding an unknown payment amount. For example, for Machine A, we need to find a two-year ordinary annuity with a PV of −$117.36 at 10 percent. Going back to Chapter 4, the two-year annuity factor is:

Annuity factor = [1 − 1/1.10^2]/.10 = 1.7355

For Machine A, then, we have:

$$\text{PV of costs} = -\$117.36 = \text{EAC} \times 1.7355$$
$$\text{EAC} = -\$117.36/1.7355$$
$$= -\$67.62$$

For Machine B, the life is three years, so we first need the three-year annuity factor:

Annuity factor = [1 − 1/1.10^3]/.10 = 2.4869

We calculate the EAC for B just as we did for A:

$$\text{PV of costs} = \$159.89 = \text{EAC} \times 2.4869$$
$$\text{EAC} = -\$159.89/2.4869$$
$$= -\$64.29$$

Based on this analysis, we should purchase B because it effectively costs $64.29 per year versus $67.62 for A. In other words, all things considered, B is cheaper. Its longer life and lower operating cost is more than enough to offset the higher initial purchase price.

equivalent annual cost (EAC)

The present value of a project's costs calculated on an annual basis.

E X A M P L E | **8.5**   **Equivalent Annual Costs**

This extended example illustrates what happens to the EAC when we consider taxes. You are evaluating two different pollution control options. A filtration system costs

$1.1 million to install and $60,000 pretax annually to operate. It would have to be replaced every five years. A precipitation system costs $1.9 million to install, but only $10,000 per year to operate. The precipitation equipment has an effective operating life of eight years. The company rents its factory and both systems are considered leasehold improvements so straight-line capital cost allowance is used throughout, and neither system has any salvage value. Which method should we select if we use a 12 percent discount rate? The tax rate is 40 percent.

We need to consider the EACs for the two approaches because they have different service lives, and they will be replaced as they wear out. The relevant information is summarized in Table 8.16.

Notice that the operating cash flow is actually positive in both cases because of the large CCA tax shields.[22] This can occur whenever the operating cost is small relative to the purchase price.

To decide which system to purchase, we compute the EACs for both using the appropriate annuity factors:

Filtration system: $-\$912,550 = EAC \times 3.6048$

EAC = $-\$253,149$ per year

Precipitation system: $-\$1,457,884 = EAC \times 4.9676$

EAC = $-\$293,479$ per year

The filtration system is the cheaper of the two, so we select it. The longer life and smaller operating cost of the precipitation system are not sufficient to offset its higher initial cost.

Setting the Bid Price

Early on, we used discounted cash flow to evaluate a proposed new product. A somewhat different (and very common) scenario arises when we must submit a competitive bid to win a job. Under such circumstances, the winner is whoever submits the lowest bid.

There is an old saw concerning this process: the low bidder is whoever makes the biggest mistake. This is called the winner's curse. In other words, if you win, there is a good chance that you underbid. In this section, we look at how to set the bid price to avoid the winner's curse. The procedure we describe is useful anytime we have to set a price on a product or service.

	Filtration System	Precipitation System
Aftertax operating cost	-$ 36,000	-$ 6,000
Annual CCATS	88,000	95,000
Operating cash flow	$ 52,000	$ 89,000
Economic life	5 years	8 years
Annuity factor (12%)	3.6048	4.9676
Present value of operating cash flow	$ 187,450	$ 442,116
Capital spending	−1,100,000	−1,900,000
Total PV of costs	-$ 912,550	-$ 1,457,884

T A B L E 8.16

Equivalent annual cost

[22] We are not using the present value of CCA tax shield formula because CCA on leasehold improvements is straight-line.

To illustrate how to set a bid price, imagine that we are in the business of buying stripped-down truck platforms and then modifying them to customer specifications for resale. A local distributor has requested bids for five specially modified trucks each year for the next four years, for a total of 20 trucks.

We need to decide what price per truck to bid. The goal of our analysis is to determine the lowest price we can profitably charge. This maximizes our chances of being awarded the contract while guarding against the winner's curse.

Suppose we can buy the truck platforms for $10,000 each. The facilities we need can be leased for $24,000 per year. The labour and material cost to do the modification works out to be about $4,000 per truck. Total cost per year would thus be

$$\$24,000 + 5 \times (\$10,000 + 4,000) = \$94,000.$$

We need to invest $60,000 in new equipment. This equipment falls in Class 8 with a CCA rate of 20 percent. It would be worth about $5,000 at the end of the four years. We also need to invest $40,000 in raw materials inventory and other working capital items. The relevant tax rate is 43.5 percent. What price per truck should we bid if we require a 20 percent return on our investment?

We start by looking at the capital spending and net working capital investment. We have to spend $60,000 today for new equipment. The aftertax salvage value is simply $5,000 assuming as usual that at the end of four years, other assets remain in Class 8. Furthermore, we have to invest $40,000 today in working capital. We get this back in four years.

We can't determine the aftertax operating income just yet because we don't know the sales price. The present value of the tax shield on CCA works out to be $11,438. The calculations are in Table 8.17 along with the other data. With this in mind, here is the key observation: The lowest possible price we can profitably charge results in a zero NPV at 20 percent. The reason is, at that price we earn exactly the required 20 percent on our investment.

Given this observation, we first need to determine what the aftertax operating income must be for the NPV to be equal to zero. To do this, we calculate the present values of the salvage and return of net working capital in Table 8.17 and set up the NPV equation.

TABLE 8.17

Setting the bid price

	Cash Flow	Year	PV at 20 %
Capital spending	−$ 60,000	0	−$60,000
Salvage	5,000	4	2,411
Additions to NWC	−40,000	0	− 40,000
	40,000	4	19,290
Aftertax operating income	$(S − 94,000)(1 − .435)$	1-4	?
Tax shield on CCA			$ 11,438
NPV			$ 0

$$PV = \frac{60,000(.20)(.435)}{.20 + .20} \times \frac{1 + .5(.20)}{1 + .20}$$
$$- \frac{5,000(.20)(.435)}{.20 + .20} \times \frac{1}{(1 + .20)^4}$$
$$= \$11,438$$

$$\text{NPV} = 0 = -\$60,000 + 2,411 - 40,000 + 19,290 + \text{PV}$$
$$\text{(annual aftertax incremental operating income)} + 11,438$$
$$\text{PV (annual aftertax incremental operating income)} = \$66,861$$

Since this represents the present value of an annuity, we can find the annual "payments,"

$$\text{PV (annuity)} = \$66,861 = P\,[1 - 1/1.20^4]/.20$$
$$P = \$25,828$$

The annual incremental aftertax operating income is $25,828. Using a little algebra we can solve for the necessary sales proceeds, S.

$$\$25,828 = (S - 94,000)(1 - .435)$$
$$\$45,713 = S - 94,000$$
$$S = \$139,713.$$

Since the contract is for five trucks, this represents $27,943 per truck. If we round this up a bit, it looks like we need to bid about $28,000 per truck. At this price, were we to get the contract, our return would be a bit more than 20 percent.

CONCEPT QUESTIONS

1. Under which circumstances do we have to worry about unequal economic lives? How do you interpret the EAC?
2. In setting a bid price, we used a zero NPV as our benchmark. Explain why this is appropriate.

8.8 | SUMMARY AND CONCLUSIONS

This chapter describes how to put together a discounted cash flow analysis. In it, we covered:

1. The identification of relevant project cash flows. We discussed project cash flows and described how to handle some issues that often come up, including sunk costs, opportunity costs, financing costs, net working capital, and erosion.
2. Preparing and using pro forma or projected financial statements. We showed how such financial statement information is useful in coming up with projected cash flows, and we also looked at some alternative definitions of operating cash flow.
3. The role of net working capital and depreciation in project cash flows. We saw that including the additions to net working capital was important because it adjusted for the discrepancy between accounting revenues and costs and cash revenues and costs. We also went over the calculation of capital cost allowance under current tax law.
4. Some special cases in using discounted cash flow analysis. Here we looked at four special issues: cost-cutting investments, replacement decisions, the unequal lives problem, and how to set a bid price.

The discounted cash flow analysis we've covered here is a standard tool in the business world. It is a very powerful tool, so care should be taken in its use. The most important thing is to get the cash flows identified in a way that makes economic sense. This chapter gives you a good start on learning to do this.

Key Terms

incremental cash flows (page 261)

stand-alone principle (page 262)

sunk cost (page 262)

opportunity cost (page 263)

erosion (page 263)

capital cost allowance (CCA) (page 265)

pro forma financial statements (page 265)

depreciation (CCA) tax shield (page 277)

equivalent annual cost (EAC) (page 288)

Chapter Review Problems and Self-Test

These problems give you some practice with discounted cash flow analysis. The answers follow.

8.1   Capital Budgeting for Project X   Based on the following information for Project X, should we undertake the venture? To answer, first prepare a pro forma income statement for each year. Second, calculate the operating cash flow. Finish the problem by determining total cash flow and then calculating NPV assuming a 20 percent required return. Use a 40 percent tax rate throughout. For help, look back at our shark attractant and power mulcher examples.

Project X is a new type of audiophile-grade stereo amplifier. We think we can sell 500 units per year at a price of $10,000 each. Variable costs per amplifier run about $5,000 per unit, and the product should have a four-year life. We require a 20 percent return on new products such as this one.

Fixed costs for the project run $610,000 per year. Further, we need to invest $1,100,000 in manufacturing equipment. This equipment belongs to Class 8 for CCA purposes. In four years, the equipment can be sold for its UCC value. We would have to invest $900,000 in working capital at the start. After that, net working capital requirements would be 30 percent of sales.

8.2   Calculating Operating Cash Flow   Mater Pasta, Ltd., has projected a sales volume of $1,432 for the second year of a proposed expansion project. Costs normally run 70 percent of sales, or about $1,002 in this case. The capital cost allowance will be $80, and the tax rate is 40 percent. What is the operating cash flow? Calculate your answer using the top-down, bottom-up, and tax shield approaches described in the chapter.

8.3   Spending Money to Save Money   For help on this one, refer back to the computerized inventory management system in Example 8.3. Here, we're contemplating a new, mechanized welding system to replace our current manual system. It costs $600,000 to get the new system. The cost will be depreciated at a 30 percent CCA rate. Its expected life is four years. The system would actually be worth $100,000 at the end of four years.

We think the new system could save us $180,000 per year pretax in labour costs. The tax rate is 44 percent. What is the NPV of buying the new system? The required return is 15 percent.

Answers to Self-Test Problems

8.1 To develop the pro forma income statements, we need to calculate the depreciation for each of the four years. The relevant CCA percentages, allowances, and UCC values for the first four years are:

Year	CCA rate	Eligible UCC	Allowance	Ending UCC
1	20.0%	$550,000	$110,000	$990,000
2	20.0	990,000	198,000	792,000
3	20.0	792,000	158,400	633,600
4	20.0	633,600	126,720	506,880

The projected income statements, therefore, are as follows:

	Year 1	2	3	4
Sales	$5,000,000	$5,000,000	$5,000,000	$5,000,000
Variable costs	2,500,000	2,500,000	2,500,000	2,500,000
Fixed costs	610,000	610,000	610,000	610,000
CCA deduction	110,000	198,000	158,400	126,720
EBIT	$1,780,000	$1,692,000	$1,731,600	$1,763,280
Taxes (40%)	712,000	676,800	692,640	705,312
Net income	$1,068,000	$1,015,200	$1,038,960	$1,057,968

Based on this information, the operating cash flows are:

	Year 1	2	3	4
EBIT	$1,780,000	$1,692,000	$1,731,600	$1,763,280
CCA deduction	110,000	198,000	158,400	126,720
Taxes	−712,000	−676,800	−692,640	−705,312
Operating cash flow	$1,178,000	$1,213,200	$1,197,360	$1,184,688

We now have to worry about the non-operating cash flows. Net working capital starts at $900,000 and then rises to 30 percent of sales, or $1,500,000. This is a $600,000 addition to net working capital.

Finally, we have to invest $1,100,000 to get started. In four years, the market and book value of this investment would be identical, $506,880. Under our usual going-concern assumption, other Class 8 assets remain in the pool. There are no tax adjustments needed to the salvage value.

When we combine all this information, the projected cash flows for Project X are:

	Year 0	1	2	3	4
Operating cash flow		$1,178,000	$1,213,200	$1,197,360	$1,184,688
Additions to NWC	−$ 900,000	−600,000			1,500,000
Capital spending	−1,100,000				506,880
Total cash flow	−$ 2,000,000	$ 578,000	$1,213,200	$1,197,360	$3,191,568

With these cash flows, the NPV at 20 percent is:

$$NPV = -\$2,000,000 + 578,000/1.2 + 1,213,200/1.2^2$$
$$+ 1,197,360/1.2^3 + 3,191,568/1.2^4$$
$$= \$1,556,227$$

So this project appears quite profitable.

8.2   We begin by calculating the project's EBIT, its tax bill, and its net income.

$$\text{EBIT} = \$1,432 - 1,002 - 80 = \$350$$
$$\text{Taxes} = \$350 \times .40 = \$140$$
$$\text{Net income} = \$350 - 140 = \$210$$

With these numbers, operating cash flow is:

$$\begin{aligned}
\text{OCF} &= \text{EBIT} + D - \text{Taxes} \\
&= \$350 + 80 - 140 \\
&= \$290
\end{aligned}$$

Using the other OCF definitions, we have:

$$\begin{aligned}
\text{Tax shield OCF} &= (S - C) \times (1 - .40) + D \times .40 \\
&= (\$1,432 - \$1,002) \times .60 + 80 \times .40 \\
&= \$290
\end{aligned}$$

$$\begin{aligned}
\text{Bottom-up OCF} &= \text{Net income} + D \\
&= \$210 + 80 \\
&= \$290
\end{aligned}$$

$$\begin{aligned}
\text{Top-down OCF} &= S - C - \text{Taxes} \\
&= \$1,432 - 1,002 - 140 \\
&= \$290
\end{aligned}$$

As expected, all of these definitions produce exactly the same answer.

8.3   The $180,000 pretax saving gives an aftertax amount of:

$$(1 - .44) \times \$180,000 = \$100,800$$

The present value of this four-year annuity amounts to:

$$\begin{aligned}
\text{PV} &= \$100,800 \times (1 - (1/1.15^4))/.15 \\
&= \$100,800 \times 2.8550 \\
&= \$287,782
\end{aligned}$$

The present value of the tax shield on the CCA is:

$$\begin{aligned}
\text{PV} &= \frac{600,000(.30)(.44)}{.15 + .30} \times \frac{(1 + .5(.15))}{1 + .15} \\
&\quad - \frac{100,000(.30)(.44)}{.15 + .30} \times \frac{1}{(1.15)^4} \\
&= 164,522 - 16,771 \\
&= \$147,750
\end{aligned}$$

The only flow left undiscounted is the salvage value of the equipment. The present value of this flow is:

$$\begin{aligned}
\text{PV} &= \$100,000 \times 1/1.15^4 \\
&= \$100,000 \times .5718 \\
&= \$57,175
\end{aligned}$$

There are no working capital consequences, so the NPV is found by adding these three flows and the initial investment.

Investment	−$600,000
PV of labour savings	287,782
PV of salvage	57,175
CCATS	147,750
NPV	−$107,293

You can verify that the NPV is −$107,293, and the return on the new welding system is only about 5.4 percent. The project does not appear to be profitable.

Questions and Problems

Basic (Questions 1–15)

1. **Calculating Net Income**   A proposed new investment has projected sales in Year 5 of $312,500. Variable costs are 50 percent of sales, and fixed costs are $50,000. CCA for the year will be $37,500. Prepare a projected income statement assuming a 40 percent tax rate.

2. **Calculating OCF**   Consider the following income statement:

Sales	$130,140
Costs	76,300
CCA	15,000
Taxes (43.5%)	?
Net income	?

   Fill in the missing numbers and then calculate the operating cash flow. What is the depreciation tax shield?

3. **OCF from Several Approaches**   A proposed new product has projected sales of $17,994, costs of $12,665, and CCA of $4,815. The tax rate is 40 percent. Calculate operating cash flow using the four different approaches described in the chapter and verify that the answer is the same in each case.

4. **Calculating Depreciation**   A new electronic process monitor costs $210,000. This cost could be depreciated at 25 percent per year (Class 9). The monitor would actually be worthless in five years. The new monitor would save us $75,000 per year before taxes and operating costs. If we require a 10 percent return, what is the NPV of the purchase? Assume a tax rate of 40 percent.

5. **NPV and NWC Requirements**   In the previous question, suppose the new monitor also requires us to increase net working capital by $15,000 when we buy it. Further suppose that the monitor could actually be worth $30,000 in five years. What is the new NPV?

6. **NPV and CCA**   In the previous question, suppose the monitor was assigned a 50 percent CCA rate. All the other facts are the same. Will the NPV be larger or smaller? Why? Calculate the new NPV to verify your answer.

7. **Identifying Relevant Costs**   Rick Bardles and Ed James are considering building a new bottling plant to meet expected future demand for their new line of tropical coolers. They are considering putting it on a plot of land they have owned for three years. They are analyzing the idea and comparing it to some others. Bardles says, "Ed, when we do this analysis, we should put in an amount for the cost of the land equal to what we paid for it. After all, it did cost us a pretty penny." James retorts, "No, I don't care how much it cost—we

have already paid for it. It is what they call a sunk cost. The cost of the land shouldn't be considered." What would you say to Bardles and James?

8.   **NPV Applications**   We believe we can sell 10,000 home security devices per year at $36 apiece. They cost $24 each to manufacture (variable cost). Fixed production costs run $36,000 per year. The necessary equipment costs $180,000 to buy and would be depreciated at a 20 percent CCA rate. The equipment would have a zero salvage value after the five-year life of the project. We need to invest $48,000 in net working capital up front; no additional net working capital investment is necessary. The discount rate is 14 percent, and the tax rate is 43.5 percent. What do you think of the proposal?

9.   **Identifying Cash Flows**   Suppose a company has $1,500 in sales during a quarter. Over the quarter, accounts receivable increased by $600. What were cash collections?

10. **Stand-Alone Principle**   Suppose a financial manager is quoted as saying: "Our firm uses the stand-alone principle. Since we treat projects like a minifirm in our evaluation process, we include financing costs, because financing costs are relevant at the firm level." Critically evaluate this statement.

11. **Relevant Cash Flows**   Perfect Plexiglass, Inc., is looking at setting up a new manufacturing plant to produce surfboards. The company bought some land six years ago for $5 million in anticipation of using it as a warehouse and distribution site, but the company decided to rent facilities from a competitor instead. The land was appraised last week for $200,000. The company wants to build its new manufacturing plant on this land; the plant will cost $7 million to build, and the site requires $500,000 in grading before it is suitable for construction. What is the proper cash flow amount to use as the initial investment in fixed assets when evaluating this project? Why?

12. **Relevant Cash Flows**   Stevinator Motorworks Corp. currently sells 10,000 compact cars per year at $8,000 each, and 25,000 luxury sedans per year at $20,000 each. The company wants to introduce a new mid-sized sedan to fill out its product line; it hopes to sell 15,000 of the cars per year at $13,000 each. An independent consultant has determined that if Stevinator introduces the new cars, it should boost the sales of its existing compacts by 7,000 units per year, while reducing the unit sales of its luxury sedans by 4,000 units per year. What is the annual cash flow amount to use as the sales figure when evaluating this project? Why?

13. **Calculating a Bid Price**   This problem is much easier if you are working with a spreadsheet. We have been requested by a large retailer to submit a bid for a new point-of-sale credit checking system. The system would be installed, by us, in 20 stores per year for three years. We would need to purchase $200,000 worth of specialized equipment. This will be depreciated at a 25 percent CCA rate. We will sell it in three years, at which time it should be worth about half of what we paid for it. Labour and material cost to install the system is about $28,000 per site. Finally, we need to invest $48,000 in working capital items. The relevant tax rate is 44 percent. What price per system should we bid if we require a 16 percent return on our investment? Try to avoid the winner's curse.

14. **EAC**   Olivaw is a leading manufacturer of positronic brains, a key component in robots. The company is considering two alternative production methods. The costs and lives associated with each are:

Year	Method 1	Method 2
0	$1,900	$2,800
1	120	180
2	120	180
3	120	180
4		180

Basic
(Continued)

Assuming that Olivaw will not replace the equipment when it wears out, which should it buy? If Olivaw is going to replace the equipment, which should it buy ($r = 10\%$)? Ignore depreciation and taxes in answering.

15. **Calculating Cash Flows and EAC**   In the previous question, suppose all the costs are before taxes and the tax rate is 40 percent. Both types of equipment would be depreciated straight-line to zero over their respective lives. What are the EACs in this case? Which is the preferred method?

16. **Cash Flows and NPV**   We project unit sales for a new household-use laser-guided cockroach search and destroy system as follows:

Intermediate
(Questions 16–24)

Year	Unit Sales
1	63,000
2	75,000
3	86,000
4	96,000
5	56,000

The new system will be priced to sell at $110 each.

The cockroach eradicator project will require $685,000 in net working capital to start, and total net working capital will rise to 35 percent of sales. The variable cost per unit is $80, and total fixed costs are $35,000 per year. The equipment necessary to begin production will cost a total of $6.9 million. This equipment is mostly industrial machinery and thus qualifies for CCA at a rate of 20 percent. In five years, this equipment will actually be worth about 30 percent of its cost.

The relevant tax rate is 45 percent, and the required return is 20 percent. Based on these preliminary estimates, what is the NPV of the project?

17. **Replacement Decisions**   An officer for a large construction company is feeling nervous. The anxiety is caused by a new excavator just released onto the market. The new excavator makes the one purchased by the company a year ago obsolete. As a result, the market value for the company's excavator has dropped significantly, from $250,000 a year ago to $100,000 now. In 10 years, it would be worth only $20,000. The new excavator costs only $200,000 and would increase operating revenues by $20,000 annually. The new equipment has a 10-year life and expected salvage value of $40,000. What should the officer do? The tax rate is 42 percent, the CCA rate, 30 percent for both excavators, and the required rate of return for the company is 12 percent.

18. **Replacement Decisions**   A university student painter is considering the purchase of a new air compressor and paint gun to replace an old paint sprayer. (Both items belong to Class 8 for CCA purposes.) These two new items cost $3,500 and have a useful life of three years, at which time they can be sold for $300. The old paint sprayer can be sold now for $100 and could be scrapped for $75 in three years. The entrepreneurial student believes that operating revenues will increase annually by $2,500. Should the purchase be made? The tax rate is 22 percent and the required rate of return is 20 percent.

**Intermediate
(Continued)**

19. **Different Lives**   The Briar Patch Golf and Country Club in Calgary is evaluating two different irrigation system options. An underground automatic irrigation system will cost $6 million to install and $20,000 pretax annually to operate. It will not have to be replaced for 20 years. An aboveground system will cost $2.5 million to install, but $60,000 per year to operate. The aboveground equipment has an effective operating life of eight years. The country club leases its land from the city and both systems are considered leasehold improvements, as a result, straight-line capital cost allowance is used throughout, and neither system has any salvage value. Which method should we select if we use a 12 percent discount rate? The tax rate is 40 percent.

20. **Comparing Mutually Exclusive Projects**   Victoria Enterprises, Inc., is evaluating alternative uses for a three-story manufacturing and warehousing building that it has purchased for $225,000. The company could continue to rent the building to the present occupants for $12,000 per year. These tenants have indicated an interest in staying in the building for at least another 15 years. Alternatively, the company could make leasehold improvements to modify the existing structure to use for its own manufacturing and warehousing needs. Victoria's production engineer feels the building could be adapted to handle one of two new product lines. The cost and revenue data for the two product alternatives follow.

	Product A	Product B
Initial cash outlay for building modifications	$ 36,000	$ 54,000
Initial cash outlay for equipment	144,000	162,000
Annual pretax cash revenues (generated for 15 years)	105,000	127,500
Annual pretax cash expenditures (generated for 15 years)	60,000	75,000

The building will be used for only 15 years for either product A or product B. After 15 years, the building will be too small for efficient production of either product line. At that time, Victoria plans to rent the building to firms similar to the current occupants. To rent the building again, Victoria will need to restore the building to its present layout. The estimated cash cost of restoring the building if product A has been undertaken is $3,750; if product B has been produced, the cash cost will be $28,125. These cash costs can be deducted for tax purposes in the year the expenditures occur.

Victoria will depreciate the original building shell (purchased for $225,000) at a CCA rate of 5 percent, regardless of which alternative it chooses. The building modifications fall into CCA class 13 and are depreciated using the straight-line method over a 15-year life. Equipment purchases for either product are in class 8 and have a CCA rate of 20 percent. The firm's tax rate is 40 percent, and its required rate of return on such investments is 12 percent.

For simplicity, assume all cash flows for a given year occur at the end of the year. The initial outlays for modifications and equipment will occur at $t = 0$, and the restoration outlays will occur at the end of year 15. Also, Victoria has other profitable ongoing operations that are sufficient to cover any losses.

Which use of the building would you recommend to management?

21. **Valuation of the Firm**   The Regina Wheat Company (RWC) has wheat fields that currently produce annual profits of $250,000. These fields are expected to produce average annual profits of $250,000 in real terms forever. RWC has no depreciable assets, so the annual cash flow is also $250,000. RWC is an

all-equity firm with 100,000 shares outstanding. The appropriate discount rate for its stock is 15 percent. RWC has an investment opportunity with a gross present value of $600,000. The investment requires a $400,000 outlay now. RWC has no other investment opportunities. Assume all cash flows are received at the end of each year. What is the price per share of RWC?

**Intermediate
(Continued)**

22. **Calculating a Bid Price** Majestic Mining Company is negotiating for the purchase of a new piece of equipment for its current operations. MMC wants to know the maximum price it should be willing to pay for the equipment. That is, how high must the price be for the equipment to have an NPV of zero? You are given the following facts:

    a. The new equipment would replace existing equipment that has a current market value of $20,000.

    b. The new equipment would not affect revenues, but before-tax operating costs would be reduced by $10,000 per year for eight years. These savings in cost would occur at year-end.

    c. The old equipment is now five years old. It is expected to last for another eight years, and to have no resale value at the end of those eight years. It was purchased for $40,000 and is being depreciated at a CCA rate of 20 percent.

    d. The new equipment will also be depreciated at a CCA rate of 20 percent. MMC expects to be able to sell the equipment for $5,000 at the end of eight years. At that time, the firm plans to reinvest in new equipment in the same CCA pool.

    e. MMC has profitable ongoing operations.

    f. The appropriate discount rate is 8 percent.

23. **Replacement with Unequal Lives** BIG Industries needs computers. Management has narrowed the choices to the SAL 5000 and the DET 1000. It would need 10 SALs. Each SAL costs $5,000 and requires $1,000 of maintenance each year. At the end of the computer's eight-year life, BIG expects to be able to sell each one for $500. On the other hand, BIG could buy eight DETs. DETs cost $7,000 each and each machine requires $700 of maintenance every year. They last for six years and have no resale value. Whichever model BIG chooses, it will buy that model forever. Ignore tax effects, and assume that maintenance costs occur at year-end. Which model should BIG buy if the cost of capital is 10 percent?

24. **Replacement with Unequal Lives** Station CJXT is considering the replacement of its old, fully depreciated sound mixer. Two new models are available. Mixer X has a cost of $216,000, a five-year expected life, and after-tax cash flow savings of $68,200 per year. Mixer Y has a cost of $345,000, a 10-year life, and aftertax cash flow of $83,400 per year. No new technological developments are expected. The cost of capital is 10 percent. Should CJXT replace the old mixer with X or Y?

25. **Abandonment Decisions** For some projects, it may be advantageous to terminate the project early. For example, if a project is losing money, you might be able to reduce your losses by scrapping the assets and terminating the project, rather than continuing to lose money all the way through to the project's completion. So consider the following project of Wing-N-A-Prayer Airlines, Inc. The company is considering a four-year project to extend airline service to Utopia. This project requires an initial investment of $90 million to buy new airplanes; the planes will be depreciated straight-line to zero over the

**Challenge
(Questions 25–28)**

project's life. An initial investment in net working capital of $8 million is required to support spare parts inventory; this cost is fully recoverable whenever the project ends. The company believes it can generate $80 million in pretax revenues with $40 million in total pretax operating costs. The tax rate is 38 percent and the discount rate is 16 percent. The market value of the airplanes over the life of the project is given below:

Year	Market Value ($ millions)
1	75
2	60
3	35
4	0

a. Assuming Wing-N-A-Prayer operates this project for four years, what is the NPV?

b. Now compute the project NPV assuming the project is abandoned after only one year, two years, or three years. What economic life for this project maximizes its value to the firm? What does this problem tell you about not considering abandonment possibilities when evaluating projects?

26. **Capital Budgeting Renovations**   Suppose we are thinking about renovating a leased office. The renovations would cost $80,000. The renovations will be depreciated straight-line to zero over the five-year remainder of the lease.

The new office would save us $15,000 per year in heating and cooling costs. Also, absenteeism should be reduced and the new image should increase revenues. These last two items would result in increased operating revenues of $15,000 annually. The tax rate is 40 percent, and the discount rate is 15 percent. Strictly from a financial perspective, should the renovations take place?

27. **Calculating Required Savings**   A proposed cost-saving device has an installed cost of $79,400. It is in Class 9 for CCA purposes. It will actually function for five years, at which time it will have no value. There are no working capital consequences from the investment, and the tax rate is 40 percent.

a. What must the pretax cost savings be for us to favour the investment? We require a 12 percent return. Hint: This one is a variation on the problem of setting a bid price.

b. Suppose the device will be worth $11,000 in salvage (before taxes). How does this change your answer?

28. **Cash Flows and Capital Budgeting Choices**   Klaatu Company has recently completed a $600,000, two-year marketing study. Based on the results, Klaatu has estimated that 10,000 of its new RUR-class robots could be sold annually over the next eight years at a price of $14,400 each. Variable costs per robot are $11,100, and fixed costs total $18 million per year.

Start-up costs include $60 million to build production facilities, $3.6 million in land, and $12 million in net working capital. The $60 million facility is made up of a building valued at $7.5 million that will belong to CCA Class 3 and $52.5 million of manufacturing equipment (belonging to CCA Class 8). At the end of the project's life, the facilities (including the land) will be sold for an estimated $12.6 million; assume the building's value will be $6 million. The value of the land is not expected to change.

Finally, start-up would also entail fully deductible expenses of $2.1 million at Year 0. Klaatu is an ongoing, profitable business and pays taxes at a 40 percent rate. Klaatu uses a 10 percent discount rate on projects such as this one. Should Klaatu produce the RUR-class robots?

Challenge (Continued)

Suggested Readings

For more on the capital budgeting decision, see:

Garrison, R.; G. R. Chesley; and R. Carroll. *Managerial Accounting,* 2nd Canadian ed. Homewood, IL: Richard D. Irwin, 1993.

Bierman, H., and S. Smidt. *The Capital Budgeting Decision,* 6th ed. New York: Macmillan, 1984.

MORE ON INFLATION AND CAPITAL BUDGETING

APPENDIX 8A

This text states that interest rates can be expressed in either nominal or real terms. For example, suppose the nominal interest rate is 12 percent and inflation is expected to be 8 percent next year. Then the real interest rate is approximately

Real rate = Nominal rate − Expected inflation rate

$$= 12\% - 8\% = 4\%.$$

Similarly, cash flows can be expressed in either nominal or real terms. Given these choices, how should one express interest rates and cash flows when performing capital budgeting?

Financial practitioners correctly stress the need to maintain consistency between cash flows and discount rates. That is, nominal cash flows must be discounted at the nominal rate. Real cash flows must be discounted at the real rate.

E X A M P L E | 8A.1 Real or Nominal?

Shields Electric forecasts the following nominal cash flows on a particular project:

	Date		
	0	1	2
Cash flow	−$1,000	$600	$650

The nominal interest rate is 14 percent, and the inflation rate is forecast to be 5 percent. What is the value of the project?

Using Nominal Quantities The NPV can be calculated as:

$$\$26.47 = -\$1,000 + \frac{\$600}{1.14} + \frac{\$650}{(1.14)^2}$$

The project should be accepted.

Using Real Quantities   The real cash flows are:

	Date		
	0	1	2
Cash flow	−$1,000	$571.43	$589.57
		$\frac{\$600}{1.05}$	$\frac{\$650}{(1.05)^2}$

The real interest rate is approximately 9 percent (14 percent − 5 percent); precisely it is 8.57143 percent.[23]

The NPV can be calculated as

$$\$26.47 = -\$1,000 + \frac{\$571.32}{1.0857143} + \frac{\$589.57}{(1.0857143)^2}$$

The NPV is the same when cash flows are expressed in real quantities. The NPV is always the same under the two different approaches.

Because both approaches always yield the same result, which one should be used? Students will be happy to learn the following rule: Use the approach that is simpler. In the Shields Electric case, nominal quantities produce a simpler calculation. That is because the problem gave us nominal cash flows to begin with.

However, firms often forecast unit sales per year. They can easily convert these forecasts to real quantities by multiplying expected unit sales each year by the product price at Date 0. (This assumes the price of the product rises at exactly the rate of inflation.) Once a real discount rate is selected, NPV can easily be calculated from real quantities. Conversely, nominal quantities complicate the example, because the extra step of converting all real cash flows to nominal cash flows must be taken.

CONCEPT QUESTIONS

1. What is the difference between the nominal and the real interest rate?
2. What is the difference between nominal and real cash flows?

APPENDIX   8B | **CAPITAL BUDGETING WITH LOTUS 1-2-3®**

Today, you are just as likely to find a computer in the average university student's room as a Walkman. The increased use of desktop PCs by students is a reflection of their popularity and success in businesses across North America. With the software that runs on them, personal computers are tools that dramatically increase the productivity of their users. One of the most useful tools for business students is spreadsheet software. Some of the popular spreadsheet packages available are Lotus 1-2-3®, Excel®, and Quattro Pro®.

Spreadsheets are almost essential for constructing a capital budgeting framework or for using pro forma financial statements. Table 8B.1 is an example of a capital budgeting framework, using the data from the Majestic Mulch and Compost Company. The framework is completely integrated, changing one of the input

---

[23] The exact calculation is 8.57143% = (1.14/1.05) − 1. It is explained in Chapter 10.

T A B L E 8B.1

The Majestic Mulch and Compost Company

Input variables:

Tax rate	40.0%	Discount rate	15.0%
CCA rate	20.0%	NWC as a % of sale	15.0%
Initial investment	$800,000		

Income statements

Year	0	1	2	3	4	5	6	7	8
Unit price		$ 120	$ 120	$ 120	$ 110	$ 110	$ 110	$ 110	$ 110
Unit sales		3,000	5,000	6,000	6,500	6,000	5,000	4,000	3,000
Revenues		$360,000	$600,000	$720,000	$715,000	$660,000	$550,000	$440,000	$330,000
Variable costs		180,000	300,000	360,000	390,000	360,000	300,000	240,000	180,000
Fixed costs		25,000	25,000	25,000	25,000	25,000	25,000	25,000	25,000
CCA		80,000	144,000	115,200	92,160	73,728	58,982	47,186	37,749
EBIT		$ 75,000	$131,000	$219,800	$207,840	$201,272	$166,018	$127,814	$ 87,251
Taxes		30,000	52,400	87,920	83,136	80,509	66,407	51,126	34,901
Net income		$ 45,000	$ 78,600	$131,880	$124,704	$120,763	$ 99,611	$ 76,688	$ 52,351

Projected cash flows

Year	0	1	2	3	4	5	6	7	8
Operating cash flows									
EBIT		$ 75,000	$131,000	$219,800	$207,840	$201,272	$166,018	$127,814	$ 87,251
CCA		80,000	144,000	115,200	92,160	73,728	58,982	47,186	37,749
Taxes		30,000	52,400	87,920	83,136	80,509	66,407	51,126	34,901
Op. cash flow		$125,000	$222,600	$247,080	$216,864	$194,491	$158,593	$123,874	$ 90,099

Net working capital

Year	0	1	2	3	4	5	6	7	8
Initial NWC	$20,000								
NWC increases		$ 34,000	36,000	$ 18,000	–$ 750	–$ 8,250	–$ 16,500	–$ 16,500	–$ 16,500
NWC recovery					–$ 49,500				
Add'ns to NWC	$20,000	$ 34,000	$ 36,000	$ 18,000	–$ 750	–$ 8,250	–$ 16,500	–$ 16,500	–$ 66,000

T A B L E 8B.1

	A	B	C	D	E	F	G	H	I	J	K	L	M	N	O	P	Q	R	S
36	Capital spending																		
37	Initial inv.		$800,000																
38	Aftertax salvage																		−$150,000
39	Net cap. spending		$800,000																−$150,000
40																			
41			0		1		2		3		4		5		6		7		8
42	Total project cash flow																		
43			−$820,000		$ 91,000		$186,600		$229,080		$217,614		$202,741		$175,093		$140,374		$306,099
44																			
45	Cumulative cash flow																		
46			−$820,000		−$729,000		−$542,400		−$313,320		−$ 95,706		$107,035		$282,128		$422,503		$728,602
47																			
48	Discounted cash flow (@15%)																		
49			−$820,000		$ 79,130		$141,096		$150,624		$124,422		$100,798		$ 75,698		$ 52,772		$100,064
50																			
51	NPV		$ 4,604																
52																			
53	IRR		15.15%																
54	PB		4.47		Cash flows														
54					−$820,000														
55					91,000														
56					186,600														
57					229,080														
58					217,614														
59					202,741														
60					175,093														
61					140,374														
62					306,099														

Cell formulas

E16: (,0) @IF(E10="1",$C$6/2*$C$5,($C$6−@SUM(D16..$E$16))*$C$5)

G32: @IF(@SUM(F32..$E$32)+$C$31<G13*$G$5,G13*$G$5−(@SUM(F32..$E$32) + $C$31),G13*$G$5−(@SUM(F32..$E$32)+$C$31))

S49: +S43/((1+$G$4)^S41)

Initial Investment	NPV	Discount Rate	NPV
Base case	$ 4,604	15.0%	$ 4,604
$750,000	$ 44,626	10.0	177,240
775,000	24,615	12.5	84,796
800,000	4,604	15.0	4,604
825,000	−15,407	17.5	−65,319
850,000	−35,418	20.0	−126,589

T A B L E 8B.2

Sensitivity analysis

variables at the top reformulates the whole problem. This is useful for sensitivity calculations as it would be tedious to recalculate each column in the framework by hand.

The highlighted cells exhibit the more complicated procedures in the framework. The first, E16, is the CCA calculation. The @IF statement is used to decide what year it is, to take into consideration the half-year effect. The second, G32, uses another @IF statement; this one is needed to assess whether there is a deficiency or excess of working capital. The last cell, S49, simply discounts the future cash flows back to Year 0 dollars.

A well-designed capital budgeting framework allows most inputs to be easily changed, simplifying sensitivity calculations. We now turn our attention to a simple sensitivity calculation, to explain the usefulness of spreadsheets.

Table 8B.2 shows two sensitivity tables: One varies the initial investment and the other varies the discount rate. Notice in the first that if the initial investment runs over budget by as little as $25,000, it makes the whole project unprofitable. The second sensitivity analysis demonstrates that the project is even more sensitive to discount rate fluctuations.

Spreadsheets are invaluable in problems such as these; they decrease the number of silly errors and make all values easier to check. They also allow for what-if analyses such as these. Knowledge of at least one spreadsheet package is almost essential for business students graduating during the 1990s.

C H A P T E R

9

Project Analysis and Evaluation

In our previous chapter, we discussed how to identify and organize the relevant cash flows for capital investment decisions. Our primary interest there was in coming up with a preliminary estimate of the net present value for a proposed project. In this chapter, we focus on assessing the reliability of such an estimate and on some additional considerations in project analysis.

We begin by discussing the need for an evaluation of cash flow and NPV estimates. We go on to develop some tools that are useful for doing so. We also examine complications and concerns that can arise in project evaluation.

9.1 | EVALUATING NPV ESTIMATES

As we discussed in Chapter 7, an investment has a positive net present value if its market value exceeds its cost. Such an investment is desirable because it creates value for its owner. The primary problem in identifying such opportunities is that most of the time we can't actually observe the relevant market value. Instead, we estimate it. Having done so, it is only natural to wonder whether our estimates are at least close to the true values. We consider this question next.

The Basic Problem

Suppose we are working on a preliminary DCF analysis along the lines we described in the previous chapter. We carefully identify the relevant cash flows, avoiding such things as sunk costs, and we remember to consider working capital requirements. We add back any depreciation; we account for possible erosion; and we pay attention to opportunity costs. Finally, we double-check our calculations, and, when all is said and done, the bottom line is that the estimated NPV is positive.

Now what? Do we stop here and move on to the next proposal? Probably not. The fact that the estimated NPV is positive is definitely a good sign, but, more than anything, this tells us we need to take a closer look.

If you think about it, there are two circumstances under which a discounted cash flow analysis could lead us to conclude that a project has a positive NPV. The first possibility is that the project really does have a positive NPV. That's the good news. The bad news is the second possibility: A project may appear to have a positive NPV because our estimate is inaccurate.

Notice that we could also err in the opposite way. If we conclude that a project has a negative NPV when the true NPV is positive, we lose a valuable opportunity.

Projected versus Actual Cash Flows

There is a somewhat subtle point we need to make here. When we say something like: "The projected cash flow in Year 4 is $700," what exactly do we mean? Does this mean we think the cash flow will actually be $700? Not really. It could happen, of course, but we would be surprised to see it turn out exactly that way. The reason is that the $700 projection is based only on what we know today. Almost anything could happen between now and then to change that cash flow.

Loosely speaking, we really mean that, if we took all the possible cash flows that could occur in four years and averaged them, the result would be $700. So, we don't really expect a projected cash flow to be exactly right in any one case. What we do expect is that, if we evaluate a large number of projects, our projections are right on the average.

Forecasting Risk

The key inputs into a DCF analysis are projected future cash flows. If these projections are seriously in error, we have a classic GIGO (garbage-in, garbage-out) system. In this case, no matter how carefully we arrange the numbers and manipulate them, the resulting answer can still be grossly misleading. This is the danger in using a relatively sophisticated technique like DCF. It is sometimes easy to get caught up in number crunching and forget the underlying nuts-and-bolts economic reality.

The possibility that we can make a bad decision because of errors in the projected cash flows is called **forecasting risk** (or estimation risk). Because of forecasting risk, there is the danger that we think a project has a positive NPV when it really does not. How is this possible? It happens if we are overly optimistic about the future and, as a result, our projected cash flows don't realistically reflect the possible future cash flows.

forecasting risk
The possibility that errors in projected cash flows lead to incorrect decisions.

Several surveys of senior financial officers of large corporations identified the excessive optimism of project sponsors as a significant problem with implementing capital budgeting. Selected comments from one survey include:

> Overly optimistic forecasting has been a continuing challenge . . . Marketing plans tend to "assume" the additional capacity will be sold; they tend to be optimistic . . . The performance of the project after completion is never (almost) as good as promised in the approval document.[1]

So far, we have not explicitly considered what to do about the possibility of errors in our forecasts, so one of our goals in this chapter is to develop some tools that are useful in identifying areas where potential errors exist and where they might be especially damaging. In one form or another, we try to assess the economic reasonableness of our estimates. We also consider how much damage can be done by errors in those estimates.

---

[1] These comments are drawn from a 1985 survey of the largest U.S. companies reported in H. Bierman, Jr., *Implementing Capital Budgeting Techniques* (Cambridge, MA: Ballinger Publishing Company, 1988), pp. 80–81.

Sources of Value

The first line of defence against forecasting risk is simply to ask: What is it about this investment that leads to a positive NPV? We should be able to point to something specific as the source of value. For example, if the proposal under consideration involved a new product, we might ask questions such as: Are we certain that our new product is significantly better than that of the competition? Can we truly manufacture at lower cost, or distribute more effectively, or identify undeveloped market niches, or gain control of a market?

These are just a few of the potential sources of value. There are many others. A key factor to keep in mind is the degree of competition in the market. It is a basic principle of economics that positive NPV investments are rare in a highly competitive environment. Therefore, proposals that appear to show significant value in the face of stiff competition are particularly troublesome, and the likely reaction of the competition to any innovations must be closely examined.

Similarly, beware of forecasts that simply extrapolate past trends without taking into account changes in technology or human behaviour. Forecasts similar to the following fall prey to the forecaster's trap:

> In 1860, several forecasters were secured from the financial community by the city of New York to forecast the future level of pollution caused by the use of chewing tobacco and horses . . . In 1850, the spit level in the gutter and manure level in the middle of the road had both averaged half an inch (approximately 1 cm). By 1860, each had doubled to a level of one inch. Using this historical growth rate, the forecasters projected levels of two inches by 1870, four inches by 1880 and 1,024 inches (22.5 metres) by 1960![2]

To avoid the forecaster's trap, the point to remember is that positive NPV investments are probably not all that common, and the number of positive NPV projects is almost certainly limited for any given firm. If we can't articulate some sound economic basis for thinking ahead of time that we have found something special, the conclusion that our project has a positive NPV should be viewed with some suspicion.

> **CONCEPT QUESTIONS**
>
> **1.** What is forecasting risk? Why is it a concern for the financial manager?
>
> **2.** What are some potential sources of value in a new project?

9.2 | SCENARIO AND OTHER WHAT-IF ANALYSES

Our basic approach to evaluating cash flow and NPV estimates involves asking what-if questions. Accordingly, we discuss some organized ways of going about a what-if analysis. Our goal in doing so is to assess the degree of forecasting risk and to identify those components most critical to the success or failure of an investment.

Getting Started

We are investigating a new project. Naturally, we begin by estimating NPV based on our projected cash flows. We call this the *base case*. Now, however, we recognize the possibility of error in those cash flow projections. After completing the base case, we wish to investigate the impact of different assumptions about the future on our estimates.

---

[2] This apocryphal example comes from L. Kryzanowski, T. Minh-Chau, and R. Seguin, *Business Solvency Risk Analysis* (Montreal: Institute of Canadian Bankers, 1990), chap. 5, p. 10.

One way to organize this investigation is to put an upper and lower bound on the various components of the project. For example, suppose we forecast sales at 100 units per year. We know this estimate may be high or low, but we are relatively certain that it is not off by more than 10 units in either direction. We would thus pick a lower bound of 90 and an upper bound of 110. We go on to assign such bounds to any other cash flow components that we are unsure about.

When we pick these upper and lower bounds, we are not ruling out the possibility that the actual values could be outside this range. What we are saying, again loosely speaking, is that it is unlikely that the true average (as opposed to our estimated average) of the possible values is outside this range.

An example is useful to illustrate the idea here. The project under consideration costs $200,000, has a five-year life, and no salvage value. Depreciation is straight-line. The required return is 12 percent, and the tax rate is 34 percent.[3] In addition, we have compiled the following information:

	Base Case	Lower Bound	Upper Bound
Unit sales	6,000	5,500	6,500
Price per unit	$ 80	$ 75	$ 85
Variable costs per unit	60	58	62
Fixed costs per year	50,000	45,000	55,000

With this information, we can calculate the base case NPV by first calculating net income:

Sales	$480,000
Variable costs	360,000
Fixed costs	50,000
Depreciation	40,000
EBIT	$ 30,000
Taxes (34%)	10,200
Net income	$ 19,800

Cash flow is thus $30,000 + 40,000 − 10,200 = $59,800 per year. At 12 percent, the five-year annuity factor is 3.6048, so the base case NPV is:

$$\text{Base case NPV} = -\$200,000 + (59,800 \times 3.6048)$$
$$= \$15,567$$

Thus, the project looks good so far.

Scenario Analysis

The basic form of what-if analysis is called **scenario analysis**. What we do is investigate the changes in our NPV estimates that result from asking questions such as: What if unit sales realistically should be projected at 5,500 units instead of 6,000?

Once we start looking at alternative scenarios, we might find that most of the plausible ones result in positive NPVs. This gives us some confidence in proceeding with the project. If a substantial percentage of the scenarios looks bad, the degree of forecasting risk is high and further investigation is in order.

scenario analysis
The determination of what happens to NPV estimates when we ask what-if questions.

---

[3] Although we use straight-line depreciation for convenience here, Chapter 2 shows that it is realistic for finding capital cost allowance for some assets in Canada. This tax rate applies for manufacturing and processing companies in some provinces.

There are a number of possible scenarios we could consider. A good place to start is the worst-case scenario. This tells us the minimum NPV of the project. If this were positive, we would be in good shape. While we are at it, we also determine the other extreme, the best case. This puts an upper bound on our NPV.

To get the worst case, we assign the least favourable value to each item. This means low values for items such as units sold and price per unit and high values for costs. We do the reverse for the best case. For our project, these values would be:

	Worst Case	Best Case
Unit sales	5,500	6,500
Price per unit	$ 75	$ 85
Variable costs per unit	62	58
Fixed costs	55,000	45,000

With this information, we can calculate the net income and cash flows under each scenario (check these for yourself):

Scenario	Net Income	Cash Flow	Net Present Value	IRR
Base case	$ 19,800	$59,800	$ 15,567	15.1%
Worst case*	−15,510	24,490	−111,719	−14.4
Best case	59,730	99,730	159,504	40.9

*We assume a tax credit is created in our worst-case scenario.

What we learn is that under the worst scenario, the cash flow is still positive at $24,490. That's good news. The bad news is that the return is −14.4 percent in this case, and the NPV is −$111,719. Since the project costs $200,000, we stand to lose a little more than half of the original investment under the worst possible scenario. The best case offers an attractive 41 percent return.

As we have mentioned, we could examine an unlimited number of different scenarios. At a minimum, we might want to investigate two intermediate cases by going halfway between the base amounts and the extreme amounts. This would give us five scenarios in all, including the base case.

Beyond this point, it is hard to know when to stop. As we generate more and more possibilities, we run the risk of paralysis by analysis. The difficulty is that no matter how many scenarios we run on our spreadsheet, all we can learn are possibilities, some good and some bad. Beyond that, we don't get any guidance as to what to do. Scenario analysis is thus useful in telling us what can happen and in helping us gauge the potential for disaster, but it does not tell us whether to take the project.

Sensitivity Analysis

sensitivity analysis
Investigation of what happens to NPV when only one variable is changed.

Sensitivity analysis is a variation on scenario analysis that is useful in pinpointing the areas where forecasting risk is especially severe. The basic idea with a sensitivity analysis is to freeze all the variables except one and see how sensitive our estimate of NPV is to changes in that one variable. The logic is exactly the same as for ceteris paribus analysis in economics.

If our NPV estimate turns out to be very sensitive to relatively small changes in the projected value of some component of project cash flow, the forecasting risk associated with that variable is high. To put it another way, NPV depends critically on the assumptions we made about this variable.

To illustrate how sensitivity analysis works, we go back to our base case for every item except unit sales. We can then calculate cash flow and NPV using the largest and smallest unit sales figures. This is very easy to do on a spreadsheet program.

Scenario	Unit Sales	Cash Flow	Net Present Value	IRR
Base case	6,000	$59,800	$15,567	15.1%
Worst case	5,500	53,200	−8,226	10.3
Best case	6,500	66,400	39,357	19.7

By way of comparison, we now freeze everything except fixed costs and repeat the analysis:

Scenario	Fixed Costs	Cash Flow	Net Present Value	IRR
Base case	$50,000	$59,800	$15,567	15.1%
Worst case	55,000	56,500	3,670	12.7
Best case	45,000	63,100	27,461	17.4

What we see here is that, given our ranges, the estimated NPV of this project is more sensitive to projected unit sales than it is to projected fixed costs. In fact, under the worst case for fixed costs, the NPV is still positive.

The results of our sensitivity analysis for unit sales can be illustrated graphically as in Figure 9.1. Here we place NPV on the vertical axis and unit sales on the horizontal axis. When we plot the combinations of unit sales versus NPV, we see that all possible combinations fall on a straight line. The steeper the resulting line is, the greater the sensitivity of the estimated NPV to the projected value of the variable being investigated.

As we have illustrated, sensitivity analysis is useful in pinpointing those variables that deserve the most attention. If we find that our estimated NPV is especially sensitive to a variable that is difficult to forecast (such as unit sales), the

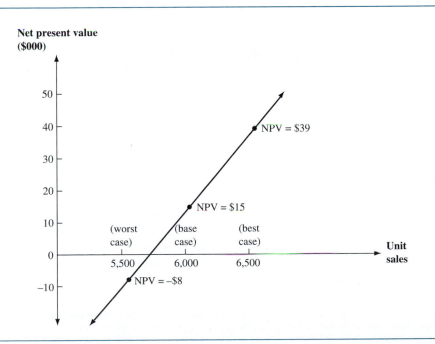

FIGURE 9.1

Sensitivity analysis for unit sales

degree of forecasting risk is high. We might decide that further market research would be a good idea in this case.

Because sensitivity analysis is a form of scenario analysis, it suffers from the same drawbacks. Scenario analysis is useful for pointing out where forecasting errors could do the most damage, but it does not tell us what to do about possible errors.

Simulation Analysis

Scenario analysis and sensitivity analysis are widely used in part because they are easily executed on spreadsheets. With scenario analysis, we let all the different variables change, but we let them take on only a small number of values. With sensitivity analysis, we let only one variable change, but we let it take on a large number of values. If we combine the two approaches, the result is a crude form of **simulation analysis**.

simulation analysis

A combination of scenario and sensitivity analyses.

Simulation analysis is potentially useful to measure risk in a complex system of variables. The technique is sometimes called *Monte Carlo simulation* and has been used successfully to test gambling strategies.

For example, researchers believed that casino gamblers could shift the odds in their favour in blackjack by varying their bets during the game. In blackjack, you play against the dealer and win if the dealer "goes bust" drawing cards that add to more than 21. The dealer must always take another card if his or her cards add to 16 or less. The probability of the dealer going bust increases as there are more face cards (worth 10) in the deck. To make the strategy work, players count all the cards as they are played and increase their bets when a high number of tens remains in the deck.

Clearly, it would have been very expensive to test this strategy in a casino using real money. Researchers developed a computer simulation of blackjack and measured hypothetical winnings. They found that the strategy worked but required a substantial stake because it often took considerable time for the winnings to occur.[4]

As our blackjack example illustrates, simulation analysis allows all variables to vary at the same time. If we want to do this, we have to consider a very large number of scenarios, and computer assistance is almost certainly needed. In the simplest case, we start with unit sales and assume that any value in our 5,500 to 6,500 range is equally likely. We start by randomly picking one value (or by instructing a computer to do so). We then randomly pick a price, a variable cost, and so on.

Once we have values for all the relevant components, we calculate an NPV. Since we won't know the project's risk until the simulation is finished, we avoid prejudging risk by discounting the cash flows at a riskless rate.[5] We repeat this sequence as much as we desire, probably several thousand times. The result is a large number of NPV estimates that we summarize by calculating the average value and some measure of how spread out the different possibilities are. For example, it would be of some interest to know what percentage of the possible scenarios result in negative estimated NPVs.

Because simulation is an extended form of scenario analysis, it has the same problems. Once we have the results, there is no simple decision rule that tells us what to do. Also, we have described a relatively simple form of simulation. To really do it right, we would have to consider the interrelationships between the different cash

---

[4] To learn more about simulation, blackjack, and what happened when the strategy was implemented in Las Vegas, read *Beat the Dealer* by Edward O. Thorp (New York: Random House, 1962).

[5] The rate on government of Canada Treasury bills is a common example of a riskless rate.

flow components. Furthermore, we assumed that the possible values were equally likely to occur. It is probably more realistic to assume that values near the base case are more likely than extreme values, but coming up with the probabilities is difficult, to say the least.

For these reasons, the use of simulation is somewhat limited in practice. A recent survey found that about 40 percent of large corporations use sensitivity and scenario analyses as compared to around 20 percent using simulation. However, recent advances in computer software and hardware (and user sophistication) lead us to believe that simulation may become more common in the future, particularly for large-scale projects.

Decision Trees

This section introduces the device of decision trees for identifying uncertain cash flows when capital budgeting decisions are sequential.

Imagine you are the treasurer of the Solar Electronics Corporation (SEC), and the engineering group has recently developed the technology for solar-powered jet engines. The marketing staff has proposed that SEC develop some prototypes and conduct test marketing of the engine. A corporate planning group, including representatives from production, marketing, and engineering, has recommended that the firm go ahead with the test and development phase. They estimate this preliminary phase would take a year and cost $100 million. Furthermore, the group believes there is a 75 percent chance that the reproduction and marketing tests could prove successful.

Based on the company's experience in the industry, it has a fairly accurate idea of how much the development and testing expenditures cost. Sales of jet engines, however, are subject to (1) uncertainty about the demand for air travel in the future, (2) uncertainty about future oil prices, (3) uncertainty about SEC's market share for engines, and (4) uncertainty about the demand for new planes. Items 2 and 4 are interrelated as future oil prices have a substantial impact on when airlines replace their existing, less-fuel-efficient fleets.

If the initial marketing tests are successful, SEC can acquire some land, build several new plants, and go ahead with full-scale production. This investment phase costs $1,500 million. Should SEC decide to go ahead with investment and production on the jet engine, the NPV at a discount rate of 15 percent is $1,517 million.

If the initial marketing tests are unsuccessful, SEC's $1,500 million investment has an NPV of −$3,611 million.

Figure 9.2 displays the problem concerning the jet engine as a decision tree. If SEC decides to conduct test marketing, there is a 75 percent probability that the test marketing will be successful. If the tests are successful, the firm faces a second decision: whether to invest $1,500 million in a project that yields $1,517 million NPV or to stop. If the tests are unsuccessful, the firm faces a different decision: whether to invest $1,500 million in a project that yields −$3,611 million NPV or to stop.

As can be seen from Figure 9.2, SEC has two decisions to make; whether to

1. Test and develop the solar-powered jet engine today.
2. Invest for full-scale production following the results of the test one year from now.

One makes decisions in reverse order with decision trees. Thus, we analyze the second-stage investment of $1,500 million first. If the tests are successful, it is

FIGURE 9.2

Decision tree (millions of dollars) for SEC. Open circles represent decision points, closed circles represent receipt of information

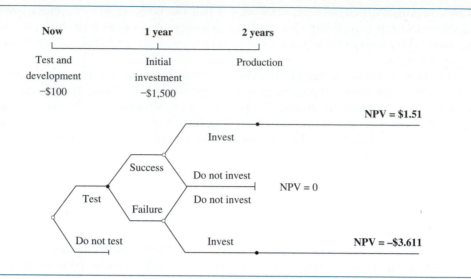

obvious that SEC should invest, because $1,517 million is greater than zero. Just as obviously, if the tests are unsuccessful, the SEC should not invest.

Now we move back to the first stage where the decision boils down to a simple question: Should SEC invest $100 million now to obtain a 75 percent chance of $1,517 million one year later? The expected payoff (in millions) evaluated at Date 1 is

$$\begin{matrix} \text{Expected} \\ \text{payoff} \end{matrix} = \begin{matrix} \text{Probability} \\ \text{of success} \end{matrix} \times \begin{matrix} \text{Payoff if} \\ \text{successful} \end{matrix} + \begin{matrix} \text{Probability} \\ \text{of failure} \end{matrix} \times \begin{matrix} \text{Payoff if} \\ \text{failure} \end{matrix}$$

$$= (0.75 \times \$1{,}517) + (0.25 \times \$0) = \$1{,}138$$

The NPV of testing computed at date zero (in millions) is

NPV = −$100 + $1,138/(1.15)

     = $890

Thus, the firm should test the market for solar-powered jet engines.[6]

| CONCEPT QUESTIONS

1. What are scenario, sensitivity, simulation, and decision tree analyses?

2. What are the drawbacks to the various types of what-if analysis?

9.3 | BREAK-EVEN ANALYSIS

It frequently turns out that the crucial variable for a project is sales volume. If we are thinking of a new product or entering a new market, for example, the hardest thing to forecast accurately is how much we can sell. For this reason, sales volume is usually analyzed more closely than other variables.

Break-even analysis is a popular and commonly used tool for analyzing the relationships between sales volume and profitability. There are a variety of different

---

[6] We have used a 15 percent discount rate for both decisions for simplification. In practice, a higher discount rate would be appropriate for the initial test marketing decision because it is riskier.

break-even measures, and we have already seen several types. All break-even measures have a similar goal. Loosely speaking, we are always asking: How bad do sales have to get before we actually begin to lose money? Implicitly, we are also asking: Is it likely that things will get that bad? To get started on this subject, we discuss fixed and variable costs.

Fixed and Variable Costs

In discussing break-even, the difference between fixed and variable costs becomes very important. As a result, we need to be a little more explicit about the difference than we have been so far.

Variable Costs   By definition, **variable costs** change as the quantity of output changes, and they are zero when production is zero. For example, direct labour costs and raw material costs are usually considered variable. This makes sense because, if we shut down operations tomorrow, there will be no future costs for labour or raw materials.

variable costs
Costs that change when the quantity of output changes.

We assume that variable costs are a constant amount per unit of output. This simply means that total variable cost is equal to the cost per unit multiplied by the number of units. In other words, the relationship between total variable cost *(VC)*, cost per unit of output *(v)*, and total quantity of output *(Q)* can be written simply as:

Variable cost = Total quantity of output × Cost per unit of output

$$VC = Q \times v$$

For example, suppose that v is \$2 per unit. If Q is 1,000 units, what will VC be?

$$VC = Q \times v$$
$$= \$1,000 \times \$2$$
$$= \$2,000$$

Similarly, if Q is 5,000 units, then VC is $5,000 \times \$2 = \$10,000$. Figure 9.3 illustrates the relationship between output level and variable costs in this case. In Figure 9.3, notice that increasing output by 1 unit results in variable costs rising by \$2, so the "rise over the run" (the slope of the line) is given by \$2/1 = \$2.

Fixed Costs   By definition, **fixed costs** do not change during a specified time period. So, unlike variable costs, they do not depend on the amount of goods or services produced during a period (at least within some range of production). For example, the lease payment on a production facility and the company president's salary are fixed costs, at least over some period.

fixed costs
Costs that do not change when the quantity of output changes during a particular time period.

Naturally, fixed costs are not fixed forever. They are fixed only during some particular time, say a quarter or a year. Beyond that time, leases can be terminated and executives retired. More to the point, any fixed cost can be modified or eliminated given enough time; so, in the long run, all costs are variable.

Notice that during the time that a cost is fixed, that cost is effectively a sunk cost because we are going to have to pay it no matter what.

Total Costs   Total costs *(TC)* for a given level of output are the sum of variable costs *(VC)* and fixed costs *(FC):*

$$TC = VC + FC$$
$$TC = v \times Q + FC$$

F I G U R E 9.3

Output level and variable costs

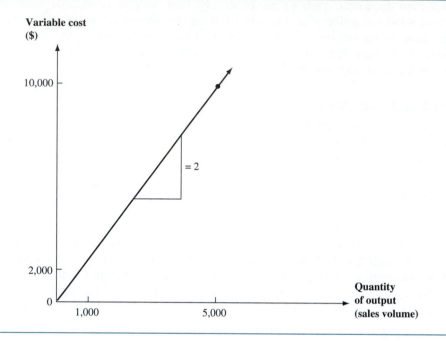

So, for example, if we have a variable cost of $3 per unit and fixed costs of $8,000 per year, our total cost is:

$$TC = \$3 \times Q + \$8,000$$

If we produce 6,000 units, our total production cost would be $3 × 6,000 + $8,000 = $26,000. At other production levels, we have:

Quantity Produced	Total Variable Cost	Fixed Costs	Total Cost
0	$ 0	$8,000	$ 8,000
1,000	3,000	8,000	11,000
5,000	15,000	8,000	23,000
10,000	30,000	8,000	38,000

marginal or incremental cost
The change in costs that occurs when there is a small change in output.

By plotting these points in Figure 9.4, we see that the relationship between quantity produced and total cost is given by a straight line. In Figure 9.4, notice that total costs are equal to fixed costs when sales are zero. Beyond that point, every one-unit increase in production leads to a $3 increase in total costs, so the slope of the line is 3. In other words, the **marginal** or **incremental cost** of producing one more unit is $3.

Accounting Break-Even

accounting break-even
The sales level that results in zero project net income.

The most widely used measure of break-even is **accounting break-even**. The accounting break-even point is simply the sales level that results in a zero project net income.

To determine a project's accounting break-even, we start with some common sense. Suppose we retail computer diskettes for $5 apiece. We can buy diskettes from a wholesale supplier for $3 apiece. We have accounting expenses of $600 in fixed

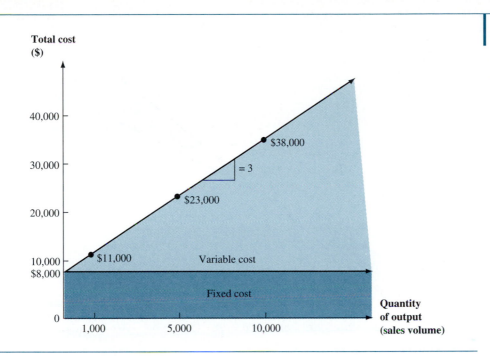

FIGURE 9.4

Output level and total costs

costs and $300 in depreciation. How many diskettes do we have to sell to break even, that is, for net income to be zero?

For every diskette we sell, we pick up $5 − 3 = $2 toward covering our other expenses. We have to cover a total of $600 + 300 = $900 in accounting expenses, so we obviously need to sell $900/$2 = 450 diskettes. We can check this by noting that, at a sales level of 450 units, our revenues are $5 × 450 = $2,250 and our variable costs are $3 × 450 = $1,350. The income statement is thus:

Sales	$2,250
Variable costs	1,350
Fixed costs	600
Depreciation	300
EBIT	$ 0
Taxes	$ 0
Net income	$ 0

Remember, since we are discussing a proposed new project, we do not consider any interest expense in calculating net income or cash flow from the project. Also, notice that we include depreciation in calculating expenses here, even though depreciation is not a cash outflow. That is why we call it accounting break-even. Finally, notice that when net income is zero, so are pretax income and, of course, taxes. In accounting terms, our revenues are equal to our costs, so there is no profit to tax.

Figure 9.5 is another way to see what is happening. This figure looks like Figure 9.4 except that we add a line for revenues. As indicated, total revenues are zero when output is zero. Beyond that, each unit sold brings in another $5, so the slope of the revenue line is 5.

From our preceding discussion, we break even when revenues are equal to total costs. The line for revenues and the line for total cost cross right where output is 450

FIGURE 9.5

Accounting break-even

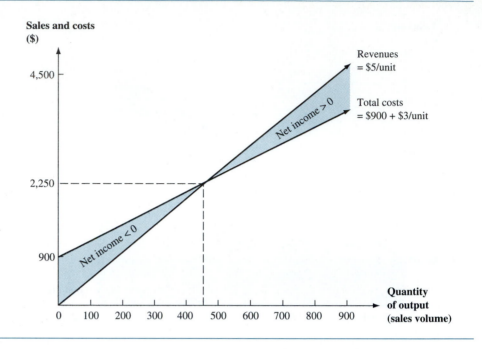

units. As illustrated, at any level below 450, our accounting profit is negative and, at any level above 450, we have a positive net income.

Accounting Break-Even: A Closer Look

In our numerical example, notice that the break-even level is equal to the sum of fixed costs and depreciation divided by price per unit less variable costs per unit. This is always true. To see why, we recall the following set of abbreviations for the different variables:

P = Selling price per unit
v = Variable cost per unit
Q = Total units sold
FC = Fixed costs
D = Depreciation
t = Tax rate
VC = Variable cost in dollars

Project net income is given by:

$$\text{Net income} = (\text{Sales} - \text{Variable costs} - \text{Fixed costs} - \text{Depreciation}) \times (1 - t)$$

$$= (S - VC - FC - D) \times (1 - t)$$

From here, it is not difficult to calculate the break-even point. If we set this net income equal to zero, we get:

$$\text{Net income} = 0 = (S - VC - FC - D) \times (1 - t)$$

Divide both sides by $(1 - t)$ to get:

$$S - VC - FC - D = 0$$

As we have seen, this says, when net income is zero, so is pretax income. If we recall that $S = P \times Q$ and $VC = v \times Q$, we can rearrange this to solve for the break-even level:

$$S - VC = FC + D$$
$$P \times Q - v \times Q = FC + D \quad\quad\quad [9.1]$$
$$(P - v) \times Q = FC + D$$
$$Q = (FC + D)/(P - v)$$

This is the same result we described earlier.

Uses for the Accounting Break-Even

Why would anyone be interested in knowing the accounting break-even point? To illustrate how it can be useful, suppose we are a small specialty ice cream manufacturer in Vancouver with a strictly local distribution. We are thinking about expanding into new markets. Based on the estimated cash flow, we find that the expansion has a positive NPV.

Going back to our discussion of forecasting risk, it is likely that what makes or breaks our expansion is sales volume. The reason is that, in this case at least, we probably have a fairly good idea of what we can charge for the ice cream. Further, we know relevant production and distribution costs with a fair degree of accuracy because we are already in the business. What we do not know with any real precision is how much ice cream we can sell.

Given the costs and selling price, however, we can immediately calculate the break-even point. Once we have done so, we might find that we need to get 30 percent of the market just to break even. If we think that this is unlikely to occur because, for example, we only have 10 percent of our current market, we know that our forecast is questionable and there is a real possibility that the true NPV is negative.

On the other hand, we might find that we already have firm commitments from buyers for about the break-even amount, so we are almost certain that we can sell more. Because the forecasting risk is much lower, we have greater confidence in our estimates. If we need outside financing for our expansion, this break-even analysis would be useful in presenting our proposal to our banker.

There are several other reasons why knowing the accounting break-even can be useful. First, managers are often concerned with the contribution a project will make to the firm's total accounting earnings. A project that does not break even in an accounting sense actually reduces total earnings.

Second, a project that just breaks even on an accounting basis loses money in a financial or opportunity cost sense. This is true because we could have earned more by investing elsewhere. Such a project does not lose money in an out-of-pocket sense. As described later, we get back exactly what we put in. For non-economic reasons, such opportunity losses may be easier to live with than out-of-pocket losses.

Complications in Applying Break-Even Analysis   Our discussion ignored several complications you may encounter in applying this useful tool. To begin, it is only in the short run that revenues and variable costs fall along straight lines. For large increases in sales, price may decrease with volume discounts while variable costs increase as production runs up against capacity limits. If you have sufficient data, you can redraw cost and revenue as curves. Otherwise, remember that the analysis is most accurate in the short run.

Further, while our examples classified costs as fixed or variable, in practice some costs are semivariable (i.e., partly fixed and partly variable). A common example is telephone expense, which breaks down into a fixed charge plus a variable cost depending on the volume of calls. In applying break-even analysis, you have to make judgments on the breakdown.

> CONCEPT QUESTIONS
> **1.** How are fixed costs similar to sunk costs?
> **2.** What is net income at the accounting break-even point? What about taxes?
> **3.** Why might a financial manager be interested in the accounting break-even point?

9.4 | OPERATING CASH FLOW, SALES VOLUME, AND BREAK-EVEN

Accounting break-even is one tool that is useful for project analysis. Ultimately, however, we are more interested in cash flow than accounting income. So, for example, if sales volume is the critical variable, we need to know more about the relationship between sales volume and cash flow than just the accounting break-even.

Our goal in this section is to illustrate the relationship between operating cash flow and sales volume. We also discuss some other break-even measures. To simplify matters somewhat, we ignore the effect of taxes.[7] We start by looking at the relationship between accounting break-even and cash flow.

Accounting Break-Even and Cash Flow

Now that we know how to find the accounting break-even, it is natural to wonder what happens with cash flow. To illustrate, suppose that Victoria Sailboats Limited is considering whether to launch its new Mona-class sailboat. The selling price would be $40,000 per boat. The variable costs would be about half that, or $20,000 per boat, and fixed costs will be $500,000 per year.

The Base Case   The total investment needed to undertake the project is $3.5 million for leasehold improvements to the company's factory. This amount will be depreciated straight-line to zero over the five-year life of the equipment. The salvage value is zero, and there are no working capital consequences. Victoria has a 20 percent required return on new projects.

Based on market surveys and historical experience, Victoria projects total sales for the five years at 425 boats, or about 85 boats per year. Should this project be launched?

---

[7] This is a minor simplification because the firm pays no taxes when it just breaks even in the accounting sense. We also use straight-line depreciation, realistic in this case for leasehold improvements, for simplicity.

To begin (ignoring taxes), the operating cash flow at 85 boats per year is:

$$
\begin{aligned}
\text{Operating cash flow} &= \text{EBIT} + \text{Depreciation} - \text{Taxes} \\
&= (S - VC - FC - D) + D - 0 \\
&= 85 \times (\$40{,}000 - 20{,}000) - \$500{,}000 \\
&= \$1{,}200{,}000 \text{ per year}
\end{aligned}
$$

At 20 percent, the five-year annuity factor is 2.9906, so the NPV is:

$$
\begin{aligned}
\text{NPV} &= -\$3{,}500{,}000 + 1{,}200{,}000 \times 2.9906 \\
&= -\$3{,}500{,}000 + 3{,}588{,}720 \\
&= \$88{,}720
\end{aligned}
$$

In the absence of additional information, the project should be launched.

Calculating the Accounting Break-Even Level   To begin looking a little more closely at this project, you might ask a series of questions. For example, how many new boats does Victoria need to sell for the project to break even on an accounting basis? If Victoria does break even, what would be the annual cash flow from the project? What would be the return on the investment?

Before fixed costs and depreciation are considered, Victoria generates $40,000 − 20,000 = $20,000 per boat (this is revenue less variable cost). Depreciation is $3,500,000/5 = $700,000 per year. Fixed costs and depreciation together total $1.2 million, so Victoria needs to sell $(FC + D)/(P − v) = \$1.2$ million/$20,000 = 60 boats per year to break even on an accounting basis. This is 25 boats less than projected sales; so, assuming that Victoria is confident that its projection is accurate to within, say, 15 boats, it appears unlikely that the new investment will fail to at least break even on an accounting basis.

To calculate Victoria's cash flow, we note that if 60 boats are sold, net income is exactly zero. Recalling from our previous chapter that operating cash flow for a project can be written as net income plus depreciation (the bottom-up definition), the operating cash flow is obviously equal to the depreciation, or $700,000 in this case. The internal rate of return would be exactly zero (why?).

The bad news is that a project that just breaks even on an accounting basis has a negative NPV and a zero return. For our sailboat project, the fact that we would almost surely break even on an accounting basis is partially comforting since our downside risk (our potential loss) is limited, but we still don't know if the project is truly profitable. More work is needed.

Sales Volume and Operating Cash Flow

At this point, we can generalize our example and introduce some other break-even measures. As we just discussed, we know that, ignoring taxes, a project's operating cash flow (OCF) can be written simply as EBIT plus depreciation:

$$
\begin{aligned}
\text{OCF} &= [(P - v) \times Q - FC - D] + D \\
&= (P - v) \times Q - FC
\end{aligned}
\tag{9.2}
$$

For the Victoria Sailboats project, the general relationship (in thousands of dollars) between operating cash flow and sales volume is thus:

$$OCF = (P - v) \times Q - FC$$
$$= (\$40 - 20) \times Q - \$500$$
$$= -\$500 + \$20 \times Q$$

What this tells us is that the relationship between operating cash flow and sales volume is given by a straight line with a slope of $20 and a *y*-intercept of −$500. If we calculate some different values, we get:

Quantity Sold	Operating Cash Flow
0	−$ 500
15	−200
30	100
50	500
75	1,000

These points are plotted in Figure 9.6. In Figure 9.6, we have indicated three different break-even points. We already covered the accounting break-even. We discuss the other two next.

Cash Flow and Financial Break-Even Points

We know that the relationship between operating cash flow and sales volume (ignoring taxes) is:

$$OCF = (P - v) \times Q - FC$$

If we rearrange this and solve it for *Q*, we get:

$$Q = (FC + OCF)/(P - v) \qquad\qquad [9.3]$$

F I G U R E 9.6

*Operating cash flow
and sales volume*

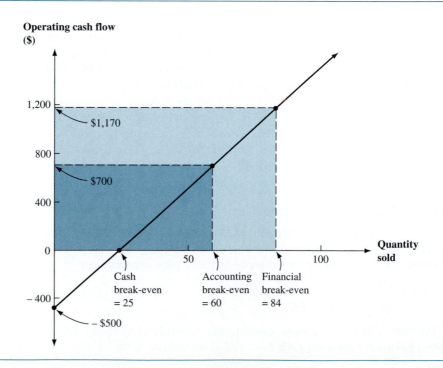

This tells us what sales volume *(Q)* is necessary to achieve any given OCF, so this result is more general than the accounting break-even. We use it to find the various break-even points in Figure 9.6.

Cash Break-Even   We have seen that our sailboat project that breaks even on an accounting basis has a net income of zero, but it still has a positive cash flow. At some sales level below the accounting break-even, the operating cash flow actually goes negative. This is a particularly unpleasant occurrence. If it happens, we actually have to supply additional cash to the project just to keep it afloat.

To calculate the **cash break-even** (the point where operating cash flow is equal to zero), we put in a zero for OCF:

$$Q = (FC + 0)/(P - v)$$
$$= \$500/\$20$$
$$= 25$$

cash break-even
The sales level where operating cash flow is equal to zero.

Victoria must therefore sell 25 boats to cover the $500 in fixed costs. As we show in Figure 9.6, this point occurs right where the operating cash flow line crosses the horizontal axis.

In this example, cash break-even is lower than accounting break-even. Equation 9.3 shows why; when we calculated accounting break-even we substituted depreciation of $700 for OCF. The formula for cash break-even sets OCF equal to zero. Figure 9.6 shows that accounting break-even is 60 boats and cash break-even, 25 boats. Accounting break-even is 35 boats higher. Since Victoria generates a $20,000 contribution per boat, the difference exactly covers the depreciation of $700 = 35 × $20.

This analysis also shows that cash break-even does not always have to be lower than accounting break-even. To see why, suppose Victoria had to make a cash outlay in Year 1 of $1 million for working capital. Accounting break-even remains at 60 boats. The new cash break-even (in thousands) is 75 boats:

$$Q = (FC + OCF)/(P - v)$$
$$= (\$500 + 1,000)/(\$20)$$
$$= 75$$

In general, retail firms and other companies that experience substantial needs for working capital relative to depreciation expenses have cash break-evens greater than accounting break-evens.

Regardless of whether the cash break-even point is more or less than the accounting break-even, a project that just breaks even on a cash flow basis can cover its own fixed operating costs, but that is all. It never pays back anything, so the original investment is a complete loss (the IRR is −100 percent).

Financial Break-Even   The last case we consider is **financial break-even**, the sales level that results in a zero NPV. To the financial manager, this is the most interesting case. What we do is first determine what operating cash flow has to be for the NPV to be zero. We then use this amount to determine the sales volume.

financial break-even
The sales level that results in a zero NPV.

To illustrate, recall that Victoria requires a 20 percent return on its $3,500 (in thousands) investment. How many sailboats does Victoria have to sell to break even once we account for the 20 percent per year opportunity cost?

The sailboat project has a five-year life. The project has a zero NPV when the present value of the operating cash flow equals the $3,500 investment. Since the cash flow is the same each year, we can solve for the unknown amount by viewing it as an ordinary annuity. The five-year annuity factor at 20 percent is 2.9906, and the OCF can be determined as follows:

$$\$3,500 = OCF \times 2.9906$$
$$OCF = \$3,500/2.9906$$
$$= \$1,170$$

Victoria thus needs an operating cash flow of $1,170 each year to break even. We can now plug this OCF into the equation for sales volume:

$$Q = (\$500 + \$1,170)/\$20$$
$$= 83.5$$

So Victoria needs to sell about 84 boats per year. This is not good news.

As indicated in Figure 9.6, the financial break-even is substantially higher than the accounting break-even point. This is often the case. Moreover, what we have discovered is that the sailboat project has a substantial degree of forecasting risk. We project sales of 85 boats per year, but it takes 84 just to earn our required return.

Overall, it seems unlikely that the Victoria Sailboats project would fail to break even on an accounting basis. However, there appears to be a very good chance that the true NPV is negative. This illustrates the danger in just looking at the accounting break-even.

Victoria can learn this lesson from the U.S. government. In the early 1970s, the U.S. Congress voted a guarantee for Lockheed Corporation, the airplane manufacturer, based on analysis that showed the L1011-TriStar would break even on an accounting basis. It subsequently turned out that the financial break-even point was much higher.

What should Victoria Sailboats do? Is the new project all wet? The decision at this point is essentially a managerial issue—a judgment call. The crucial questions are:

1. How much confidence do we have in our projections?
2. How important is the project to the future of the company?
3. How badly will the company be hurt if sales do turn out low?

What options are available to the company?

We consider questions such as these in a later section. For future reference, our discussion of different break-even measures is summarized in Table 9.1.

CONCEPT QUESTIONS

1. If a project breaks even on an accounting basis, what is its operating cash flow?
2. If a project breaks even on a cash basis, what is its operating cash flow?
3. If a project breaks even on a financial basis, what do you know about its discounted payback?

9.5 | OPERATING LEVERAGE

We have discussed how to calculate and interpret various measures of break-even for a proposed project. What we have not explicitly discussed is what determines these points and how they might be changed. We now turn to this subject.

The general expression. Ignoring taxes, the relation between operating cash flow (OCF) and quantity of output or sales volume (Q) is

$$Q = \frac{FC + OCF}{P - v}$$

where

$\qquad FC$ = Total fixed costs

$\qquad P$ = Price per unit

$\qquad v$ = Variable cost per unit

As shown next, this relation can be used to determine the accounting, cash, and financial break-even points.

The accounting break-even point. Accounting break-even occurs when net income is zero. Operating cash flow (OCF) is equal to depreciation when net income is zero, so the accounting break-even point is:

$$Q = \frac{FC + D}{P - v}$$

A project that always just breaks even on an accounting basis has a payback exactly equal to its life, a negative NPV, and an IRR of zero.

The cash break-even point. Cash break-even occurs when operating cash flow (OCF) is zero; the cash break-even point is thus:

$$Q = \frac{FC}{P - v}$$

A project that always just breaks even on a cash basis never pays back, its NPV is negative and equal to the initial outlay, and the IRR is −100%.

The financial break-even point. Financial break-even occurs when the NPV of the project is zero. The financial break-even point is thus:

$$Q = \frac{FC + OCF^*}{P - v}$$

where OCF* is the level of OCF that results in a zero NPV. A project that breaks even on a financial basis has a discounted payback equal to its life, a zero NPV, and an IRR just equal to the required return.

T A B L E   9.1

Summary of break-even measures

The Basic Idea

Operating leverage is the degree to which a project or firm is committed to fixed production costs. A firm with low operating leverage has low fixed costs (as a proportion of total costs) compared to a firm with high operating leverage. Generally, projects with a relatively heavy investment in plant and equipment have a relatively high degree of operating leverage. Such projects are said to be capital intensive.

Any time we are thinking about a new venture, there are normally alternative ways of producing and delivering the product. For example, Victoria Sailboats can purchase the necessary equipment and build all the components for its sailboats in-house. Alternatively, some of the work could be farmed out to other firms. The first option involves a greater investment in plant and equipment, greater fixed costs and depreciation, and, as a result, a higher degree of operating leverage.

operating leverage
The degree to which a firm or project relies on fixed costs.

Implications of Operating Leverage

Regardless of how it is measured, operating leverage has important implications for project evaluation. Fixed costs act like a lever in the sense that a small percentage change in operating revenue can be magnified into a large percentage change in operating cash flow and NPV. This explains why we call it operating leverage.

The higher the degree of operating leverage, the greater is the potential danger from forecasting risk. The reason is that relatively small errors in forecasting sales volume can get magnified or "levered up" into large errors in cash flow projections.

From a managerial perspective, one way of coping with highly uncertain projects is to keep the degree of operating leverage as low as possible. This generally has the effect of keeping the break-even point (however measured) at its minimum level. We illustrate this point after discussing how to measure operating leverage.

Measuring Operating Leverage

One way of measuring operating leverage is to ask: If the quantity sold rises by 5 percent, what will be the percentage change in operating cash flow? In other words, the **degree of operating leverage** (DOL) is defined such that

degree of operating leverage
The percentage change in operating cash flow relative to the percentage change in quantity sold.

$$\text{Percentage change in OCF} = \text{DOL} \times \text{Percentage change in } Q$$

Based on the relationship between OCF and Q, DOL can be written as:[8]

$$\text{DOL} = 1 + FC/\text{OCF}$$

The ratio FC/OCF simply measures fixed costs as a percentage of total operating cash flow. Notice that zero fixed costs would result in a DOL of 1, implying that changes in quantity sold would show up one for one in operating cash flow. In other words, no magnification or leverage effect would exist.

To illustrate this measure of operating leverage, we go back to the Victoria Sailboats project. Fixed costs were $500 and $(P - v)$ was $20, so OCF was:

$$\text{OCF} = -\$500 + 20 \times Q$$

Suppose Q is currently 50 boats. At this level of output, OCF is $-\$500 + 1,000 = \$500$.

If Q rises by 1 unit to 51, then the percentage change in Q is $(51 - 50)/50 = .02$, or 2%. OCF rises to $520, a change of $(P - v) = \$20$. The percentage change in OCF is $(\$520 - 500)/500 = .04$, or 4%. So a 2 percent increase in the number of boats sold leads to a 4 percent increase in operating cash flow. The degree of operating leverage must be exactly 2.00. We can check this by noting that:

$$\begin{aligned} \text{DOL} &= 1 + FC/\text{OCF} \\ &= 1 + \$500/\$500 \\ &= 2 \end{aligned}$$

This verifies our previous calculations.

Our formulation of DOL depends on the current output level, Q. However, it can handle changes from the current level of any size, not just one unit. For example, suppose Q rises from 50 to 75, a 50 percent increase. With DOL equal to 2, operating cash flow should increase by 100 percent, or exactly double. Does it? The answer is yes, because, at a Q of 75, OCF is:

---

[8] To see this, note that, if Q goes up by 1 unit, OCF goes up by $(P - v)$. The percentage change in Q is $1/Q$, and the percentage change in OCF is $(P - v)/\text{OCF}$. Given this, we have:

$$\text{Percentage change in OCF} = \text{DOL} \times \text{Percentage change in } Q$$
$$(P - v)/\text{OCF} = \text{DOL} \times 1/Q$$
$$\text{DOL} = (P - v) \times Q/\text{OCF}$$

Also, based on our definition of OCF:

$$\text{OCF} + FC = (P - v) \times q$$

Thus, DOL can be written as:

$$\begin{aligned} \text{DOL} &= (\text{OCF} + FC)/\text{OCF} \\ &= 1 + FC/\text{OCF} \end{aligned}$$

$$-\$500 + \$20 \times 75 = \$1,000$$

Notice that operating leverage declines as output *(Q)* rises. For example, at an output level of 75, we have:

$$DOL = 1 + \$500/1,000$$
$$= 1.50$$

The reason DOL declines is that fixed costs, considered as a percentage of operating cash flow, get smaller and smaller, so the leverage effect diminishes.[9]

What do you think DOL works out to at the cash break-even point, an output level of 25 boats? At the cash break-even point, OCF is zero. Since you cannot divide by zero, DOL is undefined.

E X A M P L E | 9.1   Operating Leverage

The Huskies Corporation currently sells gourmet dog food for $1.20 per can. The variable cost is 80 cents per can, and the packaging and marketing operation has fixed costs of $360,000 per year. Depreciation is $60,000 per year. What is the accounting break-even? Ignoring taxes, what will be the increase in operating cash flow if the quantity sold rises to 10 percent more than the break-even point?

The accounting break-even is $420,000/.40 = 1,050,000 cans. As we know, the operating cash flow is equal to the $60,000 depreciation at this level of production, so the degree of operating leverage is:

$$DOL = 1 + FC/OCF$$
$$= 1 + \$360,000/\$60,000$$
$$= 7$$

Given this, a 10 percent increase in the number of cans of dog food sold increases operating cash flow by a substantial 70 percent.

To check this answer, we note that if sales rise by 10 percent, the quantity sold rises to 1,050,000 × 1.1 = 1,555,000. Ignoring taxes, the operating cash flow is 1,155,000 × .40 − $360,000 = $102,000. Compared to the $60,000 cash flow we had, this is exactly 70 percent more: $102,000/60,000 = 1.70. ▌

Operating Leverage and Break-Even

We illustrate why operating leverage is an important consideration by examining the Victoria Sailboats project under an alternative scenario. At a *Q* of 85 boats, the degree of operating leverage for the sailboat project under the original scenario is:

$$DOL = 1 + FC/OCF$$
$$= 1 + \$500/1,200$$
$$= 1.42$$

Also, recall that the NPV at a sales level of 85 boats was $88,720, and that the accounting break-even was 60 boats.

An option available to Victoria is to subcontract production of the boat hull assemblies. If it does, the necessary investment falls to $3.2 million, and the fixed

---

[9] Students who have studied economics will recognize DOL as an elasticity. Recall that elasticities vary with quantity along demand and supply curves. For the same reason, DOL varies with unit sales, *Q*.

operating costs fall to $180,000. However, variable costs rise to $25,000 per boat since subcontracting is more expensive than doing it in-house. Ignoring taxes, evaluate this option.

For practice, see if you don't agree with the following:

$$\text{NPV at 20\% (85 units)} = \$74,720$$
$$\text{Accounting break-even} = 55 \text{ boats}$$
$$\text{Degree of operating leverage} = 1.16$$

What has happened? This option results in slightly lower estimated net present value, and the accounting break-even point falls to 55 boats from 60 boats.

Given that this alternative has the lower NPV, is there any reason to consider it further? Maybe there is. The degree of operating leverage is substantially lower in the second case. If we are worried about the possibility of an overly optimistic projection, we might prefer to subcontract.

There is another reason we might consider the second arrangement. If sales turned out better than expected, we always have the option of starting to produce in-house later. As a practical matter, it is much easier to increase operating leverage (by purchasing equipment) than to decrease it (by selling equipment).[10] As we discuss later, one of the drawbacks to discounted cash flow is that it is difficult to explicitly include options of this sort, even though they may be quite important.

Complications in Applying Operating Leverage   As in our discussion of the break-even point, we ignore taxes. In practice, however, taxes are not zero above the accounting break-even point. The most common approach is to continue to ignore taxes and use the same formula. This is perfectly correct as long as you recognize that DOL has the same interpretation but is defined slightly differently. Our definition of operating leverage is the percentage change in operating cash flow for a percentage change in unit sales.

$$\text{DOL} = 1 + FC/\text{OCF}$$
$$= (\text{OCF} + FC)/\text{OCF}$$

From Equation 9.2 we have the definition of OCF:

$$\text{OCF} = (P - v) \times Q - FC$$

If we ignore depreciation along with taxes, OCF and EBIT are identical. So DOL becomes percentage change in EBIT for a percentage change in unit sales.[11] This modified definition focusses on EBIT and so is not affected by taxes.[12]

---

[10] In the extreme case, if firms were able to readjust the ratio of variable and fixed costs continually, there would be no increased risk associated with greater operating leverage.

[11] To prove this, we substitute for OCF:

$$\text{DOL} = \frac{(P - v) \times Q}{(P - v) \times Q - FC}$$

This last expression is simply the formula for DOL that you may come across in other texts, percentage change in EBIT divided by percentage change in sales. Assume that sales increase by 1 unit so: $Q_2 - Q_1 = 1$.

$$\frac{(\text{EBIT}_2 - \text{EBIT}_1)/\text{EBIT}_1}{(Q_2 P - Q_1 P)/Q_1 P} = \frac{[(P - v)Q_2 - FC - (P - v)Q_1 - FC]/\text{EBIT}_1}{1/Q}$$

$$(P - v)Q_1/\text{EBIT}_1 = \frac{(P - v)Q_1}{(P - v)Q_1 - FC}$$

[12] An alternative, less commonly used approach is to redefine the break-even and DOL formulas to take taxes into account. Problems 27 and 28 at the end of the chapter show the aftertax formulas.

CONCEPT QUESTIONS
1. What is operating leverage?
2. How is operating leverage measured?
3. What are the implications of operating leverage for the financial manager?

9.6 | ADDITIONAL CONSIDERATIONS IN CAPITAL BUDGETING

Our final task for this chapter is a brief discussion of two additional considerations in capital budgeting: managerial options and capital rationing. Both of these can be very important in practice, but, as we will see, explicitly dealing with either of them is difficult.

Managerial Options and Capital Budgeting

In our capital budgeting analysis thus far, we have more or less ignored the possibility of future managerial actions. Implicitly, we assumed that once a project is launched, its basic features cannot be changed. For this reason, we say that our analysis is static (as opposed to dynamic).

In reality, depending on what actually happens in the future, there are always ways to modify a project. We call these opportunities **managerial options**. There are a great number of these options. The way a product is priced, manufactured, advertised, and produced can all be changed, and these are just a few of the possibilities. We discuss some of the most important ones in the next few sections.

managerial options
Opportunities that managers can exploit if certain things happen in the future.

Contingency Planning   The various what-if procedures, particularly the break-even measures, in this chapter have another use. We can also view them as primitive ways of exploring the dynamics of a project and investigating managerial options. What we think about are some of the possible futures that could come about and what actions we might take if they do.

For example, we might find that a project fails to break even when sales drop below 10,000 units. This is a fact that is interesting to know, but the more important thing is to go on and ask: What actions are we going to take if this actually occurs? This is called **contingency planning**, and it amounts to an investigation of some of the managerial options implicit in a project.

There is no limit to the number of possible futures or contingencies that we could investigate. However, there are some broad classes, and we consider these next.

contingency planning
Taking into account the managerial options that are implicit in a project.

The Option to Expand   One particularly important option that we have not explicitly addressed is the option to expand. If we truly find a positive NPV project, there is an obvious consideration. Can we expand the project or repeat it to get an even larger NPV? Our static analysis implicitly assumes that the scale of the project is fixed.

For example, if the sales demand for a particular product were to greatly exceed expectations, we might investigate increasing production. If this is not feasible for some reason, we could always increase cash flow by raising the price. Either way, the potential cash flow is higher than we have indicated because we have implicitly assumed that no expansion or price increase is possible. Overall, because we ignore the option to expand in our analysis, we underestimate NPV (all other things being equal).

The Option to Abandon   At the other extreme, the option to scale back or even abandon a project is also quite valuable. For example, if a project does not break even on a cash flow basis, it can't even cover its own expenses. We would be better off if we just abandoned it. Our DCF analysis implicitly assumes that we would keep operating even in this case.

In reality, if sales demand were significantly below expectations, we might be able to sell some capacity or put it to another use. Maybe the product or service could be redesigned or otherwise improved. Regardless of the specifics, we once again underestimate NPV if we assume the project must last for some fixed number of years, no matter what happens in the future.

Take the case of Solar Electronics Corporation discussed earlier in the chapter. It was assumed that after making the initial investment to produce solar engines and confronted with low demand, SEC would lose money. The pessimistic worst-case scenario leads to an NPV of −$3,611 million. This is an unlikely eventuality. Instead, it is more plausible to assume that SEC would try to sell its initial investment— patents, land, buildings, machinery, and prototypes—for $1,000 million. For example, faced with low demand, suppose SEC could scrap the initial investment. In this case, it would lose $500 million of the original investment. This is much better than what would happen if it produced the solar jet engines and generated a negative NPV of $3,611 million.

Corporations frequently make changes in their plans when confronted with changing market conditions. One of the most stunning flip-flops in marketing history occurred when the Coca-Cola Company publicly apologized for scrapping old Coke, a 99-year-old product. Henceforth, the company said, the old Coca-Cola would be revived as Coca-Cola Classic. By reviving the old Coke, the Coca-Cola Company undid an abandonment decision that had taken four-and-one-half years of planning and market research. Coke's original plan to abandon the old Coke and to replace it with new Coke was intended to break what for several years had been Pepsi's biggest advantage in the market: its ability to win taste contests. However, Coca-Cola's decision after two months to revive the old Coke came because of the unwillingness of a large number of consumers to go along with idea of a new Coke.

The Option to Wait   Implicitly, we have treated proposed investments as if they were go or no-go decisions. Actually, there is a third possibility. The project can be postponed, perhaps in hope of more favourable conditions. We call this the option to wait.

For example, suppose an investment costs $120 and has a perpetual cash flow of $10 per year. If the discount rate is 10 percent, the NPV is $10/.10 − 120 = −$20, so the project should not be undertaken now. However, this does not mean we should forget about the project forever, because in the next period, the appropriate discount rate could be different. If it fell to, say, 5 percent, the NPV would be $10/.05 − 120 = $80, and we would take it.

More generally, as long as there is some possible future scenario under which a project has a positive NPV, the option to wait is valuable.

The Tax Option   Investment decisions may trigger favourable or unfavourable tax treatment of existing assets. This can occur because, as you recall from Chapter 2, capital cost allowance calculations are based on assets in a pooled class. Tax liabilities for recaptured CCA and tax shelters from terminal losses occur only when an asset class is liquidated either by selling all the assets or writing the undepreciated capital cost below zero. As a result, management has a potentially valuable tax option.

For example, suppose your firm is planning to replace all its company delivery vans at the end of the year. Because of unfavourable conditions in the used vehicle market, prices are depressed and you expect to realize a loss. Since you are replacing the vehicles, as opposed to closing out the class, no immediate tax shelter results from the loss. If your company is profitable and the potential tax shelter sizable, you could exercise your tax option by closing out Class 10. To do this, you could lease the new vehicles or set up a separate firm to purchase the vehicles.

Options in Capital Budgeting: An Example   Suppose we are examining a new project. To keep things relatively simple, we expect to sell 100 units per year at $1 net cash flow apiece into perpetuity. We thus expect the cash flow to be $100 per year.

In one year, we will know more about the project. In particular, we will have a better idea of whether it is successful or not. If it looks like a long-run success, the expected sales could be revised upward to 150 units per year. If it does not, the expected sales could be revised downward to 50 units per year.

Success and failure are equally likely. Notice that with an even chance of selling 50 or 150 units, the expected sales are still 100 units as we originally projected.

The cost is $550, and the discount rate is 20 percent. The project can be dismantled and sold in one year for $400, if we decide to abandon it. Should we take it?

A standard DCF analysis is not difficult. The expected cash flow is $100 per year forever and the discount rate is 20 percent. The PV of the cash flows is $100/.20 = $500, so the NPV is $500 − 550 = −$50. We shouldn't take it.

This analysis is static, however. In one year, we can sell out for $400. How can we account for this? What we have to do is to decide what we are going to do one year from now. In this simple case, there are only two contingencies that we need to evaluate, an upward revision and a downward revision, so the extra work is not great.

In one year, if the expected cash flows are revised to $50, the PV of the cash flows is revised downward to $50/.20 = $250. We get $400 by abandoning the project, so that is what we will do (the NPV of keeping the project in one year is $250 − 400 = −$150).

If the demand is revised upward, the PV of the future cash flows at Year 1 is $150/.20 = $750. This exceeds the $400 abandonment value, so we would keep the project.

We now have a project that costs $550 today. In one year, we expect a cash flow of $100 from the project. In addition, this project would either be worth $400 (if we abandon it because it is a failure) or $750 (if we keep it because it succeeds). These outcomes are equally likely, so we expect it to be worth ($400 + 750)/2, or $575.

Summing up, in one year, we expect to have $100 in cash plus a project worth $575, or $675 total. At a 20 percent discount rate, this $675 is worth $562.50 today, so the NPV is $562.50 − 50 = $12.50. We should take it.

The NPV of our project has increased by $62.50. Where did this come from? Our original analysis implicitly assumed we would keep the project even if it was a failure. At Year 1, however, we saw that we were $150 better off ($400 versus $250) if we abandoned. There was a 50 percent chance of this happening, so the expected gain from abandoning is $75. The PV of the amount is the value of the option to abandon, $75/1.20 = $62.50.

Strategic Options   Companies sometimes undertake new projects just to explore possibilities and evaluate potential future business strategies. This is a little like testing the water by sticking a toe in before diving. When McDonald's of Canada decided to open a restaurant in Moscow, strategic considerations likely dominated immediate cash flow analysis.

Because the Russian ruble is not convertible, dollars were invested but no profits can be taken out in the foreseeable future. McDonald's strategic view is based on obtaining a potentially valuable option to spread its Golden Arches across the Commonwealth of Independent States from St. Petersburg to Vladivostok. In the words of McDonald's Canada executive, Ron Cohen:

> If you are going to begin doing business in a country and you're looking at the long term, the last thing you want to do is offend the very people that you're there to serve. So our idea was "let's open up a ruble restaurant to serve Soviets first" because that's what they want. What we want might be to generate hard currency, but we can take care of that later on.[13]

strategic options

Options for future, related business products or strategies.

Such projects are difficult to analyze using conventional DCF because most of the benefits come in the form of **strategic options**, that is, options for future, related business moves. Projects that create such options may be very valuable, but that value is difficult to measure. Research and development, for example, is an important and valuable activity for many firms precisely because it creates options for new products and procedures.

To give another example, a large manufacturer might decide to open a retail outlet as a pilot study. The primary goal is to gain some market insight. Because of the high start-up costs, this one operation won't break even. However, based on the sales experience from the pilot, we can then evaluate whether or not to open more outlets, to change the product mix, to enter new markets, and so on. The information gained and the resulting options for actions are all valuable, but coming up with a reliable dollar figure is probably not feasible.

We have seen that incorporating options into capital budgeting analysis is not easy. What can we do about them in practice? The answer is that we can only keep them in the back of our minds as we work with the projected cash flows. We tend to underestimate NPV by ignoring options. The damage might be small for a highly structured, very specific proposal, but it might be great for an exploratory one such as a gold mine.[14] The value of a gold mine depends on management's ability to shut it down if the price of gold falls below a certain point, and the ability to reopen it subsequently if conditions are right.[15]

capital rationing

The situation that exists if a firm has positive NPV projects but cannot find the necessary financing.

Capital Rationing

Capital rationing is said to exist when we have profitable (positive NPV) investments available but we can't get the needed funds to undertake them. For example, as division managers for a large corporation, we might identify $5 million in excellent projects, but find that, for whatever reason, we can spend only $2 million. Now what? Unfortunately, for reasons we discuss next there may be no truly satisfactory answer.

soft rationing

The situation that occurs when units in a business are allocated a certain amount of financing for capital budgeting.

Soft Rationing   The situation we have just described is **soft rationing**. This occurs when, for example, different units in a business are allocated some fixed amount of

---

[13] P. Foster, "McDonald's Excellent Soviet Venture?" *Canadian Business,* May 1991, pp. 51–69.
[14] We have more to say about options in capital budgeting in Chapter 20.
[15] M. J. Brennan and E. S. Schwartz, "A New Approach to Evaluating Natural Resource Investments," *Midland Corporate Financial Journal* 3 (Spring 1985).

money each year for capital spending. Such an allocation is primarily a means of controlling and keeping track of overall spending. The important thing about soft rationing is that the corporation as a whole isn't short of capital; more can be raised on ordinary terms if management so desires.

If we face soft rationing, the first thing to do is try to get a larger allocation. Failing that, then one common suggestion is to generate as large a net present value as possible within the existing budget. This amounts to choosing those projects with the largest benefit/cost ratio (profitability index).

Strictly speaking, this is the correct thing to do only if the soft rationing is a one-time event; that is, it won't exist next year. If the soft rationing is a chronic problem, something is amiss. The reason goes all the way back to Chapter 1. Ongoing soft rationing means we are constantly by-passing positive NPV investments. This contradicts our goal of the firm. When we are not trying to maximize value, the question of which projects to take becomes ambiguous because we no longer have an objective goal in the first place.

E X A M P L E | 9.2   Soft Rationing

Hiram Finnegan Ltd. applies a 12 percent cost of capital to two investment opportunities.

Project	Cash Flows ($000,000) C_0	C_1	C_2	PV at 12% of Cash Flows Subsequent to Initial Investment ($000,000)	Profitability Index	NPV at 12% ($000,000)
1	−20	70	10	70.5	3.53	50.5
2	−10	15	40	45.3	4.53	35.3

For example, the profitability index is calculated for Project 1 as follows: The present value of the cash flows after the initial investment is:

$$\$70.5 = \frac{\$70}{1.12} + \frac{\$10}{(1.12)^2}$$

The profitability index is calculated by dividing the result of the equation by the initial investment of $20. This yields:

$$3.53 = \$70.5/\$20$$

Imagine that the firm has a third project as well as the first two. Project 3 has the following cash flows:

Project	Cash Flows ($000,000) C_0	C_1	C_2	PV at 12% of Cash Flows Subsequent to Initial Investment ($000,000)	Profitability Index	NPV at 12% ($000,000)
3	−10	−5	60	43.4	4.34	33.4

Further, imagine that the projects of Hiram Finnegan Ltd. are independent, but the firm has only $20 million to invest. Because Project 1 has an initial investment of $20 million, the firm cannot select both this project and another one. Conversely, because Projects 2 and 3 have initial investments of $10 million each, both these projects can be chosen. In other words, the cash constraint forces the firm to choose either Project 1 or Projects 2 and 3.

What should the firm do? Individually, Projects 2 and 3 have lower NPVs than Project 1 has. However, when the NPVs of Projects 2 and 3 are added together, they are higher than the NPV of Project 1. Thus, common sense dictates that Projects 2 and 3 shall be accepted. What does our conclusion have to say about the NPV rule or the PI rule? When faced with limited funds we cannot rank projects according to their NPVs. Instead, we should rank them according to the ratio of present value to initial investment. This is the PI rule. Both Project 2 and Project 3 have higher PI ratios than Project 1. Thus, they should be ranked ahead of Project 1 when capital is rationed.

Note that the PI rule does not work if funds are also limited beyond the initial time period. For example, if heavy cash outflows elsewhere in the firm were to occur at Date 1, Project 3 might need to be rejected. In other words, the profitability index cannot handle capital rationing over multiple time periods.

What we have done is to consider all feasible sets of projects involving a total outlay of $20 million. In this example, there are only two such sets: Project 1 alone and Projects 2 and 3 combined. We choose the set that maximizes NPV.

hard rationing

The situation that occurs when a business cannot raise financing for a project under any circumstances.

Hard Rationing   With **hard rationing**, a business cannot raise capital for a project under any circumstances. For large, healthy corporations, this situation probably does not occur very often. This is fortunate because with hard rationing our DCF analysis breaks down, and the best course of action is ambiguous.

The reason that DCF analysis breaks down has to do with the required return. Suppose we say our required return is 20 percent. Implicitly, we are saying we will take a project with a return that exceeds this. However, if we face hard rationing, we are not going to take a new project no matter what the return on that project is, so the whole concept of a required return is ambiguous. About the only interpretation we can give this situation is that the required return is so large that no project has a positive NPV in the first place.

Hard rationing can occur when a company experiences financial distress, meaning that bankruptcy is a possibility. Also, a firm may not be able to raise capital without violating a preexisting contractual agreement. We discuss these situations in greater detail in a later chapter.

CONCEPT QUESTIONS

1. Why do we say that our standard discounted cash flow analysis is static?

2. What are managerial options in capital budgeting? Give some examples.

3. What is capital rationing? What types are there? What problems does it create for discounted cash flow analysis?

9.7 | SUMMARY AND CONCLUSIONS

In this chapter, we looked at some ways of evaluating the results of a discounted cash flow analysis. We also touched on some problems that can come up in practice. We saw that:

1. Net present value estimates depend on projected future cash flows. If there are errors in those projections, our estimated NPVs can be misleading. We called this forecasting risk.

2. Scenario and sensitivity analyses are useful tools for identifying which variables are critical to a project and where forecasting problems can do the most damage.

3. Break-even analysis in its various forms is a particularly common type of scenario analysis that is useful for identifying critical levels of sales.

4. Operating leverage is a key determinant of break-even levels. It reflects the degree to which a project or a firm is committed to fixed costs. The degree of operating leverage tells us the sensitivity of operating cash flow to changes in sales volume.

5. Projects usually have future managerial options associated with them. These options may be very important, but standard discounted cash flow analysis tends to ignore them.

6. Capital rationing occurs when apparently profitable projects cannot be funded. Standard discounted cash flow analysis is troublesome in this case because NPV is not necessarily the appropriate criterion anymore.

The most important thing to carry away from reading this chapter is that estimated NPVs or returns should not be taken at face value. They depend critically on projected cash flows. If there is room for significant disagreement about those projected cash flows, the results from the analysis have to be taken with a grain of salt.

Despite the problems we have discussed, discounted cash flow is still the way of attacking problems, because it forces us to ask the right questions. What we learn in this chapter is that knowing the questions to ask does not guarantee that we get all the answers.

Key Terms

forecasting risk (page 307)
scenario analysis (page 309)
sensitivity analysis (page 310)
simulation analysis (page 312)
variable costs (page 315)
fixed costs (page 315)
marginal or incremental cost (page 316)
accounting break-even (page 316)
cash break-even (page 323)

financial break-even (page 323)
operating leverage (page 325)
degree of operating leverage (page 326)
managerial options (page 329)
contingency planning (page 329)
strategic options (page 332)
capital rationing (page 332)
soft rationing (page 332)
hard rationing (page 334)

Chapter Review Problems and Self-Test

Use the following base case information to work the self-test problems. You can check your answers just below.

A project under consideration costs $500,000, has a five-year life, and has no salvage value. Depreciation is straight-line to zero. The required return is 15 percent, and the tax rate is 34 percent. Sales are projected at 400 units per year. Price per unit is $3,000, variable cost per unit is $1,900, and fixed costs are $250,000 per year.

9.1   Scenario Analysis   Suppose you think that the preceding unit sales, price, variable cost, and fixed cost projections are accurate to within 5 percent. What are the upper and lower bounds for these projections? What is the base case NPV? What are the best and worst case scenario NPVs?

9.2   **Break-Even Analysis**   Given the base case projections in the previous problem, what are the cash, accounting, and financial break-even sales levels for this project? Ignore taxes in answering.

Answers to Self-Test Problems

9.1   We can summarize the relevant information as follows:

	Base Case	Lower Bound	Upper Bound
Unit sales	400	380	420
Price per unit	$ 3,000	$ 2,850	$ 3,150
Variable costs per unit	1,900	1,805	1,995
Fixed costs	250,000	237,500	262,500

The depreciation is $100,000 per year, so we can calculate the cash flows under each scenario. Remember that we assign high costs and low prices and volume under the worst case and just the opposite for the best case.

Scenario	Unit Sales	Price	Variable Cost	Fixed Costs	Cash Flow
Base	400	$3,000	$1,900	$250,000	$159,400
Best	420	3,150	1,805	237,500	250,084
Worst	380	2,850	1,995	262,500	75,184

At 15 percent, the five-year annuity factor is 3.35216, so the NPVs are:

Base-case NPV $= -\$500,000 + 3.35216 \times \$159,400 = \ \$ \ 34,334$

Best-case NPV $= -\$500,000 + 3.35216 \times \$250,084 = \ \$338,320$

Worst-case NPV $= -\$500,000 + 3.35216 \times \$75,184 = -\$247,972$

9.2   In this case, we have $250,000 in cash fixed costs to cover. Each unit contributes $3,000 − 1,900 = $1,100 toward doing so. The cash break-even is thus $250,000/1,100 = 227 units. We have another $100,000 in depreciation, so the accounting break-even is ($250,000 + $100,000)/1,000 = 318 units.
To get the financial break-even, we need to find the OCF such that the project has a zero NPV. As we have seen, the five-year annuity factor is 3.35216 and the project costs $500,000, so the OCF must be such that:

$500,000 = OCF \times 3.35216$

So, to break even on a financial basis, the project's cash flow must be $500,000/3.35216, or $149,158 per year. If we add this to the $250,000 in cash fixed costs, we get a total of $399,158 that we have to cover. At $1,100 per unit, we need to sell $399,158/$1,100 = 363 units.

Questions and Problems

Basic
(Questions 1–17)

1.   **Calculating Costs and Break-Even**   NoNox manufactures gasoline additives. The variable materials cost is $0.72 per pint and the variable labour cost is $1.90 per pint.

a. What is the variable cost per unit?

b. Suppose NoNox incurs fixed costs of $510,000 during a year when total production is 350,000 pints. What are the total costs for the year?

c. If the selling price is $4.25 per unit, does NoNox break even on a cash basis? If depreciation is $160,000 per year, what is the accounting break-even point?

2. **Computing Average Cost**   Wonderful Widgets Corporation can manufacture widgets for $8.90 in variable raw materials cost and $29 in variable labour expense. Widgets sell for $46 each. Last year, production was 90,000 widgets. Fixed costs were $700,000. What were total production costs? What is the marginal cost per widget? What is the average cost? If the company is considering a one-shot order for an extra 4,000 widgets, what is the minimum acceptable total revenue from the order? Explain.

Basic
(Continued)

3. **Scenario Analysis**   Up-or-Down, Inc., has the following estimates for its new gear assembly project: price = $250 per unit; variable costs = $135 per unit; fixed costs = $8 million; quantity = 100,000 units. Suppose the company believes all of its estimates are accurate only to within ± 15 percent. What values should the company use for the four variables above when it performs its base-case scenario analysis? What about the worst-case scenario?

4. **Sensitivity Analysis**   For the company in the previous problem, suppose management is most concerned about the impact of its price estimate on the project's profitability. How could you answer this question for Up-or-Down? Describe how you would calculate your answer. What values would you use for the other forecast variables?

5. **Sensitivity Analysis and Break-Even**   We are evaluating a project that costs $960,000, has a six-year life, and no salvage value. Assume depreciation is straight-line to zero over the life of the project. Sales are projected at 150,000 units per year. Price per unit is $19.95, variable cost per unit is $12.00, and fixed costs are $750,000 per year. The tax rate is 35 percent and we require a 12 percent return on this project.
   a. Calculate the accounting break-even point. What is the degree of operating leverage at the accounting break-even point?
   b. Calculate the base-case cash flow and NPV. What is the sensitivity of NPV to changes in the sales figure? Explain what your answer tells you about a 500-unit decrease in projected sales.
   c. What is the sensitivity of OCF to changes in the variable cost figure? Explain what your answer tells you about a $1.00 decrease in estimated variable costs.

6. **Scenario Analysis**   In the previous question, suppose the projections given for price, quantity, variable costs, and fixed costs are all accurate to within ± 10 percent. Calculate the best-case and worst-case NPV figures.

7. **Calculating Break-Even**   In each of the following cases, calculate the accounting break-even and the cash flow break-even points. Ignore any tax effects in calculating the cash flow break-even.

Unit Price	Unit Variable Cost	Fixed Costs	Depreciation
$8,000	$6,500	$18,000,000	$12,000,000
60	35	40,000	180,000
5	3	250	400

8. **Calculating Break-Even**   In each of the following cases, find the unknown quantity.

Accounting Break-Even	Unit Price	Unit Variable Cost	Fixed Costs	Depreciation
45,000	$40	$25	$ 275,000	$?
150,000	?	60	3,000,000	1,500,000
7,500	90	?	175,000	125,000

9.   **Calculating Break-Even**   A project has the following estimated data: price = $50 per unit; variable costs = $25 per unit; fixed costs = $2,500; required return = 15 percent; initial investment = $4,500; life = three years. Ignoring the effect of taxes, what is the accounting break-even quantity? The cash flow break-even quantity? The financial break-even quantity? What is the degree of operating leverage at the financial break-even level of output?

10.   **Using Break-Even Analysis**   Consider a project with the following data: accounting break-even quantity = 14,500 units; cash flow break-even quantity = 10,000 units; life = five years; fixed costs = $100,000; variable costs = $10 per unit; required return = 10 percent. Ignoring the effect of taxes, find the financial break-even quantity.

11.   **Calculating Operating Leverage**   At an output level of 25,000 units, you calculate that the degree of operating leverage is 3. If output rises to 30,000 units, what will the percentage change in operating cash flow be? Will the new level of operating leverage be higher or lower? Explain.

12.   **Leverage**   In the previous problem, suppose fixed costs are $100,000. What is the operating cash flow at 30,000 units? The degree of operating leverage?

13.   **Operating Cash Flow and Leverage**   A proposed project has fixed costs of $75,000 per year. The operating cash flow at 5,000 units is $200,000. Ignoring the effect of taxes, what is the degree of operating leverage? If units sold rise from 5,000 to 5,600, what will be the increase in operating cash flow? What is the new degree of operating leverage?

14.   **Forecasting Risk**   What is forecasting risk? In general, would the degree of forecasting risk be greater for a new product or a cost-cutting proposal? Why?

15.   **Options and NPV**   What is the option to abandon? The option to expand? Explain why we tend to underestimate NPV when we ignore these options.

16.   **Cash Flow and Leverage**   At an output level of 8,000 units, you have calculated the degree of operating leverage is 1.5. The cash flow is $6,000 in this case. Ignoring the effect of taxes, what are fixed costs? What will the cash flow be if output rises to 9,000 units? If output falls to 7,000 units?

17.   **Leverage**   In the previous problem, what will be the new degree of operating leverage in each case?

18.   **Break-Even Intuition**   A co-worker claims that looking at all this marginal this and incremental that is just a bunch of nonsense, and states: "Listen, if our average revenue doesn't exceed our average cost, then we will have a negative cash flow, and we will go broke!" How do you respond?

19.   **Break-Even Intuition**   Consider a project with a required return of $r\%$ that costs $I and will last for N years. The project uses straight-line depreciation to zero over the N-year life; there are no salvage value or net working capital requirements.

   a. At the accounting break-even level of output, what is the IRR of this project? The payback period? The NPV?
   b. At the cash flow break-even level of output, what is the IRR of this project? The payback period? The NPV?
   c. At the financial break-even level of output, what is the IRR of this project? The payback period? The NPV?

20.   **Break-Even and Taxes**   If you were to include the effect of taxes in break-even analysis, what do you think would happen to the cash, accounting, and financial break-even points?

21. **Sensitivity Analysis** Consider a three-year project with the following information: initial fixed asset investment = $450,000; straight-line depreciation to zero over the three-year life; zero salvage value; price = $17; variable costs = $12; fixed costs = $250,000; quantity sold = 100,000; tax rate = 34 percent. How sensitive is OCF to changes in quantity sold?

Intermediate
(Continued)

22. **Operating Leverage** In the previous problem, what is the degree of operating leverage at the given level of output? What is the degree of operating leverage at the accounting break-even level of output?

23. **Project Analysis** You are considering a new product launch. It will cost $720,000, have a four-year life, and have no salvage value; depreciation is straight-line to zero. Sales are projected at 75 units per year; price per unit will be $20,000, variable cost per unit will be $14,000, and fixed costs are $175,000 per year. The required return on the project is 8 percent and the relevant tax rate is 35 percent.

    a. Based on your experience, you think the unit sales, variable cost, and fixed cost projections above are probably accurate to within ± 12 percent. What are the upper and lower bounds for these projections? What is the base-case NPV? What are the best-case and worst-case scenarios?

    b. Evaluate the sensitivity of your base-case NPV to changes in fixed costs.

    c. What is the cash break-even level of output for this project (ignore taxes)?

    d. What is the accounting break-even level of output for this project? What is the degree of operating leverage at the accounting break-even point? How do you interpret this number?

24. **Abandonment Value** We are examining a new project. We expect to sell 2,000 units per year at $35 net cash flow apiece for the next 10 years. In other words, the annual operating cash flow is projected to be $35 × 2,000 = $70,000 per year. The relevant discount rate is 17 percent, and the initial investment required is $345,000.

    a. What is the base-case NPV?

    b. After the first year, the project can be dismantled and sold for $300,000. If expected sales are revised based on the first year's performance, when would it make sense to abandon the investment? In other words, at what level of expected sales would it make sense to abandon the project?

    c. Explain how the $300,000 abandonment value can be viewed as the opportunity cost of keeping the project in one year.

25. **Abandonment** In the previous problem, suppose you think it is likely that expected sales will be revised up to 2,800 if the first year is a success and revised downward to 1,200 if the first year is not a success.

    a. If success and failure are equally likely, what is the NPV of the project? Consider the possibility of abandonment in answering.

    b. What is the value of the option to expand?

26. **Abandonment and Expansion** In the previous problem, suppose the scale of the project can be doubled in one year in the sense that twice as many units can be produced and sold. Naturally, expansion would only be desirable if the project is a success. This implies that if the project is a success, projected sales after expansion will be 5,600. Again assuming that success and failure are equally likely, what is the NPV of the project? Note that abandonment is still an option if the project is a failure. What is the value of the option to expand here?

27. **Break-Even and Taxes**   This problem concerns the effect of taxes on the various break-even measures.

   a. Show that, when we consider taxes, the general relationship between operating cash flow (OCF) and sales volume (Q) can be written as:

$$Q = \frac{FC + \dfrac{(OCF - T \times D)}{(1 - T)}}{(P - v)}$$

   b. Use the expression in part (a) to find the cash, accounting, and financial break-even points for the Victoria Sailboats example in the chapter. Assume a 38 percent tax rate.

   c. In part (b), the accounting break-even should be the same as before. Why? Verify this algebraically.

28. **Operating Leverage and Taxes**   Show that if we consider the effect of taxes, the degree of operating leverage can be written as:

$$DOL = 1 + [FC \times (1 - T) - T \times D]/OCF$$

Notice that this reduces to our previous result if $T = 0$. Can you interpret this in words?

29. **Integrative Minicase**   Consider a project to supply the highway department of your regional municipality with 25,000 tons of rock salt annually to drop on winter roads. You will need an initial $1,250,000 investment in processing equipment to get the project started; the project will last for five years. The accounting department estimates that annual fixed costs will be $200,000 and that variable costs should be $90 per ton; accounting will depreciate the initial fixed asset investment straight-line over the five-year project life. It also estimates a salvage value of $100,000. The marketing department estimates that the regional municipality will let the contract at a selling price of $120 per ton. The engineering department estimates you will need an initial net working capital investment of $90,000. You require a 14 percent return and face a marginal tax rate of 38 percent on this project.

   a. What is the estimated OCF for this project? The NPV? Should you pursue this project?

   b. Suppose you believe the accounting department's cost and salvage value projections are only accurate to within ± 15 percent; the marketing department's price estimate is accurate only to within ± 10 percent; and the engineering department's net working capital estimate is accurate only to within ± 5 percent. What is your worst-case scenario for this project? Your best-case scenario? Do you still want to pursue the project?

   c. Now, suppose you're confident about your own projections, but you're a little unsure about the regional municipality's actual rock salt requirement. What is the sensitivity of the project OCF to changes in the quantity supplied? What about the sensitivity of NPV to quantity supplied? Using the sensitivity number you calculated, is there some minimum level of output below which you wouldn't want to operate? Why?

   d. Use the results so far to find the accounting, cash flow, and financial break-even quantities for the rock salt project.

   e. Use your analysis to this point to find the degree of operating leverage for the rock salt project at the base-case output level of 25,000. How does this

Challenge
(Continued)

number compare to the sensitivity figure you found in part *c*? Verify that either approach will tell you the same OCF figure at any new quantity level.

30. Conduct a break-even analysis for the Atlantic Lumber Traders case at the end of Chapter 3. Interpret your results for Lynn Thomas, the banker.

Suggested Readings

For a more in-depth (and highly readable) discussion of break-even analysis and operating leverage, see:

Viscione, J. A. *Financial Analysis: Tools and Concepts.* New York: National Association of Credit Management, 1984, chap. 4.

For an interesting application of break-even analysis, see:

Reinhardt, U. E. "Break-Even Analysis for Lockheed's TriStar: An Application of Financial Theory." *Journal of Finance* 28, September 1973.

The following articles are classics on the subject of risk analysis in investment decisions:

Hertz, D. B. "Risk Analysis in Capital Investment." *Harvard Business Review* 42 (January–February 1964).

_____ . "Investment Policies that Pay Off." *Harvard Business Review* 46 (January–February 1968).

A trade book on competitive strategy and advantage is:

Porter, M. E. *Competitive Advantage: Creating and Sustaining Superior Performance.* New York: The Free Press, 1985.

RISK AND RETURN

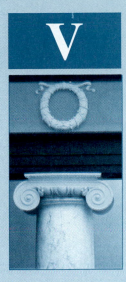

CHAPTER 10 | **Some Lessons from Capital Market History**
This chapter begins with a description of investors' historical experiences in Canadian capital markets since 1948. It describes the lessons that financial managers can learn from studying capital market history and introduces the important concept of an efficient capital market.

CHAPTER 11 | **Return, Risk, and the Security Market Line**
This chapter describes the nature of the risk-return trade-off facing investors and firms. It shows how to use the risk-return trade-off to determine the required return on an investment.

Some Lessons from Capital Market History

Thus far, we haven't had much to say about what determines the required return on an investment. In one sense, the answer is very simple: The required return depends on the risk of the investment. The greater the risk is, the greater is the required return.

Having said this, we are left with a somewhat more difficult problem. How can we measure the amount of risk present in an investment? Put another way, what does it mean to say that one investment is riskier than another? Obviously, we need to define what we mean by risk if we are going to answer these questions. This is our task in the next two chapters.

From the last several chapters, we know that one of the responsibilities of the financial manager is to assess the value of proposed real asset investments. In doing this, it is important to know what financial investments have to offer. Going further, we saw in Chapter 2 that the cash flow of a firm equals the cash flow to creditors and shareholders. So the returns and risks of financial investments provide information on the real investments firms undertake.

Our goal in this chapter is to provide a perspective on what capital market history can tell us about risk and return. The most important thing to get out of this chapter is a feel for the numbers. What is a high return? What is a low one? More generally, what returns should we expect from financial assets and what are the risks from such investments? This perspective is essential for understanding how to analyze and value risky investment projects.

We start our discussion on risk and return by describing the historical experience of investors in Canadian financial markets. In 1931, for example, the stock market lost about 33 percent of its value. Just two years later, the stock market gained 51 percent. In more recent memory, the market lost about 23 percent of its value in the month of October 1987 alone. What lessons, if any, can financial managers learn from such shifts in the stock market? We explore the last half-century of market history to find out.

Not everyone agrees on the value of studying history. On the one hand, there is philosopher George Santayana's famous comment, "Those who do not remember the past are condemned to repeat it." On the other hand, there is industrialist Henry Ford's equally famous comment, "History is more or less bunk." Nonetheless, based on recent events, perhaps everyone would agree with Mark Twain when he observed, "October. This is one of the peculiarly dangerous months to speculate in stocks in. The others are July, January, September, April, November, May, March, June, December, August, and February."

Two central lessons emerge from our study of market history: First, there is a reward for bearing risk. Second, the greater the potential reward, the greater is the risk. To understand these facts about market returns, we devote much of this chapter to reporting the statistics and numbers that make up modern capital market history in Canada. Canadians also invest in the United States so we include some discussion of U.S. markets. In the next chapter, these facts provide the foundation for our study of how financial markets put a price on risk.

10.1 | RETURNS

We wish to discuss historical returns on different types of financial assets. We do this after briefly discussing how to calculate the return from investing.

Dollar Returns

If you buy an asset of any sort, your gain (or loss) from that investment is called the return on your investment. This return usually has two components: First, you may receive some cash directly while you own the investment. This is called the income component of your return. Second, the value of the asset you purchase often changes. In this case, you have a capital gain or capital loss on your investment.[1]

To illustrate, suppose Canadian Atlantic Enterprises has several thousand shares of stock outstanding. You purchased some of these shares at the beginning of the year. It is now year-end, and you want to determine how well you have done on your investment.

Over the year, a company may pay cash dividends to its shareholders. As a shareholder in Canadian Atlantic Enterprises, you are a part owner of the company. If the company is profitable, it may choose to distribute some of its profits to shareholders (we discuss the details of dividend policy in Chapter 16). So, as the owner of some stock, you receive some cash. This cash is the income component from owning the stock.

In addition to the dividend, the other part of your return is the capital gain or capital loss on the stock. This part arises from changes in the value of your investment. For example, consider the cash flows illustrated in Figure 10.1. The stock is selling for $37 per share. If you buy 100 shares, you have a total outlay of $3,700. Suppose that, over the year, the stock paid a dividend of $1.85 per share. By the end of the year, then, you would have received income of:

Dividend = $1.85 × 100 = $185

Also, the value of the stock rises to $40.33 per share by the end of the year. Your 100 shares are worth $4,033, so you have a capital gain of:

Capital gain = ($40.33 − $37) × 100 = $333

On the other hand, if the price had dropped to, say, $34.78, you would have a capital loss of:

Capital loss = ($34.78 − $37) × 100 = −$222

---

[1] The aftertax dollar returns would be reduced by taxes levied differently for dividends and capital gains as we discussed in Chapter 2.

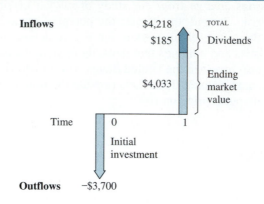

Notice that a capital loss is the same thing as a negative capital gain.

The total dollar return on your investment is the sum of the dividend and the capital gain:

Total dollar return = Dividend income + Capital gain (or loss)   [10.1]

In our first example, the total dollar return is thus given by:

Total dollar return = $185 + 333 = $518

If you sold the stock at the end of the year, the total amount of cash you would have would be your initial investment plus the total return. In the preceding example, then:

Total cash if stock is sold = Initial investment + Total return
                            = $3,700 + 518   [10.2]
                            = $4,218

As a check, notice that this is the same as the proceeds from the sale of the stock plus the dividends:

Proceeds from stock sale + Dividends = $40.33 × 100 + $185
                                     = $4,033 + 185
                                     = $4,218

Suppose you hold on to your Canadian Atlantic stock and don't sell it at the end of the year. Should you still consider the capital gain as part of your return? Isn't this only a paper gain and not really a cash flow if you don't sell it?

The answer to the first question is a strong yes, and the answer to the second is an equally strong no. The capital gain is every bit as much a part of your return as the dividend, and you should certainly count it as part of your return. That you actually decided to keep the stock and not sell (you don't realize the gain) is irrelevant because you could have converted it to cash if you wanted to. Whether you choose to do so or not is up to you.

After all, if you insisted on converting your gain to cash, you could always sell the stock at year-end and immediately reinvest by buying the stock back. There is no net difference between doing this and just not selling (assuming, there are no tax consequences from selling the stock). Again, the point is that whether you actually cash out or reinvest by not selling doesn't affect the return you earn.

Percentage Returns

It is usually more convenient to summarize information about returns in percentage terms, rather than dollar terms, because that way your return doesn't depend on how much you actually invest. The question we want to answer is: How much do we get for each dollar we invest?

To answer this question, let P_t be the price of the stock at the beginning of the year and let D_t be the dividend paid on the stock during the year. Consider the cash flows in Figure 10.2. These are the same as those in Figure 10.1, except we have now expressed everything on a per-share basis.

In our example, the price at the beginning of the year was $37 per share and the dividend paid during the year on each share was $1.85. As we discussed in Chapter 6, expressing the dividend as a percentage of the beginning stock price results in the dividend yield:

Dividend yield = D_t/P_t

$= \$1.85/\$37 = .05 = 5\%$

This says that, for each dollar we invest, we get 5 cents in dividends.

The other component of our percentage return is the capital gains yield. Recall (from Chapter 6) that this is calculated as the change in the price during the year (the capital gain) divided by the beginning price:

Capital gains yield = $(P_{t+1} - P_t)/P_t$

$= (\$40.33 - 37)/\$37$

$= \$3.33/\$37$

$= 9\%$

So, per dollar invested, you get 9 cents in capital gains.

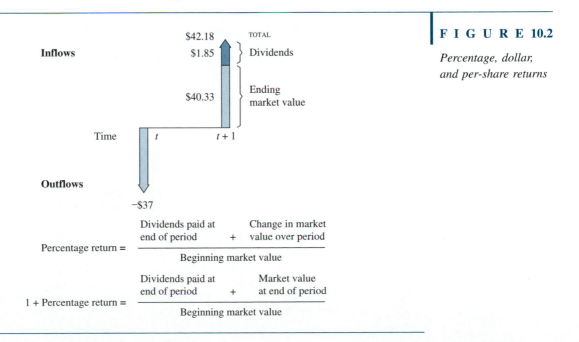

FIGURE 10.2

Percentage, dollar, and per-share returns

348 PART V | Risk and Return

Putting it together, per dollar invested, we get 5 cents in dividends and 9 cents in capital gains, a total of 14 cents. Our percentage return is 14 cents on the dollar, or 14 percent.

To check this, notice that you invested $3,700 and ended with $4,218. By what percentage did your $3,700 increase? As we saw, you picked up $4,218 − 3,700 = $518. This is a $518/$3,700 = 14% increase.

<hr />

E X A M P L E | **10.1** **Calculating Returns**

Suppose you buy some stock for $25 per share. At the end of the year, the price is $35 per share. During the year, you got a $2 dividend per share. This is the situation illustrated in Figure 10.3. What is the dividend yield? The capital gains yield? The percentage return? If your total investment was $1,000, how much do you have at the end of the year?

Your $2 dividend per share works out to a dividend yield of:

Dividend yield $= D_{t+1}/P_t$

$$= \$2/\$25 = .08 = 8\%$$

The per-share capital gain is $10, so the capital gains yield is:

Capital gains yield $= (P_{t+1} - P_t)/P_t$

$$= (\$35 - 25)/\$25$$
$$= \$10/\$25$$
$$= 40\%$$

The total percentage return is thus 48 percent.

If you had invested $1,000, you would have $1,480 at the end of the year, a 48 percent increase. To check this, note that your $1,000 would have bought you $1,000/25 = 40 shares. Your 40 shares would then have paid you a total of 40 × $2 = $80 in cash dividends. Your $10 per-share gain would give you a total capital gain of $10 x 40 = $400. Add these together, and you get the $480. |

<hr />

F I G U R E 10.3

Cash flow—an investment example

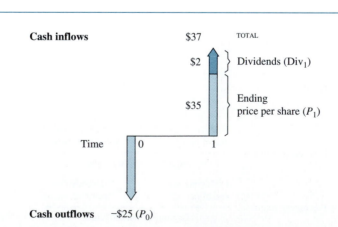

| CONCEPT QUESTIONS

1. What are the two parts of total return?
2. Why are unrealized capital gains or losses included in the calculation of returns?
3. What is the difference between a dollar return and a percentage return? Why are percentage returns more convenient?

10.2 | INFLATION AND RETURNS

So far, we haven't worried about inflation in calculating returns. Since this is an important consideration, we consider the impact of inflation next.

Real versus Nominal Returns

The returns we calculated in the previous section are called **nominal returns** because they weren't adjusted for inflation. Returns that have been adjusted to reflect inflation are called **real returns**.

nominal return
Return on an investment not adjusted for inflation.

To see the effect of inflation on returns, suppose that prices are currently rising by 5 percent per year. In other words, the inflation rate is 5 percent. We are considering an investment that will be worth $115.50 in one year. It costs $100 today.

real return
Return adjusted for the effects of inflation.

We start by calculating the percentage return. In this case, there is no income component, so the return is the capital gains yield of ($115.50 − 100)/$100 = 15.50%. Once again, we've ignored the effect of inflation, so this 15.50 percent is the nominal return.

What is the impact of inflation here? To answer, suppose pizzas cost $5 apiece at the beginning of the year. With $100, we can buy 20 pizzas. Since the inflation rate is 5 percent, pizzas will cost 5 percent more, or $5.25, at the end of the year. If we take the investment, how many pizzas can we buy at the end of the year? Measured in pizzas instead of dollars, what is our return?

Our $115.50 from the investment buys us $115.50/$5.25 = 22 pizzas. This is up from 20 pizzas, so our pizza return is (22 − 20)/20 = 10%. What this illustrates is that even though the nominal return on our investment is 15.5 percent, our buying power has gone up only 10 percent because of inflation. Put another way, we are really only 10 percent richer. In this case, we say the real return is 10 percent.

Alternatively, with 5 percent inflation, each of the $115.50 nominal dollars we get is worth 5 percent less in real terms, so the real dollar value of our investment in a year is:

$$\$115.50/1.05 = \$110$$

What we have done is to deflate the $115.50 by 5 percent. When we give up $100 in current buying power to get the equivalent of $110, our real return is again 10 percent. Because we have removed the effect of future inflation here, this $110 is said to be measured in current dollars.

The difference between nominal and real returns is important and bears repeating:

> Your nominal return on an investment is the percentage change in the number of dollars you have.
>
> Your real return on an investment is the percentage change in how much you can buy with your dollars, in other words, the percentage change in your buying power.

The Fisher Effect

Fisher effect

Relationship among nominal returns, real returns, and inflation.

Our discussion of real and nominal returns illustrates a relationship often called the **Fisher effect**. Since investors are ultimately concerned with what they can buy with their money, they require compensation for inflation. Let R stand for the nominal return and r stand for the real return. The Fisher effect tells us that the relationship between nominal returns, real returns, and inflation can be written as:

$$(1 + R) = (1 + r) \times (1 + h) \qquad [10.3]$$

where h is the inflation rate.

From the previous example, the nominal return was 15.50 percent and the inflation rate was 5 percent. What was the real return? We can determine it by plugging in these numbers:

$$(1 + .1550) = (1 + r) \times (1 + .05)$$
$$(1 + r) = (1.1550)/(1.05) = 1.10$$
$$r = 10\%$$

This real return is the same as we had before. If we take another look at the Fisher effect, we can rearrange things a little as follows:

$$(1 + R) = (1 + r)(1 + h)$$
$$R = r + h + r \times h \qquad [10.4]$$

What this tells us is that the nominal return has three components: First, there is the real return on the investment, r. Second, there is the compensation for the decrease in the value of the money originally invested because of inflation, h. The third component represents compensation for the fact that the dollars earned on the investment are also worth less because of the inflation.

This third component is usually small, so it is often dropped. The nominal rate is then approximately equal to the real rate plus the inflation rate:

$$R \approx r + h \qquad [10.5]$$

E X A M P L E | 10.2   The Fisher Effect

If investors require a 10 percent real return, and the inflation rate is 8 percent, what must be the approximate nominal rate? The exact nominal rate?

First, the nominal rate is approximately equal to the sum of the real rate and the inflation rate: $10\% + 8\% = 18\%$. From the Fisher effect, we have

$$(1 + R) = (1 + r) \times (1 + h)$$
$$= (1.10) \times (1.08)$$
$$= 1.1880$$

Therefore, the nominal rate is actually closer to 19 percent. ▎

Note that financial rates, such as interest rates, discount rates, and rates of return, are almost always quoted in nominal terms. To remind you of this, we henceforth use the symbol R instead of r in most of our subsequent discussions about such rates.

| CONCEPT QUESTIONS

1. What is the difference between a nominal and a real return? Which is more important to a typical investor?

2. What is the Fisher effect?

10.3 | THE HISTORICAL RECORD

Capital market history is of great interest to investment consultants who advise institutional investors on portfolio strategy. The data set we use is in Table 10.1. It was assembled by the Alexander Group drawing on two major studies: Roger Ibbotson and Rex Sinquefield conducted a famous set of studies dealing with rates of return in U.S. financial markets. James Hatch and Robert White examined Canadian returns.[2] Our data presents year-to-year historical rates of return on five important types of financial investments. The returns can be interpreted as what you would have earned if you held portfolios of the following:

1. Canadian common stocks. The common stock portfolio is based on a sample of the largest companies (in total market value of outstanding stock) in Canada.[3]

2. U.S. common stocks. The U.S. common stock portfolio consists of 500 of the largest U.S. companies. The full historical series is given in U.S. dollars. A separate series presents U.S. stock returns in Canadian dollars adjusting for shifts in exchange rates.

3. Small stocks. The small stock portfolio is composed of the small capitalization Canadian stocks as compiled by Nesbitt Burns.

4. Long bonds. The long bond portfolio has high-quality, long-term corporate, provincial, and government of Canada bonds.

5. Canada Treasury bills. The T-bill portfolio has Treasury bills with a three-month maturity.

These returns are not adjusted for inflation or taxes; thus, they are nominal, pretax returns.

In addition to the year-to-year returns on these financial instruments, the year-to-year percentage change in the Statistics Canada Consumer Price Index (CPI) is also computed. This is a commonly used measure of inflation, so we can calculate real returns using this as the inflation rate.

The five asset classes included in Table 10.1 cover a broad range of investments popular with Canadian individuals and financial institutions. We include U.S. stocks since Canadian investors often invest abroad—particularly in the United States.[4]

---

[2] The two classic studies are R. G. Ibbotson and R. A. Sinquefield, *Stocks, Bonds, Bills, and Inflation* (Charlottesville, VA: Financial Analysts Research Foundation, 1982) and J. Hatch and R. White, *Canadian Stocks, Bonds, Bills, and Inflation: 1950–1983* (Charlottesville, VA: Financial Analysts Research Foundation, 1985). Additional sources used by the Alexander Group are Nesbitt Burns for small capitalization stocks, ScotiaMcLeod for long bonds, and Statistics Canada CANSIM for rates of exchange and inflation.

[3] From 1956 on, the TSE 300 is used. For earlier years, the Alexander Group used a sample provided by the TSE.

[4] Chapter 22 discusses exchange rate risk and other risks of foreign investments.

Annual market index returns: 1948–94

Date	Cdn Stock	Small Stocks	T-bills	Long Bonds	S&P 500 ($US)	S&P 500 ($CDN)	CPI
48	12.25		0.40	−0.08	5.50	5.50	8.88
49	23.85		0.45	5.18	18.79	22.15	1.09
50	51.69		0.51	1.74	31.71	39.18	5.91
51	25.44		0.71	−7.89	24.02	15.00	10.66
52	0.01		0.95	5.01	18.37	13.68	−1.38
53	2.56		1.54	5.00	−0.99	−0.99	0.00
54	39.37		1.62	12.23	52.62	52.62	0.00
55	27.68		1.22	0.13	31.56	35.51	0.47
56	12.68		2.63	−8.87	6.56	2.35	3.24
57	−20.58		3.76	7.94	−10.78	−8.51	1.79
58	31.25		2.27	1.92	43.36	40.49	2.64
59	4.59		4.39	−5.07	11.96	10.54	1.29
60	1.78		3.66	12.19	0.46	5.15	1.27
61	32.75		2.86	9.16	26.89	32.85	0.42
62	−7.09		3.81	5.03	−8.73	−5.77	1.67
63	15.60		3.58	4.58	22.80	23.19	1.64
64	25.43		3.73	6.16	16.48	15.75	2.02
65	6.68		3.79	0.05	12.45	12.58	3.16
66	−7.07		4.89	−1.05	−10.06	−9.33	3.45
67	18.09		4.38	−0.48	23.98	23.61	4.07
68	22.45		6.22	2.14	11.06	10.26	3.91
69	−0.81		6.83	−2.86	−8.50	−8.50	4.79
70	−3.57	−11.69	6.89	16.39	4.01	−1.96	1.31
71	8.01	15.83	3.86	14.84	14.31	13.28	5.16
72	27.38	44.72	3.43	8.11	18.98	18.12	4.91
73	0.27	−7.82	4.78	1.97	−14.66	−14.58	9.36
74	−25.93	−26.89	7.68	−4.53	−26.47	−26.87	12.30
75	18.48	41.00	7.05	8.02	37.20	40.72	9.52
76	11.02	22.77	9.10	23.64	23.84	22.97	5.87
77	10.71	39.93	7.64	9.04	−7.18	0.65	9.45
78	29.72	44.41	7.90	4.10	6.56	15.50	8.44
79	44.77	46.04	11.04	−2.83	18.44	16.52	9.69
80	30.13	42.86	12.23	2.18	32.42	35.51	11.20
81	−10.25	−15.10	19.11	−2.09	−4.91	−5.57	12.20
82	5.54	4.55	15.27	45.82	21.41	25.84	9.23
83	35.49	44.30	9.39	9.61	22.51	24.07	4.51
84	−2.39	−2.33	11.21	16.90	6.27	12.87	3.77
85	25.07	38.98	9.70	26.68	32.16	39.82	4.38
86	8.95	12.33	9.34	17.21	18.47	16.96	4.19
87	5.88	−5.47	8.20	1.77	5.23	−0.96	4.12
88	11.08	5.46	8.94	11.30	16.81	7.21	3.96
89	21.37	10.66	11.95	15.17	31.49	27.74	5.17
90	−14.80	−27.32	13.28	4.32	−3.17	−3.06	5.00
91	12.02	18.51	9.90	23.30	30.55	30.05	3.78
92	−1.43	13.01	6.65	11.57	7.67	18.42	2.14
93	32.55	52.26	5.63	22.09	10.00	14.40	1.70
94	−0.18	−9.21	4.76	−7.39	1.34	7.48	0.23
Mean	12.73	15.67	6.15	7.01	13.25	14.09	4.52
Standard Deviation	16.81	24.40	4.17	10.20	16.22	16.60	3.54

Source: The Alexander Group.

IN THEIR OWN WORDS . . .

Roger Ibbotson on Capital Market History

The financial markets are perhaps the most carefully documented human phenomena in history. Every day, approximately 2,000 NYSE stocks are traded, and at least 5,000 more are traded on other exchanges and in over-the-counter markets. Bonds, commodities, futures, and options also provide a wealth of data. These data daily fill a dozen pages of *The Wall Street Journal* (and numerous other newspapers), and these pages are only summaries of the day's transactions. A record actually exists of every transaction, providing not only a real-time data base, but a historical record extending back, in many cases, more than a century.

The global market adds another dimension to this wealth of data. The Japanese stock market trades a billion shares on active days, and the London exchange reports trades on over 10,000 domestic and foreign issues a day. [The Toronto Stock Exchange ranks 12th in the world in dollar volume as we saw in Chapter 1.]

The data generated by these transactions are quantifiable, quickly analyzed and disseminated, and made easily accessible by computer. Because of this, finance has increasingly come to resemble one of the exact sciences. The use of financial market data ranges from the simple, such as using the S&P 500 to measure the performance of a portfolio, to the incredibly complex. For example, only a generation ago, the bond market was the staidest province on Wall Street. Today, it attracts swarms of traders seeking to exploit arbitrage opportunities—small temporary mispricings—using real-time data and supercomputers to analyze them.

Financial market data are the foundation for the extensive empirical understanding we now have of the financial markets. The following is a list of some of the principal findings of such research: Risky securities, such as stocks, have higher average returns than riskless securities such as Treasury bills. Stocks of small companies have higher average returns than those of larger companies. Long-term bonds have higher average yields and returns than short-term bonds. The cost of capital for a company, project, or division can be predicted using data from the markets. Because phenomena in the financial markets are so well measured, finance is the most readily quantifiable branch of economics. Researchers are able to do more extensive empirical research than in any other economic field, and the research can be quickly translated into action in the marketplace.

Roger Ibbotson is Professor in the Practice of Management at the Yale School of Management. He is the founder and president of Ibbotson Associates, a major supplier of financial data bases to the financial services industry. An outstanding scholar, he is best known for his original estimates of the historical rates of return realized by investors in different markets and for his research on new issues.

A First Look

Before looking closely at the different portfolio returns, we take a look at the "big picture." Figure 10.4 shows what happened to $1 invested in two of these portfolios at the beginning of 1948. The growth in value for each portfolio over the 47-year period ending in 1994 is given separately. Notice that to get everything on a single graph, some modification in scaling is used. As is commonly done with financial series, the vertical axis is scaled such that equal distances measure equal percentage (as opposed to dollar) changes in values.[5]

Looking at Figure 10.4, we see that the common stock investments did better than Treasury bills. Every dollar invested in Canadian stocks grew to $163.27 over the 47 years. At the other end, the T-bill portfolio grew to only $15.96 and the long

---

[5] In other words, the scale is logarithmic.

F I G U R E 10.4

Returns to a $1 investment; 1948–94

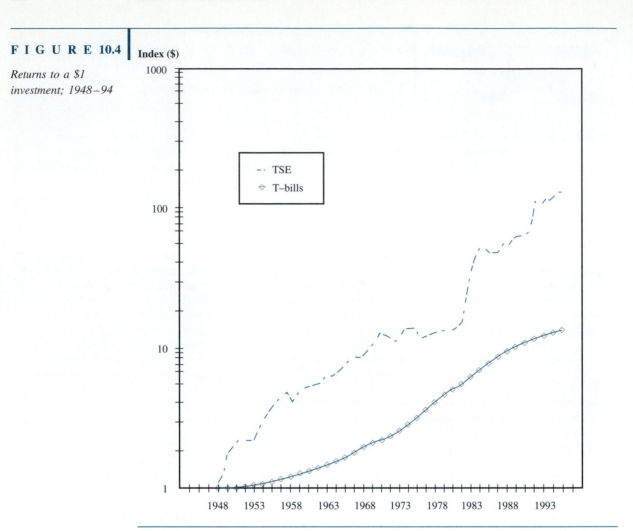

Index ($)

bonds did only slightly better with an ending value of $19.74. These values are less than impressive when we consider the inflation over this period. As illustrated, the increase in the price level was such that $7.79 is needed just to replace the original $1.

Given the historical record as discussed so far, why would anybody buy anything other than common stocks? If you look closely at Figure 10.4, you will probably see the answer. The T-bill portfolio grew more slowly than did the stock portfolio, but it also grew much more steadily. The common stocks ended up on top, but as you can see, they grew erratically at times. For example, comparing Canadian stocks with T-bills, the stocks had a smaller return than long-term government bonds in the 19 years during this period.

A Closer Look

To illustrate the variability of the different investments, we look at a few selected years in Table 10.1. For example, looking at the long-term bonds, we see the largest historical return (45.82 percent) occurred not so long ago (in 1982). This was a good year for bonds. The largest single-year return in the table is a very healthy 52.26

percent for the small stocks in 1993. In the same year, T-bills returned only 5.63 percent. In contrast, the largest Treasury bill return was 19.11 percent in 1981.

> **CONCEPT QUESTIONS**
> 1. With 20-20 hindsight, what was the best investment for the period 1981–82?
> 2. Why doesn't everyone just buy common stocks as investments?
> 3. What was the smallest return observed over the 47 years for each of these investments? When did it occur?
> 4. How many times did large Canadian stocks (common stocks) return more than 30 percent? How many times did they return less than 20 percent?
> 5. What was the longest winning streak (years without a negative return) for large Canadian stocks? For long-term bonds?
> 6. How often did the T-bill portfolio have a negative return?

10.4 | AVERAGE RETURNS: THE FIRST LESSON

As you've probably begun to notice, the history of capital market returns is too complicated to be of much use in its undigested form. We need to begin summarizing all these numbers. Accordingly, we discuss how to consider the detailed data. We start by calculating average returns.

Calculating Average Returns

The obvious way to calculate the average returns on the different investments in Table 10.1 is simply to add the yearly returns and divide by 47. The result is the historical average of the individual values.

For example, if you add the returns for the Canadian common stocks for the 47 years, you get about 5.98. The average annual return is thus 5.98/47 = 12.73%. You interpret this 12.73 percent just like any other average. If you picked a year at random from the 47-year history and you had to guess what the return in that year was, the best guess is 12.73 percent.

Average Returns: The Historical Record

Table 10.2 shows the average returns computed from Table 10.1. As shown, in a typical year, the small stocks increased in value by 15.67 percent. Notice also how much larger the stock returns are than the bond returns.

These averages are, of course, nominal since we haven't worried about inflation. Notice that the average inflation rate was 4.52 percent per year over this 47-year span. The nominal return on Canada Treasury bills was 6.15 percent per year. The average real return on Treasury bills was thus approximately 1.63 percent per year; so the real return on T-bills has been quite low historically.

At the other extreme, common stocks (both U.S. and Canadian) had an average real return of about 13% − 4.5% = 8.5%, which is relatively large. If you remember the Rule of 72 (Chapter 5), then a quick "back of the envelope" calculation tells us that 8.5 percent real growth doubles your buying power about every eight years.

Risk Premiums

Now that we have computed some average returns, it seems logical to see how they compare with each other. Based on our discussion so far, one such comparison

Investment	Average Return
Canadian common stocks	12.73%
U.S. common stocks (Cdn $)	13.25
Long bonds	7.01
Treasury bills	6.15
Small stocks	15.67*
Inflation	4.52

*Average return for small stocks is based on data from 1970 to 1994.

involves government-issued securities. These are free of much of the variability we see in, for example, the stock market.

The government of Canada borrows money by issuing debt securities in different forms. The ones we focus on are Treasury bills. These have the shortest time to maturity of the different government securities. Because the government can always raise taxes to pay its bills, this debt is virtually free of any default risk over its short life. Thus, we call the rate on such debt the risk-free return, and we use it as a kind of benchmark.

A particularly interesting comparison involves the virtually risk-free return on T-bills and the very risky return on common stocks. The difference between these two returns can be interpreted as a measure of the excess return on the average risky asset (assuming that the stock of a large Canadian corporation has about average risk compared to all risky assets).

We call this the excess return because it is the additional return we earn by moving from a relatively risk-free investment to a risky one. Because it can be interpreted as a reward for bearing risk, we call it a **risk premium**.

risk premium

*The excess return
required from an
investment in a risky
asset over a risk-free
investment.*

From Table 10.2, we can calculate the risk premiums for the different investments. We report only the nominal risk premium in Table 10.3 because there is only a slight difference between the historical nominal and real risk premiums. The risk premium on T-bills is shown as zero in the table because we have assumed that they are riskless.

The First Lesson

Looking at Table 10.3, we see that the average risk premium earned by a typical Canadian common stock is around 7 percent: 12.73 − 6.15 = 6.58. This is a significant reward. The fact that it exists historically is an important observation, and it is the basis for our first lesson: Risky assets, on average, earn a risk premium. Put another way, there is a reward for bearing risk.

Investment	Average Return	Risk Premium
Canadian common stocks	12.73%	6.58%
U.S. common stocks (cdn $)	14.09	7.94
Long bonds	7.01	0.86
Small stocks	15.67*	9.52
Inflation	4.52	−1.63
Treasury bills	6.15	0.0

*Average return for small stocks is based on data from 1970 to 1994.

Why is this so? Why, for example, is the risk premium for common stocks so much larger than the risk premium for long bonds? More generally, what determines the relative sizes of the risk premiums for the different assets? The answers to these questions are at the heart of modern finance, and the next chapter is devoted to them. For now, part of the answer can be found by looking at the historical variability of the returns of these different investments. So, to get started, we now turn our attention to measuring variability in returns.

CONCEPT QUESTIONS

1. What do we mean by excess return and risk premium?
2. What was the nominal risk premium on long bonds?
3. What is the first lesson from capital market history?

10.5 | THE VARIABILITY OF RETURNS: THE SECOND LESSON

We have already seen that the year-to-year returns on common stocks tend to be more volatile than the returns on, say, long-term bonds. Next we discuss measuring this variability so we can begin examining the subject of risk.

Frequency Distributions and Variability

To get started, we can draw a frequency distribution for the common Canadian stock returns similar to the one in Figure 10.5. What we have done here is to count the number of times the annual return on the common stock portfolio falls within each 5 percent range. For example, in Figure 10.5, the height of 1 in the range −30 percent to −25 percent means that 1 of the 47 annual returns was in that range.

Now we need to measure the spread in returns. We know, for example, that the return on Canadian common stocks in a typical year was 12.7 percent. We now want to know how far the actual return deviates from this average in a typical year. In other words, we need a measure of how volatile the return is. The **variance** and its square root, the **standard deviation**, are the most commonly used measures of volatility. We describe how to calculate them next.

variance
The average squared deviation between the actual return and the average return.

standard deviation
The positive square root of the variance

The Historical Variance and Standard Deviation

The variance essentially measures the average squared difference between the actual returns and the average return. The bigger this number is, the more the actual returns tend to differ from the average return. Also, the larger the variance or standard deviation is, the more spread out the returns are.

The way we calculate the variance and standard deviation depends on the situation. In this chapter, we are looking at historical returns; so the procedure we describe here is the correct one for calculating the historical variance and standard deviation. If we were examining projected future returns, the procedure would be different. We describe this procedure in the next chapter.

To illustrate how we calculate the historical variance, suppose a particular investment had returns of 10 percent, 12 percent, 3 percent, and −9 percent over the last four years. The average return is $(.10 + .12 + .03 − .09)/4 = 4\%$. Notice that the return is never actually equal to 4 percent. Instead, the first return deviates from the average by $.10 − .04 = .06$, the second return deviates from the average by $.12 − .04 = .08$, and so on. To compute the variance, we square each of these deviations, add

F I G U R E 10.5 *Frequency distribution of returns on Canadian common stocks*

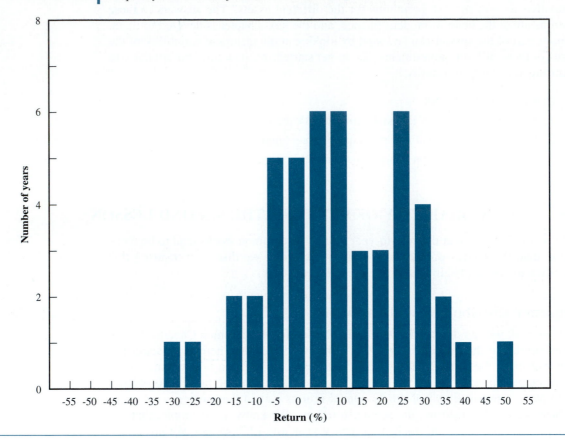

them up, and divide the result by the number of returns less one, or three in this case. This information is summarized in the following table:

	(1) Actual Returns	(2) Average Return	(3) Deviation (1) − (2)	(4) Squared Deviation
	.10	.04	.06	.0036
	.12	.04	.08	.0064
	.03	.04	−.01	.0001
	−.09	.04	−.13	.0169
Totals	.16		.00	.0270

In the first column, we write down the four actual returns. In the third column, we calculate the difference between the actual returns and the average by subtracting out 4 percent. Finally, in the fourth column, we square the numbers in column 3 to get the squared deviations from the average.

The variance can now be calculated by dividing .0270, the sum of the squared deviations, by the number of returns less one. Let Var(R) or σ^2 (read this as sigma squared) stand for the variance of the return:

$$\text{Var}(R) = \sigma^2 = .027/(4 - 1) = .009$$

The standard deviation is the square root of the variance. So, if SD(R) or σ stands for the standard deviation of return:

$$SD(R) = \sigma = \sqrt{.009} = .09487$$

The square root of the variance is used because the variance is measured in squared percentages and, thus, is hard to interpret. The standard deviation is an ordinary percentage, so the answer here could be written as 9.487 percent.

In the preceding table, notice that the sum of the deviations is equal to zero. This is always the case, and it provides a good way to check your work. In general, if we have T historical returns, where T is some number, we can write the historical variance as:

$$Var(R) = (1/(T-1))\,[(R_1 - \bar{R})^2 + \ldots + (R_T - \bar{R})^2] \qquad [10.6]$$

This formula tells us to do just what we did above: Take each of the T individual returns $(R_1, R_2, \ldots)$ and subtract the average return, $\bar{R}$; square the result, and add them up; finally, divide this total by the number of returns less one $(T-1)$. The standard deviation is always the square root of $Var(R)$.

E X A M P L E ⏐ 10.3   Calculating the Variance and Standard Deviation

Suppose Northern Radio Comm and the Canadian Empire Bank have experienced the following returns in the last four years:

Year	Northern Radio Comm Returns	Canadian Empire Bank Returns
1992	−.20	.05
1993	.50	.09
1994	.30	−.12
1995	.10	.20

What are the average returns? The variances? The standard deviations? Which investment was more volatile?

To calculate the average returns, we add the returns and divide by four. The results are:

Northern Radio Comm average return = $\bar{R}$ = .70/4 = .175

Canadian Empire Bank average return = $\bar{R}$ = .22/4 = .055

To calculate the variance for Northern Radio Comm, we can summarize the relevant calculations as follows:

Year	(1) Actual Returns	(2) Average Returns	(3) Deviation (1) − (2)	(4) Squared Deviation
1992	−.20	.175	−.375	.140625
1993	.50	.175	.325	.105625
1994	.30	.175	.125	.015625
1995	.10	.175	−.075	.005625
Totals	.70		.00	.267500

Since there are four years of returns, we calculate the variances by dividing .2675 by $(4-1) = 3$:

	Northern Radio Comm	Canadian Empire Bank
Variance (σ^2)	.2675/3 = .0892	.0529/3 = .0176
Standard deviation (σ)	$\sqrt{.0892} = .2987$	$\sqrt{.0176} = .1327$

T A B L E 10.4

Historical returns and standard deviations; 1948–94

	Average Return	Standard Deviation
Canadian common stocks	12.73%	16.81%
U.S. common stocks (Cdn $)	14.09	16.60
Long bonds	7.01	10.20
Small stocks*	15.67	24.40
Inflation	4.52	3.54
Treasury bills	6.15	4.17

*Entries for small stocks based on data from 1970 to 1994

For practice, check that you get the same answer as we do for Canadian Empire Bank. Notice that the standard deviation for Northern Radio Comm, 29.87 percent, is a little more than twice Canadian Empire's 13.27 percent; Northern Radio Comm is thus the more volatile investment.[6]

The Historical Record

Table 10.4 summarizes much of our discussion of capital market history so far. It displays average returns, standard deviations, and frequency distributions of annual returns on a common scale. In Table 10.4, notice, for example, that the standard deviation for the Canadian common stock portfolio (16.81 percent per year) is about four times larger than the T-bill portfolio's standard deviation (4.17 percent per year). We return to these figures momentarily.

Normal Distribution

normal distribution

A symmetric, bell-shaped frequency distribution that can be defined by its mean and standard deviation.

For many different random events in nature, a particular frequency distribution, the **normal distribution** (or bell curve), is useful for describing the probability of ending up in a given range. For example, the idea behind grading on a curve comes from the fact that exam scores often resemble a bell curve.

Figure 10.6 illustrates a normal distribution and its distinctive bell shape. As you can see, this distribution has a much cleaner appearance than the actual return distributions illustrated in Table 10.4. Even so, like the normal distribution, the actual distributions do appear to be at least roughly mound-shaped and symmetrical. When this is true, the normal distribution is often a very good approximation.[7]

Also, keep in mind that the distributions in Table 10.4 are based on only 47 yearly observations while Figure 10.6 is, in principle, based on an infinite number. So, if we had been able to observe returns for, say, 1,000 years, we might have filled in a lot of the irregularities and ended up with a much smoother picture. For our purposes, it is enough to observe that the returns are at least roughly normally distributed.

The usefulness of the normal distribution stems from the fact that it is completely described by the average and standard deviation. If you have these two numbers, there is nothing else to know. For example, with a normal distribution, the probability

---

[6] Since our two stocks have different average returns, it may be useful to look at their risks in comparison to the average returns. The coefficient of variation shows this. It equals (Standard deviation)/(Average return).

[7] It is debatable whether such a smooth picture would necessarily always be a normal distribution. But we assume it would be normal to make the statistical discussion as simple as possible.

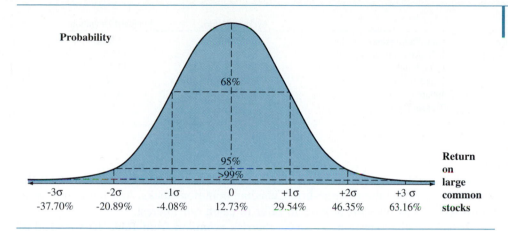

FIGURE 10.6

The normal distribution. Illustrated returns are based on the historical return and standard deviation for a portfolio of large common stocks.

that we end up within one standard deviation of the average is about two-thirds. The probability that we end up within two standard deviations is about 95 percent. Finally, the probability of being more than three standard deviations away from the average is less than 1 percent. These ranges and the probabilities are illustrated in Figure 10.6.

To see why this is useful, recall from Table 10.4 that the standard deviation of returns on Canadian common stocks is 16.81 percent. The average return is 12.73 percent. So, assuming that the frequency distribution is at least approximately normal, the probability that the return in a given year is in the range −4.08 percent to 29.54 percent (12.73 percent plus or minus one standard deviation, 16.81 percent) is about two-thirds. This range is illustrated in Figure 10.6. In other words, there is about one chance in three that the return is outside the range. This literally tells you that, if you buy stocks in larger companies, you should expect to be outside this range in one year out of every three. This reinforces our earlier observations about stock market volatility. However, there is only a 5 percent chance (approximately) that we would end up outside the range −20.89 percent to 46.35 percent (12.73 percent plus or minus 2 × 16.81%). These points are also illustrated in Figure 10.6.

The Second Lesson

Our observations concerning the year-to-year variability in returns are the basis for our second lesson from capital market history. On average, bearing risk is handsomely rewarded, but in a given year, there is a significant chance of a dramatic change in value. Thus, our second lesson is: The greater the potential reward, the greater is the risk.

To reinforce the second lesson, Table 10.5 shows the average returns and standard deviations on different investments for the recent 20-year period, 1975–94. Notice that we have added a new investment, small Canadian stocks. Small stocks illustrate the second lesson over again as this investment has both the highest return and the largest standard deviation.

Using Capital Market History

Based on the discussion in this section, you should begin to have an idea of the risks and rewards from investing. For example, suppose Canada Treasury bills are paying

T A B L E 10.5

Historical returns and standard deviations, 1975–94

	Average Return	Standard Deviation
Canadian common stocks	13.69%	15.85%
U.S. common stocks (Cdn. $)	17.36	13.74
Long bonds	12.02	12.43
Small stocks	18.88	23.76
Inflation	5.93	3.35
Treasury bills	9.91	3.37

about 8 percent. Suppose further we have an investment that we think has about the same risk as a portfolio of large-firm Canadian common stocks. At a minimum, what return would this investment have to offer to catch our interest.

To answer this question, we select the risk premium from Table 10.3 instead of Table 10.5 for two reasons: Table 10.3 represents a longer sample period and the larger risk premium is more conservative in this application. From Table 10.3, the risk premium on Canadian common stocks has been 6.6 percent historically, so a reasonable estimate of our required return would be this premium plus the T-bill rate, 8% + 6.6% = 14.6%. This may strike you as high, but, if we were thinking of starting a new business, the risks of doing so might resemble investing in small-company stocks. In this case, the risk premium must be considerably more than 6.6 percent so we might require as much as 20 percent from such an investment at a minimum.

We discuss the relationship between risk and required return in more detail in the next chapter. For now, you should notice that a projected internal rate of return (IRR) on a risky investment in the 15 to 25 percent range isn't particularly outstanding. It depends on how much risk there is. This, too, is an important lesson from capital market history.

E X A M P L E | 10.4   Investing in Growth Stocks

The phrase *growth stock* is frequently a euphemism for *small-company stock*. Are such investments suitable for elderly, conservative investors? Before answering, you should consider the historical volatility. For example, from the historical record, what is the approximate probability that you could actually lose 10 percent or more of your money in a single year if you buy a portfolio of such companies?

Looking back at Table 10.5, the average return on small stocks is 18.9 percent and the standard deviation is 23.8 percent. Assuming the returns are approximately normal, there is about a one-third probability that you could experience a return outside the range −4.9 percent to 42.7 percent (18.9 plus or minus 23.8 percent).

Because the normal distribution is symmetric, the odds of being above or below this range are equal. There is thus a one-sixth chance (half of one-third) that you could lose more than 4.9 percent. So you should expect this to happen once in every six years, on average. Such investments can thus be very volatile, and they are not well-suited for those who cannot afford the risk.[8]

---

[8]Some researchers argue that elderly investors should hold equities to protect against outliving their assets: M. A. Milevsky, K. H. and C. Robinson, "Asset Allocation via the Conditional First Exit Time or How to Avoid Outliving Your Money," York University Working Paper, 1994.

1. In words, how do we calculate a variance? A standard deviation?

2. With a normal distribution, what is the probability of ending up more than one standard deviation below the average?

3. Assuming that long-term bonds have an approximately normal distribution, what is the approximate probability of earning 17 percent or more in a given year? With T-bills, what is this probability?

4. What is the first lesson from capital market history? The second?

10.6 | CAPITAL MARKET EFFICIENCY

Capital market history suggests that the market values of stocks and bonds can fluctuate widely from year to year. Why does this occur? At least part of the answer is that prices change because new information arrives, and investors reassess asset values based on that information.

The behaviour of market prices has been extensively studied. A question that has received particular attention is whether prices adjust quickly and correctly when new information arrives. A market is said to be efficient if this is the case. To be more precise, in an **efficient capital market**, current market prices fully reflect available information. By this we simply mean that, based on available information, there is no reason to believe the current price is too low or too high.

efficient capital market
Market in which security prices reflect available information.

The concept of market efficiency is a rich one, and much has been written about it. A full discussion of the subject goes beyond the scope of our study of corporate finance. However, because the concept figures so prominently in studies of market history, we briefly describe the key points here.

Price Behaviour in an Efficient Market

To illustrate how prices behave in an efficient market, suppose the F-Stop Camera Corporation (FCC) has, through years of secret research and development, developed a camera that doubles the speed of available autofocussing systems. FCC's capital budgeting analysis suggests that launching the new camera is a highly profitable move; in other words, the NPV appears to be positive and substantial. The key assumption thus far is that FCC has not released any information about the new system; so the fact of its existence is only inside information.

Now consider a share of stock in FCC. In an efficient market, its price reflects what is known about FCC's current operations and profitability, and it reflects market opinion about FCC's potential for future growth and profits. The value of the new autofocussing system is not reflected, however, because the market is unaware of its existence.

If the market agrees with FCC's assessment of the value of the new project, FCC's stock price rises when the decision to launch is made public. For example, assume the announcement is made in a press release on Wednesday morning. In an efficient market, the price of shares in FCC adjusts quickly to this new information. Investors should not be able to buy the stock on Wednesday afternoon and make a profit on Thursday. This would imply that it took the stock market a full day to realize the implication of the FCC press release. If the market is efficient, on Wednesday afternoon the price of FCC shares already reflects the information contained in that morning's press release.

Figure 10.7 presents three possible stock price adjustments for FCC. In Figure 10.7, Day 0 represents the announcement day. As illustrated, before the announcement, FCC's stock sells for $140 per share. The NPV per share of the new system is, say, $40, so the new price would be $180 once the value of the new project is fully reflected.

The solid line in Figure 10.7 represents the path taken by the stock price in an efficient market. In this case, the price adjusts immediately to the new information and no further changes in the price of the stock occur. The broken line in Figure 10.7 depicts a delayed reaction. Here it takes the market eight days or so to fully absorb the information. Finally, the dotted line illustrates an overreaction and subsequent adjustments to the correct price.

The broken line and the dotted line in Figure 10.7 illustrate paths that the stock price might take in an inefficient market. If, for example, stock prices don't adjust immediately to new information (the broken line), buying stock immediately following the release of new information and then selling it several days later would be a positive NPV activity because the price is too low for several days after the announcement.

efficient markets hypothesis (EMH)

The hypothesis is that actual capital markets, such as the TSE, are efficient.

The Efficient Markets Hypothesis

The **efficient markets hypothesis (EMH)** asserts that well-organized capital markets such as the TSE and the NYSE are efficient markets, at least as a practical matter. In other words, an advocate of the EMH might argue that while inefficiencies may exist, they are relatively small and not common.

F I G U R E 10.7

Reaction of stock price to new information in efficient and inefficient markets

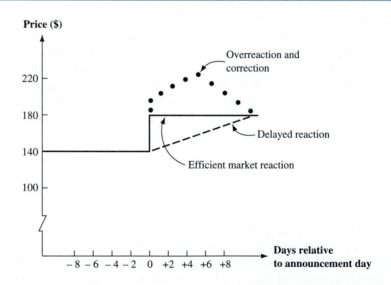

Efficient market reaction: The price instantaneously adjusts to and fully reflects new information; there is no tendency for subsequent increases and decreases.
Delayed reaction: The price partially adjusts to the new information; 10 days elapse before the price completely reflects the new information.
Overreaction: The price overadjusts to the new information; it "overshoots" the new price and subsequently corrects.

IN THEIR OWN WORDS . . .

Richard Roll on Market Efficiency

The concept of an efficient market is a special application of the "no free lunch" principle. In an efficient financial market, costless trading policies will not generate "excess" returns. After adjusting for the riskiness of the policy, the trader's return will be no larger than the return of a randomly selected portfolio, at least on average. This is often thought to imply something about the amount of "information" reflected in asset prices. However, it really doesn't mean that prices reflect all information nor even that they reflect publicly available information. Instead, it means that the connection between unreflected information and prices is too subtle and tenuous to be easily or costlessly detected. Relevant information is difficult and expensive to uncover and evaluate. Thus, if costless trading policies are ineffective, there must exist some traders who make a living by "beating the market." They cover their costs (including the opportunity cost of their time) by trading.

The existence of such traders is actually a necessary precondition for markets to become efficient. Without such professional traders, prices would fail to reflect everything that is cheap and easy to evaluate. Efficient market prices should approximate a random walk, meaning that they will appear to fluctuate more or less randomly. Prices can fluctuate nonrandomly to the extent that their departure from randomness is expensive to discern. Also, observed price series can depart from apparent randomness due to changes in preferences and expectations, but this is really a technicality and does not imply a "free-lunch" relative to current investor sentiments.

Richard Roll is Allstate Professor of Finance at UCLA. He is a preeminent financial researcher, and he has written extensively in almost every area of modern finance. He is particularly well known for his insightful analyses and great creativity in understanding empirical phenomena.

When a market is efficient, there is a very important implication for market participants: All investments in an efficient market are zero NPV investments. The reason is not complicated. If prices are neither too low nor too high, the difference between the market value of an investment and its cost is zero; hence, the NPV is zero. As a result, in an efficient market, investors get exactly what they pay for when they buy securities, and firms receive exactly what their stocks and bonds are worth when they sell them.

What makes a market efficient is competition among investors. Many individuals spend their lives trying to find mispriced stocks. For any given stock, they study what has happened in the past to the stock price and its dividends. They learn, to the extent possible, what a company's earnings have been, how much it owes to creditors, what taxes it pays, what businesses it is in, what new investments are planned, how sensitive it is to changes in the economy, and so on.

Not only is there a great deal to know about any particular company, but there is also a powerful incentive for knowing it; namely, the profit motive. If you know more about some company than other investors in the marketplace, you can profit from that knowledge by investing in the company's stock if you have good news and selling it if you have bad news.

The logical consequences of all this information being gathered and analyzed is that mispriced stocks will become fewer and fewer. In other words, because of competition among investors, the market is becoming increasingly efficient. A kind of equilibrium comes into being where there is just enough mispricing around for those who are best at identifying it to make a living at it. For most other investors, the activity of information gathering and analysis does not pay.

Some Common Misconceptions about the EMH

No idea in finance has attracted as much attention as that of efficient markets, and not all the attention has been flattering. Rather than rehash the arguments here, we are content to observe that some markets are more efficient than others. For example, financial markets on the whole are probably much more efficient than real asset markets.

Having said this, much of the criticism of the EMH is misguided because it is based on a misunderstanding of what the hypothesis says and what it doesn't say. For example, when the notion of market efficiency was first publicized and debated in the popular financial press, it was often characterized by words to the effect that throwing darts at the financial page will produce a portfolio that can be expected to do as well as any managed by professional security analysts.[9]

Confusion over statements of this sort has often led to a failure to understand the implications of market efficiency. For example, sometimes it is wrongly argued that market efficiency means it doesn't matter how you invest your money because the efficiency of the market protects you from making a mistake. However, a random dart thrower might wind up with all the darts sticking into one or two high-risk stocks that deal in genetic engineering. Would you really want all your money in two such stocks?

Efficiency does imply that the price a firm obtains when it sells a share of its stock is a fair price in the sense that it reflects the value of that stock given the information available about it. Shareholders do not have to worry that they are paying too much for a stock with a low dividend or some other sort of characteristic because the market has already incorporated that characteristic into the price. We sometimes say that the information has been "priced out."

The concept of efficient markets can be explained further by replying to a frequent objection. It is sometimes argued that the market cannot be efficient because stock prices fluctuate from day to day. If the prices are right, the argument goes, then why do they change so much and so often? From our prior discussion, these price movements are in no way inconsistent with efficacy. Investors are bombarded with information every day. The fact that prices fluctuate is, at least in part, a reflection of that information flow. In fact, the absence of price movements in a world that changes as rapidly as ours would suggest inefficiency.

Market Efficiency—Forms and Evidence

It is common to distinguish between three forms of market efficiency. Depending on the degree of efficiency, we say that markets are either weak form efficient, semistrong form efficient, or strong form efficient. The difference between these forms relates to what information is reflected in prices.

We start with the extreme case. If the market is strong form efficient, then all information of every kind is reflected in stock prices. In such a market, there is no such thing as inside information. Thus, in our previous FCC example, we apparently were assuming the market was not strong form efficient.

---

[9] See B. G. Malkiel, *A Random Walk Down Wall Street,* 2nd college ed. (New York: Norton, 1981).

Casual observation, particularly in recent years, suggests that inside information exists and it can be valuable to possess. Whether it is lawful or ethical to use that information is another issue. In any event, we conclude that private information about a particular stock may exist that is not currently reflected in the price of the stock. For example, prior knowledge of a takeover attempt could be very valuable.[10]

The second form of efficiency, semistrong efficiency, is the most controversial. In a market that is semistrong form efficient, all public information is reflected in the stock price. The reason this form is controversial is that it implies that a security analyst who tries to identify mispriced stocks using, for example, financial statement information is wasting time because that information is already reflected in the current price.

Studies of semistrong form efficiency include event studies that measure whether prices adjust rapidly to new information following the efficient markets pattern in Figure 10.7. Announcements of mergers, dividends, earnings, capital expenditures, and new issues of securities are a few examples. Although there are exceptions, event study tests for major exchanges including the TSE and NYSE generally support the view that these markets are semistrong efficient. In fact, the tests suggest these markets are gifted with a certain amount of foresight. By this, we mean that news tends to leak out and be reflected in stock prices even before the official release of the information.

If the market is efficient in the semistrong form, no matter what publicly available information mutual fund managers rely on to pick stocks, their average returns should be the same as those of the average investor in the market as a whole. Researchers have tested mutual fund performance against a market index and found that, on average, fund managers have no special ability to beat the market.[11] This supports semistrong form efficiency.

The third form of efficiency, weak form efficiency, suggests that, at a minimum, the current price of a stock reflects its own past prices. In other words, studying past prices in an attempt to identify mispriced securities is futile if the market is weak form efficient. Research supporting weak form efficiency suggests that successive price changes are consistent with a random walk where deviations from expected return are random. Tests on both the TSE and NYSE support weak form efficiency, although the results are more conclusive for the NYSE. This form of efficiency might seem rather mild; however, it implies that searching for patterns in historical prices that identify mispriced stocks does not work (this practice is quite common).

Although the bulk of the evidence supports the view that major markets such as the TSE and NYSE are reasonably efficient, we would not be fair if we did not note the existence of selected contrary results often termed anomalies. The most striking anomaly is the seasonality of stock prices. For instance, the January effect is the well-documented tendency for firms with small capitalizations to have abnormally high returns in the first five days of that month in both the United States and Canada.[12] While the effect is small relative to commissions on stock purchases and sales, investors who have decided to buy small capitalization stocks can exploit the anomaly by buying in December rather than in January.

---

[10] The movie, *Wall Street,* realistically illustrates how valuable the information can be.

[11] This does not imply that mutual funds are bad investments for individuals. Though these funds fail to achieve consistently better returns than some market indexes, they do permit investors to diversify.

[12] The effect is international and has been documented in most stock exchanges around the world occurring immediately after the close of the tax year. See V. Jog, "Stock Pricing Anomalies: Canadian Experience," *Canadian Investment Review,* Fall 1988.

In addition, the stock market crash of October 19, 1987, is extremely puzzling. The NYSE dropped by more than 20 percent and the TSE by more than 11 percent on a Monday following a weekend during which little surprising news was released. A drop of this magnitude for no apparent reason is not consistent with market efficiency. One theory sees the crash as evidence consistent with the bubble theory of speculative markets. That is, security prices sometimes move wildly above their true values. Eventually, prices fall back to their original level, causing great losses for investors. The tulip craze of the 17th century in Holland and the South Sea Bubble in England the following century are perhaps the two best-known bubbles.

In summary, what does research on capital market history say about market efficiency? At risk of going out on a limb, the evidence does seem to tell us three things: First, prices do appear to respond very rapidly to new information, and the response is at least not grossly different from what we would expect in an efficient market. Second, the future of market prices, particularly in the short run, is very difficult to predict based on publicly available information. Third, if mispriced stocks do exist, there is no obvious means of identifying them. Put another way, simple-minded schemes based on public information will probably not be successful.[13]

E X A M P L E | 10.5   **The EMH and the Accounting Veil**

The accounting profession provides firms with a significant amount of leeway in their reporting practices. Firms and their accountants have frequently been accused of misusing this leeway in hopes of boosting earning and stock prices.

However, accounting choice should not affect stock price if two conditions hold. First, enough information must be provided in the annual report so financial analysts can recast earnings under their own choice of accounting methods. Second, the market must be efficient in the semistrong form. In other words, the market must appropriately use all this accounting information to "lift the accounting veil" in determining the market price.

One example in which this occurred involved the Northland Bank. Before its failure in 1985, the bank used questionable accounting to cover up its exposure to bad energy loans in western Canada. According to the Estey Commission, which investigated the bank failure, "The financial statements became gold fillings covering cavities in the assets and in the earnings of the bank." Yet, research on stock prices prior to the collapse has shown that stock market investors were aware the bank was highly risky.[14]

CONCEPT QUESTIONS

1. What is an efficient market?
2. What are the forms of market efficiency?
3. What evidence exists that major stock markets are efficient?
4. Explain anomalies in the efficient market hypothesis.

---

[13] The suggested readings for this chapter give references to the large body of U.S. and Canadian research on efficient markets.
[14] R. Giammarino, E. Schwartz, and J. Zechner, "Market Valuation of Bank Assets and Deposit Insurance in Canada," *Canadian Journal of Economics* 22 (February 1989), pp. 109–26.

10.7 | SUMMARY AND CONCLUSIONS

This chapter explores the subject of capital market history. Such history is useful because it tells us what to expect in the way of returns from risky assets. We summed up our study of market history with two key lessons:

1. Risky assets, on average, earn a risk premium. There is a reward for bearing risk.

2. The greater the risk from a risky investment, the greater is the required reward.

These lessons have significant implications for financial managers. We consider these implications in the chapters ahead.

We also discussed the concept of market efficiency. In an efficient market, prices adjust quickly and correctly to new information. Consequently, asset prices in efficient markets are rarely too high or too low. How efficient capital markets (such as the TSE and NYSE) are is a matter of debate, but, at a minimum, they are probably much more efficient than most real asset markets.

Key Terms

nominal returns (page 349)

real returns (page 349)

Fisher effect (page 350)

risk premium (page 356)

variance (page 357)

standard deviation (page 357)

normal distribution (page 360)

efficient capital market (page 363)

efficient markets hypothesis (EMH) (page 364)

Chapter Review Problems and Self-Test

10.1   Recent Return History   Use Table 10.1 to calculate the average return over the last five years for Canadian common stocks, small stocks, and Treasury bills.

10.2   More Recent Return History   Calculate the standard deviations using information from Problem 10.1. Which of the investments was the most volatile over this period?

Answers to Self-Test Problems

10.1   We calculate the averages as follows:

Year	TSE	Small	T-Bills
1990	− 0.1480	− 0.2732	0.1328
1991	0.1202	0.1851	0.0990
1992	− 0.0143	0.1301	0.0665
1993	0.3255	0.5226	0.0563
1994	− 0.0018	− 0.0921	0.0476
Average	0.05632	0.0945	0.08044

10.2   We first need to calculate the deviations from the average returns. Using the averages from Problem 10.1, we get:

Year	TSE	Small	T-Bills
1990	− 0.2043	− 0.3677	0.0524
1991	0.0639	0.0906	0.0186
1992	− 0.0706	0.0356	− 0.0139
1993	0.2692	0.4281	− 0.0241
1994	− 0.0581	− 0.1866	− 0.0328
Total	0.0000	0.0000	0.0000

We square these deviations and calculate the variances and standard deviations:

Year	TSE	Small	T-Bills
1990	0.0417	0.1352	0.0027
1991	0.0041	0.0082	0.0003
1992	0.0050	0.0013	0.0002
1993	0.0725	0.1833	0.0006
1994	0.0034	0.0348	0.0011
Variance	0.0317	0.0907	0.0012
Standard Deviation	0.1779	0.3012	0.0351

To calculate the variances we added up the squared deviations and divided by four, the number of returns less one. Notice that the small stocks had substantially greater volatility with a smaller average return. Once again, such investments are risky, particularly over short periods.

Questions and Problems

Basic
(Questions 1–20)

1. **Calculating Returns**   Suppose a stock had an initial price of $54 per share, paid a dividend of $1.75 per share during the year, and had an ending price of $46. Compute the percentage total return.

2. **Calculating Yields**   In Problem 1, what was the dividend yield? The capital gains yield?

3. **Return Calculations**   Rework Problems 1 and 2 assuming that the ending price is $65.

4. **Calculating Real Rates of Return**   If Treasury bills are currently paying 8 percent and the inflation rate is 6 percent, what is the approximate real rate of interest? The exact real rate?

5. **Inflation and Nominal Returns**   Suppose the real rate is 2.5 percent and the inflation rate is 7 percent. What rate would you expect to see on a Treasury bill?

6. **Nominal and Real Returns**   An investment offers an 18 percent return over the coming year. Mary Moneybags thinks the total real return on this investment will only be 14 percent. What does Mary believe the inflation rate will be over the next year?

7. **Nominal versus Real Returns**   Say you own an asset that had a total return last year of 14 percent. If the inflation rate last year was 5 percent, what was your real return?

8. **Inflation and Real Returns**   In Problem 7, what was your real return if the inflation rate was 16 percent last year? Is your answer possible? Explain.

9. **Calculating Returns**   Suppose you bought an 11 percent coupon bond one year ago for $965.00. The bond sells for $925.00 today.

   a. What was your total dollar return on this investment over the past year?

   b. What was your total nominal rate of return on this investment over the past year?

c. If the inflation rate last year was 4 percent, what was your total real rate of return on this investment?

**Basic
(Continued)**

10. **Nominal versus Real Returns**   What was the average annual return on Canadian common stocks from 1948 through 1994:

     a. In nominal terms?
     b. In real terms?

11. **Bond Returns**   What is the historical real return on long-term bonds?

12. **Calculating Returns and Variability**   Using the following returns, calculate the average returns, the variances, and the standard deviations for X and Y.

	Returns	
Year	X	Y
1	14%	22%
2	3	−5
3	−6	−15
4	11	28
5	9	17

13. **Risk Premiums**   Refer to Table 10.1 in the text and look at the period from 1980–1986.

     a. Calculate the average returns for small stocks and T-bills over this time period.
     b. Calculate the standard deviation of the returns for small stocks and T-bills over this time period.
     c. Calculate the observed risk premium in each year for the small stocks versus the T-bills. What was the average risk premium over this period? What was the standard deviation of the risk premium over this period?
     d. Is it possible for the risk premium to be negative before an investment is undertaken? Can the risk premium be negative after the fact? Explain.

14. **Calculating Returns and Variability**   You've observed the following returns on Jayson Corporation's stock over the past five years: 5 percent, −11 percent, 2 percent, 27 percent, 7 percent.

     a. What was the average return on Jayson's stock over this five-year period?
     b. What was the variance of Jayson's returns over this period? The standard deviation?

15. **Calculating Real Returns and Risk Premiums**   For Problem 14, suppose the average inflation rate over this period was 4.5 percent, and the average T-bill rate over the period was 4.8 percent.

     a. What was the average real return on Jayson's stock?
     b. What was the average nominal risk premium on Jayson's stock?

16. **Calculating Real Rates**   Using the information in Problem 15, what was the average real risk-free rate over this time period? What was the average real risk premium?

17. **Effects of Inflation**   Look at Table 10.1 and Figure 10.4 in the text. When were T-bill rates at their highest over the period 1948–94? Why do you think they were so high during this period? What relationship underlies your answer?

18. **EMH and NPV**   Explain why a characteristic of an efficient market is that investments in that market have zero NPVs.

Basic
(Continued)

19. **EMH**   A stock market analyst is able to identify mispriced stocks by comparing the average price for the last 10 days to the average price for the last 60 days. If this is true, what do you know about the market?

20. **Intuition and EMH**   If a market is semistrong form efficient, is it also weak form efficient? Explain.

Intermediate
(Questions 21–27)

21. **Negative Rates**   Is a negative real rate of interest possible ahead of time? After the fact? How about a negative inflation rate? Explain.

22. **Calculating Investment Returns**   You bought one of VanWyck Manufacturing Co.'s 8 percent coupon bonds one year ago for $1,078.50. These bonds make annual payments and mature six years from now. Suppose you decide to sell your bonds today, when the required return on the bonds is 10 percent. If the inflation rate was 3.8 percent over the past year, what would be your total real return on investment?

23. **Using Return Distributions**   Suppose the return on long-term government bonds is normally distributed. Based on the historical record, what is the approximate probability that your return will be less than −4 percent in a given year? What range of returns would you expect to see 95 percent of the time? 99 percent of the time?

24. **Using Return Distributions**   Assuming the return from holding small-company stocks is normally distributed, what is the approximate probability that your money will double in value in a single year? What about triple in value?

25. **Distributions**   In Problem 24, what is the probability that the return is less than −100 percent (think)? What are the implications for the distribution of returns?

26. **EMH**   What are the implications of the efficient markets, hypothesis for investors who buy and sell stocks in an attempt to "beat the market"?

27. **EMH and Speculation**   Critically evaluate the following statements: "Playing the stock market is like gambling. Such speculative investing has no social value, other than the pleasure people get from this form of gambling."

Challenge
(Questions 28–31)

28. **Using Probability Distributions**   Suppose the returns on common stocks are normally distributed. Based on the historical record, use the cumulative normal probability table in the appendix of Chapter 20 to determine the probability that in any given year you will lose money by investing in common stock.

29. **Using Probability Distributions**   Suppose the returns on long-term bonds and T-bills are normally distributed. Based on the historical record, use the cumulative normal probability table in the appendix of Chapter 20 to answer the following questions:

  a. What is the probability that in any given year, the return on long-term bonds will be greater than 10 percent? Less than 0 percent?

  b. What is the probability that in any given year, the return on T-bills will be greater than 10 percent? Less than 0 percent?

  c. In 1974, the return on long-term corporate bonds was −4.53 percent. How likely is it for this low of a return to recur at some point in the future? T-bills had a return of 7.68 percent in this same year. How likely is it for this high of a return on T-bills to recur at some point in the future?

30. **Misconceptions about the EMH**   There are several celebrated investors and stockpickers frequently mentioned in the financial press who have recorded

huge returns on their investments over the past two decades. Is the success of these particular investors an invalidation of the EMH? Explain.

Challenge (Continued)

31. **Interpreting Efficient Markets** For each of the following scenarios, discuss whether profit opportunities exist from trading in the stock of the firm under the conditions that (1) the market is not weak form efficient, (2) the market is weak form but not semistrong form efficient, (3) the market is semistrong form but not strong form efficient, and (4) the market is strong form efficient.

a. The stock price has risen steadily each day for the past 30 days.

b. The financial statements for a company were released three days ago, and you believe you've uncovered some anomalies in the company's inventory and cost control reporting techniques that are understating the firm's true liquidity strength.

c. You observe that the senior management of a company has been buying a lot of the company's stock on the open market over the past week.

Suggested Readings

An important record of the performance of financial investments in Canadian capital markets can be found in:

Hatch, J. E., and R. W. White. *Canadian Stocks, Bonds, Bills, and Inflation: 1950–1983.* Charlottesville, VA: Financial Analysts Research Foundation, 1985.

The corresponding study for the United States is:

Ibbotson, R. G., and R. A. Sinquefield. *Stocks, Bonds, Bills and Inflation (SBBI).* Charlottesville, VA: Financial Analysts Research Foundation, 1982. Updated in *SBBI 1994 Yearbook.* Chicago: Ibbotson Associates, 1995.

Two good reviews of research on efficient markets in Canada are:

Z. Bodie, A. Kane, A. Marcus, S. Perrakis, and P. J. Ryan. *Investments.* 1st Canadian ed. Homewood, IL: Richard D. Irwin, 1993.

W. F. Sharpe, G. J. Alexander, and D. J. Fowler, *Investments.* 1st Canadian ed. Scarborough, ON: Prentice-Hall, 1993.

A useful source of highly readable current Canadian capital markets research is the *Canadian Investment Review.*

Return, Risk, and the Security Market Line

In our last chapter, we learned some important lessons from capital market history. Most importantly, there is a reward, on average, for bearing risk. We called this reward a *risk premium*. The second lesson is that this risk premium is larger for riskier investments. The principle that higher returns can be earned only by taking greater risks appeals to our moral sense that we cannot have something for nothing. This chapter explores the economic and managerial implications of this basic idea.

Thus far, we have concentrated mainly on the return behaviour of a few large portfolios. We need to expand our consideration to include individual assets. Accordingly, the purpose of this chapter is to provide the background necessary for learning how the risk premium is determined for individual assets.

When we examine the risks associated with individual assets, we find two types of risk: systematic and unsystematic. This distinction is crucial because, as we see, systematic risks affect almost all assets in the economy, at least to some degree, while a particular unsystematic risk affects at most a small number of assets. We then develop the principle of diversification, which shows that highly diversified portfolios tend to have almost no unsystematic risk.

The principle of diversification has an important implication: To a diversified investor, only systematic risk matters. It follows that in deciding whether to buy a particular individual asset, a diversified investor is concerned only with that asset's systematic risk. This is a key observation, and it allows us to say a great deal about the risks and returns on individual assets. In particular, it is the basis for a famous relationship between risk and return called the security market line, or SML. To develop the SML, we introduce the equally famous beta coefficient, one of the centerpieces of modern finance. Beta and the SML are key concepts because they supply us with at least part of the answer to the question of how to determine the required return on an investment.

11.1 | EXPECTED RETURNS AND VARIANCES

In our previous chapter, we discussed how to calculate average returns and variances using historical data. We now begin to discuss how to analyze returns and variances when the information we have concerns future possible returns and their possibilities.

Expected Return

We start with a straightforward case. Consider a single period of time, say, a year. We have two stocks, L and U, with the following characteristics: Stock L is expected to have a return of 25 percent in the coming year. Stock U is expected to have a return of 20 percent for the same period.

In a situation like this, if all investors agreed on the expected returns, why would anyone want to hold Stock U? After all, why invest in one stock when the expectation is that another will do better? Clearly, the answer must depend on the risk of the two investments. The return on Stock L, although it is expected to be 25 percent, could actually be higher or lower.

For example, suppose the economy booms. In this case, we think Stock L would have a 70 percent return. If the economy enters a recession, we think the return would be −20 percent. Thus, we say there are two *states of the economy*, meaning that these are the only two possible situations. This setup is oversimplified, of course, but it allows us to illustrate some key ideas without a lot of computation.

Suppose we think a boom and a recession are equally likely to happen, a 50-50 chance of each. Table 11.1 illustrates the basic information we have described and some additional information about Stock U. Notice that Stock U earns 30 percent if there is a recession and 10 percent if there is a boom.

Obviously, if you buy one of these stocks, say Stock U, what you earn in any particular year depends on what the economy does during that year. However, suppose the probabilities stay the same through time. If you hold U for a number of years, you'll earn 30 percent about half the time and 10 percent the other half. In this case, we say that your **expected return** on Stock U, $E(R_U)$, is 20 percent:

$$E(R_U) = .50 \times 30\% + .50 \times 10\% = 20\%$$

In other words, you should expect to earn 20 percent from this stock, on average.

For Stock L, the probabilities are the same, but the possible returns are different. Here we lose 20 percent half the time, and we gain 70 percent the other half. The expected return on L, $E(R_L)$, is thus 25 percent:

$$E(R_L) = .50 \times -20\% + .50 \times 70\% = 25\%$$

Table 11.2 illustrates these calculations.

In our previous chapter, we defined the risk premium as the difference between the return on a risky investment and a risk-free investment, and we calculated the historical risk premiums on some different investments. Using our projected returns, we can calculate the *projected* or *expected risk premium* as the difference between the expected return on a risky investment and the certain return on a risk-free investment.

For example, suppose risk-free investments are currently offering 8 percent. We say the risk-free rate, which we label as R_f, is 8 percent. Given this, what is the

expected return
Return on a risky asset expected in the future.

State of the Economy	Probability of State of the Economy	Security Returns if State Occurs	
		L	U
Recession	0.5	−20%	30%
Boom	0.5	70	10
	1.0		

T A B L E 11.1

States of the economy and stock returns

T A B L E 11.2

Calculation of
expected return

(1) State of Economy	(2) Probability of State of Economy	Stock L		Stock U	
		(3) Rate of Return if State Occurs	(4) Product (2) × (3)	(5) Rate of Return if State Occurs	(6) Product (2) × (5)
Recession	0.5	−.20	−.10	.30	.15
Boom	0.5	.70	.35	.10	.05
	1.0		$E(R_L) = 25\%$		$E(R_U) = 20\%$

projected risk premium on Stock U? On Stock L? Since the expected return on Stock U, $E(R_U)$, is 20 percent, the projected risk premium is:

$$\text{Risk premium} = \text{Expected return} - \text{Risk-free rate} \qquad [11.1]$$
$$= E(R_U) - R_f$$
$$= 20\% - 8\%$$
$$= 12\%$$

Similarly, the risk premium on Stock L is 25% − 8% = 17%.

In general, the expected return on a security or other asset is simply equal to the sum of the possible returns multiplied by their probabilities. So, if we have 100 possible returns, we would multiply each one by its probability and add the results. The result would be the expected return. The risk premium would be the difference between this expected return and the risk-free rate.

A useful generalized equation for expected return is:

$$E(R) = \sum_j O_j \times P_j \qquad [11.2]$$

where

O_j = value of the *j*th outcome

P_j = associated probability of occurrence

$\sum_j$ = the sum over all *j*

E X A M P L E | 11.1   Unequal Probabilities

Look back at Tables 11.1 and 11.2. Suppose you thought that a boom would only occur 20 percent of the time instead of 50 percent. What are the expected returns on Stocks U and L in this case? If the risk-free rate is 10 percent, what are the risk premiums?

The first thing to notice is that a recession must occur 80 percent of the time (1 − .20 = .80) because there are only two possibilities. With this in mind, Stock U has a 30 percent return in 80 percent of the years and a 10 percent return in 20 percent of the years. To calculate the expected return, we again just multiply the possibilities by the probabilities and add up the results:

$$E(R_U) = .80 \times 30\% + .20 \times 10\% = 26\%$$

		Stock L			Stock U		
(1) State of Economy	(2) Probability of State of Economy	(3) Rate of Return if State Occurs	(4) Product (2) × (3)		(5) Rate of Return if State Occurs	(6) Product (2) × (5)	
Recession	.80	−.20	−.16		.30	.24	
Boom	.20	.70	.14		.10	.02	
			$E(R_L) = -2\%$			$E(R_U) = 26\%$	

T A B L E 11.3

Expected return calculation

Table 11.3 summarizes the calculations for both stocks. Notice that the expected return on L is −2 percent.

The risk premium for Stock U is 26% − 10% = 16% in this case. The risk premium for Stock L is negative: −2% − 10% = −12%.

Calculating the Variance

To calculate the variances of the returns on our two stocks, we determine the squared deviations from the expected return. We then multiply each possible squared deviation by its probability. We add these, and the result is the variance. The standard deviation, as always, is the square root of the variance.

Generalized equations for variance and standard deviation are

$$\sigma^2 = \sum_j [O_j - E(R)]^2 \times P_j \qquad [11.3]$$

$$\sigma = \sqrt{\sigma^2}$$

To illustrate, Stock U has an expected return of $E(R_U) = 20\%$. In a given year, it could actually return either 30 percent or 10 percent. The possible deviations are thus 30% − 20% = 10% or 10% − 20% = −10%. In this case, the variance is:

Variance = σ^2 = .50 × (10%)^2 + .50 × (−10%)^2 = .01

The standard deviation is the square root of this: = .10 = 10%

Standard deviation = $\sigma = \sqrt{.01}$ = .10 = 10%

Table 11.4 summarizes these calculations for both stocks. Notice that Stock L has a much larger variance.

When we put the expected return and variability information for our two stocks together, we have:

	Stock L	Stock U
Expected return, E(R)	25%	20%
Variance, σ^2	.2025	.0100
Standard deviation, σ	45%	10%

Stock L has a higher expected return, but U has less risk. You could get a 70 percent return on your investment in L, but you could also lose 70 percent. Notice that an investment in U always pays at least 10 percent.

You've probably noticed that the way we calculated expected returns and variances here is somewhat different from the way we did it in the last chapter. The

T A B L E 11.4

Calculation of variance

(1) State of Economy	(2) Probability of State of Economy	(3) Return Deviation from Expected Return	(4) Squared Return Deviation from Expected Return	(5) Product (2) × (4)
Stock L				
Recession	0.5	$-.20 - .25 = -.45$	$(-.45)^2 = .2025$	.10125
Boom	0.5	$.70 - .25 = .45$	$(.45)^2 = .2025$	.10125
				$\sigma_L^2 = .2025$
Stock U				
Recession	0.5	$.30 - .20 = .10$	$(.10)^2 = .01$	.005
Boom	0.5	$.10 - .20 = -.10$	$(-.10)^2 = .01$	.005
				$\sigma_U^2 = .010$

reason is that, in Chapter 10, we were examining actual historical returns, so we estimated the average return and the variance based on some actual events. Here, we have projected future returns and their associated probabilities, so this is the information with which we must work.

E X A M P L E | 11.2   More Unequal Probabilities

Going back to Example 11.1, what are the variances on the two stocks once we have unequal probabilities? The standard deviations?

We can summarize the needed calculations as follows:

(1) State of Economy	(2) Probability of State of Economy	(3) Return Deviation from Expected Return	(4) Squared Return Deviation from Expected Return	(5) Product (2) × (4)
Stock L				
Recession	.80	$-.20 - (-.02) = -.18$	.0324	.02592
Boom	.20	$.70 - (-.02) = .72$	.5184	.10368
				$\sigma_L^2 = .12960$
Stock U				
Recession	.80	$.30 - .26 = .04$	.0016	.00128
Boom	.20	$.10 - .26 = -.16$	.0256	.00512
				$\sigma_U^2 = .00640$

Based on these calculations, the standard deviation for L is $\sigma_L = \sqrt{.1296} = 36$ percent. The standard deviation for U is much smaller, $\sigma_U = \sqrt{.0064} = .08$ or 8 percent.

CONCEPT QUESTIONS

1. How do we calculate the expected return on a security?
2. In words, how do we calculate the variance of the expected return?

11.2 | PORTFOLIOS

portfolio

Group of assets such as stocks and bonds held by an investor.

Thus far in this chapter, we have concentrated on individual assets considered separately. However, most investors actually hold a **portfolio** of assets. All we mean by this is that investors tend to own more than just a single stock, bond, or other asset. Given that this is so, portfolio return and portfolio risk are of obvious relevance. Accordingly, we now discuss portfolio expected returns and variances.

Portfolio Weights

There are many equivalent ways of describing a portfolio. The most convenient approach is to list the percentages of the total portfolio's value that are invested in each portfolio asset. We call these percentages the **portfolio weights**.

For example, if we have $50 in one asset and $150 in another, our total portfolio is worth $200. The percentage of our portfolio in the first asset is $50/$200 = .25. The percentage of our portfolio in the second asset is $150/$200, or .75. Our portfolio weights are thus .25 and .75. Notice that the weights have to add up to 1.00 since all of our money is invested somewhere.[1]

portfolio weights
Percentage of a portfolio's total value in a particular asset.

Portfolio Expected Returns

Let's go back to Stocks L and U. You put half your money in each. The portfolio weights are obviously .50 and .50. What is the pattern of returns on this portfolio? The expected return?

To answer these questions, suppose the economy actually enters a recession. In this case, half your money (the half in L) loses 20 percent. The other half (the half in U) gains 30 percent. Your portfolio return, R_P, in a recession is thus:

$$R_P = .50 \times (-20\%) + .50 \times 30\% = 5\%$$

Table 11.5 summarizes the remaining calculations. Notice that when a boom occurs, your portfolio would return 40 percent:

$$R_P = .50 \times 70\% + .50 \times 10\% = 40\%$$

As indicated in Table 11.5, the expected return on your portfolio, $E(R_P)$, is 22.5 percent.

We can save ourselves some work by calculating the expected return more directly. Given these portfolio weights, we could have reasoned that we expect half of our money to earn 25 percent (the half in L) and half of our money to earn 20 percent (the half in U). Our portfolio expected return is thus:

$$E(R_P) = .50 \times E(R_L) + .50 \times E(R_U)$$
$$= .50 \times 25\% + .50 \times 20\%$$
$$= 22.5\%$$

This is the same portfolio expected return we had before.

(1) State of Economy	(2) Probability of State of Economy	(3) Portfolio Return if State Occurs	(4) Product (2) × (3)
Recession	.50	½ × (−20%) + ½ × (30%) = 5%	2.5%
Boom	.50	½ × (70%) + ½ × (10%) = 40%	20.0
			$E(R_P) = \overline{22.5\%}$

T A B L E 11.5

Expected return on an equally weighted portfolio of Stock L and Stock U

---

[1] Some of it could be in cash, of course, but we would just consider the cash to be one of the portfolio assets.

This method of calculating the expected return on a portfolio works no matter how many assets are in the portfolio. Suppose we had n assets in our portfolio, where n is any number. If we let x_i stand for the percentage of our money in asset i, the expected return is:

$$E(R_P) = x_1 \times E(R_1) + x_2 \times E(R_2) + \ldots + x_n \times E(R_n) \qquad [11.4]$$

This says that the expected return on a portfolio is a straightforward combination of the expected returns on the assets in that portfolio. This seems somewhat obvious, but, as we examine next, the obvious approach is not always the right one.

E X A M P L E | 11.3   **Portfolio Expected Return**

Suppose we have the following projections on three stocks:

State of Economy	Probability of State	Returns		
		Stock A	Stock B	Stock C
Boom	.40	10%	15%	20%
Bust	.60	8	4	0

What would be the expected return on a portfolio with equal amounts invested in each of the three stocks? What would the expected return be if half the portfolio were in A, with the remainder equally divided between B and C?

From our earlier discussions, the expected returns on the individual stocks are (check these for practice):

$E(R_A) = 8.8\%$

$E(R_B) = 8.4\%$

$E(R_C) = 8.0\%$

If a portfolio has equal investments in each asset, the portfolio weights are all the same. Such a portfolio is said to be equally weighted. Since there are three stocks, the weights are all equal to 1/3. The portfolio expected return is thus:

$$E(R_P) = (\tfrac{1}{3}) \times 8.8\% + (\tfrac{1}{3}) \times 8.4\% + (\tfrac{1}{3}) \times 8.0\% = 8.4\%$$

In the second case, check that the portfolio expected return is 8.4 percent. |

Portfolio Variance

From our previous discussion, the expected return on a portfolio that contains equal investment in Stocks U and L is 22.5 percent. What is the standard deviation of return on this portfolio? Simple intuition might suggest that half the money has a standard deviation of 45 percent and the other half has a standard deviation of 10 percent, so the portfolio's standard deviation might be calculated as:

$$\sigma_P = .50 \times 45\% + .50 \times 10\% = 27.5\%$$

Unfortunately, this approach is incorrect.

Let's see what the standard deviation really is. Table 11.6 summarizes the relevant calculations. As we see, the portfolio's variance is about .031, and its standard deviation is less than we thought—it's only 17.5 percent. What is illustrated here is that the variance on a portfolio is not generally a simple combination of the variances of the assets in the portfolio.

(1) State of Economy	(2) Probability of State of Economy	(3) Portfolio Return if State Occurs	(4) Squared Deviation from Expected Return	(5) Product (2) × (4)
Recession	.50	5%	$(.05 - .225)^2 = .030625$	.0153125
Boom	.50	40%	$(.40 - .225)^2 = .030625$	.0153125
			$\sigma_p^2 =$	.030625

$$\sigma_p = \sqrt{.030625} = 17.5\%$$

T A B L E 11.6

Variance on an equally weighted portfolio of Stock L and Stock U

We can illustrate this point a little more dramatically by considering a slightly different set of portfolio weights. Suppose we put $\frac{2}{11}$ (about 18 percent) in L and the other $\frac{9}{11}$ (about 82 percent) in U. If a recession occurs, this portfolio would have a return of:

$$R_P = \left(\frac{2}{11}\right) \times (-20\%) + \left(\frac{9}{11}\right) \times (30\%) = 20.91\%$$

If a boom occurs, this portfolio would have a return of:

$$R_P = \left(\frac{2}{11}\right) \times (70\%) + \left(\frac{9}{11}\right) \times (10\%) = 20.91\%$$

Notice that the return is the same no matter what happens. No further calculations are needed: This portfolio has a zero variance. Apparently, combining assets into portfolios can substantially alter the risks faced by the investor. This is a crucial observation, and we explore its implications in the next section.

Portfolio Standard Deviation and Diversification

How diversification reduces portfolio risk as measured by the portfolio standard deviation is worth exploring in some detail.[2] The key concept is *correlation*, which provides a reading on the extent to which the returns on two assets move together. If correlation is positive, we say that Assets A and B are positively correlated; if it is negative, we say they are negatively correlated; and if it is zero, the two assets are uncorrelated.

Figure 11.1 shows these three benchmark cases for two assets, A and B. The graphs on the left side plot the separate returns on the two securities through time. Each point on the graphs on the right side represents the returns for both A and B over a particular time interval. The figure shows examples of different values for the correlation coefficient, CORR (R_a, R_b), that range from −1.0 to 1.0.

To show how the graphs are constructed, we need to look at points 1 and 2 (on the upper left graph) and relate them to point 3 (on the upper right graph). Point 1 is a return on Company B and point 2 is a return on Company A. They both occur over the same time period, say, for example, the month of June. Both returns are above

[2] The ideas in this section were first developed systematically in an article written in 1952 by Harry Markowitz, "Portfolio Selection," *Journal of Finance* 7 (March 1952), pp. 77–91. His work laid the foundation for the development of the capital asset pricing model principally by William F. Sharpe, "Capital Asset Prices: A Theory of Market Equilibrium under Conditions of Risk," *Journal of Finance* 19 (1964), pp. 425–42. These pioneers of modern portfolio theory were awarded the Nobel Prize in Economics in 1991.

F I G U R E   11.1

Examples of different correlation coefficients

The graphs on the left-hand side of the figure plot the separate returns on the two securities through time. Each point on the graphs on the right-hand side represents the returns for both *A* and *B* over a particular time period.

Perfect positive correlation
Corr $(R_A, R_B) = 1$

Returns

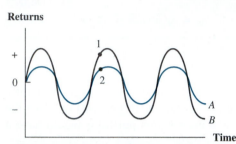

Return on B

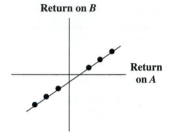

Return on *A*

Both the return on Security *A* and the return on Security *B* are higher than average at the same time. Both the return on Security *A* and the return on Security *B* are lower than average at the same time.

Perfect negative correlation
Corr $(R_A, R_B) = -1$

Returns

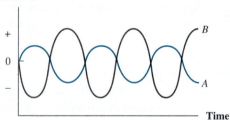

Return on B

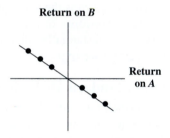

Return on *A*

Security *A* has a higher-than-average return when Security *B* has a lower-than-average return, and vice versa.

Zero correlation
Corr $(R_A, R_B) = 0$

Returns

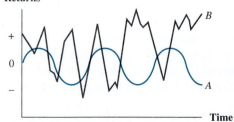

Return on B

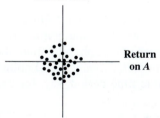

Return on *A*

The return on Security *A* is completely unrelated to the return on Security *B*.

average. Point 3 represents the returns on both stocks in June. Other dots in the upper right graph represent the returns on both stocks in other months.

Because the returns on Security B have bigger swings than the returns on Security A, the slope of the line in the upper right graph is greater than one. Perfect positive correlation does not imply that the slope is one. Rather, it implies that all points lie exactly on the line. Less-than-perfect positive correlation implies a positive slope, but the points do not lie exactly on the line. An example of less-than-perfect positive correlation is provided in the left side of Figure 11.2. As before, each point in the graph represents the returns on both securities in the same month. In a graph like this, the closer the points lie to the line, the closer the correlation is to one. In other words, a high correlation between the two returns implies that the graph has a tight fit.[3]

Less-than-perfect negative correlation implies a negative slope, but the points do not lie exactly on the line as shown on the right side of Figure 11.2.

E X A M P L E | 11.4   Correlation between Stocks U and L

What is the correlation between Stocks U and L from our earlier example if we assume the two states of the economy are equally probable? Table 11.2 shows the returns on each stock in recession and boom states.

	Stock L	Stock U
Recession	−.20	.30
Boom	.70	.10

Figure 11.3 plots the line exactly the same way as we plotted the graphs on the right sides of Figures 11.1 and 11.2. You can see from the figure that the line has a negative

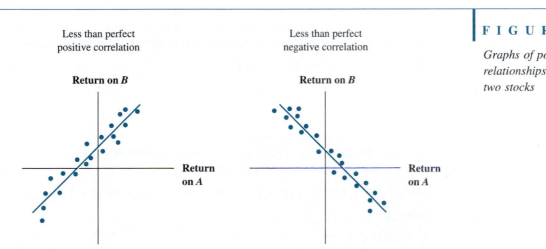

FIGURE 11.2

Graphs of possible relationships between two stocks

---

[3] If we measure the correlation by regression analysis, the *correlation coefficient* is the square root of *R* squared, the regression coefficient of determination. For a perfect fit, *R* squared is one and the correlation coefficient is also one.

F I G U R E 11.3

Correlation between stocks U and L

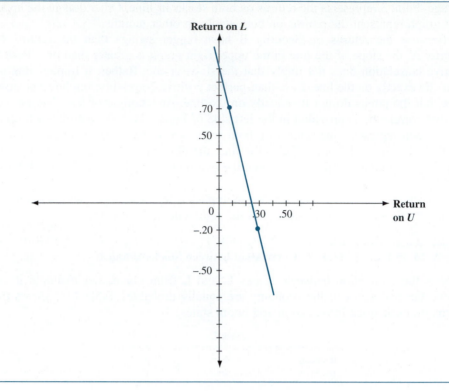

slope and all the points lie exactly on the line. (Since we only have two outcomes for each stock, the points must plot exactly on a straight line.) You can conclude that the correlation between Stocks U and L is equal to −1.0.

Our discussion of correlation provides us with a key building block of a formula for portfolio standard variance and its square root, portfolio standard deviation.

$$\sigma^2{}_P = x^2{}_L\sigma^2{}_L + x^2{}_U\sigma^2{}_U + 2x_Lx_U\text{CORR}_{L,U}\sigma_L\sigma_U \qquad [11.5]$$

$$\sigma_P = \sqrt{\sigma_P^2}$$

Recall that x_L and x_U are, respectively, the portfolio weights for Stocks U and L. $\text{CORR}_{L,U}$ is the correlation of the two stocks.

We can use the formula to check our previous calculation of portfolio standard deviation for a portfolio invested 50 percent in each stock.

$$= (.5)^2 \times (.45)^2 + (.5)^2 \times (.10)^2 + (2) \times (.5) \times (.5) \times (.45) \times (.10) \times (-1.0)$$

$$= .030625$$

$$= \sqrt{.030625} = 17.5\%$$

These are the same results we got in Table 11.6.

E X A M P L E | 11.5   **The Zero-Variance Portfolio**

Can you find a portfolio of Stocks U and L with zero variance? Earlier, we showed that investing ²⁄₁₁ (about 18) percent of the portfolio in L and the other ⁹⁄₁₁ (about 82 percent) in U gives the same expected portfolio return in either recession or boom. As a result, the portfolio variance and standard deviation should both be zero. We can check this with the formula for portfolio variance.

$$\sigma^2{}_P = \left(\frac{2}{11}\right)^2 \times (.45)^2 + \left(\frac{9}{11}\right)^2 \times (.10)^2 + 2 \times \left(\frac{2}{11}\right) \times \left(\frac{9}{11}\right) \times (.45) \times (.10) \times (-1.0)$$

$$= .006694 + .006694 - .013388$$

$$= 0$$

You can see that the portfolio variance (and standard deviation) are zero because the weights were chosen to make the negative third term exactly offset the first two positive terms. This third term is called the *covariance term* because the product of the correlation times the two security standard deviations is the covariance of U and L.[4]

To explore how the portfolio standard deviation depends on correlation, Table 11.7 recalculates the portfolio standard deviation changing the correlation between U and L, yet keeping the portfolio weights and all the other input data unchanged. When the correlation is perfectly negative, $CORR_{U,L} = -1.0$, the portfolio standard deviation is 0 as we just calculated. If the two stocks were uncorrelated ($CORR_{L,U} = 0$), the portfolio standard deviation becomes 11.5708 percent. And, with perfect positive correlation ($CORR_{L,U} = +1.0$) the portfolio standard deviation is 16.3636 percent.

When the returns on the two assets are perfectly correlated, the portfolio standard deviation is simply the weighted average of the individual standard deviations. In this special case:

$$16.3636 = \left(\frac{2}{11}\right) \times 45\% + \left(\frac{9}{11}\right) \times 10\%$$

With perfect correlation, all possible portfolios lie on a straight line between U and L in expected return/standard deviation space as shown in Figure 11.4. In this polar case, there is little benefit from diversification. But, as soon as correlation is less than perfectly positive, $CORR_{L,U} = +1.0$, diversification reduces risk.

As long as CORR is less than +1.0, the standard deviation of a portfolio of two securities is *less* than the weighted average of the standard deviations of the individual securities.

Stock L	$x_L = 2/11$	$\sigma_L = 45\%$	$E(R_L) = 25\%$	**T A B L E 11.7**
Stock U	$x_U = 9/11$	$\sigma_U = 10\%$	$E(R_U) = 20\%$	
$E(R_L) = (2/11) \times 25\% + 9/11 \times 20\% = 20.91\%$				*Portfolio standard deviation and correlation*

$CORR_{L,U}$ Portfolio	Standard Deviation of Portfolio σ_P
1. −1.0	0.0000%
2. 0.0	11.5708%
3. +1.0	16.3636%

---

[4] As the number of stocks in the portfolio increases beyond the two in our example, the number of covariance terms increases geometrically. In general, for a portfolio of N securities, the number of covariance terms is $(N^2 - N)/2$. For example, a 10 stock portfolio has 45 covariance terms.

FIGURE 11.4

Opportunity sets composed of holdings in Stock L and Stock U

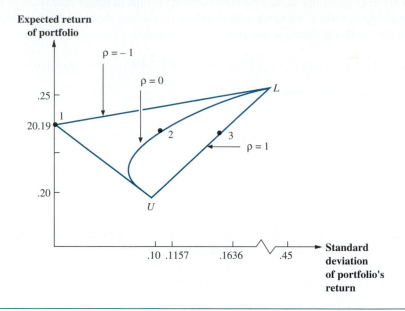

Figure 11.4 shows this important result by graphing all possible portfolios of U and L for the three cases for $CORR_{L,U}$, given in Table 11.7. The portfolios marked 1, 2, and 3 in Figure 11.4 all have an expected return of 20.91 percent as calculated in Table 11.7. Their standard deviations also come from Table 11.7. The other points on the respective lines or curves are derived by varying the portfolio weights for each value of $CORR_{L,U}$. Each line or curve represents all the possible portfolios of U and L for a given correlation. Each is called an *opportunity set* or *feasible set*. The lowest opportunity set representing $CORR_{L,U} = 1.0$ always has the largest standard deviation for any return level. Once again, this shows how diversification reduces risk as long as correlation is less than perfectly positive.

Diversification and the Efficient Set

Suppose U and L actually have a correlation of about +0.70. The opportunity set is graphed in Figure 11.5. In this figure, we have marked the minimum variance portfolio, MV. No risk-averse investor would hold any portfolio with expected return below MV. For example, no such investor would invest 100 percent in Stock U because such a portfolio has lower expected return and higher standard deviation than the minimum variance portfolio. We say that portfolios such as U are dominated by the minimum variance portfolio. (Since standard deviation is the square root of variance, the minimum variance portfolios also have minimum standard deviations as shown in Figures 11.4 and 11.5.) Though the entire curve from U to L is called the *feasible set,* investors only consider the curve from MV to L. This part of the curve is called the *efficient set.*

E X A M P L E | 11.6   Benefits of Foreign Investment

Research on diversification extends our discussion of historical average returns and risks in Chapter 10 to include foreign investment portfolios. It turns out that the feasible set looks like Figure 11.5 where points like U and L represent portfolios

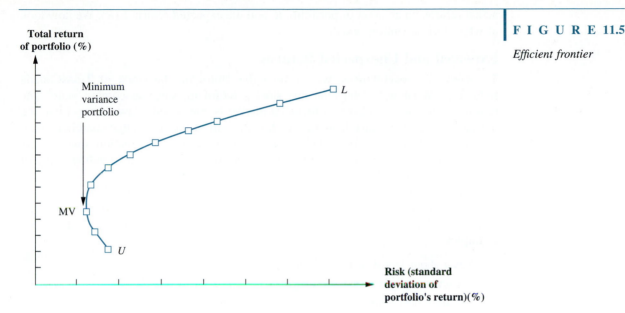

FIGURE 11.5

Efficient frontier

instead of individual stocks. Portfolio U represents 100 percent investment in Canadian equities and Portfolio L represents 100 percent in foreign equities. The domestic stock portfolio is less risky than the foreign portfolio. Does this mean Canadian portfolio managers should invest entirely in Canada?

The answer is no because the minimum variance portfolio with approximately 20 percent foreign content dominates portfolio U, the 100 percent domestic portfolio. Going from 0 percent to around 20 percent foreign content actually reduces portfolio standard deviation due to the diversification effect. Increasing the foreign content beyond around 20 percent increases portfolio risk. Recognizing this point led pension managers to lobby successfully in 1992 for an increase in allowable foreign content to 20 percent.[5]

CONCEPT QUESTIONS

1. What is a portfolio weight?
2. How do we calculate the expected return on a portfolio?
3. Is there a simple relationship between the standard deviation on a portfolio and the standard deviation of the assets in the portfolio?

11.3 | ANNOUNCEMENTS, SURPRISES, AND EXPECTED RETURNS

Now that we know how to construct portfolios and evaluate their returns, we begin to describe more carefully the risks and returns associated with individual securities. Thus far, we have measured volatility by looking at the differences between the

---

[5] These data come from H. S. Marmer, "International Investing: A New Canadian Perspective," *Canadian Investment Review,* Spring, 1991, pp. 47–53. Some analysts argue that an efficient portfolio should have more than 20 percent Canadian content. See J. McDonald and M. Cheung, "Is the 20% Foreign Cap Limiting Your Returns?" *Canadian Investment Review,* Summer 1994, pp. 33–37.

actual returns on an asset or portfolio, *R,* and the expected return, E(*R*). We now look at why those deviations exist.

Expected and Unexpected Returns

To begin, for concreteness, we consider the return on the stock of TransCanada Industries. What will determine this stock's return in, say, the coming year? The return on any stock traded in a financial market is composed of two parts: First, the normal or expected return from the stock is the part of the return that shareholders in the market predict or expect. This return depends on the information shareholders have that bears on the stock, and it is based on the market's understanding today of the important factors that influence the stock in the coming year.

The second part of the return on the stock is the uncertain or risky part. This is the portion that comes from unexpected information that is revealed within the year. A list of all possible sources of such information is endless, but here are a few examples:

News about TransCanada's research.

Government figures released on gross national product (GNP).

The imminent bankruptcy of an important competitor.

The news that TransCanada's sales figures are higher than expected.

A sudden, unexpected drop in interest rates.

Based on this discussion, one way to write the return on TransCanada's stock in the coming year would be:

$$\text{Total return} = \text{Expected return} + \text{Unexpected return} \qquad [11.6]$$
$$R = E(R) + U$$

where *R* stands for the actual total return in the year, E(*R*) stands for the expected part of the return, and *U* stands for the unexpected part of the return. What this says is that the actual return, *R,* differs from the expected return, E(*R*), because of surprises that occur during the day.

Announcements and News

We need to be careful when we talk about the effect of news items on the return. For example, suppose that TransCanada Industries' business is such that the company prospers when GNP grows at a relatively high rate and suffers when GNP is relatively stagnant. In deciding what return to expect this year from owning stock in TransCanada, shareholders either implicitly or explicitly must think about what the GNP is likely to be for the year.

When the government actually announces GNP figures for the year, what will happen to the value of TransCanada Industries stock? Obviously, the answer depends on what figure is released. More to the point, however, the impact depends on how much of that figure is new information.

At the beginning of the year, market participants have some idea or forecast of what the yearly GNP will be. To the extent that shareholders had predicted the GNP, that prediction is already factored into the expected part of the return on the stock, E(*R*). On the other hand, if the announced GNP is a surprise, the effect is part of *U,* the unanticipated portion of the return.

As an example, suppose shareholders in the market had forecast that the GNP increase this year would be 0.5 percent. If the actual announcement this year is exactly 0.5 percent, the same as the forecast, the shareholders didn't really learn anything, and the announcement isn't news. There would be no impact on the stock price as a result. This is like receiving confirmation of something that you suspected all along; it doesn't reveal anything new.

A common way of saying that an announcement isn't news is to say that the market has already "discounted" the announcement. The use of the word *discount* here is different from the use of the term in computing present values, but the spirit is the same. When we discount a dollar in the future, we say it is worth less to us because of the time value of money. When we discount an announcement or a news item, we mean it has less of an impact on the market because the market already knew much of it.

For example, going back to TransCanada Industries, suppose the government announced that the actual GNP increase during the year was 1.5 percent. Now shareholders have learned something, namely, that the increase is 1 percentage point higher than they had forecast. This difference between the actual result and the forecast, 1 percentage point in this example, is sometimes called the *innovation* or the *surprise*.

An announcement, then, can be broken into two parts, the anticipated or expected part and the surprise or innovation:

$$\text{Announcement} = \text{Expected part} + \text{Surprise} \qquad [11.7]$$

The expected part of any announcement is the part of the information that the market uses to form the expectation $E(R)$, of the return on the stock. The surprise is the news that influences the unanticipated return on the stock, U.

To take another example, if shareholders knew in January that the president of the firm was going to resign, the official announcement in February would be fully expected and would be discounted by the market. Because the announcement was expected before February, its influence on the stock would have occurred before February. The announcement itself contains no surprise, and the stock's price shouldn't change when it is actually made.

Our discussion of market efficiency in the previous chapter bears on this discussion. We are assuming that relevant information that is known today is already reflected in the expected return. This is identical to saying that the current price reflects relevant publicly available information. We are thus implicitly assuming that markets are at least reasonably efficient in the semistrong form sense.

Henceforth, when we speak of news, we mean the surprise part of an announcement and not the portion that the market has expected and, therefore, already discounted.

CONCEPT QUESTIONS
1. What are the two basic parts of a return?
2. Under what conditions does an announcement have no effect on common stock prices?

11.4 | RISK: SYSTEMATIC AND UNSYSTEMATIC

The unanticipated part of the return, that portion resulting from surprises, is the true risk of any investment. After all, if we always receive exactly what we expect, the investment is perfectly predictable and, by definition, risk-free. In other words, the risk of owning an asset comes from surprises—unanticipated events.

There are important differences, though, among various sources of risk. Look back at our previous list of news stories. Some of these stories are directed specifically at TransCanada Industries, and some are more general. Which of the news items are of specific importance to TransCanada Industries?

Announcements about interest rates or GNP are clearly important for nearly all companies, whereas the news about TransCanada Industries' president, its research, or its sales are of specific interest to TransCanada Industries. We distinguish between these two types of events however because, as we shall see, they have very different implications.

Systematic and Unsystematic Risk

systematic risk

A risk that influences a large number of assets. Also market risk.

The first surprise, the one that affects a large number of assets, we label **systematic risk**. A systematic risk is one that influences a large number of assets, each to a greater or lesser extent. Because systematic risks are market-wide effects, they are sometimes called *market risks*.

The second type of surprise we call **unsystematic risk**. An unsystematic risk is one that affects a single asset or a small group of assets. Because these risks are unique to individual companies or assets, they are sometimes called *unique* or *asset-specific risks*. We use these terms interchangeably.

unsystematic risk

A risk that affects at most a small number of assets. Also unique or asset-specific risks.

As we have seen, uncertainties about general economic conditions, such as GNP, interest rates, or inflation, are examples of systematic risks. These conditions affect nearly all companies to some degree. An unanticipated increase or surprise in inflation, for example, affects wages and the costs of the supplies that companies buy; it affects the value of the assets that companies own; and it affects the prices at which companies sell their products. Forces such as these, to which all companies are susceptible, are the essence of systematic risk.

In contrast, the announcement of an oil strike by a company primarily affects that company and, perhaps, a few others (such as primary competitors and suppliers). It is unlikely to have much of an effect on the world oil market, however, or on the affairs of companies not in the oil business.

Systematic and Unsystematic Components of Return

The distinction between a systematic risk and an unsystematic risk is never really as exact as we make it out to be. Even the most narrow and peculiar bits of news about a company ripple through the economy. This is true because every enterprise, no matter how tiny, is a part of the economy. It's like the tale of a kingdom that was lost because one horse lost a shoe. This is mostly hairsplitting, however. Some risks are clearly much more general than others. We'll see some evidence on this point in just a moment.

The distinction between the types of risk allows us to break down the surprise portion, U, of the return on TransCanada Industries stock into two parts. As before, we break the actual return down into its expected and surprise components:

$$R = E(R) + U$$

We now recognize that the total surprise for TransCanada Industries, U, has a systematic and an unsystematic component, so:

$$R = E(R) + \text{Systematic portion} + \text{Unsystematic portion.} \qquad [11.8]$$

Because it is traditional, we use the Greek letter epsilon, ϵ, to stand for the unsystematic portion. Since systematic risks are often called market risks, we use the letter m to stand for the systematic part of the surprise. With these symbols, we can rewrite the total return:

$$R = E(R) + U$$
$$= E(R) + m + \epsilon$$

The important thing about the way we have broken down the total surprise, U, is that the unsystematic portion, ϵ, is more or less unique to TransCanada Industries. For this reason, it is unrelated to the unsystematic portion of return on most other assets. To see why this is important, we need to return to the subject of portfolio risk.

CONCEPT QUESTIONS

1. What are the two basic types of risk?
2. What is the distinction between the two types of risk?

11.5 | DIVERSIFICATION AND PORTFOLIO RISK

We've seen earlier that portfolio risks can, in principle, be quite different from the risks of the assets that make up the portfolio. We now look more closely at the riskiness of an individual asset versus the risk of a portfolio of many different assets. We once again examine some market history to get an idea of what happens with actual investments in capital markets.

The Effect of Diversification: Another Lesson from Market History

In our previous chapter, we saw that the standard deviation of the annual return on a portfolio of several hundred large common stocks has historically been about 20 percent per year, for both the New York and Toronto Stock Exchanges (see Table 10.4, for example). Does this mean the standard deviation of the annual return on a typical stock is 20 percent? As you might suspect by now, the answer is no. This is an extremely important observation.

To examine the relationship between portfolio size and portfolio risk, Table 11.7A illustrates typical average annual standard deviations for equally weighted portfolios that contain different numbers of randomly selected NYSE securities.[6]

In Column 2 of Table 11.7A, we see that the standard deviation for a "portfolio" of one security is about 49 percent. What this means is that, if you randomly selected a single NYSE stock and put all your money into it, your standard deviation of return would typically have been a substantial 49 percent per year. If you were to randomly select two stocks and invest half your money in each, your standard deviation would have been about 37 percent on average, and so on.

The important thing to notice in Table 11.7A is that the standard deviation declines as the number of securities is increased. By the time we have 100 randomly chosen stocks, the portfolio's standard deviation has declined by about 60 percent,

---

[6] These figures are from Table 1 in Meir Statman, "How Many Stocks Make a Diversified Portfolio?" *Journal of Financial and Quantitative Analysis* 22 (September 1987), pp. 353–64. They were derived from E. J. Elton and M. J. Gruber, "Risk Reduction and Portfolio Size: An Analytic Solution," *Journal of Business* 50 (October 1977), pp. 415–37.

T A B L E 11.7A

Standard deviations of annual portfolio returns

(1) Number of Stocks in Portfolio	(2) Average Standard Deviation of Annual Portfolio Returns	(3) Ratio of Portfolio Standard Deviation to Standard Deviation of a Single Stock
1	49.24%	1.00
2	37.36	0.76
4	29.69	0.60
6	26.64	0.54
8	24.98	0.51
10	23.93	0.49
20	21.68	0.44
30	20.87	0.42
40	20.46	0.42
50	20.20	0.41
100	19.69	0.40
200	19.42	0.39
300	19.34	0.39
400	19.29	0.39
500	19.27	0.39
1,000	19.21	0.39

from 49 to about 20 percent. With 500 securities, the standard deviation is 19.49 percent, similar to the 21 percent we saw in our previous chapter for the large common stock portfolio. The small difference exists because the portfolio securities and time periods examined are not identical.

Table 11.8 shows standard deviations for selected Canadian companies listed on the TSE measured over a recent period.[7] For example, a portfolio invested 100 percent in the stock of the Bank of Montreal had a standard deviation of annual returns of around 20 percent. Bralorne Resources had a much higher standard deviation of about 65 percent. Diversification over 300 large TSE stocks reduced the standard deviation to around 18 percent over this period.

The Principle of Diversification

Figure 11.6 illustrates the point we've been discussing. What we have plotted is the standard deviation of return versus the number of stocks in the portfolio. Notice in Figure 11.6 that the benefit in risk reduction from adding securities drops as we add more and more. By the time we have 10 securities, the portfolio standard deviation has dropped from 49.2 to 23.9 percent, most of the effect is already realized, and by the time we get to 30 or so, there is very little remaining benefit.

principle of diversification

Principle stating that spreading an investment across a number of assets eliminates some, but not all, of the risk.

Figure 11.6 illustrates two key points: First, the **principle of diversification** (discussed earlier) tells us that spreading an investment across many assets eliminates some of the risk. The shaded area in Figure 11.6, labelled diversifiable risk, is the part that can be eliminated by diversification.

The second point is equally important. A minimum level of risk cannot be eliminated simply by diversifying. This minimum level is labelled nondiversifiable risk in Figure 11.6. Taken together, these two points are another important lesson

---

[7] The standard deviations were first calculated for monthly data spanning 84 months on the Laval Tape and then annualized.

Algonquin Mercantile	36.03%	
Argyll Energy	60.62	
Bralorne Resources	65.13	
Bell Canada Enterprises	13.86	
Bank of Montreal	20.09	
Bank of Nova Scotia	22.17	
Alcan Aluminum	27.71	
BCTEL	12.82	
TSE 300	18.36	

T A B L E 11.8

Standard deviations for selected TSE companies, annual returns

Source: Calculated from the Laval Tape. This computer tape is produced by Laval University annually.

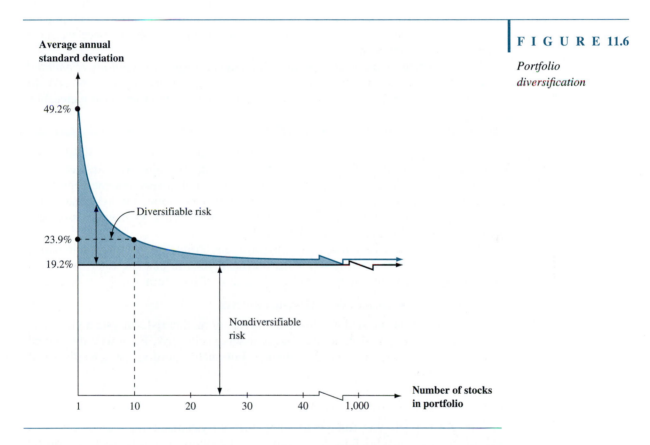

F I G U R E 11.6

Portfolio diversification

from capital market history: Diversification reduces risk, but only up to a point. Put another way, some risk is diversifiable and some is not.

Diversification and Unsystematic Risk

From our discussion of portfolio risk, we know that some of the risk associated with individual assets can be diversified away and some cannot. We are left with an obvious question: Why is this so? It turns out that the answer hinges on the distinction we made earlier between systematic and unsystematic risk.

By definition, an unsystematic risk is one that is particular to a single asset or, at most, a small group. For example, if the asset under consideration is stock in a single company, the discovery of positive NPV projects such as successful new products and innovative cost savings tend to increase the value of the stock. Unanticipated lawsuits, industrial accidents, strikes, and similar events tend to decrease future cash flows and thereby reduce share values.

Here is the important observation: If we only held a single stock, the value of our investment would fluctuate because of company-specific events. If we held a large portfolio, on the other hand, some of the stocks in the portfolio would go up in value because of positive company-specific events and some would go down in value because of negative events. The net effect on the overall value of the portfolio is relatively small, however, as these effects tend to cancel each other out.

Now we see why some of the variability associated with individual assets is eliminated by diversification. By combining assets into portfolios, the unique or unsystematic events—both positive and negative—tend to wash out once we have more than just a few assets.

This important point bears repeating: *Unsystematic risk is essentially eliminated by diversification, so a relatively large portfolio has almost no unsystematic risk.* In fact, the terms *diversifiable risk* and *unsystematic risk* are often used interchangeably.

Diversification and Systematic Risk

We've seen that unsystematic risk can be eliminated by diversifying. What about systematic risk? Can it also be eliminated by diversification? The answer is no because, by definition, a systematic risk affects almost all assets to some degree. As a result, no matter how many assets we put into a portfolio, the systematic risk doesn't go away. Thus, for obvious reasons, the terms *systematic risk* and *nondiversifiable risk* are used interchangeably.

Because we have introduced so many different terms, it is useful to summarize our discussion before moving on. What we have seen is that the total risk of an investment, as measured by the standard deviation of its return, can be written as:

$$\text{Total risk} = \text{Systematic risk} + \text{Unsystematic risk} \qquad [11.9]$$

Systematic risk is also called nondiversifiable risk or market risk. Unsystematic risk is also called diversifiable risk, unique risk, or asset-specific risk. For a well-diversified portfolio, the unsystematic risk is negligible. For such a portfolio, essentially all of the risk is systematic.

Risk and the Sensible Investor

Having gone to all this trouble to show that unsystematic risk disappears in a well-diversified portfolio, how do we know that investors even want such portfolios? Suppose they like risk and don't want it to disappear?

We must admit that, theoretically at least, this is possible, but we argue that it does not describe what we think of as the typical investor. Our typical investor is *risk averse*. Risk-averse behaviour can be defined in many ways, but we prefer the following example: A fair gamble is one with zero expected return; a risk-averse investor would prefer to avoid fair gambles.

Why do investors choose well-diversified portfolios? Our answer is that they are risk averse, and risk-averse people avoid unnecessary risk, such as the unsystematic risk on a stock. If you do not think this is much of an answer to why investors choose well-diversified portfolios and avoid unsystematic risk, consider whether you would take on such a risk. For example, suppose you had worked all summer and had saved $5,000, which you intended to use for your university expenses. Now, suppose someone came up to you and offered to flip a coin for the money: heads, you would double your money, and tails, you would lose it all.

Would you take such a bet? Perhaps you would, but most people would not. Leaving aside any moral question that might surround gambling and recognizing that some people would take such a bet, it's our view that the average investor would not.

To induce the typical risk-averse investor to take a fair gamble, you must sweeten the pot. For example, you might need to raise the odds of winning from 50-50 to 70-30 or higher. The risk-averse investor can be induced to take fair gambles only if they are sweetened so that they become unfair to the investor's advantage.

> CONCEPT QUESTIONS
> 1. What happens to the standard deviation of return for a portfolio if we increase the number of securities in the portfolio?
> 2. Why is some risk diversifiable? Why is some risk not diversifiable?
> 3. Why can't systematic risk be diversified away?
> 4. Explain the concept of risk aversion.

11.6 | SYSTEMATIC RISK AND BETA

The question that we now begin to address is: What determines the size of the risk premium on a risky asset? Put another way, why do some assets have a larger risk premium than other assets? The answer to these questions, as we discuss next, is also based on the distinction between systematic and unsystematic risk.

The Systematic Risk Principle

Thus far, we've seen that the total risk associated with an asset can be decomposed into two components: systematic and unsystematic risk. We have also seen that unsystematic risk can be essentially eliminated by diversification. The systematic risk present in an asset, on the other hand, cannot be eliminated by diversification.

Based on our study of capital market history, we know that there is a reward, on average, for bearing risk. However, we now need to be more precise about what we mean by risk. The **systematic risk principle** states that the reward for bearing risk depends only on the systematic risk of an investment. The underlying rationale for this principle is straightforward: Because unsystematic risk can be eliminated at virtually no cost (by diversifying), there is no reward for bearing it. Put another way, the market does not reward risks that are born unnecessarily.

The systematic risk principle has a remarkable and very important implication: *The expected return on an asset depends only on that asset's systematic risk.* There is an obvious corollary to this principle: No matter how much total risk an asset has, only the systematic portion is relevant in determining the expected return (and the risk premium) on that asset.

systematic risk principle
Principle stating that the expected return on a risky asset depends only on that asset's systematic risk.

Measuring Systematic Risk

Since systematic risk is the crucial determinant of an asset's expected return, we need some way of measuring the level of systematic risk for different investments. The specific measure that we use is called the **beta coefficient**, for which we will use the Greek symbol β. A beta coefficient, or beta for short, tells us how much systematic

beta coefficient
Amount of systematic risk present in a particular risky asset relative to an average risky asset.

risk a particular asset has relative to an average asset. By definition, an average asset has a beta of 1.0 relative to itself. An asset with a beta of .50, therefore, has half as much systematic risk as an average asset; an asset with a beta of 2.0 has twice as much. These different levels of beta are illustrated in Figure 11.7. You can see that high beta assets display greater volatility over time.

Table 11.9 contains the estimated beta coefficients for the stocks of some well-known companies. The range of betas in Table 11.9, from about .40 to about 1.6, spans most of the range for stocks of large Canadian corporations. Betas outside this range occur, but they are less common.

Remember that the expected return, and thus the risk premium, on an asset depends only on its systematic risk. Because assets with larger betas have greater systematic risks, they have greater expected returns. Thus, in Table 11.9, an investor who buys stock in Bell Canada Enterprises with a beta of .51, should expect to earn less, on average, than an investor who buys stock in Seagram, with a beta of about 1.14.

E X A M P L E | 11.7   Total Risk versus Beta

Consider the following information on two securities. Which has greater total risk? Which has greater systematic risk? Greater unsystematic risk? Which asset has a higher risk premium?

	Standard Deviation	Beta
Security A	40%	.50
Security B	20	1.50

From our discussion in this section, Security A has greater total risk, but it has substantially less systematic risk. Since total risk is the sum of systematic and unsystematic risk, Security A must have greater unsystematic risk. Finally, from the systematic risk principle, Security B has a higher risk premium and a greater expected return, despite the fact that it has less total risk.

F I G U R E 11.7

Volatility: High and low betas

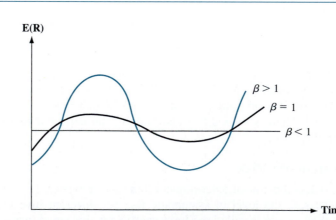

	Beta Coefficient (β_i)
Bell Canada Enterprises	0.51
Labatt	0.68
Imperial Oil	0.42
Du Pont Canada	0.85
Imasco	0.99
BCTEL	0.69
Northern Telecom	0.88
Seagram	1.14
Bombardier	1.57

T A B L E 11.9

Beta coefficients for selected companies

Source: ScotiaMcLeod Inc., 1995.

Portfolio Betas

Earlier, we saw that the riskiness of a portfolio does not have any simple relationship to the risks of the assets in the portfolio. A portfolio beta, however, can be calculated just like a portfolio expected return. For example, looking at Table 11.9, suppose you put half of your money in Bell Canada Enterprises and half in Du Pont Canada. What would the beta of this combination be? Since BCE has a beta of .51 and Du Pont has a beta of .85, the portfolio's beta, β_P, would be:

$$\beta_P = .50 \times \beta_{BCE} + .50 \times \beta_{DuPont}$$
$$= .50 \times .51 + .50 \times .85$$
$$= 0.68$$

In general, if we had a large number of assets in a portfolio, we would multiply each asset's beta by its portfolio weight and then add the results to get the portfolio's beta.

E X A M P L E | 11.8   Portfolio Betas

Suppose we had the following investments:

Security	Amount Invested	Expected Return	Beta
Stock A	$1,000	8%	.80
Stock B	2,000	12	.95
Stock C	3,000	15	1.10
Stock D	4,000	18	1.40

What is the expected return on this portfolio? What is the beta of this portfolio? Does this portfolio have more or less systematic risk than an average asset?

To answer, we first have to calculate the portfolio weights. Notice that the total amount invested is $10,000. Of this, $1,000/$10,000 = 10% is invested in Stock A. Similarly, 20 percent is invested in Stock B, 30 percent is invested in Stock C, and 40 percent is invested in Stock D. The expected return, $E(R_P)$, is thus:

$$E(R_P) = .10 \times E(R_A) + .20 \times E(R_B) + .30 \times E(R_C) + .40 \times E(R_D)$$
$$= .10 \times 8\% + .20 \times 12\% + .30 \times 15\% + .40 \times 18\%$$
$$= 14.9\%$$

Similarly, the portfolio beta, β_P, is:

$$\beta_P = .10 \times \beta_A + .20 \times \beta_B + .30 \times \beta_C + .40 \times \beta_D$$
$$= .10 \times .80 + .20 \times .95 + .30 \times 1.10 + .40 \times 1.40$$
$$= 1.16$$

This portfolio thus has an expected return of 14.9 percent and a beta of 1.16. Since the beta is larger than 1.0, this portfolio has greater systematic risk than an average asset.

CONCEPT QUESTIONS

1. What is the systematic risk principle?
2. What does a beta coefficient measure?
3. How do you calculate a portfolio beta?
4. Does the expected return on a risky asset depend on that asset's total risk? Explain.

11.7 | THE SECURITY MARKET LINE

We're now in a position to see how risk is rewarded in the marketplace. To begin, suppose Asset A has an expected return of $E(R_A) = 20\%$ and a beta of $\beta_A = 1.6$. Furthermore, the risk-free rate is $R_f = 8\%$. Notice that a risk-free asset, by definition, has no systematic risk (or unsystematic risk), so a risk-free asset has a beta of 0.

Beta and the Risk Premium

Consider a portfolio made up of Asset A and a risk-free asset. We can calculate some different possible portfolio expected returns and betas by varying the percentages invested in these two assets. For example, if 25 percent of the portfolio is invested in Asset A, the expected return is:

$$E(R_P) = .25 \times E(R_A) + (1 - .25) \times R_f$$
$$= .25 \times 20\% + .75 \times 8\%$$
$$= 11.0\%$$

Similarly, the beta on the portfolio, β_P, would be:

$$\beta_P = .25 \times \beta_A + (1 - .25) \times 0$$
$$= .25 \times 1.6$$
$$= .40$$

Notice that, since the weights have to add up to 1, the percentage invested in the risk-free asset is equal to 1 minus the percentage invested in Asset A.

One thing that you might wonder about is whether it is possible for the percentage invested in Asset A to exceed 100 percent. The answer is yes. This can happen if the investor borrows at the risk-free rate. For example, suppose an investor has $100 and borrows an additional $50 at 8 percent, the risk-free rate. The total investment in Asset A would be $150, or 150 percent of the investor's wealth. The expected return in this case would be:

$$E(R_P) = 1.50 \times E(R_A) + (1 - 1.50) \times R_f$$
$$= 1.50 \times 20\% - .50 \times 8\%$$
$$= 26.0\%$$

The beta on the portfolio would be:

$$\beta_P = 1.50 \times \beta_A + (1 - 1.50) \times 0$$
$$= 1.50 \times 1.6$$
$$= 2.4$$

We can calculate some other possibilities as follows:

Percentage of Portfolio in Asset A	Portfolio Expected Return	Portfolio Beta
0%	8%	0.0
25	11	0.4
50	14	0.8
75	17	1.2
100	20	1.6
125	23	2.0
150	26	2.4

In Figure 11.8A, these portfolio expected returns are plotted against the portfolio betas. Notice that all the combinations fall on a straight line.

The Reward-to-Risk Ratio   What is the slope of the straight line in Figure 11.8A? As always, the slope of a straight line is equal to the "rise over the run." As we move out of the risk-free asset into Asset A, the beta increases from zero to 1.6 (a "run" of 1.6). At the same time, the expected return goes from 8 to 20 percent, a "rise" of 12 percent. The slope of the line is thus 12%/1.6 = 7.50%.

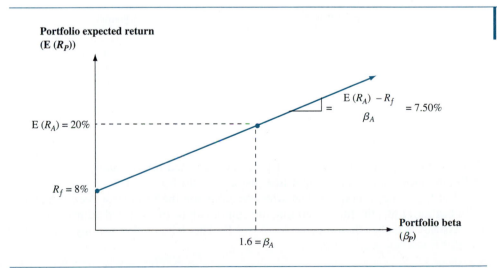

FIGURE 11.8A

Portfolio expected returns and betas for Asset A

Notice that the slope of our line is just the risk premium on Asset A, $E(R_A) - R_f$, divided by Asset A's beta, β_A:

$$\text{Slope} = \frac{[E(R_A) - R_f]}{\beta_A}$$

$$= \frac{[20\% - 8\%]}{1.6} = 7.50\%$$

What this tells us is that Asset A offers a reward-to-risk ratio of 7.50 percent.[8] In other words, Asset A has a risk premium of 7.50 percent per unit of systematic risk.

The Basic Argument   Now suppose we consider a second asset, Asset B. This asset has a beta of 1.2 and an expected return of 16 percent. Which investment is better, Asset A or Asset B? You might think that, once again, we really cannot say. Some investors might prefer A; some investors might prefer B. Actually, however, we can say: A is better because, as we demonstrate, B offers inadequate compensation for its level of systematic risk, at least relative to A.

To begin, we calculate different combinations of expected returns and betas for portfolios of Asset B and a risk-free asset just as we did for Asset A. For example, if we put 25 percent in Asset B and the remaining 75 percent in the risk-free asset, the portfolio's expected return would be:

$$E(R_P) = .25 \times E(R_B) + (1 - .25) \times R_f$$

$$= .25 \times 16\% + .75 \times 8\%$$

$$= 10.0\%$$

Similarly, the beta on the portfolio, β_P, would be:

$$\beta_P = .25 \times \beta_B + (1 - .25) \times 0$$

$$= .25 \times 1.2$$

$$= .30$$

Some other possibilities are as follows:

Percentage of Portfolio in Asset B	Portfolio Expected Return	Portfolio Beta
0%	8%	0.0
25	10	0.3
50	12	0.6
75	14	0.9
100	16	1.2
125	18	1.5
150	20	1.8

When we plot these combinations of portfolio expected returns and portfolios betas in Figure 11.8B, we get a straight line just as we did for Asset A.

The key thing to notice is that when we compare the results for Assets A and B, as in Figure 11.8C, the line describing the combinations of expected returns and betas for Asset A is higher than the one for Asset B. This tells us that for any given level

---

[8] This ratio is sometimes called the Treynor index, after one of its originators.

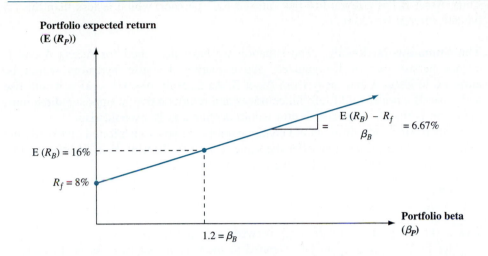

F I G U R E 11.8B

Portfolio expected returns and betas for Asset B

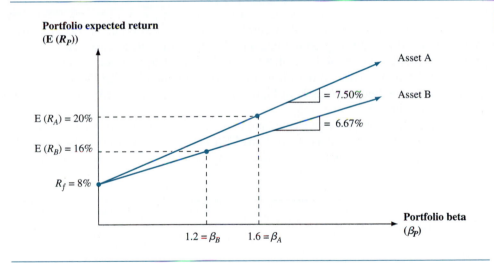

F I G U R E 11.8C

Portfolio expected returns and betas for both assets

of systematic risk (as measured by β), some combination of Asset A and the risk-free asset always offers a larger return. This is why we were able to state that Asset A is a better investment than Asset B.

Another way of seeing that A offers a superior return for its level of risk is to note that the slope of our line for Asset B is:

$$\text{Slope} = \left[\frac{E(R_B) - R_f}{\beta_B} \right]$$

$$= \frac{[16\% - 8\%]}{1.2} = 6.67\%$$

Thus, Asset B has a reward-to-risk ratio of 6.67 percent, which is less than the 7.5 percent offered by Asset A.

The Fundamental Result   The situation we have described for Assets A and B cannot persist in a well-organized, active market, because investors would be attracted to Asset A and away from Asset B. As a result, Asset A's price would rise and Asset B's price would fall. Since prices and returns move in opposite directions, the result is that A's expected return would decline and B's would rise.

This buying and selling would continue until the two assets plotted on exactly the same line, which means they offer the same reward for bearing risk. In other words, in an active, competitive market, we must have:

$$\frac{E(R_A) - R_f}{\beta_A} = \frac{E(R_B) - R_f}{\beta_B}$$

This is the fundamental relationship between risk and return.

Our basic argument can be extended to more than just two assets. In fact, no matter how many assets we had, we would always reach the same conclusion: *The reward-to-risk ratio must be the same for all the assets in the market.* This result is really not so surprising. What it says, for example, is that, if one asset has twice as much systematic risk as another asset, its risk premium is simply twice as large.

Since all the assets in the market must have the same reward-to-risk ratio, they all must plot on the same line. This argument is illustrated in Figure 11.9. As shown, Assets A and B plot directly on the line and thus have the same reward-to-risk ratio. If an asset plotted above the line, such as C in Figure 11.9, its price would rise, and its expected return would fall until it plotted exactly on the line. Similarly, if an asset plotted below the line, such as D in Figure 11.9, its expected return would rise until it too plotted directly on the line.

The arguments we have presented apply to active, competitive, well-functioning markets. The financial markets, such as the TSE and NYSE, best meet these criteria. Other markets, such as real asset markets, may or may not. For this reason, these

F I G U R E 11.9

Expected returns and systematic risk

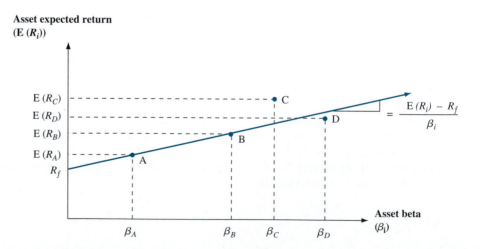

The fundamental relationship between beta and expected return is that all assets must have the same reward-to-risk ratio [E $(R_i) - R_f]/\beta_i$. This means they would all plot on the same straight line. Assets A and B are examples of this behaviour. Asset C's expected return is too high; Asset D's is too low.

concepts are most useful in examining financial markets. We thus focus on such markets here. However, as we discuss in a later section, the information about risk and return gleaned from financial markets is crucial in evaluating the investments that a corporation makes in real assets.

E X A M P L E | 11.9   **Beta and Stock Valuation**

An asset is said to be overvalued if its price is too high given its expected return and risk. Suppose you observe the following situation:

Security	Beta	Expected Return
SWMS Company	1.3	14%
Insec Company	.8	10

The risk-free rate is currently 6 percent. Is one of the two preceding securities overvalued relative to the other?

    To answer, we compute the reward-to-risk ratio for both. For SWMS, this ratio is $(14\% - 6\%)/1.3 = 6.15\%$. For Insec, this ratio is 5 percent. What we conclude is that Insec offers an insufficient expected return for its level of risk, at least relative to SWMS. Since its expected return is too low, its price is too high. To see why this is true, recall that the dividend valuation model presented in Chapter 6 treats price as the present value of future dividends.

$$P_o = \frac{D_1}{(r - g)}$$

Projecting the dividend stream gives us D_1 and g. If the required rate of return is too low, the stock price will be too high. For example, suppose $D_1 = \$2.00$ and $g = 7$ percent. If the expected rate of return on the stock is wrongly underestimated at 10 percent, the stock price estimate is \$66.67. This price is too high if the true expected rate of return is 14 percent. At this higher rate of return, the stock price should fall to \$28.57. In other words, Insec is overvalued relative to SWMS, and we would expect to see its price fall relative to SWMS's. Notice that we could also say that SWMS is undervalued relative to Insec. |

Calculating Beta

The beta of a security measures the responsiveness of that security's return to the return on the market as a whole. To calculate beta, we draw a line relating the expected return on the security to different returns on the market. This line, called the *characteristic line* of the security, has slope equal to the stock's beta.

    Consider Figure 11.10, which displays returns for both a hypothetical company and the market as a whole.[9] Each point represents a pair of returns over a particular month. The vertical dimension measures the return on the stock over the month and the horizontal dimension that of the TSE 300. (The TSE 300 is considered a reasonable proxy for the general market.)

    Figure 11.10 also shows the line of *best fit* superimposed on these points. In practical applications, this line is calculated from regression analysis. As one can see from the graph, the slope is 1.28. Because the average beta is 1, this indicates the stock's beta of 1.28 is higher than that for the average stock.

---

[9] As we mentioned in Chapter 10, the return on a security includes both the dividend and the capital gain (or loss).

FIGURE 11.10

Graphic representation of beta

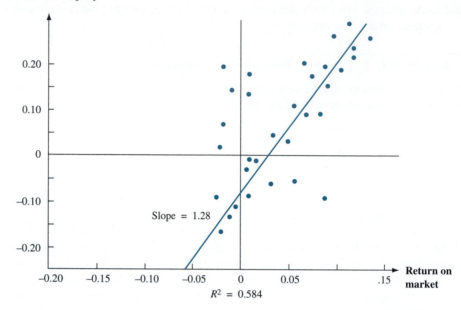

Return on company

Slope = 1.28

$R^2 = 0.584$

Return on market

The goal of a financial analyst is to determine the beta that a stock will have in the future, because this is when the proceeds of an investment are received. Of course, past data must be used in regression analysis. Thus, it is incorrect to think of 1.28 as the beta of our example company. Rather it is our estimate of the firm's beta from past data.

The bottom of Figure 11.10 indicates that the company's R^2 over the time period is 0.584. What does this mean? R^2 measures how close the points in the figure are to the characteristic line. The highest value for R^2 is 1, a situation that would occur if all points lay exactly on the characteristic line. This would be the case where the security's return is determined only by the market's return without the security having any independent variation. The R^2 is likely to approach one for a large portfolio of securities. For example, many widely diversified mutual funds have R^2s of 0.80 or more. The lowest possible R^2 is zero, a situation occurring when two variables are entirely unrelated to each other. Those companies whose returns are pretty much independent of returns on the stock market would have R^2s near zero.

The risk of any security can be broken down into unsystematic and systematic risk. Whereas beta measures the amount of systematic risk, R^2 measures the *proportion* of total risk that is systematic. Thus, a low R^2 indicates that most of the risk of a firm is unsystematic.[10]

---

[10] Standard computer packages generally provide confidence intervals (error ranges) for beta estimates. One has greater confidence in beta estimates where the confidence interval is small. While stocks with high R^2s generally have small confidence intervals, it is the size of the confidence interval, not the R^2 itself, that is relevant here. Because expected return is related to systematic risk, the R^2 of a firm is of no concern to us once we know the firm's beta. This often surprises students trained in statistics, because R^2 is an important concept for many other purposes.

Company	Beta
Bombardier Inc.	1.57
Canada Malting	0.60
Cara Operations A	0.97
Celanese Canada	0.57
Corporate Foods	1.01
Du Pont Canada	0.85
Gendis Inc.	0.44
Hawker Siddeley	0.58
Imasco Ltd.	0.99
Imperial Oil A	0.42
Labatt (John)	0.68
Loblaw Companies	0.74
Maple Leaf Foods	0.75
Molson Companies	0.67
Moore Corporation	1.29
Northern Telecom	0.88
Oshawa Group A	0.90
Quebecor Inc.	0.80
Rothmans Inc.	0.28
Schneider Corp.	0.37
Seagram Corp.	1.14
Shaw Industries	0.63
Shell Canada	0.51
UAP Inc.	0.19
Weston (George)	0.68

T A B L E 11.10

Estimates of stock betas. Based on monthly returns from 1989–94.

Source: Scotia McLeod, 1995.

The mechanics for calculating betas are quite simple. People in business frequently estimate beta by using commercially available computer programs. Certain handheld calculators are also able to perform the calculation. In addition, a large number of services sell or even give away estimates of beta for different firms. Table 11.10 presents a page from a set of betas for industrial companies calculated by Scotia McLeod estimated from monthly data over the 60-month period from 1989 to 1994. The Toronto Stock Exchange Index is used as the market index.

In their estimation procedure, Scotia McLeod analysts apparently made a number of assumptions consistent with Canadian research on the capital asset pricing model.[11] First, they chose monthly data, as do many financial economists. On the one hand, statistical problems frequently arise when time intervals shorter than a month are used. On the other hand, important information is lost when longer intervals are employed. Thus, the choice of monthly data can be viewed as a compromise.

Second, Scotia McLeod analysts used just under five years of data, the result of another compromise. Due to changes in production mix, production techniques, management style, and/or financial leverage, a firm's nature adjusts over time. A long time period for calculating beta implies many out-of-date observations. Conversely, a short time period leads to statistical imprecision, because few monthly observations are used.

---

[11] See J. Hatch and M. J. Robinson, *Investment Management in Canada,* 2nd ed. (Scarborough: Prentice Hall Canada, 1989), pp. 492–96 for a review of Canadian tests of the capital asset pricing model.

CONCEPT QUESTIONS
1. What is the statistical procedure employed for calculating beta?
2. Why do financial analysts use monthly data when calculating beta?
3. What is R^2?

The Security Market Line

security market line (SML)
Positively sloped straight line displaying the relationship between expected return and beta.

The line that results when we plot expected returns and beta coefficients is obviously of some importance, so it's time we gave it a name. This line, which we use to describe the relationship between systematic risk and expected return in financial markets, is usually called the **security market line (SML)**. After NPV, the SML is arguably the most important concept in modern finance.

Market Portfolios   It will be very useful to know the equation of the SML. There are many different ways that we could write it, but one way is particularly common. Suppose we were to consider a portfolio made up of all of the assets in the market. Such a portfolio is called a *market portfolio,* and we write the expected return on this market portfolio as $E(R_M)$.

Since all the assets in the market must plot on the SML, so must a market portfolio made of those assets. To determine where it plots on the SML, we need to know the beta of the market portfolio, β_M. Because this portfolio is representative of all the assets in the market, it must have average systematic risk. In other words, it has a beta of one. We could therefore write the slope of the SML as:

$$\text{SML slope} = \frac{[E(R_M) - R_f]}{\beta_M} = \frac{[E(R_M) - R_f]}{1} = E(R_M) - R_f$$

market risk premium
Slope of the SML, the difference between the expected return on a market portfolio and the risk-free rate.

The term $E(R_M) - R_f$ is often called the **market risk premium** since it is the risk premium on a market portfolio.

capital asset pricing model (CAPM)
Equation of the SML showing relationship between expected return and beta.

The Capital Asset Pricing Model   To finish up, if we let $E(R_i)$ and β_i stand for the expected return and beta, respectively, on any asset in the market, we know it must plot on the SML. As a result, we know that its reward-to-risk ratio is the same as the overall market's:

$$\frac{[E(R_i) - R_f]}{\beta_i} = E(R_M) - R_f$$

If we rearrange this, we can write the equation for the SML as:

$$E(R_i) = R_f + [E(R_M) - R_f] \times \beta_i \qquad [11.10]$$

This result is identical to the famous **Capital Asset Pricing Model (CAPM)**[12]

---

[12] Our discussion leading up to the CAPM is actually much more closely related to a more recently developed theory, known as the arbitrage pricing theory (APT). The theory underlying the CAPM is a great deal more complex than we have indicated here, and the CAPM has a number of other implications that go beyond the scope of this discussion. As we present here, the CAPM and the APT have essentially identical implications, so we don't distinguish between them. Appendix 11A presents another way to develop the CAPM.

What the CAPM shows is that the expected return for a particular asset depends on three things:

1. *The pure time value of money.* As measured by the risk-free rate, R_f, this is the reward for merely waiting for your money, without taking any risk.
2. *The reward for bearing systematic risk.* As measured by the market risk premium $[E(R_M) - R_f]$, this component is the reward the market offers for bearing an average amount of systematic risk in addition to waiting.
3. *The amount of systematic risk.* As measured by β_i, this is the amount of systematic risk present in a particular asset, relative to an average asset.

Figure 11.11 summarizes our discussion of the SML and the CAPM. As before, we plot the expected return against beta. Now we recognize that, based on the CAPM, the slope of the SML is equal to the market risk premium $[E(R_M) - R_f]$. This concludes our presentation of concepts related to the risk-return trade-off. For future reference, Table 11.11 summarizes the various concepts in the order we discussed them.

E X A M P L E | **11.10**   **Risk and Return**

Suppose the risk-free rate is 4 percent, the market risk premium is 8.6 percent, and a particular stock has a beta of 1.3. Based on the CAPM, what is the expected return on this stock? What would the expected return be if the beta were to double?

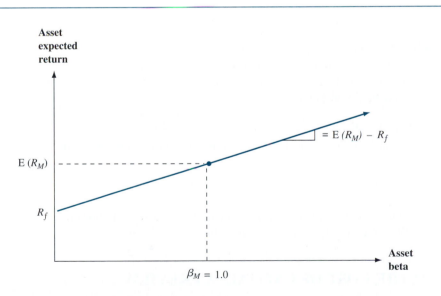

F I G U R E 11.11

The security market line (SML)

The slope of the security market line is equal to the market risk premium; i.e., the reward for bearing an average amount of systematic risk. The equation describing the SML can be written:

$$E(R_i) = R_f + \beta_i \times [E(R_M) - R_f]$$

which is the capital asset pricing model (CAPM).

T A B L E 11.11

Summary of risk and return

Total risk. The *total risk* of an investment is measured by the variance or, more commonly, the standard deviation of its return.

Total return. The *total return* on an investment has two components: the expected return and the unexpected return. The unexpected return comes about because of unanticipated events. The risk from investing stems from the possibility of unanticipated events.

Systematic and unsystematic risks. *Systematic risks* (also called market risks) are unanticipated events that affect almost all assets to some degree because they are economywide. *Unsystematic risks* are unanticipated events that affect single assets or small groups of assets. Unsystematic risks are also called *unique* or *asset-specific risks.*

The effect of diversification. Some, but not all, of the risk associated with a risky investment can be eliminated by diversification. The reason is that unsystematic risks, which are unique to individual assets, tend to wash out in a large portfolio; systematic risks, which affect all of the assets in a portfolio to some extent, do not.

The systematic risk principle and beta. Because unsystematic risk can be freely eliminated by diversification, the *systematic risk principle* states that the reward for bearing risk depends only on the level of systematic risk. The level of systematic risk in a particular asset, relative to average, is given by the *beta* of that asset.

The reward-to-risk ratio and the security market line. The *reward-to-risk ratio* for asset i is the ratio of its risk premium $E(R_i) - R_f$ to its beta, β_i:

$$\frac{E(R_i) - R_f}{\beta_i}$$

In a well-functioning market, this ratio is the same for every asset. As a result, when asset expected returns are plotted against asset betas, all assets plot on the same straight line, called the *security market line* (SML).

The capital asset pricing model. From the SML, the expected return on asset i can be written:

$$E(R_i) = R_f + [E(R_M) - R_f] \times \beta_i$$

This is the *capital asset pricing model* (CAPM). The expected return on a risky asset thus has three components: The first is the pure time value of money (R_f), the second is the market risk premium $[E(R_M) - R_f]$, and the third is the beta for that asset, β_i.

With a beta of 1.3, the risk premium for the stock would be $1.3 \times 8.6\%$, or 11.18 percent. The risk-free rate is 4 percent, so the expected return is 15.18 percent. If the beta doubles to 2.6, the risk premium would double to 22.36 percent, so the expected return would be 26.36 percent.

CONCEPT QUESTIONS

1. What is the fundamental relationship between risk and return in well-functioning markets?
2. What is the security market line? Why must all assets plot directly on it in a well-functioning market?
3. What is the capital asset pricing model (CAPM)? What does it tell us about the required return on a risky investment?

11.8 | THE SML AND THE COST OF CAPITAL: A PREVIEW

Our goal in studying risk and return is twofold: First, risk is an extremely important consideration in almost all business decisions, so we want to discuss just what risk is and how it is rewarded in the market. Our second purpose is to learn what determines the appropriate discount rate for future cash flows. We briefly discuss this second subject now; we discuss it in more detail in Chapter 14.

The Basic Idea

The security market line tells us the reward for bearing risk in financial markets. At an absolute minimum, any new investment that our firm undertakes must offer an expected return that is no worse than what the financial markets offer for the same risk. The reason for this is simply that our shareholders can always invest for themselves in the financial markets.

The only way we benefit our shareholders is by finding investments with expected returns that are superior to what the financial markets offer for the same risk. Such an investment has a positive NPV. So, if we ask what the appropriate discount rate is, the answer is that we should use the expected return offered in financial markets on investments with the same systematic risk.

In other words, to determine whether an investment has a positive NPV, we essentially compare the expected return on that new investment to what the financial market offers on an investment with the same beta. This is why the SML is so important; it tells us the going rate for bearing risk in the economy.

The Cost of Capital

The appropriate discount rate on a new project is the minimum expected rate of return an investment must offer to be attractive. This minimum required return is very often called the **cost of capital** associated with the investment. It is called this because the required return is what the firm must earn on its capital investment in a project just to break even. It can thus be interpreted as the opportunity cost associated with the firm's capital investment.

cost of capital
The minimum required return on a new investment.

Notice that when we say an investment is attractive if its expected return exceeds what is offered in financial markets for investments of the same risk, we are effectively using the internal rate of return (IRR) criterion that we developed and discussed in Chapter 7. The only difference is that now we have a much better idea of what determines the required return on an investment. This understanding will be critical when we discuss cost of capital and capital structure in Part VII.

> CONCEPT QUESTIONS
> 1. If an investment has a positive NPV, would it plot above or below the SML? Why?
> 2. What is meant by the term *cost of capital?*

arbitrage pricing theory (APT)
An equilibrium asset pricing theory that is derived from a factor model by using diversification and arbitrage. It shows that the expected return on any risky asset is a linear combination of various factors.

11.9 | ARBITRAGE PRICING THEORY

The CAPM and the **arbitrage pricing theory (APT)** are alternative models of risk and return. One advantage of the APT is that it can handle multiple factors that the CAPM ignores. Although the bulk of our presentation in this chapter focussed on the one-factor model, a multifactor model is probably more reflective of reality.

The APT assumes that stock returns are generated according to factor models. For example, we have described a stock's return as

Total return = Expected return + Unexpected return

$$R = E(R) + U$$

In APT, the unexpected return is related to several market factors. Suppose there are three such factors: unanticipated changes in inflation, GNP, and interest rates. The total return can be expanded as

$$R = R + \beta_I F_I + \beta_{GNP} F_{GNP} + \beta_r F_r + \epsilon \qquad [11.11]$$

The three factors F_I, F_{GNP}, and F_r represent systematic risk because these factors affect many securities. The term ϵ is considered unsystematic risk because it is unique to each individual security.

Under this multifactor APT, we can generalize from three to K factors to express the relationship between risk and return as:

$$E(R) = R_F + E[(R_1) - R_F]\beta_1 + E[(R_2) - R_F]\beta_2 \qquad [11.12]$$
$$+ E[(R_3) - R_F]\beta_3 + \ldots E[(R_K) - R_F]\beta_K$$

In this equation, β_1 stands for the security's beta with respect to the first factor, β_2 stands for the security's beta with respect to the second factor, and so on. For example, if the first factor is inflation, β_1 is the security's inflation beta. The term $E(R_1)$ is the expected return on a security (or portfolio) whose beta with respect to the first factor is one and whose beta with respect to all other factors is zero. Because the market compensates for risk, $E((R_1) - R_F)$ is positive in the normal case.[13] (An analogous interpretation can be given to $E(R_2)$, $E(R_3)$, and so on.)

The equation states that the security's expected return is related to its factor betas. The argument is that each factor represents risk that cannot be diversified away. The higher a security's beta with regard to a particular factor, the higher is the risk that the security bears. In a rational world, the expected return on the security should compensate for this risk. The preceding equation states that the expected return is a summation of the risk-free rate plus the compensation for each type of risk that the security bears.

As an example, consider a Canadian study where the factors were

1. The rate of growth in industrial production (INDUS).
2. The changes in the slope of the term structure of interest rates (the difference between the returns and short-term Canada bonds) (TERMS).
3. The default risk premium for bonds (measured as the difference between the yield on long-term Canada bonds and the yield on the ScotiaMcleod corporate bond index) (RISKPREM).
4. The inflation (measured as the growth of the consumer price index) (INFL).
5. The value-weighted return on the market portfolio (TSE 300) (MKRET).[14]

Using the period 1970–84, the empirical results of the study indicated that expected monthly returns on a sample of 100 TSE stocks could be described as a function of the risk premiums associated with these five factors.

Because many factors appear on the right side of the APT equation, the APT formulation explained expected returns in this Canadian sample more accurately than did the CAPM. However, as we mentioned earlier, one cannot easily determine which

---

[13] Actually $(R_i - R_F)$ could be negative in the case where factor i is perceived as a hedge of some sort.

[14] E. Otuteye, "How Economic Forces Explain Canadian Stock Returns," *Canadian Investment Review,* Spring 1991, pp. 93–99. An earlier Canadian study supportive of APT is L. Kryzanowski and M. C. To, "General Factor Models and the Structure of Security Returns," *Journal of Financial and Quantitative Analysis,* March 1983, pp. 31–52.

are the appropriate factors. The factors in this study were included for reasons of both common sense and convenience. They were not derived from theory.

> CONCEPT QUESTION
> 1. What is the main advantage of the APT over the CAPM?

11.10 | SUMMARY AND CONCLUSIONS

This chapter covered the essentials of risk. Along the way, we introduced a number of definitions and concepts. The most important of these is the security market line, or SML. The SML is important because it tells us the reward offered in financial markets for bearing risk. Once we know this, we have a benchmark against which to compare the returns expected from real asset investments and to determine if they are desirable.

Because we covered quite a bit of ground, it's useful to summarize the basic economic logic underlying the SML as follows:

1. Based on capital market history, there is a reward for bearing risk. This reward is the risk premium on an asset.
2. The total risk associated with an asset has two parts: systematic risk and unsystematic risk. Unsystematic risk can be freely eliminated by diversification (this is the principle of diversification), so only systematic risk is rewarded. As a result, the risk premium on an asset is determined by its systematic risk. This is the systematic risk principle.
3. An asset's systematic risk, relative to average, can be measured by its beta coefficient, β_i. The risk premium on an asset is then given by its beta coefficient multiplied by the market risk premium $[E(R_M) - R_f] \times \beta_i$.
4. The expected return on an asset, $E(R_i)$, is equal to the risk-free rate, R_f, plus the risk premium:

$$E(R_i) = R_f + [E(R_M) - R_f] \times \beta_i$$

This is the equation of the SML, and it is often called the capital asset pricing model (CAPM).

This chapter completes our discussion of risk and return and concludes Part V of our book. Now that we have a better understanding of what determines a firm's cost of capital for an investment, the next several chapters examine more closely how firms raise the long-term capital needed for investment.

Key Terms

expected return (page 375)
portfolio (page 378)
portfolio weight (page 379)
systematic risk (page 390)
unsystematic risk (page 390)
principle of diversification (page 392)
systematic risk principle (page 395)
beta coefficient (page 395)

security market line (SML) (page 406)
market risk premium (page 406)
capital asset pricing model (CAPM) (page 406)
cost of capital (page 409)
arbitrage pricing theory (APT) (page 409)

Chapter Review Problems and Self-Test

11.1 Expected Return and Standard Deviation This problem gives you some practice calculating measures of prospective portfolio performance. There are two assets and three states of nature:

(1) State of Economy	(2) Probability of State of Economy	(3) Stock A Rate of Return if State Occurs	(4) Stock B Rate of Return if State Occurs
Recession	.10	−.20	.30
Normal	.60	.10	.20
Boom	.30	.70	.50

What are the expected returns and standard deviations for these two stocks?

11.2 Portfolio Risk and Return In the previous problem, suppose you have $20,000 total. If you put $6,000 in Stock A and the remainder in Stock B, what would the expected return and standard deviation on your portfolio be?

11.3 Risk and Return Suppose you observe the following situation:

Security	Beta	Expected Return
Cooley, Inc.	1.6	19%
Moyer Company	1.2	16

If the risk-free rate is 8 percent, are these securities correctly priced? What would the risk-free rate have to be if they are correctly priced?

11.4 CAPM Suppose the risk-free rate is 8 percent. The expected return on the market is 14 percent. If a particular stock has a beta of .60, what is its expected return based on the CAPM? If another stock has an expected return of 20 percent, what must its beta be?

Answers to Self-Test Problems

11.1 The expected returns are just the possible returns multiplied by the associated probabilities:

$$E(R_A) = .10 \times (-.20) + .60 \times (.10) + .30 \times (.70) = 25\%$$

$$E(R_B) = .10 \times (.30) + .60 \times (.20) + .30 \times (.50) = 30\%$$

The variances are given by the sums of the squared deviations from the expected returns multiplied by their probabilities:

$$\sigma^2_A = .10 \times (-.20 - .25)^2 + .60 \times (.10 - .25)^2 + .30 \times (.70 - .25)^2$$
$$= .10 \times (-.45)^2 + .60 \times (-.15)^2 + .30 \times (.45)^2$$
$$= .10 \times .2025 + .60 \times .0225 + .30 \times .2025$$
$$= .0945$$
$$\sigma^2_B = .10 \times (.30 - .30)^2 + .60 \times (.20 - .30)^2 + .30 \times (.50 - .30)^2$$
$$= .10 \times (.00)^2 + .60 \times (-.10)^2 + .30 \times (.20)^2$$
$$= .10 \times .00 + .60 \times .01 + .30 \times .04$$
$$= .0180$$

The standard deviations are thus:

$$\sigma_A = \sqrt{.0945} = 30.74\%$$

$$\sigma_B = \sqrt{.0180} = 13.42\%$$

11.2   The portfolio weights are $6,000/20,000 = .30$ and $14,000/20,000 = .70$. The expected return is thus:

$$E(R_P) = .30 \times E(R_A) + .70 \times E(R_B)$$
$$= .30 \times 25\% + .70 \times 30\%$$
$$= 28.50\%$$

Alternatively, we could calculate the portfolio's return in each of the states:

(1) State of Economy	(2) Probability of State of Economy	(3) Portfolio Return if State Occurs
Recession	.10	$30 \times (-.20) + .70 \times (.30) = .15$
Normal	.60	$30 \times (.10) + .70 \times (.20) = .17$
Boom	.30	$.30 \times (.70) + .70 \times (.50) = .56$

The portfolio's expected return is:

$$E(R_P) = .10 \times (.15) + .60 \times (.17) + .30 \times (.56) = 28.50\%$$

This is the same as we had before.   The portfolio's variance is:

$$\sigma^2{}_P = .10 \times (.15 - .285)^2 + .60 \times (.17 - .285)^2 + .30 \times (.56 - .285)^2$$
$$= .03245$$

So the standard deviation is $\sqrt{.03245} = 18.01\%$

11.3   If we compute the reward-to-risk ratios, we get $(19\% - 8\%)/1.6 = 6.875\%$ for Cooley versus 6.67 percent for Moyer. Relative to Cooley, Moyer's expected return is too low, so its price is too high. If they are correctly priced, they must offer the same reward-to-risk ratio. The risk-free rate would have to be such that:

$$(19\% - R_f) / 1.6 = (16\% - R_f) / 1.2$$

With a little algebra, we find that the risk-free rate must be 7 percent:

$$(19\% - R_f) = (16\% - R_f)(1.6 / 1.2)$$
$$19\% - 16\% \times \left(\frac{4}{3}\right) = R_f - R_f \times \left(\frac{4}{3}\right)$$
$$R_f = 7\%$$

11.4   Since the expected return on the market is 14 percent, the market risk premium is $14\% - 8\% = 6\%$ (the risk-free rate is 8 percent). The first stock has a beta of .60, so its expected return is $8\% + .60 \times 6\% = 11.6\%$.   For the second stock, notice that the risk premium is $20\% - 8\% = 12\%$. Since this is twice as large as the market risk premium, the beta must be exactly equal to 2. We can verify this using the CAPM:

$$E(R_i) = R_f + [E(R_M) - R_f] \times \beta_i$$

$$20\% = 8\% + (14\% - 8\%) \times \beta_i$$

$$\beta_i = \frac{12\%}{6\%}$$

$$= 2.0$$

Questions and Problems

Basic
(Questions 1–24)

1. **Determining Portfolio Weights**   What are the portfolio weights for a portfolio that has 50 shares of stock that sells for $30 per share and 20 shares of a stock that sells for $45 per share?

2. **Portfolio Expected Return**   You own a portfolio that has $500 invested in Stock A and $1,000 invested in Stock B. If the expected returns on these stocks are 20 percent and 14 percent respectively, what is the expected return on the portfolio?

3. **Portfolio Expected Return**   You own a portfolio that is 40 percent invested in Stock X, 35 percent in Stock Y, and 25 percent in Stock Z. The expected returns on these three stocks are 8 percent, 15 percent, and 25 percent respectively. What is the expected return on the portfolio?

4. **Portfolio Expected Return**   You have $100,000 to invest in a stock portfolio. Your choices are Stock H with an expected return of 22 percent and Stock L with an expected return of 12 percent. If your goal is to create a portfolio with an expected return of 18 percent, how much money will you invest in Stock H? In Stock L?

5. **Calculating Expected Return**   Based on the following information, calculate the expected return.

State of Economy	Probability of State of Economy	Rate of Return if State Occurs
Recession	0.25	0.05
Boom	0.75	0.25

6. **Calculating Expected Return**   Based on the following information, calculate the expected return.

State of Economy	Probability of State of Economy	Rate of Return if State Occurs
Recession	0.10	−0.05
Normal	0.70	0.12
Boom	0.20	0.30

7. **Calculating Returns and Deviations**   Based on the following information, calculate the expected return and standard deviation for the two stocks.

State of Economy	Probability of State of Economy	Stock A Rate of Return	Stock B Rate of Return
Recession	0.15	0.02	−0.15
Normal	0.60	0.09	0.18
Boom	0.25	0.18	0.50

8. **Calculating Expected Returns**   A portfolio is invested 30 percent in Stock G, 50 percent in Stock J, and 20 percent in Stock K. The expected returns on these

stocks are 10 percent, 20 percent, and 30 percent, respectively. What is the portfolio's expected return? How do you interpret your answer?

Basic
(Continued)

9. **Returns and Deviations**   Consider the following information:

State of Economy	Probability of State of Economy	Stock A Rate of Return	Stock B Rate of Return	Stock C Rate of Return
Boom	0.65	0.12	0.16	0.25
Bust	0.35	0.10	0.04	0.00

a. What is the expected return on an equally weighted portfolio of these three stocks?

b. What is the variance of a portfolio invested 25 percent in A and B, and 50 percent in C?

10. **Returns and Deviations**   Consider the following information:

State of Economy	Probability of State of Economy	Stock A Rate of Return	Stock B Rate of Return	Stock C Rate of Return
Boom	0.20	0.10	0.35	0.20
Good	0.50	0.07	0.15	0.10
Poor	0.25	0.04	−0.05	0.00
Bust	0.05	0.00	−0.40	−0.08

a. Your portfolio is invested 30 percent in A and C, and 40 percent in B. What is the portfolio expected return?

b. What is the variance of this portfolio? The standard deviation?

11. **Types of Risk**   In broad terms, why is some risk diversifiable? Why are some risks nondiversifiable? Does it follow that an investor can control the level of unsystematic risk in a portfolio, but not the level of systematic risk?

12. **Announcements and Security Prices**   Suppose the government announces that, based on a just-completed survey, the growth rate in the economy is likely to be 2 percent in the coming year as compared to 5 percent for the year just completed. Would security prices increase, decrease, or stay the same following this announcement? Does it make any difference whether the 2 percent figure was anticipated by the market or not? Explain.

13. **Systematic versus Unsystematic Risk**   Classify the following events as mostly systematic or mostly unsystematic. Is the distinction clear in every case?

a. Short-term interest rates increase unexpectedly.

b. The interest rate a company pays on its short-term debt borrowing is increased by its bank.

c. Oil prices unexpectedly decline.

d. An oil tanker ruptures creating a large oil spill.

e. A manufacturer loses a multimillion dollar product liability suit.

f. A Supreme Court of Canada decision substantially broadens producer liability for injuries suffered by product users.

14. **Announcements and Risk**   Classify the following events on whether they might cause stocks in general to change price, and whether they might cause Big Widget Corp.'s stock to change price.

a. The government announces that inflation unexpectedly jumped by 2 percent last month.

b. Big Widget's quarterly earnings report just issued generally fell in line with analysts' expectations.

c. The government reports that economic growth last year was at 3 percent, which generally agreed with most economists' forecasts.

d. The directors of Big Widget die in a plane crash.

e. A new budget introduces changes to the tax code that will increase the top marginal corporate tax rate. The legislation had been anticipated in a white paper released six months earlier.

15. **Calculating Portfolio Betas**   You own a stock portfolio invested 20 percent in Stock Q, 40 percent in Stock R, 25 percent in Stock S, and 15 percent in Stock T. The betas for these four stocks are 1.10, 0.95, 1.40, and 0.70, respectively. What is the portfolio beta?

16. **Calculating Portfolio Betas**   You own a portfolio equally invested in a risk-free asset and two stocks. If one of the stocks has a beta of 1.20 and the total portfolio is equally as risky as the market, what must the beta be for the other stock in your portfolio?

17. **Using CAPM**   A stock has a beta of 0.9, the expected return on the market is 15 percent, and the risk-free rate is 7 percent. What must the expected return on this stock be?

18. **Using CAPM**   A stock has an expected return of 12 percent, the risk-free rate is 6 percent, and the market risk premium is 5 percent. What must the beta of this stock be?

19. **Using CAPM**   A stock has an expected return of 15 percent, its beta is 1.25, and the risk-free rate is 5 percent. What must the expected return on the market be?

20. **Using CAPM**   A stock has an expected return of 10 percent, a beta of 0.5, and the expected return on the market is 16 percent. What must the risk-free rate be?

21. **Using CAPM**   A stock has a beta of 0.80 and an expected return of 11 percent. A risk-free asset currently earns 8 percent.

a. What is the expected return on a portfolio that is equally invested in the two assets?

b. If a portfolio of the two assets has a beta of .45, what are the portfolio weights?

c. If a portfolio of the two assets has an expected return of 10 percent, what is its beta?

d. If a portfolio of the two assets has a beta of 1.75, what are the portfolio weights? How do you interpret the weight for the two assets in this case? Explain.

22. **Using the SML**   Asset W has an expected return of 20 percent and a beta of 1.25. If the risk-free rate is 6 percent, complete the following table for portfolios of Asset W and the risk-free asset. Illustrate the relationship between portfolio expected return and portfolio beta by plotting the expected returns against the betas. What is the slope of the line that results?

Percentage of Portfolio in Asset W	Portfolio Expected Return	Portfolio Beta
0%		
25		
50		
75		
100		
125		
150		

Basic (Continued)

23. **Reward-to-Risk Ratios** Stock M has a beta of 1.2 and an expected return of 20 percent. Stock N has a beta of 0.9 and an expected return of 16 percent. If the risk-free rate is 5 percent and the market risk premium is 12.3 percent, are these stocks correctly priced? Which one is undervalued? Overvalued?

24. **Reward-to-Risk Ratios** In the previous problem, what would the risk-free rate have to be for the two stocks to be correctly priced?

Intermediate (Questions 25–33)

25. **Expected Portfolio Returns** If a portfolio has a positive investment in every asset, can the expected return on the portfolio be greater than that on every asset in the portfolio? Can it be less than that on every asset in the portfolio? If you answer yes to one or both of these questions, give an example to support your answer.

26. **Individual Asset Variance and Diversification** True or false: The most important characteristic in determining the variance of a well-diversified portfolio is the variances of the individual assets in the portfolio. Explain.

27. **Portfolio Risk** If a portfolio has a positive investment in every asset, can the standard deviation on the portfolio be less than that on every asset in the portfolio? What about the portfolio beta?

28. **Portfolio Returns** Using information from the previous chapter on capital market history, what was the return on a portfolio that was equally invested in Canadian stocks and long-term bonds? What was the return on a portfolio that was equally invested in small stocks and Treasury bills?

29. **CAPM** Using the CAPM, show that the ratio of the risk premiums on two assets is equal to the ratio of their betas.

30. **Portfolio Returns and Deviations** Given the following information on a portfolio of three stocks:

State of Economy	Probability of State of Economy	Stock A Rate of Return	Stock B Rate of Return	Stock C Rate of Return
Boom	0.20	0.20	0.30	1.00
Normal	0.70	0.10	0.05	0.30
Bust	0.10	0.00	−0.20	−0.80

a. If your portfolio is invested 30 percent in A and B and 40 percent in C, what is the portfolio expected return? The variance? The standard deviation?
b. If the expected T-bill rate is 5.25 percent, what is the expected risk premium on the portfolio?
c. If the expected inflation rate is 5 percent, what is the expected real return on the portfolio? What is the expected real risk premium on the portfolio?

31. **Analyzing a Portfolio** You want to create a portfolio equally as risky as the market, and you have $200,000 to invest. Given this information, fill in the rest of the table below.

Asset	Investment ($)	Beta
Stock A	$60,000	1.20
Stock B	$60,000	0.85
Stock C	??	1.40
Risk-free asset	??	??

32. **Analyzing a Portfolio** You have $100,000 to invest in either Stock D, Stock F, or a risk-free asset. You must invest all of your money. Your goal is to create a portfolio that has an expected return of 10 percent and is only 60 percent as risky as the overall market. If D has an expected return of 20 percent and a

beta of 1.50, F has an expected return of 15 percent and a beta of 1.15, and the risk-free rate is 5 percent, how much money will you invest in Stock F?

33. **Systematic versus Unsystematic Risk**   Given the following information on stocks A and B:

State of Economy	Probability of State of Economy	Stock A Rate of Return	Stock B Rate of Return
Recession	0.15	0.14	−0.18
Normal	0.60	0.24	0.10
Boom	0.25	0.28	0.40

The market risk premium is 8 percent and the risk-free rate is 6 percent. Which stock has the most systematic risk? Which one has the most unsystematic risk? Which stock is "riskier"? Explain.

34. **Beta Coefficients**   Is it possible that a risky asset could have a beta of zero? Explain. From the CAPM, what is the expected return on such an asset? Is it possible that a risky asset could have a negative beta? What does the CAPM predict about the expected return on such an asset? Can you give an explanation for your answer?

35. **SML**   Suppose you observe the following situation:

Security	Beta	Expected Return
Abel Co.	1.15	18%
Baker Co.	0.80	15

Assume these securities are correctly priced. Based on the CAPM, what is the expected return on the market? What is the risk-free rate?

Suggested Readings

For greater detail on the subject of risk and return see chapters 8, 9, and 10 of:

Ross, S. A.; R. W. Westerfield; and J. J. Jaffe. *Corporate Finance,* 2nd ed. Homewood, IL: Richard D. Irwin, 1990.

Two intuitive discussions of APT are:

Bower, D. H.; R. S. Bower; and D. Logue. "A Primer on Arbitrage Pricing Theory." *Midland Corporate Finance Journal,* Fall 1984.

Roll, R., and S. Ross. "The Arbitrage Pricing Theory Approach to Strategic Portfolio Planning." *Financial Analysts Journal,* May–June 1984.

Discussions of Canadian tests of APT are found in:

Bodie, Z., A. Kane, A. J. Marcus, S. Perrakis, and P. J. Ryan, *Investments,* 1st Canadian Ed. Homewook, IL: Richard D. Irwin, 1993.

Hatch, J. E., and M. J. Robinson. *Investment Management in Canada,* 2nd ed. Scarborough: Prentice Hall Canada, 1989.

Otuteye, E. "How Economic Forces Explain Canadian Stock Returns." *Canadian Investment Review,* Spring 1991.

Sharpe, W. F., G. J. Alexander, and D. J. Fowler, *Investments,* 1st Canadian ed. Scarborough, OT: Prentice Hall Canada, 1993.

DERIVATION OF THE CAPITAL ASSET PRICING MODEL

Up to this point, we have assumed that all assets on the efficient frontier are risky. Alternatively, an investor could easily combine a risky investment with an investment in a riskless or risk-free security, such as a Canada Treasury bill. Using the equation for portfolio variance (Equation 11.5) we can find the variance of a portfolio with one risky and one risk-free asset:

$$\sigma^2_P = x^2_L\sigma^2_L + x^2_U\sigma^2_U + 2x_Lx_U\text{CORR}_{L,U}\sigma_L\sigma_U \qquad [11.5]$$

However, by definition, the risk-free asset (say, L in this example) has no variability so the equation for portfolio standard deviation reduces to:

$$\sigma^2_P = x^2_U\sigma^2_U$$

$$\sigma_P = \sqrt{\sigma^2_P} = x_U\sigma_U$$

The relationship between risk and return for one risky and one riskless asset is represented on a straight line between the risk-free rate and a pure investment in the risky asset as shown in Figure 11A.1. The line extends to the right of the point representing the risky asset when we assume the investor can borrow at the risk-free rate to take a leveraged position of more than 100 percent in the risky asset.

To form an optimal portfolio, an investor is likely to combine an investment in the riskless asset with a portfolio of risky assets. Figure 11A.1 illustrates our discussion by showing a risk-free asset and four risky assets: $A, X, Q,$ and $Y.$ If there is no riskless asset, the efficient set is the curve from X to $Y.$ With a risk-free asset, it is possible to form portfolios like 1, 2, and 3 combining Q with the risk-free asset. Portfolios 4 and 5 combine the riskless asset with $A.$

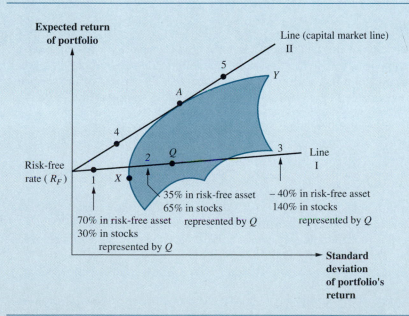

Expected return of portfolio

Line (capital market line)
II

5
Y
A
4
Q
2
3
Line
I

Risk-free rate (R_F)
1
X

35% in risk-free asset
65% in stocks
represented by Q

−40% in risk-free asset
140% in stocks
represented by Q

70% in risk-free asset
30% in stocks
represented by Q

Standard deviation of portfolio's return

FIGURE 11A.1

Relationship between expected return and standard deviation for an investment in a combination of risky securities and the riskless asset.

Portfolio Q is composed of 30 percent BCE 45 percent Bank of Montreal 25 percent Northern Telecom

The graph illustrates an important point. With riskless borrowing and lending, the portfolio of risky assets held by any investor would always be point *A*. Regardless of the investor's tolerance for risk, he or she would never choose any other point on the efficient set of risky assets. Rather, an investor with a high aversion to risk would combine the securities of *A* with riskless assets. The investor would borrow the riskless asset to invest more funds in A had he or she low aversion to risk. In other words, all investors would choose portfolios along Line II, called the *capital market line.*

To move from our description of a single investor to market equilibrium, financial economists imagine a world where all investors possess the same estimates of expected returns, variance, and correlations. This assumption is called *homogeneous expectations.*

If all investors have homogeneous expectations, Figure 11A.1 becomes the same for all individuals. All investors sketch out the same efficient set of risky assets because they are working with the same inputs. This efficient set of risky assets is represented by the curve *XAY.* Because the same risk-free rate applies to everyone, all investors view point *A* as the portfolio of risky assets to be held. In a world with homogeneous expectations, all investors would hold the portfolio of risky assets represented by point *A.*

If all investors choose the same portfolio of risky assets, *A,* then *A* must be the market portfolio. This is because, in our simplified world of homogeneous expectations, no asset would be demanded (and priced) if it were not in portfolio A. Since all assets have some demand and non-zero price, *A* has to be the market portfolio including all assets.

The variance of the market portfolio can be represented as:

$$\sigma^2{}_P = \sum_{i=1}^{N} \sum_{j=1}^{N} x_i x_j \sigma_{ij} \qquad [11.11]$$

where we define σ_{ij} as the covariance of i with j if $i \neq j$ and σ_{ij} is the variance or $\sigma^2{}_i$ if $i = j$.

$$\sigma_{ij} = \text{CORR}_{i,j}\, \sigma_i \sigma_j$$

Using a little elementary calculus, we can represent a security's systematic risk (the contribution of security i to the risk of the market portfolio) by taking the partial derivative of the portfolio risk with respect to a change in the weight of the security. This measures the change in the portfolio variance when the weight of the security is increased slightly. For security 2,

$$\frac{\delta\sigma^2{}_P}{\delta x_2} = 2\sum_{j=1}^{N} x_j \sigma_{i2} = 2[x_1 \text{COV}(R_1,R_2) + x_2\sigma^2{}_2 + x_3\,\text{COV}(R_3,R_2) \qquad [11.12]$$

$$+ \ldots + x_N \text{COV}(R_N,R_2)]$$

The term within brackets in (11A.2) is COV (R_2,R_M). This shows that systematic risk is proportional to a security's covariance with the market portfolio.

The final step is to standardize systematic risk by dividing by the variance of the market portfolio. The result is β_2 as presented in the text.

$$\beta_2 = \frac{\text{COV}(R_2,R_M)}{\sigma^2(R_M)} \qquad [11.13]$$

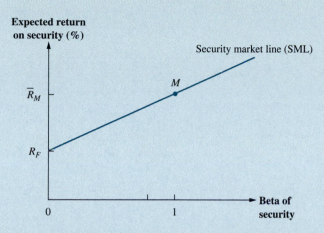

Relationship between expected return on an individual security and beta of the security.

R_F is the risk-free rate. $\bar{R}_M$ is the expected return on the market portfolio.

If you consult any basic statistics text, you will see that this formula is identical to the β_2 obtained from a regression of R_2 on R_M.

We can now redraw Figure 11A.1 in expected return-β space, as shown in Figure 11A.2. The vertical axis remains the same, but on the horizontal axis we replace total risk (σ) with systematic risk as measured by β. We plot the two points on the capital market line from Figure 11A.1: R_F with $\beta = 0$ and M (the market portfolio represented by A) with a $\beta = 1$. To see that $B_M = 1$, substitute portfolio M for i in Equation 11A.3.

$$\beta_M = \frac{COV(R_M, R_M)}{\sigma^2(R_M)}$$

$$= \frac{CORR_{M,M}\sigma_M\sigma_M}{\sigma^2(R_M)}$$

$$= \frac{1.0 \times \sigma^2_M}{\sigma^2(R_M)}$$

$$\beta_M = 1.0$$

The result is the security market line shown in Figure 11A.2. We can use the slope-intercept method to find that the intercept of the SML is R_F and the slope is $(R_M - R_F)$. The equation for the SML is:

$$E(R) = R_F + \beta (R_M - R_F)$$

And this completes the derivation of the capital asset pricing model.

LONG-TERM FINANCING

VI

CHAPTER 12 | Long-Term Financing: An Introduction

This chapter describes the main features of long-term financing and corporate securities. It begins with a discussion of long-term debt, preferred stock, and common stock and then covers the historical patterns of long-term financing.

CHAPTER 13 | Issuing Securities to the Public

This chapter describes how securities are issued and discusses the different underwriting methods. Chapter 13 also discusses the direct and indirect costs associated with issuing securities.

C H A P T E R

Long-Term Financing:
An Introduction

Corporate securities such as stocks and bonds can be a perplexing subject. Frequently, the concepts are simple and logical, but the language is unfamiliar and rich in jargon. Many of the terms and ideas we describe in this chapter and the next have appeared elsewhere in our book. Our task here and in the next several chapters is to assemble these pieces into a reasonably complete picture of long-term corporate financing.

In this chapter, we describe the main features of long-term financing and corporate securities. We begin with a look at long-term debt, preferred stock, and common stock. We go on to briefly consider patterns of the different kinds of long-term financing. We defer to a later chapter our discussion of the institutional, legal, and regulatory complexities involved in selling securities to the public.

One consequence of debt financing is the possibility of bankruptcy. Events preceding bankruptcy are referred to as *financial distress*. Because the prospect of bankruptcy is an important consideration in long-term financing, we conclude this chapter with a discussion of financial distress, bankruptcy, and reorganization.

12.1 | CORPORATE LONG-TERM DEBT

In this section, we begin our discussion of corporate debt by describing in some detail the basic terms and features that make up a typical long-term corporate debt. We discuss additional issues associated with long-term debt in subsequent sections.

Securities issued by corporations may be classified roughly as *equity securities* and *debt securities*. At its crudest level, a debt represents something that must be repaid; it is the result of borrowing money. When corporations borrow, they promise to make regularly scheduled interest payments and to repay the original amount borrowed (that is, the principal). The person or firm making the loan is called the *creditor* or *lender*. The corporation borrowing the money is called the *debtor* or *borrower*.

From a financial point of view, the main differences between debt and equity are the following:

1. Debt is not an ownership interest in the firm. Creditors generally do not have voting power.

2. The corporation's payment of interest on debt is considered a cost of doing business and is fully tax deductible.

3. Unpaid debt is a liability of the firm. If it is not paid, the creditors can legally claim the assets of the firm. This action can result in liquidation or reorganization, two of the possible consequences of bankruptcy. Thus, one of the costs of issuing debt is the possibility of financial failure. This possibility does not arise when equity is issued.

Long-Term Debt: The Basics

Ultimately, all long-term debt securities are promises by the issuing firm to pay the principal when due and to make timely interest payments on the unpaid balance. Beyond this, a number of features distinguish these securities from one another. We discuss some of these features next.

The maturity of a long-term debt instrument refers to the length of time the debt remains outstanding with some unpaid balance. Debt securities can be short-term (maturities of one year or less) or long-term (maturities of more than one year).[1]

Debt securities are typically called *notes, debentures,* or *bonds.* Strictly speaking, a bond is a secured debt, but, in common usage, the word *bond* refers to all kinds of secured and unsecured debt. We use the term generically to refer to long-term debt.

The two major forms of long-term debt are public-issue and privately placed. We concentrate on public-issue bonds. Most of what we say about them holds true for private-issue, long-term debt as well. The main difference between public-issue and privately placed debt is that the latter is directly placed with a lender and not offered to the public. Since this is a private transaction, the specific terms are up to the parties involved.

There are many other dimensions to long-term debt, including such things as security, call features, sinking funds, ratings, and protective covenants. The following table illustrates these features for a hypothetical bond. If some of these terms are unfamiliar, have no fear. We discuss them all next.

Features of a hypothetical bond

Terms		Explanation
Amount of issue	$50 million	The company will issue $50 million of bonds.
Date of issue	4/15/96	The bonds will be sold on April 15, 1996.
Maturity	4/15/26	The principal will be paid in 30 years.
Face value	$1,000	The denomination of the bonds is $1,000.
Annual coupon	10.50	The denomination of the bonds is $1,000. Each bondholder will receive $105 per bond per year.
Offer price	100	The offer price will be 100% of the $1,000 face value per bond.
Yield to maturity	10.50%	If the bond is held to maturity, bondholders will receive a stated annual rate of return equal to 10.5%.
Coupon payment	10/15, 4/14	Coupons of $105/2 = $52.50 will be paid on these dates.
Security	None	The bonds are debentures.

[1] There is no universally agreed-upon distinction between short-term and long-term debt. In addition, people often refer to intermediate-term debt, which has a maturity of more than 1 year and less than 3 to 5, or even 10, years.

Features of a hypothetical bond		
Terms		Explanation
Sinking fund	Annual	The firm will make annual payments toward the sinking fund.
Call provision	Not callable before 4/15/06	The bonds have a deferred call feature.
Call price	$1,100	After 10 years, the company can buy back the bonds for $1,100 per bond.
Rating	CBRS A++	This is CBRS's highest rating. The bonds have the lowest probability of default.

Many of these features are detailed in the bond indenture, so we discuss this now.

The Indenture

indenture

Written agreement between the corporation and the lender detailing the terms of the debt issue.

The **indenture** is the written agreement between the corporation (the borrower) and its creditors. It is sometimes referred to as the deed of trust.[2] Usually, a trustee (a trust company) is appointed by the corporation to represent the bondholders. The trust company must (1) make sure the terms of the indenture are obeyed, (2) manage the sinking fund (described later), and (3) represent the bondholders in default, that is, if the company defaults on its payments to them.

The bond indenture is a legal document. It can run several hundred pages and generally makes for very tedious reading. It is an important document, however, because it generally includes the following provisions:

1. The basic terms of the bonds.
2. The amount of the bonds issued.
3. A description of property used as security if the bonds are secured.
4. The repayment arrangements.
5. The call provisions.
6. Details of the protective covenants.

We discuss these features next.

Terms of a Bond   Corporate bonds usually have a face value (that is, a denomination) of $1,000. This is called the *principal value,* and it is stated on the bond certificate. So, if a corporation wanted to borrow $1 million, 1,000 bonds would have to be sold. The par value (that is, initial accounting value) of a bond is almost always the same as the face value.

registered form

Registrar of company records ownership of each bond; payment is made directly to the owner of record.

Corporate bonds are usually in **registered form**. For example, the indenture might read as follows: Interest is payable semiannually on July 1 and January 1 of each year to the person in whose name the bond is registered at the close of business on June 15 or December 15, respectively.

This means the company has a registrar who records the ownership of each bond and records any changes in ownership. The company pays the interest and principal by cheque mailed directly to the address of the owner of record. A corporate bond may be registered and may have attached coupons. To obtain an interest payment, the owner must separate a coupon from the bond certificate and send it to the company registrar (the paying agent).

---

[2] The words *loan agreement* or *loan contract* are usually used for privately placed debt and term loans.

Alternatively, the bond could be in **bearer form**. This means the certificate is the basic evidence of ownership, and the corporation pays the bearer. Ownership is not otherwise recorded, and, as with a registered bond with attached coupons, the holder of the bond certificate detaches the coupons and sends them to the company to receive payment.

> **bearer form**
> *Bond issued without record of the owner's name; payment is made to whoever holds the bond.*

There are two drawbacks to bearer bonds: First, they are difficult to recover if they are lost or stolen. Second, because the company does not know who owns its bonds, it cannot notify bondholders of important events. The bearer form of ownership does have the advantage of easing transactions for investors who trade their bonds frequently.

Security Debt securities are classified according to the collateral and mortgages used to protect the bondholder.

Collateral is a general term that, strictly speaking, means securities (for example, bonds and stocks) pledged as security for payment of debt. For example, collateral trust bonds often involve a pledge of common stock held by the corporation. This pledge is usually backed by marketable securities. However, the term *collateral* often is used much more loosely to refer to any form of security.

Mortgage securities are secured by a mortgage on the real property of the borrower. The property involved may be real estate, transportation equipment, or other property. The legal document that describes a mortgage on real estate is called a mortgage trust indenture or trust deed.

Sometimes mortgages are on specific property, for example, a railroad car. This is called a chattel mortgage. More often, blanket mortgages are used. A blanket mortgage pledges all the real property owned by the company.[3]

Bonds frequently represent unsecured obligations of the company. A **debenture** is an unsecured bond, where no specific pledge of property is made. The term **note** is generally used for such instruments if the maturity of the unsecured bond is less than 10 or so years when it is originally issued. Debenture holders only have a claim on property not otherwise pledged; in other words, the property that remains after mortgages and collateral trusts are taken into account.

> **debenture**
> *Unsecured debt, usually with a maturity of 10 years or more.*

> **note**
> *Unsecured debt, usually with a maturity under 10 years.*

At the current time, most public bonds issued by industrial and finance companies are debentures. However, most utility and railroad bonds are secured by a pledge of assets.

Seniority In general terms, *seniority* indicates preference in position over other lenders, and debts are sometimes labelled as "senior" or "junior" to indicate seniority. Some debt is *subordinated,* as in, for example, a subordinated debenture.

In the event of default, holders of subordinated debt must give preference to other specified creditors. Usually, this means the subordinated lenders are paid off from cash flow and asset sales only after the specified creditors have been compensated. However, debt cannot be subordinated to equity.

Repayment Bonds can be repaid at maturity, at which time the bondholder receives the stated or face value of the bonds, or they may be repaid in part or in entirety before maturity. Early repayment in some form is more typical and is often handled through a sinking fund.

---

[3] Real property includes land and things "affixed thereto." It does not include cash or inventories.

sinking fund
Account managed by the bond trustee for early bond redemption.

A **sinking fund** is an account managed by the bond trustee for the purpose of repaying the bonds. The company makes annual payments to the trustee, who then uses the funds to retire a portion of the debt. The trustee does this by either buying up some of the bonds in the market or calling in a fraction of the outstanding bonds. We discuss this second option in the next section.

There are many different kinds of sinking fund arrangements. The fund may start immediately or be delayed for 10 years after the bond is issued. The provision may require the company to redeem all or only a portion of the outstanding issue before maturity. From an investor's viewpoint, a sinking fund reduces the risk that the company will be unable to repay the principal at maturity. Since it involves regular purchases, a sinking fund improves the marketability of the bonds.

call provision
Agreement giving the corporation the option to repurchase the bond at a specified price before maturity.

The Call Provision　A **call provision** allows the company to repurchase or "call" part or all of the bond issue at stated prices over a specified period. Corporate bonds are usually callable.

Generally, the call price is more than the bond's stated value (that is, the par value). The difference between the call price and the stated value is the **call premium**. The call premium may also be expressed as a percentage of the bond's face value. The amount of the call premium usually becomes smaller over time. One arrangement is to initially set the call premium equal to the annual coupon payment and then make it decline to zero the closer the call date is to maturity.

call premium
Amount by which the call price exceeds the par value of the bond.

Call provisions are not usually operative during the first part of a bond's life. This makes the call provision less of a worry for bondholders in the bond's early years. For example, a company might be prohibited from calling its bonds for the first 10 years. This is a **deferred call**. During this period, the bond is said to be **call protected**. Appendix 12A discusses call provisions and bond refunding in detail.

deferred call
Call provision prohibiting the company from redeeming the bond before a certain date.

Protective Covenants　A **protective covenant** is that part of the indenture or loan agreement that limits certain actions a company might otherwise wish to take during the term of the loan. Covenants are designed to reduce the agency costs faced by bondholders. By controlling company activities, they reduce the risk of the bonds.

For example, common covenants limit the dividends the firm can pay and require bondholder approval for any sale of major assets. This means that, if the firm is headed for bankruptcy, it cannot sell all the assets and pay a liquidating dividend to stockholders leaving the bondholders with only a corporate shell. Protective covenants can be classified into two types: negative covenants and positive (or affirmative) covenants.

call protected
Bond during period in which it cannot be redeemed by the issuer.

A *negative covenant* is a "thou shalt not." It limits or prohibits actions that the company may take. Here are some typical examples:

1. The firm must limit the amount of dividends it pays according to some formula.
2. The firm cannot pledge any assets to other lenders.
3. The firm cannot merge with another firm.
4. The firm cannot sell or lease any major assets without approval by the lender.
5. The firm cannot issue additional long-term debt.

protective covenant
Part of the indenture limiting certain transactions that can be taken during the term of the loan, usually to protect the lender's interest.

A *positive covenant* is a "thou shalt." It specifies an action that the company agrees to take or a condition the company must abide by. Here are some examples:

1. The company must maintain its working capital at or above some specified minimum level.

2. The company must periodically furnish audited financial statements to the lender.

3. The firm must maintain any collateral or security in good condition.

This is only a partial list of covenants; a particular indenture may feature many different ones.

> CONCEPT QUESTIONS
> **1.** What are the distinguishing features of debt as compared to equity?
> **2.** What is the indenture? What are protective covenants? Give some examples.
> **3.** What is a sinking fund?

12.2 | BOND RATINGS

Firms frequently pay to have their debt rated. The two leading bond rating firms in Canada are Canadian Bond Rating Service (CBRS) and Dominion Bond Rating Service (DBRS). Moody's and Standard & Poor's (S&P) are the largest U.S. bond raters and they often rate Canadian companies that raise funds in U.S. bond markets.[4] The debt ratings are an assessment of the creditworthiness of the corporate issuer. The definitions of creditworthiness used by bond rating agencies are based on how likely the firm is to default and the protection creditors have in the event of a default.

Remember that bond ratings only concern the possibility of default. In Chapter 4, we discussed interest rate risk, which we defined as the risk of a change in the value of a bond from a change in interest rates. Bond ratings do not address this issue. As a result, the price of a highly rated bond can still be quite volatile.

Bond ratings are constructed from information supplied by the corporation. The rating classes and information concerning them are shown in this table and Table 12.1.

	Investment Quality Bond Ratings			Low Quality, Speculative and/or Junk					
	High Grade		Medium Grade	Low Grade		Very Low Grade			
Dominion Bond Rating Service Limited	AAA	AA	A BBB	BB	B	CCC	CC	C	N/R
Canadian Bond Rating Service	A++	A+	A B++	B+	B	C	D	N/R	

The highest rating a firm can have is AAA or A++, and such debt is judged to be the best quality and to have the lowest degree of risk. This rating is not awarded very often; AA or A+ ratings indicate very good quality debt and are much more common. Investment grade bonds are bonds rated at least BBB. The lowest ratings are for debt that is in default.

In the 1980s, a growing part of corporate borrowing took the form of low-grade, or junk, bonds particularly in the United States. If they are rated at all, such low-grade bonds are rated below investment grade by the major rating agencies. Junk bonds are also called *high-yield* bonds as they yield an interest rate 3 to 5 percentage points (300 to 500 basis points) higher than that of AAA-rated debt. Original issue junk bonds have never been a major source of funds in Canadian capital markets. Their niche has been filled in part by preferred shares and to a lesser extent, income bonds. In recent years, some Canadian corporations with large debt financing needs have issued bonds below investment grade in the United States.

---

[4] They also rate bonds issued by the individual provinces.

T A B L E 12.1	**AAA**	Bonds which are rated AAA are of the highest investment quality. The degree of protection afforded principal and interest is of the highest order. Earnings are relatively stable, the structure of the industry in which the company operates is very strong, and the outlook for future profitability is extremely favourable. There are few qualifying factors present which would detract from the performance of the company, and the strength of liquidity ratios is unquestioned for the industry in which the company operates.
Descriptions of ratings used by Dominion Bond Rating Service	**AA**	Bonds rated AA are of superior investment quality, and protection of interest and principal is considered high. In many cases, they differ from bonds rated AAA to a small degree.
	A	Bonds rated A are upper medium grade securities. Protection of interest and principal is still substantial, but the degree of strength is less than with AA-rated companies. Companies in this category may be more susceptible to adverse economic conditions.
	BBB	Bonds rated BBB are medium-grade securities. Protection of interest and principal is considered adequate, but the company may be more susceptible to economic cycles, or there may be other adversities present which reduce the strength of these bonds.
	BB	Bonds rated BB are lower-medium-grade obligations and are considered mildly speculative and below average. The degree of protection afforded interest and principal is uncertain, particularly during periods of economic recession, and the size of the company may be relatively small.
	B	Bonds rated B are "middle" speculative. Uncertainty exists as to the ability of the company to pay interest and principal on a continuing basis in the future, especially in periods of economic recession.
	CCC	Bonds rated CCC are considered highly speculative and are in danger of default of interest and principal. The degree of adverse elements present is more severe than bonds rated B.
	CC	Bonds rated CC are in default of either interest or principal, and other severe adverse elements are present.
	C	C is the lowest rating provided. Bonds rated C differ from bonds rated CC with respect to the relative liquidation values.
	NR	For certain companies, we may complete the editorial, yet not rate the company formally, in which case we would rate it NR, or "not rated."

High or Low   In addition to the above, our ratings may be modified by the quotation "high" or "low" to indicate the relative standing within a rating classification.

Highest Rating   Please note the rating quoted at the top left of the front page of a report indicates the rating of the highest order or securities issued by the company.

Source: Used with permission of Dominion Bond Rating Service.

CONCEPT QUESTIONS

1. What is a junk bond?
2. What does a bond rating say about the risk of fluctuations in a bond's value from interest rate changes?

12.3 | SOME DIFFERENT TYPES OF BONDS

Thus far, we have considered "plain vanilla" bonds. In this section, we look at some more unusual types, the products of financial engineering: stripped bonds, floating-rate bonds, and others.

Financial Engineering

When financial managers or their investment bankers design new securities or financial processes, their efforts are referred to as financial engineering.[5] Successful

---

[5] For more on financial engineering, see John D. Finnerty, "Financial Engineering in Corporate Finance: An Overview," in *The Handbook of Financial Engineering,* eds. C. W. Smith and C. W. Smithson (New York: Harper Business, 1990).

IN THEIR OWN WORDS . . .

Edward I. Altman on Junk Bonds

One of the most important developments in corporate finance over the last 15 years has been the re-emergence of publicly owned and traded low-rated corporate debt. Originally offered to the public in the early 1900s to help finance some of our emerging growth industries, these high yield/high risk bonds virtually disappeared after the rash of bond defaults during the Depression. Recently, however, the junk bond market has been catapulted from an insignificant element in the corporate fixed income market to one of the fastest growing and most controversial types of financing mechanisms.

The term *junk* emanates from the dominant type of low-rated bond issues outstanding prior to 1977, when the "market" consisted almost exclusively of original issue investment grade bonds that fell from their lofty status to a higher default risk, speculative grade level. These so-called "fallen angels" amounted to about $8.5 billion in 1977. At the beginning of 1994, fallen angels comprised about 17 percent of the $200 billion publicly owned junk bond market.

Beginning in 1977, issuers began to go directly to the public to raise capital for growth purposes. Early users of junk bonds were energy-related firms, cable TV companies, airlines, and assorted other industrial companies. This type of financing is a form of securitization of what heretofore was the sole province of private placements financed by banks and insurance companies. The emerging growth company rationale coupled

with relatively high returns to early investors helped legitimize this sector. Most investment banks ignored junk bonds until 1983–1984, when their merits and profit potential became more evident.

Synonymous with the market's growth was the emergence of the investment banking firm, Drexel Burnham Lambert and its junk bond wizard, Michael Milken. Drexel established a potent network of issuers and investors and rode the wave of new financing and the consequent surge in secondary trading to become one of the powerful investment banks in the late 1980s. The incredible rise in power of this firm was followed by an equally incredible fall resulting first in government civil and criminal convictions and huge fines for various misdealings and finally the firm's total collapse and bankruptcy in February 1990.

By far the most important and controversial aspect of junk bond financing was its role in the corporate restructuring movement from 1985–1989. High leverage transactions and acquisitions, such as leveraged buyouts (LBOs), which occur when a firm is taken private, and leveraged recapitalizations (debt for equity swaps), transformed the face of corporate America, leading to a heated debate as to the economic and social consequences of firms being transformed from public to private enterprises with debt/equity ratios of at least 6:1.

These transactions involved increasingly large companies, and the multibillion dollar takeover became fairly common, finally capped by

the huge $25+ billion RJR Nabisco LBO in 1989. LBOs were typically financed with about 60 percent senior bank and insurance company debt, about 25–30 percent subordinated public debt (junk bonds), and 10–15 percent equity. The junk bond segment is sometimes referred to as "mezzanine" financing because it lies between the "balcony" senior debt and the "basement" equity.

These restructurings resulted in huge fees to advisors and underwriters and huge premiums to the old shareholders who were bought out, and they continued as long as the market was willing to buy these new debt offerings at what appeared to be a favorable risk-return tradeoff. The bottom fell out of the market in the last six months of 1989 due to a number of factors including a marked increase in defaults, government regulation against S&Ls holding junk bonds, fears of higher interest rates and a recession, and, finally, the growing realization of the leverage excesses of certain ill-conceived restructurings.

The default rate rose dramatically to 4 percent in 1989 and then skyrocketed in 1990 and 1991 to 10.1 percent and 10.3 percent, respectively, with about $19 billion of defaults in 1991. By the end of 1990, the pendulum of growth in new junk bond issues and returns to investors swung dramatically downward as prices plummeted and the new issue market all but dried up. The year 1991 was a pivotal year in that despite record defaults, bond prices and new issues

continued

rebounded strongly as the prospects for the future brightened.

In the early 1990s, the financial market was questioning the very survival of the junk bond market. The answer was a resounding "yes," as the amount of new issues soared to record annual levels of $38 billion in 1992 and an incred-ible almost $50 billion in 1993. Coupled with plummeting default rates (under 1.5 percent in 1993) and returns in these years between 15 and 20 percent, the risk-return characteristics have been extremely favourable. The junk bond market in the mid-1990s is a quieter one compared to the 1980s, but, in terms of growth and returns, it is healthier than ever before.

Edward I. Altman is Max L. Heine Professor of Finance and Vice Director of the Salomon Center at the Stern School of Business of New York University. He is widely recognized as one of the world's experts on bankruptcy and credit analysis as well as the high-yield or "junk" bond market.

financial engineering reduces and controls risk and minimizes taxes. It also seeks to reduce financing costs of issuing and servicing debt as well as costs of complying-with rules laid down by regulatory authorities. Financial engineering is a response to the trends we discussed in Chapter 1, globalization, deregulation, and greater competition in financial markets.

When applied to debt securities, financial engineering creates exotic, hybrid securities that have many features of equity but are treated as debt. For example, suppose a corporation issues a perpetual bond with interest payable solely from corporate income if, and only if, earned. Whether this is really a debt or not is hard to say and is primarily a legal and semantic issue. Courts and taxing authorities would have the final say.

Obviously, the distinction between debt and equity is very important for tax purposes. So one reason that corporations try to create a debt security that is really equity is to obtain the tax benefits of debt and the bankruptcy benefits (lower agency costs) of equity.

As a general rule, equity represents an ownership interest, and it is a residual claim. This means equity holders are paid after debtholders. As a result of this, the risks and benefits associated with owning debt and equity are different. To give just one example, the maximum reward for owning a straight debt security is ultimately fixed by the amount of the loan, whereas there is no necessary upper limit to the potential reward from owning an equity interest.

Financial engineers can alter this division of claims by selling bonds with *warrants* attached giving bondholders options to buy stock in the firm. These warrants allow holders to participate in future rewards beyond the face value of the debt. We discuss other examples of financial engineering throughout this chapter. It is also featured in the following chapter on how securities are issued and in Chapter 20 on options and corporate securities.

Stripped Bonds

stripped bond

A bond that makes no coupon payments, thus initially priced at a deep discount.

A bond that pays no coupons must be offered at a price that is much lower than its stated value. Such bonds are called **stripped bonds**.[6]

Suppose the DDB Company issues a $1,000 face value five-year stripped bond. The initial price is set at $497. It is straightforward to check that, at this price, the bonds yield 15 percent to maturity. The total interest paid over the life of the bond is $1,000 − 497 = $503.

---

[6] A bond issued with a very low coupon rate (as opposed to a zero coupon rate) is an original issue, discount (OID) bond.

For tax purposes, the issuer of a stripped bond deducts interest every year even though no interest is actually paid. Similarly, the owner must pay taxes on interest accrued every year as well, even though no interest is actually received.[7] This second tax feature makes taxable stripped bonds less attractive to taxable investors. However, they are still a very attractive investment for tax-exempt investors with long-term dollar-denominated liabilities, such as pension funds, because the future dollar value is known with relative certainty. Stripped coupons, discussed in Chapter 5, are attractive to individual investors for tax-sheltered registered retirement savings plans (RRSPs). Recall from Chapter 5 (Example 5.7) that stripped bonds start life as normal coupon bonds. Investment dealers engage in bond stripping when they sell the principal and coupons separately.

Floating-Rate Bonds

The conventional bonds we have talked about in this chapter have fixed-dollar obligations because the coupon rate is set as a fixed percentage of the par value. Similarly, the principal is set equal to the par value. Under these circumstances, the coupon payment and principal are fixed.

With *floating-rate bonds (floaters),* the coupon payments are adjustable. The adjustments are tied to the Treasury bill rate or another short-term interest rate. For example, in 1993, the Royal Bank had outstanding $250 million of floating-rate notes maturing in 2083. The coupon rate was set at 0.40 percent more than the bankers acceptance rate.

Floating rate bonds were introduced to control the risk of price fluctuations as interest rates change. The bond pricing mathematics of Chapter 6 showed that a bond with a coupon equal to the market yield is priced at par. In practice, the value of a floating-rate bond depends on exactly how the coupon payment adjustments are defined. In most cases, the coupon adjusts with a lag to some base rate, and so the price can deviate from par within some range. For example, suppose a coupon-rate adjustment is made on June 1. The adjustment might be based on the simple average of Treasury bill yields during the previous three months. In addition, the majority of floaters have the following features:

1. The holder has the right to redeem his or her note at par on the coupon payment date after some specified amount of time. This is called a put provision, and it is discussed later.

2. The coupon rate has a floor and a ceiling, meaning the coupon is subject to a minimum and a maximum.

Other Types of Bonds

Since bonds are financial contracts, the possible features are limited only by the imagination of the parties involved. As a result, bonds can be fairly exotic, particularly some more recent issues. We discuss a few of the more common features and types next.

Income bonds are similar to conventional bonds, except that coupon payments are dependent on company income. Specifically, coupons are paid to bondholders only if the firm's income is sufficient. In Canada, income bonds are usually issued by firms in the process of reorganization to try to overcome financial distress. The firm

[7] The way the yearly interest on a stripped bond is calculated is governed by tax law and is not necessarily the true compound interest.

can skip the interest payment on an income bond without being in default. Purchasers of income bonds receive favourable tax treatment on interest received. *Real return bonds* have coupons and principal indexed to inflation to provide a stated real return. In 1993, the federal government issued a *stripped real return bond* packaging inflation protection in the form of zero coupon bond.[8]

A *convertible bond* can be swapped for a fixed number of shares of stock anytime before maturity at the holder's option. Convertibles are debt/equity hybrids that allow the holder to profit if the issuer's stock price rises.

A **retractable bond** or *put bond* allows the holder to force the issuer to buy the bond back at a stated price. As long as the issuer remains solvent, the put feature sets a floor price for the bond. It is, therefore, just the reverse of the call provision and is a relatively new development. We discuss convertible bonds, call provisions, and put provisions in more detail in Chapter 20.

A given bond may have many unusual features. To give just one example, Merrill Lynch created a popular bond called a *liquid yield option note,* or LYON ("lion"). A LYON has everything but the "kitchen sink"; this bond is a callable, puttable, convertible, zero coupon, subordinated note. In 1991, Rogers Communications Inc. issued the first LYON in Canada. Valuing a bond of this sort can be quite complex, and we have more to say about it in Chapter 20.

retractable bond
Bond that may be sold back to the issuer at a prespecified price before maturity.

> CONCEPT QUESTIONS
> 1. Why might an income bond be attractive to a corporation with volatile cash flows? Can you think of a reason why income bonds are not more popular?
> 2. What do you think the effect of a put feature on a bond's coupon would be? How about a convertibility feature? Why?

12.4 | PREFERRED STOCK

preferred stock
Stock with dividend priority over common stock, normally with a fixed dividend rate, often without voting rights.

Preferred stock differs from common stock because it has preference over common stock in the payment of dividends and in the distribution of corporation assets in the event of liquidation. Preference means the holders of the preferred shares must receive a dividend (in the case of an ongoing firm) before holders of common shares are entitled to anything. If the firm is liquidated, preferred shareholders rank behind all creditors but ahead of common stockholders.

Preferred stock is a form of equity from a legal, tax, and regulatory standpoint. In the last decade, chartered banks were important issuers of preferred stock as they moved to meet higher capital requirements. Importantly, however, holders of preferred stock generally have no voting privileges.

Stated Value

Preferred shares have a stated liquidating value. The cash dividend is described in dollars per share. For example, Bank of Montreal's "$2.25" translates easily into a dividend yield of 9 percent of $25 stated value.

Cumulative and Non-Cumulative Dividends

A preferred dividend is not like interest on a bond. The board of directors may decide not to pay the dividends on preferred shares, and their decision may have nothing to do with the current net income of the corporation.

---
[8] B. Critchley, "Indexing Gives These Bonds a Real Return," *Financial Post,* November 27, 1993, p. 17.

Dividends payable on preferred stock are either cumulative or non-cumulative; most are cumulative. If preferred dividends are cumulative and are not paid in a particular year, they are carried forward as an *arrearage*. Usually both the cumulated (past) preferred dividends plus the current preferred dividends must be paid before the common shareholders can receive anything.

Unpaid preferred dividends are not debts of the firm. Directors elected by the common shareholders can defer preferred dividends indefinitely. However, in such cases:

1. Common shareholders must also forgo dividends.
2. Holders of preferred shares are often granted voting and other rights if preferred dividends have not been paid for some time.

Because preferred shareholders receive no interest on the cumulated dividends, some have argued that firms have an incentive to delay paying preferred dividends.

Is Preferred Stock Really Debt?

A good case can be made that preferred stock is really debt in disguise, a kind of equity bond. Preferred shareholders receive a stated dividend only, and, if the corporation is liquidated, preferred shareholders get a stated value. Often, preferreds carry credit ratings much like bonds. Furthermore, preferred stock is sometimes convertible into common stock. Preferred stocks are often callable by the issuer and the holder often has the right to sell the preferred stock back to the issuer at a set price.

In addition, in recent years, many new issues of preferred stock have had obligatory sinking funds. Such a sinking fund effectively creates a final maturity since the entire issue is ultimately retired. For example, if a sinking fund required that 2 percent of the original issue be retired each year, the issue would be completely retired in 50 years.

On top of all of this, preferred stocks with adjustable dividends have been offered in recent years. For example, a CARP is a cumulative, adjustable rate, preferred stock. There are various types of floating-rate preferreds, some of which are quite innovative in the way the dividend is determined. For example, dividends on Royal Bank of Canada First Preferred Shares Series C are set at $2/3$ of the bank's average Canadian prime rate with a floor dividend of 6.67 percent per year.

For all these reasons, preferred stock seems to be a lot like debt. In comparison to debt, the yields on preferred stock can appear very low. For example, the Royal Bank has another preferred stock with a $2.25 stated dividend. In September 1995, the market price of the $2.25 Royal Bank preferred was about $27⅞. This is a $2.25/$27⅞ = 8.07% yield, less than the yield on Royal Bank long-term debt (about 9 percent at that time). Also at that time, long-term government of Canada bonds were yielding just under 8.5 percent.

Despite the apparently low yields, corporate investors have an incentive to hold the preferred stock issued by other corporations rather than holding their debt because 100 percent of the dividends they receive are exempt from income taxes. Individual investors do not receive this tax break, so most preferred stock in Canada is purchased by corporate investors.[9] Corporate investors pay a premium for preferred stock because of the tax exclusion on dividends; as a consequence, the yields are low.

---

[9] Individual investors do receive a watered down dividend tax credit for preferred dividends, but these shares remain generally more attractive to corporate investors.

Preferred Stock and Taxes

Turning to the issuers' point of view, a tax loophole encourages corporations that are lightly taxed or not taxable due to losses or tax shelters to issue preferred stock. Such low-tax companies can make little use of the tax deduction on interest. However, they can issue preferred stock and enjoy lower financing costs because preferred dividends are significantly lower than interest payments.

In 1987, the federal government attempted to close this tax loophole by introducing a tax of 40 percent of the preferred dividends to be paid by the issuer of preferred stock. The tax is refunded (through a deduction) to taxable issuers only. The effect of this (and associated) tax change was to narrow but not close the loophole.

Table 12.2 shows how Zero Tax Ltd., a corporation not paying any income taxes, can issue preferred shares attractive to Full Tax Ltd., a second corporation taxable at a combined federal and provincial rate of 45 percent. The example assumes that Zero Tax is seeking $1,000 in financing through either debt or preferred stock and that Zero Tax can issue either debt with a 10 percent coupon or preferred stock with a 6.7 percent dividend.[10]

Table 12.2 shows that with preferred stock financing, Zero Tax pays out 6.7% × $1,000 = $67.00 in dividends and 40% × $67.00 = $26.80 in tax on the dividends for a total aftertax outlay of $93.80. This represents an aftertax cost of $93.80/$1,000 = 9.38%. Debt financing is more expensive with an outlay of $100 and an aftertax yield of 10 percent. So Zero Tax is better off issuing preferred stock.

From the point of view of the purchaser, Full Tax Ltd., the preferred dividend is received tax free for an aftertax yield of 6.7 percent. If it bought debt issued by Zero Tax instead, Full Tax would pay income tax of $45 for a net aftertax receipt of $55 or 5.5 percent. So again, preferred stock is better than debt.

Of course, if we change the example to make the issuer fully taxable, the aftertax cost of debt drops to 5.5 percent making debt financing more attractive. This reinforces our point that the tax motivation for issuing preferred stock is limited to lightly taxed companies.

T A B L E 12.2

Tax loophole on preferred stock

	Preferred	Debt
Issuer: Zero Tax Ltd.		
Preferred dividend/interest paid	$67.00	$100.00
Dividend tax at 40%	26.80	0.00
Tax deduction on interest	0.00	0.00
Total financing cost	$93.80	$100.00
Aftertax cost	9.38%	10.00%
Purchaser: Full Tax Ltd.		
Beforetax income	$67.00	$100.00
Tax	0.00	45.00
Aftertax income	$67.00	$ 55.00
Aftertax yield	6.70%	5.50%

[10] We set the preferred dividend at around two thirds of the debt yield to reflect market practice as exemplified by the Royal Bank issue discussed earlier. Further discussion of preferred stock and taxes is in I. Fooladi, P. A. McGraw and G. S. Roberts, "Preferred Share Rules Freeze Out the Individual Investor," *CA Magazine*, April 11, 1988, pp. 38–41.

Beyond Taxes

For fully taxed firms, the fact that dividends are not an allowable deduction from taxable corporate income is the most serious obstacle to issuing preferred stock, but there are several reasons beyond taxes why preferred stock is issued.

We can start by discussing some supply factors. First, regulated public utilities can pass the tax disadvantage of issuing preferred stock on to their customers because of the way pricing formulas are set up in regulatory environments. Consequently, a substantial amount of straight preferred stock is issued by utilities.

Second, firms issuing preferred stock can avoid the threat of bankruptcy that might otherwise exist if debt were relied on. Unpaid preferred dividends are not debts of a corporation, and preferred shareholders cannot force a corporation into bankruptcy because of unpaid dividends.

A third reason for issuing preferred stock concerns control of the firm. Since preferred shareholders often cannot vote, preferred stock may be a means of raising equity without surrendering control.

On the demand side, most preferred stock is owned by corporations. Corporate income from preferred stock dividends enjoys a tax exemption, which can substantially lessen the tax disadvantage of preferred stock. Some of the new types of adjustable-rate preferred stocks are highly suited for corporations needing short-term investments for temporarily idle cash.

CONCEPT QUESTIONS

1. What is preferred stock?
2. Why is it arguably more like debt than equity?
3. Why is it attractive for firms that are not paying taxes to issue preferred stock?
4. What are two reasons unrelated to taxes why preferred stock is issued?

12.5 | COMMON STOCK

The term **common stock** means different things to different people, but it is usually applied to stock that has no special preference either in dividends or in bankruptcy. A description of the common stock of Canadian Tire Corporation Limited on January 1, 1994, is presented in the following table.[11]

common stock
Equity without priority for dividends or in bankruptcy.

Shareholders' Equity at the Book Value of Canadian Tire Corporation Limited—January 1, 1994 ($ in thousands)

Common shares and other shareholders' equity	
Common shares, authorized 3,450,000 shares	
issued 3,450,000 shares	$ 178
Class A Non-voting Shares	
authorized 100,000,000 shares	318,380
issued 88,223,527	
Less 1,484,528 treasury shares	−24,237
Total share capital	$ 278,502
Accumulated foreign currency translation adjustment	9,403
Retained earnings	904,608
Total shareholders' equity	$1,208,332

---

[11] Canadian Tire has no preferred stock. Data are from *Financial Post* Card, 1994.

shareholders or stockholders
Owners of equity in a corporation.

Owners of common stock in a corporation are referred to as **shareholders** or **stockholders**. They receive stock certificates for the shares they own. While there can be a stated value on each stock certificate called the par value, more typically in Canada, there is no particular par value assigned to stock.

Common shareholders are protected by limited liability. If the company goes bankrupt, the creditors cannot seek payment of the firm's debt from its common stockholders. On the other hand, the common stockholders are the residual claimants and almost always lose 100 percent of their investment if the firm goes bankrupt.

Authorized versus Issued Common Stock

Shares of common stock are the fundamental ownership units of the corporation. The articles of incorporation of a new corporation must state the number of shares of common stock the corporation is authorized to issue.

The board of directors of the corporation, after a vote of the shareholders, can amend the articles of incorporation to increase the number of shares authorized; there is no legal limit to the number of shares that can be authorized this way. In 1994, Canadian Tire had authorized and issued 3.45 million common shares. For Class A non-voting shares, 100 million were authorized and, of these, 1,484,528 were held as unissued treasury stock so the firm had actually issued 88,223,527 Class A non-voting shares. There is no requirement that all of the authorized shares ever be issued.

Retained Earnings

retained earnings
Corporate earnings not paid out as dividends.

book value
Accounting per share value of firm's equity. Also net worth.

Canadian Tire pays out around one quarter to one half of its net income as dividends; the rest is retained in the business and is called **retained earnings**. The cumulative amount of retained earnings (since original incorporation) was $904,608 million in 1994.

As you saw earlier, the sum of accumulated retained earnings, share capital, and adjustments to equity is the total shareholders' equity of the firm, which is usually referred to as the firm's **book value** of equity (or net worth). The book value of equity represents the amount contributed directly and indirectly to the corporation by equity investors (in an accounting sense).

To illustrate some of these definitions, suppose Western Redwood Corporation was formed in 1973 with 10,000 shares of stock issued and sold for $1 per share. By 1995, the company had been profitable and had retained profits of $100,000. The stockholders' equity of Western Redwood Corporation in 1995 is as follows:

Western Redwood Corporation Equity Accounts—1995	
Common stock (10,000 shares outstanding)	$ 10,000
Retained earnings	100,000
Total shareholders' equity	$110,000

Book value per share $110,000/10,000 = $11.

Now suppose the company has profitable investment opportunities and decides to sell 10,000 shares of new stock to raise the necessary finance. The current market price is $20 per share. The following table shows the effects of the sale of stock on the balance sheet:

Western Redwood Corporation—1995 after Sales of Stock	
Common stock (20,000 shares outstanding)	$210,000
Retained earnings	100,000
Total shareholders' equity	$310,000

Book value per share $310,000/20,000 = $15.50.
What happened?

1. Since 10,000 shares of new stock were issued at a book value of $20, a total of $200,000 was added to common stock.
2. The book value per share increased because the market price of the new stock was higher than the book value.

Market Values versus Book Values

The total book value of equity for Canadian Tire in 1994 was $1,208,332,000. The company had outstanding 3.45 million voting and 88,223,527 non-voting (Class A) shares so that the total number of outstanding shares was 91,673,527.

The book value per share was thus equal to:

$$\frac{\text{Total common shareholders' equity}}{\text{Shares outstanding}} = \frac{\$1,208,332,000}{\$88,223,527} = \$13.18$$

Canadian Tire is a publicly owned company. Its two classes of common stock trade on the Toronto Stock Exchange (TSE) and the Montreal Stock Exchange (MSE), and thousands of shares change hands every day. The market prices of both classes of Canadian Tire shares were between $11.63 and $20.50 per share during 1994. Thus, the market prices were generally more than the book value.

Shareholders' Rights

The conceptual structure of the corporation assumes that shareholders elect directors who, in turn, hire management to carry out their directives. Shareholders, therefore, control the corporation through their right to elect the directors. Generally, only shareholders have this right.

Directors are elected each year at an annual meeting. Despite the exceptions we discuss later, the general idea is "one share, one vote" (not one shareholder, one vote). Corporate democracy is thus very different from our political democracy. With corporate democracy, the "golden rule" prevails absolutely.[12]

Directors are elected at an annual shareholders' meeting by a vote of the holders of a majority of shares present and entitled to vote. However, the exact mechanism for electing directors differs across companies. The two most important methods are cumulative voting and straight voting; we discuss these in Appendix 12B.

Outside Canada and the United States, other factors besides proportionate ownership can be important in electing directors. For example, in 1989, a well-known U.S. takeover specialist, T. Boone Pickens, acquired more than 20 percent of the shares of Koito, an important auto parts manufacturer in Japan. When Pickens requested that three executives from his firm be appointed to the Koito board, Tamotsu Aoyama, a Koito director replied, "It is necessary to build a trusting relationship first. In Japan, it is not possible to just say, 'I'm a major shareholder' and get a seat on the board right away."[13]

Other Rights   The value of a share of common stock in a corporation is directly related to the general rights of shareholders. In addition to the right to vote for directors, shareholders usually have the following rights:

---

[12] The golden rule: Whosoever has the gold makes the rules.
[13] *Globe and Mail,* April 27, 1989.

1. The right to share proportionally in dividends paid.
2. The right to share proportionally in assets remaining after liabilities have been paid in a liquidation.
3. The right to vote on stockholder matters of great importance, such as a merger, usually done at the annual meeting or a special meeting.

In addition, stockholders sometimes have the right to share proportionally in any new stock sold. This is called the *preemptive right,* and we discuss it in some detail in the next chapter.

Essentially, a preeemptive right means that a company wishing to sell stock must first offer it to the existing stockholders before offering it to the general public. The purpose is to give a stockholder the opportunity to protect his or her proportionate ownership in the corporation.

Dividends

dividends

Return on capital of corporation paid by company to share-holders in either cash or stock.

A distinctive feature of corporations is that they have shares of stock on which they are authorized by law to pay dividends to their shareholders. **Dividends** paid to shareholders represent a return on the capital directly or indirectly contributed to the corporation by the shareholders. The payment of dividends is at the discretion of the board of directors.

Some important characteristics of dividends include the following:

1. Unless a dividend is declared by the board of directors of a corporation, it is not a liability of the corporation. A corporation cannot default on an undeclared dividend. As a consequence, corporations cannot become bankrupt because of nonpayment of dividends. The amount of the dividend and even whether it is paid are decisions based on the business judgment of the board of directors.
2. The payment of dividends by the corporation is not a business expense. Dividends are not deductible for corporate tax purposes. In short, dividends are paid out of aftertax profits of the corporation.
3. Dividends received by individual shareholders are partially sheltered by a dividend tax credit discussed in detail in Chapter 2. As you saw earlier in our discussion of preferred stock, corporations that own stock in other corporations are permitted to exclude 100 percent of the dividend amounts they receive from taxable Canadian corporations. The purpose of this provision is to avoid the double taxation of dividends.

Classes of Stock

Some firms have more than one class of common stock.[14] Often, the classes are created with unequal voting rights. Recall that Canadian Tire Corporation, for example, has two classes of common stock both publicly traded. The voting common stock was distributed as follows in 1990: 61 percent to three offspring of the company founder and the rest divided among Canadian Tire dealers, pension funds, and the general public. The non-voting, Canadian Tire A stock was more widely held.

There are many other Canadian corporations with restricted (non-voting) stock. Such stock made up around 15 percent of the market values of TSE listed shares at the end of 1989. Non-voting shares must receive dividends no lower than dividends on voting shares. Some companies pay a higher dividend on the non-voting shares. In 1990, Canadian Tire paid $.40 per share on both classes of stock.

---

[14] This section draws heavily on Elizabeth Maynes, Chris Robinson, and Alan White, "How Much Is a Share Vote Worth?" *Canadian Investment Review,* Spring 1990, pp. 49–56.

A primary reason for creating dual classes of stock has to do with control of the firm. If such stock exists, management of a firm can raise equity capital by issuing non-voting or limited-voting stock while maintaining control.

Because it is only necessary to own 51 percent of the voting stock to control a company, non-voting shareholders could be left out in the cold in the event of a takeover bid for the company. To protect the non-voting shareholders, most companies have a "coattail" provision giving non-voting shareholders either the right to vote or to convert their shares into voting shares that can be tendered to the takeover bid. In the Canadian Tire case, all Class A shareholders become entitled to vote and the coattail provision is triggered if a bid is made for "all or substantially all" of the voting shares.

The effectiveness of the coattail provision was tested in 1986 when the Canadian Tire Dealers Association offered to buy 49 percent of the voting shares from the founding Billes family. In the absence of protection, the non-voting shareholders stood to lose substantially. The dealers bid at a large premium for the voting shares that were trading at $40 before the bid. The non-voting shares were priced at $14. Further, since the dealers were the principal buyers of Canadian Tire products, control of the company would have allowed them to adjust prices to benefit themselves over the non-voting shareholders.

The key question was whether the bid triggered the coattail. The dealers and the Billes family argued that the offer was for 49 percent of the stock not for "all or substantially all" of the voting shares. In the end, the Ontario Securities Commission ruled that the offer was unfair to the holders of the A shares and its view was upheld in two court appeals.

As a result, investors believe that coattails have protective value but remain skeptical that they afford complete protection. In May 1995, Canadian Tire voting stock traded at a 14 percent premium over non-voting stock.

CONCEPT QUESTIONS
1. What is a company's book value?
2. What rights do shareholders have?
3. Why do some companies have two classes of stock?

12.6 | PATTERNS OF LONG-TERM FINANCING

We have looked at different types of long-term financing. We now examine the relative importance of different sources of long-term financing and how these sources are used. Figures 12.1 and 12.2 show how the assets and liabilities of Canadian industrial corporations have evolved through the 1980s and predict their future.

Looking first at assets in Figure 12.1 in 1988 and 1998, you can see that fixed asset investment growth is predicted under the pressures of technological change and global competition. Increasing environmental consciousness will speed replacement of old equipment.

Comparing fixed assets with shareholders' equity in Figure 12.2 shows that internally generated funds, net income less dividends plus depreciation, are not enough to finance fixed assets.[15] The deficit in long-term financing is made up from new common stock and long-term debt.

---

[15] Net income less dividends equals retained earnings and is included in shareholders' equity. Depreciation is not shown explicitly in Figure 12.2 as fixed assets are stated net of depreciation.

FIGURE 12.1

Composition of Canadian industrial corporations' assets*

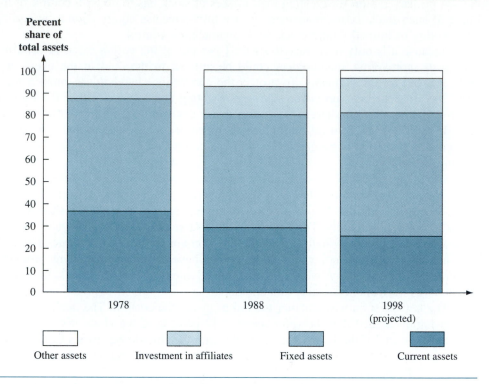

*Corporations with assets of $10 million or more.
Source: J. Grant, M. Webb, and P. Hendrick, "Financing Corporate Canada in the 1990s," *Canadian Investment Review,* Spring 1990, pp. 9–14.

Figure 12.2 also shows that debt/equity ratios of Canadian industrial corporations have remained relatively stable in contrast to the growing reliance on debt financing in the United States. A slight decline in the proportionate use of debt financing is predicted throughout the 1990s.

Returning to Figure 12.1, you can see that, in addition to fixed assets, these financing sources will likely be used for investment in affiliates. Increasing globalization of markets and international competition will force companies to become larger and more international.

CONCEPT QUESTIONS

1. What are the major growth areas in assets requiring financing?
2. What are the major sources of corporate financing? What trends have emerged in recent years?

12.7 | LONG-TERM FINANCING UNDER FINANCIAL DISTRESS AND BANKRUPTCY

One of the consequences of using debt is the possibility of financial distress, which can be defined in several ways:

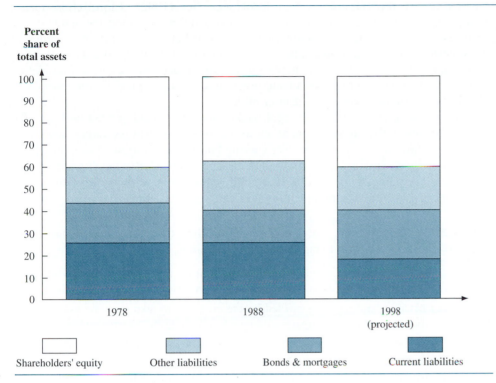

F I G U R E 12.2

*Composition of
Canadian industrial
corporations'
liabilities**

*Corporations with assets of $10 million or more.
Source: J. Grant, M. Webb, and P. Hendrick, "Financing Corporate Canada in the 1990s." *Canadian Investment Review,*
Spring 1990, pp. 9–14.

1. *Business failure.* Although this term usually refers to a situation where a business has terminated with a loss to creditors, even an all-equity firm can fail.[16]

2. *Legal bankruptcy.* Firms bring petitions to a federal court for bankruptcy. **Bankruptcy** is a legal proceeding for liquidating or reorganizing a business.

3. *Technical insolvency.* Technical insolvency occurs when a firm defaults on a current legal obligation; for example, it does not pay a bill. Technical insolvency is a short-term condition that may be reversed to avoid bankruptcy.

4. *Accounting insolvency.* Firms with negative net worth are insolvent on the books. This happens when the total book liabilities exceed the book value of the total assets.

bankruptcy
*A legal proceeding for
liquidating or
reorganizing a
business. Also, the
transfer of some or all
of a firm's assets to its
creditors.*

For future reference, we define bankruptcy as the transfer of some or all of the firm's assets to creditors. We now very briefly discuss what happens in financial distress and some of the relevant issues associated with bankruptcy.[17]

Liquidation and Reorganization

Firms that cannot or choose not to make contractually required payments to creditors have two basic options: liquidation or reorganization. Both of these options are

---

[16] Dun & Bradstreet Canada Ltd. compiles failure statistics in "The Canadian Business Failure Record."
[17] Our discussion of bankruptcy procedures is based on the 1992 Insolvency Act.

liquidation
Termination of the firm as a going concern.

reorganization
Financial restructuring of a failing firm to attempt to continue operations as a going concern.

covered under the Bankruptcy and Insolvency Act (1992). **Liquidation** means termination of the firm as a going concern, and it involves selling the assets of the firm. The proceeds, net of selling costs, are distributed to creditors in order of established priority. **Reorganization** is the option of keeping the firm a going concern; it often involves issuing new securities to replace old securities. Liquidation or reorganization is the result of a bankruptcy proceeding. Which occurs depends on whether the firm is worth more dead or alive.

Before the early 1990s, most legal bankruptcies in Canada ended with liquidation. More recently, more frequent cases of financial distress along with new bankruptcy laws are encouraging restructuring and reorganizations. For example, in 1992 Olympia & York's cash flow was not enough to cover its interest and principal payments. The company decided to seek court protection to allow it to restructure its assets and avoid formal bankruptcy liquidation.

Bankruptcy Liquidation   Liquidation occurs when the court directs sale of all assets of the firm. The following sequence of events is typical:

1. A petition is filed in a federal court. Corporations may file a voluntary petition, or involuntary petitions may be filed against the corporation by creditors.
2. A trustee-in-bankruptcy is elected by the creditors to take over the assets of the debtor corporation. The trustee attempts to liquidate the assets.
3. When the assets are liquidated, after payment of the bankruptcy administration costs, the proceeds are distributed among the creditors.
4. If any assets remain, after expenses and payments to creditors, they are distributed to the shareholders.

The distribution of the proceeds of the liquidation occurs according to the following priority. The higher a claim is on this list, the more likely it is to be paid. In many of these categories, we omit various limitations and qualifications for the sake of brevity.

1. Administrative expenses associated with the bankruptcy.
2. Other expenses arising after the filing of an involuntary bankruptcy petition but before the appointment of a trustee.
3. Wages, salaries, and commissions.
4. Contributions to employee benefit plans.
5. Consumer claims.
6. Government tax claims.
7. Unsecured creditors.
8. Preferred stockholders.
9. Common stockholders.

Two qualifications to this list are in order: The first concerns secured creditors. Such creditors are entitled to the proceeds from the sale of the security and are outside this ordering. However, if the secured property is liquidated and provides cash insufficient to cover the amount owed, the secured creditors join with unsecured creditors in dividing the remaining liquidated value. In contrast, if the secured property is liquidated for proceeds greater than the secured claim, the net proceeds are used to pay unsecured creditors and others.

The second qualification is that, in reality, courts have a great deal of freedom in deciding what actually happens and who actually gets what in the event of bankruptcy; as a result, the priority just set out is not always followed.

The 1988 restructuring of Dome Petroleum is an example. Declining oil prices in 1986 found Dome already in difficulties after a series of earlier debt rescheduling. Dome's board believed that if the company went into bankruptcy, secured creditors could force disposal of assets at fire sale prices producing losses for unsecured creditors and shareholders. One estimate obtained at the time projected that unsecured creditors would receive at best 15 cents per dollar of debt under liquidation. As a result, the board sought and received court and regulatory approval for sale of the company as a going concern to Amoco Canada. Unsecured creditors eventually received 45 cents on the dollar.

Bankruptcy Reorganization The general objective of corporate reorganization is to plan to restructure the corporation with some provision for repayment of creditors. A typical sequence of events follows:

1. A voluntary petition can be filed by the corporation, or an involuntary petition can be filed by creditors.
2. A federal judge either approves or denies the petition. If the petition is approved, a time for filing proofs of claims is set. A stay of proceedings of 30 days is effected against all creditors.
3. In most cases, the corporation (the "debtor in possession") continues to run the business.
4. The corporation is required to submit a reorganization plan.
5. Creditors and shareholders are divided into classes. A class of creditors accepts the plan if a majority of the class (in dollars or in number) agrees to the plan. The secured creditors must vote before the unsecured creditors.
6. After acceptance by creditors, the plan is confirmed by the court.
7. Payments in cash, property, and securities are made to creditors and shareholders. The plan may provide for the issuance of new securities.

The corporation may wish to allow the old shareholders to retain some participation in the firm. Needless to say, this may involve some protest by the holders of unsecured debt.

So-called prepackaged bankruptcies are a relatively new phenomenon. What happens is that the corporation secures the necessary approval of a bankruptcy plan by a majority of its creditors first, and then it files for bankruptcy. As a result, the company enters bankruptcy and re-emerges almost immediately. In some cases, the bankruptcy procedure is needed to invoke the "cram down" power of the bankruptcy court. Under certain circumstances, a class of creditors can be forced to accept a bankruptcy plan even if they vote not to approve it, hence the remarkably descriptive phrase *cram down.*

Agreements to Avoid Bankruptcy

A firm can default on an obligation and still avoid bankruptcy. Because the legal process of bankruptcy can be lengthy and expensive, it is often in everyone's best interest to devise a "work out" that avoids a bankruptcy filing. Much of the time creditors can work with the management of a company that has defaulted on a loan contract. Voluntary arrangements to restructure the company's debt can be and often are made. This may involve *extension,* which postpones the date of payment, or *composition,* which involves a reduced payment.

CONCEPT QUESTIONS
1. What is bankruptcy?
2. What is the difference between liquidation and reorganization?

12.8 | SUMMARY AND CONCLUSIONS

The basic sources of long-term financing are long-term debt, preferred stock, and common stock. This chapter describes the essential features of each.

1. We emphasize that common shareholders have
   a. Residual risk and return in a corporation
   b. Voting rights
   c. Limited liability if the corporation elects to default on its debt and must transfer some or all of the assets to the creditors.
2. Preferred stock has some of the features of debt and some features of common equity. Holders of preferred stock have preference in liquidation and in dividend payments compared to holders of common equity.
3. Long-term debt involves contractual obligations set out in indentures. There are many kinds of debt, but the essential feature is that debt involves a stated amount that must be repaid. If the debt is not repaid, the firm is in default and must reorganize or liquidate. Interest payments on debt are considered a business expense and are tax deductible.
4. Firms need financing for capital expenditures, working capital, and other uses. Most of the financing is provided from internally generated cash flow. Only about 20 percent of financing comes from new long-term debt and new external equity. In recent years, new external equity has actually been negative, implying that repurchases exceed new sales in aggregate.
5. The use of debt creates the possibility of financial distress. We discuss the options available to a firm and its creditors in this circumstance, and we describe the payment priority in the event of liquidation of the firm.

Key Terms

indenture (page 426)
registered form (page 426)
bearer form (page 427)
debenture (page 427)
note (page 427)
sinking fund (page 428)
call provision (page 428)
call premium (page 428)
deferred call (page 428)
call protected (page 428)
protective covenant (page 428)
stripped bond (page 432)
retractable bond (page 434)
preferred stock (page 434)

common stock (page 437)
shareholders or stockholders (page 438)
retained earnings (page 438)
book value (page 438)
dividends (page 440)
bankruptcy (page 443)
liquidation (page 444)
reorganization (page 444)
bond refunding (page 448)
cumulative voting (page 457)
straight voting (page 457)
proxy (page 458)

Questions and Problems

1. **Equity Accounts**   The Nosh Company equity accounts in 1995 are as follows: **Basic (Questions 1–9)**

Common stock (1,500 shares outstanding)	$ 1,500
Retained earnings	100,000
Total	$101,500

Suppose the company decides to issue 1,000 shares of new stock. The current price is $100 per share. Show the effect on the different accounts. What is the market/book ratio after the share issue?

2. **Changes in Accounts**   In the previous question, suppose the company buys 100 shares of its own stock. What is this stock called? What would happen to the accounts shown?

3. **Preferred Stock**   Which has a higher yield, preferred stock or corporate bonds? Why is there a difference? Who are the main investors in preferred stock? Why?

4. **Debt versus Equity**   What are the main differences between corporate debt and equity? Why do some clever firms try to issue equity in the guise of debt? Why might preferred stock be called an "equity bond"?

5. **Patterns of Financing**   The Babel Tower Company has $5 million of positive NPV projects of which it would like to take advantage. Based on the historical pattern of long-term financing for Canadian industrial firms, which financing strategy is Babel likely to use?

6. **Bankruptcy**   What basic options does a firm have if it cannot (or chooses not to) make a contractually required payment such as interest? Describe them.

7. **Bankruptcy**   A petition for the reorganization of the Dew Drop Inn Company has been filed under the Insolvency Act. The trustees estimate the firm's liquidation value, after considering costs, is $100 million. Alternatively, the trustees, using the analysis of the PH Consulting firm, predict that the reorganized business will generate $16 million annual cash flows in perpetuity. The discount rate is 20 percent. Should Dew Drop be liquidated or reorganized? Why?

8. **Absolute Priority Rule**   In the event of corporate liquidation proceedings, rank the following claimants of the firm from highest to lowest in order of their priority for being paid:
    a. Preferred stockholders.
    b. Revenue Canada.
    c. Unsecured debtholders.
    d. The company pension plan.
    e. Common stockholders.
    f. Employee wages.
    g. The law firm representing the company in the bankruptcy proceedings.

9. **Terms of Indentures**   What is the effect of each of the following provisions on the coupon rate for a newly issued bond? Give a brief explanation in each case.
    a. A floating-rate coupon.
    b. A call provision.
    c. A put provision.

Basic (Continued)

d. A convertibility provision.

e. Real property collateral.

f. A maximum dividend payout covenant.

Intermediate (Question 10)

10. **Stripped Bonds**   Suppose your company needs to raise $10 million and you want to issue 20-year bonds for this purpose. The required return on your bond issue will be 10 percent, and you're evaluating two issue alternatives: a 10 percent annual coupon bond and a stripped bond. Your company's tax rate is 35 percent.

a. How many of the coupon bonds would you need to issue to raise the $10 million? How many of the stripped bonds would you need to issue?

b. In 20 years, what will your company's repayment of principal be if you issue the coupon bonds? What if you issue the stripped bonds?

c. Based on your answers in *(a)* and *(b)*, why would you ever want to issue the stripped bonds? To answer, calculate the firm's aftertax cash outflows for the first year under the two different scenarios. Assume amortization rules apply for the stripped bonds.

d. Verify that the NPVs of the cash flows from the two alternative bond issues are the same.

Suggested Readings

The following provide some evidence on the financial structure of industrial corporations:

Kester, W. C. "Capital and Ownership Structure: A Comparison of the United States and Japanese Manufacturing Corporations." *Financial Management* 15 (Spring 1986).

Grant, J.; M. Webb; and P. Hendrick. "Financing Corporate Canada in the 1990s." *Canadian Investment Review,* Spring 1990.

For a highly readable discussion of voting and non-voting shares in Canada, see:

Elizabeth Maynes; Chris Robinson; and Alan White. "How Much Is a Share Vote Worth?" *Canadian Investment Review,* Spring 1990.

CALLABLE BONDS AND BOND REFUNDING | APPENDIX 12A

bond refunding
The process of replacing all or part of an issue of outstanding bonds.

The process of replacing all or part of an issue of outstanding bonds is called **bond refunding**.[18] As we have discussed, most corporate debt is callable. Typically, the first step in a bond refunding is to take advantage of this feature to call the entire issue of bonds at the call price.

Why would a firm want to refund a bond issue? One reason is obvious. Suppose a firm issues long-term debt with, say, a 12 percent coupon. Sometime after the issue, interest rates decline, and the firm finds that it could pay an 8 percent coupon and raise the same amount of money. Under such circumstances, the firm may wish to

---

[18] Our discussion focusses on refunding bonds. The analysis also applies to refunding preferred stock.

refund the debt. Notice that, in this case, refunding a bond issue is just a way of refinancing a higher-interest loan with a lower-interest one.

In the following discussion, we take a brief look at several issues concerning bond refunding and the call feature. First, what is the cost to the firm of a call provision? Second, what is the value of a call provision? Third, given that the firm has issued callable bonds, when should they be refunded?[19]

The Call Provision

Common sense tells us that call provisions have value. First, almost all publicly issued bonds have such a feature. Second, a call clearly works to the advantage of the issuer. If interest rates fall and bond prices go up, the issuer has an option to buy back the bond at a bargain price.

On the other hand, all other things being equal, bondholders dislike call provisions. The reason is again obvious. If interest rates do fall, the bondholder's gain is limited because of the possibility that the bond will be called away. As a result, bondholders take the call provision into account when they buy, and they require compensation in the form of a higher coupon rate.

This is an important observation. A call provision is not free. Instead, the firm pays a higher coupon than otherwise. Whether paying this higher coupon rate is a good idea or not is the subject we turn to next.

Cost of the Call Provision

To illustrate the effect of a call feature on a bond's coupon, suppose Kraus Intercable Company intends to issue some perpetual bonds with a face value of $1,000. We stick with perpetuities because doing so greatly simplifies some of the analysis without changing the general results.

The current interest rate on such bonds is 10 percent; Kraus, therefore, sets the annual coupon at $100. Suppose there is an equal chance that by the end of the year interest rates will either:

1. Fall to 6⅔ percent. If so, the bond price will increase to $100/.067 = $1,500.
2. Increase to 20 percent. If so, the bond price will fall to $100/.20 = $500.

Notice that the bond could sell for either $500 or $1,500 with equal probability, so the expected price is $1,000. Note also that the lower interest rate is actually .0666 . . . , not .067. We use the exact rate in all the calculations in this section.

We now consider the market price of the bond assuming it is not callable, P_{NC}. This is simply equal to the expected price of the bond next year plus the coupon, all discounted at the current 10 percent interest rate:

$$P_{NC} = [\text{First-year coupon} + \text{Expected price at the end of year}]/1.10$$

$$= [\$100 + \$1,000]/1.10$$

$$= \$1,000$$

---

[19] For a more in-depth discussion of the subjects discussed in this appendix, see John D. Finnerty, Andrew J. Kalotay, and Francis X. Farrell, Jr., *The Financial Manager's Guide to Evaluating Bond Refunding Opportunities,* The Institutional Investor Series in Finance and Financial Management Association Survey and Synthesis Series (Cambridge, MA: Ballinger Publishing Company, 1988). Our discussion is based in part on Alan Kraus, "An Analysis of Call Provisions and the Corporate Refunding Decision," *Midland Corporate Finance Journal,* Spring 1983.

Thus, the bond sells at par.

Now suppose the Kraus Intercable Company decides to make the issue callable. To keep things as simple as possible, we assume the bonds must be called in one year or never. To call the bonds, Kraus has to pay the $1,000 face value plus a call premium of $150 for a total of $1,150. If Kraus wants the callable bond to sell for par, what coupon, C, must be offered?

To determine the coupon, we need to calculate what the possible prices are in one year. If interest rates decline, the bond will be called, and the bondholder will get $1,150. If interest rates rise, the bond will not be called, and it will thus be worth $C/.20$. So the expected price in one year is $.50 \times (C/.20) + .50 \times (\$1,150)$. If the bond sells for par, the price, P_C, is $1,000 and we have that:

$$P_C = \$1,000 = [\text{First-year coupon} + \text{Expected price at end of year}]/1.10$$

$$= [\$C + \{.50 \times (\$C/.20) + .50 \times (\$1,150)\}]/1.10$$

If we solve this for C, we find that the coupon has to be

$$C = \$525/3.5 = \$150$$

This is substantially higher than the $100 we had before and illustrates that the call provision is not free.

What is the cost of the call provision here? To answer, we can calculate what the bond would sell for it if were not callable and had a coupon of $150:

$$P_{NC} = [\text{First-year coupon} + \text{Expected price at end of year}]/1.10$$

$$= [\$150 + \{.50 \times (\$150/.20) + .50 \times (\$150/.067)\}]/1.10$$

$$= \$1,500$$

What we see is that the call provision effectively costs $500 per bond in this simple case because Kraus could have raised $1,500 per bond instead of $1,000 if the bonds were not callable.

Value of the Call Provision

We have seen what Kraus has to pay to make this bond issue callable. We now need to see what the value is to Kraus from doing so. If the value is more than $500, the call provision has a positive NPV and should be included. Otherwise, Kraus should issue non-callable bonds.

If Kraus issues a callable bond and interest rates drop to 6 2/3 percent in a year, then Kraus can replace the 15 percent bond with a non-callable perpetual issue that carries a coupon of $6\frac{2}{3}$ percent. The interest saving in this case is $150 - 66.67 = \$83.33$ per year every year forever (since these are perpetuities). At an interest rate of $6\frac{2}{3}$ percent, the present value of the interest savings is $83.33/.067 = \$1,250$.

To do the refunding, Kraus has to pay a $150 premium, so the net present value of the refunding operation in one year is $1,250 - 150 = \$1,100$ per bond. However, there is only a 50 percent chance that the interest rate will drop, so we expect to get $.50 \times \$1,100 = \$550$ from refunding in one year. The current value of this amount is $550/1.1 = \$500$. So we conclude that the value of the call feature to Kraus is $500.

It is *not* a coincidence that the cost and the value of the call provision are identical. All this says is that the NPV of the call feature is zero; the bondholders demand a coupon that exactly compensates them for the possibility of a call.

The Refunding Issue

In our preceding example, we saw that Kraus gained $1,100 per bond from the refunding operation if the interest rate fell. We now need to decide when, in general, a firm should refund an outstanding bond issue. The answer to this question can get fairly complicated, so we stick with our simplified case for the first pass and then consider a more realistic one. In particular, we continue to assume that

1. The bonds in question are perpetuities.

2. There are no taxes.

3. There are no refunding costs other than the call premium and the refunding is instantaneous. There is no overlap period when both issues are outstanding.

4. The bonds must be called now or never.[20]

When Should Firms Refund Callable Bonds?

The following notation is useful in analyzing the refunding issue:

c_o = coupon rate on the outstanding bonds
c_N = coupon rate on the new issue, equal to the current market rate
CP = call premium per bond

We assume that the face value is $1,000 per bond. If we replace the old issue, then we save $(c_o - c_N) \times 1,000$ in interest per bond every year forever.

The current interest rate is c_N, so the present value of the interest saving is $(c_o - c_N) \times \$1,000/c_N$. It costs CP to call the bond, so the NPV per bond of the refunding operation can be written simply as:

$$\text{NPV} = (c_o - c_N)/c_N \times \$1,000 - CP \qquad [12\text{A}.1]$$

With our Kraus example, the bonds were originally issued with a 15 percent coupon. The going interest rate fell to 6⅔ percent, and the call premium was $150. The NPV of the refunding is:

$$
\begin{aligned}
\text{NPV} &= (c_o - c_N)/c_n \times \$1,000 - CP \\
&= (.15 - .067)/.067 \times \$1,000 - \$150 \\
&= 1.25 \times \$1,000 - \$150 \\
&= \$1,100 \text{ per bond}
\end{aligned}
$$

This is as we had before (ignoring a slight rounding error): the present value of the interest savings from calling the bond is $1,250. Subtract the call premium of $150, and you have the NPV of calling the bond of $1,100 per bond.

E X A M P L E | **12A.1**   **Who Ya Gonna Call?**

Toastdusters, Inc., has an outstanding perpetuity with a 10 percent coupon rate. This issue must be called now or never. If it is called, it will be replaced with an issue that

---

[20] The last of these assumptions cannot be easily eliminated. The problem is that when we call a bond in, we forever destroy the option to call it in later. Conceivably, it might be better to wait and call later in hopes of even lower interest rates. This is the same issue that we discussed in Chapter 9, when we discussed options in capital budgeting, in particular, the option to wait.

has a coupon rate of 8 percent, equal to the current interest rate. The call premium is $200 per bond. Should refunding commence? What is the NPV of a refunding?

Assuming a $1,000 face value, the interest saving would be $100 − 80 = $20 per bond, per year, forever. The present value of this saving is $20/.08 = $250 per bond. Since the call premium is $200 per bond, refunding should commence: The NPV is $50 per bond.

E X A M P L E | 12A.2   **Spreadsheet-Based Refunding Framework**

The Nipigon Lake Mining Company has a $20 million outstanding bond issue bearing a 16 percent coupon that it issued in 1986. The bonds mature in 2001 but are callable in 1992 for a 6 percent call premium. Nipigon Lake's investment banker has assured it that up to $30 million of new nine-year bonds maturing in 2001 can be sold carrying an 11 percent coupon. To eliminate timing problems with the two issues, the new bonds will be sold a month before the old bonds are to be called. Nipigon Lake would have to pay the coupons on both issues during this month but can defray some of the cost by investing the issue at 8.5 percent, the short-term interest rate. Flotation costs for the $20 million new issue would total $1,125,000 and Nipigon Lake's marginal tax rate is 40 percent. Construct a framework to determine whether it is in Nipigon Lake's best interest to call the previous issue.

In constructing a framework to analyze a refunding operation, there are three steps: cost of refunding, interest savings, and the NPV of the refunding operation. All work described here is illustrated in Table 12A.1.

T A B L E 12A.1 | *Bond refunding worksheet*

	A	B	C	D	E	F	G	H	I	J	K	L	M	N
1														
2														
3														
4								Amount		Amount	Time	6.6 Percent		
5								Beforetax		Aftertax	Period	PV Factor		PV
6	**PV Cost of Refunding**													
7	Call premium									$1,200,000	0	1.0000		$1,200,000
8	Flotation costs on new issue									1,125,000	0	1.0000		1,125,000
9	Tax savings on new issue flotation costs									−90,000	1-5	4.1445		−373,005
10	Extra interest on old issue						$ 266,667			160,000	0	1.0000		160,000
11	Interest on short-term investment						−141,667			−85,000	0	1.0000		−85,000
12	Total aftertax investment													$2,026,995
13														
14	**Interest savings for the refunded issue: t = 1 − 9**													
15	Interest on old bond						3,200,000			1,920,000				
16	Interest on new bond						2,200,000			1,320,000				
17	Net interest savings						$1,000,000			$ 600,000	1-9	6.6276		$3,976,560
18														
19	**NPV for refunding operation**													
20	NPV = PV of interest savings − PV of cost refunding													$1,949,565
21														
22														

Cost of Refunding   The first step in this framework consists of calculating the call premium, the flotation costs and the related tax savings, and any extra interest that must be paid or can be earned.

Call premium = $0.06 \times (\$20,000,000) = \$1,200,000$

Note that a call premium is not a tax-deductible expense.

Flotation Costs   Although flotation costs are a one-time expense, for tax purposes they are amortized over the life of the issue, or five years, whichever is less. For Nipigon Lake, flotation costs amount to $1,125,000. This results in an annual expense for the first five years after the issue.

$\$1,125,000/5 = \$225,000$

Flotation costs produce an annual tax shield of $90,000.

$\$225,000 \times (0.4) = \$90,000$

The tax savings on the flotation costs are a five-year annuity and would be discounted at the aftertax cost of debt ($11\%(1 - .40) = 6.6\%$). This amounts to a savings of $373,005. Therefore, the total flotation costs of issuing debt are:

Flotation costs	$1,125,000
PV of tax savings	−373,005
Total aftertax cost	$ 751,995

Additional Interest   Extra interest paid on old issue:

$\$20,000,000 \times (16\% \times \frac{1}{2}) = \$266,667$

Aftertax: $\$266,667 \times (1 - .40) = \$160,000$

By investing the proceeds of the new issue at short-term interest rates, some of this expense can be avoided.

$\$20,000,000 \times (8.5\% \times \frac{1}{12}) = \$141,667$

Aftertax $\$141,667 \times (1 - .40) = \$85,000$

The total additional interest is:

Extra interest paid	$160,000
Extra interest earned	−85,000
Total additional interest	$ 75,000

These three items amount to a total aftertax investment of:

Call premium	$1,200,000
Flotation costs	751,995
Additional interest	75,000
Total investment	$2,026,995

Interest Savings on New Issue

Interest on old bond = $\$20,000,000 \times 16\% = \$3,200,000$

Interest on new bond = $\$20,000,000 \times 11\% = \$2,200,000$

Annual savings = $1,000,000

Aftertax savings = $1,000,000 × (1 − .40) = $600,000

PV of annual savings over nine years = $600,000 × 6.6276 = $3,976,560

NPV for the Refunding Operation

Interest savings	$ 3,976,560
Investment	−2,026,995
NPV	$ 1,949,565

Nipigon Lake can save almost $2 million by proceeding with a call on its old bonds. The interest rates used in this example follow closely the actual interest rates during the 1980s. The example illustrates why firms would want to include a call provision when interest rates are very high.

Should Firms Issue Callable Bonds?

We have seen that the NPV of the call provision at the time a bond is issued is likely to be zero. This means that whether or not the issue is callable is a matter of indifference; we get exactly what we pay for, at least on average.[21]

A company prefers to issue callable bonds only if it places a higher value on the call option than do the bondholders. We consider three reasons a company might use a call provision:

1. Superior interest rate predictions.
2. Taxes.
3. Financial flexibility for future investment opportunities.

Superior Interest Rate Forecasting The company may prefer the call provision because it assigns a higher probability to a fall in the coupon rate it must pay than the bondholders do. For example, managers may be better informed about a potential improvement in the firm's credit rating. In this way, company insiders may know more about interest rate decreases than the bondholders.

Whether or not the companies truly know more than the creditors about future interest rates is debatable, but the point is they may think they do and thus prefer to issue callable bonds.

Taxes Call provisions may have tax advantages to both bondholders and the company. This is true if the bondholder is taxed at a lower rate than the company.

We have seen that callable bonds have higher rates than non-callable bonds. Because the coupons are a deductible interest expense to the corporation, if the corporate tax rate is higher than that of the individual holder, the corporation gains more in interest savings than the bondholders lose in extra taxes. Effectively, Revenue Canada pays for a part of the call provision in reduced tax revenues.

Future Investment Opportunities As we have seen, bond indentures contain protective covenants that restrict a company's investment opportunities. For example, protective covenants may limit the company's ability to acquire another company or to sell certain assets (for example, a division of the company). If the covenants are

---

[21] This zero NPV will hold exactly for some Canadian corporate bonds that carry a covenant requiring the issuer to pay a call premium called a *Canada call*. Determined *at the time the bonds are called,* this exactly offsets any advantage from lower interest rates: D. J. Fowler, A. Kaplan, and W. A. Mackenzie, "A Note on Call Premiums on U.S. and Canadian Corporate Debt," York University Working Paper, April 1995.

sufficiently restrictive, the cost to the shareholders in lost net present value can be large.

If bonds are callable, though, by paying the call premium, the company can buy back the bonds and take advantage of a superior investment opportunity.

CONCEPT QUESTIONS

1. Why might a corporation call in a bond issue? What is this action called?
2. What is the effect on a bond's coupon rate from including a call provision? Why?

Appendix Review Problems and Self-Test

12A.1 **Call Provisions and Bond Values** Timberlake Industries has decided to float a perpetual bond issue. The coupon will be 8 percent (the current interest rate). In one year, there is an even chance that interest rates will be 5 percent or 20 percent. What will the market value of the bonds be if they are non-callable? If they are callable at par plus $80.

12A.2 **Call Provisions and Coupon Rates** If the Timberlake bond in Problem A.1 is callable and sells for par, what is the coupon, C? What is the cost of the call provision in this case?

Answers to Appendix Self-Test Problems

12A.1 If the bond is not callable, in one year it will be worth either $80/.05 = $1,600 or $80/.2 = $400. The expected price is $1,000. The PV of the $1,000 and the first $80 coupon is $1,080/1.08 = $1,000, so the bond will sell for par.

   If the bond is callable, either it will be called at $1,080 (if rates fall to 5 percent) or it will sell for $400. The expected value is ($1,080 + 400)/2 = $740. The PV is ($740 + 80)/1.08 = $759.26.

12A.2 In one year, the bond either will be worth $C/.20$ or it will be called for $1,080. If the bond sells for par, then:

$$\$1,000 = [C + .5(C/.20) + .5(\$1,080)]/1.08$$

$$\$540 = [C + .5(C/.20)]$$

$$= 3.5C$$

The coupon, C, must be $540/3.5 = $154.29.

If the bond had a coupon of $154.29 and was not callable, in one year it would be worth either $154.29/.05 = $3,085.71 or $154.29/.20 = $771.43. There is an even chance of either of these, so we expect a value of $1,928.57. The bond would sell today for ($1,928.57 + 154.29)/1.08 = $1,928.57. The cost of the call provision is thus $928.57. This is quite a bit, but, as we see in a later chapter, this stems from the fact that interest rates are quite volatile in this example.

Appendix Questions and Problems

1. **NPV and Refunding** Atfan, Inc., has an outstanding callable perpetuity bond with an 18 percent coupon rate. This issue must be called now or never. If it is

**Basic
(Questions 1–8)**

Basic
(Continued)
called, it will be replaced with an issue that has a coupon rate of 15 percent, equal to the current interest rate. The call premium is $180 per bond. Should Atfan refund its outstanding bond issue? What is the NPV of the refunding?

2. **Interest Rates and Refunding**   In the previous problem, what would the current rate have to be for Atfan to be indifferent to refunding or not?

3. **Setting the Coupon Rate**   Supersoft Corporation has decided to finance its expansion with a perpetual bond issue. The current interest rate is 8 percent. In one year, there is an equal chance that interest rates will either be 6 percent or 10 percent. If this is a callable bond issue and the call premium to be paid is $80 per bond, what does the coupon rate have to be for the bond to sell at par?

4. **Setting the Call Premium**   In the previous problem, suppose you want to set the coupon rate on this issue at 8 percent. What would the call premium have to be for the bond to sell at par?

5. **Pricing Callable Bonds**   In the previous problem, suppose you set the coupon rate at 8 percent and the call premium at $125. What will the issue sell for?

6. **Call Provision Costs**   In the previous problem, what is the cost of the call provision to the firm?

7. **NPV and Refunding**   Your company has an outstanding perpetual bond issue with a face value of $50 million and a coupon rate of 12 percent. The bonds are callable at par plus a $150 call premium per bond; in addition, any new bond issues of your firm will incur fixed costs of $9 million. The bonds must be called now or never. What would the current interest rate have to be for you to be indifferent to a refunding operation?

8. **NPV and Maturity**   In the previous problem, suppose that bonds in question make annual coupon payments and have 10 years to maturity, rather than being perpetual bonds. If current rates are 9 percent and the bonds must be called now or never, what is the NPV of the refunding operation?

Challenge
(Questions 9–11)
9. **NPV and Maturity**   In Problem 8, what would the current interest rate have to be for you to be indifferent to a refunding operation?

10. **Refunding and Taxes**   In Problem 1, suppose Atfan is in the 35 percent tax bracket. The call premium is a tax-deductible business expense, as is interest paid on the old and new bonds. What is the NPV of the refunding? Note that the appropriate discount rate will be the aftertax borrowing rate. What is the net result of including tax effects on the NPV of refunding operations? Explain.

11. **Call Protection and Yield to Call**   This question addresses one issue involved in the quoting of yields on callable bonds. Suppose you observe a 10 percent coupon bond making annual payments with 10 years to maturity and a current market price of $1,175.00.

    a. What is the yield to maturity (YTM) on this bond?

    b. Now suppose this bond is call protected for the next two years, after which it can be refunded at par value. If the bond is expected to be called as soon as the call protection ends, what is the return on your investment (hint: find the IRR of the cash flows)? This rate is called the *yield to call* (YTC). Why is it so much lower than the YTM?

    c. What call premium, if available, would you demand so that your YTC is the same as your YTM in this case?

CORPORATE VOTING

To illustrate the two different voting procedures, imagine that a corporation has two shareholders: Smith with 20 shares and Jones with 80 shares. Both want to be directors. Jones, however, does not want Smith to be a director. We assume that four directors are to be elected.

Cumulative Voting The effect of **cumulative voting** is to permit minority participation.[22] If cumulative voting is permitted, the total number of votes that each shareholder may cast is determined first. This is usually calculated as the number of shares (owned or controlled) multiplied by the number of directors to be elected.

With cumulative voting, the directors are elected all at once. In our example, this means that the top four vote getters will be the new directors. A shareholder can distribute votes however he or she wishes.

Will Smith get a seat on the board? If we ignore the possibility of a five-way tie, the answer is yes. Smith casts $20 \times 4 = 80$ votes, and Jones casts $80 \times 4 = 320$ votes. If Smith gives all his votes to himself, he is assured of a directorship. The reason is that Jones can't divide 320 votes among four candidates in such a way as to give all of them more than 80 votes, so Smith would finish fourth at worst.

In general, if there are N directors up for election, $1/(N + 1)$ percent of the stock (plus one share) would guarantee you a seat. In our current example, this is $1/(4 + 1) = 20\%$. So the more seats that are up for election at one time, the easier (and cheaper) it is to win one.

Straight Voting With **straight voting**, the directors are elected one at a time. Each time, Smith can cast 20 votes and Jones can cast 80. As a consequence, Jones elects all the candidates. The only way to guarantee a seat is to own 50 percent plus one share. This also guarantees that you would win every seat, so it's really all or nothing.

cumulative voting *Procedure where a shareholder may cast all votes for one member of the board of directors.*

straight voting *Procedure where a shareholder may cast all votes for each member of the board of directors.*

E X A M P L E | **12B.1 Buying the Election**

Stock in JRJ Corporation sells for $20 per share and features cumulative voting. There are 10,000 shares outstanding. If three directors are up for election, how much does it cost to ensure yourself a seat on the board?

The question here is how many shares of stock it will take to get a seat. The answer is 2,501, so the cost is $2,501 \times \$20 = \$50,020$. Why 2,501? Because there is no way the remaining 7,499 votes can be divided among three people to give all of them more than 2,501 votes. For example, suppose two people receive 2,502 votes and the first two seats. A third person can receive at most $10,000 - 2,502 - 2,502 - 2,501 = 2,495$, so the third seat is yours.

As we've illustrated, straight voting can "freeze out" minority shareholders; that is the rationale for cumulative voting. But devices have been worked out to minimize its impact.

---

[22] By minority participation, we mean participation by shareholders with relatively small amounts of stock.

One such device is to stagger the voting for the board of directors. With staggered elections, only a fraction of the directorships are up for election at a particular time. Thus, if only two directors are up for election at any one time, it takes $1/(2 + 1) = 33.33\%$ of the stock to guarantee a seat. Overall, staggering has two basic effects:

1. Staggering makes it more difficult for a minority to elect a director when there is cumulative voting because there are fewer to be elected at one time.
2. Staggering makes takeover attempts less likely to be successful because it is more difficult to vote in a majority of new directors.

We should note that staggering may serve a beneficial purpose. It provides "institutional memory," that is, continuity on the board of directors. This may be important for corporations with significant long-range plans and projects. |

proxy

Grant of authority by shareholder allowing for another individual to vote his or her shares.

Proxy Voting   A **proxy** is the grant of authority by a shareholder to someone else to vote his or her shares. For convenience, much of the voting in large public corporations is actually done by proxy.

As we have seen, with straight voting, each share of stock has one vote. The owner of 10,000 shares has 10,000 votes. Many companies have hundreds of thousands or even millions of shareholders. Shareholders can come to the annual meeting and vote in person, or they can transfer their right to vote to another party.

Obviously, management always tries to get as many proxies transferred to it as possible. However, if the shareholders are not satisfied with management, an outside group of shareholders can try to obtain votes via proxy. They can vote by proxy to replace management by adding enough directors. This is called a *proxy fight*.

Appendix Review Problem and Self-Test

Cumulative versus Straight Voting
The Krishnamurti Corporation has 500,000 shares outstanding. There are four directors up for election. How many shares would you need to own to guarantee that you will win a seat if straight voting is used? If cumulative voting is used? Ignore possible ties.

Answer to Self-Test Problem

If there is straight voting, you need to own half the shares, or 250,000. In this case, you could also elect the other three directors. With cumulative voting, you need $1/(N + 1)$ percent of the shares, where N is the number of directors up for election. With four directors, this is 20 percent, or 100,000 shares.

Appendix Problem

Voting for Directors   The shareholders of Vycom, Inc., need to elect five new directors to the board. There are 750,000 shares of common stock outstanding. How many shares do you need to own to guarantee yourself a seat on the board if:

  a. The company uses cumulative voting procedures?
  b. The company uses straight voting procedures?

C H A P T E R

Issuing Securities to the Public

In Chapter 12, we looked at the different types of corporate securities. This chapter examines how corporations sell those securities to the investing public. The general procedures we describe apply to both debt and equity, but we place more emphasis on equity.

Issuing securities involves the corporation in a number of decisions. We briefly comment on how the majority of Canadian corporations have been deciding and on how these trends are changing in response to globalization of financial markets, deregulation, and increasing competition. The rest of the chapter explores these decisions in more depth.

Since issuing securities, like giving birth, is a specialized activity not undertaken on a daily basis, issuing corporations generally seek assistance from an investment dealer. The dealer acts as a midwife to assist in bringing the new securities safely into the world. Depending on the type of security and the alternatives chosen, assistance from the investment dealer may include a variety of services, such as advice on which securities to issue, how to structure and price the deal, and how to comply with disclosure requirements set by regulators. In addition, investment dealers offer various forms of protection to the issuer against receiving substantially less than the issue price or failing to sell the entire issue.

Early in the discussions with its investment dealer, the issuer decides whether to issue securities in the domestic market or in foreign markets. In 1990, Canadian corporations raised $16.7 billion in new capital. Seventy-two percent was raised in domestic markets.[1] This emphasis on domestic issues held for both debt and equity issues in 1990. Over the last decade, however, globalization has brought growth in foreign debt financing by Canadian corporations with more than half of the debt raised from foreign lenders.

The new securities could be a primary market, public issue sold directly to the public with the help of an investment dealer. Once registered with provincial regulatory authorities, the newly issued securities may be traded on secondary markets—stock exchanges or over the counter.[2] In contrast, in a private placement, debt or equity (common or preferred shares) is sold directly to a small number of buyers.

---

[1] Statistics on capital markets are from B. Critchley and J. Murphy, "DS Wins Laurels Again," *Financial Post,* August 5, 1991, p. 13. The figures exclude rights offerings later discussed in detail.
[2] Primary and secondary markets are discussed in Chapter 1.

459

The advantages for the issuer in a private placement are less stringent disclosure requirements and faster completion of the offer. Further, since the issuer is obtaining financing from a small group of knowledgeable investors, it is easier to renegotiate debt covenants should this become necessary. On the other hand, privately placed securities lack marketability and so are less attractive to investors. For this reason, privately placed debt often carries a higher yield. In 1990, public issues made up slightly less than three-quarters of total Canadian domestic security issues.

In a public offering of debt or equity, the investment dealer generally acts as an *underwriter* taking on some, or all, of the pricing risk in the new issue. The underwriter does this by buying the issue and reselling it. The underwriter takes all the pricing risk in a special type of public offering called a bought deal.

Instead of marketing to the general public, a corporation can sell common stock to its existing shareholders by what is called a rights offer. Rights offerings are usually cheaper and faster than underwritten public offerings in part because they are marketed to a narrower audience that already has shown interest in the stock. Through the 1970s, rights offerings were easily the most popular method of raising new equity in Canada.

In 1983, the Ontario Securities Commission introduced a streamlined reporting and registration system for large companies that issue securities regularly called *Prompt Offering Prospectus or POP*. With deregulation and the advantage of POP, growing competition among underwriters promoted dramatic growth in the popularity of bought deals over rights offers.[3] At the close of the 1980s, the majority of equity dollars raised in Canada used POP and were bought deals.

13.1 | THE PUBLIC ISSUE

A firm issuing securities must satisfy a number of requirements set out by provincial regulations and statutes and enforced by provincial securities commissions. Regulation of the securities market in Canada is carried out by provincial commissions and through provincial securities acts. However, only five of the provinces have commissions, due in large part to an absence of exchanges in some provinces. This is in contrast to the United States, where regulation is handled by a federal body, the Securities and Exchange Commission (SEC). The goal of the regulators is to promote the efficient flow of information about securities and the smooth functioning of securities markets.

All companies listed on the Toronto Stock Exchange come under the jurisdiction of the Ontario Securities Commission (OSC). The Securities Act of 1980 sets forth the provincial regulations for all new securities issues involving the province of Ontario and the Toronto Stock Exchange. The OSC administers the act. Other provinces have similar legislation and regulating bodies; however, the OSC is the most noteworthy because of the scope of the TSE.[4] In general terms, OSC rules seek to ensure that investors receive all material information on new issues in the form of a registration statement and prospectus.

The OSC's responsibilities for efficient information flow go beyond new issues. It continues to regulate the trading of securities after they have been issued to ensure adequate disclosure of information. Recently, the OSC broadened disclosure rules for

---

[3] Changes in regulations relaxed the requirement that chartered banks use only rights offerings and this also reduced their popularity.

[4] The TSE is Canada's largest exchange and its dollar trading ranked 12th in the world behind the NYSE (number 1) and London (number 2) in 1994. Chapter 6 discusses equity markets in more detail.

asset transactions between related parties. An example of a related party transaction is the sale of assets by one company to a sister company controlled by the same holding company. The revised Policy 9.1 required the majority of minority shareholders to approve these and other major transactions that are not at arms length. The OSC argued that this change is important because a significant portion of Canadian capital markets consists of closely controlled companies that are able to magnify their influence through networks of cross ownership.

Another informational role of the OSC is gathering and publishing *insider reports* filed by major shareholders, officers, and directors of TSE-listed firms. To ensure efficient functioning of markets, the OSC oversees the training and supervision that investment dealers provide for their personnel. It also monitors investment dealers' capital positions. Increasing market volatility and the popularity of bought deals where the dealer assumes all the price risk make capital adequacy important.

13.2 | THE BASIC PROCEDURE FOR A NEW ISSUE

There is a series of steps involved in issuing securities to the public. In general terms, the basic procedure is as follows:

1. Management's first step in issuing any securities to the public is to obtain approval from the board of directors. In some cases, the number of authorized shares of common stock must be increased. This requires a vote of the shareholders.

2. The firm must prepare and distribute copies of a preliminary **prospectus** to the OSC and to potential investors. The preliminary prospectus contains some of the financial information that will be contained in the final prospectus; it does not contain the price at which the security will be offered. The preliminary prospectus is sometimes called a **red herring**, in part because bold red letters are printed on the cover warning that the OSC has neither approved nor disapproved of the securities. The OSC studies the preliminary prospectus and notifies the company of any changes required. This process is usually completed within about two weeks.

3. Once the revised, final prospectus meets with the OSC's approval, a price is determined, and a full-fledged selling effort gets under way. A final prospectus must accompany the delivery of securities or confirmation of sale, whichever comes first.

prospectus
Legal document describing details of the issuing corporation and the proposed offering to potential investors.

red herring
Preliminary prospectus distributed to prospective investors in a new issue of securities.

Tombstone advertisements are used by underwriters during and after the waiting period. The tombstone contains the name of the company whose securities are involved. It provides some information about the issue, and it lists the investment dealers (the underwriters) who are involved with selling the issue. We discuss the role of the investment dealers in selling securities more fully later.

The investment dealers are divided into groups called *brackets* on the tombstone and prospectus, and the names of the dealers are listed alphabetically within each bracket. The brackets are a kind of pecking order. In general, the higher the bracket, the greater is the underwriter's prestige.

While an underwriter's prestige is important for a *seasoned new issue* by a well-known company already traded on the TSE, it is even more critical for the first public equity issue referred to as an **initial public offering (IPO),** or an unseasoned new issue. An IPO occurs when a company decides to go public. Researchers have found that IPOs with prestigious underwriters perform better. This is likely because

initial public offering (IPO)
A company's first equity issue made available to the public. Also an unseasoned new issue.

investors believe that prestigious underwriters, jealous of their reputations, shun questionable IPOs.

The POP System

In 1982, the SEC approved its shelf registration system designed to reduce repetitive filing requirements for large companies. In 1983, the OSC introduced the POP system with a similar goal. The five provinces with securities commissions all have compatible legislation allowing certain securities issuers prompt access to capital markets without preparing a full preliminary and final prospectus before a distribution.

The POP system, accessible only by large companies, lets issuers file annual and interim financial statements regardless of whether they issue securities in a given year. To use the POP system, issuers must have not only reported for 36 months but also complied with the continuous disclosure requirements. Because the OSC has an extensive file of information on these companies, only a short prospectus is required when securities are issued. As we stated earlier, POP offerings in the form of bought deals became quite popular in the late 1980s.

In 1991, securities regulators in Canada and the SEC in the United States introduced a Multi-Jurisdictional Disclosure System (MJDS). Under MJDS, large issuers in the two countries are allowed to issue securities in both countries under disclosure documents satisfactory to regulators in the home country. This is an important simplification of filing requirements for certain large Canadian companies. In 1991, for example, Rogers Communications Inc. completed a $270 million (U.S.) debt issue initiating MJDS.[5] In 1995, the OSC extended MJDS to issuers in G7 countries outside the United States. This will save a foreign company in say, Germany, from duplicate filings and from restating its financial statements to follow Canadian rules.

> CONCEPT QUESTIONS
> 1. What are the basic procedures in selling a new issue?
> 2. What is a preliminary prospectus?
> 3. What is the POP system and what advantages does it offer?

13.3 | THE CASH OFFER

If the public issue of securities is a cash offer, underwriters are usually involved. Underwriters perform the following services for corporate issuers:

Formulating the method used to issue the securities.

Pricing the new securities.

Selling the new securities.

syndicate
A group of underwriters formed to reduce the risk and help to sell an issue.

Typically, the underwriter buys the securities for less than the offering price and accepts the risk of not being able to sell them. Because underwriting involves risk, underwriters combine to form an underwriting group called a **syndicate** or a *banking group* to share the risk and help to sell the issue.

In a syndicate, one or more managers arrange or co-manage the offering. This manager is designated as the lead manager and typically has the responsibility for

---

[5] David Payne, "Accounting Watch," *Director*, September 1991, and Barry Critchley, "New Rates Open Up Cross-Border Financing," *Financial Post*, September 23, 1991, pp. 11–20.

packaging and executing the deal. The other underwriters in the syndicate serve primarily to distribute the issue.

The difference between the underwriter's buying and the offering price is called the **spread** or *discount*. It is the basic compensation received by the underwriter.

In Canada, firms often establish long-term relationships with their underwriters. With the growth in popularity of bought deals, competition among underwriters has increased. At the same time, mergers among investment dealers have reduced the number of underwriters. For example, RBC Dominion Securities grew through merger with six other investment dealers and a major capital injection by the Royal Bank.

Types of Underwriting

Two basic types of underwriting are possible in a cash offer: regular underwriting and a bought deal.

With **regular underwriting** the banking group of underwriters buys the securities from the issuing firm and resells them to the public for the purchase price plus an underwriting spread. Regular underwriting includes an out clause that gives the banking group the option to decline the issue if the price drops dramatically. In this case, the deal is usually withdrawn. The issue might be repriced and/or reoffered at a later date. **Firm commitment underwriting** is like regular underwriting without the out clause.

A close counterpart to regular underwriting is called **best efforts underwriting**. The underwriter is legally bound to use its best efforts to sell the securities at the agreed-on offering price. Beyond this, the underwriter does not guarantee any particular amount of money to the issuer. This form of underwriting is more common with initial public offerings (IPOs).

Bought Deal

In a **bought deal**, the issuer sells the entire issue to one investment dealer or to a group that attempts to resell it. As in firm commitment underwriting, the investment dealer assumes all the price risk. The dealer usually markets the prospective issue to a few large, institutional investors. Issuers in bought deals are large, well-known firms qualifying for the use of POP to speed up OSC filings. For these reasons, bought deals are usually executed swiftly. Bought deals are the most popular form of underwriting in Canada today.

Recently, the Investment Dealers Association of Canada and the OSC took another look at bought deals. Some investment dealers criticized bought deals for excluding retail investors from access to many new issues. There was also concern that the rush to market bought deals could prevent investment dealers from due diligence investigation.

A related concern was what happens if the underwriter cannot sell all the issue at the agreed-on offer price. In this case, it may have to lower the price on the unsold shares. With a bought deal, the issuer receives the agreed-on amount, and all the risk associated with selling the issue is transferred to the underwriter. Unlike regular underwriting, the investment dealer does not have an out clause. The additional risk in a bought deal became apparent in the fall of 1987 when three Canadian investment dealers attempted to sell stock in British Petroleum PLC to individual Canadian investors. With the crash of 1987, the investment dealers lost millions on their BP shares.[6]

---

[6] *Globe and Mail*, March 15, 1988.

spread
Compensation to the underwriter, determined by the difference between the underwriter's buying price and offering price.

regular underwriting
The purchase of securities from the issuing company by an investment banker for resale to the public.

firm commitment underwriting
Underwriter buys the entire issue, assuming full financial responsibility for any unsold shares.

best efforts underwriting
Underwriter sells as much of the issue as possible, but can return any unsold shares to the issuer without financial responsibility.

bought deal
One underwriter buys securities from an issuing firm and sells them directly to a small number of investors.

A recent study of bought deals from 1984 to 1992 is reassuring on these concerns. It finds that what happened with British Petroleum was not typical. Shares sold in bought deals fared at least as well as stock issued through regular underwriting.[7]

The Selling Period

While the issue is being sold to the public, the underwriting group agrees not to sell securities for less than the offering price until the syndicate dissolves. The principal underwriter is permitted to buy shares if the market price falls below the offering price. The purpose would be to support the market and stabilize the price from temporary downward pressure. If this issue remains unsold after a time (for example, 30 days), members can leave the group and sell their shares at whatever price the market allows.

The Overallotment Option

Many underwriting contracts contain an overallotment option or *Green Shoe provision* that gives the members of the underwriting group the option to purchase additional shares at the offering price less fees and commissions.[8] The stated reason for the overallotment option is to cover excess demand and oversubscriptions. The option has a short maturity, around 30 days, and is limited to about 10 percent of the original number of shares issued.

The overallotment option is a benefit to the underwriting syndicate and a cost to the issuer. If the market price of the new issue rises immediately, the overallotment option allows the underwriters to buy additional shares from the issuer and immediately resell them to the public.

The Investment Dealers

Investment dealers are at the heart of new security issues. They provide advice, market the securities (after investigating the market's receptiveness to the issue), and provide a guarantee of the amount an issue will raise (with a bought deal).

Table 13.1 lists the largest underwriters in Canada based on the total dollars in securities offerings (debt and equity) managed in 1990.[9] As indicated, RBC Dominion Securities was the leading manager of underwritten public securities offerings in 1990 with 130 issues and a total of $5.3 billion managed. In Parts B and C of Table 13.1, we have broken out debt and equity issues separately. From our discussion in Chapter 12, it is not surprising that debt issues are much more common than equity issues.

Table 13.2 gives an international perspective by looking at non-Canadian issues. Notice how U.S. underwriters dominate international equity underwritings while European and Japanese firms rank in the top four positions in the much larger international bond market. CIBC-Wood Gundy ranked in the top 25 underwriters for equities, but no Canadian firm made the top 25 in international bond markets.

---

[7] L. P. Schwartz, "Bought Deals: The Devil That You Know," *Canadian Investment Review,* Spring 1994, pp. 21–26.

[8] The term *Green Shoe provision* sounds quite exotic, but the origin is relatively mundane. It comes from the Green Shoe Company, which once granted such an option.

[9] We created these tables from the *Financial Post* by using its formula that divides the total amount underwritten among members of the underwriting group with a bonus to the lead manager. Our figures include corporate and government debt and corporate equity issues.

A. Canada (combined debt and equity)				
Rank			Dollar Volume (millions)	Number of Issues
1990	1989			
1	1	RBC Dominion	5,333	130
2	3	ScotiaMcLeod	4,726	105
3	2	Wood Gundy	4,393	113
4	4	Merrill Lynch	2,575	39
5	5	Burns, Fry	2,461	61
6	8	Nesbitt, Thomson	2,286	68
7		CS First Boston	1,801	24
8		Union Bank of Switzerland	1,311	19
9	10	Richardson Greenshields	1,177	46
10	7	Gordon Capital	1,080	41
B. Canada (debt issues)				
1	1	RBC Dominion	4,363	93
2	2	ScotiaMcLeod	4,210	79
3	3	Wood Gundy	3,790	86
4	4	Merrill Lynch	2,574	38
5	5	Burns, Fry	1,989	45
6	6	Nesbitt, Thomson	1,826	42
7	8	CS First Boston	1,801	24
8	10	Union Bank of Switzerland	1,311	19
9		Salomon Brothers	962	13
10	9	Richardson Greenshields	858	32
C. Canada (equity issues)				
1	1	RBC Dominion	970	37
2	2	Gordon Capital	674	24
3	3	Wood Gundy	603	27
4	4	ScotiaMcLeod	516	26
5	8	Burns, Fry	472	16
6	6	Nesbitt, Thomson	460	26
7	7	Trilon Securities	406	22
8	10	Levesque, Beaubien	361	26
9	9	Richardson Greenshields	319	14
10	5	TD Securities	304	10

T A B L E 13.1

Top 10 underwriters for 1990

Source: From figures in the *Financial Post*, August 5, 1991, p. 13.

The Offering Price and Underpricing

Determining the correct offering price is the most difficult thing an underwriter must do. The issuing firm faces a potential cost if the offering price is set too high or too low. If the issue is priced at less than the true market price, the issuer's existing shareholders experience an opportunity loss when they sell their shares for less than they are worth. If the issue is priced too high, it may be unsuccessful and have to be withdrawn. Of course, this is the underwriter's problem under a bought deal.

Underpricing is fairly common. It obviously helps new shareholders earn a higher return on the shares they buy. However, the existing shareholders of the issuing firm are not helped by underpricing. To them it is an indirect cost of issuing new securities. In the case of an IPO, underpricing reduces the proceeds received by the original owners.

T A B L E 13.2

Top 25 underwriters,
1991–1992

Ranking				
1991	January–June 1992	International Equities	Dollar Volume (millions)	Number of Issues
1	1	Goldman Sachs	$ 3,077.4	37
7	2	Morgan Stanley	2,439.4	33
4	3	Lehman Brothers	1,315.0	21
5	4	Merrill Lynch	1,011.0	18
9	5	Banco Roberts	931.8	1
2	6	S.G. Warburg Group	888.0	7
3	7	Credit Suisse/CSFB Group	869.5	17
10	8	Paribas	833.5	6
—	9	J.P. Morgan Securities	745.2	4
6	10	Salomon Brothers	325.1	7
—	11	Banque Indosuez	298.3	4
—	12	Rothschild's Continuation Holdings	255.0	2
24	13	Crédit Lyonnais	239.0	2
17	14	Donaldson, Lufkin & Jenrette	224.6	6
15	15	PaineWebber	144.4	13
18	16	Baring Brothers	141.0	1
—	17	Acciones y Valores de México	133.7	2
—	18	Bear Stearns	130.1	3
—	19	Oppenheimer	120.9	3
—	20	Commerce International Merchant Bank	104.4	1
16	21	Wood Gundy	95.3	3
14	22	Skandinaviska Enskilda Bank Group	93.6	1
—	23	Den Danske Bank	82.1	2
13	24	Barclays Bank	73.4	1
—	25	Swiss Bank Corp.	73.0	2
		International Bonds*		
3	1	Deutsche Bank	$13,627.5	53
1	2	Nomura International Group	12,057.7	53
2	3	Credit Suisse/CSFB Group	11,538.4	59
9	4	Paribas	8,856.4	39
8	5	Merrill Lynch	8,448.1	37
7	6	Union Bank of Switzerland	7,800.2	37
15	7	J.P. Morgan Securities	6,910.0	26
6	8	Goldman Sachs	6,588.3	28
11	9	Yamaichi Securities	5,994.0	44
5	10	Swiss Bank Corp.	5,795.4	46
4	11	Daiwa Securities	5,785.4	44
12	12	Nikko Securities	5,501.2	35
17	13	Crédit Lyonnais	5,236.8	19
19	14	Crédit Commercial de France	4,200.2	17
10	15	Morgan Stanley	4,175.1	18
18	16	Industrial Bank of Japan	4,096.4	15
13	17	Salomon Brothers	3,677.6	15
14	18	Dresdner Bank	2,868.7	9
28	19	Banque Nationale de Paris	2,478.5	10
—	20	Citicorp	2,442.2	11
16	21	S.G. Warburg Group	2,429.6	11
34	22	Lehman Brothers	2,310.2	16
21	23	Commerzbank	2,253.1	11
20	24	Hambros Bank	2,073.4	26
26	25	ABN Amro Bank	1,994.1	14

*This table ranks international bond underwriters in the broadest sense. It includes all Euromarket deals, as well as "foreign" bonds syndicated in domestic markets outside an issuer's home country.
Source: *Institutional Investor,* September 1992. Used with permission.

The Decision to Go Public

When a private company grows to a certain size, it may consider the advantages of going public by issuing common stock through an IPO. One important advantage is that public firms have greater access to new capital once their shares are valued on secondary markets. Further, publicly traded firms must meet OSC and other disclosure requirements that reduce information risk for potential investors. In addition, going public makes it possible for the firm's principal owners to sell some of their shares and diversify their personal portfolios while retaining control of the company.

Going public also has disadvantages. Public firms are subject to stricter disclosure and other potentially costly regulatory requirements. They have to be careful to abide by OSC Policy 9.1 against self-dealing. Senior management must spend considerable time explaining the company's activities and plans to investment analysts who follow its newly listed shares.

On balance, most large companies in Canada are public. When a firm decides to go public, it does so through an IPO.

Pricing IPOs

Because the firm has no record as a public company, pricing an IPO is a big challenge. Research on IPOs in the United States and Canada reveals firms that provide a greater amount of high-quality information are able to set higher prices on their IPOs. Different information variables are listed in Table 13.3. Firms that disclose past, favourable accounting information enjoy higher IPO prices. Of the accounting variables listed in Table 13.3, book value of assets had the most impact for Canadian firms. This suggests larger firms have an advantage in going public.

A related advantage, information intermediation, links higher offering prices to firms that use auditors and underwriters with top reputations. When issuers use such top quality (and more expensive) intermediaries, the market attaches more weight to favourable projections in their prospectuses. This reputation effect may be waning as investment dealers and accounting firms become fewer, larger, and more alike through mergers.

Investors recognize that an IPO's original owners have the best information about the company's future prospects. But the owners also have an interest in maximizing the IPO price. To resolve this *moral hazard* problem, investors look for signals that original owners have favourable inside information. If owners believed

Variable	Empirical Evidence*	
Direct disclosures		**T A B L E 13.3**
Sales and earnings from existing operations	+ or 0	
Book value of existing assets	+	*What determines*
Information intermediation		*subscription prices?*
High quality (good reputation) intermediation services	+	
Signals of inside information		
Entrepreneurial ownership retention	+ or 0	
Use of proceeds for risky investments	+	
Stated dividend policy	0	

*Expressed as positive (+), neutral (0), or negative (−).
Source: W. Rotenberg, "Pricing Initial Public Equity Offerings: Who Wins, Who Loses, and Why?" *Canadian Investment Review*, Spring 1990, pp. 17–26.

the firm had excellent opportunities, they would retain more stock themselves. They would also use the IPO proceeds to invest in risky capital projects designed to generate positive NPVs out of the firm's opportunities. Table 13.3 shows that research on U.S. and Canadian IPOs generally supports these arguments.

So far, we have discussed setting the offer price. The issue of underpricing, raised earlier, relates the offer price to the IPO's price after the offering period is over. Table 13.4 summarizes a series of studies on IPOs in the United States and Canada. It shows that IPOs are underpriced compared to their prices in the aftermarket immediately after the offering period. Figure 13.1 shows that underpricing is also cyclical. The greatest underpricing occurred in hot market periods such as 1980–1981 when prices skyrocketed immediately after issue.

Why Does Underpricing Exist?

Based on the evidence we've examined, an obvious question is: Why does underpricing continue to exist? As we discuss, there are various explanations, but to date, there is a lack of complete agreement among researchers as to which is correct.

We present some pieces of the underpricing puzzle by stressing two important caveats to our discussion: First, the average figures we have examined tend to obscure the fact that much of the apparent underpricing is attributable to the smaller, more highly speculative issues. Smaller firms tend to have offering prices of less than $3 per share, and such *penny stocks* (as they are sometimes termed) can be very risky investments. Arguably, they must be significantly underpriced, on average, just to attract investors, and this is one explanation for the underpricing phenomenon.

The second caveat is that relatively few IPO buyers actually get the initial high average returns observed in IPOs, and many actually lose money. Although it is true that, on average, IPOs have positive initial returns, a significant fraction of them have price drops. Furthermore, when the price is too low, the issue is often oversubscribed. This means investors cannot buy all the shares they want, and the underwriters allocate the shares among investors.

The average investor finds it difficult to get shares in a successful offering (one where the price increases) because there are not enough shares to go around. On the other hand, an investor blindly submitting orders for IPOs finds that he or she tends to get more shares in issues that go down in price.

This is another example of a winner's curse, and it is thought to be another reason IPOs have such a large average return. When the average investor wins and gets his or her entire allocation, it may be because those who knew better avoided the issue. The only way underwriters can counteract the winner's curse and attract the

T A B L E 13.4	Sample	Sample Period	Average Underpricing
Initial aftermarket performance: the evidence	10,626 U.S. IPOs	1960–90	15.26%
	100 Canadian IPOs	1971–83	9.3
	116 IPOs	1984–87	4.3

Source: Roger G. Ibbotson, Jody L. Sindelar, and Jay R. Ritter, "Initial Public Offerings," *Journal of Applied Corporate Finance,* Summer 1988, pp. 37–45; Roger G. Ibbotson, Jody L. Sindelar, and Jay R. Ritter, "Initial Public Offerings," *Journal of Applied Corporate Finance,* Spring 1994; V. M. Jog and A. C. Riding, "Underpricing in Canadian IPOs," *Financial Analysts Journal,* November/December 1987, pp. 48–55; and J. M. Friedlan, "Understanding the IPO Market," *CGA Magazine,* March 1994, pp. 42–68.

F I G U R E 13.1 *Average initial returns by month for SEC-registered initial public offerings: 1960–1992*

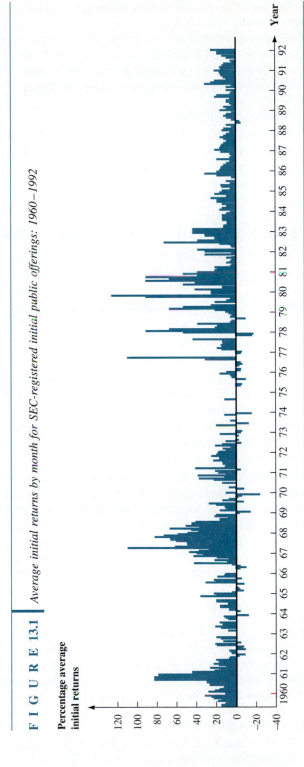

Source: Roger G. Ibbotson, Jody L. Sindelar, and Jay R. Ritter, "Initial Public Offerings," *Journal of Applied Corporate Finance*, Summer 1988, pp. 37–45, and Roger G. Ibbotson, Jody L. Sindelar, and Jay R. Ritter, "Initial Public Offerings," *Journal of Applied Corporate Finance*, Spring 1994.

Source: Roger G. Ibbotson, Jody L. Sindelar, and Jay R. Ritter, "Initial Public Offerings," *Journal of Applied Corporate Finance*, Summer 1988, pp. 37–45, and Roger G. Ibbotson, Jody L. Sindelar, and Jay R. Ritter, "Initial Public Offerings," *Journal of Applied Corporate Finance*, Spring 1994.

average investor is to underprice new issues (on average) so that the average investor still makes a profit.

A final reason for underpricing is that the underpricing is a kind of insurance for the investment dealers. Conceivably, an investment dealer could be sued successfully by angry customers if it consistently overpriced securities. Underpricing guarantees that, at least on average, the customers come out ahead.

> CONCEPT QUESTIONS
>
> 1. Suppose a stockbroker phones you out of the blue and offers to sell "all the shares you want" of a new issue. Do you think the issue will be more or less underpriced than average?
> 2. What factors determine the degree of mispricing?

13.4 | NEW EQUITY SALES AND THE VALUE OF THE FIRM

It seems reasonable to believe that new long-term financing is arranged by firms after positive net present value projects are put together. As a consequence, when the announcement of external financing is made, the firm's market value should go up. Interestingly, this is not what happens. Stock prices tend to decline following the announcement of a new equity issue, and they tend to rise following a debt announcement. A number of researchers have studied this issue. Plausible reasons for this strange result include:

1. *Managerial information.* If management has superior information about the market value of the firm, it may know when the firm is overvalued. If it does, it attempts to issue new shares of stock when the market value exceeds the correct value. This benefits existing shareholders. However, the potential new shareholders are not stupid, and they anticipate this superior information and discount it in lower market prices at the new issue date.

2. *Debt usage.* Issuing new equity may reveal that the company has too much debt or too little liquidity. One version of this argument is that the equity issue is a bad signal to the market. After all, if the new projects are favourable ones, why should the firm let new shareholders in on them? As you read earlier, in IPOs it is regarded as a positive signal when the original owners keep larger amounts of stock for themselves. Taking this argument to the limit, the firm could just issue debt and let the existing shareholders have all the gain.

3. *Issue costs.* As we discuss next, there are substantial costs associated with selling securities.

The drop in value of the existing stock following the announcement of a new issue is an example of an indirect cost of selling securities. This drop might typically be on the order of 3 percent for an industrial corporation so, for a large company, it can be a substantial amount of money. Later, we label this drop the *abnormal return* in our discussion of the costs of new issues.

> CONCEPT QUESTIONS
>
> 1. What are some possible reasons that the price of stock drops on the announcement of a new equity issue?
> 2. Explain why we might expect a firm with a positive NPV investment to finance it with debt instead of equity.

13.5 | THE COSTS OF ISSUING SECURITIES

Issuing securities to the public isn't free, and the costs of different methods are important determinants of which method is used. These costs associated with *floating* a new issue are generically called *flotation* costs. In this section, we take a closer look at the flotation costs associated with equity sales to the public.

The costs of selling stock fall into six categories: (1) the spread, (2) other direct expenses, (3) indirect expenses, (4) abnormal returns (discussed earlier), (5) underpricing, and (6) the overallotment option. We look at these costs first for United States and then for Canadian equity sales.

The Costs of Issuing Securities	
Spread	The spread consists of direct fees paid by the issuer to the underwriting syndicate—the difference between the price the issuer receives and the offer price.
Other direct expenses	These are direct costs, incurred by the issuer, that are not part of the compensation to underwriters. These costs include filing fees, legal fees, and taxes—all reported on the prospectus.
Indirect expenses	These costs are not reported on the prospectus and include the costs of management time spent working on the new issue.
Abnormal returns	In a seasoned issue of stock, the price drops on average by 3 percent on the announcement of the issue.
Underpricing	For initial public offerings, losses arise from selling the stock below the correct value.
Overallotment (Green Shoe) option	The Green Shoe option gives the underwriters the right to buy additional shares at the offer price to cover overallotments.

Table 13.5 reports the direct costs of new equity issues in 1983 for publicly traded U.S. firms. These are all seasoned offerings; the percentages in Table 13.5 are as reported in the prospectuses of the issuing companies. These costs only include the spread (underwriter discount) and other direct costs, including legal fees, accounting fees, printing costs, SEC registration costs, and taxes. Not included are indirect expenses, abnormal returns, underpricing, and the overallotment option.

As indicated in Table 13.5, the direct costs alone can be very large, particularly for smaller (less than $10 million) issues. For this group, the direct costs, as reported by the companies, average a little more than 10 percent. This means the company, net of costs, receives 90 percent of the proceeds of the sale on average. On a $10 million issue, this is $1 million in direct expenses—a substantial cost.

Table 13.5 tells only part of the story. For IPOs, the effective costs can be much greater because of the indirect costs. Table 13.6 reports both the direct costs of going public and the degree of underpricing based on IPOs that occurred on the Toronto

Gross Proceeds ($ millions)	Direct Costs Reported on Prospectus (percent)
$ 0–10	10.10%
10–20	7.02
20–50	4.89
50–100	3.99
100–200	3.71
200–	3.30

T A B L E 13.5

Flotation costs as a percentage of gross proceeds in 1983 for underwritten new issues of equity by publicly traded firms

Source: R. Hansen, "Evaluating the Costs of a New Equity Issue," *Midland Corporate Finance Journal* 4, no. 1 (Spring 1986), p. 45.

T A B L E 13.6	Spread	5.96%
Costs of going public in Canada: 1971–83	Other direct expenses	0.98
	Underpricing (first day trading return)	11.60
	Total	18.54%

Source: I. Krinsky and W. Rotenberg, "The Valuation of Public Offerings," *Contemporary Accounting Research* 5, no. 2, pp. 501–15.

Stock Exchange between 1971 and 1983. These figures understate the total cost because the study did not consider indirect expenses, abnormal returns, or the overallotment option.

The total expenses of going public over these years averaged 18.54 percent. This is roughly comparable to U.S. averages for 1977–82 of 21.22 percent for firm commitment underwriting and 31.87 percent for best efforts underwriting. Comparing the two studies suggests that the U.S. costs were higher mainly due to greater underpricing. Once again, we see that the costs of selling securities can be quite large.

Overall, three conclusions emerge from our discussion of underwriting:

1. Substantial economies of size are evident. Larger firms can raise equity more easily.

2. The cost associated with underpricing can be substantial and can exceed the direct costs.

3. The issue costs are higher for an initial public offering than for a seasoned offering.

> CONCEPT QUESTIONS
> 1. What are the different costs associated with security offerings?
> 2. What lessons do we learn from studying issue costs?

IPOs in Practice: The Case of Air Canada

In October 1988, the government of Canada sold 30.8 million shares of Air Canada stock in a successful partial privatization.[10] The IPO was priced at $8 per share and generated $234 million after flotation costs. The airline, government owned since its inception as Trans-Canada Air Lines in 1937, was to remain under government majority ownership, but the government promised to refrain from taking an active role in management. At the time, the airline industry was enjoying strong growth in revenue passenger miles domestically and more moderate growth in international markets. Deregulation improved flexibility and was expected to benefit Air Canada. Net income was volatile due to fluctuating fuel prices but had hit a high of $46 million in 1987.

The shares issued were voting shares but non-Canadian shareholders were restricted from voting more than 25 percent of the shares. The proceeds of the issue were roughly split between retiring debt and purchase of new aircraft along with other capital expenditures. Underwriters in the top bracket were RBC Dominion Securities, Inc., Wood Gundy Inc., ScotiaMcLeod Inc., Nesbitt Thomson Deacon Ltd., Richardson Greenshields of Canada Limited, Burns Fry Limited, Merrill Lynch

---

[10] This section draws on two cases by the late Cecil R. Dipchand, "Air Canada (A) and (B)," Halifax: Dalhousie University, 1990.

Canada Inc., Levesque Beaubien Inc., and Pemberton Securities Inc. Twenty-seven other investment dealers also participated in the underwriting. The selling arrangement took the form of regular underwriting with the agreement containing an out clause. The underwriters also had an overallotment option up to a maximum of 10 percent of the original number of shares.

When we apply the theory of underpricing to Air Canada, we find that several factors combined to moderate underpricing. Since Air Canada was relatively large, with total assets of $3.1 billion at book value in June 1988, underpricing should be more moderate than for a smaller issue. Other factors expected to moderate underpricing were availability of detailed historical financial information and inclusion of high-quality underwriters. The company's plans to use half the proceeds for capital investment in risky assets was also expected to boost the issue price.

In the actual event, the predictions of theory were accurate; immediate underpricing was not evident. The stock price declined from the issue price of $8 to a low of $7 in the month after issue. The decline was likely due to a general market drop. In January 1989, both the TSE and Air Canada turned upward and the stock rose to more than $13 in June 1989. Market analysts noted that the federal government remained true to its promise not to interfere in the company's affairs. Debt levels were reduced to be comparable to those of large U.S. airlines while profitability was good.

In June 1989, the federal government decided to sell its remaining shares at an issue price of $12. The government benefited from market timing as the price was up by 50 percent from the initial IPO. The offering was sold in July 1989. By August 11, 1989, the price rose to a peak of $14.88. The return to investors immediately after the issue was ($14.88 − $12)/$12 = 24 percent. So in the second offering, or tranche, underpricing was significant.

To measure the effect of underpricing, suppose the shares in the second tranche could have been sold for around 12 percent underpricing instead of 24 percent. We pick 12 percent because it is approximately the average amount of underpricing reported in Table 13.6. With 12 percent underpricing, the issue price would have been $13.44 (($13.44 − $12)/$12 = .12). Assuming that other flotation costs had stayed the same, the government would have netted an additional $59 million (41 million shares × ($13.44 − 12)).

The longer-term performance of Air Canada has not been as favourable. By October 1989, the price declined to less than the $12 offering price. In September 1992, Air Canada stock was trading at $3.80. By May 1995, the stock was up to $6. Air Canada's longer-term performance is typical of the mixed record of IPOs.

Privatization: A Financial Innovation

Globalization of financial markets in the 1980s went hand in hand with deregulation in making privatizations attractive. Large institutional investors sought international diversification to reduce risk and enhance returns. Privatizations offered these investors shares in large, well-known companies and underpricing made them attractive. As a result, many privatizations involved record amounts.

The government of Canada received over $700 million in the two Air Canada issues. At the time of writing, the federal government successfully raised $2 billion by selling Canadian National Railway. The CN deal was the largest ever privatization in Canada. The numbers are impressive but substantially less than, for example, the $4.76 billion (U.S.) raised when British Telecom (the British government-owned telephone company) went public in 1984. However, these issues pale in comparison to what NTT (Nippon Telephone and Telegraph, the Japanese telephone company) raised in 1987. In November 1987, NTT sold 1.95 million shares at a price of 2.55 *million* yen each. At the then-prevailing exchange rate, this was roughly $19,000 (U.S.) per share. The total issue amount was thus on the order of $37 billion (U.S.) What is even more remarkable is that NTT had already sold 1.95 million shares in February of the same year.

More major privatizations are expected as Eastern European countries restructure their planned systems into market economies. Many enterprises in these countries will require years of restructuring after they go private. As a result, there is not likely to be much high-quality information about future prospects. The transfer to private ownership may not take the form of a sale of stock. Instead, it may be more efficient to auction the unrestructured enterprises to the highest bidder. In any event, it is certain that participants in these privatizations will carefully study the experience of Air Canada and other similar cases.[11]

13.6   I   RIGHTS

When new shares of common stock are sold to the general public, the proportional ownership of existing shareholders is likely reduced. However, if a preemptive right is contained in the firm's articles of incorporation, the firm must first offer any new issue of common stock to existing shareholders. If the articles of incorporation do not include a preemptive right, the firm has a choice of offering the issue of common stock directly to existing shareholders or to the public. In some industries, regulatory authorities set rules concerning rights. For example, before the Bank Act of 1980, chartered banks were required to raise equity exclusively through rights offerings.

An issue of common stock offered to existing shareholders is called a *rights offering*. In a rights offering, each shareholder is issued one right for every share owned. The rights give the shareholder an option to buy a specified number of new shares from the firm at a specified price within a specified time, after which time the rights are said to expire.

The terms of the rights offering are evidenced by certificates known as rights. Such rights are often traded on securities exchanges or over the counter.

The Mechanics of a Rights Offering

To illustrate the various considerations a financial manager has in a rights offering, we examine the situation faced by the National Power Company, whose abbreviated initial financial statements are given in Table 13.7.

As indicated in Table 13.7, National Power earns $2 million after taxes and has 1 million shares outstanding. Earnings per share are thus $2, and the stock sells for $20, or 10 times earnings (that is, the price-earnings ratio is 10). To fund a planned expansion, the company intends to raise $5 million of new equity funds by a rights offering.

To execute a rights offering, the financial management of National Power has to answer the following questions:

1. What should the price per share be for the new stock?
2. How many shares will have to be sold?
3. How many shares will each shareholder be allowed to buy?

---

[11] For more on privatization in Eastern Europe, see Roy C. Smith, "Privatization Programs of the 1980s: Lessons for the Treuhandstalt," Working paper, Salomon Brothers Center, New York University, 1990.

Balance Sheet			
Assets		Shareholders' Equity	
		Common stock	$ 5,000,000
		Retained earnings	10,000,000
Total	$15,000,000	Total	$15,000,000

Income Statement	
Earnings before taxes	$ 3,333,333
Taxes (40%)	1,333,333
Net income	2,000,000
Earnings per share	2
Shares outstanding	1,000,000
Market price per share	20
Total market value	$20,000,000

T A B L E 13.7

National Power Company financial statements before rights offering

Also, management would probably want to ask:

4. What is the likely effect of the rights offering on the per share value of the existing stock?

It turns out that the answers to these questions are highly interrelated. We get to them in a moment.

The early stages of a rights offering are the same as for the general cash offer. The difference between a rights offering and a general cash offer lies in how the shares are sold. As we discussed earlier, in a cash offer, shares are sold to retail and institutional investors through investment dealers. With a rights offer, National Power's existing shareholders are informed that they own one right for each share of stock they own. National Power then specifies how many rights a shareholder needs to buy one additional share at a specified price.

To take advantage of the rights offering, shareholders have to exercise the rights by filling out a subscription form and sending it, along with payment, to the firm's subscription agent. Shareholders of National Power actually have several choices: (1) exercise and subscribe to the entitled shares, (2) sell the rights, or (3) do nothing and let the rights expire. This third action is inadvisable, as long as the rights have value.

Number of Rights Needed to Purchase a Share

National Power wants to raise $5 million in new equity. Suppose the subscription price is set at $10 per share. How National Power arrived at that price is something we discuss later, but notice that the subscription price is substantially less than the current $20 per share market price.

At $10 per share, National Power will have to issue 500,000 new shares. This can be determined by dividing the total amount of funds to be raised by the subscription price:

$$\text{Number of new shares} = \text{Funds to be raised/Subscription price} \qquad [13.1]$$
$$= \$5,000,000/\$10 = 500,000 \text{ shares}$$

Because stockholders always get one right for each share of stock they own, 1 million rights would be issued by National Power. To determine how many rights are needed to buy one new share of stock, we can divide the number of existing outstanding shares of stock by the number of new shares:

$$\text{Number of rights needed to buy a share of stock} = \text{Old shares/New shares} \quad [13.2]$$
$$= 1{,}000{,}000/500{,}000 = 2 \text{ rights}$$

Thus, a shareholder needs to give up two rights plus $10 to receive a share of new stock. If all the shareholders do this, National Power could raise the required $5 million.

It should be clear that the subscription price, the number of new shares, and the number of rights needed to buy a new share of stock are interrelated. For example, National Power can lower the subscription price. If so, more new shares will have to be issued to raise $5 million in new equity. Several alternatives are worked out here:

Subscription Price	New Shares	Rights Needed to Buy a Share of Stock
$20	250,000	4
10	500,000	2
5	1,000,000	1

The Value of a Right

Rights clearly have value. In the case of National Power, the right to be able to buy a share of stock worth $20 for $10 is definitely worth something.

Suppose a shareholder of National Power owns two shares of stock just before the rights offering. This situation is depicted in Table 13.8. Initially, the price of National Power is $20 per share, so the shareholder's total holding is worth 2 × $20 = $40. The National Power rights offer gives shareholders with two rights the opportunity to purchase one additional share for $10. The additional share does not carry a right.

The shareholder who has two shares receives two rights. The holding of the shareholder who exercises these rights and buys the new share would increase to three shares. The total investment would be $40 + 10 = $50 (the $40 initial value plus the $10 paid to the company).

The shareholder now holds three shares, all of which are identical because the new share does not have a right and the rights attached to the old shares have been exercised. Since the total cost of buying these three shares is $40 + 10 = $50, the price per share must end up at $50/3 = $16.67 (rounded to two decimal places).

Table 13.9 summarizes what happens to National Power's stock price. If all shareholders exercise their rights, the number of shares increases to 1 million + .5

T A B L E 13.8

The value of rights: the individual shareholder

Initial Position	
Number of shares	2
Share price	$20
Value of holding	$40
Terms of Offer	
Subscription price	$10
Number of rights issued	2
Number of rights for a new share	2
After Offer	
Number of shares	3
Value of holdings	$50
Share price	$16.67
Value of a right	
Old price − New price	$20 − 16.67 = $3.33

Initial Position	
Number of shares	1 million
Share price	$20
Value of firm	$20 million
Terms of Offer	
Subscription price	$10
Number of rights issued	1 million
Number of rights for a share	2
After Offer	
Number of shares	1.5 million
Share price	$16.67
Value of firm	$25 million
Value of one right	$20 − 16.67 = $3.33

T A B L E 13.9

National Power Company rights offering

million = 1.5 million. The value of the firm increases to $20 million + 5 million = $25 million. The value of each share thus drops to $25 million/1.5 million = $16.67 after the rights offering.

The difference between the old share price of $20 and the new share price of $16.67 reflects the fact that the old shares carried rights to subscribe to the new issue. The difference must be equal to the value of one right, that is, $20 − 16.67 = $3.33.

Although holding no shares of outstanding National Power stock, an investor who wants to subscribe to the new issue can do so by buying some rights. Suppose an outside investor buys two rights. This costs $3.33 × 2 = $6.67 (to account for previous rounding). If the investor exercises the rights at a subscription price of $10, the total cost would be $10 + 6.67 = $16.67. In return for this expenditure, the investor receives a share of the new stock, which, as we have seen, is worth $16.67.

E X A M P L E | 13.1   Exercising Your Rights

In the National Power example, suppose the subscription price was set at $8. How many shares have to be sold? How many rights would you need to buy a new share? What is the value of a right? What will the price per share be after the rights offer?

To raise $5 million, $5 million/$8 = 625,000 shares need to be sold. There are 1 million shares outstanding, so it will take 1 million/625,000 = 8/5 = 1.6 rights to buy a new share of stock (you can buy five new shares for every eight you own). After the rights offer, there will be 1.625 million shares, worth $25 million all together, so the per share value is $25/1.625 = $15.38 each. The value of a right is the $20 original price less the $15.38 ending price, or $4.62. |

Theoretical Value of a Right

We can summarize the discussion with an equation for the theoretical value of a right during the rights-on period:

$$R_o = (M_o − S)/(N + 1) \qquad [13.3]$$

where

M_o = common share price during the rights-on period
S = subscription price
N = number of rights required to buy one new share

We can illustrate the use of Equation 13.3 by checking our answer for the value of one right in Example 13.1.

$$R_o = (\$20 - 8)/(1.6 + 1) = \$4.62$$

This is the same answer we got earlier.

Ex Rights

ex rights

Period when stock is selling without a recently declared right, normally beginning four business days before the holder-of-record date.

holder-of-record date

The date on which existing shareholders on company records are designated as the recipients of stock rights. Also the date of record.

National Power's rights have substantial value. In addition, the rights offering would have a large impact on the market price of National Power's stock price. It would drop by $3.33 on the day when the shares trade **ex rights**.

The standard procedure for issuing rights involves the firm's setting a **holder-of-record date**. Following stock exchange rules, the stock typically goes ex rights four trading days before the holder-of-record date. If the stock is sold before the ex rights date—rights-on, with rights, or cum rights—the new owner receives the rights. After the ex-rights date, an investor who purchases the shares will not receive the rights. This is depicted for National Power in Figure 13.2

As illustrated, on September 30, National Power announced the terms of the rights offering, stating that the rights would be mailed on, say, November 1 to stockholders of record as of October 15. Since October 11 is the ex-rights date, only those shareholders who own the stock on or before October 10 receive the rights.

E X A M P L E | 13.2   Exercising Your Rights: Part II

The Lagrange Point Company has proposed a rights offering. The stock currently sells for $40 per share. Under the terms of the offer, stockholders are allowed to buy one new share for every five that they own at a price of $25 per share. What is the value of a right? What is the ex-rights price?

You can buy five rights on shares for $5 \times \$40 = \$200$ and then exercise the rights for another $25. Your total investment is $225, and you end up with six ex-rights shares. The ex-rights price per share is $\$225/6 = \$37.50$ per share. The rights are thus worth $\$40 - 37.50 = \$2.50$ apiece.

Using Equation 13.3 we have:

$$R_o = (\$40 - 25)/(5 + 1) = \$2.50 \quad |$$

F I G U R E 13.2

Ex-rights stock prices: the effect of rights-on stock prices

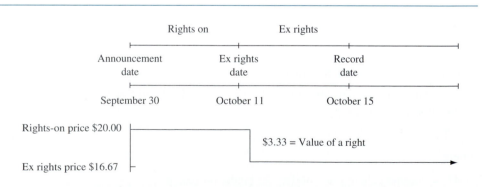

In a rights offering, there is a date of record, which is the last day that a shareholder can establish legal ownership. However, stocks are sold ex rights four business days before the record date. Before the ex rights day, the stock sells rights on, which means the purchaser receives the rights.

Value of Rights after Ex-Rights Date

When the stock goes ex rights, we saw that its price drops by the value of one right. Until the rights expire, holders can buy one share at the subscription price by exercising N rights. In equation form:[12]

$$M_e = M_o - R_o \qquad\qquad [13.4]$$
$$R_e = (M_e - S)/N \qquad\qquad [13.5]$$

where M_e = common share price during the ex-rights period.

Checking the formula using Example 13.2 gives

$$M_e = \$40 - 2.50 = \$37.50$$
$$R_e = (\$37.50 - 25)/5 = \$2.50$$

E X A M P L E | 13.3   Right on or Rights-On?

In Example 13.2, suppose you could buy the rights for only $0.25 instead of the $2.50 we calculated. What could you do?

You can get rich quick, because you have found a money machine. Here's the recipe: Buy five rights for $1.25. Exercise them and pay $25 to get a new share. Your total investment to get one ex rights share is $5 \times \$0.25 + \$25 = \$26.25$. Sell the share for $37.50 and pocket the $11.25 difference. Repeat as desired.

A variation on this theme actually occurred in the course of a rights offering by a major Canadian chartered bank in the mid-1980s. The bank's employee stock ownership plan had promoted share ownership by tellers and clerical staff who were unfamiliar with the workings of rights offerings. When they received notification of the rights offering, many employees did not bother to respond until they were personally solicited by other, more sophisticated employees who bought the rights for a fraction of their value. We do not endorse the ethics behind such transactions. But the incident does show why it pays for everyone who owns stock to understand the workings of rights offers. |

The Underwriting Arrangements

Rights offerings are typically arranged using **standby underwriting**. In standby underwriting, the issuer makes a rights offering, and the underwriter makes a firm commitment to "take up" (that is, purchase) the unsubscribed portion of the issue. The underwriter usually gets a **standby fee** and additional amounts based on the securities taken up.

Standby underwriting protects the firm against undersubscription. This can occur if investors throw away rights or if bad news causes the market price of the stock to fall to less than the subscription price.

In practice, a small percentage (less than 10 percent) of shareholders fail to exercise valuable rights. This can probably be attributed to ignorance or vacations. Furthermore, shareholders are usually given an **oversubscription privilege** enabling them to purchase unsubscribed shares at the subscription price. The oversubscription privilege makes it unlikely that the corporate issuer would have to turn to its underwriter for help.

standby underwriting
Agreement where the underwriter agrees to purchase the unsubscribed portion of the issue.

standby fee
Amount paid to underwriter participating in standby underwriting agreement.

oversubscription privilege
Allows shareholders to purchase unsubscribed shares in a rights offering at the subscription price.

---

[12] During the ex-rights period, a right represents a short-lived option to buy the stock. Equation 13.5 gives the minimum value of this option. The market value of rights is generally higher as explained in our discussion of options in Chapter 20.

Effects on Shareholders

Shareholders can exercise their rights or sell them. In either case, the shareholder does not win or lose by the rights offering. The hypothetical holder of two shares of National Power has a portfolio worth $40. If the shareholder exercises the rights, he or she ends up with three shares worth a total of $50. In other words, by spending $10, the investor's holding increases in value by $10, which means the shareholder is neither better nor worse off.

On the other hand, if the shareholder sells the two rights for $3.33 each, he or she would obtain $3.33 × 2 = $6.67 and end up with two shares worth $16.67 and the cash from selling the right:

$$
\begin{aligned}
\text{Shares held} &= 2 \times \$16.67 = \$33.33 \\
\text{Rights sold} &= 2 \times \$3.33\ \ = \underline{\$\ 6.67} \\
\text{Total} &= \hspace{3.2em} \$40.00
\end{aligned}
$$

The new $33.33 market value plus $6.67 in cash is exactly the same as the original holding of $40. Thus, shareholders cannot lose or gain from exercising or selling rights.

It is obvious that after the rights offering, the new market price of the firm's stock would be lower than it was before the rights offering. As we have seen, however, shareholders have suffered no loss because of the rights offering. Thus, the stock price decline is very much like a stock split, a device that is described in Chapter 16. The lower the subscription price, the greater is the price decline of a rights offering. It is important to emphasize that because shareholders receive rights equal in value to the price drop, the rights offering does not hurt shareholders.

There is one last issue. How do we set the subscription price in a rights offering? If you think about it, in theory, the subscription price really does not matter. It has to be less than the market price of the stock for the rights to have value, but, beyond this, the price is arbitrary. In principle, it could be as low as we cared to make it as long as it is not zero.

In practice, however, the subscription price is typically 20 to 25 percent less than the prevailing stock price. Once we recognize market inefficiencies and frictions, a subscription price too close to the share price may result in undersubscription due simply to market imperfections.

Cost of Rights Offerings

Until the early 1980s, rights offerings were the most popular method of raising new equity in Canada for seasoned issuers. (Obviously, you cannot use rights offerings for IPOs.) The reason was lower flotation costs from the simpler underwriting arrangements. In the late 1980s and early 1990s, with the advent and popularity of POP, bought deals replaced rights offers as the prevalent form of equity issue.

In the United States, firms use general cash offers much more often than rights offerings. This reliance on general cash offers has caused considerable debate among researchers because, as in Canada, rights offerings are usually much cheaper in flotation costs. One recent study has found that firms making underwritten rights offers suffered substantially larger price drops than did firms making underwritten cash offers.[13] This is a hidden cost, and it may be part of the reason that underwritten rights offers are uncommon in the United States.

---

[13] Robert S. Hansen, "The Demise of the Rights Issue," *The Review of Financial Studies* 1 (Fall 1988), pp. 289–309.

CONCEPT QUESTIONS

1. How does a rights offering work?
2. What are the questions that financial management must answer in a rights offering?
3. How is the value of a right determined?
4. When does a rights offering affect the value of a company's shares?
5. Does a rights offer cause a share price decrease? How are existing shareholders affected by a rights offer?

13.7 | DILUTION

A subject that comes up quite a bit in discussions involving the selling of securities is **dilution**. Dilution refers to a loss in existing shareholders' value. There are several kinds:

1. Dilution of percentage ownership.
2. Dilution of market value.
3. Dilution of book value and earnings per share.

The difference between these three types can be a little confusing and there are some common misconceptions about dilution, so we discuss it in this section.

dilution

Loss in existing shareholders' value, in terms of either ownership, market value, book value, or EPS.

Dilution of Proportionate Ownership

The first type of dilution can arise whenever a firm sells shares to the general public. For example, Joe Smith owns 5,000 shares of Merit Shoe Company. Merit Shoe currently has 50,000 shares of stock outstanding; each share gets one vote. Smith thus controls 10 percent (5,000/50,000) of the votes and gets 10 percent of the dividends.

If Merit Shoe issues 50,000 new shares of common stock to the public via a general cash offer, Smith's ownership in Merit Shoe may be diluted. If Smith does not participate in the new issue, his ownership drops to 5 percent (5,000/100,000). Notice that the value of Smith's shares is unaffected; he just owns a smaller percentage of the firm.

Because a rights offering would ensure Joe Smith an opportunity to maintain his proportionate 10 percent share, dilution of the ownership of existing shareholders can be avoided by using a rights offering.

Dilution of Value: Book versus Market Values

We now examine dilution of value by looking at some accounting numbers. We do this to illustrate a fallacy concerning dilution; we do not mean to suggest that accounting dilution is more important than market value dilution. As we illustrate, quite the reverse is true.

Suppose Provincial Telephone Company (PTC) wants to build a new switching facility to meet future anticipated demands. PTC currently has 1 million shares outstanding and no debt. Each share is selling for $5, and the company has a $5 million market value. PTC's book value is $10 million total, or $10 per share.

PTC has experienced a variety of difficulties in the past, including cost overruns, regulatory delays, and below normal profits. These difficulties are reflected in the fact that PTC's market-to-book ratio is $5/$10 = .50 (successful firms rarely have market prices less than book values).

Net income for PTC is currently $1 million. With 1 million shares, earnings per share (EPS) are $1, and the return on equity (ROE) is $1/$10 = 10%.[14] PTC thus sells for five times earnings (the price/earnings ratio is five). PTC has 200 shareholders, each of whom hold 5,000 shares each. The new plant will cost $2 million, so PTC has to issue 400,000 new shares ($5 × 400,000 = $2,000,000). There will thus be 1.4 million shares outstanding after the issue.

The ROE on the new plant is expected to be the same as for the company as a whole. In other words, net income is expected to go up by .10 × $2 million = $200,000. Total net income will thus be $1.2 million. The following things would occur:

1. With 1.4 million shares outstanding, EPS would be $1.2/1.4 = $.857 per share, down from $1.
2. The proportionate ownership of each old shareholder drops to 5,000/1.4 million = .36 percent from .50 percent.
3. If the stock continues to sell for five times earnings, the value would drop to 5 × .857 = $4.29, a loss of $.71 per share.
4. The total book value is the old $10 million plus the new $2 million for a total of $12 million. Book value per share falls to $12 million/1.4 million = $8.57 per share.

If we take this example at face value, dilution of proportionate ownership, accounting dilution, and market value dilution all occur. PTC's stockholders appear to suffer significant losses.

A Misconception   Our example appears to show that selling stock when the market-to-book ratio is less than 1 is detrimental to the stockholders. Some managers claim that this dilution occurs because EPS goes down whenever shares are issued where the market value is less than the book value.

When the market-to-book ratio is less than 1, increasing the number of shares does cause EPS to go down. Such a decline in EPS is accounting dilution, and accounting dilution always occurs under these circumstances.

Is it furthermore true that market value dilution will also necessarily occur? The answer is no. There is nothing incorrect about our example, but why the market value has decreased is not obvious. We discuss this next.

The Correct Arguments   In this example, the market price falls from $5 per share to $4.29. This is true dilution, but why does it occur? The answer has to do with the new project. PTC is going to spend $2 million on the new switching facility. However, as shown in Table 13.10, the total market value of the company is going to rise from $5 million to $6 million, an increase of only $1 million. This simply means that the NPV of the new project is −$1 million. With 1.4 million shares, the loss per share is $1/1.4 = .71, as we calculated before.

So, true dilution takes place for the shareholders of PTC because the NPV of the project is negative, not because the market-to-book ratio is less than 1. This negative NPV causes the market price to drop, and the accounting dilution has nothing to do with it.

[14] Return on equity (ROE) is equal to earnings per share divided by book value per share or, equivalently, net income divided by common equity. We discuss this and other financial ratios in some detail in Chapter 3.

	(1) Initial	After (2) Dilution	(3) No Dilution
Number of shares	1,000,000	1,400,000	1,400,000
Book value (B)	$10,000,000	$12,000,000	$12,000,000
Book value per share	$10	$8.57	$8.57
Market value	$5,000,000	$6,000,000	$8,000,000
Market price (P)	$5	$4.29	$5.71
Net income	$1,000,000	$1,200,000	$1,600,000
Return on equity (ROE)	0.10	0.10	0.13
Earnings per share (EPS)	$1	$0.86	$1.14
EPS/P	0.20	0.20	0.20
P/EPS	5	5	5
P/B	0.5	0.5	0.67
PROJECT			
Cost $2,000,000		NPV = −$1,000,000	NPV = $1,000,000

T A B L E 13.10

New issues and dilution: the case of Provincial Telephone Company

Suppose that the new project had a positive NPV of $1 million. The total market value would rise by $2 + 1 = $3 million. As shown in Table 13.10 (third column), the price per share rises to $5.71. Notice that accounting dilution still occurs because the book value per share still falls, but there is no economic consequence to that fact. The market value of the stock rises.

The $.71 increase in share value comes about because of the $1 million NPV, which amounts to an increase in value of about $.71 per share. Also, as shown, if the ratio of price to EPS remains at 5, EPS must rise to $5.71/5 = $1.14. Total earnings (net income) rises to $1.14 per share × 1.4 million shares = $1.6 million. Finally, ROE would rise to $1.6 million/$12 million = 13.33%.

CONCEPT QUESTIONS

1. What are the different kinds of dilution?

2. Is dilution important?

13.8 | ISSUING LONG-TERM DEBT

The general procedures followed in a public issue of bonds are the same as those for stocks. The issue must be registered with the OSC and any other relevant provincial securities commissions, there must be a prospectus, and so on. The registration statement for a public issue of bonds, however, is different from the one for common stock. For bonds, the registration statement must indicate an indenture.

Another important difference is that debt is more likely to be issued privately. There are two basic forms of direct private long-term financing: term loans and private placement.

Term loans are direct business loans. These loans have maturities of between one and five years. Most term loans are repayable during the life of the loan. The lenders include chartered banks, insurance companies, trust companies, and other lenders that specialize in corporate finance. The interest rate on a term loan may be either a fixed or floating rate.

Term loan lenders are regulated by the Office of the Superintendent of Financial Institutions (OSFI); trust companies are also governed by provincial regulators.

term loans
Direct business loans of, typically, one to five years.

Unlike the OSC in its securities regulation, OSFI does not approve each loan as it is made. Instead, it examines selected loans after they are made as it periodically inspects financial institutions. OSFI is responsible to ensure that financial institutions have sufficient capital for the risky loans on their books. In 1985, two western banks failed, and the Canada Deposit Insurance Corporation (CDIC) paid the depositors about $700 million. A few years later, Canadian chartered banks had to write off billions in bad loans to lesser developed countries. As a result, banking regulators around the world, including OSFI, implemented stricter capital rules.

private placements

Loans, usually long term in nature, provided directly by a limited number of investors.

Private placements are very similar to term loans except that the maturity is longer. Unlike term loans, privately placed debt usually employs an investment dealer. The dealer facilitates the process but does not underwrite the issue. A private placement does not require a full prospectus. Instead, the firm and its investment dealer only need to draw up an offering memorandum briefly describing the issuer and the issue. Most privately placed debt is sold to exempt purchasers. These are large insurance companies, pension funds, and other institutions, which, as sophisticated market participants, do not require the protection provided by studying a full prospectus.

The important differences between direct private long-term financing—term loans and private debt placements—and public issues of debt are:

1. Registration costs are lower for direct financing. A term loan avoids the cost of OSC registration. Private debt placements require an offering memorandum, but this is cheaper than preparing a full prospectus.

2. Direct placement is likely to have more restrictive covenants.

3. It is easier to renegotiate a term loan or a private placement in the event of a default. It is harder to renegotiate a public issue because hundreds of holders are usually involved.

4. Life insurance companies and pension funds dominate the private-placement segment of the bond market. Chartered banks are significant participants in the term loan market.

5. The costs of distributing bonds are lower in the private market because fewer buyers are involved and the issue is not underwritten.

The interest rates on term loans and private placements are usually higher than those on an equivalent public issue. This reflects the trade-off between a higher interest rate and more flexible arrangements in the event of financial distress, as well as the lower costs associated with private placements.

An additional, and very important, consideration is that the flotation costs associated with selling debt are much less than the costs associated with selling equity.

CONCEPT QUESTIONS

1. What is the difference between private and public bond issues?
2. A private placement is likely to have a higher interest rate than a public issue. Why?

13.9 | SUMMARY AND CONCLUSIONS

This chapter looks at how corporate securities are issued. The following are the main points:

1. The costs of issuing securities can be quite large. They are much lower (as a percentage) for larger issues.

2. The bought deal type of underwriting is far more prevalent for large issues than regular underwriting. This is probably connected to the savings available through Prompt Offering Prospectuses and concentrated selling efforts.

3. The direct and indirect costs of going public can be substantial. However, once a firm is public it can raise additional capital with much greater ease.

4. Rights offerings are cheaper than general cash offers. Even so, most new equity issues in the United States are underwritten general cash offers. In Canada, the bought deal is cheaper and dominates the new issue market.

Key Terms

prospectus (page 461)

red herring (page 461)

initial public offering (IPO) (page 461)

syndicate (page 462)

spread (page 463)

regular underwriting (page 463)

firm commitment underwriting (page 463)

best efforts underwriting (page 463)

bought deal (page 463)

ex rights (page 478)

holder-of-record date (page 478)

standby underwriting (page 479)

standby fee (page 479)

oversubscription privilege (page 479)

dilution (page 481)

term loans (page 483)

private placements (page 484)

Chapter Review Problems and Self-Test

13.1 **Flotation Costs**   The L5 Corporation is considering an equity issue to finance a new space station. A total of $10 million in new equity is needed. If the direct costs are estimated at 6 percent of the amount raised, how large does the issue need to be? What is the dollar amount of the flotation cost?

13.2 **Rights Offerings**   The Hadron Corporation currently has 4 million shares outstanding. The stock sells for $50 per share. To raise $30 million for a new particle accelerator, the firm is considering a rights offering at $20 per share. What is the value of a right in this case? The ex rights price?

Answers to Self-Test Problems

13.1 The firm needs to net $10 million after paying the 6 percent flotation costs. So the amount raised is given by:

Amount raised × (1 − .06) = $10 million

Amount raised = $10/.94   = $10.638 million

The total flotation cost is thus $638,000.

13.2 To raise $30 million at $20 per share, $30 million/$20 = 1.5 million shares will have to be sold. Before the offering, the firm is worth 4 million × $50 = $200 million. The issue raised $30 million and there will be 5.5 million shares outstanding. The value of an ex rights share will therefore be $230/5.5 = $41.82. The value of a right is thus $50 − 41.82 = $8.18.

Questions and Problems

Basic
(Questions 1–11)

1. **Rights Offerings**   Kilroy Co. is proposing a rights offering. Presently there are 20,000 shares outstanding at $45 each. There will be 5,000 new shares offered at $35 each.

    a. What is the new market value of the company?
    b. How many rights are associated with one of the new shares?
    c. What is the ex-rights price?
    d. What is the value of a right?
    e. Why might a company have a rights offering rather than a general cash offer?

2. **Rights Offerings**   The Clifford Corporation has announced a rights offer to raise $30 million for a new journal, the *Journal of Financial Excess*. This journal will review potential articles after the author pays a non-refundable reviewing fee of $3,000 per page. The stock currently sells for $30 per share, and there are 7,125,000 shares outstanding.

    a. What is the maximum possible subscription price? What is the minimum?
    b. If the subscription price is set at $20 per share, how many shares must be sold? How many rights will it take to buy one share?
    c. What is the ex rights price? What is the value of a right?
    d. Show how a shareholder with 1,000 shares before the offering and no desire (or money) to buy additional shares is not harmed by the rights offer.

3. **Rights**   Adonis Shoe Co. has concluded that additional equity financing will be needed to expand operations and that the needed funds are best obtained through a rights offering. It has correctly concluded that as a result of the rights offering, share price will fall from $75 to $67.50 ($75 is the rights-on price; $67.50 is the ex-rights price, also known as the *when-issued* price). The company is seeking $15 million in additional funds with a per-share subscription price equal to $50. How many shares were there before the offering? (Assume that the increment to the market value of the equity equals the gross proceeds from the offering.)

4. **Underwriting versus Rights**   Ren-Stimpy International is planning to raise fresh equity capital by selling a large new issue of common stock. Ren-Stimpy is currently a publicly traded corporation, and it is trying to choose between an underwritten cash offer and a rights offering (not underwritten) to current shareholders. Ren-Stimpy management is interested in minimizing the selling costs and has asked you for advice on the choice of issue methods. What is your recommendation and why?

5. **IPO Investment and Underpricing**   In 1980, a certain professor of finance bought 12 initial public offerings of common stock. He held each of these for approximately one month and then sold. The investment rule he followed was to submit a purchase order for every firm commitment initial public offering of oil and gas exploration companies. There were 22 of these offerings, and he submitted a purchase order for approximately $1,000 of stock for each of the companies. With 10 of these, no shares were allocated to this assistant professor. With 5 of the 12 offerings that were purchased, fewer than the requested number of shares were allocated.

    The year 1980 was very good for oil and gas exploration company owners: on average, of the 22 companies that went public, the stocks were selling for 80 percent above the offering price a month after the initial offering date. The assistant professor looked at his performance record and found the $8,400

Basic
(Continued)

invested in the 12 companies had grown to $10,000, a return of only about 20 percent (commissions were negligible). Did he have bad luck, or should he have expected to do worse than the average initial public offering investor? Explain.

6.   **IPO Underpricing**   Analyze the following statement: Because initial public offerings of common stock are always underpriced, an investor can make money by purchasing shares in these offerings.

7.   **IPO Underpricing**   The Bread Co. and the Butter Co. have both announced IPOs at $20 per share. One of these is undervalued by $4, the other is overvalued by $2, but you have no way of knowing which is which. You plan on buying 1,000 shares of each issue. If an issue is underpriced, it will be rationed, and only half your order will be filled. If you *could* get 1,000 shares in Bread and 1,000 shares in Butter, what would your profit be? What profit do you actually expect? What principle have you illustrated?

8.   **Calculating Flotation Costs**   The Beavis Corporation needs to raise $25 million to finance its expansion into new markets. The company will sell new shares of equity via a general cash offering to raise the needed funds. If the offer price is $40 per share and the company's underwriters charge a 6 percent spread, how many shares need to be sold?

9.   **Calculating Flotation Costs**   In the previous problem, if the filing fee and associated administrative expenses of the offering are $350,000, how many shares need to be sold now?

10.   **Calculating Flotation Costs**   The Utopia Poultry Co. has just gone public. Under a firm commitment agreement, Utopia received $9 for each of the 2 million shares sold. The initial offering price was $10 per share, and the stock rose to $12 per share in the first few minutes of trading. Utopia paid $150,000 in direct legal and other costs, and $70,000 in indirect costs. What was the flotation cost as a percentage of funds raised?

11.   **Price Dilution**   Jensen, Inc., has 25,000 shares of stock. Each share is worth $30, and the company's market value of equity is $750,000. Suppose the firm issues 10,000 new shares at the following prices: $30, $20, and $10. What will the effect be of each of these alternative offering prices on the existing price per share?

12.   **Dilution**   Mynor & Mayjor, Inc., wishes to expand its facilities. The company currently has 5 million shares outstanding and no debt. The stock sells for $50 per share, but the book value per share is $75. Net income for Mynor & Mayjor is currently $15 million. The new facility will cost $40 million, and it will increase net income by $1.5 million.

Intermediate
(Questions 12–19)

   a. Assuming a constant price-earnings ratio, what will the effect be of issuing new equity to finance the investment? To answer, calculate the new book value, the new total earnings, the new EPS, the new stock price, and the new market-to-book ratio. What is going on here?

   b. What would the new net income for Mynor & Mayjor have to be for the stock price to remain unchanged?

13.   **Dilution**   The Crawford Mining Corporation wants to diversify its operations. Some recent financial information for the company is shown below.

Stock price	$ 60
Number of shares	3,000
Total assets	$700,000
Total liabilities	$500,000
Net income	$ 15,000

Crawford Mining is considering an investment that has the same P/E ratio as the firm. The cost of the investment is $75,000, and it will be financed with a new equity issue. The return on the investment will equal Crawford's current ROE. What will happen to the book value per share, the market value per share, and the EPS? What is the NPV of this investment? Does dilution occur?

14. **Dilution** In the previous problem, what would the ROE on the investment have to be if we want the share price after the offering to be $60 per share (assume the P/E ratio still remains constant)? What is the NPV of this investment? Does any dilution occur?

15. **Rights** The ABC Company is considering a rights offer. The company has determined that the ex-rights price will be $35. The current price is $50 per share, and there are 8 million shares outstanding. The rights offer would raise a total of $80 million. What is the subscription price?

16. **Value of a Right** Show that the value of a right can be written as

$$\text{Value of a Right} = P_{RO} - P_X = (P_{RO} - P_S)/(N + 1)$$

where P_{RO}, P_S, and P_X stand for the rights-on price, the subscription price, and the ex-rights price, respectively, and N is the number of rights needed to buy one new share at the subscription price.

17. **Selling Rights** Heckman Corp. wants to raise $1.11 million via a rights offering. The company currently has 250,000 shares of common stock outstanding that sell for $30 per share. Its underwriter has set a subscription price of $12 per share and will charge Heckman a 7.5 percent spread. If you currently own 5,000 shares of stock in the company and decide not to participate in the rights offering, how much money can you get for selling your rights?

18. **Valuing a Right** Monolith Manufacturing Co. has announced a rights offer. The company has announced it will take four rights to buy a new share in the offering at a subscription price of $20. At the close of business the day before the ex-rights day, the company's stock sells for $40 per share. The next morning, you notice that the stock sells for $36 per share and the rights sell for $3 each. Are the stock and/or the rights correctly price on the ex-rights day? Describe a transaction where you could use these prices to create an immediate profit.

19. **Analysis of an IPO** The following material contains the cover page and summary of the prospectus for the initial public offering of the Pest Investigation Control Corporation (PICC), which is going public tomorrow with a firm commitment initial public offering managed by the investment banking firm of Erlanger and Ritter. Answer the following questions:

  a. Assume that you know nothing about PICC other than the information contained in the prospectus. Based on your knowledge of finance, what is your prediction for the price of PICC tomorrow? Provide a short explanation of why you think this will occur?

  b. Assume you have several thousand dollars to invest. When you get home from class tonight, you find that your stockbroker, whom you have not talked to for weeks, has called. She has left a message that PICC is going public tomorrow and that she can get you several hundred shares at the offering price if you call her back first thing in the morning. Discuss the merits of this opportunity.

PROSPECTUS   PICC
200,000 shares
PEST INVESTIGATION CONTROL CORPORATION
Of the shares being offered hereby, all 200,000 are being sold by the Pest Investigation Control Corporation, Inc. ("the Company"). Before the offering there has been no public market for the shares of PICC, and no guarantee can be given that any market will develop.

These securities have not been approved or disapproved by the OSC nor has the commission passed upon the accuracy or adequacy of this prospectus. Any representation to the contrary is a criminal offense.

	Price to Public	Underwriting Discount	Proceeds to Company*
Per share	$11.00	$1.10	$9.90
Total	$2,200,000	$220,000	$1,980,000

*Before deducting expenses estimated at $27,000 and payable by the company.

This is an initial public offering. The common shares are being offered, subject to prior sale, when, as, and if delivered to and accepted by the Underwriters and subject to approval of certain legal matters by their Counsel and by Counsel for the Company. The Underwriters reserve the right to withdraw, cancel, or modify such offer and to reject offers in whole or in part.

Erlanger and Ritter, Investment Bankers
July 12, 1995
Prospectus Summary

The Company	The Pest Investigation Control Corporation (PICC) breeds and markets toads and tree frogs as ecologically safe insect-control mechanisms.
The Offering	200,000 shares of common stock, no par value.
Listing	The Company will seek listing on the Toronto Stock Exchange.
Shares Outstanding	As of June 30, 1995, 400,000 shares of common stock were outstanding. After the offering, 600,000 shares of common stock will be outstanding.
Use of Proceeds	To finance expansion of inventory and receivables and general working capital, and to pay for country club memberships for certain finance professors.

Selected Financial Information
(amounts in thousands except per-share data)

	Fiscal Year Ended June 30		
	1993	1994	1995
Revenues	$60.00	$120.00	$240.00
Net earnings	3.80	15.90	36.10
Earnings per share	0.01	0.04	0.09

	As of June 30, 1995	
	Actual	As Adjusted for This Offering
Working capital	$ 8	$1,961
Total assets	511	2,464
Stockholders' equity	423	2,376

Suggested Readings

For further reading on underwriting in Canada and the role of the OSC see:

Ontario Securities Commission Annual Reports.

Hatch, J., and M. J. Robinson. *Investment Management in Canada,* 2nd ed. Scarborough: Prentice Hall Canada, 1989, chaps. 4 and 7.

For summaries of recent research, see:

Friedlan, J. M. "Understanding the IPO Market," *CFA Magazine,* March 1994, pp. 42–68.

Ibbotson, Roger G.; Jody L. Sindelar; and Jay R. Ritter. "Initial Public Offerings." *Journal of Applied Corporate Finance,* Spring 1994.

Rotenberg, W. "Pricing Initial Public Equity Offerings, Who Wins, Who Loses, and Why?" *Canadian Investment Review,* Spring 1990.

COST OF CAPITAL AND LONG-TERM FINANCIAL POLICY

Cost of Capital

Suppose you have just become the president of a large company and the first decision you face is whether to go ahead with a plan to renovate the company's warehouse distribution system. The plan will cost the company $50 million, and it is expected to save $12 million per year after taxes over the next six years.

This is a familiar problem in capital budgeting. To address it, you would determine the relevant cash flows, discount them, and, if the net present value is positive, take on the project; if the NPV is negative, you would scrap it. So far so good, but what should you use as the discount rate?

From our discussion of risk and return, you know that the correct discount rate depends on the riskiness of the warehouse distribution system. In particular, the new project would have a positive NPV only if its return exceeds what the financial markets offer on investments of similar risks. We called this minimum required return the cost of capital associated with the project.

Thus, to make the right decision as president, you must examine the returns that investors expect to earn on the securities represented in the pool of funds that would finance the project. You then use this information to arrive at an estimate of the project's cost of capital. Our primary purpose in this chapter is to describe how to do this. There are a variety of approaches to this task, and a number of conceptual and practical issues arise.

One of the most important concepts we develop is the weighted average cost of capital (WACC). This is the cost of capital for the firm as a whole, and it can be interpreted as the required return on the overall firm. In discussing the WACC, we recognize the fact that a firm normally raises capital in a variety of forms and that these different forms of capital may have different costs associated with them.

We also recognize in this chapter that taxes are an important consideration in determining the required return on an investment, because we are always interested in valuing the aftertax cash flows from a project. We therefore discuss how to incorporate taxes explicitly into our estimates of the cost of capital.

14.1 | THE COST OF CAPITAL: SOME PRELIMINARIES

In Chapter 11, we developed the security market line (SML) and used it to explore the relationship between the expected return on a security and its systematic risk. We concentrated on how the risky returns from buying securities looked from the viewpoint of, for example, a shareholder in the firm. This helped us understand more about the alternatives available to an investor in the capital markets.

In this chapter, we turn things around and look more closely at the other side of the problem, which is how these returns and securities look from the viewpoint of the companies that issue them. Note that the return an investor in a security receives is the cost of that security to the company that issued it.

Required Return versus Cost of Capital

When we say that the required return on an investment is, say, 10 percent, we usually mean the investment has a positive NPV only if its return exceeds 10 percent. Another way of interpreting the required return is to observe that the firm must earn 10 percent on the investment just to compensate its investors for the use of the capital needed to finance the project. This is why we could also say that 10 percent is the cost of capital associated with the investment.

To illustrate the point further, imagine that we were evaluating a risk-free project. In this case, how to determine the required return is obvious: We look at the capital markets and observe the current rate offered by risk-free investments, and we use this rate to discount the project's cash flows. Thus, the cost of capital for a risk-free investment is the risk-free rate.

If this project were risky, then, assuming that all the other information is unchanged, the required return is obviously higher. In other words, the cost of capital for this project, if it is risky, is greater than the risk-free rate, and the appropriate discount rate would exceed the risk-free rate.

We henceforth use the terms *required return, appropriate discount rate,* and *cost of capital* more or less interchangeably because, as the discussion in this section suggests, they all mean essentially the same thing. The key fact to grasp is that the cost of capital associated with an investment depends on the risk of that investment. This is one of the most important lessons in corporate finance, so it bears repeating: *The cost of capital depends primarily on the use of the funds, not the source.*

It is a common error to forget this crucial point and fall into the trap of thinking that the cost of capital for an investment depends primarily on how and where the capital is raised.

Financial Policy and Cost of Capital

We know that the particular mixture of debt and equity that a firm chooses to employ—its capital structure—is a managerial variable. In this chapter, we take the firm's financial policy as given. In particular, we assume the firm has a fixed debt/equity ratio that it maintains. This *D/E* ratio reflects the firm's target capital structure. How a firm might choose that ratio is the subject of our next chapter.

From our discussion, we know that a firm's overall cost of capital reflects the required return on the firm's assets as a whole. Given that a firm uses both debt and equity capital, this overall cost of capital is a mixture of the returns needed to compensate its creditors and its shareholders. In other words, a firm's cost of capital reflects both its cost of debt capital and its cost of equity capital. We discuss these costs separately in the following sections.

CONCEPT QUESTIONS

1. What is the primary determinant of the cost of capital for an investment?
2. What is the relationship between the required return on an investment and the cost of capital associated with that investment?

14.2 I THE COST OF EQUITY

cost of equity

The return that equity investors require on their investment in the firm.

We begin with the most difficult question on the subject of cost of capital: What is the firm's overall **cost of equity**? The reason this is a difficult question is that there is no way of directly observing the return that the firm's equity investors require on their investment. Instead, we must somehow estimate it. This section discusses two approaches to determining the cost of equity: the dividend growth model approach and the security market line (SML) approach.

The Dividend Growth Model Approach

The easiest way to estimate the cost of equity capital is to use the dividend growth model that we developed in Chapter 6. Recall that, under the assumption that the firm's dividend will grow at a constant rate, g, the price per share of the stock, P_0, can be written as:

$$P_0 = \frac{D_0 \times (1 + g)}{[R_E - g]} = \frac{D_1}{[R_E - g]}$$

where D_0 is the dividend just paid, and D_1 is the next period's projected dividend. Notice that we have used the symbol R_E (the E stands for equity) for the required return on the stock.

As we discussed in Chapter 6, we can arrange this to solve for R_E as follows:

$$R_E = (D_1/P_0) + g \qquad [14.1]$$

Since R_E is the return that the shareholders require on the stock, it can be interpreted as the firm's cost of equity capital.

Implementing the Approach   To estimate R_E using the dividend growth model approach, we obviously need three pieces of information: P_0, D_0, and g.[1] Of these, for a publicly traded, dividend-paying company, the first two can be observed directly, so they are easily obtainable. Only the third component, the expected growth rate in dividends, must be estimated.

For example, suppose Provincial Telephone Company, a large public utility, paid a dividend of $4 per share last year. The stock currently sells for $60 per share. You estimate the dividend will grow steadily at 6 percent per year into the indefinite future. What is the cost of equity capital for Provincial Telephone? Using the dividend growth model, the expected dividend for the coming year, D_1 is:

$$D_1 = D_0 \times (1 + g)$$
$$= \$4 \times (1.06)$$
$$= \$4.24$$

Given this, the cost of equity, R_E, is:

$$R_E = D_1/P_0 + g$$
$$= \$4.24/\$60 + .06$$
$$= 13.07\%$$

The cost of equity is thus 13.07%.

---

[1] Notice that if we have D_0 and g, we can simply calculate D_1 by multiplying D_0 by $(1 + g)$.

Estimating g To use the dividend growth model, we must come up with an estimate for g, the growth rate. There are essentially two ways of doing this: (1) use historical growth rates, or (2) use analysts' forecasts of future growth rates. Analysts' forecasts are available from the research departments of investment dealers. Naturally, different sources have different estimates, so one approach might be to obtain multiple estimates and then average them.

Alternatively, we might observe dividends for the previous, say, five years, and calculate the compound growth rate. For example, suppose we observe the following for the James Bay Company:

Year	Dividend
1991	$1.10
1992	1.20
1993	1.35
1994	1.40
1995	1.55

The compound growth rate, g, is the rate at which $1.10 grew to $1.55 during four periods of growth.

$$\$1.10 \ (1 + g)^4 = \$1.55$$

$$\$1.10 \ (\$1.55) = 0.7097 = 1/(1 + g)^4$$

$$g = 8.95\%$$

If historical growth has been volatile, the compound growth rate would be sensitive to our choice of beginning and ending years. In this case, it is better to calculate the year-to-year growth rates and average them.

Year	Dividend	Dollar Change	Percentage Change
1991	$1.10	—	—
1992	1.20	$.10	9.09%
1993	1.35	.15	12.50
1994	1.40	.15	3.70
1995	1.55	.15	10.71

Notice that we calculated the change in the dividend on a year-to-year basis and then expressed the change as a percentage. Thus, in 1992 for example, the dividend rose from $1.10 to $1.20, an increase of $.10. This represents a $.10/1.10 = 9.09% increase.

If we average the four growth rates, the result is (9.09 + 12.50 + 3.70 + 10.71)/4 = 9%, so we could use this as an estimate for the expected growth rate, g. In this case, averaging annual growth rates gives about the same answer as the compound growth rate. Other more sophisticated statistical techniques could be used, but they all amount to using past dividend growth to predict future dividend growth.[2]

An Alternative Approach Another way to find g starts with earnings retention. Consider a business whose earnings next year are expected to be the same as earnings this year unless a net investment is made. The net investment will be positive only if some earnings are not paid out as dividends, that is, only if some earnings are retained. This leads to the following equation:

$$\begin{matrix} \text{Earnings} \\ \text{next} \\ \text{year} \end{matrix} = \begin{matrix} \text{Earnings} \\ \text{this} \\ \text{year} \end{matrix} + \begin{matrix} \text{Retained} \\ \text{earnings} \\ \text{this year} \end{matrix} \times \begin{matrix} \text{Return on} \\ \text{retained} \\ \text{earnings} \end{matrix}$$

---

[2] Statistical techniques for calculating g include linear regression, geometric averaging, and exponential smoothing.

The increase in earnings is a function of both the retained earnings and the return on retained earnings.

We now divide both sides of the equation by earnings this year yielding

$$\frac{\text{Earnings next year}}{\text{Earnings this year}} = \frac{\text{Earnings this year}}{\text{Earnings this year}} + \frac{\dfrac{\text{Retained earnings}}{\text{this year}}}{\text{Earnings this year}} \times \begin{array}{c}\text{Return on}\\\text{retained}\\\text{earnings}\end{array}$$

The left side of the last equation is simply one plus the growth rate in earnings, which we write as $1 + g$.[3] The ratio of retained earnings to earnings is called the **retention ratio**. Thus we can write:

$1 + g = 1 + \text{Retention ratio} \times \text{Return on retained earnings}$

It is difficult for a financial analyst to determine the return to be expected on currently retained earnings, because the details on forthcoming projects are not generally public information. However, it is frequently assumed that the projects selected in the current year have the same risk and therefore the same anticipated return as projects in other years. Here, we can estimate the anticipated return on current retained earnings by the historical **return on equity** or **ROE**. After all, ROE is simply the return on the firm's entire equity, which is the return on the cumulation of all the firm's past projects.

We now have a simple way to estimate growth:

$g = \text{Retention ratio} \times \text{ROE}.$

retention ratio
Retained earnings divided by net income.

return on equity (ROE)
Net income after interest and taxes divided by average common shareholders' equity.

Advantages and Disadvantages of the Approach
Whichever way we estimate g, the primary advantage of the dividend growth model approach is its simplicity. It is both easy to understand and easy to use. There are a number of associated practical problems and disadvantages.

First and foremost, the dividend growth model is most applicable to companies that pay dividends. For companies that do not pay dividends, we can use the model and estimate g from earnings/growth. This is equivalent to assuming that one day dividends will be paid. Either way, the key underlying assumption is that the dividend grows at a constant rate. As our previous example illustrates, this will never be exactly the case. More generally, the model is really only applicable to cases where reasonably steady growth is likely to occur.

A second problem is that the estimated cost of equity is very sensitive to the estimated growth rate. An upward revision of g by just 1 percentage point, for example, increases the estimated cost of equity by at least a full percentage point. Since D_1 would probably be revised upwards as well, the increase would actually be somewhat larger than that.

Finally, this approach really does not explicitly consider risk. Unlike the SML approach (which we consider next), there is no direct adjustment for the riskiness of the investment. For example, there is no allowance for the degree of certainty or uncertainty surrounding the estimated growth rate in dividends. As a result, it is difficult to say whether or not the estimated return is commensurate with the level of risk.[4]

[3] Previously g referred to growth in dividends. However, the growth in earnings is equal to the growth rate in dividends in this context, because we assume the ratio of dividends to earnings is held constant.
[4] There is an implicit adjustment for risk because the current stock price is used. All other things being equal, the higher the risk, the lower the stock price. Further, the lower the stock price, the greater the cost of equity, again assuming all the other information is the same.

The SML Approach

In Chapter 11, we discussed the security market line (SML). Our primary conclusion was that the required or expected return on a risky investment depends on three things:

1. The risk-free rate, R_f.
2. The market risk premium, $E(R_M) - R_f$.
3. The systematic risk of the asset relative to average, which we called its beta coefficient, β.

Using the SML, the expected return on the company's equity, $E(R_E)$, can be written as:

$$E(R_E) = R_f + \beta_E \times [E(R_M) - R_f]$$

where β_E is the estimated beta for the equity. For the SML approach to be consistent with the dividend growth model, we drop the expectation sign, E, and henceforth write the required return from the SML, R_E, as:

$$R_E = R_f + \beta_E \times [R_M - R_f] \tag{14.2}$$

Implementing the Approach   To use the SML approach, we need a risk-free rate, R_f, an estimate of the market risk premium, $R_M - R_f$, and an estimate of the relevant beta, β_E. In Chapter 10 (Table 10.3), we saw that one estimate of the market risk premium (based on large capitalization Canadian common stocks) is around 7 percent. Three-month Canada Treasury bills are paying about 7.3 percent as this is written, so we use this as our risk-free rate. Beta coefficients for publicly traded companies are widely available. Appendix 11A showed how to calculate betas from historical returns.

To illustrate, in Chapter 11, we saw that Northern Telecom, had an estimated beta of .88 (Table 11.10). We could thus estimate Northern Telecom's cost of equity as:

$$R_{ntl} = R_f + \beta_{ntl} \times [R_M - R_f]$$

$$= 7.3\% + .88 \times (7.0\%)$$

$$= 13.46\%$$

Thus, using the SML approach, Northern Telecom's cost of equity is about 13.5 percent.

Advantages and Disadvantages of the Approach   The SML approach has two primary advantages: First, it explicitly adjusts for risk. Second, it is applicable to companies other than those with steady dividend growth. Thus, it may be useful in a wider variety of circumstances.

There are drawbacks, of course. The SML approach requires that two things be estimated, the market risk premium and the beta coefficient. To the extent that our estimates are poor, the resulting cost of equity is inaccurate. For example, our estimate of the market risk premium, 7 percent, is based on about 47 years of returns on a particular portfolio of stocks. Using different time periods or different stocks could result in very different estimates.

Finally, as with the dividend growth model, we essentially rely on the past to predict the future when we use the SML approach. Economic conditions can change very quickly, so, as always, the past may not be a good guide to the future. In the best of all worlds, the two approaches (dividend growth model and SML) are both applicable and both result in similar answers. If this happens, we might have some confidence in our estimates. We might also wish to compare the results to those for other, similar companies as a reality check.

E X A M P L E | **14.1**   **The Cost of Equity**

At the time of writing, stock in BC Telecom was trading on the TSE at $24\frac{3}{8}$. BC Telecom had a beta of 0.69.[5] The market risk premium historically has been around 7 percent, and the risk-free rate at this time was 7.3 percent. BC Telecom's last dividend was $1.24 per share, and some analysts expected the dividend would grow at 5 percent indefinitely. What is BC Telecom's cost of equity capital?

We can start by using the SML. Doing this, we find that the expected return on the common stock of BC Telephone is:

$$R_E = R_f + \beta_E \times [R_M - R_f]$$
$$= 7.31 + 0.69 \times 7\%$$
$$= 12.13\%$$

This suggests that 12.13 percent is BC Telecom's cost of equity. We next use the dividend growth model. The projected dividend is $D_0 \times (1 + g) = \$1.24 \times (1.05) = \$1.30$ so the expected return using this approach is:

$$R_E = D_1/P_0 + g$$
$$= \$1.30/\$24.375 + .05$$
$$= 10.09\%$$

Our two estimates are reasonably close, so we might just average them to find that BC Telecom's cost of equity is approximately 11 percent. When the two answers differ significantly, you should use the one in which you have the greater confidence. If the inputs are fairly reliable for the SML, it should be preferred over the growth model, which may not apply to all companies. |

The Cost of Equity in Rate Hearings

Suppose that Provincial Hydro, a regulated utility, has just applied for increases in the rates charged some of its customers. One test that regulators apply is called the "fair rate of return" rule. This means that they determine the fair rate of return on capital for the company and allow an increase in rates only if the company can show that revenues are insufficient to achieve this fair rate. For example, suppose a company had capital in the form of equity of $100 and net income of $9 providing a return of 9 percent. If the fair rate of return were 10 percent, the company would be allowed a rate increase sufficient to generate one additional dollar of net income.

Regulatory authorities determine the fair rate of return after hearing presentations by the company and by consumer groups. Since a higher fair rate of return helps make the case for rate increases, it is no surprise to find that consultants engaged by the company argue for a higher fair rate and consultants representing consumer groups argue for a lower fair rate. Because the fair rate of return depends on capital market conditions, consultants use the dividend growth approach and the SML approach along with other techniques.

---

[5] This beta was calculated by ScotiaMcLeod and reported along with other selected betas in Table 11.9.

Suppose that Provincial Hydro has presented the regulators with a cost of equity of 14 percent. You are a consultant for a consumer group. What flaws would you look for?

If you think that the cost of equity is too high, you should challenge the assumed growth rate in dividends. Also, the market risk premium used in the SML may be too high.[6] We saw in Chapter 10 that the market risk premium is lower if measured over a more recent period. If you are clever at working with these models and can remain unruffled when testifying, you may have career potential as a financial consultant.

> CONCEPT QUESTIONS
> **1.** What do we mean when we say that a corporation's cost of equity capital is 16 percent?
> **2.** What are two approaches to estimating the cost of equity capital?

14.3 | THE COSTS OF DEBT AND PREFERRED STOCK

In addition to ordinary equity, firms use debt and, to a lesser extent, preferred stock to finance their investments. As we discuss next, determining the costs of capital associated with these sources of financing is much easier than determining the cost of equity.

The Cost of Debt

The **cost of debt** is the return that the firm's long-term creditors demand on new borrowing. In principle, we could determine the beta for the firm's debt and then use the SML to estimate the required return on debt just as we estimate the required return on equity. This isn't really necessary, however.

cost of debt
The return that lenders require on the firm's debt.

Unlike a firm's cost of equity, its cost of debt can normally be observed either directly or indirectly, because the cost of debt is simply the interest rate the firm must pay on new borrowing, and we can observe interest rates in the financial markets. For example, if the firm already has bonds outstanding, then the yield to maturity on those bonds is the market-required rate on the firm's debt.

Alternatively, if we knew that the firm's bonds were rated, say, A, we can simply find out what the interest rate on newly issued A-rated bonds is. Either way, there is no need to actually estimate a beta for the debt since we can directly observe the rate we want to know.

There is one thing to be careful about, though. The coupon rate on the firm's outstanding debt is irrelevant here. That just tells us roughly what the firm's cost of debt was back when the bonds were issued, not what the cost of debt is today.[7] This is why we have to look at the yield on the debt in today's marketplace. For consistency with our other notation, we use the symbol R_D for the cost of debt.

---

[6] If you were the consultant for the company, you should counter that, at the time of writing, long-term bonds issued by Canadian utilities were yielding around 9 percent. Since equity is riskier than bonds, the cost of equity should be higher than 9 percent.
[7] The firm's cost of debt based on its historic borrowing is sometimes called the *embedded debt cost*.

E X A M P L E | **14.2**   **The Cost of Debt**

At the time of writing, Bell Canada had a bond outstanding with 28 years to maturity and a coupon rate of 9.40 percent. The bond was currently selling for 106.25 percent of its face value, or $106.25. What is Bell Canada's cost of debt?

Going back to Chapter 6, we need to calculate the yield to maturity on this bond. Using the approximation formula from Chapter 6:

$$\text{Yield} = \frac{\text{Coupon} + (\text{Face value} - \text{Price})/\text{Maturity}}{(\text{Price} + \text{Face value})/2}$$

$$= \frac{9.40 + (100 - 106.25)/28}{(100 + 106.25)/2}$$

$$= \frac{9.18}{103.13}$$

$$\text{Yield} = 8.90\%$$

The approximate yield is 8.90 percent. You can check that the yield to maturity is about 8.79 percent, assuming annual coupons. Bell Canada's cost of debt, R_D, is thus 8.79 percent.[8] |

The Cost of Preferred Stock

Determining the cost of fixed rate preferred stock is quite straightforward. As we discussed in Chapters 5 and 6, this type of preferred stock has a fixed dividend paid every period forever, so a share of preferred stock is essentially a perpetuity. The cost of preferred stock, R_P, is thus:

$$R_P = D/P_0 \qquad\qquad\qquad [14.3]$$

where D is the fixed dividend and P_0 is the current price per share of the preferred stock. Notice that the cost of preferred stock is simply equal to the dividend yield on the preferred stock. Alternatively, preferred stocks are rated in much the same way as bonds, so the cost of preferred stock can be estimated by observing the required returns on other, similarly rated shares of preferred stock.

E X A M P L E | **14.3**   **BC Tel's Cost of Preferred Stock**

On May 8, 1995, BC Tel preferred stock traded on the TSE with a dividend of $1.21 annually and a price of $18⅜. What is BC Tel's cost of preferred stock?

The cost of preferred stock is:

$$R_P = D/P_0$$

$$= \$1.21/18.375$$

$$= 6.59\%$$

So BC Tel's cost of preferred stock appears to be about 6.6 percent. |

> CONCEPT QUESTIONS
> 1. How can the cost of debt be calculated?
> 2. How can the cost of preferred stock be calculated?
> 3. Why is the coupon rate a bad estimate of a firm's cost of debt?

---

[8] For simplicity, we assume bond coupons are paid annually.

14.4 | THE WEIGHTED AVERAGE COST OF CAPITAL

Now that we have the costs associated with the main sources of capital that the firm employs, we need to worry about the specific mix. As we mentioned earlier, we take this mix (the firm's capital structure) as given for now.

One of the implications of using WACC for a project is that we are assuming that money is raised in the optimal proportions. For instance, if the optimal weight for debt is 25 percent, raising $100 million means that $25 million will come from new debt and $75 million from common and preferred shares. Practically speaking, the firm would not raise these sums simultaneously by issuing both debt and equity. Instead, the firm may issue just debt, or just equity, which, at that point, has the effect of upsetting the optimal debt ratio. Issuing just one type of security and temporarily upsetting the optimal weights presents no problem as long as a subsequent issue takes the firm back to the optimal ratio for which it is striving. The point is that the firm's capital structure weights may fluctuate within some range in the short term, but the target weights should always be used in computing WACC.

In Chapter 3, we mentioned that financial analysts frequently focus on a firm's total capitalization, which is the sum of its long-term debt and equity. This is particularly true in determining the cost of capital; short-term liabilities are often ignored in the process. Some short-term liabilities such as accounts payable and accrued wages rise automatically with sales increases and have already been incorporated into cash flow estimates. We ignore them in calculating the cost of capital to avoid the error of double counting. Other current liabilities, short-term bank borrowing for example, are excluded because they support seasonal needs and are not part of the permanent capital structure.[9]

The Unadjusted Weighted Average Cost of Capital

We use the symbol E (for equity) to stand for the market value of the firm's equity. We calculate this by taking the number of shares outstanding and multiplying it by the price per share. Similarly, we use the symbol D (for debt) to stand for the market value of the firm's debt. For long-term debt, we calculate this by multiplying the market price of a single bond by the number of bonds outstanding.

For multiple bond issues (as there normally would be), we repeat this calculation for each and then add the results. If there is debt that is not publicly traded (because it was privately placed with a life insurance company, for example), we must observe the yields on similar, publicly traded debt and estimate the market value of the privately held debt using this yield as the discount rate.

Finally, we use the symbol V (for value) to stand for the combined market value of the debt and equity:

$$V = E + D \qquad [14.4]$$

If we divide both sides by V, we can calculate the percentages of the total capital represented by the debt and equity:

$$100\% = E/V + D/V \qquad [14.5]$$

These percentages can be interpreted just like portfolio weights, and they are often called the capital structure weights.

---

[9] If a firm used short-term bank loans as part of its permanent financing, we would include their cost as part of the cost of debt.

For example, if the total market value of a company's stock were calculated as $200 million and the total market value of the company's debt were calculated as $50 million, the combined value would be $250 million. Of this total, E/V = $200/250 = 80%, so 80 percent of the firm's financing is equity and the remaining 20 percent is debt.

At this point, we have some weights (the debt and equity percentages) and some expected returns (the costs of debt and equity). We use this information to calculate the firm's overall cost of capital in the same way that we calculated a portfolio's expected return in Chapter 11: We multiply the required returns by their weights and then add them. In this context, the result is called the unadjusted **weighted average cost of capital (WACC)**:

weighted average cost of capital (WACC)
The weighted average of the costs of debt and equity.

$$\text{WACC (unadjusted)} = (E/V) \times R_E + (D/V) \times R_D \qquad [14.6]$$

where R_E and R_D are the required returns on (or the costs of) equity and debt, respectively.

We emphasize here that the correct way to proceed is to use the market values of the debt and equity. Under certain circumstances, such as a privately owned company, it may not be possible to get reliable estimates of these quantities. Even for publicly traded firms, market value weights present some difficulties. If there is a major shift in stock or bond prices, market value weights may fluctuate significantly so that WACC is quite another number by the time a weekend is over. In fact, because practitioners encounter some of these difficulties in computing WACC using market value weights, book values are usually the best alternative.

Taxes and the WACC

There is one final issue associated with the WACC. We called the preceding result the unadjusted WACC because we haven't considered taxes. Recall that we are always concerned with aftertax cash flows. If we are determining the discount rate appropriate to those cash flows, the discount rate also needs to be expressed on an aftertax basis.

As we discussed previously in various places in this book (and as we discuss later), the interest paid by a corporation is deductible for tax purposes. Payments to shareholders, such as dividends, are not. What this means, effectively, is that the government pays some of the interest provided the firm expects to have positive taxable income. Thus, in determining an aftertax discount rate, we need to distinguish between the pretax and the aftertax cost of debt.

To illustrate, suppose a firm borrows $1 million at 9 percent interest. The corporate tax rate is 40 percent. What is the aftertax interest rate on this loan? The total interest bill would be $90,000 per year. This amount is tax deductible, however, so the $90,000 interest reduces our tax bill by .40 × $90,000 = $36,000. The aftertax interest bill is thus $90,000 − 36,000 = $54,000. The aftertax interest rate is $54,000/$1 million = 5.4%.

Notice that, in general, the aftertax interest rate is simply equal to the pretax rate multiplied by one minus the tax rate. For example, using the preceding numbers, we find that the aftertax interest rate is 9% × (1 − .40) = 5.4%.

If we use the symbol T_C to stand for the corporate tax rate, the aftertax rate that we use in our WACC calculation can be written as $R_D \times (1 - T_C)$. Thus, once we consider the effect of taxes, the WACC is:

$$\text{WACC} = (E/V) \times R_E + (D/V) \times R_D \times (1 - T_C) \qquad [14.7]$$

From now on, when we speak of the WACC, this is the number we have in mind.

This WACC has a very straightforward interpretation. It is the overall return that the firm must earn on its existing assets to maintain the value of its stock. It is also the required return on any investments by the firm that have essentially the same risks as existing operations. So, if we were evaluating the cash flows from a proposed expansion of our existing operations, this is the discount rate we would use.

E X A M P L E | 14.4   **Calculating the WACC**

The B. B. Lean Company has 1.4 million shares of stock outstanding. The stock currently sells for $20 per share. The firm's debt is publicly traded and was recently quoted at 93 percent of face value. It has a total face value of $5 million, and it is currently priced to yield 11 percent. The risk-free rate is 8 percent, and the market risk premium is 7 percent. You've estimated that Lean has a beta of .74. If the corporate tax rate is 40 percent, what is the WACC of Lean Co.?

We can first determine the cost of equity and the cost of debt. From the SML, the cost of equity is $8\% + .74 \times 7\% = 13.18\%$. The total value of the equity is 1.4 million $\times$ $20 = $28 million. The pretax cost of debt is the current yield to maturity on the outstanding debt, 11 percent. The debt sells for 93 percent of its face value, so its current market value is $.93 \times 5 million = $4.65 million. The total market value of the equity and debt together is $28 + 4.65 = $32.65 million.

From here, we can calculate the WACC easily enough. The percentage of equity used by Lean to finance its operations is $28/$32.65 = 85.76\%$. Because the weights have to add up to 1, the percentage of debt is $1 - .8576 = 14.24\%$. The WACC is thus:

$$\text{WACC} = (E/V) \times R_E + (D/V) \times R_D \times (1 - T_C)$$
$$= .8576 \times 13.18\% + .1424 \times 11\% \times (1 - .40)$$
$$= 12.24\%$$

B. B. Lean thus has an overall weighted average cost of capital of 12.24 percent.

Solving the Warehouse Problem and Similar Capital Budgeting Problems

Now we can use the WACC to solve the warehouse problem that we posed at the beginning of the chapter. However, before we rush to discount the cash flows at the WACC to estimate NPV, we need to make sure we are doing the right thing.

Going back to first principles, we must find an alternative in the financial markets that is comparable to the warehouse renovation. To be comparable, an alternative must be of the same risk as the warehouse project. Projects that have the same risk are said to be in the same risk class.

The WACC for a firm reflects the risk and the target capital structure of the firm's existing assets as a whole. As a result, strictly speaking, the firm's WACC is the appropriate discount rate only if the proposed investment is a replica of the firm's existing operating activities.

In broader terms, whether or not we can use the firm's WACC to value the warehouse project depends on whether the warehouse project is in the same risk class as the firm. We assume that this project is an integral part of the overall business of the firm. In such cases, it is natural to think that the cost savings are as risky as the general cash flows of the firm, and the project is thus in the same risk class as the overall firm. More generally, projects like the warehouse renovation that are intimately related to the firm's existing operations are often viewed as being in the same risk class as the overall firm.

We can now see what the president should do. Suppose the firm has a target debt/equity ratio of $\frac{1}{3}$. In this case, E/V is .75 and D/V is .25. The cost of debt is 10 percent, and the cost of equity is 20 percent. Assuming a 40 percent tax rate, the WACC is:

$$\text{WACC} = (E/V) \times R_E + (D/V) \times (R_D \times (1 - T_C))$$
$$= .75 \times 20\% + .25 \times 10\% \times (1 - .40)$$
$$= 16.5$$

Recall that the warehouse project had a cost of $50 million and expected aftertax cash flows (the cost savings) of $12 million per year for six years. The NPV is thus:

$$\text{NPV} = -\$50 + \$12/(1 + \text{WACC})^1 + \ldots + \$12/(1 + \text{WACC})^6$$

Since the cash flows are in the form of an ordinary annuity, we can calculate this NPV using 16.5 percent (the WACC) as the discount rate as follows:

$$\text{NPV} = -\$50 + \$12 \times [1 - (1/(1 + 0.165)^6)]/0.165$$
$$= -\$50 + \$12 \times 3.6365$$
$$= -\$6.36$$

Should the firm take on the warehouse renovation? The project has a negative NPV using the firm's WACC. This means the financial markets offer superior projects in the same risk class (namely, the firm itself). The answer is clear: The project should be rejected.

For future reference, Table 14.1 summarizes our discussion of the WACC.

T A B L E 14.1

Summary of capital cost calculations

The Cost of Equity, R_E

□ Dividend growth model approach (from Chapter 6):
$R_E = D_1/P_0 + g$,
where D_1 is the expected dividend in one period, g is the dividend growth rate, and P_0 is the current stock price.

□ SML approach (from Chapter 11):
$R_E = R_f + (R_M - R_f) \times \beta_E$,
where R_f is the risk-free rate, R_M is the expected return on the overall market, and β_E is the systematic risk of the equity.

The Cost of Debt, R_D

□ For a firm with publicly held debt, the cost of debt can be measured as the yield to maturity on the outstanding debt. The coupon rate is irrelevant. Yield to maturity is covered in Chapter 6.

□ If the firm has no publicly traded debt, the cost of debt can be measured as the yield to maturity on similarly rated bonds (bond ratings are discussed in Chapter 12).

The Weighted Average Cost of Capital, *WACC*

□ The firm's WACC is the overall required return on the firm as a whole. It is the appropriate discount rate to use for cash flows similar in risk to the overall firm.

□ The WACC is calculated as
$\text{WACC} = E/V \times R_E + D/V \times R_D \times (1 - T_C)$,
where T_C is the corporate tax rate, E is the market value of the firm's equity, D is the market value of the firm's debt, and $V = E + D$. Note that E/V is the percentage of the firm's financing (in market value terms) that is equity, and D/V is the percentage that is debt.

E X A M P L E | 14.5   **Using the WACC**

A firm is considering a project that will result in initial cash savings of $5 million at the end of the first year. These savings will grow at the rate of 5 percent per year. The firm has a debt/equity ratio of 0.5, a cost of equity of 29.2 percent, and a cost of debt of 10 percent. The cost-saving proposal is closely related to the firm's core business, so it is viewed as having the same risks as the overall firm. Should the firm take on the project?

Assuming a 40 percent tax rate, the firm should take on this project if it costs less than $30.36 million. To see this, first note that the PV is:

$$PV = \$5 \text{ million}/[\text{WACC} - 0.05]$$

This is an example of a growing perpetuity as discussed in Chapter 6. The WACC is:

$$
\begin{aligned}
\text{WACC} &= (E/V) \times R_E + (D/V) \times R_D \times (1 - T_C) \\
&= 2/3 \times 29.2\% + 1/3 \times 10\% \times (1 - .40) \\
&= 21.47\%
\end{aligned}
$$

The PV is thus:

$$PV = \$5 \text{ million}/[.2147 - .05] = \$30.36 \text{ million}$$

The NPV is positive only if the cost is less than $30.36 million. |

> CONCEPT QUESTIONS
> 1. How is the WACC calculated?
> 2. Why do we multiply the cost of debt by $(1 - T_C)$ when we compute the WACC?
> 3. Under what conditions is it correct to use the WACC to determine NPV?

14.5 | DIVISIONAL AND PROJECT COSTS OF CAPITAL

As we have seen, using the WACC as the discount rate for future cash flows is only appropriate when the proposed investment is similar to the firm's existing activities. This is not as restrictive as it sounds. If we were in the pizza business, for example, and we were thinking of opening a new location, the WACC is the discount rate to use. The same is true of a retailer thinking of opening a new store, a manufacturer thinking of expanding production, or a consumer products company thinking of expanding its markets.

Nonetheless, despite the usefulness of the WACC as a benchmark, there are clearly situations where the cash flows under consideration have risks distinctly different from those of the overall firm. We consider how to cope with this problem next.

The SML and the WACC

When we are evaluating investments with risks substantially different from the overall firm, the use of the WACC can potentially lead to poor decisions. Figure 14.1 illustrates why.

In Figure 14.1, we have plotted an SML corresponding to a risk-free rate of 7 percent and a market risk premium of 8 percent. To keep things simple, we consider an all-equity company with a beta of 1. As we have indicated, the WACC and the cost of equity are exactly equal to 15 percent for this company since there is no debt.

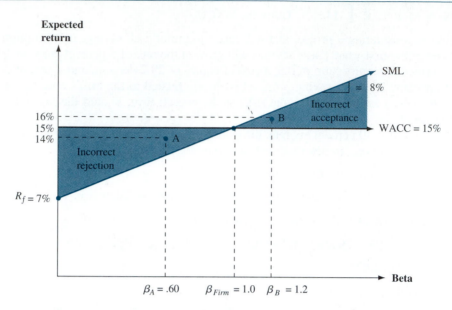

If a firm uses its WACC to make accept/reject decisions for all types of projects, it will have a tendency toward incorrectly accepting risky projects and incorrectly rejecting less risky projects.

Suppose our firm uses its WACC to evaluate all investments. This means any investment with a return of greater than 15 percent is accepted and any investment with a return of less than 15 percent is rejected. We know from our study of risk and return, however, that a desirable investment is one that plots above the SML. As Figure 14.1 illustrates, using the WACC for all types of projects can result in the firm incorrectly accepting relatively risky projects and incorrectly rejecting relatively safe ones.

For example, consider point A. This project has a beta of .6 compared to the firm's beta of 1.0. It has an expected return of 14 percent. Is this a desirable investment? The answer is yes, because its required return is only:

$$\text{Required return} = R_f + \beta \times (R_M - R_f)$$
$$= 7\% + .60 \times 8\%$$
$$= 11.8\%$$

However, if we use the WACC as a cutoff, this project would be rejected because its return is less than 15 percent. This example illustrates that a firm using its WACC as a cutoff tends to reject profitable projects with risks less than those of the overall firm.

At the other extreme, consider point B. This project offers a 16 percent return, which exceeds the firm's cost of capital. This is not a good investment, however, because its return is inadequate, given its level of systematic risk. Nonetheless, if we use the WACC to evaluate it, it appears to be attractive. So the second error that arises if we use the WACC as a cutoff is that we tend to make unprofitable investments with risks greater than the overall firm. As a consequence, through time, a firm that uses its WACC to evaluate all projects has a tendency to both accept unprofitable investments and become increasingly risky.

Divisional Cost of Capital

The same type of problem with the WACC can arise in a corporation with more than one line of business. Imagine, for example, a corporation that has two divisions, a regulated telephone company and a high-tech communications company. The first of these (the telephone company) has relatively low risk; the second has relatively high risk. Companies like this spanning several industries are very common in Canada.

In this case, the firm's overall cost of capital is really a mixture of two different costs of capital, one for each division. If the two divisions were competing for resources, and the firm used a single WACC as a cutoff, which division would tend to be awarded greater funds for investment?

The answer is that the riskier division would tend to have greater returns (ignoring the greater risk), so it would tend to be the winner. The less glamourous operation might have great profit potential that ends up being ignored. Large corporations in Canada and the United States are aware of this problem and many work to develop separate divisional costs of capital.

The Pure Play Approach

We've seen that using the firm's WACC inappropriately can lead to problems. How can we come up with the appropriate discount rates in such circumstances? Because we cannot observe the returns on these investments, there generally is no direct way of coming up with a beta, for example. Instead, what we must do is examine other investments outside the firm that are in the same risk class as the one we are considering and use the market-required returns on these investments as the discount rate. In other words, we determine what the cost of capital is for such investments by locating some similar investments in the marketplace.

For example, going back to our telephone division, suppose we wanted to come up with a discount rate to use for that division. What we can do is to identify several other phone companies that have publicly traded securities. We might find that a typical phone company has a beta of .40, AA-rated debt, and a capital structure that is about 50 percent debt and 50 percent equity. Using this information, we could develop a WACC for a typical phone company and use this as our discount rate.

Alternatively, if we are thinking of entering a new line of business, we would try to develop the appropriate cost of capital by looking at the market-required returns on companies already in that business. In the language of Bay Street, a company that focusses only on a single line of business is called a *pure play*. For example, if you wanted to bet on the price of crude oil by purchasing common stocks, you would try to identify companies that dealt exclusively with this product because they would be the most affected by changes in the price of crude oil. Such companies would be called pure plays on the price of crude oil.

What we try to do here is to find companies that focus as exclusively as possible on the type of project in which we are interested. Our approach, therefore, is called the **pure play approach** to estimating the required return on an investment.

pure play approach
Use of a WACC that is unique to a particular project.

The pure play approach is also useful in finding the fair rate of return for utility companies. Going back to our earlier example, we use the pure play approach if Provincial Hydro is not a public company. Because almost all electric utilities in Canada are crown corporations, consultants for the two sides use Canadian telephone companies and U.S. public utilities for comparison.

In Chapter 3, we discussed the subject of identifying similar companies for comparison purposes. The same problems that we described there come up here. The most obvious one is that we may not be able to find any suitable companies. In this case, how to determine a discount rate objectively becomes a very difficult question. Alternatively, a comparable company may be found but the comparison complicated by a different capital structure. In this case, we have to adjust the beta for the effect of leverage. Appendix 14A on adjusted present value (APV) explains how to do this.[10] The important thing is to be aware of the issue so we at least reduce the possibility of the kinds of mistakes that can arise when the WACC is used as a cutoff on all investments.

The Subjective Approach

Because of the difficulties that exist in objectively establishing discount rates for individual projects, firms often adopt an approach that involves making subjective adjustments to the overall WACC. To illustrate, suppose a firm has an overall WACC of 14 percent. It places all proposed projects into four categories as follows:

Category	Examples	Adjustment Factor	Discount Rate
High risk	New products	+6%	20%
Moderate risk	Cost savings, expansion of existing lines	+0	14
Low risk	Replacement of existing equipment	−4	10
Mandatory	Pollution control equipment	n.a.*	n.a.

*n.a. = Not applicable

The effect of this crude partitioning is to assume that all projects either fall into one of three risk classes or else they are mandatory. In this last case, the cost of capital is irrelevant since the project must be taken. Examples are safety and pollution control projects. With the subjective approach, the firm's WACC may change through time as economic conditions change. As this happens, the discount rates for the different types of projects also change.

Within each risk class, some projects presumably have more risk than others, and the danger of incorrect decisions still exists. Figure 14.2 illustrates this point. Comparing Figures 14.1 and 14.2, we see that similar problems exist, but the magnitude of the potential error is less with the subjective approach. For example, the project labelled A would be accepted if the WACC were used, but it is rejected once it is classified as a high-risk investment. What this illustrates is that some risk adjustment, even if it is subjective, is probably better than no risk adjustment.

It would be better, in principle, to determine the required return objectively for each project separately. However, as a practical matter, it may not be possible to go much beyond subjective adjustments because either the necessary information is unavailable or else the cost and effort required are simply not worthwhile.

> CONCEPT QUESTIONS
> 1. What are the likely consequences if a firm uses its WACC to evaluate all proposed investments?
> 2. What is the pure play approach to determining the appropriate discount rate? When might it be used?

---

[10] Another approach is to develop an accounting beta using a formula that makes beta a function of the firm's financial ratios.

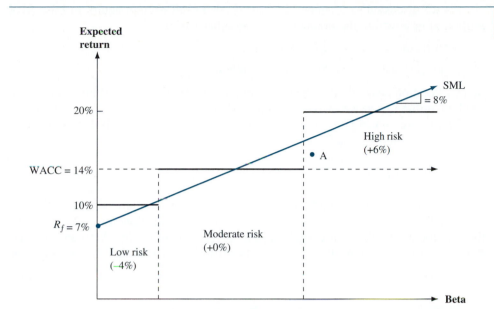

FIGURE 14.2

The security market line (SML) and the subjective approach

With the subjective approach, the firm places projects into one of several risk classes. The discount rate used to value the project is then determined by adding (for high risk) or subtracting (for low risk) an adjustment factor to or from the firm's WACC.

14.6 | FLOTATION COSTS AND THE WEIGHTED AVERAGE COST OF CAPITAL

So far, we have not included issue or flotation costs in our discussion of the weighted average cost of capital. If a company accepts a new project, it may be required to issue or float new bonds and stocks. This means the firm incurs some costs that we call flotation costs. The nature and magnitude of flotation costs are discussed in some detail in Chapter 13.

Sometimes it is suggested that the firm's WACC should be adjusted upward to reflect flotation costs. This is really not the best approach because, once again, the required return on an investment depends on the risk of the investment, not the source of the funds. This is not to say that flotation costs should be ignored. Because these costs arise as a consequence of the decision to undertake a project, they are relevant cash flows. We therefore briefly discuss how to include them in a project analysis.

The Basic Approach

We start with a simple case. The Spatt Company, an all-equity firm, has a cost of equity of 20 percent. Since this firm is 100 percent equity, its WACC and its cost of equity are the same. Spatt is contemplating a large-scale $100 million expansion of its existing operations. The expansion would be funded by selling new stock.

Based on conversations with its investment dealer, Spatt believes its flotation costs would run 10 percent of the amount issued. This means that Spatt's proceeds from the equity sale would be only 90 percent of the amount sold. When flotation costs are considered, what is the cost of the expansion?

As we discussed in Chapter 13, Spatt needs to sell enough equity to raise $100 million after covering the flotation costs. In other words:

$100 million = (1 − .10) × Amount raised

Amount raised = $100/.90 = $111.11 million

Spatt's flotation costs are thus $11.11 million, and the true cost of the expansion is $111.11 million once we include flotation costs.

Things are only slightly more complicated if the firm uses both debt and equity. For example, suppose Spatt's target capital structure is 60 percent equity, 40 percent debt. The flotation costs associated with equity are still 10 percent, but the flotation costs for debt are less, say 5 percent.

Earlier, when we had different capital costs for debt and equity, we calculated a weighted average cost of capital using the target capital structure weights. Here, we do much the same thing. We can calculate a weighted average flotation cost, f_A, by multiplying the equity flotation cost, f_E, by the percentage of equity (E/V) and the debt flotation cost, f_D, by the percentage of debt (D/V) and then adding the two together:

$$f_A = (E/V) \times f_E + (D/V) \times f_D \qquad [14.8]$$
$$= 60\% \times .10 + 40\% \times .05$$
$$= 8\%$$

The weighted average flotation cost is thus 8 percent. What this tells us is that for every dollar in outside financing needed for new projects, the firm must actually raise $1/(1 − .08) = $1.087. In our previous example, the project cost is $100 million when we ignore flotation costs. If we include them, the true cost is $100/(1 − f_A) = $100/.92 = $108.7 million.

In taking issue costs into account, the firm must be careful not to use the wrong weights. The firm should use the target weights, even if it can finance the entire cost of the project with either debt or equity. The fact that a firm can finance a specific project with debt or equity is not directly relevant. If a firm has a target debt/equity ratio of 1, for example, but chooses to finance a particular project with all debt, it has to raise additional equity later to maintain its target debt/equity ratio. To take this into account, the firm should always use the target weights in calculating the flotation cost.[11]

E X A M P L E | 14.6   Calculating the Weighted Average Flotation Cost

The Weinstein Corporation has a target capital structure that is 80 percent equity, 20 percent debt. The flotation costs for equity issues are 20 percent of the amount raised; the flotation costs for debt issues are 6 percent. If Weinstein needs $65 million for a new manufacturing facility, what is the true cost once flotation costs are considered?

We first calculate the weighted average flotation cost, f_A:

$$f_A = (E/V) \times f_E + (D/V) \times f_D$$
$$= 80\% \times .20 + 20\% \times .06$$
$$= 17.2\%$$

The weighted average flotation cost is thus 17.2 percent. The project cost is $65 million when we ignore flotation costs. If we include them, the true cost is $65/(1 −

---

[11] Since flotation costs may be amortized for tax purposes, there is a tax adjustment as explained in Appendix 14A.

f_A) = \$65/.828 = \$78.5 million, again illustrating that flotation costs can be a considerable expense.

Flotation Costs and NPV

To illustrate how flotation costs can be included in an NPV analysis, suppose the Tripleday Printing Company is currently at its target debt/equity ratio of 100 percent. It is considering building a new \$500,000 printing plant. This new plant is expected to generate aftertax cash flows of \$73,150 per year forever. There are two financing options:

1. A \$500,000 new issue of common stock. The issuance costs of the new common stock would be about 10 percent of the amount raised. The required return on the company's new equity is 20 percent.

2. A \$500,000 issue of 30-year bonds. The issuance costs of the new debt would be 2 percent of the proceeds. The company can raise new debt at 10 percent. The company faces a 40 percent combined federal/provincial tax rate.

What is the NPV of the new printing plant?

To begin, since printing is the company's main line of business, we use the company's weighted average cost of capital to value the new printing plant:

$$\text{WACC} = (E/V) \times R_E + (D/V) \times R_D \times (1 - T_C)$$
$$= .50 \times 20\% + .50 \times 10\% \times (1 - .40)$$
$$= 13.0\%$$

Since the cash flows are \$73,150 per year forever, the PV of the cash flows at 13.0 percent per year is:

$$\text{PV} = \$73,150/.13 = \$562,692$$

If we ignore flotation costs, the NPV is:

$$\text{NPV} = \$562,692 - 500,000 = \$62,692$$

The project generates an NPV greater than zero, so it should be accepted.

What about financing arrangements and issue costs? Since new financing must be raised, the flotation costs are relevant. From the information just given, we know that the flotation costs are 2 percent for debt and 10 percent for equity. Since Tripleday uses equal amounts of debt and equity, the weighted average flotation cost, f_A, is:

$$f_A = (E/V) \times f_E + (D/V) \times f_D$$
$$= .50 \times 10\% + .50 \times 2\%$$
$$= 6\%$$

Remember that the fact that Tripleday can finance the project with all debt or equity is irrelevant. Because Tripleday needs \$500,000 to fund the new plant, the true cost, once we include flotation costs, is \$500,000/(1 − f_A) = \$500,000/.94 = \$531,915. Since the PV of the cash flows is \$562,692, the plant has an NPV of \$562,692 − 531,915 = \$30,777, so it is still a good investment. However, its return is lower than we initially might have thought.

CONCEPT QUESTIONS

1. What are flotation costs?
2. How are flotation costs included in an NPV analysis?

14.7 | CALCULATING WACC FOR BOMBARDIER

We illustrate the practical application of the weighted average cost of capital by calculating it for a prominent Canadian company. Bombardier is a large, multinational manufacturer of transportation equipment and motorized consumer products as well as aerospace and defence products. Bombardier's revenue for 1994 was $4.77 billion with net income of $175.6 million.

As we pointed out, WACC calculations depend on market values as observed on a particular date. In this application, market values for Bombardier were observed on May 10, 1995.[12] Other information comes from annual statements at Bombardier's year-end on January 31, 1994.

Estimating Financing Proportions

Table 14.2 shows an abbreviated balance sheet for Bombardier. Recall from our earlier discussion that when calculating the cost of capital, it is common to ignore short-term financing, such as payables and accruals. We also ignore short-term debt unless it is a permanent source of financing. As both current assets and current liabilities are ignored for our purposes, increases (or decreases) in current liabilities are netted against changes in current assets. Leases are included in long-term debt for the purposes of this analysis.

As a multinational company, Bombardier does business in many countries and in many currencies. Its financing reflects its multinational nature. As you can see in Table 14.3, Bombardier and its subsidiaries have issued bonds in Swiss francs, French francs, Austrian schillings, U.S. dollars, and Canadian dollars. The company has issued fixed coupon and floating-rate debt. Some of the bonds pay interest at a rate linked to LIBOR, the London Interbank Offer Rate. As described in more detail in Chapter 22, LIBOR is a base rate for international transactions similar to the prime rate for domestic floating-rate debt. Table 14.3 also indicates that "following an agreement with a financial institution" certain debt issued in Canadian dollars is payable in U.S. dollars. These agreements are currency swaps and are also described in more detail in Chapter 22.

Ideally, we should calculate the market value of all sources of financing and determine the relative weights of each source. The difficulty of finding the market value of some non-traded bonds for Bombardier requires us to use book values for

T A B L E 14.2

Book value balance sheet on January 31, 1994 ($ millions)

Assets		Liabilities and Equity	
Current	$3,517	Current	$1,746
Long-term	976	Deferred taxes and other	111
		Long-term debt	1,254
		Equity	
		Preferred shares	33
		Common equity	
		Common shares	699
		Retained earnings	650
Total	$4,493	Total	$4,493

[12] "The Markets," *Financial Post*, May 11, 1995.

Bombardier, Inc.	
• Debentures, 8.3%, maturing in July 2003, with a nominal value of $150,000,000	$ 150.0
• Notes with a sinking fund, maturing in September 2003, with a nominal value of U.S. $69,000,000 at 6.06%, and a nominal value of U.S. $31,000,000 at 6.32%	132.7
• Debentures, 11.10%, maturing in May 2001, with a nominal value of $100,000,000	100.0
• Notes, 6%, maturing in April 1998, with a value of 30,275,000 Swiss francs (32,015,000 Swiss francs as at January 31, 1993)	27.5
• Notes, LIBOR rate plus at most 15/100 of 1%, with a nominal value of U.S. $25,000,000, maturing in September 1994, and a nominal value of U.S. $50,000,000 maturing in February 1995, 3.25% to 3.50% (3.71% to 3.81% as at January 31, 1993)	99.5
• Term loan, 3.58%, maturing in August 1997, with a nominal value of U.S. $75,000,000	99.5
• Notes, 4.75% to 5.2%, matured in 1993	
Learjet, Inc.	
• Notes, 6.94%, maturing in June 2000, with a nominal value of U.S. $50,000,000	66.4
• Loan, 9.02%, maturing in May 1998, with a nominal value of U.S. $25,000,000	33.2
• Notes, 12.31%, maturing in November 1995 with a nominal value of $29,175,000. Following an agreement with a financial institution, this debt is effectively payable for U.S. $25,000,000, with interest at 9.55%.	29.2
Bombardier-Rotax GmbH	
• Loans, 4.63% to 7.75%, payable in Austrian schillings, maturing from 1995 to 1998	18.7
Société ANF-Industrie S.A.	
• Loans, 5% to 13%, payable in French francs, maturing from 1995 to 1996	20.1
Bombardier-Concarril, S.A. de C.V.	
• Loans interest at LIBOR rate plus 1%, payable in U.S. $ maturing in December 2006, 4.5% (4.69% as at January 31, 1993)	13.1
Bombardier-Nordtrac OY	
• Loans, 5% to 10.4%, payable in Finnish marks, maturing from 1995 to 2001	13.0
Amounts payable under capital leases, 5.95% to 15%, maturing from 1995 to 2006	7.3
Other, bearing interest up to 10.4%, payable in various currencies, maturing from 1995 to 2005	25.8
	836.0
Exchange adjustment arising from hedging foreign currencies to U.S. dollars	4.0
	840.0
Amounts due within one year	63.5
Total Bombardier	
BCG	
Bombardier Capital, Inc.	
• Notes, 8.14%, maturing in July 1997, with a nominal value of U.S. $50,000,000. Following an agreement with a financial institution, the effective rate interest is at LIBOR plus 1.14%	66.4
• Notes, 8.51%, maturing in July 1999, with a nominal value of U.S. $100,000,000. Following an agreement with a financial institution, the effective rate interest is at LIBOR plus 1.04%	132.7
Bombardier Real Estate Ltd.	
• Mortgage bonds, 7.54% to 11%, maturing from 2001 to 2016	60.9
	260.0
Amounts due within one year	1.5
Total BCG	258.5
Total	$1035.0

T A B L E 14.3

Bombardier's long-term debt, 1994

The repayment requirements on the long-term debt during the next five fiscal years ending January 31 are as follows.

	Bombardier, Inc. Consolidated
1995	$ 65.0
1996	129.4
1997	21.0
1998	194.4
1999	78.1

Source: *Bombardier Annual Report, 1994.*

debt. It is much more important to use the market value for the calculation of equity weights than for debt, as the market value of common equity differs markedly from the book value.

Market Value Weights for Bombardier

To find the market value weights of preferred and common stock we find the total market value of each. The market values are calculated as the number of shares times the share price. The figures for Bombardier, as of January 31, 1994, were 1,324,200 preferred shares and 164,974,351 common shares. Multiplying each by its price gives:

Security	Book Value	Market Price	Market Value
Interest-bearing debt	$1,365	—	$1,365
Preferred stock	33	$25	33
Class A & B common	1,349	$29	4,784
			$6,182

Proportions	Dollars	Market Value Weights
Debt	$1,365	22.08%
Preferred stock	33	0.54
Common stock	4,784	77.38
	$6,182	100.00%

As you can see from the market value weights, Bombardier uses common equity and debt for the majority of its financing needs, preferred stock is almost insignificant.[13]

Cost of Debt

The beforetax cost of debt for Bombardier is its marginal cost of debt or the amount it would have to pay to issue debt now. We estimate the cost of debt using the yield to maturity on 15-year corporate debt in May 1995, 9.25 percent. To convert to an aftertax cost, we use the average tax rate for Bombardier during 1994, 15.25 percent.

$$R_D = \text{YTM}(1 - Tc) = 9.25\%(1 - .1525) = 7.84\%$$

Cost of Preferred Stock

We use current market values for Bombardier's preferred stock to determine the cost of this source of capital. Bombardier's preferred stock carries a dividend of $1.88 and is priced at $25.

$$R_P = D_P/P_P = \$1.88/\$25 = 7.50\%$$

Cost of Common Stock

To determine the cost of common stock for Bombardier, we use both the dividend valuation model and CAPM. We then average these two figures.

To calculate the cost of equity using the dividend valuation model, we need a growth rate for Bombardier. A geometric regression would be the most accurate; however, a geometric average is simpler and nearly as accurate. We use EPS figures to determine the growth rate for Bombardier.

---

[13] The adjustments we discuss make the debt figure different from the one in Table 14.2.

Year	EPS
1994	2.24
1993	1.70
1992	1.46
1991	1.41
1990	1.36
1989	0.78
1988	1.00
1987	0.64
1986	0.33
1985	0.17
1984	0.15

Dividend Valuation Model Growth Rate

$$(1 + g)^{10} = (2.24/0.15)$$

$$1 + g = (14.93)^{1/11}$$

$$g = 31.04\%$$

The geometric growth rate over the period 1984–94 was 31.04 percent. This rather high growth rate is likely a supernormal one in the language of Chapter 6. Since the formula calls for a normal growth rate continuing indefinitely, we adjust the calculated growth rate downward by 50 percent to get:[14]

$50\% \times 31.045 = 15.52\%$.

Dividend valuation model $= D_1/P_0 + g$

To get next year's dividend, D_1, we adjust the current dividend of $.40 for projected growth:

$D_1 = D_0(1 + g) = \$.40\,(1.1552) = \$.46$

$P_0 = \$29$

$R_E = D_1/P_0 + g$

$\quad = \$.46/29 + .1552$

$\quad = 17.11\%$

CAPM

$\beta = 1.56$

Market risk premium $= 6.58\%$ [15]

Risk free rate $= 7.30\%$

$RE = R_f + \beta\,(\text{Market risk premium})$

$\quad = 7.30\% + 1.57(6.58\%)$

$\quad = 17.63\%$

Cost of common stock $= (17.11\% + 17.63\%)/2$

$\quad\quad\quad\quad\quad = 17.37\%$

---

[14] We could justify the 50 percent adjustment by looking at analysts' forecasts for Bombardier's future growth.

[15] We use the beta calculated by ScotiaMcLeod and the market risk premium from Chapter 10 for the period 1948–94. For the most recent 20 years (1975–94), the market risk premium in Chapter 10 was far lower at 3.78 percent. Using this figure in the CAPM, the cost of equity for Bombardier is only 13.23 percent.

In this case, the dividend valuation model and the CAPM produce very similar answers, so we can just average them to find the cost of equity.

Bombardier's WACC

To find the weighted average cost of capital, we weight the cost of each source by the weights:

$$\text{WACC} = (E/V)R_E + (P/V)R_P + (D/V)R_D$$

$$= .7738(17.37\%) + .0054(7.50\%) + .2208(7.84\%)$$

$$= 15.21\%$$

Our analysis shows that in May 1994 Bombardier's weighted average cost of capital was around 15 percent.

14.8 I SUMMARY AND CONCLUSIONS

This chapter discussed cost of capital. The most important concept is the weighted average cost of capital (WACC) that we interpreted as the required rate of return on the overall firm. It is also the discount rate appropriate for cash flows that are similar in risk to the overall firm. We described how the WACC can be calculated as the weighted average of different sources of financing. We also illustrated how it can be used in certain types of analyses.

In addition, we pointed out situations in which it is inappropriate to use the WACC as the discount rate. To handle such cases, we described some alternative approaches to developing discount rates such as the pure play approach. We also discussed how the flotation costs associated with raising new capital can be included in an NPV analysis.

Key Terms

cost of equity (page 494)

retention ratio (page 496)

return on equity (ROE) (page 496)

cost of debt (page 499)

weighted average cost of capital (WACC) (page 502)

pure play approach (page 507)

adjusted present value (APV) (page 523)

Chapter Review Problems and Self-Test

14.1   Calculating the Cost of Equity   Suppose that stock in Boone Corporation has a beta of .90. The market risk premium is 7 percent, and the risk-free rate is 8 percent. Boone's last dividend was $1.80 per share, and the dividend is expected to grow at 7 percent indefinitely. The stock currently sells for $25. What is Boone's cost of equity capital?

14.2   Calculating the WACC   In addition to the information in the previous problem, suppose Boone has a target debt/equity ratio of 50 percent. Its cost of debt is 8 percent, before taxes. If the tax rate is 40 percent, what is the WACC?

14.3   Flotation Costs   Suppose that in the previous question Boone is seeking $40 million for a new project. The necessary funds have to be raised externally.

Boone's flotation costs for selling debt and equity are 3 percent and 12 percent, respectively. If flotation costs are considered, what is the true cost of the new project?

Answers to Self-Test Problems

14.1 We start with the SML approach. Based on the information given, the expected return on Boone's common stock is:

$$R_E = R_f + \beta_E \times [R_M - R_f]$$

$$= 8\% + .9 \times 7\%$$

$$= 14.3\%$$

We now use the dividend growth model. The projected dividend is $D_0 \times (1 + g)$ = $1.80 \times (1.07)$ = $1.926, so the expected return using this approach is:

$$r = D_1/P_0 + g$$

$$= \$1.926/25 + .07$$

$$= 14.704\%$$

Since these two estimates, 14.3 percent and 14.7 percent, are fairly close, we average them. Boone's cost of equity is approximately 14.5 percent.

14.2 Since the target debt/equity ratio is .50, Boone uses $.50 in debt for every $1.00 in equity. In other words, Boone's target capital structure is ⅓ debt and ⅔ equity. The WACC is thus:

$$\text{WACC} = (E/V) \times R_E + (D/V) \times R_D \times (1 - T_C)$$

$$= 2/3 \times 14.5\% + 1/3 \times 8\% \times (1 - .40)$$

$$= 11.267\%$$

14.3 Since Boone uses both debt and equity to finance its operations, we first need the weighted average flotation cost. As in the previous problem, the percentage of equity financing is ⅔, so the weighted average cost is:

$$f_A = (E/V) \times f_E + (D/V) \times f_D$$

$$= 2/3 \times 12\% + 1/3 \times 3\%$$

$$= 9\%$$

If Boone needs $40 million after flotation costs, the true cost of the project is $40/(1 - f_A) = $40/.91 = $43.96 million.

Questions and Problems

Basic
(Questions 1–19)

1. **Calculating Cost of Equity**   The Chilton Oil Co. just issued a dividend of $2.50 per share on its common stock. The company is expected to maintain a constant 6 percent growth rate in its dividends indefinitely. If the stock sells for $50 a share, what is the company's cost of equity?

2. **Calculating Cost of Equity**   The Bedrock Corporation's common stock has a beta of 1.25. If the risk-free rate is 4 percent and the expected return on the market is 12 percent, what is Bedrock's cost of equity capital?

3. **Calculating Cost of Equity**   Stock in Eddy Industries has a beta of .90. The market risk premium is 9.5 percent, and T-bills are currently yielding 5 percent. Eddy's most recent dividend was $3.75 per share, and dividends are expected to

grow at a 3 percent annual rate indefinitely. If the stock sells for $32.50 per share, what is your best estimate of Eddy's cost of equity?

4. **Estimating the Dividend Growth Rate**   Suppose Winchell Broadcasting Company just issued a dividend of $0.90 per share on its common stock. The company paid dividends of $0.45, $0.58, $0.69, and $0.80 per share in the four previous years. If the stock currently sells for $17.50, what is your best estimate of the company's cost of equity capital?

5. **Calculating Cost of Preferred Stock**   Colossus Bank has an issue of preferred stock with a $5 stated dividend that just sold for $80 per share. What is the bank's cost of preferred stock?

6. **Calculating Cost of Debt**   DC Utilities, Inc., is trying to determine its cost of debt. The utility has a debt issue outstanding with 12 years to maturity that is quoted at 93 percent of face value. The issue makes semiannual payments and has an embedded cost of 6 percent annually. What is the utility's pretax cost of debt? If the tax rate is 35 percent, what is the aftertax cost of debt?

7. **Calculating Cost of Debt**   Keefe Electronics issued a 20-year, 9 percent semiannual bond seven years ago. The bond currently sells for 108 percent of its face value. The company's tax rate is 38 percent.
   a. What is the pretax cost of debt?
   b. What is the aftertax cost of debt?
   c. Which is more relevant, the pretax or the aftertax cost of debt? Why?

8. **Calculating Cost of Debt**   For the firm in Problem 7, suppose the book value of the debt issue is $50 million. In addition, the company has a second debt issue on the market, a stripped bond with nine years left to maturity; the book value of this issue is $30 million and the bond sells for 48 percent of par. What is the company's total book value of debt? The total market value? What is your best estimate of the aftertax cost of debt now?

9. **Calculating WACC**   Corrado Construction Corporation has a target capital structure of 35 percent common stock, 10 percent preferred stock, and 55 percent debt. Its cost of equity is 18 percent, the cost of preferred stock is 8 percent, and the cost of debt is 10 percent. The relevant tax rate is 35 percent.
   a. What is Corrado's WACC?
   b. The company president has approached you about Corrado's capital structure. He wants to know why the company doesn't use more preferred stock financing, since it costs less than debt. What would you tell the president?

10. **Taxes and WACC**   Merton Manufacturing has a target debt/equity ratio of .60. Its cost of equity is 20 percent and its cost of debt is 12 percent. If the tax rate is 34 percent, what is Merton's WACC?

11. **Finding the Target Capital Structure**   Gauss Corporation's weighted average cost of capital is 9.75 percent. The company's cost of equity is 16 percent and its cost of debt is 10.25 percent. The tax rate is 39 percent. What is Gauss Corporation's target debt/equity ratio?

12. **Book Value versus Market Value**   Veetek Enterprises has 12.8 million shares of common stock outstanding. The current share price is $29, and the book value per share is $18. Veetek also has two bond issues outstanding. The first bond issue has a face value of $100 million, a 7 percent coupon, and sells for 94 percent of par. The second issue has a face value of $75 million, a 5.5

percent coupon, and sells for 87 percent of par. The first issue matures in 13 years, the second in 8 years.

**Basic
(Continued)**

a. What are Veetek's capital structure weights on a book value basis?

b. What are Veetek's capital structure weights on a market value basis?

c. Which are more relevant, the book or market value weights? Why?

13. **Calculating the WACC**   In Problem 12, suppose the most recent dividend was $2 and the dividend growth rate is 8 percent. Assume the overall cost of debt is the average of that implied by the two outstanding debt issues. Both bonds make semiannual payments. The tax rate is 35 percent. What is the company's WACC?

14. **WACC**   Huesenberg Products has a target debt/equity ratio of 2. Its WACC is 14 percent and the tax rate is 35 percent.

a. If Husenberg's cost of equity is 19 percent, what is its pretax cost of debt?

b. If instead you know that the aftertax cost of debt is 7 percent, what is the cost of equity?

15. **Finding the WACC**   Given the following information for Valley Power Co., find the WACC. Assume the company's tax rate is 35 percent.

Debt:	2,500 7.75 percent coupon bonds outstanding, $1,000 par value, eight years to maturity, selling for 103 percent of par; the bonds make annual payments.
Common stock:	75,000 shares outstanding selling for $50 per share; the beta is .85.
Preferred stock:	10,000 shares of 5 percent preferred stock outstanding, currently selling for $80 per share.
Market:	5 percent market risk premium and 6 percent risk-free rate.

16. **Finding the WACC**   Bluefield Corporation has 5 million shares of common stock outstanding, 750,000 shares of 7 percent preferred stock outstanding, and 250,000 11 percent semiannual bonds outstanding, par value $1,000 each. The stock currently sells for $40 per share and has a beta of 1.2, the preferred stock currently sells for $75 per share, and the bonds have 15 years to maturity and sell for 93.5 percent of par. The market risk premium is 6 percent, T-bills are yielding 4 percent, and Bluefield's tax rate is 34 percent.

a. What is the firm's market value capital structure?

b. If Bluefield is evaluating a new investment project that has the same risk as the firm's typical project, what rate should it use to discount the project's cash flows?

17. **SML and WACC**   An all-equity firm is considering the following projects:

Project	Beta	Expected Return (%)
W	0.60	13
X	0.85	14
Y	1.15	18
Z	1.50	20

The T-bill rate is 6 percent, and the expected return on the market is 16 percent.

a. Which projects have a higher expected return than the firm's 16 percent cost of capital?

b. Which projects should be accepted?

c. Which projects would be incorrectly accepted or rejected if the firm's overall cost of capital is used as a hurdle rate?

**Basic
(Continued)**

18. **Calculating Flotation Costs**   Suppose your company needs $2.4 million to build a new assembly line. Your target debt/equity ratio is .50. The flotation cost for new equity is 14 percent, but the flotation cost for debt is only 4 percent. Your boss has decided to fund the project by borrowing money, since the flotation costs are lower and the needed funds are relatively small.

    a. What do you think about the rationale behind borrowing the entire amount?
    b. What is your company's weighted average flotation cost?
    c. What is the true cost of building the new assembly line after taking flotation costs into account? Does it matter in this case that the entire amount is being raised from debt?

19. **Calculating Flotation Costs**   Norton & Company needs to raise $5 million to start a new project and will raise the money by selling new bonds. The company has a target capital structure mix of 50 percent common stock, 10 percent preferred stock, and 40 percent debt. Flotation costs for issuing new common stock are 13 percent, for new preferred stock, 6 percent, and for new debt, 3 percent. What is the true initial cost figure Norton should use when evaluating its project?

**Intermediate
(Questions 20–27)**

20. **Cost of Equity Estimation**   What are the advantages of using the dividend growth model for determining the cost of equity capital? What are the disadvantages? What specific piece of information needs to be estimated to find the cost of equity using this model? What are some of the ways in which you could get this estimate?

21. **SML Cost of Equity Estimation**   What are the advantages of using the SML approach to finding the cost of equity capital? What are the disadvantages? What are the specific pieces of information needed to use this method? Are all of these variables observable, or do they need to be estimated? What are some of the ways in which you could get these estimates?

22. **Cost of Debt Estimation**   How do you determine the appropriate cost of debt for a company? Does it make a difference if the company's debt is privately placed as opposed to being publicly traded? How would you estimate the cost of debt for a firm whose only debt issues are privately held by institutional investors?

23. **Cost of Capital**   Suppose Tom O'Bedlam, president of Bedlam Products, Inc., has hired you to determine the firm's cost of debt and cost of equity capital.

    a. The stock currently sells for $50 per share, and the dividend per share will probably be about $5. Tom argues: "It will cost us $5 per share to use the stockholders' money this year, so the cost of equity is equal to 10 percent ($5/$50). What's wrong with this conclusion?
    b. Based on the most recent financial statements, Bedlam Products' total liabilities are $8 million. Total interest expense for the coming year will be about $1 million. Tom therefore reasons: "We owe $8 million, and we will pay $1 million interest. Therefore, our cost of debt is obviously $1 million/$8 million = 12.5 percent." What's wrong with this conclusion?
    c. Based on his own analysis, Tom is recommending that the company increase its use of equity financing, because "Debt costs 12.5 percent, but equity only costs 10 percent; thus equity is cheaper." Ignoring all the other problems, what do you think about the conclusion that the cost of equity is less than the cost of debt?

24. **SML and NPV** Both Dow Chemical Company, a large natural gas user, and Superior Oil, a major natural gas producer, are thinking of investing in natural gas wells near Edmonton. Both are all-equity financed companies. Dow and Superior are both looking at identical projects. They've analyzed their respective investments, which would involve a negative cash flow now and positive expected cash flows in the future. These cash flows would be the same for both firms. No debt would be used to finance the projects. Both companies estimate that their project would have a net present value of $1 million at an 18 percent discount rate and a −$1.1 million NPV at a 22 percent discount rate. Dow has a beta of 1.25, while Superior has a beta of 0.75. The expected risk premium on the market is 8 percent, and risk-free bonds are yielding 12 percent. Should either company proceed? Should both? Explain.

Intermediate (Continued)

25. **Divisional Costs of Capital** Under what circumstances would it be appropriate for a firm to use different costs of capital for its different operating divisions? If the overall firm WACC is used as the hurdle rate for all divisions, would the riskier divisions or the more conservative divisions tend to get most of the investment projects? Why? If you were to try to estimate the appropriate cost of capital for different divisions, what problems might you encounter? What are two techniques you could use to develop a rough estimate for each division's cost of capital?

26. **WACC and NPV** A firm is considering a project that will result in initial aftertax cash savings of $9 million at the end of the first year, and these savings will grow at a rate of 5 percent per year indefinitely. The firm has a target debt/equity ratio of 3, a cost of equity of 22 percent, and an aftertax cost of debt of 10 percent. The cost-saving proposal is somewhat riskier than the usual projects the firm undertakes; management uses the subjective approach and applies an adjustment factor of +3 percent to the cost of capital for such risky projects. Under what circumstances should the firm take on the project?

27. **Flotation Costs** Navier and Stokes, Inc., recently issued new securities to finance an expansion project. The project cost $2 million and the company paid $150,000 in flotation costs. In addition, the equity issued had a flotation cost of 12 percent of the amount raised, while the debt issued had a flotation cost of 5 percent of the amount raised. If Navier and Stokes issued new securities in the same proportion as its target capital structure, what is the company's target debt/equity ratio?

28. **Flotation Costs and NPV** Modern Piping Corporation manufactures plastic plumbing supplies. It is currently at its target debt/equity ratio of .75. It's considering building a new $12 million manufacturing facility. This new plant is expected to generate aftertax cash flows of $2 million in perpetuity. There are three financing options:

Challenge (Questions 28–29)

1. A new issue of common stock. The flotation costs of the new common stock would be 15 percent of the amount raised. The required return on the company's new equity is 19 percent.
2. A new issue of 20-year bonds. The flotation costs of the new bonds would be about 3.5 percent of the proceeds. If the company issues these new bonds at an annual coupon rate of 11 percent, they will sell at par.
3. Increased use of accounts payable financing. Since this financing is part of the company's ongoing daily business, it has no flotation costs and the company assigns it a cost that is the same as the overall firm WACC.

Management has a target ratio of accounts payable to long-term debt of .25. (Assume there is no difference between the pretax and aftertax accounts payable cost.)

What is the NPV of the new plant? Assume Modern Piping has a 35 percent tax rate.

29. **Project Evaluation** This is a comprehensive project evaluation problem bringing together much of what you have learned in this and previous chapters. Suppose you have been hired as a financial consultant to Acme Electronics, Inc., a large, publicly traded firm that is the market share leader in virtual reality modules (VRMs). The company is looking at setting up a manufacturing plant overseas to produce a new line of VRMs. This will be a five-year project. The company bought some land six years ago for $5 million in anticipation of using it as a toxic dump site for waste chemicals, but it built a piping system to safely discard the chemicals instead. The land was appraised last week for $200,000. The company wants to build its new manufacturing plant on this land; the plant will cost $8 million to build. The following market data on Acme's securities are current:

Debt:	10,000 9 percent coupon bonds outstanding, 10 years to maturity, selling for 88 percent of par. The bonds have a $1,000 par value each and make semi-annual payments.
Common stock:	400,000 shares outstanding selling for $30 per share; the beta is 1.2.
Preferred stock:	20,000 shares of 6 percent preferred stock outstanding, selling for $90 per share.
Market:	6 percent expected market risk premium; 4 percent risk-free rate.

Acme uses G. M. Wharton as its lead underwriter. Wharton charges Acme spreads of 12 percent on new common stock issues, 7 percent on new preferred stock issues, and 4 percent on new debt issues. Wharton has included all direct and indirect issuance costs (along with its profit) in setting these spreads. Wharton has recommended to Acme that it raise the funds needed to build the plant by issuing some new shares of common stock. Acme's tax rate is 34 percent.

a. Calculate the project's initial Time 0 cash flow, taking into account all side effects.

b. The new VRM project is somewhat riskier than a typical project for Acme, primarily because the plant is being located overseas. Management has told you to use an adjustment factor of 2 percent to account for this increased riskiness. Calculate the appropriate discount rate to use when evaluating Acme's project.

c. The manufacturing plant has an eight-year tax life, and Acme uses straight-line depreciation. At the end of the project (i.e., the end of Year 5) the plant can be scrapped for $1 million. What is the aftertax salvage value of this manufacturing plant?

d. The project requires $600,000 in initial net working capital investments to get going. The company will incur $1 million in annual fixed costs. The plan is to manufacture 40,000 VRMs per year and sell them at $250 per machine; the variable production costs are $150 per VRM. What is the annual operating cash flow (OCF) from this project?

e. Acme's comptroller is primarily interested in the impact of Acme's investments on the bottom line of reported accounting statements. What will you tell her is the accounting break-even quantity of VRMs sold for this project?

f. Finally, Acme's president wants you to throw all your calculations, assumptions, and everything else into the report for the chief financial officer; all he wants to know is what the VRM project's internal rate of return (IRR) and net present value (NPV) are. What will you report?

Suggested Readings

The following article contains an excellent discussion of some of the subtleties of using the WACC for project evaluation:

Miles, J., and R. Ezzel. "The Weighted Average Cost of Capital, Perfect Capital Markets and Project Life: A Clarification." *Journal of Financial and Quantitative Analysis* 15 (September 1980).

For a good discussion on how to use the SML in project evaluation, see:

Weston, J. F. "Investment Decisions Using the Capital Asset Pricing Model." *Financial Management*, Spring 1973.

ADJUSTED PRESENT VALUE

APPENDIX 14A

Adjusted present value (APV) is an alternative to WACC in analyzing capital budgeting proposals. Under APV, we first analyze a project under all-equity financing and then add the additional effects of debt. This can be written as

Adjusted present value = All-equity value + Additional effects of debt

adjusted present value (APV)
Base case net present value of a project's operating cash flows plus present value of any financing benefits.

We illustrate the APV methodology with a simple example.[16] Suppose BDE is considering a $10 million project that will last five years. Projected operating cash flows are $3 million annually. The risk-free rate is 10 percent and the cost of equity is 20 percent. This is often called the cost of unlevered equity because we assume initially that the firm has no debt.

All-Equity Value

Assuming that the project is financed with all equity, its value is

$$-\$10,000,000 + \$3,000,000 \times [1 - 1/(1.20)^5]/.20 = -\$1,028,164$$

An all-equity firm would clearly reject this project because the NPV is negative. And equity flotation costs (not considered yet) would only make the NPV more negative. However, debt financing may add enough value to the project to justify acceptance. We consider the effects of debt next.

---

[16] To make it easier to illustrate what is new in APV, we simplify the project details by assuming the operating cash flows are an annuity. Most Canadian projects generate variable cash flows due to the CCA rules. This is handled within APV by finding the the present value of each source of cash flow separately exactly as presented in Chapter 8.

Additional Effects of Debt

BDE can obtain a five-year, balloon payment loan for $7.5 million after flotation costs. The interest rate is the risk-free cost of debt of 10 percent. The flotation costs are 1 percent of the amount raised. We look at three ways in which debt financing alters the NPV of the project.

Flotation Costs

The formula introduced in the chapter gives us the flotation costs.

$$\$7,500,000 = (1 - .01) \times \text{Amount raised}$$

$$\text{Amount raised} = \$7,500,000/.99 = \$7,575,758$$

So flotation costs are $75,758 and in the text we added these to the initial outlay reducing NPV.

The APV method refines the estimate of flotation costs by recognizing that they generate a tax shield. Flotation costs are paid immediately but are deducted from taxes by amortizing over the life of the loan. In this example, the annual tax deduction for flotation costs is $75,758/5 years = $15,152. At a tax rate of 40 percent, the annual tax shield is $15,152 \times .40 = $6,061.

To find the net flotation costs of the loan, add the present value of the tax shield to the flotation costs.

$$\text{Net flotation costs} = -\$75,758 + \$6,061 \times [1 - 1/(1.10)^5]/.10$$
$$= -\$75,758 + \$22,976 = -\$52,782$$

The net present value of the project after debt flotation costs but before the benefits of debt is

$$-\$1,028,164 - \$52,782 = -\$1,080,946$$

Tax Subsidy

The loan of $7.5 million is received at Date 0. Annual interest is $750,000 ($7,500,000 \times .10). The interest cost after tax is $450,000 ($750,000 \times (1 - .40)). The loan has a balloon payment of the full $7.5 million at the end of five years. The loan gives rise to three sets of cash flows—the loan received, the annual interest cost after taxes, and the repayment of principal. The net present value of the loan is simply the sum of three present values.

$$\text{NPV(Loan)} = + \begin{matrix} \text{Amount} \\ \text{borrowed} \end{matrix} - \begin{matrix} \text{Present value} \\ \text{of after tax} \\ \text{interest payments} \end{matrix} - \begin{matrix} \text{Present value} \\ \text{of loan} \\ \text{repayments} \end{matrix}$$

$$= + \$7,500,000 - \$450,000 \times [1 - 1/(1.10)^5]/.10$$
$$- \$7,500,000/(1.10)^5$$
$$= + \$7,500,000 - \$1,705,854$$
$$- \$4,656,910$$
$$= \$1,137,236$$

The NPV of the loan is positive, reflecting the interest tax shield.[17]

---

[17] The NPV (Loan) must be zero in a no-tax world, because interest provides no tax shield there. To check this intuition, we calculate

$$0 = +\$7,500,000 - \$750,000 [1 - 1/(1.10)^5]/.10 - \$7,500,000/(1.10)^5$$

The adjusted present value of the project with this financing is:

APV = All-equity value − Flotation costs of debt + NPV (Loan)

$56,290 = −$1,028,164 − $52,782 + $1,137,236

Though we previously saw that an all-equity firm would reject the project, a firm would accept the project if a $7.5 million loan could be obtained.

Because this loan discussed was at the market rate of 10 percent, we have considered only two of the three additional effects of debt (flotation costs and tax subsidy) so far. We now examine another loan where the third effect arises.

Non-market Rate Financing

In Canada a number of companies are fortunate enough to obtain subsidized financing from a governmental authority. Suppose the project of BDE is deemed socially beneficial and a federal governmental agency grants the firm a $7.5 million loan at 8 percent interest. In addition, the agency absorbs all flotation costs. Clearly, the company would choose this loan over the one we previously calculated. At 8 percent interest, the annual interest payments are $7,500,000 × .08 = $600,000. The aftertax payments are $360,000 = $600,000 × (1 − .40). Using the equation we developed,

$$\text{NPV (Loan)} = + \begin{array}{c} \text{Amount} \\ \text{borrowed} \end{array} - \begin{array}{c} \text{Present value} \\ \text{of aftertax} \\ \text{interest payments} \end{array} - \begin{array}{c} \text{Present value} \\ \text{of loan} \\ \text{repayments} \end{array}$$

$$= + \$7,500,000 - \$360,000 \times [1 - 1/(1.10)^5]/.10$$

$$- \$7,500,000/(1.10)^5$$

$$= + \$7,500,000 - \$1,364,683$$

$$- \$4,656,910$$

$$= \$1,478,407$$

Notice that we still discount the cash flows at 10 percent when the firm is borrowing at 8 percent. This is done because 10 percent is the fair, marketwide rate. That is, 10 percent is the rate at which one could borrow without benefit of subsidization. The net present value of the subsidized loan is larger than the net present value of the earlier loan because the firm is now borrowing at the below-market rate of 8 percent. Note that the NPV (Loan) calculation captures both the tax effect and the non-market rate effect.

The net present value of the project with subsidized debt financing is:

APV = All-equity value − Flotation costs of debt + NPV (Loan)

$450,243 = −$1,028,164   − 0   + $1,478,407

Subsidized financing has enhanced the NPV substantially. The result is that the government debt subsidy program will likely achieve its result—encouraging the firm to invest in the kind of project the government agency wishes to encourage.

This example illustrates the adjusted (APV) approach. The approach begins with the present value of a project for the all-equity firm. Next, the effects of debt are added in. The approach has much to recommend it. It is intuitively appealing because individual components are calculated separately and added together in a simple way. And, if the debt from the project can be specified precisely, the present value of the debt can be calculated precisely.

APV and Beta

The APV approach discounts cash flows from a scale-enhancing project at the cost of unlevered equity, which is also the cost of capital for the all-equity firm. Because in this chapter we are considering firms that have debt, this unlevered equity does not exist. One must somehow use the beta of the levered equity (which really exists) to calculate the beta for the hypothetical unlevered firm. Then the SML line can be employed to determine the cost of equity capital for the unlevered firm.

We now show how to compute the unlevered firm's beta from the levered equity's beta. To begin, we treat the case of no corporate taxes to explain the intuition behind our results. However, corporate taxes must be included to achieve real-world applicability. We therefore consider taxes in the second case.

No Taxes

In the previous two chapters, we defined the value of the firm to be equal to the value of the firm's debt plus the value of its equity. For a levered firm, this can be represented as $V_L = B + S$. Imagine an individual who owns all the firm's debt and all its equity. In other words, this individual owns the entire firm. What is the beta of his or her portfolio of the firm's debt and equity?

As with any portfolio, the beta of this portfolio is a weighted average of the betas of the individual items in the portfolio. Hence, we have

$$\beta_{Portfolio} = \beta_{Levered\,firm} = \frac{Debt}{Debt + Equity} \times \beta_{Debt}$$
$$+ \frac{Equity}{Debt + Equity} \times \beta_{Equity}$$

[14A.1]

where β_{Equity} is the beta of the equity of the *levered* firm. Notice that the beta of debt is multiplied by Debt/(Debt + Equity), the percentage of debt in the capital structure. Similarly, the beta of equity is multiplied by the percentage of equity in the capital structure. Because the portfolio is the levered firm, the beta of the portfolio is equal to the beta of the levered firm.

The previous equation relates the betas of the financial instruments (debt and equity) to the beta of the levered firm. We need an extra step, however, because we want to relate the betas of the financial instruments to the beta of the firm had it been *unlevered*. Only in this way can we apply APV, because APV begins by discounting the project's cash flows for an all-equity firm.

Ignoring taxes, the cash flows to both the debtholders and the equityholders of a levered firm are equal to the cash flows to the equityholders of an otherwise identical unlevered firm. Because the cash flows are identical for the two firms, the betas of the two firms must be equal as well.

Because the beta of the unlevered firm is equal to Equation 14A.1, we have

$$\beta_{Unlevered\,firm} = \frac{Debt}{Debt + Equity} \times \beta_{Debt} + \frac{Equity}{Debt + Equity} \times \beta_{Equity}$$

The beta of debt is very low in practice. If we make the common assumption that the beta of debt is zero, we have the no-tax case:

$$\beta_{Unlevered\,firm} = \frac{Equity}{Debt + Equity} \times \beta_{Equity}$$

[14A.2]

Because Equity/(Debt + Equity) must be below 1 for a levered firm, it follows that $\beta_{Unlevered\,firm} < \beta_{Equity}$. In words, the beta of the unlevered firm must be less than the beta of the equity in an otherwise identical levered firm. This is consistent with our work on capital structure. We showed there that leverage increases the risk of equity. Because beta is a measure of risk, it is sensible that leverage increases the beta of equity.

Real-world corporations pay taxes whereas the above results are for no taxes. Thus, although the previous discussion presents the intuition behind an important relationship, it does not help apply the APV method in practice. We examine the tax case next.

Corporate Taxes

It can be shown that the relationship between the beta of the unlevered firm and the beta of the levered equity in the corporate-tax case is:[18]

$$\beta_{Unlevered\,firm} = \frac{\text{Equity}}{\text{Equity} + (1 - T_c) \times \text{Debt}} \times \beta_{Equity} \qquad [14A.3]$$

Equation 14A.3 holds when (1) the corporation is taxed at the rate of T_C and (2) the debt has a zero beta.

Because Equity/(Equity + $(1 - T_C)$ × Debt) must be less than 1 for a levered firm, it follows that $\beta_{Unlevered\,firm} < \beta_{Equity}$. The corporate-tax case of (14A.3) is quite similar to the no-tax case of (14A.2), because the beta of levered equity must be greater than the beta of the unlevered firm in either case. The intuition that leverage increases the risk of equity applies in both cases.

However, notice that the two equations are not equal. It can be shown that leverage increases the equity beta less rapidly under corporate taxes. This occurs

---

[18] This result holds if the beta of debt equals zero. To see this, note that

$$V_U + T_C B = V_L = B + S \qquad (a)$$

where

V_U = value of unlevered firm

V_L = value of levered firm

B = value of debt in a levered firm

S = value of equity in a levered firm

As we stated in the text, the beta of the levered firm is a weighted average of the debt beta and the equity beta:

$$\frac{B}{B + S} \times \beta_B + \frac{S}{B + S} \times \beta_S$$

where β_B and β_S are the betas of the debt and the equity of the levered firm, respectively. Because $V_L = B + S$, we have

$$\frac{B}{V_L} \times \beta_B + \frac{S}{V_L} \times \beta_S \qquad (b)$$

The beta of the leveraged firm can *also* be expressed as a weighted average of the beta of the unlevered firm and the beta of the tax shield:

$$\frac{V_U}{V_U + T_C B} \times \beta_U + \frac{T_C B}{V_U + T_C B} \times \beta_B$$

where β_U is the beta of the unlevered firm. This follows from Equation a. Because $V_L = V_U + T_C B$, we have

$$\frac{V_U}{V_L} \times \beta_U + \frac{T_C B}{V_L} \times \beta_B \qquad (c)$$

We can equate (b) and (c) because both represent the beta of a levered firm. Equation a tells us that $V_U = S + (1 - T_C) \times B$. Under the assumption that $\beta_B = 0$, equating (b) and (c) and using Equation a yields Equation 14A.3.

because, under taxes, leverage creates a riskless tax shield, thereby lowering the risk of the entire firm.

E X A M P L E | 14A.1   Applying APV

Trans Canada Industries is considering a scale-enhancing project. The market value of the firm's debt is $100 million, and the market value of the firm's equity is $200 million. The debt is considered riskless. The corporate tax rate is 34 percent. Regression analysis indicates that the beta of the firm's equity is 2. The risk-free rate is 10 percent, and the expected market premium is 8.5 percent. What is the project's discount rate in the hypothetical case that Trans Canada is all equity?

We can answer this question in two steps.

1. *Determining beta of hypothetical all-equity firm.* Using Equation 14A.3, we have:

Unlevered beta: $\dfrac{\$200 \text{ million}}{\$200 \text{ million} + (1 - 0.34) \times \$100 \text{ Million}} \times 2 = 1.50$

2. *Determining discount rate.* We calculate the discount rate from the SML as:

Discount rate: $R_S = R_f + \beta \times [E(R_M) - R_f]$

$$22.75\% = 10\% + 1.50 \times 8.5\%$$

Thus, the APV method says that the project's NPV should be calculated by discounting the cash flows at the all-equity rate of 22.75 percent. As we discussed earlier in this chapter, the tax shield should then be added to the NPV of the cash flows, yielding APV. |

The Project Is Not Scale-Enhancing

This example assumed that the project is scale-enhancing, doing what the firm does already on a larger scale. So, we began with the beta of the firm's equity. If the project is not scale-enhancing, one could begin with the equity betas of firms in the industry of the project. For each firm, the hypothetical beta of the unlevered equity could be calculated by Equation 14A.3. The SML could then be used to determine the project's discount rate from the average of these betas.

Comparison of WACC and APV

In Chapter 14, we provided two approaches to capital budgeting for firms that use debt financing. Both WACC and APV attempt the same task: to value projects when debt financing is allowed. However, as we have shown, the approaches are markedly different in technique. Because of this, it is worthwhile to compare the two approaches.[19]

WACC is an older approach that has been used extensively in business. APV is a newer approach that, while attracting a large following in academic circles, is used less commonly in business. Over the years, we have met with many executives in firms using both approaches. They have frequently pointed out to us that the cost of equity, the cost of debt, and the proportions of debt and equity can easily be calculated for a firm as a whole.

---

[19] In some circumstances faced by multinational firms, APV breaks down. See L. Booth, "Capital Budgeting Frameworks for the Multinational Corporation," *Journal of International Business Studies,* Fall 1982, pp. 113–23.

Some projects are scale enhancing with the same risk as the whole firm. An example is a fast-food chain adding more company-owned outlets. In this case, it is straightforward to calculate the project's NPV with WACC. However, both the proportions and the costs of debt and equity are different for the project than for the firm as a whole if the project is not scale enhancing. WACC is more difficult to use in that case.

As a result, firms may switch between approaches using WACC for scale-enhancing projects and APV for special situations. For example, an acquisition of a firm in a completely different industry is clearly not scale-enhancing. So when Campeau Corporation, originally a real estate firm, acquired Federated Department Stores, APV analysis would have been appropriate because Federated was in a different industry. Also, the acquisition was through a leveraged buyout involving a large (with hindsight, too large) amount of debt and the APV approach values the NPV of the loan.

| CONCEPT QUESTIONS
| 1. What are the steps in using adjusted present value (APV) to value a project?
| 2. Compare APV with WACC. In what situations is each best applied?

Appendix Questions and Problems

A.1 **APV Problem** A mining company has discovered a small silver deposit neighbouring its existing mine site. It has been estimated that there is a 10-year supply of silver in the deposit that would return $11.25 million annually to the firm. The estimated cost of developing the site is $53 million and could be financed by the issuance of shares. The firm has experienced significant growth, and this is reflected in a cost of equity of 18 percent. After analyzing the returns to the project, the firm's chief financial officer (CFO) recommends to the board not to continue with it as it is not profitable to the firm. However, in speaking with an investment dealer the following week, the CFO is told that it would be possible to float bonds for up to $35 million carrying a coupon of 15 percent. The flotation costs for debt and equity are both 1 percent and the marginal tax rate for the firm is 40 percent. Is it profitable for the firm to continue with the project now?

A.2 **APV Problem** What would be the marginal benefit to the mining company if it could obtain a government loan for $35 million at 12 percent that has a balloon payment for the full amount at the end of 10 years? Assume there are no flotation costs for this loan.

CHAPTER

15

Financial Leverage and Capital Structure Policy

Thus far, we have taken the firm's capital structure as given. Debt/equity ratios don't just drop on firms from the sky, of course, so now it's time to wonder where they do come from. Going back to Chapter 1, we call decisions about a firm's debt/equity ratio capital structure decisions.[1]

For the most part, a firm can choose any capital structure it wants. If management so desired, a firm could issue some bonds and use the proceeds to buy back some stock, thereby increasing the debt/equity ratio. Alternatively, it can issue stock and use the money to pay off some debt, thereby reducing the debt/equity ratio. These activities that alter the firm's existing capital structure are called capital *restructurings*. In general, such restructurings occur whenever the firm substitutes one capital structure for another while leaving the firm's assets unchanged.

Since the assets of a firm are not directly affected by a capital restructuring, we can examine the firm's capital structure decision separately from its other activities. This means a firm can consider capital restructuring decisions in isolation from its investment decisions. In this chapter then, we ignore investment decisions and focus on the long-term financing, or capital structure, question. We consider only long-term financing because, as we explained in Chapter 14, short-term sources of financing are excluded in calculating capital structure weights.

What we see in this chapter is that capital structure decisions can have important implications for the value of the firm and its cost of capital. We also find that important elements of the capital structure decision are easy to identify, but precise measures of these elements are generally not obtainable. As a result, we are able to give only an incomplete answer to the question of what the best capital structure might be for a particular firm at a particular time.

15.1 | THE CAPITAL STRUCTURE QUESTION

How should a firm choose its debt/equity ratio? Here, as always, we assume that the guiding principle is to choose the action that maximizes the value of a share of stock. As we discuss next, however, when it comes to capital structure decisions, this is

---

[1] It is conventional to refer to decisions regarding debt and equity as capital structure decisions. However, the term *financial structure* would be more accurate, and we use the terms interchangeably.

530

essentially the same thing as maximizing the value of the firm, and, for convenience, we frame our discussion in terms of firm value.

Firm Value and Stock Value: An Example

The following example illustrates that the capital structure that maximizes the value of the firm is the one that financial managers should choose for the shareholders, so there is no conflict in our goals. To begin, suppose the market value of the J. J. Sprint Company is $1,000. The company currently has no debt, and J. J. Sprint's 100 shares sell for $10 each. Further suppose that J. J. Sprint restructures itself by borrowing $500 and then paying out the proceeds to shareholders as an extra dividend of $500/100 = $5 per share.

This restructuring changes the capital structure of the firm with no direct effect on the firm's assets. The immediate effect is to increase debt and decrease equity. However, what would be the final impact of the restructuring? Table 15.1 illustrates three possible outcomes in addition to the original no-debt case. Notice that in scenario II the value of the firm is unchanged at $1,000. In scenario I, firm value rises by $250; it falls by $250 in scenario III. We haven't yet said what might lead to these changes. For now, we just take them as possible outcomes to illustrate a point.

Since our goal is to benefit the shareholders, we next examine, in Table 15.2, the net payoffs to the shareholders in these scenarios. For now we ignore the impact of taxes on dividends, capital gains and losses. We see that, if the value of the firm stays the same, then shareholders experience a capital loss that exactly offsets the extra dividend. This is outcome II. In outcome I, the value of the firm increases to $1,250 and the shareholders come out ahead by $250. In other words, the restructuring has an NPV of $250 in this scenario. The NPV in scenario III is −$250.

The key observation to make here is that the change in the value of the firm is the same as the net effect on the shareholders. Financial managers can therefore try to find the capital structure that maximizes the value of the firm. Put another way, the NPV rule applies to capital structure decisions, and the change in the value of the overall firm is the NPV of a restructuring. Thus, J. J. Sprint should borrow $500 if it expects outcome I. The crucial question in determining a firm's capital structure is, of course, which scenario is likely to occur.

| | No Debt | Debt Plus Dividend | | |
		I	II	III
Debt	$ 0	$ 500	$ 500	$500
Equity	1,000	750	500	250
Firm value	$1,000	$1,250	$1,000	$750

T A B L E   15.1

Possible firm values: No debt versus debt plus dividend

| | Debt plus Dividend | | |
	I	II	III
Equity value reduction	−$250	−$500	−$750
Dividends	500	500	500
Net effect	+$250	$ 0	−$250

T A B L E   15.2

Possible payoffs to shareholders: Debt plus dividend

Capital Structure and the Cost of Capital

In Chapter 14, we discussed the concept of the firm's weighted average cost of capital (WACC). Recall that the WACC tells us that the firm's overall cost of capital is a weighted average of the costs of the various components of the firm's capital structure. When we described the WACC, we took the firm's capital structure as given. Thus, one important issue that we want to explore in this chapter is what happens to the cost of capital when we vary the amount of debt financing or the debt/equity ratio.

A primary reason for studying the WACC is that the value of the firm is maximized when the WACC is minimized. To see this, recall that the WACC is the discount rate that is appropriate for the firm's overall cash flows. Because values and discount rates move in opposite directions, minimizing the WACC maximizes the value of the firm's cash flows.

Thus, we want to choose the firm's capital structure so that the WACC is minimized. For this reason, we say that one capital structure is better than another if it results in a lower weighted average cost of capital. Further, we say that a particular debt/equity ratio represents the *optimal capital structure* if it results in the lowest possible WACC. This is sometimes called the firm's *target* capital structure as well.

> CONCEPT QUESTIONS
>
> 1. Why should financial managers choose the capital structure that maximizes the value of the firm?
> 2. What is the relationship between the WACC and the value of the firm?
> 3. What is an optimal capital structure?

15.2 | THE EFFECT OF FINANCIAL LEVERAGE

The previous section describes why the capital structure that produces the highest firm value (or the lowest cost of capital) is the one most beneficial to shareholders. In this section, we examine the impact of financial leverage on the payoffs to stockholders. As you may recall, financial leverage refers to the extent to which a firm relies on debt. The more debt financing a firm uses in its capital structure, the more financial leverage it employs.

As we describe, financial leverage can dramatically alter the payoffs to shareholders in the firm. Remarkably, however, financial leverage may not affect the overall cost of capital. If this is true, then a firm's capital structure is irrelevant because changes in capital structure won't affect the value of the firm. We return to this issue a little later.

The Impact of Financial Leverage

We start by illustrating how financial leverage works. For now, we ignore the impact of taxes. Also, for ease of presentation, we describe the impact of leverage in its effects on earnings per share (EPS) and return on equity (ROE). These are, of course, accounting numbers, and, as such, are not our primary concern. Using cash flows instead of these accounting numbers would lead to precisely the same conclusions, but a little more work would be needed. We discuss the impact on market values in a subsequent section.

	Current	Proposed
Assets	$8,000,000	$8,000,000
Debt	0	4,000,000
Equity	8,000,000	4,000,000
Debt/equity ratio	0	1
Share price	$ 20	$ 20
Shares outstanding	400,000	200,000
Interest rate	10%	10%

T A B L E   15.3

Current and proposed capital structures for the Trans Can Corporation

Financial Leverage, EPS, and ROE: An Example   The Trans Can Corporation currently has no debt in its capital structure. The CFO, Kim Morris, is considering a restructuring that would involve issuing debt and using the proceeds to buy back some of the outstanding equity. Table 15.3 presents both the current and proposed capital structures. As shown, the firm's assets have a value of $8 million, and there are 400,000 shares outstanding. Because Trans Can is an all-equity firm, the price per share is $20.

The proposed debt issue would raise $4 million; the bonds would be issued at par with a coupon rate of 10 percent for a required return on debt of 10 percent. Since the stock sells for $20 per share, the $4 million in new debt would be used to purchase $4 million/$20 = 200,000 shares, leaving 200,000. After the restructuring, Trans Can would have a capital structure that was 50 percent debt, so the debt/equity ratio would be 1. Notice that, for now, we assume the stock price remains at $20.

To investigate the impact of the proposed restructuring, Morris has prepared Table 15.4, that compares the firm's current capital structure to the proposed capital structure under three scenarios. The scenarios reflect different assumptions about the firm's EBIT. Under the expected scenario, the EBIT is $1 million. In the recession scenario, EBIT falls to $500,000. In the expansion scenario, it rises to $1.5 million.

To illustrate some of the calculations in Table 15.4, consider the expansion case. EBIT is $1.5 million. With no debt (the current capital structure) and no taxes, net income is also $1.5 million. In this case, there are 400,000 shares worth $8 million total. EPS is therefore $1.5 million/400,000 = $3.75 per share. Also, since accounting return on equity (ROE) is net income divided by total equity, ROE is $1.5 million/$8 million = 18.75%.[2]

With $4 million in debt (the proposed capital structure), things are somewhat different. Since the interest rate is 10 percent, the interest bill is $400,000. With EBIT of $1.5 million, interest of $400,000, and no taxes, net income is $1.1 million. Now there are only 200,000 shares worth $4 million total. EPS is therefore $1.1 million/200,000 = $5.50 per share versus the $3.75 per share that we calculated earlier. Furthermore, ROE is $1.1 million/$4 million = 27.5 percent. This is well above the 18.75 percent we calculated for the current capital structure. So our example in Table 15.4 shows how increased debt can magnify ROE when profitability is good.

Greater use of debt also magnifies ROE in the other direction. To see this, look at the recession case in Table 15.4. Under the current capital structure, EPS falls to

---

[2] ROE is discussed in some detail in Chapter 3.

T A B L E 15.4

Capital structure scenarios for the Trans Can Corporation

	Recession	Expected	Expansion
Current Capital Structure: No Debt			
EBIT	$500,000	$1,000,000	$1,500,000
Interest	0	0	0
Net income	$500,000	$1,000,000	$1,500,000
ROE	6.25%	12.50%	18.75%
EPS	$ 1.25	$ 2.50	$ 3.75
Proposed Capital Structure: Debt = $4 million			
EBIT	$500,000	$1,000,000	$1,500,000
Interest	400,000	400,000	400,000
Net income	$100,000	$ 600,000	$1,100,000
ROE	2.50%	15.00%	27.50%
EPS	$ .50	$ 3.00	$ 5.50

$1.25 in a recession bringing ROE down to 6.25 percent. With more debt under the proposed capital structure, EPS is only $.50 and ROE drops to 2.50 percent. In brief, Table 15.4 shows that using more debt makes EPS and ROE more risky.

Degree of Financial Leverage   As our example shows, financial leverage measures how much earnings per share (and ROE) respond to changes in EBIT. It is the financial counterpart to operating leverage that we discussed in Chapter 2. We can generalize our discussion of financial leverage by introducing a formula for the degree of financial leverage:

$$\text{Degree of financial leverage} = \text{DFL} = \frac{\text{Percentage change in EPS}}{\text{Percentage change in EBIT}} \quad [15.1]$$

Like the degree of operating leverage, DFL varies for different ranges of EPS and EBIT. To illustrate the formula, we calculate DFL for Trans Can for an EBIT of $1 million. There are two calculations, one for the current and one for the proposed capital structure. Starting with the current capital structure:

$$\text{DFL} = \frac{(\$3.75 - 2.50)/2.50}{(\$1,500,000 - 1,000,000)/1,000,000}$$
$$= \frac{.50}{.50}$$
$$\text{DFL} = 1.0$$

So for the existing capital structure, the degree of financial leverage is 1.0. For the proposed capital structure:

$$\text{DFL} = \frac{(\$5.50 - 3.00)/3.00}{(\$1,500,000 - 1,000,000)/1,000,000}$$
$$\text{DFL} = \frac{.83}{.50}$$
$$\text{DFL} = 1.67$$

The proposed capital structure includes debt and this increases the degree of financial leverage. Calculating DFL adds precision to our earlier observation that increasing financial leverage magnifies the gains and losses to shareholders. We can now say that EPS increases or decreases by a factor of 1.67 times the percentage increase or decrease in EBIT.

Many analysts use a convenient alternative formula for DFL:

$$DFL = \frac{EBIT}{EBIT - Interest} \qquad [15.2]$$

We recalculate DFL for the proposed capital structure at EBIT of $1 million to show that the new formula gives the same answer.

$$DFL = \frac{\$1,000,000}{\$1,000,000 - 400,000}$$

$$DFL = \frac{\$1,000,000}{\$600,000}$$

$$DFL = 1.67$$

EPS versus EBIT   The impact of leverage is evident when the effect of the restructuring on EPS and ROE is examined. In particular, the variability in both EPS and ROE is much larger under the proposed capital structure. This illustrates how financial leverage acts to magnify gains and losses to shareholders.

In Figure 15.1, we take a closer look at the effect of the proposed restructuring. This figure plots earnings per share (EPS) against earnings before interest and taxes (EBIT) for the current and proposed capital structures. The first line, labelled "No debt," represents the case of no leverage. This line begins at the origin, indicating that EPS would be zero if EBIT were zero. From there, every $400,000 increase in EBIT increases EPS by $1 (because there are 400,000 shares outstanding).

The second line represents the proposed capital structure. Here, EPS is negative if EBIT is zero. This follows because $400,000 of interest must be paid regardless of the firm's profits. Since there are 200,000 shares in this case, the EPS is −$2 per share as shown. Similarly, if EBIT were $400,000, EPS would be exactly zero.

The important thing to notice in Figure 15.1 is that the slope of the line in this second case is steeper. In fact, for every $400,000 increase in EBIT, EPS rises by $2, so the line is twice as steep. This tells us that EPS is twice as sensitive to changes in EBIT because of the financial leverage employed.

Another observation to make in Figure 15.1 is that the lines intersect. At that point, EPS is exactly the same for both capital structures. To find this point, note that EPS is equal to EBIT/400,000 in the no-debt case. In the with-debt case, EPS is (EBIT − $400,000)/200,000. If we set these equal to each other, EBIT is:

EBIT/400,000 = (EBIT − 400,000)/200,000

EBIT = 2 × (EBIT − $400,000)

EBIT = $800,000

When EBIT is $800,000, EPS is $2 per share under either capital structure. This is labelled as the indifference point in Figure 15.1. If EBIT is above this level, leverage is beneficial; if it is below this point, it is not.

There is another, more intuitive way of seeing why the indifferent point is $800,000. Notice that, if the firm has no debt and its EBIT is $800,000, its net income is also $800,000. In this case, the ROE is 10 percent. This is precisely the same as the interest rate on the debt, so the firm earns a return that is just sufficient to pay the interest.

Financial leverage,
EPS, and EBIT for the
Trans Can
Corporation

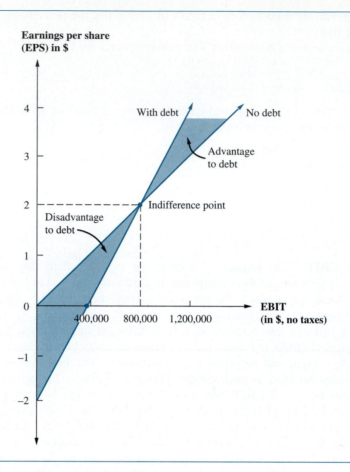

E X A M P L E | 15.1   **Indifference EBIT**

The MPD Corporation has decided in favour of a capital restructuring. Currently, MPD uses no debt financing. Following the restructuring, however, debt would be $1 million. The interest rate on the debt would be 9 percent. MPD currently has 200,000 shares outstanding, and the price per share is $20. If the restructuring is expected to increase EPS, what is the minimum level for EBIT that MPD's management must be expecting? Ignore taxes in answering.

To answer, we calculate EBIT at the indifferent point. At any EBIT above this, the increased financial leverage increases EPS, so this tells us the minimum level for EBIT. Under the old capital structure, EPS is simply EBIT/200,000. Under the new capital structure, the interest expense is $1 million × .09 = $90,000. Furthermore, with the $1 million proceeds, MPD could repurchase $1 million/$20 = 50,000 shares of stock, leaving 150,000 outstanding. EPS is thus (EBIT − $90,000)/150,000.

Now that we know how to calculate EPS under both scenarios, we set them equal to each other and solve for the indifference point EBIT:

EBIT/200,000 = (EBIT − $90,000)/150,000

EBIT = (4/3) × (EBIT − $90,000)

EBIT = $360,000

Check that, in either case, EPS is $1.80 when EBIT is $360,000. Management at MPD is apparently of the opinion that EPS will exceed $1.80. |

Corporate Borrowing and Homemade Leverage

Based on Tables 15.3 and 15.4 and Figure 15.1, Morris draws the following conclusions:

1. The effect of financial leverage depends on Trans Can's EBIT. When EBIT is expected to increase, leverage is beneficial.
2. Under the expected scenario, leverage increases the returns to shareholders, both as measured by ROE and EPS.
3. Shareholders are exposed to more risk under the proposed capital structure since the EPS and ROE are more sensitive to changes in EBIT in this case.
4. Because of the impact that financial leverage has on both the expected return to shareholders and the riskiness of the stock, capital structure is an important consideration.

The first three of these conclusions are clearly correct. Does the last conclusion necessarily follow? Surprisingly, the answer is not necessarily—at least in a world of perfect capital markets where individual investors can borrow at the same rate as corporations. As we discuss next, the reason is that shareholders can adjust the amount of financial leverage by borrowing and lending on their own. This use of personal borrowing to alter the degree of financial leverage is called **homemade leverage**.

We now assume perfect markets and illustrate that it actually makes no difference whether or not Trans Can adopts the proposed capital structure, because any shareholder who prefers the proposed capital structure can simply create it using homemade leverage. To begin, the first part of Table 15.5 shows what would happen to an investor who buys $2,000 worth of Trans Can stock if the proposed capital structure were adopted. This investor purchases 100 shares of stock. From Table 15.4, EPS will either be $.50, $3.00, or $5.50, so the total earnings for 100 shares is either $50, $300, or $550 under the proposed capital structure.

Now, suppose that Trans Can does not adopt the proposed capital structure. In this case, EPS is $1.25, $2.50, or $3.75. The second part of Table 15.5 demonstrates how a shareholder who preferred the payoffs under the proposed structure can create them using personal borrowing. To do this, the shareholder borrows $2,000 at 10 percent on his or her own. Our investor uses this amount, along with the original

homemade leverage *The use of personal borrowing to change the overall amount of financial leverage to which the individual is exposed.*

	Recession	Expected	Expansion
Proposed Capital Structure			
EPS	$ .50	$ 3.00	$ 5.50
Earnings for 100 shares	50.00	300.00	550.00
Net cost = 100 shares at $20 = $2,000			
Original Capital Structure and Homemade Leverage			
EPS	$ 1.25	$ 2.50	$ 3.75
Earnings for 200 shares	250.00	500.00	750.00
Less: Interest on			
$2,000 at 10%	200.00	200.00	200.00
Net earnings	$ 50.00	$300.00	$550.00
Net cost = 200 shares at $20/share − Amount borrowed = $4,000 − 2,000 = $2,000			

TABLE 15.5

Proposed capital structure versus original capital structure with homemade leverage

$2,000, to buy 200 shares of stock. As shown, the net payoffs are exactly the same as those for the proposed capital structure.

How did we know to borrow $2,000 to create the right payoffs? We are trying to replicate Trans Can's proposed capital structure at the personal level. The proposed capital structure results in a debt/equity ratio of 1. To replicate it at the personal level, the shareholder must borrow enough to create this same debt/equity ratio. Since the shareholder has $2,000 in equity invested, borrowing another $2,000 creates a personal debt/equity ratio of 1.

This example demonstrates that investors can always increase financial leverage themselves to create a different pattern of payoffs. It thus makes no difference whether or not Trans Can chooses the proposed capital structure.

E X A M P L E | 15.2   Unlevering the Stock

In our Trans Can example, suppose management adopts the proposed capital structure. Further suppose that an investor who owned 100 shares preferred the original capital structure. Show how this investor could "unlever" the stock to re-create the original payoffs.

To create leverage, investors borrow on their own. To undo leverage, investors must lend money. For Trans Can, the corporation borrowed an amount equal to half its value. The investor can unlever the stock by simply lending money in the same proportion. In this case, the investor sells 50 shares for $1,000 total and then lends out the $1,000 at 10 percent. The payoffs are calculated in the following table.

	Recession	Expected	Expansion
EPS (proposed structure)	$ .50	$ 3.00	$ 5.50
Earnings for 50 shares	25.00	150.00	275.00
Plus: Interest on $1,000	100.00	100.00	100.00
Total payoff	$125.00	$250.00	$375.00

These are precisely the payoffs the investor would have experienced under the original capital structure.

> CONCEPT QUESTIONS
> 1. What is the impact of financial leverage on shareholders?
> 2. What is homemade leverage?
> 3. Why is Trans Can's capital structure irrelevant?

15.3 | CAPITAL STRUCTURE AND THE COST OF EQUITY CAPITAL

We have seen that there is nothing special about corporate borrowing because investors can borrow or lend on their own. As a result, whichever capital structure Trans Can chooses, the stock price is the same. Trans Can's capital structure is thus irrelevant, at least in the simple world we examined.

M&M Proposition I
The value of the firm is independent of its capital structure.

Our Trans Can example is based on a famous argument advanced by two Nobel laureates, Franco Modigliani and Merton Miller, whom we henceforth call M&M. What we illustrated for the Trans Can Company is a special case of **M&M Proposition I.**[3] M&M Proposition I states that it is completely irrelevant how a firm chooses to arrange its finances.

---

[3] Each firm will earn $EBIT each year indefinitely. No EBIT growth is projected.

M&M Proposition I: The Pie Model

One way to illustrate M&M Proposition I is to imagine two firms that are identical on the left side of the balance sheet. Their assets and operations are exactly the same. Each firm earns $EBIT every year indefinitely. No EBIT growth is projected. The right sides are different because the two firms finance their operations differently. We can view the capital structure question as a pie model. Why we chose this name is apparent in Figure 15.2. Figure 15.2 gives two possible ways of cutting up this pie between the equity slice, *E,* and the debt slice, *D:* 40–60 percent and 60–40 percent. However, the size of the pie in Figure 15.2 is the same for both firms because the value of the assets is the same. This is precisely what M&M Proposition I states: The size of the pie doesn't depend on how it is sliced.

Proposition I is expressed in the following formula:

$$V_u = EBIT/R_E{}^u = V_L = E_L + D_L \qquad\qquad [15.3]$$

where

V_u = Value of the unlevered firm

V_L = Value of the levered firm

EBIT = Perpetual operating income

$R_E{}^u$ = Equity required return for the unlevered firm

E_L = Market value of equity

D_L = Market value of debt

The Cost of Equity and Financial Leverage: M&M Proposition II

Although changing the capital structure of the firm may not change the firm's total value, it does cause important changes in the firm's debt and equity. We now examine what happens to a firm financed with debt and equity when the debt/equity ratio is changed. To simplify our analysis, we continue to ignore taxes.

M&M Proposition II   In Chapter 14, we saw that if we ignore taxes the weighted average cost of capital, WACC, is:

$$WACC = (E/V) \times R_E + (D/V) \times R_D$$

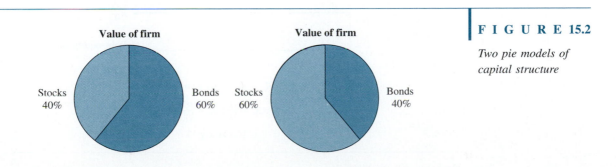

Value of firm   **Value of firm**

Stocks   Bonds   Stocks   Bonds
40%   60%   60%   40%

F I G U R E 15.2

Two pie models of capital structure

where $V = E + D$. We also saw that one way of interpreting the WACC is that it is the required return on the firm's overall assets. To remind us of this, we use the symbol R_A to stand for the WACC and write:

$$R_A = (E/V) \times R_E + (D/V) \times R_D$$

If we rearrange this to solve for the cost of equity capital, we see that:

$$R_E = R_A + (R_A - R_D) \times (D/E) \qquad\qquad [15.4]$$

M&M Proposition II

A firm's cost of equity capital is a positive linear function of its capital structure.

This is the famous **M&M Proposition II**, which tells us that the cost of equity depends on three things, the required rate of return on the firm's assets, R_A, the firm's cost of debt, R_D, and the firm's debt/equity ratio, D/E.

Figure 15.3 summarizes our discussion thus far by plotting the cost of equity capital, R_E, against the debt/equity ratio. As shown, M&M Proposition II indicates that the cost of equity, R_E, is given by a straight line with a slope of $(R_A - R_D)$. The y-intercept corresponds to a firm with a debt/equity ratio of zero, so $R_A = R_E$ in that case. Figure 15.3 shows that, as the firm raises its debt/equity ratio, the increase in leverage raises the risk of the equity and, therefore, the required return or cost of equity (R_E).

Notice in Figure 15.3 that the WACC doesn't depend on the debt/equity ratio; it's the same no matter what the debt/equity ratio is. This is another way of stating M&M Proposition I: The firm's overall cost of capital is unaffected by its capital structure. As illustrated, the fact that the cost of debt is lower than the cost of equity is exactly offset by the increase in the cost of equity from borrowing. In other words, the change in the capital structure weights (E/V and D/V) is exactly offset by the change in the cost of equity (R_E), so the WACC stays the same.

F I G U R E 15.3

The cost of equity and the WACC; M&M Propositions I and II with no taxes

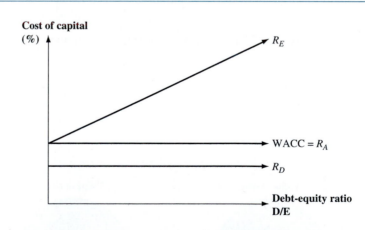

$$R_E = R_A + (R_A - R_D) \times (D/E) \text{ by Proposition II}$$

$$\text{WACC} = \left(\frac{E}{V}\right) R_E + \left(\frac{D}{V}\right) R_D$$

$$V = D + E$$

IN THEIR OWN WORDS . . .

Merton H. Miller on Capital Structure—M&M 30 Years Later

How difficult it is to summarize briefly the contribution of these papers was brought home to me very clearly after Franco Modigliani was awarded the Nobel Prize in Economics, in part—but, of course, only in part—for the work in finance. The television camera crews from our local stations in Chicago immediately descended upon me. "We understand," they said, "that you worked with Modigliani some years back in developing these M&M theorems, and we wonder if you could explain them briefly to our television viewers." "How briefly?" I asked. "Oh, take 10 seconds," was the reply.

Ten seconds to explain the work of a lifetime! Ten seconds to describe two carefully reasoned articles, each running to more than 30 printed pages and each with 60 or so long footnotes! When they saw the look of dismay on my face, they said: "You don't have to go into details. Just give us the main points in simple, common-sense terms."

The main point of the cost-of-capital article was, in principle at least, simple enough to make. It said that in an economist's ideal world, the total market value of all the securities issued by a firm would be governed by the earning power and risk of its underlying real assets and would be independent of how the mix of securities issued to finance it was divided

between debt instruments and equity capital. Some corporate treasurers might well think that they could enhance total value by increasing the proportion of debt instruments because yields on debt instruments, given their lower risk, are, by and large, substantially below those on equity capital. But, under the ideal conditions assumed, the added risk to the shareholders from issuing more debt will raise required yields on the equity by just enough to offset the seeming gain from use of low cost debt.

Such a summary would not only have been too long, but it relied on shorthand terms and concepts that are rich in connotations to economists, but hardly so to the general public. I thought, instead, of an analogy that we ourselves had invoked in the original paper. "Think of the firm," I said, "as a gigantic tub of whole milk. The farmer can sell the whole milk as is. Or he can separate out the cream and sell it at a considerably higher price than the whole milk would bring. (Selling cream is the analog of a firm selling low-yield and hence high-priced debt securities.) But, of course, what the farmer would have left would be skim milk, with low butter-fat content and that would sell for much less than whole milk. Skim milk corresponds to the levered equity. The M&M proposition says that if there were no costs of separation (and, of course, no government

dairy support programs), the cream plus the skim milk would bring the same price as the whole milk."

The television people conferred among themselves for a while. They informed me that it was still too long, too complicated, and too academic. "Have you anything simpler?" they asked. I thought for another way that the M&M proposition is presented which stresses the role of securities as devices for "partitioning" a firm's payoffs among the group of its capital suppliers. "Think of the firm," I said, "as a gigantic pizza, divided into quarters. If now, you cut each quarter in half into eighths, the M&M proposition says that you will have more pieces, but not more pizza."

Once again widespread conversation. This time, they shut the lights off. They folded up their equipment. They thanked me for my cooperation. They said they would get back to me. But I knew that I had somehow lost my chance to start a new career as a packager of economic wisdom for TV viewers in convenient 10-second sound bites. Some have the talent for it; and some just don't.

Merton H. Miller is Robert R. McCormick Distinguished Service Professor at the University of Chicago Graduate School of Business. He is famous for his path-breaking work with Franco Modigliani on corporate capital structure, cost of capital, and dividend policy. He received the Nobel Prize in Economics for his contributions shortly after this essay was prepared.

E X A M P L E | 15.3   **The Cost of Equity Capital**

The Ricardo Corporation has a weighted average cost of capital (unadjusted) of 12 percent. It can borrow at 8 percent. Assuming that Ricardo has a target capital structure of 80 percent equity and 20 percent debt, what is its cost of equity? What is the cost of equity if the target capital structure is 50 percent equity (D/E of 1.0)? Calculate the unadjusted WACC using your answers to verify that it is the same.

According to M&M Proposition II, the cost of equity, R_E, is:

$$R_E = R_A + (R_A - R_D) \times (D/E)$$

In the first case, the debt/equity ratio is .2/.8 = .25, so the cost of the equity is:

$$R_E = 12\% + (12\% - 8\%) \times (.25)$$
$$= 13\%$$

In the second case, check that the debt/equity ratio is 1.0, so the cost of equity is 16 percent.

We can now calculate the unadjusted WACC assuming that the percentage of equity financing is 80 percent and the cost of equity is 13 percent:

$$\text{WACC} = (E/V) \times R_E + (D/V) \times R_D$$
$$= .80 \times 13\% + .20 \times 8\%$$
$$= 12\%$$

In the second case, the percentage of equity financing is 50 percent and the cost of equity is 16 percent. The WACC is:

$$\text{WACC} = (E/V) \times R_E + (D/V) \times R_D$$
$$= .50 \times 16\% \times .50 \times 8\%$$
$$= 12\%$$

As we calculated, the WACC is 12 percent in both cases. |

The SML and M&M Proposition II

In our previous chapter, we discussed the use of the security market line (SML) to estimate the cost of equity capital. If we now combine the SML and M&M Proposition II, we can develop a particularly valuable insight into the cost of equity. Using the SML, we can write the required return on the firm's assets as:

$$R_A = R_f + (R_M - R_f) \times \beta_A$$

The beta coefficient in this case, β_A, is called the firm's asset beta, and it is a measure of the systematic risk of the firm's assets. It is also called the unlevered beta because it is the beta that the stock would have if the firm had no debt.

The cost of equity from the SML is:

$$R_E = R_f + (R_M - R_f) \times \beta_E$$

When this is combined with M&M Proposition II, it is straightforward to show the relationship between the equity beta, β_E, and the asset beta, β_A, is:[4]

$$\beta_E = \beta_A \times (1 + D/E) \qquad\qquad [15.5]$$

The term $(1 + D/E)$ here is the same as the equity multiplier described in Chapter 3, except here it is measured in market values instead of book values. In fact, from the Du Pont identity, we saw that the firm's return on assets (ROA) was equal to its return on equity (ROE) multiplied by the equity multiplier. Here we see a very similar result: The risk premium on the firm's equity is equal to the risk premium on the firm's assets multiplied by the equity multiplier.

We are now in a position to examine directly the impact of financial leverage on the firm's cost of equity. Rewriting things a bit, we see the equity beta has two components:

$$\beta_E = \beta_A + \beta_A \times (D/E)$$

The first component, β_A, is a measure of the riskiness of the firm's assets. Since this is determined primarily by the nature of the firm's operations, we say it measures the **business risk** of the equity. The second component, $\beta_A \times (D/E)$, depends on the firm's financial policy. We therefore say it measures the **financial risk** of the equity.

The total systematic risk of the firm's equity thus has two parts: business risk and financial risk. As we have illustrated, the firm's cost of equity rises when it increases its use of financial leverage because the financial risk of the stock increases. Shareholders require compensation in the form of a larger risk premium, thereby increasing the firm's cost of equity capital.

business risk
The equity risk that comes from the nature of the firm's operating activities.

financial risk
The equity risk that comes from the financial policy (i.e., capital structure) of the firm.

> CONCEPT QUESTIONS
>
> 1. What does M&M Proposition I state?
> 2. What are the two determinants of a firm's cost of equity?

15.4 | M&M PROPOSITIONS I AND II WITH CORPORATE TAXES

Debt has two distinguishing features that we have not taken into proper account: First, as we have mentioned in a number of places, interest paid on debt is tax deductible. This is good for the firm, and it may be an added benefit to debt financing. Second, failure to meet debt obligations can result in bankruptcy. This is not good for the firm, and it may be an added cost of debt financing. Since we haven't explicitly considered either of these two features of debt, we may get a different answer about capital structure once we do. Accordingly, we consider taxes in this section and bankruptcy in the next one.

---

[4] To see this, assume the firm's debt has a beta of zero. This means that $R_D = R_f$. If we substitute for R_A and R_D in M&M Proposition II, we see that:

$$
\begin{aligned}
R_E &= R_A + (R_A - R_D) \times (D/E) \\
&= [R_f + \beta_A \times (R_M - R_f)] + ([R_f + \beta_A \times (R_M - R_f)] - R_f) \times (D/E) \\
&= R_f + (R_M - R_f) \times \beta_A \times (1 + D/E)
\end{aligned}
$$

Thus, the equity beta, β_E, equals the asset beta, β_A, multiplied by the equity multiplier, $(1 + D/E)$.

We can start by considering what happens to M&M Propositions I and II when we look at the effect of corporate taxes. To do this, we examine two firms, Firm U (unlevered) and Firm L (levered). These two firms are identical on the left side of the balance sheet, so their assets and operations are the same.

We assume EBIT is expected to be $1,000 every year forever for both firms. The difference between them is that Firm L has issued $1,000 worth of perpetual bonds on which it pays 8 percent interest every year. The interest bill is thus .08 × $1,000 = $80 every year forever. Also, we assume the corporate tax rate is 30 percent.

For our two firms, U and L, we can now calculate the following:

	Firm U	Firm L
EBIT	$1,000	$1,000
Interest	0	80
Taxable income	$1,000	$ 920
Taxes (30%)	300	276
Net income	$ 700	$ 644

The Interest Tax Shield

To simplify things, we assume depreciation is equal to zero. We also assume capital spending is zero and there are no additions to NWC. In this case, the cash flow from assets is simply equal to EBIT − Taxes. For firms U and L we thus have:

Cash Flow from Assets	Firm U	Firm L
EBIT	$1,000	$1,000
− Taxes	300	276
Total	$ 700	$ 724

We immediately see that capital structure is now having some effect because the cash flows from U and L are not the same even though the two firms have identical assets.

To see what's going on, we can compute the cash flow to stockholders and bondholders.

Cash Flow	Firm U	Firm L
To stockholders	$700	$644
To bondholders	0	80
Total	$700	$724

What we are seeing is that the total cash flow to L is $24 more. This occurs because L's tax bill (which is a cash outflow) is $24 less. The fact that interest is deductible for tax purposes has generated a tax saving equal to the interest payment ($80) multiplied by the corporate tax rate (30 percent): $80 × .30 = $24. We call this tax saving the **interest tax shield**.

interest tax shield

The tax saving attained by a firm from interest expense.

Taxes and M&M Proposition I

Since the debt is perpetual, the same $24 shield would be generated every year forever. The aftertax cash flow to L would thus be the same $700 that U earns plus the $24 tax shield. Since L's cash flow is always $24 greater, Firm L is worth more than Firm U by the value of this perpetuity.

Because the tax shield is generated by paying interest, it has the same risk as the debt, and 8 percent (the cost of debt) is therefore the appropriate discount rate. The value of the tax shield is thus:

$$PV = \$24/.08 = .30 \times 1,000 \times .08/.08 = .30(1,000) = \$300$$

As our example illustrates, the value of the tax shield can be written as:

Value of the interest tax shield $= (T_C \times R_D \times D)/R_D$

$$= T_C \times D \qquad\qquad [15.6]$$

We have now come up with another famous result, M&M Proposition I with corporate taxes. We have seen that the value of Firm L, V_L, exceeds the value of Firm U, V_U, by the present value of the interest tax shield, $T_C \times D$. M&M Proposition I with taxes therefore states that:

$$V_L = V_U + T_C \times D \qquad\qquad [15.7]$$

The effect of borrowing is illustrated in Figure 15.4. We have plotted the value of the levered firm, V_L, against the amount of debt, D. M&M Proposition I with corporate taxes implies that the relationship is given by a straight line with a slope of T_C and a y-intercept of V_U.

In Figure 15.4, we have also drawn a horizontal line representing V_U. As indicated, the distance between the two lines is $T_C \times D$, the present value of the tax shield.

Suppose the cost of capital for Firm U is 10 percent. We call this the **unlevered cost of capital**, and because it is traditional, we use the Greek letter *rho* (ρ) to represent it. We can think of ρ as the cost of the capital the firm would have if it had no debt. Firm U's cash flow is $700 every year forever, and since U has no debt, the appropriate discount rate is $\rho = 10\%$. The value of the unlevered firm, V_U, is simply:

unlevered cost of capital
The cost of capital of a firm that has no debt.

$$\begin{aligned} V_U &= \text{EBIT} \times (1 - T_C)/\rho \\ &= 700/.10 \\ &= \$7,000 \end{aligned}$$

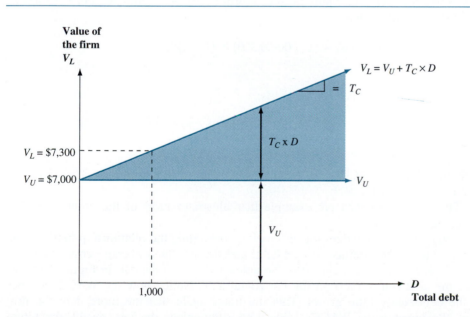

FIGURE 15.4

M&M Proposition I with taxes

The value of the firm increases as total debt increases because of the interest tax shield. This is the basis of M&M Proposition I with taxes.

The value of the levered firm, V_L, is:

$$V_L = V_U + T_C \times D$$
$$= \$7,000 + .30 \times \$1,000$$
$$= \$7,300$$

As Figure 15.4 indicates, the value of the firm goes up by \$.30 for every \$1 in debt. In other words, the NPV per dollar in debt is \$.30. It is difficult to imagine why any corporation would not borrow to the absolute maximum under these circumstances.

The result of our analysis in this section is that, once we include taxes, capital structure definitely matters. However, we immediately reach the illogical conclusion that the optimal capital structure is 100 percent debt.

Taxes, the WACC, and Proposition II

The conclusion that the best capital structure is 100 percent debt also can be seen by examining the weighted average cost of capital. From our previous chapter, we know that, once we consider the effect of taxes, the WACC is:

$$WACC = (E/V) \times R_E + (D/V) \times R_D \times (1 - T_C)$$

To calculate this WACC, we need to know the cost of equity. M&M Proposition II with corporate taxes states that the cost of equity is:

$$R_E = \rho + (\rho - R_D) \times (D/E) \times (1 - T_C) \qquad [15.8]$$

To illustrate, we saw a moment ago that Firm L is worth \$7,300 total. Since the debt is worth \$1,000, the equity must be worth \$7,300 − 1,000 = \$6,300. For Firm L, the cost of equity is thus:

$$R_E = .10 + (.10 - .08) \times (\$1,000/\$6,300) \times (1 - .30)$$
$$= 10.22\%$$

The weighted average cost of capital is:

$$WACC = \$6,300/\$7,300 \times 10.22\% + \$1,000/\$7,300 \times 8\% \times (1 - .30)$$
$$= 9.6\%$$

Without debt, the WACC is 10 percent; with debt, it is 9.6 percent. Therefore, the firm is better off with debt.

This is a comprehensive example that illustrates most of the points we have discussed thus far.

Figure 15.5 summarizes our discussion concerning the relationship between the cost of equity, the aftertax cost of debt, and the weighted average cost of capital. For reference, we have included ρ, the unlevered cost of capital. In Figure 15.5, we have the debt/equity ratio on the horizontal axis. Notice how the WACC declines as the debt/equity ratio grows. This illustrates again that the more debt the firm uses, the lower is its WACC. Table 15.6 summarizes the key results for future reference.

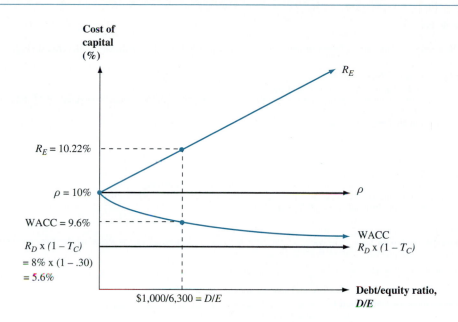

FIGURE 15.5

The cost of equity and the WACC; M&M Propositions I and II with taxes.

$R_E = \rho + (\rho - R_D) \times (D/E) \times (1 - T_C)$ by Proposition II with taxes

$$\text{WACC} = \left(\frac{E}{V}\right) \times R_E + \left(\frac{D}{V}\right) \times R_D \times (1 - T_C)$$

E X A M P L E | 15.4   The Cost of Equity and the Value of the Firm

You are given the following information for the Format Company:

EBIT = $166.67
T_C = .40
D = $500
ρ = .20

The cost of debt capital is 10 percent. What is the value of Format's equity? What is the cost of equity capital for Format? What is the WACC?

This one's easier than it looks. Remember that all the cash flows are perpetuities. The value of the firm if it had no debt, V_U, is:

$V_U = \text{EBIT} \times (1 - T_C)/\rho$
  = 100/.20
  = $500

From M&M Proposition I with taxes, we know that the value of the firm with debt is:

$V_L = V_U + T_C \times D$
  = $500 + .40 \times $500
  = $700

T A B L E   15.6

Modigliani and Miller summary

The no tax case

☐ Proposition I: The value of the firm leveraged (V_L) is equal to the value of the firm unleveraged (V_U):

$V_L = V_U$

Implications of Proposition I:
1. A firm's capital structure is irrelevant.
2. A firm's weighted average cost of capital (WACC) is the same no matter what mixture of debt and equity is used to finance the firm.

☐ Proposition II: The cost of equity, R_E, is

$R_E = R_A + (R_A - R_D) \times D/E,$

where R_A is the WACC, R_D is the cost of debt, and D/E is the debt/equity ratio.

Implications of Proposition II:
1. The cost of equity rises as the firm increases its use of debt financing.
2. The risk of the equity depends on two things, the riskiness of the firm's operations *(business risk)* and the degree of financial leverage *(financial risk)*.

With taxes

☐ Proposition I with taxes: The value of the firm levered (V_L) is equal to the value of the firm unlevered (V_U) plus the present value of the interest tax shield:

$V_L = V_U + T_C \times D$

where T_C is the corporate tax rate and D is the amount of debt.

Implications of Proposition I:
1. Debt financing is highly advantageous, and, in the extreme, a firm's optimal capital structure is 100 percent debt.
2. A firm's weighted average cost of capital (WACC) decreases as the firm relies on debt financing.

☐ Proposition II with taxes: The cost of equity, R_E, is

$R_E = R_U + (R_U - R_D) \times (D/E) \times (1 - T_C),$

where R_U is the *unlevered cost of capital,* that is, the cost of capital for the firm if it had no debt. Unlike Proposition I, the general implications of Proposition II are the same whether there are taxes or not.

Since the firm is worth $700 total and the debt is worth $500, the equity is worth $200.

$$E = V_L - D$$
$$= \$700 - 500$$
$$= \$200$$

Thus, from M&M Proposition II with taxes, the cost of equity is:

$$R_E = \rho + (\rho - R_D) \times (D/E) \times (1 - T_C)$$
$$= .20 + (.20 - .10) \times (\$500/200) \times (1 - .40)$$
$$= 35\%$$

Finally, the WACC is:

$$\text{WACC} = (\$200/700) \times 35\% + (\$500/700) \times 10\% \times (1 - .40)$$
$$= 14.29\%$$

Notice that this is substantially lower than the cost of capital for the firm with no debt ($\rho = 20\%$), so debt financing is highly advantageous.

CONCEPT QUESTIONS

1. What is the relationship between the value of an unlevered firm and the value of a levered firm once we consider the effect of corporate taxes?

2. If we only consider the effect of taxes, what is the optimum capital structure?

15.5 | BANKRUPTCY COSTS

One limit to the amount of debt a firm might use comes in the form of *bankruptcy costs*. Bankruptcy costs are a form of the agency costs of debt introduced in Chapter 1. As the debt/equity ratio rises, so too does the probability that the firm could be unable to pay its bondholders what was promised to them. When this happens, ownership of the firm's assets is ultimately transferred from the shareholders to the bondholders. This was our definition of bankruptcy (in Chapter 12).

In principle, a firm is bankrupt when the value of its assets equals the value of the debt. When this occurs, the value of equity is zero and the shareholders turn over control of the firm to the bondholders. When this takes place, the bondholders hold assets whose value is exactly equal to what is owed on the debt. In a perfect world, there are no costs associated with this transfer of ownership, and the bondholders don't lose anything.

This idealized view of bankruptcy is not, of course, what happens in the real world. Ironically, it is expensive to go bankrupt. As we discuss, the costs associated with bankruptcy may eventually offset the tax-related gains from leverage.

Direct Bankruptcy Costs

When the value of a firm's assets equals the value of its debt, the firm is economically bankrupt in the sense that the equity has no value. However, the formal means of turning over the assets to the bondholders is a legal process, not an economic one. There are legal and administrative costs to bankruptcy, and it has been remarked that bankruptcies are to lawyers what blood is to sharks.

Because of the expenses associated with bankruptcy, bondholders won't get all that they are owed. Some fraction of the firm's assets disappear in the legal process of going bankrupt. These are the legal and administrative expenses associated with the bankruptcy proceeding. We call these costs **direct bankruptcy costs**.

These direct bankruptcy costs are a disincentive to debt financing. When a firm goes bankrupt, suddenly, a piece of the firm disappears. This amounts to a bankruptcy tax. So a firm faces a trade-off: Borrowing saves a firm money on its corporate taxes, but the more a firm borrows, the more likely it is that the firm becomes bankrupt and has to pay the bankruptcy tax.

Indirect Bankruptcy Costs

Because it is expensive to go bankrupt, a firm spends resources to avoid doing so. When a firm is having significant problems in meeting its debt obligations, we say it is experiencing financial distress. Some financially distressed firms ultimately file for bankruptcy, but most do not because they are able to recover or otherwise survive.

The costs of avoiding a bankruptcy filing by a financially distressed firm are one example of **indirect bankruptcy costs**. We use the term **financial distress costs** to

direct bankruptcy costs *The costs that are directly associated with bankruptcy, such as legal and administrative expenses.*

indirect bankruptcy costs *The difficulties of running a business that is experiencing financial distress.*

financial distress costs *The direct and indirect costs associated with going bankrupt or experiencing financial distress.*

refer generically to the direct and indirect costs associated with going bankrupt and/or avoiding a bankruptcy filing.

The problems that come up in financial distress are particularly severe, and the financial distress costs are thus larger, when the shareholders and the bondholders are different groups. Until the firm is legally bankrupt, the shareholders control it. They, of course, take actions in their own economic interests. Since the shareholders can be wiped out in a legal bankruptcy, they have a very strong incentive to avoid a bankruptcy filing.

The bondholders, on the other hand, are primarily concerned with protecting the value of the firm's assets and try to take control away from shareholders. They have a strong incentive to seek bankruptcy to protect their interests and keep shareholders from further dissipating the assets of the firm. The net effect of all this fighting is that a long, drawn-out, and potentially quite expensive, legal battle gets started.

Long before the wheels of justice begin to turn, the assets of the firm lose value because management is busy trying to avoid bankruptcy instead of running the business. Further, as they get desperate, managers may adopt go-for-broke strategies that increase the risk of the firm. A good example of this occurred in the failure of two banks in Western Canada in 1985. Because they were allowed to stay in business although they were economically insolvent, the banks had nothing to lose by taking great risks. Taxpayers will have to pay the bill to shore up the resources of the Canada Deposit Insurance Corporation.

When firms are on the brink of bankruptcy, normal operations are disrupted, and sales are lost. Valuable employees leave, potentially fruitful programs are dropped to preserve cash, and otherwise profitable investments are not taken.

These are all indirect bankruptcy costs, or costs of financial distress. Whether or not the firm ultimately goes bankrupt, the net effect is a loss of value because the firm chose to use too much debt in its capital structure. This possibility of loss limits the amount of debt a firm chooses to use.

Agency Costs of Equity

Bankruptcy costs are agency costs of debt that increase with the amount of debt a firm uses. Agency costs of equity can result from shirking by owner-managers and work in the opposite direction. The idea is that when a firm run by an owner-entrepreneur issues debt, the entrepreneur has an incentive to work harder because he or she retains the claim to all the payoffs beyond the fixed interest on the debt. If the firm issues equity instead, the owner-entrepreneur's stake is diluted. In this case, the entrepreneur has more incentive to work shorter hours and to consume more perquisites (a big office, a company car, more expense account meals) than if the firm issues debt.

Agency costs of equity are likely to be more significant for smaller firms where the dilution of ownership by issuing equity is significant. Underpricing of new equity issues, especially IPOs, discussed in Chapter 13, is shareholders' response to the agency costs of equity. In effect, underpricing passes most of these agency costs back to owner-entrepreneurs. The final effect is that firms may use more debt than otherwise.

In the 1980s, it was argued that *leveraged buyouts (LBOs)* significantly reduced the agency costs of equity. In an LBO, a purchaser (usually a team of existing management) buys out the shareholders at a price above the current market. In other words, the company goes private since the stock is placed in the hands of only a few people. Because the managers now own a substantial chunk of the business, they are likely to work harder than when they were simply employees. The track record of LBOs is at best mixed, so the jury is still out.

> CONCEPT QUESTIONS
> 1. What are direct bankruptcy costs?
> 2. What are indirect bankruptcy costs?
> 3. What are the agency costs of equity?

15.6 | OPTIMAL CAPITAL STRUCTURE

Our previous two sections have established the basis for an optimal capital structure. A firm borrows because the interest tax shield is valuable. At relatively low debt levels, the probability of bankruptcy and financial distress is low, and the benefit from debt outweighs the cost. At very high debt levels, the possibility of financial distress is a chronic, ongoing problem for the firm, so the benefit from debt financing may be more than offset by the financial distress costs. Based on our discussion, it would appear that an optimal capital structure exists somewhere between these extremes.

The Static Theory of Capital Structure

The theory of capital structure that we have outlined is called the **static theory of capital structure**. It says that firms borrow up to the point where the tax benefit from an extra dollar in debt is exactly equal to the cost that comes from the increased probability of financial distress. We call this the static theory because it assumes the firm's assets and operations are fixed and it only considers possible changes in the debt/equity ratio.

The static theory is illustrated in Figure 15.6, which plots the value of the firm, V_L, against the amount of debt, D. In Figure 15.6, we have drawn lines corresponding to three different stories. The first is M&M Proposition I with no taxes. This is the horizontal line extending from V_U, and it indicates that the value of the firm is unaffected by its capital structure. The second case, M&M Proposition I with corporate taxes, is given by the upward-sloping straight line. These two cases are exactly the same as the ones we previously illustrated in Figure 15.4.

The third case in Figure 15.6 illustrates our current discussion: The value of the firm rises to a maximum and then declines beyond that point. This is the picture that we get from our static theory. The maximum value of the firm, V_L^*, is reached at D^*, so this is the optimal amount of borrowing. Put another way, the firm's optimal capital structure is composed of D^*/V_L^* in debt and $(1 - D^*/V_L^*)$ in equity.

The final thing to notice in Figure 15.6 is that the difference between the value of the firm in our static theory and the M&M value of the firm with taxes is the loss in value from the possibility of financial distress. Also, the difference between the static theory value of the firm and the M&M value with taxes is the gain from leverage, net of distress costs.[5]

static theory of capital structure *Theory that a firm borrows up to the point where the tax benefit from an extra dollar in debt is exactly equal to the cost that comes from the increased probability of financial distress.*

---

[5] Another way of arriving at Figure 15.6 is to introduce personal taxes on interest and equity disbursements. Interest is taxed more heavily than dividends and capital gains in Canada. This creates a tax disadvantage to leverage that partially offsets the corporate tax advantage to debt. This argument is developed later.

F I G U R E 15.6

*The static theory of
capital structure. The
optimal capital
structure and the
value of the firm.*

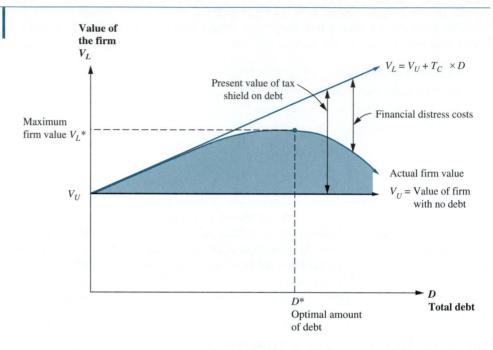

According to the static theory, the gain from the tax shield on debt is offset by financial distress costs. An optimal capital structure exists that just balances the additional gain from leverage against the added financial distress cost.

Optimal Capital Structure and the Cost of Capital

As we discussed earlier, the capital structure that maximizes the value of the firm is also the one that minimizes the cost of capital. Figure 15.7 illustrates the static theory of capital structure in the weighted average cost of capital and the costs of debt and equity. Notice in Figure 15.7 that we have plotted the various capital costs against the debt/equity ratio, *D/E*.

Figure 15.7 is much the same as Figure 15.5 except that we have added a new line for the WACC. This line, which corresponds to the static theory, declines at first. This occurs because the aftertax cost of debt is cheaper than equity, at least initially, so the overall cost of capital declines.

At some point, the cost of debt begins to rise and the fact that debt is cheaper than equity is more than offset by the financial distress costs. At this point, further increases in debt actually increase the WACC. As illustrated, the minimum WACC occurs at the point *D*/E**, just as we described earlier.

Optimal Capital Structure: A Recap

With the help of Figure 15.8, we can recap (no pun intended) our discussion of capital structure and cost of capital. As we have noted, there are essentially three cases. We will use the simplest of the three cases as a starting point and then build up to the static theory of capital structure. Along the way, we will pay particular attention to the connection between capital structure, firm value, and cost of capital.

F I G U R E 15.7

The static theory of capital structure. The optimal capital structure and the cost of capital.

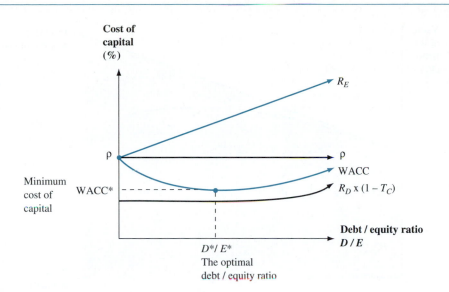

According to the static theory, the WACC falls initially because of the tax advantage to debt. Beyond the point D^*/E^*, it begins to rise because of financial distress costs.

Figure 15.8 illustrates the original Modigliani and Miller (M&M) no-tax, no-bankruptcy argument in Case I. This is the most basic case. In the top part, we have plotted the value of the firm, V_L, against total debt, D. When there are no taxes, bankruptcy costs, or other real-world imperfections, we know that the total value of the firm is not affected by its debt policy, so V_L is simply constant. The bottom part of Figure 15.8 tells the same story in terms of the cost of capital. Here, the weighted average cost of capital, WACC, is plotted against the debt to equity ratio, D/E. As with total firm value, the overall cost of capital is not affected by debt policy in this basic case, so the WACC is constant.

Next, we consider what happens to the original M&M arguments once taxes are introduced. As Case II illustrates, we now see that the firm's value critically depends on its debt policy. The more the firm borrows, the more it is worth. From our earlier discussion, we know this happens because interest payments are tax deductible, and the gain in firm value is just equal to the present value of the interest tax shield.

In the bottom part of Figure 15.8, notice how the WACC declines as the firm uses more and more debt financing. As the firm increases its financial leverage, the cost of equity does increase, but this increase is more than offset by the tax break associated with debt financing. As a result, the firm's overall cost of capital declines.

To finish our story, we include the impact of bankruptcy of financial distress costs to get Case III. As shown in the top part of Figure 15.8, the value of the firm will not be as large as we previously indicated. The reason is that the firm's value is reduced by the present value of the potential future bankruptcy costs. These costs grow as the firm borrows more and more, and they eventually overwhelm the tax advantage of debt financing. The optimal capital structure occurs at D^*, the point at which the tax saving from an additional dollar in debt financing is exactly balanced

F I G U R E 15.8

The capital structure question

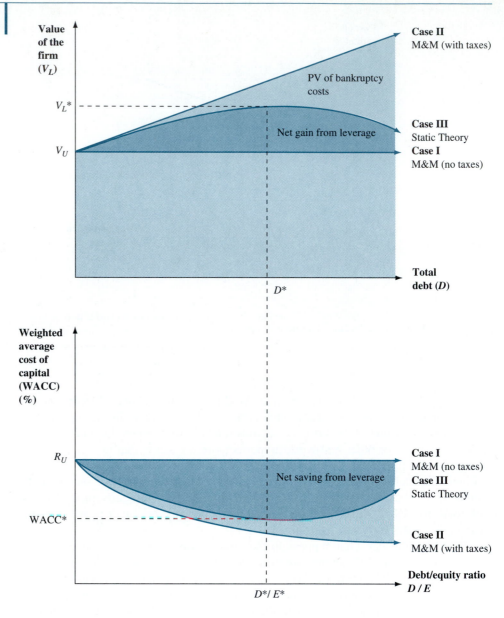

Case I

With no taxes or bankruptcy costs, the value of the firm and its weighted average cost of capital are not affected by capital structures.

Case II

With corporate taxes and no bankruptcy costs, the value of the firm increases and the weighted average cost of capital decreases as the amount of debt goes up.

Case III

With corporate taxes and bankruptcy costs, the value of the firm V_L^* reaches a maximum at D^*, the optimal amount of borrowing. At the same time, the weighted average cost of capital, WACC*, is minimized at D^*/E^*.

by the increased bankruptcy costs associated with the additional borrowing. This is the essence of the static theory of capital structure.

The bottom part of Figure 15.8 presents the optimal capital structure in terms of the cost of capital. Corresponding to D^*, the optimal debt level, is the optimal debt to equity ratio, D^*/E^*. At this level of debt financing, the lowest possible weighted average cost of capital, WACC*, occurs.

Capital Structure: Some Managerial Recommendations

The static model that we described is not capable of identifying a precise optimal capital structure, but it does point out two of the more relevant factors: taxes and financial distress. We can draw some limited conclusions concerning these.

Taxes   First, the tax benefit from leverage is obviously important only to firms that are in a tax-paying position. Firms with substantial accumulated losses get little value from the tax shield. Furthermore, firms that have substantial tax shields from other sources, such as depreciation, get less benefit from leverage.

Also, not all firms have the same tax rate. The higher the tax rate, the greater the incentive to borrow.

Financial Distress   Firms with a greater risk of experiencing financial distress borrow less than firms with a lower risk of financial distress. For example, all other things being equal, the greater the volatility in EBIT, the less a firm should borrow.

In addition, financial distress is more costly for some firms than others. The costs of financial distress depend primarily on the firm's assets. In particular, financial distress costs are determined by how easily ownership to those assets can be transferred.

For example, a firm with mostly tangible assets that can be sold without great loss in value has an incentive to borrow more. If a firm has a large investment in land, buildings, and other tangible assets, it has less financial distress than a firm with a large investment in research and development. Research and development typically has less resale value than land; thus, most of its value disappears in financial distress.

> CONCEPT QUESTIONS
> 1. Describe the trade-off that defines the static theory of capital structure?
> 2. What are the important factors in making capital structure decisions?

15.7 | THE PIE AGAIN

Although it is comforting to know that the firm might have an optimal capital structure when we take account of such real-world matters as taxes and financial distress costs, it is disquieting to see the elegant, original M&M intuition (that is, the no-tax version) fall apart in the face of them.

Critics of the M&M theory often say it fails to hold as soon as we add in real-world issues and that the M&M theory is really just that, a theory that doesn't have much to say about the real world that we live in. In fact, they would argue that it is the M&M theory that is irrelevant, not capital structure. As we discuss next, however, taking that view blinds critics to the real value of the M&M theory.

The Extended Pie Model

To illustrate the value of the original M&M intuition, we briefly consider an expanded version of the pie model that we introduced earlier. In the extended pie model, taxes just represent another claim on the cash flows of the firm. Since taxes are reduced as leverage is increased, the value of the government's claim (G) on the firm's cash flows decreases with leverage.

Bankruptcy costs are also a claim on the cash flows. They come into play as the firm comes close to bankruptcy and has to alter its behaviour to attempt to stave off the event itself, and they become large when bankruptcy actually occurs. Thus, the value of the cash flows to this claim (B) rises with the debt/equity ratio.

The extended pie theory simply holds that all of these claims can be paid from only one source, the cash flows (CF) of the firm. Algebraically, we must have:

CF = Payments to shareholders + Payments to bondholders

　　+ Payments to the government

　　+ Payments to bankruptcy courts and lawyers

　　+ Payments to any and all other claimants to the cash flow of the firm

The extended pie model is illustrated in Figure 15.9. Notice that we have added a few slices for the other groups. Notice also the relative size of the slices as the firm's use of debt financing is increased.

With this list, we have not even begun to exhaust the potential claims to the firm's cash flows. To give an unusual example, everyone reading this book has an economic claim to the cash flows of General Motors Corporation (GM). After all, if you are injured in an accident, you might sue GM, and, win or lose, GM expends some of its cash flow in dealing with the matter. For GM, or any other company, there should thus be a slice of the pie representing the potential lawsuits.

This is the essence of the M&M intuition and theory: The value of the firm depends on the total cash flow of the firm. The firm's capital structure just cuts that cash flow up into slices without altering the total. What we recognize now is that the stockholders and the bondholders may not be the only ones who can claim a slice.

F I G U R E 15.9

The extended pie model

Lower financial leverage

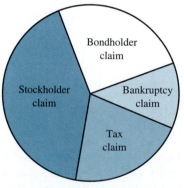

Higher financial leverage

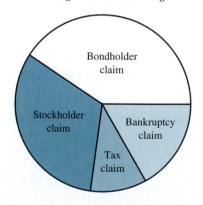

In the extended pie model, the value of all the claims against the firm's cash flows is not affected by capital structure, but the relative value of claims changes as the amount of debt financing is increased.

Marketed Claims versus Non-marketed Claims

With our extended pie model, there is an important distinction between claims such as those of shareholders and bondholders, on the one hand, and those of the government and potential litigants in lawsuits on the other. The first set of claims are *marketed claims,* and the second set are *non-marketed claims.* A key difference is that the marketed claims can be bought and sold in financial markets and the non-marketed claims cannot be.

When we speak of the value of the firm, we are generally referring just to the value of the marketed claims, V_M, and not the value of the non-marketed claims, V_N. If we write V_T for the total value of all the claims against a corporation's cash flows, then:

$$V_T = E + D + G + B + \ldots$$
$$= V_M + V_N$$

The essence of our extended pie model is that this total value, V_T, of all the claims to the firm's cash flows is unaltered by capital structure. However, the value of the marketed claims, V_M, may be affected by changes in the capital structure.

By the pie theory, any increase in V_M must imply an identical decrease in V_N. The optimal capital structure is thus the one that maximizes the value of the marketed claims, or, equivalently, minimizes the value of non-marketed claims such as taxes and bankruptcy costs.

CONCEPT QUESTIONS

1. What are some of the claims to a firm's cash flows?
2. What is the difference between a marketed claim and a non-marketed claim?
3. What does the extended pie model say about the value of all the claims to a firm's cash flows?

15.8 | OBSERVED CAPITAL STRUCTURES

No two firms have identical capital structures. Nonetheless, we see some regular elements when we start looking at actual capital structures. We discuss a few of these next.

Figure 15.10 shows the trend in debt-to-equity ratios (measured at book values) for large industrial corporations in Canada and the United States. Notice that the debt ratios in Canada are quite a bit lower. Although most corporations have debt in their capital structures, they still pay substantial amounts of taxes. Thus, it is clear that corporations have not issued debt up to the point that tax shelters have been completely used up, and we conclude that there must be limits to the amount of debt corporations can issue.

Some large corporations in the United States tested those limits in the 1980s. Use of leverage by large U.S. corporations increased substantially in the 1980s in part due to leveraged buyouts.[6] In certain well-known cases, Donald Trump and Robert Campeau are two examples, leverage became excessive. Figure 15.10 shows that the trend toward higher leverage did not extend to Canada. Why Canadian firms use

[6] For example, Ben Bernanke, "Is There Too Much Corporate Debt?" *Business Review* of the Federal Reserve Bank of Philadelphia, September–October 1989, pp. 3–13, reports that the debt of non-financial corporations rose 70 percent between 1983 and 1988, more than two-thirds faster than the growth in GNP.

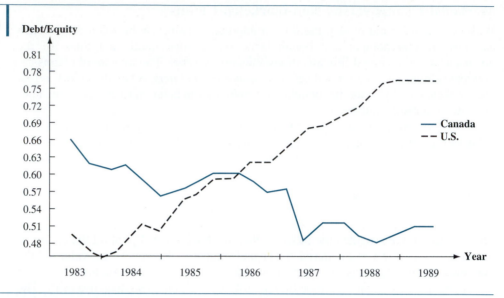

FIGURE 15.10

Canadian and U.S. debt-to-equity ratios for industrial corporations

Source: J. Grant, M. Webb, and P. Hendrick, "Financing Corporate Canada in the 1990s," *Canadian Investment Review,* Spring 1990, p. 10.

proportionately less debt is a controversial question. One possible explanation is the difference in personal taxes. In Canada, the dividend tax credit reduces personal taxes on equity distributions and reduces the tax advantage of debt financing.

A second regularity is apparent when we compare capital structures across industries. Table 15.7 shows Canadian debt/equity ratios for selected industries measured at book values. You can see rather large differences in the use of debt among industries. Steel mills, for example, carry about twice as much debt as manufacturers of communication equipment. This is consistent with our discussion of the costs of financial distress. Steel mills have large tangible assets while communication equipment firms carry significant intangible assets in the form of research and development.

Further, because different industries have different operating characteristics, for example, EBIT volatility and asset types, there does appear to be some connection between these characteristics and capital structure. Our story involving tax savings and financial distress costs is undoubtedly part of the reason, but, to date, there is no fully satisfactory theory that explains these regularities.

In practice, firms (and lenders) also look at the industry's debt/equity ratio as a guide. This practice creates a market for Dun & Bradstreet (our source in Table 15.7), a commercial supplier of ratios to financial analysts and bankers. If the industry is sound, the industry average provides a useful benchmark. Of course, if the entire industry is in distress, the average leverage is likely too high. For example, in 1989, the average debt/equity ratio of 3.206 for fishing and trapping was probably too high.

CONCEPT QUESTIONS

1. Do Canadian corporations rely heavily on debt financing? What about U.S. corporations?

2. What regularities do we observe in capital structures?

Industry	Ratio	Companies
Retail Trade	2.214	85,890
Auto accessories and parts	3.048	2,929
Food stores	1.828	12,859
Gas service stations	2.576	6,878
Manufacturers	1.253	41,801
Agricultural implements	2.739	230
Cement	0.814	20
Industrial chemicals	2.041	139
Men's clothing	1.424	738
Women's clothing	1.883	1,313
Communication equipment	0.635	503
Distilleries	1.032	25
Industrial electrical equipment	0.898	223
Fish products	4.053	468
Glass and glass products	1.101	195
Motor vehicles and parts	1.149	463
Paint and varnish	0.956	131
Paper products	0.939	246
Petroleum refineries	0.985	80
Pharmaceuticals	0.686	141
Pulp and paper mills	1.446	111
Rubber products	1.202	156
Sawmills and planing mills	2.160	1,236
Soap and cleaning compounds	0.745	125
Steel and iron mills	1.389	111
Textile products	1.431	706
Wineries	0.877	41
Wood products	1.929	465
Construction	3.005	59,286
Services	2.631	120,965
Mining	1.318	7,797
Agriculture, forestry, and fishery	1.828	23,030
Agriculture	1.890	17,435
Fishing and trapping	3.206	1,550
Forestry	1.368	4,045

T A B L E 15.7

Book value debt/equity ratios for selected industries in Canada, 1989

Source: Dun & Bradstreet, *Key Business Ratios of Canadian Businesses,* 1989.

15.9 | SUMMARY AND CONCLUSIONS

The ideal mixture of debt and equity for a firm—its optimal capital structure—is the one that maximizes the value of the firm and minimizes the overall cost of capital. If we ignore taxes, financial distress costs, and any other imperfections, we find that there is no ideal mixture. Under these circumstances, the firm's capital structure is simply irrelevant, as we see in M&M Proposition I and II.

If we consider the effect of corporate taxes, we find that capital structure matters a great deal. This conclusion is based on the fact that interest is tax deductible and thus generates a valuable tax shield. Unfortunately, we also find that the optimal capital structure is 100 percent debt, which is not something we observe for healthy firms.

We next introduced costs associated with bankruptcy, or, more generally, financial distress. These costs reduce the attractiveness of debt financing. We concluded that an optimal capital structure exists when the net tax saving from an additional dollar in interest just equals the increase in expected financial distress costs. This is the essence of the static theory of capital structure.

When we examine actual capital structures, we find two regularities: First, firms in Canada typically do not use great amounts of debt, but they pay substantial taxes. This suggests there is a limit to the use of debt financing to generate tax shields. Second, firms in similar industries tend to have similar capital structures, suggesting that the nature of their assets and operations is an important determinant of capital structure.

Key Terms

homemade leverage (page 537)

M&M Proposition I (page 538)

M&M Proposition II (page 540)

business risk (page 543)

financial risk (page 543)

interest tax shield (page 544)

unlevered cost of capital (page 545)

direct bankruptcy costs (page 549)

indirect bankruptcy costs (page 549)

financial distress costs (page 549)

static theory of capital structure (page 551)

Chapter Review Problems and Self-Test

15.1   **EBIT and EPS**   Suppose the GNR Corporation has decided in favour of a capital restructuring that involves increasing its existing $5 million in debt to $25 million. The interest rate on the debt is 12 percent and is not expected to change. The firm currently has 1 million shares outstanding, and the price per share is $40. If the restructuring is expected to increase the ROE, what is the minimum level for EBIT that GNR's management must be expecting? Ignore taxes in your answer.

15.2   **M&M Proposition II (no taxes)**   The Pro Bono Corporation has a WACC of 20 percent. Its cost of debt is 12 percent. If Pro Bono's debt/equity ratio is 2, what is its cost of equity capital? If Pro Bono's equity beta is 1.5, what is its asset beta? Ignore taxes in your answer.

15.3   **M&M Proposition I (with corporate taxes)**   The Deathstar Telecom Company (motto: "Reach out and clutch someone") expects an EBIT of $4,000 every year forever. Deathstar can borrow at 10 percent.

Suppose that Deathstar currently has no debt and its cost of equity is 14 percent. If the corporate tax rate is 30 percent, what is the value of the firm? What will the value be if Deathstar borrows $6,000 and uses the proceeds to buy up stock?

Answers to Self-Test Problems

15.1   To answer, we can calculate the break-even EBIT. At any EBIT more than this, the increased financial leverage increases EPS. Under the old capital structure, the interest bill is $5 million × .12 = $600,000. There are 1 million shares of stock, so, ignoring taxes, EPS is (EBIT − $600,000)/1 million.

Under the new capital structure, the interest expense is $25 million × .12 = $3 million. Furthermore, the debt rises by $20 million. This amount is sufficient to repurchase $20 million/$40 = 500,000 shares of stock, leaving 500,000 outstanding. EPS is thus (EBIT − $3 million)/500,000.

Now that we know how to calculate EPS under both scenarios, we set them equal to each other and solve for the break-even EBIT;

$$(EBIT − \$600,000)/1 \text{ million} = (EBIT − \$3 \text{ million})/500,000$$
$$(EBIT − \$600,000) = 2 × (EBIT − \$3 \text{ million})$$
$$EBIT = \$5,400,000$$

Check that, in either case, EPS is $4.80 when EBIT is $5.4 million.

15.2 According to M&M Proposition III (no taxes), the cost of equity is:

$$R_E = R_A + (R_A − R_D) × (D/E)$$
$$= 20\% + (20\% − 12\%) × 2$$
$$= 36\%$$

Also, we know that the equity beta is equal to the asset beta multiplied by the equity multiplier:

$$\beta_E = \beta_A × (1 + D/E)$$

In this case, D/E is 2 and β_E is 1.5, so the asset beta is 1.5/3 = .50.

15.3 With no debt, Deathstar's WACC is 14 percent. This is also the unlevered cost of capital. The aftertax cash flow is $4,000 × (1 − .30) = $2,800, so the value is just $V_U = \$2,800/.14 = \$20,000$.

After the debt issue, Deathstar is worth the original $20,000 plus the present value of the tax shield. According to M&M Proposition I with taxes, thepresent value of the tax shield is $T_c × D$, or .30 × $6,000 = $1,800, so the firm is worth $20,000 + 1,800 = $21,800.

Questions and Problems

1. **EBIT and Leverage** Debreu, Inc., has no debt outstanding and a total market value of $60,000. Earnings before interest and taxes (EBIT) are projected to be $5,000 if economic conditions are normal. If there is strong expansion in the economy, then EBIT will be 40 percent higher. If there is a recession, then EBIT will be 50 percent lower. Debreu is considering a $24,000 debt issue with a 10 percent interest rate. The proceeds will be used to buy up shares of stock. There are currently 1,000 shares outstanding. Ignore taxes for this problem.

   a. Calculate earnings per share (EPS) under each of the three economic scenarios before any debt is issued. Also, calculate the percentage changes in EPS when the economy expands or enters a recession.
   b. Repeat part *(a)* assuming that Debreu goes through with recapitalization. What do you observe?

2. **EBIT, Taxes, and Leverage** Repeat parts *(a)* and *(b)* in Problem 1 assuming Debreu has a tax rate of 35 percent.

3. **ROE and Leverage** Suppose the company in Problem 1 has a market-to-book ratio of 1.0.

   a. Calculate return on equity (ROE) under each of the three economic scenarios before any debt is issued. Also, calculate the percentage changes in ROE for economic expansion and recession.
   b. Repeat part *(a)* assuming the firm goes through with the proposed recapitalization.

Basic (Questions 1–15)

    c. Repeat parts *(a)* and *(b)* of this problem assuming the firm has a tax rate of 35 percent.

4. **Break-even EBIT**   Schwietzer Corporation is comparing two different capital structures, an all-equity plan (Plan I) and a levered plan (Plan II). Under Plan I, Schwietzer would have 300,000 shares of stock outstanding. Under Plan II, there would be 200,000 shares of stock outstanding and $6 million in debt outstanding. The interest rate on the debt is 9 percent and there are no taxes.

    a. If EBIT is $900,000, which plan will result in the higher EPS?

    b. If EBIT is $2.1 million, which plan will result in the higher EPS?

    c. What is the break-even EBIT? What is EPS at this level of EBIT?

5. **M&M and Stock Value**   In Problem 4, use M&M Proposition I to find the price per share of equity under each of the two proposed plans. What is the value of the firm?

6. **Break-even EBIT and Leverage**   The Milhone Co. is comparing two different capital structures. Plan I would result in 750 shares of stock and $8,750 in debt. Plan II would result in 900 shares of stock and $3,500 in debt. The interest rate on the debt is 8 percent.

    a. Ignoring taxes, compare both of these plans to an all-equity plan assuming that EBIT will be $2,500. The all-equity plan would result in 1,000 shares of stock outstanding. Which of the three plans has the highest EPS? The lowest?

    b. In part *(a)*, what are the break-even levels of EBIT for each plan compared to an all-equity plan? Is one higher than the other? Why?

    c. Ignoring taxes, when will EPS be identical for Plans I and II?

    d. Repeat parts *(a)*, *(b)*, and *(c)* assuming that the corporate tax rate is 38 percent. Are the break-even levels of EBIT different from before? Why or why not?

7. **Leverage and Stock Value**   Ignoring taxes in Problem 6, what is the price per share of the equity under Plan I? Plan II? What principle is illustrated by your answers?

8. **Homemade Leverage**   Buckner and Durham Inc., a prominent waste management firm, is debating whether to convert its all-equity capital structure to one that is 30 percent debt. Currently, there are 400 shares outstanding and the price per share is $75. EBIT is expected to remain at $1,000 per year forever. The interest rate on new debt is 11 percent, and there are no taxes.

    a. Mr. Smith, a shareholder of the firm, owns 80 shares of stock. What is his cash flow under the current capital structure, assuming the firm has a dividend payout rate of 100 percent?

    b. What will Mr. Smith's cash flow be under the proposed capital structure of the firm? Assume that he keeps all 80 of his shares.

    c. Suppose Buckner and Durham does convert, but Mr. Smith prefers the current all-equity capital structure. Show how he could unlever his shares of stock to re-create the original capital structure.

    d. Using your answer in part *(c)*, explain why Buckner and Durham's choice of capital structure is irrelevant.

9. **Homemade Leverage and WACC**   ABC Co. and XYZ Co. are identical firms in all respects except for their capital structure. ABC is all-equity financed with $250,000 in stock. XYZ uses both stock and perpetual debt; its stock is

worth $125,000 and the interest rate on its debt is 10 percent. Both firms expect EBIT to be $37,500. Ignore taxes.

**Basic
(Continued)**

   a. Ms. Jones owns $25,000 worth of XYZ's stock. What rate of return is she expecting?

   b. Show how Ms. Jones could generate exactly the same cash flows and rate of return by investing in ABC and using homemade leverage.

   c. What is the cost of equity for ABC? What is it for XYZ?

   d. What is the WACC for ABC? For XYZ? What principle have you illustrated?

10. **M&M**   Super Safe Corp. uses no debt. The weighted average cost of capital is 12 percent. If the current market value of the equity is $30 million and there are no taxes, what is EBIT?

11. **M&M and Taxes**   In the previous question, suppose the corporate tax rate is 34 percent. What is EBIT in this case? What is the WACC? Explain.

12. **Calculating WACC**   Brinkman Industries has a debt/equity ratio of 1.5. Its WACC is 11.5 percent, and its cost of debt is 8 percent. The corporate tax rate is 35 percent.

   a. What is Brinkman's cost of equity capital?

   b. What is Brinkman's unlevered cost of equity capital?

   c. What would the cost of equity be if the debt/equity ratio was 1.0? What if it was 0.5? What if it was zero?

13. **Calculating WACC**   Stringlet Corp. has no debt but can borrow at 10 percent. The firm's WACC is currently 14 percent and the tax rate is 39 percent.

   a. What is Stringlet's cost of equity?

   b. If the firm converts to 40 percent debt, what will its cost of equity be?

   c. If the firm converts to 70 percent debt, what will its cost of equity be?

   d. What is Stringlet's WACC in part *(a)*? In part *(b)*?

14. **M&M and Taxes**   Stefaniak & Co. expects its EBIT to be $25,000 every year forever. The firm can borrow at 9 percent. Stefaniak currently has no debt and its cost of equity is 15 percent. If the tax rate is 35 percent, what is the value of the firm? What will the value be if Stefaniak borrows $50,000 and uses the proceeds to buy up shares?

15. **M&M and Taxes**   In Problem 14, what is the cost of equity after recapitalization? What is the WACC? What are the implications for the firm's capital structure decision?

16. **Business and Financial Risk**   Explain what is meant by business and financial risk. Suppose Firm A has greater business risk than Firm B. Is it true that Firm A also has a higher cost of equity capital? Explain.

**Intermediate
(Questions 16–21)**

17. **Risk and Capital Costs**   How would you answer in the following debate?

   Q: Isn't it true that the riskiness of a firm's equity will rise if it increases its use of debt financing?

   A: Yes, that's the essence of M&M Proposition II.

   Q: And isn't it true that, as a firm increases its use of borrowing, the likelihood of default increases, thereby increasing the risk of the firm's debt?

   A: Yes.

   Q: In other words, increased borrowing increases the risk of the equity *and* the debt?

**Intermediate
(Continued)**

A: That's right.

Q: Well, given that the firm only uses debt and equity financing, and given that the risks of both are increased by increased borrowing, does it not follow that increasing debt increases the overall risk of the firm and therefore decreases the value of the firm?

A: ??

18. **Optimal Capital Structure**   Is there an easily identifiable debt/equity ratio that will maximize the value of a firm? Why or why not?

19. **Capital Structures**   Refer to the observed capital structures given in Table 15.7 of the text. What do you notice about the types of industries with respect to their average debt/equity ratios? Are certain types of industries more likely to be highly leveraged than others? What are some possible reasons for this observed segmentation? Do the operating results and tax history of the firms play a role? How about their future earnings prospects? Explain.

20. **M&M**   Clines Manufacturing has an expected EBIT of $2,880 in perpetuity, a tax rate of 35 percent, and a debt/equity ratio of 0.5. The firm has $8,000 in outstanding debt at an interest rate of 7 percent, and its WACC is 10.6 percent. What is the value of the firm according to M&M Proposition I with taxes? Should Clines change its debt/equity ratio if the goal is to maximize the value of the firm? Explain.

21. **Firm Value**   Corrado Corporation expects an EBIT of $12,000 every year forever. Corrado currently has no debt, and its cost of equity is 22 percent. The firm can borrow at 14 percent. If the corporate tax rate is 38 percent, what is the value of the firm? What will the value be if Corrado converts to 50 percent debt? 100 percent debt?

**Challenge
(Questions 22–25)**

22. **Weighted Average Cost of Capital**   Assuming a world of corporate taxes only, show that the WACC can be written as: $\text{WACC} = R_U \times [1 - T_c (D/V)]$.

23. **Cost of Equity and Leverage**   Assuming a world of corporate taxes only, show that the cost of equity, R_E, is as given in the chapter by M&M Proposition II with corporate taxes.

24. **Business and Financial Risk**   Assume a firm's debt is risk-free, so that the cost of debt equals the risk-free rate, R_f. Define β_A as the firm's *asset* beta, that is, the systematic risk of the firm's assets. Define β_E to be the beta of the firm's equity. Use the capital asset pricing model (CAPM) along with M&M Proposition II to show that: $\beta_E = B_A \times (1 + D/E)$, where D/E is the debt/equity ratio. Assume the tax rate is zero.

25. **Stockholder Risk**   Suppose a firm's business operations are such that they mirror movements in the economy as a whole very closely, i.e., the firm's asset beta is 1.0. Use the result of Problem 24 to find the equity beta for this firm for debt/equity ratios of 0, 1, 5, and 20. What does this tell you about relationship between capital structure and shareholder risk? How is the shareholders' required return on equity affected? Explain.

Suggested Readings

The classic articles on capital structure are:

Modigliani, F., and M. H. Miller. "The Cost of Capital, Corporate Finance, and the Theory of Investment." *American Economic Review* 48 (June 1958).

_____ . "Corporation Income Taxes and the Cost of Capital: A Correction." *American Economic Review* 53 (June 1963).

Some research on capital structure is summarized in:

> Smith, C. "Raising Capital: Theory and Evidence." *Midland Corporate Finance Journal,* Spring 1986.

The text of Stewart Myers's 1984 presidential address to the American Finance Association is in the following article. It summarizes the academic insights on capital structure until the early 1980s and points out directions for future research:

> Myers, S. "The Capital Structure Puzzle." *Midland Corporate Finance Journal,* Fall 1985.

CAPITAL STRUCTURE AND PERSONAL TAXES

Up to this point, we considered corporate taxes only. Unfortunately, Revenue Canada does not let us off that easily. As we saw in Chapter 2, income to individuals is taxed at different rates. For individuals in the top brackets, some kinds of personal income can be taxed more heavily than corporate income.

Earlier, we showed that the value of a levered firm equals the value of an identical unlevered firm, V_U plus the present value of the interest tax shield $T_C \times D$.

$$V_L = V_U + T_C \times D$$

This approach considered only corporate taxes. In a classic paper, Miller derived another expression for the value of the levered firm taking into account personal taxes.[7] In Equation 15A.1, T_b is the personal tax rate on ordinary income, such as interest and T_S is the personal tax rate on equity distributions—dividends and capital gains.[8]

$$V_L = V_U + \left[1 - \frac{(1 - T_C) \times (1 - T_S)}{(1 - T_b)} \right] \times B \qquad \text{[15A.1]}$$

---

[7] M. H. Miller, "Debt and Taxes," *Journal of Finance* 32 (May 1977), pp. 261–75.

[8] Stockholders receive

$(\text{EBIT} - r_B B) \times (1 - T_C) \times (1 - T_S)$

Bondholders receive

$r_B B \times (1 - T_B)$

Thus, the total cash flow to all stakeholders is

$(\text{EBIT} - r_B B) \times (1 - T_C) \times (1 - T_S) + r_B B \times (1 - T_b)$

which can be rewritten as

$$\text{EBIT} \times (1 - T_C) \times (1 - T_S) + r_B B \times (1 - T_b) \times \left[1 - \frac{(1 - T_C) \times (1 - T_S)}{1 - T_b} \right] \qquad \text{(a)}$$

The first term in Equation [a] is the cash flow from an unlevered firm after all taxes. The value of this stream must be V_U the value of an unlevered firm. An individual buying a bond for B receives $r_B B \times (1 - T_b)$ after all taxes. Thus, the value of the second term in (a) must be

$$B \times \left[1 - \frac{(1 - T_C) \times (1 - T_S)}{1 - T_b} \right]$$

Therefore, the value of the stream in (a), which is the value of the levered firm, must be

$$V_U + \left[1 - \frac{(1 - T_C) \times (1 - T_S)}{1 - T_b} \right] \times B$$

F I G U R E 15A.1

*Gains from financial
leverage with both
corporate and
personal taxes.*

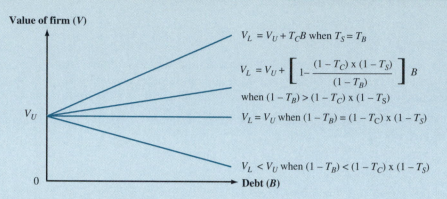

T_C is the corporate tax rate.
T_B is the personal tax rate on interest.
T_S is the personal tax rate on dividends and other equity distributions.
Both personal taxes and corporate taxes are included. Bankruptcy costs and agency costs are ignored. The effect of debt on firm value depends on T_S, T_C, and T_B.

Value of the Firm with Personal and Corporate Taxes

If the personal tax rates on interest (T_b) and on equity distributions (T_S) happen to be the same, then our new, more complex expression (Equation 15A.1) simplifies to Equation 15.7, which is the result when there are no personal taxes. It follows that introducing personal taxes does not affect our valuation formula as long as equity distributions are taxed identically to interest at the personal level.

However, the gain from leverage is reduced when equity distributions are taxed more lightly than interest, that is when T_S is less than T_b. Here, more taxes are paid at the personal level for a levered firm than for an unlevered firm. In fact, imagine that $(1 - T_C) \times (1 - T_S) = 1 - T_b$. Formula 15A.1 tells us there is no gain from leverage at all! In other words, the value of the levered firm is equal to the value of the unlevered firm. The reason there is no gain from leverage is that the lower corporate taxes for a levered firm are exactly offset by higher personal taxes. These results are presented in Figure 15A.1.

E X A M P L E | **15A.1   Financial Leverage with Personal Taxes**

Acme Industries anticipates a perpetual pretax earning stream of $100,000 and faces a 45 percent corporate tax rate. Investors discount the earnings stream after corporate taxes at 15 percent. The personal tax rate on equity distributions is 30 percent and the personal tax rate on interest is 47 percent. Acme currently has an all-equity capital structure but is considering borrowing $120,000 at 10 percent.

The value of the all-equity firm is:[9]

$$V_U = \frac{\$100,000 \times (1 - .45)}{0.15} = \$366,667$$

---

[9] Alternatively, we could have said that investors discount the earnings stream after both corporate and personal taxes at 10.5% = 15% (1 − .30):

$$V_U = \frac{\$100,000 \times (1 - .45) \times (1 - .30)}{.105} = \$366,667$$

The value of the levered firm is

$$V_L = \$366,667 + \frac{[1 - (1 - .45) \times (1 - .30)]}{(1 - .47)} \times \$120,000 = \$399,497$$

The advantage to leverage here is $399,497 - $366,667 = $32,830. This is much smaller than the $54,000 = .45 \times $120,000 = T_C \times B$, which would have been the gain in a world with no personal taxes.

Acme had previously considered the choice years earlier when $T_B = 60$ percent and $T_S = 18$ percent. Here

$$V_L = \$366,667 + \frac{[1 - (1 - .45) \times (1 - .18)]}{(1 - .60)} \times \$120,000 = \$351,367$$

In this case, the value of the levered firm, V_L, is $351,367 which is less than the value of the unlevered firm, $V_U = $366,667. Hence, Acme was wise not to increase leverage years ago. Leverage causes a loss of value because the personal tax rate on interest is much higher than the personal tax rate on equity distributions. In other words, the reduction in corporate taxes from leverage is more than offset by the increase in taxes from leverage at the personal level.

Figure 15A.1 summarizes the different cases we considered. Which one is the most applicable to Canada? While the numbers are different for different firms in different provinces, Chapter 2 showed that interest income is taxed at the full marginal rate, around 47 percent including surtaxes for the top bracket. Equity distributions take the form of either dividends or capital gains and both are taxed more lightly than interest. As we showed in Chapter 2, dividend income is sheltered by the dividend tax credit.

While the exact numbers depend on the type of portfolio chosen, our first scenario for Acme is a reasonable tax scenario for Canadian investors and companies.[10] In Canada, personal taxes reduce, but do not eliminate, the advantage to corporate leverage.

This result is still unrealistic. It suggests that firms should add debt, moving out on the second line from the top in Figure 15A.1, until 100 percent leverage is reached. Firms do not do this. One reason is that interest on debt is not the firm's only tax shield. Investment tax credits, capital cost allowance, and depletion allowances give rise to tax shields regardless of the firm's decision on leverage. Because these other tax shields exist, increased leverage brings with it a risk that income will not be high enough to utilize the debt tax shield fully. The result is that firms use a limited amount of debt.[11]

Of course, as we argued in the chapter, the costs of bankruptcy and financial distress are another reason healthy firms do not use 100 percent debt financing.

CONCEPT QUESTIONS

1. How does considering personal taxes on interest and equity distributions change the M&M conclusions on optimal debt?
2. Explain in words the logic behind Miller's theory of capital structure.
3. How does this theory apply in Canada?

---

[10] Support for this scenario comes from M. H. Wilson, "Draft Legislation, Regulations, and Explanatory Notes Respecting Preferred Share Financing," Department of Finance, Ottawa, April 1988.

[11] This argument was first advanced by H. DeAngelo and R. Masulis, "Optimal Capital Structure under Corporate and Personal Taxation," *Journal of Financial Economics*, March 1980, pp. 3–30.

Appendix Questions and Problems

A.1 Miller's model introduces personal taxes into the theory of capital structure. With both personal and corporate taxes, we got the same indifference result as with no taxes. Explain why.

A.2 This question is a follow-up on Question A.1 on Miller's model. In comparing this approach to M&M with corporate taxes, you can see that in one case both models imply that firms should use 100 percent debt financing. Explain how this conclusion occurs in each case. Why does it not occur in practice?

Dividends and Dividend Policy

CHAPTER

16

Dividend policy is an important subject in corporate finance, and dividends are a major cash outlay for many corporations. In 1994 alone, for example, Toronto Stock Exchange firms paid out in excess of $20 billion in cash dividends. At the same time, however, only 590 of the 1,250 listed companies, or about 47 percent, paid regular dividends.[1]

At first glance, it may seem obvious that a firm would always want to give as much as possible back to its shareholders by paying dividends. It might seem equally obvious, however, that a firm can always invest the money for its shareholder instead of paying it out. The heart of the dividend policy question is just this: Should the firm pay out money to its shareholders, or should the firm take that money and invest it for its shareholders?

It may seem surprising, but much research and economic logic suggest that dividend policy doesn't matter. In fact, it turns out that the dividend policy issue is much like the capital structure question. The important elements are not difficult to identify, but the interactions between those elements are complex and no easy answer exists.

Dividend policy is controversial. Many implausible reasons are given for why dividend policy might be important, and many of the claims made about dividend policy are economically illogical. Even so, in the real world of corporate finance, determining the most appropriate dividend policy is considered an important issue. It could be that financial managers who worry about dividend policy are wasting time, but it could be true that we are missing something important in our discussions.

In part, all discussions of dividends are plagued by the "two-handed lawyer" problem. Former U.S. President Harry S. Truman, while discussing the legal implications of a possible presidential decision, asked his staff to set up a meeting with a lawyer. Supposedly, Truman said, "But I don't want one of those two-handed lawyers." When asked what a two-handed lawyer was, he replied, "You know, a lawyer who says, 'On the one hand I recommend you do so and so because of the following reasons, but on the other hand I recommend that you don't do it because of these other reasons.' "

---

[1] *Toronto Stock Exchange Review,* January 1995. Regular dividends are declared annually and paid quarterly in contrast with extra dividends paid on an occasional basis.

569

Unfortunately, any sensible treatment of dividend policy appears to be written by a two-handed lawyer (or, in fairness, several two-handed financial economists). On the one hand, there are many good reasons for corporations to pay high dividends; on the other hand, there are also many good reasons to pay low dividends or no dividends.

We cover three broad topics that relate to dividends and dividend policy in this chapter. First, we describe the various kinds of dividends and how dividends are paid. Second, we consider an idealized case in which dividend policy doesn't matter. We then discuss the limitations of this case and present some practical arguments for both high- and low-dividend payouts. Finally, we conclude the chapter by looking at some strategies that corporations might employ to implement a dividend policy.

16.1 | CASH DIVIDENDS AND DIVIDEND PAYMENT

dividend

Payment made out of a firm's earnings to its owners, either in the form of cash or stock.

distribution

Payment made by a firm to its owners from sources other than current or accumulated earnings.

The term **dividend** usually refers to cash paid out of earnings. If a payment is made from sources other than current or accumulated retained earnings, the term **distribution** rather than dividend is sometimes used. However, it is acceptable to refer to a distribution from earnings as a dividend and a distribution from capital as a liquidating dividend. More generally, any direct payment by the corporation to the shareholders may be considered a dividend or a part of dividend policy. Figure 16.1 shows how the dividend decision is part of distributing the firm's cash flow over different uses.

Dividends come in several different forms. The basic types of cash dividends are:

1. Regular cash dividends.
2. Extra dividends.
3. Liquidating dividends.

Later in the chapter, we discuss dividends that are paid in stock instead of cash, and we also consider an alternative to cash dividends, stock repurchase.

FIGURE 16.1

Distribution of corporate cash flow

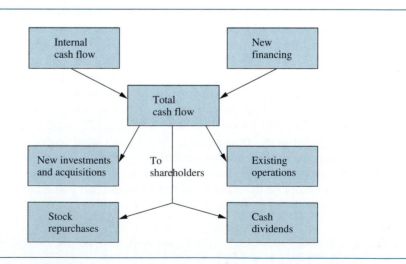

Cash Dividends

The most common type of dividend is a cash dividend. Commonly, public companies pay **regular cash dividends** four times a year. As the name suggests, these are cash payments made directly to shareholders, and they are made in the regular course of business. In other words, management sees nothing unusual about the dividend and no reason it won't be continued.

Sometimes firms pay a regular cash dividend and an extra cash dividend. By calling part of the payment extra, management is indicating it may or may not be repeated in the future.

Finally, a *liquidating dividend* usually means that some or all of the business has been liquidated, that is, sold off. Debt covenants, discussed in Chapter 12, offer the firm's creditors protection against liquidating dividends that could violate their prior claim against assets and cash flows.

However it is labelled, a cash dividend payment reduces corporate cash and retained earnings, except in the case of a liquidating dividend (where capital may be reduced).

regular cash dividend
Cash payment made by a firm to its owners in the normal course of business, usually made four times a year.

Standard Method of Cash Dividend Payment

The decision to pay a dividend rests in the hands of the board of directors of the corporation. When a dividend has been declared, it becomes a debt of the firm and cannot be rescinded easily. Sometime after it has been declared, a dividend is distributed to all shareholders as of some specific date.

Commonly, the amount of the cash dividend is expressed in dollars per share *(dividends per share)*. As we have seen in other chapters, it is also expressed as a percentage of the market price (the *dividend yield*) or as a percentage of earnings per share (the *dividend payout*).

Dividend Payment: A Chronology

The mechanics of a dividend payment can be illustrated by the example in Figure 16.2 and the following description:

declaration date
Date on which the board of directors passes a resolution to pay a dividend.

1. **Declaration date**. On January 15, the board of directors passes a resolution to pay a dividend of $1 per share on February 16 to all holders of record as of January 30.

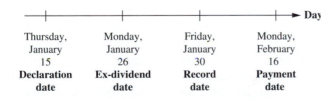

Thursday, January 15	Monday, January 26	Friday, January 30	Monday, February 16
Declaration date	**Ex-dividend date**	**Record date**	**Payment date**

F I G U R E 16.2

Procedure for dividend payment

1. *Declaration date:* The board of directors declares a payment of dividends.
2. *Ex-dividend date:* A share of stock goes ex dividend on the date the seller is entitled to keep the dividend; under TSE rules, shares are traded ex dividend on and after the fourth business day before the record date.
3. *Record date:* The declared dividends are distributable to shareholders of record on a specific date.
4. *Payment date:* The dividend cheques are mailed to shareholders of record.

ex-dividend date

Date four business days before the date of record, establishing those individuals entitled to a dividend.

2. **Ex-dividend date**. To make sure that dividend cheques go to the right people, brokerage firms and stock exchanges establish an ex-dividend date. This date is four business days before the date of record (discussed next). If you buy the stock before this date, then you are entitled to the dividend. If you buy on this date or after, then the previous owner gets it.

   The ex-dividend date convention removes any ambiguity about who is entitled to the dividend. Since the dividend is valuable, the stock price is affected when it goes "ex." We examine this effect later.

   In Figure 16.2, Monday, January 26, is the ex-dividend date. Before this date, the stock is said to trade "with dividend" or "cum dividend." Afterwards the stock trades "ex dividend."

date of record

Date on which holders of record are designated to receive a dividend.

3. **Date of record**. Based on its records, the corporation prepares a list on January 30 of all individuals believed to be stockholders as of this date. These are the *holders of record* and January 30 is the *date of record*. The word *believed* is important here. If you buy the stock just before this date, the corporation's records may not reflect that fact because of mailing or other delays. Without some modification, some of the dividend cheques would get mailed to the wrong people. This is the reason for the ex-dividend day convention.

date of payment

Date the dividend cheques are mailed.

4. **Date of payment**. The dividend cheques are mailed on February 16.

More on the Ex-Dividend Date

The ex-dividend date is important and is a common source of confusion. We examine what happens to the stock when it goes ex, meaning that the ex-dividend date arrives. To illustrate, suppose we have a stock that sells for $10 per share. The board of directors declares a dividend of $1 per share, and the record date is Thursday, June 14. Based on our previous discussion, we know that the ex date will be four business (not calendar) days earlier on Friday, June 8.

If you buy the stock on Thursday, June 7, right as the market closes, you'll get the $1 dividend because the stock is trading cum dividend. If you wait and buy it right as the market opens on Friday, you won't get the $1 dividend. What will happen to the value of the stock overnight?

If you think about it, the stock is obviously worth about $1 less on Friday morning, so its price will drop by this amount between close of business on Thursday and the Friday opening. In general, we expect the value of a share of stock to go down by about the dividend amount when the stock goes ex dividend. The key word here is *about*. Since dividends are taxed, the actual price drop might be closer to some measure of the aftertax value of the dividend. Determining this value is complicated because of the different tax rates and tax rules that apply for different buyers. The series of events described here is illustrated in Figure 16.3.

The amount of the price drop is a matter for empirical investigation. Researchers have argued that, due to personal taxes, the stock price should drop by less than the dividend.[2] For example, consider the case with no capital gains taxes. On the day before a stock goes ex dividend, shareholders must decide either to buy the stock

---

[2] The original argument was advanced and tested for the United States by N. Elton and M. Gruber, "Marginal Stockholder Tax Rates and the Clientele Effect," *Review of Economics and Statistics* 52 (February 1970). Canadian evidence (discussed briefly later in this chapter) is from J. Lakonishok and T. Vermaelen, "Tax Reform and Ex-Dividend Day Behavior," *Journal of Finance* 38 (September 1983) pp. 1157–80, and L. D. Booth and D. J. Johnston, "The Ex-Dividend Day Behavior of Canadian Stock Prices: Tax Changes and Clientele Effects," *Journal of Finance* 39 (June 1984), pp. 457–76.

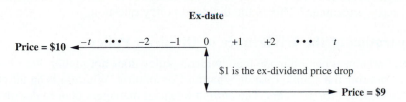

Ex-date

Price = $10 $-t$ ••• -2 -1 0 $+1$ $+2$ ••• t

$1 is the ex-dividend price drop

Price = $9

F I G U R E 16.3

*Price behaviour
around ex-dividend
date for a $1 cash
dividend*

The stock price will fall by the amount of the dividend on the ex date (time 0). If the dividend is $1 per share, the price will be equal to $10 − $1 = $9 on the ex date:

Before ex date (−1) dividend = 0   Price = $10
Ex-date (0) dividend = $1   Price = $9

immediately and pay tax on the forthcoming dividend, or to buy the stock tomorrow, thereby missing the dividend. If all investors are in a 30 percent bracket for dividends and the quarterly dividend is $1, the stock price should fall by $.70 on the ex-dividend date. If the stock price falls by this amount on the ex-dividend date, then purchasers receive the same return from either strategy.

E X A M P L E | 16.1   "Ex" Marks the Day

The board of directors of Divided Airlines has declared a dividend of $2.50 per share payable on Tuesday, May 30, to shareholders of record as of Tuesday, May 9. Cal Icon buys 100 shares of Divided on Tuesday, May 2, for $150 per share. What is the ex date? Describe the events that will occur with regard to the cash dividend and the stock price.

The ex date is four business days before the date of record, Tuesday, May 9, so the stock will go ex on Wednesday, May 3. Cal buys the stock on Tuesday, May 2, so Cal has purchased the stock cum dividend. In other words, Cal gets $2.50 × 100 = $250 in dividends. The cheque is mailed on Tuesday, May 30. When the stock does go ex on Wednesday, its value drops overnight by about $2.50 per share (or maybe a little less due to personal taxes). |

CONCEPT QUESTIONS
1. What are the different types of cash dividends?
2. What are the mechanics of the cash dividend payment?
3. How should the price of a stock change when it goes ex dividend?

16.2 | DOES DIVIDEND POLICY MATTER?

To decide whether or not dividend policy matters, we first have to define what we mean by dividend policy. All other things being the same, of course dividends matter. Dividends are paid in cash, and cash is something that everybody likes. The question we are discussing here is whether the firm should pay out cash now or invest the cash and pay it out later. Dividend policy, therefore, is the time pattern of dividend payout.

In particular, should the firm pay out a large percentage of its earnings now or a small (or even zero) percentage? This is the dividend policy question.

An Illustration of the Irrelevance of Dividend Policy

A powerful argument can be made that dividend policy does not matter. We illustrate this by considering the simple case of Wharton Corporation. Wharton is an all-equity firm that has existed for 10 years. The current financial managers plan to dissolve the firm in two years. The total cash flows that the firm will generate, including the proceeds from liquidation, are $10,000 in each of the next two years.

Current Policy: Dividends Set Equal to Cash Flow   At the present time, dividends at each date are set equal to the cash flow of $10,000. There are 100 shares outstanding, so the dividend per share will be $100. In Chapter 6, we stated that the value of the stock is equal to the present value of the future dividends. Assuming a 10 percent required return, the value of a share of stock today, P_0, is:

$$P_0 = D_1/(1 + R)^1 + D_2/(1 + R)^2$$
$$= \$100/1.10 + \$100/1.10^2 = \$173.55$$

The firm as a whole is thus worth $100 \times \$173.55 = \$17,355$.

Several members of the board of Wharton have expressed dissatisfaction with the current dividend policy and have asked you to analyze an alternative policy.

Alternative Policy: Initial Dividend Is Greater than Cash Flow   Another policy is for the firm to pay a dividend of $110 per share on the first date, which is, of course, a total dividend of $11,000. Because the cash flow is only $10,000, an extra $1,000 must somehow be raised. One way to do it is to issue $1,000 of bonds or stock at Date 1. Assume that stock is issued. The new shareholders desire enough cash flow at Date 2 so that they earn the required 10 percent return on their Date 1 investment.[3]

What is the value of the firm with this new dividend policy? The new shareholders invest $1,000. They require a 10 percent return, so they demand $1,000 $\times$ 1.10 = $1,100 of the Date 2 cash flow, leaving only $8,900 to the old stockholders. The dividends to the old shareholders would be:

	Date 1	Date 2
Aggregate dividends to old stockholders	$11,000	$8,900
Dividends per share	110	89

The present value of the dividends per share is therefore:

$$P_0 = \$110/1.10 + \$89/1.10^2 = \$173.55$$

This is the same present value as we had before.

The value of the stock is not affected by this switch in dividend policy even though we had to sell some new stock just to finance the dividend. In fact, no matter what pattern of dividend payout the firm chooses, the value of the stock is always the same in this example. In other words, for the Wharton Corporation, dividend policy makes no difference. The reason is simple: Any increase in a dividend at some point in time is exactly offset by a decrease somewhere else, so the net effect, once we account for time value, is zero.

---

[3] The same results would occur after an issue of bonds, though the arguments would be less easily presented.

Homemade Dividends   There is an alternative and perhaps more intuitively appealing explanation about why dividend policy doesn't matter in our example. Suppose individual investor X prefers dividends per share of $100 at both Dates 1 and 2. Would he or she be disappointed when informed that the firm's management is adopting the alternative dividend policy (dividends of $110 and $89 in the two dates, respectively)? Not necessarily, because the investor could easily reinvest the $10 of unneeded funds received on Date 1 by buying more Wharton stock. At 10 percent, this investment grows to $11 at Date 2. Thus, the investor would receive the desired net cash flow of $110 − 10 = $100 at Date 1 and $89 + 11 = $100 at Date 2.

Conversely, imagine Investor Z, preferring $110 of cash flow at Date 1 and $89 of cash flow at Date 2, finds that management pays dividends of $100 at both Dates 1 and 2. This investor can simply sell $10 worth of stock to boost his or her total cash at Date 1 to $110. Because this investment returns 10 percent, Investor Z gives up $11 at Date 2 ($10 × 1.1), leaving him with $100 − 11 = $89.

Our two investors are able to transform the corporation's dividend policy into a different policy by buying or selling on their own. The result is that investors are able to create **homemade dividends**. This means dissatisfied shareholders can alter the firm's dividend policy to suit themselves. As a result, there is no particular advantage to any one dividend policy that the firm might choose.

Many corporations actually assist their stockholders in creating homemade dividend policies by offering *automatic dividend reinvestment plans* (ADPs or DRIPs). As the name suggests, with such a plan, shareholders have the option of automatically reinvesting some or all of their cash dividends in shares of stock.

Under a new issue dividend reinvestment plan, investors buy new stock issued by the firm. They receive a small discount on the stock, usually under 5 percent. This makes dividend reinvestment very attractive to investors who do not need cash flow from dividends. Since the 5 percent discount compares favourably with issue costs for new stock discussed in Chapter 13, dividend reinvestment plans are popular with large companies that periodically seek new common stock.[4]

Investment dealers also use financial engineering to create homemade dividends (or homemade capital gains). Called **stripped common shares**, these vehicles entitle holders to receive either all the dividends from one or a group of well-known companies or an installment receipt that packages any capital gain in the form of a call option. The option gives the investor the right to buy the underlying shares at a fixed price and so is valuable if the shares appreciate beyond that price.

homemade dividends
Idea that individual investors can undo corporate dividend policy by reinvesting dividends or selling shares of stock.

stripped common shares
Common stock on which dividends and capital gains are repackaged and sold separately.

A Test   Our discussion to this point can be summarized by considering the following true/false test questions:

1. True or false: Dividends are irrelevant.
2. True or false: Dividend policy is irrelevant.

The first statement is surely false, and the reason follows from common sense. Clearly, investors prefer higher dividends to lower dividends at any single date if the dividend level is held constant at every other date. To be more precise regarding the first question, if the dividend per share at a given date is raised while the dividend per share at each other date is held constant, the stock price rises. The reason is that the present value of the future dividends must go up if this occurs. This action can be

---

[4] Reinvested dividends are still taxable.

accomplished by management decisions that improve productivity, increase tax savings, strengthen product marketing, or otherwise improve cash flow.

The second statement is true, at least in the simple case we have been examining. Dividend policy by itself cannot raise the dividend at one date while keeping it the same at all other dates. Rather, dividend policy merely establishes the trade-off between dividends at one date and dividends at another date. Once we allow for time value, the present value of the dividend stream is unchanged. Thus, in this simple world, dividend policy does not matter, because managers choosing either to raise or to lower the current dividend do not affect the current value of their firm. However, we have ignored several real-world factors that might lead us to change our minds; we pursue some of these in subsequent sections.

CONCEPT QUESTIONS

1. How can an investor create a homemade dividend?
2. Are dividends irrelevant?

16.3 | REAL-WORLD FACTORS FAVOURING A LOW PAYOUT

The example we used to illustrate the irrelevance of dividend policy ignored taxes and flotation costs. In other words, we assumed perfect capital markets in which these and other imperfections did not exist. In this section, we see that these factors might lead us to prefer a low-dividend payout.

Taxes

The logic we used to establish that dividend policy does not affect firm value ignored the real-world complication of taxes. In Canada, both dividends and capital gains are taxed at effective rates less than the marginal tax rates.

For dividends, we showed in Chapter 2 that individual investors face a lower tax rate due to the dividend tax credit. Capital gains in the hands of individuals are taxed at 75 percent of the marginal tax rate. Since taxation only occurs when capital gains are realized, capital gains are very lightly taxed in Canada. On balance, capital gains are subject to lower taxes than dividends.

A firm that adopts a low-dividend payout reinvests the money instead of paying it out. This reinvestment increases the value of the firm and of the equity. All other things being equal, the net effect is that the capital gains portion of the return is higher in the future. So, the fact that capital gains are taxed favourably may lead us to prefer this approach.

This tax disadvantage of dividends doesn't necessarily lead to a policy of paying no dividends. Suppose a firm has some excess cash after selecting all positive NPV projects. The firm might consider the following alternatives to a dividend:

1. *Select additional capital budgeting projects.* Because the firm has taken all the available positive NPV projects already, it must invest its excess cash in negative NPV projects. This is clearly a policy at variance with the principles of corporate finance and represents an example of the agency costs of equity introduced in Chapter 1. Still, research suggests that some companies are guilty of doing this.[5] It is frequently argued that managers who adopt negative NPV projects are ripe for takeover, leveraged buyouts, and proxy fights.

[5] M. C. Jensen, "Agency Costs of Free Cash Flows, Corporate Finance and Takeovers," *American Economic Review*, May 1986, pp. 323–29.

2. *Repurchase shares.* A firm may rid itself of excess cash by repurchasing shares of stock. In the United States, investors can treat profits on repurchased stock as capital gains and pay lower taxes than they would if the cash were distributed as a dividend. In Canada, funds distributed through stock repurchases may be considered dividends for tax purposes. For this reason, share repurchases are not always an attractive alternative to a dividend for tax purposes.

3. *Acquire other companies.* To avoid the payment of dividends, a firm might use excess cash to acquire another company. This strategy has the advantage of acquiring profitable assets. However, a firm often incurs heavy costs when it embarks on an acquisition program. In addition, acquisitions are invariably made above the market price. Premiums of 20 to 80 percent are not uncommon. Because of this, a number of researchers have argued that mergers are not generally profitable to the acquiring company, even when firms are merged for a valid business purpose.[6] Therefore, a company making an acquisition merely to avoid a dividend is unlikely to succeed.

4. *Purchase financial assets.* The strategy of purchasing financial assets in lieu of a dividend payment can be illustrated with the following example.

Suppose the Regional Electric Company has $1,000 of extra cash. It can retain the cash and invest it in Treasury bills yielding 8 percent, or it can pay the cash to shareholders as a dividend. Shareholders can also invest in Treasury bills with the same yield. Suppose, realistically, that the tax rate is 44 percent on ordinary income like interest on Treasury bills for both the company and individual investors and the individual tax rate on dividends is 30 percent. What is the amount of cash that investors have after five years under each policy?

If dividends are paid now, shareholders will receive $1,000 before taxes, or $1,000 \times (1 - .30) = $700 after taxes. This is the amount they invest. If the rate on T-bills is 8 percent, before taxes, then the aftertax return is $8\% \times (1 - .44) = 4.48\%$ per year. Thus, in five years, the shareholders have:

$$\$700 \times (1 + 0.0448)^5 = \$871.49$$

If Regional Electric Company retains the cash, invests in Treasury bills, and pays out the proceeds five years from now, then $1,000 will be invested today. However, since the corporate tax rate is 44 percent, the aftertax return from the T-bills will be $8\% \times (1 - .44) = 4.48\%$ per year. In five years, the investment will be worth:

$$\$1,000 \times (1 + 0.0448)^5 = \$1,244.99$$

If this amount is then paid out as a dividend, after taxes the stockholders receive:

$$\$1,244.99 \times (1 - .30) = \$871.49$$

In this case, dividends are the same after taxes whether the firm pays them now or later after investing in Treasury bills. The reason is that the firm invests exactly as profitably as the shareholders do on an aftertax basis.

This example shows that for a firm with extra cash, the dividend payout decision depends on personal and corporate tax rates. All other things the same, when personal tax rates are higher than corporate tax rates, a firm has an incentive to reduce

---

[6] The original hypothesis comes from R. Roll, "The Hubris Hypothesis of Corporate Takeovers," *Journal of Business* (1986). Chapter 21 presents some Canadian examples.

dividend payouts. This would have occurred if we changed our example to have the firm invest in preferred stock instead of T-bills. (Recall from Chapter 12 that corporations enjoy a 100 percent exclusion of dividends from taxable income.) However, if personal tax rates on dividends are lower than corporate tax rates (for investors in lower tax brackets or tax-exempt investors), a firm has an incentive to pay out any excess cash in dividends.

These examples show that dividend policy is not always irrelevant when we consider personal and corporate taxes. To continue the discussion, we go back to the different tax treatment of dividends and capital gains.

Expected Return, Dividends, and Personal Taxes   We illustrate the effect of personal taxes by considering a situation where dividends are taxed and capital gains are not taxed—a scenario that is not unrealistic for many Canadian individual investors. We show that a firm that provides more return in the form of dividends has a lower value (or a higher pretax required return) than one whose return is in the form of untaxed capital gains.

Suppose every shareholder is in the top tax bracket (tax rate on dividends of 30 percent) and is considering the stocks of Firm G and Firm D. Firm G pays no dividend, and Firm D pays a dividend. The current price of the stock of Firm G is $100, and next year's price is expected to be $120. The shareholder in Firm G thus expects a $20 capital gain. With no dividend, the return is $20/$100 = 20%. If capital gains are not taxed, the pretax and aftertax returns must be the same.[7]

Suppose the stock of Firm D is expected to pay a $20 dividend next year. If the stocks of Firm G and Firm D are equally risky, the market prices must be set so that their aftertax expected returns are equal. The aftertax return on Firm D thus has to be 20 percent.

What will be the price of stock in Firm D? The aftertax dividend is $20 × (1 − .30) = $14, so our investor has a total of $114 after taxes. At a 20 percent required rate of return (after taxes), the present value of this aftertax amount is:

Present value = $114/1.20 = $95.00

The market price of the stock in Firm D thus must be $95.00.

Some Evidence on Dividends and Taxes in Canada

Is our example showing higher pretax returns for stocks that pay dividends realistic for Canadian capital markets? Since tax laws change from budget to budget, we have to exercise caution in interpreting research results. Before 1972, capital gains were untaxed in Canada (as in our simplified example). Research suggests stocks that paid dividends had higher pretax returns prior to 1972. From 1972 to 1977, the same study detected no difference in pretax returns.[8]

In 1985, the lifetime exemption on capital gains was introduced. Recent research found that investors anticipated this tax break for capital gains and bid up the prices of stocks with low dividend yields. Firms responded by lowering their dividend payouts. This all ended in 1994 when the federal budget ended the capital gains

---

[7] Under current tax law, if the shareholder in Firm G does not sell the shares for a gain, it will be an unrealized capital gain, which is not taxed.
[8] I. G. Morgan, "Dividends and Stock Price Behaviour in Canada," *Journal of Business Administration* 12 (Fall 1989).

exemption.[9] We suspect that from the viewpoint of individual investors, higher dividends require larger pretax returns.

Another way of measuring the effective tax rates on dividends and capital gains in Canada is to look at ex-dividend day price drops. We showed earlier that, ignoring taxes, a stock price should drop by the amount of the dividend when it goes ex dividend. This is because the price drop offsets what investors lose by waiting to buy the stock until it goes ex dividend. If dividends are taxed and capital gains are tax free, the price drop should be lower, equal to the aftertax value of the dividend. However, if gains are taxed too, the price drop needs to be adjusted for the gains tax. An investor who waits for the stock to go ex-dividend buys at a lower price and hence has a larger capital gain when the stock is sold later.

All this allowed researchers to infer tax rates from ex-dividend day behaviour. The study concludes that marginal investors who set prices are taxed more heavily on dividends than on capital gains.[10] This supports our argument: Individual investors likely look for higher pretax returns on dividend paying stocks.

Flotation Costs

In our example illustrating that dividend policy doesn't matter, we saw that the firm could sell some new stock if necessary to pay a dividend. As we mentioned in Chapter 13, selling new stock can be very expensive. If we include flotation costs in our argument, then we find that the value of the stock decreases if we sell new stock.

More generally, imagine two firms that are identical in every way except that one pays out a greater percentage of its cash flow in the form of dividends. Since the other firm plows back more, its equity grows faster. If these two firms are to remain identical, the one with the higher payout has to sell some stock periodically to catch up. Since this is expensive, a firm might be inclined to have a low payout.

Dividend Restrictions

In some cases, a corporation may face restrictions on its ability to pay dividends. For example, as we discussed in Chapter 12, a common feature of a bond indenture is a covenant prohibiting dividend payments above some level.

> CONCEPT QUESTIONS
> 1. What are the tax benefits of low dividends?
> 2. Why do flotation costs favour a low payout?

16.4 | REAL-WORLD FACTORS FAVOURING A HIGH PAYOUT

In this section, we consider reasons a firm might pay its shareholders higher dividends even if it means the firm must issue more shares of stock to finance the dividend payments.

---

[9] B. Amoako-adu, "Capital Gains Tax and Equity Values: Empirical Test of Stock Price Reaction to the Introduction and Reduction of Capital Gains Tax Exemption, *Journal of Banking and Finance* 16 (1992), pp. 275–87; F. Adjaoud and D. Zeghal, "Taxation and Dividend Policy in Canada: New Evidence," *FINECO* (2nd Semester) 1993, pp. 141–54.

[10] L. Booth and D. Johnston, "Ex-Dividend Day Behaviour." Their research also showed that interlisted stocks, traded on exchanges in both the United States and Canada, tended to be priced by U.S. investors and not be affected by Canadian tax changes. J. Lakonishok and T. Vermaelen, "Tax Reforms and Ex-Dividend Day Behavior," *Journal of Finance*, September 1983, pp. 1157–58, gives a competing explanation in terms of tax arbitrage by short-term traders.

In a classic textbook, Benjamin Graham, David Dodd, and Sidney Cottle have argued that firms should generally have high-dividend payouts because:

1. "The discounted value of near dividends is higher than the present worth of distant dividends."
2. Between "two companies with the same general earning power and same general position in an industry, the one paying the larger dividend will almost always sell at a higher price."[11]

Two factors favouring a high-dividend payout have been mentioned frequently by proponents of this view: the desire for current income and the resolution of uncertainty.

Desire for Current Income

It has been argued that many individuals desire current income. The classic example is the group of retired people and others living on fixed incomes, the proverbial "widows and orphans." It is argued that this group is willing to pay a premium to get a higher dividend yield. If this is true, it lends support to the second claim by Graham, Dodd, and Cottle.

It is easy to see, however, that this argument is not relevant in our simple case. An individual preferring high current cash flow but holding low-dividend securities could easily sell shares to provide the necessary funds. Similarly, an individual desiring a low current cash flow but holding high-dividend securities can just reinvest the dividend. This is just our homemade dividend argument again. Thus, in a world of no transaction costs, a high current dividend policy would be of no value to the shareholder.

The current income argument may have relevance in the real world. Here the sale of low-dividend stocks would involve brokerage fees and other transaction costs. Such a sale might also trigger capital gains taxes. These direct cash expenses could be avoided by an investment in high-dividend securities. In addition, the expenditure of the stockholder's own time when selling securities and the natural (but not necessarily rational) fear of consuming out of principal might further lead many investors to buy high-dividend securities.

Even so, to put this argument in perspective, remember that financial intermediaries such as mutual funds can (and do) perform these repackaging transactions for individuals at very low cost. Such intermediaries could buy low-dividend stocks, and, by a controlled policy of realizing gains, they could pay their investors at a higher rate.

Uncertainty Resolution

We have just pointed out that investors with substantial current consumption needs prefer high current dividends. In another classic treatment, Professor Myron Gordon has argued that a high-dividend policy also benefits stockholders because it resolves uncertainty.[12]

According to Gordon, investors price a security by forecasting and discounting future dividends. Gordon then argues that forecasts of dividends to be received in the

[11] G. Graham, D. Dodd, and S. Cottle, *Security Analysis* (New York: McGraw-Hill, 1962).
[12] M. Gordon, *The Investment, Financing and Valuation of the Corporation* (Homewood, IL: Richard D. Irwin, 1961).

distant future have greater uncertainty than do forecasts of near-term dividends. Because investors dislike uncertainty, the stock price should be low for those companies that pay small dividends now in order to remit higher dividends later.

Gordon's argument is essentially a "bird-in-hand" story. A $1 dividend in a shareholder's pocket is somehow worth more than that same $1 in a bank account held by the corporation. By now, you should see the problem with this argument. A shareholder can create a bird in hand very easily just by selling some stock.

Tax and Legal Benefits from High Dividends

Earlier, we saw that dividends were taxed more heavily than capital gains for individual investors. This fact is a powerful argument for a low payout. However, a number of other investors do not receive unfavourable tax treatment from holding high-dividend yield, rather than low-dividend yield, securities.

Corporate Investors A significant tax break on dividends occurs when a corporation owns stock in another corporation. A corporate shareholder receiving either common or preferred dividends is granted a 100 percent dividend exclusion.[13] Since the 100 percent exclusion does not apply to capital gains, this group is taxed unfavourably on capital gains.

As a result of the dividend exclusion, high-dividend, low capital gains stocks may be more appropriate for corporations to hold. As we discuss elsewhere, this is why corporations hold a substantial percentage of the outstanding preferred stock in the economy. This tax advantage of dividends also leads some corporations to hold high-yielding stocks instead of long-term bonds because there is no similar tax exclusion of interest payments to corporate bondholders.

Tax-Exempt Investors We have pointed out both the tax advantages and disadvantages of a low-dividend payout. Of course, this discussion is irrelevant to those in zero tax brackets. This group includes some of the largest investors in the economy, such as pension funds, endowment funds, and trust funds.

There are some legal reasons for large institutions to favour high-dividend yields: First, institutions such as pension funds and trust funds are often set up to manage money for the benefit of others. The managers of such institutions have a *fiduciary responsibility* to invest the money prudently. It has been considered imprudent in courts of law to buy stock in companies with no established dividend record.

Second, institutions such as university endowment funds and trust funds are frequently prohibited from spending any of the principal. Such institutions might, therefore, prefer high-dividend yield stocks so they have some ability to spend. Like widows and orphans, this group thus prefers current income. Unlike widows and orphans, in terms of the amount of stock owned, this group is very large and its market share is expanding rapidly.

Overall, individual investors (for whatever reason) may have a desire for current income and may thus be willing to pay the dividend tax. In addition, some very large investors such as corporations and tax-free institutions may have a very strong preference for high-dividend payouts.

---

[13] For preferred stock, we assume the issuer has elected to pay the refundable withholding tax on preferred dividends.

CONCEPT QUESTIONS
1. Why might some individual investors favour a high dividend payout?
2. Why might some nonindividual investors prefer a high dividend payout?

16.5 | A RESOLUTION OF REAL-WORLD FACTORS?

In the previous sections, we presented some factors that favour a low-dividend policy and others that favour high dividends. In this section, we discuss two important concepts related to dividends and dividend policy: the information content of dividends and the clientele effect. The first topic illustrates both the importance of dividends in general and the importance of distinguishing between dividends and dividend policy. The second topic suggests that, despite the many real-world considerations we have discussed, the dividend payout ratio may not be as important as we originally imagined.

Information Content of Dividends

To begin, we quickly review some of our earlier discussion. Previously, we examined three different positions on dividends:

1. Based on the homemade dividend argument, dividend policy is irrelevant.
2. Because of tax effects for individual investors and new issues costs, a low-dividend policy is the best.
3. Because of the desire for current income and related factors, a high-dividend policy is the best.

If you wanted to decide which of these positions is the right one, an obvious way to get started would be to look at what happens to stock prices when companies announce dividend changes. You would find with some consistency that stock prices rise when the current dividend is unexpectedly increased, and they generally fall when the dividend is unexpectedly decreased. What does this imply about any of the three positions just stated?

At first glance, the behaviour we describe seems consistent with the third position and inconsistent with the other two. In fact, many writers have argued this. If stock prices rise on dividend increases and fall on dividend decreases, isn't the market saying it approves of higher dividends?

Other authors have pointed out that this observation doesn't really tell us much about dividend policy. Everyone agrees that dividends are important, all other things being equal. Companies only cut dividends with great reluctance. Thus, a dividend cut is often a signal that the firm is in trouble.

More to the point, a dividend cut is usually not a voluntary, planned change in dividend policy. Instead, it usually signals that management does not think the current dividend policy can be maintained. As a result, expectations of future dividends should generally be revised downward. The present value of expected future dividends falls and so does the stock price.

In this case, the stock price declines following a dividend cut because future dividends are generally lower, not because the firm changes the percentage of its earnings it will pay out in the form of dividends.

Dividend Signalling in Practice

To give a particularly dramatic example, consider what happened to Consolidated Edison, the largest investor-owned U.S. electric utility, in the second quarter of 1974. Faced with poor operating results and problems associated with the OPEC oil embargo, Con Ed announced after the market closed that it was omitting its regular quarterly dividend of 45 cents per share. This was somewhat surprising given Con Ed's size, prominence in the industry, and long dividend history. Also, Con Ed's earnings at that time were sufficient to pay the dividend, at least by some analysts' estimates.

The next morning was not pleasant. Sell orders were so heavy that a market could not be established for several hours. When trading finally got started, the stock opened at about $12 per share, down from $18 the day before. In other words, Con Ed, a very large company, lost about one-third of its market value overnight. As this case illustrates, shareholders can react very negatively to unanticipated cuts in dividends.

In a similar vein, an unexpected increase in the dividend signals good news. Management raises the dividend only when future earnings, cash flow, and general prospects are expected to rise enough so that the dividend does not have to be cut later. A dividend increase is management's signal to the market that the firm is expected to do well. The stock reacts favourably because expectations of future dividends are revised upward, not because the firm has increased its payout. Since the firm has to come up with cash to pay dividends, this kind of signal is more convincing than calling a press conference to announce good earnings prospects.

Management behaviour is consistent with the notion of dividend signalling. In 1989, for example, the Bank of Montreal's earnings per share dropped from $4.89 the previous year to $.04 due to increased loan loss provisions for LDC debt. Yet the annual dividend was increased slightly from $2.00 to $2.12 per share. The payout ratio skyrocketed to 5,300 percent ($2.12/$.04). Management signalled the market that earnings would recover in 1990, which they did.[14]

In both these cases, the stock price reacts to the dividend change. The reaction can be attributed to changes in the amount of future dividends, not necessarily a change in dividend payout policy. This signal is called the **information content effect** of the dividend. The fact that dividend changes convey information about the firm to the market makes it difficult to interpret the effect of dividend policy of the firm.

information content effect
The market's reaction to a change in corporate dividend payout.

The Clientele Effect

In our earlier discussion, we saw that some groups (wealthy individuals, for example) have an incentive to pursue low-payout (or zero-payout) stocks. Other groups (corporations, for example) have an incentive to pursue high-payout stocks. Companies with high payouts thus attract one group and low-payout companies attract another.

Table 16.1 shows the dividends paid by the companies in the TSE 35 Index, some of the biggest companies listed on the exchange. In June 1994, only two of

---

[14] Broader evidence that investors regard dividend announcements as important signals is in J. E. Hatch and M. J. Robinson, *Investment Management in Canada,* 2nd ed. (Scarborough: Prentice Hall Canada, 1989), chapter 14.

T A B L E 16.1 | Toronto 35 dividends monthly summary for June 1994

Company Name	Symbol	Shares	Price	Close QMV	Toronto 35 % Weight	Dividends per share	Earnings per share	P/E per share	Yield per share	Dividend Declared Amount	Payable	Record	Ex-Div
1 Telus Corporation	AGT	1,000	$15.625	$ 15,625.00	1.41%	0.92	1.53	10.21	5.89%	.23	Jul 15	Jun 23	Jun 17
2 Alcan Aluminum	AL	1,500	31.250	48,875.00	4.23	0.41	-0.73	N/A	1.31	.075 US	Jun 20	May 20	May 16
3 BCE Inc	B	2,000	45.000	90,000.00	8.13	2.68	-2.35	N/A	5.96	.67	Jul 15	Jun 15	Jun 9
4 Bombardier Cl B	BBD.B	1,000	19.625	19,625.00	1.77	0.31	1.18	16.63	1.58	.078125	Jul 31	Jul 15	Jul 11
5 Bank of Montreal	BMO	1,400	23.500	32,900.00	2.97	1.20	2.81	8.36	5.11	.30	May 30	May 10	May 4
6 Bank of Nova Scotia	BNS	1,000	25.000	25,000.00	2.26	1.16	1.72	14.53	4.64	.29	Jul 27	Jul 5	Jun 28
7 Canadian Imperial Bank	CM	1,500	29.625	44,437.50	4.01	1.32	3.22	9.20	4.46	.33	Jul 28	Jun 28	Jun 22
8 Canadian Pacific Ltd	CP	2,000	$20.375	$ 40,750.00	3.68%	0.32	-0.62	N/A	1.57%	.08	Jul 28	Jun 27	Jun 21
9 Canadian Tire Cl A	CTR.A	2,000	11.250	22,500.00	2.03	0.40	0.92	12.23	3.56	.10	Sep 1	Jul 31	Jul 25
10 Canadian Oxy Petroleum	CXY	700	24.250	16,975.00	1.53	0.40	0.22	110.23	1.65	.10	Jul 1	Jun 3	May 30
11 Dofasco Inc.	DFS	1,000	18.625	18,625.00	1.68	0.40	1.54	12.09	2.15	.10	Jul 1	Jun 9	Jun 3
12 Echo Bay Mines	ECO	1,000	15.000	15,000.00	1.35	0.10	0.19	78.95	0.67	.0375 US	Jun 30	Jun 15	Jun 9
13 Imperial Oil	IMO	500	40.500	20,250.00	1.83	1.80	1.53	26.47	4.44	.45	Jul 1	Jun 3	May 30
14 Imasco Ltd	IMS	1,000	33.500	33,500.00	3.02	1.56	3.36	9.97	4.66	.39	Jun 30	May 31	May 25
15 Lac Minerals	LAC	1,500	$11.500	$ 17,250.00	1.56%	0.08	-0.52	N/A	0.70%	.03 US	Jun 3	May 18	May 12
16 Laidlaw Inc Cl B	LDM.B	1,500	9.250	13,875.00	1.25	0.16	-1.44	N/A	1.73	.04	May 15	Apr 29	Apr 25
17 MacMillan Bloedel	MB	1,000	17.375	17,375.00	1.57	0.60	0.13	133.65	3.45	.15	Sep 15	Aug 19	Aug 15
18 Moore Corp	MCL	1,000	23.250	23,250.00	2.10	1.30	-1.00	N/A	5.59	.235 US	Jul 5	Jun 3	May 30
19 Inco Limited	N	1,000	33.500	33,500.00	3.02	0.55	-0.14	N/A	1.64	.10 US	Jun 1	May 2	Apr 26
20 National Bank	NA	1,000	8.750	8,750.00	0.79	0.40	1.04	8.41	4.57	.10	Aug 1	Jun 28	Jun 22
21 Noranda Inc	NOR	1,000	23.625	23,625.00	2.13	1.00	0.02	1181.25	4.23	.25	Jun 15	May 27	May 20
22 Northern Telecom	NTL	1,000	$38.500	$ 38,500.00	3.48%	0.49	-4.38	N/A	1.27%	.09 US	Jun 30	Jun 9	Jun 3
23 Nova Corp of Alberta	NVA	3,000	10.750	32,250.00	2.91	0.24	0.73	14.73	2.23	.06	Aug 15	Jul 29	Jul 25
24 Placer Dome	PDG	2,100	29.625	62,212.50	5.62	0.35	0.73	40.58	1.18	.065 US	Jun 27	May 27	May 20
25 Power Corp	POW	1,000	19.750	19,750.00	1.78	0.70	1.30	15.19	3.54	.175	Jun 30	Jun 9	Jun 3
26 Rogers Commun. Cl B	RCI.B	1,500	19.875	29,812.50	2.69	0.00	-2.40	N/A	0.00	—	—	—	—
27 Renaissance Energy	RES	1,500	28.875	43,312.50	3.91	0.00	0.64	45.12	0.00	—	—	—	—
28 Ranger Oil	RGO	3,000	9.125	27,375.00	2.47	0.11	0.23	39.67	1.21	.08 US	Apr 15	Mar 25	Mar 21
29 Royal Bank	RY	2,000	$26.750	$ 53,500.00	4.83%	1.16	0.67	39.93	4.34%	.29	Aug 24	Jul 25	Jul 19
30 TransAlta Corporation	TA	2,000	14.125	28,250.00	2.55	0.98	1.21	11.67	6.94	.245	Jul 1	Jun 1	May 26
31 Toronto-Dominion Bank	TD	2,000	19.875	39,750.00	3.59	0.80	1.59	12.50	4.03	.20	Jul 31	Jun 16	Jun 10
32 Teck Corp Cl B	TEK.B	1,000	22.875	22,875.00	2.07	0.20	0.45	50.83	0.87	.10	Jun 30	Jun 15	Jun 9
33 Thomson Corporation	TOC	2,000	15.250	30,500.00	2.75	0.62	0.60	25.42	4.07	.113 US	Jun 15	May 13	May 9
34 TransCanada PipeLines	TRP	1,000	16.375	16,375.00	1.48	0.92	1.65	9.92	5.62	.23	Jul 29	Jun 30	Jun 24
35 Seagram Co (The)	VO	2,000	$41.750	$ 83,500.00	7.54	0.77	1.20	34.79	1.84	.14 US	Jun 30	Jun 15	Jun 9
Total		**50,700**		**$1,107,650.00**	**100.00%**								

Index =	206.54	P/E = 49.27
Divisor =	5362.98	Yield % = 3.05

E.A.I.=	4.19
D.A.I.=	6.29

Source: TSE Review, June 1994. Used with permission.

these companies paid no dividends: Rogers Communication and Renaissance Energy, although mining stocks such as Echo Bay Mines and LAC Minerals paid low dividends. The highest dividend yield was 6.94 percent offered by TransAlta, a utility firm. Banks also paid relatively high dividends.

Groups of investors attracted to different payouts are called *clienteles,* and what we have described is a **clientele effect**. The clientele effect argument states that different groups of investors desire different levels of dividends. When a firm chooses a particular dividend policy, the only effect is to attract a particular clientele. If a firm changes its dividend policy, it just attracts a different clientele.

What we are left with is a simple supply and demand argument. Suppose that 40 percent of all investors prefer high dividends, but only 20 percent of the firms pay high dividends. Here the high-dividend firms are in short supply; thus, their stock prices rise. Consequently, low-dividend firms would find it advantageous to switch policies until 40 percent of all firms have high payouts. At this point, the *dividend market* is in equilibrium. Further changes in dividend policy are pointless because all of the clienteles are satisfied. The dividend policy for any individual firm is now irrelevant.

To see if you understand the clientele effect, consider the following statement: "In spite of the theoretical argument that dividend policy is irrelevant or that firms should not pay dividends, many investors like high dividends. Because of this fact, a firm can boost its share price by having a higher dividend payout ratio." True or false?

The answer is false if clienteles exist. As long as enough high-dividend firms satisfy the dividend-loving investors, a firm won't be able to boost its share price by paying high dividends.

clientele effect
Stocks attract particular groups based on dividend yield and the resulting tax effects.

CONCEPT QUESTIONS

1. How does the market react to unexpected dividend changes? What does this tell us about dividends? About dividend policy?
2. What is a dividend clientele? All things considered, would you expect a risky firm with significant but highly uncertain growth prospects to have a low- or high-dividend payout?

16.6 | ESTABLISHING A DIVIDEND POLICY

How do firms actually determine the level of dividends that they pay at a particular time? As we have seen, there are good reasons for firms to pay high dividends and there are good reasons to pay low dividends.

We know some things about how dividends are paid in practice. Firms don't like to cut dividends. We saw this with Bank of Montreal earlier. As Table 16.2 shows,

Stock	Year Dividend Payments Began
Bank of Montreal	1829
Bank of Nova Scotia	1833
Royal Bank	1870
Bell Canada	1881

T A B L E 16.2

Paying dividends

two chartered banks, Bank of Montreal and Bank of Nova Scotia, have been paying dividends for over 150 years.

In the next section, we discuss a particular dividend policy strategy. In doing so, we emphasize the real-world features of dividend policy. We also analyze an alternative to cash dividends, a stock repurchase.

Residual Dividend Approach

Earlier, we noted that firms with higher dividend payouts have to sell stock more often. As we have seen, such sales are not very common and they can be very expensive. Consistent with this, we assume that the firm wishes to minimize the need to sell new equity. We also assume that the firm wishes to maintain its current capital structure.[15]

If a firm wishes to avoid new equity sales, then it has to rely on internally generated equity to finance new, positive NPV projects.[16] Dividends can only be paid out of what is left over. This leftover is called the *residual,* and such a dividend policy would be called a **residual dividend approach**.

residual dividend approach
Policy where a firm pays dividends only after meeting its investment needs while maintaining a desired debt-to-equity ratio.

With a residual dividend policy, the firm's objective is to meet its investment needs and maintain its desired debt/equity ratio before paying dividends. To illustrate, imagine that a firm has $1,000 in earnings and a debt/equity ratio of .50. Notice that, since the debt/equity ratio is .50, the firm has 50 cents in debt for every $1.50 in value. The firm's capital structure is thus ⅓ debt and ⅔ equity.

The first step in implementing a residual dividend policy is to determine the amount of funds that can be generated without selling new equity. If the firm reinvests the entire $1,000 and pays no dividend, equity increases by $1,000. To keep the debt/equity ratio at .50, the firm must borrow an additional $500. The total amount of funds that can be generated without selling new equity is thus $1,000 + 500 = $1,500.

The second step is to decide whether or not a dividend will be paid. To do this, we compare the total amount that can be generated without selling new equity ($1,500 in this case) with planned capital spending. If funds needed exceed funds available, no dividend is paid. In addition, the firm will have to sell new equity to raise the needed finance or else (more likely) postpone some planned capital spending.

If funds needed are less than funds generated, a dividend will be paid. The amount of the dividend is the residual, that is, that portion of the earnings not needed to finance new projects. For example, suppose we have $900 in planned capital spending. To maintain the firm's capital structure, this $900 must be financed ⅔ equity and ⅓ debt. So, the firm actually borrows ⅓ × $900 = $300. The firm spends ⅔ × $900 = $600 of the $1,000 in equity available. There is a $1,000 − 600 = $400 residual, so the dividend is $400.

In sum, the firm has aftertax earnings of $1,000. Dividends paid are $400. Retained earnings are $600, and new borrowing totals $300. The firm's debt/equity ratio is unchanged at .50.

---

[15] As in our discussion of the cost of capital in Chapter 14, the capital structure should be measured using market value weights.

[16] Our discussion of sustainable growth in Chapter 4 is relevant here. We assumed there that a firm has a fixed capital structure, profit margin, and capital intensity. If the firm raises no new equity and wishes to grow at some target rate, there is only one payout ratio consistent with these assumptions.

Dividend policy under the residual approach

Row	(1) Aftertax Earnings	(2) New Investment	(3) Additional Debt	(4) Retained Earnings	(5) Additional Stock	(6) Dividends
1	$1,000	$3,000	$1,000	$1,000	$1,000	$ 0
2	1,000	2,000	667	1,000	333	0
3	1,000	1,500	500	1,000	0	0
4	1,000	1,000	333	667	0	333
5	1,000	500	167	333	0	667
6	1,000	0	0	0	0	1,000

The relationship between physical investment and dividend payout is presented for six different levels of investment in Table 16.3 and illustrated in Figure 16.4. The first three rows of the table can be discussed together, because in each case no dividends are paid.

In row 1, for example, note that new investment is $3,000. Additional debt of $1,000 and equity of $2,000 must be raised to keep the debt/equity ratio constant. Since this latter figure is greater than the $1,000 of earnings, all earnings are retained. Additional stock to be raised is also $1,000. In this example, since new stock is issued, dividends are not simultaneously paid out.

In rows 2 and 3, investment drops. Additional debt needed goes down as well since it is equal to ⅓ of investment. Because the amount of new equity needed is still greater than or equal to $1,000, all earnings are retained and no dividends are paid.

We finally find a situation in row 4 where a dividend is paid. Here, total investment is $1,000. To keep our debt/equity ratio constant, ⅓ of this investment, or $333, is financed by debt. The remaining ⅔, or $667, comes from internal funds, implying that the residual is $1,000 − 667 = $333. The dividend is equal to this $333 residual.

Relationship between dividends and investment in residual dividend policy

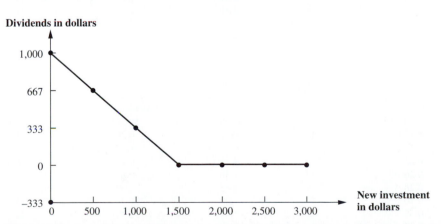

This figure illustrates that a firm with many investment opportunities will pay small amounts of dividends and a firm with few investment opportunities will pay relatively large amounts of dividends.

In this case, note that no additional stock is issued. Since the needed investment is even lower in rows 5 and 6, new debt is reduced further, retained earnings drop, and dividends increase. Again, no additional stock is issued.

Given our discussion, we expect those firms with many investment opportunities to pay a small percentage of their earnings as dividends and other firms with fewer opportunities to pay a high percentage of their earnings as dividends. This result appears to occur in the real world. Young, fast-growing firms commonly employ a low payout ratio, whereas older, slower-growing firms in more mature industries use a higher ratio.

We see this pattern somewhat in Table 16.4 where Imperial Oil and the Bank of Montreal are slower-growing firms with high payouts; Northern Telecom and Canadian Tire are faster growing firms with a pattern of low payouts. The Bank of Montreal had a steady payout in most of the years, but the payout exceeded 100 percent on one occasion in 1989. This illustrates that firms adjust their payouts if needed to avoid or soften dividend cuts. We discuss this next.

Dividend Stability

The key point of the residual dividend approach is that dividends are paid only after all profitable investment opportunities are exhausted. Of course, a strict residual approach might lead to a very unstable dividend policy. If investment opportunities in

T A B L E 16.4 | *The stability of dividends*

	EPS	DPS	Payout	EPS	DPS	Payout
			High Payout Firms			
		Imperial Oil			*Bank of Montreal*	
1984	$ 3.32	$1.45	44%	$3.37	$1.96	58%
1985	3.91	1.65	42	3.75	1.96	52
1986	2.69	1.60	59	3.70	1.96	53
1987	4.55	1.65	39	4.42	2.00	NA
1988	3.06	1.80	59	4.89	2.00	41
1989	2.54	1.80	71	0.04	2.12	5300
1990	2.58	1.80	70	4.20	2.12	50
1991	0.84	1.80	214	4.63	2.12	46
1992	1.01	1.80	178	4.76	2.12	45
1993	1.44	1.80	125	5.18	2.24	43
			Low Payout Firms			
		Northern Telecom			*Canadian Tire*	
1984	$ 1.32	$0.20	14%	$0.35	$0.20	57%
1985	1.63	0.25	15	0.49	0.20	41
1986	1.23	0.20	16	1.01	0.20	20
1987	1.39	0.23	17	1.10	0.20	18
1988	0.70	0.26	37	1.38	0.23	18
1989	1.47	0.28	19	1.65	0.30	19
1990	1.80	0.30	17	1.60	0.38	25
1991	2.03	0.32	16	1.41	0.40	28
1992	2.17	0.34	16	0.80	0.40	50
1993	−3.54	0.36	NA	0.90	0.40	44

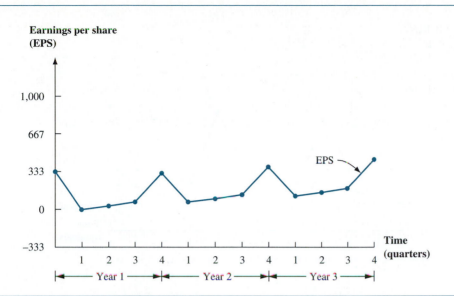

one period are quite high, dividends would be low or zero. Conversely, dividends might be high in the next period if investment opportunities are considered less promising.

Consider the case of Big Department Stores, Inc., a retailer whose annual earnings are forecasted to be equal from year to year but whose quarterly earnings change throughout the year. They are low in each year's first quarter because of the post-Christmas business slump. Although earnings increase only slightly in the second and third quarters, they advance greatly in the fourth quarter as a result of the Christmas season. A graph of this firm's earnings is presented in Figure 16.5.

The firm can choose between at least two types of dividend policies. First, each quarter's dividend can be a fixed fraction of that quarter's earnings. Here, dividends vary throughout the year. This is a cyclical dividend policy. Second, each quarter's dividend can be a fixed fraction of yearly earnings, implying that all dividend payments would be equal. This is a stable dividend policy. These two types of dividend policies are displayed in Figure 16.6.

Corporate executives generally agree that a stable policy is in the interest of the firm and its stockholders. Dividend stability complements investor objectives of information content, income, and reduction in uncertainty. Institutional investors often follow "prudence" tests that restrict investment in firms that do not pay regular dividends. For all these reasons a stable dividend policy is common. For example, looking back at Table 16.4, the dividends paid by these large Canadian firms are much less volatile through time than their earnings.

A Compromise Dividend Policy

In practice, many firms appear to follow what amounts to a compromise dividend policy. Such a policy is based on five main goals:

1. Avoid cutting back on positive NPV projects to pay a dividend.
2. Avoid dividend cuts.

F I G U R E 16.6

Alternative dividend policies for Big Department Stores, Inc.

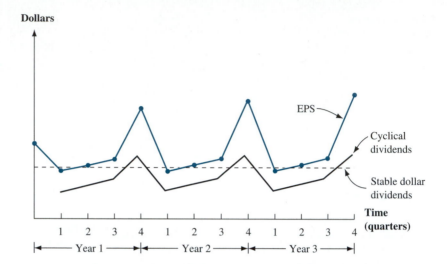

Cyclical dividend policy: Dividends are a constant proportion of earnings at each pay date.
Stable dividend policy: Dividends are a constant proportion of earnings over an earnings cycle.

3. Avoid the need to sell equity.
4. Maintain a target debt/equity ratio.
5. Maintain a target dividend payout ratio.

These goals are ranked more or less in order of their importance. In our strict residual approach, we assumed that the firm maintained a fixed debt/equity ratio. Under the compromise approach, that debt/equity ratio is viewed as a long-range goal. It is allowed to vary in the short run if necessary to avoid a dividend cut or the need to sell new equity.

In addition to a strong reluctance to cut dividends, financial managers tend to think of dividend payments in terms of a proportion of income, and they also tend to think investors are entitled to a "fair" share of corporate income. This share is the long-run **target payout ratio**, and it is the fraction of the earnings that the firm expects to pay as dividends under ordinary circumstances. Again, this is viewed as a long-range goal, so it might vary in the short run if needed. As a result, in the long run, earnings growth is followed by dividend increases, but only with a lag.

One can minimize the problems of dividend instability by creating two types of dividends: regular and extra. For companies using this approach, the regular dividend would likely be a relatively small fraction of permanent earnings, so that it could be sustained easily. Extra dividends would be granted when an increase in earnings was expected to be temporary.

Since investors look on an extra dividend as a bonus, there is relatively little disappointment when an extra dividend is not repeated.

target payout ratio

A firm's long-term desired dividend-to-earnings ratio.

CONCEPT QUESTIONS

1. What is a residual dividend policy?
2. What is the chief drawback to a strict residual policy? What do many firms do in practice?

16.7 | STOCK REPURCHASE: AN ALTERNATIVE TO CASH DIVIDENDS

When a firm wants to pay cash to its shareholders, it normally pays a cash dividend. Another way is to **repurchase** its own stock. Stock repurchasing has been a major financial activity, and it appears that it will continue to be one.

repurchase
Another method used to pay out a firm's earnings to its owners, which provides more preferable tax treatment than dividends.

Cash Dividends versus Repurchase

Imagine an all-equity company with excess cash of $300,000. The firm pays no dividends, and its net income for the year just ended is $49,000. The market value balance sheet at the end of the year is represented below.

Market Value Balance Sheet
(before paying out excess cash)

Excess cash	$ 300,000	$ 0	Debt
Other assets	700,000	1,000,000	Equity
Total	$1,000,000	$1,000,000	

There are 100,000 shares outstanding. The total market value of the equity is $1 million, so the stock sells for $10 per share. Earnings per share (EPS) were $49,000/100,000 = $.49, and the price/earnings ratio (P/E) is $10/$.49 = 20.4.

One option the company is considering is a $300,000/100,000 = $3 per share extra cash dividend. Alternatively, the company is thinking of using the money to repurchase $300,000/$10 = 30,000 shares of stock.

If commissions, taxes, and other imperfections are ignored in our example, the share holders shouldn't care which option is chosen. Does this seem surprising? It shouldn't, really. What is happening here is that the firm is paying out $300,000 in cash. The new balance sheet is represented below.

Market Value Balance Sheet
(after paying out excess cash)

Excess cash	$ 0	$ 0	Debt
Other assets	700,000	700,000	Equity
Total	$700,000	$700,000	

If the cash is paid out as a dividend, there are still 100,000 shares outstanding, so each is worth $7.

The fact that the per-share value fell from $10 to $7 isn't a cause for concern. Consider a shareholder who owns 100 shares. At $10 per share before the dividend, the total value is $1,000.

After the $3 dividend, this same shareholder has 100 shares worth $7 each, for a total of $700, plus 100 × $3 = $300 in cash, for a combined total of $1,000. This just illustrates what we saw earlier: A cash dividend doesn't affect a shareholder's wealth if there are no imperfections. In this case, the stock price simply fell by $3 when the stock went ex dividend.

Also, since total earnings and the number of shares outstanding haven't changed, EPS is still 49 cents. The price/earnings ratio (P/E), however, falls to $7/.49 = 14.3. Why we are looking at accounting earnings and P/E ratios will be apparent just below.

Alternatively, if the company repurchases 30,000 shares, there will be 70,000 left outstanding. The balance sheet looks the same.

Market Value Balance Sheet
(after share repurchase)

Excess cash	$ 0	$ 0	Debt
Other assets	700,000	700,000	Equity
Total	$700,000	$700,000	

The company is worth $700,000 again, so each remaining share is worth $700,000/70,000 = $10 each. Our shareholder with 100 shares is obviously unaffected. For example, if the shareholder were so inclined, he or she could sell 30 shares and end up with $300 in cash and $700 in stock, just as if the firm pays the cash dividend. This is another example of a homemade dividend.

In this second case, EPS goes up since total earnings are the same while the number of shares goes down. The new EPS will be $49,000/70,000 = $.70 per share. However, the important thing to notice is that the P/E ratio is $10/$.70 = 14.3, just as it was following the dividend.

This example illustrates the important point that, if there are no imperfections, a cash dividend and a share repurchase are essentially the same thing. This is just another illustration of dividend policy irrelevance when there are no taxes or other imperfections.

Real-World Considerations in a Repurchase

In the real world, there are some accounting differences between a share repurchase and a cash dividend, but the most important difference is in the tax treatment. A repurchase has a significant tax advantage over a cash dividend. A dividend is taxed, and a shareholder has no choice about whether or not to receive the dividend. In a repurchase, a shareholder pays taxes only if (1) the shareholder actually chooses to sell and (2) the shareholder has a taxable capital gain on the sale.

Normally, at any time, about one-third of TSE listed companies have announced their intentions to repurchase stock through the exchange. This means they plan to buy up to 5 percent of their stock for their treasury. Because of the favourable tax treatment of capital gains (even after the 1994 repeal of the life time gains exemption), a repurchase is a very sensible alternative to an extra dividend.

Selling its own shares back to a company repurchasing stock for treasury, as we just described, is not the only possibility. A Canadian investor could sell shares to another company making a tender offer to take over a target firm. In this case, the Income Tax Act requires investors to report a deemed dividend equal to the excess of the amount repurchased over book value. This removes the tax advantage of stock repurchases over dividends (and incidentally, shows that Revenue Canada does not dispute our view that dividends are taxed more heavily than gains). Share repurchases can be used to achieve other corporate goals such as altering the firm's capital structure or as a takeover defence.

Share Repurchase and EPS

You may read in the popular financial press that a share repurchase is beneficial because earnings per share increase. As we have seen, this will happen. The reason is simply that a share repurchase reduces the number of outstanding shares, but it has no effect on total earnings. As a result, EPS rises.

However, the financial press may place undue emphasis on EPS figures in a repurchase agreement. In our example above, we saw that the value of the stock wasn't affected by the EPS change. In fact, the price/earnings ratio was exactly the same when we compared a cash dividend to a repurchase.

Since the increase in earnings per share is exactly tracked by the increase in the price per share, there is no net effect. Put another way, the increase in EPS is just an accounting adjustment that reflects (correctly) the change in the number of shares outstanding.

In the real world, to the extent that repurchases benefit the firm, we would argue that they do so primarily because of the tax considerations we discussed above.

> CONCEPT QUESTIONS
> 1. Why might a stock repurchase make more sense than an extra cash dividend?
> 2. Why don't all firms use stock repurchases instead of cash dividends?

16.8 | STOCK DIVIDENDS AND STOCK SPLITS

Another type of dividend is paid out in shares of stock. This type of dividend is called a **stock dividend**. A stock dividend is not a true dividend because it is not paid in cash. The effect of a stock dividend is to increase the number of shares that each owner holds. Since there are more shares outstanding, each is simply worth less.

A stock dividend is commonly expressed as a percentage; for example, a 20 percent stock dividend means that a shareholder receives one new share for every five currently owned (a 20 percent increase). Since every shareholder owns 20 percent more stock, the total number of shares outstanding rises by 20 percent. As we see in a moment, the result would be that each share of stock is worth about 20 percent less.

A **stock split** is essentially the same thing as a stock dividend, except that a split is expressed as a ratio instead of a percentage. When a split is declared, each share is split to create additional shares. For example, in a three-for-one stock split, each old share is split into three new shares.

stock dividend
Payment made by a firm to its owners in the form of stock, diluting the value of each share outstanding.

stock split
An increase in a firm's shares outstanding without any change in owner's equity.

Some Details on Stock Splits and Stock Dividends

Stock splits and stock dividends have essentially the same impacts on the corporation and the shareholder: They increase the number of shares outstanding and reduce the value per share. The accounting treatment is not the same, however. Under TSE rules, the maximum stock dividend is 25 percent, anything larger is considered a stock split.

Example of a Stock Dividend   The Peterson Company, a consulting firm specializing in difficult accounting problems, has 10,000 shares of stock, each selling at $66. The total market value of the equity is $66 × 10,000 = $660,000. With a 10 percent stock dividend, each stockholder receives one additional share for each 10 presently owned, and the total number of shares outstanding after the dividend is 11,000.

Before the stock dividend, the equity portion of Peterson's balance sheet might look like this:

Common stock (10,000 shares outstanding)	$210,000
Retained earnings	290,000
Total owners' equity	$500,000

The amount of the stock dividend is transferred from retained earnings to common stock. Since 1,000 new shares are issued, the common stock account is increased by $66,000 (1,000 shares at $66 each). Total owners' equity is unaffected by the stock dividend because no cash has come in or out, so retained earnings is reduced by the entire $66,000. The net effect of these machinations is that Peterson's equity accounts now look like this:

Common stock (11,000 shares outstanding)	$276,000
Retained earnings	224,000
Total owners' equity	$500,000

Example of a Stock Split   A stock split is conceptually similar to a stock dividend, but it is commonly expressed as a ratio. For example, in a three-for-two split, each shareholder receives one additional share of stock for each two held originally, so a three-for-two split amounts to a 50 percent stock dividend. Again, no cash is paid out, and the percentage of the entire firm that each shareholder owns is unaffected.

The accounting treatment of a stock split is a little different (and simpler) from that of a stock dividend. Suppose Peterson decides to declare a two-for-one stock split. The number of shares outstanding doubles to 20,000. The owner's equity after the split is the same as before the split except the new number of shares is noted.

Common stock (20,000 shares outstanding)	$210,000
Retained earnings	290,000
Total owners' equity	$500,000

Value of Stock Splits and Stock Dividends

The laws of logic tell us that stock splits and stock dividends can (1) leave the value of the firm unaffected, (2) increase its value, or (3) decrease its value. Unfortunately, the issues are complex enough that one cannot easily determine which of the three relationships holds.

The Benchmark Case   A strong case can be made that stock dividends and splits do not change either the wealth of any shareholder or the wealth of the firm as a whole. In our prior example, the equity was worth a total of $660,000. With the stock dividend, the number of shares increased to 11,000, so it seems that each would be worth $660,000/11,000 = $60.

For example, a shareholder who had 100 shares worth $66 each before the dividend would have 110 shares worth $60 each afterwards. The total value of the stock is $6,600 either way; so the stock dividend doesn't really have any economic affect.

With the stock split, there were 20,000 shares outstanding, so each should be worth $660,000/20,000 = $33. In other words, the number of shares doubles and the price halves. From these calculations, it appears that stock dividends and splits are just paper transactions.

Although these results are relatively obvious, there are reasons that are often given to suggest that there may be some benefits to these actions. The typical financial manager is aware of many real-world complexities, and, for that reason, the stock split or stock dividend decision is not treated lightly in practice.

trading range
Price range between highest and lowest prices at which a stock is traded.

Popular Trading Range   Proponents of stock dividends and stock splits frequently argue that a security has a proper **trading range**. When the security is priced above this level, many investors do not have the funds to buy the common trading unit called a *round lot (usually 100 shares)*.

Although this argument is a popular one, its validity is questionable for a number of reasons. Mutual funds, pension funds, and other institutions have steadily increased their trading activity since World War II and now handle a sizable percentage of total trading volume (over half of the trading volume on both the TSE and NYSE). Because these institutions buy and sell in huge amounts, the individual share price is of little concern. Furthermore, we sometimes observe share prices that are quite large without appearing to cause problems.

Finally, there is evidence that stock splits may actually decrease the liquidity of the company's shares. Following a two-for-one split, the number of shares traded should more than double if liquidity is increased by the split. This doesn't appear to happen, and the reverse is sometimes observed.

Regardless of the impact on liquidity, firms do split their stock. Some managers believe that keeping the share price within a range attractive to individual investors helps promote Canadian ownership.

Reverse Splits

A less frequently encountered financial manoeuvre is the **reverse split**. In a one-for-three reverse split, each investor exchanges three old shares for one new share. As mentioned previously with reference to stock splits and stock dividends, a case can be made that a reverse split changes nothing substantial about the company.

reverse split
Procedure where a firm's number of shares outstanding is reduced.

Given real-world imperfections, three related reasons are cited for reverse splits. First, transaction costs to shareholders may be less after the reverse split. Second, the liquidity and marketability of a company's stock might be improved when its price is raised to the popular trading range. Third, stocks selling below a certain level are not considered respectable, meaning that investors underestimate these firms' earnings, cash flow, growth, and stability. Some financial analysts argue that a reverse split can achieve instant respectability. As with stock splits, none of these reasons is particularly compelling, especially the third one.

There are two other reasons for reverse splits. First, stock exchanges have minimum price per share requirements. A reverse split may bring the stock price up to such a minimum. Second, companies sometimes perform reverse splits and, at the same time, buy out any shareholders who end up with less than a certain number of shares. This second tactic can be abusive if used to force out minority shareholders.

CONCEPT QUESTIONS
1. What is the effect of a stock split on shareholder wealth?
2. How does the accounting treatment of a stock split differ from that used with a small stock dividend?

16.9 | SUMMARY AND CONCLUSIONS

In this chapter, we discussed the types of dividends and how they are paid. We then defined dividend policy and examined whether or not dividend policy matters. Finally, we illustrated how a firm might establish a dividend policy and described an important alternative to cash dividends, a share repurchase.

In covering these subjects, we saw that:

1. Dividend policy is irrelevant when there are no taxes or other imperfections because shareholders can effectively undo the firm's dividend strategy. A

shareholder who receives a dividend greater than desired can reinvest the excess. Conversely, the shareholder who receives a dividend that is smaller than desired can sell extra shares of stock.

2. Individual shareholder income taxes and new issue flotation costs are real-world considerations that favour a low-dividend payout. With taxes and new issue costs, the firm should pay out dividends only after all positive NPV projects have been fully financed.

3. There are groups in the economy that may favour a high payout. These include many large institutions such as pension plans. Recognizing that some groups prefer a high payout and some prefer a low payout, the clientele effect supports the idea that dividend policy responds to the needs of shareholders. For example, if 40 percent of the shareholders prefer low dividends and 60 percent of the shareholders prefer high dividends, approximately 40 percent of companies will have a low-dividend payout, while 60 percent will have a high payout. This sharply reduces the impact of any individual firm's dividend policy on its market price.

4. A firm wishing to pursue a strict residual dividend payout will have an unstable dividend. Dividend stability is usually viewed as highly desirable. We therefore discussed a compromise strategy that provides for a stable dividend and appears to be quite similar to the dividend policies many firms follow in practice.

5. A stock repurchase acts much like a cash dividend, but can have a significant tax advantage. Stock repurchases are therefore a very useful part of over-all dividend policy.

To close our discussion of dividends, we emphasize one last time the difference between dividends and dividend policy. Dividends are important, because the value of a share of stock is ultimately determined by the dividends that are paid. What is less clear is whether or not the time pattern of dividends (more now versus more later) matters. This is the dividend policy question, and it is not easy to give a definitive answer to it.

Key Terms

dividend (page 570)
distribution (page 570)
regular cash dividend (page 571)
declaration date (page 571)
ex-dividend date (page 572)
date of record (page 572)
date of payment (page 572)
homemade dividend (page 575)
stripped common shares (page 575)
information content effect (page 583)

clientele effect (page 585)
residual dividend approach (page 586)
target payout ratio (page 590)
repurchase (page 591)
stock dividend (page 593)
stock split (page 593)
trading range (page 594)
reverse split (page 595)

Chapter Review Problems and Self-Test

16.1 Residual Dividend Policy The Rapscallion Corporation practices a strict residual dividend policy and maintains a capital structure of 40 percent debt, 60 percent equity. Earnings for the year are $2,500. What is the maximum amount of capital spending possible without new equity? Suppose that planned investment outlays for the coming year are $3,000. Will Rapscallion be paying a dividend? If so, how much?

16.2 Repurchase versus Cash Dividend Trantor Corporation is deciding whether to pay out $300 in excess cash in the form of an extra dividend or a share repurchase. Current earnings are $1.50 per share and the stock sells for $15. The market value balance sheet before paying out the $300 is as follows:

Market Value Balance Sheet
(before paying out excess cash)

Excess cash	$ 300	$ 400	Debt
Other assets	1,600	1,500	Equity
Total	$1,900	$1,900	

Evaluate the two alternatives in the effect on the price per share of the stock, the EPS, and the P/E ratio.

Answers to Self-Test Problems

16.1 Rapscallion has a debt/equity ratio of .40/.60 = ⅔. If the entire $2,500 in earnings were reinvested, $2,500 × ⅔ = $1,667 in new borrowing would be needed to keep the debt/equity unchanged. Total new financing possible without external equity is thus $2,500 + 1,667 = $4,167.

If planned outlays are $3,000, this amount can be financed 60 percent with equity. The needed equity is thus $3,000 × .60 = $1,800. This is less than the $2,500 in earnings, so a dividend of $2,500 − 1,800 = $700 would be paid.

16.2 The market value of the equity is $1,500. The price per share is $15, so there are 100 shares outstanding. The cash dividend would amount to $300/100 = $3 per share. When the stock goes ex dividend, the price drops by $3 per share to $12. Put another way, the total assets decrease by $300, so the equity value goes down by this amount to $1,200. With 100 shares, this is $12 per share. After the dividend, EPS is the same, $1.50, but the P/E ratio is $12/1.50 = 8 times.

With a repurchase, $300/15 = 20 shares would be bought up, leaving 80. The equity again is worth $1,200 total. With 80 shares, this is $1,200/80 = $15 per share, so the price doesn't change. Total earnings for Trantor must be $1.5 × 100 = $150. After the repurchase, EPS is higher at $150/80 = $1.875. The P/E ratio, however, is still $15/1.875 = 8 times.

Questions and Problems

1. **Dividends and Taxes** York University pays no taxes on capital gains, dividend income, and interest payments received on investments in its endowment fund. Would it be irrational to find low-dividend, high-growth stocks in its portfolio? Would it be irrational to find preferred shares in its portfolio? Explain.

Basic (Questions 1–15)

2.   **Dividends and Taxes**   Zetaoid, Inc., has declared a $1.50 per share dividend. Suppose capital gains are not taxed, but dividends are taxed at 28 percent. New Revenue Canada regulations require that taxes be withheld at the time the dividend is paid. Zetaoid sells for $30 per share and the stock is about to go ex dividend. What do you think the ex-dividend price will be?

3.   **Stock Dividends**   The owners' equity accounts for RKM International are shown below:

Common stock ($1 par value)	$ 3,000
Capital surplus	60,000
Retained earnings	240,000
Total owners' equity	$303,000

a. If RKM stock currently sells for $20 per share and a 15 percent stock dividend is declared, how many new shares will be distributed? Show how the equity accounts above would change.

b. If RKM declared a 50 percent stock dividend, how would the accounts change?

4.   **Stock Splits**   For the company in Problem 3, show how the equity accounts would change if:

a. RKM declares a 10-for-1 stock split. How many shares are outstanding now?

b. RKM declares a 1-for-3 reverse stock split. How many shares are outstanding now?

5.   **Stock Splits and Stock Dividends**   Cardassian Capital Corporation (CCC) currently has 250,000 shares of stock outstanding that sell for $50 per share. Assuming no market imperfections or tax effects exist, what will the share price be after:

a. CCC has a 7-for-4 stock split?

b. CCC has a 10 percent stock dividend?

c. CCC has a 37.5 percent stock dividend?

d. CCC has a 3-for-5 reverse stock split?

e. Determine the new number of shares outstanding in parts *(a)–(d).*

6.   **Determining the Ex-Dividend Date**   On Tuesday, December 8, Hometown Power Co.'s board of directors declares a dividend of 75 cents per share payable on Wednesday, January 17, to shareholders of record as of Wednesday, January 3. When is the ex-dividend date? If a shareholder buys stock before that date, who gets the dividends on those shares, the buyer or the seller?

7.   **Regular Dividends**   The balance sheet for Columbia Netware Corp. is shown below in market value terms. There are 4,000 shares of stock outstanding.

Assets		Liabilities and Equity	
Cash	$ 6,000	Equity	$100,000
Fixed assets	94,000		

The company has declared a dividend of $1.25 per share. The stock goes ex dividend tomorrow. Ignoring any tax effects, what is the stock selling for today? What will it sell for tomorrow? What will the balance sheet above look like after the dividends are paid?

8. **Share Repurchase**   In the previous problem, suppose Columbia Netware has announced it is going to repurchase $5,000 worth of stock. What effect will this transaction have on the equity of the firm? How many shares will be outstanding? What will the price per share be after the repurchase? Ignoring tax effects, show how the share repurchase is effectively the same as a cash dividend.

Basic (Continued)

9. **Stock Dividends**   The market value balance sheet for Klein Manufacturing is shown below. Klein has declared a 10 percent stock dividend. The stock goes ex dividend tomorrow (the chronology for a stock dividend is similar to a cash dividend). There are 5,000 shares of stock outstanding. What will the ex-dividend price be?

Assets		Liabilities and Equity	
Cash	$100,000	Debt	$150,000
Fixed assets	250,000	Equity	200,000

10. **Stock Dividends**   The company with the common equity accounts shown below has declared a 6 percent stock dividend at a time when the market value of its stock is $8 per share. What effects on the equity accounts will the distribution of the stock dividend have?

Common stock ($1 par value)	$ 375,000
Capital surplus	2,450,000
Retained earnings	5,225,000
Total owners' equity	$8,050,000

11. **Stock Splits**   In the previous problem, suppose the company instead decides on a five-for-one stock split. The firm's 40-cent per share cash dividend on the new (post-split) shares represents an increase of 12.5 percent over last year's dividend on the presplit stock. What effect does this have on the equity accounts? What was last year's dividend per share?

12. **Residual Dividend Policy**   The Byarite Company uses a residual dividend policy. A debt/equity ratio of 0.5 is considered optimal. Earnings for the period just ended were $250, and a dividend of $180 was declared. How much in new debt was borrowed? What were total capital outlays?

13. **Residual Dividend Policy**   Franklin Corporation has declared an annual dividend of $1 per share. For the year just ended, earnings were $3 per share.
   a. What is Franklin's payout ratio?
   b. Suppose Franklin has 8 million shares outstanding. Borrowing for the coming year is planned at $10 million. What are planned investment outlays assuming a residual dividend policy? What target capital structure is implicit in these calculations?

14. **Residual Dividend Policy**   Straightway Corporation follows a strict residual dividend policy. Its debt/equity ratio is 2.
   a. If earnings for the year are $125,000, what is the maximum amount of capital spending possible with no new equity?
   b. If planned investment outlays for the coming year are $500,000, will Straightway pay a dividend? If so, how much?
   c. Does Straightway maintain a constant dividend payout? Why or why not?

Basic
(Continued)

15. **Residual Dividend Policy**   Omar Products, Inc., predicts that earnings in the coming year will be $24 million. There are 5 million shares, and Omar Products maintains a debt/equity ratio of 0.75.

   a. Calculate the maximum investment funds available without issuing new equity and the increase in borrowing that goes along with it.
   b. Suppose the firm uses a residual dividend policy. Planned capital expenditures total $28 million. Based on this information, what will the dividend per share amount be?
   c. In part (b), how much borrowing will take place? What is the addition to retained earnings?
   d. Suppose Omar Products plans no capital outlays for the coming year. What will the dividend be under a residual policy? What would new borrowing be?

Intermediate
(Questions 16–25)

16. **Homemade Dividends**   You own 1,625 shares of stock in WordSoft Corporation. You will receive a 65-cent per share dividend in one year. In two years, WordSoft will pay a liquidating dividend of $25 per share. The required return on WordSoft stock is 16 percent. What is the current share price of your stock (ignoring taxes)? If you would rather have equal dividends in each of the next two years, show how you can accomplish this by creating homemade dividends. Hint: Dividends will be in the form of an annuity.

17. **Homemade Dividends**   In the previous problem, suppose you want only $50 total in dividends the first year. What will your homemade dividend be in two years?

18. **Stock Repurchase**   Stowe Corporation is evaluating an extra dividend versus a share repurchase. In either case, $3,000 would be spent. Current earnings are $4 per share, and the stock currently sells for $40 per share. There are 250 shares outstanding. Ignore taxes and other imperfections in answering the first two questions.

   a. Evaluate the two alternatives in terms of the effect on the price per share of the stock and shareholder wealth.
   b. What will be the effect on Stowe's EPS and P/E ratio under the two different scenarios?
   c. In the real world, which of these actions would you recommend? Why?

19. **Alternative Dividends**   Some corporations, like one British company that offers its large shareholders free crematorium use, pay dividends in kind (that is, offer their services to shareholders at below-market cost). Should mutual funds invest in stocks that pay these dividends in kind? (The fundholders do not receive these services.)

20. **Dividend Policy**   If increases in dividends tend to be followed by (immediate) increases in share prices, how can it be said that dividend policy is irrelevant?

21. **Changes in Dividends**   Last month, Central Virginia Power Company, which has been having trouble with cost overruns on a nuclear power plant that it had been building, announced it was "temporarily suspending payments due to the cash flow crunch associated with its investment program." The company's stock price dropped from $28.50 to $25 when this announcement was made. How would you interpret this change in the stock price (that is, what caused it)?

22. **DRIPs**   The DRK Corporation has recently developed a dividend reinvestment plan (DRIP). The plan allows investors to reinvest cash dividends automatically

Intermediate
(Continued)

in DRK in exchange for new shares of stock. Over time, investors in DRK will be able to build their holdings by reinvesting dividends to purchase additional shares of the company.

Over 1,000 companies offer dividend reinvestment plans. Most companies with DRIPs charge no brokerage or service fees. In fact, the shares of DRK will be purchased at a 10 percent "discount" from the market price.

A consultant for DRK estimates that about 75 percent of DRK's shareholders will take part in this plan. This is somewhat higher than the average.

Evaluate DRK's dividend reinvestment plan. Will it increase shareholder wealth? Discuss the advantages and disadvantages involved here.

23. **Dividend Policy** For initial public offerings of common stock, 1993 was a very big year, with over $43 billion raised in the process. Relatively few of these firms paid cash dividends. Why do you think that most chose not to pay cash dividends?

24. **Dividend Policy** Consider the following article from the *Philadelphia Bulletin,* April 16, 1976:

The Dividend Question at Clark Equipment

If you're one of the 13,000 shareholders of Clark Equipment Co., you can look forward to an increase in the $1.60 annual dividend—but don't spend the money yet.

Says Leonard M. Savoie, vice president and controller, "We'll have to raise it some day. There's a lot of pressure for an increase."

The $1.60 rate has been in effect since 1973. What with the ravages of inflation, the purchasing power of the $1.60 is considerably less than in 1973.

But an increase isn't likely soon, Bert E. Phillips, president and chief executive, strongly indicated. The two officials of the Buchanan, Michigan, maker of materials-handling and construction equipment were in town yesterday for a meeting with the Financial Analysts of Philadelphia at the Racquet Club.

Two Reasons

Clark's first-quarter earnings weren't "very good," according to Phillips, who said the first half "will likely be somewhat depressed" too. That's no time to raise the dividend.

On top of that, Phillips thinks that Clark can reinvest the money in the business at a higher rate than shareholders could on their own.

That's unlikely to cut much ice with shareholders who depend on dividends. But Phillips thinks it's foolish for a company to pay a higher dividend and then have to borrow the money it needs for expansion and modernization of its plants.

In effect, he told analysts, that's borrowing to pay dividends.

Traditionally, Clark has been paying out between 45 percent and 50 percent of earnings in dividends. Phillips hopes to be able to persuade directors to let the payout ratio shrink as earnings pick up later this year and the next, as he expects.

Some directors might resist, worrying about the "little old lady in tennis shoes out in Iowa" who wants an increase in the $1.60 dividend, according to Phillips.

Said Phillips, "I think she died, but they don't know it yet."

Next year might be different, the Clark official indicated.

"We think the downturn has bottomed," Phillips said, "and that the second half (of 1976) will see improvement as the whole capital-goods sector comes back to a healthier state." Sales and earnings of capital-goods producers like Clark generally lag behind the economy by six to nine months.

Omen

Clark's shipments of forklifts and other industrial trucks declined throughout 1975. But in the past few months, according to Phillips, shipments have been "trending upward, and we expect this to continue gradually over the remainder of the year." Construction machinery, however, continues flat.

In 1975, Clark earned $46.6 million, or $3.43 per share, on sales of $1.4 billion. Some Wall Street analysts are forecasting 1976 earnings between $3.60 and $4 per share.

Evaluate "The Dividend Question at Clark" in light of what you have learned about dividend policy. In particular:

a. What do you think of the two reasons for not raising the $1.60 dividend this year?

b. What do you think of "borrowing to pay dividends"?

c. Should Clark base its dividend policy on the payout ratio? On the dividend per share?

d. How much should the company worry about investors like the "little old lady from Iowa"?

25. **Residual Policy versus a Compromise**   What is the chief drawback to a strict residual dividend policy? Why is this a problem? How does a compromise policy work? How does it differ from a strict residual policy?

26. **Expected Return, Dividends, and Taxes**   The Upstart Company and the Downdraft Company are two firms whose business risk is the same but have different dividend policies. Upstart pays no dividend, while Downdraft has an expected dividend yield of 5.5 percent. Suppose the capital gains tax rate is zero, while the income tax rate is 35 percent. Upstart has an expected earnings growth rate of 18 percent annually, and its stock price is expected to grow at this same rate. If the aftertax expected returns on the two stocks are equal (since they are in the same risk class), what is the pretax required return on Downdraft's stock?

27. **Dividends and Taxes**   As discussed in the text, in the absence of market imperfections and tax effects we would expect the share price to decline by the amount of the dividend payment when the stock goes ex dividend. Once we consider the role of taxes, however, this is not necessarily true. One model that has been proposed that incorporates tax effects into determining the ex-dividend price[17] is

$$(P_0 - P_X)/D = (1 - T_P)/(1 - T_G)$$

where P_0 is the price just before the stock goes ex, P_x is the ex-dividend share price, D is the amount of the dividend per share, T_P is the relevant marginal personal tax rate, and T_G is the effective marginal tax rate on capital gains.

a. If $T_P = T_G = 0$, how much will the share price fall when the stock goes ex?

b. If $T_P = 28$ percent and $T_G = 0$, how much will the share price fall?

c. If $T_P = 39$ percent and $T_G = 28$ percent, how much will the share price fall?

d. Suppose the only owners of stock are corporations. Recall that corporations get at least a 70 percent exemption from taxation on the dividend income

---

[17] N. Elton and M. Gruber, "Marginal Stockholder Tax Rates and the Clientele Effect," *Review of Economics and Statistics* 52 (February 1970).

they receive, but they do not get such an exemption on capital gains. If the corporation's income and capital gains tax rates are both 34 percent, what does this model predict the ex-dividend share price will be?

e. What does this problem tell you about real-world tax considerations and the dividend policy of the firm?

Challenge
(Continued)

Suggested Readings

Our dividend irrelevance argument is based on a classic article:

Miller, M. H., and F. Modigliani. "Dividend Policy, Growth and the Valuation of Shares." *Journal of Business* 34, (October 1961).

Higgins describes the residual dividend approach in:

Higgins, R. C. "The Corporate Dividend-Saving Decision." *Journal of Financial and Quantitative Analysis* 7, (March 1972).

The following examine taxes and dividends in Canada:

Adjaoud, F., and D. Zeghal. "Taxation and Dividend Policy in Canada: New Evidence." *FINECO* (2nd Semester) 1993, pp. 141–54.

Amoako-adu, B. "Capital Gains Tax and Equity Values: Empirical Test of Stock Price Reaction to the Introduction and Reduction of Capital Gains Tax Exemption. *Journal of Banking and Finance* 16 (1992), pp. 275–87.

Lakonishok, J., and T. Vermaelen. "Tax Reform and Ex-Dividend Day Behavior." *Journal of Finance* 38 (September 1983).

Booth, L. D., and D. J. Johnston. "The Ex-Dividend Day Behavior of Canadian Stock Prices: Tax Changes and Clientele Effects." *Journal of Finance* 39 (June 1984).

Morgan, I. G. "Dividends and Stock Price Behaviour in Canada." *Journal of Business Administration* 12 (Fall 1980).

Evidence that investors regard dividend announcements as important signals is in

Hatch, J. E., and M. J. Robinson. *Investment Management in Canada,* 2nd ed. Scarborough: Prentice Hall Canada, 1989, chap. 14.

SHORT-TERM FINANCIAL PLANNING AND MANAGEMENT

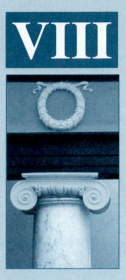

CHAPTER 17 | Short-Term Finance and Planning

To this point, we have described the decisions of long-term finance, including capital budgeting, capital structure, and dividend policy. This chapter introduces some aspects of short-term finance. Short-term finance is the analysis of decisions made when the relevant cash flows all occur in the near future. The focus of short-term finance is on current assets and current liabilities.

CHAPTER 18 | Cash and Liquidity Management

Why do firms hold any cash? This is the question Chapter 18 answers, and it discusses some very good reasons for firms doing so. This chapter shows how firms can keep investments in cash low while still operating effectively.

CHAPTER 19 | Credit and Inventory Management

This chapter looks at a firm's decision to grant credit. Granting credit can result in increased sales for the firm, but this benefit must be balanced against the extra costs of a credit sale. How to evaluate this trade-off is the essence of credit management. The chapter also looks at inventory management trade-offs. It pays special attention to new developments such as just-in-time inventory.

CHAPTER

17

Short-Term Finance and Planning

To this point, we have described many of the decisions of long-term finance, for example, capital budgeting, dividend policy, and financial structure. In this chapter, we begin to discuss short-term finance. Short-term finance is primarily concerned with the analysis of decisions that affect current assets and current liabilities.

Financial managers spend major blocks of time daily on short-term financial management. What types of questions fall under the general heading of short-term finance? To name just a very few:

1. What is a reasonable level of cash to keep on hand (in a bank) to pay bills?
2. How much should the firm borrow short-term?
3. How much credit should be extended to customers?
4. How much inventory should the firm carry?

Answering these questions is central to the financial manager's job. Short-term financial management is often an important part of entry-level jobs for new finance graduates.[1]

Frequently, the term *net working capital* is associated with short-term financial decision making. As we describe in Chapter 2 and elsewhere, net working capital is the difference between current assets and current liabilities. Often, short-term financial management is called *working capital management*. These terms mean the same thing.

There is no universally accepted definition of short-term finance. The most important difference between short-term and long-term finance is the timing of cash flows. Short-term financial decisions typically involve cash inflows and outflows that occur within a year or less. For example, short-term financial decisions are involved when a firm orders raw materials, pays in cash, and anticipates selling finished goods in one year for cash. In contrast, long-term financial decisions are involved when a firm purchases a special machine that reduces operating costs over, say, the next five years.

This chapter introduces the basic elements of short-term financial decisions. We begin by discussing the short-term operating activities of the firm. We then identify some alternative short-term financial policies. Finally, we outline the basic elements in a short-term financial plan and describe short-term financing instruments.

---

[1] N. C. Hill and W. L. Sartoris, *Short-Term Financial Management* (New York: Macmillan, 1988), p. 3.

17.1 | TRACING CASH AND NET WORKING CAPITAL

In this section, we examine the components of cash and net working capital as they change from one year to the next. We have already discussed various aspects of this subject in Chapters 2, 3, and 4. We briefly review some of that discussion as it relates to short-term financing decisions. Our goal is to describe the short-term operating activities of the firm and their impact on cash and working capital.

To begin, recall that *current assets* are cash and other assets expected to convert to cash within the year. Current assets are presented in the balance sheet in order of their accounting liquidity—the ease with which they can be converted to cash and the time it takes to do so. Four of the most important items found in the current asset section of a balance sheet are cash, marketable securities (or cash equivalents), accounts receivable, and inventories.

Analogous to their investment in current assets, firms use several kinds of short-term debt, called *current liabilities*. Current liabilities are obligations expected to require cash payment within one year (or within the operating period if it is different from one year). The three major items found as current liabilities are accounts payable; expenses payable, including accrued wages and taxes; and notes payable.

Because we want to focus on changes in cash, we start by defining cash in terms of the other elements of the balance sheet. This lets us isolate the cash account and explore the impact on cash from the firm's operating and financing decisions. The basic balance sheet identity can be written as:

$$\text{Net working capital} + \text{Fixed assets} = \text{Long-term debt} + \text{Equity} \qquad [17.1]$$

Net working capital is cash plus other current assets less current liabilities; that is,

$$\text{Net working capital} = (\text{Cash} + \text{Other current assets}) \qquad [17.2]$$
$$- \text{Current liabilities}$$

If we substitute this for net working capital in the basic balance sheet identity and rearrange things a bit, cash is:

$$\text{Cash} = \text{Long-term debt} + \text{Equity} + \text{Current liabilities} \qquad [17.3]$$
$$- \text{Current assets (other than cash)} - \text{Fixed assets}$$

This tells us in general terms that some activities naturally increase cash and some activities decrease it. We can list these along with an example of each as follows:

Activities that Increase Cash

  Increasing long-term debt (borrowing long-term).
  Increasing equity (selling some stock).
  Increasing current liabilities (getting a 90-day loan).
  Decreasing current assets other than cash (selling some inventory for cash).
  Decreasing fixed assets (selling some property).

Activities that Decrease Cash

  Decreasing long-term debt (paying off a long-term debt).
  Decreasing equity (repurchasing some stock).
  Decreasing current liabilities (paying off a 90-day loan).
  Increasing current assets other than cash (buying some inventory for cash).
  Increasing fixed assets (buying some property).

Notice that our two lists are exact opposites. For example, floating a long-term bond issue increases cash (at least until the money is spent). Paying off a long-term bond issue decreases cash.

As we discussed in Chapter 3, those activities that increase cash are sources of cash. Those activities that decrease cash are uses of cash. Looking back at our list, sources of cash always involve increasing a liability (or equity) account or decreasing an asset account. This makes sense because increasing a liability means we have raised money by borrowing it or by selling an ownership interest in the firm. A decrease in an asset means we have sold or otherwise liquidated an asset. In either case, there is a cash inflow.

Uses of cash are just the reverse. A use of cash involves decreasing a liability by paying it off, perhaps, or an increase in assets from purchasing something. Both of these activities require that the firm spend some cash.

E X A M P L E | 17.1   Sources and Uses

Here is a quick check of your understanding of sources and uses: If accounts payable goes up by $100, is this a source or use? If accounts receivable goes up by $100, is this a source or use?

Accounts payable are what we owe our suppliers. This is a short-term debt. If it rises by $100, we have effectively borrowed the money, so this is a source of cash. Receivables is what our customers owe to us, so an increase of $100 means that we loaned the money; this is a use of cash. |

CONCEPT QUESTIONS

1. What is the difference between net working capital and cash?

2. Will net working capital always increase when cash increases?

3. List five potential uses of cash.

4. List five potential sources of cash.

17.2 | THE OPERATING CYCLE AND THE CASH CYCLE

The primary concern in short-term finance is the firm's short-run operating and financing activities. For a typical manufacturing firm, these short-run activities might consist of the following sequence of events and decisions:

Events	Decisions
1. Buying raw materials	1. How much inventory to order?
2. Paying cash	2. Borrow or draw down cash balance?
3. Manufacturing the product	3. What choice of production technology?
4. Selling the product	4. Should credit be extended to a particular customer?
5. Collecting cash	5. How to collect?

These activities create patterns of cash inflows and cash outflows. These cash flows are both unsynchronized and uncertain. They are unsynchronized because, for example, the payment of cash for raw materials does not happen at the same time as the receipt of cash from selling the product. They are uncertain because future sales and costs are not known with certainty.

Defining the Operating and Cash Cycles

We can start with a simple case. One day, call it Day 0, you purchase $1,000 worth of inventory on credit. You pay the bill 30 days later, and, after 30 more days, someone buys the $1,000 in inventory for $1,400. Your buyer does not actually pay for another 45 days. We can summarize these events chronologically as follows:

Day	Activity	Cash effect
0	Acquire inventory	none
30	Pay for inventory	−$1,000
60	Sell inventory on credit	none
105	Collect on sale	+$1,400

The Operating Cycle   There are several things to notice in our example: First, the entire cycle, from the time we acquire some inventory to the time we collect the cash, takes 105 days. This is called the **operating cycle**.

As we illustrate, the operating cycle is the length of time it takes to acquire inventory, sell it, and collect for it. This cycle has two distinct components. The first part is the time it takes to acquire and sell the inventory. This 60-day span (in our example) is called the **inventory period**. The second part is the time it takes to collect on the sale, 45 days in our example. This is called the **accounts receivable period**.

Based on our definitions, the operating cycle is obviously just the sum of the inventory and receivables periods:

$$\text{Operating cycle} = \text{Inventory period} + \text{Accounts receivable period} \qquad [17.4]$$
$$105 \text{ days} = 60 \text{ days} + 45 \text{ days}$$

What the operating cycle describes is how a product moves through the current asset accounts. It begins life as inventory, it is converted to a receivable when it is sold, and it is finally converted to cash when we collect from the sale. Notice that, at each step, the asset is moving closer to cash.

The Cash Cycle   The second thing to notice is that the cash flows and other events that occur are not synchronized. For example, we didn't actually pay for the inventory until 30 days after we acquired it. This 30-day period is called the **accounts payable period**. Next, we spend cash on Day 30, but we don't collect until Day 105. Somehow or the other, we have to arrange to finance the $1,000 for 105 − 30 = 75 days. This period is called the **cash cycle**.

The cash cycle, therefore, is the number of days that pass until we collect the cash from a sale, measured from when we actually pay for the inventory. Notice that, based on our definitions, the cash cycle is the difference between the operating cycle and the accounts payable period:

$$\text{Cash cycle} = \text{Operating cycle} - \text{Accounts payable period} \qquad [17.5]$$
$$75 \text{ days} = 105 \text{ days} - 30 \text{ days}$$

Figure 17.1 depicts the short-term operating activities and cash flows for a typical manufacturing firm by looking at the cash flow time line. As shown, the **cash flow time line** is made up of the operating cycle and the cash cycle. In Figure 17.1, the need for short-term financial management is suggested by the gap between the cash inflows and cash outflows. This is related to the length of the operating cycle and accounts payable period.

operating cycle
The time period between the acquisition of inventory and when cash is collected from receivables.

inventory period
The time it takes to acquire and sell inventory.

accounts receivable period
The time between sale of inventory and collection of the receivable.

accounts payable period
The time between receipt of inventory and payment for it.

cash cycle
The time between cash disbursement and cash collection.

cash flow time line
Graphical representation of the operating cycle and the cash cycle.

*Cash flow time line
and the short-term
operating activities of
a typical
manufacturing firm*

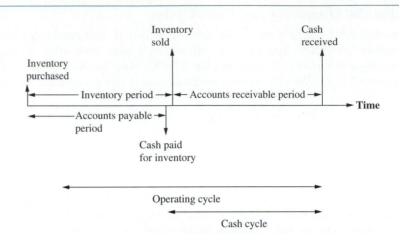

The operating cycle is the time period from inventory purchase until the receipt of cash. (Sometimes the operating cycle includes the time from placement of the order until arrival of the stock.) The cash cycle is the time period from when cash is paid out to when cash is received.

The gap between short-term inflows and outflows can be filled either by borrowing or by holding a liquidity reserve in the form of cash or marketable securities. Alternatively, the gap can be shortened by changing the inventory, receivable, and payable periods. These are all managerial options that we discuss in this and subsequent chapters.

The Operating Cycle and the Firm's Organization Chart Before we look at detailed examples of operating and cash cycles, realism dictates a look at the people involved in implementing a firm's policies. This is important because short-term financial management in a large corporation involves non-financial managers as well and there is potential for conflict as each manager looks at only part of the picture.[2] As you can see in Table 17.1, selling on credit involves the credit manager, the marketing manager, and the controller. Of these three, only two are responsible to the vice president of finance as the marketing function has its own vice president in most large corporations. If the marketing function is trying to land a new account, it may seek more liberal credit terms as an inducement. Since this may increase the firm's investment in receivables or its exposure to the bad debt risk, conflict may result. To resolve such conflict, the firm must look beyond personalities to the ultimate impact on shareholder wealth.

Calculating the Operating and Cash Cycles

In our example, the lengths of time that made up the different periods were obvious. When all we have is financial statement information, however, we have to do a little more work. We illustrate these calculations next.

_____

[2] This discussion draws on Hill and Sartoris, *Short-Term Financial Management,* chap. 1.

Title	Short-Term Financial Management Duties	Assets/Liabilities Influenced
Cash manager	Collection, concentration, disbursement; short-term investments; short-term borrowing; banking relations	Cash, marketable securities, short-term loans
Credit manager	Monitoring and control of accounts receivable; credit policy decisions	Accounts receivable
Marketing manager	Credit policy decisions	Accounts receivable
Purchasing manager	Decisions on purchases, suppliers; may negotiate payment terms	Inventory, accounts payable
Production manager	Setting of production schedules and materials requirements	Inventory, accounts payable
Payables manager	Decisions on payment policies and on whether to take discounts	Accounts payable
Controller	Accounting information on cash flows; reconciliation of accounts payable; application of payments to accounts receivable	Accounts receivable, accounts payable

T A B L E 17.1

Managers who deal with short-term financial problems

Source: Ned C. Hill and William L. Sartoris, *Short-Term Financial Management,* 2nd ed. (New York: Macmillan Publishing Company, 1992), p. 15.

To begin, we need to determine various things like how long it takes, on average, to sell inventory and how long it takes, on average, to collect. We start by gathering some balance sheet information such as the following (in thousands):

Item	Beginning	Ending	Average
Inventory	$2,000	$3,000	$2,500
Accounts receivable	1,600	2,000	1,800
Accounts payable	750	1,000	875

Also, from the most recent income statement, we might have the following figures (in thousands):

Net sales	$11,500
Cost of goods sold	8,200

We now need to calculate some financial ratios. We discussed these in some detail in Chapter 3; here we just define them and use them as needed.

The Operating Cycle First, we need the inventory period. We spent $8.2 million on inventory (our cost of goods sold). Our average inventory was $2.5 million. We thus turned our inventory over 8.2/2.5 times during the year:[3]

Inventory turnover = Cost of goods sold/Average inventory

= $8.2 million/$2.5 million = 3.28 times

---

[3] Notice that we have used the cost of goods sold in calculating inventory turnover. Sales is sometimes used instead. Also, rather than average inventory, ending inventory is often used. See Chapter 3 for some examples.

Loosely speaking, this tells us that we bought and sold off our inventory 3.28 times during the year. This means that, on average, we held our inventory for:

Inventory period = 365 days/Inventory turnover

= 365/3.28 = 111.3 days

So the inventory period is about 111 days. On average, in other words, inventory sat for about 111 days before it was sold.[4]

Similarly, receivables averaged $1.8 million, and sales were $11.5 million. Assuming that all sales were credit sales, the receivables turnover is:[5]

Receivables turnover = Credit sales/Average accounts receivable

= $11.5 million/$1.8 million = 6.4 times

If we turn over our receivables 6.4 times, then the receivables period is:

Receivables period = 365 days/Receivables turnover

= 365/6.4 = 57 days

The receivables period is also called the *days' sales in receivables* or the *average collection period.* Whatever it is called, it tells us that our customers took an average of 57 days to pay.

The operating cycle is the sum of the inventory and receivables periods:

Operating cycle = Inventory period + Accounts receivables period

= 111 days + 57 days = 168 days

This tells us that, on average, 168 days elapse between the time we acquire inventory, sell it, and collect for the sale.

The Cash Cycle   We now need the payables period. From the information just given, average payables were $875,000, and cost of goods sold was again $8.2 million. Our payables turnover is thus:

Payables turnover = Cost of goods sold/Average payables

= $8.2 million/$.875 million = 9.4 times

The payables period is:

Payables period = 365 days/Payables turnover

= 365/9.4 = 39 days

Thus, we took an average of 39 days to pay our bills.

Finally, the cash cycle is the difference between the operating cycle and the payables period:

Cash cycle = Operating cycle − Accounts payables period

= 168 days − 39 days = 129 days

So, on average, there is a 129-day delay from the time we pay for merchandise and the time we collect on the sales.

---

[4] This measure is conceptually identical to the days' sales in inventory we discussed in Chapter 3.

[5] If less than 100 percent of our sales are credit sales, we would just need a little more information, namely, credit sales for the year. See Chapter 3 for more discussion of this measure.

E X A M P L E | 17.2   **The Operating and Cash Cycles**

You have collected the following information for the Slowpay Company.

Item	Beginning	Ending
Inventory	$5,000	$7,000
Accounts receivable	1,600	2,400
Accounts payable	2,700	4,800

Sales for the year just ended were $50,000, and cost of goods sold was $30,000. How long does it take Slowpay to collect on its receivables? How long does merchandise stay around before it is sold? How long does Slowpay take to pay its bills?

We can first calculate the three turnover ratios:

Inventory turnover = $30,000/$6,000 = 5 times

Receivables turnover = $50,000/$2,000 = 25 times

Payables turnover = $30,000/$3,750 = 8 times

We use these to get the various periods:

Inventory period = 365/5 = 73 days

Receivables period = 365/25 = 14.6 days

Payables period = 365/8 = 45.6 days

All told, Slowpay collects on a sale in 14.6 days, inventory sits around for 73 days, and bills get paid after about 46 days. The operating cycle here is the sum of the inventory and receivables: 73 + 14.6 = 87.6 days. The cash cycle is the difference between the operating cycle and the payables period: 87.6 − 45.6 = 42 days. |

Interpreting the Cash Cycle

Our examples show how the cash cycle depends on the inventory, receivables, and payables periods. Taken one at a time, the cash cycle increases as the inventory and receivables periods get longer. It decreases if the company is able to stall payment of payables lengthening the payables period. Suppose a firm could purchase inventory, sell its product, collect receivables (perhaps selling for cash) and then pay suppliers all on the same day. This firm would have a cash cycle of zero days.

Some firms may meet this description but it is hard to think of many examples. Most firms have a positive cash cycle. Such firms require some additional financing for inventories and receivables. The longer the cash cycle, the more financing is required, other things being equal. Since bankers are conservative and dislike surprises, they monitor the firm's cash cycle. A lengthening cycle may indicate obsolete, unsalable inventory or problems in collecting receivables. Unless these problems are detected and solved, the firm may require emergency financing or face insolvency.

Our calculations of the cash cycle used financial ratios introduced in Chapter 3. We can use some other ratio relationships from Chapter 3 to see how the cash cycle relates to profitability and sustainable growth. A good place to start is with the Du Pont equation for profitability as measured by return on assets (ROA):

$$ROA = \text{Profit margin} \times \text{Total asset turnover}$$

Total asset turnover = Sales/Total assets

Go back to the case of the firm with a lengthening cash cycle. Increased inventories and receivables that caused the cash cycle problem also reduce total asset turnover. The result is lower profitability. In other words, with more assets tied up over a longer cash cycle, the firm is less efficient and therefore less profitable. And, as if its troubles were not enough already, this firm suffers a drop in its sustainable growth rate.

Chapter 4 (in the discussion of Equation 4.5) showed that total asset turnover is directly linked to sustainable growth. Reducing total asset turnover lowers sustainable growth. This makes sense because our troubled firm must divert its financial resources into financing excess inventory and receivables.[6]

CONCEPT QUESTIONS

1. What does it mean to say that a firm has an inventory turnover ratio of 4?
2. Describe the operating cycle and cash cycle. What are the differences?
3. Explain the connection between a firm's accounting-based profitability and its cash cycle.

17.3 | SOME ASPECTS OF SHORT-TERM FINANCIAL POLICY

The short-term financial policy that a firm adopts is reflected in at least two ways:

1. *The size of the firm's investment in current assets.* This is usually measured relative to the firm's level of total operating revenues. A *flexible* or accommodative short-term financial policy would maintain a relatively high ratio of current assets to sales. A *restrictive* short-term financial policy would entail a low ratio of current assets to sales.[7]
2. *The financing of current assets.* This is measured as the proportion of short-term debt (that is, current liabilities) and long-term debt used to finance current assets. A restrictive short-term financial policy means a high proportion of short-term debt relative to long-term financing, and a flexible policy means less short-term debt and more long-term debt.

If we take these two areas together, a firm with a flexible policy would have relatively large investment in current assets. It would finance this investment with relatively less in short-term debt. The net effect of a flexible policy is thus a relatively high level of net working capital. Put another way, with a flexible policy, the firm maintains a larger overall level of liquidity.

The Size of the Firm's Investment in Current Assets

Flexible short-term financial policies with regard to current assets include such actions as:

1. Keeping large balances of cash and marketable securities.
2. Making large investments in inventory.
3. Granting liberal credit terms, which result in a high level of accounts receivable.

[6] Further discussion of the cash cycle is in L. Kryzanowski, *Business Solvency Risk Analysis* (Montreal: Institute of Canadian Bankers, 1990), chap. 10.
[7] Some people use the term *conservative* in place of flexible and the term *aggressive* in place of restrictive.

Restrictive short-term financial policies would just be the opposite of these:

1. Keeping low cash balances and little investment in marketable securities.
2. Making small investments in inventory.
3. Allowing little or no credit sales, thereby minimizing accounts receivable.

Determining the optimal investment level in short-term assets requires an identification of the different costs of alternative short-term financing policies. The objective is to trade off the cost of a restrictive policy against the cost of a flexible one to arrive at the best compromise.

Current asset holdings are highest with a flexible short-term financial policy and lowest with a restrictive policy. So flexible short-term financial policies are costly in that they require a greater investment in cash and marketable securities, inventory, and accounts receivable. However, we expect future cash inflows to be higher with a flexible policy. For example, sales are stimulated by the use of a credit policy that provides liberal financing to customers. A large amount of finished inventory on hand ("on the shelf") provides a quick delivery service to customers and may increase sales. Similarly, a large inventory of raw materials may result in fewer production stoppages because of inventory shortages.[8]

A more restrictive short-term financial policy probably reduces future sales levels below those that would be achieved under flexible policies. It is also possible that higher prices can be charged to customers under flexible working capital policies. Customers may be willing to pay higher prices for the quick delivery service and more liberal credit terms implicit in flexible policies.

Managing current assets can be thought of as involving a trade-off between costs that rise and costs that fall with the level of investment. Costs that rise with increases in the level of investment in current assets are called **carrying costs**. The larger the investment a firm makes in its current assets, the higher its carrying costs are. Costs that fall with increases in the level of investment in current assets are called **shortage costs**.

In a general sense, carrying costs are the opportunity costs associated with current assets. The rate of return on current assets is very low when compared to other assets. For example, the rate of return on Treasury bills is usually considerably less than the rate of return firms would like to achieve overall. (Treasury bills are an important component of cash and marketable securities.)

Shortage costs are incurred when the investment in current assets is low. If a firm runs out of cash, it is forced to sell marketable securities. Of course, if a firm runs out of cash and marketable securities to sell, it may have to borrow, sell assets at fire-sale prices, or default on an obligation. This situation is called a *cash out*. A firm loses customers if it runs out of inventory (a *stock out*) or if it cannot extend credit to customers.

More generally, there are two kinds of shortage costs:

1. *Trading or order costs.* Order costs are the costs of placing an order for more cash (brokerage costs, for example) or more inventory (production set-up costs, for example).
2. *Costs related to lack of safety reserves.* These are costs of lost sales, lost customer goodwill, and disruption of production schedules.

carrying costs
Costs that rise with increases in the level of investment in current assets.

shortage costs
Costs that fall with increases in the level of investment in current assets.

---

[8] While this statement is true for distributors and retailers, many manufacturing industries are reducing inventory through new technology. We discuss this approach, called just-in-time inventory (or production), in Chapter 19.

The top part of Figure 17.2 illustrates the basic trade-off between carrying costs and shortage costs. On the vertical axis, we have costs measured in dollars and, on the horizontal axis, we have the amount of current assets. Carrying costs start at zero when current assets are zero and then climb steadily as current assets grow. Shortage costs start very high and then decline as we add current assets. The total cost ofholding current assets is the sum of the two. Notice how the combined costs reach a minimum at CA*. This is the optimum level of current assets.

Current asset holdings are highest under a flexible policy. This is one in which the carrying costs are perceived to be low relative to shortage costs. This is Case A in Figure 17.2. In comparison, under restrictive current asset policies, carrying costs are perceived to be high relative to shortage costs. This is Case B in Figure 17.2.

Alternative Financing Policies for Current Assets

In previous sections, we looked at the basic determinants of the level of investment in current assets, and we thus focussed on the asset side of the balance sheet. Now we turn to the financing side of the question. Here we are concerned with the relative amounts of short-term and long-term debt, assuming the investment in current assets is constant.

An Ideal Case   We start with the simplest possible case: an ideal economy. In such an economy, short-term assets can always be financed with short-term debt, and long-term assets can be financed with long-term debt and equity. In this economy, net working capital is always zero.

Consider a simplified case for a grain elevator operator. Grain elevator operators buy crops after harvest, store them, and sell them during the year. They have high inventories of grain after the harvest and end up with low inventories just before the next harvest.

Bank loans with maturities of less than one year are used to finance the purchase of grain and the storage costs. These loans are paid off from the proceeds of the sale of grain.

The situation is shown in Figure 17.3. Long-term assets are assumed to grow over time, whereas current assets increase at the end of the harvest and then decline during the year. Short-term assets end up at zero just before the next harvest. Current (short-term) assets are financed by short-term debt, and long-term assets are financed with long-term debt and equity. Net working capital—current assets minus current liabilities—is always zero. Figure 17.3 displays a sawtooth pattern that we see again when we get to our discussion on cash management in the next chapter. For now, we need to discuss some alternative policies for financing current assets under less idealized conditions.

Different Policies in Financing Current Assets   In the real world, it is not likely that current assets would ever drop to zero. For example, a long-term rising level of sales results in some permanent investment in current assets. Moreover, the firm's investments in long-term assets may show a great deal of variation.

A growing firm can be thought of as having a total asset requirement consisting of the current assets and long-term assets needed to run the business efficiently. The total asset requirement may exhibit change over time for many reasons, including (1) a general growth trend, (2) seasonal variation around the trend, and (3) unpredictable day-to-day and month-to-month fluctuations. This situation is depicted in Figure

Short-term financial policy: the optimal investment in current assets.

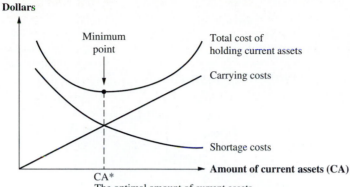

Dollars

Minimum point

Total cost of holding current assets

Carrying costs

Shortage costs

Amount of current assets (CA)

CA*
The optimal amount of current assets.
This point minimizes costs.

Carrying costs increase with the level of investment in current assets. They include the costs of maintaining economic value and opportunity costs. Shortage costs decrease with increases in the level of investment in current assets. They include trading costs and the costs related to being short of the current asset (for example, being short of cash). The firm's policy can be characterized as flexible or restrictive.

A. Flexible policy

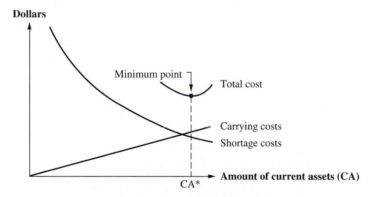

Dollars

Minimum point

Total cost

Carrying costs
Shortage costs

Amount of current assets (CA)

CA*

A flexible policy is most appropriate when carrying costs are low relative to shortage costs.

B. Restrictive policy

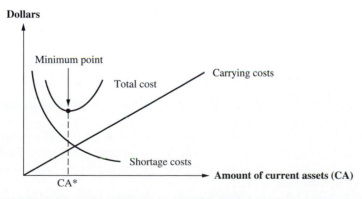

Dollars

Minimum point

Carrying costs

Total cost

Shortage costs

Amount of current assets (CA)

CA*

A restrictive policy is most apropriate when carrying costs are high relative to shortage costs.

*Financing policy for
an ideal economy*

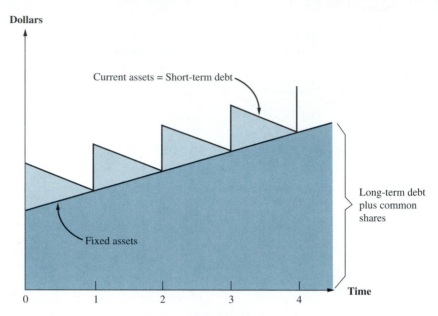

In an ideal world, net working capital is always zero because short-term assets are financed by short-term debt.

F I G U R E 17.4

*The total asset
requirement over time*

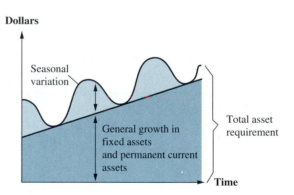

17.4. (We have not tried to show the unpredictable day-to-day and month-to-month variations in the total asset requirement.)

When long-term financing covers more than the total asset requirements, the firm has excess cash available for investment in marketable securities. Policy F, the flexible policy in Figure 17.5, always implies a short-term cash surplus and a large investment in net working capital.

When long-term financing does not cover the total asset requirement, the firm must use short-term borrowing to make up the deficit. In Figure 17.5, Policy R, the

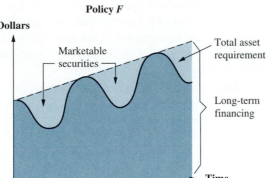

FIGURE 17.5

Alternative asset financing policies

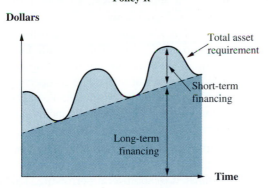

Policy R uses long-term financing for permanent asset requirements only and short-term borrowing for seasonal variations.

restrictive policy, implies a persistent need for short-term borrowing. Whenever current assets rise because of seasonal variations, the firm borrows short-term to finance the growth. As these assets are worked off, the firm repays the short-term debt out of the proceeds.

Which Is Best?

What is the most appropriate amount of short-term borrowing? There is no definitive answer. Several considerations must be included in a proper analysis:

1. *Cash reserves.* The flexible financial policy implies surplus cash and little short-term borrowing. This policy reduces the probability that a firm would experience financial distress. Firms may not have to worry as much about meeting recurring, short-run obligations. However, this higher level of liquidity comes at a price. Investments in cash and marketable securities generally produce lower returns than investments in real assets. For example, suppose the

firm invests any temporary excess liquidity in Treasury bills. The price of a Treasury bill is simply the present value of its future cash flow. It follows that, since present value and the cost of a Treasury bill are equal, Treasury bills are always zero net present value investments. If the firm followed another policy, the funds tied up in Treasury bills and other zero NPV short-term financial instruments could be invested to produce a positive NPV.

2. *Maturity hedging.* Most firms attempt to match the maturities of assets and liabilities. They finance inventories with short-term bank loans and fixed assets with long-term financing. Firms tend to avoid financing long-lived assets with short-term borrowing. This type of maturity mismatching is inherently more risky for two reasons: First, the cost of the financing is more uncertain because short-term interest rates are more volatile than longer rates. For example, in 1981, many short-term borrowers faced financial distress when short-term rates exceeded 20 percent.

   Second, maturity mismatching necessitates frequent refinancing and this produces rollover risk, the risk that renewed short-term financing may not be available. A recent example is the financial distress faced in 1992 by Olympia & York (O&Y), a real estate development firm privately owned by the Reichmann family of Toronto. O&Y's main assets were office towers including First Canadian Place in Toronto and Canary Wharf outside London, England. Financing for these long-term assets was short-term bank loans and commercial paper. In early 1992, investor fears about real estate prospects prevented O&Y from rolling over its commercial paper. To avoid default, the company turned to its bankers to negotiate emergency longer-term financing and, when that failed, had to file for bankruptcy protection.

3. *Relative interest rates.* Short-term interest rates are usually lower than long-term rates. This implies that it is, on the average, more costly to rely on long-term borrowing as compared to short-term borrowing. This is really a statement about the yield curve we introduced in Appendix 6B. What we are saying is that the yield curve is normally upward sloping.

Policies F and R that we show in Figure 17.5 are, of course, extreme cases. With F, the firm never does any short-term borrowing; with R, the firm never has a cash reserve (an investment in marketable securities). Figure 17.6 illustrates these two policies along with a compromise, Policy C.

With this compromise approach, the firm borrows short-term to cover peak financing needs, but it maintains a cash reserve in the form of marketable securities during slow periods. As current assets build up, the firm draws down this reserve before doing any short-term borrowing. This allows for some run-up in current assets before the firm has to resort to short-term borrowing.

Current Assets and Liabilities in Practice

Table 17.2 shows current assets made up 36 percent of all assets for Canadian industrial firms in 1989. Short-term financial management deals with a significant portion of the balance sheet for this sample of large firms. For small firms, especially in the retailing and service sectors, current assets make up an even larger portion of total assets.

The table also reveals a decrease in current assets over the 1980s. This suggests that Canadian firms are managing current assets more closely. In the language of the previous section (as illustrated in Figure 17.2 through 17.5) Canadian industrial firms

Dollars

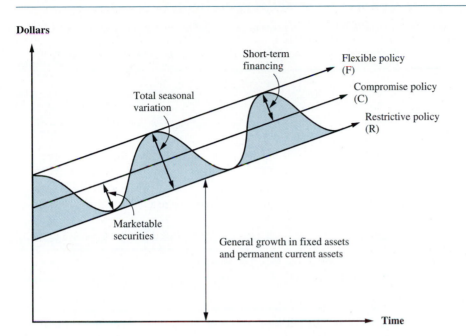

FIGURE 17.6

A compromise financing policy

With a compromise policy, the firm keeps a reserve of liquidity, which it uses to initially finance seasonal variations in current asset needs. Short-term borrowing is used when the reserve is exhausted.

	1989	1984	1979
Current Assets			
Cash and marketable securities	5.0%	6.5%	7.2%
Accounts receivable	14.8	16.9	19.3
Inventory	15.1	20.2	23.7
Other	1.1	0.8	0.8
Total current assets	36.0%	44.4%	51.0%
Current Liabilities			
Short-term debt	8.1%	6.6%	7.0%
Accounts payable	13.8	16.7	18.4
Income tax payable	0.6	1.2	1.9
Current portion of long-term debt	0.7	0.7	0.6
Other	1.1	1.1	1.4
Total current liabilities	24.3%	26.3%	29.3%

TABLE 17.2

Current assets and current liabilities as a percentage of total assets for Canadian firms, 1989

Source: *Industrial Corporations Financial Statistics* (Ottawa: Statistics Canada, 1992).

are moving away from flexible policies and toward a more restrictive approach to current assets. One important reason is that management is applying new techniques such as just-in-time inventory and on-line cash management, which we discuss in the next two chapters.

Current liabilities are also declining as a percent of total assets according to Table 17.2. Firms are practicing maturity hedging as they match lower current liabilities

T A B L E   17.3 | *Current assets and current liabilities as a percentage of total assets for selected industries, 1990*

	Printing and Publishing	Industrial Chemicals	Iron and Steel	Aircraft and Missiles
Current Assets				
Cash	3.2%	1.2%	3.7%	1.2%
Marketable securities	2.2	0.8	5.6	2.7
Accounts receivable	13.8	14.4	15.8	15.4
Inventory	7.1	11.2	18.9	40.2
Other current assets	4.5	3.5	1.6	1.5
Total current assets	30.8%	31.1%	45.6%	61.0%
Current Liabilities				
Notes payable	3.7%	6.9%	3.7%	3.9%
Accounts payable	5.7	6.6	10.2	8.8
Accruals and other current liabilities	8.7	9.7	12.2	38.3
Total current liabilities	18.1%	23.2%	26.1%	51.0%

Source: Ned C. Hill and William L. Sartoris, *Short-Term Financial Management,* 2nd ed. (New York: Macmillan, 1992), p. 12.

with decreased current assets. In addition to these differences over time, there are differences between industries in policies on current assets and liabilities.

The cash cycle is longer in some industries; various products and industry practices require different levels of inventory and receivables. This is why we saw in Chapter 3 that industry average ratios are not the same. As you can see in Table 17.3, levels of current assets and liabilities differ across four selected industries.[9] For example, the aircraft industry carries more than twice the amount of inventory of the other industries. Does this mean aircraft manufacturers are less efficient? Most likely, the higher inventory consists of airplanes under construction. Because building planes takes more time than most printing processes, it makes sense that aircraft manufacturers carry higher inventories than printing and publishing firms.

> **CONCEPT QUESTIONS**
>
> 1. What keeps the real world from being an ideal one where net working capital could always be zero?
> 2. What considerations determine the optimal size of the firm's investment in current assets?
> 3. What considerations determine the optimal compromise between flexible and restrictive net working capital policies?
> 4. How are industry differences reflected in working capital policies?

17.4 | THE CASH BUDGET

cash budget

A forecast of cash receipts and disbursements for the next planning period.

The **cash budget** is a primary tool in short-run financial planning. It allows the financial manager to identify short-term financial needs and opportunities. Importantly, the cash budget helps the manager explore the need for short-term borrowing. The idea of the cash budget is simple: It records estimates of cash receipts (cash in) and disbursements (cash out). The result is an estimate of the cash surplus or deficit.

---

[9] This example uses U.S. data and is drawn from Hill and Sartoris, *Short-Term Financial Management,* chap. 1.

Sales and Cash Collections

We start with an example for the Fun Toys Corporation for which we prepare a quarterly cash budget. We could just as well use a monthly, weekly, or even daily basis. We choose quarters for convenience and also because a quarter is a common short-term business planning period.

All of Fun Toys' cash inflows come from the sale of toys. Cash budgeting for Fun Toys must therefore start with a sales forecast for the next year, by quarters:

	Q1	Q2	Q3	Q4
Sales (in millions)	$200	$300	$250	$400

Note that these are predicted sales, so there is forecasting risk here because actual sales could be more or less. Also, Fun Toys started the year with accounts receivable equal to $120.

Fun Toys has a 45-day receivables or average collection period. This means that half of the sales in a given quarter are collected the following quarter. This happens because sales made during the first 45 days of a quarter are collected in that quarter. Sales made in the second 45 days are collected in the next quarter. Note that we are assuming that each quarter has 90 days, so the 45-day collection period is the same as a half-quarter collection period.

Based on the sales forecasts, we now need to estimate Fun Toys' projected cash collections. First, any receivables that we have at the beginning of a quarter would be collected within 45 days, so all of them are collected sometime during the quarter. Second, as we discussed, any sales made in the first half of the quarter are collected, so total cash collections are:

$$\text{Cash collections} = \text{Beginning accounts receivable} + \tfrac{1}{2} \times \text{Sales} \qquad [17.6]$$

For example, in the first quarter, cash collections would be the beginning receivables of $120 plus half of sales, $\tfrac{1}{2} \times \$200 = \$100$, for a total of $220.

Since beginning receivables are all collected along with half of sales, ending receivables for a particular quarter would be the other half of sales. First-quarter sales are projected at $200, so ending receivables are $100. This would be the beginning receivables in the second quarter. Cash collections in the second quarter are thus $100 plus half of the projected $300 in sales, or $250 total.

Continuing this process, we can summarize Fun Toys' projected cash collections as shown in Table 17.4. In this table, collections are shown as the only source of cash. Of course, this need not be the case. Other sources of cash could include asset sales, investment income, and receipts from planned long-term financing.

	Q1	Q2	Q3	Q4
Beginning receivables	$120	$100	$150	$125
Sales	200	300	250	400
Cash collections	220	250	275	325
Ending receivables	100	150	125	200

T A B L E 17.4

Cash collections for Fun Toys (in millions)

Notes: Collections = Beginning receivables + ½ × Sales

Ending receivables = Beginning receivables + Sales − Collections

= ½ × Sales

Cash Outflows

Next, we consider the cash disbursements or payments. These come in four basic categories:

1. *Payments of accounts payable.* These are payments for goods or services rendered from suppliers, such as raw materials. Generally, these payments are made sometime after purchases.
2. *Wages, taxes, and other expenses.* This category includes all other regular costs of doing business that require actual expenditures. Depreciation, for example, is often thought of as a regular cost of business, but it requires no cash outflow, and is not included.
3. *Capital expenditures.* These are payments of cash for long-lived assets.
4. *Long-term financing expenses.* This category, for example, includes interest payments on long-term outstanding debt and dividend payments to shareholders.

Fun Toys' purchases from suppliers (in dollars) in a quarter are equal to 60 percent of next quarter's predicted sales. Fun Toys' payments to suppliers are equal to the previous quarter's purchases, so the accounts payable period is 90 days. For example, in the quarter just ended, Fun Toys ordered .60 × $200 = $120 in supplies. This would actually be paid in the first quarter (Q1) of the coming year.

Wages, taxes, and other expenses are routinely 20 percent of sales; interest and dividends are currently $20 per quarter. In addition, Fun Toys plans a major plant expansion (a capital expenditure) of $100 in the second quarter. If we put all this information together, the cash outflows are as shown in Table 17.5.

The Cash Balance

The predicted net cash inflow is the difference between cash collections and cash disbursements. The net cash inflow for Fun Toys is shown in Table 17.6. What we see immediately is that there is a cash surplus in the first and third quarters and a cash deficit in the second and fourth.

We assume that Fun Toys starts the year with a $20 cash balance. Furthermore, Fun Toys maintains a $10 minimum cash balance to guard against unforeseen contingencies and forecasting errors. So we start the first quarter with $20 in cash. This increases by $40 during the quarter, and the ending balance is $60. Of this, $10 is reserved as a minimum, so we subtract it out and find that the first-quarter surplus is $60 − 10 = $50.

Fun Toys starts the second quarter with $60 in cash (the ending balance from the previous quarter). There is a net cash inflow of −$110, so the ending balance is $60

TABLE 17.5 *Cash disbursements for Fun Toys (in millions)*	Q1	Q2	Q3	Q4
Payment of accounts (60% of sales)	$120	$180	$150	$240
Wages, taxes, other expenses	40	60	50	80
Capital expenditures	0	100	0	0
Long-term financing expenses (interest and dividends)	20	20	20	20
Total	$180	$360	$220	$340

	Q1	Q2	Q3	Q4
Total cash collections	$220	$250	$275	$325
Total cash disbursements	180	360	220	340
Net cash inflow	$ 40	−$110	$ 55	−$ 15

T A B L E 17.6

Net cash inflow for Fun Toys (in millions)

	Q1	Q2	Q3	Q4
Beginning cash balance	$ 20	$ 60	−$ 50	$ 5
Net cash inflow	40	−110	55	−15
Ending cash balance	$ 60	−$ 50	$ 5	−$ 10
Minimum cash balance	−10	−10	−10	−10
Cumulative surplus (deficit)	$ 50	−$ 60	−$ 5	−$ 20

T A B L E 17.7

Cash balance for Fun Toys (in millions)

− 110 = −$50. We need another $10 as a buffer, so the total deficit is −$60. These calculations and those for the last two quarters are summarized in Table 17.7.

Beginning in the second quarter, Fun Toys has a cash shortfall of $60. This occurs because of the seasonal pattern of sales (higher toward the end of the second quarter), the delay in collections, and the planned capital expenditure.

The cash situation at Fun Toys is projected to improve to a $5 deficit in the third quarter, but, by year's end, Fun Toys still has a $20 deficit. Without some sort of financing, this deficit would carry over into the next year. We explore financing sources in the next section.

For now, we can make the following general comments on Fun Toys' cash needs:

1. Fun Toys' large outflow in the second quarter is not necessarily a sign of trouble. It results from delayed collections on sales and a planned capital expenditure (presumably a worthwhile one).

2. The figures in our example are based on a forecast. Sales could be much worse (or better) than the forecast.

CONCEPT QUESTIONS

1. How would you do a sensitivity analysis (discussed in Chapter 9) for Fun Toys' net cash balance?

2. What could you learn from such an analysis?

17.5 | A SHORT-TERM FINANCIAL PLAN

To illustrate a completed short-term financial plan, we assume Fun Toys arranges to borrow any needed funds on a short-term basis. The interest rate is 20 percent APR, and it is compounded on a quarterly basis. From Chapter 5, we know that the rate is 20%/4 = 5% per quarter. We assume that Fun Toys starts the year with no short-term debt.

From Table 17.7, Fun Toys has a second-quarter deficit of $60 million. We have to borrow this amount. Net cash inflow in the following quarter is $55 million. We now have to pay $60 × .05 = $3 million in interest out of that, leaving $52 million to reduce the borrowing.

We still owe $60 − 52 = $8 million at the end of the third quarter. Interest in the last quarter is thus $8 × .05 = $.4 million. In addition, net inflows in the last quarter are −$15 million, so we have to borrow $15.4 million, bringing our total borrowing up to $15.4 + 8 = $23.4 million. Table 17.8 extends Table 17.7 to include these calculations.

Notice that the ending short-term debt is just equal to the cumulative deficit for the entire year, $20, plus the interest paid during the year, $3 + .4 = $3.4, for a total of $23.4.

Our plan is very simple. For example, we ignored the fact that the interest paid on the short-term debt is tax deductible. We also ignored the fact that the cash surplus in the first quarter would earn some interest (which would be taxable). We could add on a number of refinements. Even so, our plan highlights the fact that in about 90 days, Fun Toys would need to borrow $60 million or so on a short-term basis. It's time to start lining up the source of the funds.

Our plan also illustrates that financing the firm's short-term needs costs more than $3 million in interest (before taxes) for the year. This is a starting point for Fun Toys to begin evaluating alternatives to reduce this expense. For example, can the $100 million planned expenditure be postponed or spread out? At 5 percent per quarter, short-term credit is expensive.

Also, if Fun Toys' sales are expected to keep growing, the $20 million plus deficit would probably also keep growing, and the need for additional financing is permanent. Fun Toys may wish to think about raising money on a long-term basis to cover this need.

As our example for Fun Toys illustrates, cash budgeting is a planning exercise because it forces the financial manager to think about future cash flows. This is important because, as we showed in Chapter 4, firms, can "grow bankrupt" if there is no planning. This is why bankers, venture capitalists, and other financing sources stress the importance of management and planning.

Short-Term Planning and Risk

After it is revised, the short-term financial plan in Table 17.8 represents Fun Toys' best guess for the future. Large firms go beyond the best guess to ask what-if questions using scenario analysis, sensitivity analysis, and simulation. We introduced

TABLE 17.8

Short-term financial plan for Fun Toys (in millions)

	Q1	Q2	Q3	Q4
Beginning cash balance	$ 20	$ 60	$ 10	$ 10.0
Net cash inflow	40	−110	55	−15.0
New short-term borrowing	—	60	—	15.4
Interest on short-term borrowing	—	—	−3	−.4
Short-term borrowing repaid	—	—	−52	—
Ending cash balance	$ 60	$ 10	$ 10	$ 10.0
Minimum cash balance	−10	−10	−10	−10.0
Cumulative surplus (deficit)	$ 50	$ 0	$ 0	$ 0.0
Beginning short-term borrowing	0	0	60	8.0
Change in short-term debt	0	60	−52	15.4
Ending short-term debt	$ 0	$ 60	$ 8	$ 23.4

these techniques in Chapter 9's discussion of project analysis. They are tools for assessing the degree of forecasting risk and identifying those components most critical to the success or failure of a financial plan.

Recall that scenario analysis involves varying the base case plan to create several others—a best case, worst case, and so on. Each produces different financing needs to give the financial manager a first look at risk.

Sensitivity analysis is a variation on scenario analysis that is useful in pinpointing the areas where forecasting risk is especially severe. The basic idea of sensitivity analysis is to freeze all the variables except one and then see how sensitive our estimate of financing needs is to changes in that one variable. If our projected financing turns out to be very sensitive to, say, sales, then we know that extra effort in refining the sales forecast would pay off.

Since the original financial plan was almost surely developed on a computer spreadsheet, scenario and sensitivity analysis are quite straightforward and widely used.

Simulation analysis combines the features of scenario and sensitivity analysis varying all the variables over a range of outcomes simultaneously. The result of simulation analysis is a probability distribution of financing needs.

Air Canada uses simulation analysis in forecasting its cash needs. The simulation is useful in capturing the variability of cash flow components in the airline industry in Canada. Bad weather, for example, causes delays and cancelled flights with unpredictable dislocation payments to travellers and crew overtime. This and other risks are reflected in a probability distribution of cash needs giving the treasurer better information for planning borrowing needs.

17.6 | SHORT-TERM BORROWING

Fun Toys has a short-term financing problem. It cannot meet the forecasted cash outflows in the second quarter from internal sources. How it finances that shortfall depends on its financial policy. With a very flexible policy, Fun Toys might seek up to $60 million in long-term debt financing.

In addition, much of the cash deficit comes from the large capital expenditure. Arguably, this is a candidate for long-term financing. Examples discussed in Chapter 13 include issuing bonds or taking a term loan from a chartered bank or other financial institution. Nonetheless, because we have discussed long-term financing elsewhere, we concentrate here on two short-term borrowing alternatives: (1) unsecured borrowing and (2) secured borrowing.

Operating Loans

The most common way to finance a temporary cash deficit is to arrange a short-term **operating loan** from a chartered bank. This is an agreement under which a firm is authorized to borrow up to a specified amount for a given period, usually one year (much like a credit card).[10] Operating loans can be either unsecured or secured by collateral. Large corporations with excellent credit ratings usually structure the facility as an unsecured line of credit. Because unsecured credit lines are backed only by projections of future cash flows, bankers offer this cash flow lending only to those with top-drawer credit.

operating loan
Loan negotiated with banks, usually by small business, for day-to-day operations.

---

[10] Descriptions of bank loans draw on L. Wynant and J. Hatch, *Banks and Small Business Borrowers* (London: University of Western Ontario, 1990).

Short-term lines of credit are classified as either *committed* or *noncommitted*. The latter is an informal arrangement. Committed lines of credit are more formal legal arrangements and usually involve a commitment fee paid by the firm to the bank (usually the fee is 0.25 percent of the total committed funds per year). A firm that pays a commitment fee for a committed line of credit is essentially buying insurance to guarantee that the bank can't back out of the agreement (absent some material change in the borrower's status).

Compensating the Bank   The interest rate on an operating loan is usually set equal to the bank's prime lending rate plus an additional percentage, and the rate usually floats. For example, suppose that the prime rate is 9 percent when the loan is initiated and the loan is at prime plus 1.5 percent. The original rate charged the borrower is 10.5 percent. If after, say, 125 days, prime increases to 9.5 percent, the company's borrowing rate goes up to 11 percent and interest charges are adjusted accordingly.

The premium charged over prime reflects the banker's assessment of the borrower's risk. Table 17.9 lists factors bankers use in assessing risk in loans to small business. Notice that risks related to management appear most often because poor management is considered the major risk with small business. There is a trend among bankers to look more closely at industry and economic risk factors. A similar set of risk factors applies to loans to large corporations.

Banks are in the business of lending mainly to low-risk borrowers. For this reason, bankers generally prefer to decline risky business loans that would require an interest rate more than prime plus 3 percent. Many of the loan requests that banks turn down are from small business, especially start-ups. Around 60 percent of these turn-downs find financing elsewhere. Federal government agencies that assist small business include the Business Development Bank of Canada and the Small Businesses Loans Act Program. The Atlantic Canada Opportunities Agency (ACOA) and

TABLE 17.9	Factor	Percent of Mentions
Factors mentioned in the credit files		(1,539 cases)
	1. Economic environment	6.1%
	Opportunities and risks	
	2. Industry environment	40.4
	Competitive conditions, prospects, and risks	
	3. Client's marketing activities	30.8
	Strategies, strengths, and weaknesses	
	4. Firm's operations management	59.5
	Strengths and weaknesses	
	5. Client's financial resources, skills, and performance	44.9
	Financial management expertise	84.8
	Historical or future profitability	41.6
	Future cash flows	20.5
	Future financing needs (beyond the current year)	
	6. Management capabilities and character	79.6
	Strengths and weaknesses	95.1
	Length of ownership of the firm	57.1
	Past management experience relevant to the business	
	7. Collateral security and the firm's net worth position	97.7
	8. Borrower's past relationship with bank	65.3

Source: Larry Wynant and James Hatch, *Banks and Small Business Borrowers* (London: University of Western Ontario, 1990), p. 136.

the Western Economic Development Program are federal programs that assist businesses in their regions. Provincial programs are also in existence.

In addition to charging interest, banks also levy fees for account activity and loan management. Small businesses may also pay application fees to cover the costs of processing loan applications. Fees are becoming increasingly important in bank compensation.[11] Fees and other details of any short-term business lending arrangements are highly negotiable. Banks generally work with firms to design a package of fees and interest.

Letters of Credit

A **letter of credit** is a common arrangement in international finance. With a letter of credit, the bank issuing the letter promises to make a loan if certain conditions are met. Typically, the letter guarantees payment on a shipment of goods provided that the goods arrive as promised. A letter of credit can be revocable (subject to cancellation) or irrevocable (not subject to cancellation if the specified conditions are met).

> **letter of credit**
> *A written statement by a bank that money will be paid, provided conditions specified in the letter are met.*

Secured Loans

Banks and other financial institutions often require security for an operating loan just as they do for a long-term loan. Table 17.9 shows that collateral security is a factor in virtually every small-business loan. Security for short-term loans usually consists of accounts receivable, inventories, or both because these are the assets most likely to retain value if the borrower goes bankrupt. Security is intended to reduce the lender's risk by providing a second "line of defense" behind the borrower's projected cash flows. To achieve this intention, the ideal collateral is Treasury bills or another asset whose value is independent of the borrower's business. We say this because, under the NPV principle, business assets derive their value from cash flow. When business is bad and cash flow low (or negative), the collateral value is greatly reduced. Several Canadian banks learned this lesson in the early 1990s when they wrote off billions in real estate loans.

In addition, banks routinely limit risk through loan conditions called **covenants**. Table 17.10 lists common covenants in Canadian small-business loans. You can see that bankers expect to have a detailed knowledge of their clients' businesses.

> **covenants**
> *A promise by the firm, included in the debt contract, to perform certain acts. A restrictive covenant imposes constraints on the firm to protect the interests of the debtholder.*

Accounts receivable financing from chartered banks typically involves assigning receivables to the lender under a general assignment of book debts. Under assignment, the bank or other lender has the receivables as security, but the borrower is still responsible if a receivable can't be collected. The lending agreement establishes a margin usually 75 percent of current (under 90 days) receivables. As the firm makes sales, it submits its invoices to the bank and can borrow up to 75 percent of their value.

> **accounts receivable financing**
> *A secured short-term loan that involves either the assignment or factoring of receivables.*

Inventory margins are set similarly to accounts receivable. Since inventory is often less liquid than receivables (bringing a lower percentage of book value in liquidations), inventory lending margins are lower, typically 50 percent.

---

[11] U.S. banks sometimes require that the firm keep some account of money on deposit. This is called a compensating balance. A *compensating balance* is some of the firm's money kept by the bank in low-interest or non-interest-bearing accounts. By leaving these funds with the bank and receiving no interest, the firm further increases the effective interest rate earned by the bank on the line of credit, thereby compensating the bank.

TABLE 17.10

Loan conditions for approved bank credits in the credit file sample

Condition	Percent of Cases* (1,382 cases)
Postponement of shareholder claims	39.8%
Life insurance on key principals	39.4
Fire insurance on company premises	35.7
Accounts receivable and inventory reporting	27.8
Limits on withdrawals and dividends	11.9
Limits on capital expenditures	10.5
Maintenance of minimum working capital levels	2.9
Restrictions on further debt	2.5
Restrictions on disposal of company assets	1.7
Maintenance of minimum cash balances	0.9
Other conditions	6.2

*Adds to more than 100 percent because of multiple responses.
Source: Larry Wynant and James Hatch, *Banks and Small Business Borrowers* (London: University of Western Ontario, 1990), p. 173.

Many small and medium-sized businesses secure their operating loans with both receivables and inventory. In this case, the lending limit fluctuates with both accounts according to the lending margins.

EXAMPLE | 17.3   Secured Borrowing for Fun Toys

Based on the cash budget we drew up earlier, the financial manager of Fun Toys has decided to seek a bank operating loan to cover the projected deficit of $60 million. The Royal Canadian National Bank has offered Fun Toys an operating loan at prime plus 1 percent to be secured by inventories. The lending officer has set a 75 percent margin on current receivables and 50 percent on inventory. Fun Toys has assured you that all its receivables are current and that two-thirds of payables were for inventory purchases. Can Fun Toys provide sufficient security for a $60 million operating loan?

Tables 17.4 and 17.5 show receivables and payables for Fun Toys for the next three quarters. Since the bank lends only against existing receivables and inventory, we use the Q1 beginning figures of $120 million for receivables and the same figure for payables. The full amount of the inventory is eligible for margining but only two-thirds of payables ($80) are inventory. We can calculate the amount that Fun Toys can secure as follows:

	Amount	×	Margin	=	Security
Receivables	$120		.75		$ 90
Inventory	80		.50		40
Total eligible security					$130

So Fun Toys could borrow up to $130 million under the margin formula and have no trouble securing a loan of $60 million.

Factoring

In addition to bank borrowing, accounts receivable financing is also possible through factoring. A factor is an independent company that acts as "an outside credit department" for the client. It checks the credit of new customers, authorizes credit, handles collections and bookkeeping. As the accounts are collected, the factor pays the client the face amount of the invoice less a 1 or 2 percent discount.[12] If any accounts are late, the factor still pays the selling firm on an average maturity date determined in advance. The legal arrangement is that the factor purchases the accounts receivable from the firm. Thus, factoring provides insurance against bad debts because any defaults on bad accounts are the factor's problem.

Factoring in Canada is conducted by independent firms whose main customers are small businesses. Factoring is popular with manufacturers of retail goods especially in the apparel business. The attraction of factoring to small businesses is that it allows outside professionals to handle the headaches of credit. To avoid magnifying those headaches, factors must offer cost savings and avoid alienating their clients' customers in the collection process.

What we have described so far is **maturity factoring** and does not involve a formal financing arrangement. What factoring does is remove receivables from the balance sheet and so, indirectly, it reduces the need for financing. It may also reduce the costs associated with granting credit. Because factors do business with many firms, they may be able to achieve scale economies, reduce risks through diversification, and carry more clout in collection.

Firms financing their receivables through a chartered bank may also use the services of a factor to improve the receivables' collateral value. In this case, the factor buys the receivables and assigns them to the bank. This is called *maturity factoring with assignment of equity*. Or the factor provides an advance on the receivables and charges interest at prime plus 2.5 to 3 percent. In advance factoring, the factor provides financing as well as other services.

maturity factoring *Short-term financing in which the factor purchases all of a firm's receivables and forwards the proceeds to the seller as soon as they are collected.*

E X A M P L E | 17.4   Cost of Factoring

For the year just ended, LuLu's Fashions had $500,000 in credit sales monthly with an average maturity of receivables of 45 days. LuLu's uses a factor to obtain funds 15 days after the sale. This means the factor is advancing funds for 45 − 15 = 30 days. The factor charges 10.5 percent interest (APR), 2.5 percent over the current prime rate of 8 percent. In addition, the factor charges a 1.5 percent fee for processing the receivables and assuming all credit risk. If LuLu's ran its own credit department, it would cost $2,000 per month in variable expenses and this is saved with factoring. What is the effective interest cost of factoring?

The costs are:

		Per Month
Interest = .105 × 30/365 × $500,000	=	$ 4,315
Factor's fee = .015 × $500,000	=	7,500
Variables expenses saved	=	−2,000
Total cost		$ 9,815

$9,815/$500,000 = 1.96 percent per month.

The effective annual rate (EAR) is $(1.0196)^{12} - 1 = 26.23$ percent.

Note that the factor takes on the risk of default by a buyer, thus providing insurance as well as immediate cash. More generally, the factor essentially takes over

[12] Our discussion of factoring draws on D. Reidy, "Factoring Smooths Banking Relationships," *Profit*, November 1991; and S. Horvitch, "Busy Days for Factoring Firms," *Financial Post*, February 15, 1991.

the firm's credit operations. This can result in a significant saving. The interest rate we calculated is therefore overstated, particularly if default is a significant possibility. ▌

Securitized Receivables—A Financial Innovation

Financial engineers have come up with a new approach to receivables financing. When a large corporation such as Sears Canada, Ltd., securitized receivables, it sold them to Sears Canada Receivables Trust (SCRT), a wholly owned subsidiary. SCRT issued debentures and commercial paper backed by a diversified portfolio of receivables. Because receivables are liquid, SCRT debt is less risky than lending to Sears Canada and the company hopes to benefit through interest savings.[13]

Inventory Loans

inventory loan

A secured short-term loan to purchase inventory.

Inventory loans, or operating loans to finance inventory, feature assignment of inventory to the lender who then advances funds according to a predetermined margin as we discussed earlier. The specific legal arrangements depend on the type of inventory. The most sweeping form is the general security agreement that registers security over all a firm's assets. Inventory as a whole can be assigned under Section 178 of the Bank Act or Bill 97 in Quebec. If the inventory consists of equipment or large, movable assets, the appropriate legal form is a chattel mortgage (commercial pledge of equipment in Quebec).

trust receipt

An instrument acknowledging that the borrower holds certain goods in trust for the lender.

The legal form of the security arrangement can be tailored to the type of inventory. For example, with large, expensive items in inventory, the security agreement is often based on **trust receipts** listing the individual items by serial numbers. Trust receipts are used to support *floor plan financing* for automobile dealers and sellers of household appliances and other equipment. The advantage of floor plan financing is that it gives the lender a systematic way to monitor the inventory as it moves through the cash cycle. As the vehicles are sold, the dealer reports the sale to the lender and repays the financing.

Warehouse financing is a similar system in which the inventory that serves as security is identified and monitored. In this case, the inventory is segregated in a designated field or public warehouse run by a third party. The warehouse issues a *warehouse receipt* providing legal evidence of the existence of the security. Because the goods are segregated, warehouse financing is not suitable for work-in-progress inventory. On the other hand, this form of financing is ideally suited for inventories that improve with age such as whiskey or wine.

Trade Credit

When a firm purchases supplies on credit, the increase in accounts payable is a source of funds and automatic financing. As compared with bank financing, trade credit has the advantage of arising automatically from the firm's business. It does not require a formal financing agreement with covenants that may restrict the borrower's business activities. Suppliers offer credit to remain competitive; in many industries, the terms of credit include a cash discount for paying within a certain period. For example, suppose a supplier offers terms of 2/10, net 30.[14] If your firm makes a $1,000

---

[13] M. Evans, "Sears Securitizes Some of Its Assets," *Financial Post,* November 19, 1991.
[14] Chapter 19 provides a full discussion of credit terms from the seller's viewpoint.

purchase, you have a choice of paying after 10 days, taking the cash discount, or paying the full $1,000 after 30 days. Or you could stretch your payables by paying the $1,000 after, say, 45 days. The longer you wait, the longer the supplier is providing you with trade credit financing.

In making your decision, you should ask whether the cash discount provides a significant incentive for early payment. The answer is yes because the implicit interest rate is extremely high.

To see why the discount is important, we calculate the cost to the buyer of not paying early. To do this, we find the interest rate that the buyer is effectively paying for the trade credit. Suppose the order is for $1,000. The buyer can pay $980 in 10 days or wait another 20 days and pay $1,000. (For the moment, we ignore the possibility of stretching.) It's obvious that the buyer is effectively borrowing $980 for 20 days and that the buyer pays $20 in interest on the loan. What's the interest rate?

This interest is ordinary discount interest, which we discussed in Chapter 5. With $20 in interest on $980 borrowed, the rate is $20/$980 = 2.0408%. This is relatively low, but remember that this is the rate per 20-day period. There are 365/20 = 18.25 such periods in a year, so the buyer is paying an effective annual rate (EAR) of:

$$EAR = (1.020408)^{18.25} - 1 = 44.6\%$$

From the buyer's point of view, this is an expensive source of financing.

Now suppose the buyer decides to stretch its payables and pay in 45 days. What is the EAR now? The interest is still $20 on $980 borrowed so the rate is still 2.0408%. What stretching changes is the length of the loan period. Since we are paying on Day 45, the loan period is now 45 − 10 = 35 days. There are 365/35 = 10.43 such periods in a year. The new EAR is:

$$EAR = (1.020408)^{10.43} - 1 = 23.5\%$$

So you can see that stretching reduces the EAR but this does not make it a recommended practice. Companies that habitually pay their suppliers late risk supplier ill will. This may impact unfavourably on delivery schedules and, in the extreme case, suppliers may cut off the firm or ship only terms of C.O.D. (cash on delivery). Late payment may also harm the firm's credit rating.

E X A M P L E | 17.5   **What's the Rate?**

Ordinary tiles are often sold 3/30, net 60. What effective annual rate does a buyer pay by not taking the discount? What would the APR be if one were quoted?

Here we have 3 percent discount interest on 60 − 30 = 30 days' credit. The rate per 30 days is .03/.97 = 3.093%. There are 365/30 = 12.17 such periods in a year, so the effective annual rate is:

$$EAR = (1.03093)^{12.17} - 1 = 44.9\%$$

The APR, as always, would be calculated by multiplying the rate per period by the number of periods:

$$APR = .03093 \times 12.17 = 37.6\% \quad |$$

An interest rate calculated like this APR is often quoted as the cost of the trade credit, and, as this example illustrates, the true cost can be seriously understated.

Money Market Financing

Large firms with excellent credit ratings can obtain financing directly from money markets. Two of the most important money market instruments for short-term financing are commercial paper and bankers acceptances.

Commercial paper consists of short-term notes issued by large and highly rated firms. Firms issuing commercial paper in Canada generally have borrowing needs over $20 million. Rating agencies, the Dominion Bond Rating Service and the Canadian Bond Rating Service discussed in Chapter 12, rate commercial paper similarly to bonds. Typically, these notes are of short maturity, ranging from 30 to 90 days with some maturities up to 365 days. Commercial paper is offered in denominations of $100,000 and up. Because the firm issues paper directly and because it usually backs the issue with a special bank line of credit, the interest rate the firm obtains is less than the rate a bank would charge for a direct loan usually by around 1 percent. Another advantage is that commercial paper offers the issuer flexibility in tailoring the maturity and size of the borrowing.

Bankers acceptances are a variant on commercial paper. When a bank accepts paper, it charges a stamping fee in return for a guarantee of the paper's principal and interest. Stamping fees vary from .20 percent to .75 percent. Bankers acceptances are more widely used than commercial paper in Canada because Canadian chartered banks enjoy stronger credit ratings than all but the largest corporations.[15] The main buyers of bankers acceptances and commercial paper are institutions including mutual funds, insurance companies, and banks.[16]

A disadvantage of borrowing through bankers acceptances or commercial paper is the risk that the market might temporarily dry up when it comes time to roll over the paper.

CONCEPT QUESTIONS

1. What are the two basic forms of short-term financing?
2. Describe two types of secured operating loans.
3. Describe factoring and the services it provides.
4. How does trade credit work? Should firms stretch their accounts payable?
5. Describe commercial paper and bankers acceptances. How do they differ?

17.7 | SUMMARY AND CONCLUSIONS

1. This chapter introduces the management of short-term finance. Short-term finance involves short-lived assets and liabilities. We trace and examine the short-term sources and uses of cash as they appear on the firm's financial statements. We see how current assets and current liabilities arise in the short-term operating activities and the cash cycle of the firm.

2. Managing short-term cash flows involves the minimizing of costs. The two major costs are carrying costs, the return forgone by keeping too much invested

---

[15] The reverse situation prevails in the United States.

[16] Our discussion of commercial paper and bankers acceptances draws on "The Canadian Commercial Paper Market, Myth and Reality," *Canadian Treasury Management Review,* March–April 1991; and D.Hogarth, "Quick Money Peps Poor Balance Sheets," *Financial Post,* December 17, 1990.

in short-term assets such as cash, and shortage costs, the cost of running out of short-term assets. The objective of managing short-term finance and doing short-term financial planning is to find the optimal trade-off between these two costs.

3. In an ideal economy, the firm could perfectly predict its short-term uses and sources of cash, and net working capital could be kept at zero. In the real world we live in, cash and net working capital provide a buffer that lets the firm meet its ongoing obligations. The financial manager seeks the optimal level of each of the current assets.

4. The financial manager can use the cash budget to identify short-term financial needs. The cash budget tells the manager what borrowing is required or what lending will be possible in the short run. The firm has available to it a number of possible ways of acquiring funds to meet short-term shortfalls, including unsecured and secured loans.

Key Terms

operating cycle (page 609)
inventory period (page 609)
accounts receivable period (page 609)
accounts payable period (page 609)
cash cycle (page 609)
cash flow time line (page 609)
carrying costs (page 615)
shortage costs (page 615)
cash budget (page 622)

operating loan (page 627)
letter of credit (page 629)
covenants (page 629)
accounts receivable financing (page 629)
maturity factoring (page 631)
inventory loan (page 632)
trust receipt (page 632)

Chapter Review Problems and Self-Test

17.1 The Operating and Cash Cycles
Consider the following financial statement information for the Glory Road Company:

Item	Beginning		Ending
Inventory	$1,543		$1,669
Accounts receivable	4,418		3,952
Accounts payable	2,551		2,673
Net sales		$11,500	
Cost of goods sold		8,200	

Calculate the operating and cash cycles.

17.2 Cash Balance for Masson Corporation
The Masson Corporation has a 60-day average collection period and wishes to maintain a $5 million minimum cash balance. Based on this and the following information, complete the cash budget. What conclusions do you draw?

MASSON CORPORATION
Cash Budget
(in millions)

	Q1	Q2	Q3	Q4
Beginning receivables	$120			
Sales	90	120	150	120
Cash collections				
Ending receivables				
Total cash collections				
Total cash disbursements	80	160	180	160
Net cash inflow				
Beginning cash balance	$ 5			
Net cash inflow				
Ending cash balance				
Minimum cash balance				
Cumulative surplus (deficit)				

Answers to Self-Test Problems

17.1   **We first need the turnover ratios.**   Note that we have used the average values for all balance sheet items and that we have based the inventory and payables turnover measures on cost of goods sold.

$$\text{Inventory turnover} = \$8,200/[(1,543 + 1,669)/2] = 5.11 \text{ times}$$
$$\text{Receivables turnover} = \$11,500/[(4,418 + 3,952)/2] = 2.75 \text{ times}$$
$$\text{Payables turnover} = \$8,200/[(2,551 + 2,673)/2] = 3.14 \text{ times}$$

We can now calculate the various periods:

$$\text{Inventory period} = 365 \text{ days}/5.11 \text{ times} = 71.43 \text{ days}$$
$$\text{Receivables period} = 365 \text{ days}/2.75 \text{ times} = 132.73 \text{ days}$$
$$\text{Payables period} = 365 \text{ days}/3.14 \text{ times} = 116.24 \text{ days}$$

So the time it takes to acquire inventory and sell it is about 71 days. Collection takes another 133 days, and the operating cycle is thus 71 + 133 = 204 days. The cash cycle is this 204 days less the payables period, 204 − 116 = 88 days.

17.2   Since Masson has a 60-day collection period, only those sales made in the first 30 days of the quarter are collected in the same quarter. Total cash collections in the first quarter thus equal $^{30}\!/_{90} = \frac{1}{3}$ of sales plus beginning receivables, or $120 + \frac{1}{3} \times \$90 = \$150$. Ending receivables for the first quarter (and the second quarter beginning receivables) are the other $\frac{2}{3}$ of sales, or $\frac{2}{3} \times \$90 = \$60$. The remaining calculations are straightforward, and the completed budget follows:

MASSON CORPORATION
Cash Budget
(in millions)

	Q1	Q2	Q3	Q4
Beginning receivables	$120	$ 60	$ 80	$100
Sales	90	120	150	120
Cash collection	150	100	130	140
Ending receivables	$ 60	$ 80	$100	$ 80
Total cash collections	$150	$100	$130	$140
Total cash disbursements	80	160	180	160
Net cash inflow	$ 70	−$ 60	−$ 50	−$ 20
Beginning cash balance	$ 5	$ 75	$ 15	−$ 35
Net cash inflow	70	−60	−50	−20
Ending cash balance	$ 75	$ 15	−$ 35	−$ 55
Minimum cash balance	−$ 5	−$ 5	−$ 5	−$ 5
Cumulative surplus (deficit)	$ 70	$ 10	−$ 40	−$ 60

The primary conclusion from this schedule is that beginning in the third quarter, Masson's cash surplus becomes a cash deficit. By the end of the year, Masson needs to arrange for $60 million in cash beyond what is available.

Questions and Problems

Basic
(Questions 1–15)

1. **Sources and Uses of Cash** For the year just ended, you have gathered the following information on the Holly Corporation:

   a. A $200 dividend was paid.
   b. Accounts payable increased by $500.
   c. Fixed asset purchases were $900.
   d. Inventories increased by $625.
   e. Long-term debt decreased by $1,200.

   Label each as a source or use of cash and describe its effect on the firm's cash balance.

2. **Changes in the Cash Account** Indicate the impact of the following corporate actions on cash, using the letter I for an increase, D for a decrease, or N when no change occurs.

   a. A dividend is paid with funds received from a sale of common stock.
   b. A piece of machinery is purchased and paid for with long-term debt.
   c. Merchandise is sold on credit.
   d. A short-term bank loan is received.
   e. Last year's taxes are paid.
   f. Common stock is issued.
   g. Raw material is purchased for inventory on credit.
   h. Interest on long-term debt is paid.
   i. Payments for previous sales are collected.
   j. Payment is made for a previous purchase.
   k. A dividend is paid.
   l. A piece of office equipment is purchased and paid for with a short-term note.
   m. Merchandise is sold on credit.
   n. Cash is paid for raw materials purchased for inventory.
   o. Marketable securities are purchased.

3. **Cash Equation** A. Rose & Company has a book net worth of $3,500. Long-term debt is $900. Net working capital, other than cash, is $1,400. Fixed assets are $2,000. How much cash does the company have? If current liabilities are $975, what are current assets?

4. **Cost of Current Assets** Loftis Manufacturing, Inc., has recently installed a just-in-time (JIT) inventory system. Describe the likely effect on the company's carrying costs, shortage costs, and operating cycle.

5. **Changes in the Operating Cycle** Indicate the effect that the following company actions would have on the operating cycle. Use the letter I to show an increase, the letter D for a decrease, and the letter N for no change.

   a. Average receivables goes up.
   b. Credit repayment times for customers are increased.
   c. Inventory turnover goes from 5 times to 10 times.
   d. Payables turnover goes from 5 times to 10 times.
   e. Receivables turnover goes from 5 times to 10 times.
   f. Payments to suppliers are speeded up.

6. **Cycles**   Is it possible for a firm's cash cycle to be longer than its operating cycle? Explain why or why not.

7. **Changes in the Cycles**   Indicate the impact of the following company actions on the cash cycle and the operating cycle. Use the letter I to show an increase, the letter D for a decrease, and the letter N for no change.

   a. The terms of cash discounts offered to customers are made more favourable.
   b. The use of cash discounts offered by suppliers is decreased; thus payments are made later.
   c. An increased number of customers pay on credit instead of with cash.
   d. Fewer raw materials than usual are purchased.
   e. A greater percentage of raw material purchases are paid for with cash.
   f. More finished goods are being produced for inventory instead of for order.

8. **Calculating Cash Collections**   The Ace Turbine Company has projected the following quarterly sales amounts for the coming year:

	Q1	Q2	Q3	Q4
Sales	$575	$625	$700	$600

   a. Accounts receivable at the beginning of the year are $300. Ace Turbine has a 72-day collection period. Calculate cash collections in each of the four quarters by completing the following:

	Q1	Q2	Q3	Q4
Beginning receivables	$	$	$	$
Sales				
Cash collections				
Ending receivables				

   b. Rework (*a*) assuming a collection period of 54 days.
   c. Rework (*a*) assuming a collection period of 36 days.

9. **Calculating Cycles**   Consider the following financial statement information for the Windbag Balloon Company:

Item	Beginning	Ending
Inventory	$4,925	$5,150
Accounts receivable	3,019	3,380
Accounts payable	7,516	7,952
Net sales	$47,115	
Cost of goods sold	22,893	

   Calculate the operating and cash cycles. How do you interpret your answer?

10. **Factoring Receivables**   Your firm has an average collection period of 48 days. Current practice is to factor all receivables immediately at a 3 percent discount. What is the effective cost of borrowing in this case? Assume that default is extremely unlikely.

11. **Calculating Payments**   Van Meter Products has projected the following sales for the coming year:

	Q1	Q2	Q3	Q4
Projected sales	$620	$550	$450	$600

Sales in the year following this one are projected to be 25 percent greater in each quarter.

**Basic
(Continued)**

a. Calculate payments to suppliers assuming that Van Meter places orders during each quarter equal to 45 percent of projected sales in the next quarter. Assume that Van Meter pays immediately. What is the payables period in this case?

	Q1	Q2	Q3	Q4
Payment of accounts	$	$	$	$

b. Rework (a) assuming a 90-day payables period.
c. Rework (a) assuming a 60-day payables period.

12. **Calculating Payments** The Kao-Teng Corporation's purchases from suppliers in a quarter are equal to 60 percent of the next quarter's forecasted sales. The payables deferral period is 60 days. Wages, taxes, and other expenses are 15 percent of sales, while interest and dividends are $30 per quarter. No capital expenditures are planned.

Projected quarterly sales are:

	Q1	Q2	Q3	Q4
Sales	$200	$300	$180	$150

Sales in the first quarter of the following year are projected at $280. Calculate Kao-Teng's cash outlays by completing the following:

	Q1	Q2	Q3	Q4
Payment of accounts	$	$	$	$
Wages, taxes, other expenses				
Long-term financing expenses (interest and expenses)	—	—	—	—
Total	$	$	$	$

13. **Calculating Cash Collections** The following is the sales budget for Eazy Graphics Printers for the first quarter of 1995:

	January	February	March
Sales budget	$80,000	$105,000	$130,000

Credit sales are collected as follows:

25 percent in the month of sale.

55 percent in the month after the sale.

20 percent in the second month after the sale.

The accounts receivable balance at the end of the previous quarter is $50,000 ($38,000 of which is uncollected December sales).

a. Compute the sales for November.
b. Compute the sales for December.
c. Compute the cash collections from sales for each month from January through March.

14. **Calculating the Cash Budget** Here are some important figures from the budget of Sturgis Products, Inc., for the second quarter of 1996:

	April	May	June
Credit	$240,000	$225,000	$276,000
Credit purchases	100,000	94,000	118,000
Cash disbursements			
Wages, taxes, and expenses	15,000	14,500	17,200
Interest	5,000	5,000	5,000
Equipment purchases	90,000	0	10,000

The company predicts that 10 percent of its sales will never be collected, 40 percent of its sales will be collected in the month of the sale, and the remaining 50 percent will be collected in the following month. Credit purchases will be paid in the month following the purchase.

In March 1996, credit sales were $250,000. Using this information, complete the following cash budget:

	April	May	June
Beginning cash balances	$300,000		
Cash receipts			
Cash collections from credit sales			
Total cash available			
Cash disbursements			
Purchases	95,000		
Wages, taxes, and expenses			
Interest			
Equipment purchases			
Total cash disbursements			
Ending cash balance			

15.   **Short-Term Policy**   Valley Piping Company and Mountain Valve Corporation are competing manufacturing firms. Use the information contained in their financial statements to answer the following questions:

a. How are the current assets of each firm financed?

b. Which firm has the larger investment in current assets on an absolute basis? On a relative basis? Which of these is more meaningful in determining working capital policy? Why?

c. Which firm is more likely to incur carrying costs, and which is more likely to incur shortage costs? Why?

VALLEY PIPING COMPANY
Balance Sheets
December 31, 1994 and 1995

	1995	1994
Assets		
Cash	$ 13,862	$ 17,339
Accounts receivable (net)	23,887	25,778
Inventory	54,867	42,287
Total current assets	$ 92,616	$ 85,404
Plant, property, and equipment	$101,543	$ 99,715
Less: accumulated depreciation	34,331	32,057
Net fixed assets	$ 67,212	$ 67,658
Prepaid expenses	$ 1,914	$ 1,791
Other assets	13,052	13,138
Total assets	$174,794	$167,991

**Basic
(Continued)**

Liabilities and Stockholders' Equity

Accounts payable	$ 6,494	$ 4,893
Notes payable	10,483	11,617
Payroll taxes and accrued expenses	7,422	7,227
Other taxes payable	9,924	8,460
Total current liabilities	$ 34,323	$ 32,197
Long-term debt	$ 22,036	$ 22,036
Total liabilities	$ 56,359	$ 54,233
Common stock	$ 38,000	$ 38,000
Paid-in capital	12,000	12,000
Retained earnings	68,435	63,758
Total stockholders' equity	$118,435	$113,758
Total liabilities and stockholders' equity	$174,794	$167,991

MOUNTAIN VALVE CORPORATION
Balance Sheets
December 31, 1994 and 1995

	1995	1994
Assets		
Cash	$ 5,794	$ 3,307
Accounts receivable (net)	26,177	22,133
Inventory	46,463	44,661
Total current assets	$78,434	$70,101
Plant, property, and equipment	$31,842	$31,116
Less: accumulated depreciation	19,297	18,143
Net fixed assets	$12,545	$12,973
Prepaid expenses	$ 763	$ 688
Other assets	1,601	1,385
Total assets	$93,343	$85,147

Liabilities and Stockholders' Equity		
Accounts payable	$ 6,008	$ 5,019
Notes payable	3,722	645
Payroll taxes and accrued expenses	4,254	3,295
Other taxes payable	5,688	4,951
Total current liabilities	$19,672	$13,910
Common stock	$20,576	$20,576
Paid-in capital	5,624	5,624
Retained earnings	48,598	46,164
	$74,798	$72,364
Less: Treasury stock	1,127	1,127
Total stockholders' equity	$73,671	$71,237
Total liabilities and stockholders' equity	$93,343	$85,147

VALLEY PIPING COMPANY
Income Statement
1995

Sales	$162,749
Other income	1,002
Total income	$163,751
Costs of goods sold	103,570
Selling and administrative costs	26,395
Depreciation	2,274
Total operating expenses	132,239
Interest paid	2,100
Pretax earnings	$ 29,412
Taxes	14,890
Net income	$ 14,522
Dividends	$ 9,845
Addition to retained earnings	4,677

MOUNTAIN VALVE CORPORATION
Income Statement
1995

Sales	$91,374
Other income	1,067
Total income	$92,441
Costs of goods sold	59,042
Selling and administrative costs	18,068
Depreciation	1,154
Total operating expenses	$78,264
Pretax earnings	$14,177
Taxes	6,838
Net income	$ 7,339
Dividends	$ 4,905
Addition to retained earnings	2,434

16. **Costs of Borrowing**   You've worked out a line of credit arrangement that allows you to borrow up to $10 million at any time. The interest rate is 0.75 percent per month. In addition, 8 percent of the amount that you borrow must be deposited in a non-interest-bearing account. Assume your bank uses compound interest on its line of credit loans.

    a. What is the effective annual interest rate on this lending arrangement?
    b. Suppose you need $3 million today and you repay it in four months. How much interest will you pay?

17. **Costs of Borrowing**   A bank offers your firm a revolving credit arrangement for up to $75 million at an interest rate of 2.5 percent per quarter. The bank uses compound interest on its revolving credit loans.

    a. What is your effective annual interest rate (an opportunity cost) of having the revolving credit arrangement if your firm does not use it during the year?
    b. What is your effective annual interest rate on the lending arrangement if you borrow $50 million immediately and repay it in one year?
    c. What is your effective annual interest rate if you borrow $75 million immediately and repay it in one year?

18. **Calculating the Cash Budget**   Streamline, Inc., has estimated sales (in millions) for the next four quarters as:

	Q1	Q2	Q3	Q4
Projected Sales	$160	$227	$269	$241

Sales in the first quarter of the year after this one are projected at $205. Accounts receivable at the beginning of the year were $65. Streamline has a 36-day collection period.

Streamline's purchases from suppliers in a quarter are equal to 55 percent of the next quarter's forecasted sales, and suppliers are normally paid in 30 days. Wages, taxes, and other expenses run about 24 percent of sales. Interest and dividends are $15 per quarter.

Streamline plans a major capital outlay in the third quarter of $150. Finally, the company started the year with a $25 cash balance and wishes to maintain a $15 minimum balance.

a. Complete a cash budget for Streamline by filling in the following:

Intermediate
(Continued)

STREAMLINE, INC.
Cash Balance (in millions)

	Q1	Q2	Q3	Q4
Beginning cash balance	$25	$	$	$
Net cash inflow				
Ending cash balance				
Minimum cash balance	15	—	—	—
Cumulative surplus (deficit)				

b. Assume Streamline can borrow any needed funds on a short-term basis at a rate of 4 percent per quarter and can invest any excess funds in short-term marketable securities at a rate of 3 percent per quarter. Prepare a short-term financial plan by filling in the following schedule. What is the net cash cost (total interest paid minus total investment income earned) for the year?

STREAMLINE, INC.
Short-Term Financial Plan
(in millions)'

	Q1	Q2	Q3	Q4
Beginning cash balance	$ 25	$	$	$
Net cash inflow				
New short-term investments				
Income on short-term investments				
Short-term investments sold				
New short-term borrowing				
Interest on short-term borrowing				
Short-term borrowing repaid				
Ending cash balance	—	—	—	—
Minimum cash balance	15	—	—	—
Cumulative surplus (deficit)				
Beginning short-term investments				
Ending short-term investments				
Beginning short-term debt				
Ending short-term debt				

19. **Cash Management Policy**   Rework Problem 18 assuming:

a. The firm maintains a minimum cash balance of $25.

b. The firm maintains a minimum cash balance of $5.

From your answers in (*a*) and (*b*), do you think the firm can boost its profit by changing its cash management policy? Are there other factors that must be considered as well? Explain.

20. **Costs of Borrowing**   In exchange for a $250 million fixed commitment line of credit, your firm has agreed to do the following:

Challenge
(Questions 20–21)

1. Pay 3 percent per quarter on any funds actually borrowed.

2. Pay an up-front commitment fee of 0.25 percent of the amount of the line.

Based on this information, answer the following:

a. Ignoring the fixed commitment fee, what is the effective annual interest rate on this line of credit?

b. Suppose your firm immediately uses $20 million of the line and pays it off in one year. What is the effective annual interest rate on this $20 million loan?

**Challenge
(Continued)**

21.   **Costs of Borrowing**   Royal Canadian Bank offers your firm a 10 percent *discount* interest loan for up to $1 million. What is the effective annual interest rate on this lending arrangement? What would the EAR be if the bank also requires an up-front commitment fee of 0.20 percent of the line?

Suggested Readings

Gallinger, G. W., and P. B. Healey. *Liquidity Analysis and Management,* 2nd ed. Reading, MA: Addison-Wesley Publishing, 1991.

Hill, N. C., and W. L. Sartoris. *Short-Term Financial Management,* 2nd ed. New York: Macmillan, 1992.

Kahl, J. G., and K. Parkinson. *Current Asset Management: Cash, Credit and Inventory.* New York: John Wiley & Sons, 1984.

Vander Weide, J., and S. F. Maier. *Managing Corporate Liquidity: An Introduction to Working Capital Management.* New York: John Wiley & Sons, 1985.

Cash and Liquidity Management

The typical large Canadian corporation holds around 3.5 percent of its assets in highly liquid form—just over 1 percent in cash and the rest in marketable securities.[1] It is reasonable to ask why firms hold these current assets. After all, cash earns no interest and marketable securities earn interest at rates less than the firm's target return on assets. For example, at the time of writing, three-month Treasury bills, a popular marketable security returned just over 6 percent. As we showed in Chapter 17, the main reason firms hold cash and marketable securities is as a liquidity reserve. In that chapter we had a lot to say about how to decide the size of the liquidity reserve.

This chapter is about how firms manage cash and marketable securities. The basic objective in cash management is to keep the investment in cash as low as possible while still operating the firm's activities efficiently and effectively. We separate cash management into three steps:

1. Determining the appropriate target cash balance. Given the target liquidity reserve, we also know the target marketable securities balance.
2. Collecting and disbursing cash efficiently.
3. Investing excess cash in marketable securities.

Determining the appropriate target cash balance involves an assessment of the trade-off between the benefit and cost of liquidity. The benefit of holding cash is the convenience in liquidity it gives the firm. The cost of holding cash is the interest income that the firm could have received from investing in Treasury bills and other marketable securities.

If the firm has achieved its target cash balance, the value it gets from the liquidity provided by its cash will be exactly equal to the value forgone in interest on an equivalent holding of Treasury bills. In other words, a firm should increase its holding of cash as long as the net present value from doing so is positive.

After the optimal amount of liquidity is determined, the financial manager must establish procedures so that collection and disbursement of cash are done as efficiently as possible. This goal usually reduces to the dictum: "Collect early and pay late." Accordingly, we discuss some ways of accelerating collections and

---

[1] *Industrial Financial Statistics* (Ottawa: Statistics Canada, 1989). Figures are for manufacturing firms with assets over $10 million.

controlling disbursements. Our examples feature large corporations and how they use computer-based cash management services offered by chartered banks.

In addition, firms must invest temporarily idle cash in short-term marketable securities. As we discussed in Chapter 1, these securities can be bought and sold in the money market. As a group, they have very little default risk and most are highly marketable. There are different types of money market securities, and we discuss a few of the most important types.

18.1 | REASONS FOR HOLDING CASH

John Maynard Keynes, in his great work, *The General Theory of Employment, Interest, and Money,* identified three reasons liquidity is important: the precautionary motive, the speculative motive, and the transaction motive. We discuss these next.

Speculative and Precautionary Motives

speculative motive
The need to hold cash to take advantage of additional investment opportunities, such as bargain purchases.

The **speculative motive** is the need to hold cash to be able to take advantage of, for example, bargain purchases that might arise, attractive interest rates, and (in the case of international firms) favourable exchange rate fluctuations.

For most firms, reserve borrowing ability and marketable securities can be used to satisfy speculative motives. Thus, for a modern firm, there might be a speculative motive for liquidity, but not necessarily for cash per se. Think of it this way: If you have a credit card with a very large credit limit, you can probably take advantage of any unusual bargains that come along without carrying any cash.

precautionary motive
The need to hold cash as a safety margin to act as a financial reserve.

This is also true, to a lesser extent, for precautionary motives. The **precautionary motive** is the need for a safety supply to act as a financial reserve. Once again, there probably is a precautionary motive for liquidity. However, given that the value of money market instruments is relatively certain and that instruments such as T-bills are extremely liquid, there is no real need to literally hold substantial amounts of cash for precautionary purposes.

The Transaction Motive

transaction motive
The need to hold cash to satisfy normal disbursement and collection activities associated with a firm's ongoing operations.

Cash is needed to satisfy the **transaction motive**, the need to have cash on hand to pay bills. Transaction-related needs come from the normal disbursement and collection activities of the firm. The disbursement of cash includes the payment of wages and salaries, trade debts, taxes, and dividends.

Cash is collected from sales, the selling of assets, and new financing. The cash inflows (collections) and outflows (disbursements) are not perfectly synchronized, and some level of cash holdings is necessary to serve as a buffer. Perfect liquidity is the characteristic of cash that allows it to satisfy the transaction motive.

As electronic funds transfers and other high-speed, paperless payment mechanisms continue to develop, even the transaction demand for cash may all but disappear. Even if it does, however, there is still a demand for liquidity and a need to manage it efficiently.

Costs of Holding Cash

When a firm holds cash in excess of some necessary minimum, it incurs an opportunity cost. The opportunity cost of excess cash (held in currency or bank deposits) is the interest income that could be earned in the next best use, such as investment in marketable securities.

Given the opportunity cost of holding cash, why would a firm hold any cash? The answer is that a cash balance must be maintained to provide the liquidity necessary for transaction needs—paying bills. If the firm maintains too small a cash balance, it may run out of cash. When this happens, the firm may have to raise cash on a short-term basis. This could involve, for example, selling marketable securities or borrowing.

Activities such as selling marketable securities and borrowing involve various costs. As we've discussed, holding cash has an opportunity cost. To determine the target cash balance, the firm must weigh the benefits of holding cash against these costs. We discuss this subject in more detail in the next section.

E X A M P L E | 18.1   Provincial Liquidity Reserves

The deputy treasurer of your province is responsible for managing liquidity reserves and financing for the province. Suppose your deputy treasurer boasts of the strong liquidity position that is always maintained. The claim is that holding cash and low-yielding marketable securities gives the province flexibility in its bond issues. The advantages are that fewer, larger bond issues allow the province to finance only when rates are favourable and to obtain scale economies in flotation costs. What do you think of this policy?

The province is incurring an opportunity cost on its liquidity holdings since they earn interest at a rate less than the province's long-term borrowing cost. While the policy makes the deputy treasurer's job easier, this does not prove that it helps taxpayers. Unless there is real evidence that the province is saving on interest costs by successful market timing and on flotation costs, the policy will have a negative net present value. |

CONCEPT QUESTIONS

1. What is the transaction motive, and how does it lead firms to hold cash?
2. What is the cost to the firm of holding excess cash?

18.2 | DETERMINING THE TARGET CASH BALANCE

Based on our general discussion of current assets in the previous chapter, the **target cash balance** involves a trade-off between the opportunity costs of holding too much cash (the carrying costs) and the costs of holding too little (the shortage costs, also called **adjustment costs**). The nature of these costs depends on the firm's working capital policy.

If the firm has a flexible working capital policy, it probably maintains a marketable securities portfolio. As we showed earlier, large Canadian corporations carry portfolios of marketable securities. In this case, the adjustment or shortage costs are the trading costs associated with buying and selling securities. If the firm has a restrictive working capital policy, it probably borrows short-term to meet cash shortages. The costs are the interest and other expenses associated with arranging a loan. The restrictive case is more realistic for small and medium-sized companies.

In the following discussion, we assume the firm has a flexible policy. Its cash management consists of moving money in and out of marketable securities. This is a very traditional approach to the subject, and it is a nice way of illustrating the costs and benefits of holding cash. Keep in mind, however, that the distinction between cash and money market investments is becoming increasingly blurred as electronic technology allows easy and fast transfers.

target cash balance
A firm's desired cash level as determined by the trade-off between carrying costs and shortage costs.

adjustment costs
The costs associated with holding too little cash. Also shortage costs.

The Basic Idea

Figure 18.1 presents the cash management problem for our flexible firm. If a firm tries to keep its cash holdings too low, it finds itself running out of cash more often than is desirable, and thus selling marketable securities (and perhaps later buying marketable securities to replace those sold) more frequently than it would if the cash balance were higher. Thus, trading costs are high when the size of the cash balance is low. These fall as the cash balance becomes larger.

In contrast, the opportunity costs of holding cash are very low if the firm holds very little cash. These costs increase as the cash holdings rise because the firm is giving up more and more in interest that could have been earned.

At point C^* in Figure 18.1, the sum of the costs is given by the total cost curve. As shown, the minimum total cost occurs where the two individual cost curves cross. At this point, the opportunity costs and the trading costs are equal. This is the target cash balance, and it is the point the firm should try to find.

Figure 18.1 is essentially the same as one in the previous chapter. However, if we use real data on holding and opportunity costs, we can come up with a precise dollar optimum investment in cash. Appendix 18A covers two models that do this in varying degrees of complexity. Here, we focus only on their implications. All other things being equal:

1. The greater the interest rate, the lower is the target cash balance.
2. The greater the trading cost, the higher is the target balance.

These are both fairly obvious from looking at Figure 18.1, but they bring out an important point on the evolution of computerized cash management techniques. In

---

F I G U R E 18.1

Costs of holding cash

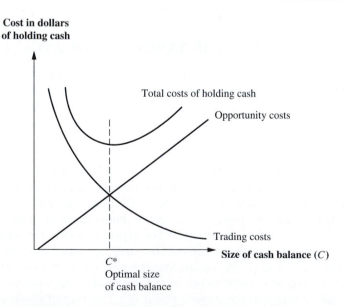

Trading costs are increased when the firm must sell securities to establish a cash balance. Opportunity costs are increased when there is a cash balance because there is no return to cash.

the early 1980s, high interest rates (the prime rate was over 22 percent) caused the cost of idle cash to skyrocket. In response, large corporations and banks invested in applying computer and communications technologies to cash management. The result was lower trading costs. With systems in place, banks are now able to offer cash management services to smaller customers.

Going beyond the simple framework of Figure 18.1, the more advanced models also show that the target cash balance should be higher for firms facing greater uncertainty in forecasting their cash needs. This makes sense because such firms need a larger cash balance as a cushion against unexpected outflows. We cover cash management under uncertainty later in the chapter.

Other Factors Influencing the Target Cash Balance

Before moving on, we briefly discuss two additional considerations that affect the target cash balance.

First, in our discussion of cash management, we assume cash is invested in marketable securities such as Treasury bills. The firm obtains cash by selling these securities. Another alternative is to borrow cash. Borrowing introduces additional considerations to cash management:

1. Borrowing is likely to be more expensive than selling marketable securities because the interest rate is likely to be higher. For example, Figure 18.7 in a later section shows that the prime rate considerably exceeds all money market rates.

2. The need to borrow depends on management's desire to hold low cash balances. A firm is more likely to have to borrow to cover an unexpected cash outflow the greater its cash flow variability and the lower its investment in marketable securities.

Second, for large firms, the trading costs of buying and selling securities are very small when compared to the opportunity costs of holding cash. For example, suppose a firm has $1 million in cash that won't be needed for 24 hours. Should the firm invest the money or leave it sitting?

Suppose the firm can invest the money overnight at the call money rate. To do this, the treasurer arranges through a chartered bank to lend funds for 24 hours to an investment dealer. According to Figure 18.7 in section 18.4, this is an annualized rate of 6.63 percent per year. The daily rate is about two basis points (.02 percent or .0002)[2].

The daily return earned on $1 million is thus $0.0002 \times \$1$ million $= \$200$. In most cases, the order cost would be much less than this. Following up on our earlier point about technology and cash management, large corporations buy and sell securities daily on terminals similar to automated bank machines so they are unlikely to leave substantial amounts of cash idle.

> ### CONCEPT QUESTIONS
> 1. What is a target cash balance?
> 2. How do changes in interest rates affect the target cash balance? Changes in trading costs?

---

[2] A basis point is 1 percent of 1 percent. Also, the annual interest rate is calculated as $(1 + R)^{365} = 1.0663$, implying a daily rate of .02 percent.

18.3 | UNDERSTANDING FLOAT

float

The difference between book cash and bank cash, representing the net effect of cheques in the process of clearing.

As you no doubt know, the amount of money you have according to your chequebook can be very different from the amount of money that your bank thinks you have. The reason is that some of the cheques you have written haven't yet been presented to the bank for payment. The same thing is true for a business. The cash balance that a firm shows on its books is called the firm's *book* or *ledger balance*. The balance shown in its bank account is called its *available* or *collected* balance. The difference between the available balance and the ledger balance is called the **float**, and it represents the net effect of cheques in the process of clearing (moving through the banking system).

Disbursement Float

Cheques written by a firm generate disbursement float, causing a decrease in its book balance but no change in its available balance. For example, suppose General Mechanics, Inc. (GMI), currently has $100,000 on deposit with its bank. On June 8, it buys some raw materials and puts a cheque in the mail for $100,000. The company's book balance is immediately reduced by $100,000 as a result.

GMI's bank, however, does not find out about this cheque until it is presented to GMI's bank for payment on, say, June 14. Until the cheque is presented, the firm's available balance is greater than its book balance by $100,000. In other words, before June 8, GMI has a zero float:

$$\text{Float} = \text{Firm's available balance} - \text{Firm's book balance}$$
$$= \$100,000 \qquad\qquad - \$100,000 \qquad\qquad = \$0$$

GMI's position from June 8 to June 14 is:

$$\text{Disbursement float} = \text{Firm's available balance} - \text{Firm's book balance}$$
$$= \$100,000 \qquad\qquad - \$0$$
$$= \$100,000$$

During this period while the cheque is clearing (moving through the mail and the banking system), GMI has a balance with the bank of $100,000. It can obtain the benefit of this cash while the cheque is clearing. For example, the available balance could be temporarily invested in marketable securities and thus earn more interest. We return to this subject a little later.

Collection Float and Net Float

Cheques received by the firm create collection float. Collection float increases book balances but does not immediately change available balances. For example, suppose GMI receives a cheque from a customer for $100,000 on October 8. Assume, as before, that the company has $100,000 deposited at its bank and a zero float. It processes the cheque through the bookkeeping department and increases its book balance by $100,000 to $200,000. However, the additional cash is not available to GMI until the cheque is deposited in the firm's bank. This occurs on, say, October 9, the next day. In the meantime, the cash position at GMI reflects a collection float of $100,000. We can summarize these events. Before October 8, GMI's position is:

$$\text{Float} = \text{Firm's available balance} - \text{Firm's book balance}$$
$$= \$100,000 \qquad\qquad - \$100,000$$
$$= \$0$$

GMI's position from October 8 to October 9 is:

$$\text{Collection float} = \text{Firm's available balance} - \text{Firm's book balance}$$
$$= \$100,000 \qquad\qquad - \$200,000$$
$$= -\$100,000$$

In general, a firm's payment (disbursement) activities generate disbursement float, and its collection activities generate collection float. The net effect, that is, the sum of the total collection and disbursement floats, is the net float. The net float at a point in time is simply the overall difference between the firm's available balance and its book balance.

If the net float is positive, the firm's disbursement float exceeds its collection float and its available balance exceeds its book balance. In other words, the bank thinks the firm has more cash than it really does. This, of course, is desirable. If the available balance is less than the book balance, the firm has a net collection float. This is undesirable because we actually have more cash than the bank thinks we do, but we can't use it.

A firm should be concerned with its net float and available balance more than its book balance. Knowing that a cheque will not clear for several days, a financial manager can keep a lower cash balance at the bank than might be true otherwise. This can generate a great deal of money.

For example, take the case of Exxon Corporation. The average daily sales of Exxon are about $248 million. If its collections could be speeded up by a single day, Exxon could free up $248 million for investing. At a relatively modest 0.02 percent daily rate, the interest earned would be on the order of $50,000 per day.

E X A M P L E | **18.2** **Staying Afloat**

Suppose you have $5,000 on deposit. You write and mail a cheque for $1,000. You receive a cheque for $2,000 and put it in your wallet to deposit the next time you use a bank machine. What are your disbursement, collection, and net floats?

After you write the $1,000 cheque, you show a balance of $4,000 on your books, but the bank shows $5,000 while the cheque is moving through the mail. This is a disbursement float of $1,000.

After you receive the $2,000 cheque, you show a balance of $6,000. Your available balance doesn't rise until you deposit the cheque. This is a collection float of −$2,000. Your net float is the sum of the collection and disbursement floats, or −$1,000.

Overall, you show $6,000 on your books, but the bank only shows $5,000 cash. The discrepancy between your available balance and your book balance is the net float (−$1,000), and it is bad for you. If you write another cheque for $5,500, it might bounce even though, net, it shouldn't. This is the reason the financial manager has to be more concerned with available balances than book balances. |

Float Management

Float management involves controlling the collection and disbursement of cash. The objective in cash collection is to speed up collections and reduce the lag between the time customers pay their bills and the time the cheques are collected. The objective in cash disbursement is to control payments and minimize the firm's costs associated with making payments.

Float can be broken down into three parts: mail float, processing float, and availability float:

1. *Mail float* is the part of the collection and disbursement process where cheques are trapped in the postal system.
2. *Processing float* is the time it takes the receiver of a cheque to process the payment and deposit it in a bank.
3. *Availability float* refers to the time required to clear a cheque through the banking system. In the Canadian banking system, availability float cannot exceed one day and is often zero so this is the least important part.

Speeding collections involves reducing one or more of these float components. Slowing disbursements involves increasing one of them. Later, we describe some procedures for managing float times; before that, we need to discuss how float is measured.

Measuring Float   The size of the float depends on both the dollars and time delay involved. For example, suppose you receive a cheque for $500 from another province each month. It takes five days in the mail to reach you (the mail float) and one day for you to get over to the bank (the processing float). The bank gives you immediate availability (so there is no availability float). The total delay is 5 + 1 = 6 days.

What is your average daily float? There are two equivalent ways of calculating the answer: First, you have a $500 float for six days, so we say the total float is 6 × $500 = $3,000. Assuming 30 days in the month, the average daily float is $3,000/30 = $100.

Second, your float is $500 for 6 days out of the month and zero the other 24 days (again assuming 30 days in a month). Your average daily float is thus:

$$\text{Average daily float} = (6 \times \$500 + 24 \times 0)/30$$
$$= 6/30 \times \$500 + 24/30 \times 0$$
$$= \$3,000/30$$
$$= \$100$$

This means that, on an average day, there is $100 that is not available to spend. In other words, on average, your book balance is $100 greater than your available balance, a $100 average collection float.

Things are only a little more complicated when there are multiple receipts. Suppose Concepts, Ltd., receives two items each month as follows:

	Amount	Days Delay	Total Float
Item 1:	$5,000,000	× 9	= $45,000,000
Item 2:	3,000,000	× 5	= 15,000,000
Total	$8,000,000		$60,000,000

The average daily float is equal to:

$$\text{Average daily float} = \text{Total float/Total days}$$
$$= \$60,000,000/30 = \$2,000,000$$

So, on an average day, $2 million is uncollected and not available.

Another way to see this is to calculate the average daily receipts and multiply by the weighted average delay. Average daily receipts are:

$$\text{Average daily receipts} = \text{Total receipts/Total days}$$
$$= \$8,000,000/30 = \$266,666.67$$

Of the $8 million total receipts, $5 million, or ⅝ of the total, is delayed for nine days. The other ⅜ is delayed for five days. The weighted average delay is thus:

$$\text{Weighted average delay} = (⅝) \times 9 \text{ days} + (⅜) \times 5 \text{ days}$$
$$= 5.625 + 1.875 = 7.50 \text{ days}$$

The average daily float is thus:

$$\text{Average daily float} = \text{Average daily receipts} \times \text{Weighted average delay}$$
$$= \$266,666.67 \times 7.50 \text{ days} = \$2,000,000$$

[18.1]

This is just as we had before.

Cost of the Float   The basic cost to the firm of collection float is simply the opportunity cost from not being able to use the cash. At a minimum, the firm could earn interest on the cash if it were available for investing.

Suppose the Lambo Corporation has average daily receipts of $1,000 and a weighted average delay of three days. The average daily float is thus 3 × $1,000 = $3,000. This means that, on a typical day, there is $3,000 that is not earning interest. Suppose Lambo could eliminate the float entirely. What would be the benefit? If it costs $2,000 to eliminate the float, what is the NPV of doing it?

After the float is eliminated, daily receipts are still $1,000. We collect the same day since the float is eliminated, so daily collections are also still $1,000. The only change occurs the first day. On that day, we catch up and collect $1,000 from the sale made three days ago. Because the float is gone, we also collect on the sales made two days ago, one day ago, and today, for an additional $3,000. Total collections today are thus $4,000 instead of $1,000.

What we see is that Lambo generates an extra $3,000 today by eliminating the float. On every subsequent day, Lambo receives $1,000 in cash just as it did before the float was eliminated. If you recall our definition of relevant cash flow, the only change in the firm's cash flow from eliminating the float is this extra $3,000 that comes in immediately. No other cash flows are affected, so Lambo is $3,000 richer.

In other words, the PV of eliminating the float is simply equal to the total float. Lambo could pay this amount out as a dividend, invest it in interest-bearing assets, or do anything else with it. If it costs $2,000 to eliminate the float, the NPV is $3,000 − 2,000 = $1,000; so Lambo should do it.

E X A M P L E | 18.3   **Reducing the Float**

Instead of eliminating the float, suppose Lambo can reduce it to one day. What is the maximum Lambo should be willing to pay for this?

If Lambo can reduce the float from three days to one day, the amount of the float will fall from $3,000 to $1,000. We see immediately that the PV of doing this is just equal to the $2,000 float reduction. Lambo should thus be willing to pay up to $2,000. |

Accelerating Collections

Based on our discussion, we can depict the basic parts of the cash collection process in Figure 18.2. The total time in this process is made up of mailing time, cheque-processing time, and the bank's cheque-clearing time. The amount of time that cash spends in each part of the cash collection process depends on where the firm's customers are located and how efficient the firm is at collecting cash.

F I G U R E 18.2

Float time line

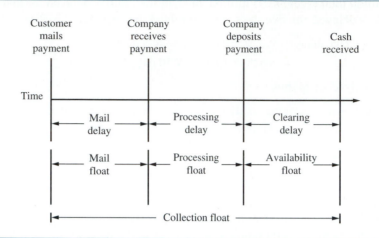

Coordinating the firm's efforts in all areas in Figure 18.2 is its cash flow information system. Tracking payments through the system and providing the cash manager with up-to-date daily cash balances and investment rates are its key tasks. Chartered banks offer cash information systems that all but put the bank on the manager's desk.[3] Linking the manager's terminal with the bank's on-line, real-time system gives the manager access to account balances and transactions and information on money market rates. This system is open 15 ½ hours a day from 7:30 A.M. through 11 P.M. Toronto time. The system also allows the manager to transfer funds and make money market investments.

Since it is the corporate equivalent of a bank machine, the cash management system has security features to prevent unauthorized use.[4] Different passwords allow access to each level of authority. For example, you could give your receivables clerk access to deposit activity files but not to payroll. Some systems use **smart cards** for security. A smart card looks like a credit card but contains a computer chip that can be programmed to grant access to certain files only. The card must be inserted into an access device attached to a personal computer and provides another safeguard in addition to a password.

We next discuss several techniques used to accelerate collections and reduce collection time: systems to expedite mailing and cheque processing and concentration banking.

smart card

Much like an automated teller machine card; it is used within corporations to control access to information by employees.

Over-the-Counter Collections

In an over-the-counter system, customers pay in person at field offices or stores. Most large retailers, utilities, and many other firms receive some payments this way. Because the payments are made at a company location, there is no mail delay. The

---

[3] Our discussion of cash management systems is based on D. W. Rogers, "Work Smart, Not Hard, A Treasurer's Guide to Electronic Banking," *Canadian Treasury Management Review,* January–February 1988, pp. 5–7; and on materials provided by a Big Six chartered bank.

[4] The bank machine comparison is literally true for commercial (mid-sized) customers of one bank that allows them to use its bank machines as a lower cost alternative to direct computer links to the firm's office.

manager of the field location is responsible for ensuring that cheques and cash collected are deposited promptly and for reporting daily deposit amounts to the head office.

As an alternative to over-the-counter collections, a company may instruct customers to mail cheques to a collection point address on its invoices. By distributing the collection points locally throughout its market area, the company avoids the delays occurring when all payments are mailed to its head office. If the collection points are field offices, the next steps are the same as for over-the-counter collections. A popular alternative, lockboxes, contracts out the collection points to a bank.

Lockboxes   **Lockboxes** are special post office boxes set up to intercept accounts receivable payments. Figure 18.3 illustrates a lockbox system. The collection process is started by business and retail customers mailing their cheques to a post office box instead of sending them to the firm. The lockbox is maintained at a local bank branch. Large corporations may maintain a number of lockboxes, one in each significant market area. The location depends on a trade-off between bank fees and savings on mailing time.

lockboxes

Special post office boxes set up to intercept and speed up accounts receivable payments.

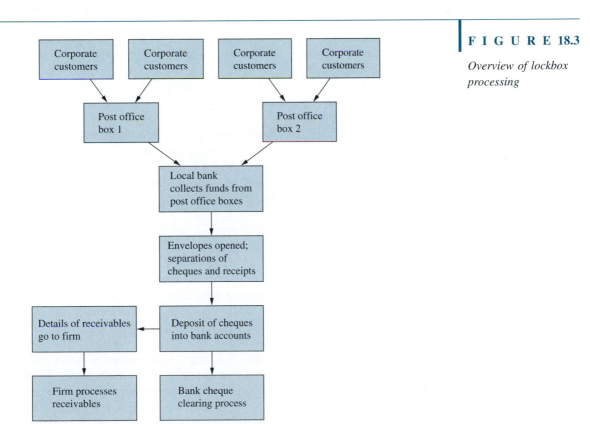

F I G U R E 18.3

Overview of lockbox processing

The flow starts when a corporate customer mails remittances to a post office box number instead of to the corporation. Several times a day the bank collects the lockbox receipts from the post office. The cheques are then put into the company bank accounts.

In the typical lockbox system, the local bank branch collects the lockbox cheques from the post office daily. The bank deposits the cheques directly to the firm's account. Details of the operation are recorded in some computer-usable form and sent to the firm.

A lockbox system reduces mailing time because cheques are received at a nearby post office instead of at corporate headquarters. Lockboxes also reduce the processing time because the corporation doesn't have to open the envelopes and deposit cheques for collection. In all, a bank lockbox should enable a firm to get its receipts processed, deposited, and cleared faster than if it were to receive cheques at its headquarters and deliver them itself to the bank for deposit and clearing.

Electronic Collection Systems

Over-the-counter and lockbox systems are standard ways to reduce mail and processing float time. They are used by almost all large Canadian firms that can benefit from them. Newer approaches focus on reducing float virtually to zero by replacing cheques with electronic funds transfer. Examples used in Canada include preauthorized payments, point-of-sale transfers, and electronic trade payables. We discuss the first two here and the third later when we look at disbursement systems.

Preauthorized payments are paperless transfers of contractual or installment payments from the customer's account directly to the firm's. Common applications are mortgage payments and installment payments for insurance, rent, cable TV, and so on. This system eliminates all invoice paperwork and the deposit and reconciliation of cheques. There is no mail or processing float. The system is presently limited mainly to annuity payments but the technology could handle any payments. One travel card company that experimented with preauthorized payment of monthly card balances found customer resistance to authorizing variable payments. Because such payments are for different amounts each month, customers still prefer to go over their statements and write cheques.

Point-of-sale systems use **debit cards** to transfer funds directly from a customer's bank account to a retailer's. A debit card works like a bank machine (ATM) card with a personal identification card (PIN) for security. Unlike a credit card, the funds are transferred immediately. Point-of-sale systems are common in Canada, especially in gas stations and supermarkets.

Cash Concentration

Using lockboxes or other collection systems helps firms collect cheques from customers and get them deposited rapidly. But the job is not finished yet since these systems give the firm cash at a number of widely dispersed branches. Until it is concentrated in a central account, the cash is of little use to the firm for paying bills, reducing loans, or investing.

With a concentration banking system, sales receipts are processed at field sales offices and banks providing lockbox services and deposited locally. Surplus funds are transferred from the various local branches to a single, central concentration account. This process is illustrated in Figure 18.4, where concentration banks are combined with over-the-counter collection and lockboxes in a total cash management system.

Large firms in Canada may manage collections through one chartered bank across the country. Chartered banks offer a concentrator account that automatically electronically transfers deposits at any branch in Canada to the firm's concentration account. These funds receive **same day value**. This means the firm has immediate use of the funds even though it takes 24 hours for a cheque to clear in Canada.[5] If the

debit card
An automated teller machine card used at the point of purchase to avoid the use of cash. As this is not a credit card, money must be available in the user's bank account.

same day value
Bank makes proceeds of cheques deposited available the same day before cheques clear.

---

[5] Since the bank is providing availability in advance of receiving funds, same day availability creates collection float for the bank. An interest charge on this float is usually included in the bank's fees.

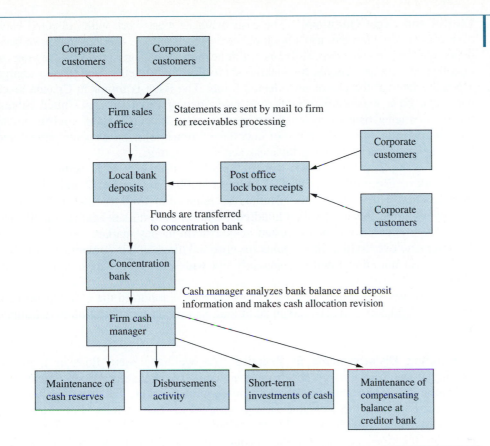

F I G U R E 18.4

*Lockboxes and
concentration banks in
a cash management
system*

concentration involves branches of more than one bank, electronic transfers take place between banks.

Once the funds are in the concentration account, the bank can make automatic transfers to pay down the firm's credit line or, if there is a surplus, to an investment account. Transfers are made in units of minimum size agreed in advance. A common practice is in units of $5,000. Mid-sized firms lacking in money market expertise may invest in bank accounts at competitive interest rates. The largest firms have the capability to purchase money market instruments electronically.

Controlling Disbursements

Accelerating collections is one method of cash management; slowing disbursements is another. This can be a sensitive area and some practices exist that we do not recommend. For example, some small firms that are short of working capital make disbursements on the "squeaky wheel principle." Payables invoices are processed before their due dates and cheques printed. When the cheques are ready, the firm's controller puts them all in a desk drawer. As suppliers call and ask for their money, the cheques come out of the drawer and go into the mail! We do not recommend the desk drawer method because it is bad for supplier relations and borders on being unethical.

Ethical and Legal Questions   The cash manager must work with collected bank cash balances and not the firm's book balance (which reflects cheques that have been deposited but not collected). If this is not done, a cash manager could be drawing on uncollected cash as a source for making short-term investments. Most banks charge a penalty rate for the use of uncollected funds. The issue is minor in Canada since there can be a maximum of only one day's deposit float. In the United States, however, smaller banks may not have good enough accounting and control procedures to be fully aware of the use of uncollected funds. This raises some ethical and legal questions for firms doing business across the border.

For example, in May 1985, Robert Fomon, chairman of E. F. Hutton (a large New York investment bank), pleaded guilty to 2,000 charges of mail and wire fraud in connection with a scheme the firm had operated from 1980 to 1982. E. F. Hutton employees wrote cheques totaling hundreds of millions of dollars against uncollected cash. The proceeds were then invested in short-term money market assets. This type of systematic overdrafting of accounts (or cheque kiting, as it is sometimes called) is neither legal nor ethical and is apparently not widespread practice among corporations.

For its part, E. F. Hutton paid a $2 million fine, reimbursed the U.S. Department of Justice $750,000, and reserved an additional $8 million for restitution to defrauded banks.

Controlling Disbursements in Practice   As we have seen, float in terms of slowing down payments comes from mail delivery, cheque-processing time, and collection of funds. As we just showed, in the United States, disbursement float can be increased by writing a cheque on a geographically distant bank. For example, a New York supplier might be paid with cheques drawn on a Los Angeles bank. This increases the time required for the cheques to clear through the banking system. Mailing cheques from remote post offices is another way firms slow disbursement. Because there are significant ethical (and legal) issues associated with deliberately delaying disbursements in these and similar ways, such strategies appear to be disappearing. In Canada, banks provide same day availability so the temptation is easy to resist.

For these reasons, the goal is to control rather than simply delay disbursements. A treasurer should try to pay payables on the last day appropriate for net terms or a discount.[6] The traditional way is to write a cheque and mail it timed to arrive on the due date. With the cash management system we described earlier, the payment can be programmed today for electronic transfer on the future due date. This eliminates paper along with guesswork about mail times.

zero-balance account

A chequing account in which a zero balance is maintained by transfers of funds from a master account in an amount only large enough to cover cheques presented.

The electronic payment is likely to come from a disbursement account, kept separate from the concentration account to ease accounting and control. Firms keep separate accounts for payroll, vendor disbursements, customer refunds, and so on. This makes it easy for the bank to provide each cost or profit centre with its own statement.

Firms use **zero-balance accounts** to avoid carrying extra balances in each disbursement account. With a zero-balance account, the firm, in cooperation with its bank, transfers in just enough funds to cover cheques presented that day. Figure 18.5 illustrates how such a system might work. In this case, the firm maintains two

---

[6] We discuss credit terms in depth in Chapter 19.

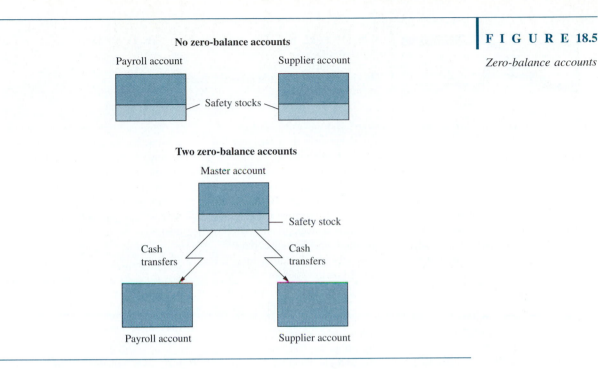

F I G U R E 18.5

Zero-balance accounts

disbursement accounts, one for suppliers and one for payroll. As shown, when the firm does not use zero-balance accounts, each of these accounts must have a safety stock of cash to meet unanticipated demands. A firm that uses zero-balance accounts can keep one safety stock in a master account and transfer in the funds to the two subsidiary accounts as needed. The key is that the total amount of cash held as a buffer is smaller under the zero-balance arrangement, thereby freeing cash to be used elsewhere.

CONCEPT QUESTIONS

1. What are collection and disbursement floats?
2. What are lockboxes? Concentration banking? Zero-balance accounts?
3. How do computer and communications technologies aid in cash management by large corporations?

18.4 | INVESTING IDLE CASH

If a firm has a temporary cash surplus, it can invest in short-term securities. As we have mentioned at various times, the market for short-term financial assets is called the money market. The maturity of short-term financial assets that trade in the money market is one year or less.

Most large firms manage their own short-term financial assets through transactions with banks and investment dealers. Some firms use money market funds that invest in short-term financial assets for a management fee. The management fee is compensation for the professional expertise and diversification provided by the fund manager. Money market funds evolved in the United States as a way of getting around ceilings on interest rates for bank deposits.

IN THEIR OWN WORDS . . .

David Rogers on Electronic Banking

The benefits corporations can derive from electronic banking are threefold. First, it helps reduce the size of the float that exists in our banking network. In the case of one insurance company, it's made about $4 million available on a daily basis for investment elsewhere. Prior to electronic banking, that money was simply not available.

Second, because disbursement requirements can be met exactly, approximately $1 million in annual overdraft interest costs have been eliminated. Third, by connecting its computer network to its bank's extensive network facilities, the company is able to provide essential financial information to its business managers and agency force in a timely manner to better help them serve their business and policyholder needs.

Perhaps the most profitable bonus of electronic banking is the elimination of a great deal of the routine and repetitive work associated with managing your cash position on a daily basis—in other words, the acquisition of time; time that ordinarily would be used to make phone calls or visits to the bank; time to think about long-range objectives; time to more thoroughly analyze short-term options; time to plan; time to invest; time to think about why you buy what you buy and where you buy what you buy; time to answer the question "How can I make more money for my company?"

Time is money—and the sooner we have the information we need to employ that money, the more money we're going to make. The technology exists to get that information, sooner. It's up to all of us to make sure we don't get left behind.

David Rogers is director of information services at London Life Insurance Company in London, Ontario. His responsibilities include the overall planning and direction of the company's information and technology strategies and operations, along with the development of strategic technology plans for the Trilon group of companies, which includes Canada Systems Group, Wellington Insurance, Royal LePage, and Triathalon Leasing, as well as London Life.
Reprinted with permission from *Canadian Treasury Management Review,* January–February 1988, pp. 5–7.

Money market funds are becoming increasingly popular in Canada. Also, Canadian chartered banks offer arrangements in which the bank takes all excess available funds at the close of each business day and invests them for the firm.

Temporary Cash Surpluses

Firms have temporary cash surpluses for various reasons. Two of the most important are the financing of seasonal or cyclical activities and the financing of planned or possible expenditures.

Seasonal or Cyclical Activities
Some firms have a predictable cash flow pattern. They have surplus cash flows during part of the year and deficit cash flows the rest of the year. For example, Toys "R" Us, a retail toy firm, has a seasonal cash flow pattern influenced by Christmas.

A firm such as Toys "R" Us may buy marketable securities when surplus cash flows occur and sell marketable securities when deficits occur. Of course, bank loans are another short-term financing device. The use of bank loans and marketable securities to meet temporary financing needs is illustrated in Figure 18.6. In this case, the firm is following a compromise working capital policy in the sense we discussed in the previous chapter.

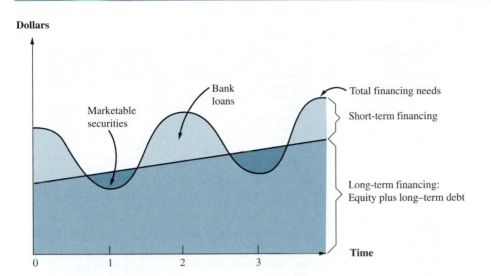

Dollars

Marketable securities

Bank loans

Total financing needs

Short-term financing

Long-term financing:
Equity plus long–term debt

Time

0   1   2   3

FIGURE 18.6

Seasonal cash demands

Time 1: A surplus cash flow exists. Seasonal demand for assets is low. The surplus cash flow is invested in short-term marketable securities.
Time 2: A deficit cash flow exists. Seasonal demand for assets is high. The financial deficit is financed by selling marketable securities and by bank borrowing.

Planned or Possible Expenditures   Firms frequently accumulate temporary investments in marketable securities to provide the cash for a plant construction program, dividend payment, and other large expenditures. Thus, firms may issue bonds and stocks before the cash is needed, investing the proceeds in short-term marketable securities and then selling the securities to finance the expenditures. Also, firms may face the possibility of having to make a large cash outlay. An obvious example would be the possibility of losing a large lawsuit. Firms may build up cash surpluses against such a contingency.

For example, on December 31, 1981, U.S. Steel Corporation (now USX Corporation) had $1.5 billion U.S. invested in marketable securities. This represented more than 11 percent of the total assets of U.S. Steel. This balance had been built up to finance a merger with Marathon Oil that was completed in March 1982.

Characteristics of Short-Term Securities

Given that a firm has some temporarily idle cash, there are a variety of short-term securities available for investing. The most important characteristics of these short-term marketable securities are their maturity, default risk, and marketability. Consistent with Chapter 10's discussion of risk and return, managers of marketable securities portfolios have an opportunity to increase expected returns in exchange for taking on higher risk. Marketable securities managers almost always resolve this trade-off in favour of low risk. Because this portfolio is a liquidity reserve, preservation of capital is generally the primary goal.

Maturity   Maturity refers to the time period over which interest and principal payments are made. From Chapter 6, we know that for a given change in the level of

FIGURE 18.7

*Money market
quotations*

Money Rates

ADMINISTERED RATES		UNITED STATES	Certificates of Deposit by dealer: 30 days, 5.79; 60 days, 5.78; 90 days, 5.77; 120 days, 5.73; 150 days, 5.67; 180 days, 5.66
Bank of Canada	6.58%	NEW YORK (AP) — Money rates for Tuesday as reported by Dow Jones Telerate:	
Canadian prime	8.25%		
MONEY MARKET RATES		Telerate interest rate index: 5.660	
(for transactions of $1-million or more)		Prime Rate: 8.75	Eurodollar rates: Overnight, 5.75-5.875; 1 month, 5.8125-5.875; 3 months, 5.8125-5.875; 6 months, 5.6875-5.75; 1 year, 5.625-5.6875
3-mo. T-bill(when-issued)	6.35%	Discount Rate: 5.25	
1-month treasury bills	6.34%	Broker call loan rate: 7.75	
2-month treasury bills	6.36%	Federal funds market rate:	
3-month treasury bills	6.38%	High 5.8125, low 5.75, last 5.75	
6-month treasury bills	6.43%		London Interbank Offered Rate: 3 months, 5.875; 6 months, 5.75; 1 year, 5.6875
1-year treasury bills	6.53%	Dealers commercial paper: 30-180 days: 5.85-5.55	
10-year Canada bonds	7.79%	Commercial paper by finance company: 30-270 days: 5.72-5.34	
30-year Canada bonds	8.26%		Treasury Bill auction results: average discount rate: 3-month as of July 10: 5.36; 6-month as of July 10: 5.22; 52-week as of June 22: 5.22
1-month banker's accept.	6.61%	Bankers acceptances dealer indications: 30 days, 5.77; 60 days, 5.74; 90 days, 5.69; 120 days, 5.62; 150 days, 5.54; 180 days, 5.52	
2-month banker's accept.	6.48%		
3-month banker's accept.	6.43%		Treasury Bill annualized rate on weekly average basis, yield adjusted for constant maturity, 1-year, as of July 10: 5.53
Commercial Paper (R-1 Low)			
1-month	6.65%	Certificates of Deposit Primary: 30 days, 4.77; 90 days, 5.00; 180 days, 5.00	
2-month	6.53%		Treasury Bill market rate, 1-year 5.17-5.15
3-month	6.46%		Treasury Bond market rate, 30-year 6.57
Call money	6.63%		
Supplied by Dow Jones Telerate Canada			

Source: *Globe and Mail,* "Report on Business," July 12, 1995, p. B14. Used with permission.

interest rates, the prices of longer maturity securities change more than those of shorter maturity securities. As a consequence, firms that invest in long-term maturity securities are accepting greater risk than firms that invest in securities with short-term maturities.

We called this type of risk interest rate risk. Firms often limit their investments in marketable securities to those maturing in less than 90 days to avoid the risk of losses in value from changing interest rates. Of course, the expected return on securities with short-term maturities is usually (but not always) less than the expected return on securities with longer maturities.

For example, suppose you are the treasurer of a firm with $10 million needed to make a major capital investment after 90 days. You have decided to invest in obligations of the government of Canada to eliminate all possible default risk. The newspaper (or your computer screen) provides you with the list of securities and rates in Figure 18.7. The safest investment is three-month Treasury bills yielding 6.35 percent. Because this matches the maturity of the investment with the planned holding period, there is no interest rate risk. After three months, the Treasury bills mature for a certain future cash flow of $10 million.[7]

If you invest instead in 10-year Canada bonds, the expected return is higher, 7.79 percent, but so is the risk. Again drawing on Chapter 6, if interest rates rise over the next three months, the bond drops in price. The resulting capital loss reduces the yield, possibly below the 6.35 percent on Treasury bills.

Default Risk   Default risk refers to the probability that interest and principal will not be paid in the promised amounts on the due dates (or not paid at all). In Chapter

---

[7] Treasury bills are sold on a discount basis so the future cash flow includes principal and interest.

6, we observed that various financial reporting agencies, such as the Dominion Bond Rating Service (DBRS) and the Canadian Bond Rating Service (CBRS), compile and publish ratings of various corporate and public securities. These ratings are connected to default risk. Of course, some securities have negligible default risk, such as Canada Treasury bills. Given the purposes of investing idle corporate cash, firms typically avoid investing in marketable securities with significant default risk.

Small variations in default risk are reflected in the rates in Figure 18.7. For example, look at the rates on three alternative 90-day (three-month) investments. Since the maturities are the same, they differ only in default risk. In increasing order of default risk, the securities are Treasury bills (6.35 percent yield), bankers acceptances (6.43 percent yield), and commercial paper (6.46 percent yield). Recall from Chapter 17 that all three are unsecured paper. Treasury bills (the least risky) are backed by the credit of the government of Canada. Commercial paper (the highest risk) is backed by the credit of the issuing large corporation. Bankers acceptances are a slightly less risky variation on commercial paper as they are guaranteed by a chartered bank as well as by the issuing corporation.

Marketability   Marketability refers to how easy it is to convert an asset to cash; so marketability and liquidity mean much the same thing. Some money market instruments are much more marketable than others. At the top of the list are Treasury bills, which can be bought and sold very cheaply and very quickly in large amounts.

Taxes   Interest earned on money market securities is subject to federal and provincial corporate tax. Capital gains and dividends on common and preferred stock are taxed more lightly, but these long-term investments are subject to significant price fluctuations and most managers consider them too risky for the marketable securities portfolio. One exception is the strategy of **dividend capture**. Under this strategy portfolio managers purchase high-grade preferred stock or blue chip common stock just before a dividend payment. They hold the stock only long enough to receive the dividend. In this way, firms willing to tolerate price risk for a short period can benefit from the dividend exclusion that allows corporations to receive dividends tax free from other Canadian corporations.

dividend capture
A strategy in which an investor purchases securities to own them on the day of record and then quickly sells them; designed to attain dividends but avoid the risk of a lengthy hold.

Some Different Types of Money Market Securities

The money market securities listed in Figure 18.7 are generally highly marketable and short-term. They usually have low risk of default. They are issued by the federal government (for example, Treasury bills), domestic and foreign banks (certificates of deposit), and business corporations (commercial paper). Of the many types, we illustrate only a few of the most common here.

Treasury bills are obligations of the federal government that mature in 1, 2, 3, 6, or 12 months. They are sold at weekly auctions and traded actively over the counter by banks and investment dealers.

Commercial paper refers to short-term securities issued by finance companies, banks, and corporations. Typically, commercial paper is unsecured.[8] Maturities range from a few weeks to 270 days. There is no active secondary market in commercial paper. As a consequence, the marketability is low; however, firms that issue

---

[8] Commercial paper and bankers acceptances are sources of short-term financing for their issuers. We discuss them in more detail in Chapter 17.

commercial paper often repurchase it directly before maturity. The default risk of commercial paper depends on the financial strength of the issuer. DBRS and CBRS publish quality ratings for commercial paper. These ratings are similar to the bond ratings we discussed in Chapter 6.

As explained earlier, bankers acceptances are a form of corporate paper stamped by a chartered bank that adds its guarantee of principal and interest.

Certificates of deposit (CDs) are short-term loans to chartered banks. Rates quoted are for CDs in excess of $100,000. There are active markets in CDs of 3-month, 6-month, 9-month, and 12-month maturities particularly in the United States.

dollar swaps

Foreign currency deposits converted back into Canadian dollars at a predetermined exchange rate by chartered banks.

Dollar swaps are foreign currency deposits that will be converted or swapped back into Canadian dollars at a predetermined rate by chartered banks. They allow the Canadian treasurer to place funds in major money markets outside Canada without incurring foreign exchange risk.

Our brief look at money markets illustrates the challenges and opportunities for treasurers in the 1990s. Securitization has produced dramatic growth in bankers acceptances and commercial paper. Currency swaps are a financial engineering product driven by globalization of financial markets.

CONCEPT QUESTIONS

1. What are some reasons firms find themselves with idle cash?
2. What are some types of money market securities?
3. How does the design of money market securities reflect the trends of securitization, globalization, and financial engineering?

18.5 | SUMMARY AND CONCLUSIONS

This chapter has described the computer-based cash management systems used by large corporations in Canada and worldwide. By moving cash efficiently and maximizing the amount available for short-term investment, the treasurer adds value to the firm. Our discussion made the following key points:

1. A firm holds cash to conduct transactions and to compensate banks for the various services they render.

2. The optimal amount of cash for a firm to hold depends on the opportunity cost of holding cash and the uncertainty of future cash inflows and outflows.

3. The difference between a firm's available balance and its book balance is the firm's net float. The float reflects the fact that some cheques have not cleared and are thus uncollected.

4. The firm can use a variety of procedures to manage the collection and disbursement of cash in such a way as to speed the collection of cash and control payments. Large firms use computerized cash management systems that include over-the-counter collections and lockboxes, concentration banking, and electronic disbursements through zero-balance accounts.

5. Because of seasonal and cyclical activities, to help finance planned expenditures, or as a contingency reserve, firms temporarily find themselves with a cash surplus. The money market offers a variety of possible vehicles for parking this idle cash.

Key Terms

speculative motive (page 646)
precautionary motive (page 646)
transaction motive (page 646)
target cash balance (page 647)
adjustment costs (page 647)
float (page 650)
smart card (page 654)

lockboxes (page 655)
debit card (page 656)
same day value (page 656)
zero-balance account (page 658)
dividend capture (page 663)
dollar swaps (page 664)

Chapter Review Problem and Self-Test

18.1 **Float Measurement**   On a typical business day, a firm writes and mails cheques totaling $1,000. These cheques clear in six days on average. Simultaneously, the firm receives $1,300. The cash is available in one day on average. Calculate the disbursement float, the collection float, and the net float. How do you interpret the answer?

Answer to Self-Test Problem

18.1 The disbursement float is 6 days × $1,000 = $6,000. The collection float is one day × −$1,300 = −$1,300. The net float is $6,000 + (−$1,300) = $4,700. In other words, at any given time, the firm typically has uncashed cheques outstanding of $6,000. At the same time, it has uncollected receipts of $1,300. Thus, the firm's book balance is typically, $4,700 less than its available balance, a positive $4,700 net float.

Questions and Problems

1. **Float**   Which would a firm prefer: a net collection float or a net disbursement float? Why?

**Basic
(Questions 1–12)**

2. **Disbursement Float**   Suppose a firm has a book balance of $2 million. At the ATM (automatic teller machine), the cash manager finds out that the bank balance is $2.5 million. What is the situation here? If this is an ongoing situation, what ethical dilemma arises?

3. **Calculating Float**   In a typical month, the Bennett Corporation receives 50 cheques totaling $84,000. These are delayed five days on average. What is the average daily float?

4. **Calculating Net Float**   Each business day, on average, a company writes cheques totaling $35,000 to pay its suppliers. The usual mail and clearing time for the cheques is six days. Meanwhile, the company is receiving payments from its customers each day, in the form of cheques, totaling $45,000. The cash from the payments is available to the firm after one day.

   a. Calculate the company's disbursement float, collection float, and net float.
   b. How would your answer to part *(a)* change if the collected funds were available in five days instead of one?

5. **Costs of Float**   Perfect Systems, Inc., receives an average of $4,000 in cheques per day. The delay in processing and clearing is typically three days. The current interest rate is 0.025 percent per day.

a. What is the company's float?

b. What is the most Perfect Systems should be willing to pay today to eliminate its float?

c. What is the highest daily fee the company should be willing to pay to eliminate its float?

6. **Float and Weighted Average Delay**   A little old lady in Pasadena (a snow bird) goes to the post office once a month and picks up two cheques, one for $8,000 and one for $5,000. The larger cheque takes three days to clear after it is deposited; the smaller one takes seven days.

a. What is the total float for the month?

b. What is the average daily float?

c. What are the average daily receipts and weighted average delay?

7. **NPV and Collection Time**   Your firm has an average receipt size of $25. A bank has approached you concerning a lockbox service that will decrease your total collection time by two days. You typically receive 15,000 cheques per day. The daily interest rate is 0.015 percent. If the bank charges a fee of $100 per day, should the lockbox project be accepted? What would the net annual savings be if the service is adopted?

8. **Using Weighted Average Delay**   A mail order firm selling to the United States processes 8,000 cheques per month. Of these, 30 percent are for $50 and 70 percent are for $75. The $50 cheques are delayed two days on average; the $75 cheques are delayed three days on average.

a. What is the average daily collection float? How do you interpret your answer?

b. What is the weighted average delay? Use the result to calculate the average daily float.

c. How much should the firm be willing to pay to eliminate the float?

d. If the interest rate is 10 percent per year, calculate the daily cost of the float.

e. How much should the firm be willing to pay to reduce the weighted average float by 1.5 days?

9. **Value of Lockboxes**   Morisson Manufacturing is investigating a lockbox system to reduce its collection time. It has determined the following:

Average number of payments per day	500
Average value of payment	$1,600
Variable lockbox fee (per transaction)	$ 0.50
Daily interest rate on money market securities	0.02%

The total collection time will be reduced by two days if the lockbox system is adopted.

a. What is the PV of adopting the system?

b. What is the NPV of adopting the system?

c. What is the net cash flow per day from adopting? Per cheque?

10. **Lockboxes and Collections**   It takes Thornton Industries about six days to receive and deposit cheques from customers. Thornton's management is considering a lockbox system to reduce its collection times. It is expected that the lockbox system will reduce receipt and deposit times to four days total. Average daily collections are $90,000, and the required rate of return is 11 percent per year.

a. What is the reduction in outstanding cash balances as a result of implementing the lockbox system?

b. What is the dollar return that could be earned on these savings?

c. What is the maximum monthly charge Thornton Industries should pay for this lockbox system?

**Basic
(Continued)**

11. **Value of Delay**   The Schooner Sail Company disburses cheques every two weeks that average $300,000 and take four days to go through the mail and clear. How much interest can the company earn annually if it delays transfer of funds from an interest-bearing account that pays 0.03 percent per day for these four days? Ignore the effects of compounding interest.

12. **NPV and Reducing Float**   Stevenson Corporation has an agreement with Canadian Montreal Bank whereby the bank handles $2 million in collections a day and requires a $400,000 compensating balance. Stevenson is contemplating cancelling the agreement and dividing its eastern region so that two other banks will handle its business. Banks A and B will each handle $1 million of collections a day, and each requires a compensating balance of $250,000. Stevenson's financial management expects that collections will be accelerated by one day if the eastern region is divided. Should the company proceed with the new system? What will be the annual net savings? Assume the T-bill rate is 8 percent annually.

13. **Lockboxes and Collection Time**   Cactus Fragrances, Inc., an Arizona company, has determined that a majority of its customers are located in the Chicago area. It therefore is considering using a lockbox system offered by a Canadian bank located in Chicago. The bank has estimated that use of the system will reduce collection time by three days. Based on the following information, should the lockbox system be adopted?

**Intermediate
(Questions 13–16)**

Average number of payments per day	450
Average value of payment	$2,000
Variable lockbox fee (per transaction)	$0.40
Annual interest rate on money market securities	6.0%

How would your answer change if there were a fixed charge of $100,000 per year in addition to the variable charge?

14. **Calculating Transactions Required**   3DBase, Inc., a large computer software distributor based in Ottawa, is planning to use a lockbox system to speed collections from its customers located primarily on the West Coast. A Vancouver-area bank branch will provide this service for an annual fee of $20,000 plus 30 cents per transaction. The estimated reduction in collection and processing time is two days. If the average customer payment in this region is $3,000, how many customers each day, on average, are needed to make the system profitable for 3DBase? Treasury bills are currently yielding 5 percent per year.

15. **Marketable Securities**   For each of the short-term marketable securities given below, provide an example of the potential disadvantages the investment has for meeting a corporation's cash management goals.

a. Treasury bills

b. Ordinary preferred stock

c. Certificates of deposit (CDs)

d. Commercial paper

e. Dollar swaps

f. 10-year Canada bonds

Intermediate
(Continued)

16. **Portfolio Weights and Investment**   Your firm has $10 million to invest for 90 days in marketable securities. Look up current money market rates in a financial newspaper.

    a. What is the yield on a portfolio with equal investments in Treasury bills, commercial paper, and bankers acceptances, all 90 days in maturity?
    b. Readjust the portfolio weights to enhance the yield by increasing interest-rate and default risk. Comment briefly on your choice.
    c. What other shift would increase yield?

Suggested Readings

We have benefitted from the following books on short-term finance:

Hill, N. C., and W. L. Sartoris. *Short-Term Financial Management,* 2nd ed. New York: Macmillan, 1992, chaps. 6–10.

Scherr, Frederick C. *Modern Working Capital Management.* Englewood Cliffs, NJ: Prentice Hall, 1989.

To keep up with Canadian practices, a good source is various issues of *Canadian Treasury Management Review,* Toronto, Royal Bank of Canada.

APPENDIX   18A | # CASH MANAGEMENT MODELS

The BAT Model

The Baumol-Allais-Tobin (BAT) model is a classic means of analyzing the cash management problem. We illustrate how this model can be used to actually establish the target cash balance. It is a straightforward model and very useful for illustrating the factors in cash management and, more generally, current asset management.

To develop the BAT model, suppose the Golden Socks Corporation starts at Time 0 with a cash balance of C = $1.2 million. Each week, outflows exceed inflows by $600,000. As a result, the cash balance drops to zero at the end of Week 2. The average cash balance is the beginning balance ($1.2 million) plus the ending balance ($0) divided by 2, or ($1.2 million + $0)/2 = $600,000 over the two-week period. At the end of Week 2, Golden Socks replaces its cash by depositing another $1.2 million.

As we have described, the cash management strategy for Golden Socks is very simple and boils down to depositing $1.2 million every two weeks. This policy is shown in Figure 18A.1. Notice how the cash balance declines by $600,000 per week. Since we bring the account up to $1.2 million, the balance hits zero every two weeks. This results in the sawtooth pattern displayed in Figure 18A.1.

Implicitly, we assume the net cash outflow is the same every day and it is known with certainty. These two assumptions make the model easy to handle. We indicate what happens when they do not hold in the next section.

If C were set higher, say, at $2.4 million, cash would last four weeks before the firm would have to sell marketable securities, but the firm's average cash balance would increase to $1.2 million (from $600,000). If C were set at $600,000, cash would run out in one week and the firm would have to replenish cash more frequently, but its average cash balance would fall from $600,000 to $300,000.

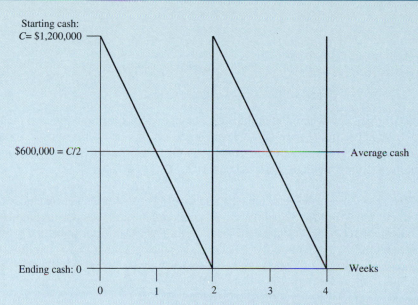

The Golden Socks Corporation starts at Time 0 with cash of $1,200,000. The balance drops to zero by the
second week. The average cash balance is $C/2 = \$1,200,000/2 = \$600,000$ over the period.

Because transaction costs must be incurred whenever cash is replenished (for
example, the brokerage costs of selling marketable securities), establishing large
initial balances lowers the trading costs connected with cash management. However,
the larger the average cash balance, the greater is the opportunity cost (the return that
could have been earned on marketable securities).

To determine the optimal strategy, Golden Socks needs to know the following
three things:

F = The fixed cost of making a securities trade to replenish cash

T = The total amount of new cash needed for transaction purposes over the
    relevant planning period, say, one year

R = The opportunity cost of holding cash; the interest rate on marketable securities

With this information, Golden Socks can determine the total costs of any particular
cash balance policy. It can then determine the optimal cash balance policy.

The Opportunity Costs   To determine the opportunity costs of holding cash, we
have to find out how much interest is forgone. Golden Socks has, on average, $\$C/2$ in
cash. This amount could be earning interest at rate R. So the total dollar opportunity
costs of cash balances are equal to the average cash balance multiplied by the interest
rate:

Opportunity costs = $(C/2) \times R$ [18A.1]

For example, the opportunity costs of various alternatives are given here
assuming that the interest rate is 10 percent:

Initial Cash Balance	Average Cash Balance	Opportunity Cost ($R = 0.10$)
C	$C/2$	$(C/2)$ x R
$4,800,000	$2,400,000	$240,000
2,400,000	1,200,000	120,000
1,200,000	600,000	60,000
600,000	300,000	30,000
300,000	150,000	15,000

In our original case where the initial cash balance is $1.2 million, the average balance is $600,000. The interest we could have earned on this (at 10 percent) is $60,000, so this is what we give up with this strategy. Notice that the opportunity cost increases as the initial (and average) cash balance rises.

The Trading Costs   To determine the total trading costs for the year, we need to know how many times Golden Socks has to sell marketable securities during the year. First, the total amount of cash disbursed during the year is $600,000 per week or $T = $600,000 × 52 weeks = $31.2 million. If the initial cash balance is set at $C = $1.2 million, Golden Socks would sell $1.2 million of marketable securities $T/C = $31.2 million/$1.2 million = 26 times per year. It costs F dollars each time, so trading costs are given by:

$31.2 million/$1.2 million $\times F = 26 \times F$

In general, the total trading costs are given by:

Trading costs $= (T/C) \times F$ [18A.2]

In this example, if F were $1,000 (an unrealistically large amount) the trading costs would be $26,000.

We can calculate the trading costs associated with some different strategies as follows:

Total Amount of Disbursements during Relevant Period	Initial Cash Balance	Trading Costs ($F = $1,000)
T	C	$(T/C) \times F$
$31,200,000	$4,800,000	$ 6,500
31,200,000	2,400,000	13,000
31,200,000	1,200,000	26,000
31,200,000	600,000	52,000
31,200,000	300,000	104,000

The Total Cost   Now that we have the opportunity costs and the trading costs, we can calculate the total cost by adding them together:

Total cost $=$ Opportunity costs $+$ Trading costs   [18A.3]
$= (C/2) \times R + (T/C) \times F$

Using these numbers, we have:

Cash Balance	Opportunity Costs	+	Trading Costs	=	Total Cost
$4,800,000	$240,000		$ 6,500		$246,500
2,400,000	120,000		13,000		133,000
1,200,000	60,000		26,000		86,000
600,000	30,000		52,000		82,000
300,000	15,000		104,000		119,000

Notice how the total cost starts at almost $250,000 and declines to about $80,000 before starting to rise again.

The Solution   We can see from the preceding schedule that a $600,000 cash balance results in the lowest total cost of the possibilities presented: $82,000. But what about $700,000 or $500,000 or other possibilities? It appears that the optimum balance is somewhere between $300,000 and $1.2 million. With this in mind, we could easily proceed by trial and error to find the optimum balance. It is not difficult to find it directly, however, so we do this next.

Take a look back at Figure 18.1. As drawn, the optimal size of the cash balance, C^*, occurs where the two lines cross. At this point, the opportunity costs and the trading costs are exactly equal. So, at C^*, we must have that:

Opportunity costs = Trading costs

$$C^*/2 \times R = (T/C^*) \times F$$

With a little algebra, we can write:

$$C^{*2} = (2T \times F)/R$$

To solve for C^*, we take the square root of both sides to get:

$$C^* = \sqrt{(2T \times F)/R} \qquad \text{[18A.4]}$$

This is the optimum initial cash balance.

For Golden Socks, we have $T = $31.2 million, $F = $1,000$, and $R = 10\%$. We can now find the optimum cash balance as:

$$C^* = \sqrt{(2 \times \$31,200,000 \times \$1,000/.10)}$$
$$= \$\sqrt{(624 \text{ billion})}$$
$$= \$789,937$$

We can verify this answer by calculating the following costs at this balance as well as a little more and a little less:

Cash Balance	Opportunity Costs	+	Trading Costs	=	Total Cost
$850,000	$42,500		$36,706		$79,206
800,000	40,000		39,000		79,000
789,937	**39,497**		**39,497**		**78,994**
750,000	37,500		41,600		79,100
700,000	35,000		44,571		79,571

The total cost at the optimum is $78,994, and it does appear to increase as we move in either direction.

E X A M P L E | 18A.1   The BAT Model

The Vulcan Corporation has cash outflows of $100 per day, seven days a week. The interest rate is 5 percent, and the fixed cost of replenishing cash balances is $10 per transaction. What is the optimal initial cash balance? What is the total cost?

The total cash needed for the year is 365 days × $100 = $36,500. From the BAT model, the optimal initial balance is:

$$C^* = \sqrt{(2T \times F)/R}$$
$$= \sqrt{2 \times \$36,500 \times \$10/.05}$$
$$= \$\sqrt{14.6 \text{ million}}$$
$$= \$3,821$$

The average cash balance is $3,821/2 = $1,911, so the opportunity cost is $1,911 × .05 = $96. Since we need $100 per day, the $3,821 balance lasts $3,821/$100 = 38.21 days. We need to resupply the account 365/38.21 = 9.6 times, so the trading (order) cost is $96. The total cost is $192.

The BAT model is possibly the simplest and most stripped-down sensible model for determining the optimal cash position. Its chief weakness is that it assumes steady, certain cash outflows. We next discuss a more involved model designed to deal with these problems. |

The Miller-Orr Model: A More General Approach

We now describe a cash management system designed to deal with cash inflows and outflows that fluctuate randomly from day to day. With this model, we again concentrate on the cash balance; in contrast to the BAT model, we assume this balance fluctuates up and down randomly and that the average change is zero.

The Basic Idea   Figure 18A.2 shows how the system works. It operates in terms of an upper limit to the amount of cash (U^*) and a lower limit (L), and a target cash balance (C^*). The firm allows its cash balance to wander around between the lower

F I G U R E 18.A2

The Miller-Orr model

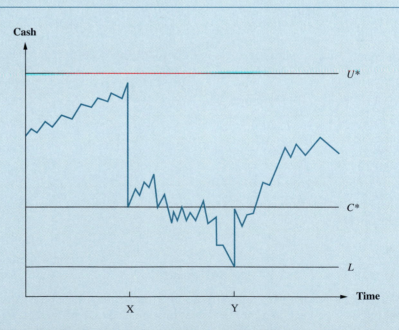

U^* is the upper control limit. L is the lower control limit. The target cash balance is C^*. As long as cash is between L and U^*, no transaction is made.

and upper limits. As long as the cash balance is somewhere between U^* and L, nothing happens.

When the cash balance reaches the upper limit (U^*), as it does at point X, the firm moves $U^* - C^*$ dollars out of the account and into marketable securities. This action moves the cash balance down to C^*. In the same way, if the cash balance falls to the lower limit (L), as it does at point Y, the firm sells $C^* - L$ worth of securities and deposits the cash in the account. This action takes the cash balance up to C^*.

Using the Model   To get started, management sets the lower limit (L). This limit is essentially a safety stock; so where it is set depends on how much risk of a cash shortfall the firm is willing to tolerate.

Like the BAT model, the optimal cash balance depends on trading costs and opportunity costs. Once again, the cost per transaction of buying and selling marketable securities, F, is assumed to be fixed. Also, the opportunity cost of holding cash is R, the interest rate per period on marketable securities.

The only extra piece of information needed is σ^2, the variance of the cash flow per period. For our purposes, the period can be anything, a day or a week, for example, as long as the interest rate and the variance are based on the same length of time.

Given L, which is set by the firm, Miller and Orr show that the cash balance target, C^*, and the upper limit, U^*, that minimize the total costs of holding cash are:[9]

$$C^* = L + (3/4 \times F \times \sigma^2/R)^{1/3} \qquad [18A.5]$$
$$U^* = 3 \times C^* - 2 \times L \qquad [18A.6]$$

Also, the average cash balance in the Miller-Orr model is:

$$\text{Average cash balance} = (4 \times C^* - L)/3 \qquad [18A.7]$$

The derivation of these expressions is relatively complex, so we do not present it here. Fortunately, as we illustrate next, the results are not difficult to use.

For example, suppose $F = \$10$, the interest rate is 1 percent per month, and the standard deviation of the monthly net cash flows is $200. The variance of the monthly net cash flows is:

$$\sigma^2 = (\$200)^2 = (\$^2)40,000$$

We assume a minimum cash balance of $L = \$100$. We can calculate the cash balance target, C^*, as:

$$\begin{aligned}
C^* &= L + (3/4 \times F \times \sigma^2/R)^{1/3} \\
&= \$100 + (3/4 \times \$10 \times (\$^2)40,000/.01)^{1/3} \\
&= \$100 + (30,000,000)^{1/3} \\
&= \$100 + 311 = \$411
\end{aligned}$$

The upper limit, U^*, is thus:

$$\begin{aligned}
U^* &= 3 \times C^* - 2 \times L \\
&= 3 \times \$411 - 2 \times \$100 \\
&= \$1,033
\end{aligned}$$

---

[9] M. H. Miller and D. Orr, "A Model of the Demand for Money by Firms," *Quarterly Journal of Economics*, August 1966.

Finally, the average cash balance is:

$$\text{Average cash balance} = (4 \times C^* - L)/3$$
$$= (4 \times \$411 - \$100)/3$$
$$= \$515$$

The advantage of the Miller-Orr model is that it improves our understanding of the problem of cash management by considering the effect of uncertainty as measured by the variation in net cash inflows.

The Miller-Orr model shows that the greater the uncertainty is (the higher σ^2 is), the greater is the difference between the target balance and the minimum balance. Similarly, the greater the uncertainty is, the higher is the upper limit and the higher is the average cash balance. These all make intuitive sense. For example, the greater the variability is, the greater is the chance of the balance dropping below the minimum. We thus keep a higher balance to guard against this happening.

| CONCEPT QUESTIONS
| **1.** What is the basic trade-off in the BAT model?
| **2.** Describe how the Miller-Orr model works.

Appendix Problems

Basic
(Questions 1–10)

1.   **Changes in Target Cash Balances**   Indicate the likely impact of each of the following on a company's target cash balance. Use the letter I to denote an increase and D to denote a decrease. Briefly explain your reasoning in each case.

   a. Commissions charged by brokers decrease.
   b. Interest rates paid on money market securities rise.
   c. The compensating balance requirement of a bank is raised.
   d. The firm's credit rating improves.
   e. The cost of borrowing increases.
   f. Direct fees for banking services are established.

2.   **Using the BAT Model**   Given the following information, calculate the target cash balance using the BAT model:

Annual interest rate	8%
Fixed order cost	$ 6
Total cash needed	$2,800

How do you interpret your answer?

3.   **Opportunity versus Trading Costs**   Goodland Corporation has an average daily cash balance of $250. Total cash needed for the year is $40,000. The interest rate is 9 percent, and replenishing the cash costs $5 each time. What are the opportunity costs of holding cash, the trading cost, and the total cost? What do you think of Goodland's strategy?

4.   **Costs and the BAT Model**   Zunder Products needs $3,000 in cash during the year for transactions and other purposes. Whenever cash runs low, it sells $750 in securities and transfers the cash in. The interest rate is 14 percent per year, and selling securities costs $80 per sale.

   a. What is the opportunity cost under the current policy? The trading cost? With no additional calculations, does Zunder keep too much or too little cash? Explain.
   b. What is the target cash balance using the BAT model?

5. **Determining Optimal Cash Balances**   The Stich Company is currently holding $600,000 in cash. It projects that over the next year its cash outflows will exceed cash inflows by $250,000 per month. How much of the current cash holding should be retained and how much should be used to increase the company's holdings of marketable securities? Each time these securities are bought or sold through a broker, the company pays a fee of $400. The annual interest rate on money market securities is 6 percent. After the initial investment of excess cash, how many times during the next 12 months will securities be sold?

Basic
(Continued)

6. **Interpreting Miller-Orr**   Sun Prime Communications, Inc., uses a Miller-Orr cash management approach with a lower limit of $25,000, an upper limit of $125,000, and a target balance of $45,000. Explain what each of these points represents and then explain how the system will work.

7. **Using Miller-Orr**   Pierce Products Corporation has a fixed cost associated with buying and selling marketable securities of $100. The interest rate is currently 0.025 percent per day, and the firm has estimated that the standard deviation of its daily net cash flows is $70. Management has set a lower limit of $1,250 on cash holdings. Calculate the target cash balance and upper limit using the Miller-Orr model. Describe how the system will work.

8. **Interpreting Miller-Orr**   Based on the Miller-Orr model, describe what will happen to the lower limit, the upper limit, and the spread (the distance between the two) if the variation in net cash flow grows. Give an intuitive explanation for why this happens. What happens if the variance drops to zero?

9. **Using Miller-Orr**   The variance of the daily cash flows for the Backwoods Whiskey Company is $1.15 million. The opportunity cost to the firm of holding cash is 10 percent per year. What should be the target cash level and the upper limit if the tolerable lower limit has been established as $30,000? The fixed cost of buying and selling securities is $500 per transaction.

10. **Using BAT**   Arbor Paper Corporation has determined that its target cash balance using the BAT model is $1,500. The total cash needed for the year is $25,000, and the order cost is $3. What interest rate must Arbor Paper be using?

CHAPTER

19

Credit and Inventory Management

When a firm sells goods and services, it can demand cash on or before the delivery date, or it can extend credit to customers and allow some delay in payment. The next few sections provide an idea of what is involved in the firm's decision to grant credit to its customers. Granting credit is investing in a customer, an investment tied to the sale of a product or service.

Why do firms grant credit? Not all do, but the practice is extremely common. The obvious reason is that offering credit is a way of stimulating sales. The costs associated with granting credit are not trivial: First, there is the chance that the customer will not pay. Second, the firm has to bear the costs of carrying the receivables. The credit policy decision thus involves a trade-off between the benefits of increased sales and the costs of granting credit. We examine this trade-off in the next sections.

This chapter also covers inventory management. Most firms hold inventories to ensure that they have finished goods to meet sales demand and raw materials and work in process when they are needed in production. Deciding how much to hold is important to managers in production and marketing. Because inventories represent a significant investment with carrying costs, the financial manager is also involved in the decision. Our discussion of inventory looks at a traditional approach that focusses on the trade-off between carrying costs and shortage costs. We also present just-in-time inventory that offers an innovative solution for large manufacturing firms.

19.1 | CREDIT AND RECEIVABLES

From an accounting perspective, when credit is granted, an account receivable is created. These receivables include credit to other firms, called *trade credit,* and credit granted consumers, called *consumer credit.* About 15 percent of all the assets of Canadian industrial firms are in the form of accounts receivable. For retail firms, the figure is much higher. So receivables obviously represent a major investment of financial resources by Canadian businesses.

Furthermore, trade credit is a very important source of financing for corporations. Looking back at Table 17.2 in Chapter 17, Canadian corporations financed about 14 percent of total assets through accounts payable, more than any other single source of short-term financing in 1989. However we look at it, receivables and receivables management are key aspects of a firm's short-term financial policy.

Components of Credit Policy

If a firm decides to grant credit to its customers, it must establish procedures for extending credit and collecting. In particular, the firm has to deal with the following components of credit policy:

1. **Terms of sale**. The terms of sale establish how the firm proposes to sell its goods and services. A basic distinction is whether the firm requires cash or extends credit. If the firm does grant credit to a customer, the terms of sale specify (perhaps implicitly) the credit period, the cash discount and discount period, and the type of credit instrument.

2. **Credit analysis**. In granting credit, a firm determines how much effort to expend trying to distinguish between customers who pay and customers who do not pay. Firms use a number of devices and procedures to determine the probability that customers will not pay, and put together, these are called *credit analysis*.

3. **Collection policy**. After credit has been granted, the firm has the potential problem of collecting the cash when it becomes due, for which it must establish a collection policy.

In the next several sections, we discuss these components of credit policy that collectively make up the decision to grant credit.

terms of sale
Conditions on which a firm sells its goods and services for cash or credit.

credit analysis
The process of determining the probability that customers will or will not pay.

collection policy
Procedures followed by a firm in collecting accounts receivable.

The Cash Flows from Granting Credit

In a previous chapter, we described the accounts receivable period as the time it takes to collect on a sale. Several events occur during that period. These are the cash flows associated with granting credit, and they can be illustrated with a cash flow diagram:

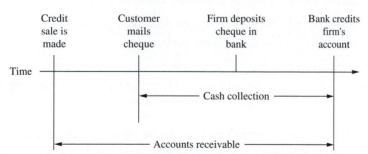

The cash flows of granting credit

As our time line indicates, the typical sequence of events when a firm grants credit is (1) the credit sale is made, (2) the customer sends a cheque to the firm, (3) the firm deposits the cheque, and (4) the firm's account is credited for the amount of the cheque.

Based on our discussion in the previous chapter, it is apparent that one of the factors influencing the receivables period is float. Thus, one way to reduce the receivables period is to speed up cheque mailing, processing, and clearing. Because we cover this subject elsewhere, we ignore float in our subsequent discussion and focus on what is likely to be the major determinant of the receivables period, credit policy. We come back to float at the end when we look at a computerized implementation of credit policy.

The Investment in Receivables

The investment in accounts receivable for any firm depends on the amount of credit sales and the average collection period. For example, if a firm's average collection period (ACP) is 30 days, at any given time there are 30 days' worth of sales outstanding. If sales run $1,000 per day, the firm's accounts receivable are equal to 30 days × $1,000 per day = $30,000.

As our example illustrates, a firm's receivables generally are equal to its average daily sales multiplied by its average collection period (ACP):

$$\text{Accounts receivable} = \text{Average daily sales} \times \text{ACP} \qquad [19.1]$$

Thus, a firm's investment in accounts receivable depends on factors that influence credit sales and collections.

We have seen the average collection period in various places, including Chapters 3 and 17. Recall that we use the terms *days' sales in receivables, receivables period,* and *average collection period* interchangeably to refer to the length of time it takes for the firm to collect on a sale.

> ### CONCEPT QUESTIONS
> **1.** What are the basic components of credit policy?
> **2.** What are the basic components of the terms of sale if a firm chooses to sell on credit?

19.2 | TERMS OF THE SALE

As we just described, the terms of a sale are made up of three distinct elements:

1. The period for which credit is granted (the credit period).
2. The cash discount and the discount period.
3. The type of credit instrument.

Within a given industry, the terms of sales are usually fairly standard, but across industries these terms vary quite a bit. In many cases, the terms of sale are remarkably archaic and literally date to previous centuries. Organized systems of trade credit that resemble current practice can be easily traced to the great fairs of medieval Europe, and they almost surely existed long before then.

Why Trade Credit Exists

Set aside the venerable history of trade credit for a moment and ask yourself why it should exist.[1] After all, it is quite easy to imagine that all sales could be for cash. From the firm's viewpoint, this would get rid of receivables carrying costs and collection costs. Bad debts would be zero (assuming the firm was careful to accept no counterfeit money).

---

[1] Our discussion draws on N. C. Hill and W. S. Sartoris, *Short-Term Financial Management,* 2nd ed. (New York: Macmillan, 1992), chap. 14.

Imagine this cash-only economy in the context of perfectly competitive product and financial markets. Competition would force companies to lower their prices to pass the savings from immediate collections on to customers. Any company that chose to grant credit to its customers would have to raise its prices accordingly to survive. A purchaser who needed financing over the operating cycle could borrow from a bank or the money market. In this perfect market environment, it would make no difference to the seller or the buyer whether credit were granted.

In practice, firms spend significant resources setting credit policy and managing its implementation. So deviations from perfect markets—market imperfections—must explain why trade credit exists. We look briefly at several imperfections and how trade credit helps to overcome them.

In practice, both the buyer and seller have imperfect information. Buyers lack perfect information on the quality of the product. For this reason, the buyer may prefer credit terms that give time to return the product if it is defective or unsuitable. When the seller offers credit, it signals potential customers that the product is of high quality and likely to provide satisfaction.[2]

In addition, in practice, any firm that grants credit or a loan lacks perfect information on the creditworthiness of the borrower. Although it is costly for a bank or other third-party lender to acquire this information, a seller that has been granting trade credit to a purchaser likely has it already. Further, the seller may have superior information on the resale value of the product serving as collateral. These information advantages may allow the seller to offer more attractive, more flexible credit terms and be more liberal in authorizing credit.

Finally, perfect markets have zero transaction costs but, in reality, it is costly to set up a bank borrowing facility or to borrow in money markets. We discussed some of the costs in Chapter 17. It may be cheaper to utilize credit from the seller.

These reasons go a long way toward explaining the popularity of trade credit. Whatever the reasons, setting credit policy involves major decisions for the firm.

The Basic Form

The easiest way to understand the terms of sale is to consider an example. For bulk candy, terms of 2/10, net 60 are common.[3] This means that customers have 60 days from the invoice date to pay the full amount. However, if payment is made within 10 days, a 2 percent cash discount can be taken.

Consider a buyer who places an order for $1,000, and assume that the terms of the sale are 2/10, net 60. The buyer has the option of paying $1,000 × (1 − .02) = $980 in 10 days, or paying the full $1,000 in 60 days.

When the terms are stated as just net 30, then the customer has 30 days from the invoice date to pay the entire $1,000, and no discount is offered for early payment.

The Credit Period

The **credit period** is the basic length of time for which credit is granted. The credit period varies widely from industry to industry, but it is almost always between 30 and 120 days. When a cash discount is offered, the credit period has two components: the net credit period and the cash discount period. In most cases, the credit period and the

credit period
The length of time that credit is granted.

---

[2] This use of signalling is very similar to dividend signalling discussed in Chapter 16. There corporations signalled the quality of projected cash flows by maintaining dividends even when earnings were down.

[3] The terms of sale cited from specific industries in this section and elsewhere are drawn from Theodore N. Beckman, *Credits and Collections: Management and Theory* (New York: McGraw-Hill, 1962).

cash discount conform to industry practice. Firms do not often deviate from the industry norm. For this reason, we focus on examples at the industry level.

The net credit period is the length of time the customer has to pay. The cash discount period, as the name suggests, is the time during which the discount is available. With 2/10, net 30, for example, the net credit period is 30 days and the cash discount period is 10 days.

The Invoice Date   The invoice date is the beginning of the credit period. An **invoice** is a written account of merchandise shipped to the buyer. For individual items, by convention, the invoice date is usually the shipping date or the billing date, *not* the date the buyer receives the goods or the bill.

Many other arrangements exist. For example, the terms of sale might be ROG, for "receipt of goods." In this case, the credit starts when the customer receives the order. This might be used when the customer is in a remote location.

End-of-month (EOM) terms are fairly common. With EOM dating, all sales made during a particular month are assumed to be made at the end of that month. This is useful when a buyer makes purchases throughout the month, but the seller bills only once a month.

For example, terms of 2/10th EOM tell the buyer to take a 2 percent discount if payment is made by the 10th of the month, otherwise the full amount is due after that. Confusingly, the end of the month is sometimes taken to be the 25th day of the month. MOM, for middle of month, is another variation.

Seasonal dating is sometimes used to encourage sales of seasonal products during the off-season. A product that is sold primarily in the spring, such as bicycles or sporting goods, can be shipped in January with credit terms of 2/10, net 30. However, the invoice might be dated May 1, so the credit period actually begins at that time. This practice encourages buyers to order early.

Length of the Credit Period   A number of factors influence the length of the credit period. One of the most important is the *buyer's* inventory period and operating cycle. All other things being equal, the shorter these are, the shorter the credit period normally is.

Based on our discussion in Chapter 17, the operating cycle has two components: the inventory period and the receivables period. The inventory period is the time it takes the buyer to acquire inventory (from us), process it, and sell it. The receivables period is the time it then takes the buyer to collect on the sale. Note that the credit period that we offer is effectively the buyer's payables period.

By extending credit, we finance a portion of our buyer's operating cycle and thereby shorten the cash cycle. When our credit period exceeds the buyer's inventory period, we are financing not only the buyer's inventory purchases but also part of the buyer's receivables.

Furthermore, if our credit period exceeds our buyer's operating cycle, we are effectively providing financing for aspects of our customer's business beyond the immediate purchase and sale of our merchandise. The reason is that the buyer has a loan from us even after the merchandise is resold, and the buyer can use that credit for other purposes. For this reason, the length of the buyer's operating cycle is often cited as an appropriate upper limit to the credit period.

A number of other factors influence the credit period. Many of these also influence our customers' operating cycles; so, once again, these are related subjects. Among the most important are:

invoice
Bill for goods or services provided by the seller to the purchaser.

1. *Perishability and collateral value.* Perishable items have relatively rapid turnover and relatively low collateral value. Credit periods are thus shorter for such goods. For example, a food wholesaler selling fresh fruit and produce might use net seven terms. Alternatively, jewelry might be sold for 5/30, net four months.

2. *Consumer demand.* Products that are well established generally have more rapid turnover. Newer or slow-moving products often have longer credit periods to entice buyers. Also, as we have seen, sellers may choose to extend much longer credit periods for off-season sales (when customer demand is low).

3. *Cost, profitability, and standardization.* Relatively inexpensive goods tend to have shorter credit periods. The same is true for relatively standardized goods and raw materials. These all tend to have lower markups and higher turnover rates, both of which lead to shorter credit periods. There are exceptions. Auto dealers, for example, generally pay for cars as they are received.

4. *Credit risk.* The greater the credit risk of the buyer, the shorter the credit period is likely to be (assuming that credit is granted at all).

5. *The size of the account.* If the account is small, the credit period is shorter. Small accounts are more costly to manage, and the customers are less important.

6. *Competition.* When the seller is in a highly competitive market, longer credit periods may be offered as a way of attracting customers.

7. *Customer type.* A single seller might offer different credit terms to different buyers. A food wholesaler, for example, might supply grocers, bakeries, and restaurants. Each group would probably have different credit terms. More generally, sellers often have both wholesale and retail customers, and they frequently quote different terms to each.

Cash Discounts

As we have seen, **cash discounts** are often part of the terms of sale. The practice of granting discounts for cash purposes goes back more than 100 years and is widespread today. One reason discounts are offered is to speed the collection of receivables. This reduces the amount of credit being offered, and the firm must trade this off against the cost of the discount.

cash discount
A discount given for a cash purchase.

Notice that when a cash discount is offered, the credit is essentially free during the discount period. The buyer only pays for the credit after the discount expires. With 2/10, net 30, a rational buyer either pays in 10 days to make the greatest possible use of the free credit or pays in 30 days to get the longest possible use of the money in exchange for giving up the discount. So, by giving up the discount, the buyer effectively gets $30 - 10 = 20$ days' credit.

Another reason for cash discounts is that they are a legal way of charging higher prices to customers that have had credit extended to them. In both Canada and the United States, the law prohibits discrimination in charging different prices to different buyers for the same product. In this sense, cash discounts are a convenient way of separately pricing the credit granted to customers.

Electronic Credit Terms   In Chapter 18, we showed how electronic disbursements saved time and money. To induce buyers to pay electronically or to give discounts to large customers, some firms offer discounts of around 1 percent for electronic payment one day after the goods are delivered. If electronic disbursement is coupled with electronic data interchange, the buyer and seller negotiate the discount and the date for payment.

Cost of the Credit   In our examples, it might seem that the discounts are rather small. With 2/10, net 30, for example, early payment gets the buyer only a 2 percent discount. Does this provide a significant incentive for early payment? The answer is yes because the implicit interest rate is extremely high.

To see why the discount is important, we will calculate the cost to the buyer of not paying early. To do this, we will find the interest rate the buyer is effectively paying for the trade credit. Suppose the order is for $1,000. The buyer can pay $980 in 10 days or wait another 20 days and pay $1,000. It's obvious that the buyer is effectively borrowing $980 for 20 days and that the buyer pays $20 in interest on the "loan." What's the interest rate?

This interest is ordinary discount interest, which we discussed in Chapter 5. With $20 in interest on $980 borrowed, the rate is $20/$980 = 2.0408%. This is relatively low, but remember that this is the rate per 20-day period. There are 365/20 = 18.25 such periods in a year, so, by not taking the discount, the buyer is paying an effective annual rate (EAR) of:

$$EAR = (1.020408)^{18.25} - 1 = 44.6\%$$

From the buyer's point of view, this is an expensive source of financing!

Given that the interest rate is so high here, it is unlikely that the seller benefits from early payment. Ignoring the possibility of default by the buyer, the decision by a customer to forgo the discount almost surely works to the seller's advantage.

E X A M P L E | 19.1   What's the Rate?

Ordinary tiles are often sold 3/30, net 60. What effective annual rate does a buyer pay by not taking the discount? What would the APR be if one were quoted?

Here we have 3 percent discount interest on 60 − 30 = 30 days' credit. The rate per 30 days is .03/.97 = 3.093%. There are 365/30 = 12.17 such periods in a year, so the effective annual rate is:

$$EAR = (1.03093)^{12.17} - 1 = 44.9\%$$

The APR, as always, would be calculated by multiplying the rate per period by the number of periods:

$$APR = .03093 \times 12.17 = 37.6\%$$

An interest rate calculated like this APR is often quoted as the cost of the trade credit, and, as this example illustrates, can seriously understate the true cost. **|**

The Cash Discount and the ACP   To the extent that a cash discount encourages customers to pay early, it shortens the receivables period and, all other things being equal, reduces the firm's investment in receivables.

For example, suppose a firm currently has terms of net 30 and an ACP of 30 days. If it offers terms of 2/10, net 30, perhaps 50 percent of its customers (in terms of volume of purchases) would pay in 10 days. The remaining customers would still take an average of 30 days to pay. What would the new average collection period (ACP) be? If the firm's annual sales are $15 million (before discounts), what happens to the investment in receivables?

If half of the customers take 10 days to pay and half take 30, the new average collection period is:

New ACP = .50 × 10 days + .50 × 30 days = 20 days

The ACP thus falls from 30 days to 20 days. Average daily sales are $15 million/365 = $41,096 per day. Receivables thus fall by $41,096 × 10 = $410,960.

Credit Instruments

The **credit instrument** is the basic evidence of indebtedness. Most trade credit is offered on *open account*. This means the only formal instrument of credit is the invoice that is sent with the shipment of goods and that the customer signs as evidence the goods have been received. Afterward, the firm and its customers record the exchange on their books of account.

At times, the firm may require the customer to sign a *promissory note*. This is a basic IOU and might be used when the order is large, when there is no cash discount involved, and when the firm anticipates a problem in collections. Promissory notes are not common, but they can eliminate controversies later about the existence of debt.

One problem with promissory notes is that they are signed after delivery of the goods. To obtain a credit commitment from a customer before the goods are delivered, a firm arranges a *commercial draft*. Typically, the firm draws up a commercial draft calling for the customer to pay a specific amount by a specified date. The draft is then sent to the customer's bank with the shipping invoices.

When immediate payment on the draft is required, it is called a *sight draft*. If immediate payment is not required, the draft is a *time draft*. When the draft is presented and the buyer accepts it—meaning the buyer promises to pay it in the future—it is called a *trade acceptance* and is sent back to the selling firm. The seller can keep the acceptance, in effect providing trade credit financing to the buyer, or sell it to someone else. The third party buying the acceptance is a money market investor. This investor is now financing the buyer and the seller receives immediate payment less discount interest.

To make the trade acceptance more salable, a chartered bank may stamp it, meaning the bank is guaranteeing payment. Then the draft becomes a *bankers acceptance*. This arrangement is common in international trade and widely used domestically. Bankers acceptances are actively traded in the money market as we discussed in Chapter 18.

A firm can also use a conditional sales contract as a credit instrument. This is an arrangement where the firm retains legal ownership of the goods until the customer has completed payment. Conditional sales contracts usually are paid in installments and have an interest cost built into them.

credit instrument
The evidence of indebtedness.

> CONCEPT QUESTIONS
> **1.** What considerations enter into the determination of the terms of sale?
> **2.** Explain what terms of "3/45, net 90" mean. What is the implicit interest rate?

19.3 | ANALYZING CREDIT POLICY

In this section, we take a closer look at the factors that influence the decision to grant credit. Granting credit makes sense only if the NPV from doing so is positive. We thus need to look at the NPV of the decision to grant credit.

Credit Policy Effects

In evaluating credit policy, there are five basic factors to consider:

1. *Revenue effects.* When the firm grants credit, there is a delay in revenue collections as some customers take advantage of the credit offered and pay later. However, the firm may be able to charge a higher price if it grants credit and it may be able to increase the quantity sold. Total revenues may thus increase.

2. *Cost effects.* Although the firm may experience delayed revenues if it grants credit, it still incurs the costs of sales immediately. Whether or not the firm sells for cash or credit, it still has to acquire or produce the merchandise (and pay for it).

3. *The cost of debt.* When the firm grants credit, it must arrange to finance the resulting receivables. As a result, the firm's cost of short-term borrowing is a factor in the decision to grant credit.[4]

4. *The probability of nonpayment.* If the firm grants credit, some percentage of the credit buyers do not pay. This can't happen, of course, if the firm sells for cash.

5. *The cash discount.* When the firm offers a cash discount as part of its credit terms, some customers choose to pay early to take advantage of the discount.

Evaluating a Proposed Credit Policy

To illustrate how credit policy can be analyzed, we start with a relatively simple case. Locust Software has been in existence for two years; it is one of several successful firms that develop computer programs. Currently, Locust sells for cash only.

Locust is evaluating a request from some major customers to change its current policy to net 30 days. To analyze this proposal, we define the following:

P = Price per unit

v = Variable cost per unit

Q = Current quantity sold per month

Q' = Quantity sold under new policy

R = Monthly required return

For now, we ignore discounts and the possibility of default. Also, we ignore taxes because they don't affect our conclusions.

NPV of Switching Policies   To illustrate the NPV of switching credit policies, suppose we had the following for Locust:

P = $49

v = $20

Q = 100

Q' = 110

---

[4] The cost of short-term debt is not necessarily the required return on receivables, although it is commonly assumed to be. As always, the required return on an investment depends on the risk of the investment, not the source of the financing. The buyer's cost of short-term debt is closer in spirit to the correct rate. We maintain the implicit assumption that the seller and the buyer have the same short-term debt cost. In any case, the time periods in credit decisions are relatively short, so a relatively small error in the discount rate does not have a large effect on our estimated NPV.

If the required return is 2 percent per month, should Locust make the switch?

Currently, Locust has monthly sales of $P \times Q = \$4,900$. Variable costs each month are $v \times Q = \$2,000$, so the monthly cash flow from this activity is:

$$\text{Cash flow (old policy)} = (P - v)Q \qquad\qquad [19.2]$$
$$= (\$49 - 20) \times 100$$
$$= \$2,900$$

This is not the total cash flow for Locust, of course, but it is all that we need to look at because fixed costs and other components of cash flow are the same whether or not the switch is made.

If Locust does switch to net 30 days on sales, the quantity sold rises to $Q' = 110$. Monthly revenues increase to $P \times Q'$, and costs are $v \times Q'$. The monthly cash flow under the new policy is thus:

$$\text{Cash flow (new policy)} = (P - v)Q' \qquad\qquad [19.3]$$
$$= (\$49 - 20) \times 110$$
$$= \$3,190$$

Going back to Chapter 8, the relevant incremental cash flow is the difference between the new and old cash flows:

$$\text{Incremental cash inflow} = (P - v)(Q' - Q)$$
$$= (\$49 - 20) \times (110 - 100)$$
$$= \$290$$

This says the benefit each month of changing policies is equal to the gross profit per unit sold $(P - v) = \$29$, multiplied by the increase in sales $(Q' - Q) = 10$. The present value of the future incremental cash flows is thus:

$$\text{PV} = [(P - v)(Q' - Q)]/R \qquad\qquad [19.4]$$

For Locust, this present value works out to be:

$$\text{PV} = (\$29 \times 10)/.02 = \$14,500$$

Notice that we have treated the monthly cash flow as a perpetuity since the same benefit would be realized each month forever.

Now that we know the benefit of switching, what's the cost? There are two components to consider: First, since the quantity sold rises from Q to Q', Locust has to produce $Q' - Q$ more units today at a cost of $v(Q' - Q) = \$20 \times (110 - 100) = \$200$. Second, the sales that would have been collected this month under the current policy $(P \times Q = \$4,900)$ are not collected. This happens because the sales made this month won't be collected until 30 days later under the new policy. The cost of the switch is the sum of these two components:

$$\text{Cost of switching} = PQ + v(Q' - Q) \qquad\qquad [19.5]$$

For Locust, this cost would be $\$4,900 + 200 = \$5,100$.

Putting it all together, the NPV of the switch is:

$$\text{NPV of switching} = -[PQ + v(Q' - Q)] + (P - v)(Q' - Q)/R \qquad\qquad [19.6]$$

For Locust, the cost of switching is $\$5,100$. As we saw, the benefit is $\$290$ per month, forever. At 2 percent per month, the NPV is:

$$NPV = -\$5,100 + \$290/.02$$
$$= -\$5,100 + 14,500$$
$$= \$9,400$$

Therefore, the switch is very profitable.

E X A M P L E | 19.2   **We'd Rather Fight than Switch**

Suppose a company is considering a switch from all cash to net 30, but the quantity sold is not expected to change. What is the NPV of the switch? Explain.

In this case, $Q' - Q$ is zero, so the NPV is just $-P \times Q$. What this says is that the effect of the switch is simply to postpone one month's collections forever, with no benefit from doing so.

A Break-Even Application   Based on our discussion thus far, the key variable for Locust is $Q' - Q$, the increase in unit sales. The projected increase of 10 units is only an estimate, so there is some forecasting risk. Under the circumstances, it's natural to wonder what increase in unit sales is necessary to break even.

Earlier, the NPV of the switch was defined as:

$$NPV = -[PQ + v(Q' - Q)] + (P - v)(Q' - Q)/R$$

We can calculate the break-even point explicitly by setting the NPV equal to zero and solving for $(Q' - Q)$:

$$NPV = 0 = -[PQ + v(Q' - Q)] + (P - v)(Q' - Q)/R \qquad [19.7]$$
$$Q' - Q = (PQ)/[(P - v)/R - v]$$

For Locust, the break-even sales increase is thus:

$$Q' - Q = \$4,900/[\$29/.02 - \$20]$$
$$= 3.43 \text{ units}$$

This tells us that the switch is a good idea as long as we are confident we can sell at least 3.43 more units.

CONCEPT QUESTIONS

1. What are the important effects to consider in a decision to offer credit?
2. Explain how to estimate the NPV of a credit policy switch.

19.4 | MORE ON CREDIT POLICY ANALYSIS

This section takes a closer look at credit policy analysis by investigating some alternative approaches and by examining the effect of cash discounts and the possibility of non-payment.

Two Alternative Approaches

Now that we know how to analyze the NPV of a proposed credit policy switch, we discuss two alternative approaches: the "one-shot" approach and the accounts receivable approach. These are very common means of analysis; our goal is to show that these two and our NPV approach are all the same. Afterward, we use whichever of the three is most convenient.

The One-Shot Approach If the switch is not made, Locust would have a net cash flow this month of $(P - v)Q = \$29 \times 100 = \$2,900$. If the switch is made, Locust would invest $vQ' = \$20 \times 110 = \$2,200$ this month and receive $PQ' = \$49 \times 110 = \$5,390$ next month. Suppose we ignore all other months and cash flows and view this as a one-shot investment. Is Locust better off with $2,900 in cash this month, or should Locust invest the $2,200 to get $5,390 next month?

The present value of the $5,390 to be received next month is $5,390/1.02 = $5,284.31; the cost is $2,200, so the net benefit is $5,284.31 - 2,200 = $3,084.31. If we compare this to the net cash flow of $2,900 under the current policy, Locust should switch. The NPV is $3,084.31 - 2,900 = $184.31.

In effect, Locust can repeat this one-shot investment every month and thereby generate an NPV of $184.31 every month (including the current one). The PV of this series of NPVs is:

$$\text{Present value} = \$184.31 + \$184.31/.02 = \$9,400$$

This PV is the same as our previous answer.

The Accounts Receivable Approach Our second approach is the one that is most commonly discussed and is very useful. By extending credit, the firm increases its cash flow through increased gross profits. However, the firm must increase its investment in receivables and bear the carrying cost of doing so. The accounts receivable approach focusses on the expense of the incremental investment in receivables compared to the increased gross profit.

As we have seen, the monthly benefit from extending credit is given by the gross profit per unit $(P - v)$ multiplied by the increase in quantity sold $(Q' - Q)$. For Locust, this benefit was $(\$49 - 20) \times (110 - 100) = \$290$ per month.

If Locust makes the switch, receivables rise from zero (since there are no credit sales) to PQ', so Locust must invest in receivables. The necessary investment has two components: The first part is what Locust would have collected under the old policy (PQ). Locust must carry this amount in receivables each month because collections are delayed by 30 days.

The second part is related to the increase in receivables that results from the increase in sales. Since unit sales increase from Q to Q', Locust must produce this quantity today even though it won't collect for 30 days. The actual cost to Locust of producing the extra quantity is equal to v per unit, so the investment necessary to provide the extra quantity sold is $v(Q' - Q)$.

In sum, if Locust switches, its investment in receivables is equal to the $P \times Q$ in revenues that are given up plus an additional $v(Q' - Q)$ in production costs:

$$\text{Incremental investment in receivables} = PQ + v(Q' - Q)$$

The required return on this investment (the carrying cost of the receivables) is R per month; so, for Locust, the accounts receivable carrying cost is:

$$\begin{aligned}
\text{Carrying cost} &= [PQ + v(Q' - Q)] \times R \\
&= [\$4,900 + 200] \times .02 \\
&= \$102 \text{ per month}
\end{aligned}$$

Since the monthly benefit is $290 and the cost per month is only $102, the net benefit per month is $290 - 102 = $188 per month. Locust earns this $188 every month, so the PV of the switch is:

$$\text{Present value} = \$188/.02$$
$$= \$9,400$$

Again, this is the same figure we previously calculated.

One of the advantages of looking at the accounts receivable approach is that it helps us interpret our earlier NPV calculation. As we have seen, the investment in receivables necessary to make the switch is $PQ + v(Q' - Q)$. If you look back at our original NPV calculation, this is precisely what we had as the cost to Locust of making the switch. Our earlier NPV calculation thus amounts to a comparison of the incremental investment in receivables to the PV of the increased future cash flows.

There is one final thing to notice. The increase in accounts receivable is PQ', and this amount corresponds to the amount of receivables shown on the balance sheet. However, the incremental investment in receivables is $PQ + v(Q' - Q)$. It is straightforward to verify that this second quantity is smaller by $(P - v)(Q' - Q)$. This difference is the gross profit on the new sales, which Locust does not actually have to put up to switch credit policies.

Put another way, whenever we extend credit to a new customer who would not otherwise pay cash, all we risk is our cost, not the full sales price. We discuss this point in greater detail later.

E X A M P L E | 19.3   Extra Credit

Looking back at Locust Software, determine the NPV of the switch if the quantity sold is projected to increase by only 5 units instead of 10. What will be the investment in receivables? What is the carrying cost? What is the monthly net benefit from switching?

If the switch is made, Locust gives up $P \times Q = \$4,900$ today. An extra five units have to be produced at a cost of $20 each, so the cost of switching is $\$4,900 + (5 \times \$20) = \$5,000$. The benefit of selling the extra five units each month is $5 \times (\$49 - 20) = \$145$. The NPV of the switch is $- \$5,000 + \$145/.02 = \$2,250$, so it's still profitable.

The $5,000 cost of switching can be interpreted as the investment in receivables. At 2 percent per month, the carrying cost is $.02 \times \$5,000 = \$100$. Since the benefit each month is $145, the net benefit from switching is $45 per month ($\$145 - \$100$). Notice that the PV of $45 per month forever at 2 percent is $\$45/.02 = \$2,250$ as we calculated. **|**

Discounts and Default Risk

We now look at cash discounts, default risk, and the relationship between the two. To get started, we define the following:

π = Percentage of credit sales that go uncollected

d = Percentage discount allowed for cash customers

P' = Credit price (the no-discount price)

The cash price (P) is equal to the credit price (P') multiplied by $(1 - d)$: $P = P' (1 - d)$ or, equivalently, $P' = P/(1 - d)$.

The situation at Locust is now a little bit more complicated. If a switch is made from the current policy of no credit, the benefit to the switch comes from both the higher price (P') and, potentially, the increased quantity sold (Q').

Furthermore, in our previous case, it was reasonable to assume that all customers took the credit since it was free. Now, not all customers take the credit because a discount is offered. In addition, of the customers who do take the credit offered, a certain percentage (π) do not pay.

To simplify the following discussion, we assume the quantity sold *(Q)* is not affected by the switch. This assumption isn't crucial, but it does cut down on the work (see Problem 23 at the end of the chapter). We also assume that all customers take the credit terms. This assumption also isn't crucial. It actually doesn't matter what percentage of our customers take the offered credit.[5]

NPV of the Credit Decision   Currently, Locust sells Q units at a price of $P = \$49$. Locust is considering a new policy that involves 30 days' credit and an increase in price to $P' = \$50$ on credit sales. The cash price remains at $49, so Locust is effectively allowing a discount of ($50 − $49)/$50 = 2% for cash.

What is the NPV to Locust of extending credit? To answer, note that Locust is already receiving $(P - v)Q$ every month. With the new, higher price, this rises to $(P' - v)Q$ assuming that everybody pays. However, since π percent of sales would not be collected, Locust collects only on $(1 - \pi) \times P'Q$; so net receipts are $[(1 - \pi) P' - v] \times Q$.

The net effect of the switch for Locust is thus the difference between the cash flows under the new policy and the old policy:

Net incremental cash flow $= [(1 - \pi)P' - v] \times Q - (P - v) \times Q$

Since $P = P' \times (1 - d)$, this simplifies to:[6]

Net incremental cash flow $= P'Q \times (d - \pi)$ [19.8]

If Locust does make the switch, the cost of the investment in receivables is just $P \times Q$ since $Q = Q'$. The NPV of the switch is thus:

$$\text{NPV} = -PQ + P'Q \times (d - \pi)/R$$ [19.9]

For example, suppose that, based on industry experience, the percentage of deadbeats (π) is 1 percent. What is the NPV of changing credit terms for Locust? We can plug in the relevant numbers as follows:

$$
\begin{aligned}
\text{NPV} &= -PQ + P'Q \times (d - \pi)/R \\
&= -\$49 \times 100 + \$50 \times 100 \times (.02 - .01)/.02 \\
&= -\$2,400
\end{aligned}
$$

Since the NPV of the change is negative, Locust shouldn't switch.

---

[5] The reason is that all customers are offered the same terms. If the NPV of offering credit is $100, assuming that all customers switch, it is $50 if only 50 percent of our customers switch. The hidden assumption is that the default rate is a constant percentage of credit sales.

[6] To see this, note that the net incremental cash flow is:

Cash flow $= [(1 - \pi) \times P' - v] \times Q - (P - v) \times Q$

$\qquad\quad = [(1 - \pi) \times P' - P] \times Q$

Since $P = P' \times (1 - d)$, this can be written as:

Net incremental cash flow $= [(1 - \pi) \times P' - (1 - d) \times P'] \times Q$

$\qquad\qquad\qquad\qquad\quad = P' \times Q \times (d - \pi)$

In our expression for NPV, the key elements are the cash discount percentage *(d)* and the default rate (π). One thing we see immediately: If the percentage of sales that goes uncollected exceeds the discount percentage, $d - \pi$ is negative. Obviously, the NPV of the switch would be negative as well. More generally, our result tells us that the decision to grant credit here is a trade-off between getting a higher price, thereby increasing sales, and not collecting on some fraction of those sales.

With this in mind, $P'Q \times (d - \pi)$ is the increase in sales less the portion of the increase that won't be collected. This increase is the incremental cash inflow from the switch in credit policy. If d is 5 percent and π is 2 percent, for example, loosely speaking, revenues are increasing by 5 percent because of the higher price, but collections rise by only 3 percent since the default rate is 2 percent. Unless $d > \pi$, we actually have a decrease in cash inflows from the switch.

A Break-Even Application   Since the discount percentage *(d)* is controlled by the firm, the key unknown is the default rate (π). What is the break-even default rate for Locust Software?

We can answer by finding the default rate that makes the NPV equal to zero.

$$\text{NPV} = 0 = -PQ + P'Q \times (d - \pi)/R$$

Rearranging things a bit:

$$PR = P'(d - \pi)$$
$$\pi = d - R \times (1 - d)$$

For Locust, the break-even default rate works out to be:

$$\pi = .02 - .02 \times (.98)$$
$$= .0004$$
$$= .04\%$$

This is quite small because the implicit interest rate Locust is charging its credit customers (2 percent discount interest per month, or about $.02/.98 = 2.0408\%$) is only slightly greater than the required return of 2 percent per month. As a result, there's not much room for defaults if the switch is going to make sense.

> CONCEPT QUESTIONS
>
> 1. What is the incremental investment that a firm must make in receivables if credit is extended?
> 2. Describe the trade-off between the default rate and the cash discount.

19.5 | OPTIMAL CREDIT POLICY

So far, we've discussed how to compute net present value for a switch in credit policy. We have not discussed the optimal amount of credit or the optimal credit policy. In principle, the optimal amount of credit is determined where the incremental cash flows from increased sales are exactly equal to the incremental costs of carrying the increased investment in accounts receivable.

The Total Credit Cost Curve

The trade-off between granting credit and not granting credit isn't hard to identify, but it is difficult to quantify precisely. As a result, we can only describe an optimal credit policy.

To begin, the carrying costs associated with granting credit come in three forms:

1. The required return on receivables.
2. The losses from bad debts.
3. The costs of managing credit and credit collections.

We have already discussed the first and second of these. Making up the third cost of managing credit are the expenses associated with running the credit department. Firms that don't grant credit have no such department and no such expense. These three costs all increase as credit policy is relaxed.

If a firm has a very restrictive credit policy, all the preceding costs are low. In this case, the firm has a shortage of credit, so there is an opportunity cost. This opportunity cost is the extra potential profit from credit sales that is lost because credit is refused. This forgone benefit comes from two sources, the increase in quantity sold, Q' versus Q, and, potentially, a higher price. These costs go down as credit policy is relaxed.

The sum of the carrying costs and the opportunity costs of a particular credit policy is called the total **credit cost curve**. We have drawn such a curve in Figure 19.1. As this figure illustrates, there is a point where the total credit cost is minimized. This point corresponds to the optimal amount of credit or, equivalently, the optimal investment in receivables.

If the firm extends more credit than this minimum, the additional net cash flow from new customers does not cover the carrying costs of the investment in receivables. If the level of receivables is less than this amount, the firm is forgoing valuable profit opportunities.

In general, the costs and benefits from extending credit depend on the characteristics of particular firms and industries. All other things being equal, for example, it is likely that firms with (1) excess capacity, (2) low variable operating costs, and (3) repeat customers extend credit more liberally than otherwise. See if you can explain why each of these contributes to a more liberal credit policy.

credit cost curve *Graphical representation of the sum of the carrying costs and the opportunity costs of a credit policy.*

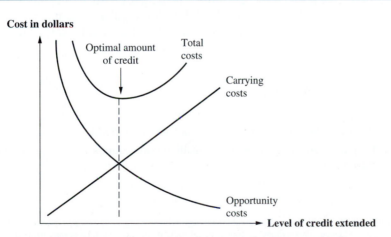

Cost in dollars

Optimal amount of credit

Total costs

Carrying costs

Opportunity costs

Level of credit extended

Carrying costs are the cash flows that must be incurred when credit is granted. They are positively related to the amount of credit extended.
Opportunity costs are the lost sales from refusing credit. These costs go down when credit is granted.

Organizing the Credit Function

captive finance company
Wholly owned subsidiary that handles credit extension and receivables financing through commercial paper.

As we stated earlier, firms selling only for cash save the expense of running a credit department. In practice, firms that do grant credit may achieve some of these savings by contracting out all or part of the credit function to a factor, an insurance company, or a **captive finance company**. Chapter 17 discussed factoring, an arrangement where the firm sells its receivables to a factor that takes on all responsibility for credit checking, authorization, and collection. The factor also guarantees payment, ruling out defaults. Factors often provide accounts receivable financing as well. Small firms may find factoring cheaper than an in-house credit department.

Firms that run internal credit operations are self-insured against default risk. An alternative is to buy credit insurance through an insurance company. The insurance company offers coverage up to a preset dollar limit for accounts. As you would expect, accounts with a higher credit rating merit higher insurance limits. Exporters may qualify for credit insurance through the Export Development Corporation, a Crown corporation of the federal government.

Large corporations commonly extend credit through a wholly owned subsidiary called a captive finance company, instead of a credit department. General Motors Corporation, for example, finances its dealers and car buyers through General Motors Acceptance Corporation (GMAC). Consumer and dealer receivables are the assets of GMAC and they are financed largely through commercial paper. Setting up the credit function as a separate legal entity has potential advantages in facilitating borrowing against receivables. Since they are segregated on the balance sheet of a captive, the receivables may make better collateral. As a result, the captive may be able to carry more debt and save on borrowing costs.[7]

A related issue in credit administration, whether through a finance captive or in-house, is the importance of having a set of written credit policies.[8] The policy covers credit terms, the information needed for credit analysis, collection procedures and the monitoring of receivables. Having the policy clearly stated helps control possible conflicts between the credit department and sales. For example, during the recession of 1991-92, some Canadian companies tightened their credit granting rules to offset the higher probability of customer bankruptcy. Other companies eased credit to promote sales and to provide flexibility for regular customers. The decision depends on the considerations we analyzed earlier. Either way, sales and credit have to work together.

> CONCEPT QUESTIONS
>
> **1.** What are the carrying costs of granting credit?
> **2.** What are the opportunity costs of not granting credit?
> **3.** Why do many large U.S. and Canadian corporations form captive finance subsidiaries?

---

[7] The trend toward securitization of receivables through wholly owned subsidiaries discussed in Chapter 17 is supporting evidence. This somewhat controversial view of finance captives comes from G. S. Roberts and J. A. Viscione, "Captive Finance Subsidiaries and the M-Form Hypothesis," *Bell Journal of Economics,* Spring 1981, pp. 285–95.

[8] Our discussion draws on "A Written Credit Policy Can Overcome a Host of Potential Problems," Joint Venture Supplement, *Financial Post,* June 20, 1991.

19.6 | CREDIT ANALYSIS

Thus far, we have focussed on establishing credit terms. Once a firm decides to grant credit to its customers, it must then establish guidelines for determining who is allowed to buy on credit as well as the credit limits to be set. Since the forces of competition often leave a firm little discretion in setting credit terms, credit managers focus on credit analysis, along with collection and receivables monitoring. Credit analysis refers to the process of deciding whether to extend credit to a particular customer. It usually involves two steps: gathering relevant information and determining creditworthiness.

When Should Credit Be Granted?

Imagine that a firm is trying to decide whether to grant credit to a customer. This decision can get complicated. For example, the answer depends on what happens if credit is refused. Will the customer simply pay cash or will the customer not make the purchase? To avoid this and other difficulties, we use some special cases to illustrate the key points.

A Onetime Sale   We start by considering the simplest case. A new customer wishes to buy one unit on credit at a price of P' per unit. If credit is refused, the customer would not make a purchase.

Furthermore, we assume that, if credit is granted, in one month, the customer either pays up or defaults. The probability of the second of these events is π. In this case, the probability (π) can be interpreted as the percentage of new customers who do not pay. Our business does not have repeat customers, so this is strictly a one-time sale. Finally, the required return on receivables is R per month and the variable cost is v per unit.

The analysis here is straightforward. If the firm refuses credit, the incremental cash flow is zero. If it grants credit, it spends v (the variable cost) this month and expects to collect $(1 - \pi)P'$ next month. The NPV of granting credit is:

$$NPV = -v + (1 - \pi)P'/(1 + R) \tag{19.10}$$

For example, for Locust Software, this NPV is:

$$NPV = -\$20 + (1 - \pi) \times \$50/(1.02)$$

With, say, a 20 percent rate of default, this works out to be:

$$NPV = -\$20 + .80 \times \$50/1.02 = \$19.22$$

Therefore, credit should be granted.

Our example illustrates an important point. In granting credit to a new customer, a firm risks its variable cost (v). It stands to gain the full price (P'). For a new customer, then, credit may be granted even if the default probability is high. For example, the break-even probability can be determined by setting the NPV equal to zero and solving for π:

$$NPV = 0 = -\$20 + (1 - \pi) \times \$50/(1.02)$$
$$(1 - \pi) = \$20/\$50 \times 1.02$$
$$\pi = 59.2\%$$

Locust should extend credit as long as there is at least a $1 - .592 = 40.8\%$ chance or better of collecting. This explains why firms with higher markups tend to have looser credit terms.

A common rule of thumb restates this information by asking, how many good accounts do we have to sell and collect to make up for the mistake of one write-off? Working with accounting numbers instead of NPVs, we can restate the break-even point as follows:

$$\text{Profit} = 0 = -\text{variable cost} \times \text{probability of loss} + \text{profit margin}$$
$$\times \text{probability of payment}$$
$$0 = -v \times \pi + (P' - v)(1 - \pi)$$

In the Locust example, we have at the break-even point:

$$\text{Profit} = 0 = -\$20 \times \pi + (\$50 - \$20)(1 - \pi)$$

With a little algebra, we can solve for $\pi = 60$ percent the same as we had earlier except for rounding error due to ignoring the present value. Notice that the break-even probability of default is simply the profit margin = $\$30/\$50 = 60\%$. This makes sense since the seller breaks even if losses offset profits. Business people interpret this as saying that for every write-off we have to sell and collect around .6 good accounts.

Finally, notice that the break-even percentage of 60 percent is much higher than the break-even percentage of .04 percent we calculated earlier, because the earlier percentage was calculated assuming that $Q = Q'$, implying there are no new customers. The percentage calculated here applies to a potential new customer only.

The important difference is that, if we extend credit to an old customer, we risk the total sales price (P), since this is what we collect if we do not extend credit. If we extend credit to a new customer, we risk only our variable cost.

E X A M P L E | 19.4   **Good and Bad Accounts at a Financial Institution**

Suppose a lending officer at a chartered bank or other financial institution lends $\$1,000$ to a customer who defaults completely. When this happens the lender has to write off the full $\$1,000$. How many good $\$1,000$ loans, paid in full and on time, does the lender have to make to offset the loss and break even on the lending portfolio?

spread

The gap between the interest rate a bank pays on deposits and the rate it charges on loans.

To answer the question, we need to know the profit margin on loans. In banking this is called the **spread** between the lending rate and the cost of funds to the bank. The spread varies over the interest rate cycle but is usually around 2 or 3 percent. Supposing the spread is 2.5 percent, the bank makes $\$25$ on every $\$1,000$ loan. This means the lender must make $\$1,000/\$25 = 40$ good loans for every write-off. Our example illustrates one reason banks are conservative lenders. Low spreads leave little room for loan losses. |

Repeat Business   A second, very important factor to keep in mind is the possibility of repeat business. We can illustrate this by extending our onetime example. We make one important assumption: A new customer who does not default the first time remains a customer forever and never defaults. If the firm grants credit, it spends v this month. Next month, it either gets nothing if the customer defaults or it gets P if the customer pays. If the customer does pay, he or she buys another unit on credit and the firm spends v again. The net cash inflow for the month is thus $P - v$. In every subsequent month, this same $P - v$ occurs as the customer pays for the previous month's order and places a new one.

It follows from our discussion that, in one month, the firm has $0 with probability π. With probability $(1 - \pi)$, however, the firm has a new customer. The value of a new customer is equal to present value of $(P - v)$ every month forever:

$$PV = (P - v)/R$$

The NPV of extending credit is therefore:

$$NPV = -v + (1 - \pi)(P - v)/R \qquad [19.11]$$

For Locust, this is:

$$NPV = -\$20 + (1 - \pi) \times (\$49 - \$20)/.02$$
$$= -\$20 + (1 - \pi) \times \$1,450$$

Even if the probability of default is 90 percent, the NPV is:

$$NPV = -\$20 + .10 \times \$1,450 = \$125$$

Locust should extend credit unless default is a virtual certainty. The reason is that it costs only $20 to find out who is a good customer and who is not. A good customer is worth $1,450, however, so Locust can afford quite a few defaults.

Our repeat business example probably exaggerates the acceptable default probability, but it does illustrate that often the best way to do credit analysis is simply to extend credit to almost anyone. It also points out that the possibility of repeat business is a crucial consideration. In such cases, the important thing is to control the amount of credit initially offered so the possible loss is limited. The amount can be increased with time. Most often, the best predictor of whether customers will pay in the future is whether they have paid in the past.

Credit Information

If a firm does want credit information on customers, there are a number of sources. Information commonly used to assess creditworthiness includes the following:

1. *Financial statements.* A firm can ask a customer to supply financial statement information such as balance sheets and income statements. Minimum standards and rules of thumb based on financial ratios like the ones we discussed in Chapter 3 can be used as a basis for extending or refusing credit.

2. *Credit reports on a customer's payment history with other firms.* Quite a few organizations sell information on the credit strength and credit history of business firms. Dun & Bradstreet Canada provides subscribers with a credit reference book and credit reports on individual firms. Ratings and information are available for a huge number of firms, including very small ones. Creditel of Canada also provides credit reporting and has the capability to send reports electronically.

   Many firms have mechanized rules that allow for automatic approval of, say, all credit requests up to a preset dollar amount for firms with high ratings. Potential customers with ratings below some minimum are automatically rejected. All others are investigated further.

3. *Banks.* Banks generally provide some assistance to their business customers in acquiring information on the creditworthiness of other firms.

4. *The customer's payment history with the firm.* The most obvious way to obtain information about the likelihood of a customer not paying is to examine whether the customer paid in the past and how much trouble collecting turned out to be.

Figure 19.2 illustrates just part of a Dun & Bradstreet credit report. As you can see, quite detailed information is available.

Credit Evaluation and Scoring

five Cs of credit
The following five basic credit factors to be evaluated: character, capacity, capital, collateral, and conditions.

No magical formulas can assess the probability that a customer will not pay. In very general terms, the classic **five Cs of credit** are the basic factors to be evaluated:

1. *Character.* The customer's willingness to meet credit obligations.
2. *Capacity.* The customer's ability to meet credit obligations out of operating cash flows.
3. *Capital.* The customer's financial reserves.
4. *Collateral.* A pledged asset in the case of default.
5. *Conditions.* General economic conditions in the customer's line of business.

credit scoring
The process of quantifying the probability of default when granting consumer credit.

Credit scoring refers to the process of calculating a numerical rating for a customer based on information collected and then granting or refusing credit based on the result. For example, a firm might rate a customer on a scale of 1 (very poor) to 10 (very good) on each of the five Cs of credit using all the information available about the customer. A credit score could then be calculated based on the total. From experience, a firm might choose to grant credit only to customers with a score of more than, say, 30.

Firms such as credit card issuers have developed elaborate statistical models for credit scoring. This approach has the advantage of being objective as compared to scoring based on judgments on the five Cs. Usually, all the legally relevant and observable characteristics of a large pool of customers are studied to find their historic relation to default rates. Based on the results, it is possible to determine the variables that best predict whether or not a customer will pay and then calculate a credit score based on those variables.

multiple discriminant analysis (MDA)
Statistical technique for distinguishing between two samples on the basis of their observed characteristics.

Computerized scoring models employ a statistical technique called **multiple discriminant analysis (MDA)** to predict which customers will be good or bad accounts.[9] Similar to regression analysis, MDA chooses a set of variables that best discriminate between good and bad credits with hindsight in a sample for which the outcomes are known. The variables are then used to classify new applications that come in. For consumer credit, for example, these variables include length of time in current job, monthly income, whether the customer's home is owned or rented, other financial obligations, and so on. For business customers, ratios are the relevant variables.

To illustrate how MDA works without getting into the derivation, suppose only two ratios explain whether a business customer is creditworthy: sales/total assets and EBIT/total assets. What MDA does is draw a line to separate good (G) from bad (B) accounts as shown in Figure 19.3. The equation for the line is:

$$\text{Score} = Z = 0.4 \times [\text{Sales/Total assets}] + 3.0 \times \text{EBIT/Total assets} \qquad [19.12]$$

For example, suppose Locust Software has a credit application from Kiwi Computers. Kiwi's financial statements reveal sales/total assets of 1.8 and EBIT/total assets of .16. We can calculate Kiwi's score as:

$$Z = 0.4 \times 1.8 + 3.0 \times .16 = 1.2$$

---

[9] Our discussion of scoring models draws on Hill and Sartoris, *Short-Term Financial Management,* chap. 14; and L. Kryzanowski et al., *Business Solvency Risk Analysis* (Montreal: Institute of Canadian Bankers, 1990), chap. 6.

F I G U R E 19.2 | *A Dunn & Bradstreet report report*

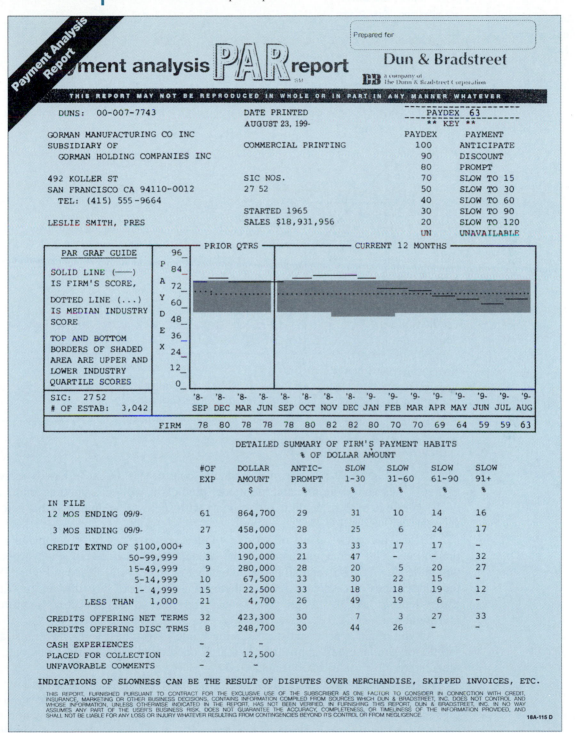

Copyright 1992, Dun & Bradstreet, Inc. All rights reserved. Reprinted with permission.

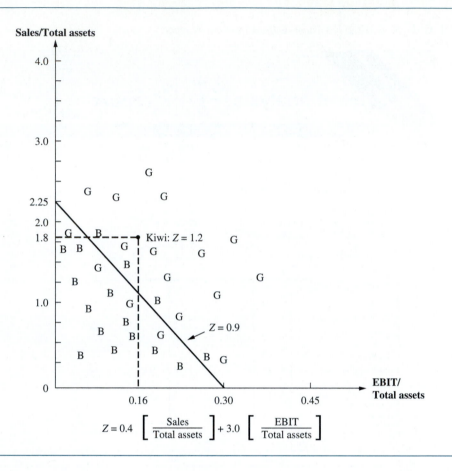

$$Z = 0.4 \left[\frac{\text{Sales}}{\text{Total assets}} \right] + 3.0 \left[\frac{\text{EBIT}}{\text{Total assets}} \right]$$

The line in Figure 19.3 is drawn at a cutoff score of .90. Because Kiwi's score is higher, it lies above the line and the model predicts it will be a good account. The decision rule is to grant credit to all accounts with scores more than 0.9, that is to all accounts above the line.

To test the track record of scoring models, researchers have compared their predictions with actual outcomes. If the models were perfect, all good accounts would be above the line and all bad accounts below it. As you can see in Figure 19.3, the model does a reasonable job but there are some errors. For this reason, firms using scoring models assign scores near the line to a gray area for further investigation.

As you might expect, statistical scoring models work best when there is a large sample of similar credit applicants. Research on scoring models bears this out: the models are most useful in consumer credit.

Because credit-scoring models and procedures determine who is and is not creditworthy, it is not surprising that they have been the subject of government regulation. In particular, the kinds of background and demographic information that can be used in the credit decision are limited. For example, suppose a consumer applicant was formerly bankrupt but has discharged all obligations. After a waiting period that varies from province to province, this information cannot be used in the credit decision.

Credit scoring is used for business customers by Canadian chartered banks. Lenders in Canadian banks and other credit analysts have access to scoring results on a popular financial analysis package called TURBOFAST™. Scoring for small business loans is a particularly promising application because the technique offers the advantages of objective analysis without taking more of the lending officer's time than could be justified for a small account.

> CONCEPT QUESTIONS
> 1. What is credit analysis?
> 2. What are the five Cs of credit?
> 3. What are credit scoring models and how are they used?

19.7 | COLLECTION POLICY

The collection policy is the final element management considers in establishing a credit policy. Collection policy involves monitoring receivables to spot trouble and obtaining payment on past-due accounts.

Monitoring Receivables

To keep track of payments by customers, most firms monitor outstanding accounts. First, a firm normally keeps track of its average collection period through time. If a firm is in a seasonal business, the ACP fluctuates during the year, but unexpected increases in the ACP are a cause for concern. Either customers in general are taking longer to pay, or some percentage of accounts receivable is seriously overdue.

The **aging schedule** is a second basic tool for monitoring receivables. To prepare one, the credit department classifies accounts by age.[10] Suppose a firm has $100,000 in receivables. Some of these accounts are only a few days old, but others have been outstanding for quite some time. The following is an example of an aging schedule.

aging schedule
A compilation of accounts receivable by the age of each account.

Aging Schedule		
Age of Account	Amount	Percent of Total Value of Accounts Receivable
0–10 days	$ 50,000	50%
11–60 days	25,000	25
61–80 days	20,000	20
Over 80 days	5,000	5
	$100,000	100%

If this firm has a credit period of 60 days, 25 percent of its accounts are late. Whether or not this is serious depends on the nature of the firm's collection and customers. Often, accounts beyond a certain age are almost never collected. "The older the receivable, the less value it is to the business and the harder it is to collect."[11] Monitoring the age of accounts is very important in such cases.

Firms with seasonal sales find the percentages on the aging schedule changing during the year. For example, if sales in the current month are very high, total receivables also increase sharply. This means the older accounts, as a percentage of total receivables, become smaller and might appear less important. Some firms have

---

[10] Aging schedules are used elsewhere in business. For example, aging schedules are often prepared for inventory items.
[11] The quotation is from S. Horvitch, "Debt Collection: When to Drop the Hammer on Delinquent Customers," *Financial Post*, March 15, 1991, p. 39.

refined the aging schedule so that they have an idea of how it should change with peaks and valleys in their sales.

Collection Effort

A firm's credit policy should include the procedures to follow for customers who are overdue. A sample set of procedures is given in Table 19.1 for an account due in 30 days. The time line is an important part of the table since experienced credit managers stress the need for prompt action.

The step at 90 days is severe: refusing to grant additional credit to the customer until arrearages are cleared up. This may antagonize a normally good customer, and it points to a potential conflict of interest between the collections department and the sales department.

After 120 days, the firm takes legal action only if the account is large. Legal action is expensive and, as we saw in Chapter 12, if the customer goes bankrupt as a result, there is usually little chance of recovering a significant portion of the credit extended. Smaller accounts are turned over to a collection agency. Agency commissions range up to 50 percent of the amount collected.

Credit Management in Practice

CO-OP Atlantic is a groceries and fuel distributor located in Moncton, New Brunswick.[12] Its credit manager, Gary Steeves, is responsible for monitoring and collecting over $450 million in receivables annually. CO-OP's customers include large grocery stores with balances of more than $1 million as well as several thousand small accounts with balances around $1,000. By installing a computerized system, CO-OP has reduced its average collection period by two days with a savings (NPV) of millions. The system improved monitoring of receivables and credit granting analysis. It also saved on labour costs in processing receivables documentation.

To make monitoring easy, treasury credit staff call up customer information from a central data base. For example, in the home fuel division, aging schedules are used

---

T A B L E   19.1

Schedule of actions to follow up late payments (Stated terms: Net 30 days)

If Payment Is Not Made By:	Action
40 days	Telephone call to customer's payables department Send duplicate invoice if needed
50 days	Second telephone call to customer's payables department
60 days	Warning letter (mild)
75 days	Warning letter (strong)
90 days	Telephone call to management level Notify that future deliveries will be made only on a COD basis until payment is made
120 days	Stop further deliveries 1. Initiate appropriate legal action if the account is large 2. Turn over to a collection agency if the account is small

Source: Ned C. Hill and William C. Sartoris, *Short-Term Financial Management,* 2nd ed. (New York: Macmillan, 1992), p. 392.

---

[12] This section draws on "High Technology Systems Boost Productivity and Bring New Efficiency to Credit Management," *Financial Post,* Joint Venture Supplement, June 20, 1991.

to identify overdue accounts that require authorization by an analyst before further deliveries can be made. Under the old manual system, this information was not available. The system also provides collections staff with a daily list of accounts due for a telephone call together with a complete history of each.

Credit analysis centres around an early warning system that examines the solvency risk of existing and new commercial accounts. The software scores the accounts based on financial ratios. By mechanizing the analysis, CO-OP is now able to score all its large commercial accounts. Under the manual system, detailed financial analysis was done on an exception basis and often came too late.

CO-OP achieved these gains in monitoring and analysis without adding any staff in the credit department. The department has the same number of people as it did in 1981 when sales were half the present level. Gary Steeves estimates automation saved the company over $100,000 in additional wages.

> **CONCEPT QUESTIONS**
>
> 1. What tools can a manager use to monitor receivables?
> 2. What is an aging schedule?
> 3. Describe collection procedures and the reasons for them.
> 4. Describe the key features of a computerized credit system.

19.8 | INVENTORY MANAGEMENT

Like receivables, inventories represent a significant investment for many firms. For a typical Canadian manufacturing operation, inventories often exceed 15 percent of assets.[13] For a retailer, inventories could represent more than 25 percent of assets. From our discussion in Chapter 17, we know that a firm's operating cycle is made up of its inventory period and its receivables period. This is one reason for discussing credit and inventory policy together. Beyond this, both credit policy and inventory policy are used to drive sales, and the two must be coordinated to ensure that the process of acquiring inventory, selling it, and collecting on the sale proceeds smoothly. For example, changes in credit policy designed to stimulate sales must be simultaneously accompanied by planning for adequate inventory.

The Financial Manager and Inventory Policy

Despite the size of an average firm's investment in inventories, the financial manager typically does not have primary control over inventory management. Instead, other functional areas such as purchasing, production, and marketing normally share decision-making authority. Inventory management has become an increasingly important specialty in its own right; often financial management has only input into the decision. For this reason, we only survey some basics of inventory and inventory policy in the sections ahead.

Inventory Types

For a manufacturer, inventory is normally classified into one of three categories: The first category is *raw material*. This is whatever the firm uses as a starting point in its production process. Raw materials might be something as basic as iron ore for a

---

[13] See Table 17.2 in Chapter 17.

steel manufacturer or something as sophisticated as disk drives for a computer manufacturer.

The second type of inventory is *work-in-progress,* which is just what the name suggests, namely, unfinished product. How large this portion of inventory is depends on the length and organization of the production process. The third and final type of inventory is *finished goods,* that is, products ready to ship or sell.

There are three things to keep in mind concerning inventory types. First, the names for the different types can be a little misleading because one company's raw materials could be another's finished goods. For example, going back to our steel manufacturer, iron ore would be a raw material, and steel would be the final product. An auto body panel stamping operation has steel as its raw material and auto body panels as its finished goods, and an automobile assembler has body panels as raw materials and automobiles as finished products.

The second thing to keep in mind is that the different types of inventory can be quite different in their liquidity. Raw materials that are commodity-like or relatively standardized can be easy to convert to cash. Work-in-progress, on the other hand, can be quite illiquid and have little more than scrap value. As always, the liquidity of finished goods depends on the nature of the product.

Finally, a very important distinction between finished goods and other types of inventories is the demand for an inventory item that becomes a part of another item is usually termed *derived* or *dependent* demand because a company's demand for the input item depends on its need for finished items. In contrast, the firm's demand for finished goods is not derived from demand for other inventory items, so it is sometimes said to be *independent.*

Inventory Costs

As we discussed in Chapter 17, two basic types of costs are associated with current assets in general and with inventory in particular. The first of these are *carrying costs.* Here, carrying costs represent all the direct and opportunity costs of keeping inventory on hand.

These include:

1. Storage and tracking costs.
2. Insurance and taxes.
3. Losses due to obsolescence, deterioration, or theft.
4. The opportunity cost of capital on the invested amount.

The sum of these costs can be substantial, roughly ranging from 20 to 40 percent of inventory value per year.

The other type of costs associated with inventory are *shortage costs.* These are costs associated with having inadequate inventory on hand. The two components are restocking costs and costs related to safety reserves. Depending on the firm's business, restocking or order costs are either the costs of placing an order with suppliers or the cost of setting up a production run. The costs related to safety reserves are opportunity losses such as lost sales and loss of customer goodwill that result from having inadequate inventory.

A basic trade-off in inventory management exists because carrying costs increase with inventory levels while shortage or restocking costs decline with inventory levels. The goal of inventory management is thus to minimize the sum of these two costs. We consider approaches to this goal in the next section.

CONCEPT QUESTIONS
1. What are the different types of inventory?
2. What are three things to remember when examining inventory types?
3. What are the basic goals of inventory management?

19.9 | INVENTORY MANAGEMENT TECHNIQUES

As we described earlier, the goal of inventory management is usually framed as cost minimization. Three techniques are discussed in this section, ranging from the relatively simple to the very complex.

The ABC Approach

The ABC is a simple approach to inventory management where the basic idea is to divide inventory into three (or more) groups. The underlying rationale is that a small portion of inventory in terms of quantity might represent a large portion in terms of inventory value. For example, this situation would exist for a manufacturer that uses some relatively expensive, high-tech components and some relatively inexpensive basic materials in producing its products.

Figure 19.4 illustrates an ABC comparison of items by their percentage of inventory value and the percentage of items represented. As Figure 19.4 shows, the A Group constitutes only 10 percent of inventory by item count, but it represents over

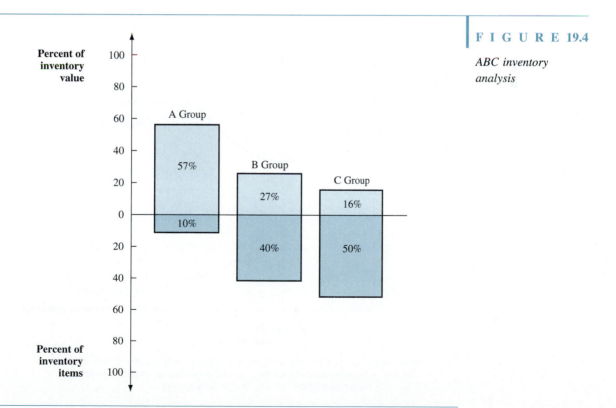

F I G U R E 19.4

ABC inventory analysis

half the value of inventory. The A Group items are thus monitored closely, and inventory levels are kept relatively low. At the other end, basic inventory items, such as nuts and bolts, also exist; because these are crucial and inexpensive, large quantities are ordered and kept on hand. These would be C Group items. The B Group is made up of in-between items.

The Economic Order Quantity (EOQ) Model

The economic order quantity (EOQ) model is the best-known approach to explicitly establishing an optimum inventory level. The basic idea is illustrated in Figure 19.5, which plots the various costs associated with holding inventory (on the vertical axis) against inventory levels (on the horizontal axis). As shown, inventory carrying costs rise as inventory levels increase, while, at the same time, restocking costs decrease. From our general discussion in Chapter 17 and our discussion of the total credit cost curve in this chapter, the general shape of the total inventory cost curve is familiar. With the EOQ model, we attempt to specifically locate the minimum total cost point, Q^*.

In our following discussion, keep in mind that the actual cost of the inventory itself is not included. The reason is that the *total* amount of inventory the firm needs in a given year is dictated by sales. What we are analyzing here is how much the firm should have on hand at any particular time. More precisely, we are trying to determine what size order the firm should place when it restocks its inventory.

F I G U R E 19.5

Costs of holding inventory

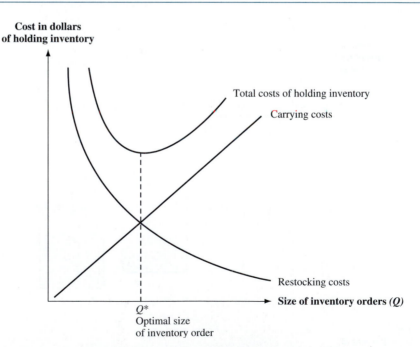

Restocking costs are increased when the firm holds a small quantity of inventory.
Carrying costs are increased when there is a large quantity of inventory on hand.
Total costs are the sum of the carrying and restocking costs.

The Carrying Costs   To develop the EOQ, we assume that the firm's inventory is sold at a steady rate until it hits zero. At that point, the firm restocks its inventory back to some optimal level. For example, suppose the Trans Can Corporation starts out today with 3,600 units of a particular item in inventory. Annual sales of this item are 46,800 units, which is about 900 per week. If Trans Can sells 900 units in inventory each week, after four weeks, all the available inventory would be sold, and Trans Can would restock by ordering (or manufacturing) another 3,600 and start over. This selling and restocking process produces the sawtooth pattern for inventory holdings shown in Figure 19.6. As this figure illustrates, Trans Can always starts with 3,600 units in inventory and ends up at zero. On average, then, inventory is half of 3,600, or 1,800 units.

Going back to Figure 19.5, we see that carrying costs are normally assumed to be directly proportional to inventory levels. Suppose we let Q be the quantity of inventory that Trans Can orders each time (3,600 units); we call this the restocking quantity. Average inventory would then just be $Q/2$, or 1,800 units. If we let CC be the carrying cost per unit per year, Trans Can's total carrying costs are as follows:

$$\text{Total carrying costs} = \text{Average inventory} \times \text{Carrying costs per unit} \qquad [19.13]$$
$$= (Q/2) \times CC$$

In Trans Can's case, if carrying costs were $0.75 per unit per year, total carrying costs would be the average inventory of 1,800 multiplied by $0.75, or $1,350 per year.

The Shortage Costs   For now, we focus only on the restocking costs. In essence, we assume the firm never actually runs short on inventory, so that costs relating to safety reserves are not important. Later, we return to this issue.

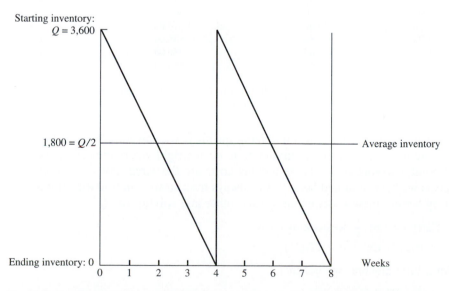

F I G U R E   19.6

Inventory holdings for the Trans Can Corporation

The Trans Can Corporation starts with inventory of 3,600 units. The quantity drops to zero by the fourth week. The average inventory is $Q/2 = 3,600/2 = 1,800$ over the period.

Restocking costs are normally assumed to be fixed. In other words, every time we place an order, there are fixed costs associated with that order (remember the cost of the inventory itself is not considered here). Suppose we let T be the firm's total unit sales per year. If the firm orders Q units each time, it needs to place a total of T/Q orders. For Trans Can, annual sales were 46,800, and the order size was 3,600. Trans Can thus places a total of $46,800/3,600 = 13$ orders per year. If the fixed cost per order is F, the total restocking cost for the year would be:

$$\text{Total restocking cost} = \text{Fixed cost per order} \times \text{Number of orders} \qquad [19.14]$$
$$= F \times (T/Q)$$

For Trans Can, order costs might be $50 per order, so the total restocking cost for 13 orders would be $50 \times 13 = \$650$ per year.

The Total Costs   The total costs associated with holding inventory are the sum of the carrying costs and the restocking costs:

$$\text{Total costs} = \text{Carrying costs} + \text{Restocking costs} \qquad [19.15]$$
$$= (Q/2) \times CC + F \times (T/Q)$$

Our goal is to find the value of Q, the restocking quantity that minimizes this cost. To see how we might go about this, we can calculate total costs for some different values of Q. For the Trans Can Corporation, we had carrying costs *(CC)* of $0.75 per unit per year, fixed costs per order *(F)* of $50 per order, and total unit sales *(T)* of 46,800 units. With these numbers, some possible total costs are (check some of these for practice):

Restocking Quantity (Q)	Carrying Costs (Q/2 × CC)	+	Restocking Costs (F × T/Q)	=	Total Costs
500	$ 187.50		$4,680.00		$4,867.50
1,000	375.00		2,340.00		2,715.00
1,500	562.50		1,560.00		2,122.50
2,000	750.00		1,170.00		1,920.00
2,500	937.50		936.00		1,873.50
3,000	1,125.00		780.00		1,905.00
3,500	1,312.50		668.60		1,981.10

Inspecting the numbers, we see that total costs start at almost $5,000, and they decline to just under $1,900. The cost-minimizing quantity appears to be approximately 2,500.

To find the precise cost-minimizing quantity, we can look back at Figure 19.5. What we notice is that the minimum point occurs right where the two lines cross. At this point, carrying costs and restocking costs are the same. For the particular types of costs we have assumed here, this is always true; so we can find the minimum point just by setting these costs equal to each other and solving for Q^*:

$$\text{Carrying costs} = \text{Restocking costs} \qquad [19.16]$$
$$(Q^*/2) \times CC = F \times (T/Q^*)$$

With a little algebra, we get that

$$Q^{*2} = \frac{2T \times F}{CC} \qquad [19.17]$$

To solve for Q^*, we take the square root of both sides to find that

$$Q^* = \sqrt{\frac{2T \times F}{CC}} \qquad [19.18]$$

This reorder quantity, which minimizes the total inventory cost, is called the *economic order quantity* (EOQ). For the Trans Can Corporation, the EOQ is

$$Q^* = \sqrt{\frac{2T \times F}{CC}} \qquad [19.19]$$

$$= \sqrt{\frac{(2 \times 46,800) \times \$50}{\$.75}}$$

$$= \sqrt{6,240,000}$$

$$= 2,498 \text{ units}$$

Thus, for Trans Can, the economic order quantity is actually 2,498 units. At this level, check that the restocking costs and carrying costs are identical (they're both $926.75).[14]

E X A M P L E | 19.5   Carrying Costs

Thiewes Shoes begins each period with 100 pairs of hiking boots in stock. This stock is depleted each period and reordered. If the carrying cost per pair of boots per year is $3, what are the total carrying costs for the hiking boots?

Inventories always start at 100 items and end at zero, so average inventory is 50 items. At an annual cost of $3 per item, total carrying costs are $150. |

E X A M P L E | 19.6   Restocking Costs

In our previous example, suppose Thiewes sells a total of 600 pairs of boots in a year. How many times per year does Thiewes restock? Suppose the restocking cost is $20 per order. What are total restocking costs?

Thiewes orders 100 items each time. Total sales are 600 items per year, so Thiewes restocks six times per year, or about every two months. The restocking costs would be 6 orders × $20 per order = $120. |

---

[14] In general, EOQ is the minimum point on the total cost curve in Figure 19.4 where the derivative of total cost with respect to quantity is zero. From Equation 19.15:

$$\frac{d\,(\text{Total cost})}{dQ} = \frac{CC}{2} - \frac{T \times F}{Q^2} = 0$$

To find the optimal value of Q, we solve this equation for Q:

$$\frac{CC}{2} = \frac{T \times F}{Q^2}$$

$$Q^2 = \frac{2T \times F}{CC}$$

$$Q = \sqrt{\frac{2T \times F}{CC}}$$

E X A M P L E | 19.6   The EOQ

Based on our previous two examples, what size orders should Thiewes place? How often will Thiewes restock? What are the carrying and restocking costs? The total costs?

We have that the total number of pairs of boots ordered for the year *(T)* is 600. The restocking cost *(F)* is \$20 per order, and the carrying cost *(CC)* is \$3. We can calculate the EOQ for Thiewes as follows:

$$\text{EOQ} = \sqrt{\frac{2T \times F}{CC}} \qquad\qquad\qquad [19.20]$$

$$= \sqrt{\frac{(2 \times 600) \times \$20}{\$3}}$$

$$= \sqrt{8{,}000}$$

$$= 89.44 \text{ units}$$

Since Thiewes sells 600 pairs per year, it restocks 600/89.44 = 6.71 times.[15] The total restocking costs are \$20 × 6.71 = \$134.16. Average inventory is 89.44/2 = 44.72 pairs of boots. The carrying costs will be \$3 × 44.72 = \$134.16, the same as the restocking costs. The total costs are thus \$268.33. |

Extensions to the EOQ Model

Thus far, we have assumed a company lets its inventory run down to zero and then reorders. In reality, a company reorders before its inventory goes to zero for two reasons: First, by always having at least some inventory on hand, the firm minimizes the risk of a stockout and the resulting losses of sales and customers. Second, when a firm does reorder, there is some time lag between placing the order and when the inventory arrives. Thus, to finish our discussion of the EOQ, we consider two extensions, safety stocks and reordering points.

Safety Stocks   A safety stock refers to the minimum level of inventory that a firm keeps on hand. Inventories are reordered whenever the level of inventory falls to the safety stock level. The top of Figure 19.7 illustrates how a safety stock can be incorporated into our EOQ model. Notice that adding a safety stock simply means the firm does not run its inventory all the way down to zero. Other than this, the situation is identical to our earlier discussion of the EOQ.

Reorder Points   To allow for delivery time, a firm places orders before inventories reach a critical level. The reorder points are the times at which the firm actually places its inventory orders. These points are illustrated in the middle of Figure 19.7. As shown, the reorder points simply occur some fixed number of days (or weeks or months) before inventories are projected to reach zero.

One of the reasons a firm keeps a safety stock is to allow for uncertain delivery times. So we can combine our reorder point and safety stock discussions in the bottom part of Figure 19.7. The result is a generalized EOQ in which the firm orders in advance of anticipated needs and also keeps a safety stock of inventory to guard against unforeseen fluctuations in demand and delivery time.

---

[15] In practice, Thiewes would order 90 pairs of boots.

F I G U R E 19.7

Safety stocks and reorder points

A. Safety stocks

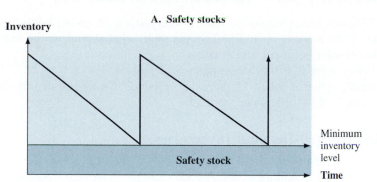

With a safety stock, the firm reorders when inventory reaches a minimum level.

B. Reorder points

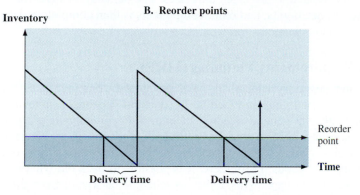

When there are lags in delivery or production times, the firm reorders when inventory reaches the reorder point.

C. Combined reorder points and safety stocks

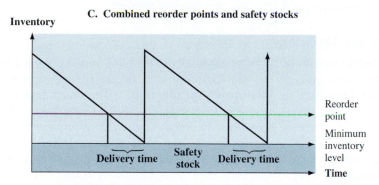

By combining safety stocks and reorder points, the firm maintains a buffer against unforeseen events.

Canadian Tire Stores uses a modified EOQ approach to set target inventory levels for the thousands of items stocked in each store. Because the company markets its stores as providing one-stop shopping, it seeks a high service level with few stockouts. Safety stocks are set accordingly. An in-store computer, on-line with the cash registers, monitors sales and automatically sends an order to the warehouse computer when the stock level drops to the reorder point.

E X A M P L E | **19.8**   **The Reorder Point for Hiking Boots**

Suppose Thiewes Shoes wishes to hold a safety stock of hiking boots equal to six days' sales. If the store is open 300 days per year, what should be the safety stock? What is the reorder point for hiking boots?

The safety stock is 6/300 × 600 pairs = 12 pairs

The reorder point is when 12 pairs are on hand. If sales are evenly distributed, there will still be 6.71 orders per year.

Managing Derived-Demand Inventories

As we described previously, the demand for some inventory types is derived from, or dependent on, other inventory needs. A good example is an auto manufacturer where the demand for finished products depends on consumer demand, marketing programs, and other factors related to projected unit sales. The demand for inventory items such as tires, batteries, headlights, and other components is then completely determined by the number of autos planned.

Materials Requirements Planning (MRP)

Production and inventory specialists have developed computer-based systems for ordering and/or scheduling production of demand-dependent inventories. These systems fall under the general heading of *material requirements planning* (MRP). The basic idea behind MRP is that, once finished goods inventory levels are set, it is possible to back out what levels of work-in-progress inventories must exist to meet the need for finished goods. From there, it is possible to back out what raw materials inventories must be on hand. This ability to schedule backward from finished goods inventories stems from the dependent nature of work-in-progress and raw materials inventories. MRP is particularly important for complicated products where a variety of components are needed to create the finished product.

Just-in-Time Inventory

just-in-time inventory (JIT)

Design for inventory in which parts, raw materials, and other work-in-process is delivered exactly as needed for production. Goal is to minimize inventory.

EOQ is a useful tool for many firms especially in the retail sector but the cutting edge of inventory management in manufacturing is a relatively new approach called **just-in-time inventory** or **just-in-time production**.[16] The basic idea is that raw materials, parts, and other work in process should be delivered at the exact time they are needed on the factory floor. Raw materials and work-in-process are no longer seen as a necessary buffer to decouple stages of production. Instead, all stages of production are recoupled and the goal is to reduce inventories of raw materials and work-in-process to zero.

At the heart of just-in-time inventory is a different approach to ordering or setup costs. Under the traditional EOQ approach, these are considered fixed. As we saw, higher ordering costs translate into larger, less frequent orders. When producing for inventory, large setup costs in switching production from one product to another mean longer production runs. Either way, the firm carries a large work-in-process inventory as the next stage of production gradually draws down the stock of

---

[16] Our discussion of just-in-time inventory draws on J. Loring, "Inventory: Taking Stock," *Canadian Business,* April 1991; E. Corcoran, "Millikwn & Co., Managing the Quality of a Textile Revolution," *Scientific American,* April 1990; and Hill and Sartoris, *Short-Term Financial Management,* chaps. 17 and 20. A good source of just-in-time production is J. D. Blackburn, ed., *Time-Based Competition: The Next Battleground in American Manufacturing* (Homewood, IL: Business One Irwin, 1991).

work-in-process. If a manufacturer produces many different products, the burden of different work-in-process for each becomes excessive.

This was the problem faced by Toyota in Japan after World War II. To be competitive, the company needed to make a mix of vehicles so no one model had a long production run. The solution was to attack setup time and reduce it dramatically by up to 75 percent. Thus, just-in-time inventory (production) was born.

Making just-in-time inventory work requires detailed materials requirements planning (MRP). As all stages of production are recoupled, careful coordination is needed. There are no longer inventory buffers to fall back on to cover planning errors or equipment downtime. This difference between the traditional approach and just-in-time inventory in resolving problems is captured in the following analogy drawn from a Japanese parable:

> The ship of enterprise floats on a lake of inventory. Problems can be thought of as rocks in the lake on which one is sailing a boat. The safety stock inventory approach is to raise the water level in the lake so that the rocks are not seen. The just-in-time approach is to chart carefully the location of the rocks and sail around them while keeping the water level at a minimum.[17]

When a manufacturer outsources parts and other work-in-process, planning must include suppliers. With the new approach, suppliers have to be capable of delivering smaller orders more often with precision timing. Suppliers need to receive high-quality information on the schedule of deliveries and to communicate continually with the buyer on the location of all shipments.

Manufacturers and suppliers use electronic data interchange (EDI) over integrated computer systems. The cash management system discussed in Chapter 18 is an example of EDI featuring communications between a firm and its bank. In implementing a just-in-time system, the firm and its supplier electronically exchange all information from the initial order to acknowledgment of the final payment.

Beyond information requirements, suppliers must meet very high quality standards. Manufacturers receive parts and use them at once so there is no room for defects. Quality control and preventive maintenance becomes very important.

Just-In-Time Inventory at GM of Canada   Since just-in-time methods were born in the automobile industry, it is not surprising that automakers in Canada are leading the way in applying it.[18] GM of Canada buys car seats for its plant at Ste.-Therese, Quebec, from Woodridge Foam Corporation. The arrangement calls for just-in-time delivery from a Quebec plant 20 kilometers away; this plant was specially set up to supply GM. A computer at GM issues orders to a Woodridge computer specifying the seats needed for vehicles about to come down the line. Ten minutes later, seat production begins. Three hours later, Woodridge loads the finished seats in delivery trucks so they can be unloaded at GM in exactly the order they are needed.

GM uses more than 900 suppliers and most of them ship daily or weekly. The reduction in inventory has been dramatic. In another GM plant in Windsor, Ontario, a huge bay was once filled with a three-month supply of door panels. The inventory is completely gone, replaced by a unit that builds the panels just in time.

The result is that inventory turns over once every 3.5 days for a turnover ratio of $365/3.5 = 104$. In 1984, under the old system, inventory turned over 24 times per year. GM saves around $1 million for each extra inventory turn.

---

[17] Hill and Sartoris, *Short-Term Financial Management,* p. 457.
[18] This section draws on Loring, "Inventory: Taking Stock," pp. 46–52.

With just-in-time inventory methods, the automobile industry suffered in the recession of 1992. But the 1981-82 recession with its high interest rates was far worse. Then the industry suffered severely from excessive inventory and the resulting carrying charges. Thus, inventory reductions through just-in-time methods are helping both the industry and its suppliers.

> CONCEPT QUESTIONS
> 1. Why do firms hold inventories?
> 2. Explain the basic idea behind the EOQ solution for inventory management.
> 3. What is just-in-time inventory? How does it differ from the more traditional EOQ approach?

19.10 | SUMMARY AND CONCLUSIONS

This chapter covered the basics of credit policy and inventory management. The major topics we discussed include:

1. The components of credit policy. We discussed the terms of sale, credit analysis, and collection policy. Under the general subject of terms of sale, the credit period, the cash discount and discount period, and the credit instrument were described.

2. Credit policy analysis. We develop the cash flows from the decision to grant credit and show how the credit decision can be analyzed in an NPV setting. The NPV of granting credit depends on five factors: revenue effects, cost effects, the cost of debt, the probability of non-payment, and the cash discount.

3. Optimal credit policy. The optimal amount of credit the firm offers depends on the competitive conditions under which it operates. These conditions determine the carrying costs associated with granting credit and the opportunity costs of the lost sales from refusing to offer credit. The optimal credit policy minimizes the sum of these two costs.

4. Credit analysis. We looked at the decision to grant credit to a particular customer. We saw that two considerations are very important: the cost relative to the selling price and the possibility of repeat business.

5. Collection policy. Collection policy is the method of monitoring the age of accounts receivable and dealing with past-due accounts. We describe how an aging schedule can be prepared and the procedures a firm might use to collect on past-due accounts.

6. Motives for holding inventory. Like cash, firms hold inventory for precautionary and speculative motives. The main reason for holding inventory is the transactions motive to have supplies for production and product to meet customer demand.

7. The economic order quantity (EOQ) model. This traditional approach to inventory sets the optimal order size and with it the average inventory, trading off ordering or setup costs against carrying costs. The optimal inventory minimizes the sum of these costs.

8. Just-in-time inventory. A new approach, JIT reduces inventory by scheduling production and deliveries of work-in-process to arrive just in time for the next stage of production. Implementation requires detailed planning with suppliers and advanced information and communications systems such as Electronic Data Interchange (EDI).

Key Terms

Chapter Review Problems and Self-Test

19.1   Credit Policy

The Cold Fusion Corporation (manufacturer of the Mr. Fusion home power plant) is considering a new credit policy. The current policy is cash only. The new policy would involve extending credit for one period. Based on the following information, determine if a switch is advisable. Also, check your answer by using the one-shot and accounts receivable approaches. The required return is 1.5 percent per period, and there are no defaults.

	Current Policy	New Policy
Price per unit	$ 150	$ 150
Cost per unit	$ 120	$ 120
Sales per period in units	2,000	2,200

19.2   Discounts and Default Risk

The ICU Binocular Corporation is considering a change in credit policy. The current policy is cash only, and sales per period are 5,000 units at a price of $95. If credit is offered, the new price would be $100 per unit and the credit would be extended for one period. Unit sales are not expected to change, and all customers would take the credit. ICU anticipates that 2 percent of its customers will default. If the required return is 3 percent per period, is the change a good idea? What if only half the customers take the offered credit?

19.3   Credit Where Credit Is Due

You are trying to decide whether or not to extend credit to a particular customer. Your variable cost is $10 per unit; the selling price is $14. This customer wants to buy 100 units today and pay in 60 days. You think there is a 10 percent chance of default. The required return is 3 percent per 60 days. Should you extend credit? Assume this is a onetime sale and the customer will not buy if credit is not extended.

19.4   The EOQ

Heusen Computer Manufacturing starts each period with 4,000 CPUs in stock. This stock is depleted each month and reordered. If the carrying cost per CPU is $1, and the fixed order cost is $10, is Heusen following an economically advisable strategy?

Answers to Self-Test Problems

19.1 If the switch is made, an extra 200 units per period would be sold at a gross profit of $150 − 120 = $30 each. The total benefit is thus $30 × 200 = $6,000 per period. At 1.5 percent per period forever, the PV is $6,000/.015 = $400,000.

   The cost of the switch is equal to this period's revenue of $150 × 2,000 units = $300,000 plus the cost of producing the extra 200 units, 200 × $120 = $24,000. The total cost is thus $324,000, and the NPV is $400,000 − 324,000 = $76,000. The switch should be made.

   For the accounts receivable approach, we interpret the $324,000 cost as the investment in receivables. At 1.5 percent per period, the carrying cost is $324,000 × 1.5% = $4,860 per period. The benefit per period we calculated as $6,000; so the net gain per period is $6,000 − $4,860 = $1,140. At 1.5 percent per period, the PV of this is $1,140/.015 = $76,000.

   Finally, for the one-shot approach, if credit is not granted, the firm generates ($150 − 120) × 2,000 = $60,000 this period. If credit is extended, the firm invests $120 × 2,200 = $264,000 today and receives $150 × 2,200 = $330,000 in one period. The NPV of this second option is $330,000/1.015 − $264,000 = $61,123.15. The firm is $61,123.15 − 60,000 = $1,123.15 better off today and in each future period by granting credit. The PV of this stream is $1,123.15 + $1,123.15/.015 = $76,000 (allowing for a rounding error).

19.2 The costs per period are the same whether or not credit is offered; so we can ignore the production costs. The firm currently sells and collects $95 × 5,000 = $475,000 per period. If credit is offered, sales rise to $100 × 5,000 = $500,000.

   Defaults will be 2 percent of sales, so the cash inflow under the new policy is .98 × $500,000 = $490,000. This amounts to an extra $15,000 every period. At 3 percent per period, the PV is $15,000/.03 = $500,000. If the switch is made, ICU would give up this month's revenues of $475,000; so the NPV of the switch is $25,000. If only half switch, then the NPV is half as large: $12,500.

19.3 If the customer pays in 60 days, then you collect $14 × 100 = $1,400. There's only a 90 percent chance of collecting this; so you expect to get $1,400 × .90 = $1,260 in 60 days. The present value of this is $1,260/1.03 = $1,223.3. Your cost is $10 × 100 = $1,000; so the NPV is $223.3. Credit should be extended.

19.4 We can answer by first calculating Heusen's carrying and restocking costs. The average inventory is 2,000 CPUs, and, since the carrying costs are $1 per CPU, total carrying costs are $2,000. Heusen restocks every month at a fixed order cost of $10, so the total restocking costs are $120. What we see is that carrying costs are large relative to reorder costs, so Heusen is carrying too much inventory.

   To determine the optimal inventory policy, we can use the EOQ model. Because Heusen orders 4,000 CPUs 12 times per year, total needs *(T)* are 48,000 CPUs. The fixed order cost is $10, and the carrying cost per unit *(CC)* is $1. The EOQ is therefore:

$$EOQ = \sqrt{\frac{2T \times F}{CC}}$$
$$= \sqrt{\frac{(2 \times 48,000) \times \$10}{\$1}}$$
$$= \sqrt{960,000}$$
$$= 979.80 \text{ units}$$

We can check this by noting that the average inventory is about 490 CPUs, so the carrying cost is $490. Heusen would have to reorder 48,000/979.8 = 49 times. The fixed reorder cost is $10, so the total restocking cost is also $490.

Questions and Problems

Basic (Questions 1–28)

1. **Credit Policy Components** What are the three components of credit policy?

2. **Terms of Sale** The conditions under which a firm proposes to grant credit are called the *terms of sale*. What elements make up the terms of sale?

3. **Cash Discounts** You place an order for 400 units of Good X at a unit price of $60. The supplier offers terms of 3/30, net 90.
   a. How long do you have to pay before the account is overdue? If you take the full period, how much should you remit?
   b. What is the discount being offered? How quickly must you pay to get the discount? If you do take the discount, how much should you remit?
   c. If you don't take the discount, how much interest are you paying implicitly? How many days' credit are you receiving?

4. **Credit Period Length** What are some of the factors that determine the length of the credit period? Why is the length of the buyers' operating cycle often considered an upper bound on the length of the credit period?

5. **Credit Period Length** In each of the following, indicate which firm would probably have a longer credit period and explain your reasoning.
   a. Firm A sells a miracle cure for baldness; Firm B sells toupees.
   b. Firm A specializes in products for landlords; Firm B specializes in products for renters.
   c. Firm A sells to customers with an inventory turnover of 10 times; Firm B sells to customers with an inventory turnover of 20 times.
   d. Firm A sells fresh fruit; Firm B sells canned fruit.
   e. Firm A sells and installs carpeting; Firm B sells rugs.

6. **Credit Instruments** Describe each of the following:
   a. Sight draft
   b. Time draft
   c. Bankers acceptance
   d. Promissory note
   e. Trade acceptance

7. **Trade Credit Forms** In what form is trade credit most commonly offered? What is the credit instrument in this case?

8. **Credit Costs** What are the costs associated with carrying receivables? What are the costs associated with not granting credit? What do we call the sum of the costs for different levels of receivables?

9. **Five Cs of Credit** What are the five Cs of credit? Explain why each is important.

10. **Size of Accounts Receivable** The Solberg Corporation has annual sales of $85 million. The average collection period is 45 days. What is Solberg's average investment in accounts receivable as shown on the balance sheet?

11. **ACP and Accounts Receivable** Macrothink, Inc., sells economic models based on the revolutionary data-free, least-squares approach. Its credit terms are 4/15, net 60. Based on experience, 40 percent of all customers will take the discount.

a. What is the average collection period for Macrothink?

b. If Macrothink sells 500 models every month at a price of $1,200 each, what is its average balance sheet amount in accounts receivable?

12. **Size of Accounts Receivable**   Robertson Products has weekly credit sales of $90,000, and the average collection period is 70 days. The cost of production is 75 percent of the selling price. What is Robertson's average accounts receivable?

13. **Terms of Sale**   A firm offers terms of 3/15, net 60. What effective annual interest rate does the firm earn when a customer does not take the discount? Without doing any calculations, explain what will happen to this effective rate if:

a. The discount is changed to 2 percent.

b. The credit period is reduced to 30 days.

c. The discount period is reduced to 10 days.

14. **ACP and Receivables Turnover**   Media Services, Inc., has an average collection period of 57 days. Its average daily investment in receivables is $250,000. What are annual credit sales? What is the receivables turnover?

15. **Size of Accounts Receivable**   Serial Semiconductors sells 6,500 of its guitar amplifiers each year at a price per unit of $500. All sales are on credit with terms of 2/10, net 45. The discount is taken by 35 percent of the customers. What is the company's accounts receivable? In reaction to its main competitor, the Phaseback Corporation, Serial Semiconductors is considering a change in its credit policy to terms of 4/10, net 45 to preserve its market share. How will this change in policy affect accounts receivable?

16. **Size of Accounts Receivable**   The Hay Lee Corporation sells on credit terms of net 30. Its accounts are on average 15 days past due. If annual credit sales are $4 million, what is the company's balance sheet amount in accounts receivable?

17. **Evaluating Credit Policy**   The Parts Emporium is a retail store that stocks electronic components and test equipment for the computer hobbyist. A new customer has placed an order for 10 novelty mood keyboards, which change color as you type according to your mood. The variable cost is $32 per unit, and the credit price is $40 each. Credit is extended for one period, and based on historical experience, about 1 out of every 8 such orders is never collected. The required return is 3 percent per period.

a. Assuming this is a onetime order, should it be filled? The customer will not buy if credit is not extended.

b. What is the break-even probability of default in part *(a)?*

c. Suppose that customers who don't default become repeat customers and place the same order every period forever. Further assume that repeat customers never default. Should the order be filled? What is the break-even probability of default?

d. Describe in general terms why credit terms will be more liberal when repeat orders are a possibility.

18. **Credit Policy Evaluation**   Vindamore, Inc., is considering a change in its cash-only sales policy. The new terms of sale would be net two months. Based on the information below, determine if Vindamore should proceed or not. Describe the buildup of receivables in this case. The required return is 1.5 percent per period.

	Current Policy	New Policy
Price per unit	$520	$520
Cost per unit	$280	$280
Unit sales per month	600	650

19. **Evaluating Credit Policy** Stricklin Manufacturing is considering a change in its terms of sale. The current policy is cash only; the new policy will involve one period's credit. Sales are 50,000 units per period at a price of $700 per unit. If credit is offered, the new price will be $790. Unit sales are not expected to change, and all customers will take the credit. Stricklin estimates that 10 percent of credit sales will be uncollectible. If the required return is 2 percent per period, is the change a good idea?

20. **Credit Policy Evaluation** The Flicker Flash Company sells 8,000 pairs of jogging shoes per month at a cash price of $67.90 per pair. The firm is considering a new policy that involves 30 days' credit and an increase in price to $70 per pair on credit sales. The cash price will remain at $67.90, and the new policy is not expected to affect the quantity sold. The discount period will be 10 days. The required return is 1 percent per month.
    a. How would the new credit terms be quoted?
    b. What is the investment in receivables required under the new policy?
    c. Explain why the variable cost of manufacturing the shoes is not relevant here.
    d. If the default rate is anticipated to be 5 percent, should the switch be made? What is the break-even credit price? The break-even cash discount?

21. **Credit Analysis** Ming Glasswares is debating whether to extend credit to a particular customer. Ming's glassware products, primarily used in the manufacture of chandelier fixtures, currently sell for $950 per unit. The variable cost is $400 per unit. The order under consideration is for seven units today; payment is promised in 60 days.
    a. If there is a 15 percent chance of default, should Ming fill the order? The required return is 1.25 percent per month. This is a onetime sale, and the customer will not buy if credit is not extended.
    b. What is the break-even probability in part (a)?
    c. This part is a little harder. In general terms, how do you think your answer to part (a) will be affected if the customer would purchase the merchandise for cash if the credit is refused? The cash price is $850 per unit.

22. **Credit Analysis** Consider the following information on two alternative credit strategies:

	Refuse Credit	Grant Credit
Price per unit	$20	$22
Cost per unit	$12	$13
Quantity sold per quarter	6,500	6,800
Probability of payment	1.0	0.90

The higher cost per unit reflects the expense associated with credit orders, and the higher price per unit reflects the existence of a cash discount. The credit period will be 90 days, and the cost of debt is 0.80 percent per month.
    a. Based on this information, should credit be granted?
    b. In part (a), what does the credit price per unit have to be to break even?
    c. In part (a), suppose we can obtain a credit report for 50 cents per customer. Assuming that each customer buys one unit and that the credit report

correctly identifies all customers who would not pay, should credit be extended?

23.   **NPV of Credit Policy Switch**   Suppose a corporation currently sells Q units per month for a cash-only price of P. Under a new credit policy that allows one month's credit, the quantity sold will be Q' and the price per unit will be P'. Defaults will be π percent of credit sales. The variable cost is v per unit and is not expected to change. The percentage of customers who will take the credit is α, and the required return is R per month. What is the NPV of the decision to switch? Interpret the various parts of your answer.

24.   **Inventory Types**   What are the different inventory types? How do the types differ? Why are some types said to have dependent demand whereas other types are said to have independent demand?

25.   **Just-in-Time Inventory**   If a company moves to a JIT inventory management system, what will happen to inventory turnover? What will happen to total asset turnover? What will happen to return on equity (ROE)? (Hint: remember the Du Pont equation from Chapter 3).

26.   **Inventory Costs**   If a company's inventory carrying costs were $5 million per year and its fixed order costs were $8 million per year, do you think the firm keeps too much inventory on hand or too little? Why?

27.   **EOQ**   Brooks Manufacturing uses 8,000 subframes per week and then reorders another 8,000. If the relevant carrying cost per subframe is $25, and the fixed order cost is $1,500, is Brook's inventory policy optimal? Why or why not?

28.   **EOQ**   The Hall Pottery Store begins each week with 250 pots in stock. This stock is depleted each week and reordered. If the carrying cost per pot is $12 per year and the fixed order cost is $900, what is the total carrying cost? What is the restocking cost? Should Hall increase or decrease its order size? Describe an optimal inventory policy for Hall in terms of order size and order frequency.

29.   **EOQ Derivation**   Prove that when carrying costs and restocking costs are as described in the chapter, the EOQ must occur when the carrying costs and restocking costs are equal.

30.   **Credit Policy Evaluation**   The Headbanger Corporation is considering a change in its cash-only policy. The new terms would be net one period. Based on the following information, determine if Headbanger should proceed or not. The required return is 2 percent per period.

	Current Policy	New Policy
Price per unit	$30	$34
Cost per unit	$18	$18
Unit sales per month	5,000	5,400

31.   **Credit Policy Evaluation**   Jordan Clothiers currently has an all-cash credit policy. It is considering a change in the credit policy by going to terms of net 30 days. Based on the following information, what do you recommend? The required return is 1.5 percent per month.

	Current Policy	New Policy
Price per unit	$30	$33
Cost per unit	$20	$21
Unit sales per month	15,000	15,000

32. **Break-Even Quantity** In Problem 30, what is the break-even quantity for the new credit policy? Assume the price under the new policy is $30 and all other values remain the same.

Challenge
(Questions 32–35)

33. **Credit Markup** In Problem 30, what is the break-even price per unit that should be charged under the new credit policy? Assume the sales figure under the new policy is 5,100 units and all other values remain the same.

34. **Credit Markup** In Problem 31, what is the break-even price per unit under the new credit policy? Assume all other values remain the same.

35. **Safety Stocks and Order Points** Woebeegon Timber, Inc., expects to sell 3,500 of its custom flannel shirts every week. The store is open seven days a week and expects to sell the same number of shirts every day. The company has an EOQ of 3,000 shirts and a safety stock of 500 shirts. Once an order is placed, it takes two days for Woebeegon to get the shirts. How many orders does the company place per year? Assume today is Monday morning before the store opens, and a shipment of shirts has just arrived. When will you place your next order?

Suggested Readings

An excellent textbook on short-term financial decisions is:

Hill, N. C., and W. L. Sartoris. *Short-Term Financial Management,* 2nd ed. New York: Macmillan, 1992.

Information on credit management in Canada is available from the Canadian Institute of Credit and Financial Management, Mississauga, Ontario.

For more on MRP, JIT, and related acronyms see Chase, Richard B., and Nicholas J. Aquilano. *Production and Operations Management,* 6th ed. Homewood, IL: Richard D. Irwin, 1992.

TOPICS IN CORPORATE FINANCE

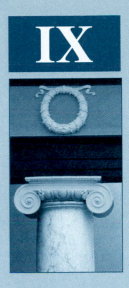

CHAPTER 20 | Options and Corporate Securities

Options are special contractual arrangements that give the owner the right to buy or to sell an asset (usually stock) at a fixed price on or before a particular date. This chapter studies options and discusses two financing instruments, warrants and convertible bonds, which are corporate securities with explicit option features.

CHAPTER 21 | Mergers and Acquisitions

Chapter 21 describes the corporate finance of mergers and acquisitions. It shows that the acquisition of one firm by another is essentially a capital budgeting decision, and the NPV framework still applies. This chapter discusses the tax, accounting, and legal aspects of mergers and acquisitions along with recent developments in areas such as takeover defences.

CHAPTER 22 | International Corporate Finance

Chapter 22 discusses international financial management. It describes the special factors that affect firms with significant foreign operations. The most important new factor that foreign operations introduce is foreign exchange rates. This chapter discusses how to deal with foreign exchange rates in financial management.

CHAPTER 23 | Leasing

Leasing is a way businesses finance plant, property, and equipment. Just about any asset that can be purchased can be leased. Leasing an asset is much like borrowing the needed funds and simply buying the asset. When is leasing preferable to long-term borrowing? This is the question we answer in Chapter 23.

Options and Corporate Securities

20

Options are a part of everyday life. "Keep your options open" is sound business advice, and "We're out of options" is a sure sign of trouble. Options are obviously valuable, but actually putting a dollar value on one is not easy. How to value options is an important topic of research, and option pricing is one of the great success stories of modern finance.

option

A contract that gives its owner the right to buy or sell some asset at a fixed price on or before a given date.

In finance, an **option** is an arrangement that gives its owner the right to buy or sell an asset at a fixed price anytime on or before a given date. The most familiar options are stock options. These are options to buy and sell shares of common stock, and we discuss them in some detail. Options on stock and other assets are examples of **derivative securities**. As the name suggests, their value is derived from the price and other features of the underlying asset. Other derivative securities are futures and swaps. We discuss futures later in this chapter and talk about swaps in Chapter 22.

derivative securities

Securities whose returns depend on the price of an underlying asset and that allow market participants to offset the exposure of their cash market positions.

In recent years, derivatives have been associated with high profile financial disasters. Well-known companies like Procter & Gamble, Gibson Greetings, and the German firm, Metallgesellschaft, have lost billions in derivatives strategies gone wrong. Losses on futures trading wiped out the capital of Barings, a venerable English merchant bank. While studying this chapter cannot make you a derivatives expert, it will provide a basic understanding of the risks and rewards of these instruments.

Almost all corporate securities have implicit or explicit option features. Furthermore, the use of such features is expanding with the growth of financial engineering. As a result, understanding securities that involve option features requires a general knowledge of the factors that determine an option's value.

This chapter starts with a description of different types of options. We identify and discuss the general factors that determine option values and show how ordinary debt and equity have optionlike characteristics. We then illustrate how option features are incorporated into corporate securities by discussing warrants, convertible bonds, and other optionlike securities.

20.1 | OPTIONS: THE BASICS

An option is a contract that gives its owner the right to buy or sell some asset at a fixed price on or before a given date. For example, an option on a building might give the holder of the option the right to buy the building for $1 million anytime on or before the Saturday before the third Wednesday in January 2010.

Options are a unique type of financial contract because they give the buyer the right, but not the obligation, to do something. The buyer uses the option only if it is profitable to do so; otherwise the option can be thrown away.

There is a special vocabulary associated with options. Here are some important definitions:

1. **Exercising the option**. The act of buying or selling the underlying asset via the option contract is called exercising the option.

2. **Striking price or exercise price**. The fixed price specified in the option contract at which the holder can buy or sell the underlying asset is called the striking price or exercise price. The striking price is often just called the *strike price*.

3. **Expiration date**. An option usually has a limited life. The option is said to expire at the end of its life. The last day on which the option can be exercised is called the expiration date.

4. **American and European options**. An American option may be exercised anytime up to the expiration date. A European option can be exercised only on the expiration date.

Puts and Calls

Options come in two basic types: puts and calls. Call options are the more common of the two and our discussion focusses mostly on calls. A **call option** gives the owner the right to buy an asset at a fixed price during a particular time period. It may help you to remember that a call option gives you the right to "call in" an asset.

A **put option** is essentially the opposite of a call option. Instead of giving the holder the right to buy some asset, it gives the holder the right to sell that asset for a fixed exercise price. If you buy a put option, you can force the seller to buy the asset from you for a fixed price and thereby "put it to him."

What about an investor who sells a call option? The seller receives money up front and has the obligation to sell the asset at the exercise price if the option holder wants it. Similarly, an investor who sells a put option receives cash up front and is then obligated to buy the asset at the exercise price if the option holder demands it.[1]

The asset involved in an option could be anything. The options that are most widely bought and sold, however, are stock options. These are options to buy and sell shares of stock. Because these are the best-known options, we study them first. As we discuss stock options, keep in mind that the general principles apply to options involving any asset, not just shares of stock.

Stock Option Quotations

In the 1970s and 1980s, organized trading in options grew from literally zero into some of the world's largest markets. The tremendous growth in interest in derivative securities resulted from the greatly increased volatility in financial markets, which we discussed in Chapter 1.[2] Exchange trading in options began in 1973 on the Chicago Board Options Exchange (CBOE). The CBOE is still the largest organized options market; options are traded in a number of other places today, including London, Paris, Tokyo, and Hong Kong.

exercising the option
The act of buying or selling the underlying asset via the option contract.

striking price
The fixed price in the option contract at which the holder can buy or sell the underlying asset. Also the exercise price or strike price.

expiration date
The last day on which an option can be exercised.

American option
An option that can be exercised at any time until its expiration date.

European option
An option that can be exercised only on the expiration date.

call option
The right to buy an asset at a fixed price during a particular period of time.

put option
The right to sell an asset at a fixed price during a particular period of time. The opposite of a call option.

---

[1] An investor who sells an option is often said to have "written" the option.

[2] Our discussion of trends in options trading draws on L. Gagnon, "Exchange-Traded Financial Derivatives in Canada: Finally Off the Launching Pad," *Canadian Investment Review*, Fall 1990, pp. 63–70, and J. Ilkiw, "From Suspicion to Optimism: the Story of Derivative Use by Pension Funds in Canada", *Canadian Investment Review*, Summer 1994, pp. 19–22.

Option trading in Canada began in 1975 on the Montreal Exchange. Today options are traded on the Montreal, Toronto, and Vancouver exchanges and cleared through Trans-Canada Options Inc. (TCO). The TCO stands between option buyers and option sellers, called writers. Put and call options involving stock in some of the best-known corporations in Canada are traded daily. Almost all such options are American (as opposed to European). Trading in Canadian options and other derivative securities has grown rapidly since 1990 as banks, pension funds, and other financial institutions gain experience with hedging techniques using derivative securities.

To get started with option specifics, we look at a simplified *Globe and Mail* quotation for a TCO option:

Series		Bid	Ask	Last
Alcan Alumin		C	$ 38 ⅜	
Ap35		3.350	3.600	3.350
MY40	P	2	2 ¼	2.050

The first thing listed here is the company identifier, Alcan Alumin. This tells us these options involve the right to buy or sell shares of stock in Alcan Aluminum. Just beside the company identifier is the closing price of the stock. As of the close of business (in Toronto), Alcan was selling for $38 ⅜ per share.

On the next line is the expiration date for the first option. AP means the option expires in April. On the next line, an option marked MY expires in May. All TCO options expire on the third Friday of the expiration month.

To the right of the expiration date is the striking price. The first Alcan Aluminum option listed here has an exercise price of $35. The second option has an exercise price of $40. The first is a call option and the second a put option marked P. Because calls are more common, all listings are assumed to be calls unless marked P. The Last column gives the closing price or last traded price for the option in pennies.

The first option listed would be described as the "Alcan Alumin. 35 call." The price for this option is $3.350. If you pay the $3.350, you have the right anytime between now and the third Friday of April to buy one share of Alcan stock for $35. Actually, trading occurs in round lots (multiples of 100 shares), so one option contract costs $3.350 × 100 = $335.

The other quotation is similar. The May 40 put option costs $2.05. If you pay $2.05 × 100 = $205.00, you have the right to sell 100 shares of Alcan stock anytime between now and the third Friday in May at a price of $40 per share.

Table 20.1 contains a more detailed TCO quote reproduced from the *Globe and Mail.* From our previous discussion, we know that these are Alcan options and that Alcan closed at $38 ⅜ per share on the TSE. Notice there are multiple striking prices instead of just one. As shown, puts and calls with striking prices ranging from 35 to 40 are available. Expiration dates range from April to October.

To check your understanding of option quotes, suppose you wanted the right to sell 100 shares of Alcan for $37.50 anytime between now and the third Friday in May. What should you tell your broker and how much will it cost you?

Since you want the right to sell the stock for $37.50, you need to buy a put option with a $37.50 exercise price. So you call your broker and place an order for one Alcan Alumin. May 37 ½ put. Since the May 37 ½ put is quoted at 0.85, you have to pay $0.85 per share, or $85 in all (plus commission).

Option Payoffs

Looking at Table 20.1, suppose you were to buy 50 Alcan Alumin. April 35 call contracts. The option is quoted at 3.350, so the contracts cost $335 each. You would

TABLE 20.1

Options quotations

Trans Canada Options

Trans Canada Options combine Montreal, Toronto and Vancouver option trading. P is a put.

Series		Bid	Ask	Last	Vol	Op Int
Agnico-Eagle			**C**	**$16**	**Opt Vol**	**75**
AP 17	P	0.950	1.150	0.850	10	
JN 14		2.400	2.650	2.350	10	41
16		1.150	1.350	1.350	10	247
18		0¼	0.450	0¼	35	45
SP 15	P	0.900	1.100	0.950	10	30
Air Canada			**C**	**$6½**	**Opt Vol**	**540**
AP 5		1½	1.650	1½	150	
MY 7		0.150	0.200	0.200	30	1687
JY 6	P	0.150	0¼	0¼	10	1060
7		0.350	0.400	0.400	330	4075
7	P	0½	0.600	0½	20	326
Alcan Alumin.			**C**	**$38⅜**	**Opt Vol**	**35**
AP 35		3.350	3.600	3.350	3	259
37½		1¼	1.400	1.550	5	1490
MY 37½		1.800	1.950	1.650	3	84
37½	P	0¾	0.850	0.850	10	364
40	P	2	2¼	2.050	5	25
JY 37½		2.650	2.900	3	2	370
40		1.450	1.600	1.600	5	452
OC 37½		3.650	3.900	3.700	2	74
Bk Nova Scotia			**C**	**$26¾**	**Opt Vol**	**7**
JY 27		0.950	1.200	0.950	7	778

Source: *Globe and Mail,* April 11, 1995, p. B21. Used with permission.

spend a total of 50 × $335 = $16,750. You wait a while, and the expiration date rolls around.

Now what? You have the right to buy Alcan stock for $35 per share. If Alcan is selling for less than $35 a share, this option isn't worth anything, and you throw it away. In this case, we say the option has finished "out of the money" since the stock price is less than the exercise price. Your $16,750 is, alas, a complete loss.

If Alcan is selling for more than $35 per share, you need to exercise your option. In this case, the option is "in the money" because the stock price exceeds the exercise price. Suppose Alcan rises to, say, $40 per share. Since you have the right to buy Alcan at $35, you make a $5 profit on each share on exercise. Each contract involves 100 shares, so you make $5 per share × 100 shares per contract = $500 per contract. Finally, you own 50 contracts, so the value of your options is a handsome $25,000. Notice that since you invested $16,750, your net profit is $8,250.

As our example indicates, the gains and losses from buying call options can be quite large. To illustrate further, suppose you had simply purchased the stock with the $16,750 instead of buying call options. You would have about $16,750/$38 ⅜ = 436 shares. We can now compare what you have when the option expires for different stock prices:

Ending Stock Price	Option Value (50 Contracts)	Net Profit (Loss)	Stock Value (436 Shares)	Net Profit (Loss)
$25	$ —	$(16,750)	$10,900	$(5,850)
30	—	(16,750)	13,080	(3,670)
35	—	(16,750)	15,260	(1,490)
40	25,000	8,250	17,440	690
45	50,000	33,250	19,620	2,870
50	75,000	58,250	21,800	5,050

The option position clearly magnifies the gains and losses on the stock by a substantial amount. The reason is that payoff on your 50 option contracts is based on $50 \times 100 = 5,000$ shares of stock instead of just 436.

In our example, if the stock price changes by only a small amount, you lose all $16,750 with the option. With the stock, you still have about what you started with. Also notice that the option can never be worth less than zero because you can always just throw it away. As a result, you can never lose more than your original investment (the $16,750 in our example).

Recognize that stock options are a zero-sum game. By this we mean that whatever the buyer of a stock option makes, the seller loses and vice versa. To illustrate, suppose that in our example you had sold 50 option contracts. You would receive $16,750 up front, and you would be obligated to sell the stock for $35 if the buyer of the option wished to exercise it. In this situation, if the stock price ends up at or less than $35, you would be $16,750 ahead. If the stock price ends up more than $35, you have to sell something for less than it is worth, so you lose the difference. For example, if the stock price were $45, you would have to sell $50 \times 100 = 5,000$ shares at $35 per share, so you would be out $45 - 35 = $10 per share, or $50,000. Because you received $16,750 up front, your net loss is $33,250. We can summarize some other possibilities as follows:

Ending Stock Price	Net Profit to Option Seller
$25	$ 16,750
30	16,750
35	16,750
40	(8,250)
45	(33,250)
50	(58,250)

Notice that the net profits to the option buyer (just calculated) are the opposites of these amounts.

Put Payoffs

Looking at Table 20.1, suppose you buy 10 Alcan Alumin. May 40 put contracts. How much does this cost (ignoring commissions)? Just before the option expires, Alcan is selling for $35 per share. Is this good news or bad news? What is your net profit?

The option is quoted at 2.050, so one contract costs $100 \times 2.05 = 205.00. Your 10 contracts total $2,050. You now have the right to sell 1,000 shares of Alcan for $40 per share. If the stock is currently selling for $35 per share, this is most definitely good news. You can buy 1,000 shares at $35 and sell them for $40. Your puts are thus worth $5 \times 1,000 = $5,000$. Since you paid $2,050, your net profit is $5,000 - 2,050 = $2,950.

CONCEPT QUESTIONS
1. What is a call option? A put option?
2. If you thought a stock was going to drop sharply in value, how might you use stock options to profit from the decline?

20.2 | FUNDAMENTALS OF OPTION VALUATION

Now that we understand the basics of puts and calls, we can discuss what determines their values. We focus on call options in the following discussion, but the same type of analysis can be applied to put options.

Value of a Call Option at Expiration

We have already described the payoffs from call options for different stock prices. To continue this discussion, the following notation is useful:

S_1 = Stock price at expiration (in one period)

S_0 = Stock price today

C_1 = Value of the call option on the expiration date (in one period)

C_0 = Value of the call option today

E = Exercise price on the option

From our previous discussion, remember that if the stock price (S_1) is not more than the exercise price (E) on the expiration date, the call option (C_1) is worth zero. In other words:

$$C_1 = 0 \text{ if } S_1 \leq E$$

Or, equivalently:

$$C_1 = 0 \text{ if } (S_1 - E) \leq 0 \tag{20.1}$$

This is the case where the option is out of the money when it expires.

If the option finishes in the money, $S_1 > E$, the value of the option at expiration is equal to the difference:

$$C_1 = S_1 - E \text{ if } S_1 > E$$

Or, equivalently:

$$C_1 = S_1 - E \text{ if } (S_1 - E) > 0 \tag{20.2}$$

For example, suppose we have a call option with an exercise price of $10. The option is about to expire. If the stock is selling for $8, we have the right to pay $10 for something worth only $8. Our option is thus worth exactly zero because the stock price is less than the exercise price on the option ($S_1 \leq E$). If the stock is selling for $12, the option has value. Since we can buy the stock for $10, it is worth ($S_1 - E$) = $12 - $10 = $2.

Figure 20.1 plots the value of a call option at expiration against the stock price. The result looks something like a hockey stick. Notice that for every stock price less than E, the value of the option is zero. For every stock price greater than E, the value of the call option is ($S_1 - E$). Also, once the stock price exceeds the exercise price, the option's value goes up dollar for dollar with the stock price.

The Upper and Lower Bounds on a Call Option's Value

Now that we know how to determine C_1, the value of the call at expiration, we turn to a somewhat more challenging question: How can we determine C_0, the value sometime before expiration? We discuss this in the next several sections. For now, we establish the upper and lower bounds for the value of a call option.

The Upper Bound What is the most a call option could sell for? If you think about it, the answer is obvious. A call option gives you the right to buy a share of stock, so it can never be worth more than the stock itself. This tells us the upper bound on a call's value: A call option always sells for less than the underlying asset. So, in our notation, the upper bound is:

$$C_0 \leq S_0 \tag{20.3}$$

F I G U R E 20.1

Value of a call option at expiration for different stock prices

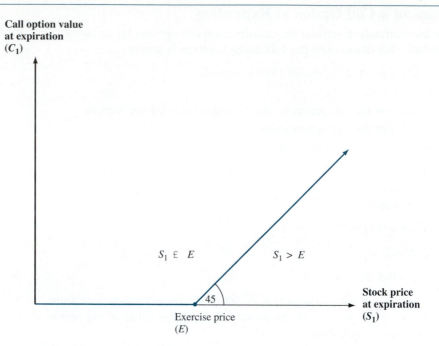

As shown, the value of a call option at expiration is equal to zero if the stock price is less than or equal to the exercise price. The value of the call is equal to the stock price minus the exercise price $(S_1 - E)$ if the stock price exceeds the exercise price. The resulting "hockey stick" shape is highlighted.

The Lower Bound   What is the least a call option could sell for? The answer here is a little less obvious. First, the call can't sell for less than zero, so $C_0 \geq 0$. Furthermore, if the stock price is greater than the exercise price, the call option is worth at least $S_0 - E$.

To see why, suppose we had a call option selling for $4. The stock price is $10, and the exercise price is $5. Is there a profit opportunity here? The answer is yes because you could buy the call for $4 and immediately exercise it by spending an additional $5. Your total cost of acquiring the stock is $4 + 5 = $9. If you turn around and immediately sell the stock for $10, you pocket a $1 certain profit.

Opportunities for riskless profits such as this one are called *arbitrages* or arbitrage opportunities. One who arbitrages is called an arbitrageur. The root for the term *arbitrage* is the same as the root for the word *arbitrate,* and an arbitrageur essentially arbitrates prices. In a well-organized market, significant arbitrages are, of course, rare.

In the case of a call option, to prevent arbitrage, the value of the call today must be greater than the stock price less the exercise price:

$$C_0 \geq S_0 - E$$

If we put our two conditions together, we have:

$$C_0 \geq 0 \text{ if } S_0 - E < 0$$
$$C_0 \geq S_0 - E \text{ if } S_0 - E \geq 0$$

[20.4]

These conditions simply say that the lower bound on the call's value is either zero or $S_0 - E$, whichever is bigger.

Our lower bound is called the **intrinsic value** of the option, and it is simply what the option would be worth if it were about to expire. With this definition, our discussion thus far can be restated as follows: At expiration, an option is worth its intrinsic value; it is generally worth more than that any time before expiration.

Figure 20.2 displays the upper and lower bounds on the value of a call option. Also plotted is a curve representing typical call option values for different stock prices before maturity. The exact shape and location of this curve depends on a number of factors. We begin our discussion of these factors in the next section.

intrinsic value
The lower bound of an option's value, or what the option would be worth if it were about to expire.

E X A M P L E | 20.1   Upper and Lower Bounds for Alcan Calls

Look back at the options listed for Alcan Aluminum in Table 20.1. Calculate the upper and lower limits for the April 37 ½ call. Does the actual price in the newspaper fall between these limits?

Alcan stock closed at $38 ⅜ and this is the upper bound. For this call, the stock price (S_0) is greater than the exercise price (E). In the jargon of options, this call is in the money. The lower bound call value is $⅞:

$$S_0 - E = \$38\,⅜ - \$37\,½ = \$⅞.$$

The actual price of this call is $1.55, which lies between the upper and lower bounds. |

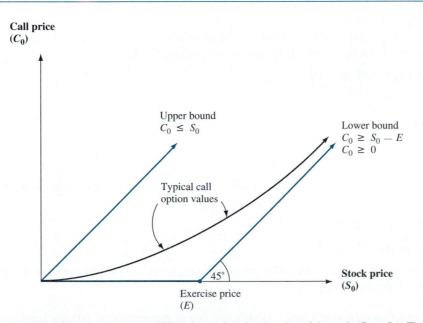

F I G U R E 20.2

Value of a call option before expiration for different stock prices

As shown, the upper bound on a call's value is given by the value of the stock ($C_0 \leq S_0$). The lower bound is either $S_0 - E$ or 0, whichever is larger. The highlighted curve illustrates the value of a call option prior to maturity for different stock prices.

A Simple Model

Option pricing can be a complex subject. Fortunately, as is often the case, many of the key insights can be illustrated with a simple example. Suppose we are looking at a call option with one year to expiration and an exercise price of $105. The stock currently sells for $100, and the risk-free rate, R_f, is 20 percent.

The value of the stock in one year is uncertain, of course. To keep things simple, suppose we know the stock price will either be $110 or $130. Importantly, we don't know the odds associated with these two prices. In other words, we know the possible values for the stock, but not the probabilities associated with those values.

Since the exercise price on the option is $105, we know the option will be worth either $110 − 105 = $5 or $130 − 105 = $25, but, once again, we don't know which. We do know one thing, however: Our call option is certain to finish in the money.

The Basic Approach   Here is the crucial observation: It is possible to duplicate exactly the payoffs on the stock using a combination of the option and the risk-free asset. How? Do the following: Buy one call option and invest $87.50 in a risk-free asset (such as a T-bill).

What will you have in a year? Your risk-free asset earns 20 percent, so it is worth $87.50 × 1.20 = $105. Your option is worth $5 or $25, so the total value is either $110 or $130, just like the stock:

Stock Value		Risk-Free Asset Value	+	Call Value	=	Total Value
$110	versus	$105	+	$ 5	=	$110
130	versus	105	+	25	=	130

As illustrated, these two strategies—buy a share of stock versus buy a call and invest in the risk-free asset—have exactly the same payoffs in the future.

Because these two strategies have the same future payoffs, they must have the same value today or else there would be an arbitrage opportunity. The stock sells for $100 today, so the value of the call option today, C_0, is:

$$\$100 = \$87.50 + C_0$$
$$C_0 = \$12.50$$

Where did we get the $87.50? This is just the present value of the exercise price on the option, calculated at the risk-free rate:

$$E/(1 + R_f) = \$105/1.20 = \$87.50$$

Thus, our example shows that the value of a call option in this simple case is given by:

$$S_0 = C_0 + E/(1 + R_f)$$
$$C_0 = S_0 - E/(1 + R_f)$$

[20.5]

In words, the value of the call option is equal to the stock price minus the present value of the exercise price.

A More Complicated Case   Obviously, our assumption that the stock price would be either $110 or $130 is a vast oversimplification. We can now develop a more realistic model by assuming the stock price can be anything greater than or equal to the exercise price. Once again, we don't know how likely the different possibilities are, but we are certain the option will finish somewhere in the money.

We again let S_1 stand for the stock price in one year. Now consider our strategy of investing $87.50 in a riskless asset and buying one call option. The riskless asset is again worth $105 in one year, and the option is worth $S_1 − \$105$, depending on what the stock price is.

When we investigate the combined value of the option and the riskless asset, we observe something very interesting:

$$\text{Combined value} = \text{Riskless asset value} + \text{Option value}$$
$$= \$105 + (S_1 − \$105)$$
$$= S_1$$

Just as we had before, buying a share of stock has exactly the same payoff as buying a call option and investing the present value of the exercise price in the riskless asset.

Once again, to prevent arbitrage, these two strategies must have the same cost, so the value of the call option is equal to the stock price less the present value of the exercise price:[3]

$$C_0 = S_0 − E/(1 + R_f)$$

Our conclusion from this discussion is that determining the value of a call option is not difficult as long as we are certain the option will finish somewhere in the money.

Four Factors Determining Option Values

If we continue to suppose that our option is certain to finish in the money, we can readily identify four factors that determine an option's value. There is a fifth factor that comes into play if the option can finish out of the money. We discuss this last factor in the next section.

For now, if we assume that the option expires in t periods, the present value of the exercise price is $E/(1 + R_f)^t$, and the value of the call is:

$$\text{Call option value} = \text{Stock value} − \text{Present value of the exercise price}$$
$$C_0 = S_0 − E/(1 + R_f)^t \qquad [20.6]$$

If we look at this expression, the value of the call obviously depends on four things:

1. *The stock price.* The higher the stock price (S_0) is, the more the call is worth. This comes as no surprise because the option gives us the right to buy the stock at a fixed price.

2. *The exercise price.* The higher the exercise price (E) is, the less the call is worth. This is also not a surprise since the exercise price is the amount we have to pay to get the stock.

3. *The time to expiration.* The longer the time to expiration is (the bigger t is), the more the option is worth. Once again, this is because the option gives us the right to buy for a fixed length of time. As the value goes up as that length of time increases.

---

[3] You're probably wondering what would happen if the stock price were less than the present value of the exercise price, resulting in a negative value for the call option. This can't happen because we are certain the stock price will be at least E since we know the stock will finish in the money. If the current price of the stock is, say, $80, the minimum return on the stock is certain to be greater than the risk-free rate, thereby creating an arbitrage opportunity. For example, if the stock were currently selling for $80, we can earn a certain return of ($105 − \$80)/\$80 = 31.25\%$. Since we can borrow at 20 percent, we earn a certain return of 11.25 percent per dollar borrowed. This, of course, is an arbitrage.

4. *The risk-free rate.* The higher the risk-free rate (R_f) is, the more the call is worth. This result is a little less obvious. Normally, we think of asset values going down as rates rise. In this case, the exercise price is a cash outflow, a liability. The current value of that liability goes down as the discount rate goes up.

CONCEPT QUESTIONS

1. What is the value of a call option at expiration?
2. What are the upper and lower bounds on the value of a call option anytime before expiration?
3. Assuming the stock price is certain to be greater than the exercise price on a call option, what is the value of the call? Why?

20.3 | VALUING A CALL OPTION

We now investigate the value of a call option when there is the possibility that the option will finish out of the money. We again examine the simple case of two possible future stock prices. This case lets us identify the remaining factor that determines an option's value.

A Simple Model: Part II

From our previous example, we have a stock that currently sells for $100. It will be worth either $110 or $130 in a year, and we don't know which. The risk-free rate is 20 percent. We are now looking at a different call option, however. This one has an exercise price of $120 instead of $105. What is the value of this call option?

This case is a little harder. If the stock ends up at $110, the option is out of the money and worth nothing. If the stock ends up at $130, the option is worth $130 − 120 = $10.

Our basic approach to determining the value of the call option is the same. We show once again that it is possible to combine the call option and a risk-free investment in a way that exactly duplicates the payoff from holding the stock. The only complication is that it's a little harder to determine how to do it.

For example, suppose we bought one call and invested the present value of the exercise price in a riskless asset as we did before. In one year, we would have $120 from the riskless investment plus an option worth either zero or $10. The total value is either $120 or $130. This is not the same as the value of the stock ($110 or $130), so the two strategies are not comparable.

Instead, consider investing the present value of $110 (the lower stock price) in a riskless asset. This guarantees us a $110 payoff. If the stock price is $110, any call options we own are worthless, and we have exactly $110 as desired.

When the stock is worth $130, our call option is worth $10. Our risk-free investment is worth $110, so we are $130 − 110 = $20 short. Since each call option is worth $10, we need to buy two of them to replicate the stock.

Thus, in this case, investing the present value of the lower stock price in a riskless asset and buying two call options exactly duplicates owning the stock. When the stock is worth $110, we have $110 from our risk-free investment. When the stock is worth $130, we have $110 from the risk-free investment plus two call options worth $10 each.

Because these two strategies have exactly the same value in the future, they must have the same value today or else arbitrage would be possible:

$$S_0 = \$100 = 2 \times C_0 + \$110/(1 + R_f)$$
$$2 \times C_0 = \$100 - \$110/1.20$$
$$C_0 = \$4.17$$

Each call option is thus worth $4.17.

E X A M P L E | 20.2   **Don't Call Us, We'll Call You**

We are looking at two call options on the same stock, one with an exercise price of $20 and one with an exercise price of $30. The stock currently sells for $35. Its future price will either be $25 or $50. If the risk-free rate is 10 percent, what are the values of these call options?

The first case (the $20 exercise price) is not difficult since the option is sure to finish in the money. We know that the value is equal to the stock price less the present value of the exercise price:

$$C_0 = S_0 - E/(1 + R_f)$$
$$= \$35 - \$20/1.1$$
$$= \$16.82$$

In the second case, the exercise price is $30, so the option can finish out of the money. At expiration, the option is worth $0 if the stock is worth $25. The option is worth $50 - 30 = $20 if it finishes in the money.

As before, we start by investing the present value of the lower stock price in the risk-free asset. This costs $25/1.1 = $22.73. At expiration, we have $25 from this investment.

If the stock price is $50, we need an additional $25 to duplicate the stock payoff. Since each option is worth $20, we need $25/$20 = 1.25 options. So, to prevent arbitrage, investing the present value of $25 in a risk-free asset and buying 1.25 call options has the same value as the stock:

$$S_0 = 1.25 \times C_0 + \$25/(1 + R_f)$$
$$\$35 = 1.25 \times C_0 + \$25/(1 + .10)$$
$$C_0 = \$9.82$$

Notice that this second option had to be worth less because it has the higher exercise price.

The Fifth Factor

We now illustrate the fifth (and last) factor that determines an option's value. Suppose that everything in our previous example is the same except the stock price can be $105 or $135 instead of $110 or $130. Notice that this change makes the stock's future price more volatile than before.

We investigate the same strategy that we used before: Invest the present value of the lower stock price ($105) in the risk-free asset and buy two call options. If the stock price is $105, as before, the call options have no value and we have $105 in all.

If the stock price is $135, each option is worth $S_1 - E = \$135 - 120 = \$15$. We have two calls, so our portfolio is worth $105 + 2 \times \$15 = \$135$. Once again, we have exactly replicated the value of the stock.

What has happened to the option's value? More to the point, the variance of the return on the stock has increased. Does the option's value go up or down? To find out, we need to solve for the value of the call just as we did before:

$$S_0 = \$100 = 2 \times C_0 + \$105/(1 + R_f)$$
$$2 \times C_0 = \$100 - \$105/1.20$$
$$C_0 = \$6.25$$

The value of the call option has gone up from $4.17 to $6.25.

Based on our example, the fifth and final factor that determines an option's value is the variance of the return on the underlying asset. Furthermore, the greater that variance is, the more the option is worth. This result appears a little odd at first, and it may be somewhat surprising to learn that increasing the risk (as measured by return variance) on the underlying asset increases the value of the option.

The reason that increasing the variance on the underlying asset increases the value of the option isn't hard to see in our example. Changing the lower stock price to $105 from $110 doesn't hurt a bit because the option is worth zero in either case. However, moving the upper possible price to $135 from $130 makes the option worth more when it is in the money.

More generally, increasing the variance of the possible future prices on the underlying asset doesn't affect the option's value when the option finishes out of the money. The value is always zero in this case. On the other hand, increasing that variance when the option is in the money only increases the possible payoffs, so the net effect is to increase the option's value. Put another way, since the downside risk is always limited, the only effect is to increase the upside potential.

In later discussion, we use the usual symbol, σ^2, to stand for the variance of the return on the underlying asset.

A Closer Look

Before moving on, it is useful to consider one last example. Suppose the stock price is $100 and it will either move up or down by 20 percent. The risk-free rate is 5 percent. What is the value of a call option with a $90 exercise price?

The stock price will either be $80 or $120. The option is worth zero when the stock is worth $80, and it's worth $120 – 90 = $30 when the stock is worth $120. We therefore invest the present value of $80 in the risk-free asset and buy some call options.

When the stock finishes at $120, our risk-free asset pays $80, leaving us $40 short. Each option is worth $30 in this case, so we need $40/$30 = 4/3 options to match the payoff on the stock. The option's value must thus be given by:

$$S_0 = 4/3 \times C_0 + \$80/1.05$$
$$C_0 = (\tfrac{3}{4}) \times (\$100 - \$76.19)$$
$$= \$17.86$$

To make our result a little bit more general, notice that the number of options you need to buy to replicate the stock is always equal to $\Delta S/\Delta C$, where ΔS is the difference in the possible stock prices and ΔC is the difference in the possible option values. In our current case, for example, ΔS would be $120 – 80 = $40 and ΔC would be $30 – 0 = $30, so $\Delta S/\Delta C$ is $40/$30 = 4/3 as we calculated.

Notice also that when the stock is certain to finish in the money, $\Delta S/\Delta C$ is always exactly equal to one, so one call option is always needed. Otherwise, $\Delta S/\Delta C$ is greater than one, so more than one call option is needed.

This concludes our discussion of option valuation. The most important thing to remember is that the value of an option depends on five factors. Table 20.2 summarizes these factors and the direction of the influence for both puts and calls. In Table 20.2, the sign in parentheses indicates the direction of the influence.[4] In other words, the sign tells us whether the value of the option goes up or down when the value of a factor increases. For example, notice that increasing the exercise price reduces the value of a call option. Increasing any of the other four factors increases the value of the call. Notice also that the time to expiration and the variance act the same for puts and calls. The other three factors have opposite signs.

We have not considered how to value a call option when the option can finish out of the money and the stock price can take on more than two values. A very famous result, the Black-Scholes option pricing model, is needed in this case. We cover this subject in the chapter appendix.

E X A M P L E | 20.3   Option Prices and Time to Expiration and Variance

According to Table 20.2, when other things are held equal, increasing either time to expiration or stock price variance raises the prices of puts and calls. Is this theory consistent with the actual option prices in Table 20.1?

We can look at time to expiration and pricing for the Alcan options. Starting with calls, all the other four factors are constant if we compare calls with the same exercise price but different expiration dates. There are four Alcan calls with a $37½ exercise price:

Call	Price (in cents)
April 37 ½	155
May 37 ½	165
July 37 ½	300
October 37 ½	370

As expected, the call prices increase with time to expiration.

To look at the effect of variance, we either need to examine the same option on different dates after the variance has changed or compare similar options on different stocks whose variances differ. In this case, we take the second approach and compare the Alcan July 40 call with a similar call on a less volatile stock, Bank of Nova Scotia, which closed at $26 ¾. Since the Alcan July 40 call is just slightly out of the money, we compare it against a similar call Bank of Nova Scotia, which is also just out of the money: the July 27.

Both these calls are listed in Table 20.1. The Alcan July 40 closed at 1.600 and the Bank of Nova Scotia July 27 at 0.95. Other things equal, call buyers were willing to pay a much higher price for the Alcan call due to its greater variance. ∎

CONCEPT QUESTIONS

1. What are the five factors that determine an option's value?
2. What is the effect of an increase in each of the five factors on the value of a call option? Give an intuitive explanation for your answer.
3. What is the effect of an increase in each of the five factors on the value of a put option? Give an intuitive explanation for your answer.

---

[4] The signs in Table 20.2 are for American options. For a European put option, the effect of increasing the time to expiration is ambiguous, and the direction of the influence can be positive or negative.

T A B L E 20.2

Five factors that determine option values

Factor	Calls	Puts
Current value of the underlying asset	(+)	(−)
Exercise price on the option	(−)	(+)
Time to expiration on the option	(+)	(+)
Risk-free rate	(+)	(−)
Variance of return on underlying asset	(+)	(+)

20.4 | EQUITY AS A CALL OPTION ON THE FIRM'S ASSETS

Now that we understand the basic determinants of an option's value, we turn to examining some of the many ways that options appear in corporate finance. One of the most important insights we gain from studying options is that the common stock in a leveraged firm (one that has issued debt) is effectively a call option on the assets of the firm. This is a remarkable observation, and we explore it next.

An example is the easiest way to get started. Suppose a firm has a single debt issue outstanding. The face value is $1,000, and the debt is coming due in a year. There are no coupon payments between now and then, so the debt is effectively a pure discount bond. In addition, the current market value of the firm's assets is $950, and the risk-free rate is 12.5 percent.

In a year, the stockholders will have a choice. They can pay off the debt for $1,000 and thereby acquire the assets of the firm free and clear, or they can default on the debt. If they default, the bondholders will own the assets of the firm.

In this situation, the shareholders essentially have a call option on the assets of the firm with an exercise price of $1,000. They can exercise the option by paying the $1,000, or they can not exercise the option by defaulting. Whether they choose to exercise obviously depends on the value of the firm's assets when the debt becomes due.

If the value of the firm's assets exceeds $1,000, the option is in the money, and the stockholders would exercise by paying off the debt. If the value of the firm's assets is less than $1,000, the option is out of the money, and the stockholders would optimally choose to default. What we now illustrate is that we can determine the values of the debt and equity using our option pricing results.

Case I: The Debt Is Risk-Free

Suppose that in one year the firm's assets will either be worth $1,100 or $1,200. What is the value today of the equity in the firm? The value of the debt? What is the interest rate on the debt?

To answer these questions, we recognize that the option (the equity in the firm) is certain to finish in the money because the value of the firm's assets ($1,100 or $1,200) always exceeds the face value of the debt. From our discussion in previous sections, we know that the option value is simply the difference between the value of the underlying asset and the present value of the exercise price (calculated at the risk-free rate). The present value of $1,000 in one year at 12.5 percent is $888.89. The current value of the firm is $950, so the option (the firm's equity) is worth $950 − 888.89 = $61.11.

What we see is that the equity, which is effectively an option to purchase the firm's assets, must be worth $61.11. The debt must therefore actually be worth

$888.89. In fact, we really didn't need to know about options to handle this example, because the debt is risk free. The reason is that the bondholders are certain to receive $1,000. Since the debt is risk free, the appropriate discount rate (and the interest rate on the debt) is the risk-free rate. Therefore, we know immediately that the current value of the debt is $1,000/1.125 = $888.89. The equity is thus worth $950 − 888.89 = $61.11 as we calculated.

Case II: The Debt Is Risky

Suppose now that the value of the firm's assets in one year will be either $800 or $1,200. This case is a little more difficult because the debt is no longer risk free. If the value of the assets turns out to be $800, the shareholders will not exercise their option and thereby default. The stock is worth nothing in this case. If the assets are worth $1,200, the stockholders will exercise their option to pay off the debt and enjoy a profit of $1,200 − 1,000 = $200.

What we see is that the option (the equity in the firm) is worth either zero or $200. The assets are worth either $1,200 or $800. Based on our discussion in previous sections, a portfolio that has the present value of $800 invested in a risk-free asset and ($1,200 − $800)/($200 − $0) = 2 call options exactly replicates the assets of the firm.

The present value of $800 at the risk-free rate of 12.5 percent is $800/1.125 = $711.11. This amount, plus the value of the two call options, is equal to $950, the current value of the firm:

$$\$950 = 2 \times C_0 + \$711.11$$
$$C_0 = \$119.44$$

Because the call option is actually the firm's equity, the value of the equity is $119.44. The value of the debt is thus $950 − 119.44 = $830.56.

Finally, since the debt has a $1,000 face value and a current value of $830.55, the interest rate is $1,000/$830.55 − 1 = 20.4%. This exceeds the risk-free rate, of course, since the debt is now risky.

E X A M P L E | 20.4   Equity as a Call Option

Swenson Software has a pure discount debt issue with a face value of $100. The issue is due in a year. At that time, the assets in the firm will be worth either $55 or $160, depending on the sales success of Swenson's latest product. The assets of the firm are currently worth $110. If the risk-free rate is 10 percent, what is the value of the equity in Swenson? The value of the debt? The interest rate on the debt?

To replicate the assets of the firm, we need to invest the present value of $55 in the risk-free asset. This costs $55/1.10 = $50. If the assets turn out to be worth $160, the option is worth $160 − 100 = $60. Our risk-free asset would be worth $55, so we need ($160 − $55)/$60 = 1.75 call options. Since the firm is currently worth $110, we have:

$$\$110 = 1.75 \times C_0 + \$50$$
$$C_0 = \$34.29$$

The equity is thus worth $34.29; the debt is worth $110 − 34.29 = $75.71. The interest rate on the debt is about $100/$75.71 − 1 = 32.1%.

CONCEPT QUESTIONS

1. Why do we say that the equity in a leveraged firm is effectively a call option on the firm's assets?
2. All other things being the same, would the stockholders of a firm prefer to increase or decrease the volatility of the firm's return on assets? Why? What about the bondholders? Give an intuitive explanation.

20.5 | WARRANTS

warrant

A security that gives the holder the right to purchase shares of stock at a fixed price over a given period of time.

A **warrant** is a corporate security that looks a lot like a call option. It gives the holder the right, but not the obligation, to buy shares of common stock directly from a company at a fixed price for a given time period. Each warrant specifies the number of shares of stock that the holder can buy, the exercise price, and the expiration date.

The differences in contractual features between the call options that trade on the Trans Canada Options Exchange and warrants are relatively minor. Warrants usually have much longer maturity periods, however. In fact, some warrants are actually perpetual and have no fixed expiration date.

sweeteners or equity kickers

A feature included in the terms of a new issue of debt or preferred shares to make the issue more attractive to initial investors.

Warrants are often called **sweeteners** or **equity kickers** because they are usually issued in combination with privately placed loans or bonds or, less commonly, with preferred shares.[5] Throwing in some warrants is a way of making the deal a little more attractive to the lender, and it is very common. In fact, the use of warrants is becoming more popular judging by the increasing number listed on the TSE.[6]

In most cases, warrants are attached to the bonds when issued. The loan agreement states whether the warrants are detachable from the bond. Usually, the warrant can be detached immediately and sold by the holder as a separate security.

For example, Navistar International is one of the world's largest manufacturers and marketers of diesel-powered trucks and replacement parts.[7] On April 14, 1985, Navistar raised $200 million by publicly issuing a combination of notes and warrants. Forty warrants were attached to each 13.25 percent senior note due in 1995. The holder was given the right to use each warrant to buy one share of common stock for $9 on any date up to and including December 31, 1990. Each unit, "note plus 40 warrants," sold for $1,000 when initially issued.

As is usually the case, the Navistar warrants were detachable, which means they could be traded separately as soon as the issue of notes and warrants was completed. The warrants first traded on July 8, 1985, when more than 1,000 of them changed hands. The closing price for the warrants was $3.50, and the price for Navistar common stock was $8.50.

Just as we had with call options, the lower limit on the value of a warrant is zero if Navistar's stock price is less than $9 per share. If the price of Navistar's common stock rises to more than $9 per share, the lower limit is the stock price minus $9. The upper limit is the price of Navistar's common stock. A warrant to buy one share of common stock cannot sell at a price more than the price of the underlying common stock.

---

[5] Warrants are also issued with publicly distributed bonds and new issues of common stock.
[6] Warrants can also be listed on the Toronto Futures Exchange. A thorough discussion of warrants is in J. E. Hatch and M. J. Robinson, *Investment Management in Canada,* 2nd ed. (Scarborough: Prentice Hall Canada Inc., 1989), chap. 16.
[7] The company was previously called International Harvester.

If Navistar stock traded for less than $9 on the warrant expiration date, the warrants would expire worthless. This is quite common—slightly fewer than half the warrants issued in Canada expired worthless.[8]

With the growth of financial engineering, warrant issuers are creating new varieties. Some warrant issues give investors the right to buy the issuers' bonds instead of their stock. In addition, warrants are issued on their own instead of as sweeteners in a bond issue. In 1991, the Toronto-Dominion Bank combined these features in a $2.7 million stand-alone issue. The TD warrants give the right to purchase debentures to be issued in the future.[9]

Echo Bay Mines Ltd. of Edmonton designed an innovative financing package including gold purchase warrants with a preferred share issue. The warrants gave the holder the right to buy gold at an exercise price of $595 (U.S.) per ounce. When the warrants were issued in 1981, gold was trading at $500 (U.S.) per ounce. A further condition restricted exercise of the warrants to cases where Echo Bay met certain production levels. As a result, how much these warrants were worth depended both on how well the company was doing and on gold prices.[10]

The Difference between Warrants and Call Options

As we have explained, from the holder's point of view, warrants are very similar to call options on common stock. A warrant, like a call option, gives its holder the right to buy common stock at a specified price. From the firm's point of view, however, a warrant is very different from a call option sold on the company's common stock.

The most important difference between call options and warrants is that call options are issued by individuals and warrants are issued by firms. When a call option is exercised, one investor buys stock from another investor. The company is not involved. When a warrant is exercised, the firm must issue new shares of stock. Each time a warrant is exercised, the firm receives some cash and the number of shares outstanding increases.

To illustrate, suppose the Endrun Company issues a warrant giving holders the right to buy one share of common stock at $25. Further suppose the warrant is exercised. Endrun must print one new stock certificate. In exchange for the stock certificate, it receives $25 from the holder.

In contrast, when a call option is exercised, there is no change in the number of shares outstanding. Suppose Bethany Enger purchases a call option on the common stock of the Endrun Company from Thomas Swift. The call option gives Enger the right to buy one share of common stock of the Endrun Company for $25.

If Enger chooses to exercise the call option, Swift is obligated to give her one share of Endrun's common stock in exchange for $25. If Swift does not already own a share, he must go into the stock market and buy one.

The call option amounts to a side bet between Enger and Swift on the value of the Endrun Company's common stock. When a call option is exercised, one investor gains and the other loses. The total number of outstanding Endrun shares remains constant, and no new funds are made available to the company.

---

[8] We should hedge this conclusion a bit since the study looked at warrants up to the mid-1970s: R. G. Storey and C. R. Dipchand, "Factors Related to the Conversion Record of Convertible Securities: The Canadian Experience, 1946–1975," *Journal of Financial Research,* Winter 1978.

[9] B. Critchley, "The Top 10 Financings, Innovative Fund-Raising in Corporate Canada for '91," *Financial Post,* December 16, 1991, p. 15.

[10] P. P. Boyle and E. F. Kirzner, "Pricing Complex Options: Echo-Bay Ltd. Gold Purchase Warrants," *Canadian Journal of Administrative Sciences* 2, no. 12 (December 1985), pp. 294–306.

IN THEIR OWN WORDS . . .

Andrew Bell on Airline Warrants

Fancy a flier on Canada's big two airlines, whose results are improving but whose stocks are languishing?

For investors who want to go all out and chance some pure speculation, there are warrants that let you buy the shares at a fixed price for a limited time.

If the underlying stock goes above the exercise price, the warrants become valuable—potentially producing big gains.

Mind you, these things are strictly for stunt pilots. Once they expire, they're worth less than a stale pack of peanuts.

Air Canada warrants let risk-takers buy the shares at $6.25, less than yesterday's closing price of $6.37 on the Toronto Stock Exchange—but there are a couple of big problems.

The warrants expire on Dec. 6, only eight months away. And the company's stock has slid 15 percent since March 29, when the

Airline warrants			
	Warrant Conditions	Price	Share Price
Air Canada	Lets holder buy one share at $6.25 anytime until the expiry date of Dec. 6, 1995.	$1.13	$6.37
PWA	Lets holder buy one share at 80¢ anytime until the expiry date of April 27, 1999. If stock trades above $1.60 for 30 days, company will buy back warrants for 10¢ on 60 days' notice.	10¢	40.5¢

Montreal-based airline announced it was raising half a billion dollars by selling non-voting shares and convertible debentures.

Existing shareholders are said to be upset with the timing of the deal and its price—the non-voting shares are to be sold at $7, below the stock's $7.50 price on March 29.

Meanwhile, **PWA Corp.** warrants offer a very different set of risks and rewards. They last for a long time—until April 1999. But the Calgary-based company has a vast amount of stock outstanding,

around 800 million shares, after debtholders accepted shares in a restructuring last year.

The warrants, which give speculators the right to buy PWA shares at 80 cents until the 1999 deadline, languished at 10 cents yesterday. The stock closed at 40.5 cents, meaning that the shares must double by early 1999 before the warrants are worth anything.

Andrew Bell is an investment reporter for the *Globe and Mail*. His work, excerpted from the *Globe and Mail*, April 6, 1995, p. B9, is reprinted here with permission.

Warrants and the Value of the Firm

Because the company is not involved in buying or selling options, puts and calls have no effect on the value of the firm. However, the firm is the original seller when warrants are involved, and warrants do affect the value of the firm. We compare the effect of call options and warrants in this section.

Imagine that Spencer Gould and Jennifer Rockefeller are two investors who together purchase six ounces of platinum at $500 per ounce. The total investment is $6 \times \$500 = \$3,000$, and each of the investors puts up half. They incorporate, print two stock certificates, and name the firm the GR Company. Each certificate represents a one-half claim to the platinum, and Gould and Rockefeller each own one certificate. The net effect of all of this is that Gould and Rockefeller have formed a company with platinum as its only asset.

The Effect of a Call Option Suppose Gould later decides to sell a call option to Franchesca Fiske. The call option gives Fiske the right to buy Gould's share for $1,800 in one year.

At the end of the year, platinum is selling for $700 per ounce, so the value of the GR Company is $6 \times \$700 = \$4,200$. Each share is worth $\$4,200/2 = \$2,100$. Fiske exercises her option, and Gould must turn over his stock certificate and receive $1,800.

How would the firm be affected by the exercise? The number of shares won't be affected. There are still two of them, now owned by Rockefeller and Fiske. The shares are still worth $2,100. The only thing that happens is that, when Fiske exercises her option, she profits by $\$2,100 - 1,800 = \$300$. Gould loses by the same amount.

The Effect of a Warrant   This story changes if a warrant is issued. Suppose Gould does not sell a call option to Fiske. Instead, Spencer Gould and Jennifer Rockefeller get together and decide to issue a warrant and sell it to Fiske. This means that, in effect, the GR Company decides to issue a warrant.

The warrant gives Fiske the right to receive a share of stock in the company at an exercise price of $1,800. If Fiske decides to exercise the warrant, the firm issues another stock certificate and gives it to Fiske in exchange for $1,800.

Suppose again that platinum rises to $700 an ounce. The firm is worth $4,200. Further suppose that Fiske exercises her warrant. Two things would occur:

1. Fiske would pay $1,800 to the firm.
2. The firm would print one stock certificate and give it to Fiske. The stock certificate represents a one-third claim on the platinum of the firm.

Fiske's one-third share seems to be worth only $\$4,200/3 = \$1,400$. This is not correct, because we have to add the $1,800 contributed to the firm by Fiske. The value of the firm increases by this amount, so:

$$\text{New value of firm} = \text{Value of platinum} + \text{Fiske's contribution to the firm}$$
$$= \$4,200 + 1,800$$
$$= \$6,000$$

Because Fiske has a one-third claim on the firm' value, her share is worth $\$6,000/3 = \$2,000$. By exercising the warrant, Fiske gains $\$2,000 - 1,800 = \$200$. This is illustrated in Table 20.3.

When the warrant is exercised, the exercise money goes to the firm. Since Fiske ends up owning one-third of the firm, she effectively gets back one-third of what she pays in. Because she really gives up only two-thirds of $1,800 to buy the stock, the effective exercise price is $2/3 \times \$1,800 = \$1,200$.

Fiske effectively pays out $1,200 to obtain a one-third interest in the assets of the firm (the platinum). This is worth $\$4,200/3 = \$1,400$. Fiske's gain, from this perspective, is $\$1,400 - 1,200 = \$200$ (exactly what we calculated earlier).

Warrant Value and Stock Value   What is the value of the common stock of a firm that has issued warrants? Let's look at the market value of the GR Company just before and just after the exercise of Fiske's warrant. Just after exercise, the balance sheet looks like this:

Cash	$1,800	Stock	$6,000
Platinum	4,200	(3 shares)	
Total	$6,000	Total	$6,000

T A B L E 20.3

Effect of a call option versus a warrant on the GR Company

	Value of Firm Based on Price of Platinum per Ounce	
	$700	$600
No Warrant or Call Option		
Gould's share	$2,100	$1,800
Rockefeller's share	2,100	1,800
Firm value	$4,200	$3,600
Call Option		
Gould's claim	$ 0	$1,800
Rockefeller's claim	2,100	1,800
Fiske's claim	2,100	0
Firm value	$4,200	$3,600
*Warrant**		
Gould's share	$2,000	$1,800
Rockefeller's share	2,000	1,800
Fiske's share	2,000	0
Firm value	$6,000	$3,600

*If the price of platinum is $700, the value of the firm is equal to the value of six ounces of platinum plus the excess dollars paid into the firm by Fiske. This amount is $4,200 + 1,800 = $6,000.

As we saw, each share of stock is worth $6,000/3 = $2,000.

Whoever holds the warrant profits by $200 when the warrant is exercised; thus, the warrant is worth $200 just before expiration. The balance sheet for the GR Company just before expiration is thus:

Platinum	$4,200		Warrant	$ 200
			Stock	4,000
			(2 shares)	
Total	$4,200		Total	$4,200

We calculate the value of the stock as the value of the assets ($4,200) less the value of the warrant ($200).

Notice that the value of each share just before expiration is $4,000/2 = $2,000 just as it is after expiration. The value of each share of stock is thus not changed by the exercise of the warrant. There is no dilution of share value from the exercise.

Earnings Dilution   Warrants and convertible bonds frequently cause the number of shares to increase. This happens (1) when the warrants are exercised and (2) when the bonds are converted. As we have seen, this increase does not lower the per share value of the stock. However, it does cause the firm's net income to be spread over a larger number of shares; thus, earnings per share decrease.

Firms with significant amounts of warrants and convertible issues outstanding generally calculate and report earnings per share on a *fully diluted basis*. This means the calculation is based on the number of shares that would be outstanding if all the warrants were exercised and all the convertibles were converted. Since this increases the number of shares, the fully diluted EPS is lower than an EPS calculated only on the basis of shares actually outstanding.

CONCEPT QUESTIONS

1. What is a warrant?
2. Why are warrants different from call options?

20.6 | CONVERTIBLE BONDS

A **convertible bond** is similar to a bond with warrants. The most important difference is that a bond with warrants can be separated into distinct securities (a bond and some warrants), but a convertible bond cannot be. A convertible bond gives the holder the right to exchange the bond for a fixed number of shares of stock anytime up to and including the maturity date of the bond.

For example, in the early 1980s, the Royal Bank issued $100 million in 12 percent convertible debentures maturing in July 1991. The convertible debentures were subordinated to the claims of depositors and counted as capital under the newly revised 1980 Bank Act. Each $1,000 debenture was convertible into 28.57 shares of stock. This means that converting the debenture was equivalent to buying stock at $35 per share:

$1,000/28.57 shares = $35 per share

The Royal Bank also issued several series of convertible preferred shares. A convertible preferred stock is the same as a convertible bond except that it has an infinite maturity date.[11]

Features of a Convertible Bond

The basic features of a convertible bond can be illustrated with an example. Crazy Eddie, a retailer of home entertainment and consumer electronic products, issues $72 million of 6 percent convertible subordinated debentures maturing in 25 years. The firm plans to use the proceeds to add new stores to its chain. In some respects, the bonds are like typical debentures. For example, they have a sinking fund and are callable after two years.

The particular feature that make the Crazy Eddie bonds interesting is that they are convertible into the common stock of Crazy Eddie anytime before maturity at a **conversion price** of $46.25 per share. Since each bond has a face value of $1,000, this means the holder of a Crazy Eddie convertible bond can exchange that bond for $1,000/$46.25 = 21.62 shares of Crazy Eddie common stock. The number of shares received for each debenture, 21.62 in this example, is called the **conversion ratio**.

When Crazy Eddie issues its convertible bonds, its common stock is trading at $38 per share. The conversion price of $46.25 is thus ($46.25 − $38)/$38 = 22% higher than the actual common stock price. This 22 percent is called the **conversion premium**. It reflects the fact that the conversion option in Crazy Eddie convertible bonds is out of the money. This conversion premium is typical.

Value of a Convertible Bond

Even though the conversion feature of the convertible bond cannot be detached like a warrant, the value of the bond can still be decomposed into its bond value and the value of the conversion feature. We discuss how this is done next.[12]

convertible bond
A bond that can be exchanged for a fixed number of shares of stock for a specified amount of time.

conversion price
The dollar amount of a bond's par value that is exchangeable for one share of stock.

conversion ratio
The number of shares per $1,000 bond received for conversion into stock.

conversion premium
Difference between the conversion price and the current stock price divided by the current stock price.

---

[11] The dividends paid are, of course, not tax deductible for the corporation. Interest paid on a convertible bond is tax deductible.

[12] Our coverage is necessarily brief. See J. C. Van Horne, *Financial Market Rates and Flows,* 2nd ed. (Englewood Cliffs, NJ: Prentice Hall, 1987), chapter 11 for a similar, in-depth treatment. See also R. A. Brealey and S. C. Myers, *Principles of Corporate Finance,* 3rd ed. (New York: McGraw-Hill, 1988), chap. 22.

straight bond value

The value of a convertible bond if it could not be converted into common stock.

Straight Bond Value   The **straight bond value** is what the convertible bond would sell for if it could not be converted into common stock. This value depends on the general level of interest rates on debentures and on the default risk of the issuer.

Suppose that straight debentures issued by Crazy Eddie are rated A, and A-rated bonds are priced to yield 10 percent. The straight bond value of Crazy Eddie convertible bonds can be determined by discounting the $60 annual coupon payment and maturity value at 10 percent, just as we did in Chapter 6:

$$\text{Straight bond value} = \$60 \times (1 - 1/1.10^{25})/.10 + \$1,000/1.10^{25}$$
$$= \$544.62 + 92.30$$
$$= \$636.92$$

The straight bond value of a convertible bond is a minimum value in the sense that the bond is always worth at least this amount. As we discuss, it is usually worth more.

conversion value

The value of a convertible bond if it was immediately converted into common stock.

Conversion Value   The **conversion value** of a convertible bond is what the bond would be worth if it were immediately converted into common stock. This value is computed by multiplying the current price of the stock by the number of shares received when the bond is converted.

For example, each Crazy Eddie convertible bond could be converted into 21.62 shares of Crazy Eddie common stock. Crazy Eddie common is selling for $38 when the bonds are issued. Thus, the conversion value is 21.62 × $38 = $821.56.

A convertible cannot sell for less than its conversion value or an arbitrage exists. If Crazy Eddie's convertible sold for less than $821.56, investors would buy the bonds and convert them into common stock and sell the stock. The arbitrage profit would be the difference between the value of the stock and the bond's conversion value.

Floor Value for a Convertible   As we have seen, convertible bonds have two floor values: the straight bond value and the conversion value. The minimum value of a convertible bond is given by the greater of these two values. For the Crazy Eddie issue, the conversion value is $821.56, while the straight bond value is $626.92. At a minimum, this bond is thus worth $821.56.

Figure 20.3 plots the minimum value of a convertible bond against the value of the stock. The conversion value is determined by the value of the firm's underlying common stock. As the value of common stock rises and falls, the conversion value rises and falls with it. For example, if the value of Crazy Eddie's common stock increases by $1, the conversion value of its convertible bonds increases by $21.62.

In Figure 20.3, we have implicitly assumed that the convertible bond is default-free. In this case, the straight bond value does not depend on the stock price, so it is plotted as a horizontal line. Given the straight bond value, the minimum value of the convertible depends on the value of the stock. When this is low, the minimum value of a convertible is most significantly influenced by the underlying value as straight debt. However, when the value of the firm is very high, the value of a convertible bond is mostly determined by the underlying conversion value. This is also illustrated in Figure 20.3.

Option Value   The value of a convertible bond always exceeds the straight bond value and the conversion value unless the firm is in default or the bondholders are forced to convert. The reason is that holders of convertibles do not have to convert immediately. Instead, by waiting, they can take advantage of whichever is greater in the future, the straight bond value or the conversion value.

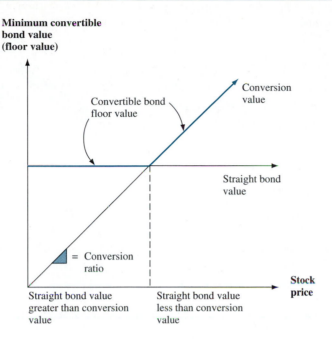

FIGURE 20.3

Minimum value of a convertible bond versus the value of the stock for a given interest rate

As shown, the minimum or "floor" value of a convertible bond is either its straight bond value or its conversion value, whichever is greater.

This option to wait has value, and it raises the value of the convertible bond over its floor value. The total value of the convertible is thus equal to the sum of the floor value and the option value. This is illustrated in Figure 20.4. Notice the similarity between this picture and the representation of the value of a call option in Figure 20.2.

CONCEPT QUESTIONS

1. What are the conversion ratio, the conversion price, and the conversion premium?
2. What three elements make up the value of a convertible bond?

20.7 | REASONS FOR ISSUING WARRANTS AND CONVERTIBLES

Until recently, bonds with warrants and convertible bonds were not well understood. Surveys of financial executives have provided the most popular textbook reasons for warrants and convertibles. Here are two of them:

1. They allow companies to issue cheap bonds by attaching sweeteners to the bonds. Sweeteners allow the coupon rate on convertibles and bonds with warrants to be set at less than the market rates on straight bonds.
2. They give companies the chance to issue common stock at a premium more than current prices in the future. In this way, convertibles and bonds with warrants represent deferred sales of common stock at relatively high prices.

*Value of a convertible
bond versus value of
the stock for a given
interest rate*

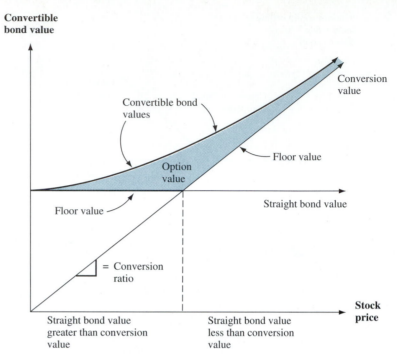

As shown, the value of a convertible bond is the sum of its floor value and its option value (highlighted region).

These justifications for convertibles and bonds with warrants are frequently mixed into free lunch explanations.

The Free Lunch Story

Suppose the RWJR Company can issue straight (non-convertible) subordinated debentures at 10 percent. It can also issue convertible bonds at 6 percent with a conversion value of $800. The conversion value means the holders can convert a convertible bond into 40 shares of common stock, which currently trades at $20.

A company treasurer who believes in free lunches might argue that convertible bonds should be issued because they represent a cheaper source of financing than either straight subordinated bonds or common stock. The treasurer points out that, if the company does poorly and the stock price does not rise to more than $20, the convertible bondholders do not convert the bonds into common stock. In this case, the company has obtained debt financing at below-market rates by attaching worthless equity kickers.

On the other hand, if the firm does well, the bondholders would convert.[13] The company issues 40 shares. Because the company receives a bond with a face value of $1,000 in exchange for issuing 40 shares of common stock, the conversion price is $25.

Effectively, if the bondholders convert, the company has issued common stock at $25 per share. This is 20 percent more than the current common stock price of $20,

---

[13]   Storey and Dipchand found that conversion occurred for two out of three issues in their sample period. The full citation is in footnote 8.

so the company gets more money per share of stock. Thus, the treasurer happily points out, regardless of whether company does well or poorly, convertible bonds are the cheapest form of financing. RWJR can't lose.

The problem with this story is that we can turn it around and create an argument showing that issuing warrants and convertibles is always a disaster. We call this the expensive lunch story.

The Expensive Lunch Story

Suppose we take a closer look at the RWJR Company and its proposal to sell convertible bonds. If the company performs badly and the stock price falls, bondholders do not exercise their conversion option. This suggests the RWJR Company should have issued common stock when prices were high. By issuing convertible bonds, the company lost a valuable opportunity.

On the other hand, if the company does well and the stock price rises, bondholders convert. Suppose the stock price rises to $40. The bondholders convert and the company is forced to sell stock worth $40 for an effective price of only $25. The new shareholders benefit. Put another way, if the company prospers, it would have been better to have issued straight debt so that the gains would not have to be shared.

Whether the convertible bonds are converted or not, the company has done worse than with straight bonds or new common stock. Issuing convertible bonds is a terrible idea.

Which is correct—the free lunch story or the expensive lunch story?

A Reconciliation

Reconciling our two stories requires only that we remember our central goal: Increase the wealth of the existing shareholders. Thus, with 20-20 hindsight, issuing convertible bonds turns out to be worse than issuing straight bonds and better than issuing common stock if the company prospers. The reason is that the prosperity has to be shared with bondholders after they convert.

In contrast, if a company does poorly, issuing convertible bonds turns out to be better than issuing straight bonds and worse than issuing common stock. The reason is that the firm benefited from the lower coupon payments on the convertible bond.

Both of our stories thus have a grain of truth; we just need to combine them. This is done in Table 20.4. Exactly the same arguments would be used in a comparison of a straight debt issue versus a bond/warrant package.

	If Firm Does Poorly	If Firm Prospers	
Convertible bonds	Low stock price and no conversion	High stock price and conversion	**T A B L E** 20.4
versus:			*The case for and against convertibles*
Straight bonds	Cheap financing because coupon rate is lower (good outcome)	Expensive financing because bonds are converted, which dilutes existing equity (bad outcome)	
Common stock	Expensive financing because the firm could have issued common stock at high prices (bad outcome)	Cheap financing because firm issues stock at high prices when bonds are converted (good outcome)	

CONCEPT QUESTIONS
1. What is wrong with the view that it is cheaper to issue a bond with a warrant or a convertible feature because the required coupon is lower?
2. What is wrong with the theory that says a convertible can be a good security to issue because it can be a way to sell stock at a price that is higher than the current stock price?

20.8   I   OTHER OPTIONS

We've discussed two of the more common optionlike securities, warrants and convertibles. Options appear in many other places. We briefly describe a few such cases in this section.

The Call Provision on a Bond

As we discussed in Chapter 12, most corporate bonds are callable. A call provision allows a corporation to buy the bonds at a fixed price for a fixed time period. In other words, the corporation has a call option on the bonds. The cost of the call feature to the corporation is the cost of the option.

Convertible bonds are almost always callable. This means a convertible bond is really a package of three securities: a straight bond, a call option held by the bondholder (the conversion feature), and a call option held by the corporation (the call provision).

Put Bonds

The owner of a put bond has the right to force the issuer to repurchase the bond at a fixed price for a fixed period of time. Such a bond is a combination of a straight bond and a put option, hence the name.

For example, Canada Savings Bonds are put bonds since the holder can force the government of Canada to repurchase them (through a financial institution acting as its agent) at 100 percent of the purchase price. The put option is exercisable at any time during the bond's life. A more exotic, financially engineered example comes from Chapter 12 where we briefly discussed a LYON, a liquid yield option note. This is a callable, putable, convertible, pure discount bond. It is thus a package of a pure discount bond, two call options, and a put option. In 1991, Rogers Communication issued the first LYON in Canada.

The Overallotment Option

In Chapter 13, we mentioned that underwriters are frequently given the right to purchase additional shares of stock from a firm in an initial public offering (IPO). We called this the overallotment option. We now recognize that this provision is simply a call option (or, more accurately, a warrant) granted to the underwriter. The value of the option is an indirect form of compensation paid to the underwriter.

Insurance and Loan Guarantees

Insurance of one kind or another is a financial feature of everyday life. Most of the time, having insurance is like having a put option. For example, suppose you have $1 million in fire insurance on an office building. One night, your building burns down, reducing its value to nothing. In this case, you would effectively exercise your put option and force the insurer to pay you $1 million for something worth very little.

Loan guarantees are a form of insurance. If you lend money to a borrower who defaults, with a guaranteed loan you can collect from someone else, often the government. For example, when you lend money to a financial institution (by making a deposit), your loan is guaranteed (up to $60,000) by the federal government provided your institution is a member of the Canada Deposit Insurance Corporation (CDIC).

The federal government, with a loan guarantee, has provided a put option to the holders of risky debt. The value of the put option is the cost of the loan guarantee. Loan guarantees are not cost-free. This point was made absolutely clear to the CDIC when two banks collapsed in western Canada in 1985.

Because the put option allows a risky firm to borrow at subsidized rates, it is an asset to the stockholders. The riskier the firm, the greater the value of the guarantee and the more it is worth to the shareholders. Researchers modified the Black-Scholes model presented in this chapter's appendix to value the put option in CDIC deposit insurance for one of the Canadian banks that failed. They found that financial markets provided early warning of bank failures as the value of the put option increased significantly before the bank failed.[14]

U.S. taxpayers learned the same lesson about loan guarantees at far greater cost in the savings and loan collapse. The cost to U.S. taxpayers of making good on the guaranteed deposits in these institutions is a staggering amount.

One result of all this is that accountants in Canada, urged on by the auditor general, are forcing government agencies to report guarantees and other contingent liabilities in their financial statements. This may induce greater caution in extending guarantees in the first place.

CONCEPT QUESTIONS
1. Explain how car insurance acts like a put option.
2. Explain why government loan guarantees are not free.

20.9 | FUTURES CONTRACTS

Futures contracts involve buying or selling an asset at some date in the future for a price fixed today. The asset may be real, a commodity future, or financial, a financial future.

futures contracts
An agreement drawn up for a fixed settlement date and price to deliver or receive an asset at a future date.

To illustrate how futures work, we take an example of a futures contract written on a Canadian government bond (CGB future). Because the value of the bond that is the delivery vehicle, and hence the value of the future, depends on the future course of interest rates, these contracts are also called **interest rate futures**.

Table 20.5 shows a listing from the *Globe and Mail* for Canadian futures, including 10-year CGB futures. The delivery month for this contract is June 1995. The delivery vehicle is a CGB with maturity of 10 years and the face value is $100,000. The listing shows the settle (closing) price for the futures contract was $103.45 per $100 of par value. Open interest shows that 21,881 contracts were outstanding at this time.

Now that we can read the numbers in the *Globe and Mail,* what are we reading about? The buyer of a futures contract owns a contract with a liquid market and can sell a similar contract to offset the position. This *netting out* is similar to options as

interest rate futures
A financial futures contract calling for the delivery of a debt security such as a T-bill or a long-term government bond.

[14] R. Giammarino, E. Schwartz, and J. Zechner, "Market Valuation of Bank Assets and Deposit Insurance in Canada," *Canadian Journal of Economics,* February 1989, pp. 109–27.

T A B L E   20.5

Futures listing

Cdn. Futures

Montreal Exchange
Futures

SeaHi	SeaLow	Mth.	Open	High	Low	Settle	Chg.	Opint

10-year Cda bonds, $100K, pts of 100%, 1 pt = $10

| 103.90 | 99.70 | Jun95 | 102.90 | 103.55 | 102.84 | 103.45 | +0.36 | 21881 |

Est sales	Prv Sales	Prv Open Int		Chg.
1396	2651	21885		−661

Source: *Globe and Mail,* April 11, 1995, p. B20. Used with permission.

we discussed earlier. However, there is one important difference between a future and an option. The buyer of an option contract can walk away from the contract by not exercising it. A buyer of a futures contract who does not subsequently sell the contract must take delivery or settle in cash.

marked to market

Daily settlement of obligations on futures positions.

Futures contracts are **marked to market** on a daily basis. To illustrate, suppose interest rates rise and the price of the CGB falls to $103.00 the next day. Because all buyers of the contract lost 45 cents, they each must turn over the 45 cents to their brokers within 24 hours. Because all sellers gained 45 cents per contract on that day, they each receive 45 cents from their brokers.[15]

Students frequently ask, "Why in the world would managers of futures exchanges ruin perfectly good contracts with these bizarre mark-to-market provisions?" Actually there is a very good reason. The mark-to-market provisions minimize the chance of default on a futures contract. If the price rises, the seller has an incentive (but not a legal right) to walk away. However, after paying the clearinghouse, the seller of a futures contract has little reason to default. If the price falls, the same argument can be made for the buyer. Because changes in the value of the underlying asset are recognized daily, there is no accumulation of loss, and the incentive to default is reduced.

hedging

A protective manoeuvre; a transaction intended to reduce the risk of loss from price fluctuations.

Hedging

cash position

The position of a portfolio when the derivative securities in that portfolio have been removed.

Now that we have determined how futures contracts work, let us talk about **hedging** Hedging offsets the firm's risk by a set of transactions in the futures markets. The basic idea is simple: determine the risk in the firm's unhedged position (often called the **cash position**). Then, take an opposite position in futures so that the two positions offset one another.

We begin our discussion of hedging with an example. Suppose Trans Canada Industries is planning to raise $10 million in long-term debt next month. The financial manager is concerned that Trans Canada may lose if interest rates rise during this period. How can Trans Canada hedge this interest rate risk?

short hedge

Protecting the value of an asset held by selling a futures contract.

Our example starts by defining the cash position. Trans Canada would lose if interest rates rise. To hedge, the financial manager should sell CGB futures. Selling futures is called a **short hedge**. The short hedge is appropriate for Trans Canada in

---

[15] Since each contract is for $100,000 face value, the 45 cents is actually $450.

this case because the seller of futures gains if interest rates rise as we saw before. Since Trans Canada is planning to raise $10 million in debt, the number of contracts to sell for a complete hedge is:[16]

Amount to be hedged/Contract face value = $10 million/$100,000 = 100 contracts

---

E X A M P L E | 20.5   Long Hedging

Suppose Imperial Investments is planning to purchase $5 million face value in long-term government of Canada bonds next month after the close of the RRSP buying season. The portfolio manager is concerned that the price of the bonds might rise over the next month if interest rates fall. What is an appropriate hedging strategy?

In this case, Imperial should set up a **long hedge**. A long hedge means buying futures contracts; it will show a profit if interest rates fall. As before, we can calculate the number of contracts as

$5 million/$100,000 = 50 contracts |

long hedge
Used to avoid increases in the price of an asset by purchasing a futures contract to protect against changes in the price of the asset.

CONCEPT QUESTIONS
1. What are the differences between futures contracts and options?
2. Give examples of hedging on futures contracts on bonds.

20.10 | SUMMARY AND CONCLUSIONS

This chapter described the basics of option valuation and discussed optionlike corporate securities. In it, we saw that:

1. Options are contracts giving the right, but not the obligation, to buy and sell underlying assets at a fixed price during a specified time period.
   The most familiar options are puts and calls involving shares of stock. These options give the holder the right, but not the obligation, to sell (the put option) or buy (the call option) shares of common stock at a given price.
   As we discussed, the value of any option depends only on five factors:
   a. The price of the underlying asset.
   b. The exercise price.
   c. The expiration date.
   d. The interest rate on risk-free bonds.
   e. The volatility of the underlying asset's value.

2. A warrant gives the holder the right to buy shares of common stock directly from the company at a fixed exercise price for a given period of time. Typically, warrants are issued in a package with privately placed bonds. Often, they can be detached afterward and traded separately.

3. A convertible bond is a combination of a straight bond and a call option. The holder can give up the bond in exchange for a fixed number of shares of stock. The minimum value of a convertible bond is given by its straight bond value or its conversion value, whichever is greater.

---

[16] A simplifying assumption is that prices (and interest rates) on CGB futures and long-term corporate bonds move together. We also assume that the maturities and coupons (durations) of the two bonds are the same.

Michael MacKenzie on Derivatives Trading and Financial System Safety

The markets for derivatives are big, are growing, and are here to stay. Canadian banks, investment dealers, and other large financial institutions have been trading in them as agents for customers and for their own account for some years. Usage has been increasing quite dramatically in the last few years, and a number of the players have recently announced that they are increasing staff and related resources to the activity.

All the main Canadian banks and trust companies have invested significant sums of money in enhancing their capacity to deal in derivative (and other securities) for their own and their clients' accounts. Up to this point, about 90 percent of the derivatives business carried on in Canada is in the hands of the major banks and the large securities dealers. In the main, the banks have been using derivatives to manage interest rate and foreign exchange risks and to control financing costs for their clients and for themselves.

More recently, the uses of derivatives have expanded markedly and now include an array of different instruments—futures, options, interest rate swaps, and various combinations of these. There has been a steady movement, particularly in the United States, to develop more and more recondite (and more highly leveraged) instruments and strategies. It has also become a worldwide business and trading activity. No major Canadian player with global aspirations can afford not to be in the business.

Financial Data The worldwide volumes of derivatives are stupendous and have been growing exponentially. This growth has been vastly greater over this period than the economic, trading, and investment growth in both the developed and developing countries of the world. It has dramatically changed the scale and nature of financial markets everywhere.

The Canadian banks provide, in their annual reports, extensive disclosures of their exposures, their strategies and uses of derivatives, and their accounting policies. All the banks state that they are not using derivatives to take speculative positions, but are using them to manage risks both for customers and for their own account. In the main, the Canadian banks have not been as aggressive as the major U.S. players and have not to any extent entered into the newer kinds of products and strategies. This will likely change as the banks respond to pressures in the market and the constant drive to increase profits.

Based on the last OSFI examinations done while I was superintendent, the Canadian banks were following, in one form or another, sets of rigorous internal and operating controls similar to those set out by the Group of Thirty in 1993 as the international standard. These controls have been given wide publicity and have generally been supported by regulators in a number of countries and are used by bank examiners.

Still, there are concerns that the necessary controls to limit credit risk, market risk, legal risk, and operations risk are not easy to develop, operate, and supervise. The derivatives business is no game for amateurs and the standards of safety required should approach those in effect for civil aviation and nuclear power stations because the leverage involved is enormous and the markets are volatile. All the examples of serious losses in recent years indicate that they can happen quickly and that relatively small movements in the values of underlyings can create large gains or losses in derivatives positions. Also, in many cases where there have been losses, those involved did not have effective controls and did not appear to have understood the risks inherent in the transactions undertaken and the strategies employed. What were held out to be risk management strategies turned out to be large speculations.

One cannot be complacent about this problem of controls. The dealing culture in trading rooms is very different than it is in traditional banking. Most importantly, the people are different; they work at incredible levels of intensity and are paid handsomely with big incentives that reward short-term profits. Many transactions, often involving very large notional amounts, have to be done quickly and the time for decisions is often very short. There is no assurance that the interests of the bank and its derivatives traders are the same—or even close!

For understandable reasons, traders, who are usually impatient young people, do not like controls, particularly when they are imposed by people who are not experts in the technicalities of the business. Traders and their positions have to be watched all the time. A great many traders hold the view that they are smarter than the markets and their judgments are not held in check by experience with the ups and downs in the business cycle.

The installation and maintenance of control processes are complex, sophisticated, and expensive. They are affordable by the big banks, but smaller institutions may not be prepared to invest in them, since they go far beyond the kinds of procedures they are used to operating with. It is difficult to imagine that there are not some institutions in the market who are induced to enter this apparently lucrative field but do not understand the importance of really strong and persistent controls that incorporate little if any tolerance for non-compliance.

Recent experience indicates that the establishment of the control culture must start at the top and include the board of directors. It is the responsibility of chief executive officers and directors to set out the institution's use of derivatives and establish quite precisely the governing appetite for risk.

It is particularly important that top management and directors of any institution or company using derivatives truly understand the business of the enterprise, what the risks are and what choices are available to manage these risks. It would appear that in the recent well-publicized instances of users suffering serious losses on derivatives, this process was not followed. In some cases, it appears that management was overly influenced by its optimistic view of the market (e.g., that interest rates would go down).

Another worry is that some of the counterparties to contracts who appear to be safe today may not be so tomorrow. This raises the issue of systemic problems if any significant bank or dealer counterparty should fail. In this connection, it should be noted that it is the banking system and the dealers who link markets around the world.

It is important to note that the G30 control recommendations apply to all traders in derivatives whether they are dealers or end users. One of the implications of this is that it is becoming extremely important for dealers acting for their clients to know these clients well and satisfy themselves that their uses of derivatives are appropriate to their businesses and are authorized by their top management and boards of directors. A number of lawsuits have recently been started by non-financial enti-

ties against the bank or securities firm who executed derivatives transactions resulting in loss. The claim generally is that the client was misled by the bank. There is a good deal of anecdotal evidence that dealers sometimes do push derivative products and strategies on customers with the promise that they are risk free.

In conclusion, I believe it is not necessary to view this whole area of derivatives with too much alarm. The odds are that the future problems with derivatives losses will be unpleasant to those concerned, but will not lead to systemic disasters. I am not therefore urging the imposition of additional overall limits to the derivatives positions that can be taken. I do think, however, that regulators and directors must be very vigilant to ensure that banks themselves do not take significant speculative positions for their own account, and that their uses of derivatives really do improve their management of risk in important ways. This will put enormous demands on them to keep up with the ongoing changes in these markets—and doing so will be anything but easy. One needs to pay attention to the concerns of some industry observers that derivatives represent "ticking time bombs."

Michael MacKenzie was Canadian superintendent of financial institutions from 1988 to 1994. His prior experience was as a senior auditor of banks with Clarkson Gordon.

4. Convertible bonds, warrants, and call options are similar, but important differences do exist:
   a. Warrants and convertible securities are issued by corporations. Call options are issued by and traded between individual investors.
   b. Warrants are usually issued privately and combined with a bond. In most cases, the warrants can be detached immediately after the issue. In some cases, warrants are issued with preferred stock, with common stock, or in publicly traded bond issues.

c. Warrants and call options are exercised for cash. The holder of a warrant gives the company cash and receives new shares of the company's stock. The holder of a call option gives another individual cash in exchange for common stock. Convertible bonds are exercised by exchange; the individual gives the company back the bond in exchange for stock.

5. Many other corporate securities have option features. Bonds with call provisions, bonds with put provisions, and debt backed by a loan guarantee are just a few examples.

6. Futures contracts involve buying or selling an asset at some date in the future for a fixed price today. The examples we discussed involved financial futures on financial assets such as Canadian government bonds. A firm may hedge risk with futures. It first determines the risk in the cash position and then takes the opposite position in futures.

Key Terms

option (page 722)

derivative security (page 722)

exercising the option (page 723)

striking price or exercise price (page 723)

expiration date (page 723)

American and European options (page 723)

call option (page 723)

put option (page 723)

intrinsic value (page 729)

warrant (page 738)

sweeteners or equity kickers (page 738)

convertible bond (page 743)

conversion price (page 743)

conversion ratio (page 743)

conversion premium (page 743)

straight bond value (page 744)

conversion value (page 744)

futures contracts (page 749)

interest rate futures (page 749)

marked to market (page 750)

hedging (page 750)

cash position (page 750)

short hedge (page 750)

long hedge (page 751)

Chapter Review Problems and Self-Test

20.1 Value of a Call Option   Stock in the Barsoom Corporation is currently selling for $20 per share. In one year, the price would either be $20 or $30. T-bills with one year to maturity are paying 10 percent. What is the value of a call option with a $20 exercise price? A $24 exercise price?

20.2 Convertible Bonds   The Kau Corporation, publisher of *Gourmand* magazine, has a convertible bond issue currently selling in the market for $900. Each bond can be exchanged for 100 shares of stock at the holder's option.

The bond has a 6 percent coupon, payable annually, and it matures in 12 years. Kau's debt is BBB-rated. Debt with this rating is priced to yield 12 percent. Stock in Kau is trading at $6 per share.

What is the conversion ratio on this bond? The conversion price? The conversion premium? What is the floor value of the bond? What is its option value?

Answers to Self-Test Problems

20.1   With a $20 exercise price, the option can't finish out of the money (it can finish "at the money" if the stock price is $20). We can replicate the stock by investing the present value of $20 in T-bills and buying one call option. Buying the T-bill would cost $20/1.1 = $18.18.

With the $24 exercise price, we start by investing the present value of the lower stock price in T-bills. This guarantees us $20 when the stock price is $20. If the stock price is $30, the option is worth $30 − 24 = $6. We have $20 from our T-bill, so we need $10 from the options to match the stock. Since each option is worth $6, we need to buy $10/$6 = 1.67 call options. Notice that the difference in the possible stock prices is $10 ($\Delta S$) and the difference in the possible option prices is $6 ($\Delta C$), so $\Delta S/\Delta C$ = 1.67.

If the stock ends up at $20, the call option is worth zero and the T-bill pays $20. If the stock ends up at $30, the T-bill again pays $20, and the option is worth $30 − 20 = $10, so the package is worth $30. Since the T-bill/call option combination exactly duplicates the payoff on the stock, it has to be worth $20 or arbitrage is possible. Using the notation from the chapter, we can calculate the value of the call option:

$$S_0 = C_0 + E/(1 + R_f)$$
$$\$20 = C_0 + \$18.18$$
$$C_0 = \$1.82$$

With the $24 exercise price, we start by investing the present value of the lower stock price in T-bills. This guarantees us $20 when the stock price is $20. If the stock price is $30, the option is worth $30 − 24 = $6. We have $20 from our T-bill, so we need $10 from the options to match the stock. Since each option is worth $6, we need to buy $10/$6 = 1.67 call options. Notice that the difference in the possible stock prices is $10 ($\Delta S$) and the difference in the possible option prices is $6 ($\Delta C$), so $\Delta S/\Delta C$ = 1.67.

To complete the calculation, the present value of the $20 plus 1.67 call options has to be worth $20 to prevent arbitrage, so:

$$\$20 = 1.67 \times C_0 + \$20/1.1$$
$$C_0 = \$1.82/1.67$$
$$= \$1.09$$

20.2   Since each bond can be exchanged for 100 shares, the conversion ratio is 100. The conversion price is the face value of the bond ($1,000) divided by the conversion ratio, $1,000/100 = $10. The conversion premium is the percentage difference between the current price and the conversion price, ($10 − $6)/$6 = 67%.

The floor value of the bond is the greater of its straight bond value or its conversion value. Its conversion value is what the bond is worth if it is immediately converted: 100 × $6 = $600. The straight bond value is what the bond would be worth if it were not convertible. The annual coupon is $60, and the bond matures in 12 years. At a 12 percent required return, the straight bond value is:

$$\text{Straight bond value} = \$60 \times (1 - 1/1.12^{12})/.12 + \$1,000/1.12^{12}$$
$$= \$371.66 + 256.68$$
$$= \$628.34$$

This exceeds the conversion value, so the floor value of the bond is $628.34. Finally, the option value is the value of the convertible in excess of its floor value. Since the bond is selling for $900, the option value is:

$$\text{Option value} = \$900 - 628.34$$
$$= \$271.66$$

Questions and Problems

Basic
(Questions 1–12)

1. **Basic Properties of Options**   What is a call option? A put option? Under what circumstances might you want to buy each? Which one has greater potential profit?

2. **Call versus Puts**   Complete the following sentence for each of these investors: The (*buyer/seller*) of a (*put/call*) option (*pays/receives*) money for the (*right/obligation*) to (*buy/sell*) a specified asset at a fixed price for a fixed length of time.

   a. A buyer of call options
   b. A buyer of put options
   c. A seller of call options
   d. A seller of put options

3. **Arbitrage and Options**   You notice that shares of stock in the Masson Corporation are going for $40 per share. Call options with an exercise price of $30 per share are selling for $5. What's wrong here?

4. **Defining Intrinsic Value**   What is the intrinsic value of a call option? How do we interpret this value?

5. **Defining Intrinsic Value**   What is the value of a put option at maturity? Based on your answer, what is the intrinsic value of a put option?

6. **Understanding Option Quotes**   Use the following option quote to answer the following questions:

Option & TSE Close	Strike Price	Calls—Last			Puts—Last		
		Jun	Jul	Aug	Jun	Jul	Aug
Dune 55	45	8	11½	14	4	5½	8

   a. Are the call options in the money? What is the intrinsic value of a Dune Company call option?
   b. One of the options is clearly mispriced. Which one? At a minimum, what should it sell for? Explain how you could profit from the mispricing.
   c. This is a little harder: What is the highest price the mispriced option should sell for? Explain.

7. **Calculating Payoffs**   Use the following option quote to answer these questions:

Option & TSE Close	Strike Price	Calls—Last			Puts—Last		
		Jun	Jul	Aug	Jun	Jul	Aug
Besley 70	80	2	2⅞	4	12	13⅞	16

   a. Suppose you buy 50 July 80 call contracts. How much will you pay, ignoring commissions?
   b. In part *a*, suppose Besley is selling for $100 per share on the expiration date. What are your options worth?
   c. Suppose you buy 10 Aug put contracts. What is your maximum gain? On the expiration date, Besley is selling for $75 per share. What are your options worth?

d. In part *c,* suppose you sold 10 Aug put contracts. What is your net gain or loss if Besley is selling for $75? For 100? What is the break-even price, that is, the stock price that results in a profit of zero?

**Basic
(Continued)**

8. **Option Value and Firm Risk**   True or false: "The unsystematic risk of a share of stock is irrelevant in valuing the stock since it can be diversified away. It is also irrelevant for valuing a call option on the stock." Explain.

9. **Calls versus Puts**   Stock in the Zinfidel Company currently sells for $30 per share. If a put option and a call option are available with $30 exercise prices, which do you think would sell for more, the put or the call? Explain.

10. **Option Value and Firm Risk**   If the risk of a stock increases, what is likely to happen to the price of call options on the stock? To the price of put options? Why?

11. **Calculating Intrinsic Value**   T-bills currently yield 7 percent. Stock in the Nostradamus Corporation is currently selling for $28 per share. There is no possibility that the stock will be worth less than $20 in one year when the options expire.
    a. What is the value of a call option with a $20 exercise price?
    b. What is the value of a call option with a $10 exercise price?
    c. What is the value of a put option with a $20 exercise price?

12. **Option Value and Interest Rates**   Suppose the interest rate on T-bills suddenly and unexpectedly rises. All other things being the same, what is the impact on call option values? On put option values?

13. **Calculating Option Values**   The price of Schome Corporation stock will be either $60 or $80 at the end of the year. Call options are available with one year to expiration. T-bills currently yield 7 percent.
    a. Suppose the current price of Schome stock is $65. What is the value of the call option if the exercise price is $55 per share?
    b. Suppose the exercise price is $65 in part *a.* What would the value of the call option be?

**Intermediate
(Questions 13–27)**

14. **Using the Price Equation**   A one-year call contract on Dilleep Company stock sells for $1,000. In one year, the stock will be worth $20 or $40 per share. The exercise price on the call option is $25. What is the current value of the stock if the risk-free rate is 6 percent?

15. **Equity as an Option**   Su-Jane Company's assets are currently worth $800. In a year, they will be worth $600 or $1,000. The risk-free rate is 8 percent. Suppose Su-Jane has an outstanding debt issue with a face value of $500.
    a. What is the value of the equity?
    b. What is the value of the debt? The interest rate on the debt?
    c. Would the value of the equity go up or down if the risk-free rate were 20 percent? Why? What does your answer illustrate?

16. **Equity as an Option**   The Wansley Corporation has a bond issue with a face value of $1,000 coming due in one year. The value of Wansley's assets is currently $1,200. Jimbo Wansley, the CEO, believes the assets in the firm will be worth $800 or $1,800 in a year. The going rate on one-year T-bills is 6 percent.
    a. What is the value of the equity? The value of the debt?
    b. Suppose Wansley can reconfigure its existing assets such that the value in a year will be $500 or $2,000. If the current value of the assets is unchanged, would the shareholders favour such a move? Why?

17. **Intuition and Option Value**   Suppose a share of stock sells for $50. The risk-free rate is 8 percent. The price of the stock in one year will be $55 or $60.

a. What is the value of a call option with a $55 exercise price?
b. What's wrong here? What would you do?

18. **Calculating Conversion Value**   A $1,000 par convertible debenture has a conversion price for common stock of $180 per share. With the common stock selling at $60, what is the conversion value of the bond?

19. **Convertible Bonds**   The following facts apply to a convertible bond:

Conversion price	$50/share
Coupon rate	9%
Par value	$1,000
Yield on non-convertible debenture of same quality	10%
Maturity	10 years
Market price of stock	$52/share

a. What is the minimum price at which the convertible should sell?
b. What accounts for the premium of the market price of a convertible over the total market value of the common stock into which it can be converted?

20. **Calculating Values for Convertibles**   You have been hired to value a new 30-year callable convertible bond. The bond has a 6 percent coupon, payable annually, and its face value is $1,000. The conversion price is $100, and the stock currently sells for $50.12.

a. What is the minimum value of the bond? Comparable non-convertible bonds are priced to yield 7 percent.
b. What is the conversion value? The conversion premium?

21. **Convertible Calculations**   Better Beta, Inc., has a convertible bond issue currently selling in the market for $840. Each bond is exchangeable anytime for 50 shares of Better Beta's common stock.

The convertible bond has an 8 percent coupon, payable semiannually. Similar non-convertible bonds are priced to yield 12 percent. The bond matures in eight years. Stock in Better Beta sells for $16 per share.

a. What are the conversion ratio, conversion price, and conversion premium?
b. What is the straight bond value? The conversion value?
c. In part b, what would the stock price have to be for the conversion value and straight bond value to be equal?
d. What is the option value of the bond?

22. **Intuition and Convertibles**   Which of the following two sets of relationships is more typical? Why? At time of issuance of convertible bonds:

	A	B
Offering price of bond	$ 900	$1,000
Bond value (straight debt)	900	950
Conversion value	1,000	900

23. **Calculating Warrant Values**   A bond with 20 detachable warrants has just been offered for sale at $1,000. The bond matures in 10 years and has an annual coupon of $80. Each warrant gives the owner the right to purchase four shares of stock at $10 per share. Ordinary bonds (no warrants) of similar quality are priced to yield 11 percent. What is the value of a warrant?

24. **Warrants and Share Value** In the previous question, what is the minimum value of the stock? What is the maximum value?

Intermediate (Continued)

25. **Warrants and the Balance Sheet** Ringworld Company has 5,000 shares of stock outstanding. The market value of Ringworld's assets is $700,000. The market value of outstanding debt is $200,000. Ringworld issued 100 warrants some time ago that are about to expire. Each warrant gives the owner the right to purchase 10 shares of stock at a price of $80 per share.

    a. What is the price per share of Ringworld stock? What is the value of a warrant?
    b. Create a market value balance sheet for just before and just after the warrants expire.
    c. What is the effective exercise price on the warrants?

26. **Hedging**

    a. How is a short hedge created?
    b. When is it wise to use a short hedge?
    c. How is a long hedge created?
    d. When is it wise to use a long hedge?

27. **Futures** Canada Wide Ltd. is engaged in a number of financial transactions that are subject to risk if interest rates change. For each transaction, state how you would hedge using Canadian government bond futures. Explain briefly.

    a. The firm holds $10 million in Canadian bonds in its pension fund portfolio. It plans to sell the bonds in six months.
    b. The firm plans to raise $50 million in long-term debt financing.
    c. The firm plans to buy $5 million in long-term Canadian bonds for the pension fund.

28. **Pricing Convertibles** You have been hired to value a new 30-year callable, convertible bond. The bond has a 6 percent coupon, payable annually. The conversion price is $100, and the stock currently sells for $50.12. The stock price is expected to grow at 10 percent per year. The bond is callable at $1,100, but, based on prior experience, it won't be called unless the conversion value is $1,300. The required return on this bond is 8 percent. What value would you assign?

Challenge (Question 28)

Case 20A: A Case of Misuse of Derivatives? Metallgesellschaft

Metallgesellschaft AG is Germany's 14th largest industrial corporation. It has operations in metals, mining, and other industrial activities, and boasts 251 subsidiaries worldwide with U.S. $15 billion in annual sales. Metallgesellschaft reported a loss of U.S. $200 million in fiscal 1993. Losses on its risky derivative securities transactions pushed this loss over the $1 billion mark.

MG Corp., a U.S. subsidiary of Metallgesellschaft, is a marketer and oil refiner. MG Corp.'s derivative strategy was an attempt to hedge away fluctuating oil price risk, but its tactics resulted in losses of close to $1.5 billion.

The specifics of MG Corp.'s derivative scheme involved fixing the prices at which it would buy and sell oil, thus generating predictable profit levels. In part one of the strategy, MG Corp. entered into long-term, fixed-price contracts to supply oil to gasoline stations and other end users. The subsidiary then entered into long-term fixed-priced contracts to buy oil. However, the quantity of oil guaranteed to be supplied to MG Corp. was not sufficient to cover the supply contracts it had entered into with the end users. This discrepancy resulted in MG Corp. purchasing oil in the open market to satisfy the remainder of its contracts, thus exposing it to fluctuations in oil prices. MG Corp. could potentially experience tremendous losses if oil prices rose. This would result in the company's need to purchase oil at prices far greater than those it would receive by way of its fixed-price contracts.

To hedge away this risk, MG Corp. entered into futures contracts through futures exchanges and OTC (over-the-counter) dealers. If oil prices rose, the gains on the derivatives contracts (as they increased in value) would offset the losses realized by MG Corp. when it purchased oil in the spot market in order to fulfill its long-term agreements. On the other hand, if oil prices fell, losses on the derivatives contracts would be offset by the gains MG Corp. would realize supplying its long-term contracts. This would guarantee MG Corp. a certain margin on its oil sales.

The hedge that MG Corp. employed was deemed an imperfect one because the derivatives contracts were short-term while the supply agreements were long-term. MG Corp. would have to renew its derivative contracts as each one expired. This renewal requirement resulted in MG Corp. being vulnerable to a widening of the gap between short-term and long-term oil prices. If short-term prices rose, MG would realize the gains on the derivatives contracts, but if short-term prices fell the company would realize losses that may not be offset by gains on the delivery of oil. This is because the two results would occur at different times.

In the fall of 1993, oil prices collapsed and the value of MG Corp.'s derivatives portfolio fell. In December 1993, Metallgesellschaft CEO Heinz Schimmelbusch was fired and came under criminal investigation for fraud and breach of trust. According to Mr. Schimmelbusch, he had been providing the company's advisory board with information on the status of the company's hedging tactics, to the best of his ability.

Two of the owners and creditors of Metallgesellschaft, Deutsche Bank and Dresdner Bank, forced the company to liquidate its derivatives position, fired the CEO, and orchestrated a bailout of the company. Creditors of the company, who now believed they had been lending to a speculator, put in approximately $2 billion to help cover its losses. Other consequences of this fiasco included the selling of some of the company's divisions and cutting of 7,500 jobs.

An analysis by Merton Miller, a Nobel Prize winning economist, revealed that MG Corp.'s marketing strategy for entering the U.S. market, called for offering gas stations and other users fixed-price contracts on oil for 5 to 10 years. At that time, due to the recent end of the Persian Gulf war, oil prices had fallen dramatically and customers were eager to lock in prices for the long term. To hedge against a rise in oil prices, MG Corp. bought futures contracts on oil to lock in its buying price of oil. While the long-term contracts were for 5 to 10 years, the futures were for three to six months. As a result, the contracts would have to be rolled over as they expired, in order to continue to hedge the long-term contracts.

According to Mr. Miller, as oil prices fell, the losses on the futures contracts would only be paper losses if the contracts were rolled over. The actual loss would not be recorded until the futures contracts were liquidated. If the contracts had been rolled over until the maturity of the long-term agreements, gains on the sale of oil would offset the loss on the futures contracts. As the value of a party's position in futures contracts deteriorates, it must deposit more funds in a margin account in order to support its investment. Mr. Miller's view is that Deutsche Bank panicked when

MG Corp.'s paper losses increased and ordered the futures contracts liquidated. The bank refused MG the use of Metallgesellschaft's $1.5 billion line of credit to cover the required deposits, to back up MG's futures investments. Pursuant to the liquidation of these contracts, oil prices rose, which resulted in losses for MG Corp.'s unhedged long-term commitments.

Deutsche Bank and Metallgesellschaft's new CEO have responded to the allegations by stating that Mr. Miller's argument works in theory, but in reality the company could not have sustained further losses on the futures positions, and the resultant increased margin requirements. The futures positions were too expensive and had to be liquidated.

Case Questions

1. Describe and illustrate the hedging strategy that the MG Corp. followed. What went wrong?
2. Was Metallgesellschaft's strategy appropriate? Describe an alternative strategy to the one used that may have had a different result (with or without the use of derivatives).
3. If the company followed Professor Miller's advice, would the outcome have been different? If yes, describe the possible outcome.
4. Mobil Oil Corp. hedges against currency and interest rate risks, but it does not hedge against oil price risk. The company feels that shareholders expect to take that risk when they purchase oil company shares. Discuss this viewpoint. Would Metallgesellschaft have been better off had it taken this approach? Do companies have the obligation to control any risk, once that risk is identifiable? Did Metallgesellschaft fully understand its risks?

Suggested Readings

For a detailed discussion of options read:

Cox, J. S., and M. Rubinstein. *Option Markets.* Englewood Cliffs, NJ: Prentice Hall, 1985. Section 7.3 analyzes corporate securities.

Hull, J. *Options, Futures, and Other Derivative Securities.* Englewood Cliffs, NJ: Prentice Hall, 1989.

To learn about interest rate options, options on bonds, see:

Hull, J., and A. White. "Buying and Selling Interest Rate Options: The New Over-the-Counter Market." *Canadian Investment Review,* Fall 1990.

Our free lunch and expensive lunch stories are adapted from Michael Brennan, who examines the conventional arguments for convertible bonds and offers a new "risk synergy" rationale in:

Brennan, M. "The Case for Convertibles." In *The Revolution in Corporate Finance,* eds. J. M. Stern and D. H. Chew. New York: Basil Blackwell, 1986.

The Metallgesellschaft case is by Stam Fountaulakis, TD Bank, and is used with permission.

APPENDIX 20A | THE BLACK-SCHOLES OPTION PRICING MODEL

In our discussion of call options in this chapter, we did not discuss the general case where the stock can take on any value and the option can finish out of the money. The general approach to valuing a call option falls under the heading of the *Black-Scholes Option Pricing Model (OPM)*, a very famous result in finance. In addition to its theoretical importance, the OPM has great practical value. Many option traders carry handheld calculators programmed with the Black-Scholes formula.

This appendix briefly discusses the Black-Scholes model. Because the underlying development is relatively complex, we present only the result and then focus on how to use it.

From our earlier discussion, when a *t*-period call option is certain to finish somewhere in the money, its value today, C_0, is equal to the value of the stock today, S_0, less the present value of the exercise price, $E/(1 + R_f)^t$:

$$C_0 = S_0 - E/(1 + R_f)^t$$

If the option can finish out of the money, this result needs modifying. Black and Scholes show that the value of a call option in this case is given by:

$$C_0 = S_0 \times N(d_1) - E/(1 + R_f)^t \times N(d_2) \qquad [20A.1]$$

where $N(d_1)$ and $N(d_2)$ are probabilities that must be calculated. This is the Black-Scholes OPM.[17]

In the Black-Scholes model, $N(d_1)$ is the probability that a standardized, normally distributed random variable (widely known as a *z* variable) is less than or equal to d_1, and $N(d_2)$ is the probability of a value that is less than or equal to d_2. Determining these probabilities requires a table such as Table 20A.1.

To illustrate, suppose we were given the following information:

S_0 = \$100

E = \$80

R_f = 1% per month

d_1 = 1.20

d_2 = .90

t = 9 months

Based on this information, what is the value of the call option, C_0?

To answer, we need to determine $N(d_1)$ and $N(d_2)$. In Table 20A.1, we first find the row corresponding to a *d* of 1.20. The corresponding probability, $N(d)$, is .8849, so this is $N(d_1)$. For d_2, the associated probability $N(d_2)$ is .8159. Using the Black-Scholes OPM, the value of the call option is thus:

$$C_0 = S_0 \times N(d_1) - E/(1 + R_f)^t \times N(d_2)$$
$$= \$100 \times .8849 - \$80/1.01^9 \times .8159$$
$$= \$88.49 - 59.68$$
$$= \$28.81$$

---

[17] Strictly speaking, the risk-free rate in the Black-Scholes model is the continuously compounded risk-free rate. Continuous compounding is discussed in Chapter 5.

T A B L E 20A.1 | *Cumulative normal distribution*

d	N(d)	d	N(d)	d	N(d)	d	N(d)	d	N(d)	d	N(d)
−3.00	.0013	−1.58	.0571	−0.76	.2236	0.06	.5239	0.86	.8051	1.66	.9515
−2.95	.0016	−1.56	.0594	−0.74	.2297	0.08	.5319	0.88	.8106	1.68	.9535
−2.90	.0019	−1.54	.0618	−0.72	.2358	0.10	.5398	0.90	.8159	1.70	.9554
−2.85	.0022	−1.52	.0643	−0.70	.2420	0.12	.5478	0.92	.8212	1.72	.9573
−2.80	.0026	−1.50	.0668	−0.68	.2483	0.14	.5557	0.94	.8264	1.74	.9591
−2.75	.0030	−1.48	.0694	−0.66	.2546	0.16	.5636	0.96	.8315	1.76	.9608
−2.70	.0035	−1.46	.0721	−0.64	.2611	0.18	.5714	0.98	.8365	1.78	.9625
−2.65	.0040	−1.44	.0749	−0.62	.2676	0.20	.5793	1.00	.8414	1.80	.9641
−2.60	.0047	−1.42	.0778	−0.60	.2743	0.22	.5871	1.02	.8461	1.82	.9656
−2.55	.0054	−1.40	.0808	−0.58	.2810	0.24	.5948	1.04	.8508	1.84	.9671
−2.50	.0062	−1.38	.0838	−0.56	.2877	0.26	.6026	1.06	.8554	1.86	.9686
−2.45	.0071	−1.36	.0869	−0.54	.2946	0.28	.6103	1.08	.8599	1.88	.9699
−2.40	.0082	−1.34	.0901	−0.52	.3015	0.30	.6179	1.10	.8643	1.90	.9713
−2.35	.0094	−1.32	.0934	−0.50	.3085	0.32	.6255	1.12	.8686	1.92	.9726
−2.30	.0107	−1.30	.0968	−0.48	.3156	0.34	.6331	1.14	.8729	1.94	.9738
−2.25	.0122	−1.28	.1003	−0.46	.3228	0.36	.6406	1.16	.8770	1.96	.9750
−2.20	.0139	−1.26	.1038	−0.44	.3300	0.38	.6480	1.18	.8810	1.98	.9761
−2.15	.0158	−1.24	.1075	−0.42	.3373	0.40	.6554	1.20	.8849	2.00	.9772
−2.10	.0179	−1.22	.1112	−0.40	.3446	0.42	.6628	1.22	.8888	2.05	.9798
−2.05	.0202	−1.20	.1151	−0.38	.3520	0.44	.6700	1.24	.8925	2.10	.9821
−2.00	.0228	−1.18	.1190	−0.36	.3594	0.46	.6773	1.26	.8962	2.15	.9842
−1.98	.0239	−1.16	.1230	−0.34	.3669	0.48	.6844	1.28	.8997	2.20	.9861
−1.96	.0250	−1.14	.1271	−0.32	.3745	0.50	.6915	1.30	.9032	2.25	.9878
−1.94	.0262	−1.12	.1314	−0.30	.3821	0.52	.6985	1.32	.9066	2.30	.9893
−1.92	.0274	−1.10	.1357	−0.28	.3897	0.54	.7054	1.34	.9099	2.35	.9906
−1.90	.0287	−1.08	.1401	−0.26	.3974	0.56	.7123	1.36	.9131	2.40	.9918
−1.88	.0301	−1.06	.1446	−0.24	.4052	0.58	.7191	1.38	.9162	2.45	.9929
−1.86	.0314	−1.04	.1492	−0.22	.4129	0.60	.7258	1.40	.9192	2.50	.9938
−1.84	.0329	−1.02	.1539	−0.20	.4207	0.62	.7324	1.42	.9222	2.55	.9946
−1.82	.0344	−1.00	.1587	−0.18	.4286	0.64	.7389	1.44	.9251	2.60	.9953
−1.80	.0359	−0.98	.1635	−0.16	.4365	0.66	.7454	1.46	.9279	2.65	.9960
−1.78	.0375	−0.96	.1685	−0.14	.4443	0.68	.7518	1.48	.9306	2.70	.9965
−1.76	.0392	−0.94	.1736	−0.12	.4523	0.70	.7580	1.50	.9332	2.75	.9970
−1.74	.0409	−0.92	.1788	−0.10	.4602	0.72	.7642	1.52	.9357	2.80	.9974
−1.72	.0427	−0.90	.1841	−0.08	.4681	0.74	.7704	1.54	.9382	2.85	.9978
−1.70	.0446	−0.88	.1894	−0.06	.4761	0.76	.7764	1.56	.9406	2.90	.9981
−1.68	.0465	−0.86	.1949	−0.04	.4841	0.78	.7823	1.58	.9429	2.95	.9984
−1.66	.0485	−0.84	.2005	−0.02	.4920	0.80	.7882	1.60	.9452	3.00	.9986
−1.64	.0505	−0.82	.2061	0.00	.5000	0.82	.7939	1.62	.9474	3.05	.9989
−1.62	.0526	−0.80	.2119	0.02	.5080	0.84	.7996	1.64	.9495		
−1.60	.0548	−0.78	.2177	0.04	.5160						

This table shows the probability *(N(d))* of observing a value less than or equal to *d*. For example, as illustrated, if *d* is −.24, then *N(d)* is .4052.

As this example illustrates, if we are given values for d_1 and d_2 (and the table), using the Black-Scholes model is not difficult. In general, however, we are not given the values of d_1 and d_2, and we must calculate them instead. This requires a little extra effort. The values for d_1 and d_2 for the Black-Scholes OPM are given by:

$$d_1 = [\ln(S_0/E) + (R_f + 1/2 \times \sigma^2) \times t]/[\sigma \times \sqrt{t}]$$
$$d_2 = d_1 - \sigma \times t \qquad\qquad [20A.2]$$

In these expressions, σ is the standard deviation of the rate of return on the underlying asset. Also, $\ln(S_0/E)$ is the natural logarithm of the current stock price divided by the exercise price (most calculators have a key labelled ln to perform this calculation).

The formula for d_1 looks intimidating, but using it is mostly a matter of "plug and chug" with a calculator. To illustrate, suppose we have the following;

$S_0 = \$70$

$E = \$80$

$R_f = 1\%$ per month

$\sigma = 2\%$ per month

$t = 9$ months

With these numbers, d_1 is:

$$d_1 = [\ln(S_0/E) + (R_f + 1/2 \times \sigma^2) \times t]/[\sigma \times \sqrt{t}]$$
$$= [\ln(.875) + (.01 + 1/2 \times .02^2) \times 9]/[.02 \times 3]$$
$$= (-.1335 + .0918]/.06$$
$$\approx -.70$$

Given this result, d_2 is:

$$d_2 = d_1 - \sigma \times \sqrt{t}$$
$$= -.70 - .02 \times 3$$
$$= -.76$$

Referring to Table 20A.1, the values for $N(d_1)$ and $N(d_2)$ are .2420 and .2236, respectively. The value of the option is thus:

$$C_0 = S_0 \times N(d_1) - E/(1 + R_f)^t \times N(d_2)$$
$$= \$70 \times .2420 - \$80/1.01^9 \times .2236$$
$$= \$.58$$

This may seem a little small, but the stock price would have to rise by $10 before the option would even be in the money.

Notice that we quoted the risk-free rate, the standard deviation, and the time to maturity in months in this example. We could have used days, weeks, or years as long as we are consistent in quoting all three of these using the same time units.

Appendix Review Problems and Self-Test

A.1   Black-Scholes OPM: Part I   Calculate the Black-Scholes price for a six-month option given the following:

$S_0 = \$80$

$E = \$70$

$R_f = 10\%$ per year

$d_1 = .82$

$d_2 = .74$

A.2 Black-Scholes OPM: Part II Calculate the Black-Scholes price for a nine-month option given the following:

$S_0 = \$80$

$E = \$70$

$\sigma = .30$ per year

$R_f = 10\%$ per year

Answers to Appendix Self-Test Problems

A.1 $C_0 = 80 \times N(.82) - 70/(1.10)^{.5} \times N(.74)$

From Table 20A.1, the values for $N(.82)$ and $N(.74)$ are .7939 and .7794, respectively. The value of the option is about $12.09. Notice that since the interest rate (and standard deviation) is quoted on an annual basis, we used a t value of .50, representing a half year, in calculating the present value of the exercise price.

A.2 We first calculate d_1 and d_2:

$$d_1 = [\ln(S_0/E) + (R_f + 1/2 \times \sigma^2) \times t]/(\sigma \times \sqrt{t}]$$
$$= [\ln(80/70) + (.10 + 1/2 \times .30^2) \times (.75)]/[.30 \times \sqrt{.75}]$$
$$= .9325$$

$$d_2 = d_1 - \sigma \times \sqrt{t}$$
$$= .9325 - .30 \times \sqrt{.75}$$
$$= .6727$$

From Table 20A.1, $N(d_1)$ appears to be roughly .825, and $N(d_2)$ is about .75. Plugging these in, we determine that the option's value is $17.12. Notice again that we used an annual t value of $9/12 = .75$ in this case.

Appendix Questions and Problems

1. **Using the OPM** Calculate the Black-Scholes option prices in each of the following cases. The risk-free rate and the variance are quoted in annual terms. Notice that the variance is given, not the standard deviation. The last three may require some thought.

Stock Price	Exercise Price	Risk-Free Rate	Maturity	Variance	Call Price
$50	$60	8%	6 months	.20	
25	15	6	9 months	.30	
50	60	8	6 months	.40	
0	10	9	12 months	.65	
90	30	7	forever	.22	
50	0	8	6 months	.44	

2. **Equity as an Option and the OPM** Anondezi Company has a discount bank loan that matures in one year and requires the firm to pay $1,000. The current market value of the firm's assets is $1,200. The annual variance for the firm's return on assets is .30, and the annual risk-free interest rate is 6 percent. Based on the Black-Scholes model, what is the market value of the firm's debt and equity?

3.　**Changes in Variance and Equity Value**　This is a challenge problem. From the previous problem, Anondezi is considering two mutually exclusive investments. Project A has an NPV of $100, and Project B has an NPV of $150. As a result of taking Project A, the variance of the firm's return on assets increases to .40. If Project B is taken, the variance falls to .25.

　　　a. What is the value of the firm's debt and equity if Project A is undertaken? If Project B is undertaken?

　　　b. Which project do the shareholders prefer? Can you reconcile your answer with the NPV rule?

　　　c. Suppose the shareholders and bondholders are in fact the same group of investors. Would this affect the answer to part *b?*

　　　d. What does this problem suggest about shareholder incentives?

Mergers and Acquisitions

There is no more dramatic or controversial activity in corporate finance than the acquisition of one firm by another or the merger of two firms. It is the stuff of headlines in the financial press, and occasionally it is an embarrassing source of scandal.

The acquisition of one firm by another is, of course, an investment made under uncertainty, and the basic principles of valuation apply. Another firm should be acquired only if doing so generates a positive net present value to the shareholders of the acquiring firm. However, because the NPV of an acquisition candidate can be difficult to determine, mergers and acquisitions are interesting topics in their own right.

Some of the special problems that come up in this area of finance include:

1. The benefits from acquisitions can depend on such things as strategic fits. Strategic fits are difficult to define precisely, and it is not easy to estimate the value of strategic fits using discounted cash flow techniques.

2. There can be complex accounting, tax, and legal effects that must be considered when one firm is acquired by another.

3. Acquisitions are an important control device for shareholders. Some acquisitions are a consequence of an underlying conflict between the interests of existing managers and shareholders. Agreeing to be acquired by another firm is one way that shareholders can remove existing managers.

4. Mergers and acquisitions sometimes involve "unfriendly" transactions. In such cases, when one firm attempts to acquire another, it does not always involve quiet negotiations. The sought-after firm often resists takeover and may resort to defensive tactics with exotic names such as poison pills or greenmail.

We discuss these and other issues associated with mergers in the next section. We begin by introducing the basic legal, accounting, and tax aspects of acquisitions.

21.1 | THE LEGAL FORMS OF ACQUISITIONS

There are three basic legal procedures that one firm can use to acquire another firm:

1. Merger or consolidation.
2. Acquisition of stock.
3. Acquisition of assets.

Although these forms are different from a legal standpoint, the financial press frequently does not distinguish between them. To make the terminology more confusing, both the Canadian and Ontario Business Corporation Acts refer to combinations of firms as **amalgamations**. In our discussion, we use the term *merger* regardless of the actual form of the acquisition.

In our discussion, we frequently refer to the acquiring firm as the *bidder*. This is the company that makes an offer to distribute cash or securities to obtain the stock or assets of another company. The firm that is sought (and perhaps acquired) is often called the *target firm*. The cash or securities offered to the target firm are the *consideration* in the acquisition.

Merger or Consolidation

A **merger** refers to the complete absorption of one firm by another. The acquiring firm retains its name and its identity, and it acquires all the assets and liabilities of the acquired firm. After a merger, the acquired firm ceases to exist as a separate business entity.

A **consolidation** is the same as a merger except that a new firm is created. In a consolidation, both the acquiring firm and the acquired firm terminate their previous legal existence and become part of a new firm. For this reason, the distinction between the acquiring and the acquired firm is not as important in a consolidation as it is in a merger.

The rules for mergers and consolidations are basically the same. Acquisition by merger or consolidation results in a combination of the assets and liabilities of acquired and acquiring firms; the only difference is whether or not a new firm is created. We henceforth use the term *merger* to refer generically to both mergers and consolidations.

There are some advantages and some disadvantages to using a merger to acquire a firm:

1. A primary advantage is that a merger is legally simple and does not cost as much as other forms of acquisition. The reason is that the firms simply agree to combine their entire operations. Thus, for example, there is no need to transfer title to individual assets of the acquired firm to the acquiring firm.

2. A primary disadvantage is that a merger must be approved by a vote of the shareholders of each firm.[1] Typically, two-thirds (or even more) of the share votes are required for approval. Obtaining the necessary votes can be time consuming and difficult. Furthermore, as we later discuss in greater detail, the cooperation of the target firm's existing management is almost a necessity for a merger. This cooperation may not be easily or cheaply obtained.

Acquisition of Stock

A second way to acquire another firm is to simply purchase the firm's voting stock in exchange for cash, shares of stock, or other securities. This process often starts as a private offer from the management of one firm to another. Regardless of how it starts, at some point the offer is taken directly to the target firm's shareholders. This can be accomplished by a tender offer. A **tender offer** is a public offer to buy shares. It is made by one firm directly to the shareholders of another firm.

---

[1] As we discuss later, obtaining majority assent is less of a problem in Canada than in the United States because fewer Canadian corporations are widely held.

If the shareholders choose to accept the offer, they tender their shares by exchanging them for cash or securities (or both), depending on the offer. A tender offer is frequently contingent on the bidder's obtaining some percentage of the total voting shares. If not enough shares are tendered, the offer might be withdrawn or reformulated.

The takeover bid is communicated to the target firm's shareholders by public announcements such as newspaper advertisements. Takeover bids may be either by **circular bid** mailed directly to the target's stockholders or by **stock exchange bid** (through the facilities of the TSE or other exchange). In either case, Ontario securities law requires that the bidder mail a notice of the proposed share purchase to shareholders. Furthermore, the management of the target firm must also respond to the bid, including their recommendation to accept or to reject the bid. For a circular bid, the response must be mailed to shareholders. If the bid is made through a stock exchange, the response is through a press release.

The following factors are involved in choosing between an acquisition by stock and a merger:

1. In an acquisition by stock, no shareholder meetings have to be held and no vote is required. If the shareholders of the target firm don't like the offer, they are not required to accept it and need not tender their shares.

2. In an acquisition by stock, the bidding firm can deal directly with the shareholders of the target firm by using a tender offer. The target firm's management and board of directors can be bypassed.

3. Acquisition by stock is occasionally unfriendly. In such cases, a stock acquisition is used in an effort to circumvent the target firm's management, which is usually actively resisting acquisition. Resistance by the target firm's management often makes the cost of acquisition by stock higher than the cost of a merger.

4. Frequently, a significant minority of shareholders holds out in a tender offer. The target firm cannot be completely absorbed when this happens, and this may delay realization of the merger benefits or otherwise be costly.

5. Complete absorption of one firm by another requires a merger. Many acquisitions by stock end up with a formal merger later.

circular bid
Corporate takeover bid communicated to the shareholders by direct mail.

stock exchange bid
Corporate takeover bid communicated to the shareholders through a stock exchange.

Acquisition of Assets

A firm can effectively acquire another firm by buying most or all of its assets. This accomplishes the same thing as buying the company. In this case, however, the target firm does not necessarily cease to exist, it just has its assets sold. The shell still exists unless its shareholders choose to dissolve it.

This type of acquisition requires a formal vote of the shareholders of the selling firm. One advantage to this approach is that there is no problem with minority shareholders holding out. However, acquisition of assets may involve transferring titles to individual assets. The legal process of transferring assets can be costly.

Acquisition Classifications

Financial analysts typically classify acquisitions into three types:

1. *Horizontal acquisition.* This is acquisition of a firm in the same industry as the bidder. The firms compete with each other in their product markets.

2. *Vertical acquisition.* A vertical acquisition involves firms at different steps of the production process. The acquisition by an airline company of a travel card company would be a vertical acquisition.

3. *Conglomerate acquisition.* When the bidder and the target firm are not related to each other, the merger is called a conglomerate acquisition. The acquisition of Federated Department Stores by Campeau Corporation, a real estate company, was considered a conglomerate acquisition.

A Note on Takeovers

Takeover is a general and imprecise term referring to the transfer of control of a firm from one group of shareholders to another. A takeover thus occurs whenever one group takes control from another.[2] This can occur in three ways: acquisitions, proxy contests, and going-private transactions. Thus, takeovers encompass a broader set of activities than just acquisitions. These activities can be depicted as follows:

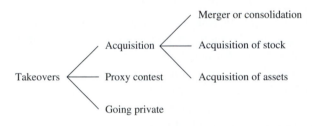

proxy contests

Attempts to gain control of a firm by soliciting a sufficient number of stockholder votes to replace existing management.

going-private transactions

All publicly owned stock in a firm is replaced with complete equity ownership by a private group.

leveraged buyouts (LBOs)

Going-private transactions in which a large percentage of the money used to buy the stock is borrowed. Often, incumbent management is involved.

As we have mentioned, a takeover achieved by acquisition occurs by merger, tender offer, or purchase of assets. In mergers and tender offers, the bidder buys the voting common stock of the target firm.

Takeovers can also occur with **proxy contests**. Proxy contests occur when a group attempts to gain controlling seats on the board of directors by voting in new directors. A proxy is the right to cast someone else's votes. In a proxy contest, proxies are solicited by an unhappy group of shareholders from the rest of the shareholders.

In **going-private transactions**, all the equity shares of a public firm are purchased by a small group of investors. Usually, the group includes members of incumbent management and some outside investors. Such transactions have come to be known generically as **leveraged buyouts (LBOs)** because a large percentage of the money needed to buy the stock is usually borrowed. Such transactions are also termed *MBOs* (management buyouts) when existing management is heavily involved. The shares of the firm are delisted from stock exchanges and no longer can be purchased in the open market.

LBOs were common in the late 1980s, and some recent ones have been quite large. As this is written, the largest acquisition in history (and possibly the single largest private transaction ever of any kind) is the 1989 LBO of RJR Nabisco, the U.S. tobacco and food products giant. The acquisition price in that buyout was an astonishing $30.6 billion. In that LBO, as with most large ones, much of the financing came from junk bond sales (see Chapter 12 for a discussion of junk bonds).

---

[2] A takeover bid has a narrowed meaning as we explained earlier. *Control* may be defined as having a majority vote on the board of directors.

20 largest mergers in Canada, 1979-89. Ranked by market value in 1989   **T A B L E 21.1**

Rank	Purchase Price ($million)	Acquiring Company	Acquired or Merged Company	Date of Acquisition	Percent Stock Acquired
1	6,600[1]	Campeau Corp.	Federated Department Stores, Cincinnati, Ohio	1988	100%
2	4,133	Dome Petroleum Ltd.	Hudson's Bay Oil & Gas Ltd.	1981	100
3	5,500	Amoco Petroleum Corp., Chicago, Illinois	Dome Petroleum Ltd.	1988	100
4	5,004[1]	Campeau Corp.	Allied Stores Corp., New York	1986	100
5	4,960	Imperial Oil Ltd.	Texaco Canada Ltd.	1989	100
6	3,091[1]	Seagram Co.	Du Pont, Wilmington, Delaware	1981	20
7	3,000[2]	Gulf Canada Corp.	Hiram Walker Resources Ltd.	1986	70
8	2,850	Olympia & York Dev.	Gulf Canada Ltd.	1985	60
9	2,600[2]	Allied Lyons PLC, UK	Hiram Walker-Gooderham & Worts	1986	51
10	2,570	Imasco Ltd.	Genstar Corp.	1986	100
11	2,600	JMB Realty Corp., Chicago, Illinois	Cadillac Fairview Ltd.	1987	100
12	1,496	Petro-Canada	Pacific Petroleums Ltd.	1979	100
13	2,600	Stone Container, Chicago, Illinois	Consolidated-Bathurst Ltd.	1989	100
14	1,600	Canada Dev. Corp.	Aquitaine Co. of Canada	1981	100
15	2,200	Noranda Inc./Trelleborg AG, Sweden	Falconbridge Ltd.	1989	100
16	1,453	Petro-Canada	Petrofina Canada Ltd.	1981	100
17	1,167	Consumers' Gas Co.	Hiram Walker-Gooderham & Worts	1980	100
18	1,421	Canadian Pacific Ltd.	CP Enterprises Ltd.	1985	30
19	1,100	CP Enterprises Ltd.	Canadian International Paper	1981	100
20	1,635	Houston Industries Inc., Houston, Texas	U.S. Cable Assets, Rogers Communications Inc.	1989	100

[1]Converted from US$.
[2]Original purchase price.
Source: *Financial Post* 500 Summer/90.

The 1980s saw a large number of mergers, acquisitions, and LBOs, many of them involving very familiar companies. In fact, the largest such transactions ever all took place in the 1980s. Table 21.1 lists the 20 largest mergers in Canada in the 1980s. While lagging behind RJR Nabisco, Campeau Corporation, the largest merger on the Canadian list, ranks number 7 in the top 20 U.S. mergers for the same period.[3] Another significant trend is foreign involvement. Three of the top 20 mergers involved Canadian firms buying U.S. companies, while 6 featured foreign firms acquiring Canadian assets.

Canadian corporations actively acquired and sold assets in 1994. Figure 21.1 shows the 15 largest deals.

CONCEPT QUESTIONS

1. What is a merger? How does a merger differ from other acquisition forms?

2. What is a takeover?

[3] W. Adams and J. W. Brock, *Dangerous Pursuits* (New York: Pantheon Books, 1989), p. 14.

Source: Kim Lockhart and Kimberly Noble, "Who's Who Behind the Year's Top Deals," Report on Business, *Globe and Mail,* January 9,1995, p. B1. Used with permission.

FIGURE 21.1

15 largest acquisitions and sales in Canada, 1994

LET'S MAKE A DEAL

Top 15 Deals of 1994

Media: Rogers buys Maclean Hunter	$3.1-billion
Gold: American Barrick buys Lac Minerals	$2.2-billion
Energy: Talisman takes over Bow Valley	$1.8-billion
Base metals: Falconbridge Nickel sells shares to public investors	$1.4-billion
Utility: Interprovincial Pipe Line buys a stake in Consumers' Gas	$1.2-billion
Real estate: Horsham and O'Connor bail out Trizec	$1.1-billion
Forest: O&Y sells paper maker Abitibi-Price in the open market	$886-million
Telecom: Alberta's Telus Corp. bids for Edmonton Tel	$720-million
Financial: Mouvement Desjardins buys Laurentian Group	$685-million
Cable TV: Shaw Communications acquires CUC Broadcasting	$646-million
Sporting goods: Nike buys Canstar Sports	$546-million
Stock brokerage: Nesbitt Thomson acquires BurnsFry	$403-million
Retail: Wal-Mart buys Woolco stores	$397-million
Natural resources: Sherritt gets fertilizer assets from Imperial Oil	$365-million
Mobile phones: Clearnet sells shares to Nextel, public	$358-million

21.2 | TAXES AND ACQUISITIONS

If one firm buys another firm, the transaction may be taxable or tax free. In a *taxable acquisition,* the shareholders of the target firm are considered to have sold their shares, and they have capital gains or losses that are taxed. In a *tax-free acquisition,* since the acquisition is considered an exchange instead of a sale, no capital gain or loss occurs at that time.

Determinants of Tax Status

The general requirements for tax-free status are that the acquisition involves two Canadian corporations subject to corporate income tax and that there be a continuity of equity interest. In other words, the shareholders in the target firm must retain an equity interest in the bidder.

The specific requirements for a tax-free acquisition depend on the legal form of the acquisition; in general, if the buying firm offers the selling firm cash for its equity, it is a taxable acquisition. If shares of stock are offered, it is a tax-free acquisition.

In a tax-free acquisition, the selling shareholders are considered to have exchanged their old shares for new ones of equal value, and no capital gains or losses are experienced.

Taxable versus Tax-Free Acquisitions

There are two factors to consider when comparing a tax-free acquisition and a taxable acquisition: the capital gains effect and the write-up effect. The *capital gains effect* refers to the fact that the target firm's shareholders may have to pay capital gains taxes in a taxable acquisition. They may demand a higher price as compensation, thereby increasing the cost of the merger. This is a cost of taxable acquisition.

The tax status of an acquisition also affects the appraised value of the assets of the selling firm. In a taxable acquisition, the assets of the selling firm are revalued or "written up" from their historic book value to their estimated current market value. This is the *write-up effect,* and it is important because the depreciation expense on the acquired firm's assets can be increased in taxable acquisitions. Remember that an increase in depreciation is a non-cash expense, but it has the desirable effect of reducing taxes.

CONCEPT QUESTIONS

1. What factors influence the choice between a taxable and a tax-free acquisition?
2. What is the write-up effect in a taxable acquisition?

21.3 | ACCOUNTING FOR ACQUISITIONS

When one firm acquires another firm, there are two possible methods of accounting for the acquisition—purchase or a pooling of interests. In the following discussion, a key point to remember is that the accounting method has no cash flow consequences.

The Purchase Method

The purchase accounting method of reporting acquisitions requires that the assets of the target firm be reported at their fair market value on the books of the bidder. With this method, an asset called *goodwill* is created for accounting purposes. Goodwill is the difference between the purchase price and the estimated fair value of the assets acquired.

To illustrate, suppose Firm A acquires Firm B, thereby creating a new firm, AB. The balance sheets for the two firms on the date of the acquisition are shown in Table 21.2. Suppose Firm A pays $18 million in cash for Firm B. The money is raised by borrowing the full amount. The fixed assets in Firm B are appraised at $14 million fair market value. Since the working capital is $2 million, the balance sheet assets are

TABLE 21.2 *Accounting for acquisitions: Purchase (in millions)*

Firm A					Firm B				
Working capital	$ 4	Equity	$20		Working capital	$ 2	Equity	$10	
Fixed assets	16				Fixed assets	8			
Total	$20		$20		Total	$10		$10	

Firm AB			
Working capital	$ 6	Debt	$18
Fixed assets	30	Equity	20
Goodwill	2		
Total	$38		$38

The market value of the fixed assets of Firm B is $14 million. Firm A pays $18 million for Firm B by issuing debt.

worth $16 million. Firm A thus pays $2 million in excess of the estimated market value of these assets. This amount is the goodwill.[4]

The last balance sheet in Table 21.2 shows what the new firm looks like under purchase accounting. Notice that:

1. The total assets of Firm AB increase to $38 million. The fixed assets increase to $30 million. This is the sum of the fixed assets of Firm A and the revalued fixed assets of Firm B ($16 million + 14 million = $30 million). Note that the tax effect of the write-up is ignored in this example.

2. The $2 million excess of the purchase price over the fair market value is reported as goodwill on the balance sheet.[5]

Pooling of Interests

Under a pooling of interests, the assets of the acquiring and acquired firms are pooled, meaning the balance sheets are just added together. Using our previous example, assume Firm A buys Firm B by giving B's shareholders $18 million worth of common stock. The result is shown in Table 21.3.

The new firm is owned jointly by all the shareholders of the previously separate firms. The accounting is much simpler here; we just add the two old balance sheets together. The total assets are unchanged by the acquisition, and no goodwill is created.

Which Is Better: Purchase or Pooling of Interests?

One important difference between purchase and pooling of interests accounting is goodwill. A firm may prefer pooling because it does not involve goodwill. Some firms do not like goodwill because the original amount must be amortized over a period of years (not to exceed 40 years).

The goodwill amortization expense must be deducted from reported income. This is a non-cash deduction, of course, but, unlike depreciation, it is not tax deductible. As a result of this expense, purchase accounting usually results in lower reported

---

T A B L E 21.3

Accounting for acquisitions: Pooling of interests (in millions)

Firm A				Firm B			
Working capital	$ 4	Equity	$20	Working capital	$ 2	Equity	$10
Fixed assets	16			Fixed assets	8		
Total	$20		$20	Total	$10		$10

Firm AB			
Working capital	$ 6	Equity	$30
Fixed assets	24		
Total	$30		$30

---

[4] Remember, there are assets such as employee talents, good customers, growth opportunities, and other intangibles that don't show up on the balance sheet. The $2 million excess pays for these.

[5] You might wonder what would happen if the purchase price were less than the estimated fair market value. Amusingly, to be consistent, it seems that the accountants would need to create a liability called ill will! Instead, the fair market value is revised downward to equal the purchase price.

income than pooling of interests accounting. Also, purchase accounting may result in a larger book value for total assets (because of the write-up in asset values). The combination of lower reported income and larger book value from purchase accounting has an unfavourable impact on accounting-based performance measures, such as return on assets (ROA) and return on equity (ROE).

Purchase accounting does not in itself affect taxes. The tax status of a merger is determined by Revenue Canada. Because the amount of tax-deductible expense is not directly affected by the method of acquisition accounting, cash flows are not affected, and the NPV of the acquisition should be the same whether pooling or purchase accounting is used. Not surprisingly, there doesn't appear to be any evidence suggesting that acquiring firms create more value under one method than the other.

> CONCEPT QUESTIONS
> 1. What is the difference between a purchase and a pooling of interests?
> 2. Why would management care about the choice if it has no effect on cash flows?

21.4 | GAINS FROM ACQUISITION

To determine the gains from an acquisition, we need to identify the relevant incremental cash flows, or, more generally, the source of value. In the broadest sense, acquiring another firm makes sense only if there is some concrete reason to believe the target firm is somehow worth more in our hands than it is worth now. As we see, there are a number of reasons this might be so.

Synergy

Suppose Firm A is contemplating acquiring Firm B. The acquisition would be beneficial if the combined firm has a greater value than the sum of the values of the separate firms. If we let V_{AB} stand for the value of the merged firm, then the merger makes sense only if:

$$V_{AB} > V_A + V_B$$

where V_A and V_B are the separate values. A successful merger thus requires that the value of the whole exceeds the sum of the parts.

The difference between the value of the combined firm and the sum of the values of the firms as separate entities is the incremental net gain from the acquisition:

$$\Delta V = V_{AB} - (V_A + V_B)$$

When ΔV is positive, the acquisition is said to generate **synergy**.

If Firm A buys Firm B, it gets a company worth V_B plus the incremental gain, ΔV. The value of Firm B to Firm A (V_B^*) is thus:

> Value of Firm B to Firm A = $V_B^* = \Delta V + V_B$

We place a * on V_B^* to emphasize that we are referring to the value of Firm B to Firm A, not the value of Firm B as a separate entity.

V_B^* can be determined in two steps: (1) estimating V_B, and (2) estimating ΔV. If B is a public company, its market value as an independent firm under existing management (V_B) can be observed directly. If Firm B is not publicly owned, its value has to be estimated based on similar companies that are. Either way, the problem of determining a value for V_B^* requires determining a value for ΔV.

synergy
The positive incremental net gain associated with the combination of two firms through a merger or acquisition.

To determine the incremental value of an acquisition, we need to know the incremental cash flows. These are the cash flows for the combined firm less what A and B could generate separately. In other words, the incremental cash flow for evaluating a merger is the difference between the cash flow of the combined company and the sum of the cash flows for the two companies considered separately. We label this incremental cash flow as ΔCF.

E X A M P L E | **21.1**   **Synergy**

Firms A and B are competitors with very similar assets and business risks. Both are all-equity firms with aftertax cash flows of $10 per year forever, and both have an overall cost of capital of 10 percent. Firm A is thinking of buying Firm B. The cash flow from the merged firm would be $21 per year. Does the merger generate synergy? What is V_B^*? What is ΔV?

The merger does generate synergy because the cash flow from the merged firm is ΔCF = $1 greater than the sum of the individual cash flows ($21 versus $20). Assuming the risks stay the same, the value of the merged firm is $21/.10 = $210. Firms A and B are each worth $10/.10 = $100, for a total of $200. The incremental gain from the merger, ΔV, is thus $210 - 200 = $10. The total value of Firm B to Firm A, V_B^*, is $100 (the value of B as a separate company) + $10 (the incremental gain) = $110.

From our discussion in earlier chapters, we know that the incremental cash flow, ΔCF, can be broken down into four parts:

$$\Delta CF = \Delta EBIT + \Delta Depreciation - \Delta Tax - \Delta CapitalRequirements$$
$$= \Delta Revenue - \Delta Cost - \Delta Tax - \Delta Capital\ Requirements$$

where ΔRevenue is the difference in revenues, ΔCost is the difference in operating costs, ΔTax is the difference in taxes, and ΔCapital Requirements is the change in new fixed assets and net working capital.

Based on this breakdown, the merger makes sense only if one or more of these cash flow components is beneficially affected by the merger. The possible cash flow benefits of mergers and acquisitions thus fall into four basic categories: revenue enhancement, cost reductions, lower taxes, and reductions in capital needs. |

Revenue Enhancement

One important reason for an acquisition is that the combined firm may generate greater revenues than two separate firms. Increases in revenue may come from marketing gains, strategic benefits, and increases in market power.

Marketing Gains   It is frequently claimed that mergers and acquisitions can produce greater operating revenues from improved marketing. For example, improvements might be made in the following areas:

1. Previously ineffective media programming and advertising efforts.
2. A weak existing distribution network.
3. An unbalanced product mix.

Strategic Benefits   Some acquisitions promise a strategic advantage. This is an opportunity to take advantage of the competitive environment if certain things occur or, more generally, to enhance management flexibility with regard to the company's future operations. In this regard, a strategic benefit is more like an option than it is a standard investment opportunity.

For example, suppose a sewing machine firm can use its technology to enter other businesses. The small-motor technology from the original business can provide opportunities to begin manufacturing small appliances and electric typewriters. Similarly, electronics expertise gained in producing typewriters can be used to manufacture electronic printers.

The word *beachhead* describes the process of entering a new industry to exploit perceived opportunities. The beachhead is to spawn new opportunities based on intangible relationships. One example is Procter & Gamble's initial acquisition of the Charmin Paper Company as a beachhead that allowed Procter & Gamble to develop a highly interrelated cluster of paper products—disposable diapers, paper towels, feminine hygiene products, and bathroom tissue.[6]

Market Power One firm may acquire another to increase its market share and market power. In such mergers, profits can be enhanced through higher prices and reduced competition for customers. In theory, such mergers are controlled by law. In practice, however, horizontal mergers are far more common in Canada than the United States due to weaker legal restrictions against combinations of competitors that might limit market competition.[7]

Cost Reductions

One of the most basic reasons to merge is that a combined firm may operate more efficiently than two separate firms. A firm can obtain greater operating efficiency in several different ways through a merger or an acquisition.

Economies of Scale Economies of scale relate to the average cost per unit of producing goods and services. As Figure 21.2 shows, when the per-unit cost of production falls as the level of production increases, an economy of scale exists.

Frequently, the phrase *spreading overhead* is used in connection with economies of scale. This expression refers to the sharing of central facilities such as corporate headquarters, top management, and computer services.

Economies of Vertical Integration Operating economies can be gained from vertical combinations as well as from horizontal combinations. The main purpose of vertical acquisitions is to make coordinating closely related operating activities easier. Benefits from vertical integration are probably the reason most forest product firms that cut timber also own sawmills and hauling equipment. Such economies may explain why some airline companies have purchased hotels and car rental companies.

Technology transfers are another reason for vertical integration. Consider the merger of General Motors Corporation and Hughes Aircraft in 1985. It seems natural that an automobile manufacturer might acquire an advanced electronics firm if the special technology of the electronics firm can be used to improve the quality of the automobile.

---

[6] This example comes from Michael Porter's *Competitive Advantage* (New York: Free Press, 1985).

[7] From the mid-1950s to the mid-1980s, only one merger in Canada was blocked under the Combines Investigation Act. In the same period, U.S. antitrust laws "prevented several hundred horizontal mergers" according to B. E. Eckbo, "Mergers and the Market for Corporate Control: the Canadian Evidence," *Canadian Journal of Economics,* May 1986, pp. 236–60.

FIGURE 21.2

Economies of scale

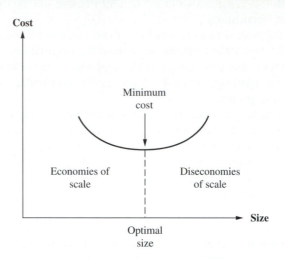

Complementary Resources   Some firms acquire others to make better use of existing resources or to provide the missing ingredient for success. Think of a ski equipment store that could merge with a tennis equipment store to produce more even sales over both the winter and summer seasons, and thereby better use store capacity.

Evidence on Market Power and Efficiency Gains   Most of the evidence on merger gains is measured in returns to shareholders. We discuss this later to see who gains in mergers. To attribute any gains from mergers to specific advantages like market share requires an industrial organization approach. A current study of Canadian mergers in the 1970s finds that gains occurred in market share, productivity, or profitability. This suggests that revenue enhancement and cost reduction are valid reasons at least for some mergers.[8]

Tax Gains

Tax gains often are a powerful incentive for some acquisitions. The possible tax gains from an acquisition include the following:

1. The use of tax losses.
2. The use of unused debt capacity.
3. The use of surplus funds.
4. The ability to write up the value of depreciable assets.

Net Operating Losses   Firms that lose money on a pretax basis do not pay taxes. Such firms can end up with tax losses that they cannot use. These tax losses are referred to as NOL (an acronym for net operating losses).

---

[8] Inefficiencies in real goods markets explain why it is sometimes cheaper to acquire resources and strategic links through mergers. J. R. Baldwin and P. K. Gorecki, "Mergers and the Competitive Process," Working Paper, Statistics Canada, 1990.

A firm with net operating losses may be an attractive merger partner for a firm with significant tax liabilities. Absent any other effects, the combined firm would have a lower tax bill than the two firms considered separately. This is a good example of how a firm can be more valuable merged than standing alone. For example, tax savings made possible by Dome Petroleum's large losses were an important attraction to Amoco when it bought Dome in 1988. Table 21.1 shows this was the third largest merger in Canada in the 1980s.

There is an important qualification to our NOL discussion. Canadian tax laws permit firms that experience periods of profit and loss to even things out through loss carry-back and carry-forward provisions. A firm that has been profitable in the past but has a loss in the current year can get refunds of income taxes paid in the three previous years. After that, losses can be carried forward for up to seven years. Thus, a merger to exploit unused tax shields must offer tax savings over and above what can be accomplished by firms via carry-overs.

Unused Debt Capacity   Some firms do not use as much debt as they are able. This makes them potential acquisition candidates. Adding debt can provide important tax savings, and many acquisitions are financed with debt. The acquiring company can deduct interest payments on the newly created debt and reduce taxes.[9]

Surplus Funds   Another quirk in the tax laws involves surplus funds. Consider a firm that has a free cash flow available after all taxes have been paid and after all positive net present value projects have been financed.

In this situation, aside from purchasing fixed income securities, the firm has several ways to spend the free cash flow, including:

1. Pay dividends.
2. Buy back its own shares.
3. Acquire shares in another firm.

We discussed the first two options in Chapter 16. We saw that an extra dividend increases the income tax paid by some investors. And, under Revenue Canada regulations, share repurchase does not always reduce the taxes paid by shareholders when compared to paying dividends.

To avoid these problems, the firm can buy another firm. By doing this, the tax problem associated with paying a dividend is avoided.

Asset Write-Ups   We have previously observed that, in a taxable acquisition, the assets of the acquired firm can be revalued. If the value of the assets is increased, tax deductions for depreciation are a gain.

Changing Capital Requirements

All firms must make investments in working capital and fixed assets to sustain an efficient level of operating activity. A merger may reduce the combined investments needed by the two firms. For example, Firm A may need to expand its manufacturing facilities while Firm B has significant excess capacity. It may be much cheaper for Firm A to buy Firm B than to build from scratch.

---

[9] While unused debt capacity can be a valid reason for a merger, hindsight shows that many mergers in the 1980s overused debt financing. We discuss this in more detail later.

In addition, acquiring firms may see ways of more effectively managing existing assets. This can occur with a reduction in working capital by more efficient handling of cash, accounts receivable, and inventory. Finally, the acquiring firm may also sell certain assets that are not needed in the combined firm.

Avoiding Mistakes

Evaluating the benefit of a potential acquisition is more difficult than a standard capital budgeting analysis because so much of the value can come from intangible, or otherwise difficult to quantify, benefits. Consequently, there is a great deal of room for error. Here are some general rules to remember:

1. *Do not ignore market values.* There is no point and little gain to estimating the value of a publicly traded firm when that value can be directly observed. The current market value represents the consensus of investors concerning the firm's value (under existing management). Use this value as a starting point. If the firm is not publicly held, the place to start is with similar firms that are publicly held.

2. *Estimate only incremental cash flows.* It is important to estimate the cash flows that are incremental to the acquisition. Only incremental cash flows from an acquisition add value to the acquiring firm. Acquisition analysis should thus focus only on the newly created, incremental cash flows from the proposed acquisition.

3. *Use the correct discount rate.* The discount rate should be the required rate of return for the incremental cash flows associated with the acquisition. It should reflect the risk associated with the use of funds, not the source. In particular, if Firm A is acquiring Firm B, Firm A's cost of capital is not particularly relevant. Firm B's cost of capital is a much more appropriate discount rate because it reflects the risk of Firm B's cash flows.

4. *Be aware of transaction costs.* An acquisition may involve substantial (and sometimes astounding) transaction costs. These include fees to investment bankers, legal fees, and disclosure requirements. Fees generated by leveraged buyouts during the 1980s amounted to $4.7 billion (U.S.)![10]

A Note on Inefficient Management

There are firms whose value could be increased with a change in management. These firms are poorly run or otherwise do not efficiently use their assets to create shareholder value. Mergers are a means of replacing management in such cases.[11]

Furthermore, the fact that a firm might benefit from a change in management does not necessarily mean that existing management is dishonest, incompetent, or negligent. Instead, just as some athletes are better than others, so might some management teams be better at running a business. This can be particularly true during times of technological change or other periods when innovations in business practice are occurring. In any case, to the extent that they can identify poorly run firms or firms that otherwise would benefit from a change in management, corporate raiders provide a valuable service to target firm shareholders and society in general.

---

[10] P. J. Regan, "Junk Bonds—Opportunity Knocks?" *Financial Analysts Journal,* May–June 1990, p. 13.

[11] Another alternative is for a firm to spin off or divest negative NPV divisions. See Chapter 9 for more discussion of the abandonment option.

Perks consumption by top management is another inefficiency that may be eliminated by acquisition. For example, Ross Johnson (former CEO of RJR Nabisco) is described as "a relentlessly cheerful rogue who reveled in all the apartments, country-club memberships, jets, Jaguars, and scotch his corporate treasuries could afford."[12]

The Negative Side of Takeovers

While most financial analysts would likely agree that corporate raiders can deliver benefits to society, there is increasing concern over whether the cost is too high. Critics of takeovers (and especially LBOs) are concerned that social costs are not counted when the post-takeover search for efficiency gains leads to plant closures and layoffs. When plants close or move, workers and equipment can be turned to other uses only at some cost to society. For example, taxpayers may need to subsidize retraining and relocation programs for workers or tax incentives for investment. In an extreme case, suppose a mine is closed in a rural area where there is no other large employer. All capital goods that cannot be moved may become worthless.

Critics of takeovers argue that they reduce trust between management and labour thus reducing efficiency and increasing costs. They point to Japan, Germany, and Korea, where there are few takeovers, as examples of more efficient economies. They argue that, as an alternative to takeovers a strong board of outside directors could maximize management's efficiency.[13]

CONCEPT QUESTIONS

1. What are the relevant incremental cash flows for evaluating a merger candidate?
2. What are some different sources of gain from acquisition?
3. Are takeovers good for society? State the main arguments on both sides.

21.5 | SOME FINANCIAL SIDE EFFECTS OF ACQUISITIONS

In addition to the various possibilities we discussed, mergers can have some purely financial side effects; that is, things that occur regardless of whether the merger makes economic sense or not. Two such effects are particularly worth mentioning: EPS growth and diversification.

EPS Growth

An acquisition can create the appearance of growth in **earnings per share (EPS)** This may fool investors into thinking the firm is doing better than it really is. What happens is easiest to see with an example.

Suppose Global Resources, Ltd., acquires Regional Enterprises. The financial positions of Global and Regional before the acquisition are shown in Table 21.4. Because the merger creates no additional value, the combined firm (Global Resources after acquiring Regional) has a value that is equal to the sum of the values of the two firms before the merger.

earnings per share (EPS)
Net income minus any cash dividends on preferred stock, divided by the number of shares of common stock outstanding.

---

[12] B. Burroughs, "Barbarians in Retreat," *Vanity Fair,* March 1993, p. 226.
[13] This section draws on C. Robinson's points in "C. Robinson versus W. Block, Are Corporate Takeovers Good or Bad? A Debate," *Canadian Investment Review,* Fall 1991, pp. 53–60; and on a piece by the late W. S. Allen, "Relegating Corporate Takeovers to the 'Campeaust' Heap: A Proposal," *Canadian Investment Review,* Spring 1990, pp. 71–76.

Both Global and Regional have 100 shares outstanding before the merger. However, Global sells for $25 per share versus $10 per share for Regional. Global therefore acquires Regional by exchanging 1 of its shares for every 2.5 Regional shares. Since there are 100 shares in Regional, it takes 100/2.5 = 40 shares in all.

After the merger, Global has 140 shares outstanding, and several things happen (see Column 3 of Table 21.4):

1. The market value of the combined firm is $3,500. This is equal to the sum of the values of the separate firms before the merger. If the market is smart, it realizes the combined firm is worth the sum of the values of the separate firms.

2. The earnings per share of the merged firm are $1.43. The acquisition enables Global to increase its earnings per share from $1 to $1.43, an increase of 43 percent.

3. Because the stock price of Global after the merger is the same as before the merger, the price/earnings ratio must fall. This is true as long as the market is smart and recognizes that the total market value has not been altered by the merger.

If the market is fooled, it might mistake the 43 percent increase in earnings per share for true growth. In this case, the price/earnings ratio of Global may not fall after the merger. Suppose the price/earnings ratio of Global remains equal to 25. Since the combined firm has earnings of $200, the total value of the combined firm increases to $5,000 (25 × $200). The per share value of Global increases to $35.71 ($5,000/140).

This is earnings growth magic. Like all good magic, it is just illusion. For it to work, the shareholders of Global and Regional must receive something for nothing. This, of course, is unlikely with so simple a trick.

Diversification

diversification

Investment in more than one asset; returns do not move proportionally in the same direction at the same time, thus reducing risk.

Diversification is commonly mentioned as a benefit to a merger. For example, U.S. Steel Corporation included diversification as a benefit in its acquisition of Marathon Oil Company, a merger that ranked in size just behind Campeau's purchase of Federated Department Stores. The problem is that diversification per se probably does not create value.

Going back to Chapter 11, diversification reduces unsystematic risk. We also saw that the value of an asset depends on its systematic risk and that diversification does not directly affect systematic risk. Since the unsystematic risk is not especially important, there is no particular benefit to reducing it.

T A B L E 21.4

Financial positions of Global Resources and Regional Enterprises

	Global Resources before Merger	Regional Enterprises before Merger	Global Resources after Merger	
			The Market Is Smart	The Market Is Fooled
Earnings per share	$ 1.00	$ 1.00	$ 1.43	$ 1.43
Price per share	$ 25.00	$ 10.00	$ 25.00	$ 35.71
Price/earnings ratio	25	10	17.5	25
Number of shares	100	100	140	140
Total earnings	$ 100	$ 100	$ 200	$ 200
Total value	$2,500	$1,000	$3,500	$5,000

Exchange ratio: 1 share in Global for 2.5 shares in Regional.

An easy way to see why diversification isn't an important benefit to mergers is to consider someone who owned stock in U.S. Steel and Marathon Oil. Such a shareholder is already diversified between these two investments. The merger doesn't do anything that the stockholders can't do for themselves.

More generally, stockholders can get all the diversification they want by buying stock in different companies. As a result, they won't pay a premium for a merged company just for the benefit of diversification.

By the way, we are not saying that U.S. Steel (now USX Corporation) made a mistake. At the time of the merger in 1982, U.S. Steel was a cash-rich company (more than 20 percent of its assets were in the form of cash and marketable securities). It is not uncommon to see firms with surplus cash articulating a "need" for diversification.

CONCEPT QUESTIONS

1. Why can a merger create the appearance of earnings growth?

2. Why is diversification by itself not a good reason for a merger?

21.6 | THE COST OF AN ACQUISITION

We've discussed some of the benefits of acquisition. We now need to discuss the cost of a merger.[14] We learned earlier that the net incremental gain to a merger is:

$$\Delta V = V_{AB} - (V_A - V_B)$$

Also, the total value of Firm B to Firm A, V_B^*, is:

$$V_B^* = V_B + \Delta V$$

The NPV of the merger is therefore:

$$NPV = V_B^* - \text{Cost to Firm A of the acquisition} \qquad [21.1]$$

To illustrate, suppose we have the following premerger information for Firm A and Firm B:

	Firm A	Firm B
Price per share	$ 20	$ 10
Number of shares	25	10
Total market value	$500	$100

Both of these firms are 100 percent equity. You estimate that the incremental value of the acquisition, ΔV, is $100.

The board of Firm B has indicated that it agrees to a sale if the price is $150, payable in cash or stock. This price for Firm B has two parts. Firm B is worth $100 as a stand-alone, so this is the minimum value that we could assign to Firm B. The second part, $50, is called the *merger premium,* and it represents the amount paid more than the stand-alone value.

Should Firm A acquire Firm B? Should it pay in cash or stock? To answer, we need to determine the NPV of the acquisition under both alternatives. We can start by noting that the value of Firm B to Firm A is:

[14] For a more complete discussion of the costs of a merger and the NPV approach, see S. C. Myers, "A Framework for Evaluating Mergers," in *Modern Developments in Financial Management,* ed. S. C. Myers (New York: Praeger Publishers, 1976).

$$V_B^* = \Delta V + V_B$$
$$= \$100 + 100 = \$200$$

The total value received by A from buying Firm B is thus $200. The question then is, how much does Firm A have to give up? The answer depends on whether cash or stock is used as the means of payment.

Case I: Cash Acquisition

The cost of an acquisition when cash is used is just the cash itself. So, if Firm A pays $150 in cash to purchase all the shares of Firm B, the cost of acquiring Firm B is $150. The NPV of a cash acquisition is:

$$NPV = V_B^* - Cost$$
$$= \$200 - 150 = \$50$$

The acquisition is, therefore, profitable.

After the merger, Firm AB still has 25 shares outstanding. The value of Firm A after the merger is:

$$V_{AB} = V_A + (V_B^* - Cost)$$
$$= \$500 + 200 - 150$$
$$= \$550$$

This is just the premerger value of $500 plus the $50 NPV. The price per share after the merger is $550/25 = $22, a gain of $2 per share.

Case II: Stock Acquisition

Things are somewhat more complicated when stock is the means of payment. In a cash merger, the shareholders in B receive cash for their stock, and, as in the previous U.S. Steel/Marathon Oil example, they no longer participate in the company. Thus, as we have seen, the cost of the acquisition is the amount of cash needed to pay off B's stockholders.

In a stock merger, no cash actually changes hands. Instead, the shareholders in B come in as new shareholders in the merged firm. The value of the merged firm is equal to the premerger values of Firms A and B plus the incremental gain from the merger, ΔV:

$$V_{AB} = V_A + V_B + \Delta V$$
$$= \$500 + 100 + 100$$
$$= \$700$$

To give $150 worth of stock for Firm B, Firm A has to give up $150 − $20 = 7.5 shares. After the merger, there are thus 25 + 7.5 = 32.5 shares outstanding and the per share value is $700 − 32.5 = $21.54.

Notice that the per-share price after the merger is lower under the stock purchase option. The reason has to do with the fact that B's shareholders own stock in the new firm.

It appears that Firm A paid $150 for Firm B. However, it actually paid more than that. When all is said and done, B's stockholders own 7.5 shares of stock in the merged firm. After the merger, each of these shares is worth $21.54. The total value of the consideration received by B's shareholders is thus 7.5 × $21.54 = $161.55.

This $161.55 is the true cost of the acquisition because it is what the sellers actually end up receiving. The NPV of the merger to Firm A is:

$$\text{NPV} = V_B^* - \text{Cost}$$
$$= \$200 - 161.55 = \$38.45$$

We can check this by noting that A started with 25 shares worth $20 each. The gain to A of $38.45 works out to be $38.45 − 25 = $1.54 per share. The value of the stock increases to $21.54 as we calculated.

When we compare the cash acquisition to the stock acquisition, we see that the cash acquisition is better in this case, because Firm A gets to keep all the NPV if it pays in cash. If it pays in stock, Firm B's stockholders share in the NPV by becoming new shareholders in A.

Cash versus Common Stock

The distinction between cash and common stock financing in a merger is an important one. If cash is used, the cost of an acquisition is not dependent on the acquisition gains. All other things being the same, if common stock is used, the cost is higher because Firm A's shareholders must share the acquisition gains with the shareholders of Firm B. However, if the NPV of the acquisition is negative, the loss is shared between the two firms.

Whether to finance an acquisition by cash or by shares of stock depends on several factors, including:[15]

1. *Sharing gains.* If cash is used to finance an acquisition, the selling firm's shareholders do not participate in the potential gains of the merger. Of course, if the acquisition is not a success, the losses are not shared, and shareholders of the acquiring firm are worse off than if stock were used.

2. *Taxes.* Acquisition by cash usually results in a taxable transaction. Acquisition by exchanging stock is generally tax free.

3. *Control.* Acquisition by cash does not affect the control of the acquiring firm. Acquisition with voting shares may have implications for control of the merged firm.

CONCEPT QUESTIONS

1. Why does the true cost of a stock acquisition depend on the gain from the merger?
2. What are some important factors in deciding whether to use stock or cash in an acquisition?

21.7 | DEFENSIVE TACTICS

Target firm managers frequently resist takeover attempts. Resistance usually starts with press releases and mailings to shareholders presenting management's viewpoint.

---

[15] All-cash transactions are much more common than all-stock transactions. In 1985, for example, only about 10 percent of U.S. acquisitions were financed solely by stock (see *Mergers and Acquisitions,* "Almanac and Review: 1985"). In Canada, two-thirds of a sample of mergers between 1963 and 1982 were for cash according to A. L. Calvet and J. Lefoll, "Information Asymmetry and Wealth Effect of Canadian Corporate Acquisitions," *Financial Review,* November 1987, pp. 415–32.

It can eventually lead to legal action and solicitation of competing bids. Managerial action to defeat a takeover attempt may make target shareholders better off if it elicits a higher offer premium from the bidding firm or another firm.

Of course, management resistance may simply reflect pursuit of self-interest at the expense of shareholders. This is a controversial subject. At times, management resistance has greatly increased the amount ultimately received by shareholders. At other times, management resistance appears to have defeated all takeover attempts to the detriment of shareholders.

In this section, we describe various defensive tactics that have been used by target firms' managements to resist unfriendly attempts. The law surrounding these defences is not settled, and some of these manoeuvres may ultimately be deemed illegal or otherwise unsuitable.

The Control Block and the Corporate Charter

control block

An interest controlling 50 percent of outstanding votes plus one; thereby it may decide the fate of the firm.

If one individual or group owns 51 percent of a company's stock, this **control block** makes a hostile takeover virtually impossible. In the extreme, one interest may own all the stock. Examples are privately owned companies such as Olympia and York Developments Ltd. and Crown corporations such as Ontario Hydro. Many Canadian companies are subsidiaries of foreign corporations that own control blocks. Many domestically owned companies have controlling shareholders.[16]

As a result, control blocks are typical in Canada although they are the exception in the United States. Table 21.5 shows that only 15 of the top 100 corporations in Canada were widely held in 1989 versus 73 for the United States.[17] One important implication is that minority shareholders need protection in Canada. One key group of minority shareholders are pension funds and other institutional investors. They are becoming increasingly vocal in opposing defensive tactic that are seen to be entrenching management at the expense of stockholders. \   discuss several examples next.

For widely held companies, their corporate charters establish the conditions that allow for takeovers. The *corporate charter* refers to the articles of incorporation and corporate by-laws that establish the governance rules of the firm. Firms can amend

T A B L E 21.5

Ownership makeup of the top 100 corporations

	Canada	United States
Widely held	15	73
Control block	50	25
Privately owned	28	2
Government owned	7	0

Source: D. H. Thain and D. S. R. Leighton, "Ownership Structure and the Board," *Canadian Investment Review,* Fall 1991, pp. 61–66.

---

[16] Important exceptions are chartered banks. As we showed in Chapter 1, the Bank Act prohibits any one interest from owning more than 10 percent of the shares.

[17] The top 100 corporations in Canada are from *Financial Post 500.* The U.S. corporations come from *Fortune 500.* The table is from D. H. Thain and D. S. R. Leighton, "Ownership Structure and the Board," *Canadian Investment Review,* Fall 1991, pp. 61–66.

their corporate charters to make acquisitions more difficult. For example, usually two-thirds of the shareholders of record must approve a merger. Firms can make it more difficult to be acquired by changing this to 80 percent or so. This is called a *supermajority amendment.*

Another device is to stagger the election of the board members. This makes it more difficult to elect a new board of directors quickly. We discuss staggered elections in Chapter 12.

Repurchase/Standstill Agreements

Managers of target firms may attempt to negotiate standstill agreements. Standstill agreements are contracts where the bidding firm agrees to limit its holdings in the target firm. These agreements usually lead to the end of takeover attempts.

Standstill agreements often occur at the same time that a targeted repurchase is arranged. In a targeted repurchase, a firm buys a certain amount of its own stock from an individual investor, usually at a substantial premium. These premiums can be thought of as payments to potential bidders to eliminate unfriendly takeover attempts. Critics of such payments view them as bribes and label them **greenmail**. Paying greenmail may harm minority shareholders if it heads off a takeover that would raise the stock price.

For example, on April 2, 1986, Ashland Oil, Inc., the largest independent oil refiner in the United States, had 28 million shares outstanding. The company's stock price the day before was $48 per share on the New York Stock Exchange. On April 2, Ashland's board of directors made two decisions:

greenmail
A targeted stock repurchase where payments are made to potential bidders to eliminate unfriendly takeover attempts.

1. The board approved management's agreement with the Belzberg family of Toronto to buy, for $51 (U.S.) a share, the Belzbergs' 2.6 million shares in Ashland. This standstill agreement ended a takeover skirmish in which the Belzberg family offered $60 per share for all of the common stock of Ashland.
2. The board authorized the company to repurchase 7.5 million shares (27 percent of the outstanding shares) of its stock. Simultaneously, the board approved a proposal to establish an employee stock ownership plan to be funded with 5.3 million shares of Ashland stock.

The result of these actions was to eliminate a takeover threat and to make Ashland invulnerable to future unfriendly takeover attempts. Earlier, Ashland had put in place a provision that said 80 percent of the stockholders have to approve a takeover (a supermajority provision). The shares of stock placed in the employee stock ownership plan are effectively controlled by management and total more than 20 percent of the shares, so no one can get the needed 80 percent approval without management's help.

Standstill agreements also occur in takeover attempts in Canada but without greenmail, which appears to be ruled out by securities laws. Even so, critics of standstill agreements argue that they often cause losses for minority shareholders by averting takeovers at a premium price.

Exclusionary Offers and Non-voting Stock

An exclusionary offer is the opposite of a targeted repurchase. Here the firm or an outside group makes an offer for a given amount of stock while excluding targeted shareholders, often holders of non-voting shares. This kind of an offer is made easier in Canada since non-voting shares are more prevalent than in the United States.[18]

A well-known example occurred in 1986 when the Canadian Tire Dealers Association offered to buy 49 percent of Canadian Tire's voting shares from the founding Billes family. The dealers' bid was at $169 per share for voting shares trading at $40 before the bid. The non-voting shares were priced at $14. Further, since the dealers were the principal buyers of Canadian Tire products, control of the company would have allowed them to adjust prices to benefit themselves over the non-voting shareholders.

The offer was voided by the Ontario Securities Commission and it appears that any future exclusionary offers are likely to be viewed as an illegal form of discrimination against one group of shareholders.

Poison Pills and Share Rights Plans

poison pill

A financial device designed to make unfriendly takeover attempts unappealing, if not impossible.

A **poison pill** is a tactic designed to repel would-be suitors. The term comes from the world of espionage. Agents are supposed to bite a pill of cyanide rather than permit capture. Presumably, this prevents enemy interrogators from learning important secrets.

In the equally colorful world of corporate finance, a poison pill is a financial device designed to make it impossible for a firm to be acquired without management's consent—unless the buyer is willing to commit financial suicide.

share rights plan

Provisions allowing existing stockholders to purchase stock at some fixed price should an outside takeover bid take place, discouraging hostile takeover attempts.

In recent years, many of the largest firms in the United States and Canada have adopted poison pill provisions of one form or another, often calling them **share rights plans** (SRPs) or something similar. Table 21.6 lists poison pills either proposed or in effect in early 1990. The table also shows the trigger level (discussed later) and the TSE weight for the company's stock. In 1990, firms with poison pills made up just less than 20 percent of the TSE market value.

SRPs differ quite a bit in detail from company to company; we describe a kind of generic approach here. In general, when a company adopts an SRP, it distributes share rights to its existing shareholders.[19] These rights allow shareholders to buy shares of stock (or preferred stock) at some fixed price.

The rights issued with an SRP have a number of unusual features. First, the exercise or subscription price on the right is usually set high enough so the rights are well out of the money, meaning the purchase price is much higher than the current stock price. The rights are often good for 10 years, and the purchase or exercise price is usually a reasonable estimate of what the stock will be worth at that time.

Second, unlike ordinary stock rights, these rights can't be exercised immediately, and they can't be bought and sold separately from the stock. Also, they can essentially be cancelled by management at any time; often, they can be redeemed (bought back) for a penny apiece, or some similarly trivial amount.

Things get interesting when, under certain circumstances, the rights are triggered. This means the rights become exercisable, they can be bought and sold separately from the stock, and they are not easily cancelled or redeemed. Typically, the rights are triggered when someone acquires 20 percent of the common stock or otherwise announces a tender offer.

---

[18] Restricted voting stock made up around 15 percent of the market values of TSE listed shares at the end of 1989. Chapter 12 discusses restricted voting stock and Canadian Tire in detail.

[19] We discuss ordinary share rights in Chapter 13.

IN THEIR OWN WORDS . . .

Espen Eckbo on the Southam-Torstar Standstill Agreement

On August 25, 1985, Southam Inc., and Torstar Corporation entered into a combined share exchange and standstill agreement. The agreement followed strong rumors that Southam was "in play" as a potential target of a takeover bid. The agreement transferred control of Southam to the managements of Southam and Torstar, resulting in market expectations that Southam was no longer in play. While there was no apparent greenmail payment involved, the empirical evidence presented below strongly indicates that news that Southam was no longer in play reduced the value of Southam's non-participating shareholders' stake in the firm by more than $100 million (in excess of general market movements) in one day.

The Southam-Torstar agreement was signed on August 25 and became public knowledge on the following day. Trading in Southam and Torstar shares was halted by the TSE on August 26 and resumed on August 27, at which time the valuation effect of the agreement showed up in the respective firms' stock prices. Southam's stock price dropped 21.1 percent from $17.75 to $14.00 over that day. The analysis shows that a 17.1 percent price drop, from $17.75 to $14.71, is due to the agreement itself, while the further price drop from $14.71 to $14.00 is caused by a movement in the stock market.

News of the agreement caused the market to almost entirely reverse its expectations of a takeover premium. While systematic evidence on unsuccessful Canadian takeovers in Canada is not available, a similar stock price reversion is typical for unsuccessful acquisition attempts in the United States following news that the target firm is no longer "in play."

Due to the important principles involved, and perhaps due to the significance of the documented-wealth transfers that took place, Southam-Torstar was eventually forced to reverse the standstill agreement by June 1990. Ironically, in preparation for this reversal, Southam adopted a "poison pill" plan, which is an alternative defence against the threat of a partial takeover. That is, the plan requires all takeover offers to be for 100 percent of Southam shares.

Since poison pill plans are also inherently discriminatory, it is noteworthy that these increasingly popular anti-takeover devices appear to pass the test of Canadian corporate laws. Perhaps shareholders' ultimate defence against self-interested managers' sophisticated strategies to prolong their tenure in office is to promote a strong sense of the need for ethics in corporate control transactions.

Espen Eckbo is chairman of the finance division at the University of British Columbia. He is a noted researcher and expert witness on takeovers. His views are excerpted, with permission from the Canadian Investment Review, Fall 1991, pp. 73–78.

When the rights are triggered, they can be exercised. Since they are out of the money, this fact is not especially important. Certain other features come into play, however. The most important is the flip-over provision.

The flip-over provision is the poison in the pill. In the event of a merger, the holder of a right can pay the exercise price and receive common stock in the merged firm worth twice the exercise price. In other words, holders of the right can buy stock in the merged firm at half price.[20]

The rights issued in connection with an SRP are poison pills because anyone trying to force a merger would trigger the rights. When this happens, all the target

---

[20] Some plans also contain flip-in provisions. These allow the holder to buy stock in the target company at half price when the target company is the surviving company in a merger. Simultaneously, the rights owned by the raider (the acquirer) are voided. A merger where the target is the surviving company is called a *reverse merger.*

T A B L E 21.6	Name	Date	Trigger Percent	TSE Weight
Poison pills in	Inco	Oct. 3/88	20%	1.83%
Canada	Pegasus	Dec. 2/88	10	0.2
	Agnico-Eagle	May 10/89	20	0.14
	Aur*	Jul. 20/89	15	0.14
	Turbo	Jul. 27/89	20.5	0.05
	Numac*	Jul. 28/89	10	0.08
	Falconbridge*	Sept. 2/89	15	N.A.
	Dominion Textile	Aug. 9/89	20	0.27
	Finning	Sept. 4/89	15	0.21
	Canada Packers	Oct. 2/89	10	0.35
	MacLean Hunter	Oct. 24/89	10	0.99
	Sherritt Gordon	Nov. 26/89	20	0.14
	Dofasco	Nov. 26/89	10	0.89
	Canadian Pacific	Dec. 6/89	10	4.55
	Alcan	Dec. 15/89	20	3.35
	Placer Dome	Jan. 5/90	15	2.76
	Nowsco Well	Jan. 5/90	15	0.14
	Franco Nevada	Jan. 15/90	N.A.	0.67
	Moore Corp.	Jan. 18/90	15	1.74
	Southam	Feb. 2/90	15	0.62
	United Coin Mines	Feb. 5/90	N.A.	N.A.
			Total Wt.	19.12%

*Not implemented.
N.A.—Not available.
Source: P. Halpern, "Poison Pills: Whose Interest Do They Serve?" *Canadian Investment Review,* Spring 1990, pp. 57–66.

firm's shareholders can effectively buy stock in the merged firm at half price. This greatly increases the cost of the merger to the bidder because the target firm's shareholders end up with a much larger percentage of the merged firm.

Notice that the flip-over provision doesn't prevent someone from acquiring control of a firm by purchasing a majority interest. It just acts to prevent a complete merger of the two firms. Even so, this inability to combine can have serious tax and other implications for the buyer.

The intention of a poison pill is to force a bidder to negotiate with management. Frequently, merger offers are made with the contingency that the rights are cancelled by the target firm.[21]

Poison pills have been heavily criticized for helping to entrench management. Supporting this view, U.S. studies have found evidence of negative share price reactions when poison pills are introduced. So far, the Canadian evidence is mixed.[22]

Going Private and Leveraged Buyouts

As we have previously discussed, going private refers to what happens when the publicly owned stock in a firm is replaced with complete equity ownership by a

---

[21] All but two of the poison pills listed in Table 21.6 have a permitted bid provision allowing a bidder to bypass management under certain circumstances. Still, even in these cases, there is a substantial deterrent to a takeover. For detailed discussion of poison pills in Canada, see P. Halpern, "Poison Pills: Whose Interest Do They Serve?" *Canadian Investment Review,* Spring 1990.

[22] P. Halpern, "Poison Pills," p. 66.

private group, which may include elements of existing management. As a consequence, the firm's stock is taken off the market (if it is an exchange-traded stock, it is delisted) and is no longer traded.

One result of going private is that takeovers via tender offer can no longer occur since there are no publicly held shares. In this sense, an LBO (or, more specifically, a management buyout or MBO) can be a takeover defence. However, it's only a defence for management. From the stockholder's point of view, an LBO is a takeover because they are bought out.

From the viewpoint of management, an LBO is a risky defence. In the RJR Nabisco LBO, F. Ross Johnson, CEO and transplanted Canadian, inadvertently put the company "in play" with a plan to go private. In the end, Johnson was outbid by the Wall Street firm of Kohlberg, Kravis, and Roberts (KKR) who paid $25 billion (U.S.) for RJR Nabisco.[23]

In an LBO, the selling shareholders are invariably paid a premium more than the market price, just as they are in a merger.[24] As with a merger, the acquirer profits only if the synergy created is greater than the premium. Synergy is quite plausible in a merger of two firms, and we delineated a number of types of synergy earlier in the chapter. However, it is much more difficult to explain synergy in an LBO, because only one firm is involved.

There are generally two reasons given for the ability of an LBO to create value: First, the extra debt provides a tax deduction, which, as earlier chapters suggest, leads to an increase in firm value. Most LBOs are on firms with stable earnings and with low to moderate debt.[25] The LBO may simply increase the firm's debt to its optimum level.

Second, the LBO usually turns the previous managers into owners, thereby increasing their incentive to work hard. The increase in debt is a further incentive because the managers must earn more than the debt service to obtain any profit for themselves.

Though it is easy to value the additional tax shields from an LBO, it is quite difficult to value the gains from increased efficiency. Nevertheless, the quest for this increased efficiency is considered to be at least as important as the tax shield in explaining the LBO phenomenon.

LBOs to Date: The Record

Since the mid-1980s, ongoing experience with LBOs has revealed some weaknesses both in the concept and the financing vehicle—junk bonds. One of the first large LBOs in the United States was Revco for $1.3 billion in 1986. Less than two years later, the company filed for bankruptcy. The failure was caused by overambitious sales growth predictions combined with a lack of funds to refurbish dilapidated stores.

Further, LBOs sometimes lead to spinoffs of assets to pay down debt. For example, Nova Corporation bought Polysar Energy & Chemical Company for $2.3

---

[23] A fascinating and highly readable account of the RJR Nabisco LBO is in B. Burrough and J. Helyar, *Barbarians at the Gate, The Fall of RJR Nabisco* (New York: Harper Perennial, 1990).

[24] H. DeAngelo, L. DeAngelo and E. M. Rice, "Going Private: Minority Freezeouts and Shareholder Wealth," *Journal of Law and Economics* 27 (1984). They show that the premiums paid to existing shareholders in U.S. LBOs and other going-private transactions are about the same as interfirm acquisitions.

[25] T. Melman, "Leveraged Buyouts: How Everyone Can Win," *Canadian Investment Review,* Spring 1990, pp. 67–70, discusses LBOs from a management perspective.

billion in 1988. To pay down the debt used to finance the deal, Nova sold $500 million in assets.[26]

Problems facing LBOs in the early 1990s are exemplified in the trials of Robert Campeau whose real estate company took over Allied Stores in 1986 and then Federated Department Stores in 1988. Table 21.1 shows that these takeovers ranked high in the Canadian list for the 1980s. The Allied takeover for $5 billion was number four and the Federated purchase at $6.6 billion, number one.

Campeau was correct; Federated Department Stores assets were undervalued at the pretakeover share price of $33 but hindsight shows that the $73.50 per share takeover price was too high. Further, the deal was overleveraged with 97 percent debt financing. With either a lower purchase price, or lower leverage, the deal might have survived.[27]

Despite an injection of $300 million from Olympia & York Developments Ltd. (then owned by the Reichmann family of Toronto), Campeau Corporation had to default on its bank loans. As a result, the National Bank of Canada took over 35 percent of Campeau's voting stock in January 1990. Shortly after, Allied and Federated filed for bankruptcy protection in the United States. Over the next year, Campeau sold just under $2 billion in Canadian real estate to try to reduce its debt to manageable levels in order to survive.[28] In January 1991, Campeau Corporation's name was changed to Candev with a 65 percent control block in the hands of Olympia & York. Robert Campeau lost his seat on the board and all but 2 percent of the company's stock.

LBO problems reflected on the high-yield or junk bonds used heavily to finance them. For example, when Allied and Federated sought bankruptcy protection in 1990, Campeau junk bonds that had a face value of $1,000 sold for $110.[29]

Only around 100 junk bond issues have appeared in the Canadian market as most Canadian takeovers have been financed with bank loans. LBO problems also affect banks that provided loans to finance them. But Canadian banks have remained sound avoiding the problems faced by some U.S. banks and S&Ls.[30]

Other Defensive Devices

As corporate takeovers become more common, other colorful terms have become popular.

- *Golden parachutes.* Some target firms provide compensation to top-level management if a takeover occurs. This can be viewed as a payment to management to make it less concerned for its own welfare and more interested in shareholders when considering a takeover bid. Alternatively, the payment can be seen as an attempt to enrich management at the shareholders' expense.

- *Crown jewels.* Firms often sell major assets—crown jewels—when faced with a takeover threat. This is sometimes referred to as the *scorched earth strategy.*

[26] This and the later discussion of LBOs and junk bonds draws on J. Cazzin, "The Road to Decline," *Macleans,* January 29, 1990; and V. Ross, "Campeau Battles to the End," *Globe and Mail,* January 29, 1992, p. 1.
[27] S. N. Kaplan, "Campeau's Acquisition of Federated, Value Destroyed or Value Added?" *Journal of Financial Economics,* December 1989, pp. 189–212.
[28] S. Horvitch, "Campeau 'Selling Itself' to Survive," *Financial Post,* July 1, 1991, p. 22.
[29] See Edward Altman in Chapter 12 for more on problems with junk bonds in the United States.
[30] L. Kryzanowski and G. S. Roberts, "LBOs Cause Few Problems for Chartered Banks," *Financial Post,* February 28, 1990.

Rogers Communications Inc.

BUSINESS

Owns and operates the largest cable television business in Canada with 15 systems.

16 radio stations.

Cellular telephone network

Video rental stores

Multilingual television station in Toronto

Cable television home shopping network.

One of two major shareholders in Unitel Communications.

FINANCIAL

Nine months 1993
Revenue: $980.5-million
Loss: $123.7-million

EMPLOYEES

7,000 in 1993.

SHARE PRICE

52-week high: $25.62
52-week low: $16.12
Yesterday: $23, up $1.50

Maclean Hunter Inc.

BUSINESS

- Cable television represents 70 per cent of company's income with 35 systems.
- Publishes 200 periodicals in 10 countries.
- Holds a controlling interest in the Toronto Sun Publishing.
- 21 radio stations
- Radio paging
- Business forms
- Commercial printing
- Consumer and trade shows

FINANCIAL

1993
Revenue: $1.7-billion
Profit: $56.6-million

EMPLOYEES

12,000 in 1993.

SHARE PRICE

52-week high: $18.75
52-week low: $10.87
Yesterday: $17.37, up $0.37

FIGURE 21.3

Features of Rogers Communications Inc. and Maclean Hunter Inc.

Source: *Globe and Mail,* February 12, 1994, p. B1. Used with permission.

- *White knight.* Target firms sometimes seek a competing bid from a friendly bidder—a white knight—who promises to maintain the jobs of existing management and to refrain from selling the target's assets.

On March 30, 1994, shareholders in Maclean Hunter tendered over 93 percent of the firm's shares to bidder Rogers Communications.[31] At $17.50 per share, the total bid was worth $3.1 billion, making it the largest ever in the communications industry; it is tied at number six with Seagram's bid for Du Pont in Table 21.1's rankings of Canada's largest mergers. Figure 21.3 shows features of the two firms and makes apparent that synergies and scale economies are important factors in this deal. Strategic positioning to develop opportunities along the information highway likely also came into play.

---

[31] Our discussion draws on J. Partridge, H. Enchin, and B. Jorgensen, "Rogers Adamant on Bid Price," *Globe and Mail,* February 12, 1994, p. B1; and J. Partridge, "Rogers Takeover Bid over the Top," *Globe and Mail,* April 1, 1994, p. B1.

IN THEIR OWN WORDS . . .

Jean-Claude Delorme on Institutional Activism

The issue of corporate democracy is receiving increasing attention by shareholders. It is only natural for institutional investors such as the Caisse de depot et placement du Quebec to be involved, considering the magnitude of funds entrusted to it and the fiduciary nature of its responsibilities. Although the Caisse's position in its investee companies is always that of a minority shareholder, it feels justified to take an active stance in the management of its investments. In so doing, the Caisse is merely following the trend initiated in recent years by other major Canadian and American fund managers.

In the United States, institutional investors are increasingly playing a counterbalancing role vis-à-vis the powerful managements of many of its widely held corporations. In Canada, the mem-

bers of the Pension Investment Association of Canada (PIAC) believe it is sound policy to actively intervene to prevent any abusive action by corporate management that runs counter to the interests of shareholders. Indeed, the North American legal and regulatory systems are introducing more and more legislation in the area of corporate governance in order to protect the interests of minority shareholders.

How the Caisse Exercises Its Responsibilities   For the Caisse, active management means either taking action when and where it is considered essential to protect its investment, or taking a stand against certain practices considered detrimental to the interests of the shareholders. Accordingly, with regard to its

corporate investment, which normally involves equity interests of between 10 and 30 percent, the Caisse looks for representation on the boards of directors in proportion to the size of its investment.

By fostering closer ties with the managements of its investee companies, not only is the Caisse better able to monitor its investments, but it is also in a position to develop a better understanding of the business itself and of the strategic direction management wishes to give to the company. As a matter of policy, however, the Caisse does not involve itself in day-to-day management operations. Rather, its interest focusses on the company's strategic orientation. It is interesting and encouraging to note that in many cases, the Caisse is

Before accepting Rogers' final bid, Maclean Hunter's board of directors explored takeover defences. They considered the white knight defence by stating that time was needed to allow competing bids. Maclean Hunter also publicly considered the possibility of selling the firm's prized U.S. cable assets—its crown jewels. Maclean Hunter has a poison pill plan and, in this case, it served its purpose, forcing Rogers to negotiate with management. When Maclean Hunter's board approved the offer, it agreed to waive the poison pill provision.

CONCEPT QUESTIONS

1. What can a firm do to make takeover less likely?
2. What is a share rights plan? Explain how the rights work.
3. What are the main problems faced by LBOs in the early 1990s?

21.8 | SOME EVIDENCE ON ACQUISITIONS

One of the most controversial issues surrounding our subject is whether mergers and acquisitions benefit shareholders. Quite a few studies have attempted to estimate the effect of mergers and takeovers on stock prices of the bidding and target firms. These

effectively invited by management itself to designate potentional representatives to the boards.

The Caisse's View on Poison Pills
The Caisse has had the opportunity in certain specific cases to come down openly against practices it considered to be abusive. The so-called poison pill arrangements are a case in point. Indeed, arrangements of that type, designed by a number of Canadian corporations to guard against acquisition bids or takeovers to which senior management is opposed, have upset a great many investors, including the Caisse.

As a shareholder and investor, the Caisse questions the advisability, as well as the propriety of measures aimed at unduly protecting senior management where it does not own the company. We believe that poison pill arrangements often remove opportunities for shareholders to realize a profit and thereby make their ownership position less attractive. This kind of action, which is also harmful to the quality of the stock market, deprives investors of their fundamental right to decide to hold onto or to sell their securities in the case of a purchase bid.

Golden Parachutes and Non-voting Shares
For the same reasons, and again consistent with a growing body of opinion amongst investors, the Caisse is concerned that unwarranted benefits such as gold parachutes are often being granted to corporate management to protect them personally in the case of hostile takeovers. This practice is unacceptable to us as it has the potential to create a situation of subjectivity or inequality for shareholders.

Also, there is growing uneasiness among shareholders in general, and professional fund managers in particular, about subordinate or non-voting shares, as such classes of securities reduce the quality of the financial markets and investors' returns. The Caisse therefore shares the view that measures aimed at eliminating these shares or limiting their consequences, should be supported.

As Canada's largest fund manager, the Caisse believes it has a responsibility to share the role of protecting the interests of Canadian minority shareholders with other institutional investors. It will always assume that responsibility with the goal of optimizing the return on its investments and in doing so, will act in the best interest of all shareholders.

Corporate Democracy: An Evolving, Dynamic Idea
The practice and implications of corporate democracy are becoming increasingly important. Corporate management and institutional investors would do well to revisit the traditional definition of the idea and to update it to suit modern times.

Jean-Claude Delorme is former chairman and CEO of the Caisse de depot et placement du Quebec in Montreal. His views are excerpted, with permission, from the *Canadian Investment Review,* Spring 1990.

are called *event studies* because they estimate abnormal stock-price changes on and around the offer-announcement date—the event. Abnormal returns are usually defined as the difference between actual stock returns and a market index, to take account of the influence of marketwide effects on the returns of individual securities.

Table 21.7 summarizes the results of numerous studies that look at the effects of merger and tender offers on stock prices in the United States. Table 21.8 shows the highpoints of three studies on mergers in Canada. Both tables are relevant because firms from one country often purchase companies in the other.

The tables show that the shareholders of target companies in successful takeovers gain substantially. Starting with U.S. takeovers in Table 21.7, when the takeover is accomplished by merger, the gains are 20 percent; when the takeover is via tender offer, the gains are 30 percent.

The Canadian studies did not distinguish among tender offers, mergers, and proxy contests in looking at target returns. The first study found a gain of 9 percent, more modest than for the United States. The other studies found that target firm shareholders in going-private transactions enjoyed an abnormal return of 23 to 25 percent, a figure consistent with U.S. results in Table 21.7.

The Canadian study of going-private transactions also looked at whether minority shareholders suffer. You can see from Table 21.8 that the answer is no.

T A B L E 21.7

Stock price changes in successful U.S. corporate takeovers

Takeover Technique	Target	Bidders
Tender offer	30%	4%
Merger	20	0
Proxy contest	8	NA*

*NA = Not applicable.
Modified from Michael C. Jensen and Richard S. Ruback, "The Market for Corporate Control: The Scientific Evidence," *Journal of Financial Economics* 11 (April 1983), pp. 7, 8. © Elsevier Science Publishers B.V. (North-Holland).

T A B L E 21.8

Abnormal returns in successful Canadian mergers

	Target	Bidder
1,930 mergers, 1964–1983*	9%	3%
119 mergers, 1963–1982†	23	11
173 going-private transactions, 1977–1989‡	25	NA
Minority buyouts	27	
Non-controlling bidder	24	

*From B. Espen Eckbo, "Mergers and the Market for Corporate Control: The Canadian Evidence," *Canadian Journal of Economics,* May 1986, pp. 236-60. The test for bidders excluded firms involved in multiple mergers.
†From A. L. Calvet and J. Lefoll, "Information Asymmetry and Wealth Effect of Canadian Corporate Acquisitions," *Financial Review,* November 1987, pp. 415–31.
‡Modified from B. Amoako-Adu and B. Smith, "How Do Shareholders Fare in Minority Buyouts?" *Canadian Investment Review,* Fall 1991, pp. 79–88.

Returns to minority shareholders hardly differ from returns that occurred when firms went private with no majority shareholder.

For both countries, these gains are a reflection of the merger premium that is typically paid by the acquiring firm. These gains are excess returns, that is, the returns over and above what the shareholders would normally have earned.

The shareholders of bidding firms do not fare as well. According to the U.S. studies summarized in Table 21.7, bidders experience gains of 4 percent in tender offers, but this gain is about zero in mergers. Canadian research places bidders' gains in a range from 3 to 11 percent.

What conclusions can be drawn from Tables 21.7 and 21.8? First, the evidence strongly suggests that the shareholders of successful target firms achieve substantial gains as a result of takeovers. The gains appear to be larger in tender offers than in mergers. This may reflect the fact that takeovers sometimes start with a friendly merger proposal from the bidder to the management of the target firm. If management rejects the offer, the bidding firm may take the offer directly to the shareholders with a tender offer. As a consequence, tender offers are frequently unfriendly.

Also, the target firm's management may actively oppose the offer with defensive tactics. This often has the result of raising the tender offer from the bidding firm; on average, friendly mergers may be arranged at lower premiums than unfriendly tender offers.

The second conclusion we can draw is that the shareholders of bidding firms earn significantly less from takeovers. The balance is more even for Canadian mergers. This may be because there is less competition among bidders in Canada. Two reasons for this are that the Canadian capital market is smaller and that federal government agencies review foreign investments.[32]

In fact, studies have found that the acquiring firms actually lose value in many mergers. These findings are a puzzle, and there are a variety of explanations:

1. Anticipated merger gains may not have been completely achieved, and shareholders thus experienced losses. This can happen if managers of bidding firms tend to overestimate the gains from acquisition as we saw happened to Campeau Corporation.

2. The bidding firms are often much larger than the target firms. Thus, even though the dollar gains to the bidder may be similar to the dollar gains earned by shareholders of the target firm, the percentage gains are much lower.[33]

3. Another possible explanation for the low returns to the shareholders of bidding firms in takeovers is simply that management may not be acting in the interest of shareholders when it attempts to acquire other firms. Perhaps, it is attempting to increase the size of the firm, even if this reduces its value per share.

4. The market for takeovers may be sufficiently competitive that the NPV of acquiring is zero because the prices paid in acquisitions fully reflect the value of the acquired firms. In other words, the sellers capture all the gain.

5. Finally, the announcement of a takeover may not convey much new information to the market about the bidding firm. This can occur because firms frequently announce intentions to engage in merger programs long before they announce specific acquisitions. In this case, the stock price in the bidding firm may already reflect anticipated gains from mergers.

CONCEPT QUESTIONS

1. What does the evidence say about the benefits of mergers and acquisitions to target company shareholders?
2. What does the evidence say about the benefits of mergers and acquisitions to acquiring company shareholders?
3. What is the evidence on whether minority shareholders are shortchanged in mergers?

21.9 | SUMMARY AND CONCLUSIONS

This chapter introduced you to the extensive literature on mergers and acquisitions. We touched on a number of issues, including:

1. Form of merger. One firm can acquire another in several different ways. The three legal forms of acquisition are merger and consolidation, acquisition of stock, and acquisition of assets.

2. Tax issues. Mergers and acquisitions can be taxable or tax-free transactions. The primary issue is whether the target firm's shareholders sell or exchange

---

[32] P. Halpern, "Poison Pills," p. 66; and A. L. Calvet and J. Lefoll, "Information Asymmetry," p. 432.
[33] This factor cannot explain the imbalance in returns in the first Canadian study in Table 21.8. In this sample, bidder and target firms were about the same size.

their shares. Generally, a cash purchase is a taxable merger, while a stock exchange is not taxable. In a taxable merger, there are capital gains effects and asset write-up effects to consider. In a stock exchange, the target firm's shareholders become shareholders in the merged firm.

3. Accounting issues. Accounting for mergers and acquisitions involves either the purchase method or the pooling of interests method. The choice between these two methods does not affect the aftertax cash flows of the combined firm. However, financial managers may prefer the pooling of interests method because the net income of the combined firm is higher than is true for the purchase method.

4. Merger valuation. If Firm A is acquiring Firm B, the benefits (ΔV) from an acquisition are defined as the value of the combined firm (V_{AB}) less the value of the firms as separate entities (V_A and V_B), or:

$$\Delta V = V_{AB} - (V_A + V_B)$$

The gain to Firm A from acquiring Firm B is the increased value of the acquired firm (ΔV) plus the value of B as a separate firm. The total value of Firm B to Firm A, V_B^*, is thus:

$$V_B^* = \Delta V + V_B$$

An acquisition benefits the shareholders of the acquiring firm if this value is greater than the cost of the acquisition. The cost of an acquisition can be defined in general terms as the price paid to the shareholders of the acquired firm. The cost frequently includes a merger premium paid to the shareholders of the acquired firm. Moreover, the cost depends on the form of payment, that is, the choice between cash or common stock.

5. The possible benefits of an acquisition come from several possible sources, including the following:

   a. Revenue enhancement.
   b. Cost reduction.
   c. Lower taxes.
   d. Changing capital requirements.

6. Some of the most colorful language of finance comes from defensive tactics in acquisition battles. *Poison pills, golden parachutes,* and *greenmail* are terms that describe various antitakeover tactics.

7. Mergers and acquisitions have been extensively studied. The basic conclusions are that, on average, the shareholders of target firms do very well, while the shareholders of bidding firms do not appear to gain anywhere near as much.

Key Terms

amalgamations (page 768)

merger (page 768)

consolidation (page 768)

tender offer (page 768)

circular bid (page 769)

stock exchange bid (page 769)

proxy contests (page 770)

going-private transactions (page 770)

leveraged buyouts (LBOs) (page 770)

synergy (page 775)

earnings per share (EPS) (page 781)

diversification (page 782)

control block (page 786)

greenmail (page 787)

poison pill (page 788)

share rights plan (page 788)

Chapter Review Problems and Self-Test

21.1   Merger Value and Cost   Consider the following information for two all-equity firms, A and B:

	Firm A	Firm B
Shares outstanding	100	50
Price per share	$ 50	$30

Firm A estimates that the value of the synergistic benefit from acquiring Firm B is $200. Firm B has indicated it would accept a cash purchase offer of $35 per share. Should Firm A proceed?

21.2   Stock Mergers and EPS   Consider the following information for two all-equity firms, A and B:

	Firm A	Firm B
Total earnings	$1,000	$400
Shares outstanding	100	80
Price per share	$ 80	$ 25

Firm A is acquiring Firm B by exchanging 25 of its shares for all the shares in B. What is the cost of the merger if the merged firm is worth $11,000? What will happen to Firm A's EPS? Its P/E ratio?

Answers to Self-Test Problems

21.1   The total value of Firm B to Firm A is the premerger value of B plus the $200 gain from the merger. The premerger value of B is $30 × 50 = $1,500, so the total value is $1,700. At $35 per share, A is paying $35 × 50 = $1,750; the merger therefore has a negative NPV of −$50. At $35 per share, B is not an attractive merger partner.

21.2   After the merger, the firm would have 125 shares outstanding. Since the total value is $11,000, the price per share is $11,000/125 = $88, up from $80. Since Firm B's stockholders end up with 25 shares in the merged firm, the cost of the merger is 25 × $88 = $2,200, not 25 × 80 = $2,000. Also, the combined firm has $1,000 + 400 = $1,400 in earnings, so EPS will be $1,400/125 = $11.2, up from $1,000/100 = $10. The old P/E ratio was $80/$10 = 8. The new one is $88/11.2 = 7.86.

Questions and Problems

1.   **Calculating Synergy**   Hallam Industries has offered $25 million cash for all the common stock in Kleen Fasteners Corporation. Based on recent market information, Kleen Fasteners is worth $22 million as an independent operation. If the merger makes economic sense for Hallam, what is the minimum estimated value of the synergistic benefits from the merger?

Basic (Questions 1–11)

2.   **Merger Accounting**   Explain the difference between purchase and pooling of interests accounting for mergers. What is the effect on cash flows from the choice of accounting method? On EPS?

3.   **The Colour of Money**   Define each of the following terms:
  a. Greenmail
  b. White knight
  c. Golden parachute

    d. Crown jewels

    e. Shark repellent

    f. Corporate raider

    g. Poison pill

    h. Tender offer

    i. Leveraged buyout (LBO)

4. **Balance Sheets for Mergers**   Consider the following premerger information about Firm X and Firm Y:

	Firm X	Firm Y
Total earnings	$ 9,000	$ 4,000
Shares outstanding	20,000	20,000
Per share values:		
Market	$ 80	$ 18
Book	$ 25	$ 12

Assume that Firm X acquires Firm Y by paying cash for all the shares outstanding at a merger premium of $5 per share. Assuming that neither firm has any debt before or after the merger, construct the postmerger balance sheet for Firm X assuming (*i*) pooling of interests accounting and (*ii*) purchase accounting methods are used.

5. **Balance Sheets for Mergers**   Assume the following balance sheets are stated at book value. Construct a postmerger balance sheet assuming that Nelson purchases Beall and the pooling of interest method of accounting is used.

Nelson Manufacturing

Current assets	$1,000	Current liabilities	$ 400
Net fixed assets	6,000	Long-term debt	1,600
		Equity	5,000
Total	$7,000		$7,000

Beall Distributors

Current assets	$1,000	Current liabilities	$ 750
Net fixed assets	3,000	Long-term debt	450
		Equity	2,800
Total	$4,000		$4,000

6. **Incorporating Goodwill**   In the previous problem, suppose the fair market value of Beall's fixed assets is $4,000 versus the $3,000 book value shown. Nelson Manufacturing pays $6,000 for Beall and raises the needed funds through an issue of long-term debt. Construct the postmerger balance sheet assuming the purchase method of accounting is used.

7. **Balance Sheets for Mergers**   The Chesterfield Cheese Company has acquired Newport Nachos, Inc., in a merger transaction. Construct the balance sheet for the new corporation if the merger is treated as a pooling of interests for accounting purposes. The balance sheets below represent the premerger values for both firms stated at their current book values.

The Chesterfield Cheese Company

Current assets	$2,000	Current liabilities	$ 500
Other assets	500	Long-term debt	1,000
Net fixed assets	3,000	Equity	4,000
Total	$5,500		$5,500

Newport Nachos, Inc.

Current assets	$ 200	Current liabilities	$ 125
Other assets	50	Long-term debt	0
Net fixed assets	750	Equity	875
Total	$1,000		$1,000

8. **Incorporating Goodwill**   In the previous problem, construct the balance sheet for the new corporation assuming the transaction is treated as a purchase for accounting purposes. The market value of Newport Nachos' fixed assets is $900; the market values for current and other assets are the same as the book values. Assume Chesterfield Cheese issues $1,300 in new long-term debt to finance the acquisition.

9. **Cash versus Stock Payment**   Cedar Publishing Corp. is analyzing the possible acquisition of Brownstone Broadcasting Company. Both firms have no debt. Cedar believes the acquisition will increase its total aftertax annual cash flows by $2.4 million indefinitely. The current market value of Brownstone is $30 million, and that of Cedar is $45 million. The appropriate discount rate for the incremental cash flows is 8 percent. Cedar is trying to decide whether it should offer 40 percent of its stock or $40 million in cash to Brownstone's shareholders.

   a. What is the cost of each alternative?
   b. What is the NPV of each alternative?
   c. Which alternative should Cedar use?

10. **EPS, P/E, and Mergers**   The shareholders of Wilton Trucking Company have voted in favor of a buyout offer from International Rail Corporation. Information about each firm is given below:

	Wilton Trucking	International Rail
Price/earnings ratio	10	26.4
Shares outstanding	60,000	150,000
Earnings	$132,000	$375,000

   Wilton shareholders will receive one share in International Rail stock for every three shares they hold in Wilton.

   a. What will the EPS of International Rail be after the merger? What will the P/E ratio be if the NPV of the acquisition is zero?
   b. What must International Rail feel is the value of the synergy between these two firms? Explain how your answer can be reconciled with the decision to go ahead with the takeover.

11. **Cash versus Stock as Payment**   Consider the following premerger information about a bidding firm (Firm B) and a target firm (Firm T). Assume both firms have no debt outstanding.

	Firm B	Firm T
Shares outstanding	1,000	250
Price per share	$ 25	$ 15

   Firm B has estimated that the value of the synergistic benefits from acquiring Firm T is $1,000.

   a. If Firm T is willing to be acquired for $18 per share in cash, what is the NPV of the merger?

b. What will the price per share of the merged firm be assuming the conditions in (a)?

c. In part (a), what is the merger premium?

d. Suppose Firm T is agreeable to a merger by exchange of stock. If B offers three of its shares for every five of T's shares, what will the price per share of the merged firm be?

e. What is the NPV of the merger assuming the conditions in (d)?

12. **Cash versus Stock as Payment**   In Problem 11, are the shareholders of Firm T better off with the cash offer or the stock offer? At what exchange ratio of B shares to T shares would the shareholders in T be indifferent between the two offers?

13. **Mergers and Taxes**   Describe the advantages and disadvantages of a taxable merger as opposed to a tax-free exchange. What is the basic determinant of tax status in a merger? Would an LBO be taxable or nontaxable? Explain.

14. **Economies of Scale in Mergers**   What does it mean to say that a proposed merger will take advantage of available economies of scale? Suppose Eastern Power Co. and Western Power Co. are located in different time zones. Both of them operate at 60 percent of capacity except for peak periods, when they operate at 100 percent of capacity. the peak periods begin at 9:00 A.M. and 5:00 P.M. local time, and last about 45 minutes. Explain why a merger between Eastern and Western might make sense.

15. **Defensive Tactics**   What types of actions might the management of a firm take to fight a hostile acquisition bid from an unwanted suitor? How do the target firm shareholders benefit from the defensive tactics of their management team? How are the target firm shareholders harmed by such actions? Explain.

16. **Effects of a Stock Exchange**   Consider the following premerger information about Firm A and Firm B:

	Firm A	Firm B
Total earnings	$1,200	$500
Shares outstanding	1,000	300
Price per share	$ 100	$ 25

Assume Firm A acquires Firm B via an exchange of stock at a price of $35 for each share of B's stock. Both A and B have no debt outstanding.

a. What will the earnings per share (EPS) of Firm A be after the merger?

b. What will Firm A's price per share be after the merger if the market is fooled by this reported earnings growth (that is, the price/earnings ratio does not change)?

c. What will the price/earnings ratio of the postmerger firm be if the market is not fooled?

d. If there are no synergy gains, what will the share price of A be after the merger? What will the price/earnings ratio be? What does your answer for the share price tell you about the amount A bid for B? Was it too high? Too low? Explain.

17. **Merger NPV**   Show that the NPV of a merger can be expressed as the value of the synergistic benefits, ΔV, less the merger premium.

18. **Calculating NPV** Galesburg Bricks is considering making an offer to purchase Whitelands Lumber. The vice president of finance has collected the following information:

Challenge
(Questions 18–19)

	Galesburg	Whitelands
Price/earnings ratio	20	14
Shares outstanding	1,500,000	150,000
Earnings	$2,000,000	$525,000

Galesburg also knows that securities analysts expect the earnings and dividends (currently $2.25 per share) of Whitelands to grow at a constant rate of 5 percent each year. Galesburg management believes that the acquisition of Whitelands will provide the firm with some economies of scale that would increase this growth rate to 7 percent per year.

a. What is the value of Whitelands to Galesburg?
b. What would Galesburg's gain be from this acquisition?
c. If Galesburg offers $53 in cash for each share of Whitelands, what would the NPV of the acquisition be?
d. What's the most Galesburg should be willing to pay in cash per share for the stock of Whitelands?
e. If Galesburg were to offer 275,625 of its shares in exchange for the outstanding stock of Whitelands, what would the NPV be?
f. Should the acquisition be attempted, and, if so, should it be as in (c) or (e)?
g. Galesburg's outside financial consultants think the 7 percent growth rate is too optimistic and a 6 percent rate is more realistic. How does this change your previous answers?

19. **Mergers** Company A is contemplating acquiring Company B. Company B's projected revenues, costs, and required investments appear in the following table. The table also shows sources for financing company B's investments if B is acquired by A. The table incorporates the following information:

Company B would immediately increase its leverage with a $110 million loan, followed by a $150 million dividend to Company A. (This operation increases the debt to equity ratio of Company B from 1/3 to 1/1.)

Company A would use $50 million of tax-loss carry-forwards available from the firm's other operations.

The terminal, total value of Company B is estimated to be $900 million in five years, and the projected debt is $300 million.

The risk-free rate and the expected rate of return on the market portfolio are 6 percent and 14 percent, respectively. Company A analysts estimated the weighted average cost of capital for their company to be 10 percent. The borrowing rate for both companies is 8 percent. The beta coefficient for the stock of Company B (at its current capital structure) is estimated to be 1.25.

The board of directors of Company A is presented with an offer for $68.75 per share for Company B, or a total of $550 million for the 8 million outstanding shares.

Evaluate the proposal. The following table may help you.

Projections for Company *B*
If Acquired by Company *A*
($ millions)

	Year 1	Year 2	Year 3	Year 4	Year 5
Sales	$800	$900	$1,000	$1,125	$1,250
Production costs	562	630	700	790	875
Depreciation	75	80	82	83	83
Other expenses	80	90	100	113	125
EBIT	$ 83	$100	$ 118	$ 139	$ 167
Interest	19	22	24	25	27
EBT	$ 64	$ 78	$ 94	$ 114	$ 140
Taxes	32	39	47	57	70
Net income	$ 32	$ 39	$ 47	$ 57	$ 70
Investments:					
Net working capital	20	25	25	30	30
Net fixed assets	15	25	18	12	7
Total	$ 35	$ 50	$ 43	$ 42	$ 37
Sources of financing:					
Net debt financing	35	16	16	15	12
Profit retention	0	34	27	27	25
Total	$ 35	$ 50	$ 43	$ 42	$ 37

Cash Flows—Company *A*

	Year 0	Year 1	Year 2	Year 3	Year 4	Year 5
Acquisition of *B*	—					
Dividends from *B*	$150	—	—	—	—	—
Tax-loss carry-forwards			$25	$25		—
Terminal value	—	—	—	—	—	—
Total	—	—	—	—	—	—

Suggested Readings

A readable book on how to quantify the value from mergers and acquisitions is:

Rappaport, A. *Creating Shareholder Value: The New Standard for Business Performance.* New York: Free Press, 1986, chap. 9.

Some good articles on mergers and acquisitions appear in:

Stern, J. M., and D. H. Chew, eds. *The Revolution in Corporate Finance.* New York: Basil Blackwell, 1986.

Canadian Investment Review, Fall 1991 issue.

Three fascinating, current paperbacks on LBOs are:

C. Bruck. *The Predators Ball, The Inside Story of Drexel Burnham, and the Rise of the Junk Bond Raiders.* New York: Penguin Books, 1989; B. Burroughs and J. Helyar. *Barbarians at the Gate, The Fall of RJR Nabisco.* New York: Harper Perennial, 1991; J. Rothchild. *Going for Broke—How Robert Campeau Bankrupted the Retail Industry, Jolted the Junk Bond Market, and Brought the Booming Eighties to a Crashing Halt.* Toronto: Simon & Schuster, 1991.

International Corporate Finance

Corporations with significant foreign operations are often called *international corporations* or *multinationals*. Such corporations must consider many financial factors that do not directly affect purely domestic firms. These include foreign exchange rates, differing interest rates from country to country, complex accounting methods for foreign operations, foreign tax rates, and foreign government intervention.

Key topics of international financial management, foreign exchange rates, for example, are also of interest to many smaller Canadian businesses. Canada has an open economy linked very closely by a free-trade agreement to its largest trading partner, the United States. There are also very important economic and financial ties to Europe, the Pacific Rim, and other major economies worldwide. To illustrate, in the Atlantic Provinces, independent fish plants that supply the Boston market also wholesale lobster to Europe. These smaller corporations do not qualify as multinationals in the league of Alcan or McCain, but their financial managers must know how to manage foreign exchange risk.

The basic principles of corporate finance still apply to international corporations; like domestic companies, they seek to invest in projects that create more value for the shareholders than they cost and to arrange financing that raises cash at the lowest possible cost. In other words, the net present value principle holds for both foreign and domestic operations, but it is usually more complicated to apply the NPV rule to foreign investments.

One of the most significant complications of international finance is foreign exchange. The foreign exchange markets provide important information and opportunities for an international corporation when it undertakes capital budgeting and financing decisions. As we discuss, international exchange rates, interest rates, and inflation rates are closely related. We spend much of this chapter exploring the connection between these financial variables.

We won't have much to say here about the role of cultural and social differences in international business. Also, we do not discuss the implications of differing political and economic systems. These factors are of great importance to international businesses, but it would take another book to do them justice. Consequently, we focus only on some purely financial considerations in international finance and some key aspects of foreign exchange markets.

22.1 | TERMINOLOGY

Chapter 1 had a lot to say about trends in world financial markets including globalization. The first step in learning about international finance is to conquer the new vocabulary. As with any specialty, international finance is rich in jargon. Accordingly, we get started on the subject with a highly eclectic vocabulary exercise.

The terms that follow are presented alphabetically, and they are not of equal importance. We chose these particular ones because they appear frequently in the financial press or because they illustrate some of the colorful language of international finance.

1. A **Belgian dentist** is a stereotype of the traditional Eurobond investor. This self-employed professional, a dentist, for instance, must report income, has a disdain for tax authorities, and likes to invest in foreign currencies. Anonymous bearer Eurobonds fit the bill nicely for this type of investor because they are unregistered and, therefore, untraceable. Such individual investors don't mind paying a premium for Eurobonds, because the bonds effectively are issued on a tax-free basis. The Belgian dentist may be an endangered species, however, and destined for replacement by the Japanese engineer.

2. The **cross-rate** is the implicit exchange rate between two currencies when both are quoted in some third currency. Usually the third currency is the U.S. dollar.

3. A **Eurobond** is a bond issued in multiple countries, but denominated in a single currency, usually the issuer's home currency. Such bonds have become an important way to raise capital for many international companies and governments. Eurobonds are issued outside the restrictions that apply to domestic offerings and are syndicated and traded mostly from London. Trading can and does occur anywhere there is a buyer and a seller.

4. **Eurocurrency** is money deposited in a financial centre outside of the country whose currency is involved. For instance, Eurodollars—the most widely used Eurocurrency—are U.S. dollars deposited in banks outside the U.S. banking system. EuroCanadian are Canadian dollar bank deposits outside Canada.

5. **Foreign bonds**, unlike Eurobonds, are issued in a single country and are usually denominated in that country's currency. Often, the country in which these bonds are issued draws distinctions between them and bonds issued by domestic issuers, including different tax laws, restrictions on the amount issued, or tougher disclosure rules.

   Foreign bonds often are nicknamed for the country where they are issued: Yankee bonds (United States), Samurai bonds (Japan), Rembrandt bonds (the Netherlands), and Bulldog bonds (Britain). Partly because of tougher regulations and disclosure requirements, the foreign-bond market hasn't grown in past years with the vigor of the Eurobond market. A substantial portion of all foreign bonds are issued in Switzerland.

6. **Gilts**, technically, are British and Irish government securities, although the term also includes issues of local British authorities and some overseas public-sector offerings.

7. The **London Interbank Offer Rate (LIBOR)** is the rate that most international banks charge one another for loans of Eurodollars overnight in the London market. LIBOR is a cornerstone in the pricing of money market issues and other short-term debt issues by both government and corporate borrowers.

Belgian dentist

Stereotype of the traditional Eurobond investor as a professional who must report income, has a disdain for tax authorities, and likes to invest in foreign currencies.

cross-rate

The implicit exchange rate between two currencies (usually non-U.S.) quoted in some third currency (usually the U.S. dollar).

Eurobond

International bonds issued in multiple countries but denominated in a single currency (usually the issuer's currency).

Eurocurrency

Money deposited in a financial centre outside of the country whose currency is involved.

foreign bonds

International bonds issued in a single country, usually denominated in that country's currency.

gilts

British and Irish government securities including issues of local British authorities and some overseas public-sector offerings.

Interest rates are frequently quoted as some spread over LIBOR, then they float with the LIBOR rate.

8. There are two basic kinds of **swaps**: interest rate and currency. An *interest rate swap* occurs when two parties exchange a floating-rate payment for a fixed-rate payment or vice versa. *Currency swaps* are agreements to deliver one currency in exchange for another. Often both types of swaps are used in the same transaction when debt denominated in different currencies is swapped. Chartered banks make an active market in arranging swaps, and swap volumes are growing rapidly.

9. **Export Development Corporation (EDC)** is a federal Crown corporation with a mandate to promote Canadian exports. EDC provides long-term financing for foreign companies that purchase Canadian exports. To qualify for EDC support, exporters must produce or market goods with a minimum Canadian content of 60 percent.

   Other government programs to support exports include the federal Programme for Export Market Development (PEMD), which reimburses part of the costs of developing export markets and a variety of provincial programs.

London Interbank Offer Rate (LIBOR)
The rate most international banks charge one another for overnight Eurodollar loans.

swaps
Agreements to the exchange of two securities or currencies.

Export Development Corporation (EDC)
Federal Crown corporation that promotes Canadian exports by making loans to foreign purchasers.

CONCEPT QUESTIONS

1. What are the differences between a Eurobond and a foreign bond?
2. What are Eurodollars?

22.2 | FOREIGN EXCHANGE MARKETS AND EXCHANGE RATES

The **foreign exchange market** is undoubtedly the world's largest financial market. It is the market where one country's currency is traded for another's. Most of the trading takes place in a few currencies: the U.S. dollar ($), the German deutsche mark (DM), the British pound sterling (£), the Japanese yen (Y), the Swiss franc (SF), and the French franc (FF). Table 22.1 lists some of the more common currencies and their symbols.

foreign exchange market
The market where one country's currency is traded for another's.

The foreign exchange market is an over-the-counter market, so there is no single location where traders get together. Instead, market participants are located in the major banks around the world. They communicate using computer terminals, telephones, and other telecommunications devices. For example, one communications network for foreign transactions is the Society for Worldwide Interbank Financial Telecommunications (SWIFT), a Belgian not-for-profit cooperative. Using data transmission lines, a bank in Toronto, the centre of Canada's foreign exchange trading, can send messages to a bank in London via SWIFT regional processing centres.

The many different types of participants in the foreign exchange market include the following:

1. Importers who pay for goods involving foreign currencies by converting foreign exchange.
2. Exporters who receive foreign currency and may want to convert to the domestic currency.
3. Portfolio managers who buy or sell foreign stocks and bonds.

T A B L E 22.1

International currency symbols

Country	Currency	Symbol
Australia	Dollar	A$
Austria	Schilling	Sch
Belgium	Franc	BF
Canada	Dollar	Can$
Denmark	Krone	DKr
Finland	Markka	FM
France	Franc	FF
Germany	Deutsche mark	DM
Greece	Drachma	Dr
India	Rupee	Rs
Iran	Rial	RI
Italy	Lira	Lit
Japan	Yen	¥
Kuwait	Dinar	KD
Mexico	Peso	Ps
Netherlands	Guilder	FL
Norway	Krone	NKr
Saudi Arabia	Riyal	SR
Singapore	Dollar	S$
South Africa	Rand	R
Spain	Peseta	Pta
Sweden	Krona	Skr
Switzerland	Franc	SF
United Kingdom	Pound	£
United States	Dollar	$

4. Foreign exchange brokers who match buy and sell orders.
5. Traders who "make a market" in foreign exchange.
6. Speculators who try to profit from changes in exchange rates.

Exchange Rates

exchange rate

The price of one country's currency expressed in another country's currency.

An **exchange rate** is simply the price of one country's currency expressed in another country's currency. In practice, almost all trading of currencies worldwide takes place in terms of the U.S. dollar. For example, both the French franc and the German mark are traded with their price quoted in U.S. dollars.

Exchange Rate Quotations   Table 22.2 reproduces exchange rate quotations as they appear in the *Globe and Mail*. Notice that the rates were supplied to the *Globe* by the Bank of Montreal, part of the over-the-counter foreign exchange market. The first portion of Table 22.2 is the cross-rates of nine main currencies. Because of the heavy volume of transactions in U.S. dollars, U.S./Canada rates appear next at the top of the second portion of Table 22.2. The first column (labeled "$1 U.S. in Cdn $") gives the number of Canadian dollars it takes to buy one unit of foreign currency. For example, the U.S./Canada spot rate is quoted at 1.3837, which means you can buy one U.S. dollar today with 1.3837 Canadian dollars.[1]

---

[1] The spot rate is for immediate trading. Forward rates are for future transactions and are discussed in detail later.

T A B L E 22.2

Exchange rate quotations

Foreign Exchange

Cross Rates

	Canadian dollar	U.S. dollar	British pound	German mark	Japanese yen	Swiss franc	French franc	Dutch guilder	Italian lira
Canada dollar	—	1.3837	2.2060	0.9820	0.016660	1.1928	0.2822	0.8766	0.000800
U.S. dollar	0.7227	—	1.5943	0.7097	0.012040	0.8620	0.2039	0.6335	0.000578
British pound	0.4533	0.6272	—	0.4451	0.007552	0.5407	0.1279	0.3974	0.000363
German mark	1.0183	1.4091	2.2464	—	0.016965	1.2147	0.2874	0.8927	0.000815
Japanese yen	60.02	83.06	132.41	58.94	—	71.60	16.94	52.62	0.048019
Swiss franc	0.8384	1.1600	1.8494	0.8233	0.013967	—	0.2366	0.7349	0.000671
French franc	3.5436	4.9033	7.8172	3.4798	0.059036	4.2268	—	3.1063	0.002835
Dutch guilder	1.1408	1.5785	2.5165	1.1202	0.019005	1.3607	0.3219	—	0.000913
Italian lira	1250.00	1729.63	2757.50	1227.50	20.825000	1491.00	352.75	1095.75	—

Mid-market rates in Toronto at noon, April 10, 1995. Prepared by the Bank of Montreal Treasury Group.

		$1 U.S. in Cdn.$ =	$1 Cdn. in U.S.$ =
U.S./Canada spot		1.3837	0.7227
1 month forward		1.3860	0.7215
2 months forward		1.3884	0.7203
3 months forward		1.3904	0.7192
6 months forward		1.3955	0.7166
12 months forward		1.4024	0.7131
3 years forward		1.4262	0.7012
5 years forward		1.4577	0.6860
7 years forward		1.5087	0.6628
10 years forward		1.5817	0.6322
Canadian dollar	High	1.3784	0.7255
in 1995:	Low	1.4267	0.7009
	Average	1.4057	0.7114

Country	Currency	Cdn. $ per unit	U.S. $ per unit
Britain	Pound	2.2060	1.5943
1 month forward		2.2097	1.5943
2 months forward		2.2128	1.5938
3 months forward		2.2150	1.5931
6 months forward		2.2192	1.5903
12 months forward		2.2202	1.5832
Germany	Mark	0.9820	0.7097
1 month forward		0.9848	0.7105
3 months forward		0.9905	0.7124
6 months forward		0.9983	0.7154
12 months forward		1.0113	0.7211
Japan	Yen	0.016660	0.012040
1 month forward		0.016748	0.012084
3 months forward		0.016869	0.012132
6 months forward		0.017210	0.012333
12 months forward		0.017751	0.012657
Algeria	Dinar	0.0319	0.0231
Antigua, Grenada and St. Lucia	E.C.Dollar	0.5134	0.3711
Argentina	Peso	1.38370	1.00000
Australia	Dollar	1.0256	0.7412
Austria	Schilling	0.13950	0.10082
Bahamas	Dollar	1.3837	1.0000
Barbados	Dollar	0.6953	0.5025
Belgium	Franc	0.04836	0.03495
Bermuda	Dollar	1.3837	1.0000
Brazil	Real	1.5392	1.1123
Bulgaria	Lev	0.0206	0.0149
Chile	Peso	0.003510	0.002536
China	Renminbi	0.1642	0.1187
Cyprus	Pound	3.1164	2.2523
Czech Rep	Koruna	0.0536	0.0387
Denmark	Krone	0.2481	0.1793
Egypt	Pound	0.4079	0.2948

Country	Currency	Cdn. $ per unit	U.S. $ per unit
Fiji	Dollar	1.0073	0.7280
Finland	Markka	0.3203	0.2315
France	Franc	0.2822	0.2039
Greece	Drachma	0.00605	0.00437
Hong Kong	Dollar	0.1789	0.1293
Hungary	Forint	0.01148	0.00829
Iceland	Krona	0.02180	0.01576
India	Rupee	0.04405	0.03184
Indonesia	Rupiah	0.000623	0.000450
Ireland	Punt	2.2236	1.6070
Israel	N Shekel	0.5134	0.3711
Italy	Lira	0.000800	0.000578
Jamaica	Dollar	0.04258	0.03077
Jordan	Dinar	2.0171	1.4577
Lebanon	Pound	0.000847	0.000612
Luxembourg	Franc	0.04836	0.03495
Malaysia	Ringgit	0.5567	0.4023
Mexico	N Peso	0.2165	0.1565
Netherlands	Guilder	0.8766	0.6335
New Zealand	Dollar	0.9202	0.6650
Norway	Krone	0.2194	0.1586
Pakistan	Rupee	0.04487	0.03243
Philippines	Peso	0.05316	0.03842
Poland	Zloty	0.5713	0.4129
Portugal	Escudo	0.00933	0.00674
Romania	Leu	0.000744	0.000537
Russia	Ruble	0.000279	0.000202
Saudi Arabia	Riyal	0.3690	0.2667
Singapore	Dollar	0.9898	0.7153
Slovakia	Koruna	0.0478	0.0345
South Africa	Rand	0.3849	0.2782
South Korea	Won	0.001809	0.001307
Spain	Peseta	0.01101	0.00796
Sudan	Dinar	0.0332	0.0240
Sweden	Krona	0.1881	0.1359
Switzerland	Franc	1.1928	0.8620
Taiwan	Dollar	0.0555	0.0401
Thailand	Baht	0.0566	0.0409
Trinidad, Tobago	Dollar	0.2430	0.1756
Turkey	Lira	0.0000327	0.0000237
Venezuela	Bolivar	0.00815	0.00589
Zambia	Kwacha	0.001785	0.001290
European Currency Unit		1.8131	1.3103
Special Drawing Right		2.1766	1.5730

The U.S. dollar closed at $1.3795 in terms of Canadian funds, down $0.0116 from Friday. The pound sterling closed at $2.1996, down $0.0477.

In New York, the Canadian dollar closed up $0.0060 at $0.7249 in terms of U.S. funds. The pound sterling was down $0.0210 to $1.5945.

Source: *Globe and Mail,* April 11, 1995, p. B8. Used with permission.

The second column in the U.S./Canada section shows the indirect exchange rate. This is the amount of U.S. currency per Canadian dollar. The U.S./Canada spot rate is quoted here at 0.7227, so you can get 0.7227 U.S. dollars for one Canadian dollar. Naturally, this second exchange rate is just the reciprocal of the first one, $1/.7227 = 1.3837$.

The rest of Table 22.2 shows exchange rates for other foreign currencies. Notice that the most important currencies are listed first: British pounds, German marks, and Japanese yen. In this part of the table, the first column, labelled "Cdn. $ per unit" gives the price of one unit of the foreign currency in Canadian dollars, the same as in the Canada/U.S. section. For example, you can buy one British pound for $2.2060 Canadian. The second column in this part of the table repeats the price of one unit of foreign currency in U.S. dollars. You can buy the same one British pound for $1.5943 U.S. dollars.

E X A M P L E | 22.1   On the Mark

Suppose you have $1,000. Based on the rates in Table 22.2, how many Japanese yen can you get? Alternatively, if a Porsche costs DM 200,000, how many dollars will you need to buy it? (DM is the abbreviation for deutsche marks.)

The exchange rate for yen is given in Canadian dollars per yen as 0.016660 (first line under Japan, first column). Your $1,000 thus gets you:

$1,000/0.016660 dollars per yen = 60,024 yen

Since the exchange rate in dollars per mark (first column) is .9820, you need:

DM 200,000 × .9820 $ per DM = $196,400

Cross-Rates and Triangle Arbitrage   Using the U.S. dollar as the common denominator in quoting exchange rates greatly reduces the number of possible cross-currency quotes. For example, with five major currencies, there would potentially be 10 exchange rates instead of just 4.[2] Also, the fact that the dollar is used throughout cuts down on inconsistencies in the exchange rate quotations.

Earlier, we defined the cross-rate as the exchange rate for a non-U.S. currency expressed in another non-U.S. currency. For example, suppose we observed the following:

FF per $1US = 10.00
DM per $1US = 2.00

Suppose the cross-rate is quoted as:

FF per DM = 4.00

What do you think?

---

[2] In discussing cross-rates, we follow Canadian practice of using the U.S. dollar. There are four exchange rates instead of five because one exchange rate would involve the exchange rate for a currency with itself. More generally, it might seem there should be 25 exchange rates with five currencies. There are 25 different combinations, but, of these, 5 involve the exchange rate of a currency for itself. Of the remaining 20, half of them are redundant because they are just the reciprocals of the exchange rate. Of the remaining 10, 6 can be eliminated by using a common denominator.

The cross-rate here is inconsistent with the exchange rates. To see this, suppose you have $100US. If you convert this to deutsche marks, you receive:

$100US × DM 2 per $1 = DM 200

If you convert this to francs at the cross-rate, you have:

DM 200 × FF 4 per DM 1 = FF 800

However, if you just convert your U.S. dollars to francs without going through deutsche marks, you have:

$100US × FF 10 per $1 = FF 1,000

What we see is that the franc has two prices, FF 10 per $1US and FF 8 per $1US, depending on how we get them.

To make money, we want to buy low, sell high. The important thing to note is that francs are cheaper if you buy them with U.S. dollars because you get 10 francs instead of just 8. You should proceed as follows:

1. Buy 1,000 francs for $100US.
2. Use the 1,000 francs to buy deutsche marks at the cross-rate. Since it takes four francs to buy a deutsche mark, you receive FF 1,000/4 = DM 250.
3. Use the DM 250 to buy U.S. dollars. Since the exchange rate is DM 2 per dollar, you receive DM 250/2 = $125, for a round-trip profit of $25.
4. Repeat steps 1 through 3.

This particular activity is called *triangle arbitrage* because the arbitrage involves moving through three different exchange rates.

$$FF\ 10/1\$$$

DM 2/1$ = $.50/DM 1   ←   DM .25/FF1 = FF 4/DM 1

To prevent such opportunities, it is not difficult to see that since a U.S. dollar buys you either 10 francs or 2 deutsche marks, the cross-rate must be:

(FF 10/$1US)/(DM 2/$1US) = FF 5/DM 1

That is, five francs per deutsche mark. If it were anything else, there would be a triangle arbitrage opportunity.

E X A M P L E | 22.2   **Shedding Some Pounds**

Suppose the exchange rates for the British pound and German mark are:

Pounds per $1US = 0.60
DM per $1US = 2.00

The cross-rate is three marks per pound. Is this consistent? Explain how to go about making some money.

The cross-rate should be DM 2.00/£ .60 = DM 3.33 per pound. You can buy a pound for DM 3 in one market, and you can sell a pound for DM 3.33 in another. So we want to first get some marks, then use the marks to buy some pounds, and then sell the pounds. Assuming you have $100US, you could:

1. Exchange U.S. dollars for marks: $100US × 2 = DM 200.
2. Exchange marks for pounds: DM 200/3 = £66.67.
3. Exchange pounds for U.S. dollars: £66.67/.60 = $111.12.

This would result in an $11.12 U.S. round-trip profit.

Types of Transactions

There are two basic types of trades in the foreign exchange market: spot trades and forward trades. A **spot trade** is an agreement to exchange currency on the spot; this actually means the transaction is completed or settled within two business days. The exchange rate on a spot trade is called the **spot exchange rate**. Implicitly, all of the exchange rates and transactions we have discussed so far have referred to the spot market.

Forward Exchange Rates   A **forward trade** is an agreement to exchange currency at some time in the future. The exchange rate used is agreed on today and is called the **forward exchange rate**. A forward trade would normally be settled sometime in the next 12 months, but some forward rates are quoted for as far as 10 years into the future.

Look back at Table 22.2 to see forward exchange rates quoted for some of the major currencies. For example, the spot exchange rate for the U.S. dollar is $1.3837. The six-month forward exchange rate is U.S.$1 = $1.3955. This means you can buy one U.S. dollar today for $1.3837, or you can agree to take delivery of a U.S. dollar in six months and pay $1.3955 at that time.

Notice that the U.S. dollar is more expensive in the forward market ($1.3955 versus $1.3837). Since the U.S. dollar is more expensive in the future than it is today, it is said to be selling at a premium relative to the Canadian dollar in the forward market. For the same reason, the Canadian dollar is said to be selling at a discount relative to the U.S. dollar. To see the discount, compare the spot and six-month forward rates in the second column. (Recall that this column shows the value of $1 Canadian in U.S. dollars.) The Canada/U.S. spot rate is 0.7227 and the six-month forward rate is 0.7166. The Canadian dollar is selling at a discount in the forward market since buyers with U.S. dollars can buy it for less six months afterward.

Why does the forward market exist? One answer is that it allows businesses and individuals to lock in a future exchange rate today, thereby eliminating any risk from unfavourable shifts in the exchange rate.

spot trade
An agreement to trade currencies based on the exchange rate today for settlement in two days.

spot exchange rate
The exchange rate on a spot trade.

forward trade
Agreement to exchange currency at some time in the future.

forward exchange rate
The agreed-on exchange rate to be used in a forward trade.

E X A M P L E | **22.3   Looking Forward**

Suppose you were expecting to receive a million British pounds in six months, and you agree to a forward trade to exchange your pounds for Canadian dollars. Based on Table 22.2, how many dollars will you get in six months? Is the pound selling at a discount or a premium relative to the dollar?

In Table 22.2, the spot exchange rate and the six-month forward rate in dollars per pound are $2.2060 = £1 and $2.2192 = £1, respectively. If you expect £1 million in six months, you will get £1 million × $2.2192 per pound = $2.2192 million. Since it is more expensive to buy a pound in the forward market than in the spot market ($2.2192 versus $2.2060), the pound is selling at a premium relative to the dollar.

E X A M P L E | **22.4**   **Looking Forward Again**

Now suppose you plan to invest $1 million in cracking the Japanese market in 12 months. To lock in your cost, you agree to a forward trade to exchange Canadian dollars for yen after 12 months. How many yen can you buy after 12 months? Is the yen selling at a forward discount or premium relative to the dollar?

From Table 22.2, first column, the spot and 12-month forward rate in dollars per yen are $0.016660 = 1¥ and $0.017751, respectively. You plan to convert $1 million in 12 months so you need to know the forward exchange rate in yen per dollar.

$1¥ = \$.017751$

$\$1 = 1/.017751 = 56.334854¥$

So your $1 million converts to ¥56,334,854. |

The spot exchange rate in yen per dollar is 1/.016660 = ¥60.024010. Either way you look at it, the yen is selling at a forward premium. It would take more dollars to buy one yen. And if you converted your funds today, instead of waiting 12 months, you would get more yen.

CONCEPT QUESTIONS

1. What is triangle arbitrage?
2. What do we mean by the six-month forward exchange rate?

22.3 | PURCHASING POWER PARITY

Now that we have discussed what exchange rate quotations mean, we can address an obvious question: What determines the level of the spot exchange rate? In addition, we know that exchange rates change through time. A related question is: What determines the rate of change in exchange rates? At least part of the answer in both cases goes by the name of **purchasing power parity (PPP)**, the idea that the exchange rate adjusts to keep purchasing power constant among currencies. As we discuss next, there are two forms of PPP, absolute and relative.

purchasing power parity (PPP)
The idea that the exchange rate adjusts to keep purchasing power constant among currencies.

Absolute Purchasing Power Parity

The basic idea behind *absolute purchasing power parity* is that a commodity costs the same regardless of what currency is used to purchase it or where it is selling. This is a very straightforward concept. If a beer costs £2 in London, and the exchange rate is £.60 per dollar, then a beer costs £2/.60 = $3.33 in Montreal. In other words, absolute PPP says $1 will buy you the same number of, say, cheeseburgers anywhere in the world.

More formally, let S_0 be the spot exchange rate between the British pound and the Canadian dollar today (Time 0). Here we are quoting exchange rates as the amount of foreign currency per dollar. Let P_{CDN} and P_{UK} be the current Canadian and British prices, respectively, on a particular commodity, say, apples. Absolute PPP simply says that:

$P_{UK} = S_0 \times P_{CDN}$

This tells us that the British price for something is equal to the Canadian price for that same something, multiplied by the exchange rate.

The rationale behind PPP is similar to that behind triangle arbitrage. If PPP did not hold, arbitrage would be possible (in principle) by moving apples from one country to another. For example, suppose apples in Halifax are selling for $4 per bushel, while in London the price is £2.40 per bushel. Absolute PPP implies that:

$$P_{UK} = S_0 \times P_{CDN}$$
$$£2.40 = S_0 \times $4$$
$$S_0 = £2.40/$4 = £.60$$

That is, the implied spot exchange rate is £.60 per dollar. Equivalently, a pound is worth $1/£.60 = $1.67.

Suppose, instead, the actual exchange rate is £.50. Starting with $4, a trader could buy a bushel of apples in Halifax, ship it to London, and sell it there for £2.40. Our trader then converts the £2.40 into dollars at the prevailing exchange rate, $S_0 = £.50$, yielding a total of £2.40/.50 = $4.80. The round-trip gain is 80 cents.

Because of this profit potential, forces are set in motion to change the exchange rate and/or the price of apples. In our example, apples would begin moving from Halifax to London. The reduced supply of apples in Halifax would raise the price of apples there, and the increased supply in Britain would lower the price of apples in London.

In addition to moving apples around, apple traders would be busily converting pounds back into dollars to buy more apples. This activity increases the supply of pounds and simultaneously increases the demand for dollars. We would expect the value of a pound to fall. This means the dollar is getting more valuable, so it will take more pounds to buy one dollar. Since the exchange rate is quoted as pounds per dollar, we would expect the exchange rate to rise from £.50.

For absolute PPP to hold, several things must be true:

1. The transactions cost of trading apples—shipping, insurance, wastage, and so on—must be zero.
2. There are no barriers to trading apples, such as tariffs, taxes, or other political barriers such as voluntary restraint agreements.
3. Finally, an apple in Halifax must be identical to an apple in London. It won't do for you to send red apples to London if the English eat only green apples.

Given the fact that the transaction costs are not zero and that the other conditions are rarely exactly met, it is not surprising that absolute PPP is really applicable only to traded goods, and then only to very uniform ones.

For this reason, absolute PPP does not imply that a Mercedes costs the same as a Ford or that a nuclear power plant in France costs the same as one in Ontario. In the case of the cars, they are not identical. In the case of the power plants, even if they were identical, they are expensive and very difficult to ship. On the other hand, we would be very surprised to see a significant violation of absolute PPP for gold.

Relative Purchasing Power Parity

As a practical matter, a relative version of purchasing power parity has evolved. *Relative purchasing power parity* does not tell us what determines the absolute level of the exchange rate. Instead, it tells what determines the *change* in the exchange rate over time.

Global Strategy on Big Mac Purchasing Power Parity

To compare currency values around the world, you need a basket of goods universally produced and sold. The magazine *The Economist* has used the Big Mac to measure this type of purchasing power parity (PPP) between countries since 1986. After all, a Big Mac is pretty much the same around the world, and it is locally produced in 68 different countries.

Canadian Dollar Under-valued
In Canada, it costs $2.86 (including taxes, with local variations). In the United States, the same Big Mac costs US$2.30. Using the Big Mac theory, the "correct" exchange rate should be C$1 = US$0.804. The actual exchange rate at the time (April 5) was C$1 = US$0.719. The Canadian dollar is undervalued by 10 percent using this measure.

On the same basis, the yen is overvalued against the U.S. dollar by more than 60 percent. European currencies are also overvalued.

The Science of Burgernomics
The Economist concedes the weaknesses of "burgernomics." It assumes there are no price barriers, so countries with farm subsidies

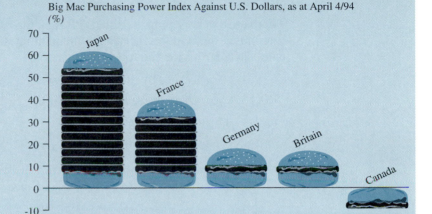

Big Mac Purchasing Power Index Against U.S. Dollars, as at April 4/94 (%)

Source: *The Economist*

and import restrictions appear over-valued. Value-added taxes in other countries inflate prices and exag-gerate overvaluation. In some countries McDonald's is a restau-rant with upper-middle-class appeal for those looking to emulate American lifestyle.

In spite of those weaknesses, the Big Mac has some validity as a quick measure of PPP.

As the magazine concludes, economics favour the appreciation

of the U.S. and Canadian dollars. Interest rates in the United States are likely to rise this year and Eu-ropean rates have fallen and will continue to fall. The Big Mac in-dex is hardly a fool-proof tool of economic forecasting, but it offers investors something to chew on.

Global Strategy is an investment fund company based in Toronto. This material is excerpted, with permission, from *Global Strategy Views*, Spring 1994, p. 9.

The Basic Idea   Suppose again that the British pound/Canadian dollar exchange rate is currently $S_0 = £.50$. Further suppose that the inflation rate in Britain is predicted to be 10 percent over the coming year and (for the moment) the inflation rate in Canada is predicted to be zero. What do you think the exchange rate will be in a year?

If you think about it, a dollar currently costs .50 pounds in Britain. With 10 percent inflation, we expect prices in Britain to generally rise by 10 percent. So we expect that the price of a dollar will go up by 10 percent and the exchange rate should rise to £.50 × 1.1 = £.55.

If the inflation rate in Canada is not zero, we need to worry about the relative inflation rates in the two countries. For example, suppose the Canadian inflation rate is predicted to be 4 percent. Relative to prices in Canada, prices in Britain are rising at a rate of 10% − 4% = 6% per year. So we expect the price of the dollar to rise by 6 percent, and the predicted exchange rate is £.50 × 1.06 = £.53.

The Result   In general, relative PPP says that the change in the exchange rate is determined by the difference in the inflation rates between the two countries. To be more specific, we use the following notation:

S_0 = Current (Time 0) spot exchange rate (foreign currency per dollar)

$E[S_t]$ = Expected exchange rate in t periods

h_{CDN} = Inflation rate in Canada

h_{FC} = Foreign country inflation rate

Based on our discussion, relative PPP says the expected percentage change in the exchange rate over the next year, $(E[S_1] - S_0)/S_0$, is:

$$(E[S_1] - S_0)/S_0 = h_{FC} - h_{CDN} \qquad [22.1]$$

In words, relative PPP simply says that the expected percentage change in the exchange rate is equal to the difference in inflation rates. If we rearrange this slightly, we get:

$$[E(S_1) = S_0 \times [1 + (h_{FC} - h_{CDN})] \qquad [22.2]$$

This result makes a certain amount of sense, but care must be used in quoting the exchange rate.

In our example involving Britain and Canada, relative PPP tells us the exchange rate rises by $h_{FC} - h_{CDN}$ = 10% − 4% = 6% per year. Assuming the difference in inflation rates doesn't change, the expected exchange rate in two years, $E[S_2]$, is therefore:

$$E[S_2] = E[S_1] \times (1 + .06)$$
$$= .53 \times 1.06$$
$$= .562$$

Notice that we could have written this as:

$$E[S_2] = .53 \times 1.06$$
$$= (.50 \times 1.06) \times 1.06$$
$$= .50 \times 1.06^2$$

In general, relative PPP, says the expected exchange rate at sometime in the future, $E[S_t]$, is:

$$E[S_t] = S_0 \times [1 + (h_{FC} - h_{CDN})]^t \qquad [22.3]$$

As we shall see, this is a very useful relationship.

Because we don't really expect absolute PPP to hold for most goods, we focus on relative PPP in the following discussion. Henceforth, when we refer to PPP without further qualification, we mean relative PPP.

E X A M P L E | **22.5**   **It's All Relative**

Suppose the Japanese exchange rate is currently 130 yen per dollar. The inflation rate in Japan over the next three years will run, say, 2 percent per year while the Canadian inflation rate will be 6 percent. Based on relative PPP, what would the exchange rate be in three years?

Since the Canadian inflation rate is higher, we expect a dollar to become less valuable. The exchange rate change would be 2% − 6% = −4% per year. Over three years, the exchange rate falls to:

$$E[S_3] = S_0 \times [1 + (h_{FC} - h_{CDN})]^3$$
$$= 130 \times [1 + (-.04)]^3$$
$$= 115.02$$

Currency Appreciation and Depreciation

We frequently hear these statements: The dollar strengthened (or weakened) in financial markets today or the dollar is expected to appreciate (or depreciate) relative to the pound. When we say the dollar strengthens or appreciates, we mean the value of a dollar rises, so it takes more foreign currency to buy a Canadian dollar.

What happens to the exchange rates as currencies fluctuate in value depends on how exchange rates are quoted. Since we are quoting them as units of foreign currency per dollar, the exchange rate moves in the same direction as the value of the dollar: It rises as the dollar strengthens, and it falls as the dollar weakens.

Relative PPP tells us the exchange rate rises if the Canadian inflation rate is lower than the foreign country's. This happens because the foreign currency depreciates in value and therefore weakens relative to the dollar.

CONCEPT QUESTIONS

1. What does absolute PPP say? Why might it not hold for many goods?
2. According to relative PPP, what determines the change in exchange rates?

22.4 | INTEREST RATE PARITY, UNBIASED FORWARD RATES, AND THE INTERNATIONAL FISHER EFFECT

The next issue we need to address is the relationship between the spot exchange rates, forward exchange rates, and interest rates. To get started, we need some additional notation:

F_t = Forward exchange rate for settlement at time t

R_{CDN} = Canadian nominal risk-free interest rate

R_{FC} = Foreign country nominal risk-free interest rate

As before, use S_0 to stand for the spot exchange rate. You can take the Canadian nominal risk-free rate, R_{CDN}, to be the T-bill rate.

Covered Interest Arbitrage

Suppose we observe the following information about Canadian and German currency in the market:

S_0 = DM 2.00 R_{CDN} = 10%

F_1 = DM 1.90 R_G = 5%

where R_G is the nominal risk-free rate in Germany. The period is one year, so F_1 is the one-year forward rate.

Do you see an arbitrage opportunity here? There is one. Suppose you have $1 to invest, and you want a riskless investment. One option you have is to invest the $1 in a riskless Canadian investment such as a one-year T-bill. If you do this, in one period your $1 will be worth:

$$\$ \text{ value in 1 period} = \$1 \times (1 + R_{CDN})$$
$$= \$1.10$$

Alternatively, you can invest in the German risk-free investment. To do this, you need to convert your $1 to deutsche marks and simultaneously exercise a forward trade to convert marks back to dollars in one year. The necessary steps would be as follows:

1. Convert your $1 to $1 × S_0 = DM 2.00.
2. At the same time, enter into a forward agreement to convert marks back to dollars in one year. Since the forward rate is DM 1.90, you get $1 for every DM 1.90 that you have in one year.
3. Invest your DM 2.00 in Germany at R_G. In one year, you have:

$$\text{DM value in 1 year} = \text{DM } 2.00 \times (1 + R_G)$$
$$= \text{DM } 2.00 \times 1.05$$
$$= \text{DM } 2.10$$

4. Convert your DM 2.10 back to dollars at the agreed-on rate of DM 1.90 = $1. You end up with:

$$\$ \text{ value in 1 year} = \text{DM } 2.10/1.90$$
$$= \$1.1053$$

Notice that the value in one year from this strategy can be written as:

$$\$ \text{ value in 1 year} = \$1 \times S_0 \times (1 + R_G)/F_1$$
$$= \$1 \times 2 \times (1.05)/1.90$$
$$= \$1.1053$$

The return on this investment is apparently 10.53 percent. This is higher than the 10 percent we get from investing in Canada. Since both investments are risk-free, there is an arbitrage opportunity.

To exploit the difference in interest rates, you need to borrow, say, $5 million at the lower Canadian rate and invest it at the higher German rate. What is the round-trip profit from doing this? To find out, we can work through the preceding steps:

1. Convert the $5 million at DM 2 = $1 to get DM 10 million.
2. Agree to exchange marks for dollars in one year at DM 1.90 to the dollar.
3. Invest the DM 10 million for one year at R_G = 5%. You end up with DM 10.5 million.
4. Convert the DM 10.5 million back to dollars to fulfill the forward contract. You receive DM 10.5 million/1.90 = $5,526,316.
5. Repay the loan with interest. You owe $5 million plus 10 percent interest, for a total of $5.5 million. You have $5,526,316, so your round-trip profit is a risk-free $26,316.

The activity that we have illustrated here goes by the name of *covered interest arbitrage*. The term *covered* refers to the fact that we are covered in the event of a change in the exchange rate because we lock in the forward exchange rate today.

Interest Rate Parity (IRP)

If we assume that significant covered interest arbitrage opportunities do not exist, there must be some relationship between spot exchange rates, forward exchange rates, and relative interest rates. To see what this relationship is, note that, in general, strategy 1—investing in a riskless Canadian investment—gives us $(1 + R_{CDN})$ for every dollar we invest. Strategy 2—investing in a foreign risk-free investment—gives us $S_0 \times (1 + R_{FC})/F_1$ for every dollar we invest. Since these have to be equal to prevent arbitrage, it must be the case that:

$$(1 + R_{CDN}) = S_0 \times (1 + R_{FC})/F_1$$

Rearranging this a bit gets us the famous **interest rate parity (IRP)** condition:

$$F_1/S_0 = (1 + R_{FC})/(1 + R_{CDN}) \qquad [22.4]$$

interest rate parity (IRP)
The condition stating that the interest rate differential between two countries is equal to the difference between the forward exchange rate and the spot exchange rate.

A very useful approximation for IRP illustrates very clearly what is going on and is not difficult to remember. If we define the percentage forward premium or discount as $(F_1 - S_0)/S_0$, IRP says this percent premium or discount is approximately equal to the difference in interest rates:

$$(F_1 - S_0)/S_0 = R_{FC} - R_{CDN} \qquad [22.5]$$

Very loosely, what IRP says is that any difference in interest rates between two countries for some period is just offset by the change in the relative value of the currencies, thereby eliminating any arbitrage possibilities. Notice that we could also write:

$$F_1 = S_0 \times [1 + (R_{FC} - R_{CDN})] \qquad [22.6]$$

In general, if we have t periods instead of just one, the IRP approximation would be written as:

$$F_t = S_0 \times [1 + (R_{FC} - R_{CDN})]^t \qquad [22.7]$$

E X A M P L E | **22.6   Parity Check**

Suppose the exchange rate for Japanese yen, S_0, is currently ¥120 = $1. If the interest rate in Canada is R_{CDN} = 10% and the interest rate in Japan is R_J = 5%, what must the forward rate be to prevent covered interest arbitrage?

From IRP, we have:

$$
\begin{aligned}
F_1 &= S_0 \times [1 + (R_J - R_{CDN})] \\
&= ¥120 \times [1 + (.05 - .10)] \\
&= ¥120 \times .95 \\
&= ¥114
\end{aligned}
$$

Notice that the yen sells at a premium relative to the dollar (why?). |

Forward Rates and Future Spot Rates

unbiased forward rates (UFR)
The condition stating that the current forward rate is an unbiased predictor of the future exchange rate.

In addition to PPP and IRP, there is one more basic relationship we need to discuss. What is the connection between the forward rate and the expected future spot rate? The **unbiased forward rates (UFR)** condition says the forward rate, F_1, is equal to the expected future spot rate, $E[S_1]$:

$$F_1 = E[S_1]$$

With t periods, UFR would be written as:

$$F_t = E[S_t]$$

Loosely, the UFR condition says that, on average, the forward exchange rate is equal to the future spot exchange rate.

If we ignore risk, the UFR condition should hold. Suppose the forward rate for the Japanese yen is consistently lower than the future spot rate by, say, 10 yen. This means that anyone who wanted to convert dollars to yen in the future would consistently get more yen by not agreeing to a forward exchange. The forward rate would have to rise to get anyone interested.

Similarly, if the forward rate were consistently higher than the future spot rate, anyone who wanted to convert yen to dollars would get more dollars per yen by not agreeing to a forward trade. The forward exchange rate would have to fall to attract such traders.

For these reasons, the forward and actual future spot rates should be equal to each other on average. What the future spot rate will actually be is uncertain, of course. The UFR condition may not hold if traders are willing to pay a premium to avoid this uncertainty. If the condition does hold, the six-month forward rate that we see today should be an unbiased predictor of what the exchange rate will actually be in six months.

Putting It All Together

We have developed three relationships, PPP, IRP, and UFR, that describe the relationships between key financial variables such as interest rates, exchange rates, and inflation rates. We now explore the implications of these relationships as a group.

Uncovered Interest Parity To start, it is useful to collect our international financial market relationships in one place:

$$\text{PPP: } E[S_1] = S_0 \times [1 + (h_{FC} - h_{CDN})]$$

$$\text{IRP: } F_1 = S_0 \times [1 + (R_{FC} - R_{CDN})]$$

$$\text{UFR: } F_1 = E[S_1]$$

uncovered interest parity (UIP)
The condition stating that the expected percentage change in the exchange rate is equal to the difference in interest rates.

We begin by combining UFR and IRP. Since $F_1 = E[S_1]$ from the UFR condition, we can substitute $E[S_1]$ for F_1 in IRP. The result is:

$$E[S_1] = S_0 \times [1 + (R_{FC} - R_{CDN})] \quad [22.8]$$

This important relationship is called **uncovered interest parity (UIP)**, and it plays a key role in our international capital budgeting discussion that follows. With t periods, UIP becomes:

$$E[S_t] = S_0 \times [1 + (R_{FC} - R_{CDN})]^t \quad [22.9]$$

The International Fisher Effect   Next, we compare PPP and UIP. Both of them have $E[S_1]$ on the left side, so their right sides must be equal. We thus have that:

$$S_0 \times [1 + (h_{FC} - h_{CDN})] = S_0 \times [1 + (R_{FC} - R_{CDN})]$$

$$h_{FC} - h_{CDN} = R_{FC} - R_{CDN}$$

This tells us that the difference in risk-free returns between Canada and a foreign country is just equal to the difference in inflation rates. Rearranging this slightly gives us the **international Fisher effect (IFE)**:

$$R_{CDN} - h_{CDN} = R_{FC} - h_{FC} \qquad\qquad [22.10]$$

The IFE says that real rates are equal across countries.[3]

    The conclusion that real returns are equal across countries is really basic economics. If real returns were higher in, say, the United States than in Canada, money would flow out of Canadian financial markets and into U.S. markets. Asset prices in the United States would rise and their returns would fall. At the same time, asset prices in Canada would fall and their returns would rise. This process acts to equalize real returns.

    Having said all this, we need to note several things: First, we really haven't explicitly dealt with risk in our discussion. We might reach a different conclusion about real returns once we do, particularly if people in different countries have different tastes and attitudes toward risk. Second, there are many barriers to the movement of money and capital around the world. Real returns might be different between two countries for long periods of time if money can't move freely between them.

    Despite these problems, we expect capital markets to become increasingly internationalized. As this occurs, any differences in real rates that do exist will probably diminish. The laws of economics have very little respect for national boundaries.

> **international Fisher effect (IFE)**
> *The theory that real interest rates are equal across countries.*

E X A M P L E | **22.7**   **Taking a High Toll**

Suppose a municipal authority is constructing a tunnel connecting two parts of a major Canadian city separated by a river. The tunnel will cost $100 million to build. Work will be complete in one year at which time the authority will pay off the present construction loan and replace it with long-term financing from capital markets. The loan will be paid off over 10 years with tolls collected from tunnel users.

    In the meantime, it is time to renew the construction loan for one year. A group of Canadian banks has offered to lend $100 million for one year at 11 percent. A Japanese bank has offered a yen loan at 7 percent. Should the authority borrow in yen for one year to save 4 percent in interest—$4 million?

    While you are considering, you come across the following information on exchange rates: the spot exchange rate is ¥110 per Canadian dollar ($0.009091 per ¥). The 12-month forward rate is ¥106 per dollar ($.0094340 per yen).

    According to the UFR condition, the forward rate shows that the yen is expected to rise in value. It follows that the authority is naive if it expects to save $4 million by borrowing in Japan. The UIP condition tells us the yen should rise by just enough

---

[3] Notice that our result here is in the approximate real rate, $R - h$ (see Chapter 10), because we used approximations for PPP and IRP. For the exact result, see Problem 22 at the end of the chapter.

so that exchange losses on paying back the loan in more expensive yen exactly offset the lower interest rate. To prove this, we compare the balloon payments at the end of one year for borrowing in Canadian dollars and in yen. If the authority borrows in Canadian dollars at 11 percent, the principal and interest at the end of one year would be $111 million.

If the borrowing is in yen, the treasurer of the authority executes the following steps:

1. Borrow the equivalent of $100 million in yen. Converting at today's spot rate, this is $100 million × 110 = ¥11 billion.

2. At the end of 12 months, the authority owes ¥11 billion × (1.07) = ¥11 billion.

3. After 12 months, the authority purchases ¥11.77 billion in the spot market to repay the loan. The cost depends on the unknown future spot rate for the yen. By borrowing in Japan, the authority is gambling that the yen will not appreciate in value by enough to cancel the gains of the lower interest rate. In other words, the authority is betting that the future cost of buying ¥11.77 billion will not exceed $111 million. This gives us a break-even future spot rate:

$$¥11.77 \text{ billion} = \$111 \text{ million} \times F_1$$
$$F_1 = 11.77 \text{ billion}/111 \text{ million}$$
$$F_1 = 106.036$$

If the authority gambles, it could break even if the future spot rate is around 106 yen per dollar. This translates to 1/106 = $.009434 per yen. If the yen appreciates more, the authority loses. Suppose the yen goes up to $.01 or 100 yen to the dollar. Then the authority has to repay ¥11.77 billion × .01 = $118 million. This is equivalent to borrowing at 18 percent!

Our advice in this case is to borrow in Canada to eliminate foreign exchange risk. Or, if there is a good reason to borrow abroad, say better access to funds, the authority should hedge in the forward market.[4] Under this approach, steps 1 and 2 are the same. With a forward contract taken out when the borrowing is initiated, the future exchange rate is locked in at ¥106 to the dollar. Due to the IRP condition, it is no coincidence that this is the break-even rate.   ▎

CONCEPT QUESTIONS

1. What is covered interest arbitrage?

2. What is the international Fisher effect?

22.5 | INTERNATIONAL CAPITAL BUDGETING

Kihlstrom Equipment, a Canadian-based international company, is evaluating an overseas investment. Kihlstrom's exports of high-tech communications equipment have increased to such a degree that it is considering building a plant in France. The project would cost FF 20 million to launch. The cash flows are expected to be FF 9 million a year for the next three years.[5]

---

[4] Currency futures offer another possible hedging vehicle. Chapter 20 discusses futures in more detail.
[5] In our discussion of Kihlstrom, all cash flows and interest rates are nominal unless we state otherwise.

IN THEIR OWN WORDS ...

Richard M. Levich on Forward Exchange Rates

What is the relationship between today's three-month forward exchange rate, which can be observed in the market, and the spot exchange rate of three months from today, which cannot be observed until the future? One popular answer is that there is no relationship. As every bank trader knows, the possibility of covered interest arbitrage between domestic and foreign securities establishes a close link between the forward premium and the interest rate differential. At any moment, a trader can check his screen and observe that the forward premium and the interest rate differentials are nearly identical, especially when Eurocurrency interest rates are used. Thus, the trader might say, "The forward rate reflects today's interest differential. It has nothing to do with expectations."

To check the second popular belief, that the forward rate reflects exchange rate expectations, takes a bit more work. Take today's three-month forward rate as of January 15 and compare it to the spot exchange rate that actually exists three months later on April 15. This produces one observation on

the forward rate as a forecaster— not enough to accept or reject a theory. The idea that the forward rate might be an unbiased predictor of the future spot rate suggests that, on average and looking at many observations, the prediction error is small. So collect more data using the forward rate of April 15 and match it with the spot rate of July 15, and then the forward rate of July 15 matched to the spot rate of October 15, and so on. Look at the data for 8 to 10 years to have a large sample of observations.

The data suggest [for full citation see Suggested Readings] that in the early 1980s when the U.S. dollar was very strong, the forward rate significantly *under*estimated the strength of the dollar, and the forward rate was a biased predictor. But from 1985 to 1987 when the dollar depreciated sharply, the forward rate tended to *over*estimate the strength of the dollar, and the forward rate was again a biased predictor, but with the opposite sign as the earlier period. Looking at all of the 1980s—you guessed it—the forward rate was on average very close to the future spot exchange rate.

There are two messages here. First, even if there were "no relationship" between the forward rate and the future spot rate, the treasurer of General Motors would want to know exactly what that "nonrelationship" was. Because if the forward rate were *consistently* 3 percent higher than, or *consistently* 5 percent lower than, the future spot rate, the treasurer would be facing a tantalizing profit opportunity. A watch that is three minutes fast or five minutes slow is a very useful watch, as long as the bias is known and consistent. And finally, the data from the 1980s have revalidated Michael Mussa's [for full citation see Suggested Readings] interpretation of the 1970s. Mussa observed that "the forward rate is an unbiased predictor of the future spot rate, [it] is close to the best available predictor ... but [it] is probably not a very good predictor.

Richard M. Levich is professor of finance and international business at New York University. He has written extensively on exchange rates and other issues in international economics and finance.

The current spot exchange rate for French francs is FF 5. Recall that this is francs per dollar, so a franc is worth $1/5 = $.20. The risk-free rate in Canada is 5 percent, and the risk-free rate in France is 7 percent. Notice that the exchange rate and the two interest rates are observed in financial markets, not estimated.[6] Kihlstrom's required return on dollar investments of this sort is 10 percent.

---

[6] For example, the interest rates might be the short-term Eurodollar and Eurofranc deposit rates offered by large money centre banks.

Should Kihlstrom take this investment? As always, the answer depends on the NPV, but how do we calculate the net present value of this project in Canadian dollars? There are two basic ways to do this:

1. *The home currency approach.* Convert all the franc cash flows into dollars, and then discount at 10 percent to find the NPV in dollars. Notice that for this approach, we have to come up with the future exchange rates to convert the future projected franc cash flows into dollars.

2. *The foreign currency approach.* Determine the required return on franc investments, and discount the franc cash flows to find the NPV in francs. Then convert this franc NPV to a dollar NPV. This approach requires us to somehow convert the 10 percent dollar required return to the equivalent franc required return.

The difference between these two approaches is primarily a matter of when we convert from francs to dollars. In the first case, we convert before estimating the NPV. In the second case, we convert after estimating NPV.

It might appear that the second approach is superior because we only have to come up with one number, the franc discount rate. Furthermore, since the first approach requires us to forecast future exchange rates, it probably seems that there is greater room for error. As we illustrate next, however, based on our results the two approaches are really the same.

Method 1: The Home Currency Approach

To convert the project future cash flows into dollars, we invoke the uncovered interest parity (UIP) relation to come up with the project exchange rates. Based on our discussion, the expected exchange rate at time t, $E[S_t]$ is:

$$E[S_t] = S_0 \times [1 + (R_{FR} - R_{CDN})]^t$$

where R_{FR} stands for the nominal risk-free rate in France. Since R_{FR} is 7 percent, R_{CDN} is 5 percent, and the current exchange rate (S_0) is FF 5:

$$E[S_t] = 5 \times [1 + (.07 - .05)]^t$$
$$= 5 \times 1.02^t$$

The projected exchange rates for the communications equipment project are thus:

Year	Expected Exchange Rate
1	FF 5 × 1.02^1 = FF 5.100
2	FF 5 × 1.02^2 = FF 5.202
3	FF 5 × 1.02^3 = FF 5.306

Using these exchange rates, along with the current exchange rate, we can convert all of the franc cash flows to dollars:

Year	(1) Cash Flow in FF	(2) Expected Exchange Rate	(3) Cash Flow in $ (1)/(2)
0	−FF 20	FF 5.000	−$4.00
1	9	5.100	1.76
2	9	5.202	1.73
3	9	5.306	1.70

To finish, we calculate the NPV in the ordinary way:

$$NPV = \$4.00 + \$1.76/1.10 + \$1.73/1.10^2 + \$1.70/1.10^3$$
$$= \$.3 \text{ million}$$

So the project appears to be profitable.

Method 2: The Foreign Currency Approach

Kihlstrom requires a nominal return of 10 percent on the dollar-denominated cash flows. We need to convert this to a rate suitable for franc-denominated cash flows. Based on the international Fisher effect, we know that the difference in the nominal rates is:

$$R_{FC} - R_{CDN} = h_{FC} - h_{CDN}$$
$$= 7\% - 5\% = 2\%$$

The appropriate discount rate for estimating the franc cash flows from the project is approximately equal to 10 percent plus an extra 2 percent to compensate for the greater franc inflation rate.

If we calculate the NPV of the franc cash flows at this rate, we get:

$$NPV_{FF} = -FF\ 20 + FF\ 9/1.12 + FF\ 9/1.12^2 + FF\ 9/1.12^3$$
$$= FF\ 1.6 \text{ million}$$

The NPV of this project is FF 1.6 million. Taking this project makes us FF 1.6 million richer today. What is this in dollars? Since the exchange rate today is FF 5, the dollar NPV of the project is:

$$NPV_\$ = NPV_{FF}/S_0 = FF\ 1.6/5 = \$.3 \text{ million}$$

This is the same dollar NPV as we previously calculated.

The important thing to recognize from our example is that the two capital budgeting procedures are actually the same and always give the same answer.[7] In this second approach, the fact that we are implicitly forecasting exchange rates is simply hidden. Even so, the foreign currency approach is computationally a little easier.

Unremitted Cash Flows

The previous example assumed that all aftertax cash flows from the foreign investment could be remitted to (paid out to) the parent firm. Actually, substantial differences can exist between the cash flows generated by a foreign project and the amount that can actually be remitted or repatriated to the parent firm.

A foreign subsidiary can remit funds to a parent in many ways, including the following:

1. Dividends.
2. Management fees for central services.
3. Royalties on the use of a trade name and patents.

---

[7] Actually, there will be a slight difference because we are using the approximate relationships. If we calculate the required return as $(1.10) \times (1 + .02) - 1 = 12.2\%$, we get exactly the same NPV. See Problem 22 for more detail.

However cash flows are repatriated, international firms must pay special attention to remittance because there may be current and future controls on remittances. Many governments are sensitive to the charge of being exploited by foreign national firms. In such cases, governments are tempted to limit the ability of international firms to remit cash flows. Funds that cannot currently be remitted are sometimes said to be blocked.

> CONCEPT QUESTIONS
>
> **1.** What financial complications arise in international capital budgeting? Describe two procedures for estimating NPV in this case.
> **2.** What are blocked funds?

22.6 I FINANCING INTERNATIONAL PROJECTS

The Cost of Capital for International Firms

An important question for firms with international investments is whether the required return for international projects should be different from that of similar domestic projects. The answer to this question depends on:

1. Segmentation of the international financial market.
2. Foreign political risk of expropriation, foreign exchange controls, and taxes.

We save political risk for later discussion and focus here on the first point.

Suppose barriers prevented shareholders in Canada from holding foreign securities. If this were the case, the financial markets of different countries would be segmented. Further suppose that firms in Canada did not face the same barriers. In such a case, a firm engaging in international investing could provide indirect diversification for Canadian shareholders that they could not achieve by investing within Canada. This could lead to lowering of the risk premium on international projects.

On the other hand, if there were no barriers to international investing for shareholders, investors could get the benefit of international diversification for themselves by buying foreign securities. Then, the project cost of capital for Canadian firms would not depend on where the project was located.

To resolve this issue, researchers have compared the variance of purely domestic stock portfolios with international portfolios. The result is that international portfolios have lower variance. Because investors are not fully diversified internationally, firms can benefit from a lower cost of capital for international projects that provide diversification services for the firms' shareholders.[8]

International Diversification and Investors

As we just saw, there is evidence that international diversification by firms presently provides a service that investors cannot obtain themselves at reasonable cost. Holding foreign securities may subject investors to increased tax, trading, and information costs. Financial engineering is aiding investors in avoiding some of these costs. As a result, as investors diversify globally, the cost of capital advantage to firms is likely to decline.

---

[8] B. H. Solnik, "Why Not Diversify Internationally Rather than Domestically?" *Financial Analysts Journal,* July–August 1974.

An *Index Participation* (IP) is a current example of a financially engineered vehicle for international diversification.[9] An IP on the Standard & Poor's 500 Stock Average, for example, gives an investor an asset that tracks this well-known U.S. market index. IPs are highly liquid, thus reducing trading costs. Information costs are also reduced since the holder need not research each of the 500 individual stocks that make up the index.

International diversification for Canadian investors is being made easier by the lowering of an important barrier. In 1992, the maximum allowable foreign holding for pension funds doubled from 10 to 20 percent. Increased demand is fueling the development of new products to exploit this opportunity.

One popular new product is the *emerging market fund,* a mutual fund investing in Latin America, Southeast Asia, China, or other emerging markets. Highly popular with investors in 1993 and 1994, emerging market funds proved highly volatile in early 1995 after the large Mexican peso devaluation.

Sources of Short- and Intermediate-Term Financing

In raising short-term and medium-term cash, Canadian international firms have a choice between borrowing from a chartered bank at the Canadian rate or borrowing EuroCanadian (or other Eurocurrency) from a bank outside Canada through the Eurocurrency market.

The Eurocurrency markets are the **Eurobanks** that make loans and accept deposits in foreign currencies. Most Eurocurrency trading involves the borrowing and lending of time deposits at Eurobanks. For example, suppose the Bank of Nova Scotia (BNS) receives a 30-day Eurodollar deposit from McCain in London. The BNS then makes a U.S. dollar-denominated loan to the Bank of Tokyo. Ultimately, the Bank of Tokyo makes a loan to a Japanese importer with invoices to pay in the United States. As our example shows, the Eurocurrency market is not a retail market. The customers are large corporations, banks, and governments.

Eurobanks
Banks that make loans and accept deposits in foreign currencies.

One important characteristic of the Eurocurrency market is that loans are made on a floating rate basis. The interest rates are set at a fixed margin above the London Interbank Offered Rate (LIBOR) for the given period and currency involved. For example, if LIBOR is 8 percent and the margin is 0.5 percent for Eurodollar loans in a certain risk class, called a *tier,* the Eurodollar borrower pays an interest rate of 8.5 percent. Eurodollar loans have maturities ranging up to 10 years.

Securitization and globalization have produced alternatives to borrowing from a Eurobank. Under a **Note Issuance Facility (NIF)**, a large borrower issues short-term notes with maturities usually three to six months but ranging to one year.[10] Banks may underwrite NIFs or sell them to investors. In the latter case, where banks simply act as an agent, the Euronotes issued are called *Euro-commercial paper (ECP)*. ECP is similar to domestic commercial paper but, because the Eurocredit market is not regulated, offers greater flexibility in available maturities and tax avoidance.

Note Issuance Facility (NIF)
Large borrowers issue notes up to one year in maturity in the Euromarket. Banks underwrite or sell notes.

The drive to escape regulation (part of the regulatory dialectic introduced in Chapter 1) explains the attraction and growth of the Euromarkets. Eurocurrency markets developed to allow borrowers and banks to operate without regulation and taxes mainly in the United States. They offer borrowers an opportunity to tap large

---

[9] G. Axford and Y. Lin, "Surprise! Currency Risk Improves International Investment," *Canadian Treasury Management Review,* Royal Bank of Canada, March–April 1990.

[10] Our discussion of NIFs draws on A. L. Melnik and S. E. Plaut, *The Short-Term Eurocredit Market* (New York: New York University Salomon Center, 1991), chap. 4.

amounts of short-term funds quickly and at competitive rates. As banking regulations—for example capital rules—become tighter, alternatives to bank borrowing, such as NIFs, are growing and sharing the Euromarket with banks.

The Eurobond Market   Eurobonds are denominated in a particular currency and are issued simultaneously in the bond markets of several countries. The prefix *Euro* means the bonds are issued outside the countries in whose currencies they are denominated. For example, a French automobile firm issues 50,000 bonds with a face value of $1,000 (U.S.) each. When the bonds are issued, they are managed by London merchant bankers and listed on the London Stock Exchange.

Most Eurobonds are bearer bonds. The ownership of the bonds is established by possession of the bond. In contrast, foreign bonds (issued by foreign borrowers in a domestic capital market) are registered. This makes Eurobonds more attractive to Belgian dentists, investors who have a disdain for tax authorities.

Most issues of Eurobonds are arranged by underwriting. However, some Eurobonds are privately placed. Eurobonds appear as straight bonds, floating-rate notes, convertible bonds, zero coupon bonds, mortgage-backed bonds, and dual-currency bonds.

> **CONCEPT QUESTIONS**
>
> 1. Can firms reduce their risk and with it their costs of capital through diversifying with international projects?
> 2. What are the main sources of short and intermediate financing in Euro-markets?
> 3. Describe a Eurobond and its advantages over a foreign bond.

22.7 | EXCHANGE RATE RISK

exchange rate risk
The risk related to having international operations in a world where relative currency values vary.

Exchange rate risk is the natural consequence of international operations in a world where relative currency values move up and down. Managing exchange rate risk is an important part of international finance. As we discuss next, there are three different types of exchange rate risk or exposure: short-run exposure, long-run exposure, and translation exposure.

Short-Run Exposure

The day-to-day fluctuations in exchange rates create short-run risks for international firms. Most such firms have contractual agreements to buy and sell goods in the near future at set prices. When different currencies are involved, such transactions have an extra element of risk.

For example, imagine you are importing imitation pasta from Italy and reselling it in Canada under the Impasta brand name. Your largest customer has ordered 10,000 cases of Impasta. You place the order with your supplier today, but you won't pay until the goods arrive in 60 days. Your selling price is $6 per case. Your cost is 8,400 Italian lira per case, and the exchange rate is currently Lit 1,500, so it takes 1,500 lira to buy $1.

At the current exchange rate, your cost in dollars from filling the order is Lit 8,400/1,500 = $5.60 per case, so your pretax profit on the order is 10,000 × ($6 − $5.60) = $4,000. However, the exchange rate in 60 days will probably be different, so your profit depends on what the future exchange rate turns out to be.

For example, if the rate goes to Lit 1,600, your cost is Lit 8,400/1,600 = $5.25 per case. Your profit goes to $7,500. If the exchange rate goes to, say, Lit 1,400, then your cost is Lit 8,400/1,400 = $6, and your profit is zero.

The short-run exposure in our example can be reduced or eliminated in several ways. The most obvious means of hedging is to enter into a forward exchange agreement to lock in an exchange rate. For example, suppose the 60-day forward rate is Lit 1,580. What is your profit if you hedge? What profit should you expect if you don't?

If you hedge, you lock in an exchange rate of Lit 1,580. Your cost in dollars is thus Lit 8,400/1,580 = $5.32 per case, so your profit is 10,000 × ($6 − $5.32) = $6,800. If you don't hedge, assuming that the forward rate is an unbiased predictor (in other words, assuming the UFR condition holds), you should expect the exchange rate to actually be Lit 1,580 in 60 days. You should expect to make $6,800.

Alternatively, if this is not feasible, you could simply borrow the dollars today, convert them into lira, and invest the lira for 60 days to earn some interest. From IRP, this amounts to entering into a forward contract.

Should the treasurer hedge or speculate? There are usually two reasons the treasurer should hedge:

1. In an efficient foreign exchange rate market, speculation is a zero NPV activity. Unless the treasurer has special information, nothing is gained from foreign exchange speculation.

2. The costs of hedging are not large. The treasurer can use forward contracts to hedge, and if the forward rate is equal to the expected spot, the costs of hedging are negligible.

More Advanced Short-Term Hedges   Of course, there are ways to hedge foreign exchange risk other than with forward contracts. Currency swaps, currency options, and other financially engineered products are taking considerable business away from the forward exchange market.[11] A currency swap is an arrangement between a borrower, a second borrower, called a **counterparty**, and a bank. The borrower and the counterparty each raise funds in a different currency and then swap liabilities. The bank guarantees the borrower's and counterparty's credit as in a bankers acceptance. The result is that the borrower obtains funds in the desired currency at a lower rate than for direct borrowing.

> **counterparty**
> *Second borrower in currency swap. Counterparty borrows funds in currency desired by principal.*

For example, in 1986 the federal government of Canada made an 80 billion yen bond issue and swapped part of it into U.S. dollars. The interest rate was six-month LIBOR and the ending liability was in U.S. dollars, not yen. The interest cost turned out to be 54 basis points below the cost of direct borrowing in the United States.

Currency options are similar to options on stock (discussed in Chapter 20) except the exercise price is an exchange rate.[12] They are exchange traded in the United States with exercise prices in various currencies including the Canadian dollar. Currency options can be exercised at any time before maturity. In the jargon of options, they are **American options**. A call option on the Canadian dollar gives the holder the right, but not the obligation, to buy C$ at a fixed exercise price in U.S.$.

> **American options**
> *A call or put option that can be exercised on or before its expiration date.*

---

[11] Our discussion of currency swaps in practice draws on B. Critchley, "Explosion of New Products Cuts Foreign Currency Risk," *Financial Post,* September 14, 1987.

[12] See Chapter 20 for a thorough introduction to options. Our discussion of currency options simplifies the description by discussing options on currency. In practice, options are written against currency futures contracts.

It increases in value as the C$ exchange rate in U.S.$ rises. A put option allows the holder to sell C$ at the exercise price. A put becomes more valuable when the C$ declines against the U.S.$.

The basic idea behind hedging with options is to take an options position opposite to the cash position. For this reason, hedge analysis starts by looking at the unhedged position of the business. For example, suppose an exporter expects to collect receivables totalling $1 million (U.S.) in 30 days. Suppose the present C$ exchange rate is $.85 (U.S.). If the rate remains at 85 cents, the exporter receives $1 million U.S./.85 = $1,176,470 (Can) after 30 days. The exporter is at risk if the exchange rate rises so that the $1 million (U.S.) buys fewer Canadian dollars. For example, if the exchange rate rises to .87, the exporter receives only $1 million U.S./.87 = $1,149,425 (Can). The loss of $27,045 comes out of profits.

Since the exporter loses if the the exchange rate rises, buying call options is an appropriate hedge. Calls on the C$ increase in value if the exchange rate rises. The profit on the calls helps offset the loss on exchange. To implement this strategy, the exporter likely seeks expert advice on how many calls to buy and, more generally, the relative cost of hedging with options rather than with forwards.

Long-Run Exposure

In the long run, the value of a foreign operation can fluctuate because of unanticipated changes in relative economic conditions. For example, imagine that we own a labor-intensive assembly operation located in another country to take advantage of lower wages. Through time, unexpected changes in economic conditions can raise the foreign wage levels to the point where the cost advantage is eliminated or even becomes negative.

Hedging long-run exposure is more difficult than hedging short-term risks. For one thing, organized forward markets don't exist for such long-term needs. Currency swaps can be arranged up to 15 years, but it is sometimes difficult to find a counterparty.

Instead, many firms try to match foreign currency inflows and outflows. The same thing goes for matching foreign currency-denominated assets and liabilities. For example, a firm that sells in a foreign country might try to concentrate its raw material purchases and labour expense in that country. That way, the dollar value of its revenues and costs move up and down together.

Similarly, a firm can reduce its long-run exchange risk by borrowing in the foreign country. Fluctuations in the value of the foreign subsidiary's assets are then at least partially offset by changes in the value of the liabilities.

Toyota took this approach and financed assembly plants in the United States in U.S. dollars during the early 1970s. Volkswagen also built plants in the United States but financed in deutsche marks. During the late 1970s, the U.S. dollar dropped against both the yen and deutsche mark. Toyota was unaffected on the financing side, but Volkswagen faced increased costs putting it at a disadvantage in selling low-end cars.

Translation Exposure

When a Canadian company calculates its accounting net income and EPS for some period, it must translate everything into dollars. This can create some problems for the accounts when there are significant foreign operations. In particular, two issues arise:

1. What is the appropriate exchange rate to use for translating each balance sheet account?

Andre Kleynhans on Managing Currency Transaction Risk at Nutri/System Ltd.

Nutri/System Ltd. is a business that offers a comprehensive weight loss solution to perennial dieters through food products, exercise, and behaviour modification counseling. In 1988, Nutri/System was sourcing a significant portion of its food product from the United States without any hedge of its exposure to the U.S. dollar. Of course, between July 1986 and late 1988, it had enjoyed the virtually unmitigated rise in the value of the Canadian dollar from the 70 cent level to around 83.5 cents, thereby escaping the negative impact of a falling dollar.

A strategic risk assessment, however, indicated the need for a hedging strategy in response to the following analysis:

Recognition that the company is exposed to U.S.$ transaction risk on its U.S.$ food purchases, which are made on a perpetual basis, as distinct from an isolated transaction basis.

Quantification of the adverse impact on the company's margins with every one cent rise in the U.S. dollar.

Recognition that a rise in costs can only be passed on in the form of price increases once every six months at best, with marketing considerations such as price points possibly precluding certain increases.

Recognition that Nutri/System is not in the business of taking significant foreign exchange positions, whether active or otherwise. This was a vital point of discussion, given that in an effort to avoid

"risk" in unfamiliar territory, executives often fail to recognize that by not actively managing their exposures, they are in effect taking a "position." In doing so, they incur significant risk in an incidental area of the business.

The objective of the exposure management strategy was to eliminate the risk of the impact of a falling Canadian dollar on the company's food margins.

With an assumption that prices could be adjusted every six months, the strategy required a hedge of the company's U.S.$ cash flows on a rolling six-month forward basis.

The simplest method of hedging the exposure would be through forward exchange contracts purchased from commercial banks. Of course, while guarding against falls in domestic currency, forward contacts preclude any participation in any subsequent rise in the currency hedged. Also due to the significant interest rate differential between Canada and the United States, a rolling six-month forward contract program would initially cost Nutri/System an average of 75 to 100 basis point premium over the current spot rates.

Ultimately Nutri/System engaged Toron Capital Markets to manage a "Dynamic Range Forward Fence" program that operates as follows:

American-style put and call options are simultaneously bought and sold in a band or "collar" or "fence" around the spot rate at the time contracts are entered into. Nutri/System therefore retains the

risk of currency movements within the fence. The program has several advantages:

The forward premium of 75 to 100 basis points inherent in forward contracts is avoided.

Some upside opportunity in currency movements is preserved, while limiting the downside risk to a level no lower than that upon which mark-ups are based.

The margin deposit required is generally only half of the credit line required by most banks. In addition, there is no requirement to provide financial statements.

Because the "Range Forward Fence" strategy was used as a superior means of hedging compared with forwards, it was logical that its performance should be measured against that alternative. For the first year of operation to February 1990, a significant benefit was measured with the Range Forward Fence program under this scale.

The use of American-style options in our range forward fence strategy lends prudence against opportunity in the management of Nutri/System's foreign exchange risk exposure.

Andre Kleynhans is vice president, finance of Nutri/Systems Ltd. He joined the company as director of finance in 1988, the beginning of the company's explosive growth from 45 retail centres to its current number in excess of 250. Kleyhans worked for a number of Canadian chartered banks in the area of corporate finance prior to joining Nutri/System. His comments here are excerpted, with permission, from the *Canadian Treasury Management Review,* November/December 1990, pp. 2–4.

2. How should balance sheet accounting gains and losses from foreign currency translation be handled?

To illustrate the accounting problem, suppose we started a small foreign subsidiary in Lilliputia a year ago. The local currency is the gulliver, abbreviated GL. At the beginning of the year, the exchange rate was GL 2 = $1Can, and the balance sheet in gullivers looked like this:

Assets	GL 1,000	Liabilities	GL 500
		Equity	500

At 2 gullivers to the dollar, the beginning balance sheet in dollars was:

Assets	$500	Liabilities	$250
		Equity	250

Lilliputia is a quiet place, and nothing at all actually happened during the year. As a result, net income was zero (before consideration of exchange rate changes). However, the exchange rate did change to 4 gullivers = $1 purely because the Lilliputian inflation rate is much higher than the U.S. inflation rate.

Since nothing happened, the accounting ending balance sheet in gullivers is the same as the beginning one. However, if we convert it to dollars at the new exchange rate, we get:

Assets	$250	Liabilities	$125
		Equity	125

Notice that the value of the equity has gone down by $125, even though net income was zero. Despite the fact that absolutely nothing really happened, there is a $125 accounting loss. How to handle this $125 loss has been a controversial accounting question.

One obvious and consistent way to handle this loss is simply to report the loss on the parent's income statement. During periods of volatile exchange rates, this kind of treatment can dramatically impact an international company's reported EPS. This is purely an accounting phenomenon; even so, such fluctuations are disliked by financial managers.

The current compromise approach to translation gains and losses is based on rules set out in Canadian Institute of Chartered Accountants (CICA) rule 1650. The rules divide a firm's foreign subsidiaries into two categories: integrated and self-sustaining. For the most part, the rules require that all assets and liabilities must be translated from the subsidiary's currency into the parent's currency using the exchange rate that currently prevails.[13] Because Canadian accountants consolidate the financial statements of subsidiaries more than 50 percent owned by the parent firm, translation gains and losses are reflected on the income statement of the parent company.

---

[13] The rules also define the current exchange rate differently for the types of subsidiaries. An integrated subsidiary uses the exchange rate observed on the last day of its fiscal year. For a self-sustaining subsidiary, the exchange rate prescribed is the average rate over the year. For detailed discussion of CICA 1650, see A. Davis and G. Pinches, *Canadian Financial Management,* 2nd ed. (New York: Harper Collins, 1991), pp. 684–86.

For a self-sustaining subsidiary, any translation gains and losses that occur are accumulated in a special account within the shareholder's equity section of the parent company's balance sheet. This account might be labelled something like "unrealized foreign exchange gains (losses)." These gains and losses are not reported on the income statement. As a result, the impact of translation gains and losses is not recognized explicitly in net income until the underlying assets and liabilities are sold or otherwise liquidated.

Managing Exchange Rate Risk

For a large multinational firm, the management of exchange rate risk is complicated by the fact that many different currencies may be involved in many different subsidiaries. It is very likely that a change in some exchange rate benefits some subsidiaries and hurts others. The net effect on the overall firm depends on its net exposure.

For example, suppose a firm has two divisions: Division A buys goods in Canada for dollars and sells them in Britain for pounds. Division B buys goods in Britain for pounds and sells them in Canada for dollars. If these two divisions are of roughly equal size in their inflows and outflows, the overall firm obviously has little exchange rate risk.

In our example, the firm's net position in pounds (the amount coming in less the amount going out) is small, so the exchange rate risk is small. However, if one division, acting on its own, were to start hedging its exchange rate risk, the overall firm's exchange risk would go up. The moral of the story is that multinational firms have to be conscious of the overall position that the firm has in a foreign currency. For this reason, exchange risk management is probably best handled on a centralized basis.

CONCEPT QUESTIONS
1. What are the different types of exchange rate risk?
2. How can a firm hedge short-run exchange rate risk? Long-run exchange rate risk?

22.8 | POLITICAL RISK

One final element of risk in international investing concerns **political risk**. Political risk refers to changes in value that arise as a consequence of political actions. This is not purely a problem faced by international firms. For example, changes in Canadian tax laws and regulations may benefit some Canadian firms and hurt others, so political risk exists nationally as well as internationally.

Some countries do have more political risk than others, however. In such cases, the extra political risk may lead firms to require higher returns on overseas investments to compensate for the risk that funds will be blocked, critical operations interrupted, and contracts abrogated. In the most extreme case, the possibility of outright confiscation may be a concern in countries with relatively unstable political environments.

Political risk also depends on the nature of the business; some businesses are less likely to be confiscated because they are not particularly valuable in the hands of a different owner. An assembly operation supplying subcomponents that only the parent company uses would not be an attractive takeover target, for example.

political risk
Risk related to changes in value that arise because of political actions.

Similarly, a manufacturing operation that requires the use of specialized components from the parent is of little value without the parent company's cooperation.

Natural resource developments, such as copper mining or oil drilling, are just the opposite. Once the operation is in place, much of the value is in the commodity. The political risk for such investments is much higher for this reason. Also, the issue of exploitation is more pronounced with such investments, again increasing the political risk.

Political risk can be hedged in several ways, particularly when confiscation or nationalization is a concern. The use of local financing, perhaps from the government of the foreign country in question, reduces the possible loss because the company can refuse to pay on the debt in the event of unfavourable political activities. Based on our previous discussion, structuring the operation so that it requires significant parent company involvement to function is another way some firms try to reduce political risk.

At the other extreme, some companies avoid the implicit threats in the methods just discussed while trying to be good corporate citizens in the host country. This approach is an international application of the view of the corporation as responsible to shareholders and stakeholders that we presented in Chapter 1.

> CONCEPT QUESTIONS
> 1. What is political risk?
> 2. What are some ways of hedging political risks?

22.9 | SUMMARY AND CONCLUSIONS

The international firm has a more complicated life than the purely domestic firm. Management must understand the connection between interest rates, foreign currency exchange rates, and inflation. It must also become aware of a large number of different financial market regulations and tax systems. This chapter is intended to be a concise introduction to some of the financial issues that come up in international investing.

Our coverage was necessarily brief. The main topics we discussed include:

1. Some basic vocabulary. We briefly defined some exotic terms such as *LIBOR, Eurodollar,* and *Belgian dentist.*

2. The basic mechanics of exchange rate quotations. We discussed the spot and forward markets and how exchange rates are interpreted.

3. The fundamental relationships between international financial variables:
   a. Absolute and relative purchasing power parity (PPP).
   b. Interest rate parity (IRP).
   c. Unbiased forward rates (UFR).

   Absolute purchasing power parity states that $1 should have the same purchasing power in each country. This means that an orange costs the same whether you buy it in Montreal or in Tokyo.

   Relative purchasing power parity means the expected percentage change in exchange rates between the currencies of two countries is equal to the difference in their inflation rates.

   Interest rate parity implies that the percentage difference between the forward exchange rate and the spot exchange rate is equal to the interest rate differential. We showed how covered interest arbitrage forces this relationship to hold.

The unbiased forward rates condition indicates that the current forward rate is a good predictor of the future spot exchange rate.

4. International capital budgeting. We showed that the basic foreign exchange relationships imply two other conditions:

  a. Uncovered interest parity.

  b. International Fisher effect.

  By invoking these two conditions, we learned how to estimate NPVs in foreign currencies and how to convert foreign currencies into dollars to estimate NPV in the usual way.

5. Exchange rate and political risk. We described the various types of exchange rate risk and discussed some commonly used approaches to managing the effect of fluctuating exchange rates on the cash flows and value of the international firm. We also discussed political risk and some ways of managing exposure to it.

Key Terms

Belgian dentist (page 806)

cross-rate (page 806)

Eurobond (page 806)

Eurocurrency (page 806)

foreign bonds (page 806)

gilts (page 806)

London Interbank Offer Rate (LIBOR) (page 806)

swaps (page 807)

Export Development Corporation (EDC) (page 807)

foreign exchange market (page 807)

exchange rate (page 808)

spot trade (page 812)

spot exchange rate (page 812)

forward trade (page 812)

forward exchange rate (page 812)

purchasing power parity (PPP) (page 813)

interest rate parity (IRP) (page 819)

unbiased forward rates (UFR) (page 820)

uncovered interest parity (UIP) (page 820)

international Fisher effect (IFE) (page 821)

Eurobanks (page 827)

Note Issuance Facility (NIF) (page 827)

exchange rate risk (page 828)

counterparty (page 829)

American options (page 829)

political risk (page 833)

Chapter Review Problems and Self-Test

22.1 Relative Purchasing Power Parity The inflation rate in Canada is projected at 6 percent per year for the next several years. The German inflation rate is projected to be 2 percent during that time. The exchange rate is currently DM 2.2. Based on relative PPP, what is the expected exchange rate in two years?

22.2 Covered Interest Arbitrage The spot and 12-month forward rates on the Swiss franc are SF 1.8 and SF 1.7, respectively. The risk-free interest rate in Canada is 8 percent, and the risk-free rate in Switzerland is 5 percent. Is there an arbitrage opportunity here? How would you exploit it?

Answers to Self-Test Problems

22.1   From relative PPP, the expected exchange rate in two years, $E[S_2]$ is:

$$E[S_2] = S_0 \times [1 + (h_G - h_{CDN})]^2$$

where h_G is the German inflation rate. The current exchange rate is DM 2.2, so the expected exchange rate is:

$$E[S_2] = DM\ 2.2 \times [1 + (.02 - .06)]^2$$
$$= DM\ 2.2 \times .96^2$$
$$= DM\ 2.03$$

22.2   From interest rate parity, the forward rate should be (approximately):

$$F_1 = S_0 \times [1 + (R_{FC} - R_{CDN})]$$
$$= 1.8 \times [1 + .05 - .08]$$
$$= 1.75$$

Since the forward rate is actually SF 1.7, there is an arbitrage opportunity.

To exploit the arbitrage, we first note that dollars are selling for SF 1.7 each in the forward market. From IRP, this is too cheap because they should be selling for SF 1.75. So we want to arrange to buy dollars with Swiss francs in the forward market. To do this, we can:

1. Today: Borrow, say, $10 million for 12 months. Convert it to SF 18 million in the spot market, and forward contract at SF 1.7 to convert it back to dollars in one year. Invest the SF 18 million at 5 percent.

2. In one year: Your investment has grown to SF 18 × 1.05 = SF 18.9 million. Convert this to dollars at the rate of SF 1.7 = $1. You have SF 18.9 million/1.7 = $11,117,647. Pay off your loan with 8 percent interest at a cost of $10 million × 1.08 = $10,800,000 and pocket the difference of $317,647.

Questions and Problems

Basic
(Questions 1–17)

1.   **Using Exchange Rates**   Take a look back at Table 22.2 to answer the following questions:

   a. If you have $100, how many Italian lira can you get?
   b. How much is one lira worth?
   c. If you have Lit 3 million (Lit stands for Italian lira), how many dollars do you have?
   d. Which is worth more: a New Zealand dollar or a Singapore dollar?
   e. Which is worth more: a Mexican peso or a Chilean peso?
   f. How many Swiss francs can you get for a Belgian franc? What do you call this rate?
   g. Per unit, which is the most valuable currency listed? The least valuable?

2.   **Using the Cross-Rate**   Use the information in Table 22.2 to answer the following questions:

   a. Which would you rather have, $100 or £100? Why?
   b. Which would you rather have, FF 100 or £100? Why?
   c. What is the cross-rate for French francs in terms of British pounds? For British pounds in terms of French francs?

3. **Forward Exchange Rates** Use the information in Table 22.2 to answer the following questions:

Basic
(Continued)

   a. What is the 180-day forward rate for the Japanese yen in yen per U.S. dollar? Is the yen selling at a premium or a discount? Explain.
   b. What is the 90-day forward rate for German deutsche marks in U.S. dollars per deutsche mark? Is the dollar selling at a premium or a discount? Explain.
   c. What do you think will happen to the value of the dollar relative to the yen and the deutsche mark, based on the information in the table? Explain.

4. **Using Spot and Forward Exchange Rates** Suppose the spot U.S./Canada exchange rate is $1.30 and the 180-day forward rate is Can$1.25.

   a. Which is worth more, a U.S. dollar or a Canadian dollar?
   b. Assuming absolute PPP holds, what is the cost in the United States of an Elkhead beer if the price in Canada is Can$1.95? Why might the beer actually sell at a different price in the United States from the price you found in (a)?
   c. Is the U.S. dollar selling at a premium or a discount relative to the Canadian dollar?
   d. Which currency is expected to appreciate in value?
   e. Which country do you think has higher interest rates—the United States or Canada? Explain.

5. **Spot versus Forward Rates** Suppose the exchange rate for the Swiss franc is quoted as SFr 1.50 on the spot market and SFr 1.53 in the 90-day forward market.

   a. Is the dollar selling at a premium or a discount relative to the franc?
   b. Does the financial market expect the franc to strengthen relative to the dollar? Explain.
   c. What do you suspect is true about relative economic conditions in the United States and Switzerland?

6. **Cross-Rates and Arbitrage** Suppose the Japanese yen exchange rate is ¥120 = $1, and the British pound exchange rate is £1 = $1.50.

   a. What is the cross-rate of ¥ per £?
   b. Suppose the cross-rate is ¥175 = £1. Is there an arbitrage opportunity here? If there is, explain how to take advantage of the mispricing.

7. **Inflation and Exchange Rates** Suppose the rate of inflation in Germany will run about 3 percent higher than the Canadian inflation rate over the next several years. All other things the same, what will happen to the deutsche mark versus dollar exchange rate? What relationship are you relying on in answering?

8. **Changes in Interest Rates and Inflation** The exchange rate for the Australian dollar is currently A$1.40. This exchange is expected to rise by 10 percent over the next year.

   a. Is the Australian dollar expected to get stronger or weaker?
   b. What do you think about the relative inflation rates in the United States and Australia?
   c. What do you think about the relative nominal interest rates in the United States and Australia? Relative real rates?

9. **Foreign Bonds** Which of the following most accurately describes a Yankee bond?

      a. A bond issued by General Motors in Japan with the interest payable in U.S. dollars.

      b. A bond issued by General Motors in Japan with the interest payable in yen.

      c. A bond issued by Toyota in the United States with the interest payable in yen.

      d. A bond issued by Toyota in the United States with the interest payable in dollars.

      e. A bond issued by Toyota worldwide with the interest payable in dollars.

10. **Interest Rate Parity**   Use Table 22.2 to answer the following questions. Suppose interest rate parity holds, and the current 6-month risk-free rate in Canada is 4 percent. What must the 6-month risk-free rate be in France? In Japan? In Switzerland?

11. **Interest Rates and Arbitrage**   The treasurer of a major Canadian firm has $12 million to invest for three months. The annual interest rate in Canada is 0.75 percent per month. The interest rate in Great Britain is 1 percent per month. The spot exchange rate is £0.60, and the three-month forward rate is £0.62. Ignoring transactions costs, in which country would the treasurer want to invest the company's funds? Why?

12. **Inflation and Exchange Rates**   Suppose the current exchange rate for the French franc is FF 5. The expected exchange rate in four years is FF 4. What is the difference in the annual inflation rates for Canada and France over this period? Assume the anticipated rate is constant for both countries. What relationship are you relying on in answering?

13. **Exchange Rate Risk**   Suppose your company imports computer modems from South Korea. The exchange rate is given in Table 22.2. You have just placed an order for 60,000 modems at a cost to you of 81,915 won each. You will pay for the shipment when it arrives in 90 days. You can sell the modems for $170 each. Calculate your profit if the exchange rate goes up or down by 10 percent over the next 90 days. What is the break-even exchange rate? What percentage rise or fall does this represent in terms of the South Korean won versus the dollar?

14. **Exchange Rates and Arbitrage**   Suppose the spot and 180-day forward rates on the deutsche mark are DM 1.70 and DM 1.75, respectively. The annual risk-free rate in Canada is 7 percent, and the annual risk-free rate in Germany is 9 percent.

      a. Is there an arbitrage opportunity here? If so, how would you exploit it?

      b. What must the 180-day forward rate be to prevent arbitrage?

15. **International Fisher Effect**   You observe that the inflation rate in the United States is 4 percent per year and that T-bills currently yield 5 percent annually. What do you estimate the inflation rate to be in:

      a. The Netherlands, if short-term Dutch government securities yield 7 percent per year?

      b. Canada, if short-term Canadian government securities yield 9 percent per year?

      c. France, if short-term French government securities yield 12 percent per year?

16. **Spot versus Forward Rates**   Suppose the spot and 90-day forward rates for the yen are ¥110 and ¥109, respectively.

      a. Is the yen expected to get stronger or weaker?

      b. What would you estimate is the difference between the inflation rates of Canada and Japan?

17. **Expected Spot Rates** Suppose the spot exchange rate for the Hungarian forint is HUF 100. Interest rates in Canada are 5 percent per year. They are quadruple that in Hungary. What do you predict the exchange rate will be in one year? In two years? In five years? What relationship are you using?

Basic
(Continued)

18. **Economic Conditions and Exchange Rates** Are the following statements true or false? Explain why.

Intermediate
(Questions 18–21)

  a. If the general price index in Great Britain rises faster than that in Canada, we would expect the pound to appreciate relative to the dollar.

  b. Suppose you are a German machine tool exporter and you invoice all of your sales in foreign currency. Further suppose the German monetary authorities begin an expansionary monetary policy. If it is certain that the easy money policy will result in higher inflation rates in Germany relative to other countries, then you should use the forward markets to protect yourself against future losses resulting from the deterioration in the value of the deutsche mark.

  c. If you could accurately estimate differences in relative inflation rates between two countries over a long period of time, while other market participants were unable to do so, you could successfully speculate in spot currency markets.

19. **Economic Policy and Exchange Rates** Some countries often encourage movements in their exchange rate relative to some other country as a short-term means of addressing foreign trade imbalances. For each of the scenarios below, evaluate the impact the announced policy change would have on a Canadian importer and a Canadian exporter doing business with the foreign country.

  a. Officials in the Canadian government announce they are comfortable with a rising deutsche mark relative to the dollar.

  b. British monetary authorities announce they feel the pound has been driven too low by currency speculators relative to its value against the dollar.

  c. The Irish government announces it will devalue the punt in an effort to stay in line with the ECU.

  d. The Brazilian government announces it will print billions of new cruzeiros and inject them into the economy, in an effort to reduce the country's 40 percent unemployment rate.

20. **International Relationships** We discussed five international capital market relationships: relative PPP, IRP, UFR, UIP, and the international Fisher effect. Which of these do you expect to hold most closely? Which do you think would be most likely to be violated?

21. **Capital Budgeting** You are evaluating a proposed expansion of an existing subsidiary located in Switzerland. The cost of the expansion would be SFr 15.75 million. The cash flows from the project would be SFr 5 million for the next four years. The dollar required return is 11 percent per year, and the current exchange rate is SFr 2.25. The going rate on Eurodollars is 8 percent per year. It is 5 percent per year on Euroswiss.

  a. What do you project will happen to exchange rates over the next four years?

  b. Based on your answer in (*a*), convert the projected franc flows into dollar flows and calculate the NPV.

  c. What is the required return on franc flows? Based on your answer, calculate the NPV in francs and then convert to dollars.

22.   **Using the Exact International Fisher Effect**   From our discussion of the Fisher effect in Chapter 10, we know that the actual relationship between a nominal rate, R, a real rate, r, and an inflation rate, h, can be written as:

$$1 + r = (1 + R)/(1 + h)$$

This is the *domestic* Fisher effect.

a. What is the nonapproximate form of the international Fisher effect?

b. Based on your answer in (a), what is the exact form for UIP? (Hint: recall the exact form of IRP and use UFR.)

c. What is the exact form for relative PPP? (Hint: combine your previous two answers.)

d. Recalculate the NPV for the Kihlstrom drill bit project (discussed in Section 22.5) using the exact forms for UIP and the international Fisher effect. Verify that you get precisely the same answer either way.

Suggested Readings

The following are good books on the modern theory of international markets:

Grabbe, J. O. *International Financial Markets*. New York: Elsevier-North Holland Publishing, 1986.

Levi, M. *International Finance*. New York: McGraw-Hill, 1983.

These two articles describe budgeting for international projects:

Lessard, D. R. "Evaluating Foreign Projects: An Adjusted Present Value Approach." In *International Financial Management,* ed. D. R. Lessard. New York: Warren, Gorham & Lamont, 1979.

Shapiro, A. S. "Capital Budgeting for the Multinational Corporation." *Financial Management* 7 (Spring 1978).

For more information on the relationship between the forward rate and the spot rate, see:

Levich, Richard M. "Is the Foreign Exchange Market Efficient?" *Oxford Review of Economic Policy* 5, no. 3 (1989).

Mussa, Michael. "Empirical Regularities in the Behavior of Exchange Rates and Theories of the Foreign Exchange Market." In *Policies for Employment, Prices and Exchange Rates,* eds. K. Bruner and A. Meltzer. Carnegie-Rochester Conference 11. Amsterdam: North-Holland, 1979.

For an up-to-date discussion of short- and intermediate-term Euromarkets see:

Melnik, A. L., and S. E. Plaut. *The Short-Term Eurocredit Market*. New York: New York University Salomon Center, 1991.

Leasing

Leasing is a way businesses finance plant, property, and equipment. Just about any asset that can be purchased can be leased. Computers and communications equipment make up the largest sector of equipment leasing in Canada. Next comes aircraft leases—big-ticket items ranging to $200 million for a 747. Leasing is popular in financing furniture and fixtures, manufacturing, transportation, and construction equipment.[1]

Although corporations do both short-term leasing and long-term leasing, this chapter is primarily concerned with long-term leasing, where long-term typically means more than five years. As we discuss in greater detail shortly, leasing an asset on a long-term basis is much like borrowing the needed funds and simply buying the asset. Thus, long-term leasing is a form of financing much like long-term debt. When is leasing preferable to long-term borrowing? This is the question we seek to answer in this chapter.[2]

23.1 | LEASES AND LEASE TYPES

A lease is a contractual agreement between two parties: the lessee and the lessor. The **lessee** is the user of the equipment; the **lessor** is the owner. Typically, a company first decides on the asset that it needs. Then it must decide how to finance the asset. If the firm decides to lease, it then negotiates a lease contract with a lessor for use of that asset. The lease agreement establishes that the lessee has the right to use the asset and, in return, must make periodic payments to the lessor, the owner of the asset. The lessor is usually either the asset's manufacturer or an independent leasing company. If the lessor is an independent leasing company, it must buy the asset from a manufacturer. The lessor then delivers the asset to the lessee, and the lease goes into effect. Some lessors play both roles. Xerox Canada Inc., for example, leases its own copying machines and also leases aircraft to Air Canada and Canadian Airlines International.

lessee

The user of an asset in a leasing agreement. Lessee makes payments to lessor.

lessor

The owner of an asset in a leasing agreement. Lessor receives payments from the lessee.

---

[1] Laura Ramsay, "Recession Adds Reason to Lease Your Equipment," *Financial Post,* November 25, 1991, p. 20.

[2] Our discussion of lease valuation is drawn, in part, from Chapter 22 of S. A. Ross, R. W. Westerfield, and J. F. Jaffe, *Corporate Finance,* 2nd ed. (Homewood, IL: Richard D. Irwin, 1990), which contains a more comprehensive treatment and discusses some subtle, but important, issues not covered here.

F I G U R E 23.1 | *Buying versus leasing*

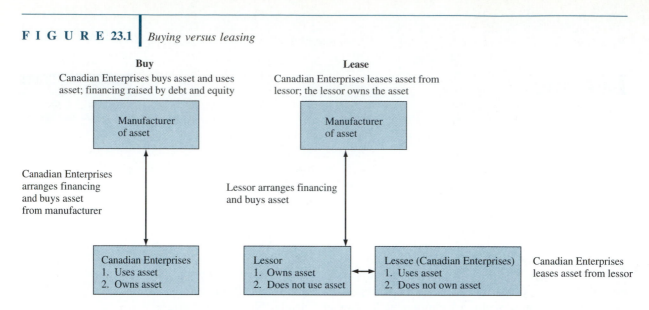

If Canadian Enterprises buys the asset, it owns the asset and uses it. If Canadian Enterprises leases the asset, the lessor owns it, but Canadian Enterprises still uses it as the lessee.

Leasing versus Buying

As far as the lessee is concerned, it is the use of the asset that is important, not necessarily who has title to it. One way to obtain the use of an asset is to lease it. Another way is obtain outside financing and buy it. Thus, the decision to lease or buy amounts to a comparison of alternative financing arrangements for the use of an asset.

You may think of leasing analysis as an extension of the capital budgeting decision. The lessee has already done capital budgeting analysis and found that buying the asset has a positive NPV. Leasing analysis investigates whether acquiring the use of the asset through leasing is better still.

Figure 23.1 compares leasing and buying. The lessee, Canadian Enterprises, might be a hospital, a law firm, or any other firm that uses computers. The lessor is an independent leasing company that purchased the computer from a manufacturer such as Hewlett-Packard Company (HP). Leases of this type, where the leasing company purchases the asset from the manufacturer, are called *direct leases*. Of course, HP might choose to lease its own computers, and many companies have set up wholly owned subsidiaries called *captive finance companies* to lease out their products.[3]

As shown in Figure 23.1, Canadian Enterprises ends up using the asset either way. The key difference is that in the case of buying, Canadian Enterprises arranges the financing, purchases the asset, and holds title to the asset. In the case of leasing, the leasing company arranges the financing, purchases the asset, and holds title to it.

---

[3] Captive finance companies (or subsidiaries) may do a number of other things, such as purchase the parent company's accounts receivable. General Motors Acceptance Corporation (GMAC) and GE Capital are examples of captive finance companies. We discuss captive finance companies in Chapter 19.

Operating Leases

Years ago, a lease where the lessee received an equipment operator along with the equipment was called an **operating lease**. Today, an operating lease (or service lease) is difficult to define precisely, but this form of leasing has several important characteristics.

First, with an operating lease, the payments received by the lessor are usually not enough to fully recover the cost of the asset. A primary reason is that operating leases are often relatively short-term. In such cases, the life of the lease can be much less than the economic life of the asset. For example, if you lease a car for two years, the car has a substantial residual value at the end of the lease, and the lease payments you make would pay off only a fraction of the original cost of the car.

A second characteristic is that an operating lease frequently requires that the lessor maintain the asset. The lessor is also responsible for any taxes or insurance. Of course, these costs would be passed on, at least in part to the lessee in the form of higher lease payments.

The third, and perhaps most interesting, feature of an operating lease is the cancellation option. This option gives the lessee the right to cancel the lease contract before the expiration date. If the option to cancel is exercised, the lessee returns the equipment to the lessor and ceases to make payments. The value of a cancellation clause depends on whether technological and/or economic conditions are likely to make the value of the asset to the lessee less than the value of the future lease payments under the lease.

To leasing practitioners, these three characteristics constitute an operating lease. However, as we see shortly, accountants use the term in a somewhat different way.

operating lease
Usually a shorter-term lease where the lessor is responsible for insurance, taxes, and upkeep. Often cancellable on short notice.

Financial Leases

Financial leases are the other major type of lease. In contrast to an operating lease, the payments made under a financial lease are usually sufficient to cover fully the lessor's cost of purchasing the asset and pay the lessor a return on the investment. For this reason, a financial lease is sometimes said to be a fully amortized or full-payout lease whereas an operating lease is said to be partially amortized.

For both operating and financial leases, formal legal ownership of the leased asset resides with the lessor. However, in terms of economic function, we see that the lessee enjoys the risk/reward of ownership in a financial lease. Operating leases, on the other hand, are more like a rental agreement.

With a financial lease, the lessee (not the lessor) is usually responsible for insurance, maintenance, and taxes. Importantly, a financial lease generally cannot be cancelled, at least not without a significant penalty. In other words, the lessee must make the lease payments or face possible legal action.

The characteristics of a financial lease, particularly the fact it is fully amortized, make it very similar to debt financing, so the name is a sensible one. Two special types of financial leases are of particular interest, *sale and leaseback* agreements and *leveraged leases*. We consider these next.

financial lease
Typically, a longer-term, fully amortized lease under which the lessee is responsible for upkeep. Usually not cancellable without penalty.

Sale and Leaseback Agreements   A sale and leaseback occurs when a company sells an asset it owns to another firm and immediately leases it back. In a sale and leaseback, two things happen:

1. The lessee receives cash from the sale of the asset.
2. The lessee continues to use the asset.

sale and leaseback

A financial lease in which the lessee sells an asset to the lessor and then leases it back.

An example of a **sale and leaseback** occurred in January 1989 when Air Canada arranged a sale and leaseback of four Boeing 767-200ER aircraft. The purchaser was a Canadian financial institution and the transaction proceeds were $260 million. Further examples include Canadian universities and hospitals that set up sale-leaseback deals for library books and medical equipment.[4] With a sale and leaseback, the lessee may have the option of repurchasing the leased assets at the end of the lease.

leveraged lease

A financial lease where the lessor borrows a substantial fraction of the cost of the leased asset.

Leveraged Leases A **leveraged lease** is a tax-oriented lease involving three parties: a lessee, a lessor, and a lender. A typical arrangement might go as follows:

1. The lessee selects the asset, gets the value of using the asset, and makes the periodic lease payments.
2. The lessor usually puts up no more than 40 to 50 percent of the financing, is entitled to the lease payments, has title to the asset, and pays interest to the lenders.
3. The lenders supply the remaining financing and receive interest payments. Thus, the arrangement on the right side of Figure 23.1 would be a leveraged lease if the bulk of the financing were supplied by creditors.

The lenders in a leveraged lease typically use a non-recourse loan. This means the lender cannot turn to the lessor in case of a default. However, the lender is protected in two ways:

1. The lender has a first lien on the asset.
2. The lender may actually receive the lease payments from the lessee. The lender deducts the principal and interest due, and forwards whatever is left to the lessor.

Leveraged leases make the most sense when the lessee is not in a position to use tax credits or capital cost allowance (CCA) deductions that come with owning the asset. By arranging for someone else to hold title, a leveraged lease passes these benefits on. The lessee can benefit because the lessor may return a portion of the tax benefits to the lessee in the form of lower lease costs.

CONCEPT QUESTIONS

1. What are the specific differences between an operating lease and a financial lease?
2. What is a sale and leaseback agreement?

23.2 | ACCOUNTING AND LEASING

Before 1979, leasing was frequently called *off balance sheet financing*. As the name implies, a firm could arrange to use an asset through a lease and not disclose the existence of the lease contract on the balance sheet. Lessees only had to report information on leasing activity in the footnotes of their financial statements.

Of course, this meant firms could acquire the use of a substantial number of assets and incur a substantial long-term financial commitment through financial

---

[4] Tax changes have subsequently restricted sale-leasebacks and we discuss this later. "Report on Business," *Globe and Mail,* January 9, 1989, p. B2; and Barry Critchley and Brian Baxter, "Why the SLB Ban?" *Financial Post,* April 28, 1989, p. B6.

T A B L E 23.1

Leasing and the balance sheet

1. *Initial balance sheet (the company buys a $100,000 truck with debt)*

Truck	$100,000	Debt	$100,000
Other assets	100,000	Equity	100,000
Total assets	$200,000	Total debt plus equity	$200,000

2. *Operating lease (the company has an operating lease for the truck)*

Truck	$ 0	Debt	$ 0
Other assets	100,000	Equity	100,000
Total assets	$100,000	Total debt plus equity	$100,000

3. *Capital (financial) lease (the company has a capital lease for the truck)*

Assets under capital lease	$100,000	Obligations under capital lease	$100,000
Other assets	100,000	Equity	100,000
Total assets	$200,000	Total debt plus equity	$200,000

In the first case, a $100,000 truck is purchased with debt. In the second case, an operating lease is used; no balance sheet entries are created. In the third case, a capital (financial) lease is used; the lease payments are capitalized as a liability, and the leased truck appears as an asset.

leases while not disclosing the impact of these arrangements in their financial statements. Operating leases, being cancellable at little or no penalty, do not involve a firm financial commitment. So operating leases did not generate much concern about complete disclosure. As a result, the accounting profession wanted to distinguish clearly between operating and financial leases to ensure that the impact of financial leases was included in the financial statements.

In 1979, the Canadian Institute of Chartered Accountants implemented new rules for lease accounting (CICA 3065). The basic idea is that all financial leases (called *capital leases* in CICA 3065) must be capitalized. This requirement means that the present value of the lease payments must be calculated and reported along with debt and other liabilities on the right side of the lessee's balance sheet.[5] The same amount must be shown as an asset on the left side of the balance sheet. Operating leases are not disclosed on the balance sheet. We discuss exactly what constitutes a financial or operating lease for accounting purposes next.

The accounting implications of CICA 3065 are illustrated in Table 23.1. Imagine a firm that has $100,000 in assets and no debt, implying that the equity is also $100,000. The firm needs a truck that costs $100,000 (it's a big truck), that it can lease or buy. The top of the table shows the balance sheet assuming that the firm borrows the money and buys the truck.

If the firm leases the truck, one of two things happen: If the lease is an operating lease, the balance sheet looks like the one in the center of the table. In this case, neither the asset (the truck) nor the liability (the lease payments) appear. If the lease is a capital (financial) lease, the balance sheet would look like the one at the bottom of the table, where the truck is shown as an asset and the present value of the lease payments is shown as a liability.

---

[5] The income statement is also affected. The asset created is amortized over the lease life and reported income is adjusted downward.

As we discussed earlier, it is difficult, if not impossible, to give a precise definition of what constitutes a financial or operating lease. For accounting purposes, a lease is declared to be a financial lease, and must therefore be disclosed, if at least one of the following criteria is met:

1. The lease transfers ownership of the property to the lessee by the end of the term of the lease.
2. The lessee has an option to purchase the asset at a price below fair market value (bargain purchase price option) when the lease expires.
3. The lease term is 75 percent or more of the estimated economic life of the asset.
4. The present value of the lease payments is at least 90 percent of the fair market value of the asset at the start of the lease.

If one or more of the four criteria is met, the lease is a capital lease; otherwise, it is an operating lease for accounting purposes.

A firm might be tempted to try and cook the books by taking advantage of the somewhat arbitrary distinction between operating leases and capital leases. Suppose a trucking firm wants to lease the $100,000 truck in our example in Table 23.1. The truck is expected to last for 15 years. A (perhaps unethical) financial manager could try to negotiate a lease contract for 10 years with lease payments having a present value of $89,000. These terms would get around criteria 3 and 4. If criteria 1 and 2 are similarly circumvented, the arrangement would be an operating lease and would not show up on the balance sheet.

There are several alleged benefits to hiding financial leases. One of the advantages to keeping leases off the balance sheet has to do with fooling financial analysts, creditors, and investors. The idea is that if leases are not on the balance sheet, they would not be noticed.

Financial managers who devote substantial effort to keeping leases off the balance sheet are probably wasting time. Of course, if leases are not on the balance sheet, traditional measures of financial leverage, such as the ratio of total debt to total assets, understates the true degree of financial leverage. As a consequence, the balance sheet appears stronger than it really is, but it seems unlikely that this type of manipulation could mislead many people.

CONCEPT QUESTIONS

1. For accounting purposes, what constitutes a capital lease?
2. How are capital leases reported?

23.3 | TAXES, REVENUE CANADA, AND LEASES

The lessee can deduct lease payments for income tax purposes if the lease is qualified by Revenue Canada. The tax shields associated with lease payments are critical to the economic viability of a lease, so Revenue Canada guidelines are an important consideration. Tax rules on leasing have changed considerably in the last few years and further changes may occur. The discussion that follows gives you a good idea of rules in force at the time of writing.

Essentially, Revenue Canada requires that a lease be primarily for business purposes and not merely for tax avoidance. In particular, Revenue Canada is on the lookout for leases that are really conditional sales agreements in disguise. The reason is that, in a lease, the lessee gets a tax deduction on the full lease payment. In a conditional sales agreement, only the interest portion of the payment is deductible. When Revenue Canada detects one or more of the following, it disallows the lease:[6]

1. The lessee automatically acquires title to the property after payment of a specified amount in the form of rentals.
2. The lessee is required to buy the property from the lessor during or at the termination of the lease.
3. The lessee has the right during or at the expiration of the lease to acquire the property at a price less than fair market value.

These rules also apply to sale-leaseback agreements. Revenue Canada auditors rule that a sale-leaseback is really a secured loan if they find one of the three terms in the sale-leaseback agreement.

Once leases are qualified for tax purposes, lessors still must be aware of further tax regulations limiting their use of CCA tax shields on leased assets. Current regulations allow lessors to deduct CCA from leasing income only. Any unused CCA tax shields cannot be passed along to other companies owned by the same parent holding company.

In addition, the 1989 federal budget introduced rules to reduce the tax advantages of sale-leaseback. The new rules place strict limits on a lessor's CCA write-offs on expensive assets such as aircraft. As a result, Canadian air carriers are turning to foreign financial institutions for lease financing for their new generation of aircraft.[7] In addition, the 1989 budget also practically ended sale-leasebacks by non-profit institutions such as universities and hospitals.

CONCEPT QUESTIONS
1. Why is Revenue Canada concerned about leasing?
2. What are some of the standards Revenue Canada uses in evaluating a lease?

23.4 | THE CASH FLOWS FROM LEASING

To begin our analysis of the leasing decision, we need to identify the relevant cash flows. The first part of this section illustrates how this is done. A key point, and one to watch for, is that taxes are a very important consideration in a lease analysis.

The Incremental Cash Flows

Consider the business decision facing TransCanada Distributors, a distribution firm that runs a fleet of company cars for its sales staff. Business has been expanding and the firm needs 50 additional cars to provide basic transportation in support of sales. The type of car required can be purchased wholesale for $10,000. TransCanada has determined that each car can be expected to generate an additional $6,000 per year in added sales for the next five years.

TransCanada has a corporate tax rate (combined federal and provincial) of 40 percent. The cars would qualify for a CCA rate of 40 percent (as rental cars) and, due

[6] For more details on these conditions, see Revenue Canada Interpretation Bulletin No. IT233R (1983) and updates.
[7] David Wagner, "Lessors Will Likely Take Changes in Stride," *Financial Post,* March 20, 1990, p. 18, and Laura Ramsay, "Canadian Aircraft Lessors Grounded by Tax Changes," *Financial Post,* April 6, 1990, p. 16.

to the hard-driving habits of TransCanada's sales staff, the cars would have no residual value after five years. Financial Lease Company has offered to lease the cars to TransCanada for lease payments of $2,500 per year for each car over the five-year period. Lease payments are made at the beginning of the year. With the lease, TransCanada would remain responsible for maintenance, insurance, and operating expenses.

Susan Smart has been asked to compare the direct incremental cash flows from leasing the cars to the cash flows associated with buying them. The first thing she realizes is that, because TransCanada has the cars either way, the $6,000 saving is realized whether the cars are leased or purchased. Thus, this cost saving, and any other operating costs or revenues, can be ignored in the analysis because they are not incremental.

On reflection, Smart concludes that there are only three important cash flow differences between leasing and buying:[8]

1. If the cars are leased, TransCanada must make a lease payment of $2,500 each year. However, lease payments are fully tax deductible, so there is a tax shield of $1,000 on each lease payment. The aftertax lease payment is $2,500 − $1,000 = $1,500. This is a cost of leasing instead of buying.[9]

2. If the cars are leased, TransCanada does not own them and cannot depreciate them for tax purposes.

Table 23.2 shows the CCA and UCC schedule for one car. Notice that Revenue Canada's half-year rule means that the eligible UCC is only $5,000 when the car is put in use in Year 0. Table 23.2 also shows the tax shield on CCA for each year. For example, in Year 0, the tax shield is $2,000 × .40 = $800. The tax shields for years 1–4 are calculated in the same way. In Year 5, the car is scrapped for a zero salvage value. We assume that the asset pool is closed at this time, so there is a tax shield on the terminal loss of $1,037 × .40 = $415.[10] All these tax shields are lost to TransCanada if it leases so they are a cost of leasing.

3. If the cars are leased, TransCanada does not have to spend $10,000 apiece today to buy them. This is a benefit to leasing.

	Year	UCC	CCA	Tax Shields
T A B L E 23.2	0	$5,000	$2,000	$ 800
	1	8,000	3,200	1,280
Tax shield on CCA for	2	4,800	1,920	768
car	3	2,880	1,152	461
	4	1,728	691	276
	5	1,037		415

---

[8] There is a fourth consequence that we do not discuss here. If the car has a non-trivial salvage value and we lease, we give up that salvage value. This is another cost of leasing instead of buying.

[9] Lease payments are made at the beginning of the year as shown in Table 23.3. Firms pay taxes later but our analysis ignores this difference for simplicity.

[10] If the pool were continued, the remaining UCC of $1,037 would be depreciated to infinity as explained in Chapter 2.

	Year						TABLE 23.3
	0	1	2	3	4	5	
Investment	$10,000						*Incremental cash flows for TransCanada from leasing one car instead of buying*
Lease payment	−2,500	−$ 2,500	−$2,500	−$2,500	$2,500		
Payment shield	1,000	1,000	1,000	1,000	1,000		
Forgone tax shield	−800	−1,280	−768	−461	−276	−$415	
Total cash flow	$ 7,700	−$ 2,780	−$2,268	−$1,961	−$1,776	−$415	

The cash flows from leasing instead of buying are summarized in Table 23.3. Notice that the cost of the car shows up with a positive sign in Year 0. This is a reflection of the fact that TransCanada saves $10,000 by leasing instead of buying.

A Note on Taxes   Susan Smart has assumed that TransCanada can use the tax benefits of the CCA allowances and the lease payments. This may not always be the case. If TransCanada were losing money, it would not pay taxes and the tax shelters would be worthless (unless they could be shifted to someone else). As we mentioned, this is one circumstance under which leasing may make a great deal of sense. If this were the case, the relevant lines in Table 23.3 would have to be changed to reflect a zero tax rate. We return to this point later.

> CONCEPT QUESTIONS
> 1. What are the cash flow consequences of leasing instead of buying?
> 2. Explain why the $10,000 in Table 23.3 has a positive sign.

23.5 | LEASE OR BUY?

From our discussion thus far, Smart's analysis comes down to this: If TransCanada Distributors leases instead of buying, it saves $10,000 today because it avoids having to pay for the car, but it must give up the cash outflows detailed in Table 23.3 in exchange. We now must decide whether getting $10,000 today and then paying back these cash flows is a good idea.

A Preliminary Analysis

Suppose TransCanada were to borrow $10,000 today and promise to make aftertax payments of the cash flows shown in Table 23.3 over the next five years. This is essentially what the firm does when it leases instead of buying. What interest rate would TransCanada be paying on this "loan"? Going back to Chapter 7, we need to find the unknown rate that solves the following equation:

$$0 = 7,700 - \frac{2,780}{1 + i} - \frac{2,268}{(1 + i)^2} - \frac{1,961}{(1 + i)^3} - \frac{1,776}{(1 + i)^4} - \frac{415}{(1 + i)^5}$$

The equation may be solved by trial and error on a Lotus 1-2-3 spreadsheet to show that the discount rate is 7.8 percent aftertax.

The cash flows of our hypothetical loan are identical to the cash flows from leasing instead of borrowing, and what we have illustrated is that when TransCanada leases the car, it effectively arranges financing at an aftertax rate of 7.8 percent.

Whether this is a good deal or not depends on what rate TransCanada would pay if it simply borrowed the money. For example, suppose the firm can arrange a five-year loan with its bank at a rate of 11 percent. Should TransCanada sign the lease or should it go with the bank?

Because TransCanada is in a 40 percent tax bracket, the aftertax interest rate would be $11 \times (1 - .40) = 6.6$ percent. This is less than the 7.8 percent implicit aftertax rate on the lease. In this particular case, TransCanada is better off borrowing the money because it gets a better rate.

We have seen that TransCanada should buy instead of lease. The steps in our analysis can be summarized as follows:

1. Calculate the incremental aftertax cash flows from leasing instead of borrowing.
2. Use these cash flows to calculate the implicit aftertax interest rate on the lease.
3. Compare this rate to the company's aftertax borrowing cost and choose the cheaper source of financing.

The most important thing about our discussion thus far is that in evaluating a lease, the relevant rate for the comparison is the company's aftertax borrowing rate. The fundamental reason is that the alternative to leasing is long-term borrowing, so the aftertax borrowing rate on such borrowing is the relevant benchmark.

Three Potential Pitfalls   There are three potential problems with the implicit rate on the lease that we calculated: First, this rate can be interpreted as the internal rate of return (IRR) on the decision to lease instead of buy, but doing so can be confusing. To see why, notice that the IRR from leasing is 7.8 percent, which is greater than TransCanada's aftertax borrowing cost of 6.6 percent. Normally, the higher the IRR the better, but we decided that leasing was a bad idea here. The reason is that the cash flows are not conventional; the first cash flow is positive and the rest are negative, which is just the opposite of the conventional case (see Chapter 7 for a discussion). With this cash flow pattern, the IRR represents the rate we pay, not the rate we earn, so the lower the IRR the better.

A second, and related, potential pitfall is that we calculated the advantage of leasing instead of borrowing. We could have done just the opposite and come up with the advantage to borrowing instead of leasing. If we did this, the cash flows would be the same, but the signs would be reversed. The IRR would be the same. Now, however, the cash flows are conventional, so we interpret the 7.8 percent IRR as saying that borrowing is better.

The third potential problem is that our implicit rate is based on the net cash flows of leasing instead of borrowing. There is another rate that is sometimes calculated that is just based on the lease payments. If we wanted to, we could note that the lease provides $10,000 in financing and requires five payments of $2,500 each. It is tempting to determine an implicit rate based on these numbers, but the resulting rate is not meaningful for making lease versus buy decisions because it ignores the CCA tax shields. It should not be confused with the implicit return on leasing instead of borrowing.

Perhaps because of these potential confusions, the IRR approach we have outlined thus far is not as widely used as an NPV-based approach that we describe next.

NPV Analysis

Now that we know the relevant rate for evaluating a lease versus buy decision is the firm's aftertax borrowing cost, an NPV analysis is straightforward. We simply discount the cash flows in Table 23.3 back to the present at TransCanada's borrowing rate of 6.6 percent as follows:

$$NPV = \$7,700 - \frac{2,780}{(1.066)} - \frac{2,268}{(1.066)^2} - \frac{1,961}{(1.066)^3} - \frac{1,776}{(1.066)^4} - \frac{415}{(1.066)^5} = -\$199$$

The NPV from leasing instead of buying is −$199, verifying our earlier conclusion that leasing is a bad idea. Once again, notice the signs of the cash flows; the first is positive, the rest are negative. The NPV that we have computed here is often called the **net advantage to leasing** and abbreviated NAL. Surveys indicate that the NAL approach is the most popular means of lease analysis in the business world.

net advantage to leasing (NAL)
The NPV of the decision to lease an asset instead of buying it.

A Misconception

In our lease versus buy analysis, it looks as if we ignored the fact that if TransCanada borrows $10,000 to buy the car, it has to repay the money with interest. In fact, we reasoned that if TransCanada leased the car, it would be better off by $10,000 today because it wouldn't have to pay for the car. It is tempting to argue that if TransCanada borrowed the money, it wouldn't have to come up with the $10,000. Instead, the firm would make a series of principal and interest payments over the next five years. This observation is true, but not particularly relevant. The reason is that if TransCanada borrows $10,000 at an aftertax cost of 6.6 percent, the present value of the aftertax loan payments is simply $10,000, no matter what the repayment schedule is (assuming that the loan is fully amortized). Thus, we could write down the aftertax loan repayments and work with these, but it would just be extra work for no gain.

E X A M P L E | 23.1   Lease Evaluation

In our TransCanada example, suppose the firm is able to negotiate a lease payment of $2,000 per year. What would be the NPV of the lease in this case?

Table 23.4 shows the new cash flows. You can verify that the NPV of the lease (net advantage to leasing) at 6.6 percent is now a substantial $1,126. |

E X A M P L E | 23.2   Lease Evaluation with a Continuing Asset Pool

In our original TransCanada example, the firm wrote off the entire book value of the cars in Year 5 as it closed the asset pool. Suppose, more generally, that TransCanada has other assets in the same class so that the unused UCC is depreciated to zero to infinity. In this case, we use the CCA tax shield formula introduced in Chapter 8 and recast our analysis in the following formula:

	Year					
	0	1	2	3	4	5
Investment	$10,000					
Lease payment	−2,000	−$ 2,000	−$2,000	−$2,000	$2,000	
Payment shield	800	800	800	800	800	
Forgone tax shield	−800	−1,280	−768	−461	−276	−$415
Total cash flow	$ 8,000	−$ 2,480	−$1,968	−$1,661	−$1,476	−$415
NAL	$ 1,126					

T A B L E 23.4

Revised NAL spreadsheet

$$\text{NPV}_{\text{lease}} = \text{NAL} = \text{Investment} - \text{PV(aftertax lease payments)} - \text{PVCCATS}$$

$$\text{NAL} = I - \sum_{t=0}^{4} \frac{L(1-T)}{(1+i)^t} - \frac{[T\,d\,I]}{i+d} \times \frac{[1+0.5i]}{1+i}$$

$$\text{NAL} = \$10,000 - \sum_{t=0}^{4} \frac{\$2,500(1-.40)}{(1+0.066)^t} - \frac{0.40 \times 0.40 \times \$10,000}{0.066+0.40} \times \frac{1.033}{1.066}$$

$$\text{NAL} = \$10,000 - \$6,627 - \$3,327$$

$$\text{NAL} = \$46$$

With the full tax shield on CCA available instead of just the write-off in Year 5, the NAL increases from the original value of −$199 to +$46.

CONCEPT QUESTIONS

1. What is the relevant discount rate for evaluating whether or not to lease an asset? Why?
2. Explain how to go about a lease versus buy analysis.

23.6 | A LEASING PARADOX

We previously looked at the lease versus buy decision from the perspective of the potential lessee, TransCanada Distributors. We now turn things around and look at the lease from the perspective of the lessor, Financial Leasing Company. The cash flows associated with the lease from the lessor's perspective are shown in Table 23.5. First, the lessor must buy each car for $10,000, so there is a $10,000 outflow today. Next, Financial Leasing depreciates the car at a CCA rate of 40 percent to obtain the CCA tax shields shown. Finally, the lessor receives a lease payment of $2,500 each year on which it pays taxes at a 40 percent tax rate. The aftertax lease payment received is $1,500.

What we see is that the cash flows to Financial Leasing (the lessor) are exactly the opposite of the cash flows to TransCanada Distributers (the lessee). This makes perfect sense because Financial Leasing and TransCanada are the only parties to the transaction, and the lease is a zero-sum game. In other words, if the lease has a positive NPV to one party, it must have a negative NPV to the other. Financial Leasing hopes that TransCanada will do the deal because the NPV would be +$199, just what TransCanada would lose.

We seem to have a paradox. In any leasing arrangement, one party must inevitably lose (or both parties exactly break even). Why would leasing occur? We know that leasing is very important in the business world, so the next section

TABLE 23.5

Cash flows to the lessor

	Year					
	0	1	2	3	4	5
Investment	−$10,000					
Lease payment	2,500	$ 2,500	$ 2,500	$ 2,500	$ 2,500	
Payment shield	−1,000	−1,000	−1,000	−1,000	−1,000	
Forgone tax shield	800	1,280	768	461	276	$415
Total cash flow	−$ 7,700	$ 2,780	$ 2,268	$ 1,961	$ 1,776	$415
NAL	$ 199					

describes some factors that we have omitted thus far from our analysis. These factors can make a lease attractive to both parties.

E X A M P L E | 23.3   **It's the Lease We Can Do**

In our TransCanada example, a lease payment of $2,500 makes the lease unattractive to TransCanada and a lease payment of $2,000 makes the lease very attractive. What payment would leave TransCanada indifferent to leasing or not leasing?

TransCanada is indifferent when the NPV from leasing is zero. For this to happen, the present value of the cash flows from leasing instead of buying would have to be −$10,000. From our previous efforts, we know the answer is to set the payments somewhere between $2,500 and $2,000. To find the exact payment, we use our spreadsheet as shown in Table 23.6. It turns out that the NPV of leasing is zero for a payment of $2,425. |

CONCEPT QUESTIONS
1. Why do we say that leasing is a zero-sum game?
2. What paradox does the first question create?

Resolving the Paradox

A lease contract is not a zero-sum game between the lessee and lessor when their effective tax rates differ. In this case, the lease can be structured so that both sides benefit. Any tax benefits from leasing can be split between the two firms by setting the lease payments at the appropriate level, and the shareholders of both firms benefit from this tax transfer arrangement. The loser is Revenue Canada.

This works because a lease contract swaps two sets of tax shields. The lessor obtains the CCA tax shields due to ownership. The lessee receives the tax shield on lease payments made. In a full-payout lease, the total dollar amounts of the two sets of tax shields may be roughly the same, but the critical difference is the timing. CCA tax shields are accelerated deductions reducing the tax burden in early years. Lease payments, on the other hand, reduce taxes by the same amount in every year. As a result, the ownership tax shields often have a greater present value provided the firm is fully taxed.

The basic logic behind structuring a leasing deal makes a firm in a high tax bracket want to act as the lessor. Low tax (or untaxed) firms are lessees because they are not able to use the tax advantages of ownership, such as CCA and debt financing. These ownership tax shields are worth less to the lessee because the lessee faces a lower tax rate or may not have enough taxable income to absorb the accelerated tax shields in the early years.

	Year					
	0	1	2	3	4	5
Investment	−$10,000					
Lease payment	−2,425	−$ 2,425	−$2,425	−$2,425	−$2,425	
Payment shield	970	970	970	970	970	
Forgone tax shield	−800	−1,280	−768	−461	−276	−$415
Total cash flow	$ 7,745	−$ 2,735	−$2,223	−$1,916	−$1,731	−$415
NAL	$ 0					

T A B L E 23.6

Indifference lease payments

Overall, less tax is paid by the lessee and lessor combined and this tax savings occurs sooner rather than later. The lessor gains on the tax side; the lessee may lose but the amount of any loss is less than the lessor gains. To make the lease attractive, the lessor must pass on some of the tax savings in the form of lower lease payments. In the end, the lessor gains by keeping part of the tax savings, the lessee gains through a lower lease payment, and Revenue Canada pays for both gains through a reduction in tax revenue.

To see how this would work in practice, recall the example of Section 23.3 and the situation of Financial Leasing. The value of the lease it proposed to TransCanada was $199. The value of the lease to TransCanada was exactly the opposite −$199. Since the lessor's gains came at the expense of the lessee, no deal could be arranged. However, if TransCanada pays no taxes and the lease payments are reduced to $2,437 from $2,500, both Financial Leasing and TransCanada find there is positive NPV in leasing.

To see this, we can rework Table 23.3 with a zero tax rate. This would be the case when TransCanada has enough alternate tax shields to reduce taxable income to zero for the foreseeable future.[11] In this case, notice that the cash flows from leasing are simply the lease payments of $2,437 because no CCA tax shield is lost and the lease payment is not tax deductible. The cash flows from leasing are thus:

	Year					
	0	1	2	3	4	5
Cost of car	$10,000					
Lease payment	−2,437	−$2,437	−$2,437	−$2,437	−$2,437	0
Cash flow	$ 7,563	−$2,437	−$2,437	−$2,437	−$2,437	0

The value of the lease for TransCanada is

$$\text{NPV} = \$7{,}563 - \$2{,}437 \times (1 - 1/1.11^4)/.11$$
$$= \$2.34$$

which is positive. Notice that the discount rate here is 11 percent because Trans-Canada pays no taxes; in other words, this is both the pretax and the aftertax rate.

From Table 23.7, the value of the lease to Financial Leasing can be worked out as +$32.

As a consequence of different tax rates, the lessee (TransCanada) gains $2.34, and the lessor (Financial Leasing) gains $32.00. Revenue Canada loses. What this example shows is that the lessor and the lessee can gain if their tax rates are different.

T A B L E 23.7

Revised cash flows to lessor

	Year					
	0	1	2	3	4	5
Cost of car	−$10,000					
Lease payment	2,437	$2,437	$2,437	$2,437	$2,437	
Payment shield	−974	−974	−974	−974	−974	
CCA tax shield	800	1,280	768	461	276	$415
Total cash flow	−$ 7,738	$2,742	$2,230	$1,923	$1,739	$415
NPV lessor	$ 32					

[11] Strictly speaking, the UCC of the cars would be carried on the books until the firm is able to claim CCA. However, the present value of the CCA tax shield would be low; so for the sake of simplicity, we ignore it here.

The lease contract allows the lessor to take advantage of the CCA and interest tax shields that cannot be used by the lessee. Revenue Canada experiences a net loss of tax revenue, and some of the tax gains to the lessor are passed on to the lessee in the form of lower lease payments.

23.7 | REASONS FOR LEASING

Proponents of leasing make many claims about why firms should lease assets rather than buy them. Some of the reasons given to support leasing are good, while some are not. We discuss here the reasons for leasing we think are good and some that we think are not so good.

Good Reasons for Leasing

If leasing is a good choice, it is probably because one or more of the following is true:

1. Taxes may be reduced by leasing.
2. The lease contract may reduce certain types of uncertainty that might otherwise decrease the value of the firm.
3. Transaction costs can be lower for a lease contract than for buying the asset.

Tax Advantages   As we have hinted in various places, by far the most important reason for long-term leasing is tax avoidance. If the corporate income tax were repealed, long-term leasing would become much less important. The tax advantages of leasing exist because firms are in different tax brackets. A potential tax shield that cannot be used by one firm can be transferred to another by leasing.

A Reduction of Uncertainty   We have noted that the lessee does not own the property when the lease expires. The value of the property at this time is called the *residual value* (or salvage value). At the time the lease contract is signed, there may be substantial uncertainty as to what the residual value of the asset is. A lease contract is a method that transfers this uncertainty from the lessee to the lessor.

Transferring the uncertainty about the residual value of an asset to the lessor makes sense when the lessor is better able to bear the risk. For example, if the lessor is the manufacturer, the lessor may be better able to assess and manage the risk associated with the residual value. The transfer of uncertainty to the lessor amounts to a form of insurance for the lessee. A lease, therefore, provides something besides long-term financing.

Transaction Costs   The costs of changing ownership of an asset many times over its useful life are frequently greater than the costs of writing a lease agreement. Consider the choice that confronts a person who lives in Vancouver but must do business in Halifax for two days. It seems obvious that it will be cheaper to rent a hotel room for two nights than it would be to buy a condominium for two days and then to sell it. Thus, transactions costs may be the major reason for short-term leases (operating leases). However, they are probably not the major reason for long-term leases.

Bad Reasons for Leasing

Leasing and Accounting Income   Leasing can have a significant effect on the appearance of the firm's financial statements. If a firm is successful at keeping its leases off the books, the balance sheet and income statement can be made to look better. As a consequence, accounting-based performance measures such as return on assets (ROA) can appear to be higher.

For example, off-the-books leases (that is, operating leases) result in an expense, namely, the lease payment. However, in the early years of the lease, the expense is usually lower in accounting terms than if the asset were purchased. If an asset is purchased with debt financing, capital cost allowance and interest expenses are subtracted from revenues to determine accounting net income. With accelerated depreciation under the CCA rules, the total of the depreciation deduction and the interest expense almost always exceeds the lease payments. Thus, accounting net income is greater with leasing.

In addition, because an operating lease does not appear on the balance sheet, total assets (and total liabilities) are lower than they would be if the firm borrowed the money and bought the asset. From Chapter 3, ROA is computed as net income divided by total assets. With an operating lease, the net income is bigger and total assets are smaller, so ROA is larger.

As we have discussed, however, the impact that leasing has on a firm's accounting statements is not likely to fool anyone. As always, what matters are the cash flow consequences. Whether or not a lease has a positive NPV has little to do with its effect on a firm's financial statements.

100 Percent Financing   It is often claimed that an advantage to leasing is that it provides 100 percent financing, whereas secured equipment loans require an initial down payment. Of course, a firm can simply borrow the down payment from another source that provides unsecured credit. Moreover, leases do usually involve a down payment in the form of an advance lease payment (or security deposit). Even when they do not, leases may implicitly be secured by assets of the firm other than those being leased (leasing may give the appearance of 100 percent financing, but not the substance).

Other Reasons for Leasing   There are, of course, many special reasons for some companies to find advantages in leasing. For example, leasing may be used to circumvent capital expenditure control systems set up by bureaucratic firms.

Leasing Decisions in Practice

The reduction-of-uncertainty motive for leasing is the one that is most often cited by corporations. For example, computers have a way of becoming technologically outdated very quickly, and computers are very commonly leased instead of purchased. In a recent U.S. survey, 82 percent of the responding firms cited the risk of obsolescence as an important reason for leasing, whereas only 57 percent cited the potential for cheaper financing.

Yet, cheaper financing based on shifting tax shields is an important motive for leasing. One piece of evidence is Canadian lessors' strong reaction to 1989 changes in tax laws restricting sale and lease-backs. Further evidence comes from a study analyzing decisions taken by Canadian railroads to lease rolling stock. The study examined 20 lease contracts and found that, in 17 cases, leasing provided cheaper financing than debt.[12]

---

[12] T. K. Mukherjee, "A Survey of Corporate Leasing Analysis," *Financial Management* 20 (Autumn 1991), pp. 96–107; C. R. Dipchand, A. C. Gudikunst, and G. S. Roberts, "An Empirical Analysis of Canadian Railroad Leases," *Journal of Financial Research* 3 (Spring 1980), pp. 57–67.

CONCEPT QUESTIONS

1. Explain why differential tax rates may be a good reason for leasing.
2. If leasing is tax-motivated, who has the higher tax bracket, the lessee or lessor?

23.8 | SUMMARY AND CONCLUSIONS

A large fraction of Canada's equipment is leased rather than purchased. This chapter describes different lease types, accounting and tax implications of leasing, and how to evaluate financial leases.

1. Leases can be separated into two types, financial and operating. Financial leases are generally longer-term, fully amortized, and not cancellable. In effect, the lessor obtains economic but not legal ownership. Operating leases are usually shorter-term, partially amortized, and cancellable; they can be likened to a rental agreement.

2. The distinction between financial and operating leases is important in financial accounting. Financial leases must be reported on a firm's balance sheet; operating leases are not. We discussed the specific accounting criteria for classifying leases as financial or operating.

3. Taxes are an important consideration in leasing, and Revenue Canada has some specific rules about what constitutes a valid lease for tax purposes.

4. A long-term financial lease is a source of financing much like long-term borrowing. We showed how to go about an NPV analysis of the leasing decision to decide whether leasing is cheaper than borrowing. A key insight was that the appropriate discount rate is the firm's aftertax borrowing rate.

5. We saw that differential tax rates can make leasing an attractive proposition to all parties. We also mentioned that a lease decreases the uncertainty surrounding the residual value of the leased asset. This is a primary reason cited by corporations for leasing.

Key Terms

lessee (page 841)
lessor (page 841)
operating lease (page 843)
financial lease (page 843)

sale and leaseback (page 844)
leveraged lease (page 844)
net advantage to leasing (NAL) (page 851)

Chapter Review Problems and Self-Test

23.1 Your company wants to purchase a new network file server for its wide-area computer network. The server costs $24,000. It will be obsolete in three years. Your options are to borrow the money at 10 percent or lease the machine. If you lease it, the payments will be $9,000 per year, payable at the beginning of each year. If you buy the server, you can apply a CCA rate of 30 percent per year. The tax rate is 40 percent. Assuming the asset pool remains open, should you lease or buy?

23.2   In the previous question again assuming the asset pool remains open, what is the NPV of the lease to the lessor? At what lease payment do the lessee and the lessor both break even?

Answers to Self-Test Problems

23.1   Because the asset pool remains open after the useful life of the network file server, we can answer this question by using the net advantage to leasing (NAL) formula shown in Example 23.2 of the text. This formula is:

$$NAL = I - \sum_{t=0}^{2} \frac{L(1-T)}{(1+i)^t} - \frac{[T\,d\,I]}{i+d} \times \frac{[1+0.5i]}{1+i}$$

We are given all the information necessary to solve for NAL:

I = the investment necessary to purchase the asset
   = $24,000

t = the number of years, beginning at zero, that the new asset would be used
   = 3 (Year 0, Year 1, and Year 2)

L = the amount of money required to lease the asset for one year
   = $9,000

T = the applicable tax rate
   = 40%

i = the applicable aftertax interest rate
   = 10%(1 − T)
   = 10%(.6)
   = 6%

d = the applicable CCA rate
   = 40%

We then plug all of these numbers into the formula:

NAL = $24,000

$$- \sum_{t=0}^{2} \frac{\$9,000(1-.40)}{(1+0.06)^t} - \frac{0.40 \times 0.30 \times \$24,000}{0.06+0.30} \times \frac{1.03}{1.06}$$

NAL = $24,000 − $15,299 − $7,774
NAL = $927

Because the NAL formula gives a positive value of $927, there is a net advantage to lease the file server.

23.2   The answer to the first part of the question is that the lessor has a NPV of −$927. The lessor has lost what the lessee has gained. To solve the second question posed in 23.2 we can again refer to the NAL formula:

$$NAL = I - \sum_{t=0}^{2} \frac{L(1-T)}{(1+i)^t} - \frac{[T\,d\,I]}{i+d} \times \frac{[1+0.5i]}{1+i}$$

We also use much of the information used to solve Problem 23.1. However, instead of using the value of $9,000 for L, we make NAL = 0 and solve for L.

We merely have to plug in the values for the information we know and rearrange the formula so that we may solve for L:

$$0 = \$24,000 - \sum_{t=0}^{2} \frac{L(1 - .40)}{(1 + 0.06)^t} - \frac{0.40 \times 0.30 \times \$24,000}{0.06 + 0.30} \times \frac{1.03}{1.06}$$

$$0 = \$24,000 - \sum_{t=0}^{2} \frac{L(0.6)}{(1.06)^t} - \$7,774$$

$$\$16,226 = \sum_{t=0}^{2} \frac{L(0.6)}{(1.06)^t}$$

$$\$16,226 = \frac{L(0.6)}{(1.06)^0} + \frac{L(0.6)}{(1.06)^1} + \frac{L(0.6)}{(1.06)^2}$$

$$\$16,226 = .600L + .566L + .534L$$

$$\$16,266 = 1.7L$$

$$L = \$9,545$$

As we can now see, some of the tax advantages of the lessee have been transferred to the lessor and they are now in a break-even situation.

Questions and Problems

Basic
(Questions 1–7)

1. **Lease or Buy**   Assuming the asset pool was closed when the network file server became obsolete, redo Self-Test Problem 23.1.

2. **Leasing**   Respond to the following remarks:
   a. Leasing reduces risk and can reduce a firm's cost of capital.
   b. Leasing provides 100 percent financing.
   c. If the tax advantages of leasing were eliminated, leasing would disappear.

3. **Balance Sheet and Leasing**   Discuss the accounting criteria for determining whether or not a lease must be reported on the balance sheet. In each case, give a rationale for the criterion.

4. **Revenue Canada and Leasing**   Discuss Revenue Canada's criteria for determining whether or not a lease is valid. In each case, give a rationale for the criterion.

5. **Off the Balance Sheet Financing**   What is meant by the phrase *off balance sheet financing?* When do leases provide such financing, and what are the accounting and economic consequences of such activity?

6. **Sale and Leaseback**   Why might a firm choose to engage in a sale and leaseback transaction? Give two reasons.

7. **Aftertax Discount Rate**   Explain why the aftertax borrowing rate is the appropriate discount rate for use in lease evaluation.

   Using the following information, work the next six problems: You work for a nuclear research laboratory that is contemplating leasing a diagnostic scanner (leasing is a very common practice with expensive, high-tech equipment). The scanner costs $810,000 and it qualifies for a 30 percent CCA rate. Because of radiation contamination, it is valueless in four years. You can lease it for $240,000 per year for four years.

**Intermediate
(Questions 8–13)**

8. **Lease or Buy**   Assume the tax rate is 40 percent. You can borrow at 10 percent pretax. Should you lease or buy?

9. **Lessor View of Leasing**   What are the cash flows from the lease from the lessor's viewpoint? Assume a 40 percent tax bracket.

10. **Break-even Lease**   What would the lease payment have to be for both lessor and lessee to be indifferent to the lease?

11. **Tax Effects on Leasing**   Assume that your company does not contemplate paying taxes for the next several years. What are the cash flows from leasing?

12. **Leasing Profits**   In the previous question, over what range of lease payments will the lease be profitable for both parties?

13. **Lease or Buy**   Rework Problem 8 assuming the scanner qualifies for a special CCA rate of 50 percent per year.

**Challenge
(Questions 14–17)**

14. **Lease or Buy**   In the Self-Test Problem 23.1, suppose the server had a projected salvage value of $2,000. How would you conduct the lease versus buy analysis?

15. **Lease or Buy**   In the Self-Test Problem 23.1, suppose the entire $24,000 is borrowed. The rate on the loan is 10 percent, and the loan would be repaid in equal installments. Create a lease versus buy analysis that explicitly incorporates the loan payments. Show that the NPV of leasing instead of buying is not changed. Why does this happen?

16. **Break-even Lease**   An asset costs $86.87. The CCA rate for this asset is 20 percent. The asset's useful life is two years. It will have no salvage value. The corporate tax rate on ordinary income is 40 percent. The interest rate on risk-free cash flows is 10 percent.

   a. What set of lease payments will make the lessee and the lessor equally well off?
   b. Show the general condition that will make the value of a lease to the lessor the negative of the value to the lessee.
   c. Assume that the lessee pays no taxes and the lessor is in the 40 percent tax bracket. For what range of lease payments does the lease have a positive NPV for both parties?

17. **Lease or Buy**   Tollufson Corporation has decided to purchase a new machine that costs $3,000. The machine will be worthless after three years. CCA for this type of machine is 40 percent. Tollufson is in the 40 percent combined tax bracket. The Royal Canadian Bank has offered Tollufson a three-year loan for $3,000. The repayment schedule is three yearly principal repayments of $1,000 and an interest charge of 14 percent on the outstanding balance of the loan at the beginning of each year. Fourteen percent is the marketwide rate of interest. Both principal repayments and interest are due at the end of each year.

   York Leasing Corporation offers to lease the same machine to Tollufson. Lease payments of $1,200 per year are due at the end of each of the three years of the lease.

   a. Should Tollufson lease the machine or buy it with bank financing?
   b. What is the annual lease payment that will make Tollufson indifferent to whether it leases the machine or purchases it?

Suggested Readings

A classic article on lease valuation is:

Myers, S., D. A. Dill, and A. J. Bautista. "Valuation of Financial Lease Contracts." *Journal of Finance,* June 1976.

A good review and discussion of leasing is contained in:

Smith, C. W., Jr., and L. M. Wakeman. "Determinations of Corporate Leasing Policy." *Journal of Finance,* July 1985.

The survey evidence mentioned in the chapter is from:

Mukherjee, Tarun K. "A Survey of Corporate Leasing Analysis." *Financial Management,* Autumn 1991.

Accounting Break-Even The sales level that results in zero project net income. (page 316)

Accounts Payable Period The time between receipt of inventory and payment for it. (page 609)

Accounts Receivable Financing A secured short-term loan that involves either the assignment or factoring of receivables. (page 629)

Accounts Receivable Period The time between sale of inventory and collection of the receivable. (page 609)

Adjusted Present Value (APV) Base case net present value of a project's operating cash flows plus present value of any financing benefits. (page 523)

Adjustment Costs The costs associated with holding too little cash. Also shortage costs. (page 647)

Agency Problem The possibility of conflicts of interest between the stockholders and management of a firm. (page 11)

Aggregation Process by which smaller investment proposals of each of a firm's operational units are added up and treated as one big project. (page 101)

Aging Schedule A compilation of accounts receivable by the age of each account. (page 699)

Amalgamations Combinations of firms that have been joined by merger, consolidation, or acquisition. (page 768)

American Options A call or put option that can be exercised on or before its expiration date. (pages 723, 829)

Annual Percentage Rate (APR) The interest rate charged per period multiplied by the number of periods per year. (page 166)

Annuity A level stream of cash flows for a fixed period of time. (page 156)

Annuity Due Annuity contract specification of payments at the beginning of each period. (page 160)

Arbitrage Pricing Theory (APT) An equilibrium asset pricing theory that is derived from a factor model by using diversification and arbitrage. It shows that the expected return on any risky asset is a linear combination of various factors. (page 409)

Average Accounting Return (AAR) An investment's average net income divided by its average book value. (page 236)

Average Tax Rate Total taxes paid divided by total taxable income. (page 40)

Balance Sheet Financial statement showing a firm's accounting value on a particular date. (page 25)

Bankruptcy A legal proceeding for liquidating or reorganizing a business. Also, the transfer of some or all of a firm's assets to its creditors. (page 443)

Bearer Form Bond issued without record of the owner's name; payment is made to whoever holds the bond. (page 427)

Belgian Dentist Stereotype of the traditional Eurobond investor as a professional who must report income, has a disdain for tax authorities, and likes to invest in foreign currencies. (page 806)

Benefit/Cost Ratio The profitability index of an investment project. (page 247)

Best Efforts Underwriting Underwriter sells as much of the issue as possible, but can return any unsold shares to the issuer without financial responsibility. (page 463)

Beta Coefficient Amount of systematic risk present in a particular risky asset relative to an average risky asset. (page 395)

Bond Refunding The process of replacing all or part of an issue of outstanding bonds. (page 448)

Book Value Accounting per share value of firm's equity. Also net worth. (page 438)

Bought Deal One underwriter buys securities from an issuing firm and sells them directly to a small number of investors. (page 463)

Business Risk The equity risk that comes from the nature of the firm's operating activities. (page 543)

CCA Tax Shield Tax saving that results from the CCA deduction, calculated as depreciation multiplied by the corporate tax rate. (page 277)

Call Option The right to buy an asset at a fixed price during a particular time period. (page 723)

Call Premium Amount by which the call price exceeds the par value of the bond. (page 428)

Call Protected   Bond during period in which it cannot be redeemed by the issuer. (page 428)

Call Provision   Agreement giving the corporation the option to repurchase the bond at a specified price before maturity. (page 428)

Capital Asset Pricing Model (CAPM)   Equation of the SML showing relationship between expected return and beta. (page 406)

Capital Budgeting   The process of planning and managing a firm's investment in fixed assets. (page 3)

Capital Cost Allowance (CCA)   Depreciation method under Canadian tax law allowing for the accelerated write-off of property under various classifications. (pages 44, 265)

Capital Gains   The increase in value of an investment over its purchase price. (page 42)

Capital Gains Yield   The dividend growth rate or the rate at which the value of an investment grows. (page 205)

Capital intensity ratio   A firm's total assets divided by its sales, or the amount of assets needed to generate $1 in sales. (page 107)

Capital Markets   Financial markets where long-term debt and equity securities are bought and sold. (page 16)

Capital Rationing   The situation that exists if a firm has positive NPV projects but cannot find the necessary financing. (page 332)

Capital Structure   The mix of debt and equity maintained by a firm. (page 3)

Captive Finance Company   Wholly owned subsidiary that handles credit extension and receivables financing through commercial paper. (page 692)

Carrying Costs   Costs that rise with increases in the level of investment in current assets. (page 615)

Cash Break-even   The sales level where operating cash flow is equal to zero. (page 323)

Cash Budget   A forecast of cash receipts and disbursements for the next planning period. (page 622)

Cash Cycle   The time between cash disbursement and cash collection. (page 609)

Cash Discount   A discount given for a cash purchase. (page 681)

Cash Flow from Assets   The total of cash flow to bondholders and cash flow to stockholders, consisting of the following: operating cash flow, capital spending, and additions to net working capital. (page 33)

Cash Flow Time Line   Graphical representation of the operating cycle and the cash cycle. (page 609)

Cash Flow to Creditors   A firm's interest payments to creditors less net new borrowings. (page 35)

Cash Flow to Shareholders   Dividends paid out by a firm less net new equity raised. (page 35)

Cash Position   The position of a portfolio when the derivative securities in that portfolio have been removed. (page 750)

Circular Bid   Corporate takeover bid that is communicated to the stockholders by direct mail. (page 769)

Clientele Effect   Stocks attract particular groups based on dividend yield and the resulting tax effects. (page 585)

Collection Policy   Procedures followed by a firm in collecting accounts receivable. (page 677)

Common-Base-Year Statement   A standardized financial statement presenting all items relative to a certain base year amount. (page 62)

Common-Size Statement   A standardized financial statement presenting all items in percentage terms. Balance sheets are shown as a percentage of assets and income statements as a percentage of sales. (page 60)

Common Stock   Equity without priority for dividends or in bankruptcy. (page 437)

Compounding   The process of accumulating interest in an investment over time to earn more interest. (page 137)

Compound Interest   Interest earned on both the initial principal and the interest reinvested from prior periods. (page 137)

Consol   A perpetual bond. (page 161)

Consolidation   A merger in which an entirely new firm is created and both the acquired and acquiring firm cease to exist. (page 768)

Contingency Planning   Taking into account the managerial options implicit in a project. (page 329)

Control Block   An interest controlling 50 percent of outstanding votes plus one; thereby it may decide the fate of the firm. (page 786)

Conversion Premium   Difference between the conversion price and the current stock price divided by the current stock price. (page 743)

Conversion Price   The dollar amount of a bond's par value that is exchangeable for one share of stock. (page 743)

Conversion Ratio   The number of shares per $1,000 bond received for conversion into stock. (page 743)

Conversion Value   The value of a convertible bond if it was immediately converted into common stock. (page 744)

Convertible Bond   A bond that can be exchanged for a fixed number of shares of stock for a specified amount of time. (page 743)

Corporation   A business created as a distinct legal entity composed of one or more individuals or entities. (page 6)

Cost of Capital   The minimum required return on a new investment. (page 409)

Cost of Debt   The return that lenders require on the firm's debt. (page 499)

Cost of Equity   The return that equity investors require on their investment in the firm. (page 494)

Counterparty   Second borrower in currency swap. Counterparty borrows funds in currency desired by principal. (page 829)

Coupons   The stated interest payments made on a bond. (page 188)

Coupon Rate   The annual coupon divided by the face value of a bond. (page 188)

Covenants   A promise by the firm, included in the debt contract, to perform certain acts. A restrictive covenant imposes constraints on the firm to protect the interests of the debtholder. (page 629)

Credit Analysis   The process of determining the probability that customers will or will not pay. (page 677)

Credit Cost Curve   Graphical representation of the sum of the carrying costs and the opportunity costs of a credit policy. (page 691)

Credit Instrument   The evidence of indebtedness. (page 683)

Credit Period   The length of time that credit is granted. (page 679)

Credit Scoring   The process of quantifying the probability of default when granting consumer credit. (page 696)

Cross-Rate   The implicit exchange rate between two currencies (usually non-U.S.) quoted in some third currency (usually the U.S. dollar). (page 806)

Cumulative Voting   Procedure where a shareholder may cast all votes for one member of the board of directors. (page 457)

Date of Payment   Date that the dividend cheques are mailed. (page 572)

Date of Record   Date on which holders of record are designated to receive a dividend. (page 572)

Debenture   Unsecured debt, usually with a maturity of 10 years or more. (page 427)

Debit Card   An automated teller machine card used at the point of purchase to avoid the use of cash. As this is not a credit card, money must be available in the user's bank account. (page 656)

Debt Capacity   The ability to borrow to increase firm value. (page 115)

Declaration Date   Date on which the board of directors passes a resolution to pay a dividend. (page 571)

Deferred Call   Call provision prohibiting the company from redeeming the bond before a certain date. (page 428)

Degree of Operating Leverage   The percentage change in operating cash flow relative to the percentage change in quantity sold. (page 326)

Derivative Securities   Securities whose returns depend on the price of an underlying asset and that allow market participants to offset the exposure of their cash market positions. (pages 19, 722)

Dilution   Loss in existing shareholders' value, in either ownership, market value, book value, or EPS. (page 481)

Direct Bankruptcy Costs   The costs that are directly associated with bankruptcy, such as legal and administrative expenses. (page 549)

Discount   Calculate the present value of some future amount. (page 143)

Discounted Cash Flow (DCF) Valuation   The process of valuing an investment by discounting its future cash flows. (page 230)

Discounted Payback Period   The length of time required for an investment's discounted cash flows to equal its initial cost. (page 234)

Discount Rate   The rate used to calculate the present value of future cash flows. (page 144)

Distribution   Payment made by a firm to its owners from sources other than current or accumulated earnings. (page 570)

Diversification   Investment in more than one asset, whose returns do not move proportionally in the same direction at the same time thus reducing risk. (page 782)

Dividends   Payment made out of a firm's earnings to its owners, either in the form of cash or stock. (pages 440, 570)

Dividend Capture   A strategy in which an investor purchases securities to own them on the day of record and then quickly sells them; designed to attain dividends but avoid the risk of a lengthy hold. (page 663)

Dividend Growth Model   Model that determines the current price of a stock as its dividend next period divided by the discount rate less the dividend growth rate. (page 200)

Dividend Payout Ratio   Amount of cash paid out to shareholders divided by net income. (page 106)

Dividend Tax Credit   Tax formula that reduces the effective tax rate on dividends. (page 41)

Dividend Yield   A stock's cash dividend divided by its current price. (page 205)

Dollar Swaps   Foreign currency deposits converted back into Canadian dollars at a predetermined exchange rate by chartered banks. (page 664)

Du Pont Identity   Popular expression breaking ROE into three parts: profit margin, total asset turnover, and financial leverage. (page 76)

Earnings Per Share   Net income minus any cash dividends on preferred stock, divided by the number of shares of common stock outstanding. (page 781)

Effective Annual Rate (EAR)   The interest rate expressed as if it were compounded once per year. (page 163)

Efficient Capital Market   Market in which security prices reflect available information. (page 363)

Efficient Markets Hypothesis (EMH)   The hypothesis is that actual capital markets, such as the TSE, are efficient. (page 364)

Equivalent Annual Cost (EAC)   The present value of a project's costs calculated on an annual basis. (page 288)

Erosion   The cash flows of a new project that come at the expense of a firm's existing projects. (page 263)

Eurobanks   Banks that make loans and accept deposits in foreign currencies. (page 827)

Eurobond   International bonds issued in multiple countries but denominated in a single currency (usually the issuer's currency). (page 806)

Eurocurrency   Money deposited in a financial centre outside of the country whose currency is involved. (page 806)

European Option   An option that can only be exercised on the expiration date. (page 723)

Exchange Rate   The price of one country's currency expressed in another country's currency. (page 808)

Exchange Rate Risk   The risk related to having international operations in a world where relative currency values vary. (page 828)

Ex-Dividend Date   Date four business days before the date of record, establishing those individuals entitled to a dividend. (page 572)

Exercising the Option   The act of buying or selling the underlying asset via the option contract. (page 723)

Expected Return   Return on a risky asset expected in the future. (page 375)

Expiration Date   The last day on which an option can be exercised. (page 723)

Export Development Corporation (EDC)   Federal Crown corporation that promotes Canadian exports by making loans to foreign purchasers. (page 807)

Ex Rights   Period when stock is selling without a recently declared right, normally beginning four business days before the holder-of-record date. (page 478)

Face Value   The principal amount of a bond that is repaid at the end of the term. Also par value. (page 188)

Financial Break-even   The sales level that results in a zero NPV. (page 323)

Financial Distress Costs   The direct and indirect costs associated with going bankrupt or experiencing financial distress. (page 549)

Financial Engineering   Creation of new securities or financial processes. (page 18)

Financial Lease   Typically, a longer-term, fully amortized lease under which the lessee is responsible for upkeep. Usually not cancellable without penalty. (page 843)

Financial Ratios   Relationships determined from a firm's financial information and used for comparison purposes. (page 63)

Financial Risk   The equity risk that comes from the financial policy (i.e., capital structure) of the firm. (page 543)

Firm Commitment Underwriting   Underwriter buys the entire issue, assuming full financial responsibility for any unsold shares. (page 463)

Fisher Effect   Relationship between nominal returns, real returns, and inflation. (page 350)

Five Cs of Credit   The following five basic credit factors to be evaluated: character, capacity, capital, collateral, and conditions. (page 696)

Fixed Costs   Costs that do not change when the quantity of output changes during a particular time period. (page 315)

Float   The difference between book cash and bank cash, representing the net effect of cheques in the process of clearing. (page 650)

Forecasting Risk   The possibility that errors in projected cash flows lead to incorrect decisions. (page 307)

Foreign Bonds   International bonds issued in a single country, usually denominated in that country's currency. (page 806)

Foreign Exchange Market   The market where one country's currency is traded for another's. (page 807)

Forward Exchange Rate   The agreed-on exchange rate to be used in a forward trade. (page 812)

Forward Trade   Agreement to exchange currency at some time in the future. (page 812)

Futures Contracts   An agreement drawn up for a fixed settlement date and price to deliver or receive an asset at a future date. (page 749)

Future Value (FV)   The amount an investment is worth after one or more periods. Also compound value. (page 137)

Generally Accepted Accounting Principles (GAAP)   The common set of standards and procedures by which audited financial statements are prepared. (page 28)

Gilts   British and Irish government securities, including issues of local British authorities and some overseas public-sector offerings. (page 806)

Going-Private Transactions   All publicly owned stock in a firm is replaced with complete equity ownership by a private group. (page 770)

Greenmail   A targeted stock repurchase where payments are made to potential bidders to eliminate unfriendly take-over attempts. (page 787)

Half-year Rule   Revenue Canada requirement to figure CCA on only one half of an asset's installed cost for its first year of use. (page 44)

Hard Rationing   The situation that occurs when a business cannot raise financing for a project under any circumstances. (page 334)

Hedging   A protective manoeuvre; a transaction intended to reduce the risk of loss from price fluctuations. (page 750)

Holder-of-Record Date   The date on which existing shareholders on company records are designated as the recipients of stock rights. Also the date of record. (page 478)

Homemade Dividends   Idea that individual investors can undo corporate dividend policy by reinvesting dividends or selling shares of stock. (page 575)

Homemade Leverage   The use of personal borrowing to change the overall amount of financial leverage to which the individual is exposed. (page 537)

Income Statement   Financial statement summarizing a firm's performance over a period of time. (page 30)

Incremental Cash Flows   The difference between a firm's future cash flows with a project or without the project. (page 261)

Indenture   Written agreement between the corporation and the lender detailing the terms of the debt issue. (page 426)

Indirect Bankruptcy Costs   The difficulties of running a business that is experiencing financial distress. (page 549)

Information Content-Effect   The market's reaction to a change in corporate dividend payout. (page 583)

Initial Public Offering (IPO)   A company's first equity issue made available to the public. Also an unseasoned new issue. (page 461)

Interest on Interest   Interest earned on the reinvestment of previous interest payments. (page 137)

Interest Rate Futures   A financial futures contract calling for the delivery of a debt security such as a T-bill or a long-term government bond. (page 749)

Interest Rate Parity (IRP)   The condition stating that the interest rate differential between two countries is equal to the difference between the forward exchange rate and the spot exchange rate. (page 819)

Interest Tax Shield   The tax saving attained by a firm from interest expense. (page 544)

Internal Growth Rate   The growth rate a firm can maintain with only internal financing. (page 114)

Internal Rate of Return (IRR)   The discount rate that makes the NPV of an investment zero. (page 238)

International Fisher Effect (IFE)   The theory that real interest rates are equal across countries. (page 821)

Intrinsic Value   The lower bound of an option's value, or what the option would be worth if it were about to expire. (page 729)

Inventory Loan   A secured short-term loan to purchase inventory. (page 632)

Inventory Period   The time it takes to acquire and sell inventory. (page 609)

Invoice   Bill for goods or services provided by the seller to the purchaser. (page 680)

Just-in-Time Inventory (JIT)   Design for inventory in which parts, raw materials, and other work-in-process is delivered exactly as needed for production. Goal is to minimize inventory. (page 710)

Lessee   The user of an asset in a leasing agreement. Lessee makes payments to lessor. (page 841)

Lessor   The owner of an asset in a leasing agreement. Lessor receives payments from the lessee. (page 841)

Letter of Credit   A written statement by a bank that money will be paid, provided conditions specified in the letter are met. (page 629)

Leveraged Buyout (LBO)   Going-private transactions in which a large percentage of the money used to buy the stock is borrowed. Often, incumbent management is involved. (page 770)

Leveraged Lease   A financial lease where the lessor borrows a substantial fraction of the cost of the leased asset. (page 844)

Liquidation   Termination of the firm as a going concern. (page 444)

Lockboxes   Special post office boxes set up to intercept and speed up accounts receivable payments. (page 655)

London Interbank Offer Rate (LIBOR)   The rate most international banks charge one another for overnight Eurodollar loans. (page 806)

Long Hedge   Used to avoid increases in the price of an asset by purchasing a futures contract to protect against changes in the price of the asset. (page 751)

Loss Carry-forward, Carry-back   Using a year's capital losses to offset capital gains in past or future years. (page 43)

Managerial Options   Opportunities that managers can exploit if certain things happen in the future. (page 329)

M&M Proposition I   The value of the firm is independent of its capital structure. (page 538)

M&M Proposition II   A firm's cost of equity capital is a positive linear function of its capital structure. (page 540)

Marginal or Incremental Cost   The change in costs that occurs when there is a small change in output. (page 316)

Marginal Tax Rate   Amount of tax payable on the next dollar earned. (page 40)

Marked to Market   Daily settlement of obligations on futures positions. (page 750)

Market Risk Premium   Slope of the SML, the difference between the expected return on a market portfolio and the risk-free rate. (page 406)

Maturity   Specified date at which the principal amount of a bond is paid. (page 188)

Maturity Factoring   Short-term financing in which the factor purchases all of a firm's receivables and forwards the proceeds to the seller as soon as they are collected. (page 631)

Merger   The complete absorption of one company by another, where the acquiring firm retains its identity and the acquired firm ceases to exist as a separate entity. (page 768)

Money Markets   Financial markets where short-term debt securities are bought and sold. (page 16)

Multiple Discriminant Analysis (MDA)   Statistical technique for distinguishing between two samples on the basis of their observed characteristics. (page 696)

Multiple Rates of Return   One potential problem in using the IRR method if more than one discount rate makes the NPV of an investment zero. (page 242)

Mutually Exclusive Investment Decisions   One potential problem in using the IRR method if the acceptance of one project excludes that of another. (page 244)

Net Acquisitions   Total installed cost of capital acquisitions minus adjusted cost of any disposals within an asset pool. (page 46)

Net Advantage to Leasing (NAL)   The NPV of the decision to lease an asset instead of buying it. (page 851)

Net Present Value (NPV)   The difference between an investment's market value and its cost. (page 229)

Net Present Value Profile   A graphical representation of the relationship between an investment's NPVs and various discount rates. (page 240)

Nominal Rate of Interest   The stated rate of interest applied to your investment. (page 136)

Nominal Return   Return on an investment not adjusted for inflation. (page 349)

Non-cash Items   Expenses charged against revenues that do not directly affect cash flow, such as depreciation. (page 31)

Normal Distribution   A symmetric, bell-shaped frequency distribution that can be defined by its mean and standard deviation. (page 360)

Note   Unsecured debt, usually with a maturity under 10 years. (page 427)

Note Issuance Facility (NIF)   Large borrowers issue notes up to one year in maturity in the Euromarket. Banks underwrite or sell notes. (page 827)

Operating Cash Flow   Cash generated from a firm's normal business activities. (page 33)

Operating Cycle   The time period between the acquisition of inventory and when cash is collected from receivables. (page 609)

Operating Lease   Usually a shorter-term lease where the lessor is responsible for insurance, taxes, and upkeep. Often cancellable on short notice. (page 843)

Operating Leverage   The degree to which a firm or project relies on fixed costs. (page 325)

Operating Loan   Loan negotiated with banks, usually by small business, for day-to-day operations. (page 627)

Opportunity Cost   The most valuable alternative that is given up if a particular investment is undertaken. (page 263)

Option   A contract that gives its owner the right to buy or sell some asset at a fixed price on or before a given date. (page 722)

Oversubscription Privilege   Allows shareholders to purchase unsubscribed shares in a rights offering at the subscription price. (page 479)

Partnership   A business formed by two or more co-owners. (page 6)

Payback Period   The amount of time required for an investment to generate cash flows to recover its initial cost. (page 232)

Percentage of Sales Approach   Financial planning method in which accounts are projected depending on a firm's predicted sales level. (page 106)

Perpetuity   An annuity in which the cash flows continue forever. (page 161)

Planning Horizon   The long-range time period the financial planning process focuses on, usually the next two to five years. (page 101)

Plowback Ratio   See Retention Ratio.

Poison Pill   A financial device designed to make unfriendly takeover attempts unappealing, if not impossible. (page 788)

Political Risk   Risk related to changes in value that arise because of political actions. (page 833)

Portfolio   Group of assets such as stocks and bonds held by an investor. (page 379)

Portfolio Weight   Percentage of a portfolio's total value in a particular asset. (page 379)

Precautionary Motive The need to hold cash as a safety margin to act as a financial reserve. (page 646)

Preferred Stock Stock with dividend priority over common stock, normally with a fixed dividend rate, often without voting rights. (page 434)

Present Value (PV) The current value of future cash flows discounted at the appropriate discount rate. (page 143)

Principle of Diversification Principle stating that spreading an investment across a number of assets eliminates some, but not all, of the risk. (page 392)

Private Placements Loans, usually long term in nature, provided directly by a limited number of investors. (page 484)

Profitability Index (PI) The present value of an investment's future cash flows divided by its initial cost. Also benefit/cost ratio. (page 247)

Pro Forma Financial Statements Financial statements projecting future years' operations. (page 265)

Prospectus Legal document describing details of the issuing corporation and the proposed offering to potential investors. (page 461)

Protective Covenant Part of the indenture limiting certain transactions that can be taken during the term of the loan, usually to protect the lender's interest. (page 428)

Proxy Grant of authority by shareholder allowing for another individual to vote his or her shares. (page 458)

Proxy Contests Attempts to gain control of a firm by soliciting a sufficient number of stockholder votes to replace existing management. (page 770)

Purchasing Power Parity (PPP) The idea that the exchange rate adjusts to keep purchasing power constant among currencies. (page 813)

Pure Play Approach Use of a WACC that is unique to a particular project. (page 507)

Put Option The right to sell an asset at a fixed price during a particular period of time. The opposite of a call option. (page 743)

Real Interest Rate The nominal interest rate minus the rate of inflation. (page 136)

Realized Capital Gains The increase in value of an investment converted to cash. (page 42)

Real Return Return adjusted for the effects of inflation. (page 349)

Recaptured Depreciation The taxable difference between adjusted cost of disposal and UCC when UCC is greater. (page 46)

Red Herring Preliminary prospectus distributed to prospective investors in a new issue of securities. (page 461)

Registered Form Registrar of company records ownership of each bond; payment is made directly to the owner of record. (page 426)

Regular Cash Dividend Cash payment made by a firm to its owners in the normal course of business, usually made four times a year. (page 571)

Regular Underwriting The purchase of securities from the issuing company by an investment banker for resale to the public. (page 463)

Regulatory Dialectic The pressures financial institutions and regulatory bodies exert on each other. (page 19)

Reorganization Financial restructuring of a failing firm to attempt to continue operations as a going concern. (page 444)

Repurchase Another method used to pay out a firm's earnings to its owners, which provides more preferable tax treatment than dividends. (page 591)

Residual Dividend Approach Policy where a firm pays dividends only after meeting its investment needs while maintaining a desired debt-to-equity ratio. (page 586)

Retained Earnings Corporate earnings not paid out as dividends. (page 438)

Retention Ratio Retained earnings divided by net income. Also called the plowback ratio. (pages 106, 496)

Retractable Bond Bond that may be sold back (put) to the issuer at a prespecified price before maturity. (page 434)

Return on Equity (ROE) Net income after interest and taxes divided by average common shareholders' equity. (page 496)

Reverse Split Procedure where a firm's number of shares outstanding is reduced. (page 595)

Risk Premium The excess return required from an investment in a risky asset over a risk-free investment. (page 356)

Sale and Leaseback A financial lease in which the lessee sells an asset to the lessor and then leases it back. (page 844)

Same Day Value Bank makes proceeds of cheques deposited available the same day before cheques clear. (page 656)

Scenario Analysis The determination of what happens to NPV estimates when we ask what-if questions. (page 309)

Security Market Line (SML) Positively sloped straight line displaying the relationship between expected return and beta. (page 406)

Sensitivity Analysis Investigation of what happens to NPV when only one variable is changed. (page 310)

Shareholders or Stockholders Owners of equity in a corporation. (page 438)

Share Rights Plan   Provisions allowing existing share-holders to purchase stock at some fixed price should an outside takeover bid take place, discouraging hostile take-over attempts. (page 788)

Shortage Costs   Costs that fall with increases in the level of investment in current assets. (page 615)

Short Hedge   Protecting the value of an asset held by selling a futures contract. (page 750)

Simple Interest   Interest earned only on the original principal amount invested. (page 137)

Simulation Analysis   A combination of scenario and sensitivity analyses. (page 312)

Sinking Fund   Account managed by the bond trustee for early bond redemption. (page 428)

Smart Card   Much like an automated teller machine card; it is used within corporations to control access to information by employees. (page 654)

Soft Rationing   The situation that occurs when units in a business are allocated a certain amount of financing for capital budgeting. (page 332)

Sole Proprietorship   A business owned by a single individual. (page 5)

Sources of Cash   A firm's activities that generate cash. (page 57)

Speculative Motive   The need to hold cash to take advantage of additional investment opportunities, such as bargain purchases. (page 646)

Spot Exchange Rate   The exchange rate on a spot trade. (page 812)

Spot Trade   An agreement to trade currencies based on the exchange rate today for settlement in two days. (page 812)

Spread   The gap between the interest rate a bank pays on deposits and the rate it charges on loans. (page 694)

Spread   Compensation to the underwriter, determined by the difference between the underwriter's buying price and offering price. (page 463)

Stakeholder   Anyone who potentially has a claim on a firm. (page 12)

Stand-Alone Principle   Evaluation of a project based on the project's incremental cash flows. (page 262)

Standard Deviation   The positive square root of the variance. (page 357)

Standby Fee   Amount paid to underwriter participating in standby underwriting agreement. (page 479)

Standby Underwriting   Agreement where the underwriter agrees to purchase the unsubscribed portion of the issue. (page 479)

Stated or Quoted Interest Rate   The interest rate expressed in terms of the interest payment made each period. Also quoted interest rate. (page 163)

Statement of Changes in Financial Position   A firm's financial statement that summarizes its sources and uses of cash over a specified period. (page 59)

Static Theory of Capital Structure   Theory that a firm borrows up to the point where the tax benefit from an extra dollar in debt is exactly equal to the cost that comes from the increased probability of financial distress. (page 551)

Stock Dividend   Payment made by a firm to its owners in the form of stock, diluting the value of each share outstanding. (page 593)

Stock Exchange Bid   Corporate takeover bid communicated to the stockholders through a stock exchange. (page 769)

Stock Split   An increase in a firm's shares outstanding without any change in owner's equity. (page 593)

Straight Bond Value   The value of a convertible bond if it could not be converted into common stock. (page 744)

Straight Voting   Procedure where a shareholder may cast all votes for each member of the board of directors. (page 457)

Strategic Options   Options for future, related business products or strategies. (page 332)

Striking Price   The fixed price in the option contract at which the holder can buy or sell the underlying asset. Also the exercise price or strike price. (page 723)

Stripped Bond   A bond that makes no coupon payments, thus initially priced at a deep discount. (page 432)

Stripped Common Shares   Common stock on which dividends and capital gains are repackaged and sold separately. (page 575)

Sunk Cost   A cost that has already been incurred and cannot be removed and therefore should not be considered in an investment decision. (page 262)

Sustainable Growth Rate   The growth rate a firm can maintain given its debt capacity, ROE, and retention ratio. (page 115)

Swaps   Agreements to the exchange of two securities or currencies. (page 807)

Sweeteners or Equity Kickers   A feature included in the terms of a new issue of debt or preferred shares to make the issue more attractive to initial investors. (page 738)

Syndicate   A group of underwriters formed to reduce the risk and help to sell an issue. (page 462)

Synergy   The positive incremental net gain associated with the combination of two firms through a merger or acquisition. (page 775)

Systematic Risk   A risk that influences a large number of assets. Also market risk. (page 390)

Systematic Risk Principle   Principle stating that the expected return on a risky asset depends only on that asset's systematic risk. (page 395)

Target Cash Balance A firm's desired cash level as determined by the trade-off between carrying costs and shortage costs. (page 647)

Target Payout Ratio A firm's long-term desired dividend-to-earnings ratio. (page 590)

Tender Offer A public offer by one firm to directly buy the shares from another firm. (page 768)

Term Loans Direct business loans of, typically, one to five years. (page 483)

Terminal Loss The difference between UCC and adjusted cost of disposal when UCC is greater. (page 46)

Terms of Sale Conditions on which a firm sells its goods and services for cash or credit. (page 677)

Trading Range Price range between highest and lowest prices at which a stock is traded. (page 594)

Transaction Motive The need to hold cash to satisfy normal disbursement and collection activities associated with a firm's ongoing operations. (page 646)

Trust Receipt An instrument acknowledging that the borrower holds certain goods in trust for the lender. (page 632)

Unbiased Forward Rates (UFR) The condition stating that the current forward rate is an unbiased predictor of the future exchange rate. (page 820)

Uncovered Interest Parity (UIP) The condition stating that the expected percentage change in the exchange rate is equal to the difference in interest rates. (page 820)

Unlevered Cost of Capital The cost of capital of a firm that has no debt. (page 545)

Unsystematic Risk A risk that affects at most a small number of assets. Also unique or asset-specific risks. (page 390)

Uses of Cash A firm's activities in which cash is spent. Also applications of cash. (page 57)

Variable Costs Costs that change when the quantity of output changes. (page 315)

Variance The average squared deviation between the actual return and the average return. (page 357)

Warrant A security that gives the holder the right to purchase shares of stock at a fixed price over a given period of time. (page 738)

Weighted Average Cost of Capital (WACC) The weighted average of the costs of debt and equity. (page 502)

Working Capital Management Planning and managing the firm's current assets and liabilities. (page 5)

Yield to Maturity (YTM) The market interest rate that equates a bond's present value of interest payments and principal repayment with its price. (page 188)

Zero-Balance Account A chequing account in which a zero balance is maintained by transfers of funds from a master account in an amount only large enough to cover cheques presented. (page 658)

Zero Coupon Bond See Stripped Bond.

Mathematical Tables

T A B L E A.1 | *Future value of $1 at the end of t periods* $= (1 + r)^t$

Interest Rate

Period	1%	2%	3%	4%	5%	6%	7%	8%	9%
1	1.0100	1.0200	1.0300	1.0400	1.0500	1.0600	1.0700	1.0800	1.0900
2	1.0201	1.0404	1.0609	1.0816	1.1025	1.1236	1.1449	1.1664	1.1881
3	1.0303	1.0612	1.0927	1.1249	1.1576	1.1910	1.2250	1.2597	1.2950
4	1.0406	1.0824	1.1255	1.1699	1.2155	1.2625	1.3108	1.3605	1.4116
5	1.0510	1.1041	1.1593	1.2167	1.2763	1.3382	1.4026	1.4693	1.5386
6	1.0615	1.1262	1.1941	1.2653	1.3401	1.4185	1.5007	1.5869	1.6771
7	1.0721	1.1487	1.2299	1.3159	1.4071	1.5036	1.6058	1.7138	1.8280
8	1.0829	1.1717	1.2668	1.3686	1.4775	1.5938	1.7182	1.8509	1.9926
9	1.0937	1.1951	1.3048	1.4233	1.5513	1.6895	1.8385	1.9990	2.1719
10	1.1046	1.2190	1.3439	1.4802	1.6289	1.7908	1.9672	2.1589	2.3674
11	1.1157	1.2434	1.3842	1.5395	1.7103	1.8983	2.1049	2.3316	2.5804
12	1.1268	1.2682	1.4258	1.6010	1.7959	2.0122	2.2522	2.5182	2.8127
13	1.1381	1.2936	1.4685	1.6651	1.8856	2.1329	2.4098	2.7196	3.0658
14	1.1495	1.3195	1.5126	1.7317	1.9799	2.2609	2.5785	2.9372	3.3417
15	1.1610	1.3459	1.5580	1.8009	2.0789	2.3966	2.7590	3.1722	3.6425
16	1.1726	1.3728	1.6047	1.8730	2.1829	2.5404	2.9522	3.4259	3.9703
17	1.1843	1.4002	1.6528	1.9479	2.2920	2.6928	3.1588	3.7000	4.3276
18	1.1961	1.4282	1.7024	2.0258	2.4066	2.8543	3.3799	3.9960	4.7171
19	1.2081	1.4568	1.7535	2.1068	2.5270	3.0256	3.6165	4.3157	5.1417
20	1.2202	1.4859	1.8061	2.1911	2.6533	3.2071	3.8697	4.6610	5.6044
21	1.2324	1.5157	1.8603	2.2788	2.7860	3.3996	4.1406	5.0338	6.1088
22	1.2447	1.5460	1.9161	2.3699	2.9253	3.6035	4.4304	5.4365	6.6586
23	1.2572	1.5769	1.9736	2.4647	3.0715	3.8197	4.7405	5.8715	7.2579
24	1.2697	1.6084	2.0328	2.5633	3.2251	4.0489	5.0724	6.3412	7.9111
25	1.2824	1.6406	2.0938	2.6658	3.3864	4.2919	5.4274	6.8485	8.6231
30	1.3478	1.8114	2.4273	3.2434	4.3219	5.7435	7.6123	10.063	13.268
40	1.4889	2.2080	3.2620	4.8010	7.0400	10.286	14.974	21.725	31.409
50	1.6446	2.6916	4.3839	7.1067	11.467	18.420	29.457	46.902	74.358
60	1.8167	3.2810	5.8916	10.520	18.679	32.988	57.946	101.26	176.03

T A B L E A.1 | *(concluded)*

					Interest Rate					
10%	12%	14%	15%	16%	18%	20%	24%	28%	32%	36%
1.1000	1.1200	1.1400	1.1500	1.1600	1.1800	1.2000	1.2400	1.2800	1.3200	1.3600
1.2100	1.2544	1.2996	1.3225	1.3456	1.3924	1.4400	1.5376	1.6384	1.7424	1.8496
1.3310	1.4049	1.4815	1.5209	1.5609	1.6430	1.7280	1.9066	2.0972	2.3000	2.5155
1.4641	1.5735	1.6890	1.7490	1.8106	1.9388	2.0736	2.3642	2.6844	3.0360	3.4210
1.6105	1.7623	1.9254	2.0114	2.1003	2.2878	2.4883	2.9316	3.4360	4.0075	4.6526
1.7716	1.9738	2.1950	2.3131	2.4364	2.6996	2.9860	3.6352	4.3980	5.2899	6.3275
1.9487	2.2107	2.5023	2.6600	2.8262	3.1855	3.5832	4.5077	5.6295	6.9826	8.6054
2.1436	2.4760	2.8526	3.0590	3.2784	3.7589	4.2998	5.5895	7.2058	9.2170	11.703
2.3579	2.7731	3.2519	3.5179	3.8030	4.4355	5.1598	6.9310	9.2234	12.166	15.917
2.5937	3.1058	3.7072	4.0456	4.4114	5.2338	6.1917	8.5944	11.806	16.060	21.647
2.8531	3.4785	4.2262	4.6524	5.1173	6.1759	7.4301	10.657	15.112	21.199	29.439
3.1384	3.8960	4.8179	5.3503	5.9360	7.2876	8.9161	13.215	19.343	27.983	40.037
3.4523	4.3635	5.4924	6.1528	6.8858	8.5994	10.699	16.386	24.759	36.937	54.451
3.7975	4.8871	6.2613	7.0757	7.9875	10.147	12.839	20.319	31.691	48.757	74.053
4.1772	5.4736	7.1379	8.1371	9.2655	11.974	15.407	25.196	40.565	64.359	100.71
4.5950	6.1304	8.1372	9.3576	10.748	14.129	18.488	31.243	51.923	84.954	136.97
5.0545	6.8660	9.2765	10.761	12.468	16.672	22.186	38.741	66.461	112.14	186.28
5.5599	7.6900	10.575	12.375	14.463	19.673	26.623	48.039	85.071	148.02	253.34
6.1159	8.6128	12.056	14.232	16.777	23.214	31.948	59.568	108.89	195.39	344.54
6.7275	9.6463	13.743	16.367	19.461	27.393	38.338	73.864	139.38	257.92	468.57
7.4002	10.804	15.668	18.822	22.574	32.324	46.005	91.592	178.41	340.45	637.26
8.1403	12.100	17.861	21.645	26.186	38.142	55.206	113.57	228.36	449.39	866.67
8.9543	13.552	20.362	24.891	30.376	45.008	66.247	140.83	292.30	593.20	1178.7
9.8497	15.179	23.212	28.625	35.236	53.109	79.497	174.63	374.14	783.02	1603.0
10.835	17.000	26.462	32.919	40.874	62.669	95.396	216.54	478.90	1033.6	2180.1
17.449	29.960	50.950	66.212	85.850	143.37	237.38	634.82	1645.5	4142.1	10143
45.259	93.051	188.88	267.86	378.72	750.38	1469.8	5455.9	19427	66521	*
117.39	289.00	700.23	1083.7	1670.7	3927.4	9100.4	46890	*	*	*
304.48	897.60	2595.9	4384.0	7370.2	20555	56348	*	*	*	*

*FVIV > 99,999.

T A B L E   A.2 | *Present value of $1 to be received after t periods = $1/(1 + r)^t$*

Interest Rate

Period	1%	2%	3%	4%	5%	6%	7%	8%	9%
1	0.9901	0.9804	0.9709	0.9615	0.9524	0.9434	0.9346	0.9259	0.9174
2	0.9803	0.9612	0.9426	0.9246	0.9070	0.8900	0.8734	0.8573	0.8417
3	0.9706	0.9423	0.9151	0.8890	0.8638	0.8396	0.8163	0.7938	0.7722
4	0.9610	0.9238	0.8885	0.8548	0.8227	0.7921	0.7629	0.7350	0.7084
5	0.9515	0.9057	0.8626	0.8219	0.7835	0.7473	0.7130	0.6806	0.6499
6	0.9420	0.8880	0.8375	0.7903	0.7462	0.7050	0.6663	0.6302	0.5963
7	0.9327	0.8706	0.8131	0.7599	0.7107	0.6651	0.6227	0.5835	0.5470
8	0.9235	0.8535	0.7894	0.7307	0.6768	0.6274	0.5820	0.5403	0.5019
9	0.9143	0.8368	0.7664	0.7026	0.6446	0.5919	0.5439	0.5002	0.4604
10	0.9053	0.8203	0.7441	0.6756	0.6139	0.5584	0.5083	0.4632	0.4224
11	0.8963	0.8043	0.7224	0.6496	0.5847	0.5268	0.4751	0.4289	0.3875
12	0.8874	0.7885	0.7014	0.6246	0.5568	0.4970	0.4440	0.3971	0.3555
13	0.8787	0.7730	0.6810	0.6006	0.5303	0.4688	0.4150	0.3677	0.3262
14	0.8700	0.7579	0.6611	0.5775	0.5051	0.4423	0.3878	0.3405	0.2992
15	0.8613	0.7430	0.6419	0.5553	0.4810	0.4173	0.3624	0.3152	0.2745
16	0.8528	0.7284	0.6232	0.5339	0.4581	0.3936	0.3387	0.2919	0.2519
17	0.8444	0.7142	0.6050	0.5134	0.4363	0.3714	0.3166	0.2703	0.2311
18	0.8360	0.7002	0.5874	0.4936	0.4155	0.3503	0.2959	0.2502	0.2120
19	0.8277	0.6864	0.5703	0.4746	0.3957	0.3305	0.2765	0.2317	0.1945
20	0.8195	0.6730	0.5537	0.4564	0.3769	0.3118	0.2584	0.2145	0.1784
21	0.8114	0.6598	0.5375	0.4388	0.3589	0.2942	0.2415	0.1987	0.1637
22	0.8034	0.6468	0.5219	0.4220	0.3418	0.2775	0.2257	0.1839	0.1502
23	0.7954	0.6342	0.5067	0.4057	0.3256	0.2618	0.2109	0.1703	0.1378
24	0.7876	0.6217	0.4919	0.3901	0.3101	0.2470	0.1971	0.1577	0.1264
25	0.7798	0.6095	0.4776	0.3751	0.2953	0.2330	0.1842	0.1460	0.1160
30	0.7419	0.5521	0.4120	0.3083	0.2314	0.1741	0.1314	0.0994	0.0754
40	0.6717	0.4529	0.3066	0.2083	0.1420	0.0972	0.0668	0.0460	0.0318
50	0.6080	0.3715	0.2281	0.1407	0.0872	0.0543	0.0339	0.0213	0.0134

T A B L E A.2 | (concluded)

					Interest Rate					
10%	12%	14%	15%	16%	18%	20%	24%	28%	32%	36%
0.9091	0.8929	0.8772	0.8696	0.8621	0.8475	0.8333	0.8065	0.7813	0.7576	0.7353
0.8264	0.7972	0.7695	0.7561	0.7432	0.7182	0.6944	0.6504	0.6104	0.5739	0.5407
0.7513	0.7118	0.6750	0.6575	0.6407	0.6086	0.5787	0.5245	0.4768	0.4348	0.3975
0.6830	0.6355	0.5921	0.5718	0.5523	0.5158	0.4823	0.4230	0.3725	0.3294	0.2923
0.6209	0.5674	0.5194	0.4972	0.4761	0.4371	0.4019	0.3411	0.2910	0.2495	0.2149
0.5645	0.5066	0.4556	0.4323	0.4104	0.3704	0.3349	0.2751	0.2274	0.1890	0.1580
0.5132	0.4523	0.3996	0.3759	0.3538	0.3139	0.2791	0.2218	0.1776	0.1432	0.1162
0.4665	0.4039	0.3506	0.3269	0.3050	0.2660	0.2326	0.1789	0.1388	0.1085	0.0854
0.4241	0.3606	0.3075	0.2843	0.2630	0.2255	0.1938	0.1443	0.1084	0.0822	0.0628
0.3855	0.3220	0.2697	0.2472	0.2267	0.1911	0.1615	0.1164	0.0847	0.0623	0.0462
0.3505	0.2875	0.2366	0.2149	0.1954	0.1619	0.1346	0.0938	0.0662	0.0472	0.0340
0.3186	0.2567	0.2076	0.1869	0.1685	0.1372	0.1122	0.0757	0.0517	0.0357	0.0250
0.2897	0.2292	0.1821	0.1625	0.1452	0.1163	0.0935	0.0610	0.0404	0.0271	0.0184
0.2633	0.2046	0.1597	0.1413	0.1252	0.0985	0.0779	0.0492	0.0316	0.0205	0.0135
0.2394	0.1827	0.1401	0.1229	0.1079	0.0835	0.0649	0.0397	0.0247	0.0155	0.0099
0.2176	0.1631	0.1229	0.1069	0.0930	0.0708	0.0541	0.0320	0.0193	0.0118	0.0073
0.1978	0.1456	0.1078	0.0929	0.0802	0.0600	0.0451	0.0258	0.0150	0.0089	0.0054
0.1799	0.1300	0.0946	0.0808	0.0691	0.0508	0.0376	0.0208	0.0118	0.0068	0.0039
0.1635	0.1161	0.0829	0.0703	0.0596	0.0431	0.0313	0.0168	0.0092	0.0051	0.0029
0.1486	0.1037	0.0728	0.0611	0.0514	0.0365	0.0261	0.0135	0.0072	0.0039	0.0021
0.1351	0.0926	0.0638	0.0531	0.0443	0.0309	0.0217	0.0109	0.0056	0.0029	0.0016
0.1228	0.0826	0.0560	0.0462	0.0382	0.0262	0.0181	0.0088	0.0044	0.0022	0.0012
0.1117	0.0738	0.0491	0.0402	0.0329	0.0222	0.0151	0.0071	0.0034	0.0017	0.0008
0.1015	0.0659	0.0431	0.0349	0.0284	0.0188	0.0126	0.0057	0.0027	0.0013	0.0006
0.0923	0.0588	0.0378	0.0304	0.0245	0.0160	0.0105	0.0046	0.0021	0.0010	0.0005
0.0573	0.0334	0.0196	0.0151	0.0116	0.0070	0.0042	0.0016	0.0006	0.0002	0.0001
0.0221	0.0107	0.0053	0.0037	0.0026	0.0013	0.0007	0.0002	0.0001	*	*
0.0085	0.0035	0.0014	0.0009	0.0006	0.0003	0.0001	*	*	*	*

*The factor is zero to four decimal places.

T A B L E A.3 | *Present value of an annuity of $1 per period for t periods = $[1 - 1/(1 + r)^t]/r$*

Number of Periods	Interest Rate								
	1%	2%	3%	4%	5%	6%	7%	8%	9%
1	0.9901	0.9804	0.9709	0.9615	0.9524	0.9434	0.9346	0.9259	0.9174
2	1.9704	1.9416	1.9135	1.8861	1.8594	1.8334	1.8080	1.7833	1.7591
3	2.9410	2.8839	2.8286	2.7751	2.7232	2.6730	2.6243	2.5771	2.5313
4	3.9020	3.8077	3.7171	3.6299	3.5460	3.4651	3.3872	3.3121	3.2397
5	4.8534	4.7135	4.5797	4.4518	4.3295	4.2124	4.1002	3.9927	3.8897
6	5.7955	5.6014	5.4172	5.2421	5.0757	4.9173	4.7665	4.6229	4.4859
7	6.7282	6.4720	6.2303	6.0021	5.7864	5.5824	5.3893	5.2064	5.0330
8	7.6517	7.3255	7.0197	6.7327	6.4632	6.2098	5.9713	5.7466	5.5348
9	8.5660	8.1622	7.7861	7.4353	7.1078	6.8017	6.5152	6.2469	5.9952
10	9.4713	8.9826	8.5302	8.1109	7.7217	7.3601	7.0236	6.7101	6.4177
11	10.3676	9.7868	9.2526	8.7605	8.3064	7.8869	7.4987	7.1390	6.8052
12	11.2551	10.5753	9.9540	9.3851	8.8633	8.3838	7.9427	7.5361	7.1607
13	12.1337	11.3484	10.6350	9.9856	9.3936	8.8527	8.3577	7.9038	7.4869
14	13.0037	12.1062	11.2961	10.5631	9.8986	9.2950	8.7455	8.2442	7.7862
15	13.8651	12.8493	11.9379	11.1184	10.3797	9.7122	9.1079	8.5595	8.0607
16	14.7179	13.5777	12.5611	11.6523	10.8378	10.1059	9.4466	8.8514	8.3126
17	15.5623	14.2919	13.1661	12.1657	11.2741	10.4773	9.7632	9.1216	8.5436
18	16.3983	14.9920	13.7535	12.6593	11.6896	10.8276	10.0591	9.3719	8.7556
19	17.2260	15.6785	14.3238	13.1339	12.0853	11.1581	10.3356	9.6036	8.9501
20	18.0456	16.3514	14.8775	13.5903	12.4622	11.4699	10.5940	9.8181	9.1285
21	18.8570	17.0112	15.4150	14.0292	12.8212	11.7641	10.8355	10.0168	9.2922
22	19.6604	17.6580	15.9369	14.4511	13.1630	12.0416	11.0612	10.2007	9.4424
23	20.4558	18.2922	16.4436	14.8568	13.4886	12.3034	11.2722	10.3741	9.5802
24	21.2434	18.9139	16.9355	15.2470	13.7986	12.5504	11.4693	10.5288	9.7066
25	22.0232	19.5235	17.4131	15.6221	14.0939	12.7834	11.6536	10.6748	9.8226
30	25.8077	22.3965	19.6004	17.2920	15.3725	13.7648	12.4090	11.2578	10.2737
40	32.8347	27.3555	23.1148	19.7928	17.1591	15.0463	13.3317	11.9246	10.7574
50	39.1961	31.4236	25.7298	21.4822	18.2559	15.7619	13.8007	12.2335	10.9617

T A B L E A.3 *(concluded)*

				Interest Rate					
10%	12%	14%	15%	16%	18%	20%	24%	28%	32%
0.9091	0.8929	0.8772	0.8696	0.8621	0.8475	0.8333	0.8065	0.7813	0.7576
1.7355	1.6901	1.6467	1.6257	1.6052	1.5656	1.5278	1.4568	1.3916	1.3315
2.4869	2.4018	2.3216	2.2832	2.2459	2.1743	2.1065	1.9813	1.8684	1.7663
3.1699	3.0373	2.9137	2.8550	2.7982	2.6901	2.5887	2.4043	2.2410	2.0957
3.7908	3.6048	3.4331	3.3522	3.2743	3.1272	2.9906	2.7454	2.5320	2.3452
4.3553	4.1114	3.8887	3.7845	3.6847	3.4976	3.3255	3.0205	2.7594	2.5342
4.8684	4.5638	4.2883	4.1604	4.0386	3.8115	3.6046	3.2423	2.9370	2.6775
5.3349	4.9676	4.6389	4.4873	4.3436	4.0776	3.8372	3.4212	3.0758	2.7860
5.7590	5.3282	4.9464	4.7716	4.6065	4.3030	4.0310	3.5655	3.1842	2.8681
6.1446	5.6502	5.2161	5.0188	4.8332	4.4941	4.1925	3.6819	3.2689	2.9304
6.4951	5.9377	5.4527	5.2337	5.0286	4.6560	4.3271	3.7757	3.3351	2.9776
6.8137	6.1944	5.6603	5.4206	5.1971	4.7932	4.4392	3.8514	3.3868	3.0133
7.1034	6.4235	5.8424	5.5831	5.3423	4.9095	4.5327	3.9124	3.4272	3.0404
7.3667	6.6282	6.0021	5.7245	5.4675	5.0081	4.6106	3.9616	3.4587	3.0609
7.6061	6.8109	6.1422	5.8474	5.5755	5.0916	4.6755	4.0013	3.4834	3.0764
7.8237	6.9740	6.2651	5.9542	5.6685	5.1624	4.7296	4.0333	3.5026	3.0882
8.0216	7.1196	6.3729	6.0472	5.7487	5.2223	4.7746	4.0591	3.5177	3.0971
8.2014	7.2497	6.4674	6.1280	5.8178	5.2732	4.8122	4.0799	3.5294	3.1039
8.3649	7.3658	6.5504	6.1982	5.8775	5.3162	4.8435	4.0967	3.5386	3.1090
8.5136	7.4694	6.6231	6.2593	5.9288	5.3527	4.8696	4.1103	3.5458	3.1129
8.6487	7.5620	6.6870	6.3125	5.9731	5.3837	4.8913	4.1212	3.5514	3.1158
8.7715	7.6446	6.7429	6.3587	6.0113	5.4099	4.9094	4.1300	3.5558	3.1180
8.8832	7.7184	6.7921	6.3988	6.0442	5.4321	4.9245	4.1371	3.5592	3.1197
8.9847	7.7843	6.8351	6.4338	6.0726	5.4509	4.9371	4.1428	3.5619	3.1210
9.0770	7.8431	6.8729	6.4641	6.0971	5.4669	4.9476	4.1474	3.5640	3.1220
9.4269	8.0552	7.0027	6.5660	6.1772	5.5168	4.9789	4.1601	3.5693	3.1242
9.7791	8.2438	7.1050	6.6418	6.2335	5.5482	4.9966	4.1659	3.5712	3.1250
9.9148	8.3045	7.1327	6.6605	6.2463	5.5541	4.9995	4.1666	3.5714	3.1250

T A B L E A.4 | *Future value of an annuity of $1 per period for t periods* $= [(1 + r)^t - 1]/r$

Number of Periods	Interest Rate								
	1%	2%	3%	4%	5%	6%	7%	8%	9%
1	1.0000	1.0000	1.0000	1.0000	1.0000	1.0000	1.0000	1.0000	1.0000
2	2.0100	2.0200	2.0300	2.0400	2.0500	2.0600	2.0700	2.0800	2.0900
3	3.0301	3.0604	3.0909	3.1216	3.1525	3.1836	3.2149	3.2464	3.2781
4	4.0604	4.1216	4.1836	4.2465	4.3101	4.3746	4.4399	4.5061	4.5731
5	5.1010	5.2040	5.3091	5.4163	5.5256	5.6371	5.7507	5.8666	5.9847
6	6.1520	6.3081	6.4684	6.6330	6.8019	6.9753	7.1533	7.3359	7.5233
7	7.2135	7.4343	7.6625	7.8983	8.1420	8.3938	8.6540	8.9228	9.2004
8	8.2857	8.5830	8.8932	9.2142	9.5491	9.8975	10.260	10.637	11.028
9	9.3685	9.7546	10.159	10.583	11.027	11.491	11.978	12.488	13.021
10	10.462	10.950	11.464	12.006	12.578	13.181	13.816	14.487	15.193
11	11.567	12.169	12.808	13.486	14.207	14.972	15.784	16.645	17.560
12	12.683	13.412	14.192	15.026	15.917	16.870	17.888	18.977	20.141
13	13.809	14.680	15.618	16.627	17.713	18.882	20.141	21.495	22.953
14	14.947	15.974	17.086	18.292	19.599	21.015	22.550	24.215	26.019
15	16.097	17.293	18.599	20.024	21.579	23.276	25.129	27.152	29.361
16	17.258	18.639	20.157	21.825	23.657	25.673	27.888	30.324	33.003
17	18.430	20.012	21.762	23.698	25.840	28.213	30.840	33.750	36.974
18	19.615	21.412	23.414	25.645	28.132	30.906	33.999	37.450	41.301
19	20.811	22.841	25.117	27.671	30.539	33.760	37.379	41.446	46.018
20	22.019	24.297	26.870	29.778	33.066	36.786	40.995	45.762	51.160
21	23.239	25.783	28.676	31.969	35.719	39.993	44.865	50.423	56.765
22	24.472	27.299	30.537	34.248	38.505	43.392	49.006	55.457	62.873
23	25.716	28.845	32.453	36.618	41.430	46.996	53.436	60.893	69.532
24	26.973	30.422	34.426	39.083	44.502	50.816	58.177	66.765	76.790
25	28.243	32.030	36.459	41.646	47.727	54.865	63.249	73.106	84.701
30	34.785	40.568	47.575	56.085	66.439	79.058	94.461	113.28	136.31
40	48.886	60.402	75.401	95.026	120.80	154.76	199.64	259.06	337.88
50	64.463	84.579	112.80	152.67	209.35	290.34	406.53	573.77	815.08
60	81.670	114.05	163.05	237.99	353.58	533.13	813.52	1253.2	1944.8

T A B L E A.4 *(concluded)*

					Interest Rate					
10%	12%	14%	15%	16%	18%	20%	24%	28%	32%	36%
1.0000	1.0000	1.0000	1.0000	1.0000	1.0000	1.0000	1.0000	1.0000	1.0000	1.0000
2.1000	2.1200	2.1400	2.1500	2.1600	2.1800	2.2000	2.2400	2.2800	2.3200	2.3600
3.3100	3.3744	3.4396	3.4725	3.5056	3.5724	3.6400	3.7776	3.9184	4.0624	4.2096
4.6410	4.7793	4.9211	4.9934	5.0665	5.2154	5.3680	5.6842	6.0156	6.3624	6.7251
6.1051	6.3528	6.6101	6.7424	6.8771	7.1542	7.4416	8.0484	8.6999	9.3983	10.146
7.7156	8.1152	8.5355	8.7537	8.9775	9.4420	9.9299	10.980	12.136	13.406	14.799
9.4872	10.089	10.730	11.067	11.414	12.142	12.916	14.615	16.534	18.696	21.126
11.436	12.300	13.233	13.727	14.240	15.327	16.499	19.123	22.163	25.678	29.732
13.579	14.776	16.085	16.786	17.519	19.086	20.799	24.712	29.369	34.895	41.435
15.937	17.549	19.337	20.304	21.321	23.521	25.959	31.643	38.593	47.062	57.352
18.531	20.655	23.045	24.349	25.733	28.755	32.150	40.238	50.398	63.122	78.998
21.384	24.133	27.271	29.002	30.850	34.931	39.581	50.895	65.510	84.320	108.44
24.523	28.029	32.089	34.352	36.786	42.219	48.497	64.110	84.853	112.30	148.47
27.975	32.393	37.581	40.505	43.672	50.818	59.196	80.496	109.61	149.24	202.93
31.772	37.280	43.842	47.580	51.660	60.965	72.035	100.82	141.30	198.00	276.98
35.950	42.753	50.980	55.717	60.925	72.939	87.442	126.01	181.87	262.36	377.69
40.545	48.884	59.118	65.075	71.673	87.068	105.93	157.25	233.79	347.31	514.66
45.599	55.750	68.394	75.836	84.141	103.74	128.12	195.99	300.25	459.45	700.94
51.159	63.440	78.969	88.212	98.603	123.41	154.74	244.03	385.32	607.47	954.28
57.275	72.052	91.025	102.44	115.38	146.63	186.69	303.60	494.21	802.86	1298.8
64.002	81.699	104.77	118.81	134.84	174.02	225.03	377.46	633.59	1060.8	1767.4
71.403	92.503	120.44	137.63	157.41	206.34	271.03	469.06	812.00	1401.2	2404.7
79.543	104.60	138.30	159.28	183.60	244.49	326.24	582.63	1040.4	1850.6	3271.3
88.497	118.16	158.66	184.17	213.98	289.49	392.48	723.46	1332.7	2443.8	4450.0
98.347	133.33	181.87	212.79	249.21	342.60	471.98	898.09	1706.8	3226.8	6053.0
164.49	241.33	356.79	434.75	530.31	790.95	1181.9	2640.9	5873.2	12941	28172.3
442.59	767.09	1342.0	1779.1	2360.8	4163.2	7343.9	22729	69377	*	*
1163.9	2400.0	4994.5	7217.7	10436	21813	45497	*	*	*	*
3034.8	7471.6	18535	29220	46058	*	*	*	*	*	*

*FVIFA > 99,999.

Answers to Selected End-of-Chapter Problems

CHAPTER 2

1. Shareholder's equity = $3,800
   Net working capital = $500
3. Addition to retained earnings = $26,200
5. Book value = $2.5M
   Market value = $3.2M
7. Net capital spending = $500K
9. Tax bill = $278,400
11. Cash flow to bondholders = $325,000
13. Operating cash flow = $500K
15. Depreciation = $1,000
17. Owner's equity = $100
    Owner's equity = $0
19. *a.* Net income = ($25,000)
    b. Operating cash flow = $100,000
21. *a.* Net income = $462
    b. Operating cash flow = $1,762
    c. Cash flow from assets = ($338)
    d. Cash flow to bondholders = $300
       Cash flow to stockholders = ($638)
27. *a.* After tax rate of return on dividends = 4.65%
    b. After tax rate of return on interest = 3.71%
    c. After tax rate of return on capital gains = 4.03%
29. CCA   Ending UCC
     $36,800 $147,200
     $66,240 $264,960
     $52,992 $211,968
     $42,394 $169,574
     $33,915 $135,660
31. CCA for 1995 = $93,750
    CCA for 1996 = $169,063
33. A. After tax income = $2,196.59
    B. After tax income = $2,502.50
    C. After tax income = $2,050.61
35. Ending UCC = $16,445

CHAPTER 3

1. *a.* No change (assuming cash purchase)
   c. Increase
   e. No change
   g. Increase
5. Current ratio = 1.28
   Quick ratio = 0.94
7. Receivables turnover = 6.95

Days' sales in receivables = 52.51 days
Average collection period = 52.51 days
9. Total debt ratio = 0.60
   Debt to equity ratio = 1.50
   Equity multiplier = 2.50
11. Return on equity = 20%
13. Cash decreased by $825
15. $500; a use of cash
21. *a.* 1.183; 1.322
    b. 0.474; 0.508
    c. 0.113; 0.123
    d. 0.044; 0.070
    e. Debt to equity ratio: 0.621; 0.448
       Equity multiplier: 1.621; 1.448
    f. Total debt ratio: 0.383; 0.310
       Long-term debt ratio: 0.190; 0.118
34. Return on equity = 21.75%
35. Interval measure = 494 days
37. P/E ratio = 9.85 times
    Dividends per share = $1.50
    Market to book ratio = 2.14 times

CHAPTER 4

1. Pro forma net income = $1,200
   Pro forma equity = $2,100
   Dividends (the plug) = $850
3. −$572.50
5. $692.80
7. $g^* = 6.36\%$
9. $837.78
13. ROA = 11.31%; ROE = 20.33%
15. $g^* = 15.94\%$
17. $g^* = 7.53\%$
19. $6,800
21. 12.28%
23. Total asset turnover = 1.887 times
25. $g^* = 1.52\%$; additional borrowing = $457
    $g_{int} = 0.86\%$
27. −$16,935
29. EFN is zero when $g = 19.15\%$
31. $g^* = 4.17\%$

CHAPTER 5

1. $1,958.56
3. PV = $260.79

PV = $3,517.62
PV = $3,363.82
PV = $83,205.57

5. $t = 9.79$; 2.32; 28.66; 6.30 years
7. $t = 8.04$ years; $t = 12.75$ years
9. 3.83 years
11. PV @ 10% = $1,688.75
    PV @ 14% = $1,559.83
    PV @ 20% = $1,394.68
13. FV @ 6% = $3,312.79
    FV @ 8% = $3,422.86
    FV @ 16% = $3,893.29
15. $10,927.98
17. $9,336.17; $12,257.77
19. $1,607.25
21. 8.24%
23. APR = 7.85%; 11.39%; 15.72%; 21.51%
25. APR = 8.65%
27. FV = $338.25; $352.05; $667.63
29. APR = 300%; EAR = 1,355.19%
31. 43 months
33. $r = 0.83\%$ per month
    APR = 10%; EAR = 10.47%
35. $38,986.47
37. $10,405.23
39. 6.05%
41. $PVA_1 = \$65,082.91$
    $PVA_2 = \$62,541.45$
43. $r_G = 8.15\%$; $r_H = 8.28\%$
45. 77 payments
47. $4,179.19
49. PV = $38,609.17
    Break-even $r = 5.98\%$
51. $3,334,927.21
53. $70,182.10
55. $3,520.05
57. FV = $197,397.39; $313,244.85
59. *a.* $1,693.61
    b. $1,812.16
61. $r = 11.11\%$, not 10%
63. Quoted rate = 13.32%
    EAR = 13.76%
65. *a.* $788
    b. $8,824.29
    c. $364.33
69. 3.63%
73. *a.* APR = 520%; EAR = 14,104.29%
    b. APR = 577.78%; EAR = 23,854.63%
    c. APR = 1,604.43%; EAR = 118,306,303%

CHAPTER 6

5. 9.22%
7. $1,097.91
9. 7.82%

11. $P_0 = \$30.29$; $P_3 = \$36.07$; $P_{15} = \$72.58$
13. Dividend yield = 4.26%
    Capital gains yield = 5%
15. 10.5%
17. $P_0 = \$22.82$
21. $\Delta P_A = -3.55\%$; $\Delta P_B = -15.37\%$
    $\Delta P_A = +3.72\%$; $\Delta P_B = +19.60\%$
23. Current yield = 10.91%
    YTM = 10.27%; Effective yield = 10.53%
25. 11.95 years
29. $P_0 = \$52.68$
31. $P_0 = \$27.84$
33. $P_0 = \$20.85$
35. $P_0 = \$17.90$
37. $P_0 = \$97.96$
39. P: current yield = 8.75%
        capital gains yield = -0.75%
    D: current yield = 6.78%
        capital gains yield = 1.22%
41. $P_M = \$17,125.37$; $P_N = \$3,551.14$
44. *a.* $P_0 = \$41.25$
    b. P_0 $38.15
45. $P_0 = \$122.61$

CHAPTER 7

1. 2.67 years
3. Payback: A = 1.56 years; B = 2.80 years
5. 4.00 years; 4.58 years; no payback at 10%
7. IRR = 16.11%
9. NPV @ 7% = $77.86; NPV @ 15% = −$167.92
    IRR = 9.20%
11. $300; $130.28; $6.48; −$86.57
13. Crossover rate = 11.24%
15. 1.119; 1.049; 0.958
17. *a.* A: 3.529 years; B: 0.889 years
    b. A: 3.965 years; B: 1.230 years
    c. A: $8,547.85; B: $3,525.79
    d. A: 15.98%; B: 24.04%
    e. A: 1.033; B: 1.088
27. Payback = 1/IRR
29. There is no crossover rate for positive NPVs
31. Worst case: NPV = −$45,231.93
    Best case: NPV = ∞
33. *a.* NPV = $41,667
    b. $g = 5.41\%$

CHAPTER 8

3. Operating cash flow = $5,123.40
5. NPV = $25,477.41
9. $900
11. $7.7M
13. $32,787 per system
15. Method 1: EAC = −$582.69; Method 2: EAC = −$811.32

17. NPV of purchasing the new excavator = –$3,620.35
19. Underground: EAC = –$695,273; Above ground: EAC = –$414,257
21. $18.67
23. 10 SALS: EAC = $18,935; 8 DETS: EAC = $18,458
25. a. NPV = –$262,347
    b. 1 year: NPV = –$155,172.41
       2 years: NPV = $1,833,532
       3 years: NPV = $1,405,572
27. a. Cost savings = $27,320.30
    b. Cost savings = $25,214.42

CHAPTER 9

1. a. $2.62
   b. $1,427,000
   c. Q_{cf} = 312,883; Q_{acc} = 411,043
5. a. Q_{acc} = 114,465; DOL = 5.688
   b. OCF = $343,625; NPV = $452,782.34
      Δ NPV/ΔS = +$21.246
   c. Δ OCF/Δv = –97,500
7. a. Q_{cf} = 12,000; Q_{acc} = 20,000
   b. Q_{cf} = 1,600; Q_{acc} = 8,800
   c. Q_{cf} = 125; Q_{acc} = 325
9. Q_{cf} = 100; Q_{acc} = 160; Q_{acc} = 179
   DOL = 2.268
11. Δ OCF = +60%; the new operating leverage is lower
13. DOL = 1.375; Increase in OCF = $33,000
    New DOL = 1.322
17. @ 9,000 units: DOL = 1.421
    @ 7,000 units: DOL = 1.615
21. Δ OCF/ΔQ = +$3.30
23. a. NPV_{worst} = –$319,471.13
       NPV_{base} = $80,706.66
       NPV_{best} = $545,987.62
    b. Δ NPV/ΔFC = –2.153
    c. 29.17 units
    d. Q_{acc} = 59.17 units; DOL = 1.972
25. a. $29,425.42
    b. $48,310.17
29. a. OCF = $436,000; NPV = $235,767.34
    b. NPV_{worst} = –$1,192,006.19
       NPV_{best} = $1,663,540.87
31. Q_{cf} = 1,559; Q_{acc} = 15,000; Q_{fin} = 21,308

CHAPTER 10

1. –11.57%
3. R = 23.61%; Dividend yield = 3.24%
   Capital gains yield = 20.37%
5. 9.68%
7. 8.57%
9. a. $70
   b. 7.25%
   c. 3.13%

12. Average: X = 6.2%; Y = 9.4%
    Standard deviation: s_X = 7.92%; s_Y = 18.47%
14. a. 6%
    b. Variance = 0.0187
       Standard deviation = 13.67%
15. a. 1.44%
    b. 1.20%
23. The probability is about ⅙
    @ 95%: R between –12.1% and +21.9%
    @ 99%: R between –20.6% and +30.4%
25. The probability is zero.
29. a. 38.4%; 24.6%
    b. 17.8%; 7.0%
    c. 12.9%; 35.7%

CHAPTER 11

1. 0.625; 0.375
3. 14.7%
5. 20.0%
7. $E(R_A)$ = 10.20%; σ_A = 5.11%
   $E(R_B)$ = 21.05%; σ_B = 20.25%
9. a. 13.12%
   b. 0.05824
15. 1.055
17. 14.2%
19. 19%
21. a. 9.5%
    b. Stock; 0.5625: risk-free asset: 0.4375
    c. 0.533
    d. Stock: 2.1875; risk-free asset: –1.1875
23. M is undervalued; N is overvalued
30. a. $E(R_P)$ = 18.75%; variance = 0.05884
       Standard deviation = 24.26%
    b. 13.50%
    c. 13.10%; 12.86%
31. Investment in C = $55,000
    Investment in risk-free asset = $25,000
    β_{rf} = 0
33. β_A = 2.1875; β_B = 0.9125
    σ_A = 4.33%; σ_B = 18.21%
35. $E(R_M)$ = 16.71%; $E(R_f)$ = 8.14%

CHAPTER 12

1. Market/book value ratio = 0.99
7. Reorganized, PV = $80M
   which is less than the $100M liquidation value

APPENDIX 12A

1. NPV = $20
3. 9%
5. $965.28
7. 9.02%

CHAPTER 13

1. *a.* $1,075,000
   b. 4
   c. $43
   d. $2
3. Number of old shares = 700,000
7. $2,000; $0
9. 674,202
11. *a.* No change
    b. Price drops $2.86 per share
    c. Price drops $5.71 per share
13. EPS falls to $4.85
    BV/share falls to $64.71
    MV/share falls to $58.24
    NPV = −$7,500
15. $14.00
17. $25,714

CHAPTER 14

1. 11.30%
3. 14.22%
5. 6.25%
7. *a.* 8.00%
   b. 4.96%
9. *a.* 10.68%
   b. Aftertax cost of debt = 6.50%
11. 1.787
13. 12.32%
15. 7.82%
17. *a.* Y and Z
    b. W and Y
    c. W would be incorrectly rejected
    Z would be incorrectly accepted
19. $5.453 million
27. 2.54
28. NPV = $440,246

CHAPTER 15

1. *a.* EPS = $2.50; $5.00; $7:00
   b. EPS = $0.17; $4.33; $7.67
3. *a.* ROE = 4.17%; 8.33%; 11.67%
   b. ROE = 0.28%; 7.22%; 12.78%
   c. ROE = 2.71%; 5.42%; 7.58%
   ROE = 0.18%; 4.69%; 8.31%
5. P = $60 per share; V = $18 million
7. P = $35 per share. This is M&M Proposition I without taxes.
9. *a.* 20%
   c. R_E: ABC = 15%; XYZ = 20%
   d. WACC: ABC = 15%; XYZ = 15%
   M&M Proposition I without taxes
11. EBIT = $5.455 million; WACC = 12%
13. *a.* 14%
    b. 15.63%
    c. 19.69%
    d. 11.82%; 10.18%

15. R_E = 17.57%; WACC = 12.91%
    M&M Proposition I with taxes
21. $33,818.18; $40,243.64; $46,669.09
25. β_E = 1.0, 2.0, 6.0, 21.0

CHAPTER 16

2. $28.92
5. *a.* $28.57
   b. $45.45
   c. $36.36
   d. $83.33
   e. 437,500; 275,000; 343,750; 150,000
7. P_0 = $25; P_X = $23.75. The equity and cash accounts will both decline by $5,000.
9. $36.36
11. The accounts are unchanged except the new par value for the stock is $0.20 per share.
    Dividends per share last year = $1.78
13. *a.* ⅓
    b. Planned outlays = $16 million
    Debt/equity ratio = 0.625
15. *a.* Maximum investment = $42 million
    Debt = $18 million
    b. $1.60
    c. Borrowing = $12 million
    Addition to retained earnings = $16 million
    d. Dividends per share = $4.80
    No new borrowing will occur
17. $41,792.25; PV = $31,101.55
27. *a.* $P_0 - P_X = D$
    b. $P_0 - P_X = 0.72D$
    c. $P_0 - P_X = 0.8472D$
    d. $P_0 - P_X = 1.361D$
    e. Tax clienteles may affect dividend policy

CHAPTER 17

3. Cash = $1,000; Current assets = $3,375
9. Operating cycle = 105.10 days
   Cash cycle = −18.21 days
13. *a.* $60,000
    b. $50,666.67
    c. January: $59,866.67
    February: $80,383.33
    March: $106,250.00
17. *a.* If it is not used the opportunity cost is zero
    b. 10.38%
    c. 10.38%
21. 11.11%; 11.14%

CHAPTER 18

3. $14,000
5. *a.* $12,000
   b. $12,000
   c. $3.00

7. NPV = $83,333
9. *a.* $1.6 million
   b. $350,000
   c. $70/day; $0.14/cheque
11. $9,360
13. NPV = $1,572,562
    NPV (with fee) = $94,104.75

CHAPTER 19

3. *a.* 90 days; $24,000
   b. 3%; 30 days; $23,280
   c. $720; 60 days
11. *a.* 42 days
    b. $600,000
13. EAR = 28.03%
    a. EAR = 17.81%
    b. EAR = 109.84%
    c. EAR = 24.90%
15. Average receivables = $291,609.59
17. *a.* NPV = $1.98 per unit
    b. 17.60%
    c. NPV = $201.33 per unit
       Break-even probability = 88.00%
27. EOQ = 7,065 units
33. P = $30.36
35. Number of orders per year = 60.83

CHAPTER 20

7. *a.* $14,375
   b. $100,000
   c. $64,000; $5,000
   d. $11,000; $16,000; $64
9. Call has higher profit potential and higher price
11. *a.* $7.48
    b. $16.82
    c. $0
13. *a.* $13.60
    b. $6.69
15. *a.* $337.04
    b. $462.96
    c. Increase. Present value of the debt decreased while firm value stays the same.
17. *a.* Zero
    b. Current stock price is too low; minimum possible return of 10% exceeds risk-free rate.
19. *a.* $1040
    b. Value of the option to convert
21. *a.* CR = 50; CP = $20; Premium = 25%
    b. SB = $797.88; CV = $800
    c. $15.96
    d. $2.12
23. $8.83
25. *a.* $96.67; $166.67
    c. $66.67

27. *a.* Long hedge
    b. Long hedge
    c. Short hedge

CHAPTER 21

1. $3 million
9. *a.* Cash cost = $40 million
      Equity cost = $42 million
   b. NPV cash = $20 million
      NPV stock = $18 million
   c. Acquire the firm for $40 million cash
10. *a.* EPS = $2.98; P/E = 22.13
    b. Synergy value Δ V = $0
11. *a.* $250
    b. $25.25
    c. $750
    d. $25.87
    e. $869.57
16. *a.* $1.54
    b. $128.21
    c. 65 times
    d. P = $97.29; P/E = 63.2 times
       The $35 bid price is a negative NPV acquisition for A; they should lower their bid.

CHAPTER 22

1. *a.* Lit 125,000
   b. 0.0800¢
   c. $2,400
   d. Singapore dollar
   e. Mexican peso
   f. S Fr .0405 / BF 1; this is a cross rate
3. *a.* ¥81.08; premium
   b. $0.7124; discount
   c. It will probably fall; fall
10. 5.08%; 3.14%; 4.03%
11. Canada: $12,364,070
    Great Britain: $12,084,434; invest in Canada
13. No change: profit = $1,308,946
    If the rate rises: profit = $2,117,200
    If the rate falls: profit = $319,414
    Break-even rate: W 481.853
15. *a.* 6%
    b. 8%
    c. 11%
17. HUF 115.00; HUF 132.25; HUF 201.14
    Relative PPP is the relationship
21. *b.* $414,671.93
    c. R = 7.67%
       NPV = $414,671.93

CHAPTER 23

8. NAL = $18,729
10. $248,498
17. *a.* Lease; NPV incremental cash flows = $205
    b. $1,333

E Q U A T I O N S   I N D E X

S U B J E C T   I N D E X